918.1 Sai 2019
St. Louis, Regis,
Brazil [2019] /
$29.99 on1103671090

___ glasses
___ discs/disks
_/_ maps
_/_ bks/pamphs

DISCARD

The Amazon p568

Ceará, Piauí & Maranhão p532

Pernambuco, Paraíba & Rio Grande do Norte p482

Sergipe & Alagoas p464

Bahia p400

Mato Grosso & Mato Grosso do Sul p362

Brasília & Goiás p334

Minas Gerais & Espírito Santo p170

São Paulo State p222

Rio de Janeiro State p128

Paraná p268

Rio de Janeiro p60

Santa Catarina p292

Rio Grande do Sul p314

Regis St Louis, Gregor Clark, Anthony Ham, Andy Symington, Robert Balkovich, Alex Egerton, Anna Kaminski, Kevin Raub

PLAN YOUR TRIP

Welcome to Brazil 6
Brazil Map 8
Brazil's Top 20 10
Need to Know 20
First Time Brazil 22
If You Like... 24
Month by Month 27
Itineraries 30
Carnaval 37
Outdoors 43
Eat & Drink Like a Local 48
Travel with Children 53
Regions at a Glance 55

ON THE ROAD

RIO DE JANEIRO **60**
Sights 61
Activities 78
Courses 83
Tours 84
Festivals & Events 85
Sleeping 85
Eating 96
Drinking & Nightlife 110
Entertainment 119
Shopping 121

RIO DE JANEIRO STATE **128**
Costa Verde **129**
Ilha Grande & Vila do Abraão 129
Paraty 137
Itatiaia Region **146**
Parque Nacional do Itatiaia 146
Visconde de Mauá 148
Penedo 150
North of Rio de Janeiro **151**
Petrópolis 151
Teresópolis 155
Nova Friburgo 157
East of Rio de Janeiro **159**
Saquarema 159

OSTILL/SHUTTERSTOCK ©

MUSEU DO ARTE CONTEMPORÂNEA P84

STEVEN FISH/SHUTTERSTOCK ©

CAIMAN, THE PANTANAL P375

NESSAFLAME/GETTY IMAGES ©

Contents

Arraial do Cabo. 162
Cabo Frio 163
Búzios 164

MINAS GERAIS & ESPÍRITO SANTO. . . 170
Minas Gerais 171
Belo Horizonte 171
Ouro Preto. 182
Mariana 190
Lavras Novas. 192
Congonhas 192
São João del Rei. 193
Tiradentes 196
Caxambu 202
Aiuruoca & the Vale do Matutu 203
Diamantina 204
Serro & Around. 208
Parque Nacional da Serra Do Cipó 209
Tabuleiro 210
Parque Natural do Caraça 210
Parque Nacional de Caparaó 211
Espírito Santo. 212
Vitória. 213
Itaúnas. 215
Guarapari & Around. 218
Domingos Martins 219
Pedra Azul 220

SÃO PAULO STATE. 222
São Paulo City 223
Paulista Coast. 259
Ubatuba. 259
São Sebastião. 262
Ilhabela 263
Iguape & Around 267

PARANÁ. 268
Curitiba 269
Morretes 274
Paranaguá 275
Ilha do Mel. 277
Iguaçu Falls & Around 282
Foz do Iguaçu 282
Parque Nacional do Iguaçu (Brazil) 289
Parque Nacional Iguazú (Argentina). 291

SANTA CATARINA 292
Ilha de Santa Catarina 293
Florianópolis. 295
North Island 298
East Coast. 300
South Island 302
The Mainland 304
Joinville 304
Blumenau 306
North of Florianópolis . . . 310
South of Florianópolis. . . 312

RIO GRANDE DO SUL. 314
Porto Alegre 316
Serra Gaúcha 320
Bento Gonçalves 320
Vale dos Vinhedos 321
Pinto Bandeira 326
Gramado 326
Cambará do Sul 328
Litoral Gaúcho 331
Torres 331
Rio Grande. 333

BRASÍLIA & GOIÁS. 334
Brasília. 335
Goiás. 349
Goiânia. 350
Cidade de Goiás. 352
Pirenópolis 354
Parque Nacional da Chapada Dos Veadeiros. 358
Alto Paraíso de Goiás . . . 359
São Jorge. 361

TAIPU DE FORA P439

ON THE ROAD

MATO GROSSO & MATO GROSSO DO SUL 362

Mato Grosso 364
Cuiabá 365
Chapada dos Guimarães 369
Parque Nacional da Chapada dos Guimarães 371
Bom Jardim 372
Poconé 373
Alta Floresta 373
The Pantanal 375
Northern Pantanal 379
Southern Pantanal 383
Mato Grosso do Sul 384
Campo Grande 384
Corumbá 389
Bonito & Around 393
Ponta Porã 398

BAHIA 400

Salvador 402
Recôncavo 427
Cachoeira & São Felix ... 427
North of Salvador 430
Praia do Forte 430
Mangue Seco 432
South of Salvador 434
Morro de São Paulo 434
Boipeba 437
Valença 438
Barra Grande 439
Itacaré 441
Ilhéus 443
Porto Seguro 447
Arraial d'Ajuda 450
Trancoso 453
Caraíva 455
Caravelas 456
West of Salvador 456
Lençóis 457
Parque Nacional da Chapada Diamantina 462

SERGIPE & ALAGOAS 464

Sergipe 466
Aracaju 466
Alagoas 470
Maceió 470
Praia do Francês 477
Penedo 478
Maragogi 480

PERNAMBUCO, PARAÍBA & RIO GRANDE DO NORTE 482

Pernambuco 483
Recife 483
Olinda 497
Fernando de Noronha 502
Paraíba 513
João Pessoa 513
Rio Grande do Norte ... 517
Natal 517
Praia da Pipa 526
São Miguel do Gostoso 530

VITORMARIGO/GETTY IMAGES ©

VALE DA LUA P358

Contents

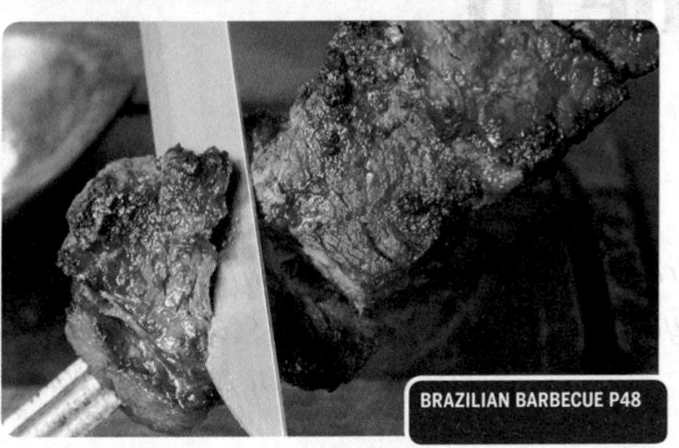

BRAZILIAN BARBECUE P48

CEARÁ, PIAUÍ & MARANHÃO 532

Ceará 533
Fortaleza 533
Canoa Quebrada 543
Icaraí de Amontada 549
Jericoacoara 550
Maranhão........... 556
São Luís............... 556
Parque Nacional dos Lençóis Maranhenses ... 564

THE AMAZON 568

Pará................ 572
Belém................ 572
Algodoal............... 585
Ilha de Marajó.......... 587
Santarém.............. 590
Floresta Nacional do Tapajós............ 596
Alter do Chão 598
Tocantins........... 602
Palmas 602
Taquarussú 605
Amazonas 606
Manaus 606
Rio Negro Basin 620
Tefé................... 627
Mamirauá Reserve...... 637
The Triple Frontier 638
Roraima 645
Boa Vista 646
Rondônia 649
Porto Velho 649
Guajará-Mirim.......... 651
Acre 652
Rio Branco............. 653
Xapuri................. 655
Brasiléia.............. 657

UNDERSTAND

Brazil Today 660
History.............. 662
Life in Brazil 674
Brazilian Rhythms 677
Football 682
Cinema & Literature ...685
Architecture 687
The Natural World 690

SURVIVAL GUIDE

Directory A–Z 702
Transportation 711
Language............717
Index............... 726
Map Legend.......... 734

SPECIAL FEATURES

Football Fever.............81
Beaches of Rio de Janeiro State 161
Pizza Paulistana..................241
Iguaçu Falls 286
Vale Europeu 308
Vale dos Vinhedos 323
Niemeyer's Brasília..................... 338
Driving the Transpantaneira.........376
Candomblé 412
Capoeira 422
Fernando de Noronha....................505
Beach Beauties......... 547
Riverboat Travel........ 582
Amazon Wildlife....... 629

Welcome to Brazil

Tropical islands, lush rainforests and rhythm-filled cities set the scene for the great Brazilian adventure.

Landscapes & Biodiversity

One of the world's most captivating places, Brazil is a country of powdery white-sand beaches, verdant rainforests and wild, rhythm-filled metropolises. Brazil's attractions extend from frozen-in-time colonial towns to otherworldly landscapes of red-rock canyons, thundering waterfalls and coral-fringed tropical islands. Add to that, Brazil's biodiversity: legendary in scope, its diverse ecosystems boast the greatest collection of plant and animal species found anywhere on earth. There are countless places in Brazil where you can spot its iconic species, which include toucans, scarlet macaws, howler monkeys, capybaras, pink dolphins, sea turtles and many more.

The Rhythms of Brazil

Wherever there's music, that carefree lust for life tends to appear – whether dancing with *cariocas* at Rio's atmospheric samba clubs or following powerful drumbeats through the streets of Salvador. There's the dancehall *forró* of the Northeast, twirling *carimbó* of the Amazon, scratch-skilled DJs of São Paulo and an endless variety of regional sounds that extends from the twangy country music of the sunbaked *sertanejo* to the hard-edged reggae of Maranhão.

Days of Adventure

Brazil offers big adventures for travelers with budgets large and small. There's horseback riding and wildlife-watching in the Pantanal, kayaking flooded forests in the Amazon, ascending rocky clifftops to panoramic views, whale-watching off the coast, surfing stellar breaks off palm-fringed beaches and snorkeling crystal-clear rivers or coastal reefs – all are part of the great Brazilian experience. No less entrancing is the prospect of doing nothing, aside from sinking toes into warm sands and soaking up a glorious stretch of beach, with a caipirinha – Brazil's national cocktail – in hand.

Joie de Vivre

Carnaval, storms through the country's cities and towns with hip-shaking samba and *frevo*, dazzling costumes and parties that last until sunup. Outside of this, *festas* (festivals) happen year-round, and provide a window into Brazil's incredible diversity. The streets are carpeted with flowers during Ouro Preto's Semana Santa (Holy Week), while in the north, Bumba Meu Boi blends indigenous, African and Portuguese folklore. Hit Blumenau's beer- and schnitzel-loving Oktoberfest, the largest outside of Germany. Several cities, such as Recife, Fortaleza and Natal even host Carnaval at other times of year.

Why I Love Brazil

By Regis St Louis, Writer

The music, the beaches, the wildlife and, most importantly, the people: it's hard not to fall for Brazil. Rio de Janeiro is one of my favorite cities: I never tire of watching the sunset from Arpoador, chasing the samba scene in Lapa or wandering the village-like streets of Santa Teresa. But Rio is just the beginning, and in Brazil there really is no end. I have fond memories spotting wildlife (especially in the Pantanal and the Amazon), making friends in small towns and finding incredible musicians in unlikely places. There's really no other country that offers so much.

For more about our writers, see p735

Above: The Pantanal (p377)

Brazil

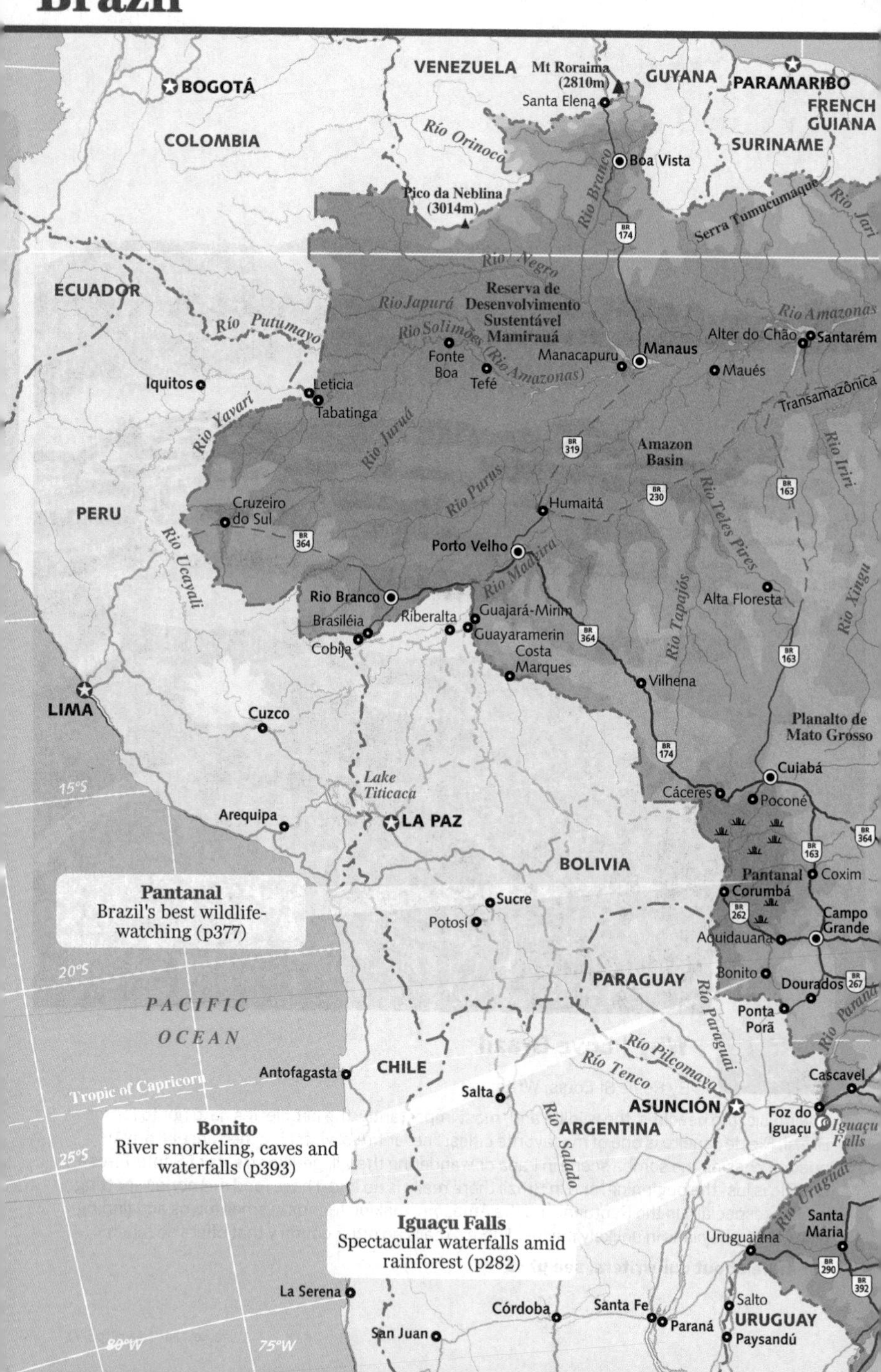

Pantanal
Brazil's best wildlife-watching (p377)

Bonito
River snorkeling, caves and waterfalls (p393)

Iguaçu Falls
Spectacular waterfalls amid rainforest (p282)

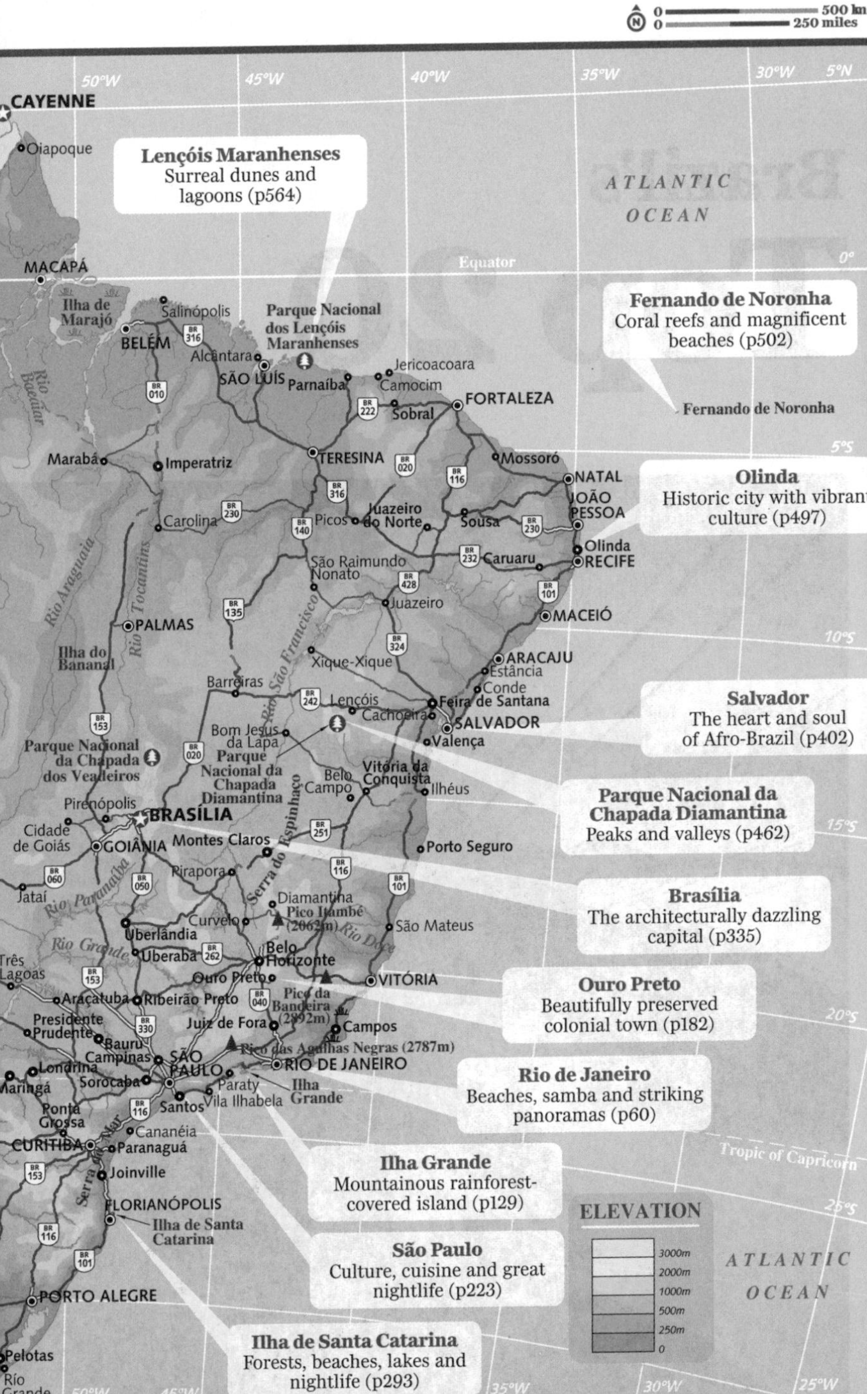

0 500 km
0 250 miles
Lençóis Maranhenses
Surreal dunes and lagoons (p564)
Fernando de Noronha
Coral reefs and magnificent beaches (p502)
Olinda
Historic city with vibrant culture (p497)
Salvador
The heart and soul of Afro-Brazil (p402)
Parque Nacional da Chapada Diamantina
Peaks and valleys (p462)
Brasília
The architecturally dazzling capital (p335)
Ouro Preto
Beautifully preserved colonial town (p182)
Rio de Janeiro
Beaches, samba and striking panoramas (p60)
Ilha Grande
Mountainous rainforest-covered island (p129)
São Paulo
Culture, cuisine and great nightlife (p223)
Ilha de Santa Catarina
Forests, beaches, lakes and nightlife (p293)
ATLANTIC OCEAN
Equator
Tropic of Capricorn
ELEVATION
3000m
2000m
1000m
500m
250m
0
CAYENNE
Oiapoque
MACAPÁ
Ilha de Marajó
BELÉM
Salinópolis
SÃO LUÍS
Alcântara
Parque Nacional dos Lençóis Maranhenses
Parnaíba
Jericoacoara
Camocim
Sobral
FORTALEZA
Fernando de Noronha
TERESINA
Imperatriz
Marabá
Mossoró
NATAL
JOÃO PESSOA
Olinda
RECIFE
Caruaru
Sousa
Juazeiro do Norte
Picos
Carolina
São Raimundo Nonato
Juazeiro
MACEIÓ
ARACAJU
Estância
Conde
PALMAS
Ilha do Bananal
Xique-Xique
Barreiras
Lençóis
Cachoeira
Feira de Santana
SALVADOR
Valença
Bom Jesus da Lapa
Parque Nacional da Chapada Diamantina
Parque Nacional da Chapada dos Veadeiros
Belo Campo
Vitória da Conquista
Ilhéus
Pirenópolis
BRASÍLIA
Cidade de Goiás
GOIÂNIA
Montes Claros
Porto Seguro
Pirapora
Jataí
Diamantina
Pico Itambé (2062m)
Curvelo
Uberlândia
São Mateus
Uberaba
Belo Horizonte
Três Lagoas
Ouro Preto
VITÓRIA
Araçatuba
Ribeirão Preto
Pico da Bandeira (2892m)
Presidente Prudente
Juiz de Fora
Campos
Bauru
Pico das Agulhas Negras (2787m)
Campinas
SÃO PAULO
RIO DE JANEIRO
Londrina
Maringá
Sorocaba
Paraty
Ilha Grande
Santos
Vila Ilhabela
Ponta Grossa
Cananéia
CURITIBA
Paranaguá
Joinville
FLORIANÓPOLIS
Ilha de Santa Catarina
PORTO ALEGRE
Pelotas
Rio Grande
Rio Araguaia
Rio Tocantins
Rio São Francisco
Rio Paranaíba
Rio Grande
Rio Doce
Serra do Espinhaço
Serra do Mar

Brazil's Top 20

1

Pão de Açúcar, Rio de Janeiro

1 Some say to come around sunset for the best views from this absurd confection of a mountain (p67). But in truth, it doesn't matter when you come; you're unlikely to look at Rio (or your own comparatively lackluster city) in the same way. From here the landscape is pure undulating green hills and golden beaches lapped by blue sea, with rows of skyscrapers sprouting along the shore. The ride up is good fun: all-glass aerial trams that whisk you up to the top. The adventurous can rock-climb their way to the summit.

Iguaçu Falls

2 No matter the number of waterfalls you've checked off your bucket list, no matter how many times you have thought you'd be just fine never seeing another waterfall again, Iguaçu Falls (p282) will stomp all over your idea of water trickling over the edge of a cliff. The thunderous roar of 275 falls crashing across the Brazil and Argentina border floors even the most jaded traveler. Loud, angry, unstoppable and impossibly gorgeous, Iguaçu will leave you stunned and slack-jawed at the absolute power of Mother Nature.

JUAN CARLOS RUIZ/500PX ©

2

ODAIRSON ANTONELLO/SHUTTERSTOCK ©

3

LAZYLLAMA/SHUTTERSTOCK ©

4

VITORMARIGO/SHUTTERSTOCK ©

Salvador

3 The world capital of Afro-Brazil, Salvador (p402) is famous for capoeira, Candomblé, Olodum, colonial Portuguese architecture, African street food and one of the oldest lighthouses in the Americas. The city's past, marked by gritty stories of Portuguese seafaring and the heartbreaking history of the African slave trade, is characterized by hardship. But today's lively Bahian capital offers a unique fusion of two vibrant cultures. The festive music and nightlife scene culminates every February when Salvador hosts one of the best Carnavals in Brazil.

Ilha Grande

4 Thanks to its isolation, Ilha Grande (p129) served for decades as a prison and leper's colony. Spared from development by this unusual history, its jungle-clad slopes and dozens of beaches are some of the best preserved in all of Brazil. Days are spent hiking through lush Atlantic rainforest, snorkeling amid aquamarine seas and cooling off in refreshing waterfalls. With no motor vehicles to spoil the party, this is one clean, green island – a true nature-lover's paradise. It's also an easy day's journey from Rio.

5

UWE BERGWITZ/SHUTTERSTOCK ©

6

MANDALA EYE/SHUTTERSTOCK ©

Ouro Preto

5 The 18th-century streets of Ouro Preto (p182) veer precipitously between one baroque masterpiece and the next. Admire the sculpted masterpieces of Aleijadinho, discover the 18th-century African king turned folk hero Chico-Rei and gaze upon opulent gilded churches. The elaborate Holy Week processions are among the country's most spectacular. From gold trading post to state capital, revolutionary hotbed to Unesco World Heritage site, Ouro Preto has been at the center of the action for more than 300 years.

Above: Igreja Nossa Senhora do Bonfim (p406)

Beers of Blumenau

6 Ubiquitous pale lagers such as Brahma and Skol certainly suffice as beat-the-heat treats, but Brazil's best brews come from greater Blumenau (p306). Heavy German immigration in the 1800s brought Reinheitsgebot, Germany's beer purity law, and these German-Brazilians aren't too fond of sharing. That means with the exception of the once-micro Eisenbahn, seriously good artisanal suds such as Schornstein Kneipe, Bierland and Das Bier don't fall too far from the tree. You'll need to venture into Santa Catarina's Vale Europeu to quench your thirst.

7

PHOTOCECHCZ/SHUTTERSTOCK ©

8

MAURICIO M FAVERO/GETTY IMAGES ©

The Pantanal

7 Few places on earth can match the wildlife-watching experience provided by the Pantanal (p375), a wondrously remote wetland in the heart of Mato Grosso. From cute capybaras to stately storks, the animal life simply abounds and is remarkably easy to see in the open marshy surroundings. There are a million reasons not to miss out on this particular eco-experience, and not least among them is that there is no better place in South America to see the elusive jaguar (pictured above left).

Fernando de Noronha

8 This archipelago (p502) of one 10km-long island and 20 smaller ones, 350km out into the Atlantic from Natal, has everything a tropical getaway should have – jaw-dropping scenery and seascapes, fine beaches, the best diving and snorkeling in the country, good surfing, memorable hikes, plentiful visible wildlife, good accommodations and restaurants – and no crowds, for visitor numbers are restricted by the limited number of plane seats available each day. Visiting Noronha is expensive, but it's worth every centavo if your budget will stretch far enough.

Jungle Trips

9 Needless to say, the best reason to visit the Amazon (p568) is to get out into the jungle: to ply the winding waterways in a canoe, hike lush leafy trails, and scan the canopy for monkeys, sloths and other creatures. The world's biggest and best-known rainforest has outdoor excursions of all sorts, and for all types of travelers: from easy nature hikes to scaling 50m trees, from luxury lodges to makeshift camps in the forest. Whatever your interest, experience, ability or budget, there's a jungle trip in the Amazon waiting to blow your mind.

EDUARDO ARRAES - WWW.FLICKR.COM/PHOTOS/DUDA_ARRAES ©

Nightlife in São Paulo

10 Rivaling the frenetic pace of New York, the modernism of Tokyo and the prices of Moscow but swamping all of them in options, São Paulo city (p223) is home to a pool of 20 million potential foodies, cocktail connoisseurs and clubbers and nearly 30,000 restaurants, bars and clubs to satiate them. From the contemporary gourmet haunts of Itaim Bibi and Jardins, to the edgy offerings of Baixo Augusta, to bohemian bars in Vila Madalena, it's a gluttonous avalanche of *bolinhos* (appetizers), booze and beats that outruns the sunrise on most nights. *Saúde!*

T PHOTOGRAPHY/SHUTTERSTOCK ©

Brasília Architecture

11 What the city of the future (p335) really needed to back up its claim to be the harbinger of Brazil's 'new dawn' was an architect capable of designing buildings that looked the part. In Oscar Niemeyer Brasilia found the right man for the job. The 'crown of thorns' Catedral Metropolitana (p337; pictured above) is a religious masterwork and the interplanetary Teatro Nacional is out of this world! Brasilia is a city overloaded with architectural gems designed by a genius inspired by the concept of a better future.

Bonito

12 Bonito (p393) is beautiful! Book yourself on a smorgasbord of aquatic adventures in the jaw-dropping surroundings of the Serra da Bodoquena and prepare for a wild wet-suited adventure like you've never experienced before. Whether you're taking your first foray into flotation on the Rio da Prata or journeying to the center of the earth at the Abismo Anhumas, Bonito is packed with unique experiences that will rank among your most cherished memories of any trip to Brazil.

Bottom: Gruta do Lago Azul (p394)

11

NICK ALBI/SHUTTERSTOCK ©

12

RICARDO NISHIOKA MORI/GETTY IMAGES ©

A.PAES/SHUTTERSTOCK ©

MICHAEL HEFFERNAN/LONELY PLANET ©

HBPRO/SHUTTERSTOCK ©

Carnaval in Rio de Janeiro

13 Get plenty of sleep before you board the plane, because once you land, it's nonstop revelry (p37) until Ash Wednesday (sort of) brings it all to a close. With nearly 500 street parties happening all over town, you will not lack for options. For the full experience, join a samba school and parade amid pounding drum corps and mechanized smoke-breathing dragons before thousands of roaring fans in the Sambódromo. Or assemble a costume and hit one of the Carnaval balls around town. The buildup starts weeks in advance.

Tiradentes

14 The colonial town of Tiradentes (p196) is so well preserved, and its natural setting so appealing, you could be excused for feeling like you've wandered onto a movie set. Cobbled lanes, flower-draped walls and some stunning colonial architecture make every step a delight – even more if you like to hike. The surrounding mountains are threaded with trails; Tiradentes' hyperactive restaurant scene serves up delicious meals, both modern and traditional; and its charming guesthouses make a relaxing spot to recharge.

Above: Igreja Matriz de Santo Antônio (p197)

Parque Nacional da Chapada Diamantina

15 A pristine outdoor wonderland of rushing waterfalls, crystal-blue pools, rugged hiking trails and natural waterslides, Chapada Diamantina (p462) is a deliciously unspoiled national park well off the beaten path – it's one of the only inland attractions in the beach-happy state of Bahia. Those who make the effort to explore the park, either on day excursions from Lençóis or on the Grand Circuit with a local guide, often count the Chapada Diamantina as one of their top outdoor travel experiences in Brazil.

MMPOP/SHUTTESTOCK ©

MARCIO JOSE BASTOS SILVA/SHUTTERSTOCK ©

MARIANO VILLAFANE/SHUTTERSTOCK ©

Parque Nacional dos Lençóis Maranhenses

16 Of all Brazil's landscape spectacles, the most unexpected has to be the Lençóis Maranhenses (p564) in Maranhão – a 70km-long, 25km-wide expanse of high dunes resembling *lençóis* (bed sheets) spread across the landscape. From around March to September (best in July and August), the dunes are partnered by thousands of crystal-clear, freshwater lagoons from rainwater filling the hollows between them. It can be visited by 4WD tour, by boat down the jungle-lined Rio Preguiças or, for the adventurous, on a three- or four-day trek right across the Lençóis.

Recife & Olinda

17 These two contrasting Northeastern neighbors with an intertwined history and shared culture make a heady double act. Recife (p483) is the big-city big sister with the skyscrapers and traffic, but also a fascinating historic center becoming ever more appealing through renovations and new museums, restaurants and cultural centers. Photogenic Olinda (p497; pictured top right) has tranquil winding lanes, colonial churches and artists' galleries. Their vibrant shared heritage comes together at Carnaval with some of Brazil's most riotous street festivities, highlighted by unique music and dance forms such as *frevo* and *maracatu*.

Alter do Chão

18 Alter do Chão (p598) truly has it all: a slice of beachfront in the heart of the rainforest. The Amazonian destination is best known for its picturesque setting, an island made entirely of fine white sand lapped by cool tea-colored water. But Alter do Chão is also a gateway to a major national forest, with massive *samaúma* trees (pictured above) and a chance to live with local rubber-tapper families. With so much to do, appealing lodging options and a great laid-back vibe, it's a place where you'll want to linger for a while – and many travelers do just that.

Santa Catarina Beaches

19 Santa Catarina (p292) is synonymous with the good life and that has a whole lot to do with its sun-toasted shores. Whether you hang out in Florianópolis (where an easy path to paradise boasts 42 idyllic beaches sitting within an hour's drive) or head south of the capital to Guarda do Embaú (one of Brazil's best surfing spots) or to Praia do Rosa (the state's most sophisticated beach resort), a powerful punch of wow will greet you the first time you dig your toes into the state's unspoiled sands.

Top: Praia do Santinho (p299)

Paraty

20 No place in Brazil offers such an enticing blend of colonial architecture and natural beauty as Paraty (p137). Located a few hours southwest of Rio on the picturesque Costa Verde, it has long been a favorite *carioca* getaway. Drop-dead gorgeous beaches and a stunning mountain backdrop jostle for attention with the multihued, cobblestoned charms of the 18th-century town center. If you get bored with sunbathing and sightseeing, cool off with a caipirinha, go hurtling down a natural waterslide nearby, or whip up a gourmet Brazilian meal at the local cooking school.

MELISSA GRUNDEMANN/SHUTTERSTOCK ©

PHOTOGRAPHY BY ULRICH HOLLMANN/GETTY IMAGES ©

Need to Know

For more information, see Survival Guide (p701)

Currency
Real (R$)

Language
Portuguese

Visas
Required for some nationalities, including holders of passports from the US, Canada and Australia.

Money
ATMS are widespread in Brazil. Credit cards are accepted at most restaurants, shops and hotels.

Cell Phones
Local SIM cards can be used in unlocked European and Australian phones, and in US phones on the GSM network.

Time
Brazil has four time zones. Rio and São Paulo are on Brasília time (GMT/UTC minus three hours).

When to Go

High Season
(Dec–Mar)

➡ Brazil's high season coincides with the northern-hemisphere winter.

➡ A hot, festive time – expect higher prices and minimum stays (typically four nights) during Carnaval.

➡ It's particularly busy in Rio and popular beach destinations.

Shoulder
(Apr & Oct)

➡ The weather is warm and dry along the coast, though it can be chilly in the south.

➡ Prices and crowds are average, though Easter week draws crowds and high prices.

Low Season
(May–Sep)

➡ Aside from July, which is a school-holiday month, you'll find lower prices and mild temperatures in the south.

➡ July to September are good months to visit the Amazon or Pantanal.

Useful Websites

Embratur (www.visitbrasil.com) Official site of Brazil's Ministry of Tourism.

Insider's Guide to Rio (www.ipanema.com) Tips and planning info, with special sections on Carnaval and gay Rio.

Rio Times (www.riotimesonline.com) English-language news and resources on Brazil.

What About São Paulo (http://whataboutsaopaulo.com) Blog exploring the highs and lows of life in Brazil's biggest city.

Lonely Planet (www.lonelyplanet.com/brazil) Destination information, hotel bookings, traveller forum and more.

Important Numbers

Brazil's country code	☎55
Ambulance	☎192
Fire	☎193
Police	☎190
International collect call	☎0800-703-2111

Exchange Rates

Argentina	R$1	R$0.10
Australia	A$1	R$2.68
Bolivia	B$1	R$0.54
Canada	C$1	R$2.93
Euro zone	€1	R$4.37
Japan	¥100	R$3.35
New Zealand	NZ$1	R$2.45
UK	UK£1	R$4.98
US	US$1	R$3.80

For current exchange rates, see www.xe.com.

Daily Costs

Budget: Less than R$200

- Dorm bed: R$40–80
- Sandwich and drink in a juice bar: R$18–25
- Long-distance buses: around R$15–18 per hour of travel

Midrange: R$200–400

- Standard double room in a hotel: R$160–300
- Dinner for two in a midrange restaurant: R$80–160
- Jungle trip: R$150–350 per day
- Admission to nightclubs and live-music venues: R$20–50
- One-way flight from Rio to Salvador/Iguaçu/Manaus: from R$470/500/550

Top end: More than R$400

- Boutique hotel: from R$500
- Upscale jungle lodges outside Manaus: R$600–1200 per night
- Dinner for two at top restaurants: R$200–500

Opening Hours

Banks 9am–3pm Monday–Friday

Bars 6pm–2am

Cafes 8am–10pm

Nightclubs 10pm–4am Thursday–Saturday

Post offices 9am–5pm Monday–Friday; some open Saturday morning

Restaurants Noon–2:30pm and 6–10:30pm

Shops 9am–6pm Monday–Friday and 9am–1pm Saturday

Arriving in Brazil

Galeão International Airport (Rio de Janeiro) Premium Ônibus 2018 (R$16, one to two hours, every 30 minutes) buses to Flamengo, Copacabana, Ipanema, Leblon and other neighborhoods. Radio taxis (set fare R$130, 45 to 90 minutes) to Copacabana and Ipanema. Metered yellow-and-blue *comum* taxis cost between R$82 and R$100. Ride-sharing services cost around R$60. Shuttle service costs R$25.

GRU Airport (São Paulo) The Airport Bus Service (www.airportbusservice.com.br; R$50) is the most efficient way to/from GRU Airport. Guarucoop (www.guarucoop.com.br) is the only taxi service allowed to operate at the airport (R$150 to Jardins or Vila Madalena, R$157 to Vila Mariana). Ride-share services cost about half as much. By train, the brand new CPTM Linha 13 (Jade) connects GRU Airport with Engenheiro Goulart station on Linha 12 (Safira) in northeast São Paulo.

Getting Around

Plane Useful for crossing Brazil's immense distances; can save days of travel; prices are generally high, but airfare promotions are frequent.

Bus Extensive services from *comun* (conventional) to *leito* (overnight sleepers) throughout the country, except for the Amazon. For timetables and bus operators, check out Busca Ônibus (www.buscaonibus.com.br).

Boat Slow, uncomfortable, but brag-worthy transport between towns in the Amazon, with trips measured in days rather than hours. You'll need a hammock, snacks, drinking water and a high tolerance for boredom.

For much more on **getting around**, see p711

First Time Brazil

For more information, see Survival Guide (p701)

Checklist

- Make sure you have your Brazilian visa if you need one.
- Inform your debit-/credit-card company of your travel plans.
- Make arrangements to be able to use your mobile phone upon arrival.
- Download essential smartphone apps (see our Top Tips section below for more on this)

What to Pack

- Good walking shoes
- A sarong (handy for the beach and as an extra towel)
- Lightweight rain jacket (for those unexpected tropical downpours)
- Brazilian electrical adaptor
- Portable water filter (to cut down on waste from plastic water bottles)
- Language phrasebook
- Insect repellent
- Sunscreen, hat and sunglasses

Top Tips for Your Trip

- Brazil is a massive country, and it's impossible to see it all. Pick one or two regions, rather than losing a lot of time transiting between far-flung parts of the country just ticking off highlights.
- If you haven't already, download WhatsApp and set up your profile. Tour operators, guides, restaurants, guesthouses and everyone else uses it. It's also the best way to stay in touch with Brazilians you meet.
- Using a ride-sharing app (like Uber, 99Taxis or Easy Taxi) to get around major towns and cities is generally faster and cheaper than using a traditional taxi.
- Brazil has many facets; decide what kind of trip you want while making your plans: wildlife-watching vs big-city nightlife, remote beaches and island-hopping vs cultural experiences etc. Customize your itinerary based on your own interests.

What to Wear

The dress code is very casual in Brazil, but it's a good idea to bring along something a bit more dressy for a night out. Given the heat and humidity, lightweight, natural, breathable fabrics are best.

On the beach, women generally wear tiny bikinis, and men wear tight swim trunks. Everyone flaunts it all, regardless of body shape and size.

Sleeping

Brazil has a wide range of lodging, covering all budgets. Reserve well in advance when booking during high season (December to March).

Hotels From simple accommodations in cookie-cutter high-rises to boutique options with ocean views in luxury buildings.

Pousadas Guesthouses running the gamut from basic to plush, with many family-run options.

Hostels Dorms and a few private rooms with communal good cheer at locations across the country.

Jungle lodges Found in the Amazon; prices are midrange to high and luxuries are few, but the wildlife-watching can be astonishing.

Safe Travel

Crime is a concern in Brazil, but if you take basic precautions, you'll minimize your risk of becoming a target.

➡ Dress down and leave expensive jewelry, watches and sunglasses at home.

➡ Carry only the money you'll need for the day.

➡ After dark, don't ever walk along empty streets, in deserted parks or on urban beaches.

➡ Use ATMs inside buildings. Before doing so, be very aware of your surroundings.

Bargaining

A little bargaining for hotel rooms should become second nature. Before you agree to take a room, ask for a better price: *'Tem desconto?'* (Is there a discount?) and *'Pode fazer um melhor preço?'* (Can you give a better price?). There's sometimes a discount for paying *à vista* (cash).

You should also bargain when shopping in markets. In unmetered taxis, be sure to agree on the price before departing.

Tipping

Hotels Tipping is optional for housekeepers, but appreciated.

Parking Usually R$2 or more; assistants do not receive wages and are dependent on tips.

Taxis Not expected but most people round up to the nearest real.

Tours It's customary to tip guides at the end of a tour, and certainly appreciated if you can give a little to the assistant or boat operator(s).

Restaurants A 10% service charge is usually included.

Phrases to Learn Before You Go

English is not widely spoken in Brazil. You'll have the best luck communicating in popular tourist destinations like Rio de Janeiro. It helps to master a few basic Portuguese phrases. You'll have a head start if you've studied Spanish, as Portuguese and Spanish share many words and grammatical structures. The pronunciation, however, is completely different, and very few Brazilians speak Spanish. Note too, that European and Brazilian Portuguese have different spelling, pronunciation and to some extent, different vocabulary.

1 **Do you speak English?**
Você fala inglês?
vo•se *faa*•laa eeng•*gles*

Staff at hostels, midrange and top-end hotels and high-end shops will often speak some English.

2 **What's the score?**
Quanto está o jogo?
kwang•to es•*taa* o *zho*•go

On big international game days, Rio residents pack into neighborhood *botecos* (small, open-air bars) to watch the game.

3 **What would you recommend?**
O que você recomenda?
o ke vo·se he·ko·*meng*·daa

Brazilian dishes are normally quite large – and some dishes are meant for two. When in doubt, ask the server to clarify.

4 **How much is it?**
Quanto custa?
kwang•to *koos*•taa

A little bargaining is expected at markets, but sellers generally don't inflate their prices so often aren't willing to haggle.

5 **Where's the best beach?**
Onde fi ca a melhor praia?
ong•de *fee*•kaa aa me•*lyorr prai*•aa

The beaches of Rio are the city's wondrous and carefree backyard and have long seduced visitors.

Etiquette

Brazilians are pretty informal, but there are a few key rules of etiquette.

Greetings When greeting or bidding goodbye to women, an air kiss is exchanged on each cheek (start to her left). Men shake hands with one another.

Dining Use a napkin or a toothpick when eating finger food. Brazilians tend to eat pizza with a knife and fork.

Touchy subjects Brazilians are exasperated by their country's corruption, but can be defensive if foreigners criticize their government or talk about poverty or religion.

If You Like...

Beaches

Brazil has some of the finest beaches on earth: you'll find idyllic island getaways, vibrant big-city beaches and rainforest-backed sands all along the coastline.

Baía do Sancho On Fernando de Noronha, this is easily one of Brazil's most gorgeous beaches. (p503)

Ilha Grande Enchanting island with gorgeous beaches, a welcome lack of cars and a laid-back island vibe. (p129)

Trancoso Cliff-backed beaches are a short stroll from this pretty Bahian village. (p453)

Jericoacoara Hip international beach scene with good activities, pousadas (guesthouses), restaurants and nightlife. (p550)

Ilhabela Dense jungle, waterfalls and picturesque beaches a few hours from São Paulo. (p263)

Florianópolis & Ilha de Santa Catarina Protected dunes and cliff- and forest-lined beaches, plus stunning lagoons in the interior. (p293)

Wildlife

Brazil is home to a staggering array of plant and animal species, with memorable wildlife-watching in the rainforests, wetlands and along the coast.

Mamirauá Reserve One of the best places in the Amazon to see wildlife and experience the wonders of the mother of all rainforests. (p637)

The Pantanal You're likely to see a great many animal species in these wildlife-rich wetlands. (p375)

Fernando de Noronha World-class diving and snorkeling amid abundant marine life. (p502)

Praia do Rosa Watch southern right whales off the coast between June and October. (p312)

Parque Nacional de Monte Pascoal Part of the bio-rich Atlantic rainforest, this park lies just south of Salvador. (p455)

Estação Biológica de Caratinga Head to this remote reserve in Minas Gerais to see some of the largest primates in the Americas. (p213)

Scenery

Blessed with verdant rainforests, thundering waterfalls, craggy mountains and tropical islands, it's easy to see why Brazilians say *'Deus e Brasileiro'* (God is Brazilian).

Rio de Janeiro The Cidade Maravilhosa (Marvelous City) lives up to its name with forested mountains and lovely beaches. (p61)

Fernando de Noronha Cliffs, rock pinnacles, beautiful bays and beaches all packed into one 10km-long island. (p502)

Iguaçu Falls Spread between Argentina and Brazil, these are some of the most spectacular waterfalls on earth. (p282)

Parque Nacional da Chapada Diamantina In the Bahian interior, you can hike across dramatic plateaus and swim in refreshing waterfalls. (p462)

Parque Nacional dos Lençóis Maranhenses An otherworldly landscape of windswept dunes and sparkling blue lagoons. (p564)

Alter do Chão Startling white-sand beaches surrounded by jungle deep in the Amazon. (p598)

Parque Nacional Serra dos Órgãos Great hiking amid dramatic mountain scenery just two hours north of Rio. (p151)

Food & Drink

Specialties in Brazil range from African-influenced stews to delectable Amazonian fish.

Ipanema & Leblon These twin beachfront neighborhoods have some of the best restaurants in Rio. (p96; p100)

MARCOS AMEND/SHUTTERSTOCK ©

KSENIA RAGOZINA/SHUTTERSTOCK ©

Top: Rock paintings, Parque Nacional da Serra da Capivara (p555)

Bottom: Church ruins, Alcântara (p564)

São Paulo With great pizzerias, sushi bars and restaurants serving first-rate Brazilian and international fare, you won't go hungry in Sampa. (p223)

Vale dos Vinhedos This scenic valley in the south is the heart of Brazil's wine-growing region, and has top restaurants as well. (p321)

SENAC Take a cooking class or simply come for the buffet, which features all the great Bahian dishes. (p410)

Belém Sample lip-numbing *tacacá* (a soup) and many delicious Amazonian fish such as the prized *tucanaré* (peacock bass). (p572)

Tiradentes Great place to feast on *mineira* cooking, particularly during its 10-day gastronomic festival. (p196)

Getting off the Beaten Path

Pre-Columbian rock art, deserted beaches, end-of-the-earth fishing villages: these are just a few of the sights you can see by heading off the tourist path.

Parque Nacional da Serra da Capivara This dramatic rocky landscape contains thousands of prehistoric rock paintings. (p555)

Peninsula de Maraú Peaceful and remote, the Bahian peninsula's quiet beaches feel far removed from the tourist crowds. (p439)

Itaúnas Charming beach town in the little-visited state of Espírito Santo, with a wildlife-filled state park nearby. (p215)

Algodoal Isolated little village on the edge of wild beaches near the mouth of the Amazon. (p585)

Reserva Extrativista Baixo Rio Branco-Jauperi Magnificent rainforest reserve 500km north of Manaus. (p623)

São Miguel das Missões Gateway to the mystical 17th-century ruins left behind by Jesuit missionaries. (p26)

Adventure

Brazil offers some memorable ways to experience its stunningly diverse landscapes, from multi-day treks across dunes to snorkeling in crystal-clear rivers.

Trekking Take the three- to four-day journey across the spectacular Lençóis Maranhenses and see the dunes by moonlight. (p564)

Hang Gliding Soar over Rio's stunning tropical landscape on a tandem glide off a mountain. (p79)

Ecotourism Bonito is a great spot for adventure, with river snorkeling, cave crawls, hiking and rappelling (abseiling). (p393)

Climbing The scenic high-country Parque Nacional do Itatiaia is a must for hikers and rock-climbers. (p146)

Tree Climbing Get an intimate view of the rainforest canopy on an ascent inside the Amazon. (p610)

Slow-Boating String up your hammock and travel the old-school way on a riverboat trip between towns in the Amazon. (p582)

Kitesurfari Go on a long-distance kitesurfing adventure in Rio Grande do Norte, complete with vehicle support. (p551)

History

You can delve into the past on a stroll through Brazil's magnificent colonial centers, some of which are Unesco World Heritage sites.

Salvador Bahia's star attraction is packed with historic churches and Afro-Brazilian culture. (p402)

Manaus Learn about indigenous culture and history at this city in the heart of the Amazon. (p606)

Ouro Preto One of Brazil's most alluring towns, hilly Ouro Preto is packed with 18th-century architectural treasures. (p182)

Olinda Remnants of lovely architecture left by the Portuguese as well as the Dutch. (p497)

Alcântara Fascinating town in Maranhão full of restored and abandoned mansions and churches. (p564)

Paraty Picturesque cobblestone village with beautifully preserved 18th-century buildings. (p137)

Museu Histórico Nacional One of the best places to learn about the presence of the Portuguese royals in Rio. (p70)

Cidade de Goiás A Unesco World Heritage site that's packed with architectural treasures from centuries past. (p352)

Festivals

Whether you prefer the colorful pageantry of Semana Santa (Holy Week) or the unbridled revelry of Carnaval, Brazil has you covered.

Carnaval Many cities throw a wild pre-Lenten bash, but Rio, Salvador, Olinda and Corumbá are among the most festive. (p37)

São Paulo Gay Pride Parade The world's biggest gay pride parade, with an estimate three to four million in attendance. (p236)

Oktoberfest Experience Brazil's European roots at this beer- and bratwurst-loving bash in Blumenau. (p306)

Bumba Meu Boi São Luís erupts with color, music and dance in this fascinating June festival. (p561)

Nightlife

Nightlife here is electric, fueled by the nation's incredible music scene. Samba, Afro-Brazilian drumming, rock and hip-hop are all essential parts of the Brazilian soundtrack.

Lapa The epicenter of Rio's nightlife is packed with bars and samba clubs, and transforms into a street party on weekends. (p118)

São Paulo There's always something afoot inside this nightlife-loving metropolis. (p223)

Pelourinho Salvador's historic center is the place to hear drum corps like Olodum laying down the heavy rhythms. (p403)

Lagoa da Conceição Live music, lake views and top-notch DJs are the big draw of this town on Ilha de Santa Catarina. (p301)

Belo Horizonte Take in the lively arts scene and buzzing nightlife of the Minas Gerais capital. (p171)

Búzios Bask on the beach by day and hit the clubs by night at this stylish resort town. (p164)

Month by Month

TOP EVENTS

Carnaval, February or March

Semana Santa, April or May

Bumba Meu Boi, June

Oktoberfest, October

Reveillon, December

January

Following the excitement of New Year's Eve, Brazil starts off the year in high gear, with steamy beach days and the buzz of pre-Carnaval revelry.

Lavagem do Bonfim

In Salvador, on the second Thursday in January, this equal-parts Catholic and Candomblé fest features a ritual washing of the church steps followed by all-night music and dancing. (p411)

February

High season is in full swing, with people-packed beaches, sold-out hotel rooms and the unbridled revelry of Carnaval. It's a festive and pricey time to travel, and advance planning is essential.

Carnaval

In February or early March, for the five days preceding Ash Wednesday, the famous bacchanalian event takes place nationwide. It's liveliest in Rio, Salvador, Olinda and Corumbá, with parades, costumes and round-the-clock merrymaking.

April

After Carnaval, prices dip, the intense heat subsides and the crowds dissipate, particularly in the north and northeast (when heavy rains continue through June). In Minas Gerais, however, Holy Week festivals keep things lively.

Semana Santa

In Ouro Preto, Holy Week (the week before Easter) is a colorful event of processions and streets 'painted' with flowers. São João del Rei's Holy Week features parades accompanied by fabulous traditional orchestras. Other well-known Holy Weeks happen in Congonhas and Cidade de Goiás.

May

May is a quiet time for tourism with cooler temperatures beginning to arrive (particularly in the south) and heavy rains still falling in the Amazon.

Festival Internacional de Balonismo

Torres springs to life for five days in early May or late April when it hosts a colorful hot-air balloon festival. Concerts, extreme sports, films and a country-style fair are among the attractions. (p332)

Virada Cultural

One of the best times to visit São Paulo is during this 24-hour cultural fest. It takes place all across town and features concerts, film screenings, art exhibitions and other events. (p236)

Festa do Divino Espírito Santo

This old-fashioned folk festival in Pirenópolis comprises medieval tournaments, dances and festivities. (p355)

June

In the south, winter arrives (with cold weather the norm through August). Tourism-related activities remain curtailed (also through winter) in the north, south and northeast, though it's a good time to visit the Pantanal.

São Paulo Pride

It's official, São Paulo throws the largest gay pride parade on earth in early June, attracting more than three million people to this massive parade. (p236)

Bumba Meu Boi

Maranhão's magnificent mythic bull festival has African, Indian and Portuguese roots and features singing, dancing, poetry and countless ox costumes. Held from 13 to 30 June. (p561)

Boi-Bumbá

In Parintins in the Amazon, this popular traditional folk festival on the last weekend of June recounts the death and resurrection of an ox, with music and dancing. (p607)

Festas Juninas

Spanning the month of June, the feast days of various saints mark some of the most important folkloric festivals in Brazil. Expect concerts, food stands, fireworks and bonfires. Bahia is one of the best places to be. (p85)

KSENIA RAGOZINA/SHUTTERSTOCK ©

ALEXANDRE ROTENBERG/SHUTTERSTOCK ©

Top: Bumba Meu Boi, Maranhão (p561).

Bottom: Reveillon (p85), Rio de Janeiro

July

After months of rain, the dry season arrives in the Amazon, making it a good

time to visit. The weather is mild (cold in the far south), but Brazilians travel during July, which is a school-holiday month.

Festitália

Italians have made many cultural contributions to the south, including this vibrant Blumenau fest featuring a week of wine, pasta and music in mid-July.

Festival Literária Internacional de Parati

This important literary festival in mid-July brings together celebrated authors from around the world. It also includes film screenings, exhibitions and musical performances. (p142)

Festival Nacional de Forró

Music lovers wanting to get off the beaten track should make their way up to the pretty beach town of Itaúnas, which hosts 10 days of concerts and dancing (to *forró* music of course). (p216)

August

The tail end of winter is a quiet time in Brazil, with fewer tourists (and limited services) in the south and north. Temperatures are pleasant in the tropics and cold in the south.

Festival de Gramado

European-style town Gramado hosts an important film festival each year, running for nine days in August. This long-running fest (around since 1973) is a showcase for Brazilian and other Latin American films. (p326)

Folclore Nordestino

Olinda's highly recommended fest celebrates music and folklore from across the Northeast in late August.

October

The tourist masses and high-season prices haven't yet arrived, though the weather is beginning to warm and cities are already livening up for the following year's Carnaval.

Círio de Nazaré

Belém's enormous annual event on the second Sunday in October brings one million to the streets to take part in the procession of one of Brazil's most important icons. (p589)

Oktoberfest

This beer-drinking extravaganza in Blumenau is the best place to connect to southern Brazil's German roots. Held mid-October. (p306)

Bienal de São Paulo

This major art event occurs in even-numbered years (next in 2020 and 2022) between October and December and showcases the work of over 120 artists from around the globe. (p237)

Rio International Film Festival

Rio's international film festival – Latin America's biggest – features more than 200 films from all over the world, shown at some 35 theaters over several weeks in October or Novmber. (p85)

November

This late spring month can be a great time to visit, as the crowds are generally small and you can often score good off-season deals (flights, accommodations).

Maceió Fest

Maceió's biggest bash of the year is much like Carnaval, with street parades, outlandish costumes, bars that are open 24 hours and a general joie de vivre among the populace, only it's held in the third week of November.

December

Summer marks the beginning of Brazil's most festive season (through February), with hot temperatures and ideal beach days. The crowds are growing and prices are rising (but typically rise even more in January and February).

Carnatal

The country's biggest 'off-season Carnaval' is this Salvador-style festival held in Natal in the first week of December. It features raucous street parties and pumping *trios elétricos* (bands playing atop mobile speaker-trucks). (p520)

Reveillon

Some two million revelers, dressed in white, pack the sands of Copacabana Beach in Rio on 31 December, where music concerts and fireworks ring in the New Year. (p85)

Itineraries

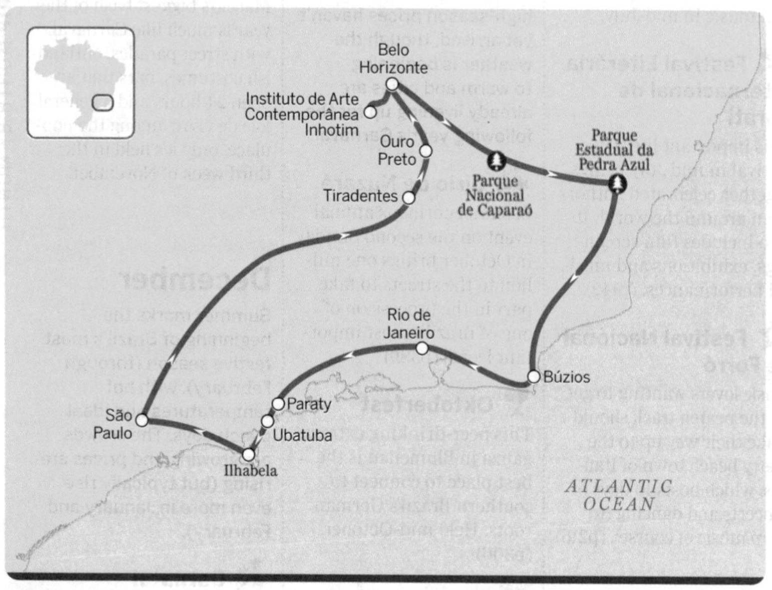

Rio & the Southeast

Gorgeous beaches, rainforest-covered islands and historic towns are just some of the things you'll experience on this loop around the Southeast.

Spend a few days discovering **Rio** and its beaches, restaurants and incredible music scene before heading to **Paraty**, a beautifully preserved town with rainforest hikes and stunning beaches nearby. Next, stop in **Ubatuba** with its jungle-clad mountains and spectacular coastal scenery. **Ilhabela** is a car-free island of beaches, forests and waterfalls. Stop in **São Paulo** for high culture, including the nation's best museums and restaurants.

Head next to exquisite **Tiradentes** and **Ouro Preto**, with some of Brazil's finest colonial architecture. Afterwards, take in a bit of friendly Mineira hospitality, good restaurants and buzzing nightlife in **Belo Horizonte**. Make a day trip to the outstanding collection of art galleries and gardens at the **Instituto de Arte Contemporânea Inhotim**, 50km southwest of Belo Horizonte.

Visit the hiker's paradise of **Parque Nacional de Caparaó**; further east, relish the dramatic beauty of **Parque Estadual da Pedra Azul**. Further south you'll find the stunning beaches and high-end dining and nightlife of **Búzios**, which makes a great final stop before heading back to Rio.

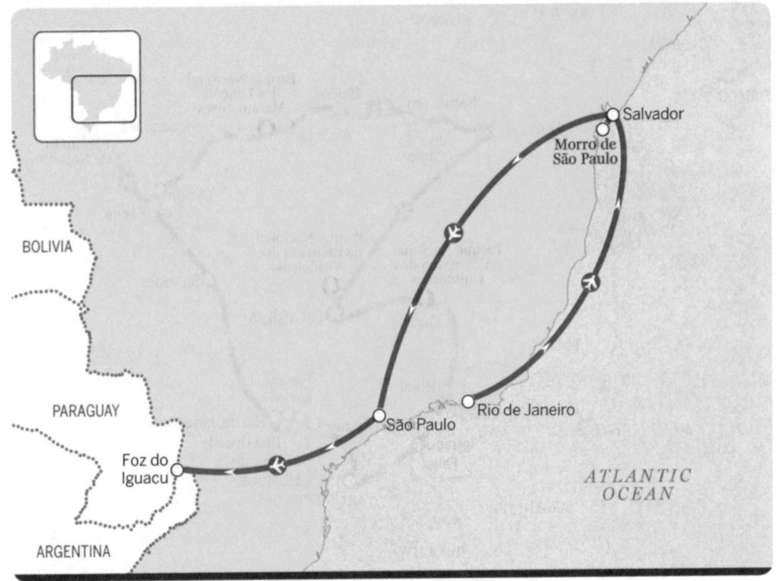

Eastern Highlights

Even on a short trip, you can take in some spectacular scenery and get a taste of Brazil's staggering diversity. With a few key flights you can maximize your time here.

Start off in the Cidade Maravilhosa, aka **Rio de Janeiro**. Spend two days taking in grand views from the forested mountaintops overlooking the city (atop Pão de Açúcar and Cristo Redentor), leaving time for relaxing on Ipanema Beach, biking along Copacabana Beach and strolling through the historic center. When evening arrives, head out for dining and drinking in Lebon (Rua Dias Ferreira is a great place to start) and be sure to check a samba club or two in nightlife-packed Lapa.

On days three and four, fly up to **Salvador** for a heady dose of Afro-Brazilian culture. Check out the brightly painted colonial buildings of the Pelourinho, take in a dazzling dance performance of the Balé Folclórico da Bahia and feast on seafood at Pelô Bistrô. Browse for handicrafts at the Mercado Modelo in Cidade Baixa, and try to catch a sunset out at Barra (the stylish eatery and bar Pereira is a good choice).

On your fifth day, make a day trip out to **Morro de São Paulo** for a slice of tropical, car-free paradise. Be sure to check out the island's 17th-century ruins, and pay a visit to a few beaches (go to Segunda Praia for dining and seaside drinks; while less visited Quarta Praia makes for an alluring retreat).

Beat the sunrise for an early-morning flight down to **Foz do Iguaçu** (via **São Paulo**). Spend the first day exploring the Brazilian side of the majestic waterfalls. Take the walkways that make up the Trilha das Cataratas (Waterfall Trail) and marvel at the view of the Garganta do Diabo (Devil's Throat). On your last day, cross to the Argentine side for a walk through rainforest along elevated walkways. Keep an eye out for shimmering butterflies, dazzling hummingbirds, eye-catching toucans and other bird species, as well as the odd monkey. In the afternoon, take a boat trip near the thundering falls. That night toast your adventures with drinks along lively Av Jorge Schimmelpfeng in Foz do Iguaçu.

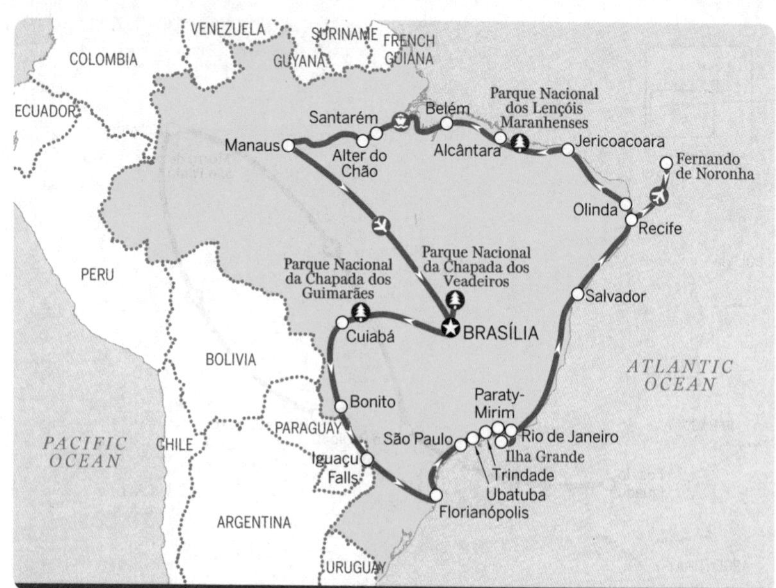

Best of Brazil

On this epic trip you'll experience the rhythm-infused towns of the Northeast, the jungles of the Amazon and the biodiversity of the Pantanal, with beaches, tropical islands and historic towns thrown into the mix.

From **São Paulo**, head east towards Rio, stopping at glorious beaches such as **Ubatuba**, **Trindade** and **Paraty-Mirim**. Leave a couple of days for hiking the rainforest paths and basking on the beaches of **Ilha Grande**. Continue northeast to **Rio de Janeiro**, for a hearty dose of nightlife, beach culture and panoramic views.

From there head north, via bus or plane, to **Salvador**, the country's Afro-Brazilian gem that's known for its colorful colonial center, drumming in the streets and lively (and numerous) festivals. Further up the coast visit historic and arts-loving **Olinda**, then catch a flight from neighboring **Recife** to the spectacular archipelago of **Fernando de Noronha**, where you find pretty beaches, snorkeling, diving and a paradise-like setting.

Back on the mainland, travel north, stopping in the backpackers' paradise of **Jericoacoara** en route to the surreal dunes in the **Parque Nacional dos Lençóis Maranhenses**, a stark contrast to the historic beauty of **Alcântara**. To the west lies **Belém**, a culturally rich city near the lush island of Ilha de Marajó. Catch a boat up the Amazon to **Santarém** and on to **Alter do Chão** for a trip into the jungle. Then continue to the burgeoning city of **Manaus**.

From Manaus, fly to **Brasília** to take in its stunning architecture, then visit **Parque Nacional da Chapada dos Veadeiros** for waterfalls, canyons and dips in natural swimming pools. Next head to **Cuiabá**, gateway to the breathtaking canyons of **Parque Nacional da Chapada dos Guimarães**. Spend a few days horseback riding and boating in the Pantanal, one of Brazil's best destinations for wildlife watching. Head south via Campo Grande to **Bonito** for crystal-clear rivers, lush forests and caves. Continue south to the awe-inspiring **Iguaçu Falls**. Before completing the circle, explore the secluded beaches and charming Germanic towns around **Florianópolis**.

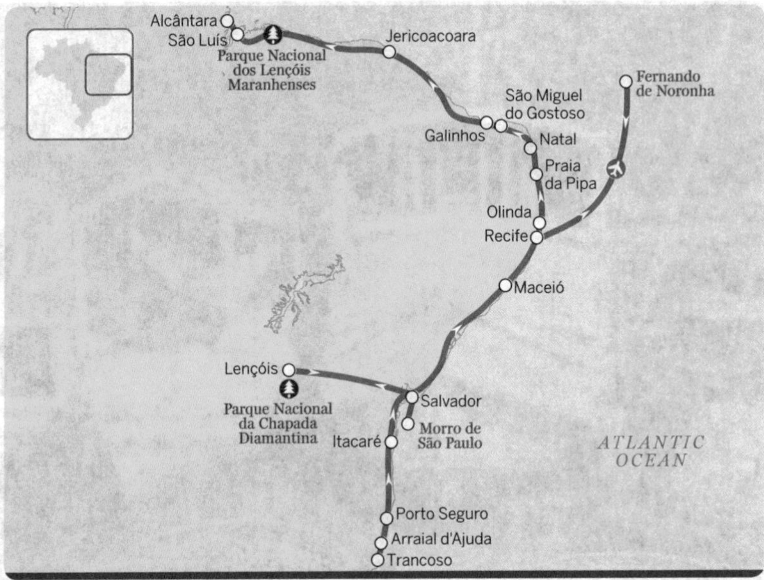

Bahia & the Northeast

Those looking for the soul of Brazil would do well to focus on the Northeast. A confluence of music, history and culture amid spectacular natural scenery makes for an unforgettable journey.

Catch a flight to **Porto Seguro**, then quickly make your way to the pretty towns of **Arraial d'Ajuda** and **Trancoso**, both blessed with great guesthouses and restaurants, festive nightlife and access to walks on a seemingly endless cliff-backed beach. Continue north to **Itacaré**, a lively town with great surf and cove beaches reached via trails through hilly rainforest. Then head on to rhythm-filled **Salvador**, Bahia's most vibrant and colorful city. From there, catch a boat to **Morro de São Paulo**, an island with enchanting beaches and a laid-back vibe. Don't miss boat rides around the island, taking in mangroves, reefs, oysters and the quiet village of Boipeba.

Detour west to the tranquil diamond-mining town of **Lençóis**, which has pretty outdoor cafes, cobblestone streets, and caves, rivers and waterfalls nearby. From here, head into the **Parque Nacional da Chapada Diamantina** for crisp mountain streams, panoramic views and an endless network of trails. Back on the coast, go north to **Maceió**, a vibrant, youthful city with gorgeous beaches nearby. Keep going north to reach **Olinda**, home to some of Brazil's best-preserved colonial buildings and a Unesco World Heritage site. From Olinda's buzzing neighbor **Recife**, fly out to **Fernando de Noronha**, an exquisite archipelago of rich marine life and splendid beaches.

Returning to the mainland, visit beautiful **Praia da Pipa**, then hit the spectacular coastline stretching from **Natal** to Jericoacoara, including the enticing coastal spots of **São Miguel do Gostoso** and **Galinhos**. In the sandy-street village of **Jericoacoara**, try your hand at sandboarding, kitesurfing and beachfront capoeira, and watch memorable sunsets. West of Jericoacoara, **Parque Nacional dos Lençóis Maranhenses** is a striking landscape of dunes, lagoons and beaches. Continue west to the reggae-charged **São Luís**, home to 18th-century buildings, seafood restaurants and buzzing nightlife. It's worth planning a trip around one of the town's many folkloric festivals. The last stop is **Alcântara**, a little-visited colonial town with remarkable architecture.

LUOMAN/GETTY IMAGES ©

FILIPE FRAZAO/SHUTTERSTOCK ©

Top: Belém (p572)

Bottom: Teatro Amazonas, Manaus (p606)

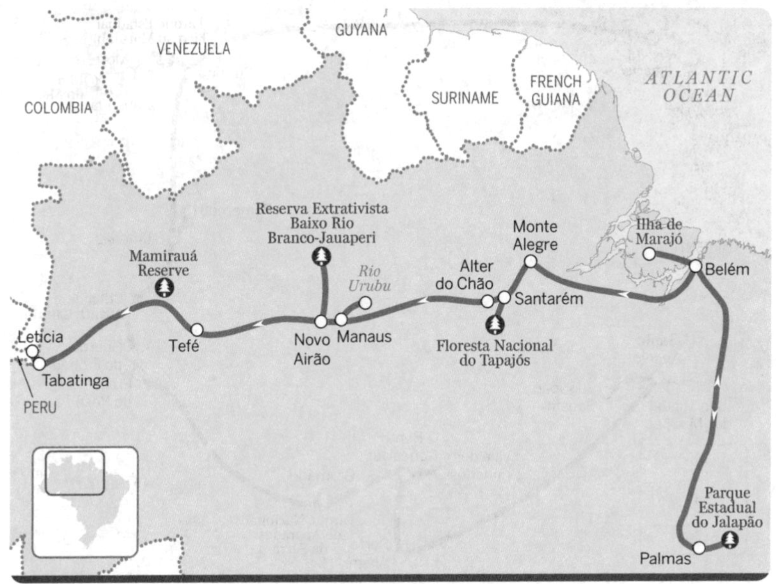

4 WEEKS Waterways of the Amazon

Few places ignite the imagination like the Amazon. The largest forest on the planet has an incredible array of plant and animal life. Surprising to many visitors, these wetlands also contain vibrant cities, architectural treasures and beautiful river beaches.

Begin in **Belém**, a culturally rich city at the mouth of the great river. Explore the revitalized riverfront docks, visit the waterfront market, sample Amazonian dishes and catch a performance at the lavish Teatro da Paz. From here, explore the forest-covered island of **Ilha de Marajó**, which has bird-filled forests, friendly locals and itinerant water buffalo roaming the streets. Back in Belém, dip south to **Palmas**, another ultraplanned city like Brasília and the jumping-off point for 4x4 tours of rugged **Parque Estadual do Jalapão**.

Get a hammock and prepare yourself for a few hardy days of boat travel up the Amazon River. Set off from Belém and stop in **Monte Alegre** to see ancient rock paintings in the sandstone hills beyond towns. Upstream is **Santarém**, a pleasant city with many nearby attractions. Also reachable is the virgin rainforest of the **Floresta Nacional do Tapajós**, where you can lodge in simple pousadas and hike through pristine forest in search of massive samaúma trees. It's also worth stopping in **Alter do Chão** for its picturesque lagoon with white-sand beaches.

Continue upriver to **Manaus**, Amazonia's largest city. Visit the city's opera house, market, indigenous museums and nature parks, and the Encontro das Águas. From here, head to the **Rio Urubu**, base yourself in ecofriendly lodges and take in great wildlife-watching opportunities. Afterwards, go west of Manaus to the small town of **Novo Airão**, the jumping-off point to the **Reserva Extrativista Baixo Rio Branco-Jauaperi**, a remote and pristine rainforest reserve where you can see a stunning array of plant and animal life.

Outside of **Tefé**, visit the **Mamirauá Reserve**, a vast rainforest reserve where you can see dolphins, sloths, macaws, various monkey species (including the rare uakari) and other wildlife. From there, continue by river to **Tabatinga**, a fascinating place where you can visit three different countries in an afternoon (Brazil, Colombia and Peru). End your trip by crossing into **Leticia** in Colombia and staying in a jungle lodge along the Rio Javari.

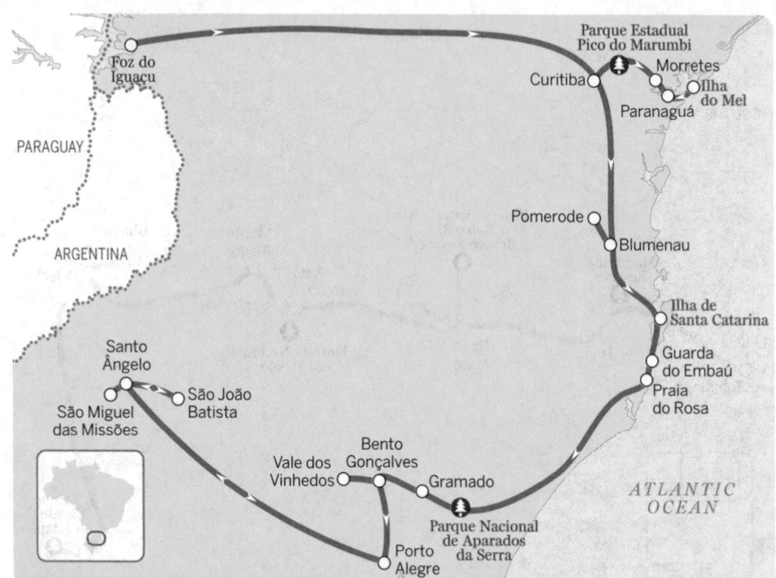

Southward Bound

This trip through Brazil's southernmost states takes in forested islands, scenic beaches, mountainous national parks, historic missions and Bavarian-style towns with largely European roots.

Start in **Foz do Iguaçu** to gaze at the most impressive waterfalls on the planet. Take short day trips to Argentina and Paraguay to get a taste of lush rainforests before heading east (by overnight bus or quick flight) to **Curitiba**, a city with an intriguing environmentally friendly design, plus pretty botanic gardens and an Oscar Niemeyer museum. Next, take the scenic train ride to the sleepy waterfront town of **Morretes**. From there you can visit the **Parque Estadual Pico do Marumbi**, a lush reserve that offers some memorable walks amid the highlands. Continue on to **Paranaguá**, the departure point to car-free **Ilha do Mel**. The forest-covered island has lovely beaches and low-key guesthouses, and is skirted by some pretty trails.

Next head to beer-loving **Blumenau** and nearby **Vale Europeu**, where **Pomerode** boasts Teutonic architecture, blond-haired residents and a local brew more Bavarian than Brazilian. Head back east to the coast and continue south to **Ilha de Santa Catarina**, a forest-covered gem of sand dunes, sparkling beaches, pretty lagoons and sleepy fishing villages. Keep going south to **Guarda do Embaú**, a bohemian seaside town with excellent surf. A short jaunt south is **Praia do Rosa**, which has pretty beaches and whale-watching.

On into Rio Grande do Sul, explore the dramatic canyon and waterfalls of **Parque Nacional de Aparados da Serra**. It's worth heading further inland to **Gramado**, a charming mountain resort where gourmet chocolates, fondue and excellent infrastructure might make you feel like you've stepped into a Swiss portal. Continue west to **Bento Gonçalves**, gateway to the award-winning vineyards of the **Vale dos Vinhedos**, set amid the rolling hills of the Serra Gaucho.

Head south to **Porto Alegre** for transport links to **Santo Ângelo**, which leads on to the Jesuit missions. From there you can visit **São Miguel das Missões**, **São João Batista** and numerous other holy sites. At trip's end, return to Porto Alegre for an onward flight.

Plan Your Trip
Carnaval

One of the world's largest parties, Carnaval – in all its colorful, hedonistic bacchanalia – is celebrated with verve in practically every town and city in Brazil. Millions of visitors come for the spectacular costume parades, rhythm-filled street parties, and merriment of every shape and form.

History

Carnaval, like Mardi Gras, originated from various pagan spring festivals. During the Middle Ages, these tended to be wild parties until tamed, in Europe, by both the Reformation and the Counter-Reformation. But not even the heavy hand of the Inquisition could squelch Carnaval in the Portuguese colony, where it came to acquire indigenous costumes and African rhythms.

Some speculate that the word *carnaval* derives from the Latin *carne vale,* meaning 'goodbye meat,' owing to the 40 days of abstinence (from meat and other worldly pleasures) that Lent entails. To compensate for the deprivation ahead, sins are racked up in advance with wild parties in honor of King Momo, the king of Carnaval.

Carnaval in Rio de Janeiro

If you haven't heard by now, Rio throws an exceptional party, with music and dancing filling the streets for days on end. The culmination of the big fest is the brilliantly colorful parade through the Sambódromo, with giant mechanized floats, pounding drummers and whirling dancers – but there's lots of action in Rio's many

Carnaval through the Year

If you can't make it to Brazil during Carnaval, you can still join the party by hitting one of the so-called out-of-season Carnavals.

Carnatal

Natal's huge out-of-season Carnatal (p520) is the country's biggest, drawing upwards of one million revelers each year. The celebration kicks off in the first week of December, with extensive street parties and Salvador-style *trios elétricos* (electrically amplified bands playing atop trucks). The big event happens outside the Arena das Dunas (p525).

Fortal

Half a million revelers celebrate Carnaval street-party style at Fortaleza's big bash (p538) in the last weekend of July. Going strong for over 25 years, Fortal brings some of Brazil's top musicians to town to play *forró, sertanejo* and other regional sounds. The main action happens in the open-air Cidade Fortal, located some 9km southeast of the city center.

CARNAVAL DATES

The following are the Carnaval dates (Friday to Shrove Tuesday) in coming years:

2020 February 21 to 25

2021 February 12 to 16

2022 February 25 to March 1

2023 February 17 to 21

neighborhoods for those seeking more than just the stadium experience.

Out-of-towners add to the mayhem, joining *cariocas* (residents of Rio) in the street parties and costumed balls erupting throughout town. There are free live concerts throughout the city (near the Arcos do Lapa, on Largo do Machado and on Praça Floriano, among other places), while those seeking a bit of decadence can head to the various balls about town. Whatever you do, prepare yourself for sleepless nights, an ample dose of caipirinhas (cane-liquor cocktails) and samba, and mingling with joyful crowds spilling out of the city.

To get more information on events during Carnaval, check *Veja* magazine's *Veja Rio* insert (sold on Sunday at newsstands) or visit Riotur (p126), the tourist organization in charge of Carnaval.

Carnaval on the Streets

Joining the *bandas* and *blocos* (street parties) is one of the best ways to have the Carioca experience. These marching parades consist of a procession of brass bands (in the case of *bandas*) or drummers and vocalists (in the case of *blocos*) followed by anyone who wants to dance through the streets. Currently there are more than 400 street parties, filling every neighborhood in town with the sound of pounding drums and old-fashioned Carnaval songs – not to mention thousands of merrymakers. For many *cariocas*, this is the highlight of Carnaval. You can don a costume (or not), learn a few songs and join in; all you have to do is show up. For Zona Sul fests, don't forget to bring your swimsuit for a dip in the ocean afterwards.

For complete listings, check the latest issues of *Veja Rio* when you arrive during Carnaval season.

AfroReggae (Av Atlântica, Copacabana; ⌚9am Carnaval Sun) A massive and hugely popular *bloco* (street party) with a heavy rhythm section that celebrates along the beachfront Av Atlântica near Rainha Elizabeth in Copacabana.

Banda de Ipanema (www.facebook.com/bandadeipanema; Praça General Osório, Ipanema; ⌚4pm 2nd Sat before Carnaval, Carnaval Sat & Carnaval Tue) This long-standing *banda* (procession) attracts a wild crowd, complete with drag queens and others in costume. Don't miss it.

Banda Simpatia é Quase Amor (www.facebook.com/pg/bloco.simpataquaseamor; Praça General Osório, Ipanema; ⌚4pm Sat before Carnaval & Carnaval Sun) A favorite Ipanema *banda*, with a 50-piece percussion band.

Barbas (www.facebook.com/blocodobarbasoficial; cnr Assis Bueno & Arnaldo Quintela, Botafogo; ⌚3:30pm Carnaval Sat) One of the oldest *bandas* of the Zona Sul parades through the streets with a 60-piece percussion band.

Carmelitas (cnr Dias de Barros & Ladeira de Santa Teresa, Santa Teresa; ⌚1pm Carnaval Fri & 8am Carnaval Tue) A crazy mixed crowd (some dressed as Carmelite nuns) parades through Santa Teresa's streets.

Céu na Terra (www.facebook.com/ceunaterracarnaval; Curvelo, Santa Teresa; ⌚8am Carnaval Sat) Follows the tracks where the *bonde* (streetcar line) once ran on a memorable celebration through Santa Teresa en route to Largo das Neves.

Cordão do Bola Preta (www.facebook.com/pg/cordaodabolapreta; Primeiro de Março, Centro; ⌚9am Carnaval Sat) The oldest and biggest *banda* still in action. Costumes are always welcome, especially those with black-and-white spots. Held near Rua Rosário.

Dois Pra Lá, Dois Pra Cá (www.facebook.com/BlocoCarnavalescoDoisPraLaDoisPraCa; Carlinhos de Jesus Dance School, Rua da Passagem 145, Botafogo; ⌚10am Carnaval Sat) This fairly long march begins at the Carlinhos de Jesus Dance School and ends at the Copacabana Palace.

Monobloco (www.facebook.com/monoblocooficial; Av Rio Branco, Centro; ⌚7am 1st Sun after Carnaval) Rise and shine! This huge *bloco* attracts upwards of 500,000 revelers who, nursing hangovers (or perhaps still inebriated), gather near Av Vargas in Centro for a final farewell to Carnaval.

Que Merda É Essa? (Garcia d'Ávila, Ipanema; ⌚1pm Carnaval Sun) This playful gathering (which means 'What the shit is this?') is a big draw

Samba school parade, Rio de Janeiro

in Ipanema. Beginning near Nascimento da Silva, it eventually makes its way along the beach.

Suvaco de Cristo (Rua Jardim Botânico, Jardim Botânico; ⏲9am Sun before Carnaval) Very popular *bloco* (whose name means 'Christ's armpit,' in reference to the open-armed Redeemer looming overhead). It also meets on Carnaval Saturday but doesn't announce the time (to avoid overcrowding), so ask around. Held near the corner of Faro.

Samba School Parades

The highlight of any Carnaval experience is attending (or participating in) a parade at the Sambódromo. There before a crowd of some 90,000 (with millions more watching on TV), each of the 12 samba schools has its 80 minutes to dance and sing through the open Oscar Niemeyer–designed stadium. The pageantry is not simply eye candy for the masses. Schools are competing for top honors in the parade, with winners announced (and a winner's parade held) on the Saturday following Carnaval.

Here's what to expect: each school enters the Sambódromo with amped energy levels, and dancers take things up a notch as they dance through the stadium. Announcers introduce the school, then the lone voice of the *puxador* (interpreter) starts the samba. Thousands more voices join him (each school has 3000 to 5000 members), and then the drummers kick in, 200 to 400 per school, driving the parade. Next come the main wings of the school, the big allegorical floats, the children's wing, the celebrities and the bell-shaped *baianas* (women dressed as Bahian aunts) twirling in elegant hoopskirts.

Costumes are fabulously lavish, with 1.5m feathered headdresses; long, flowing capes that sparkle with sequins; and rhinestone-studded G-strings.

The whole procession is also an elaborate competition. A handpicked set of judges chooses the best school on the basis of many components, including percussion, the *samba do enredo* (theme song), harmony between percussion, song and dance, choreography, costumes, story line, floats and decorations. The dance championship is hotly contested, with the winner becoming not just the pride of Rio but all of Brazil.

The Sambódromo parades start with the *mirins* (young samba-school members) on the evening of Carnaval Friday, and

JONATHAN GREGSON/LONELY PLANET ©

Traditional Bahian dress at Carnaval, Salvador (p411)

continue on through Saturday night when the Group A samba schools strut their stuff. Sunday and Monday are the big nights, when the Grupo Especial – the 12 best samba schools in Rio – parade: six on Sunday night, and six more on Monday night. The following Saturday, the six top schools do it again in the Parade of Champions, which generally has more affordable tickets than on the big nights. Each event starts at 9pm and runs until 4am.

Most visitors stay for three or four schools, and come to see their favorite in action (every self-respecting Carioca has a school they support, just as they have a favorite football team). If you're really gung-ho, wear your school's colors and learn the theme song (the words are found on each of the school's websites) so you can sing along when it marches through the Sambódromo.

Don't take a bus to or from the Sambódromo. It's safer to take a taxi or the metro (Praça Onze or Central stations), which runs around the clock during Carnaval until 11pm Tuesday. It's also a great opportunity to check out the paraders commuting in costume.

Tickets

Getting tickets at legitimate prices can be tough. Liesa (http://liesa.globo.com), the official samba-school league, begins selling tickets in December or January, most of which get immediately snatched up by travel agencies then later resold at higher prices. Check with Riotur about where you can get them, as the official outlet can vary from year to year. At face value, tickets run from R$160 to R$500, though you'll probably have to pay about twice that (or more) if you buy just before Carnaval. The best sectors, in order of preference, are sectors 9, 7, 11, 5 and 3. The first two (9 and 7) have great views and are in the center, which is the liveliest place to be.

By Carnaval weekend, most tickets are sold out, but there are lots of scalpers. If you buy a ticket from a scalper (no need to worry about looking for them – they'll find you!), make sure you get both the plastic ticket with the magnetic strip and the ticket showing the seat number. The tickets for different days are color coded, so double-check the date as well.

If you haven't purchased a ticket but still want to go, during Carnaval you can show up at the Sambódromo at around midnight. This is when you can get grandstand tickets for about R$50 from scalpers outside the gate. Make sure you check which sector your ticket is for. Most ticket sellers will try to pawn off their worst seats.

And if you can't make it during Carnaval proper, there's always the cheaper Parade of Champions the following Saturday.

Open-Air Concerts

Lapa becomes a major focal point during Carnaval. In front of the Arcos da Lapa, the Praça Cardeal Câmara transforms into an open-air stage, with concerts running through Carnaval. About six different bands play samba each night during this event, which is called Rio Folia. The music starts at 10pm and runs past 2am, though revelers pack Lapa until well past sunrise.

Samba-School Rehearsals

Around August or September, rehearsals start at the *escolas de samba* (samba schools or clubs). Rehearsals usually take place in the *favelas* (slums) and are open to visitors. Salgueiro (p121) and Mangueira (p121) are among the easiest schools to get to.

JOINING A SAMBA SCHOOL

Those who have done it say no other part of Carnaval quite compares to donning a costume and dancing through the Sambódromo before roaring crowds. Anyone with the desire and a little extra money to spare can march in the parade. Most samba schools are happy to have foreigners join one of the wings. To get the ball rolling, you'll need to contact your chosen school in advance; they'll tell you the rehearsal times and when you need to be in the city (usually a week or so before Carnaval). Ideally, you should memorize the theme song as well.

The biggest investment, aside from the airfare to Rio, is buying a *fantasia* (costume), which will cost upwards of R$1000. If you speak some Portuguese, you can contact a school directly; some Rio travel agencies can also arrange this.

Carnaval Balls

Carnaval balls are giant, often costumed, parties with live music and dancing, and an ambience that runs the gamut from staid and formal to wild and tawdry. The most famous ball is held at the Copacabana Palace. It's a black-tie affair, and tickets run R$1100 to R$3200.

Popular, less pricey balls (under R$150) are held at nightspots like Rio Scenarium.

Tickets go on sale about two weeks beforehand, and the balls are held nightly during Carnaval. The *Veja Rio* insert in *Veja* magazine has details.

Carnaval in Salvador

Although Rio's Carnaval hogs all the attention, Salvador hosts its own magnificent bash. In fact, this is one of the largest Carnavals in Brazil, attracting over two million revelers at last count.

Carnaval in Salvador usually kicks off Thursday night, with the mayor handing King Momo the keys to the city at Campo Grande (though in recent years it's happened at Praça Castro Alves). It all comes to an end on Ash Wednesday, with a handful of street parades giving a final afternoon send-off.

As elsewhere in Brazil, music plays a key role in the celebration, and in Salvador that means *axé,* an Afro-Bahian musical genre that incorporates a wide range of sounds, from samba-reggae and *forró* (a Northeastern two-step) to calypso and fast-passed *frevo* (a fast, syncopated, brass-band beat). It's the undisputed pop anthem during Carnaval in Salvador, and in many other parts of the Northeast.

Trios Elétricos & Blocos

An integral element of the Salvadoran party is the *trio elétrico* – a long, colorfully decorated truck that's covered with oversized speakers. Small stages perch up top, with a band pumping out the rhythms as the *trio* slooowly winds through town. Hundreds of thousands line the streets of the parade route, packing in tightly – indeed, moving freely becomes a Sisyphean task.

Each *trio* is the centerpiece of a *bloco,* the gathering of revelers that surrounds the trucks. Those who want to be a part of the *bloco* pay anywhere from R$100 to upwards of R$700 (depending on the popularity of the *bloco*); this gives access to the *cordão,* the safer, roped-off area guarded by security personnel that surrounds the *trio. Bloco* members receive an *abadá,* an outfit (usually T-shirt and shorts) that identifies them as part of the group.

Those who don't want to pay to join a *bloco* can always choose to *fazer pipoca* (be popcorn) in the street. Once you get over the initial crush of the surrounding crowds, you can enjoy a wide variety of music and be spared the hassle involved with picking up the *abadá*.

You can also escape some of the madness by buying a day in a *camarote,* the walled-off, roadside bleachers with their own facilities. Head to the Bahiatursa (p425) tourist office for information on *camarote* tickets.

Afoxés & Blocos Afros

Sprinkled between each of the *blocos* – and densely concentrated in the Pelourinho, where there are no *trio elétricos* – are *afoxés,* groups that parade to the rhythms, songs and dances found in Candomblé (the polytheistic Afro-Brazilian religion). Years ago, *afoxé* groups would perform a ritual in

MESQUITAFMS/SHUTTERSTOCK ©

Olinda Carnaval (p499)

the *terreiro* (house of worship) before hitting the streets. Today this is not mandatory, and many *afoxé* members don't worship the *orixás* (the gods that the groups celebrate).

One of the most famous *afoxé* groups around today is the Filhos de Gandhy, founded in 1949. The bloco's founding members felt Gandhi, an Indian activist, was an important symbol of peace; their nonviolent approach earned the *bloco* respect in the eyes of the authorities, which took a largely repressive stance toward Afro-Brazilian culture in the early 20th century. The *bloco* also helped pave the way for numerous other *afoxés*. Today the Filhos are the largest *afoxé*, with more than 10,000 members. They wear blue-and-white outfits with white turbans, shimmering sashes and blue-and-white beaded necklaces. Like some other *afoxés*, the group plays the serene rhythms of *ijexá* (a style of African-influenced music), and sprays the crowd with perfume.

Blocos afros also play an intrinsic role in the Carnaval festivities in Salvador. These are groups that celebrate African or Afro-Brazilian heritage in both costumes and themes. The most famous *bloco afro* performing today is Olodum, a group widely credited for creating samba-reggae during Carnaval in 1986. Today the powerful drum corps parades with some 200 drummers, a handful of singers and thousands of costumed members.

Parade Routes

There are three main Carnaval circuits: the beachside Barra to Rio Vermelho circuit (where most tourists hang out), the narrow Campo Grande to Praça Castro Alves circuit, and the Pelourinho (no *trios* here, mostly concerts and parading drum corps). Some neighborhoods also hold their own parties. Bahiatursa and Emtursa publish a schedule of events with a route map.

Carnaval in Other Cities

Most foreign travelers tend to join the party in Rio or Salvador, but there are scores of other places to rack up a few sins Brazilian-style before Ash Wednesday (or perhaps the week after) brings the revelry to a close.

Recife Costumed re-enactments, diverse music, ample audience participation (bring a costume) and huge street parties, including the Galo da Madrugada, which gathers over two million celebrants on the official Carnaval opening on Saturday morning.

Olinda Spontaneous, inclusive and playful; lasts 11 days and begins with a parade of more than 400 'Virgins' – men in drag.

Porto Seguro Similar to Salvador's Carnaval; lasts a full week, ending the Saturday after Ash Wednesday.

Florianópolis One of Brazil's most gay-friendly Carnavals (after Rio); the biggest and best bash in the South.

São Paulo While less riotous than most, São Paulo's Carnaval celebrations include a spectacular parade in its own Sambódromo; fewer crowds and lower prices are appealing.

Corumbá This small town near the Bolivian border goes wild during Carnaval, with massive, Rio-style parades, complete with samba schools.

Ouro Preto The cobblestone lanes of town transform into one vast street party in Minas Gerais.

Paraty Famed for its Bloco da Lama, when revelers plaster themselves with mud and dance through the streets.

São João del Rei The party never seems to end during this rollicking good time in Minas with countless *blocos* taking to the streets.

Plan Your Trip
Outdoors

Brazil's coastline, its forests and mountainous interior set the stage for fresh-air adventures. Wildlife-watching is world class in the Pantanal and the Amazon. There are hundreds of great surf spots all along the Atlantic, while the chapadas (tablelands) are good destinations for hikes and treks. Other big draws include rock climbing, canyoning, paragliding and diving.

Wildlife Encounters

Home to an astounding variety of creatures great and small, Brazil is one of the world's best places for seeing wildlife.

Mamirauá Reserve (p637) Spot five species of monkey, toucans, sloths, river dolphins and caimans deep in the Amazon jungle.

Cristalino Lodge (p376) Take a day trip or overnight at this lodge, home to an awe-inspiring collection of wildlife.

Fernando de Noronha (p502) Swim with sea turtles in this heavenly archipelago.

The Pantanal (p375) Look for wildlife (including jaguars) while boating near Porto Jofre.

Praia do Rosa (p312) Watch southern right whales – mothers and calves – from the beach.

Parque Nacional do Superagüi (p281) Spy an amazing variety of birds on a boat trip around the mangroves and Atlantic rainforest.

Reserva Extrativista Baixo Rio Branco-Jauperi (p620) Immerse yourself in Amazonian animal life at this remote location.

Alter do Chão (p598) Hear the squawk of tropical birds while paddling across the Lago Verde.

Estação Biológica de Caratinga (p213) Encounter the largest primate in the Americas, the endangered *muriqui* (woolly spider monkey).

Top Activities

Wildlife-Watching

See monkeys, macaws, capybaras, caimans, toucans, jaguars and dozens of other species on a wildlife-watching trip in the Amazon or the Pantanal.

Hang Gliding

Take to the skies off Pedra Bonita in Rio de Janeiro.

Surfing

Ride the excellent breaks off Itacaré in Bahia.

Diving & Snorkeling

Dive amid abundant coral and marine life off Fernando de Noronha, or snorkel the crisp rivers around Bonito.

Rock Climbing

Take on challenging routes surrounded by craggy peaks in the Serra dos Órgãos in Rio state.

Hiking

Take the five- to eight-day Grand Circuit trek in the beautiful mountainous setting of Parque Nacional da Chapada Diamantina. Or hike to waterfalls set in a picturesque valley of the Parque Nacional da Chapada dos Veadeiros.

DEA E BRUNO/SHUTTERSTOCK ©

Hiking, Parque Nacional da Chapada dos Veadeiros (p358)

Hiking

Hiking in Brazil is highly popular. It's best done during the cooler months of April to October. During the summer, the tropical sun heats the rock to oven temperatures and turns the jungles into steamy saunas. If you plan to hike in the Amazon, aim to come when the water levels are low (roughly August to December); at other times the forest is flooded and virtually all your activities will be by canoe.

There are lots of great places to hike in Brazil, both in the national and state parks and along the coastline, and especially in the Southeast and South. Outstanding areas include the following:

Floresta da Tijuca, Rio de Janeiro (Map p86; ☎21 2492-2250; www.parquedatijuca.com.br; Estrada da Cascatinha 850, Alto da Boa Vista; ⏲8am-5pm) FREE Atlantic rainforest, peaks and ocean views inside the city limits. You can even arrange hikes up Corcovado to the open-armed Cristo Redentor (though it's best to go with a guide).

Parque Nacional da Chapada Diamantina, Bahia (p462) Spectacular day hikes and multiday treks; Lençóis is a good base.

Parque Nacional da Serra dos Órgãos, Rio de Janeiro state (p152) Hiking amid peaks and forest; a couple of hours north of Rio.

Parque Nacional do Itatiaia, Rio de Janeiro state (p146) Climbing, trekking and wildlife-watching amid mountains and rainforest.

Parque Nacional da Chapada dos Veadeiros, Goiás (p358) Vast, 650-sq-km park in high-altitude cerrado with scenic day hikes taking in waterfalls, swimming holes and lunar landscapes.

Parque Nacional de Caparaó, Minas Gerais (p211) Summit hikes to the highest mountains in the south, including Pico da Bandeira (2892m).

Parque Estadual Pico do Marumbi, Paraná (p274) Well-signposted network of old pioneer trails.

Parque Nacional de Aparados da Serra, Rio Grande do Sul (p328) Scenic hikes amid waterfalls and pine forest, and observation points overlooking steep canyons.

Parque Nacional da Serra Geral, Rio Grande do Sul (p329) Intriguing rock formations, natural pools and dramatic canyon views are all part of the scenery of this gem in the deep south.

Parque Nacional da Serra do Cipó, Minas Gerais (p209) Huge mountain park with lush river valleys, adventure activities, and short and multiday hikes.

Ilha Grande, Rio de Janeiro state (p129) Atlantic rainforest hikes to gorgeous beaches and tiny villages.

Serra de São José, Minas Gerais (p196) Short hikes through protected Atlantic rainforest in the mountains near Tiradentes.

Manaus, Amazonas (p606) Best place to book a multiday 'survival tour' with rainforest hiking, fishing for dinner, building shelters and sleeping in hammocks.

Parque Nacional dos Lençóis Maranhenses, Maranhão (p564) For a different perspective, consider the three-day trek across the otherworldly dune landscapes. You can overnight in tiny oasis villages along the way.

Surfing

Surfing is very popular, and several Brazilian pros are usually to be found in the top 20 of the world rankings.

There's surf virtually all along the coast, with particularly good waves in the South. The best surf beaches are in Santa Catarina state; the Brazilian championships are held here at Praia da Joaquina, on Ilha de Santa Catarina. São Francisco do Sul, Ilha do Mel, Ubatuba, Ilhabela, Maresias and the Boiçucanga area all serve up good waves.

A top destination for serious surfers are the beaches west of Rio de Janeiro. Just past Barra da Tijucca and Recreio is Macumba Beach; its left and right breaks draw both longboarders and beginners. After Macumba is lovely Prainha, which is widely considered the best surf spot in the area, with waves reaching 3m on good days. If it's too packed, you can continue on to Grumari, where the swell isn't as good but the crowds are thinner.

Further out, but still in Rio state, you'll find Saquarema, Itacoatiara (across the bay south of Niteroi), Búzios and Ilha Grande. The waves are best in the Brazilian winter (from June to August).

On other beaches surfing is still a way of life, and boogie boarding is popular too. Renting boards can be difficult outside of popular tourist areas, though. If you plan to do a lot of surfing in less traveled places, you'll need to bring your own board.

Further to the north, Itacaré, Sítio, Praia da Pipa and Fernando de Noronha are among the better spots.

A curious event is the national *pororoca* (tidal bore) surf championship held at São Domingos do Capim at the time of the full moon nearest the March equinox. The waves here are formed by the tidal bore on a tributary of the Rio Amazonas, a long way from the ocean. Waves can reach a few meters in height, and the rides are legendary (the record is a 12.5km, 37-minute ride).

For something completely different, you can join the naturists at nude surfing in Tambaba, Paraíba. There's even a nude surfing festival held in August.

SURFING VOCABULARY

Despite their reputation for aggressiveness in the water, once on land Brazilian surfers are fairly keen on meeting foreign surfers and hearing about their travels. Some will even lend you a board if you ask politely.

body board – boogie board

onda – wave

Pode me emprestar sua prancha por favor? – Could I borrow your board please?

prancha – surfboard

quebrar – to break

surfista – surfer

Tem ondas? – Are there any waves?

Vamos pegar ondas – Let's go surfing

vento – wind

Stand-Up Paddleboarding

Stand-up paddleboards are increasingly popular in Brazil. You can rent them and go for a paddle in Rio (off the beaches of Copacabana, Ipanema or Barra) and in Bahia (Itacaré and Arraial d'Ajuda), among other places.

Other unique experiences:

Alter do Chão, the Amazon (p598) Standing atop a board and taking in the scenery is a memorable way to visit the surprising white-sand beaches of Ilha do Amor near this Amazonian town located deep inland.

Bonito, Mato Grosso do Sul (p393) Paddle beside gentle waterfalls and marvel at the surrounding tropical paradise just south of the ecotourism mecca of Bonito.

Ilha do Mel, Paraná (p277) Get a full-body workout while paddling off this lovely forested island in Brazil's south.

Paraty, Rio de Janeiro state (p142) Few coastlines are as lovely as the Costa Verde located a few hours southwest of Rio de Janeiro – and one of the best ways to see it is from atop the water.

Windsurfing

Windsurfing has caught on in Brazil. In Rio you can rent equipment at Barra da Tijuca, but there are better conditions, and again equipment to rent, northeast of Rio at Búzios. In São Paulo state there's good windsurfing at Ilhabela and around Boiçucanga. But Brazil's hard-core windsurfing mecca can be found much further north, along the Ceará coast, northwest of Fortaleza, where constant, regular, strong trade winds blow from July to December. Jericoacoara is one of the best spots in the country for windsurfing. Near Fortaleza, the beaches of Praia do Futuro and Praia de Iracema are also popular spots.

Kitesurfing

Kitesurfing is hugely popular in the northeast. The most popular destinations lie west of Fortaleza, including Cumbuco, Jericoacoara, and Icaraí de Amontada. The conditions are also excellent in Rio Grande do Norte, especially in Sao Miguel de Gostoso. It's possible to rent gear and take classes in all of these places. Longer, multiday kitesurf safaris link many of these destinations together.

Diving & Snorkeling

The *mergulho* (diving) here doesn't match the Caribbean, but it's worthwhile if you're keen. By far the best diving in the country is in the Fernando de Noronha archipelago (p502), where there's excellent visibility (up to 40m), warm seas and abundant marine life, including 15 coral species and more than 200 fish species. There are several reputable dive operators.

Other good places for diving:

Arraial do Cabo, Rio de Janeiro state (p162) Astonishing combination of clear waters full of marine life, plus wrecks and caves for experienced divers. It's often rated one of the top three dive spots in Brazil.

Ponta do Seixas, near João Pessoa in Paraíba (p513) Diving amid coral reefs in clear seas near the easternmost point of Brazil.

Lagoa Misteriosa, near Bonito (p395) Freshwater cave-diving. Visibility is at its best from May through September.

The snorkeling is also quite good on Fernando de Noronha and there are places where sea turtles appear at high tide. Snorkel-by-boat excursions are available. Other spots in the northeast worth including in a snorkeling itinerary include Porto do Galinhos and Tamandaré; both have tidal pools full of colorful tropical fish.

For something completely different, nothing compares to the experience of snorkeling in the crystal-clear rivers around Bonito and Bom Jardim and seeing some of the Pantanal's most famous (and tastiest!) fish: pintados, pacus and dourados.

You can also go snorkeling on boat excursions from Morro de São Paulo (p434) and **Parque Nacional Marinho de Abrolhos** in Bahia (p457), and Maceió (p470) and Maragogi (p480) in Alagoas.

Rock Climbing

Climbing in Brazil is best in the cooler, drier months, from April to October. Brazil has lots of fantastic climbs, ranging from beginner level to routes yet to be conquered. Rio de Janeiro is the hub of Brazilian climbing, with some 350 documented climbs within an hour's drive of the city. You can even climb inside the city limits. The ascent up Pão de Açúcar has dozens of routes, from easy to quite challenging. Rio is also the best place to set up a climb if you're heading further afield.

Other places famous for rock climbing:

Parque Nacional Serra dos Órgãos, Rio de Janeiro state (p151) A rock-climber's paradise with scores of great climbs, including a grade III ascent up the iconic Dedo do Deus (God's Finger).

Pedra Azul, Espírito Santo (p220) The state's best rock climbing. One of the best views around is on a climb up this magnificent rock face (which is best followed by a refreshing dip in one of the state park's natural pools).

Parque Nacional do Itatiaia, Rio de Janeiro state (p146) Offers some memorable climbs including thrilling ascents up Agulhas Negras, the park's highest peak.

Parque Nacional de Caparaó, Minas Gerais (p211)Home to some of Brazil's tallest mountains, this park is a major draw for climbers from near and far.

Kayaking & Canoeing

There are some great places to get out on the water, paddle in hand, and take in the Brazilian landscape. Foremost among them is the Amazon, where you can go canoeing through the flooded forest and winding *igarapés* (creek or small river in the Amazon). You can also go kayaking off Ilha Grande and Paraty in Rio de Janeiro state, on excursions in the Pantanal, and from Itacaré and other beach destinations in the Northeast.

Other destinations include the following:

Lagoa de Guarairas, near Praia da Pipa (p527) There's fine kayaking through the mangroves.

Lagoa da Conceição, Ilha de Santa Catarina (p301) Serene kayaking spots.

Morretes, Paraná (p274) This river town is another fine destination for kayakers, and is also the departure point for a fun cheap outing by inner tube along the Rio Nhundiaquara.

Parque Nacional do Iguaçu (p282) While there are many activities you can do in the Parque Nacional do Iguaçu, one of the best ways to spend a sun-drenched afternoon is taking in the tranquil forested scenery on a paddling excursion on a peaceful lagoon, like those off the Trilha das Bananeiras (p291).

Hang Gliding & Paragliding

Rio de Janeiro (p79) is probably one of the world's most scenic places to go hang gliding, offering memorable tandem flights over tropical rainforest with views of the beach and island-filled ocean in the distance. Another place you can do tandem hang gliding is Rio da Barra, near Trancoso in Bahia.

Paragliding *(parapente)* can also be arranged in Rio, as well as in the northeast, over the red cliffs and brilliant sea of Canoa Quebrada.

Horseback Riding

In Minas Gerais you can ride stretches of the old gold road, the Estrada Real, or take a five-day horse trek from the state capital, Belo Horizonte, to its most famous historic town, Ouro Prêto. Many guesthouses in the Pantanal also offer horseback rides – a fine way to see even more wildlife while exploring this biologically rich (but vast) region.

Other memorable destinations for rides include the following:

Pedra Azul, Espírito Santo (p220) Take in the dramatic play of light on this massive outcropping while riding on one-of-a-kind Fjorde horses from Norway.

LAZYLLAMA/SHUTTERSTOCK ©

Hang gliding, Parque Nacional da Tijuca (p64)

Paraty, Rio de Janeiro state (p142) The best place to arrange a ride taking in lush rainforests, villages and a waterfall or two.

Cambará do Sul, Rio Grande do Sul (p329) Take in the stunning vistas inside the Cânion Pedra do Segredo on a ride in Brazil's cowboy-loving south.

Lençóis, Bahia (p458) Magnificent rides amid the forests and mountains of Chapada Diamantina. Serious riders can even arrange multiday excursions.

Fishing

Fishing in the interior of Brazil is fantastic. The Rio Araguaia in Goiás and Tocantins states is known as a fishing paradise with a large variety of fish, including the pintado, dourado and the legendary *tucunaré* (peacock bass) – which unfortunately is heavily fished and faces declining numbers. Fishing for piranha is not undertaken by serious anglers, though is good fun. Fishing is brilliant in the Pantanal too, and is allowed from February to October.

Plan Your Trip

Eat & Drink Like a Local

Rank it up there with *festas* (parties) and *futebol* (football): dining is one of life's great pleasures for Brazilians. No matter the setting – juice counter, produce market, neighborhood bar or high-end restaurant – Brazilians have a wealth of culinary temptations. Every region has its specialties, though there are many crowd-pleasers found all across the country.

Top Brazilian Dishes

Feijoada completa

Plan for a long, digestive nap after indulging in this rich stew of black beans mixed with pork and beef. It's served with rice, crunchy pork cracklings, fresh shredded kale, fluffy *farofa* (toasted cassava flour) and orange slices, which are meant to 'cut through the calories' and aid in digestion.

Moqueca

A rich seafood stew with coconut milk, tomatoes, onions, cilantro and *dendê* (palm) oil. Served with *peixe* (fish), *camarão* (shrimp) or a combination of the two.

Picanha

Brazil's favorite cut of beef comes from the cow's rump; it's eaten pinkish, salty and fresh from the grill. One worth waiting for at the *churrascaria* (traditional barbecue restaurant).

Vatapá

An Afro-Brazilian puree of dried smoked shrimp, ground peanuts (and sometimes cashews), *malagueta* peppers, ginger, coconut milk and *dendê* oil.

Food Experiences

Meals of a Lifetime

Maní (p246) A São Paulo stunner – and one of the country's best restaurants.

Taypá (p347) Fabulous upscale Peruvian cooking in Brazil's futuristic capital.

Ostradamus (p303) Beautiful Ilha de Santa Catarina waterfront setting matched by some of the country's best seafood.

Flor do Luar (p622) Fantastic Amazonian cuisine, best followed with a swim off the dock.

Rocka Beach Lounge (p168) A beachside icon in Búzios with a creative, seafood-accented menu.

Cruzeiro do Pescador (p528) One-of-a-kind dining experience complete with garden-grown produce and plenty of culinary creativity.

Cheap Treats

Acarajé Made of mashed then deep-fried black-eyed peas and topped with dried shrimp, these Bahian fritters make a delectable street snack.

Agua de coco Coconut water, sometimes served straight from the nut. The perfect refreshment after a day on the beach.

Açaí This addictive, deep-purple, vitamin-rich berry from the Amazon is a staple of both Tupi people and Brazilian bodybuilders.

Sucos Apart from açaí, there's a staggering variety of juices and combinations on offer at Brazil's ubiquitous juice bars.

Petiscos Appetizers that come in many varieties, from *pasteis* (fried pastries stuffed with shrimp, cheese and other goodies) to *bolinhos de bacalhau* (codfish balls).

Tapioca A mixture of cassava flour and shredded coconut, fried into a kind of crepe that's then filled with savory or sweet ingredients.

Dare to Try

Tacacá Soup popular in the Amazon region with dried shrimp, juice from the *tucupí* (a manioc root) and lip-tingling jambu leaves.

Camarão na moranga Shrimp in a creamy sauce that's baked inside a pumpkin.

Tutu à mineira A classic from Minas Gerais featuring mashed beans often served with sausage or salt-dried beef.

Vitamina de abacate Pureed avocado with milk, served milkshake-style at most juice bars.

Siri recheado A crabmeat mixture with onions, tomatoes, cilantro and peppers served in empty crab shells.

Agulhas fritas Small needlefish served fried; a popular bar snack all along the coast.

Bacalhau à bras A Portuguese dish featuring shredded salted codfish mixed with scrambled eggs and shoestring potatoes.

Cabrito assado Roasted kid (goat).

Rabada ensopada Oxtail stew.

Cupim The tender prized meat from the hump of a *zebu* (Brahma steer); available at top-end *churrascarias* (grilled barbecue restaurants).

Carangueijo à marajoara A dish from Marajó Island, consisting of crabmeat in a sauce of tomato and coconut, served with spices.

Local Specialties

Food

Bahia & the Northeast

Bahian cuisine was developed by enslaved peoples toiling in the region's sugar plantations. The African origins appear in dishes such as *moqueca,* a delicious seafood stew with coconut milk; spicy *malagueta* peppers; and *dendê* (palm) oil. On the streets of Bahia you can't escape the smell of *acarajé* (fritters made with black-eyed peas and shrimp fried in *dendê* oil).

BONCHAN/GETTY IMAGES ©

Moqueca (seafood stew)

By contrast, drier inland areas of the Northeast known as the Sertão produce *carne seca* or *carne de sol,* beef that has been salted and dried. Squash, which manages to survive in difficult growing conditions, is also very popular.

The Amazon

Amazonian cuisine is strongly influenced by the region's native Tupi people, who live largely on manioc, freshwater fish, yams and beans, and fruit. *Caldeirada* is a popular fish stew not unlike bouillabaisse, and *pato no tucupí* is a regional favorite made with duck, garlic, lip-tingling *jambú* leaves and the juice of both lemons and manioc roots. Fish like *tambaquí* and *pirarucú* are technically protected species, but those you see on menus come from fish farms – so you can safely order them without worry of contributing to their decline.

MENU DECODER

Ao vapor Steamed

Cardápio Menu

Cozido Boiled

Cru Raw

Entrada starter or appetizer

Especialidade local Local specialty

Frito Fried

Grelhado Grilled

Lista de bebidas Drinks list

Na brasa Broiled

Petiscos Snacks or appetizers

Prato do dia (or prato feito) Dish of the day

Prato principal Main course

Salada Salad

Sobremesa Dessert

Sopa Soup

The Central West

Occupying the prairie-like *cerrado,* the Central West is dominated by sprawling *fazendas* (ranches) that produce pork and beef, as well as staples such as corn, rice, kale and manioc. The region's rivers offer up the meaty dourado fish, the pintado (a type of catfish) and the infamous piranha. The Pantanal is also a goldmine for fish lovers with outstanding pintado and pacú. Unfortunately, overfishing has led to a decline in all of these fish species, though none are currently listed as threatened in the Central West.

Rio, São Paulo & the Southeast

Rio offers excellent food from every region. Feijoada, a bean-and-meat stew served with rice, farofa (toasted cassava flour), kale and sliced orange, is the city's contribution to the national cuisine. It is traditionally served on Saturday.

São Paulo, the gastronomic capital of Brazil, has both Michelin-starred dining rooms and humble ethnic restaurants that reflect the city's many immigrant communities. You'll find outstanding Japanese, Lebanese and Italian food, and the wood-fired pizza is world class.

In the mountainous state of Minas Gerais, pork is popular, as is the kale-like *couve,* which is sautéed in oil with garlic and onions. *Frango ao molho pardo* (chicken stewed in its own blood with vegetables) sounds gruesome but tastes delicious.

The South

Italian and German food rules the day in the South. Expect to see lots of sausage and sauerkraut in the German enclaves of Joinville and Blumenau. Brazilian wine, the quality of which improves year by year, comes from grapes lovingly imported from Italy and planted in the accommodating soil of Rio Grande do Sul.

The far south is *gaúcho* (Brazilian cowboy) country, and grilled-beef restaurants are excellent here. The region preserves another cowboy tradition – *erva maté* (a tea-like beverage).

Pan-Brazilian Fusion

Like much of the world, Brazil has undergone a kind of culinary renaissance in the last decade. One result has been a new, high-end, pan-Brazilian fusion cuisine, which showcases native ingredients, from the Amazonian fruits of the north to the grass-fed beef of the south. In major cities, you can find unique combinations that fuse Brazilian elements with Asian, French, Italian and other Latin American recipes.

Drinks

Brazilians love to drink – and by that we don't just mean alcohol. The juice bar is a Brazilian institution, and you can try a wide range of varieties, including plenty of flavors rarely found outside of Brazil.

Juices

Brazilian *sucos* (juices) are divine. Staples include known quantities such as mango, orange, papaya, banana, passion fruit, watermelon and avocado. Then there are the Amazonian fruits like açaí, *graviola* (custard apple), *cupuaçu* (pear-like fruit) and *fruta do conde* (sugar-apple fruit).

Fresh *agua de côco* (coconut juice) is available across the country and is highly recommended.

REBECA MELLO/GETTY IMAGES ©

Bolinhos de bacalhau (codfish balls)

Cocktails

The caipirinha is the unofficial Brazilian national drink. Ingredients are simple – *cachaça* (a high-proof sugarcane alcohol) with crushed lime, sugar and ice – but the results are sublime. You can replace the *cachaça* with vodka (to make a caipirosca) or sake (to create caipisakes) and the lime with a variety of fruit, including passion fruit, pineapple, mango, kiwi or the cherry-like *pitanga*.

Beer

Brazilians enjoy their beer served *bem gelada* (icy cold). Bohemia and Original are among the best national brands, though there are a growing number of (better) microbrews, including Jeffrey from Rio, Dogma from São Paulo and Seasons from Rio Grande do Sul.

Chope (sho-pee) is a pale-blond pilsner draft that's lighter and generally superior to mainstream canned or bottled beers.

Coffee, Maté & Guaraná

Brazil produces some exceptional coffees, and premium single-origin roasts are at long last available in some specialty coffeehouses in São Paulo, Rio and some other big cities. Espresso is also widely available in more upscale establishments, and just about everywhere in São Paulo, which boasts a highly evolved coffee culture (chalk it up to the influence of Italian immigrants).

Brazilians traditionally prefer their coffee to be quite strong, near boiling hot and 'as sweet as love.' In the morning they take it with milk (*café com leite*). For the rest of the day, it's *cafezinhos,* regular coffee served either in a drinking glass or an espresso-sized coffee cup and often presweetened. It is sold in stand-up bars, and dispensed free in large thermoses in restaurants, at hotel reception desks and in offices to keep the general population perky the whole day through.

A good cup of tea is harder to come by, but *erva maté* (called simply *maté*) is a potential alternative. It's available throughout the country and is usually served cold and cloyingly sweet. Only in the state of Rio Grande do Sul is it drunk hot.

Made from an Amazonian berry, guaraná 'champagne' rivals Coca Cola as

IVANMATEEV/GETTY IMAGES ©

Caipirinha cocktail

Brazil's favorite soft drink. It's served cold, carbonated and sweet, and it's reputed to have all sorts of health-giving properties.

How to Eat & Drink

When to Eat

Café da manhã (breakfast) Breakfast is typically a minimal affair. Brazilians tend to have a small *café* (coffee) with milk and a sweet or savory baked good. Juice bars are extremely popular spots to grab a bite to start off the day.

Almoço (lunch) The noontime meal has traditionally been one of the biggest of the day, though on weekdays, locals might just grab something light. Those with a bigger appetite might opt for a *prato feito,* an inexpensive and filling plate of rice, beans and chicken, steak, pork or fish. Many higher-end restaurants serve an *almoço executivo* (executive lunch), which features one or two different dishes at more affordable prices than during the evening. For variety, the *por quilo* (per kilo) restaurant is a Brazilian institution. At these self-serve buffet-style places, you can sample salads, cooked dishes, fresh grilled meats, sushi and desserts. After a plate is loaded up with food, it's weighed, and patrons are charged by the gram.

Lanche (late-afternoon or evening snack) When hunger strikes in the late afternoon – perhaps after a day on the beach – Brazilians head to juice bars for a *suco* (juice) and a *salgado* (savory snack), such as *pão de queijo* (cheese bread), *empada de camarão* (shrimp pasty) or *kibe* (a deep-fried whole-wheat snack with ground beef in the center). Snacking is perfectly acceptable at any time of the day or night, as is a quick *cafezinho* (sweetened strong espresso-sized coffee).

Jantar (dinner) Evening meals are often a big event, at least in urban areas, and provide opportunities to linger over multiple courses. Standard dining times are between 7pm and 10pm, though some places open at 6pm (and busier places stay open right through the day from around noon to 10pm or later).

Where to Eat

Lanchonete Snack bar or diner-style eatery for a casual meal; one step up from fast food.

Bar Drinking places nearly always serve food, and the range of bar snacks can be quite extensive (though it usually entails plenty of fried fare).

Botequim Brazilian-style pub where friends gather over ice-cold beer and filling snacks and meals.

Por kilo restaurante The pay-by-weight restaurant typically charges from R$45 to R$80 per kilogram. Offerings generally include fresh salads and veggies, rice, beans, grilled meat and fish, plus regional specialties.

Churrascaria Restaurant specializing in grilled meats. These are usually all-the-meat-you-can-eat experiences, with the food served *rodízio*-style, meaning servers make the rounds through the restaurant bringing fresh cuts to your table. Experienced diners decline all but the best selections.

Rodízios Restaurants serving pizza and *massa* (pasta) are also popular, and *rodízio*-style means the cooks whip a variety of dishes, which are served as they come out of the oven.

Plan Your Trip

Travel with Children

Long distances in Brazil can make family travel challenging, but the rewards are considerable: endless fun on sun-kissed beaches, walks in rainforests, boat and train rides, and abundant wildlife-watching opportunities. Best of all is the warm reception from Brazilians themselves – who go out of their way to make kids feel welcome.

Brazil for Kids

Brazil is a family-friendly country that has a wide range of attractions for kids. Travelling with kids does require some advance planning, but most Brazilians will do their best to make sure they are well looked after.

Eating Out

Dining out isn't usually a problem, even for fussy eaters. Ubiquitous *por-kilo* (per kilogram; self-serve restaurants that sell food by weight) places are a good place for a meal: children will have a huge range of options, and you can get in and out without a lot of fuss. Familiar food – pizza, burgers, ice cream – is widely available, and sometimes takes fun new forms (pizza with chocolate, or with bananas and cinnamon). Food courts in shopping malls are excellent spots for quick meals.

Juice bars are handy for snack breaks. At these ubiquitous spots, you can order dozens of tangy juices, as well as grilled burgers, sandwiches, *pão de queijo* (cheese-filled bread) and other bites.

Most sit-down restaurants will have a *cadeira alta* (high chair), though few have menus for kids. Portions, however, are huge, so kids can share what their parents order. Bring crayons, paper or other amusement, as Brazilian restaurants don't provide them.

Best Regions for Kids

Rio de Janeiro state

Funicular rides and scenic views in Rio city, island-exploring on vehicle-free Ilha Grande, wandering cobblestone streets and taking schooner cruises off Paraty. You can even get a taste of mountain scenery in Parque Nacional do Itatiaia, and visit imperial sites in Petrópolis.

Minas Gerais

Time-travel to the 18th century in the colonial mountain town of Ouro Preto, which is near an old gold mine you can visit. You can also ride an old steam train from São João del Rei to Tiradentes. Don't miss the Santuário do Caraça to swims in waterfalls and see the maned wolf come in at night.

Bahia

Lots of great food, music and street entertainment in Salvador. Catch the hydrofoil to car-free Morro de São Paulo for pretty beaches, a zip line and panoramic views from a hilltop lighthouse. Head inland for the canyons, waterfalls and swimming holes of Parque Nacional da Chapada Diamantina.

Transportation

Given the great size of Brazil, transport presents challenges. You'll either spend long hours on buses or have to rely on pricier flights. Sticking to one or two regions is the best way to keep your holiday hassle-free. Renting a car can save you cash and help you move about more efficiently (though you'll need to bring your own car seats).

Children typically fly free or pay half-fare for flights if under two, and pay 10% to 25% of the fare if age two to 12. On buses, it's all or nothing: they ride free if sitting on a lap and full fare if they take up a seat.

Children's Highlights

The Coast

Ilha Grande, Rio de Janeiro state (p129)A tropical rainforest-covered island, an old abandoned prison, boat trips, snorkeling, lovely beaches, howler monkeys – and all of it completely free from traffic.

Balneário Camboriú Santa Catarina (p310)This resort town has many attractions , including an aerial tram, beaches and a roller coaster, all close to the Beto Carrero World (p311) amusement park.

Arraial d'Ajuda, Bahia (p450)This low-key town for beach lovers has the usual coastal attractions, plus you can rent a buggy for exploring sandy coastal paths around the area.

The Jungle

Foz do Iguaçu & Around, Paraná (p282)The thundering waterfalls are quite family friendly, with discount entry for kids and various wildlife adventures and boating activities. Kids stay and eat free all over town.

Serra Verde Express, Paraná (p275) This memorable train ride traverses lush forests with sweeping views down to the coast.

JUNGLE LODGES

Many jungle lodges near Manaus offer fairly low-impact excursions, making them good for families with kids. High-water season may be best, as you do more canoeing than hiking. Black-water areas have far fewer mosquitoes and much lower risk of malaria.

Bonito, Mato Grosso do Sul (p393)Bonito has caves, lush rainforests, treetop canopy walks and crystal-clear rivers that you snorkel down.

Nature & Wildlife Encounters

Parque Lage, Rio de Janeiro (p65) This lush space in Rio has short walking trails, plus a playground, a small fishpond and a good outdoor cafe; it's also a great spot to see monkeys.

Pousada Santuário do Caraça, Minas Gerais (p211) Watching wolves arrive for a nightly feeding in an enchanting corner of southeastern Brazil.

Pantanal Nature, Cuiabá (p379) Spying monkeys, caiman, macaws and loads of other wildlife with this top-notch operator that offers special family trips.

Planning

For general information and advice on traveling with young ones, check out Lonely Planet's *Travel with Children.*

When to Go

To beat the worst of the crowds, but still enjoy warm beach weather, plan on coming from November through January or late March and April.

What to Bring

- If renting a car, bring your own car seats as availability is unreliable with most rental agencies.
- Diapers (nappies) are widely available in Brazil. You may not easily find creams, baby foods or familiar medicines outside larger cities. Bring insect repellent, sunscreen and other essentials, as prices for these items are much higher here.
- Baby food is available in most supermarkets.

Accommodations

Children under five typically stay free, while under 12s often pay half-price. Cribs (cots) are not always available, so have an alternative plan before arriving. Babysitters are readily available in most hotels.

Health & Safety

For trips outside of the main coastal cities, enquire about vaccines and antimalarial medications (particularly for the Amazon).

Regions at a Glance

The great challenge of Brazil, with its vast size and incredible diversity, is deciding where to go. Rio figures high on most itineraries, with nightlife, beaches and scenery. Tropical islands and the historic colonial towns of Minas Gerais lie nearby. The Northeast offers a mix of picturesque towns, beaches and outdoor adventures, and its vibrant cities (Salvador, Olinda) offer a window into rich Afro-Brazilian culture. The South, meanwhile, has notable European influence (Oktoberfest, vineyards, mountain towns) and stellar highlights such as Iguaçu falls and the Ilha de Santa Catarina. For outstanding wildlife-watching, visit the Pantanal (Cuiabá in Mato Grosso is a major gateway) and the Amazon. Other Brazilian hits include modernist architecture in Brasília, otherworldly dune landscapes in Maranhão, and the jaw-dropping island beauty of Fernando de Noronha.

Rio de Janeiro

Scenery
Nightlife
Culture

Mountains & Beaches

Rainforest-covered peaks, sparkling beaches and an island-dotted coastline – Rio's setting is breathtaking, especially when viewed from panoramic heights atop Corcovado or Pão de Açúcar.

Sounds of Samba

Rio's dizzying nightlife includes open-air bars, stylish nightclubs and old-school dance halls dominated by the addictive rhythms of samba.

Historic Treasures

At first glance, Rio's downtown is a bustling hive of commerce. Look deeper, though, to discover surprising landmarks including 18th-century baroque churches, a former royal palace and an extravagant opera house.

p60

Rio de Janeiro State

Beaches
Outdoor Adventure
History

Sun, Surf & Sand

For easy access to dreamy beaches, Rio state is as good as it gets, from gleaming white dunes to island-studded bays backed by jungle-clad mountains.

Hiking & Climbing Paradise

The crags of Itatiaia and the Serra dos Órgãos are the twin capitals of Brazilian rock climbing; meanwhile hikers thrill to the trails of Serra da Bocaina and Ilha Grande.

The Golden Road & Imperial Past

Near Paraty, the Caminho do Ouro once brought gold from Minas Gerais, while Dom Pedro II's Petrópolis palace was the 19th-century seat of Brazilian power.

p128

Minas Gerais & Espírito Santo

History
Food
Outdoors

Baroque Grandeur

With an incredible density of historical monuments, Minas' historic towns are showcases for the uniquely Brazilian baroque style.

A Bountiful Feast

From Espírito Santo's delectable seafood stews to Minas' hearty wood-fired ranch fare, this is foodie paradise. Don't forget the obligatory shot of smooth Minas *cachaça*, Brazil's best.

Wildlife & Waterfalls

With natural pools and waterfalls, Minas' cerrado ecosystem is a hiker's dream. To the east, awe-inspiring mountains rise up, and patches of Atlantic rainforest shelter endangered woolly spider monkeys.

p170

São Paulo State

Food & Drink
Beaches
Landscapes

Culinary Powerhouse

São Paulo city holds its own with any gastronomic capital in the southern hemisphere. Cutting-edge Brazilian chefs such as Alex Atala (D.O.M.) and Helena Rizzo (Maní) have received worldwide acclaim.

The Green Coast

From the rainforest-lined coast of Ubatuba to the sophisticated getaway of Ilhabela, São Paulo's coastline is part of Brazil's Costa Verde (Green Coast), a world-class stretch of postcard-perfect beaches and islands.

Scenic Setting

Wide swaths of Mata Atlântica rainforest, modest but wonderful Serra de Mantiqueira peaks and sun-kissed sands: São Paulo is easy on the eyes.

p222

Paraná

Scenery
Nature
Architecture

Photogenic Panoramas

Besides the spectacular Iguaçu Falls, splendid scenery awaits elsewhere, most notably on the car-free island of Ilha do Mel, and the superb Serra Verde Express train, which snakes past lush mountains from Curitiba to the historic town of Morretes.

Waterfalls, Islands & Rainforest

Iguaçu Falls offers impressive hiking and adventure excursions amid subtropical rainforest, while isolated Parque Nacional do Superagüi and Parque Estadual Marumbi boast abundant bird and plant life.

A Complex Past

Morretes, Paranaguá and Curitiba's Largo da Ordem are cobblestoned glimpses into Brazil's colonial past.

p268

Santa Catarina

Beaches
Culture
Microbreweries

Seductive Shorelines

Whether you seek solitude, surf or socializing, Santa Catarina has the sands for you. The state has outstanding surfing, laid-back fishing villages and sophisticated resort towns.

European History

Nowhere is Brazil's rich melting pot more evident than Santa Catarina's interior, where German architecture, Italian food and distinctly European faces will leave you wondering if you've left the country.

Brew Culture

Brazil's best microbrews hail from Blumenau and its environs, offering the chance to sample beers unavailable in most other parts of the country.

p292

Rio Grande do Sul

Landscapes
Wine Tasting
Culture

Canyonlands

Parque Nacional de Aparados da Serra and Parque Nacional da Serra Geral offer southern Brazil's most striking landscape. Magnificent deep-cutting canyons have earned the region the nickname of the 'Brazilian Grand Canyon.'

Venerable Vineyards

Around 90% of Brazilian wine comes from the Vale dos Vinhedos, a little touch of Tuscany in the heart of Cowboy Country that defies notions of typical Brazil.

Gaúcho Traditions

With its *chimarrão* (*maté* tea), *churrasco* (grilled meat) and traditional Farroupilha dress, Rio Grande do Sul's *gaúcho* (cowboy) culture lives on in this unique region.

p314

Brasília & Goiás

Architecture
Scenery
Culture

A Capital Idea

Niemeyer's genius proved that a little concrete and a creative mind were all that was needed to make Brasília a must-see for building buffs.

Striking Panoramas

The breathakingly beautiful cerrado (savanna) is the perfect frame for heavenly sunsets on the *planalto* (plateau), especially at the otherworldly Vale da Lua in the Chapada dos Veadeiros.

Medieval Mischief

Pirenópolis converts itself from a kooky artist's enclave into a center of historical re-creation, as the town goes medieval during the Festa do Divino Espírito Santo (Cavalhadas).

p334

Mato Grosso & Mato Grosso do Sul

Aquatic Adventure
Wildlife-Watching
Fishing

Surreal Snorkeling

Squeeze into your wetsuit and let the current take you on a fish-watching adventure in the aquatic playgrounds of Bonito and Nobres.

Animal Encounters

The Pantanal has incredible wildlife-watching, with capybaras, anacondas, macaws, capuchins, giant river otters and even jaguars among the many species to see.

Catch Your Dinner

Sling your hook for some of the world's best fishing in the waterways of Mato Grosso and maybe pick up a pacu!

p362

Bahia

Beaches
Outdoor Adventure
Culture

Bahian Beauty

Featuring more than 900km of coastline, the state of Bahia is renowned for its gorgeous beaches, idyllic island getaways and surfing hot spots.

Hiking & Trekking

Head inland to see one of Brazil's finest national parks, Chapada Diamantina, which has great hiking and trekking, plus waterfalls, natural swimming holes and other idyllic spots to cool off.

Afro-Brazilian Star

Salvador is the center of Afro-Brazilian culture: capoeira and Candomblé, glittering churches, and pounding drums on cobblestone streets. Nearby Cachoeira is renowned for its woodcarving traditions.

p400

Sergipe & Alagoas

Scenery
History
Seafood

Coastal Allure

Alagoas' star attraction is its coastline, with its white-sand beaches and aquamarine waters. Top picks include Praia do Francês, Praia do Gunga and buzzing Maceió. The Galés marine reserve off the coast of Maragogi is a favorite for snorkelers.

Colonial Remnants

These neighboring states have a number of colonial highlights, including the grand churches of historic Penedo, cobblestone Laranjeiras and hilltop São Cristóvão.

Dining & Dancing

Seafood lovers won't want to miss the open-air restaurants of Aracaju, which specialize in fresh crabs; many also serve up live *forró* music, which makes a great ending to a crab feast.

p464

Pernambuco, Paraíba & Rio Grande do Norte

Beaches
Festivals
Outdoor Activities

Endless Sands

The 1000km coast curving round Brazil's northeastern corner has seemingly endless sands fronting tropical waters. Bask on the beach, sip coconuts and enjoy great meals in laid-back beach bars.

Carnaval, Northeastern Style

During Carnaval, head to Recife and Olinda for their euphoric explosions of color, music and fun.

Shoreline Adventures

This is the place for swimming, snorkeling, surfing, kitesurfing or buggy-riding. Fernando de Noronha, an archipelago getaway 350km offshore, has Brazil's best diving.

p482

Ceará, Piauí & Maranhão

Scenery
Outdoor Activities
Cities & Towns

Dunes & Bays

The setting is spectacular: a sequence of long, dune-backed sweeps and small, palm-lined bays all along the tropical shoreline. There's also the unique dune-and-lagoon mosaic of the Lençóis Maranhenses.

Sun-Drenched Adventures

You can do most things you've dreamed of in, on and beside the water, with steady winds providing some of the world's best conditions for kitesurfing.

Coastal Enclaves

Hang out at legendary Jericoacoara, enjoy the urban vibes of Fortaleza or head to end-of-road beach villages like Atins or Icaraí de Amontada for a tropical escape.

p532

The Amazon

Wildlife-Watching
Adventure
Culture

Biodiversity Hot Spot

The Amazon is a fabled setting for wildlife-watching. You can stay in upscale rainforest resorts or community-run ecotourism outfits, both great bases for seeing wildlife.

Rainforest Experiences

The world's greatest rainforest offers memorable adventures, from tree-climbs through dense canopy, to silent canoe paddles across flooded forest. You can also take multiday boat trips between towns.

Amazonian Riches

Belém and Manaus are the best places to sample Amazonian cuisine, hear unique musical styles and browse colorful markets. There are even beach towns in the interior and on the coast.

p568

On the Road

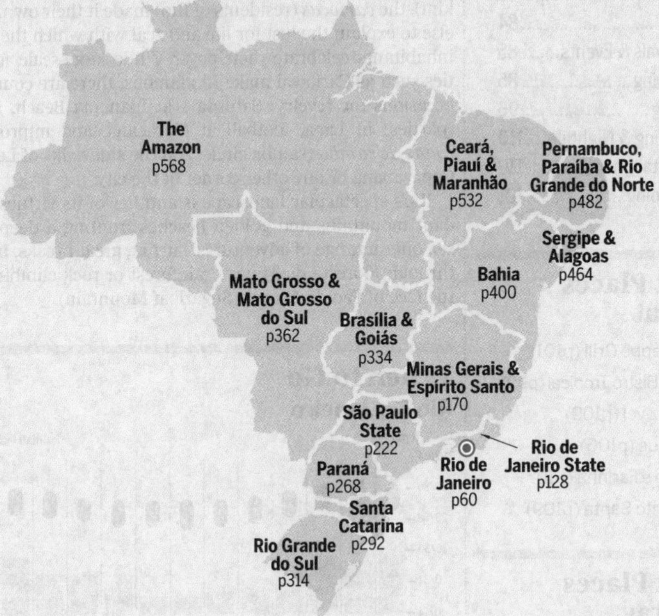

The Amazon p568

Ceará, Piauí & Maranhão p532

Pernambuco, Paraíba & Rio Grande do Norte p482

Sergipe & Alagoas p464

Bahia p400

Mato Grosso & Mato Grosso do Sul p362

Brasília & Goiás p334

Minas Gerais & Espírito Santo p170

São Paulo State p222

Rio de Janeiro State p128

Paraná p268

Rio de Janeiro p60

Santa Catarina p292

Rio Grande do Sul p314

Rio de Janeiro

☎21 / POP 6.5 MILLION

Includes ➡

History 61
Sights 61
Activities 78
Courses 83
Tours 84
Festivals & Events 85
Sleeping 85
Eating 96
Drinking & Nightlife 110
Entertainment 119
Shopping 121

Best Places to Eat

- ➡ Giuseppe Grill (p101)
- ➡ Zazá Bistrô Tropical (p99)
- ➡ Aprazível (p109)
- ➡ Oteque (p106)
- ➡ Ferro e Farinha (p107)
- ➡ Espírito Santa (p109)

Best Places to Stay

- ➡ Casa Beleza (p95)
- ➡ Hotel Santa Teresa (p96)
- ➡ Pouso Verde (p89)
- ➡ Maze Inn (p91)
- ➡ Belmond Copacabana Palace (p90)

Why Go?

Planted between lush, forest-covered mountains and breathtaking beaches, the *Cidade Maravilhosa* (Marvelous City) has many charms at its disposal.

Although joie de vivre is a French invention (as is the bikini), the *cariocas* (residents of Rio) made it their own. How else to explain the lust for life and zeal with which the city's inhabitants celebrate their days? While large-scale festivities such as Carnaval make Rio famous, there are countless occasions for revelry: Saturdays at Ipanema Beach, *festas* (parties) in Lapa, football at Maracanã, and impromptu *rodas de samba* (samba circles) on the sidewalks of Leblon, Copacabana or any other corner of the city.

Rio's spectacular landscape is another of its virtues. Verdant mountains and golden beaches fronting a deep blue sea offer a range of adventures: surfing great breaks, hiking through Floresta da Tijuca's rainforest or rock climbing up the face of Pão de Açúcar (Sugarloaf Mountain).

When to Go

Rio De Janeiro

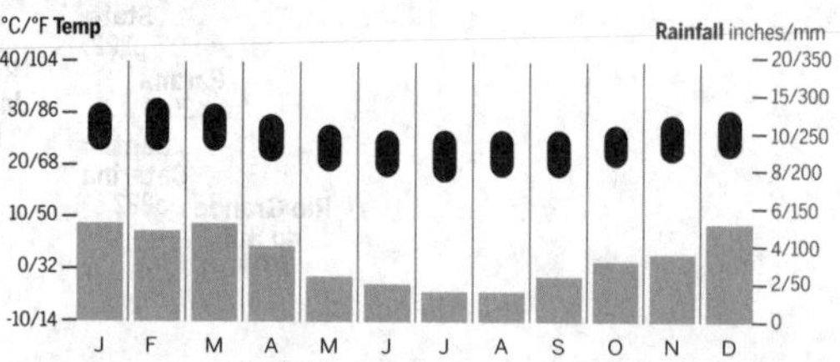

Dec–Feb Steamy beach days and a packed festival calendar, including the Carnaval buildup.

Apr & May Cooler but sunny days, fewer crowds and lower prices.

Jun Low season, lower temperatures and sometimes misty days, but great lodging discounts.

History

Portuguese explorer Gonçalo Coelho was the first European to land in Rio. In January 1502 he entered a huge bay, which he allegedly mistook for a river, thus bequeathing the future city its lasting moniker. Portuguese settlement proceeded in fits and starts, but by the 17th century Rio was Brazil's third-most important settlement (after Salvador da Bahia and Recife-Olinda). African slaves streamed in and the sugar plantations thrived. Even more slaves were brought in to work in the gold mines of Minas Gerais during the 18th century.

In 1807 the Portuguese prince regent (later known as Dom João VI) and his entire court of 15,000 set sail for Brazil to escape the impending invasion of Napoleon Bonaparte.

Dom João fell in love with Brazil. He declared Rio the capital of the United Kingdom of Portugal, Brazil and the Algarve, and became the only European monarch to rule from a New World colony.

At the end of the 19th century the city's population exploded as a result of European immigration and internal migration (mostly of ex-slaves from the declining coffee and sugar regions).

The early 1920s to the late 1950s were Rio's golden age. With the inauguration of the grand hotels, Rio became a romantic, exotic destination for Hollywood celebrities and high society.

During the 1960s, modern skyscrapers rose in the city, and some of Rio's most beautiful buildings were lost. During the same period, the favelas (slums, informal communities) of Rio grew to critical mass, with immigrants from poverty-stricken areas of the Northeast swelling the number of Rio's urban poor. The Cidade Maravilhosa began to lose its gloss as crime and violence increased.

As Rio entered the new millennium, social problems continued to plague the city, with violence claiming thousands of lives – particularly in the favelas. Rio's middle and upper classes seemed mostly resigned to life behind gated and guarded condos, while poverty and violence surged in communities nearby.

In the buildup to the 2014 World Cup and 2016 Summer Olympics, large investments have been used to revitalize Rio's waterfront port, vastly expand its metro system and create new museums and cultural spaces around town. Unfortunately, the post-Olympic crash hit hard, bringing a flailing economy and surging unemployment in its wake.

Sights

Rio has much more than just pretty beaches. From the bohemian lanes of old Santa Teresa to the village charm of Urca, Rio's colonial streets, magnificent churches and leafy plazas provide urban wanderers with days of exploration.

Rio's historic center, its lake (Lagoa Rodrigo de Freitas), the lush Jardim Botânico (Botanical Gardens) and the Atlantic rainforest that trims many parts of the city make for some fascinating discovery. There are also fantastic overlooks from Pão de Açúcar and Cristo Redentor, tranquil islands in the bay, wildly beautiful beaches to the west, and vibrant markets, with vendors peddling everything from vintage samba recordings to tangy *jabuticaba* (a native fruit).

Ipanema & Leblon

Truly among the world's most enchanting addresses, Ipanema and Leblon are blessed with a magnificent beach, and open-air cafes, bars and restaurants scattered along tree-lined streets. Here you'll find a mix of wealthy *cariocas*, young and old, gay and straight.

★Ipanema Beach BEACH

(Map p66; Av Vieira Souto) One long stretch of sun-drenched sand, Ipanema Beach is demarcated by *postos* (posts), which mark off subcultures as diverse as the city itself. *Posto* 9, right off Rua Vinícius de Moraes, is where Rio's most lithe and tanned bodies migrate. The area is also known as Cemetério dos Elefantes because of the handful of old leftists, hippies and artists who sometimes hang out there. In front of Rua Farme de Amoedo is Praia Farme, the stomping ground for gay society.

Praia de Leblon BEACH

(Map p66; Av Delfim Moreira) Separated from Ipanema by the gardens and canal of Jardim de Alah, Leblon Beach attracts families and has a slightly more sedate vibe than its eastern counterpart. Parents with little ones may want to check out Baixo Bebê, between *postos* 11 and 12, where you'll find a small playground on the sand as well as other young families.

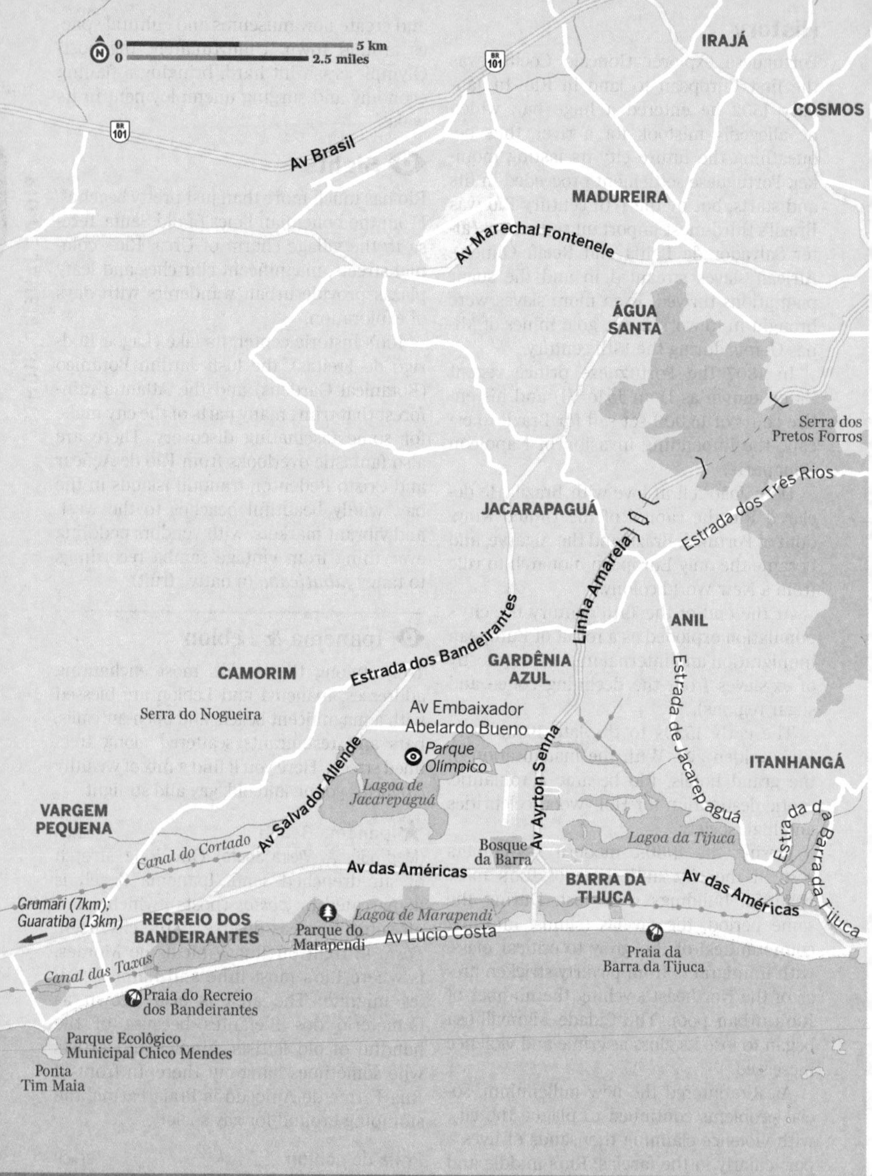

Rio de Janeiro Highlights

❶ **Copacabana Beach** (p65) Basking in the sunshine followed by drinks at an oceanfront kiosk.

❷ **Pão de Açúcar** (p67) Admiring the Cidade Maravilhosa from the craggy heights.

❸ **Ipanema Beach** (p61) Frolicking in the waves and watching the parade of passing people.

❹ **Cristo Redentor** (p68) Taking the cog train up Corcovado for stunning views beneath the open-armed statue of Christ the Redeemer.

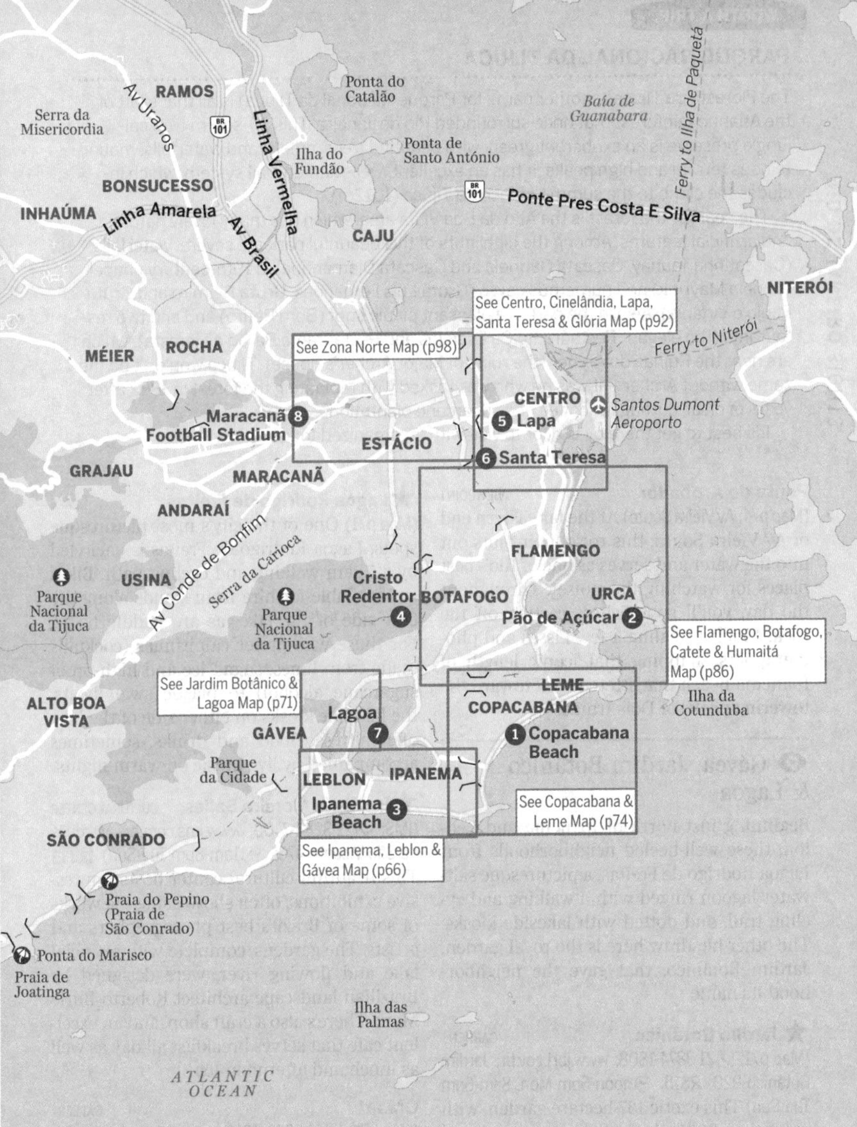

❺ **Lapa** (p76) Finding the perfect beat at a samba club in Brazil's most musically charged neighborhood.

❻ **Santa Teresa** (p73) Catching the *bonde* (cable car) up to Santa Teresa and taking a scenic stroll through this village-like neighborhood.

❼ **Lagoa** (p114) Taking a run or a spin around the pretty lagoon, followed by drinks at Palaphita Kitch on the waterfront.

❽ **Maracanã Football Stadium** (p77) Feeling the roar of the crowds inside this hallowed stadium.

WORTH A TRIP

PARQUE NACIONAL DA TIJUCA

The Floresta da Tijuca (another name for Parque Nacional da Tijuca) is all that's left of the Atlantic rainforest that once surrounded Rio de Janeiro. This 39-sq-km tropical-jungle preserve is an exuberant green, with beautiful trees, creeks and waterfalls, mountainous terrain and high peaks. It has an excellent, well-marked trail system, which includes the climb to the summit of Pico da Tijuca (1012m).

The heart of the forest is the Alto da Boa Vista area, which has many lovely natural and artificial features. Among the highlights of this beautiful park are several waterfalls (Cascatinha Taunay, Cascata Gabriela and Cascata Diamantina), a 19th-century chapel (Capela Mayrink) and numerous caves (Gruta Luís Fernandes, Gruta Belmiro and Gruta Paulo e Virgínia). Also in the park is a pleasant picnic spot (Bom Retiro) and and two restaurants (the elegant Restaurante Os Esquilos and Restaurante Barão a Floresta), which are near the Ruínas do Archer (the ruins of Major Archer's house). Tijuca wouldn't be the same without Archer – it was he who was tasked with replanting the forest in 1862 after years of clear-cutting for coffee and sugarcane plantations.

It's best to get there by taxi, or to visit with an organized tour.

Ponta do Arpoador VIEWPOINT

(Map p74; Av Vieira Souto) At the far eastern end of Av Vieira Souto, this rocky point juts out into the water and serves as one of Rio's best places for watching the sunset. Throughout the day, you'll spot fishers casting off the rock, couples stealing a few kisses and photographers snapping that iconic length of Ipanema Beach that stretches off toward the towering peaks of Dois Irmãos.

Gávea, Jardim Botânico & Lagoa

Beginning just north of Ipanema and Leblon, these well-heeled neighborhoods front Lagoa Rodrigo de Freitas, a picturesque saltwater lagoon ringed with a walking and cycling trail, and dotted with lakeside kiosks. The other big draw here is the royal garden, Jardim Botânico, that gave the neighborhood its name.

★Jardim Botânico GARDENS

(Map p71; 21 3874-1808; www.jbrj.gov.br; Jardim Botânico 920; R$15; noon-6pm Mon, 8am-6pm Tue-Sun) This exotic 137-hectare garden, with more than 8000 plant species, was designed by order of the Prince Regent Dom João (later to become Dom João VI) in 1808. The garden is quiet and serene on weekdays and blossoms with families on weekends. Highlights of a visit here include the row of palms (planted when the garden first opened), the Amazonas section, the lake containing the huge Vitória Régia water lilies and the enclosed **orquidário**, home to 600 species of orchids.

★Lagoa Rodrigo de Freitas LAKE

(Map p71) One of the city's most picturesque spots, Lagoa Rodrigo de Freitas is encircled by a 7.2km walking and cycling path. Bikes are available for hire from stands along the east side of the lake, as are paddle boats. For those who prefer caipirinhas (cocktails made from limes, sugar, ice and high-proof sugarcane alcohol) to plastic swan boats, the lakeside kiosks on either side of the lake offer alfresco food and drinks, sometimes accompanied by live music on warm nights.

★Instituto Moreira Salles CULTURAL CENTER

(IMS; 21 3284-7400; www.ims.com.br; Marquês de São Vicente 476; 11am-8pm Tue-Sun) FREE This beautiful cultural center hosts impressive exhibitions, often showcasing the works of some of Brazil's best photographers and artists. The gardens, complete with artificial lake and flowing river, were designed by Brazilian landscape architect Roberto Burle Marx. There's also a craft shop, and an excellent cafe that serves breakfast all day as well as lunch and afternoon tea.

OM.art GALLERY

(Map p71; 21 2239-9019; www.om.art.br; Jardim Botânico 997; 10am-7pm Tue-Fri, to 6pm Sat) In the Jockey Club, this avant-garde gallery opened to much acclaim in 2018. Expect challenging multimedia shows and big installations that often incorporate interactive components. Film, music, sculpture and photography have all featured in past exhibitions. OM.art was founded by artist and designer Oskar Metsavaht, the creator of the well-known Osklen brand.

Parque Lage PARK

(Map p71; ☎21 2334-4088; www.eavparque lage.rj.gov.br; Jardim Botânico 414; ⏲8am-5pm Apr-Nov, to 6pm Dec-Mar) FREE This beautiful park lies at the base of the Floresta da Tijuca, about 1km from Jardim Botânico. It has English-style gardens, little lakes, and a mansion that houses the **Escola de Artes Visuais** (School of Visual Arts), which hosts free art exhibitions and occasional performances. The park is a tranquil place and the cafe here offers a fine setting for a coffee or a meal.

Carpintaria GALLERY

(Map p71; ☎21 3875-5554; www.fdag.com.br/carpintaria; Jardim Botânico 971, Jockey Club; ⏲10am-7pm Tue-Fri, to 6pm Sat) One of several new galleries in the Jockey Club, Carpintaria stages exhibitions by both Brazilian and foreign artists. It's a great place to see sculpture, painting and mixed media by up-and-coming stars on the art circuit.

Parque da Catacumba PARK

(☎21 2247-9949; Av Epitácio Pessoa; ⏲8am-5pm Tue-Sun) FREE On the edge of Lagoa Rodrigo de Freitas, across a busy road, this park and sculptural garden has a short but steep trail to the **Mirante do Sacopã**. It's a 15-minute walk along a 600m forest-lined path to the lookout, which has memorable views from its perch 130m above the lake. For a bit more excitement, you can scale a rock-climbing wall, go rappelling (abseiling) or take a treetop walk offered by **Lagoa Aventuras** (☎21 4105-0079; www.lagoaaventuras.com.br; Av Epitácio Pessoa 3000; zip line R$20, climbing wall R$25, treetop walk R$35, rappelling R$130; ⏲9:30am-4:30pm Tue-Sun; 👪).

Parque da Cidade PARK

(☎21 2512-2353; www.rio.rj.gov.br/cultura; Estrada de Santa Marinha 505; ⏲8am-5pm Tue-Sun) On the outer reaches of Gávea, this lush park of native Mata Atlântica rainforest and replanted secondary forest provides a refreshing escape from the heavy traffic on nearby Rua Marques de São Vicente. Local residents come to jog here, to go for long walks with their dogs and to let their kids run about at the large playground.

Planetário PLANETARIUM

(☎21 2088-0536; www.planetariodorio.com.br; Av Padre Leonel Franca 240; adult/child R$13/6.50, incl cúpula session R$26/13; ⏲9am-5pm Tue-Fri, 2:30-8pm Sat, 2-6pm Sun) Gávea's stellar attraction, the Planetário features a museum, a *praça dos telescópios* (telescopes' square) and a couple of state-of-the-art operating *cúpulas* (domes), each capable of projecting more than 6000 stars onto its walls. Forty-minute sessions in the domes take place on weekends and holidays. Visitors can also take a peek at the night sky through the telescopes on Wednesdays and Saturdays from 7:30pm to 8:30pm (6:30pm to 7:30pm from June to August).

Copacabana & Leme

Framed by mountains and deep blue sea, Rio's most beautiful beach curves 4.5km from end to end. No longer a symbol of Rio's glamour, Copacabana is a fascinating but chaotic place, its art deco buildings, aging beachfront hotels and sleepy side streets forming the backdrop to a wildly democratic mix of tourists, elderly middle-class *cariocas*, and favela dwellers (who live in the hillsides surrounding the neighborhood). Despite its faults, the neighborhood has its charms: old-school *botecos* (small open-air bars), eclectic restaurants, vibrant street life and the handsome beach still entrance many visitors.

★Copacabana Beach BEACH

(Map p74; Av Atlântica) A magnificent confluence of land and sea, the long, scalloped beach of Copacabana extends for some 4km, with a flurry of activity along its length: over-amped soccer players singing their team's anthem; *cariocas* (Rio residents) and tourists lining up for caipirinhas at kiosks; favela kids showing off their soccer skills; and beach vendors shouting out their wares among the tanned beach bodies.

Forte de Copacabana FORT

(Map p74; ☎21 2521-1032; Av Atlântica & Rua Francisco Otaviano; adult/child R$6/free, Tue free; ⏲10am-7:30pm Tue-Sun) Built in 1914 on the promontory of the old Our Lady of Copacabana chapel, the fort of Copacabana was one of Rio's premier defenses against attack. You can still see its original features, including walls that are up to 12m thick, defended by Krupp cannons. Inside is a museum with several floors of exhibits tracing the early days of the Portuguese colony through to the mid-19th century. The views out across the full length of Copacabana are striking.

There are several cafes here with fine vantage points, including **Cafe Colombo** (Map p74; ☎21 3201-4049; www.confeitariacolombo.com.br; Forte de Copacabana, Praça Coronel Eugênio Franco; mains R$25-47; ⏲10am-8pm Tue-Sun).

Ipanema, Leblon & Gávea

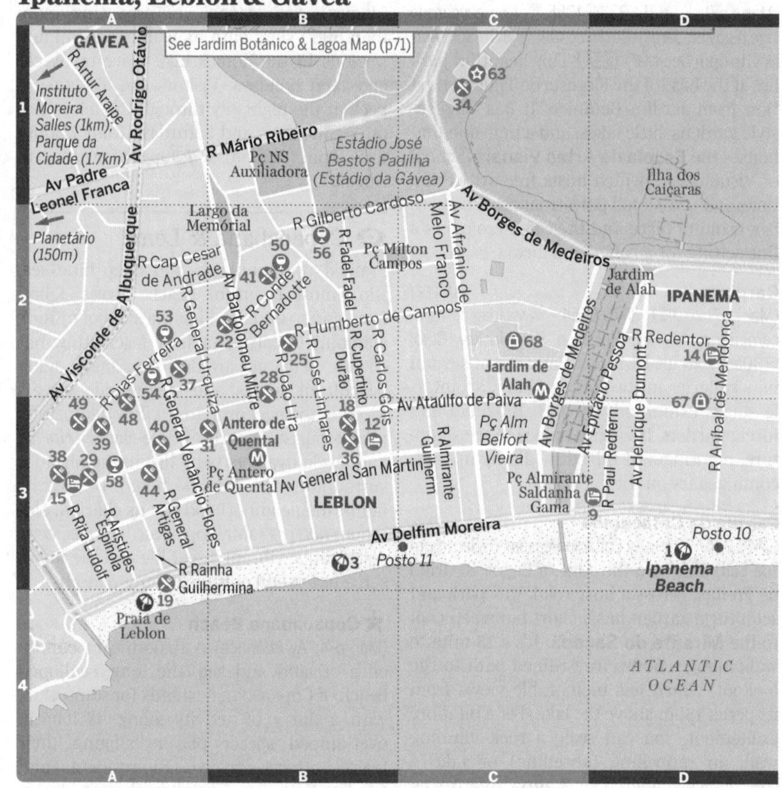

Forte Duque de Caxias FORT
(Forte do Leme; Map p74; ☎21 3223-5076; www.cep.eb.mil.br/visitacao; Praça Almirante Júlio de Noronha; adult/child R$4/free; ⏲9:30am-4:30pm Tue-Sun) More commonly known as Forte do Leme, this military base is open to the public. Visitors can walk to the top of Morro do Leme (Leme Mountain) along a steep 800m trail that passes through Atlantic rainforest. At the top stands an 18th-century fort affording magnificent views of Pão de Açúcar (Sugarloaf Mountain) and the Cagarras Islands.

Museu da Imagem e Som MUSEUM
(Map p74; www.mis.rj.gov.br; Av Atlântica, near Miguel Lemos) If work on this new museum is ever complete, Copacabana will finally have an outstanding rainy-day attraction. The building, designed by celebrated New York firm Diller Scofidio + Renfro (who also designed NYC's High Line), will feature high-tech interactive galleries devoted to the great Brazilian music and film that have played such a pivotal role in the nation's culture. Performance halls and an open-air rooftop amphitheater (for outdoor films) will be other highlights.

Botafogo & Humaitá

Just north of Copacabana, Botafogo and Humaitá are desirable neighborhoods with vibrant nightlife, cutting-edge restaurants and a few intriguing museums and galleries in the area's old mansions.

Museu do Índio MUSEUM
(Map p86; ☎21 3214-8700; www.museudoindio.gov.br; Rua das Palmeiras 55; ⏲9am-5:30pm Tue-Fri, 1-5pm Sat & Sun) FREE Though closed for renovations at the time of research, the small Museu do Índio features multimedia exhibitions on Brazil's northern tribes and

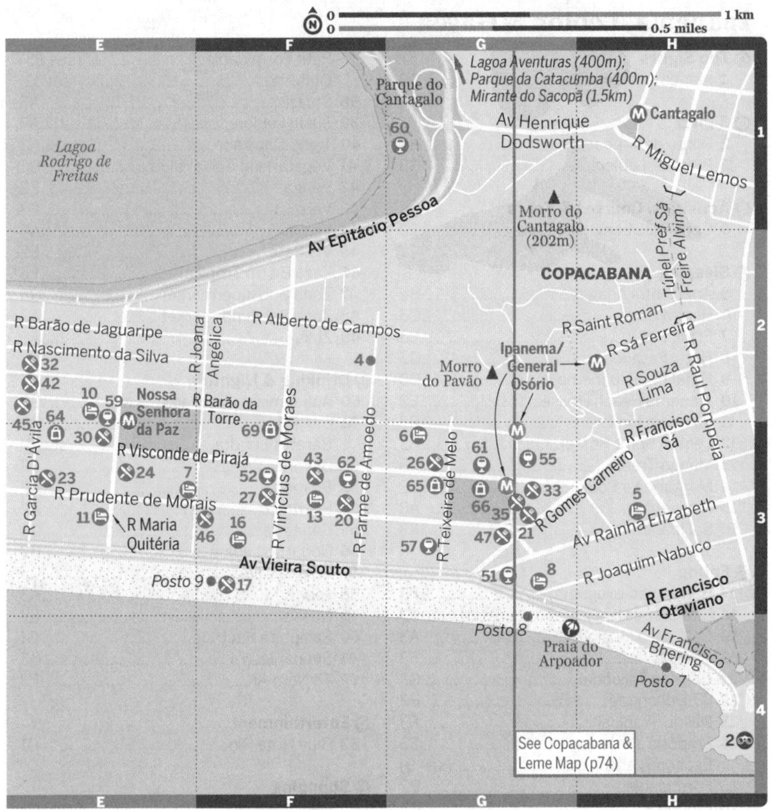

provides an excellent introduction to the economic, religious and social life of Brazil's indigenous people. Next to native food and medicinal plants, the four life-size dwellings in the courtyard were actually built by four different tribes.

Urca

The tranquil, shady streets of Urca offer a pleasant escape from the urban bustle of other parts of the city. An eclectic mix of building styles and manicured gardens lines its streets, where local residents like to stroll. Along the sea wall, which forms the northwestern perimeter of Pão de Açúcar, fishers cast for dinner as couples lounge beneath palm trees, taking in views of Baía de Guanabara and Cristo Redentor off in the distance. Tiny Praia Vermelha, in the south, has one of Rio's finest beach views. A short but scenic walking trail begins from here.

★Pão de Açúcar MOUNTAIN

(Sugarloaf Mountain; Map p86; ☎21 2546-8400; www.bondinho.com.br; Av Pasteur 520, Urca; adult/child R$85/42; ⏲8am-8pm) Seen from the peak of Pão de Açúcar, Rio is undoubtedly a *Cidade Maravilhosa* (Marvelous City). There are many good times to make the ascent, but sunset on a clear day is the most rewarding. Two cable cars connect to the summit, 395m above Rio. At the top, the city unfolds beneath you, with Corcovado mountain and Cristo Redentor (Christ the Redeemer) off to the west, and Copacabana Beach to the south.

Praia Vermelha BEACH

(Map p86; Praça General Tibúrcio, Urca) Beneath Morro da Urca, narrow Praia Vermelha has superb views of the rocky coastline. Its coarse sand gives the beach the name *vermelha* (red). Because the beach is protected by the headland, the water is usually calm.

Ipanema, Leblon & Gávea

Top Sights

1 Ipanema Beach ... D3

Sights

2 Ponta do Arpoador ... H4
3 Praia de Leblon ... B3

Activities, Courses & Tours

4 Caminhos Language Centre ... F2

Sleeping

5 Aparthotel Adagio ... H3
6 Bonita ... G3
7 El Misti ... E3
8 Hotel Fasano ... G3
9 Hotel Praia Ipanema ... D3
10 Ipanema Beach House ... E2
11 Ipanema Inn ... E3
12 Lemon Spirit Hostel ... B3
13 Mango Tree ... F3
14 Margarida's Pousada ... D2
15 Ritz Leblon ... A3
16 Sol Ipanema ... F3

Eating

17 Barraca do Uruguai ... F3
18 Bibi Crepes ... B3
19 Café de la Musique ... A3
20 Cafeína ... F3
21 Casa da Feijoada ... G3
22 CT Boucherie ... B2
23 Delírio Tropical ... E3
24 Empório Jardim na Praia ... E3
Espaço 7zero6 ... (see 9)
25 Formidable ... B2
26 Frontera ... G3
27 Garota de Ipanema ... F3
28 Giuseppe Grill ... B2
29 Graviola ... A3
Joana ... (see 7)
30 Koni Store ... E3
31 Kurt ... B3
32 La Carioca Cevicheria ... E2
33 La Veronese ... G3
34 Lagoon ... C1
35 Mercearia da Praça ... G3
36 Okanossa ... B3
37 Pabu Izakaya ... A2
Petit Formidable ... (see 25)
Quitéria ... (see 11)
38 Stuzzi ... A3
39 Sushi Leblon ... A3
40 Talho Capixaba ... A3
41 Vegetariano Social Club ... B2
42 Venga! ... E2
43 Vero ... F3
44 Vezpa ... A3
45 Via Sete ... E2
46 Zazá Bistrô Tropical ... F3
47 Zona Sul Supermarket ... G3
48 Zona Sul Supermarket ... A3
49 Zuka ... A3

Drinking & Nightlife

50 Academia da Cachaça ... B2
51 Bar Astor ... G3
Baretto-Londra ... (see 8)
52 Barzin ... F3
53 Belmonte ... A2
54 Brewteco ... A2
55 Canastra ... G3
56 Cobal do Leblon ... B2
57 Galeria Café ... G3
58 Jobi ... A3
59 Nosso ... E2
60 Palaphita Kitch ... G1
61 Shenanigan's ... G3
62 Tô Nem Aí ... F3

Entertainment

63 Blue Note Rio ... C1

Shopping

Chocolate Q ... (see 42)
64 Gilson Martins ... E3
65 Havaianas ... G3
66 Hippie Fair ... G3
Isabela Capeto ... (see 54)
Lenny Niemeyer ... (see 42)
67 Livraria da Travessa ... D3
Maria Oiticica ... (see 68)
Osklen ... (see 59)
68 Shopping Leblon ... C2
69 Toca do Vinícius ... F3
Void General Store ... (see 58)

Flamengo & Around

Following the curve of the bay north is Parque do Flamengo, home to cycling trails, sports fields, and several monuments and museums. Inland from there, the neighborhoods of Flamengo, Catete and Glória hide history in their battered streets, including the former presidential home.

West of there, Cosme Velho is the starting point (by cog train) to the open-armed Cristo Redentor, one of Rio's most recognizable features.

★ **Cristo Redentor** MONUMENT

(Christ the Redeemer; ☎ 21 2558-1329; www.tremdocorcovado.rio; cog train station, Cosme Velho 513; adult/child R$75/49; ⏲ 8am-7pm) Standing atop Corcovado (which means 'hunchback'), Cristo Redentor gazes out over Rio, a placid expression on his well-crafted face. The mountain rises straight up from the city to 710m, and at night the brightly lit 38m-high open-armed statue – all 1145 tons of him – is visible from nearly every part of the city.

Corcovado lies within the Parque Nacional da Tijuca. The most popular way to reach the statue is to take the red narrow-gauge train that departs every 30 minutes, and takes approximately 20 minutes to reach the top. Note that same-day tickets are not available from the cog train station. Buy tickets online or from an authorized seller around Rio (the website lists numerous places to buy under 'Selling Points'); you must select a date and time when purchasing. To reach the cog station, take any 'Cosme Velho' bus: you can take bus 583 from Copacabana, Ipanema or Leblon.

You can also go by Parque da Tijuca–authorized van to visit the monument. These depart from three locations around town: Copacabana (in front of Praça do Lido from 8am to 4pm; adult/child R$74/48), Largo do Machado (8am to 4pm; adult/child R$74/48) and Paineiras, a few kilometres north of the statue (8:30am to 5pm; adult/child R$41/15).

Parque do Flamengo PARK

(Map p86; Av Infante Dom Henrique) Officially called Parque Brigadeiro Eduardo Gomes, Parque do Flamengo was the result of a landfill project that leveled the São Antônio hill in 1965. It now spreads all the way from downtown Rio through Glória, Catete and Flamengo, and on around to Botafogo. The 1.2 sq km of land reclaimed from the sea now sees every manner of outdoor activity by *cariocas* (residents of Rio).

Cyclists and rollerbladers glide along the myriad paths, while the park's many football fields and sports courts are framed against the sea. On Sundays and holidays, the avenues through the park are closed to vehicle traffic from 7am to 6pm.

Designed by famous Brazilian landscaper Burle Marx (who also landscaped Brasília), the park features some 170,000 trees of 300 different species. There are two indoor attractions in the park: the Museu de Arte Moderna (p72) and the **Monumento Nacional aos Mortos da II Guerra Mundial** (Monument to the Dead of World War II).

Museu da República MUSEUM

(Map p86; ☎21 2127-0324; http://museudarepublica.museus.gov.br; Rua do Catete 153; R$6, Wed & Sun free; ⏰10am-5pm Tue-Fri, 11am-6pm Sat & Sun) The Museu da República, located in the Palácio do Catete, has been wonderfully restored. Built between 1858 and 1866, and easily distinguished by the bronze condors on its eaves, the palace was home to the president of Brazil from 1896 until 1954, when President Getúlio Vargas committed suicide here. The museum has a good collection of art and artifacts from the Republican period, and also houses a small cafe, an art-house cinema and a bookstore.

Centro Cultural Oi Futuro ARTS CENTER

(Map p86; ☎21 3235-5815; www.oifuturo.org.br; Dois de Dezembro 63; ⏰11am-5pm Tue-Sun) FREE One of Rio's most visually exciting additions is this futuristic space on the edge of Flamengo. Within 2000 sq meters of exhibition area spread across six floors, the center features temporary multimedia installations that run the gamut from architecture and urban design to pop art, photojournalism and eye-catching video art.

Museu de Folclore Edison Carneiro MUSEUM

(Map p86; ☎21 3826-4434; www.cnfcp.gov.br; Rua do Catete 179; ⏰11am-6pm Tue-Fri, 3-6pm Sat & Sun) FREE Created in 1968, this museum is an excellent introduction to Brazilian folk art, particularly that from the Northeast. Its permanent collection comprises 1400 pieces, and includes Candomblé costumes, ceramic figurines and religious costumes used in festivals. The museum also features a folklore library and a small shop that sells handicrafts, books and folk music. The museum is located next door to the Palácio do Catete.

Centro & Praça Mauá

Rio's bustling commercial district, Centro is a blend of high-rise office buildings with baroque churches, wide plazas and cobblestone streets, remnants of its grand past. North of Centro is Praça Mauá, a waterfront plaza that has become the symbol of Rio's renaissance. The once derelict streets here have been revitalized with new museums, an aquarium and a photogenic mural-lined promenade.

★Museu Histórico Nacional MUSEUM
(Map p92; ☎21 3299-0324; http://mhn.museus.gov.br; off General Justo, near Praça Marechal Âncora; adult/child R$10/5, Sun free; ⏰10am-5:30pm Tue-Fri, 1-5pm Sat & Sun) Housed in the colonial arsenal, which dates from 1764, the impressive Museu Histórico Nacional contains relics relating to the history of Brazil from its founding to its early days as a republic. Highlights include gilded imperial coaches, the throne of Dom Pedro II, massive oil paintings depicting the horrific war with Paraguay and a full-sized model of a colonial pharmacy.

★Museu de Arte do Rio MUSEUM
(MAR; Map p92; ☎21 3031-2741; www.museudeartedorio.org.br; Praça Mauá 5; adult/child R$20/10, Tue free; ⏰10am-5pm Tue-Sun) Looming large over Praça Mauá, the MAR is an icon for the rebirth of Rio's once derelict port. The huge museum hosts wide-ranging exhibitions that focus on Rio in all its complexity – its people, landscapes, beauty, challenges and conflicts. Start off by taking the elevator to the top (6th) floor, and absorbing the view over the bay. There's also an excellent restaurant here. Then work your way down through the galleries, taking in a mix of international and only-in-Rio exhibitions.

Museu do Amanhã MUSEUM
(Map p92; www.museudoamanha.org.br; Rodrigues Alves 1; adult/child R$20/free, Tue free; ⏰10am-6pm Tue-Sun) Designed by famed Spanish architect Santiago Calatrava, this thoughtfully conceived science museum has interactive exhibitions on outer space, the earth and its biodiversity, humans (and our impact on the world), and the major global trends and challenges that lie in the future. In all the museum takes a somewhat pessimistic view of the human species and its long-ranging impact on everything around it.

Boulevard Olímpico AREA
(Map p92) Rio's formerly derelict port district has been reborn as a wide promenade lined with massive street art. A handful of renowned artists has painted spectacular murals on the old warehouses, though Brazilian artist Eduardo Kobra (www.eduardokobra.com) deserves special mention for his jaw-dropping work entitled *Etnias* (Ethnicities). The massive mural stretches for 190m and features photogenic portraits of indigenous people from around the globe.

The boulevard stretches from Praça Mauá to AquaRio, and the tracks for the VLT run down the center, so watch your step. Near the east end of the promenade, you'll find a few food trucks selling sandwiches, craft beer and ice cream, with shaded tables out front. Further west along the boulevard, there are benches where you can take in the street art as well as lookouts that provide glimpses over the bay.

AquaRio AQUARIUM
(☎21 3613-0700; www.aquariomarinhodorio.com.br; Av Rodrigues Alves 379; adult/child R$100/50; ⏰10am-6pm) The largest aquarium in South America is Rio's newest major downtown attraction. You can get an up-close look at some 350 different species (there are more than 8000 animals in all), spread among two dozen different tanks. The highlight is a 3.5-million-liter aquarium with a tunnel through the middle that gives fine views of sharks, rays and shimmering schools of fish gliding past.

CRAB CULTURAL CENTER
(Centro Sebrae de Referência do Artesanato Brasileiro; Map p92; ☎21 3380-1850; www.crab.sebrae.com.br; Praça Tiradentes 69; ⏰10am-5pm Tue-Sat) FREE Inside a beautifully restored mansion overlooking Praça Tiradentes, this exhibition hall is dedicated to Brazilian crafts from across the country. Several small exhibitions are staged here, and there's also a ground-floor restaurant and an airy upstairs cafe. The real reason to come, however, is to browse the exceptional handicrafts for sale in the shop (p124).

Cais do Valongo ARCHAEOLOGICAL SITE
(Map p92; Barão de Tefé) Unearthed in 2011, the Valongo Wharf was the first arrival point for an estimated 900,000 enslaved peoples brought to Brazil after long, harrowing voyages from Africa. Those who survived the journey were sold in markets, while those who didn't were buried without ceremony in mass graves nearby. The heartbreaking tragedy of the Atlantic slave trade remained a topic little broached for many years, and this newly designated archaeological site is an important reference for coming to grips with this aspect of the nation's history.

Instituto de Pesquisa e Memória Presto Novos MUSEUM
(Map p98; ☎21 96465-9983; www.pretosnovos.com.br; Pedro Ernesto 32; ⏰1-6pm Tue-Fri, 11am-2pm Sat) FREE When Mercedes Guimarães was doing construction work on her house

Jardim Botânico & Lagoa

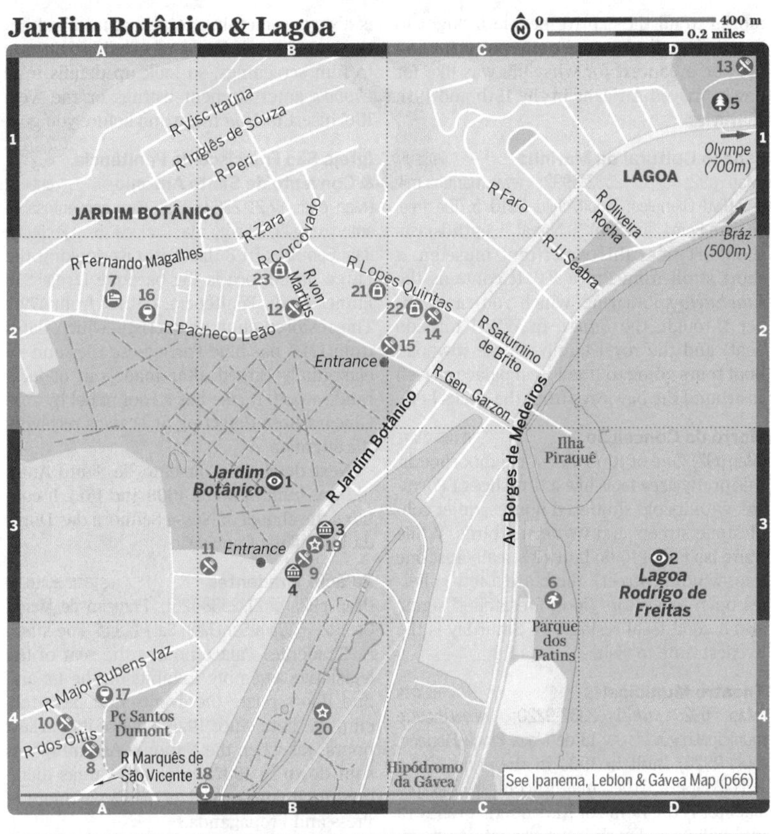

Jardim Botânico & Lagoa

Top Sights
1 Jardim Botânico B3
2 Lagoa Rodrigo de Freitas D3

Sights
3 Carpintaria B3
4 OM.art B3
5 Parque Lage D1

Activities, Courses & Tours
6 Helisight C3

Sleeping
7 Pouso Verde A2

Eating
8 Braseiro da Gávea A4
9 Casa Camolese B3
10 Guimas A4
11 Jarbô B3
12 La Bicyclette B2
13 Plage Café D1
14 Prana Vegetariano C2
15 Puro C2

Drinking & Nightlife
16 Bar do Horto A2
17 Hipódromo A4
18 Palaphita Gávea B4

Entertainment
19 Clube Manouche B3
20 Jockey Club Brasileiro B4

Shopping
21 Dona Coisa B2
22 Gabinete C2
23 O Sol B2

in 1996, workers uncovered huge quantities of human fragments. After discussions with a historian, she learned the site had been the burial place of enslaved Africans. She halted work and turned her house into this small museum, cultural center and memorial to all the captive people brought to Brazil. The displays are quite powerful and provide a context for what life was like for newly arrived Africans in the 18th and 19th centuries.

Espaço Cultural da Marinha MUSEUM
(Map p92; ☎21 2532-5992; www.marinha.mil.br; Blvd Olímpico; adult/child R$10/5, Tue free; ⏲11am-5pm Tue-Sun) Naval enthusiasts shouldn't miss this waterfront museum, a short stroll from Praça XV. It contains the *Riachuelo* submarine, which you can wander through, the *Bauru* (a WWII torpedo boat) and the royal family's large rowboat. Boat tours going to Ilha Fiscal palace as well as around the bay leave from the docks here.

Morro da Conceição HISTORIC SITE
(Map p92) One of Rio's oldest neighborhoods, this pretty area feels like a tiny slice of Portugal, with its old shuttered houses, quiet cobblestone streets and twittering birds. While there isn't a lot to do here (it's really just one long winding street), there are a few galleries open to visitors (look for 'atelier' signs) and a good local restaurant. Saturday is the liveliest time to visit.

Theatro Municipal THEATER
(Map p92; ☎21 2332-9220; www.theatromunicipal.rj.gov.br; Av 13 de Maio, Praça Floriano; tours R$20) Built in 1905 in the style of the Paris Opera, the magnificent Municipal Theater is the home of Rio's opera, orchestra and ballet. Its lavish interior contains many beautiful details – including the stage curtain painted by Italian artist Eliseu Visconti that features portraits of 75 major figures from the arts, such as Carlos Gomes, Wagner and Rembrandt.

Guided multilingual tours lasting 45 minutes are offered from Tuesday to Friday (at noon, 2:30pm and 4pm) and on Saturday (at 11am, noon, 1pm and 4pm). Call ahead to confirm availability of an English-speaking guide. It's also well worth coming for a performance.

Centro Cultural Banco do Brasil CULTURAL CENTER
(CCBB; Map p92; ☎21 3808-2020; www.culturabancodobrasil.com.br; Primeiro de Março 66, Centro; ⏲9am-9pm Wed-Mon) FREE Housed in a beautifully restored 1906 building, the Centro Cultural Banco do Brasil hosts some of Rio's top exhibitions. Facilities include a cinema, two theaters and a permanent display of the evolution of currency in Brazil. There is always something going on, from exhibitions and lunchtime and evening concerts to film screenings, so look up details in *O Globo's* entertainment listings or the 'Veja Rio' insert in *Veja* magazine before you go.

Igreja São Francisco da Penitência & Convento de Santo Antônio CHURCH
(Map p92; ☎21 2262-0129; www.conventosantoantonio.org.br; Largo da Carioca 5; ⏲church 8am-6pm Mon-Fri, 8-11am Sat) Overlooking the Largo da Carioca is the baroque Igreja São Francisco da Penitência, dating from 1726. The restored church's sacristy, which dates from 1745, has blue Portuguese tiles and an elaborately carved altar made out of jacaranda wood. It also has a roof panel by José Oliveira Rosa depicting St Francis receiving the stigmata.

Next door, the Convento de Santo Antônio was built between 1608 and 1615. It contains the chapel of Nossa Senhora das Dores da Imaculada Conceição.

Palácio Tiradentes HISTORIC BUILDING
(Map p92; ☎21 2588-1251; Primeiro de Março, Centro; ⏲10am-5pm Mon-Sat) FREE The stately Tiradentes Palace houses the seat of the legislative assembly. Exhibits on the 1st and 2nd floors relate the events that have taken place here since 1926. One of its darkest hours was when the National Assembly was shut down in 1937 under the Vargas dictatorship; it later served as the Department of Press and Propaganda.

Mosteiro de São Bento CHURCH
(Map p92; ☎21 2206-8100; www.mosteirodesaobentorio.org.br; Dom Gerardo 68; ⏲6:30am-6:30pm) This is one of the finest colonial churches in Brazil. It was built between 1617 and 1641 on Morro de São Bento, and has an excellent view over the city. The simple facade hides a baroque interior richly decorated in gold. Among its historic treasures are wood carvings designed by Frei Domingos da Conceição and made by Alexandre Machado, and paintings by José de Oliveira Rosa.

Museu de Arte Moderna MUSEUM
(MAM; Map p92; ☎21 3883-5600; www.mamrio.org.br; Av Infante Dom Henrique 85, Parque do Flamengo; adult/child R$14/free; ⏲noon-6pm Tue-Fri, 11am-6pm Sat & Sun) At the northern end of Parque do Flamengo, the Museu de Arte Moderna is immediately recognizable by its striking postmodern edifice designed by Affonso Eduardo Reidy. The landscaping of Burle Marx is no less impressive. Inside, the

design feels a bit dated, but it's still worth a visit for the superb collection of Brazilian artists, which includes works by Bruno Giorgi, Di Cavalcanti and Maria Martins.

Paço Imperial HISTORIC BUILDING
(Map p92; ☎21 2215-2093; www.amigosdopacoimperial.org.br; Praça XV/Quinze de Novembro 48, Centro; ⏲noon-7pm Tue-Sun) FREE The former imperial palace was originally built in 1743 as a governor's residence. Later it became the home of Dom João and his family when the Portuguese throne transferred the royal seat of power to the colony. In 1888 Princesa Isabel proclaimed the Freedom from Slavery Act from the palace's steps. The building was neglected for many years but has been restored and now hosts excellent changing exhibitions and concerts. There's also a good cafe and a restaurant here.

Ilha Fiscal HISTORIC BUILDING
(Map p92; ☎21 2233-9165; tours R$30; ⏲tours 12:30pm, 2pm & 3:30pm Thu-Sun) This eye-catching lime-green neo-Gothic palace sitting in Baía de Guanabara looks like something out of a child's fairy-tale book. It was designed by engineer Adolfo del Vecchio and completed in 1889. Originally used to supervise port operations, the palace is famous as the location of the last Imperial Ball on November 9, 1889. Today it's open for guided tours, which leave from the dock near Praça XV (Quinze) de Novembro. Purchase tickets from the Espaço Cultural da Marinha.

Museu Nacional de Belas Artes MUSEUM
(Map p92; ☎21 3299-0600; www.mnba.gov.br; Rio Branco 199; adult/student R$8/4, Sun free; ⏲10am-6pm Tue-Fri, 1-5pm Sat & Sun) Rio's fine-arts museum houses more than 18,000 original paintings and sculptures, some of which date back to works brought over from Portugal by Dom João VI in 1808. One of its most important galleries is the **Galeria de Arte Brasileira**, which includes 20th-century classics, such as Cândido Portinari's *Café*. Other galleries display Brazilian folk art, African art and furniture, as well as contemporary exhibits. Audio guides are available (R$8).

Centro de Arte Hélio Oiticica MUSEUM
(Map p92; ☎21 2242-1012; Luis de Camões 68; ⏲noon-6pm Mon-Sat) FREE This avant-garde museum is set in a 19th-century neoclassical building that originally housed the Conservatory of Music and Dramatic Arts. Today the center displays permanent works by the artist, theoretician and poet Hélio Oiticica, as well as bold contemporary art exhibitions, well-tuned to Oiticica's forward-leaning aesthetics.

Praça Floriano PLAZA
(Map p92; Rio Branco, Cinelândia) The heart of modern Rio, the Praça Floriano (known to *cariocas* simply as Cinelândia) comes to life at lunchtime and after work when its outdoor cafes fill with a beer-swilling office crowd. The square is also Rio's political marketplace and is a major meeting point for protestors.

Praça XV (Quinze) de Novembro HISTORIC SITE
(Map p92; near Primeiro de Março, Centro) The first residents on this historic site were Carmelite fathers who built a convent here in 1590. It later came under the property of the Portuguese crown and became Largo do Paço, which surrounded Paço Imperial, the royal palace. The square was later renamed Praça XV (Quinze) de Novembro after Brazil declared itself a republic on November 15, 1822.

Santa Teresa

Set on a hill overlooking the city, Santa Teresa, with its cobbled streets and aging mansions, retains the charm of days past and is Rio's most atmospheric neighborhood. Currently the residence of a new generation of artists and bohemians, Santa Teresa has colorful restaurants and bars and a lively weekend scene around Largo do Guimarães and Largo das Neves.

Museu Chácara do Céu MUSEUM
(Map p92; ☎21 3970-1093; www.museuscastromaya.com.br; Murtinho Nobre 93; adult/child R$6/free, Wed free; ⏲noon-5pm Wed-Mon) The former mansion of art patron and industrialist Raymundo Ottoni de Castro Maya contains a small but diverse array of modern art, formerly Ottoni's private collection, which he bequeathed to the nation. In addition to works by Portinari, Di Cavalcanti and Lygia Clark, the museum displays furniture and Brazilian maps dating from the 17th and 18th centuries, and hosts temporary exhibitions.

Parque das Ruínas VIEWPOINT
(Map p92; ☎21 2215-0621; www.facebook.com/parquedasruinas; Murtinho Nobre 169; ⏲8am-6pm Tue-Sun) FREE This park contains the ruins – exterior brick walls and a newly built staircase – of the mansion belonging to Brazilian heiress Laurinda Santos Lobo. Her house

Copacabana & Leme

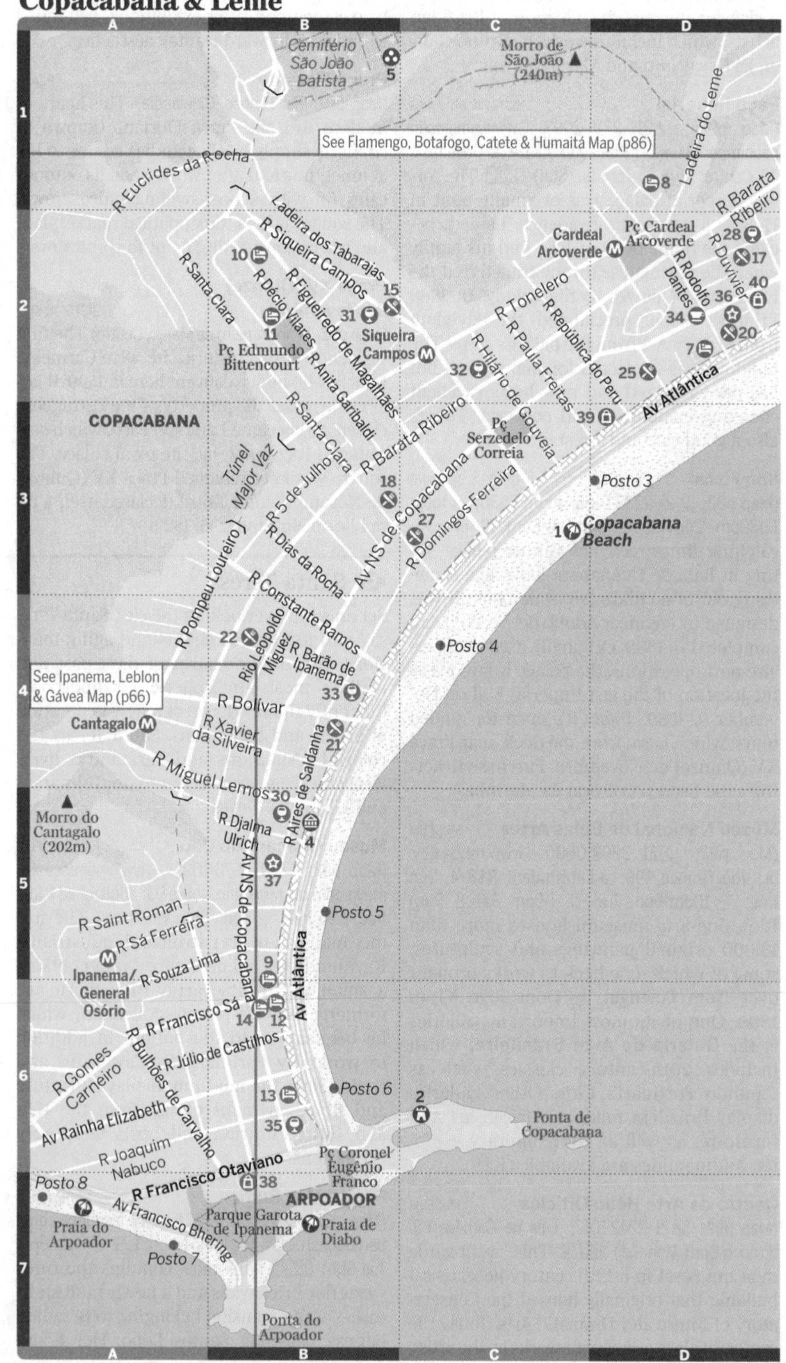

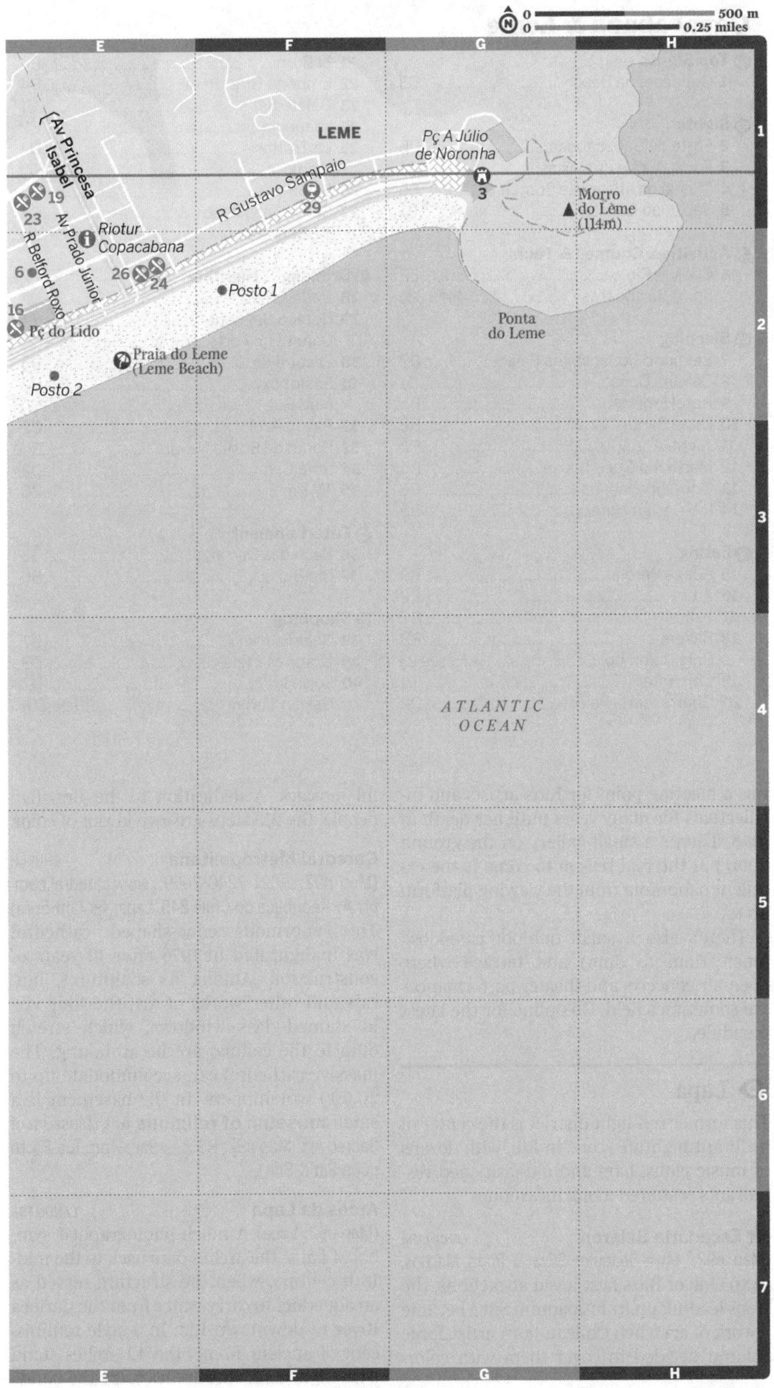
0 500 m
0 0.25 miles
E
F
G
H
1
2
3
4
5
6
7
LEME
Pç A Júlio de Noronha
Av Princesa Isabel
R Gustavo Sampaio
29
3
Morro do Leme (114m)
19
23
Av Prado Júnior
Riotur Copacabana
R Belford Roxo
6
26
24
Posto 1
16
Pç do Lido
Ponta do Leme
Praia do Leme (Leme Beach)
Posto 2
ATLANTIC OCEAN

Copacabana & Leme

Top Sights
1 Copacabana Beach C3

Sights
2 Forte de Copacabana C6
3 Forte Duque de Caxias G1
4 Museu da Imagem e Som B5
5 São João Batista B1

Activities, Courses & Tours
6 Cook in Rio E2
Spirit Surfboards .... (see 38)

Sleeping
7 Belmond Copacabana Palace D2
8 Cabana Copa D1
9 Hotel Emiliano B5
10 Hotel Santa Clara B2
11 Jucati B2
12 Marta Rio Guesthouse B6
13 Orla Copacabana B6
14 Rio Design Hotel B6

Eating
15 Adega Pérola B2
16 Amir E2
17 Azumi D2
18 Bakers B3
Cafe Colombo .... (see 2)
19 Cervantes E1
20 Churrascaria Palace D2
21 El Born B4
22 Empório Grão-Pará B4
23 Galeto Sat's E1
24 Joaquina E2
25 La Trattoria D2
Momo .... (see 7)
26 Salomé E2
27 Santa Satisfação C3
TT Burger .... (see 38)

Drinking & Nightlife
28 Bodega D2
29 Boteco Belmonte F1
Cafe 18 do Forte .... (see 2)
30 Escondido B5
31 Fosfobox B2
Mud Bug .... (see 20)
32 Pavão Azul C2
33 Ponto da Bossa Nova B4
34 Sofá Café D2
35 TV Bar B6

Entertainment
36 Beco das Garrafas D2
37 Bip Bip B5

Shopping
38 Galeria River B7
39 Gilson Martins D3
40 Loja Fla D2
Osklen Surfing .... (see 38)

was a meeting point for Rio's artists and intellectuals for many years until her death in 1946. There's a small gallery on the ground floor, but the real reason to come is the excellent panorama from the viewing platform up top.

There's also a small outdoor cafe-kiosk (open 11am to 6pm) and terrace where open-air concerts and theater performances are sometimes held. Go online for the latest schedule.

Lapa

This former red-light district is the center of a vibrant nightlife scene in Rio, with dozens of music clubs, bars and old-fashioned restaurants scattered along its avenues.

★ **Escadaria Selarón** LANDMARK
(Map p92; btwn Joaquim Silva & Pinto Martins, Lapa) One of Rio's best-loved attractions, the steps leading up from Joaquim Silva became a work of art when Chilean-born artist Jorge Selarón decided to cover them with colorful mosaics. A dedication to the Brazilian people, the 215 steps are a vivid riot of color.

Catedral Metropolitana CHURCH
(Map p92; 21 2240-2669; www.catedral.com.br; Av República do Chile 245, Lapa; 7am-5pm) This enormous cone-shaped cathedral was inaugurated in 1976 after 12 years of construction. Among its sculptures, murals and other works of art, the four vivid stained-glass windows, which stretch 60m to the ceiling, are breathtaking. The massive cathedral can accommodate up to 20,000 worshippers. In the basement is a small **museum of religious art** (Museum of Sacred Art; Map p92; R$5; 9am-4pm Tue-Fri, to noon Sat & Sun).

Arcos da Lapa LANDMARK
(Map p92; Lapa) A much-photographed symbol of Lapa, the arches date back to the mid-18th century, when the structure served as an aqueduct to carry water from the Carioca River to downtown Rio. In a style reminiscent of ancient Rome, the 42 arches stand 64m high. Today the arches carry the bonde

cable car on its way between Centro and Santa Teresa. Located near Av Mem de Sá.

Zona Norte

The North Zone has a handful of attractions, including the Sambódromo, Maracanã Football Stadium and the sprawling market amusement of Feira Nordestina. You'll also find the Quinta da Boa Vista, a large park that was once the estate of the Portuguese royal family.

★Maracanã Football Stadium STADIUM
(Map p98; 21 2334-1705; www.suderj.rj.gov.br/maracana.asp; Av Maracanã, São Cristóvão) Rio's Maracanã stadium is hallowed ground among football lovers. The massive arena has been the site of legendary victories and crushing defeats. Maracanã played a starring role in the 2014 World Cup when it hosted major games, including the final between Germany and Argentina. The stadium also staged the opening and closing ceremonies of the 2016 Summer Olympics. No matter who takes the field, the 78,800-seat arena comes to life in spectacular fashion on game days.

Feira Nordestina MARKET
(Northeastern Fair; Map p98; 21 2580-5335; www.facebook.com/feiradesaocristovaooficial; Campo de São Cristóvão; R$5, Tue-Thu free; 10am-6pm Tue-Sat, to 8pm Sun) This enormous fair (32,000 sq meters, with over 600 stalls) is not to be missed. It showcases the culture of the Northeast of Brazil, with *barracas* (food stalls) selling Bahian dishes as well as beer and *cachaça* (sugarcane alcohol), which flows in great abundance here. The best time to go is at the weekend, when you can catch live bands playing *forró* (popular music of northeast Brazil), plus samba groups and comedy troupes, Música Popular Brasileira (MPB) and *rodas de capoeira* (capoeira circles).

Sambódromo STADIUM
(Map p98; www.sambadrome.com; Marques do Sapuçai) The epicenter of Rio's Carnaval, the Sambódromo was designed by Oscar Niemeyer and completed in 1984. During big parades, come here for fantastic views from the stands of the elaborate floats, whirling dancers and pounding drum corps. The open-air arena received a makeover for the 2016 Olympics, with improved sight lines and a more symmetrical design in keeping with Niemeyer's original vision.

TAKE THE BONDE

The **bonde** (Map p92; return ticket R$20; 9am-5pm Mon-Fri, 10am-5:30pm Sat, 11am-4:30pm Sun; M Carioca) is the last of the historic streetcars that once crisscrossed the city. Its romantic clatter through the cobbled streets is the archetypal sound of bohemian Santa Teresa. Currently the *bonde* travels every 15 to 20 minutes from the cable-car station in **Centro** (Map p92; Lélio Gama 65) over the scenic Arcos da Lapa and as far as Largo do Guimarães in the heart of Santa Teresa.

After a tragic accident in 2011 the *bonde* was taken out of commission while much-needed improvements to the track were made. After more than four years the line reopened – but now it only travels 1.7km of its 10km of track. Although work on further sections of the track has been promised, the project's estimated cost (around R$100 million) makes it unlikely that the *bonde* will continue beyond Largo do Guimarães any time soon.

Quinta da Boa Vista PARK
(Map p98; 21 3938-6900; 8am-6pm) Quinta da Boa Vista was the estate of the Portuguese imperial family until the Republic was proclaimed. Today it's a large and busy park with gardens and lakes. On weekends it's crowded with football games and families from the Zona Norte. Sadly, a devastating fire in 2018 destroyed the former imperial mansion, which housed one of Brazil's most important historical collections; Museu Nacional and Museu da Fauna. Countless archaeological treasures were lost. The **Rio Zoo** (Jardim Zoológico; Map p98; 21 3030-2141; www.riozoo.com.br; Quinta da Boa Vista; R$20; 10am-5pm Fri-Sun) is 200m west.

Barra da Tijuca & Western Rio

West of Leblon, Barra da Tijuca is a sprawling suburb with a long, pretty beach. Apart from the area near the new Jardim Oceânico metro stop, to get around here you'll generally need a car. Other beaches dot the coast, and get wilder and less populated the further west you go.

WORTH A TRIP

BEACHES WEST OF RIO

Although Copacabana and Ipanema are Rio's most famous stretches of sand, there are many inviting beaches to the west, some in spectacular natural settings.

The first major beach you'll reach heading west of Leblon is **Praia do Pepino** in São Conrado. It's near where the hang gliders land, and it's not the cleanest beach around. Further west is the small, lovely but well-concealed **Praia da Joatinga**, reachable by a steep path down a rocky hillside. Be aware of the tides, so you don't get stranded.

Although it gets crowded on weekends, **Praia do Recreio dos Bandeirantes** is almost deserted during the week. The large rock acts as a natural breakwater, creating a calm bay. The 2km-long stretch of sand is popular with families.

The secluded 700m-long **Praia da Prainha** lies just past Recreio. It's one of the best surfing beaches in Rio, so it's always full of surfers. Waves come highly recommended here.

Praia de Grumari, the most isolated and unspoiled beach close to the city, is quiet during the week and packed on weekends with *cariocas* looking to get away from city beaches. It is a gorgeous setting, surrounded by mountains and lush vegetation.

From Grumari, a narrow road climbs over a jungle-covered hillside toward **Praia de Guaratiba**. West of here you'll get a good view of the **Restinga da Marambaia** (the vegetation-rich strip between the beach and the mainland), closed off to the public by a naval base. *Cariocas* enjoy eating lunch at several of the seafood restaurants in the area.

Praia da Barra da Tijuca BEACH

(Av Sernambetiba, Recreio dos Bandeirantes) The best thing about Barra is the beach. It stretches for 18km, with the blue sea lapping at the shore. The first few kilometers of its eastern end are filled with bars and seafood restaurants.

Sítio Burle Marx GARDENS

(☎212410-1412; visitas.srbm@iphan.gov.br; Estrada Roberto Burle Marx 2019, Guaratiba; R$10; ⊙tours 9:30am & 1:30pm Tue-Sat) This 35-hectare estate was once the home of Brazil's most famous landscape architect, Roberto Burle Marx. The estate's lush vegetation includes thousands of plant species, some of which are rare varieties from different corners of the globe. A 17th-century **Benedictine chapel** also lies on the estate, along with Burle Marx's original farmhouse and studio, where you can see displays of paintings, furniture and sculptures by the talented designer. Tours are by appointment only.

Casa do Pontal MUSEUM

(☎21 2490-4013; www.museucasadopontal.com.br; Estrada do Pontal 3295, Recreio dos Bandeirantes; permanent collection/temporary exhibits R$12/4; ⊙9:30am-5pm Tue-Sun) Owned by French designer Jacques Van de Beuque, this impressive museum containing some 4500 pieces has one of the best folk-art collections in Brazil. The assorted artifacts are grouped according to theme, including rural life, popular festivals, religion and erotic art. The grounds of the museum are surrounded by lush vegetation.

Activities

Tropical rainforest, towering peaks and sparkling beaches set the stage for a wide range of adventures in this outdoors-loving city. Hiking, rock climbing, hang gliding, surfing and cycling are only a few ways to spend a sun-drenched afternoon.

Walking, Jogging & Cycling

Splendid views and the sounds of the ever-present ocean are just two features of the many good walking and jogging paths of the Zona Sul. Parque do Flamengo (p69) has plenty of paths stretching between city and bay. Further south, Lagoa Rodrigo de Freitas (p64) has a 7.2km track for cyclists, joggers and in-line skaters. At the lakeside Parque dos Patins you can rent bicycles (R$15 per hour), tricycles or quadricycles (around R$30 per hour). A popular option is to take the seaside path from Leme to Barra da Tijuca. You can also cycle along paths from Copacabana up to Parque do Flamengo. Sunday is the best day to go, as the road is closed to traffic but open to the city's many outdoor enthusiasts.

The short **Pista Cláudio Coutinho** (Map p86; off Praça General Tibúrcio, Urca; ⊙6am-sunset), between the mountains and the sea at Praia Vermelha in Urca, is open to walkers and joggers from 7am to 6pm daily.

Hiking & Climbing

In addition to access to nearby national parks such as Parque Nacional da Serra dos Órgãos and Parque Nacional do Itatiaia, Rio has many trails through the rainforest of Parque Nacional da Tijuca. Visitors can also take part in hikes around Corcovado, Morro da Urca, Parque Lage and other areas.

Rio is the center of rock climbing in Brazil, and has hundreds of documented climbs within an hour's drive of the city.

Jungle Me HIKING
(☎21 4105-7533; www.jungleme.com.br; tours from R$195; 👪) This top-notch outfit offers excellent hiking tours through Parque Nacional da Tijuca led by knowledgeable guides. The eight-hour Tijuca Circuit (Peaks & Waterfalls tour) offers challenging walks up several escarpments with stunning views of Rio, followed by a refreshing dip in a waterfall. The Prainha & Grumari tour consists of a hike between scenic beaches in Rio's little-visited western reaches.

Crux Eco CLIMBING
(☎21 3322-8765, 21 99392-9203; www.cruxeco.com.br; 👪) This reputable outfit offers a huge range of excursions and outdoor adventures. You can arrange a mountaineering adventure up Pão de Açúcar (R$470) or climb Corcovado, go rappelling (abseiling) down waterfalls, head off on full-day hikes through Floresta da Tijuca, or go on cycling and kayaking trips.

Rio Adventures HIKING
(☎21 3587-3282; www.rioadventures.com; hiking/climbing/rafting tours from R$180/370/450) Offering a range of outdoor activities, Rio Adventures leads hikes through Parque Nacional da Tijuca, including short treks up Pico Tijuca and more challenging ascents up Pedra Bonito. It also runs sightseeing tours, rock climbs, rafting excursions to Paraibuna River (175km northwest of Rio), and parachuting and paragliding trips.

Climb in Rio CLIMBING
(☎21 99328-5904; www.climbinrio.com; half-/full-day climbs from R$350/600) This respected agency offers half- and full-day climbing trips led by experienced guides. Navigating more than 400 routes around Rio and the state, this is a good pick for climbing junkies.

Cycling

There are more than 300km of bike paths around Rio. The best places to ride are around Lagoa Rodrigo de Freitas, along Barra da Tijuca and the oceanfront from Leblon to Leme. This last path also connects to Praia de Botafogo and Parque do Flamengo, running all the way to Centro. In the Floresta da Tijuca, a 6km cycle path runs from Cascatinha Taunay waterfall to Açude museum.

On Sundays the beach road from Leblon to Leme closes to vehicle traffic, as does the road through Parque do Flamengo. You can rent bikes from a stand along the east and west sides of Lagoa Rodrigo de Freitas for R$15 per hour.

Hang Gliding

If you weigh less than 100kg (about 220lb) and have a spare R$500, you can do the fantastic hang glide off 510m Pedra Bonita – one of the giant granite slabs that tower above Rio – onto Pepino Beach in São Conrado. Flights last about seven to 10 minutes, and no experience is necessary. Guest riders are secured in a kind of pouch that is attached to the hang glider. The winds are quite safe here and accidents are rare.

The price includes pickup and drop-off at your hotel.

Just Fly HANG GLIDING
(☎21 3593-4362; www.justflyinrio.blogspot.com; R$520) Go hang gliding with Paulo Celani, a highly experienced tandem flyer with more than 6000 flights to his credit.

RIO FOR CHILDREN

Brazilians are very family-oriented. Some hotels let children stay free, although the age limit varies. Babysitters are readily available and most restaurants have high chairs.

There's plenty of good spade-and-sandbucket fun to be had on Rio's beaches, particularly Leblon's *posto* 12, known as Baixo for its mini-playground and all the moms and tots around. Other amusement for kids includes rainforest walks in Parque Lage (p65), pedal boats on Lagoa, biking (and triking) from Parque dos Patins (on the west side of Lagoa), aquatic wonders at AquaRio (p70), ziplines and canopy walks at Lagoa Aventuras (p65), plus snacking at juice bars and markets all around town.

CP DC PRESS/SHUTTERSTOCK ©

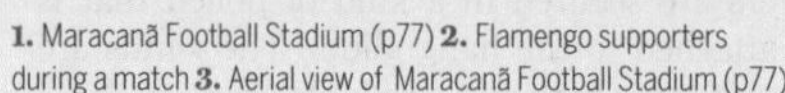
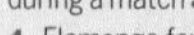

1. Maracanã Football Stadium (p77) **2.** Flamengo supporters during a match **3.** Aerial view of Maracanã Football Stadium (p77) **4.** Flamengo fans

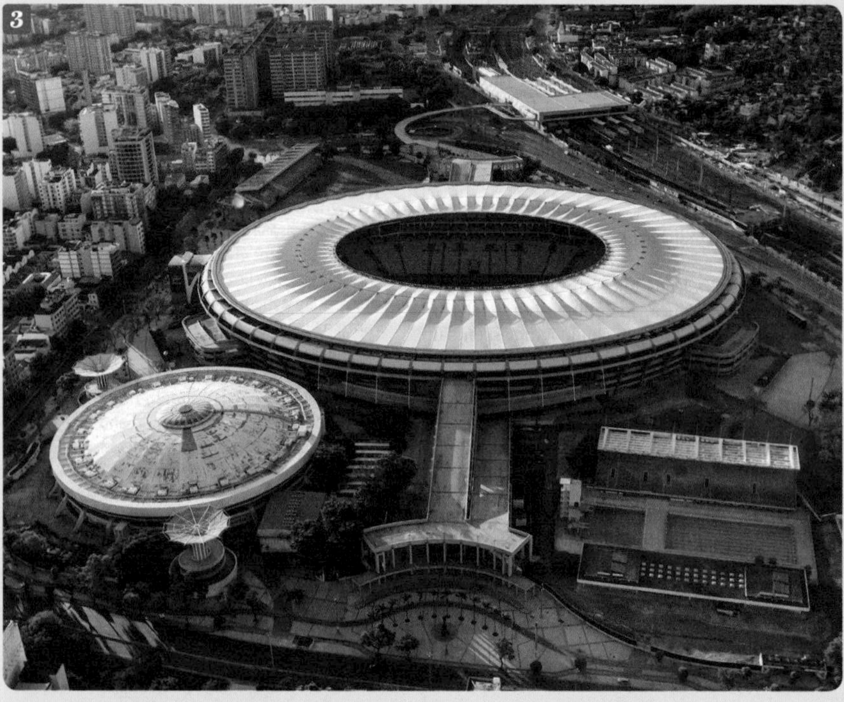

MARCELLO74/SHUTTERSTOCK ©

A.RICARDO/SHUTTERSTOCK ©

Football Fever

Rio's Maracanã (p77) is one of the world's most famous football arenas. It's also Brazil's largest sports arena, seating over 78,000 fans. In the last decade the stadium has been in the spotlight during both the 2014 World Cup and the 2016 Summer Olympics.

The Spectacle

A game at Maracanã is a must-see. Matches here rate among the most exciting in the world, and the fans among the most colorful. The devoted pound huge samba drums, spread vast flags across great swaths of the stadium, dance in the aisles, and detonate smoke bombs in team colors. You'll hear – and feel – the deafening roar when the home team takes the field, and a wall of sound and palpable air of near hysteria will hit you when a player pounds the ball into the back of the net. Things are only slightly calmer since alcohol was banned inside the stadium back in 2003 – though with pressure from FIFA, an exception to the law was put in place for the 2014 World Cup.

The Clubs

Rio is home to four major club teams – Flamengo, Fluminense, Vasco da Gama and Botafogo – each with a diehard local following. Apart from a couple of short breaks for the Christmas and New Year holiday and Carnaval, professional club competitions go on all year. The major event in Rio's sporting calendar is the *classico,* when the four hometown teams play each other. Expect intense and bitter rivalry, matched in excitement only by encounters between Rio and São Paulo clubs.

Maracanã Tour

A must for football fans, the **tour** (☎21 98341-1949; www.tourmaracana.com.br; Av Maracanã, São Cristóvão; tour guided/unguided R$60/50; ⌚9am-4:30pm) takes you through the press box, the grandstand, into the locker rooms and then through the tunnel out onto the field. You'll also visit a room that pays tribute to Brazilian legends who made history here, like Pelé and Garrincha. Tours ($60) take place from 9am to 4pm; on game days the last tour starts four hours before kickoff.

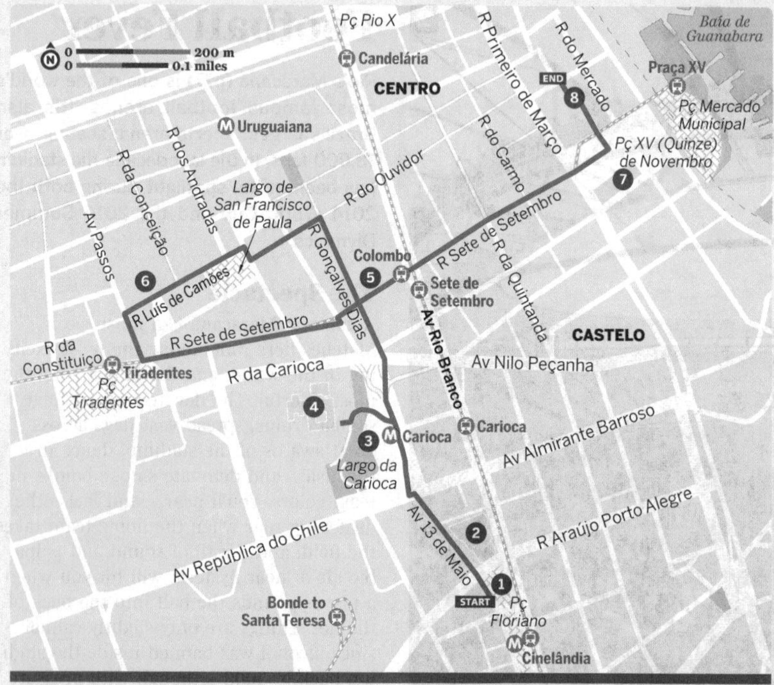

City Walk
Historic Centro

START PRAÇA FLORIANO
END TRAVESSA DO COMÉRCIO
LENGTH 3KM; FOUR HOURS

A mélange of historic buildings and skyscrapers, Centro is a fine place to experience the city away from its beaches and mountains. Do this tour during the week, as the area's deserted (and unsafe) on weekends.

Start at the ❶ **Praça Floriano** (p73), known to *cariocas* simply as Cinelândia, a scenic plaza set with several outdoor cafes. The square is also Rio's political marketplace and is a major meeting point for protestors. On the north side, the neoclassical ❷ **Theatro Municipal** (p72) is one of the city's finest buildings, particularly after its recent R$65 million renovation. Home of Rio's opera, orchestra and ballet, it has a lavish interior containing many beautiful details. If you time your visit right, you can take one of the guided tours.

Stroll north along Av 13 de Maio. You'll pass through the ❸ **Largo da Carioca**, a bustling area with a small market. On the hill is ❹ **Igreja São Francisco da Penitência** (p72), an 18th-century church with a jaw-dropping gilded interior. Reach the church via stairs or elevator near the Carioca metro station.

After taking in the views, walk over to narrow Rua Gonçalves Dias to reach ❺ **Confeitaria Colombo** (p107) for caffeine, pastries and art nouveau surroundings.

From Rua Gonçalves Dias, turn left on Rua do Ouvidor, following it to Largo de San Francisco de Paula. One block further is the ❻ **Real Gabinete Português de Leitura**, a historic reading room that seems straight out of 19th-century Portugal.

Turn right when exiting and pass Praça Tiradentes, before heading left over to Rua Sete de Setembro. Follow it until it ends near the ❼ **Paço Imperial** (p73). Once the seat of the Portuguese rulers in Brazil, the building today houses cafes and intriguing art exhibitions.

Leaving the Paço, cross Praça XV (Quinze) de Novembro and take the narrow lane beneath the arch. You'll walk along one of Centro's oldest lanes, **Travessa do Comércio**, full of open-air restaurants and bars. It's a fitting ending to a day's wander.

Tandem Fly HANG GLIDING
(☎21 9996-6341, 21 2422-0941; www.riotandemfly.com.br; flight R$500) Two brothers – both very experienced pilots – run this outfit; they also give lessons for those who want to learn how to fly solo.

Asa Delta Flight in Rio HANG GLIDING
(☎21 99693-8800; www.facebook.com/asadeltaflightrio; tandem flight R$490) With more than 20 years' experience, Ricardo Hamond has earned a solid reputation as a safety-conscious and extremely professional pilot; he has flown more than 12,000 tandem flights.

Surfing

Rio has some fine options when it comes to surfing, with great breaks just outside the city. If you're not ready to leave the Zona Sul, there are a few options, including fairly consistent breaks in front of *posto* (post) 10 in Ipanema and *posto* 11 in Leblon. Copacabana gets an OK break between *postos* 4 and 5. You'll find better waves near the spit of land dividing Copacabana from Ipanema. On the east side, off Praia do Diabo, there are right and left breaks that can reach up to 2m high, but it's not a good spot for beginners. On the other side of the rocks is Arpoador, which is generally more consistent, with fast, hollow breaks to the left ranging from 0.5m to 3m. The big drawback here is that the place gets crowded, making maneuvering extremely difficult. To beat the crowds, go early on weekday mornings.

If you're serious about surfing, you'll want to head down to the beaches west of Rio. Just past Barra da Tijuca and Recreio is **Macumba Beach**; its left and right breaks draw both longboarders and beginners. After Macumba is pretty **Prainha**, which is widely considered the best surf spot in the area, with waves reaching 3m on good days. If it's too packed, you can continue to **Grumari**, where the swell isn't as good but the crowds are thinner.

You can also get out on the water on a stand-up paddle board.

For boards and other gear, visit **Galeria River** (Map p74; www.galeriariver.com.br; Francisco Otaviano 67, Arpoador; ⏲9am-8pm Mon-Sat, 10am-7pm Sun) or **Spirit Surfboards** (Map p74; Galeria River, Francisco Otaviano 67, Arpoador; surfboard hire per day from R$60; ⏲10am-6pm Mon-Sat). You can also rent boards on the beach and from hostels such as Mango Tree (p85). You can hire paddle boards by the half hour from outfits located at the southern end of Copacabana Beach. You can also rent a kayak off the beach in Praia Vermelha in Urca.

> **COOK IN RIO**
>
> Run by Simone Almeida, **Cook in Rio** (Map p74; ☎21 98894-9857; www.cookinrio.com; 2nd fl, Belfort Roxo 161, Copacabana) is a hands-on one-day course that shows you how to prepare either *moqueca* (seafood stew) or *feijoada* (black bean and pork stew), along with appetizers and side dishes, dessert and a masterful caipirinha. The best part is that you'll get to devour your creations afterwards.

Courses

Caminhos Language Centre LANGUAGE
(Map p66; ☎21 2267-6552; www.caminhoslanguages.com; Farme de Amoedo 135, Ipanema; private class per hour R$90, 4-week 80hr course R$1800) Offers competitively priced Portuguese classes, with intensive group classes – four hours a day for five days for R$450. Profits go toward its social project Mais Caminhis (www.maiscaminhos.org).

Maracatu Brasil MUSIC
(Map p86; ☎21 2557-4754; www.maracatubrasil.com.br; 2nd fl, Ipiranga 49, Laranjeiras; ⏲11am-8pm Mon-Sat) This is the best place in Rio to study percussion, and students have the opportunity to perform in music events throughout the city. Instructors here offer courses in a number of different drumming styles: Amazonian rhythms, samba, conga drums, Candomblé and much more, plus private lessons in guitar and other instruments.

Rio Samba Dancer DANCING
(☎21 98229-2843; www.riosambadancer.com; group/private class US$20/60, private class for 2/3 people US$65/90) English-speaking dance instructor Hélio Ricardo offers private and group dance classes in samba or *forró* (a popular music of the Northeast). To try out your new moves, take a samba class and night tour combo: you'll get a one-hour crash course, then head out to Lapa for a night of dancing in a club (US$60 per person, including guide, transportation and club admissions).

WORTH A TRIP

EXPLORING THE BAY

To the east of Centro lies Rio's scenic bay. Unfortunately, it's too polluted for swimming, but it makes a fine backdrop for a boat ride to Ilha de Paquetá or Niterói.

Ilha de Paquetá

This car-free island provides a pleasant escape from the city's bustle. Transport is by foot, bicycle (there are hundreds for rent) or horse-drawn carts. There's a certain decadent charm to the colonial buildings, unassuming beaches and businesses catering to local tourism. The place gets crowded on weekends. Boats leave from near Praça XV (Quinze) de Novembro in Centro. The ferry takes 70 minutes and will cost you R$12.20 for a return trip. There are 12 departures daily, roughly every 90 minutes from about 7am.

Niterói

Across the bay from Rio, the city of Niterói's principal attraction is the photogenic Museu do Arte Contemporânea (. The cruise across the bay, however, is perhaps just as valid a reason for leaving Rio. The ferry costs R$12.20 return and leaves near Praça XV (Quinze) de Novembro in Centro; it's usually full of commuters. Once you reach the dock, the immediate area is a busy commercial district, full of pedestrians and crisscrossing intersections. From here catch bus 47B to the MAC (McDermott Athletic Centre), 2.1km south, or simply return on the next ferry.

Tours

Favela Tour CULTURAL

(☎21 3322-2727; www.favelatour.com.br; tours R$95) Marcelo Armstrong's insightful tour pioneered favela (slum, informal community) tourism. His three-hour excursion in Rocinha provides a fascinating insight into life inside the favela. You'll also stop in a community school, with funding from his tours helping to support various social projects.

Paulo Amendoim CULTURAL

(☎21 99747-6860; www.favelatourrio.com; tours R$75) Recommended guide Paulo Amendoim is the former president of Rocinha's residents' association. He seems to know everyone in the favela, and leads a warm and personalized three-hour tour that helps visitors see beyond the stereotypes.

Free Walker Tours WALKING

(Map p92; ☎21 97101-3352; www.freewalkertours.com) This well-organized outfit runs a free walking tour that takes in a bit of history and culture in downtown Rio. You'll visit the Travessa do Comércio, Praça XV (Quinze) do Novembre, Cinelândia, the Arcos da Lapa and the Selarón steps, among other places. Although it's free, the guide asks for tips at the end: R$50 is fair for the insightful three-hour walk.

Sail in Rio BOATING

(Map p86; ☎21 99998-3709; www.sailinrio.com; Av Pasteur 333, Iate Clube do Rio de Janeiro; sailing tours from R$250) This recommended outfit offers memorable sailing tours around Rio. When the weather cooperates, there are daily departures (at 11am) from the yacht club in Urca. You can also arrange your own private sailings with up to 10 people; you choose the date and help design the itinerary (private sailings cost R$1500 for three hours, R$1800 for five hours).

Bem Brasil CRUISE

(Map p92; www.bembrasilrio.com; Marina da Glória, Glória; cruises from R$75) Runs popular booze cruises in the bay from a two-story yacht every Monday night at 11pm. Also hosts big, fun parties in Rio venues, including Barzin (p111) on a Tuesday night and Palaphita Gávea (p114) on a Thursday.

Rio Street Art Tour CULTURAL

(☎21 99762-8083; www.riostreetarttour.com; tours R$60-120) Nina Chini Gani's street-art tours take small groups on foot or by van to explore Rio's vibrant urban-art scene. Tours last two to four hours, and cover Zona Sul, Zona Norte and the revitalized Port Zone. Nina's encyclopedic knowledge of Rio's urban artists gives guests a deeper understanding of the artworks while providing an alternative introduction to the city.

Brazil Expedition TOURS
(☎21 99998-2907; www.brazilexpedition.com; all-day city tours R$160) Friendly English-speaking guides run a variety of traditional tours around Rio, including trips to Cristo Redentor, hikes in Parque Nacional da Tijuca, game-day trips to Maracanã football stadium, street-art tours and favela (slum, informal community) tours.

Rio Secret Spots OUTDOORS
(☎21 99991-7477; www.riosecretspots.com; tours from R$200) Leads small-group tours by car out to beautiful hidden beaches west of Rio, as well as many other lovely spots beyond the city. Aside from the cliff-top panoramas, hidden lagoons and captivating unpeopled beaches in a quasi-tropical paradise, the tour includes some great photos from your trip (using a GoPro and a drone).

Helisight SCENIC FLIGHTS
(Map p71; ☎21 2542-7935; www.helisight.com.br; 6/15/30min flight per person R$350/880/1220) Offering helicopter tours since 1991, Helisight has seven itineraries, all giving gorgeous views over the city. There's a three-person minimum. Helipad locations are at the edge of Lagoa and on Morro da Urca, the first cable-car stop up Pão de Açúcar.

Festivals & Events

Aside from Carnaval, there are many other exciting events happening throughout the year.

Festas Juninas CULTURAL
(Jun) The June Festival is one of the most important folkloric festivals in Brazil. In Rio it's celebrated in various public plazas throughout the month, primarily on June 13 (Dia de Santo Antônio), June 24 (Dia de São João) and June 29 (Dia de São Pedro).

Portas Abertas ART
(www.facebook.com/artedeportasabertas; Santa Teresa) Santa Teresa's artists open their studios and the neighborhood becomes a living installation for a weekend each year in winter. Dates have varied between June and September, making it rather difficult to plan for.

Rio International Film Festival FILM
(www.festivaldorio.com.br; Oct or Nov) The festival is one of the biggest in Latin America. Some 250 films from more than 60 countries are shown at 20-odd theaters. Runs over two weeks.

Reveillon & Festa de Iemanjá NEW YEAR
(Copacabana; Dec 31) New Year's Eve (Reveillon) in Rio is celebrated by millions of people. Tons of fireworks explode in the sky over Copacabana. New Year's Day coincides with the festival of Iemanjá, the sea goddess. Wearing white, the faithful carry a statue of Iemanjá to the beach and launch flowers and other offerings into the sea.

Sleeping

Rio has a wide mix of lodging options, including boutique hotels, hostels, B&Bs and plenty of cookie-cutter high-rise accommodations. If you want to be in the heart of the action and don't mind paying for it, stay in Ipanema or Leblon, where there are beautiful beaches and excellent restaurants, shopping and nightlife. Copacabana has many more options (and better prices), plus a great beach and many restaurants and bars.

For a nonbeach alternative, take a peek at Santa Teresa's colonial guesthouses – the neighborhood is also close to the nightlife of Lapa. Other northern neighborhoods along the metro line (Botafogo, Flamengo and Catete) generally have cheaper options than the beachside southern neighborhoods.

Hotel rates are 30% higher during summer (from December to mid-March) and prices double or triple for New Year's Eve and Carnaval, when most places, including hostels, also require four- or seven-day minimum bookings.

Ipanema & Leblon

Mango Tree HOSTEL $
(Map p66; ☎21 3083-5031; www.mangotreehzzzzzostel.com; Prudente de Morais 594, Ipanema; dm R$40-55, d with/without bathroom R$220/160;) In a cheery yellow house in Ipanema, this well-run hostel offers rooms with two-toned wood floors and a welcoming atmosphere. The back terrace with a bar provides open-air space for unwinding, and it's a great spot to meet other travelers. There's a kitchen, surfboard rental and plenty of activities on offer (including boat parties, surf outings and street art tours).

El Misti HOSTEL $
(Map p66; ☎21 2246-1070; www.elmistihostelipanema.com; Joana Angélica 47; dm/d from R$45/250;) An excellent base in Ipanema, the friendly El Misti has simple, well-maintained dorm rooms (sleeping four to 12) as well as a few private rooms (two

Flamengo, Botafogo, Catete & Humaitá

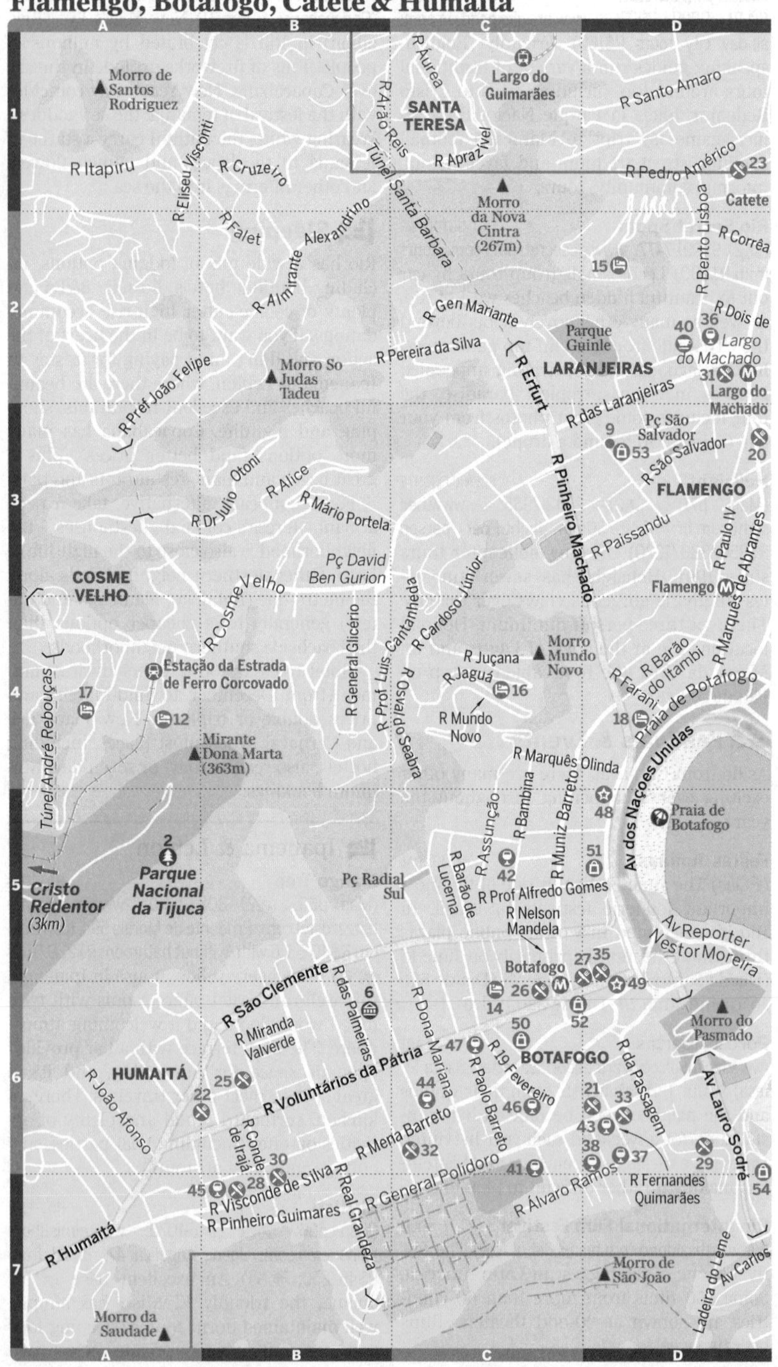

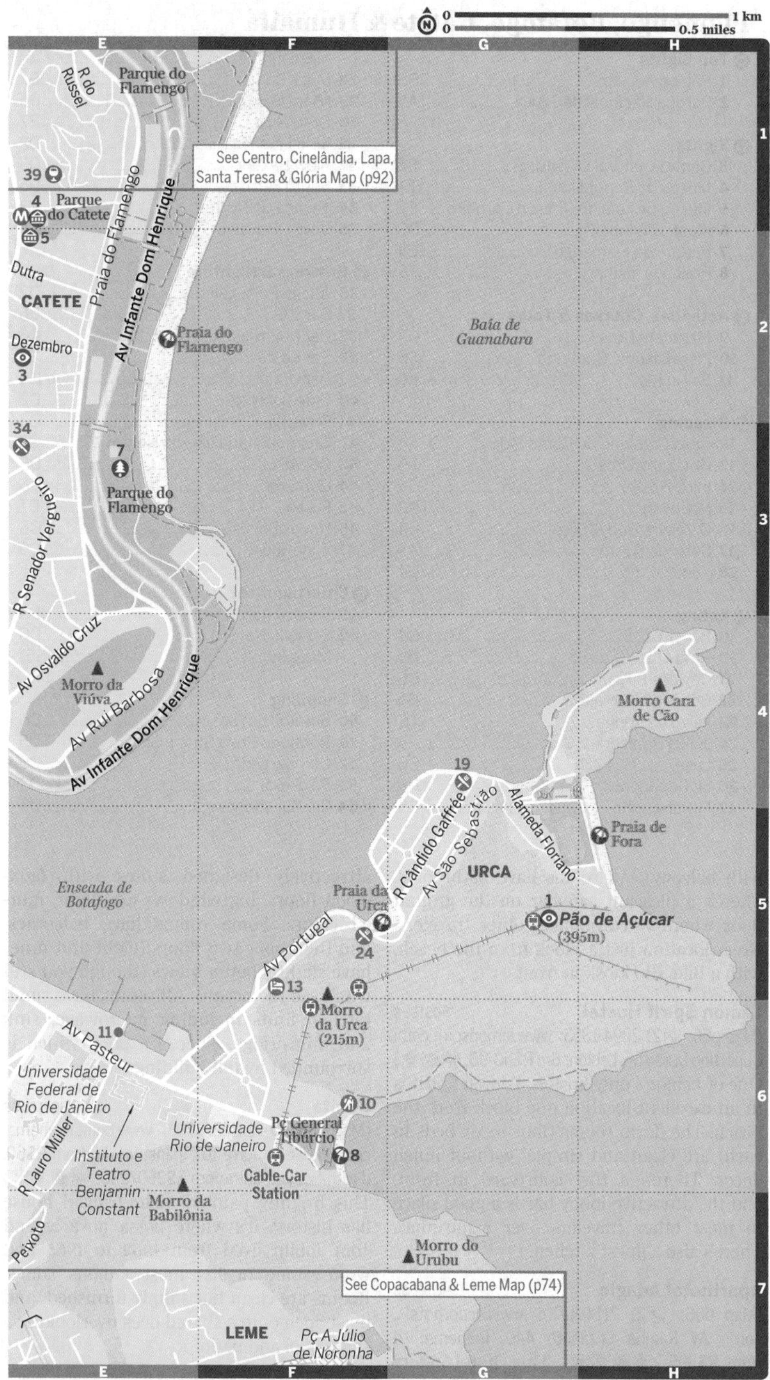

0 1 km
0 0.5 miles
E
F
G
H
1
2
3
4
5
6
7
R do Russel
Parque do Flamengo
See Centro, Cinelândia, Lapa, Santa Teresa & Glória Map (p92)
39
4
Parque do Catete
5
Dutra
CATETE
Praia do Flamengo
Av Infante Dom Henrique
Praia do Flamengo
Baía de Guanabara
Dezembro
3
34
7
Parque do Flamengo
R Senador Vergueiro
Av Osvaldo Cruz
Morro da Viúva
Av Rui Barbosa
Av Infante Dom Henrique
Morro Cara de Cão
19
R Cândido Gaffrée
Av São Sebastião
Alameda Floriano
Praia de Fora
URCA
Enseada de Botafogo
Praia da Urca
1
Pão de Açúcar
(395m)
24
Av Portugal
13
Morro da Urca
(215m)
11
Av Pasteur
Universidade Federal de Rio de Janeiro
10
Universidade Rio de Janeiro
Pç General Tibúrcio
8
R Lauro Müller
Instituto e Teatro Benjamin Constant
Cable-Car Station
Morro da Babilônia
Peixoto
Morro do Urubu
See Copacabana & Leme Map (p74)
LEME
Pç A Júlio de Noronha

Flamengo, Botafogo, Catete & Humaitá

Top Sights
1 Pão de Açúcar ... G5
2 Parque Nacional da Tijuca ... A5

Sights
3 Centro Cultural Oi Futuro ... E2
4 Museu da República ... E1
5 Museu de Folclore Edison Carneiro ... E2
6 Museu do Índio ... B6
7 Parque do Flamengo ... E3
8 Praia Vermelha ... F6

Activities, Courses & Tours
9 Maracatu Brasil ... D3
10 Pista Cláudio Coutinho ... F6
11 Sail in Rio ... E6

Sleeping
12 Casa Caminho do Corcovado ... A4
13 Hotelinho Urca ... F5
14 Injoy Hostel ... C6
15 Maze Inn ... D2
16 O Veleiro Bed & Breakfast ... C4
17 Solar do Cosme ... A4
18 Yoo2 ... D4

Eating
19 Bar Urca ... G4
20 Brou ... D3
21 Ceviche RJ ... D6
22 Cobal do Humaitá ... B6
23 Ferro e Farinha ... D1
24 Julius Brasserie ... F5
25 Lasai ... B6
26 Le Depanneur ... C6
27 Marchezinho ... D5
Maze Inn ... (see 15)
28 Meza Bar ... B7
29 Miam Miam ... D6
30 Oteque ... B7
31 Sírio Libaneza ... D2
32 Slow Bakery ... C6
33 South Ferro ... D6
34 Tacacá do Norte ... E3
35 Void – House of Food ... D5

Drinking & Nightlife
36 Adega Portugália ... D2
37 Bar 1928 ... D6
38 Bar Bukowski ... D6
39 Bar do Zé ... E1
Bar Urca ... (see 19)
40 Café Secreto ... D2
41 Caverna ... C6
42 Champanharia Ovelha Negra ... C5
43 CoLAB ... D6
44 Comuna ... C6
45 Fuska 2.0 ... B7
46 Hocus Pocus ... C6
47 WineHouse ... C6

Entertainment
48 Espaço Itaú ... D5
49 Estação Net Rio ... D6
Maze Inn ... (see 15)

Shopping
50 Baratos da Ribeiro ... C6
51 Botafogo Praia Shopping ... D5
52 Comparsaria ... C6
53 Pé de Boi ... D3
54 Rio Sul Shopping ... D6

with balcony). All rooms have bathrooms. There's a pleasant cafe-bar on the ground floor where you can meet other travelers. Great location just a block from the beach, with a Bike Rio kiosk in front.

Lemon Spirit Hostel HOSTEL $
(Map p66; 21 2294-1853; www.lemonspirit.com; Cupertino Durão 56, Leblon; dm R$50-90;) One of Leblon's only hostels, Lemon Spirit is in an excellent location one block from the beach. The dorm rooms (four to six beds in each) are clean and simple, without much decor. There's a tiny courtyard in front, and the attractive lobby bar is a good place to meet other travelers over caipirinhas. There's also a guest kitchen.

Aparthotel Adagio HOTEL $$
(Map p66; 21 2114-8100; www.accorhotels.com; Av Rainha Elizabeth 440, Ipanema; d from R$395;) This hotel offers attractively designed suites with faux-wood floors, big windows and light, muted colors. Some rooms have balconies, and the upper two floors (eight and nine) have slightly better views (though you still won't see the ocean). All rooms have small kitchen units including microwave, sink and mini-fridge. There's a pool, which is surrounded by tall buildings.

Bonita HOSTEL $$
(Map p66; 21 2227-1703; www.bonitaipanema.com; Barão da Torre 107, Ipanema; dm from R$60, d with/without bathroom R$360/230;) This brightly painted, palm-fringed house has history: it's where bossa nova legend Tom Jobim lived from 1962 to 1965 and wrote some of his most famous songs. Rooms are clean but simply furnished, and most open onto a shared deck overlooking a small pool and patio.

Ipanema Beach House HOSTEL $$
(Map p66; ☎21 3202-2693; www.beachhouseipanema.com; Barão da Torre 485, Ipanema; dm R$60-85, d with/without bathroom from R$270/220;) The location is fabulous, in a converted two-story house with a beautiful pool and yard, just a short stroll to the beach. The private rooms, while small, are bright and attractively furnished, and the common areas are quite enticing. On the downside, space is tight in the dorms (with three-tiered bunk beds), and the wait for the communal bathrooms can be long.

Margarida's Pousada POUSADA $$
(Map p66; ☎21 2239-1840; www.margaridaspousada.com; Barão da Torre 600, Ipanema; d from R$280, apt from R$360;) Those seeking something smaller and cozier than a high-rise hotel should try this superbly located Ipanema pousada (guesthouse). You'll find 11 simply furnished rooms scattered about the low-rise building; the best have small verandas. Margarida also rents out several private, fully equipped apartments nearby.

★**Hotel Fasano** HOTEL $$$
(Map p66; ☎21 3202-4000; www.fasano.com.br; Av Vieira Souto 80, Ipanema; d R$2500-5100;) Designed by Philippe Starck, the Fasano has fabulously designed rooms with hardwood floors, handsome furnishings (including chairs designed by Sergio Rodrigues) and eye-catching flourishes (oversized ear-shaped mirrors pay homage to Salvador Dalí). The best rooms have balconies overlooking the crashing waves of Ipanema Beach. The rooftop pool (open to guests only) is breathtaking, and the seafood-focused restaurant is outstanding.

Hotel Praia Ipanema HOTEL $$$
(Map p66; ☎21 2141-4949; www.praiaipanema.com; Av Vieira Souto 706, Ipanema; d R$550-1200, ste R$950-1600;) With a view of Ipanema Beach, this popular 16-story hotel offers trim, comfortable rooms, each with a balcony. The design is sleek and modern, with off-white tile floors, recessed lighting and artwork on the walls. Stretch out on the molded white lounge chairs next to the rooftop pool or enjoy a meal: the penthouse restaurant, Espaço 7zero6 (p99), is excellent.

Ipanema Inn HOTEL $$$
(Map p66; ☎21 2523-6092; www.ipanemainn.com.br; Maria Quitéria 27, Ipanema; d R$580-720;) Located just a short stroll from the beach, the Ipanema Inn is a simple hotel whose rooms have off-white ceramic tile floors and simple wood furnishings; some rooms are disappointingly small. *Superiores* (front-facing rooms) don't have ocean views, but if you lean far enough out the window, you'll get a glimpse of the beachfront.

Ritz Leblon HOTEL $$$
(Map p66; ☎21 2540-4940; www.ritzhotel.com.br; Av Ataúlfo de Paiva 1280, Leblon; r R$580-910, ste from R$1280;) In one of Rio's most desirable areas, this stylish low-key hotel has attractive, uniquely designed rooms and common areas that give it a boutique feel. The best rooms have kitchen units and balconies – some offering partial ocean views – and all have artwork, good lighting and spotless bedrooms.

Sol Ipanema HOTEL $$$
(Map p66; ☎21 2525-2020; www.solipanema.com.br; Av Vieira Souto 320, Ipanema; d R$690-820;) Occupying prime real estate facing Ipanema Beach, the tall, slender Sol Ipanema features contemporary rooms decorated in creams and earth tones, with dark-wood furnishings and good lighting. Pricier rooms have magnificent, unobstructed ocean views but are otherwise identical to the standard rooms.

Gávea, Jardim Botânico & Lagoa

Pouso Verde GUESTHOUSE $$
(Map p71; ☎21 2529-2942; www.pousoverde.com; Caminhoá 14, Jardim Botânico; s/d from R$260/300) On a quiet cobblestone street in a charming corner of Jardim Botânico, Pouso Verde has elegant, comfortably furnished rooms, the best of which have views of Cristo Redentor (Christ the Redeemer). The historic house, dating back to the 1890s, is packed with artwork, and the owners go out of their way to make guests feel at home. Excellent breakfasts.

Copacabana & Leme

Cabana Copa HOSTEL $
(Map p74; ☎21 97154-9473; www.cabanacopa.com.br; Travessa Guimarães Natal 10, Copacabana; dm R$40-60, d R$150-180;) Top hostel honors go to this Greek-Brazilian-run gem in a colonial-style '50s house tucked away in a Copacabana cranny. Four- to 10-bed dorms prevail throughout the home, which is chock-full of original architectural details and a hodgepodge of funky floorings. There's a lively bar and common areas.

Jucati APARTMENT $$
(Map p74; ☎21 2547-5422; www.edificiojucati.com.br; Tenente Marones de Gusmão 85, Copacabana; d/q from R$240/300;) On a tranquil street overlooking a small park, Jucati has large, simply furnished serviced apartments with tile floors and small but serviceable kitchens. Most apartments have just one bedroom with a double bed, and a living room with either a bunk bed (*beliche*) or pull-out sofa bed. The small covered courtyard is a fine spot to unwind.

Hotel Santa Clara HOTEL $$
(Map p74; ☎21 2256-2650; www.hotelsantaclara.com.br; Décio Vilares 316, Copacabana; d R$300-400;) Along one of Copacabana's most peaceful streets you'll find this attractive three-story hotel with a white stucco facade and blue shutters. The front-facing upstairs *(luxo)* rooms are best, with wood floors and balconies. The rooms in back are quieter, but also attractively designed with a wallpaper-covered feature wall and oversized hanging paper lanterns.

The on-site restaurant, 316 Bistro, serves *moqueca* and other Brazilian dishes, including a few creative vegetarian options (mains around R$28).

Orla Copacabana HOTEL $$
(Map p74; ☎21 2525-2425; www.orlahotel.com.br; Av Atlântica 4122, Copacabana; d R$400-750;) The Spanish-owned Orla Copacabana has some attractive, understated rooms, but the beach-facing location is the real draw. The standard rooms are too cramped, so it's not worth staying here unless you book one of the deluxe rooms, with their unobstructed ocean views.

The rooftop terrace offers fabulous views, though the adjoining plunge pool is tiny.

Rio Design Hotel BOUTIQUE HOTEL $$
(Map p74; ☎21 3222-8800; www.riodesignhotel.com; Francisco Sá 17, Copacabana; r R$475-590;) This stylish 13-story hotel demonstrates real design smarts. Rooms have tile floors, artful lighting and big windows, and each floor is decorated in a different style. The staff is friendly and there's a small dip pool on the rooftop, as well as a sauna and shoebox-sized fitness center that don't see much action.

Marta Rio Guesthouse B&B $$
(Map p74; ☎21 2521-8568; www.martarioguesthouse.com; Francisco Sá 5, Copacabana; d R$350-580;) Marta, a gracious host with an innate sense of hospitality, opens up her home and rents out six comfortable rooms at this split-level penthouse overlooking the beach. The highlight is undoubtedly the outdoor veranda, which has gorgeous views over Copacabana.

★**Hotel Emiliano** LUXURY HOTEL $$$
(Map p74; ☎21 3503-6600; www.emiliano.com.br; Av Atlântica 3804; d R$1600-2300;) Rio's loveliest new hotel sits on a prime spot fronting Copacabana's southern shore. The rooms have a modernist aesthetic, with jacaranda wood furniture, artful lighting and tropical photographs by the artist Leonardo Finotti. The small rooftop pool and bar (for guests only) is a fabulous retreat, and the ground-floor restaurant serves outstanding cuisine – including a decadent weekend brunch (R$195 including drinks).

Other thoughtful touches include high-end bath products by Santapele, a free pair of Havaianas flip flops, plus fruit and a free cocktail (enjoy it on the roof) upon arrival.

Belmond Copacabana Palace HOTEL $$$
(Map p74; ☎21 3500-0292; www.belmond.com; Av Atlântica 1702, Copacabana; d from R$1850;) Rio's most famous hotel has hosted heads of state, rock stars and other prominent personalities – Queen Elizabeth once stayed here, as did the Rolling Stones. The dazzling white facade dates from the 1920s, when it became a symbol of the city. Today accommodations range from deluxe rooms to spacious suites with balconies.

The pool is the loveliest in Rio, and the restaurants are top-notch.

Botafogo & Urca

★**Yoo2** BOUTIQUE HOTEL $$
(Map p86; ☎21 3445-2000; www.yoo2.com; Praia de Botafogo 242; d from R$350;) Yoo2, which opened in 2016, has taken a generic high-rise and transformed it into a captivating 138-room hotel with an avant-garde style. Glass elevators ascend up an interior adorned with street art, while the rooftop pool and bar offer 360° vistas over a jaw-dropping stretch of the city. Rooms are spacious and most have alluring views.

You can hire bikes, and the ground-floor restaurant is a fine place to try local microbrews while dining on creative Brazilian fusion fare (mains R$58 to R$77).

O Veleiro Bed & Breakfast GUESTHOUSE $$
(Map p86; ☎21 2554-8980; www.oveleiro.com; Mundo Novo 1440, Botafogo; d R$260-395;) Surrounded by Atlantic rainforest, O Veleiro is a delightfully set guesthouse located on a cobblestone road uphill from Botafogo. The rooms are small and adequately furnished but the backyard is the real attraction, with hammocks, a small pool and pretty views (plus the occasional marmoset visitor).

On the downside, it's a bit of a trudge to get down to Botafogo (even more so on the way back uphill), but for a tranquil escape that's still inside central Rio, this is a decent option.

Injoy Hostel GUESTHOUSE $$
(Map p86; ☎21 3593-6662; www.injoyhostel.com; Estácio de Coimbra 80, Botafogo; dm R$43-59, d R$160-250;) Despite the name, this place feels less like a hostel and more like a small guesthouse. Injoy has a mix of private doubles and cozy dorms set in a lovely house at the end of a tree-lined lane. Rooms are modern, very clean and well maintained, and each is named after a major city, with iconic photos from the destination decorating one wall. Friendly staff.

Hotelinho Urca GUESTHOUSE $$
(Map p86; ☎21 3449-8867; www.hotelinho.com; Marechal Cantuária 10, Urca; r R$280-390;) One of the few lodging options in Urca, this quiet, low-key guesthouse has a range of clean, well-equipped rooms with attractive wood floors. The sunny veranda has views over the bay and is the best feature; there's also a tiny dip pool. Hotelinho Urca also rents several apartments nearby.

Flamengo & Around

★Maze Inn GUESTHOUSE $
(Map p86; ☎21 2558-5547; www.jazzrio.com; Casa 66, Tavares Bastos 414, Catete; s/d R$120/140, with panoramic view R$160/180) Set in the Tavares Bastos favela, the Maze Inn is a fantastic place to overnight for those looking for an alternative view of Rio. The rooms are uniquely decorated with original artworks by English owner and Renaissance man Bob Nadkarni, while the veranda offers stunning views of the bay and Pão de Açúcar (Sugarloaf Mountain).

Discovery Hostel HOSTEL $
(Map p92; ☎21 3449-0672; www.discoveryhostel.com; Benjamin Constant 26, Catete; dm/d R$54/190;) One of Rio's most socially minded hostels, Discovery is a great place to meet other travelers. While it's not on the beach, the attractive converted house is convenient for exploring the nightlife of Lapa, and it's an easy stroll to the metro. In addition to dorm rooms (a minus for the triple bunks), the hostel has a couple of colorful private rooms.

There's a bar, a lounge and a small plant-lined patio. The staff organizes many activities for guests.

Solar do Cosme GUESTHOUSE $$
(Map p86; ☎21 3596-0585; www.solardocosme.com; Ladeira do Ascurra 124, Cosme Velho; d/tr/q/apt R$200/260/320/420;) Nestled at the foothill of Corcovado, this tranquil guesthouse earns high marks from guests for its verdant surroundings as well as the kindhearted hosts, who are happy to share tips on making the most of Rio. The rooms are tidy and well maintained, and the lush grounds add to the value.

On the downside, it's a long way from the beach, though it's a short walk to the railway station leading up to Cristo Redentor.

Casa Caminho do Corcovado B&B $$
(Map p86; ☎21 2265-2124; www.casacaminhodocorcovado.com.br; Filinto de Almeida 283, Cosme Velho; d from R$240;) On the Corcovado hillside, this idyllic place is surrounded by tropical rainforest, and feels like a peaceful escape from the city. Friendly, knowledgeable hosts offer just two attractive rooms and one bungalow overlooking the garden; the place is in high demand so book early. There are fine views, and a relaxing air pervades.

Centro & Praça Mauá

Belga Hotel HOTEL $$
(Map p92; ☎21 2263-9086; www.belgahotel.com.br; Rua dos Andradas 129; d R$130-320) In a beautifully restored building from the 1920s, this classy hotel is helping to breathe new life into an overlooked corner of downtown. The Belgian-owned pioneer has simple but comfortably priced rooms that are excellent value for the money (the best are the 'executive' rooms with French doors opening onto decorative balconies).

The Belgian bistro (p108) on the ground floor is not to be missed.

Centro, Cinelândia, Lapa, Santa Teresa & Glória

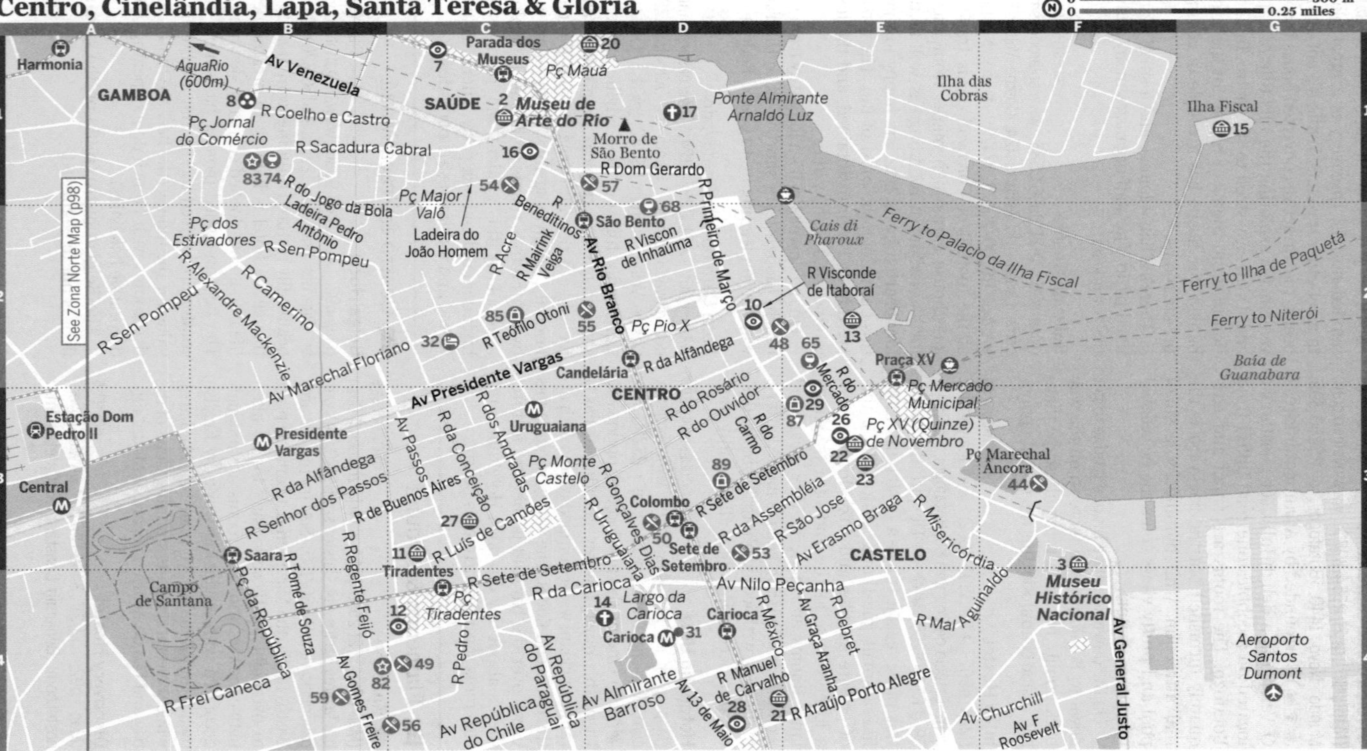

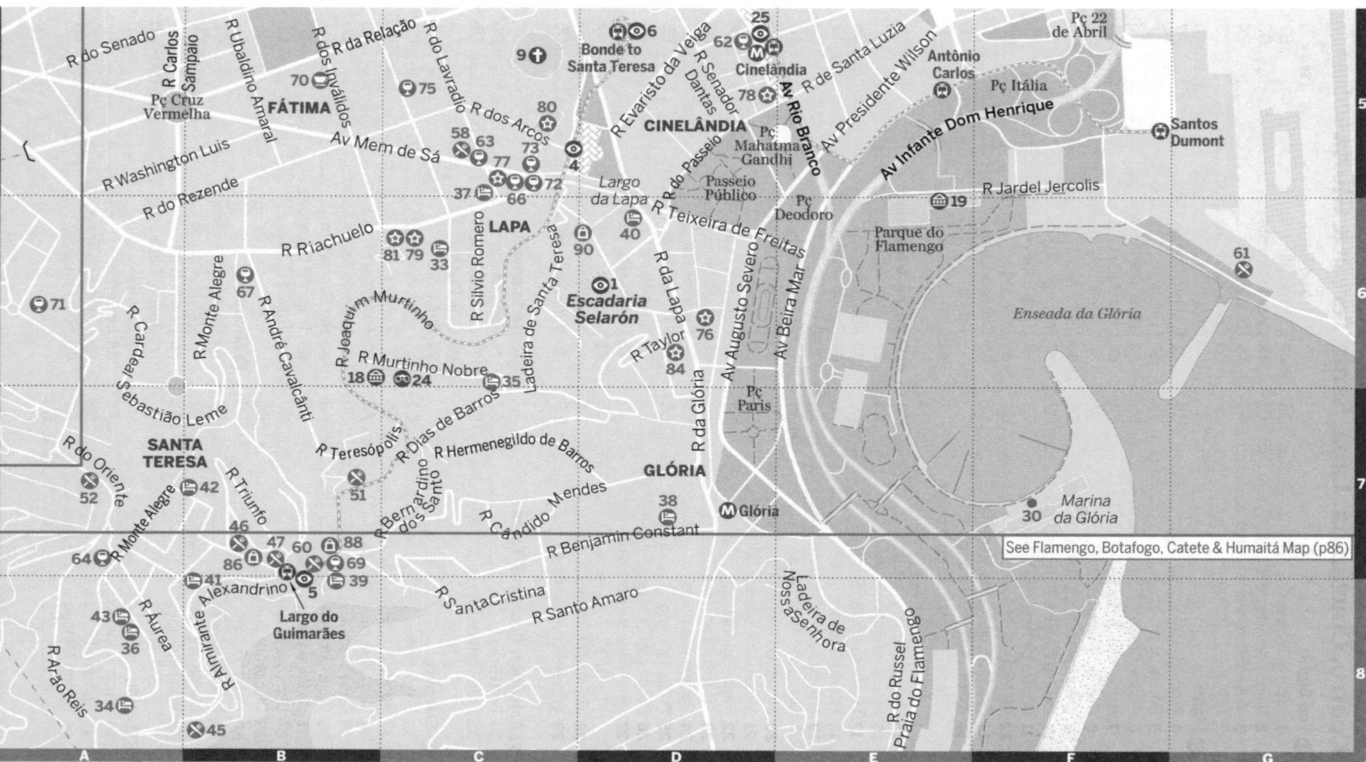
R do Senado
R Carlos Sampaio
Pç Cruz Vermelha
R Ubaldino Amaral
FÁTIMA
R dos Inválidos
R da Relação
R do Lavradio
R dos Arcos
Av Mem de Sá
R Washington Luis
R do Rezende
R Riachuelo
LAPA
R Silvio Romero
Bonde to Santa Teresa
R Evaristo da Veiga
R Senador Dantas
Cinelândia
CINELÂNDIA
Av Rio Branco
R de Santa Luzia
Av Presidente Wilson
Antônio Carlos
Pç Itália
Pç 22 de Abril
Av Infante Dom Henrique
Santos Dumont
Pç Mahatma Gandhi
R do Passeio
Passeio Público
Largo da Lapa
R Teixeira de Freitas
Pç Deodoro
R Jardel Jercolis
Parque do Flamengo
Enseada da Glória
Escadaria Selarón
Ladeira de Santa Teresa
R da Lapa
R Taylor
Av Augusto Severo
Av Beira Mar
Pç Paris
R da Glória
GLÓRIA
Glória
Marina da Glória
See Flamengo, Botafogo, Catete & Humaitá Map (p86)
R Monte Alegre
R André Cavalcânti
R Joaquim Murtinho
R Murtinho Nobre
R Cardeal Sebastião Leme
SANTA TERESA
R do Oriente
R Teresópolis
R Dias de Barros
R Hermenegildo de Barros
R Bernardino dos Santo
R Cândido Mendes
R Benjamin Constant
R Triunfo
R Monte Alegre
R Alexandrino
Largo do Guimarães
R Almirante Alexandrino
R Áurea
R Arão Reis
R Santa Cristina
R Santo Amaro
Ladeira de Nossa Senhora
R do Russel
Praia do Flamengo
A
B
C
D
E
F
G
5
6
7
8

Centro, Cinelândia, Lapa, Santa Teresa & Glória

Top Sights
1 Escadaria Selarón ... D6
2 Museu de Arte do Rio ... C1
3 Museu Histórico Nacional ... F3

Sights
4 Arcos da Lapa ... C5
5 Bonde ... B8
6 Bonde Station ... D5
7 Boulevard Olímpico ... C1
8 Cais do Valongo ... B1
9 Catedral Metropolitana ... C5
10 Centro Cultural Banco do Brasil ... D2
11 Centro de Arte Hélio Oiticica ... C3
12 CRAB ... C4
13 Espaço Cultural da Marinha ... E2
14 Igreja São Francisco da Penitência & Convento de Santo Antônio ... D4
15 Ilha Fiscal ... G1
16 Morro da Conceição ... C1
17 Mosteiro de São Bento ... D1
18 Museu Chácara do Céu ... B6
19 Museu de Arte Moderna ... E6
Museu de Arte Sacra ... (see 9)
20 Museu do Amanhã ... D1
21 Museu Nacional de Belas Artes ... D4
22 Paço Imperial ... E3
23 Palácio Tiradentes ... E3
24 Parque das Ruínas ... C6
25 Praça Floriano ... D5
26 Praça XV (Quinze) de Novembro ... E3
27 Real Gabinete Português de Leitura ... C3
28 Theatro Municipal ... D4
29 Travessa do Comércio ... E3

Activities, Courses & Tours
30 Bem Brasil ... F7
31 Free Walker Tours ... D4

Sleeping
32 Belga Hotel ... C2
33 Books Hostel ... C6
34 Casa Beleza ... A8
35 Casa Bianca ... C6
36 Casa Cool Beans ... A8
37 Da Lapa Design Hotel ... C5
38 Discovery Hostel ... D7
39 Discovery Suites ... B8
40 Hotel 55 Rio ... D6
41 Hotel Santa Teresa ... B8
42 Mama Shelter ... B7
43 Villa Laurinda ... A8

Eating
44 Ancoramar ... F3
45 Aprazível ... B8
46 Bar do Mineiro ... B7
Belga ... (see 32)
Bistrô do Paço ... (see 22)
47 Cafe do Alto ... B7
48 Cais do Oriente ... D2
49 Casa Momus ... C4
50 Confeitaria Colombo ... D3
Cristóvão ... (see 50)
51 Espírito Santa ... B7
52 Galeria Bazá ... A7
53 Govardhana Harí ... D3
54 Imaculada ... C1
55 L'Atelier du Cuisinier ... D2
56 Lilia ... C4
57 Mironga ... D1
58 Nova Capela ... C5
59 Refeitório ... B4
60 Sobrenatural ... B7
Térèze ... (see 41)
61 Xian ... G6

Drinking & Nightlife
62 Amarelinho ... D5
63 Antônio's ... C5
64 Bar do Gomes ... A7
Bar dos Descasados ... (see 41)
65 Bar Léo ... E2
66 Booze Bar ... C5
67 Buraco da Lacraia ... B6
68 Cine Botequim ... D2
69 Explorer Bar ... B7
70 Fazenda Paradiso Café ... B5
71 Goya-Beira ... A6
72 Leviano Bar ... C5
73 Sarau ... C5
74 The Week ... B1
75 Vaca Atolada ... C5

Entertainment
76 Beco do Rato ... D6
77 Carioca da Gema ... C5
78 Cine Odeon ... D5
79 Clube dos Democráticos ... C6
Favela Hype ... (see 86)
80 Fundição Progresso ... C5
81 Lapa 40 Graus ... C6
82 Rio Scenarium ... B4
83 Trapiche Gamboa ... B1
84 TribOz ... D6

Shopping
85 Casa Naara ... C2
CRAB ... (see 12)
86 Favela Hype ... B7
Galeria Bazá ... (see 52)
87 Granado ... E3
88 La Vereda ... B7
89 Livraria da Travessa ... D3
90 Loja Pence ... D6

Santa Teresa & Lapa

Da Lapa Design Hotel HOTEL $
(Map p92; 21 2252-4237; www.dalapahotel.com.br; Rua do Lavradio 200, Lapa; dm R$54-75, d R$200;) Set in lively Lapa, this kooky and colorful little hostel will wow you with its arty vibe and communal atrium. Breakfast is complimentary, and there's a seating area in the atrium for all to enjoy. And, of course, party central is right on the doorstep!

Books Hostel HOSTEL $
(Map p92; 21 3437-3783; www.bookshostel.com; Francisco Muratori 10, Lapa; dm R$45-75;) In the heart of Lapa and true to the nature of the neighborhood, this party hostel is the appetizer for your crazy night out. Dorms have eye-catching graffiti art and there's a social bar styled like a barraca (stall) – rooms overlooking it don't allow for much sleep. All bathrooms are shared, and only some rooms have air-conditioning.

★**Casa Beleza** POUSADA $$
(Map p92; 21 98288-6764; www.casabeleza.com; Laurinda Santos Lobo 311, Santa Teresa; r R$290-470, villas R$650;) This lovely property dates to the 1930s and was once a governor's mansion. Tropical gardens overlook the picturesque pool, and you can sometimes spot toucans and monkeys in the surrounding foliage. It's a small and peaceful operation, with just four guest rooms and one peacefully set villa (complete with rooftop deck offering panoramic views).

The kind multilingual family that runs the *pousada* lives on-site.

Discovery Suites GUESTHOUSE $$
(Map p92; 21 3264-9665; www.discoverysuitesrio.com; Almirante Alexandrino 399, Santa Teresa; r from R$260;) Run by the same folks behind the charming Explorer Bar (p118) next door, Discovery Suites has bright, stylish rooms with nicely framed artwork, colorful textiles, vintage furnishings, comfortable beds and sparkling modern bathrooms. The veranda is a fine spot to relax while taking in views over Santa Teresa.

It's also in a great location near the neighborhood's shops, eateries and *bonde* (streetcar) stop. The entrance is on Corrêa de Sá.

Mama Shelter BOUTIQUE HOTEL $$
(Map p92; 21 3980-0300; www.mamashelter.com; Paschoal Carlos Magno 5, Santa Teresa; r R$320-650;) Part of a budget-minded boutique-hotel chain, Mama Shelter has 55 colorful rooms, each with whimsical touches and bursting with personality. Lush greenery surrounds the property, and the various terraces make fine places to enjoy the tropical setting. The airy restaurant serves a mix of Brazilian classics and creatively topped pizzas, and the stylish bar is a destination in its own right.

Mama Shelter is in a good location within walking distance of Santa Teresa's epicenter, about 400m from Largo de Guimarães.

Hotel 55 Rio BOUTIQUE HOTEL $$
(Map p92; 21 3883-2030; www.55rio.com.br; Visconde de Maranguape 9, Centro; d R$200-250, ste R$475) This stylish boutique hotel is located just a few minutes' walk from Escadaria Selarón (p76), the Arcos da Lapa (p76) and the nightlife hot spots of Av Mem de Sá. The hotel's stunning facade was recently restored, and although the original hotel was built more than 100 years ago, today's incarnation (reopened in 2016) features ultramodern design throughout.

Villa Laurinda GUESTHOUSE $$
(Map p92; 21 2507-2216; www.villalaurinda.net; Laurinda Santos Lobo 98, Santa Teresa; d with/without bathroom from R$260/210;) In a converted 1888 Victorian house, Villa Laurinda presents a serene portrait of life in Santa Teresa. At the entrance there's a lovely pool, ringed with tropical foliage and mango trees. The rooms are simply designed, with wide-plank floors, and range from small to large; three of the rooms share a bathroom (others are en suite).

Casa Bianca GUESTHOUSE $$
(Map p92; 21 3233-1563; www.guesthousebianca.com; Murtinho Nobre 35, Santa Teresa; r R$270-350;) This beautiful 1930s-era mansion down the road from Parque das Ruinas (p73) has lovely details: stained-glass windows, tall ceilings, a marble staircase and period furnishings. Rooms are attractively set, with wood floors and antique fixtures; two have excellent views, and one of these has a private veranda. It's a quiet place with just three rooms. The friendly owner lives on-site.

Casa Cool Beans GUESTHOUSE $$
(Map p92; 21 2262-0552; www.casacoolbeans.com; Laurinda Santos Lobo 136, Santa Teresa; s/d R$300/350;) Your expectations will easily be exceeded at this discreet 10-room B&B, where the American owner's mantra focuses on personalized service.

Each colorful room in the renovated 1930s Spanish-style villa was designed by a different Brazilian artist; book room 9 for the best views. It also has a spacious sundeck and an enticing pool. No children allowed.

★Hotel Santa Teresa BOUTIQUE HOTEL **$$$**
(Map p92; ☎21 3380-0200; www.santateresahotelrio.com; Almirante Alexandrino 660, Santa Teresa; d from R$950;) What is probably the finest boutique hotel in Rio is set in a lavishly restored building that was part of a coffee plantation in the 19th century. It includes artfully designed rooms, an award-winning restaurant (p109), a full-service spa, a stylish bar and a pool with fine views over the city.

The design incorporates a certain tropical elegance, with art and artifacts from across Brazil on display in common areas and in some rooms.

Barra da Tijuca & Western Rio

Rio Surf 'N Stay HOSTEL **$**
(☎21 3418-1133; www.riosurfnstay.com; Raimundo Veras 1140, Recreio dos Bandeirantes; dm/d from R$65/196;) Just a short stroll to the fine surf off Macumba Beach, this converted house, which is owned by a New Zealander and a Brazilian, is the go-to spot for anyone who has come to Rio to learn to surf. The dorm rooms (sleeping four or five people) and private doubles are comfortably furnished, and the hosts make everyone feel at home.

LSH Lifestyle HOTEL **$$**
(☎21 3609-1140; www.lshhotel.net; Professor Coutinho Fróis 10; d from R$450;) In an excellent location near Praia do Pepê, this lavish 122-room hotel has handsome interiors (designed by notable American architect David Rockwell), good service and excellent amenities. The rooms are strikingly modern, with floor-to-ceiling windows, spacious bathrooms and verandas. The best suites have their own private outdoor Jacuzzis overlooking the beach.

Eating

Rio has an impressive array of restaurants, serving up Brazilian regional cuisine along with international and fusion fare. In general, Ipanema and Leblon have Rio's best dining, though every neighborhood has its gems.

Rio's quintessential dining experiences include feasting at a *churrascaria* (all-you-can-eat barbecued-meat restaurant), joining the fashion parade at a sidewalk cafe in Ipanema, chowing on local favorites at a neighborhood *boteco* (small open-air bar) and lingering over the views from a restaurant patio up in Santa Teresa.

To eat on the cheap, try per-kilo places and juice bars. Self-caterers should check out Rio's many *feiras* (produce markets).

Ipanema

Joana PIZZA **$**
(Map p66; ☎21 98201-8044; www.facebook.com/joanapizzabar; Joana Angélica 47; pizzas R$24-30; ⏲6pm-midnight Tue-Sun;) One block up from Ipanema Beach, this hip little spot with a small terrace fires up some of the best thin-crust pizzas in the Zona Sul. The creative toppings steal the show: grilled pumpkin and eggplant with cherry tomatoes (the Veggie), or thin slices of marinated steak with fresh goat cheese and mint (the Churrasco Turco).

Delírio Tropical BRAZILIAN **$**
(Map p66; ☎21 3624-8164; www.delirio.com.br; Garcia d'Ávila 48; salads R$18-27; ⏲11am-9pm Mon-Sat;) Delírio Tropical serves a tempting array of salads, which you can enhance by adding grilled trout, salmon carpaccio, filet mignon and other items. The open layout has a pleasant, casual ambience, but you'll need to go early to beat the lunchtime crowds.

Barraca do Uruguai SNACKS **$**
(Map p66; Posto 9, Ipanema Beach; sandwiches R$14-20; ⏲noon-5pm) Of the many *barracas* (food stalls) on Ipanema Beach, Uruguai is a long-term favorite and serves scrumptious grilled chicken, beef and sausage sandwiches, plus *agua de côco* (coconut water), caipirinhas, beers and other refreshments. Look for the blue-and-white striped Uruguayan flag flying high over the beach.

Vezpa PIZZA **$**
(Map p66; www.vezpa.com.br; Av Ataúlfo de Paiva 1063; pizza slices from R$11; ⏲noon-2am Sun-Thu, to 4am Fri & Sat) Vezpa is a New York–style pizza place in Leblon, with brick walls and high ceilings, where you can order pizza by the slice. The crusts are thin and crunchy and there are decent selections on hand – try the mozzarella with tomatoes and basil. Vezpa also has many other locations, including in Ipanema (on Farme de Amoedo) and Copacabana (on Djalma Ulrich).

FOOD MARKETS

The *feiras* (produce markets) that pop up in different locations throughout the week are the best places to shop for juicy mangoes, papayas, pineapples and other fruits. For an authentic slice of homegrown *carioca* commerce, nothing beats wandering through a market and taking in the action. The best time to go is from 9am to noon; the *feiras* end by 2pm or 3pm. You can also stop in at Ipanema's Hippie Fair (p121) on Sunday for delectable Bahian fare.

Cobal do Humaitá (Map p86; Voluntários da Pátria 446, Botafogo; ⌚8am-10pm) is the city's largest farmers market, and sells plenty of veggies and fruit; it also has cafes and restaurants, and a huge open-air pavilion for alfresco dining. **Cobal do Leblon** (Map p66; ☎21 2529-2222; Gilberto Cardoso; ⌚6pm-1am Tue-Sun) has Fruit stalls, as well as infdoor-outdoor restaurants and bars. You can also check out the following:

Copacabana Markets are held Wednesday on Praça Edmundo Bittencourt, Thursday on Ministro Viveiros de Castro and Ronald de Carvalho, Saturday on General Azevedo Pimentel and Sunday on Praça Serzedelo Correia.

Gávea Friday market on Praça Santos Dumont.

Glória Sunday market on Av Augusto Severo.

Ipanema Markets are held Monday on Henrique Dumont, Tuesday on Praça General Osório and Friday on Praça NS da Paz.

Jardim Botânico Saturday market on Frei Leandro.

Leblon Thursday market on General Urquiza.

Leme Monday market on Gustavo Sampaio.

Santa Teresa Friday market on Felicio dos Santos.

Urca Sunday market on Praça Tenente Gil Guilherme.

La Veronese PIZZA $

(Map p66; ☎21 2247-3152; www.laveronese.com.br; Visconde de Pirajá 29; mini pizzas from R$5; ⌚8:30am-7pm Tue-Fri, to 6pm Sat, 9am-2:30pm Sun) If Rio is destroying your budget, head to this friendly stand-up snack counter for one of the best deals in the Zona Sul: the R$5 mini pizza with crispy crust is excellent value, and you can top it off with a few strangely addictive *palmeiras* (palm-shaped cookies).

La Carioca Cevicheria PERUVIAN $$

(Map p66; ☎21 2522-8184; www.lacarioca.com.br; Garcia d'Ávila 173; sharing plates R$31-51; ⌚6:30pm-1am Mon, noon-1am Tue-Sun) True to its name, this Peruvian place specializes in ceviche and serves more than a dozen varieties of the tangy, tender seafood dish. Other great plates for sharing include the *pulpo andino* (crispy octopus with potato salad and baked red pepper), *tiraditos* (fresh, thinly sliced fish) and *lomo saltado* (stir-fried steak and spices).

Take a seat on the inviting front terrace and don't forget to order a pisco sour; they're the best you'll find this side of Machu Picchu.

Quitéria BRAZILIAN $$

(Map p66; ☎21 2267-4603; www.ipanemainn.com.br/en/quiteria; Maria Quitéria 27; mains around R$53, lunch buffet weekday/weekends R$39/53; ⌚7am-11pm) Inside the Ipanema Inn (p89), this humble-looking place serves delectable contemporary Brazilian cooking. Seasonal, high-quality ingredients feature in the extensive lunch buffet, which draws mostly locals. By night the à la carte menu offers hits such as nicely turned out pork ribs with mashed baroa potatoes and cashew sauce, or grilled catch of the day with creamy rice and black-eyed beans.

Mercearia da Praça BRAZILIAN $$

(Map p66; ☎21 3986-1400; www.facebook.com/merceariadapracaipanema; Praça General Osório; mains R$45-80; ⌚11am-midnight Mon, 9am-midnight Tue-Sun) This photogenic newcomer evokes more than a hint of old-world Portugal with its tiled walls, bottle-filled shelves and gourmet items tantalizingly displayed in glass counters. Creamy *bacalhau* (codfish), duck with rice and octopus salad are best followed by a rich *pastel de nata* (custard tart). The buzzing space also functions as a deli and a wine shop.

Zona Norte

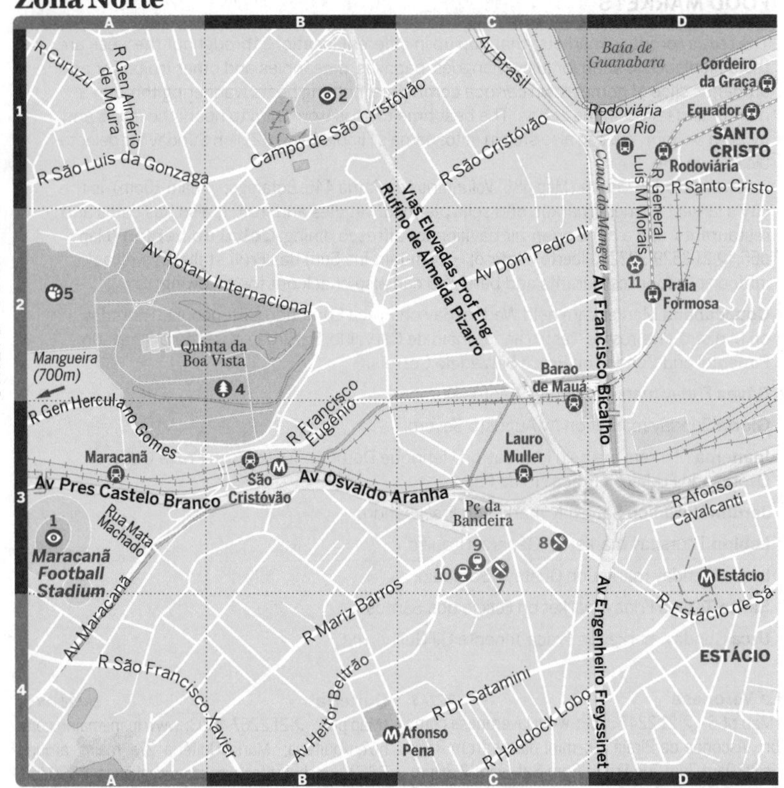

Empório Jardim na Praia BISTRO **$$**
(Map p66; ☎21 2513-5151; www.emporiojardimrio.com.br; Maria Quitéria 62; mains R$36-68; ⏰8am-10pm; 📶🍴) This charming cafe, which arrived in Ipanema in 2018, was an instant hit thanks to its excellent anytime menu of rich quiches, huge ingredient-packed salads and mouthwatering sandwiches on Empório's house-baked breads. You can start off the morning (or take an afternoon coffee break) over flaky croissants, éclairs and fruit-topped tarts at the bakery counter. Excellent vegetarian options, too.

Venga! SPANISH **$$**
(Map p66; ☎21 2247-0234; www.venga.com.br; Garcia d'Ávila 147; small plates R$20-46; ⏰noon-midnight; 🍴) A festive spot to eat and drink, Venga! was Rio's first authentic tapas bar when it opened back in 2009. Classic wood details and a good soundtrack set the scene for noshing on *patatas bravas* (spicy potatoes), *pulpo a la Gallega* (grilled octopus), *gambas al ajillo* (garlic prawns) and other Iberian hits. Match those small plates with a glass of Spanish rioja.

There are other Venga! locations in town, including in Leblon, Copacabana and Jardim Botânico.

Frontera BUFFET **$$**
(Map p66; ☎21 3289-2350; www.frontera.com.br; Visconde de Pirajá 128; food per kg R$65-70; ⏰11:30am-11pm) Run by a Dutch chef, Frontera offers more than 60 plates at its lunch buffet, which features a mouthwatering assortment of grilled meats, baked casseroles and seafood pastas, plus grilled vegetables, salads, fresh fruits and desserts. Sushi and the dessert counter costs extra. Dark woods and vintage travel posters give it a cozier feel than most per-kilo places.

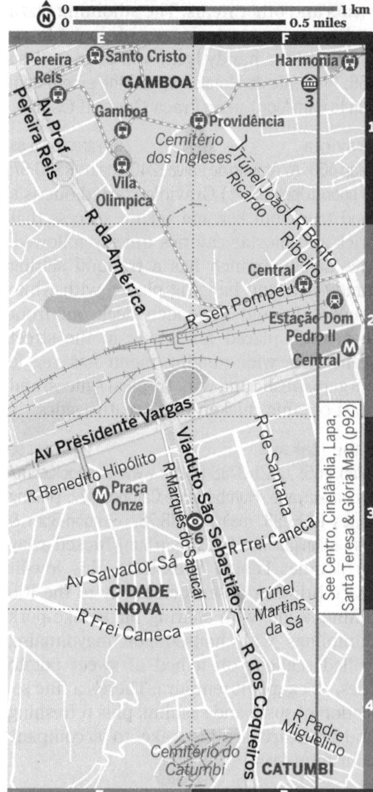

Via Sete INTERNATIONAL **$$**
(Map p66; ☎21 2512-8100; www.viasete.com.br; Garcia d'Ávila 125; mains R$46-92; ⏰noon-midnight; 📶) This restaurant on upscale Garcia d'Ávila serves a good selection of salads, burgers and unique appetizers such as calamari in manioc crust, as well as excellent grilled dishes like tuna steak, rump steak, Black Angus and a fish of the day. You choose the side dishes and sauce to accompany your meal.

Garota de Ipanema BRAZILIAN **$$**
(Map p66; ☎21 2522-0340; Vinícius de Moraes 49; mains R$64-133; ⏰noon-2am) A mix of visitors and neighborhood regulars pack the tables at the former bar where 'The Girl from Ipanema' composers Tom Jobim and Vinícius de Moraes once held court. Although the food is fairly standard Brazilian fare, one dish stands out: the *picanha Brasileira* (R$133 for two), a scrumptious skillet of sliced sirloin brought sizzling to your table.

Zona Norte

Top Sights
1 Maracanã Football Stadium A3

Sights
2 Feira Nordestina B1
3 Instituto de Pesquisa e Memória Presto Novos F1
4 Quinta da Boa Vista B2
5 Rio Zoo A2
6 Sambódromo F3

Eating
7 Aconchego Carioca C3
8 Bar Kalango C3

Drinking & Nightlife
9 Hop Lab C3
10 Noo Cachaçaria C3

Entertainment
11 Unidos da Tijuca D2

★Zazá Bistrô Tropical FUSION **$$$**
(Map p66; ☎21 2247-9101; www.zazabistro.com.br; Joana Angélica 40; mains R$65-87; ⏰7pm-midnight Mon-Thu, from noon Fri-Sun) Inside an art-filled and whimsically decorated converted house, Zazá serves beautifully prepared dishes with Asian accents, and uses organic ingredients when possible. Favorites include chicken curry with jasmine rice, flambéed prawns with risotto, and grilled fish served with caramelized plantain. Don't miss brilliantly creative cocktails like the Caramba Carambola, with Amazonian gin (or vodka), carambola (star fruit), ginger, mint and lemon.

Upstairs, diners lounge in shoeless comfort on throw pillows amid flickering candles. You can also sit at one of the tables out the front.

Espaço 7zero6 BRAZILIAN **$$$**
(Map p66; ☎21 2141-4992; www.espaco7zero6.com.br; Av Vieira Souto 706; set brunch R$100; ⏰noon-midnight Mon-Thu, 8am-2pm & 6pm-midnight Fri-Sun) From its location on the top floor of the Hotel Praia Ipanema (p89), this place has a jaw-dropping view of Ipanema Beach. The dinner menu features Brazilian classics, but the best time to come is for the weekend brunch, when the restaurant spreads a banquet of tropical fruits, yogurt, freshly baked breads and pastries, egg dishes and even waffles.

Casa da Feijoada BRAZILIAN $$$
(Map p66; ☎21 2247-2776; www.restaurantecasadafeijoada.com.br; Prudente de Morais 10B; feijoada R$95; ⏲noon-midnight Mon-Sat, to 11pm Sun) Admirers of Brazil's iconic *feijoada* (black bean and salted pork stew served with rice) needn't wait until Saturday, the time it's traditionally eaten, to experience this meaty meal. The casual Casa da Feijoada serves the rich dish every day of the week.

Leblon

Petit Formidable CAFE $
(Map p66; www.formidablebistrot.com.br; João Lira 148; pastries from R$10; ⏲cafe 8am-6pm, bakery 7am-6pm) Next to the Formidable bistro (p101), this tiny bakery and cafe fires up delicious croissants, *pains au chocolat*, éclairs, mille-feuilles and other delicacies. The cafe also serves eggs Benedict, croque monsieurs (toasted ham and cheese sandwiches) and other light fare.

Vegetariano Social Club VEGAN $
(Map p66; ☎21 2294-5200; www.vegetarianosocialclube.com.br; Conde Bernadotte 26L; buffet lunch R$38, mains R$28-36; ⏲noon-11pm Mon-Sat, to 5:30pm Sun; ☑) Vegetarians interested in sampling Brazil's signature dish should visit this small charmer on a Wednesday or a Sunday, when tofu *feijoada* is served. At other times, this 100% vegan eatery serves a 10-dish lunch buffet, while the evening à la carte menu features pizzas, vegetable sandwiches, oat pancakes with shiitake mushrooms and delicious salads.

Kurt DESSERTS $
(Map p66; ☎21 2294-0599; www.confeitariakurt.com.br; General Urquiza 117B; desserts R$14-17; ⏲8am-7pm Mon-Fri, 9am-6pm Sat) Extremely popular and going strong since 1942, Kurt has an array of irresistible temptations: flaky strudels, berry crumbles, and palm-sized tortes with strawberries and kiwifruit. There are a few outdoor tables where you can nibble on pastries and take in the street scene.

Zona Sul Supermarket SUPERMARKET $
(Map p66; ☎21 2259-4699; www.zonasul.com.br/; Dias Ferreira 290; ⏲24hr, except 9pm Sun to 6am Mon) A Rio institution for over 50 years, Zona Sul Supermarket has branches all over the city. This one in Leblon is the best of the bunch, with fresh-baked breads, imported cheeses and olives, wines, cured meats and other items. The adjoining pizza and lasagna counter serves decent plates. There's also a handy **Ipanema branch** (Map p66; Prudente de Morais 49; ⏲24hr, except 9pm Sun to 6am Mon) near Praça General Osório.

Graviola INTERNATIONAL $$
(Map p66; Av Ataúlfo de Paiva 1240; mains R$30-57; ⏲noon-10pm; 📶☑) Graviola started out as a food truck but became such a success that brick-and-mortar eateries quickly followed. The Leblon branch has a tranquil setting amid ferns and hanging plants, with white brick walls and a wooden deck out front that's well placed for taking in the street scene. The wide-ranging menu has veggie burgers, fresh tuna with tropical sauces, and roast organic chicken with creative sides.

Pabu Izakaya JAPANESE $$
(Map p66; ☎21 3738-0416; www.facebook.com/pabuizakayario; Humberto de Campos 827; sharing plates R$16-38, mains R$48-78; ⏲noon-3pm & 6pm-midnight Mon-Sat, 1-11pm Sun) Tucked away on a quiet Leblon backstreet, this low-lit space brings a dose of creativity to the Rio dining scene, with sharing plates like pork dumplings with house-made mayonnaise, grilled scallops on a bed of sweet potato fries, or eggplant tempura. There's a fine selection of sushi and sashimi, plus refreshing and/or heartwarming sake to accompany your mini feast.

Stuzzi ITALIAN $$
(Map p66; ☎21 2274-4017; www.stuzzibar.com.br; Dias Ferreira 48; sharing plates R$29-55, mains R$52-76; ⏲7pm-1am Tue, to 3am Wed-Sat, to midnight Sun) This buzzing, uberpopular Leblon spot specializes in creative Italian tapas (such as roast lamb croquettes, and goat cheese, fig and honey bruschetta) and expertly mixed cocktails. The lively, candelit tables on the sidewalk are the place to be; come early to score one.

Talho Capixaba SANDWICHES $$
(Map p66; ☎21 2512-8760; www.talhocapixaba.com.br; Av Ataúlfo de Paiva 1022; sandwiches R$21-40, mains R$38-60; ⏲7am-10pm; ☑) This deli and gourmet grocer is one of the city's best. In addition to lunchtime specials (roast duck, lasagna, grilled salmon), you'll find pastas, salads and antipasti here. The star of the show is Talho's sandwich selection, with quality ingredients piled high on house-baked baguettes, ciabattas and rye bread. You can dine inside or at the sidewalk tables in front.

★Giuseppe Grill BRAZILIAN $$$
(Map p66; ☎21 2249-3055; www.bestfork.com.br; Bartolomeu Mitre 370; mains R$88-150; ⏰noon-4pm & 7pm-midnight Mon-Thu, noon-1am Fri & Sat, noon-11pm Sun) One of Rio's best restaurants, Giuseppe Grill aims for perfection and it rarely disappoints. Chargrilled meat and fish plates are outstanding, as are Brazilian classics like *bobó de camarão* (manioc paste with dried shrimp and coconut milk). The setting is all class, with black-garbed waitstaff, dark-wood tables and artful touches (an open kitchen, a soaring bar that reaches to the ceiling and a Zen-like wall of water near the entrance).

★Zuka INTERNATIONAL $$$
(Map p66; ☎21 3205-7154; www.zuka.com.br; Dias Ferreira 233; mains R$76-120; ⏰7pm-1am Mon, noon-4pm & 7pm-1am Tue-Fri, 1pm-midnight Sat & Sun) One of Rio's best restaurants, Zuka prepares mouthwatering cuisine. Try zingy ceviche with Brazilian *piquinho* pepper or the confection-like delicacy of Zuka's original foie gras to start, followed by tender octopus over a roast potato crisp, honey-glazed duck breast with Moroccan couscous, grilled fish of the day with truffle sauce, or one of many other outstanding dishes.

Sushi Leblon JAPANESE $$$
(Map p66; ☎21 2512-7830; www.sushileblon.com/; Dias Ferreira 256; mains R$68-122, sushi rolls R$25-38; ⏰noon-4pm & 7pm-midnight) Leblon's top sushi destination boasts a Zen-like ambience, with a handsome dark-wood sushi counter setting the stage for succulent cuisine. In addition to sashimi and sushi, you'll find grilled *namorado* (a type of perch) with passion fruit *farofa* (a garnish of manioc flour sautéed with butter), sea-urchin ceviche and refreshing sake to complement your meal.

Formidable BISTRO $$$
(Map p66; ☎21 2239-7632; www.formidablebistrot.com.br; João Lira 148; mains R$56-86; ⏰noon-11pm) Something of a secret culinary spot in Leblon, Formidable is a charming bistro with only a handful of tables inside (and a few tables out front). It has a chalkboard menu featuring beautifully executed French bistro classics such as *bœuf bourguignon* (beef stew braised in red wine), *magret de canard* (seared duck breast) and *thon béarnaise* (grilled tuna with *béarnaise* sauce).

CT Boucherie FUSION $$$
(Map p66; ☎21 2529-2329; www.ctboucherie.com.br; Dias Ferreira 636; mains R$94-124; ⏰noon-4pm & 7pm-midnight) Created by Claude Troisgros, Rio's most famous chef, this innovative Leblon restaurant takes the idea of the *churrascaria* (traditional barbecue restaurant) and turns it on its head. Instead of all-you-can-eat meat, you order a main course – say a beautifully turned out rack of lamb, duck breast or grilled fish – and you get as many sides as you wish, served *rodizio*-style fresh from the kitchen.

Gávea, Jardim Botânico & Lagoa

★Casa Camolese BRAZILIAN $$
(Map p71; ☎21 3514-8200; www.casacamolese.com.br; Jardim Botânico 983; mains R$42-70; ⏰noon-midnight Mon-Sat, to 11pm Sun; ✎) One of the most talked about openings in recent years is this beautifully designed eating, drinking and entertainment space overlooking the Jockey Club Brasileiro. Camolese is home to a microbrewery, a cafe, a live-music spot and a spacious restaurant, with soaring ceilings, glass walls and an elegant plant-trimmed terrace – the best place to be on clear nights.

Start off with classic appetizers, like codfish balls or paprika-dusted octopus, then tuck into seafood pasta in white-wine sauce, grilled Angus steaks or veg-friendly options like creamy polenta with mushrooms.

The restaurant is accessed via a small lane opposite the main entrance to the botanical gardens.

Prana Vegetariano VEGETARIAN $$
(Map p71; ☎21 2245-7643; www.pranavegetariano.com; Lopes Quintas 37, Jardim Botânico; mains around R$40; ⏰noon-4pm Mon-Sat; ✎) A short stroll from the Jardim Botânico's north exit, this very friendly vegetarian restaurant has garnered quite a following for its deliciously healthy meat-free plates. The small menu changes daily (check the website to see what's cooking), and features creative and filling lunch combinations, as well as great juices and smoothies, and decadent desserts.

Jarbô FRENCH $$
(Map p71; ☎21 2259-2924; www.jarbocafe.com; Jardim Botânico 1008; mains R$38-67; ⏰noon-6:30pm Mon, 8am-6:30pm Tue-Sun; 📶✎) Just outside the entrance to the Jardim Botânico (but inside the gates off the busy roadway), Jarbô is a great anytime favorite, with a wide-ranging menu encompassing tartines (open-faced sandwiches), eggs Benedict,

SNACK SPOTS

Ipanema and Leblon have some enticing places for grabbing a quick bite, indulging in a bit of dessert or simply lingering over a coffee at a sidewalk cafe.

Vero (Map p66; ☎21 3497-8754; Visconde de Pirajá 229; ice creams R$11-16, pizza slices R$13-16; ⊙10am-12:30am; ☑) This artisanal Italian-run gelateria whips up Rio's best ice cream. You'll find more than two dozen rich and creamy temptations, including *gianduia* (chocolate with hazelnut), *caramelo com flor de sal* (caramel with sea salt), *figo com amêndoas* (fig with almond) and classic flavors such as *morango* (strawberry).

Café de la Musique (Map p66; ☎21 97273-7467; www.facebook.com/cafedelamusiquebeach; Av Delfim Moreira; mains R$32-64; ⊙8am-10pm Sun-Thu, to midnight Fri & Sat) Bringing a dash of style to the Leblon beachfront, the Café de la Musique serves high-end cocktails (R$35 to R$40) to a fashionable crowd. You can sit and watch the surf roll in from well-placed lounge chairs, or grab a table and dine alfresco on salads, sandwiches and seafood (ceviche, marinated octopus, *moqueca*).

Okanossa (Map p66; ☎21 3204-4055; www.facebook.com/okanossa; Cupertino Durão 79; mains R$22-36; ⊙9am-7:30pm Tue-Sat, 10am-5pm Sun & Mon; ☑) This tiny cafe has a loyal local following for its excellent coffees, all-organic fare and decent vegetarian and vegan dishes – not to mention the friendly welcome. Try a tapioca with goat cheese and pesto (they're made with beet, so they're pink!) or for something more filling, opt for a tartine (open-faced sandwich), heart-of-palm ravioli or the day's changing special (like falafel with tahini).

Cafeína (Map p66; ☎21 2521-2194; www.cafeina.com.br; Farme de Amoedo 43; pastas R$35-57, sandwiches R$25-46; ⊙8am-10pm; ☜) In the heart of Ipanema, this inviting cafe with sidewalk tables is a fine spot to have an espresso while watching the city stroll by. You'll also find freshly made sandwiches, salads, pastas, quiches and some very rich desserts.

Koni Store (Map p66; ☎21 2521-9348; www.koni.com.br; Maria Quitéria 77; hand rolls R$16-22; ⊙11am-midnight Sun-Thu, to 2am Fri & Sat) The Koni craze shows no sign of abating. The recipe is simple: *temakis* (seaweed hand rolls) stuffed with salmon, tuna, shrimp, roast beef or a combination of ingredients, which are then devoured at one of the tiny bistro tables.

Bibi Crepes (Map p66; ☎21 2259-4948; www.bibisucos.com.br; Cupertino Durão 81; crepes R$24-38; ⊙noon-1am Sun-Thu, to 2am Fri & Sat) This small, open-sided restaurant attracts a young, garrulous crowd who enjoy the more than two dozen sweet and savory crepes available, as well as design-your-own salads (choose from 40 different toppings). Come early to beat the lunch crowds.

Gorgonzola-topped salads or fancier fare like beet and goat cheese ravioli or duck confit.

It's set in a lovely colonial building and has outdoor seating on a peaceful veranda.

Lagoon BRAZILIAN **$$**

(Map p66; ☎21 2529-5300; www.lagoon.com.br; Av Borges de Medeiros 1424; mains R$35-75; ⊙noon-2am) This lakefront eating and entertainment complex houses a handful of restaurants, plus a cinema, a bar and a live-music venue. The best tables are on the 2nd floor, and offer photogenic views over Lagoa Rodrigo de Freitas. Italian, seafood, bistro fare and traditional Brazilian cooking are among the options. No matter where you sit, you can order from any of the menus.

The back of the complex, by the lake, usually has food trucks (burgers, snacks and microbrews), plus reclaimed wood loungers and tables where you can take in the relaxing views.

Plage Café CAFE **$$**

(Map p71; ☎21 2535-7336; www.plagecafe.com.br; off Jardim Botânico 414; mains R$32-54; ⊙9am-6pm Mon-Fri, to 5pm Sat & Sun; ☜☑) Inside the lush Parque Lage, this beautifully located cafe serves an expansive array of dishes, including eggs Benedict and roasted eggplant lasagna, as well as sandwiches and lighter fare such as yogurt with house-made granola or salad Niçoise. It's an ideal spot for taking in Rio's tropical verdure, with views of Cristo Redentor.

Bráz PIZZA $$
(☎21 3563-4670; www.brazpizzaria.com.br; Maria Angélica 129; pizzas R$54-88; ⊙6:30pm-midnight) The much-touted pizzeria from São Paulo has had a huge following with *cariocas* (Rio residents) since opening in the city in 2007. Perfect crusts and superfresh ingredients are two of the components that make Bráz one of the best pizza spots in town. This is no secret, however, so arrive early and plan on having a few quiet *chopes* (draft beers) on the front patio before scoring a table.

La Bicyclette CAFE $$
(Map p71; ☎21 3256-9052; www.labicyclette.com.br; Pacheco Leão 320; sandwiches R$19-42; ⊙8:30am-9pm Mon-Fri, to 8pm Sat & Sun; 📶☎) La Bicyclette whips up creative sandwiches (named after Parisian neighborhoods), hearty quiches, salads and desserts. Vegetarians can opt for the Olympia, with goat cheese, olives, capers and cherry tomatoes. Bakery items are superb, and there's ample outdoor seating for a coffee break. It's located across from the headquarters of media giant Globo.

Braseiro da Gávea BRAZILIAN $$
(Map p71; ☎21 2239-7494; www.braseirodagavea.com.br; Praça Santos Dumont 116; sandwiches around R$24, mains for 2 people R$60-120; ⊙11:30am-1am Sun-Thu, to 3am Fri & Sat) This family-style place serves large portions of its popular *linguiça* (garlicky pork sausage) appetizers, *picanha* (rump steak) and *galetos* (grilled chicken). On weekends the open-air spot fills with the din of conversation and the aroma of freshly poured *chope* (draft beer). As the evening wanes, a younger crowd takes over, drinking late into the night.

Puro BRAZILIAN $$$
(Map p71; ☎21 3284-5377; www.purorestaurante.com.br; Visconde de Carandaí 43; mains R$62-86, multicourse lunch menu R$49; ⊙noon-5pm & 7pm-midnight Mon-Fri, 12:30-5pm & 7pm-1am Sat, 12:30-10pm Sun) Puro offers consistently excellent food and service in the upmarket Jardim Botânico neighborhood. Chef Pedro Siqueira's menu features traditional Brazilian dishes that have been given modern updates. Head to the top floor for open-air views over the botanical gardens – it's a fine setting for dishes such as roasted lamb with rice, octopus and smoked pork belly, or oven-baked fish of the day.

Olympe FUSION $$$
(☎21 2539-4542; www.olympe.br; Custódio Serrão 62; 5-/7-course tasting menu R$390/450; ⊙7:30-11pm Mon-Thu & Sat, noon-4pm & 7:30-11pm Fri) 🍃 Thomas Troisgros, one of Rio's top chefs, dazzles guests with unforgettable meals at this award-winning restaurant set in a peaceful villa on a quiet, tree-lined street. Originally from France, Troisgros mixes the Old World with the New in dishes such as scallops with *tucupí* (a manioc root from the Amazon) or *açaí*-crusted lamb loin, followed perhaps by caramelized passion-fruit soufflé.

Vegetarians can also opt for a five-course tasting menu (R$390). Wine pairings are available.

Guimas BRAZILIAN $$$
(Map p71; ☎21 2259-7996; www.restauranteguimas.com.br; José Roberto Macedo Soares 5; mains R$64-86; ⊙noon-1am) An upscale *carioca boteco* (small open-air bar) with a creative flair, Guimas has been going strong since 1981. Winning dishes include the *bacalhau à brás* (codfish mixed with potatoes, eggs and onions), shrimp risotto and the juicy *picanha wessel* (grilled rump steak). There's outdoor seating in front.

Copacabana & Leme

Momo ICE CREAM $
(Map p74; Av Atlântica 1702, Copacabana; small/large ice cream R$16/22; ⊙noon-11pm) A few steps from the entrance to the Belmond Copacabana Palace, Momo is a cheery gelateria serving the neighborhood's best ice cream. All the classics are on hand, as well as tropical flavors such as mango and *maracujá* (passion fruit). Grab an outdoor table in front to take in the passing people parade.

Cervantes BRAZILIAN $
(Map p74; ☎21 2275-6147; www.restaurantecervantes.com.br; Barata Ribeiro 7; sandwiches R$25-42; ⊙noon-4am Tue-Thu, to 6am Fri & Sat, to 2am Sun) A Copacabana institution, the late-night Cervantes attracts *cariocas* who come to feast on the trademark filet mignon and pineapple sandwiches. This popular branch on busy Barata Ribeiro brings a mostly standing-room-only crowd. For the sit-down restaurant, head a few steps around the corner to Av Prado Junior 335.

Galeto Sat's BRAZILIAN $$
(Map p74; ☎21 2275-6197; Barata Ribeiro 7; mains R$30-76, lunch specials R$34; ⊙11am-5am) One of Rio's best roast-chicken spots, laid-back Galeto Sat's has earned many fans since it opened back in 1962. Grab a seat along the mirrored, tiled wall, order a *chope*

(draft beer) and enjoy the scent of grilled spit-roasted birds before tucking into a filling meal. Price-wise you can't beat the *galeto completo,* a R$55 chicken feast for two.

★Salomé BISTRO $$

(Map p74; ☎21 2541-2416; www.facebook.com/salomebistro; Av Atlântica 994; mains R$48-65; ⏰6:30pm-midnight Tue-Thu, noon-midnight Fri-Sun;) Run by the same people behind Ipanema's enormously popular Canastra (p111), Salomé brings a dash of style to the Leme beachfront. The easy-going open-sided bistro has vintage mirrors and curious wall hangings, potted palms and atmospheric lighting – though on fine days, the outdoor tables are the best place to enjoy high-quality small plates, grilled meats and seafood, and wines by the glass.

While small, the menu has plenty of variety, from grilled octopus to Moroccan lamb tagine with couscous. You'll also find seafood linguine, duck breast with eggplant caviar and salads with warm Saint-Marcellin cheese.

★El Born SPANISH $$

(Map p74; ☎21 3496-1780; www.barelborn.com.br; Bolívar 17; tapas R$13-57, sandwiches R$25-31; ⏰5pm-2am Mon-Fri, from 4pm Sat & Sun) Named after Barcelona's hippest foodie neighborhood, El Born fires up some of Rio's best tapas plates, such as Galician-style octopus, spicy prawns and tender Iberian ham. The setting channels a bit of old-world Spain, with rustic stone and brick walls, outdoor tables on the sidewalk, and ample bar seating, which is a fine spot for watching the dexterous bartenders in action.

Don't order too much. Waiters emerge from the kitchen and make the rounds with freshly cooked tapas plates; if you see something you like, take it!

Adega Pérola TAPAS $$

(Map p74; ☎21 2255-9425; www.facebook.com/adegaperolariodejaneiro; Siqueira Campos 138; sharing plates R$24-46; ⏰11am-1am Mon-Thu, to 2am Fri & Sat) Going strong since 1957, this atmospheric bottle-lined eating and drinking den serves outstanding Spanish and Portuguese small plates, including marinated octopus, whole sardines, stuffed olives, codfish balls, fried squid and marinated shrimp. Just step inside and check out the culinary bounty on the long front counter.

Joaquina BRAZILIAN $$

(Map p74; ☎21 2275-8569; Av Atlântica 974; mains R$40-58; ⏰11:30am-midnight;) Joaquina has much to recommend it: a great ocean-facing location with outdoor seating, excellent caipirinhas that don't stint on the fresh fruit, and tasty Brazilian fare at fair prices. On Sundays Joaquina serves *feijoada* (bean-and-meat stew; R$50); on Saturdays it's oxtail rice (R$40). Arrive early before it runs out. Other hits: *moqueca* for one, shrimp risotto and vegetarian *feijoada.*

Santa Satisfação BRAZILIAN $$

(Map p74; ☎21 2255-9349; www.santasatisfacao.com; Santa Clara 36C; mains R$41-62; ⏰10am-11pm Mon-Sat) Oozing farmhouse charm, this always-packed bistro is worth forking out a bit extra for its outstanding daily lunch specials (R$37) of upscale Brazilian comfort food and sophisticated sandwiches. Among the favorites: pasta with Gorgonzola and sliced filet mignon, caprese salad, and open-faced ham and Brie sandwiches.

La Trattoria ITALIAN $$

(Map p74; ☎21 2255-3319; www.latrattoria.com.br; Fernando Mendes 7A; mains R$47-80; ⏰noon-11pm) Set with checkered tablecloths, exposed brick and decorations from the Old World, La Trattoria has been a neighborhood favorite since 1976. Shrimp dishes are the Italian family's specialty: many diners have been won over by the *camarões com spaghetti ao funghi tartufado* (shrimp with spaghetti and truffles).

Empório Grão-Pará AMAZONIAN $$

(Map p74; ☎21 3489-0262; Barão de Ipanema 94; mains R$25-50; ⏰9am-9pm Sun-Thu, to 10pm Fri & Sat) A creative addition to the Copacabana food scene, this small snack bar serves delicacies from the north, including pure *açaí* (a berry-like fruit), *casquinha de caranguejo* (crabmeat served in its shell), *pato no tucupí* (duck in a spicy manioc sauce) and the wild-tasting *tacacá,* a dish with lip-numbing jambu leaves, manioc and shrimp.

TT Burger BURGERS $$

(Map p74; ☎21 96458-8674; www.ttburger.com.br; Francisco Otaviano 67; burgers R$42-48; ⏰noon-midnight Sun-Thu, to 2am Fri & Sat;) The son of famed local chef Claude Troisgros runs this high-end Brooklyn-style burger outpost, and has gained a strong following for his delicious burgers (the guava ketchup is outstanding), sweet potato fries, milkshakes and craft beers. It's a charming spot, with subway tiles, framed photos, wood floors and a small front deck. TT also fires up a respectable veggie burger.

There are several other locations around Rio, including on Leblon's main drag (Av Ataúlfo de Paiva).

Bakers CAFE $$
(Map p74; ☎21 3209-1212; www.thebakers.com.br; Santa Clara 86; desserts R$9-15, sandwiches R$29-40, mains R$47-64; ⏰9am-8pm; 📶) The Bakers is a fine spot for flaky croissants, banana Danishes, apple strudels and other treats. There are also waffles, omelets, salads, gourmet sandwiches (such as prosciutto and mozzarella on ciabatta), quiches (including ricotta with sun-dried tomatoes), pastas, and heartier fare such as filet mignon with Gorgonzola sauce or grilled salmon with risotto and passion-fruit sauce.

Amir MIDDLE EASTERN $$
(Map p74; ☎21 2275-5596; www.amirrestaurante.com.br; Ronald de Carvalho 55C; mains R$48-62, sandwiches R$23-39; ⏰noon-midnight Mon-Sat, to 11pm Sun) At Amir you'll enter a world of delicate aromas amid a brightly painted interior complete with Middle Eastern decorative touches. Daytime crowds come for good-value set menus (around R$29), while at night the à la carte menu features all the favorites, including delicious platters of hummus, *kaftas* (spiced meat patties), falafel, kibbe and salads.

★Churrascaria Palace CHURRASCARIA $$$
(Map p74; ☎21 2541-5898; www.churrascariapalace.com.br; Rodolfo Dantas 16; all you can eat R$140; ⏰noon-midnight; 🍷) This elegantly set dining room is one of the best *churrascarias* (traditional barbecue restaurants) in town. Aside from juicy, high-quality cuts of meat, the included buffet nearly steals the show with fresh oysters, grilled heart of palm, sushi and sashimi, rice with wild mushrooms and goji berries, codfish casseroles, smoked fish, grilled prawns and octopus and amazing salads.

Azumi JAPANESE $$$
(Map p74; ☎21 2295-1098; Ministro Viveiros de Castro 127; meals R$90-220, lunch specials from R$50; ⏰noon-3pm & 7pm-midnight) Hands down, Azumi serves some of the best traditional Japanese cuisine in Rio. This laid-back sushi bar certainly has its fans – both in the *nisei* community and from abroad. Azumi's *sushiman* (sushi chef) masterfully prepares delectable sushi and sashimi, and the tempuras and soups are also excellent. Be sure to ask what's in season.

THE KIOSKS OF COPACABANA

The *quiosque* (kiosk) has long been a presence on the beachfront of Rio. It's where cold drinks and snacks are doled out to *cariocas* (residents of Rio) on the move, and where plastic tables and chairs provide a fine vantage point for contemplating the watery horizon. In recent years Copacabana Beach has seen a new crop of flashy kiosks replacing the old-fashioned wooden ones. Now it's possible to get a decent meal (the kitchens are cleverly concealed underground), an ice-cold draft beer or gourmet snacks without ever leaving the sand.

The new kiosks are sprinkled all along Copacabana Beach, with most options roughly between Rua Siqueira Campos and the Belmond Copacabana Palace hotel.

Botafogo & Urca

Slow Bakery BAKERY $
(Map p86; ☎21 3563-8638; www.theslowbakery.com.br; São João Batista 93, Botafogo; sandwiches R$24-29; ⏰9am-7pm Tue-Fri, 9am-3pm Sat; 📶🍷) The sourdough revolution has yet to take hold in Rio, so this modern bakery is something of a pioneer. A range of superb sourdough loaves are baked on-site and available both for takeaway purchase and as chunky sandwiches that can be enjoyed at the simple tables that line the place. The menu also includes salads, pastries and excellent coffee.

Ceviche RJ CEVICHE $$
(Map p86; ☎21 3549-7077; www.facebook.com/cevicherj; Arnaldo Quintela 66B, Botafogo; ceviche around R$35; ⏰noon-4pm & 6pm-midnight Wed-Fri, 1pm-midnight Sat, 1-11pm Sun) This simple Peruvian-run restaurant serves arguably the best ceviche in Rio. Although there is some seating inside the restaurant, most diners sit outside in what is essentially a car park. The sublime ceviche is the compulsory order, but a few other classic Peruvian dishes are available, alongside a selection of decent craft beers and a handful of wines.

Marchezinho CAFE $$

(Map p86; www.facebook.com/marchezinho; Voluntários da Pátria 46, Botafogo; sandwiches R$28-38; ⏲9am-1am Mon-Wed, to 2am Thu & Fri, 10am-2am Sat) This multipurpose space operates as a cafe, bar and minimarket. The owner's French roots show through on the menu and store shelves, with the excellent cheese, bread and coffee. The carefully selected ingredients and produce are exclusively Brazilian, however, with most coming from small local producers. Come for creative tapas, delectable sandwiches, craft beers and first-rate cocktails.

South Ferro ASIAN, PIZZA $$

(Map p86; 21 3986-4323; www.facebook.com/pg/SouthFerro; Arnaldo Quintela 23, Botafogo; mains R$41-62; ⏲11:30am-3pm Mon, 11:30am-3pm & 6:30-11pm Tue-Sat;) Chef Sei Shiroma made his name with Ferro e Farinha, widely regarded as Rio's best pizza place. South Ferro, Shiroma's second restaurant, adds a healthy pinch of Asian spice in vegetable dumplings, tempura, fish curry and outstanding bowls of ramen. You'll also find a few pizza selections and well-made cocktails (R$32).

The barely marked entrance leads into a cozy but industrial space with exposed bulbs, concrete floors and street-art-style paintings adorning the walls.

Meza Bar TAPAS $$

(Map p86; 21 3239-1951; www.mezabar.com.br; Capitão Salomão 69, Humaitá; tapas R$16-42; ⏲6pm-1am) Humaitá's see-and-be-seen hot spot serves delectable, Brazilian-slanted tapas to a sophisticated and trendy crowd. Creative cocktails and delightful staff round out the fun.

Void – House of Food INTERNATIONAL $$

(Map p86; 21 3593-3326; www.avoid.com.br; Voluntários da Pátria 31, Botafogo; snacks R$18-36; ⏲noon-midnight;) This venue has two halves: on one side is Void, a store and cafe/bar selling sneakers, T-shirts, baseball caps, brownies and drinks. On the other side of the divide is House of Food, a 'guest kitchen' hosting chefs, cooks and general food enthusiasts on daily rotation. The menus are heavy on international street food and food-truck classics.

Le Depanneur CAFE $$

(Map p86; 21 2537-5250; www.ledep.com.br; Voluntários da Pátria 86, Botafogo; sandwiches R$27-36; ⏲8am-10pm Sun-Thu, to 11pm Fri & Sat;) This buzzing cafe and deli serves juices, waffles, crepes, salads, antipasti plates and specialty sandwiches. On weekends the large plant-trimmed front patio fills with brunching locals and makes a good people-watching perch. There's also a self-serve bakery with croissants and other goodies, and plenty of other provisions for picnickers.

Julius Brasserie EUROPEAN $$

(Map p86; 21 3518-7117; Av Portugal 986, Urca; mains R$67-85; ⏲noon-midnight Tue-Sat, noon-6pm Sun) This elegant Dutch-Brazilian-run restaurant in Urca turns out a creative mix of grilled meats (rack of lamb, duck breast), seafood (shrimp curry with black rice), pastas and risottos in a quiet location on the edge of Praia da Urca. It makes a great lunch or dinner spot, followed by a stroll around the neighborhood.

Miam Miam BRAZILIAN $$

(Map p86; 21 2244-0125; www.miammiam.com.br; General Goés Monteiro 34, Botafogo; mains R$62-82; ⏲noon-3:30pm & 7pm-midnight Mon-Fri, 1pm-midnight Sat) Exposed brick walls and a mishmash of retro furnishings set the scene for dining in style at Botafogo's culinary darling. Chef Roberta Ciasca serves her own brand of comfort food, which means smoked trout with roasted potatoes, pork with basmati rice and pineapple, eggplant lasagna with sheep's milk yogurt, and other unique dishes.

★**Lasai** GASTRONOMY $$$

(Map p86; 21 3449-1834; www.lasai.com.br; Conde de Irajá 191, Humaitá; prix fixe R$350; ⏲7:30-10pm Tue-Fri, 1-10pm Sat) Inside an elegant early-20th-century house in Humaitá, Lasai dazzles critics and foodies with its deliciously inventive cuisine. The award-winning *carioca* chef Rafa Costa e Silva earned his chops in some of the world's best dining rooms (including Mugaritz in Spain), and he puts his skills to brilliant use here. Reservations are essential.

There's no set menu: dishes are based on whatever is fresh for the day (and some ingredients are grown in the chef's own garden).

Oteque GASTRONOMY $$$

(Map p86; 21 3486-5758; www.oteque.com; Conde de Irajá 581; 8-course tasting menu R$250; ⏲7:30-11:30pm Tue-Sat) Much to the delight of *cariocas*, celebrated São Paulo chef Alberto Landgraf recently moved to Rio and opened this small, beautifully designed restaurant, complete with a theatrically lit open kitchen. The menu changes daily but features exquisite seafood (grilled octopus, scallops, monkfish, oysters) artfully prepared with Brazilian accents like hearts of palm and *tucupi* (a sauce made from wild manioc).

There's an extensive wine cellar, with wine pairings available.

Bar Urca BRAZILIAN $$$
(Map p86; ☎21 2295-8744; Cândido Gaffrée 205, Urca; mains R$57-170; ⊙noon-3pm & 7-11pm Mon-Sat, noon-8pm Sun) Upstairs from Bar Urca's popular snack stand you'll find an elegantly set dining room with memorable views across the bay. The seafood is first rate, with scrumptious *caldeirada* (seafood stew), *moqueca* (Bahian fish stew) and grilled octopus on the menu. Bar Urca's most famous dish is *camarão na moranga:* shrimp cooked in creamy sauce and served in a pumpkin (R$219 for two people).

Flamengo & Around

Sírio Libaneza MIDDLE EASTERN $
(Map p86; ☎21 2146-4915; Largo do Machado 29, Loja 16-19; snacks R$6-28; ⊙8am-11pm Mon-Sat; Wi-Fi) Always packed, this bustling place serves tasty and cheap Syrian-Lebanese cuisine and great juices. Try the hearty *kibe de forno* (an oven-baked ground-beef dish with spices), a hummus platter or *kafta* (spiced meat patty), followed by baklava and other sweets. It's inside the Galleria Condor on Largo do Machado.

Tacacá do Norte AMAZONIAN $
(Map p86; ☎21 2205-7545; Barão do Flamengo 35, Flamengo; tacacá R$27; ⊙9am-11pm Mon-Sat) In the Amazonian state of Pará, people order their *tacacá* late in the afternoon from their favorite street vendor. In Rio, you don't have to wait until the sun is setting. The fragrant soup of manioc paste, lip-numbing leaves of *jambú* (a Brazilian vegetable), and fresh and dried shrimp isn't for everyone. But then again, neither is the Amazon.

This simple lunch counter also serves savory bowls of *açaí* (berry-like fruit), which is how folks in the Amazon eat it; it's quite different from the sweet juice versions served everywhere else in Rio.

★**Ferro e Farinha** PIZZA $$
(Map p86; Andrade Pertence 42; pizzas R$40-50; ⊙7-11:30pm Tue-Sat, from 6:30pm Sun) Sei Shiroma, an expat from NYC, and a dexterous team of dough handlers serve Rio's best pizza at this atmospheric and delightfully ramshackle spot in Catete. Seats are few, with just a handful of bar stools crowding around the pizza makers and oven at center stage, plus a few outdoor tables, so go early to try to beat the crowds.

Maze Inn INDIAN $$
(Map p86; ☎21 97967-8270; www.themazerio.com/en/hoje-tem-curry; Casa 66, Tavares Bastos 414; buffet R$59; ⊙12:30-3:30pm Sun) For an alternative taste of Rio, head up to Tavares Bastos for an amazing feast of Indian cuisine. Chef Bruno Dantas Nadkarni learned from his Indian relatives how to make outstanding samosas, pork vindaloo and *bhịngan bharta* (made with roasted eggplant), among other dishes. Come on Sundays for a full spread of delicacies from the subcontinent.

Brou BRAZILIAN $$
(Map p86; ☎21 2556-0618; www.facebook.com/casa.brou; Senador Vergueiro 2, Flamengo; mains lunch R$18-30, dinner R$32-56; ⊙11:30am-3pm & 6pm-midnight) A brilliant new addition to Flamengo, this bright and attractive eating and drinking spot features a daytime menu of creative salads topped with grilled veggies, salmon or roast meat, as well as quiches and soups. By night, crowds come for nicely prepared prime rib, grilled octopus and thin-crust pizzas fired up in a wood-burning oven.

True to its name, Brou is a brew-lover's paradise, with more than 20 brews on tap. You'll get a card when you come in, which you can then use to pour your own drafts. This clever new incarnation of pay by weight allows you to sample a wide range of local and Brazilian microbrews.

Centro & Praça Mauá

Confeitaria Colombo BRAZILIAN $
(Map p92; ☎21 2505-1500; www.confeitariacolombo.com.br; Gonçalves Dias 34; pastries R$11-16, sandwiches R$22-46; ⊙9am-7pm Mon-Fri, to 5pm Sat) Stained-glass windows, brocaded mirrors and marble countertops create a lavish setting for coffee or a meal here. Dating from the late 19th century, the Confeitaria Colombo serves desserts – including a good *pastel de nata* (custard tart) – befitting its elegant decor.

The restaurant above, **Cristóvão** (Map p92; Gonçalves Dias 34; buffet per person R$100; ⊙11:30am-4pm), spreads an extensive buffet of Brazilian dishes for those wanting to further soak up the splendor.

Bistrô do Paço CAFE $

(Map p92; ☎21 2262-3613; www.bistro.com.br; Praça XV/Quinze de Novembro 48, Paço Imperial, Centro; mains R$22-45; ⏰noon-7pm) On the ground floor of the Paço Imperial, this informal restaurant offers a tasty assortment of quiches, salads, soups and other light fare. Save room for the delicious pies and cakes.

★**Xian** ASIAN $$

(Map p92; ☎21 2303-7080; www.xianrio.com.br; top fl, Almirante Silvio de Noronha 365, Bossa Nova Mall; mains R$65-90; ⏰noon-11pm Mon-Thu, to midnight Fri & Sat, noon-10pm Sun; 📶) One of Rio's loveliest new additions is this spacious, theatrically decorated dining room, open-air cocktail bar and nightclub, all set rather dramatically on the edge of the bay. Come for mouthwatering seafood and tender meats with Asian accents, such as fresh oysters with ponzu sauce, salmon truffle tartar or marinated pork ribs with miso.

Dishes are great for sharing, and go nicely with the brilliant cocktail menu. The stunning views over the bay make this a magical place to be at sunset.

L'Atelier du Cuisinier FRENCH $$

(Map p92; ☎21 3179-0024; www.latelierdu cuisinier.com.br; Teófilo Otoni 97; mains R$45-60, multicourse lunch R$86-120; ⏰noon-2pm Mon-Fri) Set in a 19th-century building just off busy Av Rio Branco, this small 24-seat place serves some of the best cuisine in Centro. The menu is tiny (just a few options each day), but beautifully executed, with French chef David Jobert creating recipes with fresh-from-the-market Brazilian ingredients.

Govardhana Harí VEGETARIAN $$

(Map p92; ☎21 2544-2636; 2nd fl, Rodrigo Silva 6; lunch R$35; ⏰11:30am-3:30pm Mon-Fri; 🌿) Amid artwork and decorations from India, the always-welcoming Hare Krishnas whip up delicious vegetarian dishes made with care. The restaurant is tucked down a narrow lane just off Rua São José and is always packed, so arrive early to get a seat.

Belga BELGIAN $$

(Map p92; www.belgahotel.com.br; Rua dos Andradas 129; mains R$48-64; ⏰6:30am-10pm Mon-Fri, 7am-3pm Sat; 📶🌿) Belgian chef Alexandre Binard heads this delightful brasserie a few blocks west of Av Rio Branco. Stop by in the morning for coffees, muffins and quiches. Later in the day, there are lunch specials, happy-hour tapas and, of course, Belgian waffles. You can also enjoy one of the delectable beers on tap (including Straffe Hendrik Tripel from Bruges).

Imaculada BRAZILIAN $$

(Map p92; ☎21 2253-3999; Ladeira do João Homem 7; mains R$32-50; ⏰11am-4pm Mon, to 10pm Tue-Sat; 📶) Located in the old neighborhood of Morro da Conceição, Imaculada is a Rio classic. The walls are adorned with artwork and the cooking doesn't disappoint. Come for daily lunch specials – *bobó de camarão* (manioc paste with dried shrimp, coconut milk and cashew nuts) on Thursdays or *feijoada* (bean-and-meat stew) on Fridays and Saturdays – and beer and appetizers at day's end.

Mironga BRAZILIAN $$

(Map p92; ☎21 2518-7727; www.mironga.com.br; Av Rio Branco 19; mains R$28-40; ⏰noon-3:30pm Mon, 11:30am-10pm Tue-Fri, noon-5:30pm Sat & Sun; 📶) With its tall ceilings, exposed Edison bulbs, lounge-like music and chunky wooden tables, Mironga channels a Brooklyn vibe, which is unsurprising given the owner has deep NYC connections. Aesthetics aside, the food is excellent, with a wide-ranging menu of Moroccan-style couscous salads, mushroom and filet mignon risotto, grilled dishes (*picanha,* salmon and chicken breast), pastas and quiches.

Cais do Oriente BRAZILIAN $$

(Map p92; ☎21 2203-0178; www.caisdo oriente-rj.com.br; Visconde de Itaboraí 8, Centro; mains R$55-75; ⏰11am-10pm Mon-Sat, to 5pm Sun) Brick walls lined with tapestries stretch high to the ceiling in this almost-cinematic 1870s mansion. Set on a brick-lined street, hidden from the masses, it blends elements of Brazilian and Mediterranean cooking in dishes such as duck breast with Brazil-nut *farofa* (garnish of manioc flour sautéed with butter) and *açaí* sauce.

Ancoramar SEAFOOD $$$

(Map p92; ☎21 2240-8378; www.ancoramar.com.br; Praça Marechal Âncora 186; mains R$72-140; ⏰11:30am-5pm Mon-Fri) Ancoramar (previously known as Albamar) has long been one of Rio's best lunchtime seafood destinations. Its top picks are fresh oysters, grilled seafood with vegetables and *moqueca* (seafood stew cooked in coconut milk) dishes. The old-fashioned green gazebo-like structure offers excellent views of Baía de Guanabara and the area of Niterói across the bay.

Santa Teresa

Galeria Bazá VEGETARIAN $

(Map p92; 21 2533-0686; www.facebook.com/galeriabaza; Rua do Oriente 414, Santa Teresa; mains R$18-25; noon-11pm Tue-Sun;) One of Santa Teresa's most creative spaces, Bazá is equal parts vegetarian cafe, handicraft gallery and live-music venue. Stop in for tasty lentil or tabbouleh salads, curry rice, black-bean burgers and veggie *moqueca*. Throughout the month you can catch live samba as well as more diverse Brazilian sounds (like *carimbó* from the Amazon).

Cafe do Alto BRAZILIAN $$

(Map p92; 21 2507-3172; www.cafedoalto.com.br; Paschoal Carlos Magno 143, Santa Teresa; mains R$25-48; noon-9pm Mon, Tue, Thu & Fri, 9am-9pm Sat & Sun;) Conveniently located a few steps from Largo do Guimarães (Santa Teresa's epicenter), Cafe do Alto whips up filling Northeastern dishes. The wide-ranging menu features *tapiocas* (crepes made from manioc flour), *casquinha de siri* (pulled crab), *xinxim de galinha* (chicken and dried shrimp with coconut, ginger and spices over rice) and other regional fare, plus lighter options, such as sandwiches.

Bar do Mineiro BRAZILIAN $$

(Map p92; 21 2221-9227; Paschoal Carlos Magno 99, Santa Teresa; mains R$65-125, weekday lunch special R$22-35; noon-2am Tue-Sat, to midnight Sun) Black-and-white photographs of legendary singers cover the walls of this old-school *boteco* (small open-air bar) in the heart of Santa Teresa. Lively crowds have been filling this spot for years to enjoy traditional Minas Gerais dishes. The *feijoada* (bean-and-meat stew served with rice) is tops, and served every day, along with appetizers, including *pasteis* (savory pastries).

★Aprazível BRAZILIAN $$$

(Map p92; 21 2508-9174; www.aprazivel.com.br; Aprazível 62, Santa Teresa; mains R$90-130; noon-11pm Thu-Sat, 11am-6pm Sun;) Hidden on a winding road high in Santa Teresa, Aprazível offers beautiful views and a lush garden setting. Grilled fish and roasted dishes showcase the country's culinary highlights from land and sea. Start with grilled heart of palms before moving on to standout main courses like delectable *moquequinha* (seafood stew), roast pork with pineapple chutney and polenta, or house-made vegetarian ravioli.

★Espírito Santa AMAZONIAN $$$

(Map p92; 21 2507-4840; www.espiritosanta.com.br; Almirante Alexandrino 264, Santa Teresa; mains R$55-98; noon-11pm) At this beautifully restored mansion, you can sit on the back terrace with its sweeping views or in the charming, airy dining room, and feast on rich, expertly prepared meat and seafood dishes from the Amazon and Northeast. Top picks include the *moqueca* (fish stew), made with pintado (a delicious river fish), and the slow-roasted pork ribs served with sweet potato.

Don't miss the creative cocktails, some of which feature juices from Amazonian fruits.

Térèze FUSION $$$

(Map p92; 21 3380-0220; www.santateresahotelrio.com; Hotel Santa Teresa, Rua Almirante Alexandrino 660, Santa Teresa; mains R$80-140; noon-3:30pm & 7:30-11pm) Under the command of chef Esteban Mateu, Térèze provides a memorable dining experience. All the elements are there, from the decadent menu to the suggested wine pairings and the superb views over the city. Choose from the likes of creamy codfish risotto with lobster bisque, suckling pig with mashed sweet potatoes and truffles, and eggplant gnocchi with cashew pesto.

Sobrenatural SEAFOOD $$$

(Map p92; 21 2224-1003; Almirante Alexandrino 432, Santa Teresa; mains for 2 R$80-155; noon-11pm Thu-Tue) The old hardwood ceiling and exposed brick set the stage for feasting on *frutas do mar* (seafood). Lines gather at weekends for crabmeat appetizers, fresh grilled fish and flavorful platters of *moqueca* (fish stew). During the week, stop by for tasty lunchtime specials. There's live music most nights.

Lapa

★Lilia BRAZILIAN $$

(Map p92; 21 3852-5423; www.facebook.com/lilia.restaurante; Rua do Senado 45; set menu R$50; 11:30am-3pm Mon-Fri, noon-4pm Sat; ; Cinelândia) You could easily miss the low-key entrance to this tranquil lunch spot. Covering the top two floors of a 19th-century building, the restaurant has an airy, creative design, with white brick walls, shelves of plants, and decorative balconies overlooking the street. The three-course menu changes daily, focusing on simple but beautifully prepared dishes; it always includes a vegetarian option.

OFF THE BEATEN TRACK

SNACKING & SIPPING NEAR PRAÇA DA BANDEIRA

Formerly a culinary desert, the district known as Praça da Bandeira has seen much new life with a spate of new restaurants and bars. These casual spots make a great setting for a snack and pub crawl. For a foodie excursion, sign up with **Eat Rio Food Tours** (www.eatrio.net; tours from US$75).

Aconchego Carioca (Map p98; ☎21 2273-1035; Barão de Iguatemi 245, Praça da Bandeira; mains for 2 people R$80-120; ⏰noon-11pm Tue-Sat, to 5pm Sun) Aconchego Carioca consistently ranks as one of the best places in town to eat traditional Brazilian cuisine. The setting, cozy and welcoming, has a casual neighborhood vibe, but attracts diners from across the city who come for *bobó de camarão* (shrimp and coconut milk stew), pork ribs with guava sauce, and a *cachaça*-tinged flan for dessert.

Bar Kalango (Map p98; ☎21 2504-0088; www.facebook.com/barkalango; Joaquim Palhares 513, Praça da Bandeira; lunch special R$35, appetizers from R$15; ⏰noon-6pm Tue, Wed, Sat & Sun, to 10pm Thu & Fri) This small, colorful bar is yet another in the growing number of watering holes and restaurants that pepper the neighborhood of Praça da Bandeira. The menu features hearty dishes from Northeast Brazil along with superior versions of traditional bar snacks. The drinks list is short, but includes the mandatory caipirinha and a range of juices.

Hop Lab (Map p98; ☎21 3217-1146; www.facebook.com/hoplab; Barão de Iguatemi 292; ⏰5pm-midnight Tue-Thu, to 2am Fri & Sat, 3-10pm Sun) This beer-lover's paradise offers 30 draft beers on rotation – more than any other bar in Rio – many of which are locally brewed. The English-speaking waiters are certified beer sommeliers, ready to provide guidance and recommendations to curious or indecisive customers. Hearty staples such as burgers and croquettes should keep the hungry drinker satisfied.

Noo Cachaçaria (Map p98; ☎021 3689-4388; www.facebook.com/noocachacaria; Barão de Iguatemi 358; ⏰5-10pm Tue-Fri, noon-11pm Sat) This cozy little bar is one of the highlights of the growing oasis of drinking dens in the otherwise drab neighborhood of Praça da Bandeira. While the impressive list of *cachaça* (sugarcane alcohol) options will appeal to connoisseurs of Brazil's national spirit, the main draw for everyone else will be the inventive snacks, sharing plates and *cachaça*-based cocktails.

★Casa Momus MEDITERRANEAN $$
(Map p92; ☎21 3852-8250; www.casamomus.com.br; Rua do Lavradio 11, Lapa; mains R$42-58; ⏰11:30am-5pm Mon, to midnight Tue & Wed, to 2am Thu-Sat) One of the best and loveliest restaurants in Lapa, Casa Momus has a small but well-executed menu of Mediterranean-influenced dishes. Start with prawn croquettes, fried polenta with spicy Gorgonzola or a Moroccan lamb *kafta* (spiced meat patty) with tabbouleh and yogurt sauce, then feast on oxtail risotto with watercress, seared tuna with couscous, grilled beef tenderloin, and other rich main courses.

Refeitório BRAZILIAN $$
(Map p92; ☎21 2252-2257; www.facebook.com/refeitoriorj; Gomes Freire 226, Lapa; 3-course lunch special R$48; ⏰11:30am-3pm; ✍) One of the neighborhood's best restaurants, Refeitório serves only set lunches. Diners choose from a small selection of beautifully prepared dishes and there's always one vegetarian option. Look for the cleaver over the unsigned entrance to the low-lit space.

Nova Capela PORTUGUESE $$
(Map p92; ☎21 2552-6228; Av Mem de Sá 96, Lapa; mains R$38-68; ⏰11am-4pm Mon, to midnight Tue-Sun) This classic, old-time eating and drinking spot opened in 1967 and is a well-known draw for neighborhood bohemians: a noisy mix of artists, musicians and party kids fill the place till early morning. Efficient waiters in ties and white coats serve up big plates of traditional Portuguese cuisine.

Start with the excellent *bolinhos de bacalhau* (codfish balls), then move on to the famous *cabrito* (goat) dishes.

🍷 Drinking & Nightlife

Ipanema, Leblon and Copacabana offer flashy nightspots as well as old-school watering holes. A youthful bar scene draws revelers to Gávea, while scenic Lagoa draws mostly couples. The narrow pedestrian streets of Centro near Praça XV (Quinze) de Novembro attract drinkers during weekday cocktail hours, and Santa Teresa is a laid-back spot for cocktails. Lapa is full of samba clubs and frenetic outdoor bars, and becomes a late-night street party on weekends.

Ipanema

★Canastra WINE BAR

(Map p66; Jangadeiros 42; ⊙6:30pm-1am Tue-Sat) Run by a trio of Frenchmen, Canastra has become one of the top nightlife destinations in Ipanema. Most nights, the crowd spills out onto the streets, and plenty of socializing *cariocas* never even make it inside. This, however, would be a mistake, as the food (cheese and charcuterie plates, grilled squid and octopus) and drinks (Brazilian wines, sangria, creative caipirinhas) is outstanding.

There's also a hidden bar downstairs – an artfully decorated speakeasy where you can escape the chattering crowds. The big night is Tuesday, when fresh oysters from Santa Catarina arrive (a fine deal at R$40 a dozen).

Nosso COCKTAIL BAR

(Map p66; ☎21 99619-0099; www.facebook.com/nossoipanema; Maria Quitéria 91, Ipanema; ⊙7pm-1am Tue-Thu, to 2am Fri & Sat, 6-11pm Sun) Located in the heart of Ipanema, this supremely stylish cocktail bar and restaurant, complete with swanky rooftop terrace, feels like it has been plucked directly from downtown Manhattan. The meticulously crafted cocktails are made with high-quality spirits and often arrive adorned with foams and dehydrated fruit slices. The menu offers equally intricate yet delicious dishes.

Bar Astor BAR

(Map p66; ☎21 2523-0085; www.barastor.com.br; Av Vieira Souto 110, Ipanema; ⊙6pm-1am Mon-Thu, 1pm-2am Fri, noon-2am Sat, noon-10pm Sun) Not visiting São Paulo? No problem. One of Sampa's best bars has now become a mainstay of post-beach revelry on prime real estate along the Ipanema shorefront. This gorgeous art deco bar does meticulously prepared caipirinhas, as well as Astor's own creative cocktails – try a Tiki Brasil, featuring mango, rangpur and Brazil nut syrup, plus *cachaça* (sugarcane alcohol).

Barzin BAR

(Map p66; www.facebook.com/barzinriolive; Vinícius de Moraes 75; ⊙noon-1am Sun, Mon, Wed & Thu, noon-4am Tue, Fri & Sat) Barzin is a popular spot for post-beach drinks; its open-sided ground-floor bar fills with animated chatter at all hours. Upstairs you can catch a changing lineup of bands playing surf rock, hip-hop and other popular Brazilian music (cover charge from R$30 to R$80). The Tuesday night parties hosted by Bem Brasil (p84) are all the rage.

Baretto-Londra LOUNGE

(Map p66; ☎21 3202-4000; www.fasano.com.br/gastronomia/baretto-londra; Av Vieira Souto 80, Hotel Fasano; ⊙8pm-2am Thu-Sat) You'll find one of Rio's most glam bars here inside the Hotel Fasano (p89), offering a vision of decadence matched by few of the city's night spots. The intimate space, designed by Philippe Starck, has an enchantingly illuminated bar, leather armchairs and divans, and a DJ spinning world electronica.

The crowd is A-list, the drinks are pricey, and unless you're a model (or have one on your arm), be prepared for a long wait at the door.

Shenanigan's IRISH PUB

(Map p66; ☎21 2267-5860; www.facebook.com/shenanigansrj; Visconde de Pirajá 112A; ⊙6pm-1am Tue-Thu, to 3am Fri & Sat, 4pm-1am Sun) Overlooking the Praça General Osório, Shenanigan's is a friendly, Irish-style pub with imported beers, exposed brick walls and a couple of tiny balconies perched above the street. Gringos and *cariocas* mix it up over games of pool and darts to the backdrop of major games on TV (Brazilian football, American football and basketball).

Leblon

Brewteco BAR

(Map p66; ☎21 3217-8280; www.brewteco.com.br; Dias Ferreira 420; ⊙10am-4pm Mon, to midnight Tue-Sat, 3:30pm-midnight Sun) A pillar of Rio's growing microbrew-loving community, Brewteco has nearly two dozen taps featuring unique craft beers – nearly all of which are from Rio. Among the rotating selections, you'll find plenty of variety: wheat beers, IPAs, American IPAs, Belgian-style Tripels, and even Russian Imperial stout.

Note that Brewteco is tiny, with only a few seats. The 'bar' is essentially the sidewalk in front of the place, where beer-sipping crowds gather.

Belmonte BAR

(Map p66; ☎21 2294-8249; Dias Ferreira 521; ⊙11am-2am) An icon in Leblon, Belmonte always

1

MICHAEL HEFFERNAN/LONELY PLANET ©

2

4

PINTAI SUCHACHAISRI/GETTY IMAGES ©

RAFA BAHIENSE/500PX ©

1. Cristo Redentor (p68) Rising 710m above Rio de Janeiro, this 1145-ton statue of Christ is visible from nearly every part of the city.

2. Copacabana Beach (p65) Tourists and locals alike enjoy caipirinhas, sunbathing and football games along this 4km of beachfront.

3. Bonde (p77) The last of the historic streetcars that once traversed the city, the bonde can take you from Centro as far as Santa Teresa.

4. Escadaria Selarón (p76) Chilean-born Jorge Selarón began covering the steps leading into Santa Teresa with colourful mosaics in 1990. All 215 are now covered, and have been featured in numerous magazine, photo and film shoots.

LAZYLLAMA/SHUTTERSTOCK ©

draws huge crowds: it's pretty much a massive street party every night, with beer-drinking revelers spilling onto the sidewalk from 8pm onward. If you can score a table, don't miss the delicious, well-priced *pasteis* (dough that's filled then deep-fried), stuffed with crab, jerked beef with cheese, shrimp, heart of palm and other tasty ingredients.

Jobi BOTECO

(Map p66; ☎21 2274-0547; www.jobileblon.com.br; Av Ataúlfo de Paiva 1166; ⏲9am-5am) A favorite since 1956, Jobi has served a lot of beer in its day, and its popularity hasn't waned. The unadorned *botequim* (bar with table service) still serves plenty; grab a seat by the sidewalk and let the night unfold. If hunger beckons, try the tasty appetizers; the *carne seca* (jerked beef) and the *bolinhos de bacalhau* (codfish croquettes) are tops.

Academia da Cachaça BAR

(Map p66; ☎21 2529-2680; www.academiadacachaca.com.br; Conde Bernadotte 26G; ⏲noon-1am) Although *cachaça* has a sordid reputation in some parts, at this bar the fiery liquor is given the respect it (nearly) deserves. Along with dishes of traditional Brazilian cooking, this pleasant indoor-outdoor spot serves more than 100 varieties of *cachaça;* you can order it straight, with honey and lime, or disguised in a fruity caipirinha.

Gávea, Jardim Botânico & Lagoa

★Palaphita Kitch LOUNGE

(Map p66; ☎21 2227-0837; www.palaphitakitch.com.br; Av Epitácio Pessoa s/n; ⏲6pm-midnight Mon-Fri, from 10am Sat & Sun) A great spot for a sundowner, Palaphita Kitch is an open-air, thatched-roof wonderland with rustic bamboo furniture, flickering tiki torches and a peaceful setting on the edge of Lagoa Rodrigo de Freitas. It's a popular spot with couples, who come for the view and the creative (but pricey) cocktails: the caipirinhas, made from unusual fruits from the Northeast and Amazonia, are a hit.

Palaphita Gávea BAR

(Map p71; ☎21 3114-0853; www.palaphitakitch.com.br; Bartolomeu Mitre 1314; ⏲6pm-1am Mon, 8pm-4am Thu, 9pm-4am Fri & Sat, 5pm-1am Sun) Overlooking the **Jockey Club Brasileiro** (Hipódromo da Gávea; Map p71; ☎21 3534-9001; www.jcb.com.br; Jardim Botânico 1003, Gávea; ⏲6-11pm Mon & Tue, 2-8pm Sat & Sun), this sprawling open-air bar and party space is a wonderful mess of rustic wooden structures, thatch-roofed bars and scattered-about handmade furniture. It draws a young, animated crowd most nights and is a great place at which to end the night. On racing days, you can even place bets here and watch the horses thunder past.

From Thursday through Saturday (11pm to 5am), DJs spinning at the attached nightclub Palaphita Privê draw dance-loving crowds from across the Zona Sul.

Hipódromo BAR

(Map p71; ☎21 2274-9720; www.restaurantehipodromo.com.br; Praça Santos Dumont 108; ⏲noon-1am) In an area commonly referred to as Baixo Gávea, Hipódromo is one of several bar-eateries responsible for the local residents' chronic lack of sleep. Most nights you'll find a college-age and twenty-something crowd celebrating here, with patrons spilling onto the facing Praça Santos Dumont.

Bar do Horto BAR

(Map p71; ☎21 3114-8439; www.dohorto.com.br; Pacheco Leão 780; ⏲noon-2am Tue-Sun) Colorful Bar do Horto is one of Jardim Botânico's most charming bars. The decor is festive and kitsch: walls covered with shimmering fabric and an interior that's festooned with brightly hued paper lanterns, butterfly appliqués, bottle-cap curtains and other recycled ephemera. At night the sidewalk tables gather a festive crowd that comes for cocktails and good cheer.

Copacabana & Leme

Bodega BAR

(Map p74; ☎21 2542-8963; www.facebook.com/bodegabebidaseantepastos; Rua Ministro Viveiros de Castro 102; ⏲5-11pm Tue-Sun) A hip little spot with furniture and fixtures made of recycled products, Bodega stocks an impressive array of craft beer from near and far (including Rio labels like Hocus Pocus and world-class Chimay from Belgium). There are also three rotating beers on tap. Match these brews with cheese platters, codfish balls, foie gras and eggplant dip, among other temptations (appetizers R$15 to R$30).

Sofá Café COFFEE

(Map p74; ☎21 2543-9107; www.sofacafe.com.br; Av NS de Copacabana 300; ⏲8am-8pm Mon-Sat) You'll find Copacabana's best coffee inside this roomy and atmospheric coffeehouse – part of a chain. You select your beans and your preferred method of preparation (Siphon, Chemex, French press, AeroPress etc), and there are plenty of iced options for those hot and steamy days.

Pavão Azul BAR

(Map p74; 21 2236-2381; Hilário de Gouveia 71, Copacabana; noon-midnight Mon-Sat, to 8pm Sun) A Copacabana classic, Pavão Azul is a simple open-sided bar where huge crowds gather on the sidewalk out front to drink ice-cold *chope* (draft beer) and chat late into the night. It's been so successful in fact that the owners have opened a similar *boteco,* Pavãzinho, across the street. Don't miss the fantastically good, inexpensive *pataniscas* (codfish fritters).

Escondido BAR

(Map p74; 21 2522-9800; Aires de Saldanha 98, Copacabana; 6pm-1am Tue-Sun) One of the top beer bars in Copacabana, Escondido has a rotating selection of microbrews such as American pale ales (IPAs), stouts and ciders, including about two dozen on draft at any one time. It's a laid-back spot to head to with friends to sample a few brews and nibble on pub grub (including huge burgers).

Mud Bug BAR

(Map p74; 21 2543-5052; www.mudbug.com.br; Rudolfo Dantas 16, Copacabana; 4pm-1am Tue & Wed, to 3am Thu-Sat, to midnight Sun) Mud Bug is a buzzing, warmly lit sports bar that has a rustic, all-wood interior where *cariocas* and foreigners mingle over football games, bar bites and a broad beer selection. There's also live music – typically classic rock – on weekends, and a jukebox at other times.

Boteco Belmonte BAR

(Map p74; 21 2239-1649; www.facebook.com/botecobelmonte; Av Atlântica 514, Leme; 11:30am-2am Mon-Wed, to 3:30am Thu-Sat, to 5pm Sun) With a peaceful beachfront location, this casual, breezy bar is a relaxing and largely local spot to enjoy a draft or a filling meal. Like the other Belmontes in town, there's a huge selection of appetizers, grilled meats, sandwiches and seafood plates to go with those perfectly frothy brews.

Ponto da Bossa Nova BAR

(Map p74; 21 2235-4616; Domingos Ferreira 215, Copacabana; 5pm-1am Tue-Thu, noon-1am Fri-Sun) On a lively street sprinkled with bars,

LGBT+ RIO

Rio has been a major destination for gay travelers since the 1950s. Back then the action was near the Copacabana Palace (now the Belmond Copacabana Palance), where you'll still find remnants of this past (look for the rainbow-hued flag). Today, however, the party has mostly moved on, with the focal point of the LGBT (lesbian, gay, bisexual, transgender) scene, especially for visitors, being in Ipanema. The beach at the end of Rua Farme de Amoedo attracts a gay crowd (again, look for the rainbow flag), while bars and cafes of nearby streets – Rua Teixeira de Melo and Rua Farme de Amoeda – have a sprinkling of gay bars and cafes.

For more info on what's happening around town, check out www.riogayguide.com or follow its twitter feed (@riogayguide) for listings of parties and other events.

Buraco da Lacraia (Map p92; 21 2242-0446; www.facebook.com/buracodalacraia; André Cavalcante 58, Lapa; R$25-55; 10pm-5:30am Fri & Sat) An icon in Lapa, this is the place for a trashy good time, with bizarre drag shows, karaoke, a darkroom and other amusements.

Cafeína (p102) A popular Ipanema cafe that attracts a mix of gay and straight folk.

Fosfobox (p116) Small underground club that attracts a mixed crowd.

Galeria Café (Map p66; 21 2523-8250; www.galeriacafe.com.br; Teixeira de Melo 31; 11pm-4am Wed-Sat, to 8pm Sun) This bar with a mixed crowd has lovely decor.

Tô Nem Aí (Map p66; 21 2247-8403; www.facebook.com/tonemairestaurante; cnr Farme de Amoedo & Visconde de Pirajá; 5pm-2am Mon-Fri, noon-3am Sat & Sun) On Ipanema's gayest street, this popular bar is a great after-beach spot.

TV Bar (Map p74; www.bartvbar.com.br; Av NS de Copacabana 1417, Shopping Cassino Atlântico, Copacabana; 11pm-5am Thu-Sat, to 3am Sun) The trendy favorite intown; DJs spin amid an audiovisual assault in the space of a former TV station.

The Week (Map p92; 21 2253-1020; www.theweek.com.br; Sacadura Cabral 135, Centro; 11:45pm-7am Sat) Rio's best gay dance club has a spacious dance fl oor, excellent DJs and go-go dancers.

this boxy, wood-lined space has a tiny outdoor patio that makes a peaceful spot for sampling appetizers such as *carne seca com aipim* (jerked beef with fried cassava) and well-made caipirinhas. True to its name, there's live bossa nova – and Música Popular Brasileira (MPB) – from time to time.

Fosfobox CLUB
(Map p74; ☎21 2548-7498; www.fosfobox.com.br; Siqueira Campos 143, Copacabana; ⏲11:30pm-6am Wed-Sat) This subterranean club is hidden under a shopping center near the metro station. Good DJs spin everything from funk to glam rock, and the crowd here is one of the more eclectic in the club scene. Admission R$20 to R$60.

Cafe 18 do Forte CAFE
(Map p74; ☎21 2523-0171; www.cafe18doforte.com.br; Av Atlântica & Francisco Otaviano; ⏲10am-8pm Tue-Sun) The best place for a coffee or a microbrew in the Forte de Copacabana (p65), this outdoor cafe serves a fine array of craft beers from Rio (Hocus Pocus, Three Monkeys, Três Cariocas), including Praya on draft (R$18). The burgers, pastas and hearty Brazilian fare (mains R$42 to R$70) go nicely with the views from the red-umbrella-shaded tables.

Botafogo & Urca

Hocus Pocus BAR
(Map p86; ☎21 4107-3107; www.facebook.com/HocusPocusDNA; Dezenove de Fevereiro 186; ⏲6pm-midnight Mon-Wed, to 2am Thu-Sat) Helping to lead Rio's craft-beer revolution, Hocus Pocus opened this beer hall in 2016 to provide its fans with easy access to its brews. There are over a dozen drafts here – including HP's finest (try the Magic Trap, a Belgian-style golden ale) as well as a few beers from other microbrewers. The buzzing barn-like setting is a great place to while away the evening.

Bar 1928 COCKTAIL BAR
(Map p86; ☎21 3586-2511; contato@bar1928.com.br; Álvaro Ramos 170, Botafogo; ⏲6:30pm-12:30am Tue-Fri, noon-1am Sat, noon-11pm Sun) Tucked away on an otherwise quiet backstreet, Bar 1928 specializes in cocktails and superior bar food. The street-side veranda gets packed early on weekends but more seating is available in a side alley and dining room. Traditional Brazilian dishes have been given a modern twist (sharing plates around R$34), and the excellent cocktails are not to be missed.

CoLAB BAR
(Map p86; ☎21 3592-0470; www.colab-rio.com; Fernandes Guimarães 66; ⏲10am-1am Tue-Sat) CoLAB is one of Botafogo's increasing number of lively bar/restaurants attracting a predominantly young crowd with a combination of international cuisine, cocktails and craft beers. The menu features curries (both Indian and Thai) as well as samosas, falafel sandwiches, burgers and other temptations. Calm by day, CoLAB picks up in the evenings – with DJs and the occasional band keeping things lively.

WineHouse WINE BAR
(Map p86; ☎21 3264-4101; www.winehouserio.com; Paulo Barreto 25; ⏲5pm-midnight Mon-Wed, to 1am Thu-Sat) WineHouse is a stylish yet unpretentious wine bar – a welcome break from Rio's traditionally expensive and starchy wine-drinking scene. A blackboard lists a dozen or so wines available by the glass and always includes a few Brazilian wines. The menu features light bites and an excellent selection of charcuterie. Arrive before 8pm on weekdays for happy-hour prices.

Comuna BAR
(Map p86; ☎21 3579-6175; www.facebook.com/comunacc; Sorocaba 585, Botafogo; ⏲noon-1am Tue-Fri, 6:30pm-1:30am Sat, 6:30pm-midnight Sun) This creative space is equal parts bar, art gallery and independent bookseller (and indie publishing house). There's always something afoot in the delightfully off-the-beaten-path locale, with workshops, music sessions, readings, exhibitions and fashion shows. It's also just a great spot for a local microbrew and a bite (try one of the award-winning burgers).

Bar Urca BAR
(Map p86; ☎21 2295-8744; Cândido Gaffrée 205, Urca; ⏲6:30am-11pm Mon-Sat, 8am-8pm Sun) This much-loved neighborhood bar and restaurant has a marvelous setting near Urca's bayside waterfront. At night, young and old crowd along the seaside wall to enjoy cold drinks, appetizers and fine views.

Fuska 2.0 BAR
(Map p86; ☎21 2266-3621; www.facebook.com/pg/fuskabar2.0; Capitão Salomão 52; ⏲8am-3am Tue-Sun) When you need a break from upmarket drinking and dining, head to Fus-

ka 2.0, a hole-in-the-wall gathering space where a fun crowd gathers at tables on the front sidewalk. There's always something going on, and you can catch live music from Thursday to Sunday nights.

Caverna BAR

(Map p86; ☎21 3507-5600; www.espacocaverna.com; Assis Bueno 26; ⏲6pm-midnight Mon-Thu, to 2am Fri, 7pm-2am Sat) Yet another reason why Botafogo may be surpassing Ipanema in the cool factor these days, this always buzzing rock-and-roll-loving bar and bistro serves microbrews and juicy burgers amid a fun and festive atmosphere (though the music rocks a little loud some nights).

Bar Bukowski CLUB

(Map p86; ☎21 2244-7303; http://barbukowski.com.br/; Álvaro Ramos 270, Botafogo; ⏲9pm-6am Fri & Sat) Paying homage to the eponymous bohemian American writer, this club has a downstairs dance floor and bar, and an upstairs level for live bands playing rock, pop and blues. It's a great scene, and usually attracts a fun crowd. There's also a pool table and darts, and you can have a go at one of the water pipes. The cover charge is R$55.

Champanharia Ovelha Negra BAR

(Map p86; ☎21 2226-1064; www.champanhariaovelhanegra.com.br; Bambina 120, Botafogo; ⏲6pm-midnight Mon-Fri) One of Rio's top happy-hour scenes, Ovelha Negra draws a mostly local crowd who come for the lively conversation and the 40 varieties of champagne and prosecco – the specialties of the house.

Flamengo & Around

Café Secreto CAFE

(Map p86; ☎21 2084-9020; www.facebook.com/cafesecretorj; Casa 8, Gago Coutinho 6; ⏲9am-6pm Mon-Fri) This excellent little coffee shop, hidden down an alleyway off bustling Largo do Machado, is well worth searching out. The expert staff – including a veteran from São Paulo's legendary Coffee Lab – offers a range of coffee beans and extraction methods, including espresso, AeroPress and Hario V60 drippers. Don't miss out on the fantastic cheese breads.

Adega Portugália BAR

(Map p86; www.adegaportugalia.com.br; Largo do Machado 30, Catete; ⏲11am-midnight) Overlooking leafy Largo do Machado, Adega Portugália has an ideal location for enjoying a bit of open-air drinking and eating in an untouristy corner of Rio. In addition to a garrulous crowd and ice-cold *chope* (draft beer), you'll fine classic bar snacks such as *bolinhos de bacalhau* (codfish croquettes) and Portuguese-style sardines.

Bar do Zé BAR

(Map p86; Barão de Guaratiba 59, Catete; ⏲6pm-midnight Mon-Sat) Hidden down a narrow cobblestone side street off Rua do Catete, Bar do Zé has bohemian charm and remains little known to most *cariocas* (Rio residents). You'll find just a few tables inside among the old bottle-lined shelves, low-playing samba on the radio and groups of friends gathered on the street out front.

Centro & Praça Mauá

Bar Léo BAR

(Map p92; ☎21 2509-5725; www.facebook.com/barleoouvidor; Rua do Ouvidor 18, Centro; ⏲11am-11pm Mon-Sat) A great place to retire after a day of exploring, Bar Léo serves ice-cold brews with just the right amount of froth. The setting on a pretty cobblestone lane makes for great people-watching, particularly in the evening when the neighboring bars spring to life.

Cine Botequim BAR

(Map p92; ☎21 2253-1414; www.cinebotequim.com.br; Conselheiro Saraiva 39; ⏲11am-11pm Mon-Fri) Vintage film posters and the odd Star Wars figurine adorn the old stone walls at this atmospherically lit space at the north end of Centro. The after-work crowd comes for Rio craft beers, an extensive appetizer menu, and screenings of big football games. DJs occasionally add to the good cheer.

Amarelinho BOTECO

(Map p92; ☎21 3549-8434; Praça Floriano 55, Cinelândia; ⏲10am-1am) Easy to spot by its bright *amarelo* (yellow) awning, Amarelinho has a splendid setting on the Praça Floriano, with the Theatro Municipal in the background. Waiters serve plenty of *chope* (draft beer) here as they wander among the crowded tables. Amarelinho is a popular lunch spot but packs in even bigger crowds for that ever-important after-work brew.

Santa Teresa

Explorer Bar COCKTAIL BAR

(Map p92; 21 3264-9665; www.explorerbar.com; Almirante Alexandrino 399, Santa Teresa; 5pm-midnight Tue-Fri, from 2pm Sat & Sun) A gorgeous multilevel garden with fairy lights is the centerpiece of this charming cocktail bar. Beautifully conceived cocktails (around R$30) showcase exotic flavors in elixirs like TLV, with orange, tamarind, ginger foam and grated nutmeg. The first-rate food menu features an eclectic mix of Sicilian seafood pasta, *sabich* (a roasted eggplant and hummus sandwich) and other globally inspired dishes (mains R$32 to R$56).

Bar dos Descasados LOUNGE

(Map p92; 21 3380-0200; Almirante Alexandrino 660, Hotel Santa Teresa, Santa Teresa; 6pm-1am Fri & Sat, 5pm-11pm Sun) This stylish bar with outdoor seating has lovely views over the city (looking north). You can enjoy decadent cocktails (including a caipirinha made with tangerines grown on the property) and savory snacks, such as salmon tartare, while pondering the A-list crowd.

Bar do Gomes BOTECO

(Map p92; 21 2232-0822; www.armazemsaothiago.com.br; Áurea 26, Santa Teresa; noon-1am Mon-Sat, to 10pm Sun) Although the sign says 'Armazém do São Thiago,' everyone calls this place Bar do Gomes. Regardless, this atmospheric drinking den with its old photographs and bottle-lined cabinets has long been a favorite meeting spot for ice-cold *chope* (draft beer) and such delicious *petiscos* (snacks) as *bolinhos de abóbora con carne seca* (pumpkin and jerked beef surrounded by deep-fried breading).

Goya-Beira BAR

(Map p92; 21 2232-5751; Largo das Neves 13, Santa Teresa; 6pm-midnight Sun-Thu, to 2am Fri & Sat) Small but charming Goya-Beira is one of Santa Teresa's treasures, and has a peaceful view onto Largo das Neves. Owner Rose Guerra prepares intriguing *cachaça* (high-proof sugarcane alcohol) infusions as well as pizzas and appetizers. Things are liveliest at weekends.

Lapa

Vaca Atolada BAR

(Map p92; 21 2221-0515; Gomes Freire 533, Lapa; 9pm-3am Tue-Sat) For an authentic samba experience, head to this simple, brightly lit, tile-covered eating and drinking den. You'll find a *samba de roda* (table with samba-playing musicians) and a local crowd that squeezes up and joins in with the songs and dance (when space allows). This is old-school Lapa: friendly, ungentrified and full of life.

Booze Bar BAR

(Map p92; www.facebook.com/boozebarrj; Av Mem de Sá 63, Lapa; 5pm-midnight Mon-Wed, to 2am Thu, to 3am Fri & Sat) Though unimaginatively named, the Booze Bar deserves high marks for bringing quality beer to Lapa. You'll find nearly a dozen intriguing microbrews on draft, as well as the bar's own signature easy-drinking pilsen. The attractive high-ceilinged space is a fine spot for a bite, offering *coxinhas* (croquettes), burgers, fish and chips, rice balls and other pub fare (mains R$22 to R$40).

Sarau BAR

(Map p92; www.facebook.com/saraurioIapa; Av Mem de Sá 64, Lapa; 6pm-4am Wed-Sun) Just past the Arcos da Lapa (p76) and tucked inside a building covered with an enormous mural, this place is hard to miss. There's live music – samba and *forró* (popular music of the Northeast) – from 8pm. It's also a great spot to have a few drinks at one of the many outdoor tables on the plaza in front and take in the vertiginous street scene.

Leviano Bar BAR

(Map p92; 21 99580-6462; www.levianobar.com.br; Av Mem de Sá 49, Lapa; 6pm-late) Near the entrance to Mem de Sá, the Leviano Bar is part of a new crop of slightly more upscale drinking and dance spots. Watch the passing people parade – and take in the great view of the Arcos da Lapa (p76) – from the outdoor area before heading to the upstairs dance floor, where DJs mix house, electro-samba, soul and reggae.

Antônio's BOTECO

(Map p92; 21 2224-4197; Av Mem de Sá 88, Lapa; 4pm-3am Mon-Fri, from noon Sat & Sun) Antônio's has lots of old-school charm with its hanging lamps, wrought-iron trim and simple wooden tables. There are a few seats on the sidewalk for taking in the pulsing street scene.

Fazenda Paradiso Café CAFE

(Map p92; 21 3852-3082; www.facebook.com/fazendaparadisocafe; Rua dos Inválidos 126; 8am-7pm Mon-Fri) This excellent family-run cafe provides true 'farm to cup' service. Several kinds of coffee (all grown on the family farm in Minas Gerais) are roasted on-site and available to purchase. Choose from preparation methods including AeroPress, Chemex and Siphon, and team with cakes, wraps, quiches and more substantial lunch dishes.

☆ Entertainment

Music & Dancing

Rio's music scene features talented performers playing in atmospheric settings to a democratic crowd. Lapa is the heart of samba, and its old clubs are a must-see for visitors.

The widest assortment of music venues is along Av Mem de Sá. *Gafieiras* (dance halls) are a big attraction in Lapa. Here you'll find restored colonial buildings hiding dance floors and large samba bands – along with their many admirers.

Rio Scenarium SAMBA

(Map p92; ☎21 3147-9000; www.rioscenarium.art.br; Rua do Lavradio 20, Lapa; R$35-60; ⏲7pm-4am Tue-Sat) One of the city's most photogenic nightspots, Rio Scenarium has three floors, each lavishly decorated with antiques. Balconies overlook the stage on the 1st floor, where dancers keep time to the jazz-infused samba, *choro* (romantic, improvised, samba-related music) or *pagode* (popular samba music) filling the air. Rio Scenarium receives much press outside Brazil, and attracts about twice as many foreigners as locals. Bring ID.

Carioca da Gema SAMBA

(Map p92; ☎21 2221-0043; www.barcariocadagema.com.br; Av Mem de Sá 79, Lapa; R$20-40; ⏲7:30pm-1:30am Sun-Tue & Thu, to 3am Fri, from 9pm Sat) Although it's now surrounded by clubs, Carioca da Gema was one of Lapa's pioneers when it opened in 2000. This small, warmly lit club still attracts some of the city's best samba bands, and you'll find a festive mixed crowd filling the dance floor most nights.

Clube dos Democráticos SAMBA

(Map p92; ☎21 2252-4611; www.clubedosdemocraticos.com.br; Rua do Riachuelo 93, Lapa; R$30-50; ⏲8pm-3am Wed, 10pm-4am Fri & Sat, 8pm-midnight Sun) Murals line the foyer of this 1867 mansion and rhythms filter down from above. Follow the sound up the marble staircase and out to a large table-filled hall, an enormous dance floor and a long stage covered with musicians. A wide range of *cariocas* gathers here to dance, revel in the music and soak up the splendor of the samba-infused setting.

Lapa 40 Graus LIVE MUSIC

(Map p92; ☎21 3970-1338; www.lapa40graus.com.br; Rua do Riachuelo 97, Lapa; R$20-50; ⏲8pm-4am Thu-Sat) This impressive multistory music venue and pool hall has tables for lounging on the 1st floor, more than a dozen pool tables on the 2nd floor, and a small stage and dancing couples on the top floor. There are usually two shows nightly. Pop, rock, samba and *choro* (romantic, improvised, samba-related music) typically kick off around 9pm.

Beco do Rato LIVE MUSIC

(Map p92; ☎21 96984-5797; www.becodorato.com.br; Joaquim Silva 11, Lapa; ⏲7pm-2am Tue-Sat, from 5pm Sun) One of Lapa's classic bohemian spots, this tiny bar in a battered part of the neighborhood has excellent live groups playing to a samba-loving crowd. The outdoor seating and informal setting are an unbeatable mix. Friendly owner Márcio Pacheco hails from Minas Gerais; to get the night started, ask him for a fiery *cachaça* (high-proof sugarcane alcohol) from his home state.

There's live music most nights starting at 8pm (from 5pm Sunday). Beco do Rato, incidentally, means 'Alley of the Rat'.

★**Bip Bip** LIVE MUSIC

(Map p74; ☎21 2267-9696; www.facebook.com/barbipbip; Almirante Gonçalves 50, Copacabana; ⏲7pm-midnight Sun-Fri) For years Bip Bip has been one of the city's favorite spots to catch a live *roda de samba* (informal samba played around a table), despite it being just a storefront with a few battered tables. As the evening progresses the tree-lined neighborhood becomes the backdrop to serious jam sessions, with music and revelers spilling into the street.

TICKET MATTERS

At most samba clubs and live-music bars (also self-serve restaurants) in Rio, you'll receive a ticket when you enter. Rather than paying for individual drinks, your ticket will be marked each time you order. At the end of the night, you'll head to the cashier and pay for your food and drinks, plus pay for any admission charge. The cashier will then give you another ticket to pass to the door attendant as you exit. Don't lose that ticket, as you'll be hit with a hefty fee (upwards of R$200). You'll see this system in many areas of Brazil.

Beco das Garrafas LIVE MUSIC

(Map p74; ☎21 2543-2962; www.becodasgarrafas.mus.br; Duvivier 37, Copacabana; entry R$30-40; ⊙shows daily from 8pm) Come to this club to connect to a small part of Brazilian history – and a big part of musical lore. It was on this lane where Tom Jobim and other innovators first unveiled bossa nova in the 1960s. Shuttered for years, the bar was brought back to life in 2014 and today hosts an excellent lineup of bossa and MPB singers.

Trapiche Gamboa SAMBA

(Map p92; ☎21 2516-0868; www.trapichegamboa.com; Sacadura Cabral 155, Gamboa; entry R$25-35; ⊙6:30pm-1am Thu, 7:30pm-3am Fri, 8:30pm-3am Sat) A charming live-samba joint, Trapiche Gamboa is set in a multistory colonial edifice in Gamboa (just north of Centro) and has a friendly, mixed crowd and decent appetizers. It's a casual affair, with samba musicians gathering around a table on the ground floor, and dancers spilling out in front of them.

It's best reached by taxi (R$40 or so from the Zona Sul).

Fundição Progresso CONCERT VENUE

(Map p92; ☎21 3212-0800; www.fundicaoprogresso.com.br; Rua dos Arcos 24, Lapa; R$50-120) This former foundry hides one of Rio's top music and theater spaces. A diverse range of shows is staged here: big-name acts, such as Manu Chao and Caetano Veloso, plus theater, video arts and ballet.

The foundation is one of Lapa's premier arts institutions; you can study dance, capoeira and circus arts here.

Cinemas

Rio remains remarkably open to foreign and independent films, documentaries and avant-garde cinema. For listings and show times pick up *O Globo*, *Jornal do Brasil* newspapers or *Veja Rio* magazine. Major shopping centers also have cinemas.

Cine Odeon CINEMA

(Centro Cultural Luiz Severiano Ribeiro; Map p92; www.cineodeon.com.br; Praça Floriano 7, Cinelândia; ⊙1:30-9pm Tue-Sun) Rio de Janeiro's landmark cinema is a remnant of the once flourishing movie-house scene that gave rise to the name Cinelândia. Following a

LIVE JAZZ

Maze Inn (Map p86; ☎21 2558-5547; www.jazzrio.info; Casa 66, Tavares Bastos 414, Catete; R$50; ⊙10pm-4am 1st Fri of month) Also known as the 'Casa do Bob' after owner Bob Nadkarni, the once-a-month event here is well worth attending. It's set in the guesthouse (p91) of the same name high up in Tavares Bastos (one of Rio's safest favelas). There's a fun mix of *cariocas* and expats, with live jazz and fantastic city views.

TribOz (Map p92; ☎21 2210-0366; www.triboz-rio.com; Conde de Lages 19, Lapa; R$15-30; ⊙6-8pm & 9pm-1am Thu-Sat) Not for lazy ears, this avant-garde jazz house known to the sonic cognoscenti is unique in Rio for its serious approach to performances. Run by an Australian ethnomusicologist, it sits in a shadier part of old Lapa in a signless mansion, which transforms into a beautiful showcase space.

Blue Note Rio (Map p66; ☎21 3799-2500; www.bluenoterio.com.br; Av Borges de Medeiros 1424; cover R$70-150) In 2017 the famed NYC jazz club opened this Rio outpost (Blue Note's first venture into South America) in an entertainment complex on the edge of Lagoa Rodrigo de Freitas. True to form, it's a classy venue with excellent acoustics that hosts a quality lineup of performers (roughly 75% from Brazil, and the other 25% international performers). Concerts typically happen Wednesday through Saturday.

Ticket prices are steep, but music aside, the service is top-notch, and there's good food (and two bars) on hand. It's located inside the Lagoon (p102) complex.

Clube Manouche (Map p71; www.casacamolese.com.br; Jardim Botânico 983; R$60-90) Downstairs from the main restaurant in Casa Camolese (p101). Clube Manouche is an intimate music bar designed in the tradition of West Village clubs in New York City. Sight lines are excellent no matter where you sit, and you can order drinks throughout the show. The club lines up some top-notch jazz artists, as well as eclectic sounds from Brazil and beyond.

There are shows three or four nights per week (typically starting around 9pm). Check the website to see what's on. Advance reservations are essential.

SAMBA SCHOOLS

Starting around September, in preparation for Carnaval, most big samba schools open their rehearsals to the public. These are large dance parties, and provide a good chance to mingle with *cariocas*. Schools typically charge R$10 to R$40 at the door (prices are higher the closer you are to Carnaval). Many samba schools are in the favelas, so use common sense when visiting.

You can visit the samba schools on a tour, or you can go by yourself. If going independently, catch a taxi there and back; there are always cabs outside the schools waiting to take people home. It's a good idea to confirm that the rehearsals are on before heading out. The most popular schools for tourists are Mangueira and Salgueiro.

Beija-Flor (21 2791-2866; www.beija-flor.com.br; Praçinha Wallace Paes Leme 1025, Nilópolis; 10pm Thu)

Grande Rio (21 2671-3585; www.academicosdogranderio.com.br; Almirante Barroso 5, Duque de Caxias; midnight Sat)

Imperatriz Leopoldinense (21 2560-8037; www.imperatrizleopoldinense.com.br; Professor Lacê 235, Ramos; 8pm Sun)

Mangueira (21 2567-3419; www.mangueira.com.br; Visconde de Niterói 1072, Mangueira; 10pm Sat)

Mocidade Independente de Padre Miguel (21 3291-8700; www.mocidadeindependente.com.br; Av Brasil 31146, Padre Miguel; 11pm Sat)

Portela (21 3207-1604; www.gresportela.org.br; Clara Nunes 81, Oswaldo Cruz; 10pm Fri)

Rocinha (21 3205-3318; www.facebook.com/gresrocinha; Bertha Lutz 80, São Conrado; 10pm Sat)

Salgueiro (21 2238-9226; www.salgueiro.com.br; Silva Teles 104, Andaraí; 10pm Sat)

Unidos da Tijuca (Map p98; 21 2516-2749; www.unidosdatijuca.com.br; Francisco Bicalho 47, Santo Cristo; 10pm Sat)

Vila Isabel (21 2578-0077; www.facebook.com/unidosdevilaisabeloficial; Blvd 28 de Setembro 382, Vila Isabel; 10pm Sat)

restoration before the 2016 Olympics, this 1926 film palace was converted into a multifunction venue. Aside from screenings of the latest Hollywood fare, the Odeon stages occasional concerts, plays and dance performances.

Espaço Itaú CINEMA

(Map p86; www.itaucinemas.com.br; Praia de Botafogo 316) A high-quality six-screen cinema that shows a wide variety of fare. You can linger before or after the film at the cafe, bookstore or various snack counters.

Estação Net Rio CINEMA

(Map p86; 21 2226-1986; www.grupoestacao.com.br; Voluntários da Pátria 35, Botafogo) This two-screen cinema in Botafogo shows a range of films – Brazilian, foreign, independent and the occasional Hollywood offering. It has a cafe inside, as well as a shop selling used records and books, with a number of works focusing on the film arts.

Shopping

Ipanema & Leblon

★Hippie Fair MARKET

(Map p66; Praça General Osório; 9am-6pm Sun) The Zona Sul's most famous market, the Hippie Fair (aka Feira de Arte de Ipanema) has artwork, jewelry, handicrafts, clothing and souvenirs for sale. Stalls in the four corners of the plaza sell tasty plates of *acarajé* (croquettes made from mashed black-eyed peas, with a sauce of *vatapá* – manioc paste, coconut and *dendê* oil – and shrimp), plus excellent desserts. Don't miss it.

Lenny Niemeyer FASHION & ACCESSORIES

(Map p66; 21 2227-5537; www.lennyniemeyer.com; Garcia d'Ávila 149; 10am-8pm Mon-Fri, to 6pm Sat) When it comes to swimwear, few designers have earned a following like Lenny Niemeyer. She creates beautiful, form-fitting bikinis and one-pieces in both classic and avant-garde styles. You'll also find plenty of other essentials for street and beach, including dresses, tops, caftans and sarongs.

Chocolate Q CHOCOLATE

(Map p66; ☎21 2274-1001; www.chocolateq.com; Shop B, Garcia d'Ávila 149; ⏲10am-8pm Mon-Sat) This is serious chocolate. Cacao beans, harvested from a single, environmentally conscious grower in Bahia, are processed into a range of exquisite dark-chocolate products (milk chocolate fans be advised, there is nothing for you here). All the bars and pastilles are beautifully packaged, with colorful illustrations of Brazilian wildlife, making them eminently gift-worthy.

Gilson Martins FASHION & ACCESSORIES

(Map p66; ☎21 2227-6178; www.shop.gilsonmartins.com.br; Visconde de Pirajá 462; ⏲9am-8pm Mon-Fri, to 7pm Sat) Designer Gilson Martins transforms the Brazilian flag and silhouettes of Pão de Açúcar (Sugarloaf Mountain) and Corcovado into eye-catching accessories in his flagship store in Ipanema. This is the place for unique glossy handbags, wallets, passport covers, key chains and iPad covers. Products are durable and use recycled and sustainable materials – and are not available outside Rio.

Maria Oiticica JEWELRY

(Map p66; ☎21 3875-8025; www.mariaoiticica.com; Av Afrânio de Melo Franco 290, Shopping Leblon; ⏲10am-10pm Mon-Sat, 1-9pm Sun) Using native materials found in the Amazon, Maria Oiticica has created some lovely handcrafted jewelry inspired by indigenous art. Seeds, plant fibers and tree bark are just some of the ingredients of her bracelets, necklaces, earrings and sandals. There are even sandals and handbags made from fish 'leather.'

Osklen CLOTHING

(Map p66; ☎21 2227-2930; www.osklen.com; Maria Quitéria 85; ⏲9am-8pm Mon-Fri, 10am-7pm Sat, 11am-5pm Sun) One of Brazil's best-known fashion labels outside the country, Osklen is notable for its stylish and well-made beachwear (particularly men's swim shorts and graphic T-shirts), sneakers and outerwear. The company was started in 1988 by outdoor enthusiast Oskar Metsavaht, the first Brazilian to scale Mont Blanc.

Livraria da Travessa BOOKS, MUSIC

(Map p66; ☎21 3205-9002; www.travessa.com.br; Visconde de Pirajá 572; ⏲9am-11pm Mon-Sat, 10am-11pm Sun) One of several branches around town, this Livraria da Travessa has a small selection of foreign-language books and periodicals, and some CDs upstairs. The buzzing 2nd-floor cafe (a branch of Bazzar) serves salads, sandwiches, quiches and desserts. There's an even larger Livraria da Travessa inside the Shopping Leblon mall (p122).

Isabela Capeto CLOTHING

(Map p66; ☎21 2540-6640; www.isabelacapeto.com.br; General Venâncio Flôres 481C, Leblon; ⏲10am-8pm Mon-Sat) One of Brazil's rising fashion stars, Isabela Capeto creates colorful apparel that is both flattering and playful. Many of her pieces are embroidered and feature add-ons of vintage lace, sequins or fabric trims. Her new shop here in leafy Leblon is the best place to see dresses and skirts that have earned her accolades in *O Globo*, *Vogue* and other publications.

Toca do Vinícius MUSIC

(Map p66; ☎21 2247-5227; www.facebook.com/casadabossanova.tocadovinicius; Vinícius de Moraes 129; ⏲11am-7pm Mon-Fri, 10am-6pm Sat, 3-6pm Sun) Bossa nova fans shouldn't miss this store. In addition to its ample CD and vinyl selection (starting at R$40) of contemporary and old performers, it also sells music scores and composition books. Around the store you'll find memorabilia from great songwriters including Vinícius de Moraes and Chico Buarque.

Void General Store FASHION & ACCESSORIES

(Map p66; ☎21 3592-7719; www.avoid.com.br; Av Ataúlfo de Paiva 1166; ⏲10am-1am Mon-Wed, to 3am Thu-Sat, 11am-1am Sun) The go-to spot for all your underground hipster needs, the tiny Void is a shop by day and a lively beer-drinking spot by night. You'll find unique jewelry, graphic T-shirts, baseball caps, sneakers (Converse, Vans) and CDs. It tends to attract a young, alternative crowd.

Havaianas SHOES

(Map p66; ☎21 3437-1479; Visconde de Pirajá 111; ⏲9am-8pm Mon-Fri, 10am-7pm Sat & Sun) This small shop is a great place to stock up on Brazil's iconic rubber sandals. You'll find a colorful variety of Havaianas for men, women and children, covering all price points (from R$35 to R$96).

Shopping Leblon SHOPPING CENTER

(Map p66; ☎21 2430-5122; www.shoppingleblon.com.br; Av Afrânio de Melo Franco 290; ⏲10am-10pm Mon-Sat, 1-9pm Sun) This glittering multistory shopping center packed with top-name Brazilian and foreign labels is the best shopping destination in Leblon. It has plenty of tempting stores that will drain your vacation funds, as well as good restaurants and a cinema.

Gávea, Jardim Botânico & Lagoa

Dona Coisa FASHION & ACCESSORIES

(Map p71; ☎21 2249-2336; www.donacoisa.com.br; Lopes Quintas 153, Jardim Botânico; ⏰10am-8:30pm Mon-Fri, to 6pm Sat) One of Rio's top boutiques, Dona Coisa sells top labels by Brazilian and international designers, including one-of-a-kind pieces you won't find elsewhere. Head upstairs to browse original objects for the home (including delicate ceramics by Heloisa Galvão) as well as skincare products by Phebo, and beautifully designed stationery by Nina Write.

The small, well-lit cafe out back serves ciabatta sandwiches, espresso drinks and decadent desserts.

Gabinete HOMEWARES

(Map p71; ☎21 3173-8828; www.gabineteduiliosartori.com.br/; Lopes Quintas 87, Jardim Botânico; ⏰11am-8pm Mon-Sat) On a street with a growing number of shops and cafes, Gabinete is a fun place to browse for unusual items – geometric jewelry made of volcanic rock, delicately fluted vases and glassware, illuminated teapot lamps, wind-up circus miniatures and earth-toned pottery – that line the artfully lit display shelves of this intriguing curiosity cabinet.

O Sol ARTS & CRAFTS

(Map p71; ☎21 2294-5149; www.osolartesanato.org.br; Corcovado 213, Jardim Botânico; ⏰9am-6pm Mon-Fri, to 1pm Sat) O Sol is run by Leste-Um, a nonprofit social-welfare organization. This delightful store displays the works of regional artists and sells Brazilian folk art made from clay, wood and porcelain. Aside from handicrafts, the store also stocks baskets, hammocks, pottery and woven rugs.

Copacabana & Leme

Gilson Martins FASHION & ACCESSORIES

(Map p74; ☎21 2235-5701; http://shop.gilsonmartins.com.br; Av Atlântica 1998, Copacabana; ⏰9am-8pm Mon-Sat, 10am-4pm Sun) Like its flagship store in Ipanema, this colorful shop sells well-crafted wallets, messenger bags, purses, key chains and other items with images of Cristo Redentor (Christ the Redeemer), the Brazilian flag and other iconic designs. Products are durable and use recycled and sustainable materials – and are not available outside of Rio.

Loja Fla FASHION & ACCESSORIES

(Map p74; ☎21 2295-5057; www.lojafla.com.br; Av NS de Copacabana 219, Copacabana; ⏰9am-7pm Mon-Fri, 10am-4pm Sat) With more than 30 million fans worldwide, Flamengo is one of the most-watched football (soccer) teams in all of Brazil. This shop sells all the Flamengo merchandise, including jerseys, logo-emblazoned soccer balls, posters, bean bags, smartphone covers, clocks, flip-flops (thongs), socks, mugs, pens, pacifiers, baby bottles and heaps of other items.

Osklen Surfing CLOTHING

(Map p74; ☎21 2513-0369; https:/osklen.com; Francisco Otaviano 67, Arpoador; ⏰9am-8pm Mon-Fri, 10am-8pm Sat, 11am-5pm Sun) The famous Brazilian beachwear brand sells its well-made board shorts, T-shirts, *sungas* (Speedo-sized male swimsuits) and a few bikinis from this attractive store in Arpoador. You can even buy a very beautiful Kronig design surfboard here, if you have a spare R$1700.

Botafogo & Urca

Baratos da Ribeiro MUSIC

(Map p86; ☎21 3547-2220; www.baratosdaribeiro.com.br; Paulino Fernandes 15, Botafogo; ⏰10am-8pm Mon-Fri, 11am-8pm Sat) Vinyl fans and bookworms flock to this cabinet of musical and literary curiosities with its extensive collection of unusual albums combined with secondhand art books, novels and other intriguing publications – including titles in English (spotted when last we passed through: the cowboy novel *Wyatt Earp* and an autobiography of Katharine Hepburn).

Comparsaria SHOES

(Map p86; ☎21 3178-2114; www.facebook.com/comparsaria; Voluntários da Pátria 45; ⏰10am-8pm Mon-Wed, to 9pm Thu & Fri, 10am-7pm Sat) This small attractive boutique stocks handsomely crafted shoes and sandals, leather bags and satchels, hats, wallets and other accessories. Production runs are limited and styles range from timeless and classic to avant-garde and utterly unwearable.

Rio Sul Shopping SHOPPING CENTER

(Map p86; ☎21 3723-9500; www.riosul.com.br; Lauro Müller 116, Botafogo; ⏰10am-10pm Mon-Sat, 3-9pm Sun) The biggest shopping center you can reach without heading to Barra da

RIO ANTIQUES FAIR

Don't miss the **Rio Antiques Fair** (Rua do Lavradio, Lapa; ⏲10am-6pm 1st Sat of month) if it's on while you're in town. The colonial buildings become a living installation as the whole street fills with antiques, clothing and craft vendors, and food stalls, with samba bands adding to the festive atmosphere.

It happens all along Rua do Lavradio, with the action often spilling over onto nearby Praça Tiradentes.

Tijuca, Rio Sul has more than 400 shops, featuring both the prominent and the obscure, plus cinemas and restaurants.

Botafogo Praia Shopping SHOPPING CENTER
(Map p86; ☎21 3171-9872; www.botafogopraiashopping.com.br; Praia de Botafogo 400, Botafogo; ⏲10am-10pm Mon-Sat, 2-9pm Sun; 📶) Botafogo's large shopping center has dozens of stores, featuring Brazilian and international designers to suit every style – and clothe every part of the body. The 3rd floor's the best for top designers: check out stores such as Maria Filó, Reserva and Hope. The mall also has a cinema and several 5th-floor restaurants with panoramic views.

Flamengo & Around

Pé de Boi ARTS & CRAFTS
(Map p86; ☎21 2285-4395; www.pedeboi.com.br; Ipiranga 55, Laranjeiras; ⏲10am-7pm Mon-Fri, to 1pm Sat) Although everything is for sale here, Pé de Boi feels more like an art gallery than a handicrafts shop, owing to the high quality of the wood and ceramic works, and the tapestries, sculptures and weavings. This is perhaps Rio's best place to see one-of-a-kind pieces by artists from Bahia, Amazonia, Minas Gerais and other parts of Brazil.

Centro & Praça Mauá

★**CRAB** ARTS & CRAFTS
(Map p92; ☎21 3380-1850; www.facebook.com/crabsebrae; Praça Tiradentes 69; ⏲10am-5pm Tue-Sat) 🍃 One of Rio's best new handicraft stores stocks an exquisite collection of pieces from every corner of Brazil. You'll find ceramics with pre-Columbian imagery found in the Serra da Capivara, lovely eco-jewelry made of seeds and nuts from indigenous groups and brightly painted folk art from the Northeast, as well as sustainably made animal-free bags, vegetable-fiber woven textiles and all-rubber footwear.

Casa Naara ARTS & CRAFTS
(Map p92; ☎21 97399-0642; www.casanaara.com.br; 2nd fl, Teófilo Otoni 134; ⏲11am-8pm Mon-Fri) This upstairs shop has loads of character, with original paintings, carved wooden folk art, artfully bound blank books, coffee from small producers and other curiosities for sale. There's a small cafe on-site, and Casa Naara hosts yoga sessions, photo courses, round-table discussions and other cultural fare (in Portuguese of course).

Granado COSMETICS
(Map p92; ☎21 2252-4136; www.granado.com.br; Primeiro de Março 14, Centro; ⏲8am-7pm Mon-Fri, 10am-2pm Sat) A classic-looking apothecary with a name that's been around since 1870, Granado incorporates Brazilian ingredients in its all-natural products. Favorites include the Castanha do Brasil line of moisturizers, shampoos and conditioners (made from chestnuts from the Amazon).

Livraria da Travessa BOOKS, MUSIC
(Map p92; ☎21 3231-8015; Sete de Setembro 54, Centro; ⏲9am-8pm Mon-Fri, to 2pm Sat) Livraria da Travessa offers a peaceful refuge from the people-packed sidewalks. There are some books in English, and an array of colorful (but pricey) coffee-table books. There's also a small in-store cafe-restaurant where you can order drinks and creatively topped focaccia sandwiches.

Santa Teresa & Lapa

Favela Hype FASHION & ACCESSORIES
(Map p92; www.facebook.com/favelahype; Paschoal Carlos Magno 103, Santa Teresa; ⏲10am-11pm Tue-Sun) This ultra-hip but very friendly gathering spot is part fashion boutique, part restaurant and (at certain times) all **party space** (Map p92; www.facebook.com/favelahype; Paschoal Carlos Magno 103, Santa Teresa; ⏲10am-11pm Tue-Sun). The art-filled shop sells swimwear, dresses, jewelry, sunglasses, ecofriendly flip-flops, floral-print button-downs (for the guys) and original artworks. Most products are made by local designers. Favela Hype also serves creative

Brazilian fare, including an excellent *feijoada* (bean-and-meat stew).

La Vereda ARTS & CRAFTS
(Map p92; ☎21 2507-0317; www.lavereda.art.br; Almirante Alexandrino 428, Santa Teresa; ⏰10am-8pm) La Vereda stocks a colorful selection of handicrafts from local artists and artisans in a spot near Largo do Guimarães. Hand-painted clay figurines by Pernambuco artists, heavy Minas ceramics, delicate sterling-silver jewelry and loosely woven tapestries cover the interior of the old store.

Galeria Bazá ARTS & CRAFTS
(Map p92; www.facebook.com/galeriabaza; Rua do Oriente 414, Santa Teresa; ⏰noon-11pm Tue-Sun) This vegan restaurant and creative cultural venue also sells Brazilian folk art, eye-catching jewelry and graphic T-shirts, with many pieces made by local artisans.

Loja Pence FASHION & ACCESSORIES
(Map p92; www.instagram.com/lojapence; Joaquim Silva 123, Lapa; ⏰10am-6pm Mon-Thu, to 11pm Fri, 11am-7pm Sat) Lapa's most creative boutique captures the bohemian spirit of the neighborhood in a wide range of clothing and accessories, all created by local designers. Check out geometric necklaces and bracelets by Linguagem Primativo, bath products by Vanzinga, swimwear by Rota do Sul, dresses by Fios e Atavios, *eco-joias* (sustainably made jewelry) by Raquel Duarte and printed shirts (for men) by Geração.

Information

DANGERS & ANNOYANCES

Crime is a perennial problem in Rio, so travel smart.

- Copacabana and Ipanema Beaches have a police presence, but robberies still occur on the sands, even in broad daylight. Don't ever take anything of value with you to the beach. Late at night, don't walk on any of the beaches.
- Lapa and Santa Teresa are other areas well worth visiting but which have their share of crime. Avoid walking on empty streets; it's safest to stick to well-trafficked areas.
- Take taxis at night to avoid walking along empty streets and beaches. That holds especially true for Centro, which becomes deserted in the evening and on weekends, and is better explored during the week.
- Cameras and backpacks attract a lot of attention. Plastic shopping bags better disguise whatever you're carrying.
- If you have the misfortune of being robbed, slowly hand over the goods. Thieves in the city are only too willing to use their weapons.

EMERGENCY & IMPORTANT NUMBERS

Report robberies to the **tourist police** (☎21 2332-2924; cnr Afrânio de Melo Franco & Humberto de Campos, Leblon; ⏰24hr); no major investigation is going to occur, but you will get a police form to give to your insurance company.

Ambulance	☎192
Fire Department	☎193
Police	☎190

MEDIA

The English-language *Rio Times* (www.riotimesonline.com) maintains a website updated weekly. *Jornal do Brasil* and *O Globo* are Brazil's leading dailies. *Veja* is the country's best-selling weekly magazine. In Rio it comes with the 'Veja Rio' insert, available on Sunday, which details entertainment options for the week ahead.

MEDICAL SERVICES

Clinica Galdino Campos (☎21 2548-9966; www.galdinocampos.com.br; Av NS de Copacabana 492, Copacabana; ⏰24hr) The best hospital for foreigners, with high-quality care and multilingual doctors (who even make outpatient calls). The clinic works with most international health plans and travel-insurance policies.

There are scores of pharmacies in town, a number of which stay open 24 hours, including **Drogaria Pacheco** (☎21 2521-2124; Visconde de Pirajá 82, Ipanema; ⏰24hr).

MONEY

ATMs are the handiest way to access money in Rio. Unfortunately, there has been an alarming rise in card cloning, with travelers returning home to find unauthorized withdrawals on their cards. This has been especially problematic with Bradesco ATMs, which you should avoid at all costs.

When possible use high-traffic ATMs inside bank buildings during banking hours. Always cover your hands when inputting your PIN, and check your account frequently to make sure you haven't been hacked.

ATMs for most card networks are widely available.

Banco do Brasil Branches with ATM in **Centro** (Av Ataúlfo de Paiva 980, Leblon), **Copacabana** (Av NS de Copacabana 1274, Copacabana; ⏰10am-4pm Mon-Fri) and **Galeão international airport** (1st fl, Terminal 1, Galeão international airport).

TOURIST INFORMATION

Riotur's multilingual website (www.visit.rio) is a good source of information. Its offices distribute maps and guides about major events; the main branch is in **Copacabana** (Map p74; ☎21 2541-7522; Av Princesa Isabel 183; ⊙9am-6pm Mon-Fri).

Riotur Office (Terminal 1, Domestic Arrivals Hall, Galeão International Airport; ⊙6am-11pm)

Riotur Office (Terminal 2, International Arrivals Hall, Galeão International Airport; ⊙6am-11pm)

Central 1746 (☎21 2271-7048, 1746; www.1746.rio.gov.br; ⊙24hr) Rio's City Hall directory assistance. Press 8 for tourist info, then 1 for English.

Getting There & Away

AIR

Aeroporto Antônio Carlos Jobim Most international flights arrive at this airport (also called Galeão), located 15km north of the city center.

Aeroporto Santos Dumont (Map p92; ☎21 3814-7222; www4.infraero.gov.br; Praça Senador Salgado Filho), used by some domestic flights, is by the bay, in the city center, 1km east of Cinelândia metro station.

BUS

Buses leave from the sleek **Rodoviária Novo Rio** (Map p98; ☎21 3213-1800; www.novorio.com.br; Av Francisco Bicalho 1), 2km northwest of Centro. There's a Riotur desk here for city info. If you're traveling without much luggage, you can get to/from the bus station using Rio's new light rail, the VLT. If you're headed south, transfer to the metro at Central.

A small booth near the exit at Novo Rio bus station organizes the yellow taxis out the front. Sample fares (with one bag) are about R$50 to the international airport, R$50 to Copacabana and Ipanema, and R$35 to Santa Teresa.

You can consult the schedule and buy tickets online at www.clickbus.com. There's a dedicated pickup booth in the front of the bus terminal. Major bus companies like **Viação 1001** (☎0800-941-3334; www.autoviacao1001.com.br) have frequent departures to São Paulo.

A handful of travel agents, including **Guanatur** (☎21 2548-3275; Dias da Rocha 16A, Copacabana; ⊙9am-6pm Mon-Fri, to noon Sat) and **Dantur** (☎21 2557-7144; www.dantur.com.br; Loja 47, Largo do Machado 29, Flamengo; ⊙9am-6:30pm Mon-Fri, to 1pm Sat), sells bus tickets; the commission is around R$8 per ticket.

Getting Around

TO & FROM THE AIRPORT

From Aeroporto Antônio Carlos Jobim (Galeão), Premium Auto Ônibus operates buses approximately every 30 to 40 minutes to Flamengo, Copacabana, Ipanema, Leblon and other neighborhoods (bus 2018; R$16). The trip takes one to two hours depending on traffic. Radio taxis charge a set fare of R$130 to Copacabana and Ipanema (45 to 90 minutes). Less-expensive metered yellow-and-blue *comum* (common) taxis cost between R$82 and R$100. Ride-sharing services cost around R$60. There's also the **Shuttle Rio** (☎21 2524-7730; www.shuttlerio.com.br; one way R$25; ⊙hourly 8am-7pm) service (R$25) from Terminals 1 and 2 to hotels in Copacabana, Ipanema and Leblon. Reserve ahead.

CAR

Driving in Rio can be a frustrating experience even if you know your way around. Traffic snarls and parking problems do not make for an enjoyable holiday.

Rental

Car-rental agencies can be found at both airports and scattered along Av Princesa Isabel in Copacabana.

At the international airport, **Hertz** (☎21 2153-2124; www.hertz.com; Av Vinte de Janeiro; ⊙24hr), **Budget** (☎21 3398-2350; www.budget.com; Av Vinte de Janeiro) and **Unidas** (☎21 97697-0407; www.unidas.com.br; Av Vinte de Janeiro; ⊙24hr) provide rentals. In Copacabana, among the many are **Hertz** (☎21 2275-3340; Av Princesa Isabel 500; ⊙8am-8pm Mon-Sat, to 2pm Sun) and **Unidas** (☎21 2543-2067; www.unidas.com.br; Av Princesa Isabel 214; ⊙8am-7:45pm Mon-Fri, to 5:45pm Sat).

PUBLIC TRANSPORTATION

Metro

Rio's **metro system** (www.metrorio.com.br; 1 ride R$4.30; ⊙5am-midnight Mon-Sat, 7am-11pm Sun) is an excellent way to get around. Its three lines are air-conditioned, clean and efficient. Line 1 goes from Ipanema-General Osório to Uruguai in the north zone. Line 2, which partly overlaps line 1, travels from Botafogo to Pavuna (passing Maracanã football stadium en route). Line 3 travels between Ipanema-General Osório and the eastern end of Barra da Tijuca at Jardim Oceânico.

You can purchase a *cartão pré-pago* (prepaid card) from a kiosk in any metro station using cash (no change given) with a minimum of R$5. You can then recharge the card at any kiosk. Free subway maps are available from most ticket booths.

During Carnaval the metro operates nonstop from 5am Saturday morning until at least 11pm on Tuesday.

Bus

Rio's new BRS (Bus Rapid System) features dedicated public-transportation corridors in Copacabana, Ipanema, Leblon and Barra. Fares on most buses are around R$3.50.

Every bus has its key destination displayed on the illuminated signboard in front. If you see the bus you want, hail it by sticking your arm straight out (drivers won't stop unless flagged down).

Light Rail

Rio's new light rail – the **VLT** (www.vltcarioca.com.br; one way R$3.80; ⌚6am-midnight) – is part of a massive urban-renewal project helping to revitalize Centro. Launched in 2016, the VLT has 26 stations in Rio, running on two different routes through downtown. For visitors, handy access is at Cinelândia (outside the metro) to Praça Mauá (to the stop labelled Parada dos Museus). To reach Praça XV (Quinze) de Novembro or Praça Tiradentes, take the Praia Formosa line, which you can access on Rua Sete de Setembro, just west of Rio Branco. The VLT also goes to Aeroporto Santos Dumont and Rodoviária Novo Rio bus station. For maps, schedules and other info, download the free **VLT Carioca** app.

Taxi & Moto-Taxi

Rio's yellow taxis are plentiful, and easy to hail, particularly by using free apps like 99Taxis or Easy Taxi. They're generally a speedy way to zip around and are usually safe. The flat rate is around R$5.50, plus around R$2.50 per kilometer (R$3 per kilometer at night and on Sunday). Radio taxis, which can be ordered in advance, are 30% more expensive than regular taxis. No one tips taxi drivers, but it's common to round up the fare.

Especial Coop Taxi (☎21 3295-9606, WhatsApp 21 99776-5347; www.facebook.com/especialcoop) has vehicles with lifts for wheelchair users. It also has its own app, Especial Coop.

If you prefer to reserve a car, a few reliable radio-taxi operators include **Transcoopass** (☎21 2209-1555; www.transcoopass.com.br), **Coopertramo** (☎21 2209-9292; www.radio-taxi.com.br), **Transcootour** (☎21 2590-2220; www.transcootour.com.br) and **Cootramo** (☎21 3976-9944; www.cootramo.com.br).

In Rocinha and some other favelas (slums, informal communities), moto-taxis (basically a lift on the back of a motorcycle) are a handy way to get around, with short rides (usually from the bottom of the favela to the top or vice versa) costing R$3. That said, given the currently unstable security situation, it's unwise to head into a favela on a moto-taxi.

TRAVELING GREEN

Rio has many kilometers of bike paths along the beach, around Lagoa and along Parque do Flamengo.

The city's public bike-sharing scheme, **Bike Rio** (www.bikeitau.com.br/bikerio), features bright-orange bikes found at over 250 stations. After registering on the website or the app (Bike Itaú), you can buy a monthly pass (R$10) or a day pass (R$5). Instructions are available in English at the stations and the bikes are released via mobile phone or app.

Many (but not all) stations also have a pay-on-the-spot option for a day pass. After you swipe your credit card you'll be given a code that you'll use to release any of the bikes. The first 60 minutes won't cost extra; after that it's R$5 per hour, though you can make an unlimited number of checkouts during your 24-hour day pass (or monthly pass).

Rio de Janeiro State

POP 17 MILLION

Includes ➡

Ilha Grande & Vila do Abraão............129
Paraty............137
Parque Nacional do Itatiaia............146
Petrópolis............151
Teresópolis............155
Nova Friburgo............157
Saquarema............159
Arraial do Cabo............162
Búzios............164

Best Places to Eat

- ➡ Rocka Beach Lounge (p168)
- ➡ Rosmarinus Officinalis (p150)
- ➡ Linguiça do Padre (p156)
- ➡ Bacalhau do Tuga (p163)
- ➡ Banana da Terra (p145)

Best Places to Stay

- ➡ Pousada da Alcobaça (p153)
- ➡ Bonito Paraiso Beach House (p134)
- ➡ Hotel Warabi (p149)
- ➡ Pousada Paraiso Açu (p153)

Why Go?

If you thought Rio was just a city, think again! Right next door, the equally enticing *state* of Rio de Janeiro is home to some of Brazil's greatest treasures, all within an easy one- to four-hour journey from the Cidade Maravilhosa (Marvelous City).

East along the coast are the dunes, lagoons, white sands and limpid blue-green waters of the Costa do Sol, an ever-popular playground for surfers, divers and suntan-seeking urban escapees.

Inland you'll find Itatiaia, Brazil's oldest national park, and the spectacular Serra dos Órgãos, whose whimsically shaped peaks test the mettle of international climbers and form the backdrop for the former imperial city of Petrópolis.

West lies the Costa Verde, a patchwork of bays, islands, waterfalls and forest-draped mountains. Highlights here include the 18th-century architecture of colonial Paraty and the vast island paradise of Ilha Grande, where dozens of hiking trails lead to more than 100 of Brazil's most secluded beaches.

When to Go

Búzios

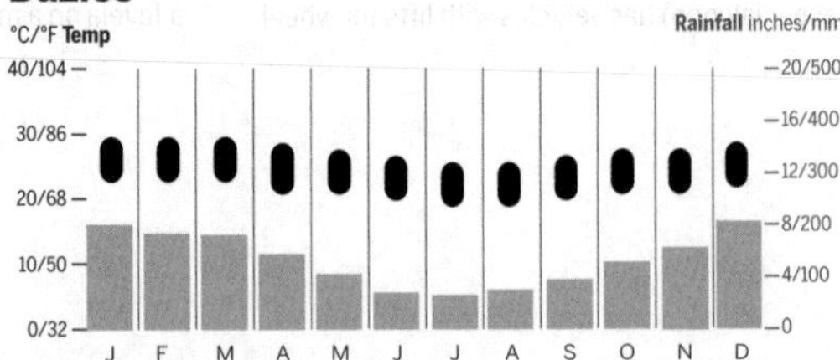

Dec–Feb Hit the beach, or escape the heat in the mountain refuges of Petrópolis and Itatiaia.

Apr & May Drier weather, perfect waves and lower prices create dream conditions along the coast.

Jul & Aug Winter brings festivals of literature and *cachaça* to Paraty's picturesque streets.

History

The Tupí and other indigenous groups inhabited modern-day Rio state for over two millennia before Europeans arrived in the 16th century. Early Portuguese activity was focused along the coast, but the discovery of gold in the late 17th century prompted construction of Brazil's first major overland thoroughfare, the Caminho do Ouro. This rugged route extended from coastal Paraty across the jungle-clad Serra da Bocaina and the Rio Paraíba valley to the gold and diamond mines of Minas Gerais, whose mineral riches were exploited using slave labor to fill Portuguese royal coffers. Another important chapter in Rio state's development was the establishment of coffee plantations here in the early 19th century, another enterprise heavily dependent on the labor of enslaved Africans. The crop was taken by mule train to new ports along the coast, and these roads were the main means of communication until the coming of the railways after 1855.

In the first decade of the 21st century, modern Rio de Janeiro state was one of Brazil's economic powerhouses, fueled by oil, a steady tourist trade and traditional industries such as steel and shipbuilding. Recent political crises have taken a heavy toll on the state's prosperity, with money laundering charges earning the state's former governor Sergio Cabral a 72-year prison sentence in 2017.

Getting There & Around

International and domestic flights fly into Rio de Janeiro's **Galeão** (Aeroporto Internacional Antônio Carlos Jobim; ☎21 3004-6050; www.riogaleao.com; Domestic Arrival Hall, Av Vinte de Janeiro) and Santos Dumont (p126) airports, linking Rio state to cities throughout Brazil and the world. Rio's long-distance bus station (p126) is a hub for virtually every bus line in the country, with fast, frequent service to nearby towns via well-maintained modern highways.

COSTA VERDE

West of Rio city is the Costa Verde (Green Coast), a captivating stretch of coastline where jungled mountainsides dotted with flowering trees dive precipitously into a blue-green sea. The sinuous shoreline here presents visitors with an ever-changing panorama of bays, islands, peaks and waterfalls. Tucked into this idyllic landscape, the 17th-century port of Paraty is famed both for its well-preserved historic center and for the legendary beauty of surrounding beaches such as Trindade and Sono. Just inland lies the Parque Nacional da Serra da Bocaina, which protects large tracts of endangered Mata Atlântica (Atlantic rainforest). Offshore lies another hiker's and beach lover's dream: Ilha Grande, a vast island with no vehicle traffic and very few settlements to disrupt its pristine natural splendor. Amazingly, all of this is right in Rio's backyard: hop a bus in the morning, and you can be spending the afternoon in tropical coastal paradise.

Ilha Grande & Vila do Abraão

☎0XX24 / POP 5000

The fabulous island retreat of Ilha Grande owes its pristine condition to its unusual history. For centuries, the island's unsavory reputation – first as a pirate's lair, then as a leper colony and penitentiary – kept developers at bay. Consequently, beautiful tropical beaches and virgin Atlantic rainforest (now protected as state parkland) abound, and the island still has only a handful of settlements.

Vila do Abraão, Ilha Grande's main town, was just a sleepy fishing village until the mid-1990s, when the infamous prison was destroyed and tourism began in earnest. Despite the influx of outsiders, Abraão, with its palm-studded beachfront and tidy orange church, remains small by mainland standards, and the prevailing rhythm is agreeably slow, thanks in large part to the absence of motorized vehicles. By day, life is all about exploring the island's dozens of trails and beaches, while evening brings half the town down to socialize by the waterfront.

Sights & Activities

From hiking to water sports, outdoor adventure options on Ilha Grande are endless.

Posted around town are maps showing 16 different signposted trails leading through the lush forest to several of the island's 102 beaches. When visiting some beaches, it's possible to hike one way and take a boat the other.

Before hitting the trail, let people at your pousada know where you're going and when you'll be back, stock up on water and bug repellent, and bring a flashlight, as darkness comes swiftly under the jungle canopy. Guides are advisable for exploring beyond the most heavily traveled routes; poorly marked trails and poisonous snakes can make things challenging.

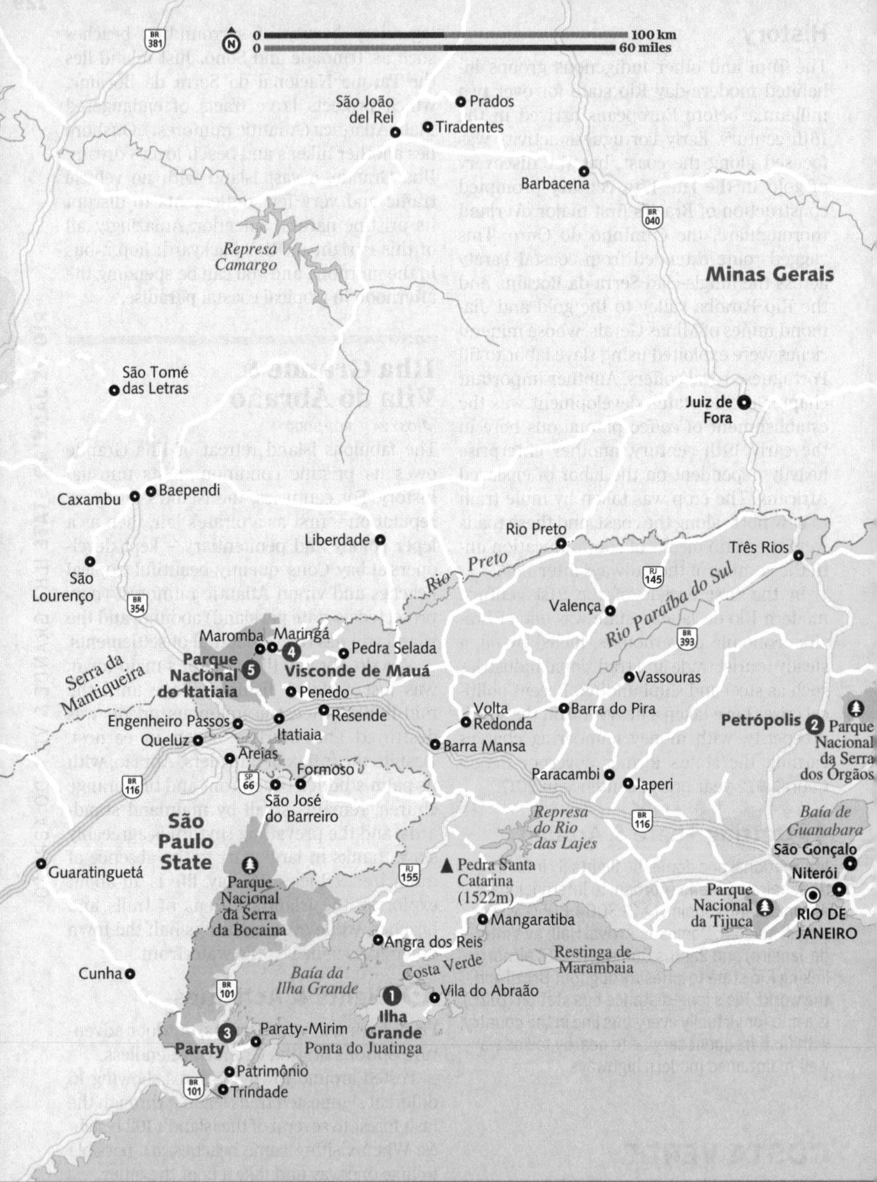

Rio de Janeiro State Highlights

1 Ilha Grande (p129) Surfing the south shore's wild waves, or chilling at the floating bar in a tranquil cove nearby.

2 Petrópolis (p151) Gliding across the polished wood floors of Brazil's 19th-century imperial palace, or discovering the wild splendor of neighboring Parque Nacional Serra dos Órgãos.

3 Paraty (p137) Snorkeling, swimming, hiking to remote coastal villages, or learning to cook gourmet Brazilian food in this beautifully preserved historic coastal town.

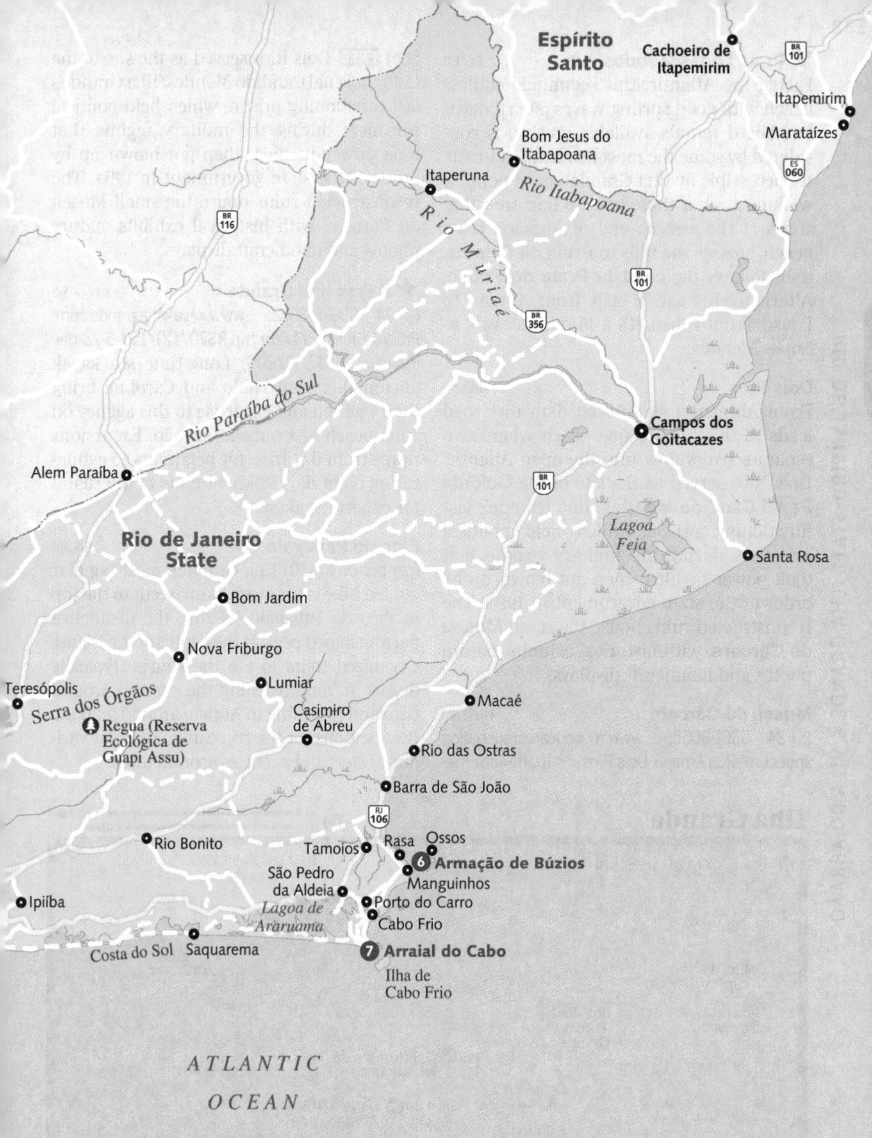

❹ **Visconde de Mauá** (p148) Relaxing to the rhythms of rushing water in this idyllic hidden valley.

❺ **Parque Nacional do Itatiaia** (p146) Swimming in natural pools at the base of waterfalls, or climbing up craggy Pico das Agulhas Negras.

❻ **Armação de Búzios** (p164) Strolling at sunset or partying all night on breezy beachfront Orla Bardot.

❼ **Arraial do Cabo** (p162) Watching for whales plying the sparkling blue-green waters.

★Praia Lopes Mendes BEACH

Facing the Atlantic, this seemingly endless beach with good surfing waves (shortboard/longboard rentals available on-site) is considered by some the most beautiful in Brazil. It's accessible by Ilha Grande's most popular walking trail, a three-hour, 6.1km trek that starts at the eastern end of Abraão's town beach, crosses the hills to **Praia de Palmas**, then follows the coast to **Praia do Pouso**. Alternatively, take a boat from Abraão to Pouso. From Pouso, it's a 15-minute walk to Lopes Mendes.

Dois Rios BEACH

From Abraão, a signposted 6km dirt road leads to this picturesque beach where two separate rivers flow into the open Atlantic. Dois Rios served as the site of the **Colônia Penal Cândido Mendes**, Ilha Grande's last functioning prison, which held political prisoners during the military regime that took power in 1964, then got blown up by order of the state government in 1994. The reconstructed ruins house the small **Museu do Cárcere**, with historical exhibits, nature photos and handicraft displays.

Museu do Cárcere MUSEUM

(☎24 3361-9055; www.museucarcereuerj.blogspot.com; Rua Amapá, Dois Rios; ⏲10am-4pm Tue-Sun) FREE Dois Rios served as the site of the Colônia Penal Cândido Mendes, Ilha Grande's last functioning prison, which held political prisoners during the military regime that took power in 1964, then got blown up by order of the state government in 1994. The reconstructed ruins house the small Museu do Cárcere, with historical exhibits, nature photos and handicraft displays.

★Kayak Ilha Grande KAYAKING

(☎24 99979-3572; www.kayakilhagrande.com; Praia da Júlia; 2/4/7hr trip R$70/110/150, 5-/8-day excursion US$600/900) Long-time sea kayak aficionados Juan Pablo and Carolina bring their passion and expertise to this agency on Júlia beach just outside Abraão. Excursions range from day trips for beginners to exhilarating eight-day, 115km circuits of the island for expert kayakers.

Pico do Papagaio HIKING

(per person R$130) Ilha Grande's most popular guided hike is the steep 6km ascent to the top of Pico do Papagaio (982m), the distinctive parrot-shaped peak at the center of the island. Organized tours to see the sunrise typically depart at 2am, reaching the summit around 6am and returning to Abraão around 9:30am. Reservations for the trip can be made at various hostels and agencies around town.

Ilha Grande

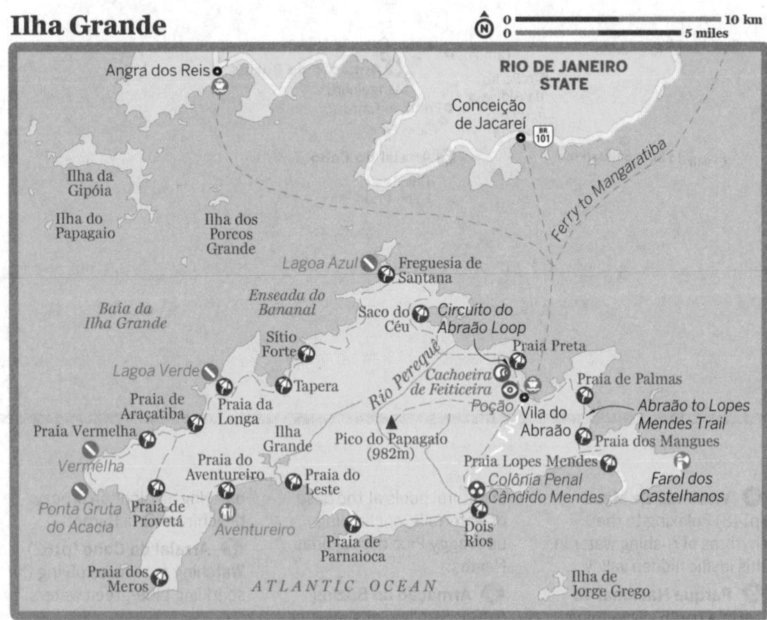

OFF THE BEATEN TRACK

THE QUIETER SIDE OF ILHA GRANDE

Almost all travelers to Ilha Grande arrive and sleep in Vila do Abraão, the island's biggest town and only major port. But there's a whole world of other options out there for people wishing to get off the beaten track.

The easiest way to broaden your perspective is to take a round-the-island boat tour. These tours typically stop at some of Ilha Grande's most beautiful and remote swimming spots, including **Praia de Caxadaço**, **Praia de Parnaioca**, **Praia do Aventureiro**, **Lagoa Verde** and **Lagoa Azul**.

To really escape the crowds and get immersed in Ilha Grande's wild natural beauty, consider staying at one of the island's more remote accommodations on beaches such as Praia Vermelha or Praia do Pouso. All can provide transportation and meals.

Pousada Lagamar (☎24 99904-6623, 24 99997-7219; www.pousadalagamar.com.br; Praia Vermelha; d with garden/sea view R$270/350, chalet R$400; ⏲closed mid-May–Jun) Owners Ezequiel and Luciana have created this family-friendly pousada at beautiful Praia Vermelha on Ilha Grande's northwestern shore. It's a perfect place to kick back in nature for a few days and settle into a simpler rhythm: swimming, snorkeling, walking the nearby trails, lounging with a good book in your hammock, and enjoying dinners of freshly caught fish. Two companies, Flexboat Natiga and Barcos da Comunidade, offer regular boat service from Angra dos Reis to Praia Vermelha; there are one to three crossings daily.

Atlântica Jungle Lodge (☎21 99999-5577; www.atlanticajunglelodge.com.br; Praia do Pouso; r R$730-955; ❄📶) Fall asleep to the sound of birds and jungle critters at this four-room ecolodge, serenely situated near the island's southeastern corner, between Pouso beach and the surrounding forest. From here, it's an easy 15-minute walk to Praia Lopes Mendes, Ilha Grande's most famous stretch of sand and surf. Guests get free use of kayaks, snorkeling equipment, beach towels and umbrellas.

Cabanas Paraiso (☎21 99608-1987; www.cabanasparaiso.com; Praia Brava de Palmas; d with shared bathroom R$220, with private bathroom R$330-480) Low-key beachfront living is the norm at these simple fan-cooled bungalows on Praia Brava de Palmas, a small beach easily accessible from the popular Abraão–Lopes Mendes trail (Lopes Mendes–bound boats can also drop you here for about R$20). Accommodations range from bare-bones units with shared bath to beachfront units with orthopedic mattresses, private bathrooms and sea-view verandas with hammocks.

Circuito do Abraão HIKING

This easy 1.7km return hike leads west of Vila do Abraão past two small beaches, **Praia Corisco** and **Praia Preta**, to the moss-covered stone ruins of **Lazareto prison**, shut down in 1954. It then continues past an old aqueduct adjoined by a large swimming hole called **Poção**, perfect for a picnic and a dip. Along the way you'll hear birds and jungle creatures, and may run into local kids jumping into the water on their way home from school.

Beyond the aqueduct, a more challenging trail leads to **Cachoeira da Feiticeira**, a lovely 15m waterfall, before continuing to the beach at **Saco do Céu**.

Elite Dive Center DIVING

(Map p134; ☎24 3361-5501, 24 99936-4181; www.elitedivecenter.com.br; Travessa Buganville, Vila do Abraão; 2 tank dive R$300) Offers courses and two-tank dives with English-speaking guides in some fantastic spots.

Tours

There are a dozen-plus tour operators in town. Most offer similar prices for boat excursions including round-the-island tours (R$130 to R$160), half-island tours (R$80 to R$110), and daily trips to prime beaches and snorkeling spots such as Lopes Mendes (schooner/speedboat R$30/40), Feiticeira (R$50) and Lagoa Azul (R$60). Other services include bike, kayak and surfboard rentals and treks with bilingual guides.

Sleeping

Vila do Abraão is swarming with pousadas, hostels and other accommodations for every budget. Prices drop by as much as 50% between April and November.

Vila do Abraão

Vila do Abraão

Activities, Courses & Tours
1 Elite Dive Center B2

Sleeping
2 Aratinga Inn C2
3 Biergarten Hostel B2
4 Holandês Hostel D2
5 Pousada Caúca C2
6 Pousada d'Pillel C2
7 Pousada Manacá C1
8 Pousada Naturalia D1

Eating
9 Banana da Terra C2
10 Biergarten B2
11 Café do Mar D1
12 Dom Mário B2
13 Las Sorrentinas D1
14 Lua e Mar C1
15 O Pescador B1

★Che Lagarto HOSTEL $
(☎24 3361-9669; www.chelagarto.com; Praia do Canto; dm R$70-90; @) Unbeatable location at the far eastern end of Abraão's main beach, a panoramic waterfront deck and a bar with free-flowing caipirinhas are the prime attractions at this hostel, part of South America's largest chain. Some boats from Conceição de Jacareí will drop you at the Aquário hostel next door; otherwise, it's a 10-minute walk from Abraão's town center.

Holandês Hostel HOSTEL $
(Map p134; ☎21 3833-7979; www.holandeshostel.com.br; Rua da Assembleia; dm R$60-70, d R$250;) Ilha Grande's HI hostel is hidden up a dead-end street on a leafy, peaceful hillside, 10 minutes above the ferry dock. Chalet-style, air-conditioned dorms (the best with hammocks and front porches) and private A-frame mini-bungalows surround a tidy, spacious garden with cobbled paths, palms, banana trees and a fish pond.

Biergarten Hostel HOSTEL $
(Map p134; ☎24 99839-9912; www.facebook.com/biergartenhostel; Getúlio Vargas 161; dm/d R$100/300;) Just a stone's throw from the boat docks, this centrally located hostel is a good bet for those who seek easy walking access to – or stumbling access *from* – Abraão's beaches and nightlife.

Pousada d'Pillel POUSADA $$
(Map p134; ☎24 3361-5075; www.ilhagrandedpillel.com.br; Bicão 51; r R$220-285;) This friendly, family-run pousada, a few blocks from the beach, has a cool, shady garden with comfortable seating under a thatched roof out back. Additional amenities include DVD players in every room, a ping-pong table and free use of snorkeling equipment.

★Bonito Paraiso Beach House POUSADA $$$
(☎24 99907-0307; www.bonitoilhagrande.com; Praia Abraãozinho; r R$430-570;) A five-minute boat ride or a 30-minute hike from Abrãao brings you to this idyllic hideaway at the end of Abraãozinho beach. Argentine owners Juan and Paolina have transformed the original beach house into a delightful pousada, with an open seaside porch where meals are served, a breezy family unit upstairs, and several doubles in a modern structure up the hill.

★Pousada Manacá POUSADA $$$

(Map p134; ☎24 3361-5404; www.ilhagrandemanaca.com.br; Rua da Praia 333; d R$360-400, tr R$440-480; ❄📶) It's worth reserving ahead and paying the small surcharge for a front room with balcony and hammock at this French-run beachfront pousada. The ample breakfast is accompanied by sea views from the pleasant front terrace; other nice touches include in-room fridges, dependable solar hot water and a central patio for lounging. Septuagenarian owner Gerard speaks five languages.

Pousada Caúca POUSADA $$$

(Map p134; ☎24 3361-5292; www.cauca.com.br; Rua Getúlio Vargas 300; d R$400-500; ❄📶) Central location and a spacious backyard are the twin draws at this pousada on Abraão's main pedestrian thoroughfare, run by the same local family for decades. A cluster of spotless air-conditioned rooms with minibar surrounds the central green space, which includes a covered breakfast area, hammocks for lounging and a pillow-strewn meditation platform.

Aratinga Inn POUSADA $$$

(Map p134; ☎24 3361-9559; www.aratingailhagrande.com.br; Rua das Flores 232; r R$430-450, chalet R$480-520; ⏲closed May, Jun & Sep; ❄📶) This cozy, gay-friendly, Australian-run pousada offers ultracomfy chalets in a garden setting. Homey touches include complimentary use of iPads, beach towels and thermoses, a generous afternoon tea, an extensive movie library and a welcoming lounge where guests can relax over music and board games and early arrivals can sip coffee or juice while awaiting their room.

Pousada Naturalia POUSADA $$$

(Map p134; ☎24 3361-9583; www.pousadanaturalia.net; Praia do Abraão 149; r R$420; ❄📶) One of Abraão's nicest top end options, this comfortable pousada under the direction of French-Vietnamese owner Laurent sits amid giant boulders on a green hillside just inland from the beach. Its 12 spacious rooms all feature pretty ocean views and solar hot water, with new queen-size beds in half the units.

Eating

Restaurants abound along Rua da Praia, Rua Getúlio Vargas and the small pedestrian street Travessa Buganville. During busy periods you'll see sweets carts being pushed about.

Banana da Terra BRAZILIAN $

(Map p134; Rua do Bicao; set meals R$20; ⏲12:30-7pm Wed-Mon) Proprietress Dona Celina, born and raised on Ilha Grande, has been delighting local palates for 35 years with her delicious home cooking. Grab a red plastic chair under the streamers on her shady patio and settle in for a *prato feito* (set meal) of fried fish, chicken or beef accompanied by rice, beans, thin-cut fries and salad. Sundays feature occasional live *forró* (popular music of the Northeast).

Biergarten BUFFET, VEGETARIAN $

(Map p134; Getúlio Vargas 161; per kg R$59; ⏲noon-10pm Wed-Mon; 🌿) The self-serve buffet at this informal vegetarian-owned eatery includes everything from brown rice and soy protein to sushi and other seafood, with plenty of vegan options and more vegetables than you'll see at most places around town.

★The Secret INTERNATIONAL $$

(☎24 99921-1124; www.facebook.com/thesecretgourmetclub; mains R$38-65; ⏲7:30-11pm) Every evening, Argentine expats Cris and Nel invite up to 10 prereserved guests into their secret garden in Abraão village for wonderful home-cooked dinners accompanied by chilled-out music and convivial conversation. Contact them via WhatsApp to check out the nightly changing offerings (typically Mediterranean, South American or vegetarian), reserve a time, get directions and learn the secret (shh!) password.

Las Sorrentinas ARGENTINE, ITALIAN $$

(Map p134; ☎24 3361-5063; www.facebook.com/Sorrentinas; Getúlio Vargas 638; mains R$40-60; ⏲6:30-10:30pm Mon-Sat) Superb homemade *sorrentinos* (ravioli-like stuffed pasta pockets) are the specialty at this breezy Argentine-run upstairs restaurant. Fillings range from gorgonzola, walnuts and mozzarella to ham, cheese and basil, accompanied by your choice of sauces. The place wins extra points for its friendly service and potent caipirinhas.

Café do Mar BRAZILIAN $$

(Map p134; ☎24 3361-9446; www.cafedomar.com; Getúlio Vargas 719; mains R$42-72; ⏲10am-11pm) This candlelit beach bar and lounge is perfect for sundown cocktails, with reasonably priced (by Ilha Grande standards!) *pratos do dia* (daily specials) and frequent barbecue nights.

O Pescador MEDITERRANEAN $$$

(Map p134; ☎24 3361-5114; www.opescadorilhagrande.wixsite.com/opescadorilhagrande;

OFF THE BEATEN TRACK

PARQUE NACIONAL DA SERRA DA BOCAINA: HIKING THE GOLD TRAIL

The historic Caminho do Ouro (Gold Trail), which connected Rio de Janeiro's coastline to the gold mines of Minas Gerais, passes through dramatic scenery in the Parque Nacional da Serra da Bocaina just north of Paraty. Paraty Tours (p142), Paraty Explorer (p142) and other operators offer two-hour day hikes covering a very small fraction of the trail, near Penha.

For a more challenging and unique experience, consider the **Trilha do Ouro** backpacking adventure, a three-day, 53km hike through the wildest reaches of the national park offered by **MW Trekking** (21 98708-4188; www.mwtrekking.com.br; per person R$860). This longer trek starts in São José do Barreiro in São Paulo state and visits a number of spectacular waterfalls en route towards Mambucaba, on the coast 45 minutes northeast of Paraty. The price includes transport to the trailhead, park fees, food, simple lodging and excellent local guide.

Rua da Praia 647; mains for 2 people R$100-150; 5pm-late Oct-Apr) The Italian-run Pescador is one of the island's best choices for a fancy beachfront dinner, with mean caipirinhas, authentic Italian risotto and Mediterranean-style fish, meat and poultry dishes such as the *grigliata mista al salmoriglio* (fish and shrimp grilled with olive oil, lemon juice and oregano).

Lua e Mar SEAFOOD $$$
(Map p134; 24 3361-5113; Praia do Canto; mains for 2 people R$95-185; 11am-11pm Thu-Tue) Candlelit tables on the sand make a tranquil place to watch the crashing waves and scurrying crabs while you enjoy tasty *moqueca* (fish stew) and other seafood dishes for two. Individual portions are available for 60% of the two-person price.

Dom Mário SEAFOOD $$$
(Map p134; 24 3361-5349; Travessa Buganville; mains for 2 people R$75-155; 5:30-10pm Tue-Sat) Long-time local chef Mário cooks up seafood specialties like *filé de peixe ao molho de maracujá* (fish fillet with passion fruit sauce) and scrumptious desserts, including his trademark caramelized bananas.

Orientation

Ferries from the mainland dock at a **cement pier** (Map p134) on the western end of Abraão's beach. Private speedboats and schooners dock at a separate **wooden pier** (Map p134) about 150m east.

In between the two piers lies the heart of Abraão village, with its main street, the cobbled Rua Alice Kuri da Silva, curving to become Rua Getúlio Vargas. West of the piers is the road to Praia Preta and the ruined Lazareto prison. East of the piers, at the far end of the town beach, Ilha Grande's most popular hiking trail leads to Praia de Palmas, Praia do Pouso and Praia Lopes Mendes.

Information

Note that there are no ATMs on the island, and although many places accept credit cards, it's still advisable to bring cash from the mainland; in a pinch, some businesses will accept foreign cash. Wi-fi is available at many accommodations but tends to be slow and intermittent.

Centro de Visitantes do Parque Estadual (State Park Visitors Center; Map p134; 24 3361-5540; Nacib Monteiro de Queiroz s/n; 8am-5pm Tue-Sun) The state park's small information office has a nice scale model of the island and its trails.

TurisAngra (Map p134; 24 3361-5760; www.angra.rj.gov.br/turisangra; Rua da Praia; 7am-7pm) At the foot of the wooden speedboat pier, Ilha Grande's official tourist office offers general information about the island.

Getting There & Away

Most boats from the mainland arrive at Vila do Abraão, the island's biggest town.

The quickest and most hassle-free way to reach the island from Rio is with a door-to-door shuttle service such as **Easy Transfer** (21 99386-3919; www.easytransferbrazil.com). This will pick you up at any hostel, hotel or pousada in Rio and deliver you to the island (R$95, 3½ to 4½ hours), with a synchronized transfer from van to speedboat in the coastal town of Conceição de Jacareí. Easy Transfer offers a similar service to Ilha Grande from Paraty (R$85, 3½ hours).

Reaching the island via public transport is slightly cheaper but more complicated, as you have to choose from multiple routes and buy two separate tickets (one for the bus, one for the boat).

Costa Verde (Map p140; 21 3907-3900; www.costaverdetransportes.com.br) runs buses from Rio to the three ports where boats for Ilha Grande depart: Conceição de Jacareí (R$56, 2½ hours, four daily), Mangaratiba (R$39, 2½ hours, four daily) and Angra dos Reis (R$56, three hours, hourly).

The most frequent boat crossings are from Conceição de Jacareí, where speedboats (R$40, 20 minutes) and schooners (R$25, 50 minutes) leave every hour or two between 8:30am and 6pm, returning from Abraão between 8am and 5:30pm. From Angra dos Reis, similar service is available by speedboat (R$50, 30 minutes) and schooner (R$25, 80 minutes). Boat companies operating along one or both routes include **Objetiva** (Map p134; 24 98112-4730, 24 3370-5584; www.objetivatour.com; Rua da Praia 677; 8am-10pm), **Angra Flex** (24 3365-2125; www.facebook.com/angraflex; Terminal Rodoviário, Av Caravelas, Angra dos Reis; 7am-5pm), **Doce Atitude** (24 99954-9477, 24 3367-1281; www.doceangraturismo.com; Av Júlio Maria 74, Angra dos Reis; 7am-7pm Mon-Sat, to 1pm Sun) and **Água Viva** (Map p134; 24 99978-4932; www.aguavivatour.com.br; Rua da Praia 26; 8am-8pm).

More affordable but less frequent are the daily ferries to Ilha Grande operated by **CCR Barcas** (Map p134; 0800-721-1012; www.grupoccr.com.br/barcas/linhas-horarios-tarifas; Cais do Abraão; 9:30-10am & 5-5:30pm), leaving from Angra dos Reis and Mangaratiba (R$17, 80 minutes from either port). Ferries depart Angra at 3:30pm weekdays and 1:30pm weekends, returning from Abraão at 10am daily. From Mangaratiba, ferries leave at 8am daily and 10pm Friday, returning from Abraão at 5:30pm daily. Extra ferries are sometimes added during high season; confirm locally before departure.

Angra is the most useful port for those traveling west from Ilha Grande. Colitur buses for Paraty (R$15, two hours, at least hourly from 6am to 11pm) leave Angra's bus station, 1.5km east of the boat docks.

Getting Around

Except for Vila do Abraão's lone garbage truck, fire engine and police vehicle, cars are prohibited, so all transport around the island is by foot or boat.

Paraty

0XX24 / POP 41,454

Backed by steep, jungled mountains plunging into an island-studded bay, Paraty enjoys one of Brazil's most spectacular settings and an exquisitely preserved colonial center, recognized as a National Historic Site since 1966. The town's pedestrianized streets are lined with elegant white buildings adorned with fanciful multihued borders and latticed windows that blend harmoniously with the natural beauty that envelops the town – it's a joy to explore (despite the ankle-twisting irregular cobblestones!)

The area surrounding Paraty is a nature-lover's paradise, offering some of southeastern Brazil's prettiest coastal and mountain scenery. Dozens of pristine beaches are easily accessible by boat or bus, while inland, the Parque Nacional da Serra da Bocaina protects a lush remnant of *mata atlântica* (Atlantic rainforest).

Throughout the year, Paraty brims with Brazilian and international vacationers. The town's cosmopolitan flavor is further enhanced by the multitude of artists, writers and chefs, both Brazilian and foreign, who have settled here.

History

Paraty was inhabited by the indigenous Guaianás when the Portuguese first arrived here in the 16th century. With the discovery of gold in Minas Gerais at the end of the 17th century, Paraty became an obligatory stopover between Rio de Janeiro and the mines, as it was the only point where the escarpment of the Serra do Mar could be scaled.

As gold poured from the interior, borne by the labor of thousands of African slaves, Paraty became a busy, important port, and wealthy Europeans built fine houses and churches. After the 1720s, a new road from Rio via the Serra dos Órgãos cut 15 days off the journey to Minas Gerais, and Paraty started to decline. In the 19th century, the local economy revived with the coffee boom, but until the mid-20th century the sea remained the only viable commercial route to Paraty. In 1954 a modern road was built through the steep Serra do Mar, passing the town of Cunha, 47km inland. Then in 1960 the coastal road from Rio, 253km away, was extended to Paraty and 330km beyond to São Paulo, ushering in a new era of tourism-based prosperity.

Sights & Activities

Hours and opening times at Paraty's historic churches seem to be in constant flux; check with the tourist office for up-to-the-minute details.

Paraty Town

Forte Defensor Perpétuo FORT
(Map p140; museum 9am-noon & 2-5pm Tue-Sun, grounds open to 7pm) FREE For sweeping

Paraty Islands & Beaches

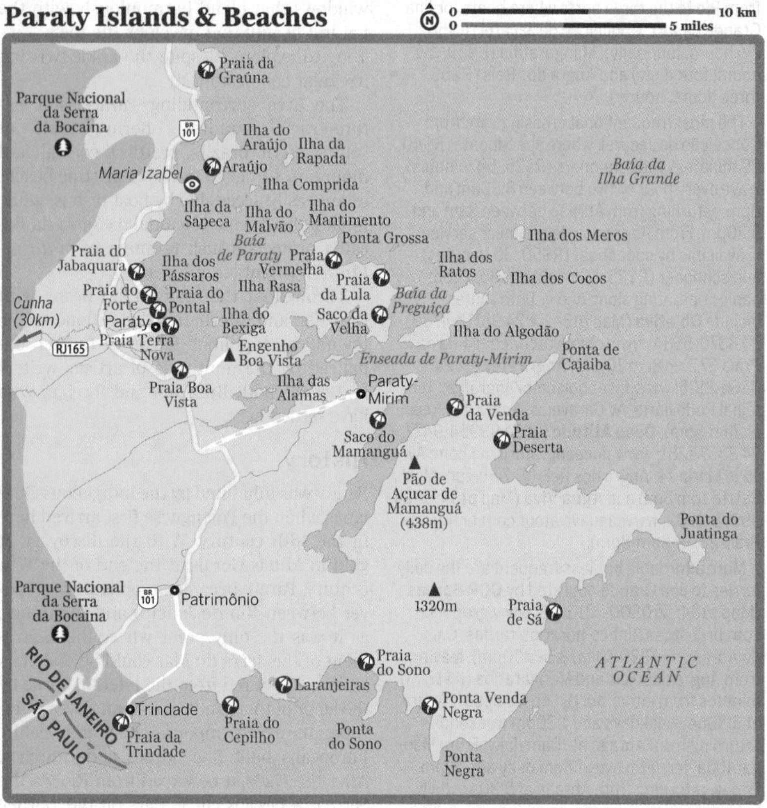

bay views, climb to this historic Portuguese fort. First built in 1703 and rebuilt in 1822, its original purpose was to defend the gold passing through Paraty's port from pirate raids. The fort's small museum has rotating exhibits on local history and culture; just heed the cryptic signs warning against descending the steep slopes ('high index of accidents with oysters'!). It's 20 minutes' walk north of town on Morro da Vila Velha (the hill past Praia do Pontal).

Igreja Santa Rita dos Pardos Libertos CHURCH
(Map p140; Praça Santa Rita; admission R$4 Wed-Sun, Tue free; ⌚9-11:45am & 2-4:45pm Tue-Sun) Built in 1722, this was the church for freed persons of mixed black and white ancestry. Nowadays it houses a tiny museum of sacred art and has some fine woodwork on the doorways and altars.

Casa da Cultura MUSEUM
(Map p140; ☎24 3371-2325; www.casadacultura paraty.org.br; Dona Geralda 194; ⌚10am-10pm Tue-Sat, to 4pm Sun) FREE In a beautiful colonial mansion, Paraty's Casa da Cultura hosts rotating exhibitions and events, with a focus on local culture. There are nice views of town from the main gallery upstairs.

Matriz NS dos Remédios CHURCH
(Map p140; Praça da Matriz; ⌚hours vary) Built in 1787 on the site of two previous 17th-century churches, this 'mother' church on Paraty's main square legendarily got financing for its construction from pirate treasure found hidden on Praia da Trindade. Opening times are extremely variable; ask at the tourist office (p145) for current hours, or go by the church directly to see if it's open.

DON'T MISS

ISLANDS & BEACHES

Paraty has some 65 islands and 300 beaches in its vicinity. To visit the less-accessible beaches, take an organized schooner tour. Multiple boats depart daily from the **Cais de Turismo** (Map p140) at the southeastern edge of the historic center; tickets average about R$65 per person.

Alternatively, you can hire one of the small motorboats at the port for a private tour. Local captains know some great spots and will take you out for around R$100 per hour, which can be a good deal if you have a large enough group.

The closest fine beaches on the coast – **Vermelha**, **Lula** and **Saco da Velha** – are all east of Paraty, roughly an hour away by boat. Good island beaches nearby include **Araújo** and **Sapeca**; many other islands have rocky shores and are private. The mainland beaches tend to be better; most have a handful of beachgoers and *barracas* (stalls) serving beer and fish.

Back in Paraty, walking north across the river, the first beach you'll reach is **Praia do Pontal**. A cluster of open-air restaurants lines its shore, but it's not great for swimming. Another 2km further north is **Praia do Jabaquara**, a spacious beach with great views and shallow waters that's ideal for kayaking and stand-up paddling.

Igreja NS do Rosário e São Benedito dos Homens Pretos CHURCH
(Map p140; cnr Dr Samuel Costa & Rua do Comércio; ⌚hours vary) Built in 1725 by and for slaves, and renovated in 1857, the church has gilded wooden altars dedicated to Our Lady of the Rosary, St Benedict and St John. Hours vary; ask for opening times at the tourist office (p145) or visit in person to see if it's open.

Around Paraty

★Praia da Trindade BEACH
About 25km south of Paraty, Trindade occupies a long sweep of stunningly beautiful coastline. Here you can lounge or hike along four of Brazil's most dazzling beaches (**Cepilho**, **Ranchos**, **Meio** and **Cachadaço**), with surging breakers, enormous boulders, vast expanses of mountain-fringed white sand, steep trails threading through the dense jungle, and a calm-watered natural swimming pool opposite the furthest beach, Cachadaço. Hourly Colitur buses (R$4.25, 45 minutes) serve Trindade from Paraty's bus station.

The town itself has the somewhat scraggly quality of a frontier outpost that's grown up too fast (indeed, 25 years ago there was only a small fishing village here), but the sizeable cluster of pousadas, hostels, camping grounds and restaurants permits an overnight stay.

★Saco de Mamanguá BAY
This gorgeous fjord-shaped inlet cuts a narrow 7km channel into the mountains southeast of Paraty. Various Paraty-based tour companies offer boat trips here. Alternatively, hire a guide for the strenuous 2km hike up the dramatic peak known as **Pão de Açúcar do Mamanguá** (438m) for excellent views of the bays and islands below.

Praia do Sono BEACH
This stunning beach, about 35km southeast of Paraty, is accessible only by foot or boat. Catch a Colitur bus to Laranjeiras (R$4.25, 40 minutes) and then follow the trail across the hills (about one hour). Paraty Tours (p142) and other local operators offer tours here.

Praia de Paraty-Mirim BEACH
For accessibility, cost and beauty, this tranquil beach 17km southeast of Paraty is hard to beat. The adjacent chapel, dating to 1686, was the first constructed by the Portuguese in the Paraty region. *Barracas* (food stalls) on the beach here serve simple meals – don't miss the *pasteis de camarão* (fried dough pockets filled with locally caught shrimp) at **Quiosque do Xico** (snacks from R$5; ⌚10am-6pm). Colitur runs buses here (R$4.25, 40 minutes) from Paraty's bus station.

Fazenda Bananal HISTORIC SITE
(☎24 3371-0039; www.fazendabananal.com.br; Estrada da Pedra Branca; adult/child R$20/10; ⌚9am-6pm) Opened in 2017, this unique park is part nature reserve, part historic site. The grounds shelter 260 species of birds, walking trails, a mini-farm where you can visit goats, calves and chickens, and a native plant garden with fruit trees from all over Brazil. The real highlight, though, is the reconstructed 19th-century farmhouse, complete with working waterwheel, where well-written bilingual exhibits trace the history of the *fazenda* (farm) through Brazil's successive gold, sugar and coffee booms.

Paraty

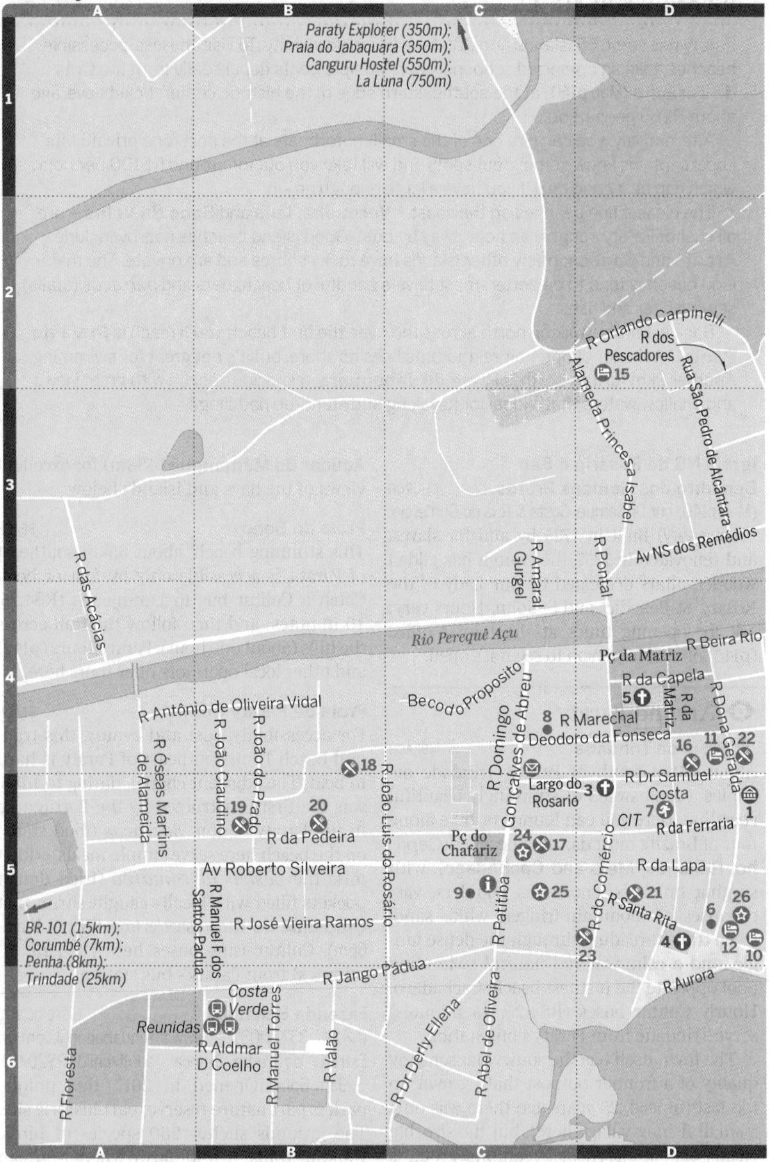

Alambique Paratiana DISTILLERY
(☎24 3371-9620; www.cachacaparatiana.com.br; Estrada da Pedra Branca; ⌚9:30am-5pm) Set beside the rushing Rio da Pedra Branca, Paratiana offers free tours of its *cachaça* distillery, where gleaming stills share space with giant casks of oak and native umburána wood and a collection of vintage bottles (including a rare one depicting soccer star Pelé). Afterwards head downstairs for free tastings. Plans are underway for an outdoor restaurant by the riverside.

Paraty

Sights

1 Casa da Cultura ... D5
2 Forte Defensor Perpétuo ... E1
3 Igreja NS do Rosário e São Benedito dos Homens Pretos ... D5
4 Igreja Santa Rita dos Pardos Libertos ... D5
5 Matriz NS dos Remédios ... D4

Activities, Courses & Tours

6 Academia de Cozinha e Outros Prazeres ... D5
7 Birds Parati ... D5
8 Paraty Adventure ... C4
9 Paraty Tours ... C5

Sleeping

10 Casa Turquesa ... D5
11 Hotel Solar dos Gerânios ... D4
12 Pousada Arte Urquijo ... D5
13 Pousada do Ouro ... E4
14 Pousada Flor do Mar ... E5
15 Pousada Morro do Forte ... D2

Eating

16 Banana da Terra ... D4
17 Casa do Fogo ... C5
18 Frida y Diego ... B4
19 Manuê ... B5
20 Maria Fulô Bistrô Natural & Tapiocaria ... B5
21 Oui Paraty ... D5
22 Punto Divino ... D4
23 Quintal das Letras ... D5

Entertainment

24 Margarida Café ... C5
25 Paraty 33 ... C5
26 Teatro Espaço ... D5

Maria Izabel DISTILLERY

(☎24 99999-9908; www.mariaizabel.com.br; Sítio Santo Antônio, Corumbê; ⊙10:30am-5pm Sat & Sun, by appointment Mon-Fri) FREE This acclaimed *cachaça* distillery, 10km north of Paraty, often places within the top 10 or 20 in nationwide competitions. Call at least a day ahead to arrange a visit, or sign up for a tour through a Paraty travel agency.

Activities

★Cachoeira Tobogã SWIMMING

In the hills 8km inland from Paraty, this natural waterslide is a blast! The slick rock face sends swimmers plunging into an idyllic pool surrounded by jungle. Tourists who value their skulls should heed the posted warnings against surfing (ie standing instead of sitting), although local teenagers have mastered the technique and it's exciting (if terrifying!) to watch. Afterwards, grab a caipirinha at Bar do Tarzan, across the swinging bridge above the falls.

From Paraty, take a local Colitur bus to Penha (R$4.25, 30 minutes), get off at the church and follow signs 100m downhill.

★ **Paraty Explorer** OUTDOORS
(☎99952-4496; www.paratyexplorer.com; Praia do Jabaquara) This agency on Jabaquara beach, run by outdoors enthusiasts Paddy (from Ireland) and Rodrigo (from Brazil), specializes in sea kayaking tours of Paraty Bay (from R$170), stand-up paddle boarding, and hiking adventures to destinations including Cachoeira Melancia, a spectacular waterfall in Serra da Bocaina National Park (R$200), the dramatic Pão de Açúcar do Mamanguá (R$300), and remote Costa Verde beaches.

Horses4u HORSEBACK RIDING
(☎24 99943-3916; www.raulparaty.wordpress.com; half-day excursion incl transfers & snacks R$190) Raul Sampaio's agency offers horseback rides high in the hills above Paraty, for novice to experienced riders. The standard two-hour excursion climbs through Atlantic rain forest into the Serra da Bocaina, reaching heights of 1400m. Participants meet Raul in Paraty for the 45-minute drive to his pasture. Long pants and closed-toe shoes are required (no shorts or sandals).

Birds Parati ECOTOUR
(Map p140; ☎24 99837-6396; www.birdsparati.com; Rua da Matriz 210) Gabriel Toledo's agency focuses on the wealth of bird-watching opportunities in and around Paraty. Outings range from sunrise explorations of Paraty's waterfront and Bird Parati's hillside reserve just inland from town, to more adventurous rafting excursions in search of the endemic black-hooded antwren and predawn climbs to the summit of Pedra da Macela, the region's highest peak.

Tours

Paraty Adventure OUTDOORS
(Map p140; ☎24 3371-6135; www.paratyadventure.com; Marechal Deodoro 12) Local resident Alessandra runs this great little agency offering off-the-beaten-track opportunities for adventure and cultural immersion. Highlights include an all-day excursion to Pedra da Macela, the region's highest peak (R$280), and multiday treks to Ponta da Juatinga, the remote fishing village where Alessandra grew up (R$2725 to R$4855, including food, boat transfers and accommodation in local homes).

Paraty Tours OUTDOORS
(Map p140; ☎24 3371-1327; www.paratytours.com.br; Roberto Silveira 5) Paraty's longest established commercial agency offers guided hiking tours (R$90 to R$300), self-guided cycling tours (R$15 to R$25 per hour, R$60 to R$100 per day), horseback riding (R$180, three hours), kayaking (R$170, four hours) and diving (R$335 to R$365, five hours) adventures. Especially popular are five-hour schooner cruises (R$60 to R$70, three daily), stopping at various beaches en route.

Festivals & Events

See www.paraty.com.br/calendario.asp for a full calendar.

Carnaval CULTURAL
(Feb/Mar) Carnaval here is a big street party – check out the Saturday procession of the **Bloco da Lama**, in which young people come in droves to cover themselves in mud and dance through the streets. See photos at www.paraty.com.br/blocodalama.

Semana Santa RELIGIOUS
(Mar/Apr) Holy Week celebrations include the beautiful **Procissão do Fogaréu**, a torchlit procession through the historic center starting just past midnight on the Thursday before Easter.

The Festa do Divino Espírito Santo (seven weeks after Easter) and Corpus Christi (in June) are also magnificent, with processions and colorful street decorations.

Estações Musicais em Paraty MUSIC
(www.paraty.com.br/estacoes-musicais-paraty; Apr-Dec) Launched in 2017 and spanning nearly nine months, this music festival brings dozens of instrumental and chamber music concerts to local churches, with additional performances at Paraty's Casa da Cultura (p138) and the hilltop Forte Defensor Perpétuo (p137).

FLIP CULTURAL
(Festa Literária Internacional de Paraty; www.flip.org.br; Av NS dos Remédios 172-240; Jul) Since launching in 2003, Paraty's international literary festival has grown into one of the year's biggest cultural events, bringing in authors from around the world for five days each July. Author panels, debates, workshops and other events take place in a big tent along the riverfront just north of the historical center.

Festival da Pinga de Paraty FOOD & DRINK
(Festival da Cachaça, Cultura e Sabores; www.festivaldapingadeparaty.com.br; Av NS dos Remédios 172-240; ⌚Aug) The Paraty region produces excellent *cachaça* (sugarcane alcohol), and in 1984 the town council inaugurated this annual celebration. Housed in a giant tent just over the bridge from the historical center, this food-and-drink-fueled party lasts for four days each August, with free live music and kiosks representing a variety of local producers.

Sleeping

From December to February, and during festivals, hotels fill up and room prices double, so reservations are advisable. The rest of the year, finding accommodations is relatively easy.

Budget-minded travelers will find several campgrounds and hostels along the Pontal and Jabaquara beachfronts (north of town, across the pedestrian bridge).

★**Happy Hammock** HOSTEL $
(☎24 99994-9527; www.facebook.com/happyhammockparaty; Ponta Grossa; dm/d R$55/200) This Swiss-run waterfront hostel sits on isolated Ponta Grossa, a 15-minute boat ride from Paraty. With no road access, limited generator-fueled electricity and gorgeous sea views, it's a dreamy end-of-the-line getaway where guests can lounge in hammocks, swim in phosphorescent waters or hike to nearby beaches before the tour boats arrive. Book dinners (R$25) and boat transfers (R$20) in advance.

Canguru Hostel HOSTEL $
(☎24 3371-1477; www.canguruhostel.com.br; Avenida Vera Cruz 46, Praia do Jabaquara; dm R$38-65; 📶) A block inland from Jabaquara beach, friendly Canguru offers a varied collection of doubles, six- to 12-bed dorms and campsites surrounding a sprawling enclosed yard. Barbecues, dance parties with live bands, and shots of *gabriela* (*cachaça* with cloves and cinnamon) from the in-house bar keep things hopping, while the free laundry service is one of several homey touches.

Hotel Solar dos Gerânios INN $$
(Map p140; ☎24 3371-1550; www.paraty.com.br/geranio; Praça da Matriz 2; s/d/tr R$120/180/240; @📶) Run by the same family for decades, this rustic place on lively Praça da Matriz is by far the best budget hotel deal in Paraty's colonial center. Wood and ceramic sculptures, stone walls and floors, columns and beamed ceilings, and a courtyard full of plants, cats and dogs all add character. Several rooms have balconies overlooking the square.

In the morning, it's wonderful to sit on the open-sided flagstoned terrace and watch hummingbirds flit about the interior garden over a breakfast of fruit, cheese, cake and fresh-squeezed OJ.

Le Gite d'Indaiatiba POUSADA $$
(☎24 99999-9923; www.legitedindaiatiba.com.br; Hwy BR-101, Km 562; d/tr R$250/300, d/tr/q bungalow R$300/350/400, loft R$600; ❄📶🏊) In a gorgeous jungle setting 16km northwest of Paraty, well-traveled hosts Olivier and Valéria serve tasty Franco-Brazilian cuisine and rent out five units with fireplaces and panoramic verandas, including two 'lofts' with air-con, large bathtubs and DVD players. Activities include horseback riding, jungle treks, and relaxing stints by the pool, waterfall and riverside sauna. See website for driving directions.

Pousada Flor do Mar POUSADA $$
(Map p140; ☎24 3371-1674; www.pousadaflordomar.com.br; Fresca 257; d R$220-340; ❄@📶) Hidden away opposite Paraty's beachfront, this simple little pousada has clean, spacious rooms, a pretty front courtyard with hammocks and couches, and one of the historic center's quietest locations.

Pousada Morro do Forte POUSADA $$$
(Map p140; ☎24 3371-1211; www.pousadamorrodoforte.com.br; Orlando Carpinelli 21; r R$385-520; ❄📶🏊) This modern pousada enjoys incomparable vistas of the town and bay from its breakfast deck and pool. Perched on the Morro do Forte, a 10-minute climb from downtown, it has 10 comfortable rooms, the best of which are the upstairs units with panoramic balconies and hammocks. The owners speak English and German.

Casa Turquesa POUSADA $$$
(Map p140; ☎24 3371-1037; www.casaturquesa.com.br; Doutor Pereira 50; ste R$1105-1600; ❄📶🏊) This luxuriously appointed, lovingly converted mansion near Paraty's waterfront is one of the most welcoming lodgings in town. Spacious rooms and suites with queen- or king-size beds and DVD players, inviting pool and lounge areas and copious breakfasts served any time of day invite guests to settle completely into relaxation mode.

Pousada do Ouro POUSADA $$$
(Map p140; ☎24 3371-4300; www.pousadaouro.com.br; Doutor Pereira 298; d R$430-760, d/tr/q ste R$950/1240/1530;) It's easy to imagine bumping into Mick Jagger, Sonia Braga or Tom Cruise here – especially when you enter the lobby and see photos of them posing in front of the pousada! This centrally located hotel has everything – bar, pool, sauna and a gorgeous garden.

Pousada Arte Urquijo POUSADA $$$
(Map p140; ☎24 3371-1362; www.urquijo.com.br; Dona Geralda 79; r R$490-610;) This cozy little pousada is obviously a labor of love for the artist owners. Downstairs common areas include a spacious lounge and bar and a small pool. Especially nice is the Sofia Suite, with its deck, flowering tree and bay view.

Eating

Paraty has many pretty restaurants, but once your feet touch the cobblestones in the picturesque historic center, prices rise.

Manuê SANDWICHES, JUICE BAR $
(Map p140; www.facebook.com/manueparaty; Rua João do Prado 1; sandwiches R$9-20, juices R$7-10; ⊙10am-11pm;) With good coffee, free wi-fi, two dozen varieties of juice and a delicious array of budget-friendly omelettes and *dobrados* (toasted flatbread sandwiches), this little eatery draws a mixed crowd of locals and tourists.

Maria Fulô Bistrô Natural & Tapiocaria VEGETARIAN $
(Map p140; ☎24 3371-5036; www.facebook.com/mariafulobistro; Rua Presidente Pedreira; mains R$15-28; ⊙noon-11pm Mon-Sat;) This cheerfully painted little restaurant just outside the historic center is a welcome refuge for both wallet and taste buds. At lunchtime, reasonably priced, healthy *pratos feitos* (set meals; R$26) rule the day; come evening, the menu shifts over to *tapiocas,* the spongy manioc-flour pancakes stuffed with various fillings that have long been a Brazilian budget staple.

Frida y Diego LATIN AMERICAN $$
(Map p140; ☎24 3371-2160; www.fridaydiegoparaty.com; Rua Benina Toledo do Prado; mains R$30-38; ⊙6pm-midnight Mon-Thu, noon-1am Fri-Sun) After years traveling and working in Peru, Argentina and elsewhere around Latin America, chef-owner Lu has poured her enthusiasm for the continent's varied cuisine into this colorful little restaurant. Twinkling lights and *forró* music accompany a menu dominated by tasty (if not 100% authentic) Mexican classics – tacos, burritos, quesadillas – supplemented by weekly specials from other Latin American lands.

La Luna ARGENTINE $$
(☎24 3371-6917; www.facebook.com/lalunaparaty; Praia do Jabaquara; mains R$44-99; ⊙11:30am-11:30pm) Steak and a prime beachfront setting are the twin attractions at this Argentine-run eatery in Jabaquara, 2km north of Paraty's historic center. Everything from sirloin to *picanha* (rump steak) comes out sizzling on iron platters, accompanied by chimichurri sauce and all the trimmings. Moonrise views are spectacular, and there are beds where little ones can lounge while parents linger at the candlelit tables.

Oui Paraty CRÊPES $$
(Map p140; ☎24 2122-2311; www.facebook.com/ouiparaty; Santa Rita 190; crepes R$35-47, other mains R$44-59; ⊙3:30-11pm Wed-Fri, 11:30am-11pm Sat & Sun) With bona fide French chef Patrick Louis in the kitchen, Oui Paraty stands out for its authentic Breton-style galettes made with buckwheat flour, alongside subtly sweet dessert offerings like nutella with caramelized bananas or crepe Suzette flambéed in Cointreau.

CHEF FOR A DAY

Tired of eating out? How about cooking your own gourmet dinner in Paraty's historic center, with the help of acclaimed local chef and cookbook author Yara Roberts?

Mixing theater with haute cuisine, chef Yara stages cooking classes in Portuguese, English, French and Spanish at her home-based culinary academy, the **Academia de Cozinha e Outros Prazeres** (Map p140; ☎24 3371-6025; www.chefbrasil.com; Dona Geralda 45; cooking class incl dinner R$310). Guests learn about Brazilian regional cuisines, assist with the cooking (optional), then sit down to a leisurely dinner and an evening of lively conversation. Groups are often international – residents of 105 different countries have participated to date! The price includes cocktails, wine, desserts and recipes.

Chef Yara also organizes multiday programs that combine cooking classes with visits to local producers. See the website for details.

Punto Divino ITALIAN **$$**
(Map p140; ☎24 3371-1348; www.facebook.com/puntodivino; Marechal Deodoro da Fonseca 129; pizza R$38-50, mains R$40-93; ⊙noon-midnight) This corner Italian restaurant serves pasta and thin-crust pizzas in its cozy main dining room and on its stone-walled back patio adorned with ferns and banana trees. Nightly live music adds a romantic touch.

Casa do Fogo BISTRO **$$**
(Map p140; ☎3371-3163, 24 98802-5903; www.casadofogo.com.br; Comendador José Luiz 404; mains R$46-89; ⊙6-11pm Mon-Sat) The name says it all here – everything's on fire! The menu focuses on seafood set ablaze with the local *cachaça:* flambéed octopus with passion fruit, honey and black rice, or fish with flambéed veggies, bananas and hearts of palm. Fruit-based desserts (pineapple, banana, mango) also face a fiery death.

★**Quintal das Letras** FUSION **$$$**
(Map p140; ☎24 3371-2616; www.pousadaliteraria.com.br/gastronomia; Rua do Comercio 362; mains R$62-96; ⊙1-11pm Sun-Thu, noon-midnight Fri & Sat) Attached to Paraty's Pousada Literária hotel, this sophisticated eatery serves regional cuisine with big city flair. From amuse-bouches like a mushroom 'cappuccino' (frothy brown soup topped with a dollop of cream) to a sterling *moqueca de peixe* for one, and divine desserts like grilled fruit or crispy fried bananas with homemade ginger ice cream, it's a class act all around.

★**Banana da Terra** SEAFOOD **$$$**
(Map p140; ☎24 3371-1725; www.restaurantebananadaterra.com.br; Dr Samuel Costa 198; mains R$85-98; ⊙6pm-midnight Mon, Wed & Thu, noon-4pm & 7pm-midnight Fri-Sun) Creative taste combinations and artistic presentation make this one of Paraty's classiest restaurants. Meat and fish dishes are supplemented by inspired vegetarian offerings such as the superb *moqueca* made with hearts of palm, peppers and bananas. Chef Ana Bueno, whose local roots go back decades, remains deeply involved in community projects, including promoting healthy, regionally sourced lunches in local schools.

Drinking & Entertainment

A slew of bars spill tables out onto the tree-shaded cobblestones of Praça da Matriz from late afternoon to the wee hours.

Margarida Café LIVE MUSIC
(Map p140; ☎24 3371-6037; www.margaridacafe.com.br; Praça do Chafariz; ⊙noon-midnight) This cavernous yet cozy bar with checkerboard tile floors and massive stone columns has great drinks and live music nightly, including MPB (Musica Popular Brasileira), bossa nova, jazz, *forró* and tango.

Paraty 33 LIVE MUSIC
(Map p140; ☎24 3371-1630; www.paraty33.com.br; Rua da Lapa 357; ⊙noon-1am Sun-Thu, to 4am Fri & Sat) With an early evening happy hour featuring MPB and bossa nova, and a late-night weekend mix of DJs and live acts, Paraty 33 is the historic center's liveliest nightspot.

Teatro Espaço THEATER
(Map p140; ☎24 3371-1575; www.ecparaty.org.br; Dona Geralda 42; admission R$55; ⊙shows 9pm Wed & Sat, plus Fri in summer) Now in its fifth decade, Paraty's internationally acclaimed Contadores de Estórias theater company presents puppetry, music and dance performances in this small playhouse.

Orientation

The historic center is small and easy to navigate, although street names and addresses can get confusing. Some streets have more than one name, and house numbers don't always follow a predictable pattern.

Information

Bradesco (Av Roberto Silveira 73-77) Multiple ATMs two blocks north of the bus station; more at Banco do Brasil next door.

CIT (Map p140; ☎24 3371-1222; www.visiteparaty.tur.br; Av Roberto Silveira 1; ⊙9am-9pm) Paraty's tourist office is perfectly positioned at the entrance to the historic center.

Hospital Municipal São Pedro de Alcântara (☎24 3371-2954; Rua São Pedro de Alcântara 1) Provides first aid and 24/7 emergency care.

Getting There & Away

The **bus station** (Map p140; Rua Jango Pádua) is 500m west of the old town. Costa Verde (p136) offers frequent services to Rio de Janeiro (R$76, 4¾ hours, 12 daily). Colitur has buses to Angra dos Reis (R$15, two hours, hourly from 5am to 8pm) and **Reunidas** (Map p140; ☎18 2102-4420; www.reunidaspaulista.com.br) buses head to São Paulo (R$78, six hours, six daily).

ITATIAIA REGION

Originally settled by northern Europeans, the Itatiaia region of northwestern Rio de Janeiro state is a curious mix. The climate is alpine temperate and the chalets are Swiss, but the vegetation is tropical and the warm smiles are pure Brazilian. There are neatly tended little farms with horses and goats, and homes with clipped lawns and flower boxes side by side with large tracts of dense forest untouched by the machete. This is a wonderful place to tramp around green hills, ride ponies up purple mountains, splash in waterfalls and hike trails without straying too far from the comforts of civilization: a fireplace, a soft bed, a bottle of wine and a well-grilled trout.

Parque Nacional do Itatiaia

☎0XX24

Established in 1937, **Parque Nacional do Itatiaia** (☎3352-1292; www.icmbio.gov.br/parnaitatiaia/en; per day foreigners/Brazilians R$33/17; ⏲8am-5pm) is Brazil's oldest national park, and one of its most ruggedly beautiful. Its lush, dark foliage contains more than 400 species of native bird and is also home to monkeys and sloths. Divided into upper and lower sections, the park features lakes, rivers, waterfalls, alpine meadows and primary and secondary Atlantic rainforests.

Don't let the tropical plants fool you; temperatures in the high country drop below freezing in June and, occasionally, the park even has a few snowy days! Bring warm clothes, even in summer.

Sights & Activities

Each section of the park (upper and lower) has its own entrance station. Park headquarters is 9km north of Itatiaia town, in the park's lower, tamer section. Here you'll find a natural history museum, along with easy trails leading to a natural swimming hole, **Lago Azul**, and three pretty waterfalls: **Maromba**, **Véu de Noiva** and **Itaporani**.

Climbing and trekking enthusiasts will want to pit themselves against the high country's more challenging peaks, cliffs and trails. The upper park's diminutive entrance station – almost two hours drive from Itatiaia town – is reached by way of a 15km extremely rugged unpaved road from a junction called **Garganta do Registro**, along Hwy BR-354 at the border between Rio and Minas Gerais states.

A guide is required for climbs to the high country's peaks. Contact the **Grupo Excursionista Agulhas Negras** (www.gean.org.br), which organizes climbs throughout the year, or see the park website ('Visitor's Guide' page) for a list of local guides; another excellent guide not on the park's list is **Levy Cardozo da Silva** (☎98812-0006; levy.ecologico@hotmail.com).

Lower Section

Centro de Visitantes MUSEUM

(Visitors Center; ⏲8am-5pm) FREE Revamped to celebrate Itatiaia's 80th anniversary in 2017, this visitors center, 5km uphill from the lower entrance, houses exhibits about the biology and natural history of Brazil's oldest national park. A Portuguese-language video with English subtitles introduces Itatiaia's many ecosystems, waterfalls, trails and shelters. Other attractions include a huge scale model of the park, a one-room display on the history of local mountaineering and a natural history museum with dioramas featuring Itatiaia's wealth of mammals, birds, butterflies and insects.

Mirante Último Adeus VIEWPOINT

Accessible via a short flight of steps off the main road, about 2.5 miles above the lower park entrance, this viewpoint commands sweeping views of Itatiaia's Atlantic rainforest and the valley of the Rio Campo Belo.

Três Picos HIKING

(lower section) One of the best hikes in Itatiaia National Park's low country is this five-hour, 15km return trip to the three mountains known as Três Picos (1600m).

Upper Section

Agulhas Negras MOUNTAIN

Parque Nacional do Itatiaia's highest peak, Agulhas Negras (2791m) gets its name – meaning 'Black Needles' – from the serrated form of its imposing ridgeline. For serious climbers, this is Itatiaia's ultimate challenge.

Prateleiras MOUNTAIN

In the upper section of Parque Nacional do Itatiaia, this jumble of massive boulders is one of the park's highest peaks (2548m) and a favorite climbing destination, with stunning views all the way down to the Atlantic Ocean.

Travessia Ruy Braga HIKING

This classic walk descends from the high country to the lower park headquarters,

Itatiaia Region

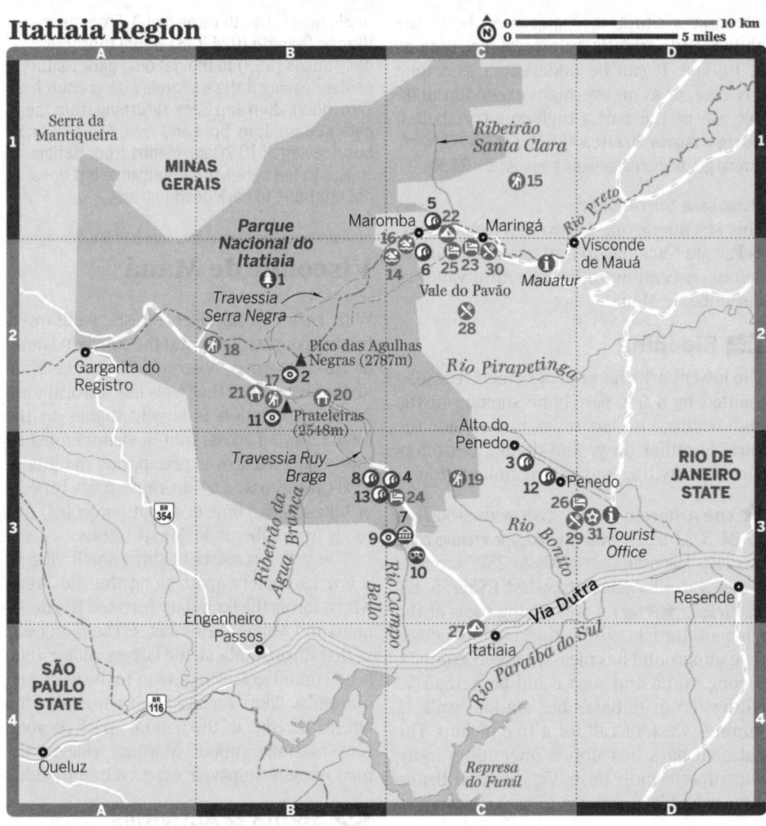

Itatiaia Region

Top Sights
1 Parque Nacional do Itatiaia B2

Sights
2 Agulhas Negras B2
3 Cachoeira de Deus C3
4 Cachoeira do Maromba C3
5 Cachoeira Santa Clara C1
6 Cachoeira Veu de Noiva C2
7 Centro de Visitantes C3
8 Itaporani Waterfall B3
9 Lago Azul C3
10 Mirante Último Adeus C3
11 Prateleiras B2
12 Três Cachoeiras C3
13 Véu de Noiva Waterfall B3

Activities, Courses & Tours
14 Cachoeira do Escorrega C2
15 Cachoeiras do Alcantilado C1
16 Poção C2
17 Travessia Ruy Braga B2
18 Travessia Serra Negra B2
19 Três Picos C3

Sleeping
20 Abrigo Água Branca B2
21 Abrigo Rebouças B2
22 Fazenda Santa Clara Camping C1
23 Hotel Bühler C2
24 Hotel do Ypê C3
25 Hotel Warabi C2
26 Pequena Suécia D3
Pousada Moriá .... (see 14)
27 Ypê Amarelo C4

Eating
28 Babel C2
29 Casa da Picanha C3
Pequena Suécia .... (see 26)
30 Rosmarinus Officinalis C2
Zorba Budda .... (see 25)

Entertainment
31 Clube Finlândia D3

allowing visitors to experience both the alpine and Atlantic rainforest ecosystems of Itatiaia. It can be undertaken as a long day hike, or as an overnight excursion making use of the park's high-country shelter, **Abrigo Água Branca** (☎24 3352-2288; www.icmbio.gov.br/parnaitatiaia/reservas; dm R$30).

Travessia Serra Negra HIKING

This strenuous one-to-two-day trek traverses Parque Nacional do Itatiaia's high country before descending to the beautiful valley of Visconde de Mauá.

Sleeping

The lower park's handful of hotels is complemented by a few bare-bone shelters in the high country. Itatiaia town, just outside the park, is rather dusty and dreary, but offers the most inviting budget accommodation.

★Ypê Amarelo CAMPGROUND, POUSADA $

(☎24 3352-1232; www.pousadaypeamarelo.com.br; João Mauricio Macedo Costa 352; campsite per person with/without breakfast R$55/35, s/d R$90/180;) A welcoming oasis at the edge of Itatiaia town, this combo pousada-campground has pleasant green grounds, a pool, sauna and soccer and basketball facilities. From Itatiaia's bus station, walk 15 minutes west, or call for a free pickup. The national park bus stop is only 200m away, and superfriendly hosts Vanessa and Bruno offer valuable assistance to park visitors.

Abrigo Rebouças HUT $

(☎24 3352-1292; www.icmbio.gov.br/parnaitatiaia/reservas; dm R$30) This hikers' shelter in the high country, with a gas stove and electricity, provides basic accommodations for up to 20 people but no food or other supplies. Reserve as far in advance as possible!

Hotel do Ypê HOTEL $$$

(☎24 3352-1453; www.hoteldoype.com.br; s/d R$350/440, chalet R$500, all with full board;) About 8.5km north of the park entrance, near the end of the road, the nicest of the lower park's hotels offers somewhat dated rooms and chalets, with several hiking trails nearby. Toucans and hummingbirds feed in abundance outside the breakfast room window; between September and Carnaval there's a Saturday barbecue (R$60 for nonguests) served outdoors around the pool.

Getting There & Away

Cidade do Aço (p151) operates buses from Rio de Janeiro to Itatiaia's bus station (R$45, 2¾ to 3¼ hours, two to three daily). From here, **Viação Penedo** (024 3381-8861) runs four daily buses (R$2) to the national park visitors center, leaving Itatiaia's Igreja Matriz church at 7am, noon, 3pm and 6pm, returning from the park at 8am, 1pm, 5pm and 7pm. An additional bus, leaving at 10:20am, climbs from Itatiaia village to the park's lower entrance but does not continue to park headquarters.

Visconde de Mauá

☎0XX24 / ELEV 1200M

With cozy chalets, deep forests, wildflower-fringed country lanes and the constant sound of rushing water, Visconde de Mauá is an idyllic river valley that feels like a world unto itself. Its isolation is largely thanks to the town's limited access routes; visitors must either switchback over precipitous mountaintops on the paved 27km route from Penedo, or take a series of rutted (but gorgeous!) dirt roads from Liberdade, Minas Gerais.

The valley consists of three small villages a few kilometers apart along the Rio Preto, which forms the boundary between Rio de Janeiro and Minas Gerais states. The road passes first through Mauá, the largest village, then heads uphill to Maringá, 6km to the west, and Maromba, 2km further on, before petering out at the edge of the national park. Beyond Alto Maringá (upper Maringá village) the road remains unpaved; expect a bumpy ride!

Sights & Activities

Rio Preto, the cascading river dividing Minas Gerais from Rio state, has several small beaches and natural pools. It's possible to kayak the rapids. Horseback riding is also available from various private operators around town. Details are available at the tourist office.

Cachoeira Santa Clara WATERFALL

Among the nicest and most accessible of Mauá's dozen or so waterfalls, this one is a 10-minute drive or a 40-minute walk northwest of Alto Maringá via the Ribeirão Santa Clara. Cross the bridge to Minas Gerais about 1km west of Alto Maringá, then continue another 1km over a hill to a left-hand fork marked with signs for the waterfall.

Cachoeira Veu de Noiva WATERFALL

This very beautiful waterfall is 300m south of the main road, just west of Maromba.

★Cachoeira do Escorrega SWIMMING

At the far western end of the valley, 2km west of Maromba on the border with Parque

Nacional do Itatiaia, this natural waterslide culminates in a gorgeous natural pool.

Cachoeiras do Alcantilado HIKING, SWIMMING
(admission R$20; ⏲8am-4pm) Reached by an unpaved 4km dirt road, this private nature preserve features well-maintained trails through farmland and forest to a series of nine waterfalls and natural pools, with shady glens for swimming. The snack bar up front sells juices and toasted *pinhões* (nuts from local araucaria trees).

Poção SWIMMING
One of the valley's finest swimming spots is this giant, 7m-deep natural pool 1km west of Maromba.

Sleeping

The valley is jam-packed with cozy, chalet-style accommodations, many equipped with fireplaces and whirlpool tubs for cool mountain evenings. Inexpensive, bare-bones rooms are also available near the bus stops in Mauá and Maromba; just ask around.

Fazenda Santa Clara Camping CAMPGROUND $
(☎24 3387-1508; www.viscondedemaua.com.br/campingsantaclaramaua.html; Estrada Maringá/Maromba, Km 1; camping per person R$35, d cabana/chalet R$110/185) Occupying a grassy slope at the convergence of the Rios Preto and Santa Clara, this campground has a natural swimming hole and snack bar, plus two-person chalets and miniscule A-frame cabanas for those without a tent. The bus stop across the river is accessible via a pedestrian bridge.

★**Hotel Warabi** POUSADA $$
(☎24 3387-1143; www.viscondedemauaturismo.com/hotel.htm; Alto Maringá, RJ; d midweek R$220-300, weekend R$350-480) Inviting features abound at this rustic hotel just above Maringá: comfy futons, *ofuro* (Japanese bath) tubs and a spacious wooden deck overlooking the swimming pool, sauna and riverside lawn. Guests also appreciate the boats for floating downstream to a local swimming hole and the stellar Japanese-Brazilian breakfasts, ranging from *pão de queijo* (balls of cheese-stuffed tapioca bread) and tropical fruit to grilled fish and delicious homemade sushi.

Pousada Moriá POUSADA, CHALET $$$
(☎24 3387-1505; www.pousadamoria.com.br; Estrada da Maromba s/n; ste R$390-425, chalet R$315-440;) At this welcoming end-of-the-road hideaway, eight chalets and three suites with whirlpool tubs straddle a hillside at the national park's edge. Cozy touches include fireplaces, electric blankets, sauna, DVD library and an ample breakfast served in a charming glass-walled cabin or on an outdoor deck within earshot of the waterfall. The owners are active in local reforestation efforts.

INDIGENOUS NAMES

Many place names in Rio state have their origins in indigenous words, including the following:

Geribá A kind of coconut palm.

Guanabara Arm of the sea.

Ipanema Place that gives bad luck or place of dangerous sea.

Itatiaia Many-pointed rock.

Mangaratiba Banana orchard.

Paraty A kind of fish.

Saquarema Lagoon without shells.

Tijuca Putrid-smelling swamp.

Hotel Bühler HOTEL $$$
(☎24 3387-1204; www.hotelbuhler.com.br; Maringá, MG; r midweek R$350-450, weekend incl half-board R$580-950; @) Founded in 1931, this German-style hotel with sprawling, verdant grounds, a stone's throw west of Maringá's restaurant row, is the valley's oldest lodging. Twenty fireplace-equipped chalets, including four larger ones suitable for families, are complemented by two swimming pools, a kids' wading pool, basketball and tennis courts, trails down to the river, a sauna and an on-site restaurant.

Eating

For over two decades, Mauá has hosted its renowned three-day culinary festival, the **Concurso Gastronômico** (www.mauagastronomico.com.br; ⏲Jun), with special emphasis on the local trout and *pinhões,* giant pine nuts from the native araucaria trees.

In Maringá, don't miss the Alameda Gastronômica, a street packed with restaurants for every taste along the Minas Gerais side of the Rio Preto. Here you'll find Italian and vegetarian eateries, a German beer garden, a jazz bistro and a restaurant whose menu revolves around local mushrooms.

Zorba Budda PIZZA $$
(☎24 3387-1170; Estrada Maringá-Marombá, Km 6, Alto Maringá, RJ; pizza from R$36; ⏲8pm-1am Fri-Sun) A Mauá institution for over two decades, this pumpkin-colored pizzeria serves two dozen varieties of wood-fired, thin-crusted beauties.

Perennial favorites include the *montanhesa* (with locally smoked trout), the *caliente* (tomato sauce, mozzarella, brie, mango slices and spicy pepper jelly) and the *selvagem* (with roasted garlic and hearts of palm).

★ **Rosmarinus Officinalis** MEDITERRANEAN **$$$**
(☎24 3387-1550; www.rosmarinus.com.br; Estrada Mauá-Maringá, Km 1; mains R$60-95; ⊙1-5pm Wed, Thu & Sun, 1-10pm Fri & Sat) Food and setting are equally enticing at this sweet little house in the woods between Mauá and Maringá. Sporting a gorgeous riverside deck, it's surrounded by meticulously tended gardens that provide veggies and herbs for some of Mauá's most memorable meals. Specialties include oatmeal-almond-breaded trout, brie-*pinhão* (giant pine nut) ravioli and a sweet tomato, basil and mascarpone dessert 'salad.'

Babel INTERNATIONAL **$$$**
(☎24 99977-0152; www.babelrestaurante.com; Vale do Pavão; mains R$68-95, tasting menu R$185; ⊙1-10pm Fri & Sat, to 6pm Sun) Perched 3.5km up a mountainside along a steep, tortuous dirt road, this intimate glass-walled restaurant serves up divine views and refined international cuisine, from risotto and homemade fettuccine to lamb, duck and filet mignon. Chefs Dani Keiko and André Murray are renowned for their desserts (tiramisu, tarte tatin, crème brûlée) and their decadent 'Tower of Babel' tasting menu.

Information

Wi-fi is spotty and sometimes slow in the valley.

Mauatur (☎24 3387-1283; www.visiteviscondedemaua.com.br; ⊙10am-6pm Mon-Thu & Sat, to 10pm Fri, to 3pm Sun) At the entrance to Mauá village, the valley's tourist information hut has brochures and photos of area accommodations and can help with bookings.

Getting There & Away

Visconde de Mauá has no bus station. Buses stop at the top of Mauá's main street and in the center of Maringá before ending their run at Maromba's town square.

All public transport into Mauá passes through Resende, a city on the national park's eastern outskirts. **Cidade do Aço** (☎24 3354-2387; www.cidadedoaco.com.br) runs buses from Rio de Janeiro to Resende (R$41, 2½ to three hours, two to six daily).

From Resende, the most useful buses into Visconde de Mauá are operated by **Viação Resendense** (24 3354-1878), which travels the length of the valley into Maromba (R$9.40, 1½ hours, three to six daily).

Penedo

☎0XX24 / POP 30,703 / ELEV 600M

Originally started as a Finnish colony in the early 20th century, Penedo has grown into a vacation resort that embraces all things non-Brazilian. In the more developed lower section of town, you'll find tourist traps capitalizing on the region's European heritage mixed in with authentic Old World influences such as the Clube Finlândia, which still hosts traditional Finnish dances the first Saturday of every month. In Alto do Penedo, the upper part of town, it's easier to appreciate the luxuriant natural beauty that lies just outside the city limits. Wherever you go, you'll be sure to appreciate the emphasis on the traditional Finnish sauna, found at most hotels.

Sights

There's some nice scenery in the hills outside town. Worthwhile sights include the waterfalls **Três Cachoeiras**, west of downtown Penedo along the main road just before it starts climbing to Alto do Penedo, and **Cachoeira de Deus**, about 20 minutes uphill from the bus turnaround in Alto do Penedo. Ask locally for directions, as signs are intermittent. About one hour of uphill **hiking** from the end of the asphalt in Alto do Penedo takes you into very dense forest with trails and opportunities to observe wildlife, including monkeys.

Sleeping & Eating

Penedo is expensive, due to the large number of weekend tourists who come up from Rio and São Paulo – but the accommodations and food are generally above average.

Pequena Suécia HOTEL **$$**
(☎24 3351-1275, 24 99330-0168; www.pequenasuecia.com.br; Toivo Suni 33; d R$220-330, ste R$315-395, chalet R$395-495; ❄📶🏊) A Penedo classic, this red house in the woods has provided luxurious amenities in a rustic setting for over half a century. The on-site **restaurant** (www.pequenasuecia.com.br/restaurante; mains R$35-69, smörgåsbricka for 2 people R$150; ⊙6-10pm Wed & Thu, 1pm-midnight Fri & Sat, 1-5pm Sun) serves surprisingly tasty Scandinavian food, the spa offers massage and shiatsu treatments, and the attached **Clube Finlândia** (☎24 3351-1374; www.clubefinlandiablog.blogspot.com; Av das Mangueiras 2601) features live jazz music.

Casa da Picanha BARBECUE **$$**
(☎24 3351-2251; www.casadapicanhapenedo.com.br; Av Brasil 525; mains per person R$45-65; ⊙11am-

11pm) Fans of classic *churrasco* (Brazilian barbecue) with all the trimmings – rice, beans, French fries, *farofa* (sautéed manioc flour garnish), kale etc – should make a beeline for this cavernous temple to grilled meat, on a backstreet parallel to Penedo's main drag. Come hungry – portions are huge!

Information

Tourist Office (☎24 3351-1704; turismo@itatiaia.rj.gov.br; Av Casa das Pedras 766; ⏲9:30am-5pm) Housed inside Penedo's town entrance portal; has brochures and information in Portuguese.

Getting There & Away

Cidade do Aço (☎0800 886-1000; www.cidadedoaco.com.br) operates direct buses from Rio to Penedo (R$45, 3¼ hours, three daily). Alternatively, take a Cidade do Aço bus from Rio to Resende (R$42, 2½ to three hours), and connect to the hourly Resende–Penedo bus (R$4.25, 45 minutes) operated by **Viação Penedo** (024 3381-8861). The latter bus services the 3km-long main street and continues to the end of the paved road.

NORTH OF RIO DE JANEIRO

The mountains north of Rio rise up with shapes so improbable and dramatic, they catch your attention even from a great distance. Landing at Galeão international airport or surveying the northern skyline from the top of Rio's Pão de Açúcar (Sugarloaf), your eye is automatically drawn to the intriguing sawtooth ridge on the horizon. In the 19th century, the allure of these mountains led Brazil's imperial family to set up a summer residence in Petrópolis, and inspired the country's first Swiss immigrants to choose Nova Friburgo as their New World home.

More recently, climbers from all over the world have become enamored of the vertiginous rocky faces of the Serra dos Órgãos (Organ Pipe Range). To this day, the cooler climate and recreational opportunities, along with the region's imperial and immigrant legacy, continue to attract visitors from Rio and beyond.

Petrópolis

☎0XX24 / POP 298,235 / ELEV 809M

A lovely mountain retreat with a decidedly European flavor, Petrópolis is where Dom Pedro II's imperial court spent the summer when Rio got too muggy, and it's still a favorite weekend getaway for *cariocas* (residents of Rio city). The city center, with its picturesque parks, bridges, canals and old-fashioned street lamps, is easily explored on foot or by horse and carriage.

The landscape surrounding Petrópolis provides another compelling reason to visit. The fantastically shaped peaks of Parque Nacional Serra dos Órgãos are just a short drive out of town, with waterfalls, swimming holes, trails and outdoor experiences suitable for everyone from families with children to world-class climbers.

Finally, there's the beer. Petrópolis and the surrounding region are packed with breweries, from Cervejaria Bohemia in the heart of town (Brazil's oldest brewery, with its own beer museum) to big industrial operations like Itaipava, to a host of up-and-coming microbreweries.

Sights & Activities

★Cervejaria Bohemia BREWERY

(www.bohemia.com.br; Alfredo Pachá 166; adult/student & senior R$36/18; ⏲noon-5pm Tue-Thu, 10am-5pm Fri & Sun, 10am-6pm Sat) Don't miss the engaging 1½-hour tour (half self-guided, half guided) at Brazil's oldest brewery, where interactive exhibits trace beer-making history and nifty touchscreens let you explore brews from dozens of countries. Tours conclude with free samples of specialty beers that are only brewed here. The on-site bar-restaurant is the only spot in Brazil you can get Bohemia on draft.

★Museu Imperial PALACE

(☎24 2233-0300; www.museuimperial.gov.br; Rua da Imperatriz 220; adult/student R$10/5; ⏲10am-5pm Tue-Sun) Petrópolis' top draw is this impeccably preserved 19th-century palace. Felt slippers provided at the entrance help protect the fine wood floors – great fun to slide around in! Displays include the 1.95kg imperial crown, with its 639 diamonds and 77 pearls, and the ruby-encrusted, feather-shaped gold pen used to sign the *Lei Aurea,* which freed Brazil's remaining slaves in 1888.

★Parque Nacional Serra dos Órgaos – Vale do Bonfim Entrance NATIONAL PARK

Up a dirt road in the foothills 20km northeast of Petrópolis, this remote entrance to Parque Nacional Serra dos Órgaos (p152) grants immediate access to a variety of trails for all fitness levels. The easiest is the short,

Petrópolis

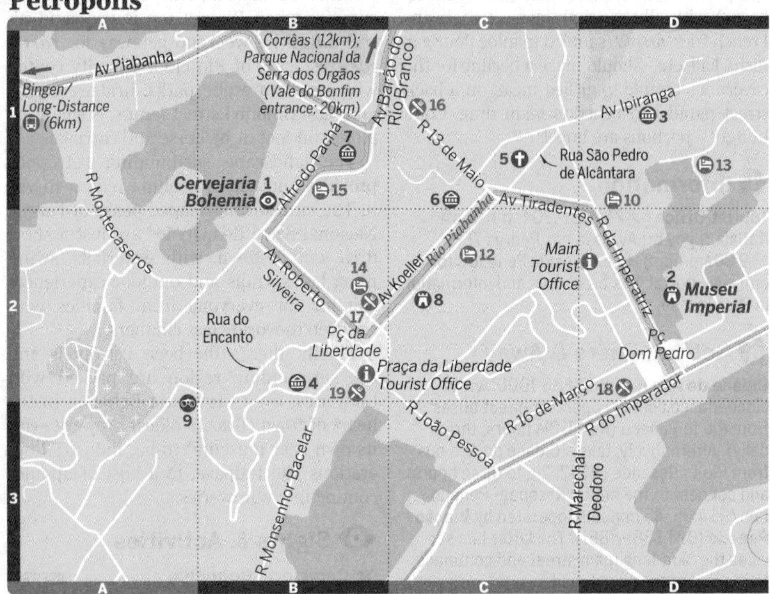

relatively flat path along the Rio do Bonfim, passing through a bamboo grove to a series of natural swimming holes – **Poço Paraiso**, **Poço das Bromélias** and **Poço dos Primatas** – all accessible within a 10- to 25-minute walk from the entrance.

Visitors seeking a longer day hike in the park's lower section can continue climbing along the trail about an hour and a half to a pair of waterfalls, **Cachoeira Véu de Noiva** and **Poco das Andorinhas**.

For a glimpse of the park's spectacular high country (extra fee and physical stamina required), nothing beats the classic hike to the top of **Morro do Açu** (2216m), a bald rocky outcrop that commands breathtaking panoramic views. Allow five to seven hours for the round trip from the park entrance.

Casa da Ipiranga HISTORIC BUILDING

(☎24 2231-8718; Av Ipiranga 716; adult/child R$10/5; ⏲2-6pm Fri-Sun) Dating to 1884, this beautifully preserved Victorian mansion retains a host of elegant features including French chandeliers, Belgian crystal mirrors, Carrara marble fireplaces and dozens of murals. The magnificent grounds are the work of Auguste Glaziou, the landscape architect who designed Rio's Quinta da Boa Vista and Passeio Público. It's open for guided tours and occasional musical and theatrical events.

Palácio Rio Negro PALACE

(Av Koeller 255; ⏲10am-6pm Tue-Sun) FREE Visitors are free to roam among the high-ceilinged, parquet-floored rooms of this grand yellow edifice, which served as a summer home for Brazil's presidents for decades before the capital moved to Brasilia. Highlights include the 2nd floor display of furniture belonging to former president Getúlio Vargas, and his colorfully tiled bathroom, complete with swimming pool-sized bathtub.

Palácio de Cristal HISTORIC BUILDING

(Alfredo Pachá; ⏲9am-6pm Sun-Tue, to 9pm Wed-Sat) FREE Built in France and imported in 1879, this ornate iron-and-glass structure was originally used as a hothouse for growing orchids. It's now a venue for various cultural events.

Casa de Santos Dumont MUSEUM

(☎24 2247-5222; Rua do Encanto 22; adult/reduced R$8/4; ⏲9am-5:30pm Tue-Sun) This charming house was the summer home of Brazil's diminutive father of aviation and inventor of the wristwatch. Photos and exhibits document Dumont's many inventions.

Catedral São Pedro de Alcântara CHURCH

(Sao Pedro de Alcântara 60; ⏲8am-6pm) Petrópolis' cathedral houses the tombs of Brazil's

Petrópolis

Top Sights
1 Cervejaria Bohemia B1
2 Museu Imperial D2

Sights
3 Casa da Ipiranga D1
4 Casa de Santos Dumont B2
5 Catedral São Pedro de Alcântara C1
6 Palácio da Princesa Isabel C1
7 Palácio de Cristal B1
8 Palácio Rio Negro C2
9 Trono de Fátima A3

Sleeping
10 Casablanca Imperial D1
11 Pousada 14 Bis F2
12 Pousada Imperial Koeler C2
13 Pousada Monte Imperial D1
14 Solar do Império B2
15 Um Hostel B1

Eating
Bordeaux .... (see 3)
16 Casa Pellegrini C1
17 Imperatriz Leopoldina B2
18 Majórica Churrascaria D2
19 Restaurante Paladar B2

last emperor, Dom Pedro II, his wife, Dona Teresa, and their daughter, Princesa Isabel. The **bell tower**, which offers fine views of the city, remained closed indefinitely at the time of research.

Trono de Fátima VIEWPOINT
Enjoy great views of Petrópolis and the surrounding mountains from this 3.5m-tall Italian sculpture of the NS de Fátima Madonna, in the hills on the western side of town.

Palácio da Princesa Isabel HISTORIC BUILDING
(Av Koeler s/n) This showy salmon-hued mansion was once home to Brazil's Princess Isabel, daughter of Emperor Pedro II and Empress Teresa Cristina. It can be viewed from the outside only.

Trekking Petrópolis OUTDOORS
(☎24 99261-8502, 24 2235-7607; www.rioserra.com.br/trekking) Organizes hiking and bird-watching trips in the nearby Mata Atlântica rainforest.

Festivals & Events

Bauernfest CULTURAL
(www.bauernfestpetropolis.com.br; ⊙late Jun) In the mid-19th century, Germans constituted the vast majority of Petrópolis's population. This Germanic legacy is celebrated with music, dancing, German food and free-flowing beer during the city's 10-day Bauernfest, centered on the Dia do Colono (city festival) on June 29.

Sleeping

★**Um Hostel** HOSTEL $
(☎24 2231-7129; www.umhostel.com.br; Padre Siqueira 325; weekday/weekend dm R$60/80, d R$150/190; ❄📶) With a prime city center location opposite the Bohemia brewery, this town-house-turned-hostel has been a Petrópolis budget traveler's dream-come-true since opening in 2017. Three quads, a double and four high-ceilinged dorms with parquet floors share a host of inviting common spaces, including a living room with fireplace and pool table, and a light-flooded upstairs bathroom with windows overlooking the park.

★**Pousada Paraiso Açu** POUSADA $$
(☎24 2221-3999; www.pousadaparaisoacu.com; Estrada do Bonfim 3511; r R$195-385, chalet R$360-550; 📶🏊) Outdoors enthusiasts need look no further than this family-run, end-of-the-road hideaway, 20km northeast of Petrópolis adjoining Parque Nacional da Serra dos Órgãos. Surrounded by mountain peaks, with an attached restaurant serving

DON'T MISS

PARQUE NACIONAL SERRA DOS ÓRGÃOS

Created in 1939, this high country **park** (☎21 2642-0579; www.icmbio.gov.br/parnaserradosorgaos; admission lower section/upper section R$32/52; ⏰8am-5pm) straddling the Serra dos Órgãos (Organ Pipe Range) just north of Rio is best known for its spectacular mountain scenery, superb climbing opportunities, and extensive trail system, including the classic 42km, three-day traverse over the mountains from Petrópolis to Teresópolis. Hiring a guide for this and other local treks is easy (the park service maintains a list of qualified guides), with May through October (the drier months) being the best time to walk.

The national park covers 118 sq km of mountainous terrain between Teresópolis and Petrópolis. The park's most distinctive features are the strangely shaped peaks of Pedra do Sino (2263m), Pedra do Açu (2230m), Agulha do Diabo (2020m), Nariz do Frade (1919m), Dedo de Deus (1651m), Pedra da Ermitage (1485m) and Dedo de Nossa Senhora (1320m). With so many peaks, it's no wonder that this is the mountain-climbing, rock-climbing and trekking center of Brazil.

The main entrance (p156) to the national park is at the south edge of the town of Teresópolis, off Hwy BR-116 from Rio, about 4km from the center. Other park entrances can be found at Vale do Bonfim (p151), (20km northeast of Petrópolis) and **Guapimirim** (in the park's southeastern corner, off the Rio–Teresópolis highway).

home-brewed Odin beer and local trout, it has cozy chalets, spacious lounging areas, a spring-fed pool, wood-fired sauna and ample recreation facilities, including a zip line and via ferrata.

Owner Marina accompanies guests on weekend hikes to swimming holes in the national park and takes kids to visit the bunnies, chickens and tangerine orchard at the adjacent mini-farm. There's a two-night minimum on weekends.

Pousada Imperial Koeler POUSADA **$$**
(☎24 2243-4330; www.pousadaimperialkoeler.com.br; Av Koeler 99; r midweek/weekend R$235/435; ❄@📶🏊) This gabled gem, dating back to 1875, is right in the heart of things, along architecturally stunning Av Koeler. Its sister hotel **Pousada Monte Imperial** (☎24 2237-1664; www.pousadamonteimperial.com.br; José Alencar 27; r midweek/weekend R$235/435; ❄📶🏊), in an old vine-covered house on the hillside above the Museu Imperial, shares the same prices. Rates get slashed nearly in half between Sunday and Thursday.

Pousada 14 Bis POUSADA **$$**
(☎24 2231-0946; www.pousada14bis.com.br; Buenos Aires 192; s/d with fan R$165/280, with air-con R$210/350; ❄📶) On a quiet residential street near the downtown bus station, the restored colonial Pousada 14 Bis has handsome, well-appointed rooms with comfortable beds. The best offer lovely wood floors and balconies overlooking the mountains or the garden out back.

Casablanca Imperial HOTEL **$$**
(☎24 2242-6662; www.casablancahotel.com.br; Avenida da Imperatriz 286; r with fan/air-con R$270/290; ❄📶🏊) The Casablanca, almost next door to the Museu Imperial, has a range of rooms – the best featuring high ceilings, old-fashioned shutters, large bathrooms with tubs and antique furnishings.

★**Pousada da Alcobaça** POUSADA **$$$**
(☎24 2221-1240; www.pousadadaalcobaca.com.br; Goulão 298, Corrêas; r R$480-680; ❄📶🏊) Midway between Petrópolis and Parque Nacional da Serra dos Órgãos, this gorgeous family-run hotel has a pool, sauna, tennis court and ample gardens crossed by a small river. The parquet-floored guest rooms, ranging from cozy under-the-eaves hideaways to larger units with garden and mountain views, are individually decorated with quilts, armchairs and colorful area rugs. There's also an excellent restaurant.

Solar do Império HOTEL **$$$**
(☎24 2103-3000; www.solardoimperio.com.br; Av Koeler 376; r R$590-950 Fri & Sat, midweek R$540-840; 📶🏊) Centrally located on Praça da Liberdade, with polished wood floors, 5m-high ceilings, grand fireplaces, a pool, sauna and spa, the meticulously restored Solar do Império will make you feel like a member of the imperial family.

Eating

Casa Pellegrini FAST FOOD **$$**
(☎24 2231-6110; www.facebook.com/CasaPellegrini; 13 de Maio 184; mains R$14-49; ⏰11am-

11:45pm Sun-Thu, to 1:30am Fri & Sat) For budget eats any time of day, this convivial downtown hole-in-the-wall is one of Petrópolis' new local favorites. Burgers, sandwiches, pizza, pasta, fried chicken, steaks and French fries all come accompanied by reasonably priced Brazilian beers, juices and caipirinhas.

Restaurante Paladar BUFFET $$
(☎24 2243-1143; www.paladarpetropolis.com.br; Barão do Amazonas 25; per kg R$70; ⏲11am-3:30pm Tue-Sun) Prices are higher than at your average *por-kilo* joint, but the atmosphere can't be beat at this classy converted mansion across from Praça da Liberdade. Watch the horse-drawn carriages clip-clop by as you enjoy classic Brazilian fare on the old-fashioned wraparound porch.

Bordeaux INTERNATIONAL $$
(☎24 2242-5711; www.bordeauxvinhos.com.br; Av Ipiranga 716; mains R$42-98, weekday lunch specials R$23-36, weekend buffet per kg $110; ⏲noon-4pm & 7-10:30pm Mon-Thu, to 11:30pm Fri & Sat, noon-5pm Sun) On the picturesque grounds of the Casa da Ipiranga, these converted stables provide a pleasant backdrop for the menu of pasta, risotto, fish and meat dishes backed up by an extensive wine cellar.

Majórica Churrascaria BARBECUE $$
(☎24 2249-2498; www.majorica.com.br; Rua do Imperador 754; lunch specials R$35-45, mains per person R$20-61; ⏲noon-11:30pm) This *churrascaria* (barbecue restaurant) near the Museu Imperial is renowned citywide for its excellent cuts of meat, accompanied by *batata pastel* (potato puffs), *farofa de banana* (toasted manioc with banana) and other delicious sides. Most dishes serve two to three people; solo travelers can request half portions. *Pratos executivos* (lunch specials served weekdays from noon to 5pm) offer superb value.

★ **Restaurante Alcobaça** BRAZILIAN $$$
(☎24 2221-1240; Goulão 298, Corrêas; mains R$81-105; ⏲1-10pm) Verdant, flowery grounds and a gorgeous mountain setting enhance the mood of relaxed elegance in the lovely glass-walled dining room of Pousada da Alcobaça (p153), 12km outside Petrópolis. The locally sourced menu revolves around trout, steak, shrimp, chicken and pasta accompanied by fruit, veggies and herbs harvested from the pousada's own organic gardens. The Saturday *feijoada* (bean-and-meat stew) is legendary.

Imperatriz Leopoldina BRAZILIAN $$$
(☎24 2103-3000; www.solardoimperio.com.br/restaurant1; Av Koeler 376; mains R$50-85; ⏲7am-11pm) Tall windows flanked by murals of monkeys, capybaras and tropical foliage create a cheerful mood at this renowned restaurant attached to the Hotel Solar do Império (p153). Chef Claudia Mascarenhas balances traditional recipes against more whimsical creations, using ingredients that range from lamb to lobster, figs to filberts. The midweek executive lunch (mains R$30) is especially good value.

ℹ Information

Petrópolis has two conveniently located tourist offices: the main branch in the **Centro de Cultura** (☎0800 024-1516, 24 2233-1217; www.petropolis.rj.gov.br/fct; Centro de Cultura Raul de Leoni, Praça Visconde de Mauá 305; ⏲9am-6pm Mon-Sat, to 2pm Sun) opposite the Museu Imperial, and at **Praça da Liberdade** (Praça da Liberdade; ⏲9am-5pm).

Bradesco (Rua do Imperador 268) One of many ATMs along Rua do Imperador.

ℹ Getting There & Away

Única/Fácil buses from Rio (R$28, 1½ hours, half-hourly from 5:30am to midnight) drop you at the Leonel Brizola bus station in Bingen, 6km outside downtown Petrópolis. To reach the **downtown bus station** (Terminal de Integração Imperatriz Leopoldina; Dr Porciúncula 58) and other city center attractions, transfer to local bus number 100 (R$4.20, 30 minutes, every 10 to 15 minutes).

Teresópolis

☎0XX21 / POP 176,060 / ELEV 871M

Do as Empress Maria Tereza used to do and escape from the steamy summer heat of Rio to the cool mountain retreat of Teresópolis, the highest city in the state, nestled in the strange, organ-pipe rock formations of the Serra dos Órgãos. The gorgeous winding road from Rio to Teresópolis climbs steeply through a padded green jungle, with bald peaks towering dramatically overhead the entire way.

Today the city's principal attraction is the surrounding landscape and its natural treasures, most notably Parque Nacional da Serra dos Órgãos, whose trails, waterfalls and mountain peaks beckon just 6km south of the city center. The **Dedo de Deus** (God's Finger) is the town symbol, a dramatic rock spire visible from all over town.

Teresópolis's Comary neighborhood has long been the training base of Brazil's national football squad; you can still occasionally catch a glimpse of the team practicing here in town.

Sights

★Parque Nacional Serra dos Órgaos – Teresópolis Entrance NATIONAL PARK

About 6km south of Teresópolis, off the BR-116 Rio–Teresópolis highway, you'll find the main (and most accessible) entrance to magnificent Parque Nacional Serra dos Órgaos (p152), which offers some of Brazil's most dramatic hiking, climbing and mountain scenery. From this point of entry, visitors can access both the park's tamer lower section – perfect for a picnic with its walking trails, waterfalls, natural swimming pools and tended lawns and gardens – and the wilder upper section, with its challenging high country trails.

From the Teresópolis entrance, the road extends into the park as far as Barragem Beija Flor. From here, lower section visitors can continue up the 800m **Trilha Mozart Catão** (one hour round trip from the park road) up to the Mirante Alexandre Oliveira (1100m) for nice views of Teresópolis – or follow the park's newest trail, the 1.2km **Trilha Cartão Postal**, up to a higher viewpoint (1320m) for spectacular perspectives on the distinctive Dedo de Deus and the entire Serra dos Órgãos range.

There are also several good day hikes for visitors who wish to explore the park's more rugged upper section. The highlight is the **Trilha Pedra do Sino** – a strenuous roundtrip of about eight hours from the end of the park road (R$52 trail fee). The trail passes **Cachoeira Veu da Noiva**, the vegetation changes from rainforest to grassland, and the reward is a panoramic view stretching all the way to Rio de Janeiro and the Baía de Guanabara.

To reach the park entrance from downtown Teresópolis, take the 'Soberbo' bus (R$4). Alternatively, take the more frequent 'Alto' bus and get off at the Praçinha do Alto, from where it's a 10-minute walk south to the park's main entrance. Both buses can be caught at multiple stops along Teresópolis' main drag, Av Almirante Lúcio Meira. A taxi ride from town to the park entrance costs about R$30.

Colina dos Mirantes VIEWPOINT

(Av Nilo Tavares, Fazendinha) Colina dos Mirantes, in the southern suburb of Fazendinha, is an especially good place to view the city and its mountain backdrop. On clear days you can see as far as Rio's Pão de Açúcar and the Baía de Guanabara.

Sleeping & Eating

Hotel Willisau HOTEL $$

(☎21 3642-6600; www.hotelwillisau.com.br; Ernesto Sansoé 143; d midweek/weekend from R$220/275; 📶) The Willisau won't win any prizes for originality or character, but the cookie-cutter faux-Swiss rooms here are comfortable enough, and the south-of-town location, equidistant from the national park entrance and the Therezópolis beer garden, affords easy access to two of the city's top attractions.

Hotel Rosa dos Ventos HOTEL $$$

(☎21 2644-9900; www.hotelrosadosventos.com.br; Estrada Tere-Fri, Km 22.6, Campanha; r/ste incl breakfast from R$695/920, with full board from R$940/1170; ❄📶🏊) Way up in the mountains, this luxurious alpine-style resort has its own lake and network of hiking trails. Magnificent views abound from the many terraces and on-site restaurants. It's 22km out of Teresópolis along the road to Nova Friburgo.

★Linguiça do Padre GRILL $$

(☎21 2641-0065; www.facebook.com/RestauranteLinguicaDoPadre; Estrada Tere-Fri, Km 33; mains for 2 people R$55-108; ⏰8am-8pm) This local favorite sits beside a rushing river just off the Teresópolis–Friburgo highway. The menu ranges from *linguiça* (spicy Portuguese sausage) sandwiches (R$8) to substantial meals featuring trout, *picanha* or roast suckling pig. Locally grown fruit also features prominently, in fresh squeezed lemonade or strawberry-orange juice (R$12 per pitcher) and strawberries with whipped cream for dessert.

Taberna Alpina INTERNATIONAL $$

(☎21 2742-0123; Duque de Caxias 131; mains per person R$23-55; ⏰8am-10pm Tue-Thu & Sun, to midnight Fri & Sat) The Taberna's cozy interior, sporting rustic log walls and wooden benches with heart-shaped cutouts, is reminiscent of the Alps. So is the menu, featuring German sausages, brown bread, goulash, smoked pork, potato salad and sauerkraut, all served alongside more typical Brazilian and Portuguese fare by old-school black-and-white-clad waiters.

Drinking & Nightlife

Vila St Gallen BEER GARDEN

(☎21 2642-1575; www.vilastgallen.com.br; Augusto do Amaral Peixoto 166; ⏰7pm-midnight Wed & Thu, noon-12:30am Fri & Sat, noon-6pm Sun) Brazilian waitstaff in faux Swiss-German attire sling the city's famed Therezópolis beer at this cavernous beer hall, built to celebrate the brewery's centennial in 2012. Weekend patrons spill into the adjacent beer garden, bistro, fondue restaurant and kitschy chapel with piped-in Gregorian chants. There's international pub grub nightly, plus occasional live music.

Information

Bradesco (Av Delfim Moreira 390) One of several ATMs near the main square.

Getting There & Away

The **bus station** (☎21 2742-2676; Rua Primeiro de Maio) is 800m southwest of the main square. **Viação Teresópolis** (☎21 2742-0606; www.viacaoteresopolis.com.br) runs buses to Rio (R$34, 1½ hours, hourly from 6am to 10pm), Petrópolis (R$20, 1½ hours, six daily from 7am to 7pm) and Nova Friburgo (R$26, two hours, five daily 7am to 7pm).

Nova Friburgo

☎0XX22 / POP 185,381 / ELEV 846M

In 1818, newly crowned Portuguese King Dom João VI started recruiting immigrants from Switzerland and Germany to come to his vast Brazilian territory. The first 30 families to arrive, from the Swiss canton of Friburg, immediately set out to create a perfect little village reminiscent of their home country in the mountains north of Rio. Traces of Swiss and German heritage remain in modern Friburgo, in the local architecture, the town's passion for floral decoration and the fair-haired, blue-eyed features of some residents. Nowadays the local economy revolves around the lingerie industry, while tourism revolves around the region's natural attractions: waterfalls, woods, trails, sunny mountain mornings and cool evenings.

Sights & Activities

Nova Friburgo's most interesting sights are a few kilometers out of town.

★Pico da Caledônia MOUNTAIN

(⏲7am-4pm) FREE For spectacular views all the way to Rio and the Baía de Guanabara, climb Pico da Caledônia (2310m), a popular local launching site for hang gliders. It's a 6km uphill hike from the Alto do Cascatinha neighborhood; local buses marked Cascatinha-Interpass (R$4.20, 15 minutes) can drop you at the trailhead. Alternatively, with a 4WD vehicle, you can drive the absurdly steep, rugged approach road. Either way, the final summit climb is via a 650-step staircase (ID required for access).

Parque Cão Sentado PARK

(☎22 99765-3876; www.facebook.com/pedradocaosentado; Hwy RJ 116, Km 91.2; trail fee R$15; ⏲9am-5pm Sat & Sun, last entry 3:30pm) Head to this park, 10km north of town, for the 30-minute climb via a moderate trail to the top of Pedra do Cão Sentado, a rock formation resembling a sitting dog that serves as Friburgo's town symbol.

THE TERESÓPOLIS–FRIBURGO SCENIC CIRCUIT

Pretty mountain vistas and European heritage are on full display along the **Circuito Turístico Tere-Fri** (www.terefri.com.br), a 68km scenic highway connecting the towns of Teresópolis and Nova Friburgo.

Starting from Teresópolis, highlights include the **Mulher de Pedra** (Woman of Stone) viewpoint at Km 12, where a distant mountain really *does* look like a reclining woman; the **Restaurante Crémerie** (☎21 99176-0167, 21 3643-5168; www.restaurantecremerie.com.br; Estrada Tere-Fri, Km 16; mains R$42-80; ⏲noon-5pm Thu, 10am-10pm Fri & Sat, noon-6pm Sun) at Km 16, where you can watch baby goats frolicking in the yard, buy local cheese or indulge in a fine French meal; the **Cachoeira dos Frades** turnoff at Km 21.5, where an unpaved side road leads through an idyllic valley to a waterfall with a swimming hole; Hotel Rosa dos Ventos (p156) at Km 22.6, one of many opulent hotels along the route; the Linguiça do Padre (p156) restaurant at Km 33, whose delicious grilled meat and fresh-squeezed juices make for the perfect roadside lunch break; and **Queijaria Suiça** (☎22 2529-4000; www.frialpalimentos.com; Estrada Tere-Fri Km 18, Conquista; ⏲9am-6pm) at Km 49, where a Swiss cheese factory sits adjacent to a small museum tracing two centuries of Swiss culture in the Friburgo area.

Additional points of interest are indicated on a handy map available throughout the region. It's easiest to drive the route in your own car, although local buses travel through here and will let you off wherever you like.

Chairlift OUTDOORS

(Teleférico; ☎22 2522-4834; Praça do Teleférico; 1-/2-section ride R$25/40; ⊙9am-5pm Tue-Sun) Brazil's longest chairlift (1.4km) runs from town up to Morro da Cruz (1800m) in two sections, offering fine panoramic views.

Lumiar Aventura OUTDOORS

(☎22 98131-6768; www.lumiaraventura.com.br) Lumiar, 34km southeast of Nova Friburgo, is a popular destination for Brazilian ecotourists, with waterfalls, walking trails and white-water adventures centered on the Encontro dos Rios – the tumultuous confluence of three local rivers. Lumiar Aventura offers a variety of guided rafting (R$96 to R$216), climbing (R$96) and trekking (R$72) adventures in the area.

Sleeping & Eating

Alê Friburgo Hostel HOSTEL $

(☎22 2526-3478; www.friburgohostel.com; Bizzotto Filho 2; dm/d R$50/130; @🛜🏊) This family-run hostel, 2km straight uphill from Friburgo's town square, compensates for its remote location with a friendly welcome and great amenities, including a pool, sauna and nice mountain views. The hostel's downtown affiliate, **Hotel Alê** (Dante Laginestra 89; dm R$60, d R$180-190; 🛜), is more convenient for those using public transit, with a mix of dorms and old-fashioned, parquet-floored private rooms.

Hotel Auberge Suisse HOTEL $$$

(☎22 2541-1270; www.aubergesuisse.com.br; Rua 10 de Outubro, Amparo; chalet from R$660; ❄🛜🏊) The luxury chalets here, 12km northeast of Nova Friburgo, all have wi-fi and minibars and most have fireplaces and DVD players. The pretty landscaped grounds include indoor and outdoor pools, a sauna and a small collection of farm animals, whose milk is used to make cheese for the excellent on-site restaurant specializing in traditional Swiss cuisine: raclette, fondue and trout.

Restaurante-Pizzeria La Bamba INTERNATIONAL $$

(☎22 2522-9869; www.facebook.com/rlabamba; Salusse 7; pizzas R$28-38, mains R$29-87; ⊙6-11pm Tue-Thu, 11am-11pm Fri & Sat, 11am-4:30pm Sun) Efficient service and a family-friendly vibe draw constant crowds to this buzzing restaurant near Nova Friburgo's chairlift. The menu ranges from pizzas and pasta to a variety of grilled meat and fish dishes.

Dona Mariquinha BUFFET $$

(☎22 2522-2309; www.facebook.com/DonaMariquinha; Monsenhor Miranda 110; all-you-can-eat lunch weekdays/weekend R$35/45; ⊙noon-3:30pm Tue-Sun, 7-9pm Mon-Fri) This friendly place features all-you-can-eat home cooking at lunchtime and all-you-can-eat soup for R$15 on weekday evenings.

★**Crescente** FRENCH $$$

(☎22 2523-4616; www.elocrescente.com.br; General Osório 21; mains R$69-98; ⊙noon-10pm Mon & Thu-Sat, noon-4pm Sun) Nova Friburgo's standout restaurant for over 25 years, this classy family-run place specializes in French-influenced cuisine accompanied by wines from a dozen countries (including Brazil). Sit in the homey parquet-floored dining room or on the back patio, enjoying locally sourced treats including lamb, duck, rabbit, seafood, herbs and fruits from the garden out back, and a tempting range of desserts.

Information

Banco do Brasil (Praça Dermeval B Moreira 10) One of several ATMs downtown.

Tourist Office (☎22 2543-6307; circuito@pmnf.rj.gov.br; Praça Dermeval B Moreira; ⊙9am-5pm Sun-Thu, to 7pm Fri & Sat) Has maps, complete lists of hotels and restaurants, and excellent multilingual staff.

Getting There & Away

Nova Friburgo is a short jaunt from Rio, via Niterói, on bus line 1001. The ride is along a picturesque, winding, misty jungle road.

Nova Friburgo has two long-distance bus stations. From the **north bus station** (Rodoviária Norte; Praça Feliciano Costa), 2.5km north of the center, **Viação Teresópolis** (☎22 2522-2708; www.viacaoteresopolis.com.br) has buses to Teresópolis (R$26, two hours, five daily). From the **south bus station** (Rodoviária Sul; Ponte da Saudade), 4km south of the center, **Viação 1001** (☎22 2522-0400; www.autoviacao1001.com.br) has buses to Rio (R$48 to R$59, 2½ hours, hourly), plus one direct bus to Cabo Frio (R$56, 3¼ hours, 7am Saturday).

Local buses (R$4.20) connect both long-distance terminals to the central **local bus station** (Praça Getúlio Vargas 333) just north of Praça Getúlio Vargas. Local buses also go to just about all the tourist attractions. Ask for details at the tourist office.

EAST OF RIO DE JANEIRO

East of Rio, the mountains recede and the coastal strip becomes flatter, punctuated by the sparkling lagoons of the Região dos Lagos (Lakes Region) and the dazzling white sands of the Costa do Sol (Sunshine Coast). Some of Rio state's most beautiful beaches are found here. Only two hours from Rio by car, the area is a weekend playground for *cariocas,* with plenty of opportunities for nightlife and outdoor recreation.

Saquarema

☎0XX22 / POP 85,175

Straddling a spit of sand between a gorgeous lagoon and the open Atlantic, and crowned by a beautiful white church, Saquarema is a laid-back little town 100km east of Rio. Polluting industries are forbidden in the municipality; the waters are clean, and fish and shrimp are abundant.

Touted as the surfing capital of Brazil, Saquarema hosts world-class competitions every year and draws a steady stream of surf devotees to its two long main beaches, Praia Itaúna and Praia da Vila. Its unmarred shoreline also attracts sport-fishing enthusiasts and sun worshippers. Even so, the town remains less touristy than neighboring coastal resorts such as Búzios, making it an agreeable, off-the-beaten-track spot to kick back for a day or two.

Sights

★Praia Itaúna BEACH

About 3km east of town is Praia Itaúna, Saquarema's most beautiful beach and one of the best surf spots in Brazil. National and international surfing competitions are held here each year, generally between May and October.

NS de Nazaré CHURCH

(NS de Nazareth; www.facebook.com/nazarethsaquarema; Praça NS de Nazaré; 8am-4pm) The stunning white church of NS de Nazaré (1837), perched on the hill near the entrance to the lagoon, is the town's focal point. From this strategic spot you can survey the long, empty beaches, the lagoon and the mountains beyond. The Mass held here on September 7 and 8 attracts around 150,000 pilgrims, second only to the NS de Nazaré celebrations of Belém (in Brazil's northern state of Pará).

Festivals & Events

Oi Rio Pro Saquarema SPORTS

(www.worldsurfleague.com/events; May) This 10-day international competition is the highlight of Saquarema's annual surfing calendar.

Sleeping & Eating

The best options are near the Itaúna beachfront, with others strung out along Praia da Vila, the long beach west of the city center.

Spazio Itaúna Hostel HOSTEL $

(☎22 2651-1746; www.spazioitauna.com.br; cnr Rua das Garças & Av Oceânica; dm R$60-70, tw R$140-165, d R$150-175, q R$270-310;) Directly opposite the beach at Itaúna, this hostel offers spotless white dorms, twins, doubles and a family unit, each with minifridge and en suite. The guest kitchen, equipped with a four-burner stove and microwave, is perfect for cooking up post-surf snacks from the Mercado Itaúna market downstairs.

Maasai Hotel Beach & Resort HOTEL $$$

(☎22 2651-1092; www.maasai.com.br; Travessa Itaúna 17; d R$400, with ocean view R$460-480;) If you're looking for cushy digs, this place is a no-brainer. Maasai has a stunning beachfront location, comfy sitting rooms, a sauna and swimming pool and a pretty bar-restaurant overlooking the water.

Casa da Praia BRAZILIAN $$

(☎22 2651-7920; www.casadapraiaitauna.com.br; Av Oceânica 1564; mains per person R$40; 10am-5pm Thu, to midnight Fri & Sat, to 10pm Sun) On Thursday and Friday afternoons, this great little beachfront place tucked behind a surf shop serves its popular *prato do surfista* (surfer's special; R$30) – grilled meat or fish accompanied by rice, beans and salad. On weekends and after hours, it's all about seafood mains, cold beers and the sound of crashing waves.

Garota de Itaúna SEAFOOD $$

(☎22 2651-2156; Av Oceânica 978; mains per person R$35-70; 11am-midnight) The Girl from Itaúna's attractions include a fabulous beachfront terrace and a wide variety of seafood specials. Hang on to your beers – the wind can be vicious. The adjacent pousada rents simple rooms (single/double R$154/220).

Information

Centro de Atendimento ao Turista (☎22 2651-2123; turismo@saquarema.rj.gov.br; Av Saquarema s/n; 9am-5pm Mon-Fri, to 1pm Sat) Overlooking the lagoon, on the Itaúna side of the downtown bridge.

LIA CALDAS/SHUTTERSTOCK ©

1. NS de Nazaré, Saquarema (p159) **2.** Arraial do Cabo (p162)
3. Ilha Grande (p129) **4.** Búzios (p164)

CRISTIAN ANTONIO LOURENCO/SHUTTERSTOCK ©

Beaches of Rio de Janeiro State

Amerigo Vespucci said it best: 'If there were an earthly paradise, it wouldn't be far from here!' Tiny Rio state offers a stunning variety of beaches. Whether you're into surfing, diving, bronzing your bod or strutting your stuff on a seaside dance floor, you'll find it here.

Ilha Grande

A nature-lover's vision of tropical paradise, Ilha Grande (p129) has more trails than motorized vehicles, and endless stretches of secluded sands. Circumnavigate the island on foot, or hop from beach to beach on the classic round-the-island boat tour.

Paraty

The spectacular mosaic of bays, islands, mountains, waterfalls and beaches of Paraty (p137) would be reason enough to visit; the colonial center's whitewashed houses, kaleidoscopic latticework and picturesque cobbled streets are like icing on the cake.

Saquarema

Laid-back and off the beaten track, Saquarema (p159) is best known to surfers, who flock here for international competitions; nonsurfers can admire its gorgeous 19th-century church, perched high on a promontory.

Arraial do Cabo

Even in Brazil, it'd be hard to find a cluster of beaches any prettier than this. Surrounded by prime diving and whale-watching spots, the white sands and blue-green waters of Arraial (p162) are downright dazzling.

Búzios

If you'd like a few chic comforts and a little nightlife to go with that perfect tan, look no further than Búzios (p164). The preferred destination of Brazil's (and half of Argentina's!) beautiful people, this scalloped peninsula full of dreamy beaches is as luxurious and as decadent as it gets.

Getting There & Away

Viação 1001 (☎22 2651-2054; www.autoviacao1001.com.br) runs buses from Rio to Saquarema throughout the day (R$35 to R$42, two hours, every hour or two). Saquarema's **bus station** (Praça Oscar Soares) is on the eastern side of the main bridge through town, about 800m north of the beach at Itaúna.

Salineira (☎22 2647-8200; www.salineira.com.br) runs four buses in each direction daily except Sunday on its B145 route between Saquarema and Cabo Frio (R$5.55, one hour). The main **bus stop** is just west across the bridge from the tourist office.

Arraial do Cabo

☎0XX22 / POP 29,304

Arraial do Cabo, 45km east of Saquarema, is surrounded by gleaming white sand dunes and offers breathtaking beaches without half the touristy fuss of neighboring Búzios. Arraial is home to a working fishing port, Porto do Forno, which lends it a welcoming working-class demeanor. Some of the best beaches – pristine swaths of gorgeous sand and bright-green waters – are within an easy 15-minute stroll of the downtown bus station, while others are just a short boat ride away. Arraial is a renowned diving destination, and it's also a good place to observe humpback whales (*Megaptera novaeangliae*), whose migration routes pass directly offshore.

Just above Praia dos Anjos beach in the town center, look for the plaque commemorating Amerigo Vespucci's landing here in 1503. Vespucci left 24 men behind to start a settlement, making Arraial one of the first European toeholds in the Americas.

Sights & Activities

Arraial's prime attractions lie along the shoreline. Centrally located Praia dos Anjos has beautiful turquoise water but a little too much boat traffic for swimming. Favorite beaches within a short walking distance of town are **Prainha** to the north of town; **Praia do Forno** (accessed by a 1km walking trail from Praia dos Anjos) to the northeast; and the vast **Praia Grande** to the west, where wilder surf races in off the open Atlantic.

There are several other stunning beaches along the mountainous peninsula just south of town. For near-aerial views, and the best sunset in the area, climb up to **Pontal do Atalaia**, a popular viewpoint at the top of the peninsula that also makes an excellent spot for **whale watching** in July and August.

Several agencies offer boat excursions to outlying beaches. The standard tour lasts about four hours. Arraial is also one of Brazil's top scuba diving spots. Tour operators who organize dives in these waters abound – the tourist office (p163) keeps a complete list.

★Ilha de Cabo Frio ISLAND

This stunning island, accessed by boat from Praia dos Anjos, is Arraial do Cabo's top day-trip destination. **Praia do Farol**, on the protected side of the island, is a gorgeous beach with fine white sand. The **Gruta Azul** (Blue Cavern), on the southwestern side of the island, is another beautiful spot. Be alert, though: the entrance to the underwater cavern is submerged at high tide.

★Embarcação Ericka Barreto BOATING

(☎22 99944-9988; www.facebook.com/EmbarcacaoErickaBarreto; Av Liberdade 501; cruise R$300) Of Arraial's many boat operators, Ericka Barreto stands out for its leisurely pace. Skipper Gaúcho's cute red boat makes a five- to seven-hour circuit of the bay (as opposed to the typical four-hour tour), stopping off at Ilha Cabo Frio and Arraial's best outlying beaches, and culminating with sunset over the Atlantic. Free soft drinks and bargain-priced *churrasco* (barbecue) are available onboard.

Sleeping & Eating

Marina dos Anjos Hostel HOSTEL $

(☎22 2622-4060; www.marinadosanjos.com.br; Bernardo Lens 145; dm R$82-95, d R$220-240; @📶) One block back from Praia dos Anjos, this hostel is a wonderful base from which to explore the area. The helpful staff rent bicycles, canoes, snorkels, surfboards and diving equipment, and help coordinate dives and boat tours. The central courtyard, with hammocks and pillows for lounging, is the venue for spontaneous evening barbecues and jam sessions.

Hotel Pousada Caminho do Sol HOTEL $$$

(☎22 2622-2029; www.caminhodosol.com.br; Miguel Angelo 55; r R$395-605; 📶🏊) Just off Praia Grande, this hotel with king-size beds, a pool, pretty interior gardens and sweeping views over the city is a big hit with visiting Brazilians looking for a romantic weekend.

Água na Boca BUFFET $

(☎22 2622-1106; Praça da Bandeira 1; per kg R$63; ⏰11:30am-5pm) A stone's throw from the bus station, this recommended self-serve includes plenty of seafood in its daily offerings.

WORTH A TRIP

A BIRD-WATCHER'S PARADISE IN RIO'S BACKYARD

Located only 80km from Rio's Galeão airport, **Guapi Assu Bird Lodge** (☎21 2745-3947; www.regua.org/visit-us/lodge; s R$705, d R$1140-1255, all incl full board;) is part of the nonprofit **Regua nature reserve** (Reserva Ecológica de Guapiaçu; ☎21 2745-3947; www.regua.org) , a 50-sq-km tract at the foot of the Serra dos Órgãos where Nicholas and Raquel Locke have dedicated their lives to restoring native ecosystems. Serious birders, or anyone who wants a genuine taste of Brazil's remarkable biodiversity, should head here. Volunteers from around the world are engaged in an ambitious reforestation project, while school kids from the local community are invited to use the reserve as a hands-on environmental education laboratory.

The comfy rooms have solar hot water, meals are served family-style around a big table and the library of nature books makes for great browsing, caipirinha in hand, after a long day of bird-watching. The artificial pond ecosystem next to the lodge draws in a stupendous array of birds, as well as families of capybaras. A network of trails surrounding the lodge offers opportunities to enter into deeper forest and visit other attractions, including a lovely waterfall. For details on reaching the lodge, see their website.

★**Bacalhau do Tuga** PORTUGUESE, SEAFOOD $$
(☎22 2622-1108; www.bacalhaudotuga.com; Santa Cruz 5, Praia dos Anjos; mains per person R$40-75; 6-11pm Tue-Thu, from 1pm Fri-Sun) From humble origins selling codfish fritters from a beachside stand in 2008, the 'Tuga' (Portuguese guy) has built this wonderful family-run restaurant near Praia dos Anjos. Superfresh ingredients are incorporated into Portuguese classics, from seafood stews to custard tarts, served alongside local specialties like *peixe com banana* (grilled fish with bananas) and superb pork ribs with barbecue sauce.

Information

You'll find a multibank ATM on Av Gov Leonel de Moura Brizola, just around the corner from the bus station.

Tourist Office (☎22 2622-1949; turismo@arraial.rj.gov.br; Pórtico de Arraial do Cabo; 8am-5pm) Housed within the town's formal entry portal, 3km northwest of the center, this office provides a helpful map. It also operates a tourist info kiosk with shorter hours (8am to 1pm Monday to Friday) at Praia dos Anjos.

Getting There & Away

Arraial do Cabo's **bus station** (Praça Castelo Branco) is situated in the town center. Direct buses operated by **Viação 1001** (☎22 2622-1488; www.autoviacao1001.com.br) run between Rio (R$57 to R$72, three hours) and Arraial every other hour.

An alternative is to catch Salineira municipal bus B150 to Cabo Frio (R$5.55, every 15 minutes), then transfer to one of the half-hourly Rio-bound buses leaving from the Cabo Frio bus station.

For Búzios, take Salineira bus 414 (R$5.55, 1½ hours, four daily).

Cabo Frio

☎0XX22 / POP 216,030

Sandwiched between sand dunes, lagoons and the sparkling Atlantic, Cabo Frio is the seventh-oldest city in Brazil. These days its historic charms and naturally gorgeous setting have been overshadowed by industry and overdevelopment, but on weekends and summer holidays its bars and beaches continue to draw throngs of happy-go-lucky Brazilians, whose merrymaking spirit is the modern city's strongest attraction.

The three main focal points for tourists are **Praia do Forte**, a stunning stretch of white sand and green waters named after the 17th-century fort at its eastern end, the historic **Bairro da Passagem** where the Portuguese first settled, and the restaurant-fringed **Canal do Itajuru**, which links nearby Lagoa de Araruama to the Atlantic Ocean.

Sights

Forte São Mateus FORT
(9am-noon & 1-5pm Apr-Nov, to 6pm Dec-Mar) FREE Forte São Mateus, a stronghold against pirates, was built between 1616 and 1620 at the eastern end of Praia do Forte to protect the lucrative brazilwood trade. Inside, photos and exhibits trace the fort's history, and visitors can gaze down into the old prison.

Museu do Surf MUSEUM
(☎22 98816-0250; www.museudosurf.com; Aníbal Amador do Vale; 5-10pm Tue-Sun) FREE A must-see for surfers, this quirky museum near the Cabo Frio waterfront traces the history of the sport through the owner's private collection of hundreds of vintage surfboards.

Sleeping & Eating

★Bravo Hostel Design HOSTEL **$$**
(☎22 2647-4244; www.bravohostel.com.br; Constantino Menelau 260; dm/d/ste R$90/400/470;) With a spectacular poolside deck overlooking bobbing boats in the harbor, this gleaming place feels like a cross between a hotel and a hostel, with a mix of en suite doubles and dorms, and a prime location on the waterfront of Cabo Frio's oldest neighborhood. Praia do Forte is a 10-minute walk away.

Pousada Boulevard POUSADA **$$$**
(☎22 2643-1456; www.pousadaboulevard.com; Marechal Floriano 237; r R$360-450;) Well placed in Cabo Frio's canalside restaurant district, this newer pousada offers amenities like satellite TV, a sauna and a plunge pool. The best five rooms have canal views.

Restaurante do Zé BARBECUE **$$**
(☎22 2643-4277; Blvd Canal 33; mains per person R$33-54; ⊙11am-midnight) The sidewalk tables at this animated eatery overlook the canal, one of the most picturesque spots in town. The house specialty is *picanha na chapa* (sizzling grilled steak).

Restaurante Galápagos SEAFOOD **$$$**
(☎22 2643-4097; Praça São Benedito 11; mains R$49-100; ⊙6pm-midnight Mon-Fri, from noon Sat & Sun) Directly opposite the picturesque 17th-century white church on Cabo Frio's most historic square, this eatery in a colonial house serves sophisticated international fare. The inventive offerings range from grilled fish with rosemary and passion fruit, to risotto with shrimp and asparagus or lobster and saffron, to lamb goulash with couscous, to beef with mashed potatoes and Madeira sauce.

Information

Bradesco (Av Assunção 904) One of several ATMs on this downtown thoroughfare.

Cabo Frio's tourist office has branches at the **bus station** (☎22 99888-8554; www.facebook.com/cabofriotur; Rodoviária Alex Novelino, Av Júlia Kubitschek; ⊙9am-5pm Mon-Fri) and along the **Canal do Itajuru** (☎22 2645-2505; Blvd Canal 319; ⊙9am-5pm Mon-Fri).

Getting There & Away

AIR

From **Aeroporto Internacional de Cabo Frio** (☎22 2647-9500; www.cabofrioairport.com.br; Estrada Velha de Arraial do Cabo), 12km southwest of town, **Azul** (☎22 2647-9515; www.voeazul.com.br) offers nonstop flights to Belo Horizonte (weekends only).

BUS

The **bus station** (Av Júlia Kubitschek) is 2km west of the center. **Viação 1001** (☎22 2643-3778; www.autoviacao1001.com.br) has services to Rio departing half-hourly from early morning to late evening (R$52 to R$66, 2¾ hours).

Bus B150, operated by **Salineira** (☎22 2647-8200; www.salineira.com.br), runs to Arraial do Cabo (R$5.55, 30 minutes) every 15 minutes from the bus stop just to your left as you exit the bus station. For Búzios, catch any Salineira bus marked 'Búzios' from the stop across the road (R$5.55, 45 minutes).

Búzios

☎0XX22 / POP 32,260

Beautiful Búzios sits on a jutting peninsula scalloped by 17 beaches. A simple fishing village until the early '60s, when it was 'discovered' by Brigitte Bardot and her Brazilian boyfriend, it's now one of Brazil's most upscale and animated seaside resorts, littered with boutiques, fine restaurants, villas, bars and posh pousadas. The Mediterranean touch introduced by the Portuguese has not been lost – indeed, the narrow cobblestone streets and picturesque waterfront contribute to Búzios' image as Brazil's St Tropez.

Búzios is not a single town but rather three settlements on the same peninsula – Ossos, Manguinhos and Armação de Búzios. Ossos (Bones), at the northern tip of the peninsula, is the oldest and most attractive. It has a pretty harbor and yacht club, plus a few hotels and bars. Manguinhos, on the isthmus, is the most commercial. Armação, in between, is the heart of town, with tourist amenities.

Sights & Activities

The biggest draws in Búzios are the natural setting plus its array of opportunities for relaxation, nightlife, shopping and ocean sports.

Cobblestoned **Rua das Pedras** (Map p166; Rua das Pedras) is Búzios' main venue for shopping, dining and evening entertainment, overflowing with revelers on weekend nights. Its eastward continuation, **Orla Bardot** (Map p166), is a delightful oceanfront promenade linking the two oldest and most picturesque sections of town (Armação and Ossos). As you walk along the beachfront, you'll notice several statues by sculptor Christina Motta, including representations of **Brigitte Bardot** (Map p166) and former Brazilian **president Juscelino Kubitschek** (Map p166), plus some remarkably realistic-looking **fishermen** (Map p166) hauling in their nets.

Búzios

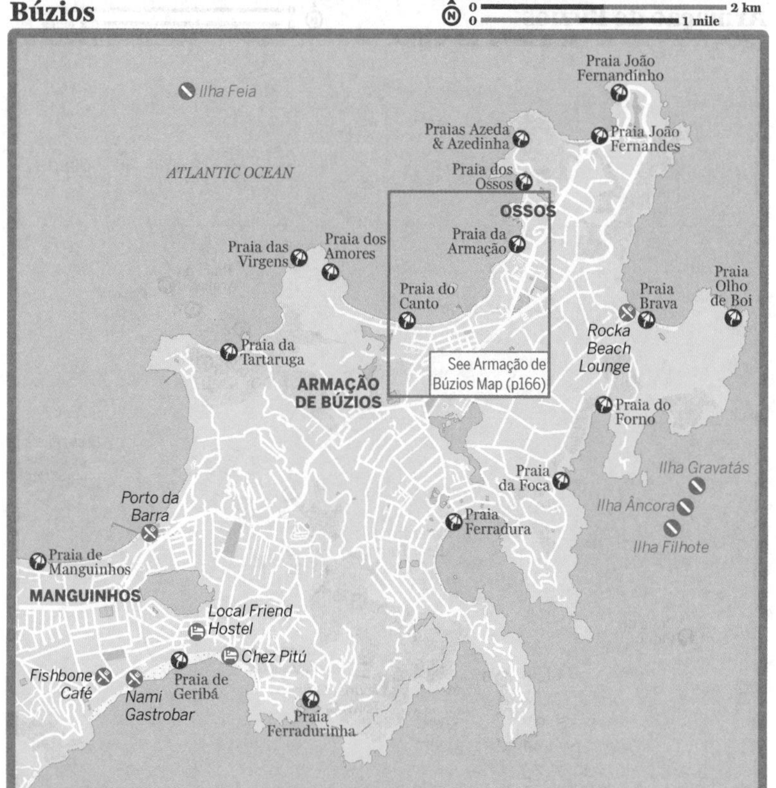

Several operators offer tours to local beaches and islands. If you'd rather explore at your own pace, Búzios' *taxis marítimos* (water taxis) are an attractive alternative, charging R$10 to R$30 per person to individual beaches around the peninsula; rates are posted on a board at Armação's **water taxi & boat tour dock** and around town.

Tour Shop Búzios TOURS
(Map p166; ☎22 2623-4733; www.tourshop.com.br; Orla Bardot 550; tours from R$60) This agency runs the Búzios Trolley, an open-sided bus that visits 12 of the peninsula's beaches daily. Additional offerings include snorkeling, diving and rafting tours, along with excursions by schooner and glass-bottomed catamaran.

Búzios Divers DIVING
(Map p166; ☎22 2623-0670; www.buziosdivers.com.br; Rua das Pedras 232; single-tank dive from R$160) Offers a full range of diving courses and excursions to dive sites around Búzios.

Sleeping

Búzios offers hundreds of places to stay, ranging from hostels to top-end hotels. Lodgings in Armação dos Búzios and along the Orla Bardot waterfront towards Ossos offer the easiest walking access to restaurants and nightlife, but there are plenty of other options at beaches around the peninsula, including Praia de Geribá and Praia João Fernandes. Búzios largely caters to couples, so hotel stays can be pricey for solo travelers. High season runs December through March, plus July.

★**Bamboo Búzios Hostel** HOSTEL $
(Map p166; ☎22 98835-0085, 22 2620-8085; www.bamboobuzioshostel.com; Rua das Pedras 25; dm R$85-120, d R$260-400; ❄@📶) Boasting a seaside perch in the thick of the Rua das Pedras nightlife zone, Búzios' most centrally located hostel offers four- to 13-bed dorms complemented by a dozen-plus private doubles and family rooms. The best units enjoy gorgeous full-on ocean views, as do the

Armação de Búzios

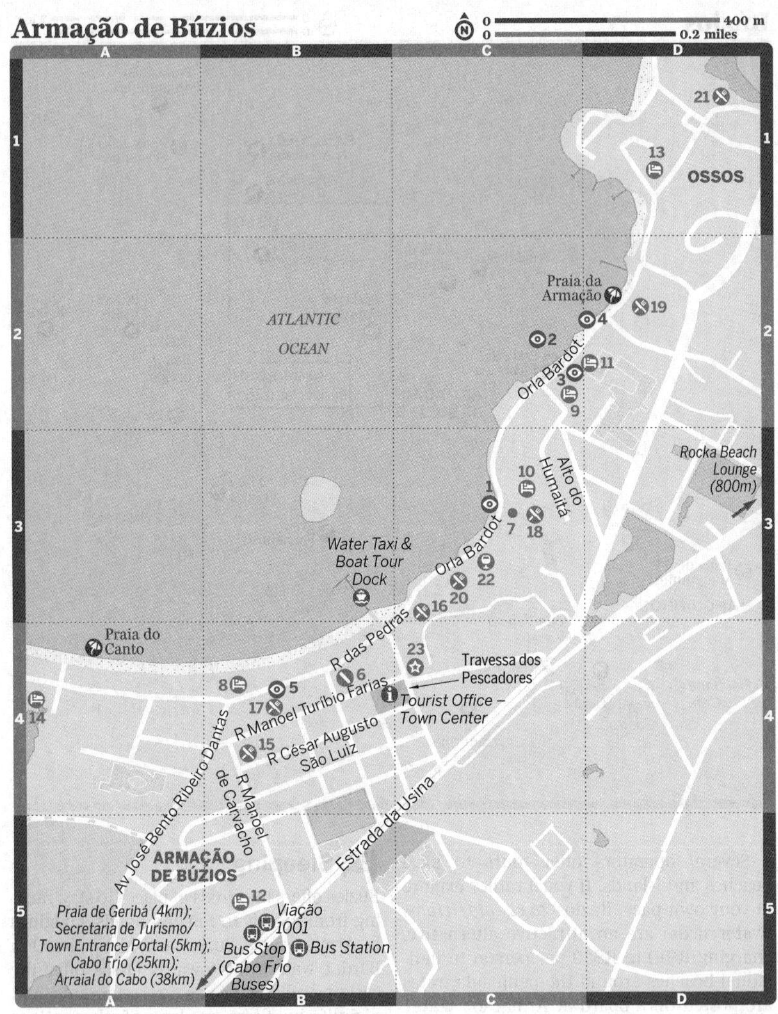

light-filled breakfast area and the deck chairs and lounging bed on the waterfront terrace.

★The Search House Búzios HOSTEL $
(☎22 2623-6628; www.thesearchhouse.com.br/buzios; Vila das Aroeiras 221, Manguinhos; dm R$60-75, d R$175-350; ❄📶) With clean white air-conditioned dorms and doubles, comfortable beds, and a dreamy backyard opening directly onto Manguinhos beach, the Search House is Búzios' best new hostel in years. The on-site bar, movie room, ping-pong table, beachside lounge chairs and sports equipment (surfboards, SUP and kite surfing gear) create a seductively festive atmosphere.

Local Friend Hostel HOSTEL $
(Map p165; ☎22 2623-0614; www.facebook.com/localfriendhostel; Av Geribá 585; dm R$50-55, d/tr/q R$160/200/270; 📶) The name says it all at this homey hostel one block from Geribá beach. After an eight-year round-the-world trip (New Zealand, Europe, United States), Rio Grande do Sul–born chef Eduardo has brought his infectious gaucho hospitality to Búzios, inviting guests to disconnect from technology and enjoy human interaction: surfing, kayaking, playing board games or joining one of his cooking classes (R$70 including dinner).

Armação de Búzios

Sights
1 Brigitte Bardot Statue C3
2 Fishermen Statues C2
3 Orla Bardot C2
4 President Juscelino Kubitschek Statue D2
5 Rua das Pedras B4

Activities, Courses & Tours
6 Búzios Divers B4
7 Tour Shop Búzios C3

Sleeping
8 Bamboo Búzios Hostel B4
9 Casa Búzios C2
10 Casas Brancas C3
11 Cesar Apartamentos D2
12 Che Lagarto Hostel B5
13 L'Escale D1
14 Villa Balthazar A4

Eating
15 Bananaland B4
16 Bar do Zé C3
17 Chez Michou Crêperie B4
18 Mistico C3
19 O Barco D2
20 Salt C3
21 Sukão D1

Drinking & Nightlife
22 Privilège C3

Entertainment
23 Gran Cine Bardot C4

Cesar Apartamentos APARTMENT **$$**
(Map p166; 22 2623-1349; www.cesarbuzios.com; Orla Bardot 974; r R$180-200, apt R$350-380, apt with sea view R$400-420;) One of Búzios' rare beachfront bargains, this family-run cluster of three modest rooms and seven more spacious upstairs apartments sleeping up to four boasts a prime Orla Bardot location. Budget-minded travelers will appreciate the motel-like cheapies downstairs; those with extra reais to spend should reserve ahead for one of the two oceanfront quads with private terraces directly overlooking the water.

★**Casa Búzios** POUSADA **$$$**
(Map p166; 22 2623-4885; www.pousadacasabuzios.com; Alto do Humaitá 1; r R$650,d/tr/q ste R$750/975/1200; P) In a dream location just off Orla Bardot, this 1940s-vintage hillside home is now a sweet pousada, offering six spacious and unique suites with high ceilings, wood and tile floors, comfortable beds and L'Occitane toiletries. Generous breakfasts are served on the poolside patio, which affords picturesque views of boats bobbing in the harbor below. There's free enclosed parking out back. Larger suites accommodate up to four people.

Villa Balthazar POUSADA **$$$**
(Map p166; 22 2623-6680; www.villabalthazar.com.br; Maria Joaquina 375; d R$495-560;) On a peaceful residential lane three blocks from Rua das Pedras, this stylish five-room pousada is a labor of love for Swedish owners Petra and Felix, who have filled the place with family heirlooms and homey touches inspired by their own world travels. Guests love the in-room DVD players, swimming pool and delicious homemade breakfasts.

L'Escale POUSADA **$$$**
(Map p166; 22 2623-2816; www.pousadalescale.com; Travessa Santana 14, Ossos; r from R$350, with sea view R$450; closed May-Sep;) Book ahead for one of the three ocean-facing rooms with terraces and hammocks at this sweet, petite Brazilian-Argentine-run pousada with a divine beachfront location in relaxed Ossos. Owners Javier and Adriana also operate the eponymous restaurant downstairs serving seafood and fresh pasta.

Casas Brancas BOUTIQUE HOTEL **$$$**
(Map p166; 22 2623-1458; www.casasbrancas.com.br; Alto do Humaitá 10; r without/with sea view from R$1315/1675, ste from R$2760; @) If you're honeymooning or just won the lottery, head straight for this top-end place on Alto do Humaitá hill. Pampering touches include stupendous ocean views from the poolside terrace (and all but the most basic rooms), massages in the on-site spa, free yoga and tai-chi classes and a choice of two restaurants: upscale Atlântico and chilled-out Deck Pizzeria.

Prices quoted here are official high-season rates; look online for better deals.

Chez Pitú POUSADA **$$$**
(Map p165; 22 2623-6460; www.chezpitu.com.br; Av Geribá 10; r from R$405, with sea view R$505-670; @) Rooms are small and somewhat dated, but nothing can diminish the Geribá beachfront location of this colorful pousada, decorated with mosaics and brightly painted French doors. The breakfast room, poolside bar and lounge chair-equipped front deck all offer tantalizing views of the ocean a few feet away. The nicest upstairs rooms sport small verandas tailor-made for watching Búzios' best sunset.

DON'T MISS

BÚZIOS' BEACHES

With nearly two dozen beaches to choose from in and around Búzios, it's hard to know where to start. In general, the southern beaches are trickier to get to, but they're prettier and have better surf. The northern beaches are more sheltered and closer to the towns.

Going counterclockwise from south of Manguinhos, the first beaches are **Geribá** and **Ferradurinha** (Little Horseshoe). These are beautiful beaches with good surf. Next on the coast is **Ferradura**, which is large enough for windsurfing, followed by **Praia da Foca** and **Praia do Forno**, which have colder water than the other beaches. **Praia Olho de Boi** (Bull's Eye) is the area's only nude beach. It's reached by a little trail from the long, clean beach of **Praia Brava**.

On the north side of the peninsula, both **João Fernandinho** and **João Fernandes** are good for snorkeling, as are **Azedinha** and **Azeda**, reached by a short trail from Ossos. **Praia dos Ossos**, **Praia da Armação**, **Praia do Canto** and **Praia dos Amores** are lovely to look at, but a bit public and not so nice for lounging on. **Praia das Virgens** and **Praia da Tartaruga** are quiet and pretty. **Praia de Manguinhos** is another town beach further west. Offshore, the islands of **Âncora**, **Gravatás**, **Filhote** and **Feia** are especially good diving destinations.

Eating

Most of the better restaurants are in or near Armação. For good seafood at more affordable prices, check out the little thatched-roof places on Ferradura and João Fernandes beaches.

Three kilometers west of town at Manguinhos, the **Porto da Barra** (Map p165; www.portodabarrabuzios.com.br; Av José Bento Ribeiro Dantas 2900, Manguinhos; ⏰10am-midnight) complex features over a dozen bars and restaurants spread out along a tree-fringed waterfront boardwalk; it's a great place for a snack and a drink at sunset.

Sukão SANDWICHES $

(Map p166; Praça dos Ossos; sandwiches R$9-29, juices R$12-16; ⏰11am-11pm) Half-liter goblets of fresh fruit juice and sandwiches piled onto four varieties of homemade bread make this Ossos corner eatery a tempting pit stop en route to the beach at Azeda or Azedinha.

Chez Michou Crêperie CRÊPES $

(Map p166; ☎22 2623-2169; www.chezmichou.com.br; Rua das Pedras 90; crepes R$19-32; ⏰noon-late Thu-Tue, from 5pm Wed) Crowds flock here not only for the sweet and savory crepes, but also for mixed drinks at the outdoor bar, sports events on the big screen TVs and the weekend DJ mixes (from 9pm).

★ **O Barco** SEAFOOD $$

(Map p166; ☎22 2629-8307; Orla Bardot 1054; mains per person R$28-45; ⏰11am-11pm Wed-Mon) This waterfront joint stakes its reputation on well-made, reasonably priced fish dishes – from fried fish with rice and salad to full-on seafood stews. Eight tables on a cute little terrace plus a few extra sidewalk seats offer excellent people-watching and ocean views. Solo diners will appreciate the menu's wealth of *pratos individuais* (individual dishes).

Bananaland BUFFET $$

(Map p166; www.facebook.com/bananalandbuzios; Manoel Turíbio de Farias 50; per kg R$94; ⏰11am-11pm) Standing out among the several deluxe self-serve eateries on this street for its wide variety of offerings, Bananaland offers something for everyone. Temptations range from *bobó de camarão*, to steak with mushrooms and Madeira wine sauce, to an enticing array of salads.

★ **Belli Belli** GASTROPUB $$$

(☎22 99871-4056; www.bellibelligastrobar.com; Porto da Barra, Av José Bento Ribeiro Dantas; mains per person R$46-99; ⏰1pm-midnight Tue-Sun) There's no more blissful spot to catch the sunset than the outdoor deck of this gastrobar in the waterfront Porto da Barra complex. While away the early evening over mixed drinks and Brazilian tapas like *bolinhos de baroa* (shrimp-stuffed potato croquettes), or linger over a late dinner of seafood, pasta and salad, soothed by gentle breezes off nearby Manguinhos beach.

★ **Rocka Beach Lounge** SEAFOOD $$$

(Map p165; ☎22 2623-6159; www.rockafish.com.br; Praia Brava; mains R$79-86; ⏰9:30am-6:30pm daily mid-Dec–mid-Mar, to 5pm Wed-Mon rest of year) People-watching and creative cuisine are the twin draws at this seafood eatery perched directly above Praia Brava. Rocka is a full-day event for most visitors, who linger long after lunchtime on the lounge chairs and beds spread out on terraced hillsides overlooking the beach. Reserve ahead for weekends.

★Mistico MEDITERRANEAN $$$
(Map p166; ☎22 2623-9046; www.abracadabrapousada.com.br; Alto do Humaitá 13; mains R$69-130; ⏲1-11pm) Perched high on the hill between Armação and Ossos, Mistico's intimate glass-walled dining room enjoys one of Búzios' finest panoramic sea views. The menu abounds in revelatory seafood dishes, from homemade squid ink gnocchi with saffron cream and grilled veggies to the *mix al mare:* Provençal-style octopus, broiled salmon, tuna tataki, lobster buns and crispy octopus balls.

Salt BRAZILIAN $$$
(Map p166; ☎22 2623-6769; www.restaurantesalt.com.br; Orla Bardot 468; mains per person R$49-82; ⏲5pm-midnight Tue-Fri, 1pm-1am Sat, 1-10pm Sun) Directly opposite the Orla Bardot boardwalk, Salt's sea-facing front terrace makes a romantic dinner spot, with a wide-ranging mixed drinks menu and a host of seafood specials, from ceviche to *moqueca* (Bahian fish and shrimp stew) to Thai curries. Save room for decadent desserts like crunchy fried bananas with passion fruit sauce and vanilla ice cream.

Nami Gastrobar JAPANESE, FUSION $$$
(Map p165; ☎22 2623-6637; www.namigastrobar.com.br; Gelbert Perissé 1023; small plates R$42-95, mains R$60-170; ⏲6-11pm Wed-Fri, 1-11pm Sat, 1-5pm Sun) Near Geribá beach, this restaurant fuses traditional Japanese cuisine with Peruvian, Mexican and other influences to create a wonderfully eclectic international dining experience. Fresh seafood takes center stage in citrusy ceviche, crunchy wasabi-salmon tacos, tempura shrimp and miso-marinated black cod, but meatier delights also abound, including delicate slices of grilled beef with sesame seeds or spare ribs with roasted corn.

Fishbone Café SANDWICHES, BAR $$$
(Map p165; ☎22 2623-7348; www.facebook.com/fishbonebuzios; Gerbert Périssé 1196, Praia de Geribá; sandwiches R$30-40, mains R$50-85; ⏲10am-sunset) At this laid-back beach club on Praia de Geribá, the menu features everything from sandwiches to salads to a delicious *caldeirada de frutos do mar* (seafood stew) – but plenty of people come just to drink, catch some rays and listen to tunes on the deck.

Bar do Zé MEDITERRANEAN $$$
(Map p166; ☎22 2623-4986; Orla Bardot 382; mains R$55-120; ⏲6pm-late Mon, 1pm-late Tue-Sun) This classy restaurant with an open-air deck facing Orla Bardot is famous for its well-mixed drinks (classic caipirinhas, freshly minted mojitos), served alongside grilled fish, risotto, steak and seafood.

Drinking & Entertainment

A slew of bars and clubs lines Rua das Pedras and Orla Bardot, with the action continuing well past midnight.

Privilège CLUB
(Map p166; ☎22 98819-0465; www.privilegebrasil.com/casa/buzios; Orla Bardot 550; ⏲11pm-late Thu-Sun) The star of Búzios' late-night scene is this sleek nightclub with two dance floors and four bars on the Orla Bardot waterfront.

Gran Cine Bardot CINEMA
(Map p166; ☎22 2623-1298; www.facebook.com/grancinebardot.buzios; Travessa dos Pescadores 88; admission R$30-32; ⏲Thu-Sun) Shows movies on weekend nights, including some in English with Portuguese subtitles. The adjacent cafe is a nice spot for snacks, coffee or caipirinhas before or after the show.

Information

Búzios' two tourist offices – at the **town entrance portal** (☎22 2623-4254; www.buzios.rj.gov.br/informacoes_turisticas; Av José Bento Ribeiro Dantas; ⏲8am-8pm) and on the **main square** (Map p166; ☎22 2623-2099; Praça Santos Dumont, Armação; ⏲8am-8pm) in Armação – distribute city maps and hotel information.

Bradesco (Av José Bento Ribeiro Dantas 254) One of several downtown ATMs.

Hospital Municipal Rodolpho Perissé (☎22 2623-7959; Estrada Búzios-Cabo Frio) Just outside the town entrance portal along the road to Cabo Frio.

Getting There & Away

The Búzios **bus station** (Map p166; Estrada da Usina 444) is a simple covered bus stop with no building attached, five blocks south of the Armação waterfront. **Viação 1001** (Map p166; ☎22 2623-2050; www.autoviacao1001.com.br; Estrada da Usina) runs buses from Búzios to Rio's Novo Rio bus station (R$70, 2¾ hours, eight daily between 6am and 8:30pm); the same company offers direct buses to Rio's Galeão airport (R$72, six daily). The ticket office is on the northern side of Estrada da Usina, diagonally across from the Rio-bound bus stop.

Passengers coming direct from Rio's airport to Búzios have to pay a small surcharge (tickets purchased at Galeão cost R$86) but are entitled to a free, convenient Viação 1001 shuttle transfer from the bus stop to any hotel in town.

Municipal buses between Búzios and Cabo Frio (R$5.55; 45 minutes) travel along Av José Bento Ribeiro Dantas and Estrada da Usina; there's a convenient **stop** (Map p166; Estrada da Usina) just outside the Viação 1001 ticket office. Buy tickets on board the bus.

Minas Gerais & Espírito Santo

POP 25 MILLION

Includes ➡

Belo Horizonte 171
Ouro Preto 182
São João del Rei 193
Tiradentes 196
Diamantina 204
Serro & Around 208
Parque Nacional da Serra Do Cipó 209
Parque Natural do Caraça 210
Parque Nacional de Caparaó 211
Itaúnas 215

Best Places to Eat

- ➡ Glouton (p179)
- ➡ Casa do Ouvidor (p188)
- ➡ Empório Santo Antônio (p200)
- ➡ Kiko & Kika (p204)

Best Places to Stay

- ➡ Pousada Santuário do Caraça (p211)
- ➡ Villa Magnolia Pousada (p194)
- ➡ Pousada do Capão (p208)
- ➡ Mandala das Águas (p204)

Why Go?

For those seeking a tangible sense of Brazilian history, no state compares with Minas Gerais. The cobblestone streets and splendid baroque monuments of Minas' colonial mining towns have seen it all, from the horrors of slavery to the fervor of Brazil's 18th-century independence movement.

Minas' natural wonders are equally alluring. The Serra do Espinhaço, a Unesco Biosphere Reserve running the length of the state, is just one of many refuges providing critical habitat for endangered species as well as exhilarating outdoor-recreation opportunities. Add to this the cosmopolitan charms of Belo Horizonte, the fabulous flavors of Minas' wood-fired cuisine, the intoxicating effects of Brazil's best *cachaça* (sugarcane alcohol) and the locals' legendary hospitality, and it's hard to resist Minas' seductive spell.

Neighboring Espírito Santo offers an attractive off-the-beaten-track counterpoint, with pretty beach and mountain scenery and some of Brazil's tastiest seafood.

When to Go

Belo Horizonte

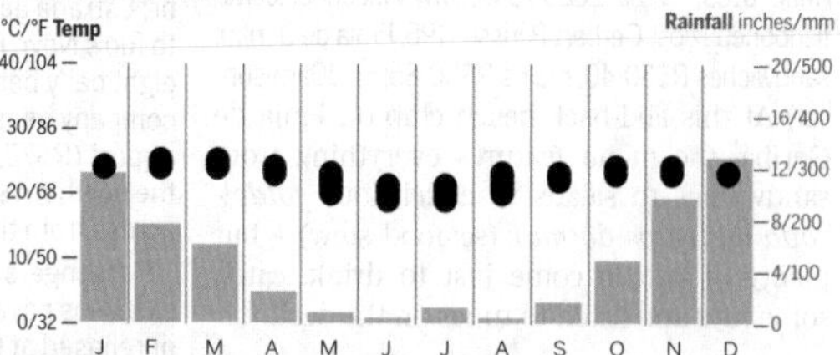

Mar & Apr Witness Brazil's most colorful Easter Week processions in Ouro Preto and São João del Rei.

Apr & May Festivals celebrate independence hero Tiradentes and Belo Horizonte's best bar food.

Jun–Aug Enjoy cool, dry weather and see cachaça production during the sugar harvest season.

History

In the late 17th century, gold was discovered in Minas Gerais, and Brazilians began flocking to Minas, while Portuguese flocked to Brazil. Slaves were brought from Bahia's sugar fields and the savannas of Angola, and, until the last quarter of the 18th century, Minas' mines were producing half the world's gold.

Minas set the gold-rush standard – crazy, wild and violent – more than 100 years before the Californian and Australian gold rushes. Licentious living, disease and famine were rampant. Much of the gold wealth was siphoned off to Portugal; among the few lasting benefits to Brazil was the creation of the beautiful, church-clad mining cities that still dot Minas' hills. Nowadays, the Estrada Real (Royal Road) that connected these *cidades históricas* has become the state's most popular tourist route.

Colonized in the 16th century, Espírito Santo became an armed region to prevent gold from being smuggled out of Minas Gerais state. Coffee plantations, the prime source of income up until the 1960s, have since been superseded by mining and shipping. The capital city, Vitória, serves as headquarters to Garoto, Brazil's famous chocolate, as well as several chemical and agribusiness concerns.

Getting There & Around

Minas' capital city Belo Horizonte is the arrival point for most travelers. Flights from Brazil and beyond land at the city's international airport, Aeroporto Internacional de Belo Horizonte, while the smaller Pampulha airport handles a few domestic flights. Belo's downtown bus station serves as a hub for long-distance ground transport. Direct buses from Rio and São Paulo also serve some of Minas' historic towns.

Vitória is Espírito Santo's transport hub. Eurico Salles Airport, with its gleaming new terminal, offers service to major cities throughout Brazil. Frequent long-distance buses connect Vitória to Rio, São Paulo and cities in neighboring Minas Gerais and Bahia, while Brazil's longest-distance passenger train offers a unique way to travel between Vitória and Belo Horizonte.

MINAS GERAIS

POP 21 MILLION

Renowned for its friendly people, wonderful food, spectacular natural setting and beautiful historical architecture, Minas Gerais is one of Brazil's most appealing and accessible states.

In the early 18th century, colonial towns like Ouro Preto, Mariana and Diamantina sprang up along the gold road linking Minas to the coast. Built on Minas' mineral wealth, they soon developed a cultural and architectural wealth all their own. Minas was the birthplace of Tiradentes, leader of Brazil's first great independence movement, and Aleijadinho, the country's finest baroque artist.

Complementing Minas' historical treasures are the state's magnificent scenery and wildlife, with a host of state and national parks providing critical habitat for endangered species such as the maned wolf and northern *muriqui*.

Belo Horizonte

0XX31 / POP 2.5 MILLION / ELEV 858M

Known to locals as Beagá (pronounced 'bay-ah-gah', Portuguese for BH), Belo Horizonte was named for its beautiful view of nearby mountains. Urban sprawl may make it a little more challenging to appreciate the natural setting nowadays, but Brazil's third-largest city still has considerable charm.

Walk down the buzzing cosmopolitan streets of the Savassi neighborhood on a Saturday evening, eat at one of the fine restaurants in Lourdes, stroll through the densely packed stalls at Mercado Central, attend the exuberant weekend street fair alongside leafy Parque Central, take in a concert at the Palácio das Artes, or visit the Inhotim art museum west of the city, and you'll see that Belo Horizonte has countless dimensions. Add to all this the friendly, welcoming nature of Beagá's people and you've got a winning combination. Stick around a few days – you might grow fond of the place.

History

In the late 19th century, as the Brazilian Republic was coming into its own, *mineiros* (residents of Minas Gerais state) began planning a new capital to replace hard-to-reach Ouro Preto, which, as a symbol of colonialism, had fallen out of favor. Belo Horizonte sprang up as an art nouveau city, influenced by the spirit of *Ordem e Progresso* (Order and Progress), the new slogan on the Brazilian flag.

In the 1940s, Belo expanded northward. Then-mayor Juscelino Kubitschek commissioned young architectural-school graduate Oscar Niemeyer to design the brand-new Pampulha district. These two men are largely responsible for the city's wide avenues, large lakes, parks and jutting skyline.

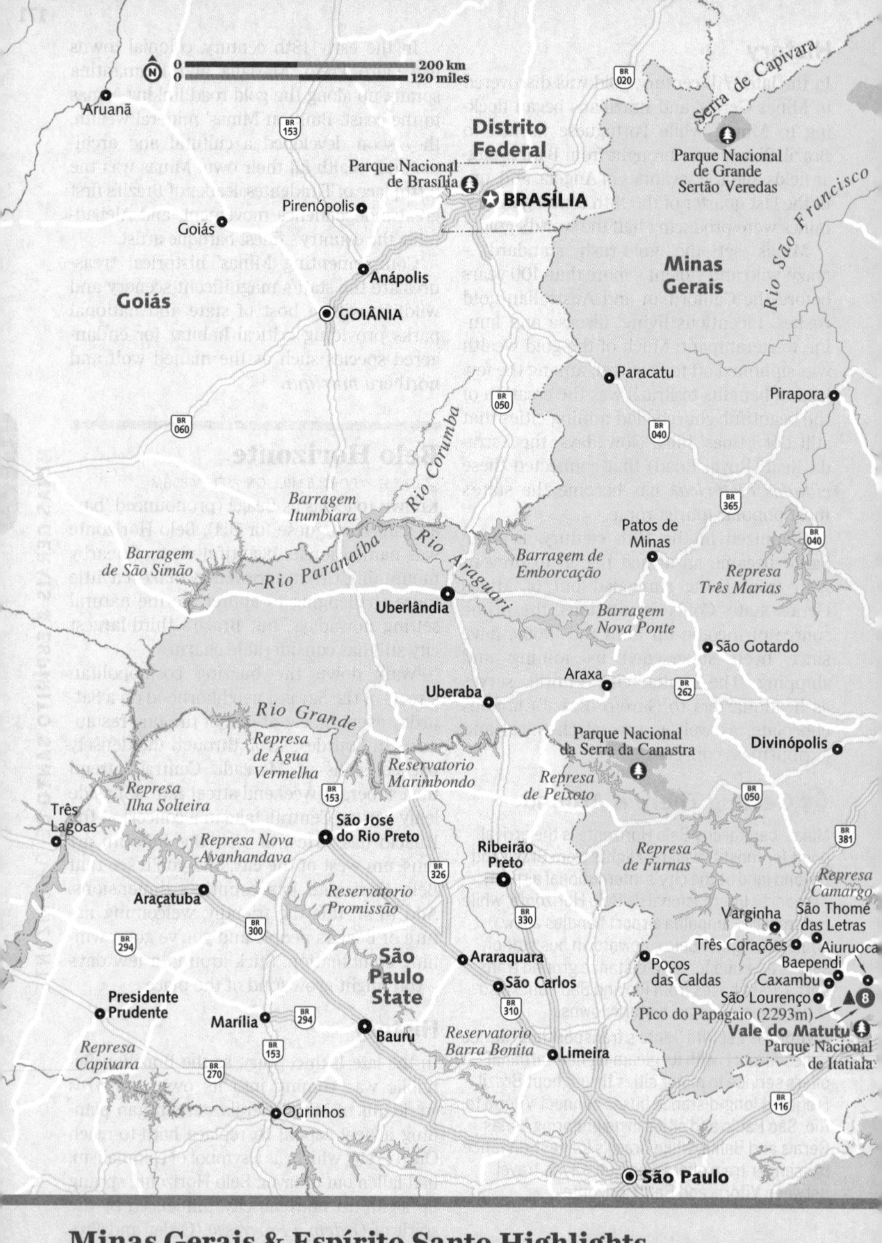

Minas Gerais & Espírito Santo Highlights

❶ **Instituto de Arte Contemporânea Inhotim** (p175) Exploring two dozen galleries of contemporary art spread out in exquisite tropical gardens.

❷ **Ouro Preto** (p182) Wandering among the picturesque cobblestone streets and baroque architectural treasures of Minas' one-time capital.

❸ **Parque Nacional de Caparaó** (p211) Climbing Brazil's third-tallest mountain, the 2892m Pico da Bandeira.

❹ **Belo Horizonte** (p171) Feasting on Minas' finest

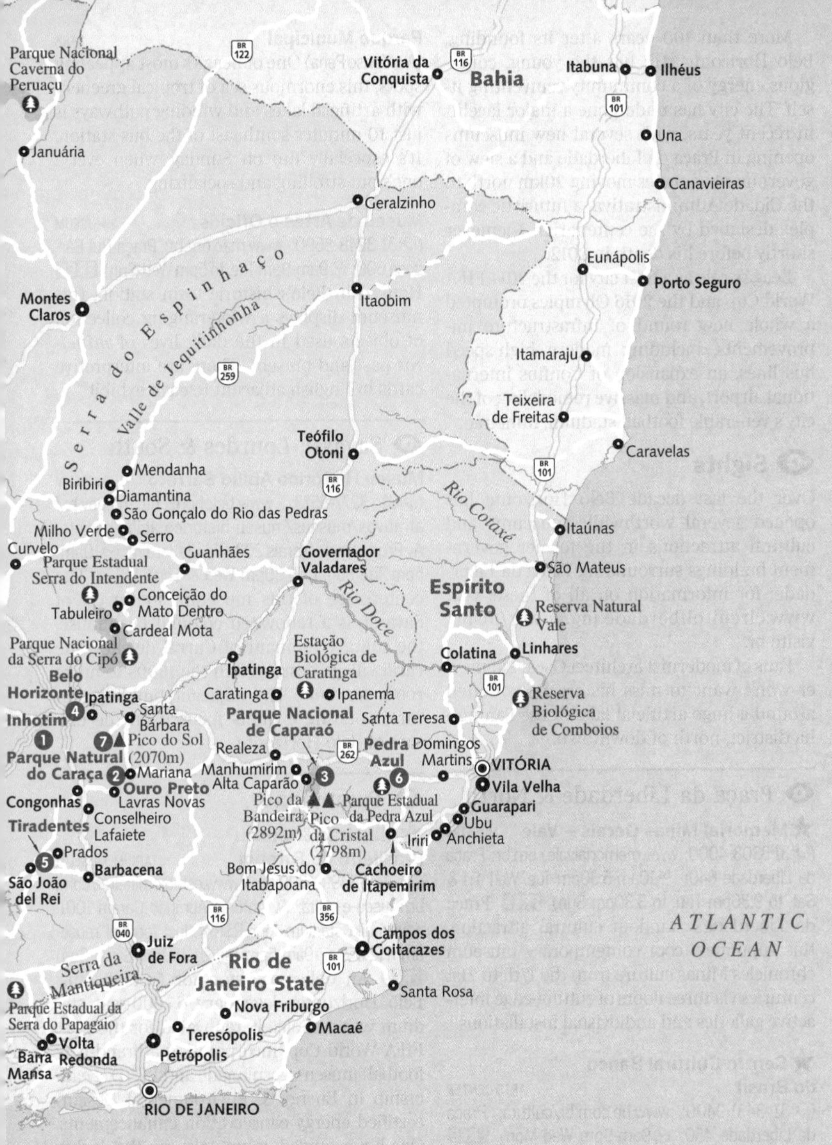

food and touring the famous Mineirão football stadium.

5 Tiradentes (p196) Catching a concert on the 18th-century church organ and hopping aboard a 19th-century steam train.

6 Pedra Azul (p220) Holding on to that rope as you traverse the steep granite base of Espírito Santo's most spectacular rock formation.

7 Parque Natural do Caraça (p210) Waiting by starlight for the maned wolves to appear at this remote mountain sanctuary.

8 Vale do Matutu (p203) Getting off the beaten track on the scenic mountain trails of this end-of-the-road valley.

More than 100 years after its founding, Belo Horizonte still has the young, contagious energy of a community reinventing itself. The city has undergone a major facelift in recent years, with several new museums opening in Praça da Liberdade and a slew of government agencies moving 20km north to the Cidade Administrativa, a futuristic complex designed by the centenarian Niemeyer shortly before his death in 2012.

Beagá's role as a host city for the 2014 FIFA World Cup and the 2016 Olympics prompted a whole new round of infrastructure improvements, including modern high-speed bus lines, an expansion of Confins international airport, and massive remodeling of the city's venerable football stadium, Mineirão.

Sights

Over the last decade Belo Horizonte has opened several worthwhile museums and cultural attractions in the former government buildings surrounding Praça da Liberdade; for information on all of these, visit www.circuitoliberdade.mg.gov.br/pt-br/visite-br.

Fans of modernist architect Oscar Niemeyer won't want to miss his creations dotted around a huge artificial lake in the Pampulha district, north of downtown.

Praça da Liberdade & North

★Memorial Minas Gerais – Vale MUSEUM

(☎31 3308-4000; www.memorialvale.com.br; Praça da Liberdade 640; ⏲10am-5:30pm Tue, Wed, Fri & Sat, to 9:30pm Thu, to 3:30pm Sun) FREE Praça da Liberdade's standout cultural attraction, this supremely cool contemporary museum chronicles Minas culture from the 17th to 21st centuries via three floors of cutting-edge interactive galleries and audiovisual installations.

★Centro Cultural Banco do Brasil ARTS CENTER

(☎31 3431-9400; www.bb.com.br/cultura; Praça da Liberdade 450; ⏲9am-9pm Wed-Mon) FREE Inaugurated in late 2013, this magnificent palace on Praça da LIberdade is one of Belo Horizonte's cultural gems. The vast 3rd-floor gallery hosts special exhibitions that rotate every couple of months, while the downstairs is dedicated to free or low-cost arts events including film, theater and dance; pick up a schedule on-site. The interior courtyard makes for a pleasant break any time of day with its cafes, stained-glass windows and retractable roof.

Parque Municipal PARK

(Av Afonso Pena) One of Beagá's most appealing spots, this enormous sea of tropical greenery with artificial lakes and winding pathways is just 10 minutes southeast of the bus station. It's especially fun on Sunday, when everyone's out strolling and socializing.

Museu de Artes e Ofícios MUSEUM

(☎31 3248-8600; www.mao.org.br; Praça Rui Barbosa 600; ⏲9am-9pm Tue, to 5pm Wed-Sun) FREE Housed in Belo's historic train station, this museum displays a wide-ranging collection of objects used in the daily lives of *mineiros* past and present. There are interpretive cards in English adjacent to each exhibit.

Savassi, Lourdes & South

Museu Histórico Abílio Barreto MUSEUM

(☎31 3277-8573; www.belohorizonte.mg.gov.br/atrativos/museus/museu-historico-abilio-barreto; Av Prudente de Morais 202, Cidade Jardim; ⏲10am-5pm Tue-Sun, to 6:30pm Wed & Thu) FREE The centerpiece of this museum, southwest of Savassi, is a renovated colonial farmhouse, the solitary remnant of Curral del Rey, the rural village destroyed in the 1890s to make room for Belo. The adjacent building features rotating exhibits focused on the culture of Belo Horizonte.

Pampulha

★Mineirão & Museu Brasileiro do Futebol STADIUM, MUSEUM

(☎31 3499-4300; www.estadiomineirao.com.br/museu-e-visita; Av Antônio Abrahão Caram 1001; adult/child stadium tour R$8/4, incl football museum R$14/7; ⏲9am-5pm Tue-Fri, to 1pm Sat & Sun) FREE An obligatory stop for football fans, Belo Horizonte's legendary 65,000-seat stadium was completely renovated for the 2014 FIFA World Cup, incorporating a brand-new football museum, esplanade and LEED (Leadership in Energy & Environmental Design) certified energy conservation enhancements. One-hour guided tours take in the locker rooms, showers, press room, stands and revamped playing field, with occasional wistful comments about Brazil's heartbreaking 7-1 World Cup loss to Germany here. Combined tickets include a self-guided museum visit, with exhibits covering the stadium's construction, famous games and players, and football history.

The stadium and museum are 10km north of Centro in Pampulha; take bus 5106 (R$3.40, 30 minutes) from Praça da Liberdade.

DON'T MISS

THE WORLD-CLASS MUSEUM IN BELO'S BACK YARD

The world's largest open-air contemporary art museum, and greater Belo Horizonte's standout attraction, **Instituto de Arte Contemporânea Inhotim** (☎31 3571-9700; www.inhotim.org.br; Rua B, 20, Brumadinho; adult/reduced R$44/22, Wed free; ⏲9:30am-4:30pm Tue-Fri, to 5:30pm Sat & Sun) is a sprawling, world-class complex of gardens dotted with 23 modern art galleries and numerous outdoor sculptures lies 50km west of the city, near Brumadinho. Much of the international artwork on view is monumental in size, with galleries custom-built to display it. The constantly expanding gardens has over 4000 different species of plants (including one of the world's most extensive collections of palm trees) and lakes with swans.

You can wander at will, or attend daily scheduled programs led by guides trained in visual arts and natural science. Ten on-site eateries serve everything from hot dogs to gourmet international fare. Wednesday's a great day to visit, as the museum is free; weekends can get crowded, but offer a wider range of guided tours.

From Tuesday through Sunday **Saritur** (☎31 3479-4300; www.saritur.com.br) runs direct buses (R$74 round trip, 1½ hours each way) from Belo Horizonte to Inhotim at 8:15am, returning at 4:30pm weekdays, 5:30pm Saturday and Sunday.

Igreja de São Francisco de Assis CHURCH
(Av Otacílio Negrão de Lima 3000; admission R$2; ⏲8am-5pm Tue-Sat, 9am-2pm Sun) On the banks of Pampulha's artificial lake, Niemayer's striking modernist church, with interior tiles and paintings by Portinari, is an architectural delight.

Casa do Baile MUSEUM
(☎31 3277-7443; www.facebook.com/casadobaile.bh; Av Otacílio Negrão de Lima 751; ⏲9am-5pm Tue-Sun) FREE This former dance hall on Pampulha's lakeshore, designed by Oscar Niemeyer with grounds by landscape architect Burle Marx, now holds all types of temporary art exhibits.

Museu de Arte da Pampulha MUSEUM
(☎31 3277-7946; www.facebook.com/map.fmc; Av Otacílio Negrão de Lima 16585; ⏲9am-6pm Tue-Sun) FREE This art museum, with its cute garden designed by landscape architect Roberto Burle Marx, originally served as a casino and shows the obvious modernist influence of Le Corbusier.

Sleeping

Large chain hotels, especially those aimed at business travelers, dominate Belo Horizonte's accommodations scene. Most drop their rates significantly on weekends. The city also has a decent lineup of hostels. For easier walking access to the city's main attractions, stay near Praça da Liberdade or elsewhere within the central zone delineated by the Av do Contorno ring road.

Praça da Liberdade & North

Samba Rooms Hostel HOSTEL $
(☎31 3267-0740; www.sambaroomshostel.com.br; Av Bias Fortes 368; dm R$49-53, d with shared/private bathroom R$110/130, q R$190; @ 📶) Within easy walking distance of Praça da Liberdade, Mercado Central and the airport bus stop, this friendly hostel in a historic building has five- to nine-bed dorms and pleasant community spaces including a parquet-floored living room, a well-equipped guest kitchen, a cluster of open-air terraces and its own resto-bar. Traffic noise from the busy boulevard below is a potential deal breaker.

Hotel Ibis HOTEL $$
(☎31 2111-1500; www.ibis.com.br; João Pinheiro 602; r R$135-215; ❄ @ 📶) Midway between downtown and Savassi, and just steps from leafy Praça da Liberdade, this ultra convenient chain hotel has comfortable if predictable rooms in an ugly high-rise behind a pretty 1930s town house. The optional breakfast (R$17) and parking (R$17) cost extra.

Othon Palace HOTEL $$
(☎31 2126-0000; www.othon.com.br; Av Afonso Pena 1050; r R$190-270; ❄ @ 📶 🏊) A high-rise relic that's definitely showing its age (right down to the vintage massage chairs in the lobby!), the four-star Othon still offers plenty of perks: a prime downtown location opposite Parque Central, a rooftop pool and bar, and amazing city, park and mountain views from front-facing rooms. Feel free to bargain – during slow periods, even suites are surprisingly affordable.

Central Belo Horizonte

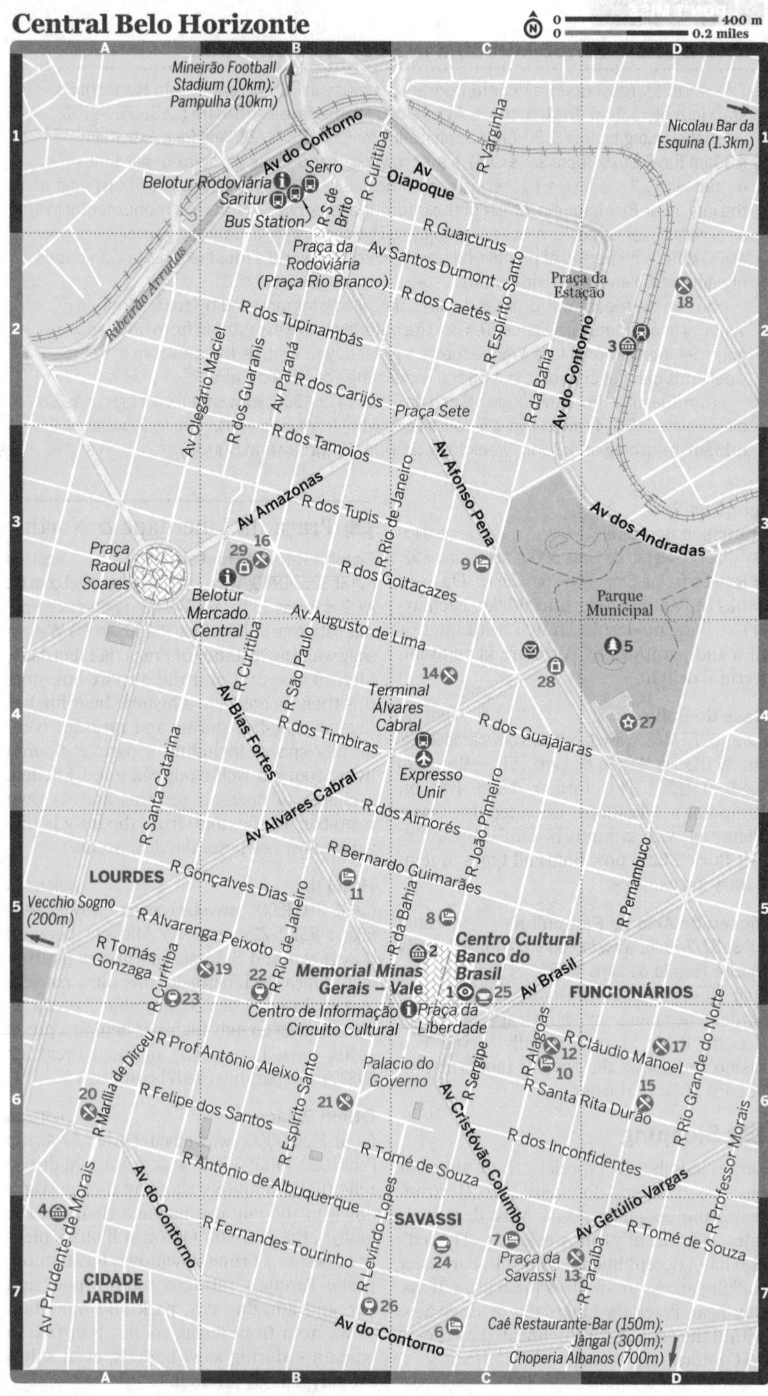

Central Belo Horizonte

Top Sights
1 Centro Cultural Banco do Brasil........ C5
2 Memorial Minas Gerais – Vale........... C5

Sights
3 Museu de Artes e Ofícios.................. D2
4 Museu Histórico Abílio Barreto..........A7
5 Parque Municipal............................. D4

Sleeping
6 Adrena Sport Hostel..........................C7
7 Hostel Savassi...................................C7
8 Hotel Ibis.. C5
9 Othon Palace.................................... C3
10 Royal Savassi Hotel.......................... C6
11 Samba Rooms Hostel.........................B5

Eating
12 Amadeus C6
13 Baiana do Acarajé.............................C7
14 Cantina do Lucas C4
Caravela....................................... (see 4)
15 Casa Amora...................................... D6
16 Casa Cheia.. B3
17 Casa Cheia Savassi........................... D6
18 Dorsé.. D2
19 Glouton B5
20 Marília Pizzeria................................. A6
21 Restaurante do Minas Tenis Clube B6

Drinking & Nightlife
22 Albanos Bar Gastronômico............... B5
23 Bar Tizé.. A5
24 Café com Letras................................ C7
25 Café com Letras – Centro Cultural C5
26 Wäls Gastropub................................ B7

Entertainment
27 Palácio das Artes D4

Shopping
28 Feira Hippie C4
29 Mercado Central B3

Savassi, Lourdes & South

★**Hostel Savassi** HOSTEL **$**
(☎31 3243-4771; www.hostelsavassi.com.br; Antônio de Albuquerque 626; dm R$45-55;) This small and cozy hostel enjoys a dream location on a pedestrianized street in the heart of Savassi. The trio of four- to 10-person dorms (two for women, one mixed) offers thoughtful features such as individual reading lights and power outlets for every bed, while the bright upstairs guest kitchen and spacious downstairs lounge and TV area invite travelers to mingle.

Adrena Sport Hostel HOSTEL **$**
(☎31 3657-9970; www.adrenasporthostel.com.br; Av Getúlio Vargas 1635A; dm R$52-55, with HI card R$47-50, d with shared/private bathroom R$125/145;) This homey HI-affiliated hostel in a 1950s Savassi town house is the brainchild of Belo Horizonte local Pedro, who also owns the adventure-sports store downstairs. Six- to 10-bed sport-themed dorms with paragliding, skateboard and climbing wall decor are complemented by a small sitting area, a welcoming kitchen-dining space and a back room where guests can linger over billiards and a beer.

Royal Savassi Hotel HOTEL **$$**
(☎31 2138-0000; www.royalsavassi.com.br; Alagoas 699; r R$200-320;) Well-positioned just east of Praça da Liberdade, this business-oriented hotel offers good online deals year-round, especially on weekends, when prices can get slashed nearly in half. Amenities include plush beds, big flat-screen TVs, minibars, a rooftop Jacuzzi and the **Amadeus** (☎31 3261-4292; Alagoas 699; per kg lunch weekday/weekend R$50/68, dinner R$95; ⊙11:30am-3pm & 6pm-12:30am Mon-Sat, noon-4pm Sun) restaurant downstairs with its sumptuous lunch buffet. Weak links include lackadaisical customer service and inconsistent wi-fi.

Pampulha

Pousada Sossego da Pampulha POUSADA **$$**
(☎31 3439-3250; www.sossegodapampulha.com.br; Av José Dias Bicalho 1258; s R$180-240, d R$230-320;) A stone's throw from Pampulha's lakeshore and the Mineirão football stadium, this pousada (guesthouse) is friendly, clean, well run and convenient for people arriving from the north. Amenities include a small pool and rooftop terrace with views of Belo Horizonte and the mountains. A taxi from Pampulha airport, 2km away, costs about R$15.

Eating

Belo Horizonte is teeming with good food for every budget. The area between Praça Sete and Praça da Liberdade is best for cheap eats, with countless *lanchonetes* (snack bars), self-serve *por kilo* restaurants and

DON'T MISS

FIVE ESSENTIAL BELO HORIZONTE EXPERIENCES

For a quintessential taste of the city, seek out at least one or two of the following:

➡ Stroll through the cheerful chaos of stalls and restaurants at Mercado Central (p181).

➡ Spend a Sunday morning at the open-air Hippie Fair (p181).

➡ Explore the 23 art galleries and magnificent grounds at the Instituto de Arte Contemporânea Inhotim (p175).

➡ Take a stadium tour and visit the football museum at Mineirão (p174).

➡ Attend a performance or stop in for an evening drink at Centro Cultural Banco do Brasil (p174).

fast-food places. Further south, the Lourdes and Savassi neighborhoods constitute the epicenter of the city's fine-dining scene.

The lion's share of the city's non-*mineira* restaurants specialize in Italian food, although you can also find a world of other flavors if you look around.

Praça da Liberdade & North

Casa Cheia BRAZILIAN **$$**

(☎31 3274-9585; www.restaurantecasacheia.com.br; Mercado Central, Loja 167; mains R$23-38; ⏰10:30am-6pm Mon-Sat, 10am-1pm Sun) This perennial Mercado Central favorite earns its name (meaning 'Full House'), with lines regularly stretching out the door. Behind the counter, a bevy of women prepare traditional *mineira* favorites on a giant stove, including *pratos do dia* (low-priced daily specials) such as the not-to-be-missed Saturday *feijoada* (Brazil's classic bean-and-meat stew). A branch in **Savassi** (☎31 3234-6921; Cláudio Manoel 784, Savassi; mains R$23-38; ⏰11am-midnight Mon-Sat, to 7pm Sun) offers the same menu and prices.

Dorsé BRAZILIAN **$$**

(☎31 3327-8516; www.facebook.com/dorsebarerestaurante; Sapucaí 271, Floresta; mains R$26-49; ⏰11:30am-midnight Tue-Fri, noon-midnight Sat, noon-6pm Sun) One of several resto-bars lining Rua Sapucaí above Belo Horizonte's train station, Dorsé is a prime spot for late afternoon drinks, snacks and gazing at sunset over the downtown skyline. Favorite menu items include grilled fish and meats, and original creations like *bruschetta mineira* – *pão de queijo* (cheese bread) topped with pork loin, *linguiça* garlicky pork sausage) ragù, or pears and gorgonzola.

Nicolau Bar da Esquina FUSION **$$**

(☎31 3318-6970; www.nicolaubardaesquina.com.br; Pouso Alegre 2217, Horto; mains R$23-49; ⏰6pm-midnight Tue-Fri, noon-midnight Sat, noon-6pm Sun) The brainchild of chef Leonardo Paixão from Belo's renowned Glouton restaurant, this buzzy newcomer northeast of downtown puts a whole new spin on the neighborhood corner bar. The attractive high-ceilinged space draws a youthful crowd for reimagined *mineira* classics like grilled pork with *canjaquinha cremosa* (creamy hominy grits) and *ora-pro-nóbis* (cactus leaves), or sandwiches of charbroiled homemade *linguiça* (garlicky pork sausage) with greens.

Cantina do Lucas BRAZILIAN, ITALIAN **$$**

(☎31 3226-7153; www.cantinadolucas.com.br; Av Augusto de Lima 233, Loja 18, Edificio Maletta; mains per person R$35-49; ⏰11:30am-2am Mon-Thu, to 3am Fri & Sat, to 1am Sun) Tucked off a busy downtown street on the ground floor of the Maletta building, this beloved local institution has been feeding *belorizontinos* into the wee hours since 1962. Vest-and-tie-clad waiters navigate through a landscape of checked tablecloths and wood paneling, hefting trays of *mineira* food and pasta. Especially popular after the Sunday Hippie Fair (p181) in nearby Parque Municipal.

Savassi, Lourdes & South

Casa Amora BUFFET **$**

(☎31 3261-5794; www.casaamora.com.br; Paraiba 941, Savassi; meals R$24-32; ⏰11:30am-3pm Mon-Fri, noon-3:30pm Sat) The concept is simple at this health-conscious lunch spot, founded by a trio of women: select one of the three daily specials (including one vegetarian option daily), add two or three side dishes of your choice, grab a glass of juice and decamp to the sunny outdoor patio or one of the cheery yellow tables up front.

Caê Restaurante-Bar BRAZILIAN $$
(☎31 2528-2244; www.caerestaurantebar.com.br; Outono 314, Sion; mains R$43-68; ⏲6-11:30pm Tue-Thu, noon-midnight Fri & Sat, noon-5pm Sun) Locally sourced ingredients and inventive twists on Brazilian and international recipes are the focus at this classy-casual restaurant opened by renowned Belo Horizonte chef Caetano Sobrinho. Mineiro cheese and meat platters share the menu with Peruvian-style ceviche, Uruguayan beef with chimichurri and grilled fish with Bahian-style *moqueca* (fish stew) and coconut *farofa* (sautéed manioc flour garnish), all accompanied by a good selection of artisanal beers.

Marília Pizzeria PIZZA $$
(☎31 3275-2027; www.mariliapizzeria.com.br; Marília de Dirceu 226; pizzas R$49-83; ⏲6:30pm-12:30am) Regularly voted one of Belo Horizonte's best pizzerias, Marília earns accolades for its chewy-crispy crust, top-quality mozzarella and deliciously fresh homemade tomato sauce. It draws a trendy, youthful crowd, with late hours and a fashionable, well-stocked bar decked out floor-to-ceiling with backlit bottles.

Restaurante do Minas Tenis Clube BUFFET $$
(☎31 3516-1310; Rua da Bahia 2244; all-you-can-eat buffet lunch weekday R$38, weekend R$59-65, dinner mains per person R$33-79; ⏲lunch 11:30am-3pm Mon-Fri, to 5pm Sat & Sun, dinner 5pm-midnight Tue-Sat) For atmosphere and price combined, it's hard to beat the noon buffet at Belo's tennis club. Gorge to your heart's content in the parquet-floored dining room or on the palm-shaded back terrace overlooking the pool and waterslides. The Saturday special is *feijoada* (Brazil's national dish), while Sunday's more elaborate buffet includes shrimp. À la carte dinners are also served.

Baiana do Acarajé BAHIAN $$
(☎31 3264-5804; www.facebook.com/baianadoacarajebh; Antônio de Albuquerque 440; acarajé R$14-28, mains for 2 people R$96-151; ⏲noon-midnight Tue-Thu, to 12:30am Fri & Sat, to 10pm Sun) A little slice of Bahia just off Praça da Savassi, this bright, lively and informal bar-restaurant specializes in tasty *acarajé* (shrimp-stuffed brown bean fritters) served alongside pricier and more substantial dishes like *moqueca* (Bahian seafood stew). A popular spot for people-watching over late-afternoon beers.

★**Glouton** FUSION $$$
(☎31 3292-4237; www.glouton.com.br; Barbara Heliodora 59; mains R$65-95; ⏲7-11:30pm Mon-Thu, noon-3pm & 7pm-12:30am Fri, noon-4pm & 7pm-12:30am Sat) This intimate brick-walled bistro with candlelit back patio is one of Belo's most romantic addresses. Award-winning chef Leonardo Paixão peppers his menu with French classics, but hits his stride with fusion recipes featuring Portuguese-Brazilian ingredients like suckling pig, codfish, manioc, okra, *malagueta* (pepper) and hearts of palm. For a perfect introduction, don't miss the delectable 10-piece *degustação de petiscos* (appetizer sampler).

Caravela PORTUGUESE $$$
(☎31 2531-3101; www.restaurantecaravela.com.br; Av Prudente de Morais 202, Cidade Jardim; mains R$67-90; ⏲11:30am-2pm Tue, 11:30am-2pm & 7pm-midnight Wed-Fri, noon-4:30pm & 7pm-midnight Sat, noon-4:30pm Sun) In 2017, Lisbon-born chef Cristóvão Laruça moved his popular Portuguese restaurant from Belo Horizonte's suburbs to this sleek space overlooking the Abilio Barreto Historical Museum's leafy courtyard. Couples and families come here to enjoy treats from across the Atlantic like *bolinhos de bacalhau* (codfish fritters) or shrimp and octopus *cataplanas* (seafood stews served with rice), followed by delicious homemade desserts.

Pampulha

★**Xapuri** BRAZILIAN $$
(☎31 3496-6198; www.facebook.com/RestauranteXapuri; Mandacarú 260, Pampulha; mains per person R$48-75; ⏲noon-11pm Tue-Sat, to 6pm Sun) Run by the affable Dona Nelsa, this long-standing local institution 15km northwest of Belo Horizonte is renowned for its fabulous *comida mineira* (typical Mineira cuisine). Everything is served at picnic tables under a thatched roof, with children's entertainment and hammocks close at hand for post-meal relaxation. The traditional wood stove blazes up front, while colorful desserts are attractively displayed in two long cases.

Drinking & Nightlife

Belo Horizonte is Brazil's self-proclaimed drinking capital, with thousands of *botecos* (neighborhood bars) sprinkled throughout the city. If you're visiting between mid-April and mid-May, don't miss the **Comida di Buteco festival** (www.comidadibuteco.com.br/belo-horizonte; ⏲mid-Apr–mid-May), in which dozens of places compete to see who makes the best bar food. Originating right here in 1999, it has since expanded to over a dozen other Brazilian cities.

Downtown, the 2nd floor of the indie-intellectual Maletta building is home to several bars with great views from the consistently packed open-air balcony. Savassi and Sion are other prime late-night destinations, packed with sidewalk pubs and trendy dance clubs.

★Café com Letras CAFE

(31 3225-9973; www.cafecomletras.com.br; Antônio de Albuquerque 781, Savassi; noon-11:30pm Mon-Wed, to midnight Thu, to 1am Fri & Sat, 5-11pm Sun;) With live jazz on Sundays, DJs Thursday through Saturday, and a bohemian buzz between sets, this bookstore-cafe is a fun place to kick back over light meals (R$25 to R$56) and drinks, browse the shelves and enjoy the free wi-fi. There's a second branch in the **Centro Cultural Banco do Brasil** (Praça da Liberdade 450, lower level; 10am-9pm) and it sponsors jazz performances citywide at the annual **Savassi Festival** (www.savassifestival.com.br; Aug).

Wäls Gastropub MICROBREWERY

(31 3582-5628; Levindo Lopes 358, Savassi; 11:30am-2:30pm & 6pm-midnight Mon-Thu, noon-2am Fri & Sat) Locals flock to this retail branch of Belo Horizonte's popular Wäls microbrewery for weekday lunch specials (R$20 to R$30) and late-night weekend carousing. The high-ceilinged, industrial-chic space serves over a dozen varieties on tap, from the bargain-priced X-Wäls lager to Hop Corn IPA to the intensely strong Quadruppel Belgian ale.

Jângal BAR

(31 3653-8947; www.jangalbh.com; Outono 523; 6pm-1am Tue-Fri, 2pm-1:30am Sat, 2-10pm Sun) This cool and colorfully lit garden bar draws regular crowds for its creative mixed drinks and nightly musical offerings that run the gamut from samba to electronica.

Choperia Albanos PUB

(www.albanos.com.br; Pium-i 611, Sion; 5pm-midnight Mon-Fri, noon-midnight Sat, noon-5pm Sun) This beloved, award-winning brewpub, with its sidewalk seating and high-ceilinged industrial interior featuring shiny vats and concrete floors, serves some of Beagá's best beer, with six varieties always on tap. There's a second branch in **Lourdes** (Rio de Janeiro 2076, Lourdes; 5pm-midnight Mon-Fri, noon-midnight Sat, noon-5pm Sun).

Bar Tizé BAR

(31 3654-7412; www.facebook.com/tizeoficial; Curitiba 2205, Lourdes; 5-10:30pm Mon & Tue, to midnight Wed-Fri, noon-midnight Sat, noon-10:30pm Sun) Since 1967, this strategically located corner bar with tables spilling onto a long island of sidewalk has been drawing crowds with ice-cold buckets of beer and award-winning *comida di buteco* (bar food).

☆ Entertainment

Belo Horizonte is a cosmopolitan town with a vibrant arts scene and plenty of nightlife. Online entertainment listings are available at www.soubh.com.br, guiabh.com.br and www.uai.com.br/entretenimento.

Palácio das Artes PERFORMING ARTS

(31 3236-7400; www.fcs.mg.gov.br/espacos-culturais/palacio-das-artes; Av Afonso Pena 1537) Near the southern end of Parque Municipal, this arts complex with multiple performance spaces and galleries is the hub of Belo's theater, dance and music-concert scene.

Bar do Museu Clube da Esquina LIVE MUSIC

(31 2512-5050, 31 99688-0558; www.bardomuseuclubedaesquina.com; Paraisópolis 738; 7:30pm-1am Tue-Fri, noon-2am Sat) Locals pack into this intimate Santa Tereza bar for live performances celebrating the legacy of the Clube da Esquina, Belo Horizonte's groundbreaking musical movement of the 1960s and '70s. Family members and musical associates of the club's revered co-founders make regular appearances.

Sports

Three football teams call Belo Horizonte home: América, Atlético Mineiro and Cruzeiro. The last of these plays regularly in the city's legendary Mineirão stadium, whose fame attained international proportions when it was selected as a venue for the 2014 FIFA World Cup and the 2016 Olympics. Buy tickets online (http://ingresso.cruzeiro.com.br) or in person at the stadium's ticket windows. Even if you don't get a chance to see a match, it's well worth touring the stadium and the attached football museum (p174).

Shopping

Don't leave Belo Horizonte without visiting its two iconic markets: the daily Mercado Central and the Sunday Feira Hippie. Locals also favor the many high-rise shopping centers downtown and Savassi's high-end boutiques.

★**Feira Hippie** MARKET

(Feira da Afonso Pena; Feira de Arte e Artesanato; Av Afonso Pena; ⊙8am-2pm Sun) A Belo Horizonte classic, this Sunday street fair attracts massive crowds searching for clothing, jewelry, street food and more. Located between Rua da Bahia and Rua das Guajajaras, and bordered by the soothing greenery of the Parque Municipal, it's a fun place to wander and enjoy a slice of city life, even if you're not shopping.

★**Mercado Central** MARKET

(☎31 3274-9497; www.mercadocentral.com.br; Av Augusto de Lima 744; ⊙7am-6pm Mon-Sat, to 1pm Sun) You'll find everything from parrots to peppers to perfume at this indoor market, a true Belo Horizonte institution. Shop for Minas cheeses and fresh produce, socialize at one of the bars or simply roam the aisles aimlessly for a wonderful slice of local life.

ℹ Orientation

Central Belo Horizonte has a grid of large *avenidas* (avenues), with another smaller grid superimposed at a 45° angle. The boundaries of the original planned city are defined by the ring road called Av do Contorno. It's a hilly town, so trips are sometimes less straightforward than they appear on the map.

The main drag is Av Afonso Pena, which runs diagonally from northwest to southeast, starting at the bus station at the northern end of downtown and running past leafy green Parque Municipal. From northwest to southeast, there are three pivotal *praças* (squares): bustling Praça Sete, just southeast of the bus station; serene Praça da Liberdade, heart of the government-turned-museum district; and trendy Praça da Savassi, the center of Belo nightlife and cafe society.

Outside of downtown, Pampulha (8km north) is the neighborhood with most cultural attractions.

ℹ Information

MEDICAL SERVICES

For an ambulance or emergency medical care, call SAMU (Serviço Médico de Atendimento de Urgência) at 192 or SEU (Serviços de Enfermagem de Urgência) at 31 3222-3322.

MONEY

Banks with ATMs are clustered downtown between Praça Sete and Parque Municipal, and along Av do Contorno in Savassi.

TOURIST INFORMATION

Belo Horizonte's municipal tourist bureau, Belotur (www.belohorizonte.mg.gov.br), is among the best in Brazil. Several branches are located around town.

Alô Turismo (☎from Belo Horizonte 156, from elsewhere 31 3429-0405; ⊙24h) Belotur's tourist-inquiry hotline.

Belotur Mercado Central (☎31 3277-4691; www.belohorizonte.mg.gov.br; Av Augusto de Lima 744; ⊙8am-4:20pm Mon & Tue, to 5:20pm Wed-Sat, to 1pm Sun) On the ground floor of Belo's famous indoor market.

Belotur Pampulha Lakeshore (☎31 3277-9987; www.belohorizonte.mg.gov.br; Av Otacílio Negrão de Lima 855, Pampulha; ⊙8am-5pm Tue-Sun) On the lakeshore in the northern suburb of Pampulha.

Belotur Rodoviária (☎31 3277-6907; www.belohorizonte.mg.gov.br; Praça Rio Branco 100; ⊙8am-5pm) On the main floor of the bus station, near the entrance.

Centro de Informação Circuito Cultural (www.circuitoliberdade.mg.gov.br/visite-br; Av Bias Fortes 50, Praça da Liberdade; ⊙9am-6pm Tue-Sun, to 9pm Thu) Information center for the museums and other cultural attractions surrounding Praça da Liberdade.

ℹ Getting There & Away

AIR

Belo Horizonte has two airports. International flights and many domestic flights use the renovated and expanded **Aeroporto Internacional de Belo Horizonte** (CNF; Aeroporto Tancredo Neves; Aeroporto Confins; ☎0800-037-1547; www.bh-airport.com.br; Rodovia LMG 800, Km 7.9, Confins), 40km north of the city. The **Aeroporto da Pampulha** (PLU; Aeroporto Carlos Drummond de Andrade; ☎31 3490-2000; www4.infraero.gov.br/aeroportos/aeroporto-de-belo-horizonte-pampulha-carlos-drummond-de-andrade; Praça Bagatelle, Pampulha), 10km north of the city center, is more conveniently located but only has limited domestic flights. Between them, the two airports serve most locations in Brazil.

BUS

Belo's long-distance **bus station** (☎31 3271-8933, 31 3271-3000; Praça Rio Branco 100) is at the northern end of downtown.

TRAIN

Companhia Vale do Rio Doce (☎0800-285-7000; www.vale.com/tremdepassageiros; Aarão Réis s/n; ⊙6am-4pm Tue-Sat, to noon Sun; 🛜) operates a daily train to Vitória (*econômica/executiva* class R$73/105) in Espírito Santo state, departing at 7:30am from Belo Horizonte's **train station** (Praça da Estação), just north of Parque Municipal, and arriving at Cariacica/Pedro Nolasco train station on Vitória's western outskirts at 8:30pm. The return run leaves Vitória at 7am, reaching Belo Horizonte at 8:10pm.

Getting Around

TO/FROM THE AIRPORT

Expresso Unir (☎31 3689-2415; www.conexaoaeroporto.com.br) runs frequent, comfortable Conexão Aeroporto buses between downtown and Belo's two airports. The *convencional* bus (R$12.70 to either airport) leaves Belo's bus station every 15 to 30 minutes between 4am and 10:30pm (slightly less frequently on weekends). Travel time is approximately 30 minutes to Pampulha airport, 70 minutes to Confins. Buses return from Confins between 5:15am and 12:20am.

Unir also runs an *executivo* bus to Confins airport (R$27.70, 50 minutes) from its **Terminal Álvares Cabral** (☎31 3224-1002; Alvares Cabral 387), just southwest of Parque Municipal, every 25 to 40 minutes between 3:30am and 9:40pm, returning from Confins between 6am and 12:30am. See the Unir website for complete schedules.

PUBLIC TRANSPORTATION

Belo Horizonte's local buses, operated by **BHTrans** (☎31 3429-0405; www.bhtrans.pbh.gov.br), are color-coded. Blue buses (R$4.05) go up and down main avenues in the city center, green express buses (R$4.05) only stop at select points, red-and-beige buses (R$4.05 or more, depending on distance) connect outlying suburbs to downtown, and yellow buses (R$2.85) have circular routes through the city.

The city's newest public transport innovation, introduced for the 2014 FIFA World Cup, is the fleet of greenish-yellow buses painted with the MOVE logo. Designed to cut travel times in half, MOVE buses enjoy the use of exclusive bus lanes and loading platforms and offer special facilities for bicycles and wheelchairs, yet still cost the same as regular city buses (R$4.05). Downtown corridors for MOVE buses run along Av Paraná and Av Santos Dumont, with the main northbound line to Pampulha traveling along Av Antônio Carlos and Av Dom Pedro I.

Ouro Preto

☎0XX31 / POP 74,659 / ELEV 1179M

Of all the exquisite colonial towns scattered around Minas Gerais, Ouro Preto is the jewel in the crown. Significant historically as a center of gold mining and government, and as the stage for Brazil's first independence movement, the city remains vital in modern times as a center for education and the arts, and is one of Brazil's most visited tourist destinations.

Built at the feet of the Serra do Espinhaço, Ouro Preto's colonial center is larger and has steeper topography than any other historical town in Minas. The narrow, crooked streets of the upper and lower towns tangle together and in places are too rough and precipitous for vehicles. Navigating the vertiginous cobblestone slopes on foot can be exhausting, but the views of 23 churches spread out across the hilly panorama are spectacular. The city is a showcase of outstanding *mineiro* art and architecture, including some of Aleijadinho's finest works.

History

Legend has it that a servant in an early expedition exploring Brazil's interior pocketed a few grains of an odd black metal he found while drinking from a river near the current site of Ouro Preto. It turned out to be gold, and the local deposits were soon discovered to be the largest in the New World.

Gold fever spread fast. In 1711, Vila Rica de Ouro Preto was founded, and in 1721 it became the capital of Minas Gerais. Gold bought the services of baroque artisans, who turned the city into an architectural gem. At the height of the gold boom in the

BUSES FROM BELO HORIZONTE

DESTINATION	COST (R$)	TIME (HR)	COMPANY
Brasília	168-230	11-12	União (www.expressouniao.com.br), Kaissara (www.kaissara.com.br)
Diamantina	97	5	Pássaro Verde (www.passaroverde.com.br)
Ouro Preto	34	2	Pássaro Verde
Rio de Janeiro	81-166	6-7	Útil (www.util.com.br), Cometa (www.viacaocometa.com.br)
Salvador	298	25	Gontijo (www.gontijo.com.br)
São João del Rei	60	3½	Viação Sandra (www.viacaosandra.com.br)
São Paulo	146-256	8-9	Cometa
Vitória	120-161	9-10	São Geraldo (www.saogeraldo.com.br), Kaissara

OFF THE BEATEN TRACK

SABARÁ

Sabará, 25km southeast of Belo Horizonte, was one of the world's wealthiest cities in the 18th century, when it produced more gold in one week than the rest of Brazil produced in a year. Now just a workaday suburb, it still retains many churches, mansions, statues, fountains and sacred art from those gold-mining days.

All colonial attractions are signposted from central Praça Santa Rita. Most charge small admission fees, and all are closed Monday. Highlights include the following:

Matriz de NS de Conceição (Praça Getúlio Vargas; 9am-noon & 2-5pm Tue-Sun) The triple-naved Matriz de NS de Conceição, finished in 1720, is a fascinating blend of Asian arts and Portuguese baroque styles.

Igreja NS do Ó (Largo NS do Ó; 9am-noon & 2-5pm Tue-Sun) Diminutive and jewel-like, decorated in gold, red and blue and dedicated to the Virgin Mary in her role as protector of pregnant women.

Igreja NS do Carmo (Rua de Carmo; 9-11:30am Tue-Sun) Aleijadinho's work predominates here, especially in the faces of São Simão and São João da Cruz.

Teatro Municipal (31 3672-7728; www.facebook.com/teatromunicipaldesabara; Rua Dom Pedro II; 8-11am & noon-5pm) FREE Sabará's elegant 19th-century opera house.

Museu do Ouro (31 3671-1848; www.museus.gov.br/tag/museu-do-ouro; Rua da Intendência 264; admission US$1; 10am-5pm Tue-Fri, noon-5pm Sat & Sun) A 1730s gold foundry filled with historical artifacts.

Igreja NS do Rosário dos Pretos (Praça Melo Viana; 8-11am & 1-5pm) Started and financed by slaves, this half-finished church now stands as a memorial to slavery's abolition.

Viação Cisne (31 3672-1222) runs buses to Sabará (*convencional/executivo* R$4.95/6.30, 40 minutes, every five to 15 minutes) from the street corner just southwest of Belo's main bus station. Return buses leave from stops along Av Victor Fantini in Sabará.

mid-18th century, there were 110,000 people (mainly slaves) in Ouro Preto, compared with 50,000 in New York and about 20,000 in Rio de Janeiro.

In theory, all gold was brought to *casas de intendéncias* (weighing stations), and a *quinto do ouro* (royal fifth) was set aside for the Portuguese crown. The greed of the Portuguese led to sedition, as the miners found it increasingly difficult to pay ever-larger gold taxes. In 1789, poets Claudio da Costa, Tomás Antônio Gonzaga, Joaquim José da Silva Xavier (nicknamed Tiradentes, meaning 'Tooth Puller,' for his dentistry skills) and others, full of French Revolutionary philosophies, hatched an uprising against Portuguese colonization known as the Inconfidência Mineira.

The rebellion was crushed in its early stages by agents of the crown. Gonzaga was exiled to Mozambique and Costa did time in prison. Tiradentes was jailed for three years, then drawn and quartered in Rio de Janeiro. His head was paraded around Ouro Preto, his house demolished and its grounds salted to ensure that nothing would grow there.

In 1897 the state capital was shifted from Ouro Preto to Belo Horizonte, decisively preserving the city's colonial flavor. In 1980, Ouro Preto was enshrined as Brazil's first Unesco World Heritage Site.

Sights

There are virtually no 20th-century buildings in this colonial town. As you wander, watch for informative historical plaques that have been placed on 150 houses around town to heighten visitors' curiosity and expand their knowledge of the city's treasures – part of a citywide cultural initiative known as Museu Aberto/Cidade Viva.

Ouro Preto is divided into parishes, each with its own Matriz (mother church). If you stand in Praça Tiradentes facing the Museu da Inconfidência (p184), the parish of Pilar is to the right (west), the parishes of Antônio Dias and Santa Efigênia to the left (east).

For a panoramic view of the churches and rooftops, head northeast out of Praça Tiradentes and walk for five minutes along Conselheiro Quintiliano towards Mariana.

Ouro Preto

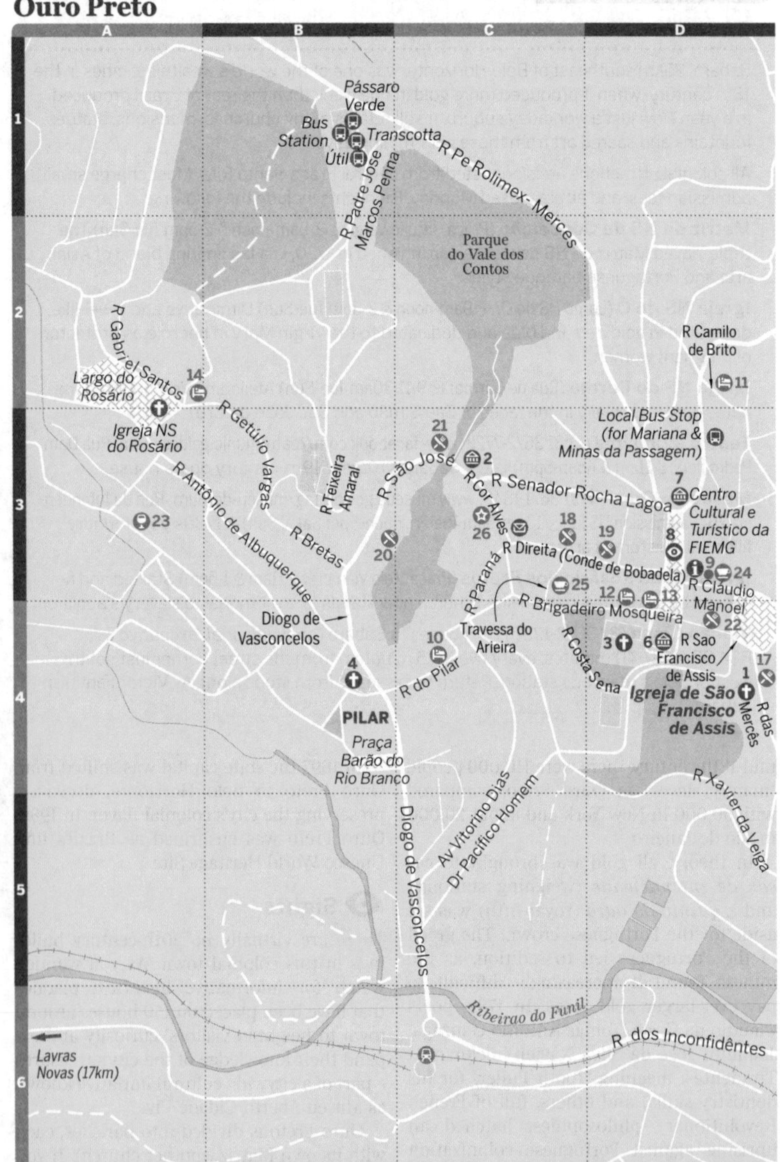

Praça Tiradentes & Around

Praça Tiradentes SQUARE
Ouro Preto's vast cobblestoned central square is surrounded by some of the city's finest museums and churches, and serves as the centerpiece for city wide festivals such as Carnaval.

Museu da Inconfidência MUSEUM
(www.museudainconfidencia.gov.br; Praça Tiradentes 139; adult/child R$10/5; 10am-6pm Tue-Sun) This historical museum is housed

Ouro Preto

Top Sights

1 Igreja de São Francisco de Assis ... D4

Sights

2 Casa dos Contos ... C3
3 Igreja NS do Carmo ... D4
4 Matriz NS do Pilar ... B4
5 Mina do Chico-Rei ... F4
6 Museu da Inconfidência ... D4
7 Museu de Ciência e Técnica da Escola de Minas ... D3
Museu do Oratório ... (see 3)
8 Praça Tiradentes ... D3

Activities, Courses & Tours

9 AGTOP ... D3

Sleeping

10 Goiabada com Queijo ... C4
11 Hotel Pousada Casa Grande ... D2
12 Pouso do Chico Rei ... D3
13 Rock in Hostel ... D3
14 Solar do Rosario ... A2
15 Trilhas de Minas Hostel ... E4

Eating

16 7 de Ouros Luderia ... E4
17 Bené da Flauta ... D4
18 Café Geraes & Escadabaixo ... C3
19 Casa do Ouvidor ... D3
20 Chafariz ... B3
21 O Passo ... C3
22 Restaurante Tiradentes ... D4

Drinking & Nightlife

23 Cervejaria Ouropretana – Loja da Fábrica ... A3
24 Império do Café ... D3
25 Villa Koa Café ... C3

Entertainment

26 Cine-Teatro Vila Rica ... C3

in Ouro Preto's old municipal headquarters and jail, an attractive building built between 1784 and 1854 on the southern side of Praça Tiradentes. It contains the tomb of Tiradentes, documents of the Inconfidência Mineira, torture instruments and important works by Manuel da Costa Ataíde and Aleijadinho (p190). Last admission is at 5pm.

Igreja NS do Carmo CHURCH

(Brigadeiro Mosqueira; admission R$3; 8:30-11:10am & 1-5pm Tue-Sat, 10am-3pm Sun) Built between 1766 and 1772, this lovely church was a group effort by the area's most important artists. It features a facade and two side altars by Aleijadinho.

Museu do Oratório MUSEUM

(31 3551-5369; www.museudooratorio.org.br; Adro da Igreja do Carmo 28; adult/reduced R$5/2.50; 9:30am-5:30pm Wed-Mon) This museum features a fabulous collection of

CHICO-REI

Brazil's first abolitionist was Chico-Rei, an African king. In the early 18th century, amid the frenzy of the gold rush, an entire tribe, king and all, was captured in Africa, sent to Brazil and sold to a mine owner in Ouro Preto.

The king, Chico-Rei, worked as the foreman of the slave miners. Working Sundays and holidays, he finally bought his freedom from the slave master, then freed his son Osmar. Together, father and son liberated the entire tribe.

This collective then bought the fabulously wealthy Encardadeira gold mine, and Chico-Rei assumed his royal functions once again, holding court in Vila Rica and celebrating African holidays in traditional costume. News of this reached the Portuguese king, who immediately prohibited slaves from purchasing their freedom. Chico-Rei is now a folk hero among black Brazilians.

hand-carved *oratórios* – miniature home altars and portable devotional shrines dating back to the 17th century. It's housed in the Casa do Noviciado, a triple-level colonial building where Aleijadinho is said to have lived while working on the adjacent Igreja NS do Carmo.

Museu de Ciência e Técnica da Escola de Minas MUSEUM

(☎31 3559-3119; www.museu.em.ufop.br; Praça Tiradentes 20; adult/reduced R$6/3; ⏲noon-5pm Tue-Sun) In the old governor's palace above Praça Tiradentes, this museum features dazzling gemstones from around the world. Even if you skip the museum itself, it's worth climbing to its front terrace for spectacular views of Praça Tiradentes backed by mountains. The attached astronomical observatory offers free shows between 8pm and 10pm on Saturday nights.

Antônio Dias Parish

★Igreja de São Francisco de Assis CHURCH

(www.museualeijadinho.com.br; Largo de Coimbra s/n; adult/reduced R$10/5; ⏲8:30-11:50am & 1:30-5pm Tue-Sun) This exquisite church is Brazil's most important piece of colonial art, after Aleijadinho's masterpiece The Prophets (p192) in Congonhas. Its entire exterior was carved by Aleijadinho himself, from the soapstone medallion to the cannon waterspouts to the Franciscan two-bar cross. The interior was painted by Aleijadinho's long-term partner, Manuel da Costa Ataíde.

Mina do Chico-Rei MINE

(☎31 99615-5297, 31 3551-1749; www.minadochicorei.com; Dom Silvério 108; admission R$25; ⏲8am-5pm) Near Matriz NS da Conceição de Antônio Dias is the abandoned mine of Chico-Rei. There's little to see as you stoop through the low passageways, but it's the perfect place to meditate on the fascinating story of this famous West African king-turned-slave-turned-king-again.

Pilar Parish

Matriz NS do Pilar CHURCH

(Praça Monsenhor Castilho Barbosa; adult/reduced R$10/5; ⏲9-10:45am & noon-4:45pm Tue-Sun) On the southwestern side of town, this is Brazil's second-most-opulent church (after Salvador's São Francisco). It has 434kg of gold and silver and is one of the country's finest showcases of artwork. Note the wild-bird chandelier holders, the scrolled church doors and the hair on Jesus (the real stuff, donated by a penitent worshipper).

Casa dos Contos MUSEUM

(São José 12; ⏲10am-5pm Tue-Sat, to 3pm Sun) FREE This 18th-century treasury building still retains its historic foundry where gold was melted down and formed into bars under the watchful eye of the Portuguese crown. It doubled as a prison for members of the Inconfidência. The renovated mansion now houses informational displays about the history of money in Brazil. The grand rooms upstairs command sweeping views over Ouro Preto's streets, while the dank, cobblestoned former *senzala* (slave quarters) below exhibits harrowing instruments of imprisonment and torture.

Santa Efigênia Parish

Igreja de Santa Efigênia dos Pretos CHURCH

(☎31 3551-5047; Santa Efigênia 396; adult/reduced R$5/2.50; ⏲8:30am-4:30pm Tue-Sun) Financed by gold from Chico-Rei's mine and built by the slave community, this mid-18th-century church honors Santa Efigênia, princess of Nubia. The exterior image of NS do Rosário is by Aleijadinho. Slaves legendarily contributed to the church coffers by washing their gold-flaked hair in baptismal fonts, or smuggling gold powder under fingernails and inside tooth cavities.

Capela do Padre Faria CHURCH
(Rua da Padre Faria s/n; adult/reduced R$5/2.50; 8:30am-4:30pm Tue-Sun) Built between 1701 and 1704 and named after one of the original *bandeirantes* (roaming adventurers who spent the 17th and 18th centuries exploring Brazil's interior), Ouro Preto's oldest chapel crowns a steep hillside at the far eastern edge of town, behind a triple-branched papal cross (1756) representing the pope's temporal, spiritual and material powers. Because of poor documentation, the artists here are anonymous.

Tours

AGTOP WALKING
(31 3559-3269; 4hr tour up to 10 people in Portuguese R$165, in English, French or Spanish R$250) Official guided city tours are available at the tourist office (p190). Note that prices quoted here are from the official table; you may be able to negotiate better rates with individual guides. The office can also help organize treks and horseback rides into the surrounding hills.

Festivals & Events

Semana Santa (Holy Week; March/April) processions in Ouro Preto are quite a spectacle (p189).

There are also festivities associated with Congado, the local expression of Afro-Christian syncretism (similar to Candomblé in Bahia or Quimbanda in Rio). The major **Congado celebrations** are for NS do Rosário (October 23 to 25, at the Capela do Padre Faria), for the New Year and for May 13 (the anniversary of abolition).

★**Carnaval** CULTURAL
(www.carnavalouropreto.com; Feb/Mar) Thanks in part to Ouro Preto's huge student population, Carnaval here is boisterous and fun. The town government hosts free live music on multiple stages in the historic center, while dozens of *blocos* (drumming and dancing processions) parade through the streets throughout the week; Balanço da Cobra and Bloco do Caixão are among the best.

Tiradentes Day CULTURAL
(Apr 21) Ouro Preto reclaims the symbolic role of state capital once a year.

CineOP FILM
(www.cineop.com.br; mid-Jun) This annual June film festival draws thousands of visitors and cinema professionals from around Brazil, with lectures, workshops and free movies shown on a big screen in Praça Tiradentes.

Festival de Inverno CULTURAL
(www.festivaldeinverno.ufop.br; Jul) This two-week winter arts festival features music, dance, theater, cinema and kids' activities at various venues throughout Ouro Preto and Mariana.

Sleeping

★**Goiabada com Queijo** HOSTEL $
(31 99435-1813, 31 3552-3816; www.facebook.com/HostelGoiabadacomQueijo; Rua do Pilar 44; dm R$40-50;) Midway between Praça Tiradentes and the train station, this sweet and simple three-room hostel is a labor of love for well-traveled owner Lidiane, who makes guests feel at home with her solid command of German and English and her enthusiasm for showing off Ouro Preto's hidden treasures.

Rock in Hostel HOSTEL $
(31 3551-3165; www.rockinhostelouropreto.com.br; Brigadeiro Musqueiro 14; dm R$50-60, d R$120-140;) Featuring a trio of simple four- to six-bed dorms and two upstairs doubles with shared bath, this hostel lacks the personal warmth of Ouro Preto's family-run hostels, but the location smack on central Praça Tiradentes couldn't be better.

Trilhas de Minas Hostel HOSTEL $
(31 3551-6367; www.trilhasdeminashostel.com; Praça Antônio Dias 21; dm R$55-60, d R$150;) With in-your-face views of NS de Conceição across the street, this three-room hostel has sunny upstairs dorm space, a guest kitchen, a wooden deck and a sweet double overlooking the permaculture garden out back. Friendly pets, local artwork and furniture built from reclaimed wood all reflect owner Jussara's passions for sustainability and animal rescue.

★**Pouso do Chico Rei** POUSADA $$
(31 3551-1274; www.pousodochicorei.com.br; Brigadeiro Musqueira 90; s R$210-250, d R$240-290, tr R$310-370, q R$400-450, s/d/tr without bathroom from R$100/175/260; @) Ouro

Preto's best midrange option, this beautifully preserved 18th-century mansion directly opposite the Carmo church is all charm, with creaky wood floors and a breakfast room full of hand-painted antique cupboards. Each room is unique, and most have period furniture and fabulous views. The three least-expensive rooms share a bathroom.

Hotel Pousada Casa Grande POUSADA **$$**
(☎31 3551-4314; www.hotelpousadacasagrande.com.br; Conselheiro Quintiliano 96; r R$190-200;) The best rooms at this pousada, 400m northeast of Praça Tiradentes along the road to Mariana, enjoy sweeping views over town. Pleasant sitting areas and terraces enhance its value-for-money appeal.

Solar do Rosario HOTEL **$$$**
(☎31 3551-5200; www.hotelsolardorosario.com.br; Getúlio Vargas 270; d R$360-720;) The four-star Solar do Rosario has an enviable position facing the Rosário church, and is the finest hotel to open in Ouro Preto in recent years. Ample rooms in the original 18th-century mansion are complemented by luxurious suites in the colonial-style modern annex and countless amenities spread over pretty terraced grounds out back, including indoor and outdoor pools and a sauna.

Eating

Ouro Preto is packed with restaurants for all budgets and tastes. Many are clustered along lively Ruas Direita and São José.

Restaurante Tiradentes BRAZILIAN, BUFFET **$**
(☎31 3551-6378; Amália Benhaus 25; all-you-can-eat R$15; ⊙11am-3pm) Travelers on a tight budget will appreciate the bargain-priced all-you-can-eat buffet at this hole-in-the-wall between Praça Tiradentes and Igreja São Francisco. Fill up on hearty *mineira* fare (meat, rice and beans) accompanied by fresh lettuce, tomatoes, cucumbers and beets from the salad table.

★**Casa do Ouvidor** BRAZILIAN **$$**
(☎31 3551-2141; www.casadoouvidor.com.br; Direita 42; mains per person R$29-69; ⊙11am-3pm & 7-10pm) Just downhill from Praça Tiradentes, Ouvidor has garnered numerous awards for its authentic *comida mineira* over the past four decades, with specialties like *tutu à mineira* (mashed beans with roast pork loin, cracklings, collard greens and boiled egg). At night, low lighting enhances the rustic charm of the ancient wood-beamed upstairs dining room. Bring an empty stomach – portions are immense!

★**O Passo** ITALIAN **$$**
(☎31 3552-5089; www.opassopizzajazz.com; São José 56; pizzas R$50-69, mains R$33-79; ⊙11:30am-midnight Sun-Thu, to 1am Fri & Sat) In a lovely 18th-century building with intimate candlelit interior, this local favorite specializes in pizza, pasta and salads complemented by a good wine list. Outside, the relaxed creekside terrace is ideal for an after-dinner drink. On Tuesday nights, don't miss the *rodizio de pizzas* (all-you-can-eat pizza; R$42). There's live jazz on Thursday and Friday evenings, and during Sunday lunch.

Chafariz BUFFET **$$**
(☎31 3551-2828; São José 167; all-you-can-eat R$58; ⊙noon-3:30pm Tue-Sun) Eclectically decorated with old photos, religious art, Brazilian flags and antiques, this local institution serves one of Minas' tastiest (if priciest) buffets. The menu showcases traditional local favorites such as *lombo* (roasted pork loin) and *feijão tropeiro* (beans with bacon, sausage, greens and manioc flour), followed by Minas cheese and *goiabada* (guava paste) for dessert. Post-meal shots of *cachaça*, coffee and *jabuticaba* liqueur are included in the price.

7 de Ouros Luderia BRAZILIAN **$$**
(☎31 3552-2682; www.facebook.com/7deourosluderia; Rua do Aleijadinho 57; all-you-can-eat R$30; ⊙11am-3pm Tue-Sun) Help yourself to a wide variety of *mineira* home cooking, including desserts, at this welcoming new self-serve near the Igreja NS de Conceição.

Café Geraes & Escadabaixo INTERNATIONAL **$$**
(☎31 3551-5097; www.opassopizzajazz.com/escadabaixo; Direita 122; mains per person R$30-55; ⊙11:45am-midnight Mon, Wed, Thu & Sun, to 1:30am Fri & Sat) Creatively prepared salads, pasta, salmon, steak and wine are the name of the game at Café Geraes, an upscale eatery on Ouro Preto's main street. Its downstairs space **Escadabaixo** serves the exact same menu, but with more of a cellar beer-hall atmosphere.

Bené da Flauta INTERNATIONAL **$$$**
(☎31 3551-1036; www.benedaflauta.com.br; São Francisco de Assis 32; mains R$36-98; ⊙noon-11pm) Occupying two levels of a gorgeous colonial *sobrado* (mansion) just below Igreja de São Francisco, this upscale restaurant is ideal for a romantic dinner, with pretty

views of Ouro Prêto's hillsides, candlelight reflecting off tall multipaned windows, and Brazilian jazz on the sound system. The menu of trout, steak, pasta and *mineira* specialties is complemented by a good wine list.

Drinking & Entertainment

At night and on weekends, students assemble in Praça Tiradentes and crowd the bars along nearby Direita.

Villa Koa Café CAFE

(☎31 98785-3100; www.villakoa.com.br; Travessa Arieira 26; ⏲11:30am-9pm Tue, Wed & Sun, to 11:30pm Thu-Sat) This back-alley cafe is perfect for chilling out between church and museum visits. The ample menu ranges from teas, espresso drinks and hot chocolate to caipirinhas, Irish coffee and artisanal beer accompanied by quiche, salad and sandwiches. There's live music most nights, with the revelry spilling out onto the cobblestones on warm evenings.

Cervejaria Ouropretana – Loja da Fábrica MICROBREWERY

(☎31 98818-0646; www.ouropretana.com.br; Benedito Valadares 250; ⏲3-9pm Tue-Fri, noon-9pm Sat) The recently launched brewpub affiliated with Ouro Preto's favorite microbrewery is a festive place for bar snacks and glasses of Ouropretana's trademark coffee lager or passion fruit and ginger IPA. It's especially boisterous on Tuesday evenings, when pint prices get slashed in half.

Império do Café CAFE

(☎31 97542-5432; www.facebook.com/Imperiodocafeop; cnr Cláudio Manoel & Praça Tiradentes; ⏲9am-7pm) Just below the tourist office, this cafe with exposed stone walls has simple food, fancy coffee drinks, and an extensive beer and wine list. It's an attractive place to pore over the map and get your bearings, though the overall vibe is touristy and the service rather lackadaisical.

Cine-Teatro Vila Rica CINEMA

(☎31 3552-5424; www.facebook.com/Cine.Teatro.Vila.Rica; Praça Reinaldo Alves de Brito 47) With an ever-changing film lineup (including frequent classic films in English), this small community movie theater and its attached cafe make for an enjoyable night out.

Orientation

Many streets in town have two names: the official one and another used by locals because the official one is too long. For example, Conde de Bobadela, the major thoroughfare descending from Praça Tiradentes, is commonly known as Rua Direita, and Conselheiro Quintiliano, the road to Mariana, is also Rua das Lajes. Adding to the confusion, street names are rarely posted.

SEMANA SANTA IN OURO PRETO

Semana Santa (Holy Week) is celebrated all over Brazil, but Ouro Preto's festivities are especially dazzling. For four days the town becomes a giant stage, starting with Thursday night's ceremonial washing of feet and the deposition of Christ from a giant cross in front of Igreja de São Francisco on Good Friday.

The most memorable event is saved for the wee hours preceding Easter Sunday. Around midnight Saturday, locals begin opening bags of colored sawdust on street corners all over town, unleashing an all-night public art project in which 3km of Ouro Preto's cobblestone streets are covered with fanciful designs, a giant carpet marking the route for the following morning's Easter processions. Until the early 1960s, Ouro Preto observed the old Portuguese tradition of decorating Easter-parade routes with flowers and leaves. More recently, colored scraps of leather, sand, coffee grounds and sawdust have become the media of choice for these *tapetes coloridos* (colored carpets).

Tourists are welcome to participate in laying out the designs, but be prepared for a late night. Things really don't get going until well after midnight. Music and general merrymaking erupt unpredictably all night long, and a few stragglers stick around till dawn to put finishing touches on Praça Tiradentes, the last spot cleared of vehicle traffic. If you prefer your beauty rest, go to bed early Saturday evening, then wake up at 5am Sunday to see the magic that's unfolded while you slept. It's like awakening to a Technicolor snowfall!

The designs – some religious, some profane – change every year and only last a few short hours. Within moments of the procession's passing, the public-works crew is out in force with brooms and shovels to clean the streets, until next year.

Information

Banco do Brasil (São José 189)

Bradesco (São José 201)

Centro Cultural e Turístico da FIEMG (☎31 3551-3637; turismo@ouropreto.mg.gov.br; Praça Tiradentes 4; ⏲8:15am-7pm) Ouro Preto's underfunded tourist office can provide general information about the city, but if you want a map, you'll need to snap a photo of the dog-eared copy on the countertop.

Getting There & Away

BUS

Long-distance buses leave from Ouro Preto's main **bus station** (☎31 3559-3252; Padre Rolim 661), a 10-minute uphill walk from Praça Tiradentes at the northwest end of town. During peak periods, buy tickets a day in advance.

Pássaro Verde (☎31 3551-1081; www.gabrasil.com.br) provides service to Belo Horizonte (R$34, two hours, hourly from 6am to 8pm); **Útil** (☎31 3551-3166; www.util.com.br) goes to Rio (R$100 to R$123, eight hours, 10am and 9:30pm daily) and São Paulo (R$154, 11 hours, 7pm daily); the São Paulo bus stops en route at São João del Rei (R$68, 3½ hours).

From the **local bus stop**, just northeast of Praça Tiradentes, **Transcotta** (☎31 3551-2385; www.transcotta.com) offers frequent service to Mariana (R$4.45, 30 minutes, every 20 minutes from 6am to 11pm), stopping at Minas de Passagem en route.

TRAIN

On weekends, the Vale mining company operates a renovated historic **tourist train** (www.vale.com/brasil/PT/business/logistics/railways/trem-turistico-ouro-preto-mariana; one-way/round trip R$46/66, air-conditioned panoramic car R$70/90) between Ouro Preto and Mariana, leaving Ouro Preto's **train station** (☎31 3551-7705; Praça Cesário Alvim) at the south edge of town once daily on Thursday and twice daily Friday, Saturday and Sunday. The 18km, one-hour journey is pretty, but slow, snaking along a river gorge the whole way. Best views are from the right side leaving Ouro Preto, and the left side leaving Mariana.

Getting Around

Viação Turin runs a small bus (R$2.70) between the bus station and Capela do Padre Faria on the east side of town, making various stops in the historic center along the way.

Mariana

☎0XX31 / POP 59,857 / ELEV 712M

Graced with fine colonial architecture and two of Minas' prettiest squares, Mariana, founded in 1696, was one of the state's earliest settlements and its first capital. Only 14km from Ouro Preto, Mariana makes an easy day trip or can even be used as a base to explore both cities. Its compact historical

ALEIJADINHO

Brazil's greatest sculptor, Antônio Francisco Lisboa (1738–1814) – known worldwide today as Aleijadinho (Little Cripple) – was born in Ouro Preto, the son of a Portuguese architect and a black slave. His nickname was given to him sometime in the 1770s, when the artist began to suffer from a terrible, debilitating disease. It might have been syphilis or possibly leprosy – either way, he lost his fingers and toes and the use of his lower legs.

Undaunted, Aleijadinho strapped hammers and chisels to his arms and continued working, advancing the art in his country from the excesses of the baroque to a finer, more graceful form known as Barroco Mineiro.

Mineiros have reason to be proud of Aleijadinho – he is a figure of international prominence in the history of art. He studied European baroque and rococo traditions through pictures, but went on to develop his own unique style, using only native materials such as soapstone and wood. Aleijadinho's angels have his stylistic signature: wavy hair, wide-open eyes and big, round cheeks.

For many years Manuel da Costa Ataíde, from nearby Mariana, successfully collaborated with Aleijadinho on several churches. Aleijadinho would sculpt the exterior and a few interior pieces, and Ataíde would paint the interior panels. With his secretly concocted vegetable dyes, Ataíde fleshed out many of Aleijadinho's creations.

Aleijadinho was buried in Ouro Preto's Matriz NS da Conceição de Antônio Dias, within 50 paces of his birth site. He was named patron of Brazilian arts by federal decree in 1973. The Prophets (p192) in Congonhas, the Igreja de São Francisco de Assis (p186) and the facade of the Igreja de NS do Carmo, both in Ouro Preto, were all carved by Aleijadinho, as were innumerable relics in Mariana, Sabará, Tiradentes and São João del Rei.

center is easier to navigate than Ouro Preto's, not only because of its smaller size, but also because the hills are less steep. The ground floors of many historic mansions have been transformed into stores, boutiques and artists' workshops where you're invited to wander at will.

Sights

All the sights are close together. Two blocks uphill from the tourist office and the Ouro Preto bus stop, Praça Minas Gerais has one of the state's most harmonious arrangements of public buildings on a single square.

Praça Gomes Freire SQUARE
One block downhill from Praça Minas Gerais, this leafy square is an inviting place to sit and watch the world go by, with a pond, a gazebo and park benches shaded by grand old trees.

Catedral Basílica da Sé CHURCH
(☎31 3558-2785; www.orgaodase.com.br; Praça Cláudio Manuel) The star attraction at Mariana's cathedral is its fantastic German organ dating from 1701, painted with designs from the then-Portuguese colony of Macau and adorned with carved wooden angels.

The cathedral was closed for restoration work in early 2016, with the first phase completed in December 2017 and the second phase initiated in early 2018. At the time of research, the church remained closed, with organ concerts suspended indefinitely.

Igreja São Francisco de Assis CHURCH
(Praça Minas Gerais) Mariana's loveliest church was designed by Aleijadinho, whose work can also be seen in the pulpits and other interior details. The gorgeous ceiling panels in the sacristy were painted by Mariana's native son Ataíde, who lies buried here with 94 others.

As of mid-2018, the church was closed indefinitely for restoration.

Museu Arquidiocesano de Arte Sacra MUSEUM
(☎31 3557-2581; Frei Durão 49; admission R$5; ⊙8:30am-noon & 1:30-5pm Tue-Fri, 9am-3pm Sat & Sun) Mariana's sacred art museum features sculptures by Aleijadinho, paintings by Ataíde and other religious objects.

Sleeping

Hotel Providência HOTEL $$
(☎31 3557-1444; www.hotelprovidencia.com.br; Dom Silvério 233; s/d R$135/255;) Guest rooms in this 1849 building, two blocks uphill from Praça Minas Gerais, are airy and inviting, with clean white sheets and lovely high ceilings. It shares a semi-Olympic-size swimming pool with the Catholic school next door.

WORTH A TRIP

DESCENDING INTO THE MINES

Halfway between Ouro Preto and Mariana, ancient gold mine **Minas da Passagem** (☎31 3557-5000; www.minasdapassagem.com.br; Rua de Mariana; adult/child R$88/44; ⊙9am-5pm) was founded by the Portuguese in 1719 and definitively decommissioned in 1985. Guided tours descend in a rickety antique cable car, covering the mine's history and local gold-extraction methods, then visiting a subterranean lake and a shrine to the many black slaves who died here dynamiting into the rock. Any Ouro Preto–Mariana bus can drop you here (R$4.45, 15 minutes from either town).

Eating & Drinking

★Lua Cheia BUFFET $
(☎31 3557-3232; Dom Viçoso 58; per kg R$36; ⊙11am-3pm Mon-Fri, to 4pm Sat & Sun) Mariana's best *por-kilo* place offers a sumptuous buffet of *mineira* cuisine – from freshly grilled meat to *feijão tropeiro* (beans mixed with toasted manioc flour, crunchy pork rind, sausage, eggs, kale, garlic and onions) – enticingly arrayed across an ample brick stovetop. There's atmospheric seating indoor and out, in the high-ceilinged colonial-style dining room or on the umbrella-shaded back patio.

Cervejaria Inconfidentes BAR
(☎31 98861-1886; https://cervejaria-inconfidentes.business.site; Praça Gomes Freire; ⊙6pm-1am Wed-Sun) With a prime location on Mariana's prettiest square, this brewpub featuring local beers has become the town's go-to nightspot since opening in 2017. There's live music Thursday through Saturday evenings.

Information

Bradesco (Av Salvador Furtado 69) There are Bradesco ATMs one block below the cathedral square.

Centro de Atenção ao Turismo (☎31 3558-2314, 31 3558-1062; www.mariana.org.br; Direita 91; ⊙8am-5pm) Mariana's tourist office offers city information and tours.

Getting There & Away

Transcotta (p190) runs frequent buses between Ouro Preto and Mariana (R$4.45, 30 minutes, at least twice hourly from 6am to 11pm). In Mariana, the **bus stop** (Ponte Liberdade) is near the northwestern corner of the historic center; in Ouro Preto catch the bus from the local bus stop northeast of Praça Tiradentes.

Mariana's long-distance **bus station** (Rodovia dos Inconfidentes) is located about 2km southwest of town. Passaro Verde runs buses to Belo Horizonte (R$39, 2¼ hours, every hour or two), and Útil operates a bus to São Paulo (R$158, 11¼ hours, daily 6:30pm). The Transcotta bus from Ouro Preto also stops here en route to downtown Mariana.

From Thursday to Sunday, Vale operates a tourist train (p190) from Mariana to Ouro Preto. Mariana's picturesque peach-and-white-colored **train station** (Av Manuel Leandro Corrêa 135) is about 400m north of the local bus stop for Ouro Preto-bound buses. There's a museum and kids' playground next door to keep everyone occupied while you wait.

Lavras Novas

☎0XX31 / POP 1500 / ELEV 1370M

Lavras Novas, named for the new gold strikes discovered here in 1704, sits on a high plateau 17km from Ouro Preto. When the gold started running out in the late 18th century, this hamlet became home to a small community of freed slaves, many of whose descendants have remained to this day. Surrounded by wide-open mountain scenery, its cobblestone main street runs between colorful single-story houses to the town's focal point, the **Igreja NS dos Prazeres**.

The rapid influx of weekend visitors from Belo Horizonte over the past decade, coupled with the paving of Lavras' access road, have led to a boom in new pousadas and ecotourism agencies; during busy holiday periods, outsiders easily outnumber locals. For lower prices and a taste of the town's traditional off-the-beaten-path tranquility, consider visiting midweek.

Activities

Several companies around town offer guided hikes and horseback-riding tours to local attractions, including the waterfalls **Três Pingos** and **Namorados**. An alternative resource for independent hikers is the rudimentary free trail map distributed at pousada Palavras Novas.

Sleeping

Palavras Novas POUSADA $$$

(☎31 99749-0033, 31 3554-2025; www.pousadapalavrasnovas.com.br; NS dos Prazeres 1110; d/chalet midweek from R$280/420, weekend from R$390/550; 📶🏊) One of Lavras Novas' first pousadas, Palavras Novas continues to seduce guests with a range of welcoming amenities: two swimming pools, nice mountain views, fireplaces, afternoon tea, whirlpool tubs, in-room DVD players, a sauna and spa – plus live music and organized hikes on weekends.

Getting There & Away

Transcotta (p190) runs daily buses to Lavras Novas (R$6.40, one hour) from in front of the Ouro Preto train station (*not* the bus station). There are three departures in each direction Monday through Friday, and one each on Saturday and Sunday.

Congonhas

☎0XX31 / POP 53,843 / ELEV 871M

This small industrial town has been saved from complete obscurity by the beautiful, brooding presence of Aleijadinho's extraordinary *The Prophets* at the Basílica do Bom Jesus de Matosinhos. The dramatic statues, arrayed artistically along the broad staircase at the foot of Congonhas' hilltop basilica, are Aleijadinho's masterpiece and Brazil's most famed work of art. For lovers of the Brazilian baroque, it's worth detouring to Congonhas just to see them. Every September, approximately 600,000 pilgrims throng the town for the **Jubileu do Senhor Bom Jesus do Matosinhos** (⏲Sep 7-14), one of Minas' great religious festivals. Holy Week processions in Congonhas are also famous, especially the dramatizations on Good Friday.

Congonhas is 72km south of Belo Horizonte, 3km off Hwy BR-040. The city grew up with the search for gold in the nearby Rio Maranhão, and the economy today is dominated by iron mining in the surrounding countryside.

Sights

The Prophets SCULPTURE

(Praça do Santuario) Already an old man, sick and crippled, Aleijadinho sculpted *The Prophets* between 1800 and 1805. Symmetrically placed in front of the **Basílica do Bom Jesus de Matosinhos**, each of the 12 Old Testament figures was carved from one or two blocks of soapstone. Each carries a message in Latin: some are hopeful prophecies, others warn of the end of the world.

Much has been written about these sculptures – their dynamic quality, the sense of movement (much like a Hindu dance or a ballet), how they complement each other and how their arrangement prevents them from being seen in isolation.

Before working on *The Prophets,* Aleijadinho carved (or supervised his assistants in carving) the wooden statues that were placed in the six little chapels below. The **chapels** themselves – also of Aleijadinho's design – and their placement on the sloping site are superb. The way the light falls on the pale sculpted domes against the dark mountain backdrop is truly beautiful.

Each chapel depicts a scene from Christ's passion, and several portray Jesus with a red mark on his neck. While little is known of Aleijadinho's politics, some local historians interpret this to mean that Aleijadinho intended to draw parallels between the martyred Christ and slain independence fighter Tiradentes. Aleijadinho's sculptures of Roman soldiers lend support to this theory – they all sport ankle boots, a shoe style favored by the colonizing Portuguese.

Museu de Congonhas MUSEUM
(☎31 3731-6747; www.museudecongonhas.org.br; Alameda Cidade de Matosinhos de Portugal; admission R$10, Wed free; ⏲9am-5pm Tue & Thu-Sun, 1-9pm Wed) Sticking out like a sore thumb amid the 18th-century streets of Congonhas, this striking modernist museum houses replicas of Aleijadinho's *The Prophets,* along with displays about his soapstone carving technique and Congonhas' history as a pilgrimage site. There's also a mixed collection of religious and modern artwork.

Sleeping & Eating

Congonhas is not an attractive city, and there's little to keep you here beyond Aleijadinho's artwork, so most visitors make it a day trip from nearby Belo Horizonte, Ouro Preto or São João del Rei. If you wish to linger, **Santíssimo Bistrô** (☎31 3731-1582; www.facebook.com/santissimobistro; Alameda Cidade Matozinhos de Portugal 77; mains R$21-40; ⏲9am-midnight Tue-Sun), attached to Congonhas' museum, is a convenient place to refuel with pasta or meat-focused Brazilian fare anytime of day. while **Circuito dos Inconfidentes** (☎31 3732-1243; www.circuitodosinconfidentes.com.br; Av Bias Fortes 1172; s R$150, d R$220-350; ❄📶🏊), a couple of blocks uphill from the basilica, offers modern, comfortable rooms with a pool, sauna and free parking garage. If you spend the night, take the opportunity to see the statues in the early-morning light, when they're especially beautiful.

Getting There & Away

Congonhas is on the direct bus route between Belo Horizonte and São João del Rei, so these two towns make the best starting points for a day trip. **Viação Sandra** (☎31 3731-1386; www.viacaosandra.com.br) serves this route several times daily (R$26, 1¼ hours from Belo Horizonte; R$34, two hours from São João). The long-distance **bus station** (Av Mauá) is just off Rua Júlia Kubitschek, 3km east of the basilica.

Getting Around

Viação Profeta (☎31 3731-3932; www.viacaoprofeta.com.br) runs buses from Congonhas' long-distance bus station to the basilica and *The Prophets* (R$3.60, 15 minutes) every 30 to 60 minutes. For the best approach and first view of the statues, get off just after the bus passes the church (as it heads downhill). The same bus returns you to the bus station, or you can take a taxi (R$15, 10 minutes).

São João del Rei

☎0XX32 / POP 90,263 / ELEV 898M

Set between mountain ridges near the southern end of the Serra do Espinhaço, São João del Rei affords a unique look at a *cidade historica* that didn't suffer a great decline when the gold boom ended in the 19th century. Present-day São João has the unselfconscious urban vitality of a modern city, which can come as a welcome contrast to the preserved-in-amber quality of neighboring Tiradentes.

Downtown there are plenty of high-rises and other trappings of 21st-century Brazil, yet unexpected colonial surprises lurk around every corner. The historic city center, which is protected by Brazil's Landmarks Commission, features two good museums, several of the country's finest churches and some gorgeous old mansions – one of which belonged to the late and still popular never-quite-president Tancredo Neves. Floodlights illuminate the churches every night, adding to the city's aesthetic appeal.

Sights

★Igreja de São Francisco de Assis CHURCH

(Padre José Maria Xavier; admission R$3; ⏲8am-5:30pm Mon-Sat, to 2:30pm Sun) This exquisite 1774 baroque church, fronted by a palm-shaded, lyre-shaped plaza, is home to two **Aleijadinho sculptures** (second altar to the left) and one of Minas' finest facades, based on Aleijadinho's design. Out back, arrows lead to politician Tancredo Neves' grave, a pilgrimage site for Brazilians. The local Ribeiro Bastos orchestra and choir perform sacred baroque music at 9:15am Sunday.

Catedral de NS do Pilar CHURCH

(Getúlio Vargas; ⏲6-11am & 1:30-8pm) Begun in 1721, São João's cathedral has exuberant gold altars and fine Portuguese tiles. Two of the city's famous orchestras can be heard here at the 7pm Mass: on Wednesday it's the Lira Sanjoanense orchestra, and on Thursday and Friday it's the Ribeiro Bastos orchestra.

Igreja de NS do Carmo CHURCH

(Praça Deputado Viegas; admission R$4; ⏲6am-noon & 1-7pm) This 18th-century church, dominating a lovely triangular *praça* (plaza), was designed by Aleijadinho, who also did the frontispiece and the sculpture around the door. In the second sacristy is a famous unfinished sculpture of Christ.

Museu Regional São João del Rei MUSEUM

(☎32 3371-7663; mrsjdr@museus.gov.br; Praça Severiano Resende s/n; ⏲9:30am-4pm Tue-Fri, 9am-1pm Sat & Sun) FREE One of the best regional museums in Minas Gerais, this 19th-century colonial mansion houses three floors of antique furniture, sacred art and assorted cultural relics.

Museu de Arte Sacra MUSEUM

(☎32 3371-7005; www.museudeartesacra.com.br; Praça Embaixador Gastão da Cunha 8; adult/reduced R$5/2.50; ⏲noon-5pm Mon-Fri, 9am-1pm Sat) In a building that served as the public jail between 1737 and 1850, this museum has a small but impressive collection of art from the city's churches.

Festivals & Events

Someone's always celebrating something in São João. There are literally dozens of festivals, both religious and secular – stop by the tourist office for a full calendar.

Carnaval RELIGIOUS

(⏲Jan-Mar) Locals boast, credibly, that their Carnaval is the best in Minas Gerais, with five dozen *blocos* (drumming and dancing processions) parading through the streets during three full weeks of festivities.

Holy Week RELIGIOUS

(⏲Mar/Apr) Semana Santa processions are especially colorful, preserving centuries-old Portuguese traditions and incorporating the music of the city's two baroque orchestras, who have been performing here uninterruptedly since the 18th century.

Semana da Inconfidência CULTURAL

(⏲Apr 15-21) Celebrates Brazil's first independence movement, culminating in a horseback procession between São João and Tiradentes.

Sleeping

Downtown São João boasts several good value, centrally located accommodations. Book ahead in December, when the town is filled with students sitting for exams, and during holidays such as Carnaval and Easter.

AZ Hostel HOSTEL $

(☎32 98854-2842, 32 99994-2709; www.azhostel.com.br; Marechal Bittencourt 73; dm/d/tr R$65/150/180; 📶) For budget travelers, this hostel is a dream come true. Smack in the heart of the historic district, only steps from the Carmo church and a buzzing nightlife strip, it offers easy walking access to all of São João's cultural attractions.

★Villa Magnolia Pousada POUSADA $$

(☎32 3373-5065; www.pousadavillamagnolia.com.br; Ribeiro Bastos 2; s/d midweek from R$180/230, weekend from R$220/280; ❄@📶🏊) A delightful refuge just across from Igreja de São Francisco, this stylishly renovated 19th-century mansion features pure cotton bedding, oversized towels, spacious rooms, a large pool, shade trees and common areas filled with art books.

Pousada Beco do Bispo POUSADA $$

(☎32 3371-8844; www.becodobispo.com.br; Irmã Eugênia Luz Pinto 93; s R$200, d R$280-330, tr R$330-380; ❄📶🏊) Tucked down a peaceful dead-end street a block from Igreja de São Francisco, this pousada has cheerful, ultracomfy rooms with queen- and king-size beds, fine cotton sheets, international TV channels and a pool with palm trees.

São João del Rei

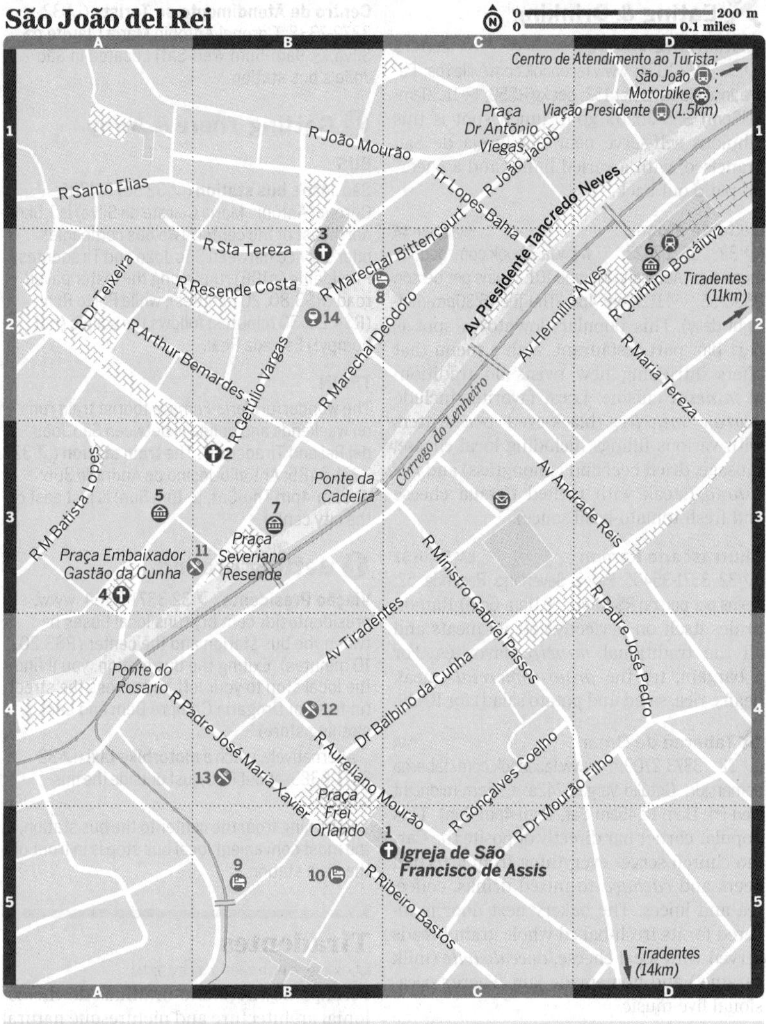

São João del Rei

Top Sights
1 Igreja de São Francisco de Assis C5

Sights
2 Catedral de NS do Pilar B3
3 Igreja de NS do Carmo B2
4 Igreja de NS do Rosário A3
5 Museu de Arte Sacra A3
6 Museu Ferroviário D2
7 Museu Regional São João del Rei B3

Sleeping
8 AZ Hostel B2
9 Pousada Beco do Bispo B5
10 Villa Magnolia Pousada B5

Eating
11 Churrascaria Ramon B3
12 Dedo de Moça B4
13 Restaurante Villeiros B4

Drinking & Nightlife
14 Taberna de Omar B2

Eating & Drinking

Restaurante Villeiros BUFFET $
(☎32 3372-1034; www.facebook.com/villeiros; Padre José Maria Xavier 132; per kg R$50; ⊙11:30am-3:30pm) São João's go-to lunch spot is this fabulous self-serve near the Igreja de São Francisco, with a varied buffet and a cheerful patio out back.

Dedo de Moça BRAZILIAN $$
(☎32 3371-7623; www.facebook.com/dedodemoca.sjdr; Aureliano Mourão 101; mains per person R$30-55; ⊙11:30am-4pm Thu-Tue, 6:30pm-midnight daily) This popular downtown spot is part bar, part restaurant, with a menu that offers intriguing new twists on traditional *mineira* cuisine. Local favorites include *acarajé mineira* (black-eyed pea fritters with various fillings including local cheese, sausage, dried beef and lemongrass) and *filé catauá* (steak with melted Catauá cheese and fresh tomato-basil sauce).

Churrascaria Ramon BARBECUE $$
(☎32 3371-3540; Praça Severiano Resende 52; mains per person R$20-40; ⊙11am-6pm) Ramon prides itself on perfectly cooked meats and all the traditional *mineira* favorites. For a bargain, try the *prato comercial* (meat, beans, rice, salad and potato salad) for R$20.

★ **Taberna de Omar** BAR
(☎32 3373-2709; www.facebook.com/tabernadomarsjdr; Getúlio Vargas 242a; ⊙6pm-midnight Wed-Fri, 11am-12:45am Sat, 11am-4pm Sun) This popular corner bar directly opposite the Carmo church serves everything from artisanal beers and *cachaça* to mixed drinks, coffee, tea and juices. The bakery next door is revered for its fresh-baked whole grain breads served with local cheese, *doce de leite* (milk caramel) and homemade jam. There's occasional live music.

Information

Bradesco (Av Hermilio Alves 190)

Centro de Atendimento ao Turista (☎32 3372-7338; Coronel Antônio Maria Clarete da Silva; ⊙9am-5pm Wed-Sat) Located in São João's bus station.

Getting There & Away

BUS

São João's **bus station** (☎32 3373-4700; Coronel Antônio Maria Clarete da Silva) is 1.5km northeast of the center. Two bus companies offer service between São João and Tiradentes. Presidente (p196) runs along the faster paved road (R$3.80, 20 minutes), while Porto Real (R$4.20, 30 minutes) follows the scenic (but bumpy!) Estrada Real.

TRAIN

The wonderful *Maria-Fumaça* tourist train runs on weekends and holidays between São João del Rei and Tiradentes. The **train station** (☎32 3371-8485; Antônio Josino de Andrade 366; ⊙9am-4pm Thu-Sat, to 1pm Sun) is just east of the city center.

Getting Around

Viação Presidente (☎32 3371-5064; www.presidentesjdr.com.br) runs local buses between the bus station and the center (R$3.20, 10 minutes). Exiting the bus station, you'll find the local stop to your left and across the street (in front of Drogaria Compre Bem and Luck's clothing store).

Alternatively, catch a **motorbike taxi** (☎32 3371-6389; about R$5) just outside the bus station.

Returning from the center to the bus station, the most convenient local bus stop is in front of the train station.

Tiradentes

☎0XX32 / POP 7807 / ELEV 927M

Perhaps nowhere else in Minas do the colonial architecture and picturesque natural setting blend so harmoniously as in Tiradentes. Quaint historic houses, fringed by exuberant wildflowers, stand out against

BUSES FROM SÃO JOÃO DEL REI

DESTINATION	COST (R$)	TIME (HR)	COMPANY
Belo Horizonte	60	3½	Viação Sandra (www.viacaosandra.com.br)
Congonhas	34	2	Viação Sandra
Ouro Preto	68	4¼	Útil (www.util.com.br)
Petrópolis	82-111	4½	Paraibuna (www.paraibunatransportes.com.br)
Rio	93-126	5½	Paraibuna
São Paulo	114-136	8½	Útil

a backdrop of pretty blue mountains threaded with hiking trails. If you can, visit midweek, when the town's abundant attractions are most easily appreciated. On weekends, the swarms of visitors who come to gawk at Tiradentes' antique stores and boutiques can make the place feel a bit like a theme park, and the sudden increase in horse-drawn carriages creates some strong aromas!

Tiradentes

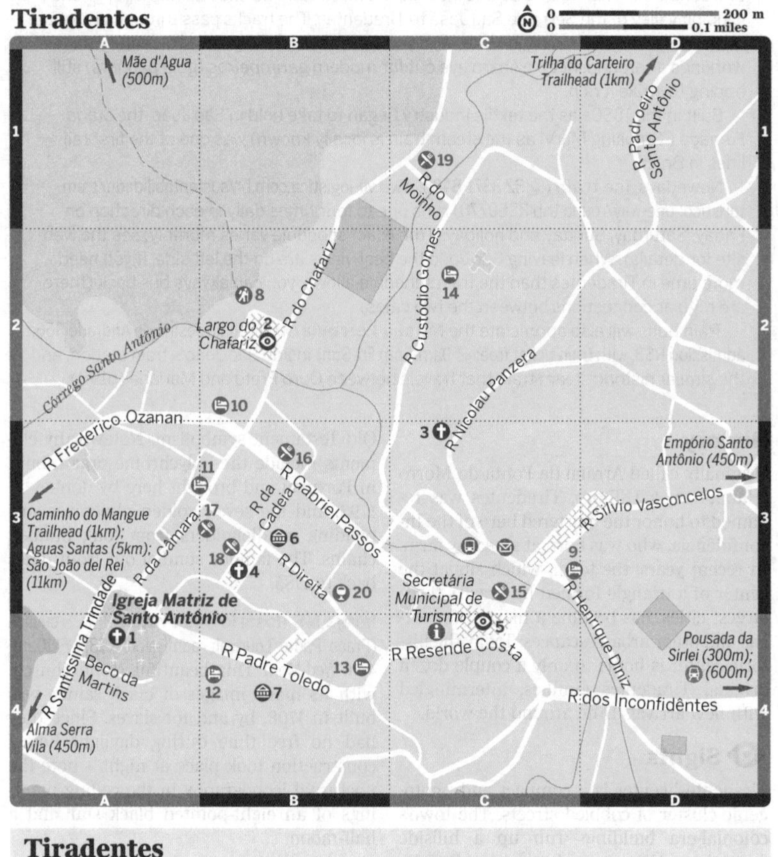

Tiradentes

Top Sights
1 Igreja Matriz de Santo Antônio A4

Sights
2 Chafariz de São José B2
3 Igreja de São Francisco de Paula C3
4 Igreja NS Rosário dos Pretos B3
5 Largo das Forras C4
6 Museu de Sant'Ana B3
7 Museu do Padre Toledo B4

Activities, Courses & Tours
8 Mãe d'Agua B2

Sleeping
9 Hotel Solar da Ponte C3
10 Pousada da Bia B2
11 Pousada do Ó B3
12 Pousada Richard Rothe B4
13 Pousada Três Portas B4
14 Pouso Alforria C2

Eating
15 Bar do Celso C3
16 Estalagem do Sabor B3
17 Gourmeco B3
18 Tragaluz B3
19 Viradas do Largo C1

Drinking & Nightlife
20 Entrepôt du Vin B3

Entertainment
Organ Concerts .... (see 1)

DON'T MISS

SMOKING MARY: MINAS' VINTAGE STEAM TRAINS

Sure, there are buses that will get you back and forth between São João del Rei and Tiradentes, but how can they compare with a trip on a 19th-century steam train in pristine condition? Hop aboard as this little engine hisses and belches its way through the winding valley of the Serra de São José to Tiradentes. The tracks pass through one of the oldest areas of gold mining in Minas and you'll see the remnants of 18th-century mine workings all around. Keep a sharp eye out for modern *garimpeiros* (gold panners) still hoping to strike it rich.

Built in the 1880s as the textile industry began to take hold in São João, the *Maria-Fumaça* ('Smoking Mary', as the steam train is locally known) was one of the first rail lines in Brazil.

Nowadays, the **train** (☎32 3371-8485; www.vli-logistica.com.br/sustentabilidade/trem-turistico; one-way/round trip R$60/70) runs one to four times daily in each direction on Friday, Saturday, Sunday and holidays (the exact schedule varies monthly; see the website for details). When leaving São João the best views are on the left side. If you need more time in Tiradentes than the train schedule allows, you can always bus back (there are regular connections between the two cities).

Train buffs will also appreciate the **Museu Ferroviário** (Antônio Josino de Andrade 366; admission R$3, with train ticket free; ⌚9am-5pm Fri-Sun) inside São João's train station, and the similar historic steam train that travels between Ouro Preto and Mariana (p190).

History

Originally called Arraial da Ponta do Morro (Hamlet on a Hilltop), Tiradentes was renamed to honor the martyred hero of the Inconfidência, who was born at a nearby farm. In recent years, the town, which sits at the center of a triangle formed by Brazil's three largest cities, has become a magnet for artists and other urban escapees. Today the historic center is home to only a couple dozen original Tiradentes families, intermingled with new arrivals from around the world.

Sights

Tiradentes' center is a compact and photogenic cluster of cobbled streets. The town's colonial-era buildings run up a hillside from the main square, **Largo das Forras**, culminating in the beautiful Igreja Matriz de Santo Antônio. From the terrace in front of the church there's a stunning view of the terracotta-tiled colonial houses, the green valley and the towering wall of stone formed by the Serra de São José. For another picture-postcard view of town, climb the hill just above the bus station to the grassy square in front of **Igreja de São Francisco de Paula** (Nicolau Panzera).

★**Igreja Matriz de Santo Antônio** CHURCH
(Padre Toledo s/n; admission R$5; ⌚9am-5pm) Named for Tiradentes' patron saint, this gorgeous church is one of Aleijadinho's last designs. The dazzling gold interior is rich in Old Testament symbolism. Noteworthy elements include the polychrome organ, built in Portugal and brought here by donkey in 1798, and the seven golden phoenixes suspending candleholders from long braided chains. The famous sundial out front dates back to 1785.

Igreja NS Rosário dos Pretos CHURCH
(Praça Padre Lourival; admission R$3; ⌚10am-4pm Wed-Mon) This beautiful stone church, with its many images of black saints, was built in 1708, by and for slaves. Since they had no free time during daylight hours, construction took place at night – note the nocturnal iconography in the ceiling paintings of an eight-pointed black star and a half-moon.

★**Mazuma Mineira** DISTILLERY
(☎32 3353-6654; www.mazuma.com.br; São Bento 300, Bichinho; ⌚9:30am-5pm Thu-Sat, Mon & Tue, to 2:30pm Sun) FREE If you've ever wondered how *cachaça* (Brazil's famous sugarcane alcohol) is made, this is a perfect place to learn. This small-scale *alambique* (distillery) with a focus on sustainable production offers free guided tours demonstrating every stage of the process, from harvesting and milling of sugarcane, to filtering and separation of the juice, to distillation at high heat in elegant copper cooling towers, to aging in casks of oak, Brazil nut or local pink jequitibá wood. It's located 7km northeast of Tiradentes.

Afterwards, taste the goods and purchase a bottle or two to bring home in the attached shop. Ideal times to observe the whole process are during the main June to August harvest season, or the secondary harvest in January and February.

Chafariz de São José FOUNTAIN
(Rua do Chafariz) Constructed in 1749 by the town council and set against a verdant backdrop, this gorgeous fountain north of Córrego Santo Antônio has three sections: one for drinking, one for washing clothes and one for watering horses. The water comes from a nearby spring, Mãe d'Agua, via an old stone pipeline.

Museu de Sant'Ana MUSEUM
(☎32 3355-2798; www.museudesantana.org.br; cnr Cadeia & Direita; adult/reduced R$5/2.50; ⏰10am-7pm Wed-Mon) This innovative museum in Tiradentes' former town jail was conceived by Belo Horizonte–based Angela Gutierrez, creator of Ouro Preto's Museu do Oratório (p185) and Belo Horizonte's Museu de Artes e Ofícios (p174). The simple but beautifully presented collection features 270 images of St Anne in wood, stone and terracotta, from the 17th century to the present. Bilingual exhibits trace the importance of St Anne imagery throughout Brazil and its evolution through the baroque and rococo periods.

Museu do Padre Toledo MUSEUM
(☎32 3355-1549; www.ufmg.br/frmfa/museu-padre-toledo; Padre Toledo 158; adult/reduced R$10/5; ⏰10am-5pm Tue-Fri, to 4:30pm Sat, 9am-3pm Sun) Dedicated to 18th-century Brazilian priest and revolutionary hero Padre Toledo, this historical museum occupies the 18-room house where Padre Toledo himself once lived and where the Inconfidentes first met. The collection features regional antiques and documents from the 18th century, along with some fine ceiling paintings artistically reflected in floor-mounted mirrors.

Activities

Mãe d'Agua HIKING
(⏰8am-4pm) Tiradentes' most popular, least challenging trail leads to this natural spring that feeds the Chafariz de São José fountain. From the top of the fountain square, cross through a simple wooden door in the old stone wall, continuing 10 minutes northwest along the viaduct into the jungle. It's a magical spot, with sun-dappled glens and monkeys cavorting in the trees.

Trilha do Carteiro HIKING
(Calçada dos Escravos) This three-hour round-trip hike climbs through open fields to a windswept saddle with gorgeous views of the *serra* (mountain range). It includes a section of the old stone-paved road built by slaves between Ouro Preto and Rio de Janeiro.

To reach the trailhead, climb from Tiradentes' bus station to Igreja de São Francisco de Paula, then follow the cobbled road north, continuing straight at the first intersection and bearing slightly left at the second (following a brown sign marked 'Serra de São José'). Shortly after passing Pousada Recanto dos Encantos on your right, take the right (uphill) fork and continue straight another few hundred meters. Bear right again to stay on the cobblestones shortly after passing Pousada da Trilha on your left, then just beyond a yellow house numbered 878 on the left, cross through a gate to find a cluster of signposts indicating the Trilha do Carteiro. Fork left on the rickety bridge over the stream and start climbing toward the saddle.

Festivals & Events

Mostra de Cinema de Tiradentes FILM
(www.mostratiradentes.com.br; ⏰Jan) Entering its third decade, Brazil's largest film festival showcases contemporary Brazilian filmmakers with nine days of world premieres, juried prizes and free open-air screenings in Largo das Forras.

Festival de Cultura e Gastronomia de Tiradentes FOOD & DRINK
(www.farturabrasil.com.br; ⏰Aug) This 10-day food festival brings world-class chefs to Tiradentes.

Sleeping

Tiradentes caters to well-heeled urban escapees and couples looking for romance. Budget-minded and solo travelers can save money by visiting midweek, when some pousadas grant discounts.

Pousada da Bia POUSADA $$
(☎32 3355-1173; www.pousadadabia.com.br; Ozanan 330; d midweek/weekend R$250/270; 📶🏊) A few steps outside the historical center, this long-standing pousada, lovingly managed by French- and English-speak-

ing owner Bia, features clean, comfortable rooms with shared verandas facing a fragrant herb garden and relaxing pool area. Breakfasts of fresh fruit, *pão de queijo* (cheese bread), homemade cakes and coffee heated on the wood stove are served in a sweet glass-walled garden house.

Pousada Três Portas POUSADA **$$**
(☎32 3355-1444; www.pousadatresportas.com.br; Direita 280a; r R$295-350;) Sitting pretty in a historic building just above Tiradentes' main square, this pousada features rooms with beautiful antiques and hardwood floors, some with four-poster beds. The cheery upstairs sitting room with fireplace enjoys nice views of town and the mountains beyond; other amenities include a covered swimming pool and sauna.

Pousada do Ó POUSADA **$$**
(☎32 3355-1699; www.pousadadoo.com.br; Rua do Chafariz 25; d midweek R$160-300, weekend R$290-390;) Set in an 18th-century house, Pousada do Ó enjoys a privileged location two blocks below the church in the heart of Tiradentes. The original pousada, featuring seven snug rooms around a small garden, is supplemented by four larger rooms in the building above. Rooms 8 and 11 are the best of the bunch.

★ **Hotel Solar da Ponte** POUSADA **$$$**
(☎32 3355-1255; www.solardaponte.com.br; Praça das Mercês; r midweek R$660-950, weekend R$825-1185;) Right in the heart of town, this magnificent re-creation of a colonial-era mansion is one of Brazil's finest hotels, with first-rate food and service across the board. Rooms have fresh flowers, beautiful antiques, and comfortable chairs and beds. There's a reading room, complete with fireplace, and complimentary afternoon tea is served in the garden.

Alma Serra Vila POUSADA **$$$**
(☎32 99837-9332, 32 3355-1521; www.almaserravila.com; Santíssima Trindade 420; d R$352-506;) A 10-minute walk above Tiradentes' Santo Antônio church brings you to this peaceful, Italian-run hillside oasis. There are no TVs in the luxuriously comfortable rooms; rather, guests are invited to relax with a book or simply soak up the divine views of the Serra São José from a hammock in the soothingly green backyard.

Pouso Alforria POUSADA **$$$**
(☎32 3355-1536; www.pousoalforria.com.br; Custódio Gomes 286; s/d R$390/430;) This classy, secluded pousada, tucked up a flagstoned driveway five minutes' walk north of the center, features eight rooms in modern style, a reading room full of art books and some nice views of the Serra de São José. English and French are spoken.

Pousada Richard Rothe POUSADA **$$$**
(☎32 3355-1333; www.pousadarichardrothe.com.br; Padre Toledo 124; r midweek/weekend R$370/400;) On a picturesque street in the historic center, this stylish pousada has spacious suites, an elegant reading room with fireplace, and a small protected forest out back where monkeys come to play at dawn.

Eating

Tempero da Ângela BUFFET **$**
(☎32 3353-7010; Rua Deputado José Bonifácio 64; all-you-can-eat R$28; ⊙noon-4pm Mon-Fri, to 5pm Sat & Sun) It's an 8km trip east of town, but you won't find a more authentic traditional *por-kilo* place anywhere in Minas Gerais. Every square centimeter of Ângela's wood stove is covered with bubbling pots of *comida mineira*, with local cheese, *goiabada* (guava paste) and *doce de leite* (milk caramel) for dessert.

Bar do Celso BRAZILIAN **$$**
(☎32 3355-1193; www.facebook.com/RestauranteBardoCelso; Largo das Forras 80a; mains R$22-43; ⊙noon-8pm Wed-Mon) On the main square, this locally run restaurant specializes in down-to-earth *mineira* fare at reasonable prices. Folks with less voracious appetites will appreciate the R$25 *prato mini*, a smaller plate designed for one person.

★ **Empório Santo Antônio** BRAZILIAN **$$**
(☎32 3355-2433; Bélica 133; mains per person R$50-64, all-you-can-eat weekend buffet R$60; ⊙noon-4pm Wed-Sun) At this edge-of-town hideaway, run by the same family for nearly two decades, everything is lovingly homemade – roast chicken, pork cheeks, artisanal *linguiça* (garlicky pork sausage), home-smoked trout and classic *mineira* specialties. The real tour de force is the sumptuous all-you-can-eat weekend buffet, which includes everything from *leitão a pururuca* (crispy roast marinated pork) to homemade cookies. Bring your appetite!

DON'T MISS

COMIDA MINEIRA: MINAS' FABULOUS FOOD

Wherever you go in Minas Gerais, you'll see signs advertising *comida mineira* – the Brazilian term for Minas' fabulous cuisine. Don't miss these culinary specialties, which you'll see throughout the state:

feijão tropeiro – beans mixed with toasted manioc flour, crunchy pork rind, sausage, eggs, kale, garlic and onions

goiabada – sweet guava paste (like thick guava jelly) eaten as a dessert; often served together with Minas cheese under the romantic name *Romeo e Julieta*

queijo Minas – the traditional cow's-milk cheese of Minas Gerais

tutu à mineira – a thick puree of mashed beans with garlic and onions, usually served alongside pork loin, crunchy pork rind, kale and/or rice

pão de queijo – chewy, cheesy and best enjoyed hot from the oven, Minas' famous cheese bread is made with tapioca flour, which accounts for its delightful consistency

Minas is also legendary for its *cachaça* (sugarcane alcohol) – don't leave the state without sampling it!

★Gourmeco ITALIAN $$

(☎32 3355-1955; www.gourmeco.com.br; Direita 10b; mains R$53-60; ⏱12:30-3:30pm & 8-10:30pm Mon, Tue & Thu-Sat, 12:30-4pm Sun; ✎) Authentic Italian antipasti, pasta and risotto dishes – including several vegetarian offerings – coupled with a prime corner location below Tiradentes' Matriz church, make this one of the best eateries in town. Pugliese Slow Food aficionado Umberto and chef Juliana whip up classics ranging from *orecchiette* (ear-shaped pasta) with Bolognese ragù or fava bean puree to panna cotta for dessert.

Tragaluz BRAZILIAN $$

(☎32 3355-1424; www.tragaluztiradentes.com.br; Direita 52; mains R$54-78; ⏱7-10:30pm Sun, Mon, Wed & Thu, to 12:30am Fri & Sat) Set in a romantic, candlelit space with exposed stone and brick walls, Tragaluz prides itself on home cooking served with artistic flair. The innovative dishes range from yam and sugar beet soup to *pintada* (the restaurant's trademark guinea fowl) with veggies, mushrooms and homemade ravioli. Divine desserts include *cachaça* mousse, lemon sorbet and fried guava paste.

Estalagem do Sabor BRAZILIAN $$

(☎32 3355-1144; Gabriel Passos 280; mains per person R$40-75; ⏱11am-5pm) One of Tiradentes' finest restaurants, Estalagem specializes in classic *comida mineira,* from *frango com quiabo* (chicken stewed with okra) to *tutu à mineira* (a thick puree of mashed beans with garlic and onions). The house specialty, *mane sem jaleco,* is a tasty, waistline-expanding concoction of rice, beans, bacon, kale, pork loin, onions, fried eggs and bananas.

Viradas do Largo BRAZILIAN $$

(☎32 3355-1111; www.viradasdolargo.com.br; Rua do Moinho 11; mains per person R$34-60; ⏱noon-10pm Wed-Mon) Tucked down a peaceful lane far from the relative bustle of downtown Tiradentes, this is one of the region's standout restaurants for traditional *comida mineira.* Crowds pack into it on weekends, spilling over into the pleasant outdoor patio and garden area.

Drinking & Entertainment

Bars with outdoor seating and occasional live music vie nightly for visitors' attention on Largo das Forras. Local *cachaça* (sugarcane alcohol) and imported wine are among the drinks of choice here.

Entrepôt du Vin WINE BAR

(☎55 99992-2050; Direita 205; ⏱2-10pm Mon-Thu, noon-midnight Fri & Sat, noon-10pm Sun) This convivial little wine bar with its 18th-century frescoed ceiling makes an agreeable spot to sip a glass or two.

★Organ Concerts CLASSICAL MUSIC

(☎32 3355-1238; Igreja Matriz de Santo Antônio, Padre Toledo s/n; adult/reduced R$40/20; ⏱8pm Fri) Friday visitors should make a beeline for the glittering gold interior of Igreja Matriz de Santo Antônio (p197) for weekly live concerts performed on the church's 18th-century organ.

Information

Bradesco (Passos 43) Has multiple ATMs near the main square.

Secretária Municipal de Turismo (32 3355-1212; turismo@tiradentes.mg.gov.br; Resende Costa 71; 9am-6pm Mon-Fri, to 5pm Sat, to 2pm Sun) Located on the main square. Provides maps, information on hotels and guided tours.

Getting There & Away

BUS

Tiradentes' **bus station** (São Francisco de Paula 71) is just north of the main square, across the stream. Two companies, Presidente (R$3.80, 20 minutes) and Porto Real (R$4.20, 30 minutes), run regular buses between Tiradentes and São João del Rei. Thanks to this friendly rivalry, you'll never wait longer than 45 minutes for a bus during daylight hours. After 7pm, only Porto Real operates, and departures are less frequent. If you miss the last bus from São João (at 10:10pm), a taxi costs about R$60.

With advance planning, it's possible to catch a bus directly from Tiradentes to Rio. Paraibuna (www.paraibunatransportes.com.br) operates a morning bus originating in São João del Rei (8am Monday to Saturday, 10am Sunday) that will pick passengers up in front of the Tiradentes train station (not the bus station); you must buy your ticket in São João and indicate that you're boarding in Tiradentes. Coming from Rio, you can do the same thing in reverse: take Paraibuna's 7am bus Monday through Saturday (or the 2pm bus on Sunday) and indicate that you want to disembark in Tiradentes when buying your ticket; make sure to inform the driver as well.

TRAIN

Tiradentes' **train station** (Praça da Estação s/n; ticket office 9am-4pm Thu-Sat, to 1pm Sun) is located about 700m southeast of the main square. A tourist train (p197) connects Tiradentes with São João del Rei.

Caxambu

0XX35 / POP 22,208 / ELEV 895M

Long before Perrier hit Manhattan singles bars, Caxambu water was being celebrated on the international circuit, winning gold medals at the 1903 Victor Emmanuel III Exposition in Rome and the St Louis International Fair of 1904. More than a century later, the famous waters continue to be sold throughout Brazil.

Caxambu remains the most venerable of several mineral spa towns in southern Minas – collectively known as the Circuito das Águas – though its turn-of-the-century glory has faded gradually toward dowdiness. Even so, it's a convenient transport hub for other southern Minas attractions, and worth a look for curiosity's sake if you're passing this way.

Activities

Parque das Águas PARK, SPRING

(35 3341-3266; www.facebook.com/ParquedasAguasdeCaxambu; admission R$5, plus individual attractions R$5-40; 7am-6pm) A rheumatic's Disneyland, this vast park in the center of town has lovely gardens, tree-shaded canals, a geyser, a spring-fed outdoor swimming pool, a chairlift climbing 800m to the Christ statue atop Morro Cristo hill, and the ornate 1912-vintage **Balneário Hidroterápico**, where you can soak in a hot bath, take therapeutic showers or relax in a sauna.

Sleeping & Eating

Palace Hotel HOTEL **$$**

(35 3341-3341; www.palacehotel.com.br; Dr Viotti 567; s/d/tr R$175/180/250;) This colonial establishment is one of the best deals in town. There's free parking, the pool out back has a waterslide, and the card-playing rooms downstairs exude a faded 19th-century charm. Half and full board are available at the on-site restaurant.

Coreto BUFFET **$**

(35 3341-6561; www.facebook.com/RestauranteCoreto; Praça 16 de Setembro 59; per kilo with/without meat R$42/33; 11am-2:30pm Mon-Fri, noon-3pm Sat & Sun) Organic salads and *mineira* cuisine cooked over the wood fire are the specialties at this self-serve opposite the bandstand in Caxambu's central square.

Information

Secretaria de Turismo (35 3341-7378; www.caxambu.mg.gov.br; Praça 16 de Setembro 24; 8am-noon & 2-6pm Mon-Fri) In the town hall, near the Parque das Águas.

Getting There & Away

From Caxambu's **bus station** (Praça Cônego José de Castilho Moreira), about 1km south of the center, Expresso Gardénia (www.expressogardenia.com.br) offers service to Belo Horizonte (R$119, six hours) at 7:40am daily and 10:40pm Sunday to Friday. Cometa (www.viacaocometa.com.br) goes to São Paulo (R$95, 6¼ hours, four daily). For Rio de Janeiro (R$70 to R$106, five to 5½ hours) and Resende (R$33 to R$49, 2½ hours), gateway to Parque Nacional de Itatiaia, Cidade do Aço (www. cidadedoaco.com.br) runs a daily *executivo* bus at 8am, plus a conventional bus at midnight.

OFF THE BEATEN TRACK

A MYSTICAL RETREAT IN SOUTHERN MINAS

If you're into mysticism or superstition, or just looking for a cheap, fun and idyllic place to relax, consider a detour to the quaint village of **São Thomé das Letras**. High on a plateau north of Caxambu, with a bird's-eye view of the surrounding farmland, São Thomé feels like a world apart. Perhaps this accounts for its reputation among Brazilian mystics as one of the seven sacred cities of the world, and the many sightings of flying saucers and extraterrestrials reported here.

The word 'Letras' in São Thomé's name refers to the mysterious inscriptions found in local caverns such as **Carimbado** and **Chico Taquara** (both 3km outside town) and the **Gruta de São Thomé**, a small cave in the heart of town. Other attractions include the nearby waterfalls **Euboise** (3km), **Prefeitura** (7km) and **Véu de Noiva** (12km) and the town's strikingly rough-hewn buildings, made from slabs of locally quarried quartzite. There are some lovely churches, including **Igreja Matriz de São Thomé** (1785) on leafy Praça da Matriz, and the raw-stone **Igreja de Pedra**, downhill toward the bus station. For great mountain views at sunset and sunrise, head up to the **lookout** 500m above town.

During the third or fourth weekend in August the three-day **Festa de Agosto** fills São Thomé's streets with live music and other festivities.

The town is filled with reasonably priced pousadas and restaurants. A couple of blocks from the Gruta de São Thomé, **Pousada Arco Iris** (☎35 3237-1212; www.pousarcoiris.com.br; João Batista Neves 225; s R$120, d R$220-320, q R$335, chalet per person R$105; ❄@📶🏊) is the most attractive place to stay, with a sauna and pool. For tasty treats in the heart of town, try the excellent per kilo *mineira* cuisine at family-run **Restaurante da Sinhá** (☎35 3237-1348; Capitão Pedro José Martins 31; per kg R$40, all-you-can-eat R$25; ⏲noon-11pm) or the wood-fired pizzas at **Ser Criativo** (☎35 3237-1266; www.facebook.com/SerCriativoPizzanaPedra; Praça Getúlio Vargas 18; pizzas from R$28, mains per person R$18-35; ⏲6pm-midnight).

Just off the main square, Praça da Matriz, São Thomé's **tourist office** (☎35 3237-1276; turismo@saotomedasletras.mg.gov.br; José Cristiano Alves 20; ⏲9am-noon & 2-5pm Mon-Sat, 9am-noon & 1-3pm Sun) provides a map of town and surrounding natural attractions.

From São Thomé's bus station, 1km north of the center, **Coutinho** (☎35 3231-3355; Av Thomé Mendes Peixoto) runs once daily (in good weather only) to/from Caxambu along a rugged but scenic dirt road (R$19, 2¼ hours, leaving São Thomé at 7:30am, returning from Caxambu at 2:15pm). For further-flung destinations such as São Paulo or Belo Horizonte, take one of Coutinho's frequent buses to Tres Corações (R$10, 1½ hours) and change there.

Aiuruoca & the Vale do Matutu

☎0XX35 / POP 7807 / ELEV 989M

About an hour east of Caxambu is the Vale do Matutu, a lush green valley flanked by waterfalls and mountains. Most prominent among the surrounding peaks is photogenic Pico do Papagaio (2293m), which forms the centerpiece of the **Parque Estadual da Serra do Papagaio**. There's some great hiking in the region. Access to the valley is via a very rough dirt road running 20km south from the small town of Aiuruoca. You could easily linger here for a few days, relaxing into the rhythms of nature, reading a good book, hiking and swimming.

Sights & Activities

Hiking destinations include the nearby waterfall **Cachoeira do Fundo** (a moderate four-hour, 10km round trip), or the valley's standout attraction, **Pico do Papagaio** (a challenging eight-hour, 13km round trip with 800m elevation gain, about R$100 per person). Guides are strongly recommended and can be arranged through Pousada Mandala das Águas (p204), **MMA Ecoturismo** (www.aiuruocaminas.com.br/mma-ecoturismo; Antônio Gonçalves 149) in Aiuruoca or the **Casarão do Matutu**, an attractive century-old building at the valley's far end that serves as headquarters for AMA-Matutu, a community organization dedicated to sustainable tourism.

Sleeping & Eating

The nicest place to stay is in the peaceful, verdant Vale do Matutu, where pousadas have sprouted like mushrooms in recent years. There are also a few basic hotels in the less exciting town of Aiuruoca.

★Mandala das Águas POUSADA **$$$**
(☎35 99948-5650; www.mandaladasaguas.com.br; Estrada Vale do Matutu; s/d/ste incl half-board R$300/400/500;) Near the valley's far end, the delightfully tranquil Mandala boasts spacious rooms, verandas with hammocks, an *ofurô* (Japanese hot tub; per two people R$100), panoramic views of Pico do Papagaio and trails to secluded swimming holes in the gorgeous river below. Hearty homemade meals feature produce from the American-Brazilian owners' garden, and the *pão de queijo* at breakfast is superb.

★Kiko & Kika BRAZILIAN **$$**
(☎35 99927-4853; www.facebook.com/kikacraik; Estrada Aiuruoca-Alagoa, Km 1.8; mains R$40-75; ⊙noon-4pm Fri & Sun, to 5pm Sat) For fine dining in a rural setting, try this sweet little restaurant just 2km south of Aiuruoca. Run by a couple with roots in France and Switzerland, it specializes in trout – both fresh and smoked – along with earthy touches such as wooden utensils and fresh herbed lemonade. Dinner is available upon request on Friday and Saturday nights (7pm to 9pm).

Getting There & Away

Aiuruoca's bus stop is on the central Praça Côn José Castilho. Viação Sandra operates buses from Caxambu (R$18, one hour, 6:20pm daily, 10am weekdays only) to Aiuruoca; buses return to Caxambu at 5:20am and 11:15am on weekdays, 5:20am on Saturday and 6:20am on Sunday.

To reach the more remote pousadas in the Vale do Matutu, you'll need your own car (beware the rough road); alternatively, call **Ajuru Taxi** (☎35 99844-1601, 35 3344-1601; www.ajuru.com.br/taxi; Antônio Gonçalves 149). Once settled in the valley, walking is the most pleasant way to get around.

Diamantina

☎0XX38 / POP 48,230 / ELEV 1113M

Isolated but fabulous, Diamantina is one of Brazil's best-preserved and least-visited colonial towns. Surrounded by desolate mountains, it was the most remote mining town in Minas and the starting point for the Estrada Real, the old road to the coast built with the sweat, blood and tears of thousands of African slaves. Diamantina's fine mansions and winding streets haven't changed much in the last 200 years. Designated a Unesco World Heritage Site in 1999, this *cidade histórica* is also the birthplace of Juscelino Kubitschek, former Brazilian president and founder of Brasília.

As with most *mineiro* cities, Diamantina is built on precipitous slopes. The bus station sits high on a bluff, so the 500m descent into town can be tough on the knees, and the return climb is a true workout. The central square is Praça Conselheiro Mota, dominated by **Santo Antônio cathedral** (⊙hours vary) – both colloquially known as Sé.

Sights

Casa de Juscelino Kubitschek MUSEUM
(☎38 3531-3607; São Francisco 241; admission R$10; ⊙8am-5pm Tue-Sat, to 1pm Sun) Casa de Juscelino Kubitschek, childhood home of the former president, is full of historical memorabilia that reflects his simple upbringing as the grandson of poor Czech immigrants. Kubitschek himself believed that his early life in Diamantina influenced him greatly.

Mercado Municipal MARKET
(Municipal Market; Praça Barão Guaicuí; ⊙6-11pm Fri, 8am-1pm Sat & Sun) Built by the army in 1835, this public market is a popular community gathering place on Friday evening, when vendors set up stalls selling typical *mineiro* food, and on Saturday and Sunday mornings, for the weekly produce and crafts markets, respectively. All three events are accompanied by live music. The building's wooden arches inspired Niemeyer's design for the presidential palace in Brasília.

Igreja de NS do Carmo CHURCH
(Rua do Carmo; ⊙hours vary) Adorned with rich, golden carvings and a gilded organ made in Diamantina, this is the town's most opulent church. Constructed between 1760 and 1765, its tower was reputedly built at the rear at the request of locally renowned personage Chica da Silva, so that she might sit in the front pews (Portuguese law at the time denied blacks the right to pass 'beyond the belltower').

Igreja de NS do Rosário dos Pretos CHURCH
(Largo do Rosário; ⊙hours vary) Downhill from the center you'll find Diamantina's

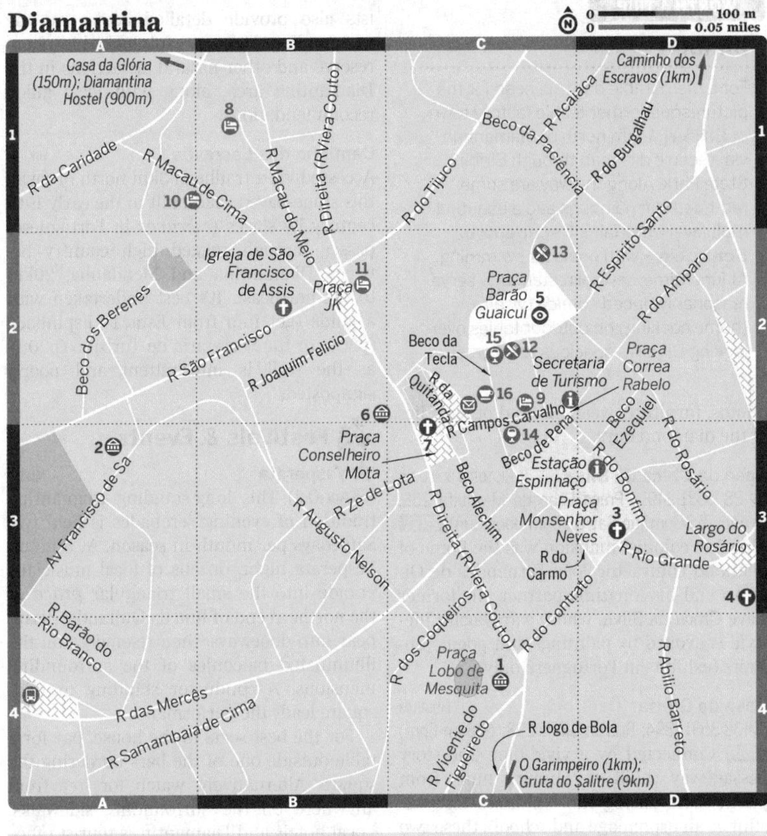

Diamantina

Sights
1 Casa da Chica da Silva C4
2 Casa de Juscelino Kubitschek A3
3 Igreja de NS do Carmo D3
4 Igreja de NS do Rosário dos Pretos D3
5 Mercado Municipal C2
6 Museu do Diamante B2
7 Santo Antônio Cathedral C3

Sleeping
8 Hotel Tijuco B1
9 Pousada Capistrana C2
10 Pouso da Chica A1
11 Relíquias do Tempo B2

Eating
12 Apocalipse Restaurante C2
13 Relicário Gastronomia C2

Drinking & Nightlife
14 A Baiúca C3
15 Capistrana Brewpub C2
16 Livraria Café Espaço B C2

oldest church, built by black slaves in 1731. Don't miss the tree out front with a cross embedded in its trunk; according to legend, it sprang up here as a divine sign to prove the innocence of an 18th-century slave who was falsely accused of stealing diamonds.

Museu do Diamante MUSEUM

(☎38 3531-1382; http://museudodiamante.museus.gov.br; Direita 14; ⏰10am-5pm Tue-Sat, 9am-1pm Sun) FREE Between Praça JK and the cathedral is the house of Padre Rolim, one of the Inconfidentes. It's now the Museu do Diamante, exhibiting religious art, old

WORTH A TRIP

BIRIBIRI

For a memorable day trip, head for the picturesque former textile factory town of **Biribiri**, 14km north of Diamantina via a scenic dirt road through Biribiri State Park. Along the way are some red-hued cliff paintings and a beautiful multilevel waterfall – **Cachoeira da Sentinela** – with pools for swimming. At lunchtime, several restaurants serve reasonably priced *comida caseira* (home cooking) on outdoor tables overlooking Biribiri's spacious town green.

photos, furniture, weapons, and other relics of the diamond days.

Casa da Chica da Silva HISTORIC BUILDING
(☎38 3531-2491; Praça Lobo de Mesquita 266; ⌚noon-5:30pm Tue-Sat, 8:30am-noon Sun) FREE This fine colonial mansion was the home of diamond contractor João Fernandes de Oliveira and his longtime partner, the former slave Chica da Silva, whose extravagant lifestyle is evoked by paintings and poems upstairs (exhibits in Portuguese only).

Casa da Glória MUSEUM
(☎38 3531-1394; Rua da Glória 298; ⌚8am-6pm) FREE Connected by a vivid-blue 2nd-story passageway (built to obscure nuns from public view during the building's 102-year stint as an orphanage and school), these two houses on opposite sides of the street once also served as the residence of Diamantina's diamond supervisors and the palace of its first bishop. Currently housing Diamantina's Institute of Geology, the place has plenty of historical character, but exhibits are limited to a ragtag collection of old photos, mineral specimens and 19th-century German maps.

Activities

Gruta do Salitre CAVING
(admission per person weekend/weekday R$20/10; ⌚9am-noon & 2-5pm Sat, 9am-noon Sun, weekdays by arrangement) This lovely quartzite cave 9km southeast of Diamantina (near the village of Curralinho) is administered by local environmental NGO Biotrópicos. To arrange a guided visit covering the cave's flora, fauna, geology and cultural history, call or stop in at Biotrópicos' Estação Espinhaço (p208) interpretive center in Diamantina, whose staff of professional conservationists also provide detailed advice on the surrounding Unesco Espinhaço biosphere reserve and other natural attractions in the Diamantina area, along with local guide recommendations.

Caminho dos Escravos HIKING
Accessed via a trailhead 3km north of town, this stone-paved road built in the early 19th century by slaves (*escravos* in Portuguese) passes through rugged high country between Diamantina and Mendanha, 20km to the northeast. It's best undertaken with a guide (get info from Estação Espinhaço (p208) or the Secretaria de Turismo (p208), as the trail is intermittent and poorly signposted.

Festivals & Events

★**Vesperata** MUSIC
(⌚Apr-Oct) This long-standing Diamantina tradition of evening serenades is held two Saturdays per month in season. At 8pm on Vesperata night, dozens of local musicians parade into the small triangular *praça* at the northern end of Rua da Quitanda, disappear into doorways, then re-emerge on the illuminated balconies of the surrounding mansions. A conductor standing in mid-square leads the performance.

For the best seats in the house, pay for a table outside one of the bars bordering the square. Alternatively, watch for free from anywhere on the surrounding sidewalks. Local hotels and Diamantina's tourist office (p208) can provide current dates.

Sleeping

Hotels can fill up on Vesperata weekends, when many require a two-night minimum stay; it's best to plan ahead. For late arrivals who only need a convenient place to lay their head, there are several no-frills hotels directly across from the bus station.

Relíquias do Tempo POUSADA **$$**
(☎38 3531-1627; www.pousadareliquiasdotempo.com.br; Macau de Baixo 104; s R$190-250, d R$255-345, tr R$340-460, q R$400-545; 📶🏊) Travel back in time at this gorgeous historical house with fantastic views, antique furniture and local artwork. Afternoon tea in the rustic dining room is a real treat. Downstairs are an old chapel, a museum of historical artifacts and a modern back annex with sauna and pool. Rooms in the original building are smaller and cheaper than the annex units.

Pousada Capistrana POUSADA $$
(☎38 3531-6560; www.pousadacapistrana.com.br; Campos Carvalho 35; s/d R$90/180; P wi-fi) Rooms here are a bit cramped, and street noise can be a problem on weekends, but the price and the location smack in the middle of Diamantina's historic district are hard to beat. There's free parking nearby.

Hotel Tijuco HOTEL $$
(☎38 3531-1022; www.hoteltijuco.com.br; Macau do Meio 211; s R$150-160, d R$210-220, ste R$250-280, q R$350; wi-fi) The once-modernist, now rather retro Tijuco is a Niemeyer creation with spacious, wood-paneled rooms and efficient chain-hotel-style service. It's well worth paying R$10 extra for a front room with veranda and panoramic views; interior units are windowless and claustrophobic. There are some good photos of Juscelino Kubitschek along the staircase.

Pouso da Chica POUSADA $$$
(☎38 3531-6190; www.pousodachica.com.br; Macau de Cima 129; s R$200-250, d R$360-460; air-con wi-fi) This well-maintained pousada near the city center offers 22 air-conditioned rooms, some in the high-ceilinged main building with original wood floors, others in chalets out back. Room prices include hearty soup cooked over the wood stove every evening.

Eating

Apocalipse Restaurante BUFFET $
(☎38 3531-3242; www.facebook.com/ApocalipseRestaurante; Praça Barão do Guaicuí 78; per kg midweek/weekend R$49/55; ⏲11am-3pm; wi-fi) Apocalipse serves an excellent international per kilo lunch in a spacious upstairs room overlooking the municipal market.

Relicário Gastronomia BRAZILIAN $$
(☎38 3531-4294; www.facebook.com/relicario-diamantina; Joaquim Gomes da Costa 59; mains R$33-53; ⏲6-11pm Tue-Thu, 6pm-midnight Fri & Sat, noon-4pm Sun) Whimsically decorated with vintage radios, telephones and sewing machines, this trendy, high-ceilinged corner spot with old vinyl records for placemats serves inventive takes on traditional *mineira* recipes. Don't miss the ever-popular *bolas de feijoada,* deep-fried croquettes made with the same yummy combination of pork, beans, kale and spices used in Brazil's national dish.

O Garimpeiro BRAZILIAN $$
(☎38 3531-1044; www.pousadadogarimpo.com.br/restaurante-o-garimpeiro; Av da Saudade 265; mains per person R$35-70; ⏲6-10pm Mon-Fri, noon-10pm Sat, noon-4pm Sun) Famous for its regional *mineira* dishes, the restaurant at Pousada do Garimpo challenges the heftiest of appetites with its house specialty *bambá do garimpo,* a high-calorie concoction dating back to the diamond-mining days that includes pork chops, beans, rice, finely chopped kale and *angu* (corn porridge). There's also an occasional all-you-can-eat weekend buffet.

Drinking & Nightlife

Diamantina's nightlife hub is the lively cluster of bars with streetside seating along Rua Quitanda and Beco da Tecla, around the corner from the cathedral. On Friday evenings from 6pm onwards, visit Diamantina's Mercado Municipal for **Sexta Nossa**, a community happy hour where locals unwind with drinks and regional food, accompanied by live samba, blues and *chorinho* (informal instrumental music).

Another classic weekend event is **Café no Beco**, held Sunday mornings along the Beco da Tecla, a pedestrianized street between the cathedral and the market square. Locals sell baked goods, play live music and offer free coffee and tea to passersby.

★**Capistrana Brewpub** MICROBREWERY
(☎38 98817-7885; www.cervejacapistrana.com; Beco da Tecla 58; ⏲5pm-late Tue-Fri & Sun, from 2pm Sat) Capistrana Brewpub, on nightlife-happy Beco da Tecla, is the retail outlet for Diamantina's home-grown Capistrana beer, including an excellent pale ale, pilsner and red ale. There's live music on Saturday night.

★**Livraria Café Espaço B** CAFE
(☎38 3531-6005; Beco da Tecla 31; ⏲9am-midnight Mon-Thu, to 2am Fri & Sat, to 2pm Sun; wi-fi) This bookstore-cafe is a relaxing spot to mingle with Diamantina's bohemian set. You can browse books (including a few in English), use the free wi-fi and linger over coffee, tea, wine and light meals.

A Baiúca BAR
(☎38 3531-3181; Quitanda 13; ⏲8am-midnight) This corner bar is a Diamantina classic, with locals popping in day and night for drinks of all kinds. It's also a prime spot to watch the Vesperata (p206).

Information

Bradesco (Praça Barão do Guaicuí) Just below the Mercado Municipal.

Estação Espinhaço (38 3531-2197; www.biotropicos.org.br; Praça Monsenhor Neves 44; 9am-noon & 2-5pm Mon-Fri, to 1pm Sat) Info center for Unesco's Espinhaço biosphere reserve, run by local environmental NGO Biotrópicos. Offers reams of advice on the area's natural attractions and can recommend guides.

Secretaria de Turismo (38 3531-9532; www.diamantina.mg.gov.br/turismo; Praça Antônio Eulálio 53; 9am-6pm Mon-Sat, to 2pm Sun) Distributes a Portuguese-language town map and guide.

Getting There & Away

From Diamantina's **bus station** (Largo Dom João), on a hilltop 750m southwest of the center, Pássaro Verde (p190) runs buses to Belo Horizonte (R$94, five hours, seven to eight daily) and to the neighboring historical town of Serro (R$24, 2¼ hours, two daily). A taxi between the bus station and the center costs around R$15.

Serro & Around

0XX38 / POP 21,435 / ELEV 781M

Founded in 1714, the colonial town of Serro snakes down a hillside in beautiful rural country south of Diamantina. While quite popular with Brazilians, this region remains little visited by foreigners and therefore retains a tranquil and traditional *mineiro* air. Its cheese is considered the best in Minas.

Heading north from Serro towards Diamantina, the tranquil high-altitude hamlets of **Milho Verde** and **São Gonçalo do Rio das Pedras** (less than 35km away) also make lovely stopovers, with access to waterfalls and hikes along some of the most scenic stretches of the original Estrada Real (the 18th-century 'Royal Road' that connected Diamantina to the Rio de Janeiro coast).

Sights

Serro's main attractions are its historic buildings, including a pair of 18th-century churches and a 19th-century baronial mansion. Hours are variable, so check with the tourist office for the latest schedule.

Capela de Santa Rita CHURCH
(admission R$3; hours vary) Serro's most striking building in town is the graceful, single-steepled Capela de Santa Rita, straight uphill from the main square via a steep series of steps. The interior features some masterful faux marble patterns painted onto the woodwork.

Chácara do Barão do Serro HISTORIC BUILDING
(hours vary) FREE Just downhill from town, the Chácara do Barão do Serro is a lovely old mansion affording a glimpse of 19th-century baronial life in Serro.

Festivals & Events

Festa de NS do Rosário CULTURAL
(Jul) In early July, Serro hosts one of Minas' oldest festivals, the Festa de NS do Rosário, dating back to 1728. Townspeople representing Brazil's three main cultural traditions parade through the streets in colorful attire: *caboclos* (the descendants of indigenous peoples and Portuguese) beat out rhythms on bows and arrows, holding mock confrontations with sword- and guitar-wielding *marujos* (Europeans), while *catopês* (Africans) speak in ancient dialect and beat on instruments symbolizing empty plates.

Sleeping & Eating

There are a few simple hotels in Serro's historic center. For a more tranquil and bucolic experience, try the pousadas in the neighboring towns of São Gonçalo and Milho Verde.

Refúgio dos Cinco Amigos POUSADA $
(38 3541-6037; www.pousadarefugio5amigos.com.br; Largo Félix Antônio 160, São Gonçalo; r per person with breakfast R$80, incl full board R$140;) This charmingly rustic Swiss-run pousada next to the church green and bus stop has been welcoming guests to São Gonçalo for over three decades. Simple but delicious meals are cooked on the wood stove, and there's a spacious reading room with a fireplace for chilly nights.

Pousada do Capão POUSADA $$
(38 3541-6068; www.pousadacapao.com; Rua da Nascente 550, São Gonçalo do Rio das Pedras; d with shared bath R$175, 2-person chalet R$220, each additional person R$70;) Six rooms with shared bath and eight chalets encircle a spacious green area at this lovely pousada just outside São Gonçalo. New owner Luis Sergio offers advice on local attractions, including hikes to numerous nearby waterfalls. Guests enjoy an ample breakfast of cheeses, juices and home-baked goods and dinners of pasta, pizza, crepes and sandwiches (R$14 to R$28) at the on-site restaurant.

Café da Praça CAFE $

(Praça João Pinheiro; snacks & light meals R$4-20; ⌚9:30am-10pm Mon-Sat) At the foot of the long staircase leading up to Igreja Santa Rita, this sweet cafe with outdoor seating serves up prime views of Serro's main square, along with fresh juices, coffee and a variety of snacks, from pizzas to *tortinhas de frango* (delicious pastries stuffed with chicken).

Information

Centro de Atendimento ao Turista (☎38 3541-2754; www.serro.mg.gov.br; Praça Dom Epaminondas; ⌚8am-noon & 1-5pm Mon-Sat, 8am-noon Sun) Serro's tourist office has a useful map of the town's old mansions and churches and also provides information about São Gonçalo and Milho Verde.

Getting There & Away

From Serro's new long-distance **bus station** (☎38 3541-1366; MG-259), 750m west of the historical center, Pássaro Verde (p190) runs buses to Diamantina (R$24, 2¼ hours, three daily), while **Serro** (☎31 3201-9662; www.serro.com.br) goes to Belo Horizonte (R$76 to R$103, five to 6¾ hours, five to six times daily) via Conceição do Mato Dentro (R$24, 1½ to 2½ hours) and Serra do Cipó (R$45, 2¾ to 4¼ hours).

TransFacil (38 3541-4091) runs from Serro to Milho Verde (one hour) and São Gonçalo do Rio das Pedras (1½ hours) twice daily Monday through Friday and once on Saturday (no Sunday service).

Parque Nacional da Serra Do Cipó

☎0XX31

Parque Nacional da Serra do Cipó, 100km northeast of Belo Horizonte, is one of the most beautiful parks in Minas. Most of the park's vegetation is *cerrado* and grassy highlands, straddling the Serra do Espinhaço that divides the water basins of the São Francisco and Doce rivers. At lower elevations there are waterfalls and lush, ferny river valleys containing a number of unique orchids. Fauna here includes maned wolves, tamarin monkeys, banded anteaters, jaguars, bats and the small, brightly colored *sapo de pijama* (pyjama frog).

The park is vast, with trails for all fitness levels, ranging from day hikes to waterfalls, viewpoints and swimming holes, to multiday traverses of the *serra*. Information is available at the park's two entrances, just outside the town of Santana do Riacho. Tour operators such as **Bela Geraes Turismo** (☎31 3718-7394; www.serradocipogeraes.com.br; MG-010, Km 96.5) offer various adventure sports, including hiking, horseback riding, mountain biking, kayaking, stand-up paddleboarding and rappelling.

Sights

Parque Nacional da Serra do Cipó – Portaria Areias NATIONAL PARK

(☎31 3718-7151; www.icmbio.gov.br/parnaserradocipo; MG-010, Km 97) FREE The park's main entrance, south of Santana do Riacho, serves as the gateway to several hiking destinations. Two especially popular day trips are the 16km round trip from headquarters to the 70m waterfall called **Cachoeira da Farofa**, and the 24km round trip to **Cânion da Bandeirinha**, an 80m-deep gorge. Shorter hikes include the 4km round trip to the **Mirante do Bem** panoramic viewpoint and the family-friendly **Circuito das Lagoas**, which affords swimming opportunities at the confluence of the Rios Bocaina and Mascate.

Staff at the entrance can provide general information but unfortunately no trail maps – you'll have to content yourself with snapping photos of their lone info booklet.

Parque Nacional da Serra do Cipó – Portaria do Retiro NATIONAL PARK

FREE The northern entrance to the park, accessed via a 3km paved road from Santana do Riacho, is the trailhead for day hikes to several points of scenic interest including the **Bambuzal** swimming hole in the Rio Cipó and three pretty waterfalls: **Cachoeira do Gavião**, **Cachoeira das Andorinhas** and **Cachoeira do Tombador**.

Sleeping & Eating

Camping Véu de Noiva CAMPGROUND $

(☎31 3718-7096; www.acmmg.com.br/veu-da-noiva; MG-010, Km 100; campsite per person R$45; 🛜🏊) Camping in the park is not permitted, but this campground along the main road 5km north of park headquarters is a great alternative. There's a freshwater swimming pool, snack bar and direct access to the lovely Véu de Noiva waterfall via a 200m footpath. Buses will drop you at the entrance upon request.

Grande Pedreira POUSADA $$

(☎31 3718-7007, 31 98492-7548; www.pousadagrandepedreira.com.br; Rua da Pedreira 82; campsite per person R$20, d midweek R$140, weekend R$170-190;) Set on a pretty green hillside across the road from the Véu de Noiva waterfall, this pousada has 15 sweet and simple rooms, most with verandas with hammocks where you can lie and admire the verdant grounds dotted with flowering trees and giant boulders. There's a big open field for camping just below.

Restaurante da Joca BRAZILIAN $
(31 98230-3855; MG-010, Km 97; all-you-can-eat buffet R$20, per kilo R$35; 11am-7pm Thu-Mon) For tasty *mineira* fare, hit this friendly, good-value per kilo joint on Santana do Riacho's main drag. Chef Joca announces each newly prepared dish ('we've got kale, people!', 'feijão tropeiro!') as she brings it out to the traditional wood stove, while her sidekick Alessandro cooks up scrumptious pork loin, sausages, chicken and buffalo steaks on the grill out front.

Getting There & Away

Serro (p209) and Saritur (p175) run buses from Belo Horizonte to the town of Santana do Riacho (R$29, 2½ hours, several daily from 6am to 4pm) just outside the park. For park headquarters, get off just before the Rio Cipó bridge at the southern edge of town, then walk or hitch 3km east down the signposted dirt road on your right. For restaurants and most lodging, stay on the bus and continue through town.

Tabuleiro

0XX31

Approximately 180km north of Belo Horizonte, in the wild high country of Unesco's Serra do Espinhaço Biosphere Reserve, is Cachoeira Tabuleiro, Brazil's third-highest waterfall. The dramatic 273m falls are protected witthin Parque Estadual Serra do Intendente (p210), a state park just outside the small town of Tabuleiro. This remote spot makes a worthwhile detour for anyone traveling north between Parque Nacional da Serra do Cipó and the historic mountain towns of Serro and Diamantina.

Sights

★ Parque Estadual Serra do Intendente PARK
(31 3868-2878; admission R$10; 8am-6pm, last entry for waterfall 2pm, for viewpoint 5pm) This remote state park, 19km west of Conceição do Mato Dentro at the end of a rugged dirt road, preserves a 13,500-hectare chunk of backcountry within Unesco's Serra do Espinhaço Biosphere Reserve. The park's centerpiece is **Cachoeira Tabuleiro**, Brazil's third-highest waterfall (273m). From the park entrance, it's a 1½-hour hike, with steep staircases and a sustained spell of boulder-hopping along the river, to reach the natural swimming pool at the base of the falls.

For a less strenuous perspective on the falls, take the 15-minute trail from the park entrance to the *mirante* (viewpoint).

Sleeping & Eating

Tabuleiro Eco Hostel HOSTEL $
(31 3654-3288; www.tabuleiro-eco-hostel8.webnode.com; Joaquim Costinha 1b, Vila do Tabuleiro; campsite/dm/d incl breakfast R$40/70/150;) About 3km east of the eponymous waterfall, Tabuleiro Eco Hostel offers grassy terraces for camping, plus dorms and private rooms in a series of colorful buildings running down the hillside. There's a small on-site cafe serving soups (R$15) and fixed-price lunches (R$20) when there's enough demand. Accommodations without breakfast cost R$15 less per person.

Getting There & Away

The first part is easy: take a Serro (p209) bus from Belo Horizonte to Conceição do Mato Dentro (R$56, 3¼ to 3¾ hours, eight to 10 daily). The trick is getting from Conceição to Tabuleiro; local buses only leave at 3pm on Monday, Wednesday and Friday, and at 2pm on Saturday, returning from Tabuleiro at 8am the same days (R$10, one hour). A one-way taxi between Conceição and Tabuleiro costs about R$80.

Parque Natural do Caraça

0XX31 / ELEV 1297M

Some 100km east of Belo Horizonte in the heart of the Serra do Espinhaço, the Parque Natural do Caraça is a blissful spot. Isolated from the rest of the world by a mountain ridge, the park encompasses 110 sq km of transition zone between the *Mata Atlântica* (Atlantic rainforest) and *cerrado* (savanna) ecosystems. The park's centerpiece, nestled in a bowl-shaped valley, is a former monastery and boarding school attended by several Brazilian presidents. Now converted to a pousada, it's still owned and run by the Catholic congregation who use the neo-Gothic church for services.

The surrounding countryside includes several mountains, including **Pico do Sol** (at 2070m, the highest point in the Serra do Espinhaço), waterfalls and natural swimming pools. The hillsides are criss-crossed with hiking trails, all marked on a helpful map provided at the park entrance.

The two towns nearest the park are Barão de Cocais and Santa Bárbara. Note that the park gate is only open from 7am to 5pm (or to 9pm for pousada guests).

Sleeping & Eating

★ Pousada Santuário do Caraça POUSADA $$$
(☎31 98978-3179; www.santuariodocaraca.com.br; s R$305-330, d R$405-440, s/d with shared bathroom R$235/315, all incl full board; @☎) Rooms at this peaceful, one-of-a-kind pousada range from simple shared-bath *quartos* off the garden courtyard to larger *apartamentos* (rooms with bathroom), the best of which are in the Ala do Santuário (Sanctuary Wing). All rates include three awesome *mineira* meals featuring local produce. The big highlight of staying here is the nightly feeding of the wolves. Advance reservations required.

Visit midweek if you can, as it's easier to see the wolves and appreciate Caraça's isolation and tranquility without the crowds of weekend escapees from Belo. During less crowded periods breakfast is served in the more intimate downstairs dining room, where you can fry your own eggs on the wood-fired stove. Kids under seven stay for free, and those aged seven to 11 stay half price, making this a superb deal for families.

Getting There & Away

Pássaro Verde (☎31 3073-7575; www.passaroverde.com.br) operates frequent buses from Belo Horizonte to Barão de Cocais (R$35, two hours, every two hours from 6am to 8:30pm). From Ouro Preto, Transcotta (p190) runs two buses Monday through Saturday to Santa Bárbara (R$34, 2½ hours, 7:25am and 1:45pm).

The daily Belo Horizonte–Vitória passenger train operated by Vale (p181) also makes a stop just outside Barão de Cocais, in Dois Irmãos (*convencional/executivo* R$22/36, leaving Belo Horizonte at 7:30am and arriving around 9am).

From Santa Bárbara, Barão de Cocais or Dois Irmãos, a taxi to Parque Natural do Caraça takes roughly 30 minutes and costs around R$100. To reserve a taxi ahead of time, call **Célio do Táxi** (☎31 99689-3098).

Parque Nacional de Caparaó

☎0XX32

This 250-sq-km national park contains southern Brazil's highest mountains, including **Pico da Cristal** (2798m), **Pico do Calçado** (2766m) and the third-highest peak in the country, **Pico da Bandeira** (2892m). Popular with climbers and hikers from all over Brazil, it affords panoramic views of the Caparaó Valley that divides Minas Gerais and Espírito Santo. The wide-open, rocky highlands that predominate here are complemented by a few lush remnants of

DON'T MISS

THE MANED WOLVES OF CARAÇA

The maned wolf – *lobo guará* in Portuguese – is South America's largest wild canine, native to the *cerrado* (savanna) environment protected within the Parque Natural do Caraça. A few years back, one of Caraça's priests had the idea of befriending the wolves, St Francis style. After two years of patient work gradually tempting them toward the church with offerings of food, he gained the wolves' trust.

Nowadays the feeding has become a nightly ritual, open to overnight guests at the Pousada Santuário do Caraça. After dinner in the monastery's old stone refectory, people drift out to the patio. The ceremonial tray of scraps for the wolves is placed on the flagstones just past sunset, while popcorn, herb tea and *cachaça* (sugarcane alcohol) are provided for the humans. Then the waiting begins.

Even on nights when a wolf never comes, the meditative pleasure of sitting under the stars, trading conversation and soaking up Caraça's tranquility is a magical experience. But wait patiently enough and you may be rewarded...with the patter of feet, the sudden hush rippling through the crowd, the scamper up the steps, and the wild eyes of this beautiful creature come to steal a quick meal and then vanish again into the night.

Mata Atlântica (Atlantic rainforest) at lower elevations.

The **park entrance** (www.icmbio.gov.br/parnacaparao; foreigner/Brazilian R$33/17; 7am-6pm) FREE is 2km steeply uphill from the nearest town, Alto do Caparaó. Between November and January there's lots of rain. The best time for clear weather is between June and August - although these are the coldest months. Bring warm clothes!

Activities

★Pico da Bandeira HIKING

The classic hike to the summit of Pico da Bandeira can be made without climbing gear or a guide, as the trail is gradual and well marked. You can drive or take a taxi to the trailhead at Tronqueira, 8km up a steep dirt road from the park entrance. Cars are prohibited beyond Tronqueira. From here, a gradual 9km climb leads to the summit. Allow about three hours for the ascent, and two hours to get back down.

If you prefer to hike with a guide, various agencies around town offer guided excursions, including predawn departures arriving at the summit in time for sunrise.

Sleeping & Eating

Alto Caparaó's lone hotel and small collection of pousadas are strung out along the town's long main street, Av Pico da Bandeira.

Hikers can make use of the national park's four rustic campgrounds: **Tronqueira** (reservaspnc@icmbio.gov.br) FREE and **Terreirão** (reservaspnc@icmbio.gov.br) FREE on the Minas Gerais side, and **Casa Queimada** (reservaspnc.es@icmbio.gov.br) FREE and **Macieira** (reservaspnc.es@icmbio.gov.br) FREE on the Espírito Santo side. All sites have flush toilets and cold showers. Bring drinking water, food and gear, and reserve sites by email.

Pousada do Bezerra POUSADA **$$**

(32 3747-2538; www.pousadadobezerra.com.br; Av Pico da Bandeira; s/d incl breakfast R$150/240;) Run by the same family for over 25 years, this friendly place just below the park entrance has a sauna for soothing weary muscles, a river-fed pool with a waterslide for kids, and an attached restaurant specializing in trout (mains for two people R$58 to R$119).

Caparaó Parque Hotel HOTEL **$$$**

(32 3747-2559; www.caparaoparquehotel.com.br; Av Pico da Bandeira; s R$295-355, d R$390-480, q R$780-835; daily Jan & Jul, Thu-Sun rest of year;) Above town near the park entrance, the region's spiffiest hotel offers comfortable rooms and chalets set amid manicured grounds. It also has two pools, a sauna, a natural swimming hole in the adjacent Rio Caparaó, an on-site restaurant and a pizzeria. It's a civilized spot to unwind after a day in the wild.

Getting There & Away

To reach Caparaó by bus from Belo Horizonte or Vitória (Espírito Santo), head first to the tiny town of Manhumirim, 25km outside the park. Pássaro Verde (www.passaroverde.com.br) operates three daily buses from Belo to Manhumirim (R$101 to R$112, 6½ to 7¼ hours). From Vitória, Águia Branca (www.aguiabranca.com.br) runs a daily 5:50pm bus direct to Manhumirim (R$52, 4½ hours).

Rio Doce (33 3314-1700; www.viacaoriodoce.com.br) runs buses from Manhumirim to Alto Caparaó (R$6.05, 55 minutes, nine daily from 6:30am to 8pm, returning 6:25am to 9:10pm). Alternatively, it's a half-hour taxi ride (about R$75). Manhumirim's **Palace Hotel** (33 3341-2255; http://palacehoteldemanhumirim1.placeweb.site; Av Lauro Célio 656; s/d R$80/120, with shared bathroom R$50/90;), diagonally across from the bus station, is perfectly adequate if you're stuck here overnight.

An alternative option from Vitória is Águia Branca's 7am bus to Manhuaçu (R$50 to R$53, 4¾ hours), where Rio Doce buses connect to Alto Caparaó (R$14, 1½ hours, eight daily).

ESPÍRITO SANTO

POP 4 MILLION

Often overlooked as a destination due to its lack of high-profile attractions, Espírito Santo is an enjoyable place to mingle with Brazilians without the hype and higher prices of neighboring Rio and Bahia states.

North of the state capital of Vitória lies idyllic Itaúnas, a beach town surrounded by sand dunes, beloved for its tranquil natural setting and its exuberant annual *forró* (popular music of the Northeast) festival. Further south, Espírito Santo's beaches cater to vacationing families from neighboring Minas Gerais. Here you'll find low-key beach resorts interspersed with fishing villages, all infused with a cheerful holiday buzz. Inland, Espírito Santo's mountains form an exquisite patchwork of jungled greenery and domed rocky

OFF THE BEATEN TRACK

SAFE HAVEN FOR AN ENDANGERED PRIMATE

The *muriqui* (woolly spider monkey), largest primate of the New World, is a stunning creature. Adult males stand roughly 1.5m tall, and their movements and physical presence can be startlingly humanlike. The animal's photogenic qualities have made it a poster child for wildlife preservation in Brazil, but actually seeing one in the wild can be challenging. At the time of writing, there were only a few thousand left in the world – including less than 500 of the rarer northern *muriqui* – down from an estimated 400,000 at the time of Portuguese colonization.

Three factors explain the *muriquis'* drastic drop in numbers: destruction of their native Mata Atlântica (Atlantic rainforest) habitat, their own docile nature (their Tupi name means 'easygoing folks') and the slow pace of their reproductive cycle. Female *muriquis* generally give birth to a single baby after a gestation period of eight months, and newborns stay with their mothers for up to three years, during which time no new mating occurs. *Muriquis* are slow moving and less combative than most other primates – indeed, they spend most of their time eating, playing and hugging each other! So they've historically been easy targets for hunters.

Estação Biológica de Caratinga (33 3322-2540; www.preservemuriqui.org.br/estacao.htm; park entry fee per person R$120, plus guide R$200; 8am-5pm), a remote and little-visited nature reserve in eastern Minas, is the easiest place to spot *muriquis* in the wild. The reserve has played a critical role in rescuing the northern *muriqui* from extinction. In 1944 there were only eight *muriquis* on record here, when local coffee farmer Feliciano Abdalla committed himself to preserving a large chunk of the native Atlantic rainforest on his property. Forty years later, the Estação Biológica was established, and in the three decades since, research and preservation efforts have led to greater understanding of the *muriqui* and an impressive resurgence of its numbers. Today there are approximately 165 northern *muriquis* living within the reserve, representing roughly a third of the world's population.

Seeing the primates in their natural habitat is an amazing experience, and visitors have a better-than-average chance of a sighting, thanks to the expert skills of local guides. To arrange a day visit, call or email the park office. Bring sturdy shoes for quick scrambles up the hillside, and don't wear red – *muriquis* take this as a sign of aggression. May is an especially good month to visit, as the *muriqui's* favorite food source, *Mabea fistulifera,* is in flower and the animals may linger in a single spot for long periods feeding on the nectar.

Ipanema and Caratinga are the transport hubs nearest the park. Pássaro Verde (www.gabrasil.com.br) runs two daily buses from Belo Horizonte to Ipanema (R$127, eight hours), and one early-morning bus from Ouro Preto to Caratinga (R$86, 5½ hours). São Geraldo (www.saogeraldo.com.br) also runs an overnight service from Vitória (Espírito Santo) to Caratinga (R$74, 5½ hours).

From either Caratinga or Ipanema, Rio Doce (p212) runs buses to the entrance of the reserve (R$19, two hours from Caratinga; R$9, one hour from Ipanema); ask to be let off at the Estação Biológica. From the bus stop on Hwy BR-474, it's a 2km walk up a dirt road to the park headquarters.

Ipanema is your best bet for an overnight stay. The centrally located hotel **Itália Palace** (33 3314-1793; www.italiapalacehotel.com; Av 7 de Setembro 383; s/d with fan R$75/125, with air-con & minibar R$125/175;) offers decent value.

outcroppings, culminating in the spectacularly scenic state park of Pedra Azul.

Even without all these scenic attractions, it would be worth visiting Espírito Santo just to eat. Local seafood specialties such as *moqueca* and *torta capixaba* (seafood frittata with olives and hearts of palm) are famous throughout Brazil.

Vitória

0XX27 / POP 363,140

Built on an island just off the Atlantic coast and connected to the mainland via a series of bridges, Espírito Santo's capital have some attractive sandy beaches and a lush backdrop of mountains descending to the sea that's vaguely reminiscent of Rio. The locals, known as *capixabas,* are warm and friendly, and the city has a flourishing economy, which means many universities, bars, restaurants and hotels.

That said, Vitória is first and foremost an industrial port city, and its aesthetic appeal is easily lost on first-time visitors. Given the city's size, it takes time to discover its diamonds in the rough – the elegant yellow 18th-century government palace, the striking hilltop convent in Vila Velha (the first place in Espírito Santo to be colonized) and the nationally famous Garoto chocolate factory – so if you're in a hurry, your best bet may be to treat Vitória as a transport hub and move on.

Sights & Activities

The city's best beaches are **Praia do Camburí** to the north, and **Praia da Costa** to the south, in the sister city of Vila Velha.

Convento da Penha CONVENT
(27 3329-0420; www.conventodapenha.org.br; Rua Vasco Coutinho; 5:15am-4:45pm Mon-Sat, from 4:15am Sun) This 16th-century convent atop the densely forested Morro da Penha is a must-see. The panoramic city views are magnificent, and the chapel (founded in 1558) isn't too bad either. It's a major pilgrimage destination – around Easter expect massive crowds paying homage to NS da Penha, some climbing the hill on their knees.

Anchieta Palace PALACE
(27 3636-1032; www.facebook.com/palacioanchieta; Praça João Clímaco; 9:30am-5pm Tue-Fri, to 4pm Sat & Sun) FREE Vitória's grandest historic building is this former Jesuit college and church, now the seat of state government. Free 40-minute guided tours include the original 16th-century foundations, artifacts discovered during renovation, and the tomb of Padre José de Anchieta (1534–97), an early missionary hailed as the 'Apostle of Brazil'. Weekend tours (50 minutes) visit additional rooms reserved for government functions on weekdays.

Parque Moscoso PARK
(Av Cleto Nunes) *Capixabas* like to walk and relax in the leafy Parque Moscoso, just west of the city center.

Garoto Chocolate Factory FOOD & DRINK
(27 3320-1000; www.garoto.com.br; Praça Meyerfreund 1; factory/museum tour R$25/5; 9am-5pm Mon-Fri, to 2pm Sat) Brazil's best chocolate is made and sold right here, at Garoto's factory and store. Reserve ahead online for a 1½-hour factory tour (in Portuguese) that includes a chocolate tasting. For a short glimpse of Garoto's history, visit the adjacent three-room museum, which houses vintage machinery, advertisements and a wonderful traveling salesman's case filled with chocolate.

Take bus 500 to Vila Velha, then transfer to bus 503, 507, 525 or 526

Sleeping & Eating

Chain hotels predominate in Vitória and offer the city's best value for money. Staying out at the beach is a much more attractive option than downtown, which is deserted after nightfall. The waterfront Praia do Canto neighborhood offers the city's best eating and nightlife. Check out the Triângulo das Bermudas, a neighborhood packed with bars, eateries and nightclubs centered on the intersection of Joaquim Lírio and João da Cruz. Crowds also gather at Curva da Jurema, populated by shacks that serve snacks and food into the wee hours.

Ibis Vitória HOTEL $$
(27 2104-4850; www.ibis.com.br; João da Cruz 385, Praia do Canto; r R$165-270;) Well-priced given its prime location, this chain hotel sits right at the edge of the Triângulo das Bermudas, Vitória's nightlife hub, and is only a few blocks from the beach. Breakfast costs R$23 extra. There's another Ibis with identical prices 1.5km north opposite the Camburí beachfront.

Senac Ilha do Boi HOTEL $$
(27 3345-0111; www.hotelilhadoboi.com.br; Bráulio Macedo 417; r from R$230;) For a night of luxury, this is an excellent choice. It's located on top of a hill with sweeping views of the surrounding bay. The service is impeccable and the amenities delightful, including a tennis court, solarium, piano bar, pools and saunas.

★ **Pirão** SEAFOOD $$$
(27 3227-1165; www.piraovitoria.com.br; Joaquim Lírio 753, Praia do Canto; mains for 2 people R$90-230; 11am-4pm & 6-11pm Mon-Fri, 11am-5pm Sat & Sun) With award-winning *moquecas* (featuring everything from whiting to shrimp to lobster) and *torta capixaba* (seafood frittata with olives and hearts of palm), Pirão has earned a

reputation as one of Vitória's finest restaurants. On warm evenings, sit outside under the awning to watch the endless parade of passersby and catch tunes from the live music venue across the street.

Information

ATMs for several banks are clustered together inside the bus station.

Espírito Santo's state government operates two conveniently located tourist information booths: in the arrivals hall at the **airport** (Via do Aeroporto; 7am-1pm & 2-7pm) and opposite track 6 at the **bus station** (Av Alexandre Buaiz 350; 7am-1pm & 2-7pm).

Getting There & Away

AIR

With a spiffy new terminal opened in 2018, **Eurico Salles Airport** (27 3235-6300; www.infraero.gov.br) is 12km northeast of the city center. Flights leave regularly for Belo Horizonte, Rio, São Paulo and other Brazilian cities.

BUS

Vitória's teeming, modern **bus station** (27 3203-3666; Av Alexandre Buaiz 350) is just west of the old town center.

TRAIN

Companhia Vale do Rio Doce (p181) runs a daily train to Belo Horizonte (*econômica/executiva* R$73/105, 13 hours) from **Estação Ferroviária Pedro Nolasco** (Av Mario Gurgel s/n, Cariacica), 5km west of downtown Vitória in Cariacica.

Getting Around

TO/FROM THE AIRPORT

Between the airport and the city center, take local bus 539 (R$3.40); buy tickets onboard. Going into Vitória, the bus is marked 'Jardim América.' Returning to the airport, it's marked 'Terminal Carapina.' Taxis from the airport cost around R$35 to Praia do Canto or R$45 to the city center. An Uber will cost about half as much.

BUS

Local buses (R$3.40) run from the various stops outside the bus station; the route is written on the side of each bus. For the center, catch any bus that goes along Av Vitória and get off after you pass the yellow Anchieta Palace on your left. For Praia do Camburí, catch any bus that goes along Av Dante Michelini. For Praia do Canto and Triângulo das Bermudas, take any bus that goes along Av Saturnino de Brito. To Vila Velha and Praia da Costa catch any bus marked Praia da Costa.

Itaúnas

0XX27 / POP 2500

Surrounded by a majestic state park and encroaching sand dunes, Itaúnas masquerades as a sleepy fishing village most of the year. However, around New Year's Eve and Carnaval (February/March), and again in July, it's a party-mad town filled with young Brazilians who come for the lively *forró* dance parties as much as for the beautiful surroundings.

Near the Bahia border 270km north of Vitória, Itaúnas is one of those rare places that manages to retain a low-key 'end of the road' feel despite the intermittent barrage of tourists. Many visitors fall under the town's easygoing spell and end up staying longer than they expected.

More than fifty years ago, sand dunes engulfed the original village of Itaúnas, which was set about 1km closer to the ocean than it is now – these days the old church tower and other ruins lie completely buried in sand, marked only by an interpretive sign.

BUSES FROM VITÓRIA

DESTINATION	COST (R$)	TIME (HR)	BUS COMPANY
Belo Horizonte	112-152	9	São Geraldo (www.saogeraldo.com.br), Kaissara (www.kaissara.com.br)
Conceição da Barra (for Itaúnas)	68-90	5-6	Águia Branca (www.aguiabranca.com.br)
Domingos Martins	14	1-1¼	Águia Branca
Guarapari	17	1¼	Planeta (www.viacaoplaneta-es.com.br)
Pedra Azul	27	2	Águia Branca
Porto Seguro	149-259	11	Águia Branca
Rio	140-255	8	Águia Branca, Kaissara
Salvador	240-270	22	Águia Branca

Sights & Activities

★Parque Estadual de Itaúnas PARK

(☎27 3762-5196; www.iema.es.gov.br/PEI; ⊙8am-5pm) FREE The 36.7-sq-km Parque Estadual de Itaúnas extends for 25km along the coast and has impressive 20m- to 30m-high sand dunes that afford magnificent views of the Atlantic Ocean and the surrounding mangrove forest and wetlands. The wilderness here is home to monkeys, sloths, *jaguatiricas* (wildcats) and sea turtles, who come onshore from September to March to lay eggs. The **park office** (pei@iema.es.gov.br; ⊙8am-5pm), in the village next to the Rio Itaúnas bridge, has informative displays about the local flora, fauna and culture, along with a souvenir shop.

Trilha das Dunas WALKING

(Dunes Trail) Just outside town, the state park's most popular hike is this 1km trail across the dunes to a cluster of beachside *barracas* (stalls selling beer and seafood). From Itaúnas, cross the bridge over the river and follow the dirt road until the dunes slope down to meet it. At the crest of the first dune, panoramic views of the ocean unfold.

Off to the right, the site of the original village of Itaúnas (now buried in sand) is clearly signposted.

Riacho Doce WALKING

Ambitious hikers can follow the long, flat beach 8km north from Itaúnas to Riacho Doce, a small river that forms the border between Espírito Santo and Bahia. You'll know you've arrived when you see the hand-painted sign on the far side '*Sorria – você está na Bahia!*' (Smile – you're in Bahia!). Near the river mouth, **Pousada do Celsão** (☎27 99951-9834; Riacho Doce; mains per person R$30; ❄) serves tasty home-cooked meals.

To return to Itaúnas, retrace your steps down the beach, or hitch a ride with one of the pickup trucks or school buses that occasionally drive the 16km road back to town.

Casinha de Aventuras OUTDOORS

(☎27 99981-9616; www.casinhadeaventuras.com.br; Av Bento Daher; ⊙9am-noon & 3-8pm Jan & Jul, 9am-noon rest of year) Near the bus stop in the center of town, this well-established outfit arranges kayaking trips along the Rio Itaúnas, horseback and dune-buggy excursions, bike rentals and more.

Festivals & Events

Reveillon on New Year's Eve draws up to 10,000 visitors each year. Carnaval also draws a festive, youthful crowd.

FENFIT DANCE

(Festival Nacional de Forró; www.forrodeitaunas.com; ⊙Jul) For 10 days in mid- to late July, Itaúnas hosts this national festival celebrating *forró* (popular music of the Northeast). Big-name performers pour in from all over Brazil, and there's music and dancing all day and night.

Sleeping

Pousada & Camping A Nave POUSADA, CAMPGROUND $

(☎27 3762-5102; www.anave.tur.br; Ítalo Vasconcelos; campsite per person R$40, s/d from R$100/140; @ 📶) Rustic rooms with carved wooden doors abound at this attractive pousada, which is a labor of love for sculptor-owner Júlio. The attached campground overlooks a mangrove forest and sand dunes at the northern edge of town.

★Casa da Praia POUSADA $$

(☎27 3762-5133, 27 99902-0533; www.pousadacasadapraiaitaunas.com.br; Dercilio Ferreira da Fonseca; r R$170-250; ❄ 📶) This backstreet hideaway is one of Itaúnas' loveliest pousadas. The guest rooms, surrounded by pretty landscaped grounds, feature cheerful colors, flower-patterned sheets and immaculate blue-and-white-tiled bathrooms. After nightfall, nothing compares to lying in a hammock on the upstairs deck, listening to the sounds of the river, the ocean and insects chirping in the balmy evening air.

Pousada Zimbaue POUSADA $$

(☎27 3762-5023, 27 98111-9159; www.guiaitaunas.com.br/zimbaue.html; Cabral da Silva 6; d R$190-250; ❄ @ 📶) Lovingly presided over by longtime owners Kelly and Felipe, this cheerful family-run pousada just off the main square has clean white sheets, colorful decor, free bicycles for guest use and a spacious common area with DVD player and internet access.

Pousada dos Corais POUSADA $$

(☎27 3762-5200; www.pousadadoscorais.com.br; Barcelos 154; d/tr R$250/310; ❄ @ 📶 🏊) If you're suffering from the heat, try this friendly pousada with its air-con rooms, comfortable sitting areas and pool.

OFF THE BEATEN TRACK

GREEN DETOURS IN ESPÍRITO SANTO

North of Vitória, Espírito Santo offers a couple of off-the-beaten-track attractions for nature lovers. Both are easily accessible by car as day trips from Vitória, or can be incorporated into a longer itinerary progressing north towards Bahia.

Reserva Natural Vale (27 3371-9702; www.vale.com/rnv; Hwy BR-101, Km 122, Linhares; 8:30am-4pm) North of Linhares towards the Bahia border, this privately protected 218-sq-km expanse of Atlantic rainforest has earned it a place on the Unesco World Heritage list for its tremendous biological diversity. Visitors can stay overnight at the reserve's simple but comfortable **lodge** (27 3371-9797; Hwy BR-101, Km 122, Linhares; s R$110-225, d R$145-260;) and explore the surrounding network of trails.

Museu de Biologia Professor Mello Leitão (27 3259-1182; www.inma.gov.br; José Ruschi 4, Santa Teresa; 8am-5pm Tue-Sun) In the pretty mountain town of Santa Teresa, 82km northwest of Vitória, this museum celebrates the work of local ecologist Augusto Ruschi (1915–86), who conducted pioneering studies on the region's remarkable variety of hummingbirds and orchids and was a strong early proponent of environmental protection in Brazil. The verdant grounds are a peaceful oasis, and offer a chance to observe many local plant and hummingbird species.

Eating

There are plenty of inexpensive eateries scattered around Itaúnas. Especially appealing are the *barracas* (food stalls) out at the beach, which serve seafood and beer with ocean views. Note that hours are seasonal and prone to change.

★Dona Pedrolina SEAFOOD $$
(27 3762-5296; www.facebook.com/restaurantedapedrolina; Lionório Lisboa de Vasconcelos 110; mains per person R$20-65; 11:30am-11pm Dec-Mar & Jul, to 6pm rest of year) At this sweet, unassuming family-run place, Dona Pedrolina prepares delicious home-cooked meals, as she's been doing for 25 years – in between lull periods working at her sewing machine on the back table. The menu includes simple *pratos feitos* (plates of the day) of fish, rice, beans and salad, alongside more elaborate offerings like *moqueca de camarão* (shrimp stew) – feeding three people for R$190.

Oficina 1 Express PIZZA $$
(27 98111-9159; Demerval Leite da Silva; pizzas R$24-49; 5:30pm-midnight daily Dec-Mar & Jul, Fri & Sat rest of year) Opposite the church square, Oficina 1 serves some of Itaúnas' best and most reasonably priced pizzas in a bright space playfully decorated with road signs, tires, car seats and the refurbished shells of vintage VW buses.

A Casa di Berê ITALIAN $$
(27 99986-1228; www.facebook.com/Bererestaurante; Lionório Lisboa de Vasconcelos 120; mains R$29-46; 5:30-11pm Tue-Sun) Grab a table on the front patio of this pretty turquoise house, suffused with the warm-hearted presence of chef-owner Berê, who specializes in delicious pastas and *parmigianas* (meats with melted cheese and homemade tomato sauce). Post-dinner treats include arabica coffee and Berê's trademark dessert, made with local white cheese and warm guava paste and topped with a sprig of mint.

Dona Tereza SEAFOOD $$
(27 3762-5031; www.facebook.com/restaurantedonaterezaitaunas; Leite da Silva; mains R$15-65; 11am-midnight Dec-Mar & Jul, to 6pm rest of year) With a breezy front terrace and menus printed on wooden boards, this long-standing Itaúnas favorite is a family affair – don't be surprised if the young grandson takes your order! The *prato feito* (listed as 'pf' on the menu) is a great deal, including fish, rice and beans for only R$15. From the central square, go one block toward the river

Drinking & Entertainment

During high season the pounding beats of *forró,* reggae and *axé* (an Afro-Brazilian pop style incorporating samba, rock, soul and other influences) spill from every open window and doorway in Itaúnas. Things don't really start swinging till after midnight, and the party lasts till dawn.

Bar da Ponte BAR
(Dermeval Leite da Silva; hours vary) Next to the Rio Itaúnas bridge, this supremely laid-back shack of a bar serves everything from

juices to caipirinhas and hosts live reggae during peak party periods.

★ **Bar Forró** LIVE MUSIC
(☎27 3762-5087; www.forrodeitaunas.com; Vasconcelos 98; ⌚hours vary) This ever-popular *forró*-themed bar with its huge dance floor is the center of the action during New Year's, Carnaval and the Festival do Forró in July.

Buraco do Tatu LIVE MUSIC
(☎27 99651-3126; www.facebook.com/buracodotatuoficial; Vasconcelos 49; ⌚hours vary) A popular venue for live *forró* during holiday periods throughout the year, the 'Armadillo's Lair' also periodically hosts other events. See the Facebook page for current goings-on.

Information

Although most businesses accept credit cards, there are no banks in Itaúnas; bring some cash. The closest town with an ATM is Conceição da Barra, 23km away down a bumpy dirt road.

Getting There & Away

The closest place you can make long-distance bus connections is in Conceição da Barra, 23km south. Águia Branca (www.aguiabranca.com.br) runs three buses daily from Vitória to Conceição (*convencional/executivo* R$68/90, five to six hours).

From Conceição a local Mar Aberto bus goes to Itaúnas (R$9.75, 40 minutes) at 7am, 12:30pm and 3:30pm daily, returning to Conceição at 8am, 1:30pm and 4:30pm. There's an additional 10:30am bus to Itaúnas on Monday and Friday throughout the year (returning at 11:30am), plus multiple extra buses in summer. If you get stuck overnight in Conceição, there are several pousadas to choose from.

To head north into Bahia, first catch an Águia Branca bus from Conceição out to São Mateus on the main highway (R$10, 45 to 55 minutes, five to eight daily). From there, buses run to Porto Seguro (*convencional/executivo* R$81/100, 6¾ hours, two to three daily).

Guarapari & Around

☎0XX27 / POP 123,166

About 60km south of Vitória, **Guarapari** is a favored resort destination for Brazilians and retains a relaxed, fun and family-friendly atmosphere. There are 23 beaches in the municipality, each with an attractive mountain backdrop.

South of Guarapari, you'll find a trio of beach communities worthy of an afternoon's jaunt, all within a 45-minute drive.

Ubu, 20km south of Guarapari, is a sleepy little seaside town with a picturesque waterfront.

Eight kilometers further south is **Anchieta**, one of Espírito Santo's oldest settlements, with a 16th-century sanctuary founded by famed Jesuit priest José de Anchieta. Every year devoted followers of Padre Anchieta participate in the **Passos de Anchieta** (Steps of Anchieta; www.abapa.org.br; ⌚Jun), a four-day, 100km pilgrimage along the beach from Vitória to Anchieta.

Continuing another 8km south of Anchieta, **Iriri** is an agreeable coastal getaway very popular with *mineiros*, who come in droves during the summer months (especially Carnaval).

Sights

Guarapari's best and longest urban beach is **Praia do Morro**, northeast of downtown, famous for the reputedly healing properties of its radioactive black monazitic sand. Closer to the center, from north to south, you'll find **Praia dos Namorados**, small but surrounded by rocks creating beautiful pools; **Praias Castanheiras** and **Areia Preta**, for more radioactive sand and crystal-clear waters; and **Praia do Meio** (Praia do Siribeira), with its gorgeous rock pools.

Top beaches immediately south of Guarapari include the long, beautiful **Praia Enseada Azul**; the stunning **Praia dos Padres**, accessible only by trail from Enseada Azul; and, at the far southern end of town, **Meaípe**, best known for its beachfront eateries.

Sleeping & Eating

★ **Recanto da Pedra** POUSADA $$
(☎28 3534-1599; www.recantodapedra.com.br; Av Beira Mar 16; s R$155-201, d R$210-265; ❄📶) Hands down the best value along this stretch of coast, Recanto da Pedra is picturesquely sited on rocks at Iriri beach's northern end. Many rooms have terraces with bird's-eye views of the curving shoreline. The attached restaurant serves excellent food (mains per person from R$36), and swimmers occasionally pop up from the water for a quick drink at the bar.

Hotel Atlântico HOTEL $$
(☎27 3361-1551; www.hotelatlanticoguarapari.com.br; Av Edísio Cirne 332; d R$250-315; ❄@📶🏊) Just across from Praia dos Namorados in the heart of Guarapari, this well-equipped hotel offers comfy rooms

with panoramic terraces, plus perks including a sauna, poolside bar and free beach umbrellas.

Restaurante do Português SEAFOOD $$
(☎28 3534-1222; Alpoim 558, Iriri; mains for 2 people from R$55; ⏲11am-9pm) Generous portions of local seafood, from fried fish to shrimp and lobster stews, are served at this unpretentious eatery half a block from Iriri's beach. *Pratos individuais* (R$17 to R$20), featuring your choice of fish, chicken, beef or pork with rice, beans and salad, offer great value for solo diners.

There are a few bare-bones rooms (R$60 per person) upstairs.

★Cantinho do Curuca SEAFOOD $$$
(☎27 3272-2000; Av Santana 96, Meaípe; mains per person R$60-180; ⏲11am-10pm Mon-Sat, to 6pm Sun) The *moqueca* (fish stew) at this beachfront eatery in Meaípe has been voted the best in Brazil multiple times. Everything from fish to squid and shrimp to bananas finds its way into the dozens of clay pots bubbling away in the cavernous kitchen. Dine with toes in the sand at one of the limited front tables facing the water.

★Moqueca do Garcia SEAFOOD $$$
(☎28 3536-5050; www.moquecadogarcia.com.br; Av Magno Ribeiro Muqui, Ubu; mains per person R$52-175; ⏲11am-10pm) Celebrating more than half a century in business, this award-winning restaurant with a spacious, airy dining room down by the mermaid statue on Ubu's waterfront serves top-notch *capixaba* cuisine. Seafood is the house specialty, from straightforward fish and shrimp *moquecas* to the let-out-all-the-stops *mariscada à Ubu* (a savory stew of shrimp, lobster, mussels, octopus and crab).

ℹ Information

There are several banks with ATMs along Joaquim da Silva Lima in Guarapari's city center.

Tourist Office (☎27 3262-8759; seltur@guarapari.es.gov.br; Jacinto Almeida 32; ⏲noon-6pm) In the center just west of the bridge. Has maps and information in Portuguese.

ℹ Getting There & Away

From Guarapari's **bus station** (Av Governador Jones dos Santos Neves 99, Várzea Nova), **Planeta** (☎27 3223-6126; www.viacaoplaneta-es.com.br) offers frequent services to Vitória (R$17, 1¼ hours), Ubu (R$5, 30 minutes), Anchieta (R$7, 40 minutes) and Iriri (R$9, one hour).

Domingos Martins

☎0XX27 / POP 34,757 / ELEV 542M

As you leave Espírito Santo's coast for the mountainous interior, the landscapes get more dramatic, the European immigrant influences more pronounced and the temperatures cooler. High season here is May to August, when Brazilians flock inland for a rare taste of winter comforts – chilly nights, fondue and a blazing fire.

Tucked into the highlands of the Serra Capixaba, the pretty little German-style town of Domingos Martins – also referred to as Campinho by locals – makes a good base for exploring the nearby forests, streams and mountains. The town's Germanic roots are evident in the bilingual signs scattered around town, the German-influenced cuisine found on many local menus and the orderly layout of the main square, a pretty gathering spot with benches, trees, well-tended flowers and an old Lutheran church.

Sights

Instituto Reserva Kautsky GARDENS
(☎27 3268-2300; www.institutokautsky.org.br; Rodovia João Ricardo Schorling, Km 2; admission R$10; ⏲8-11:30am & 1-5pm) Flora lovers should head out to this lovely mountainside reserve, established by dedicated botanist Roberto Kautsky, who cultivated more than 100 species of orchids at his home at the southern end of town. To arrange a visit, phone weekdays between 8am and 5pm, or send an email.

Festivals & Events

Sommerfest CULTURAL
(www.facebook.com/SommerfestDomingosMartins; ⏲late Jan) In late January or early February, Domingos Martins celebrates its German heritage with music, dance and food during the four-day Sommerfest.

Festival Internacional de Inverno MUSIC
(www.festivaldm.com.br; ⏲Jul) In the second half of July, the annual Festival Internacional de Inverno is a 10-day gathering of Brazilian and international musicians who offer daily classes and nightly concerts on Domingos Martins' main square.

Sleeping & Eating

Pousada Pouso do Barão POUSADA $$
(☎27 3268-1028; www.pousodobarao.net.br; Roberto Carlos Kautsky 346; d R$190-300, per additional person R$80; P 📶) At this converted family

home within a five-minute walk of downtown Domingos Martins, owners Ilton and Fátima offer five spotless rooms including two smaller doubles, a wheelchair-accessible triple and a pair of spacious upstairs units sleeping four to six. The walls are adorned with Fátima's own Bauernmalerei (traditional German painting), and there's free parking on-site.

★**Choperia Fritz Frida** GERMAN **$$**
(☎27 3268-1808; www.facebook.com/fritzfrida restaurante; Av Presidente Vargas 782; mains R$48-98; ⏲11am-11pm Sun, Mon, Wed & Thu, to 2am Fri & Sat) This half-timbered building overlooking Domingos Martins' main square serves old German favorites such as sausages, sauerkraut and Wiener schnitzel, along with fondue, pizza and locally brewed Trarko beer. Half portions cost 70% of the full portion price.

Drinking

★**Cervejaria Barba Ruiva** MICROBREWERY
(☎27 3268-1223; www.facebook.com/Barba-RuivaCervejaria; Rodovia João Ricardo Schorling, Km 1; ⏲6pm-midnight Fri, 11am-midnight Sat, 11am-5pm Sun) At the sign of the red-bearded lumberjack, Espírito Santo's very first brewpub (opened in 2016) is a welcome addition to Domingos Martins' social scene. Its award-winning IPA is the star attraction in a quintet of homebrews, while bar snacks and frequent live music keep things hopping all weekend long.

Information

Casa da Cultura (☎27 3268-2550; www.domingosmartins.es.gov.br; Av Presidente Vargas 531; ⏲8am-5pm Tue-Fri, 10am-4pm Sat & Sun) Domingo Martins' unofficial tourist office, offering a wealth of advice about Domingos Martins and the surrounding area. The museum upstairs features photos, documents and household objects dating from 1847, when Pomeranians first settled this colony.

Getting There & Away

Águia Branca (www.aguiabranca.com.br) runs direct buses (R$14, one to 1¼ hours, seven to 10 daily) along the 42km route from Vitória to Domingos Martins' **bus station** (☎27 3268-1243; Rua Bernardino Monteiro). Upon request, any bus between Vitória and Belo Horizonte will also stop on the main highway just outside the town entrance gate, where you can call a taxi (27 99917-4959) for the 3km ride to the town square (R$15).

Pedra Azul

Towering dramatically above the surrounding green hills, 50km west of Domingos Martins along Hwy BR-262, is one of Espírito Santo's quintessential attractions – Pedra Azul (500m). This massive rock outcropping, tinted by a bluish moss that changes color with the sun's shifting rays, makes for some fabulous photo ops and forms the centerpiece of its own state park, with hiking trails, natural swimming pools and some of Espírito Santo's best rock climbing.

Locals regularly come up here from the nearby city of Vitória to spend an entire weekend in nature – but even if you only visit on a day trip, it's well worth the detour.

Sights & Activities

★**Parque Estadual da Pedra Azul** PARK
(☎27 3248-1156; www.iema.es.gov.br/PEPAZ; Rota do Lagarto, Km 2.3; ⏲8am-5pm Tue-Sun, last entry 2:30pm) FREE If you've made it to Espírito Santo, don't miss this gorgeous state park. A two- to three-hour self-guided walk affords magnificent views of Pedra Azul and the surrounding forest and farmland, with stops at the rock's nine natural pools. Bring a swimsuit and sturdy shoes – the climb is moderately difficult, and there's a short section where ropes are used to scale a steep rock face. Arrive early on weekends and holidays, as trail access is limited to 150 people.

Rock climbing, another popular Pedra Azul pursuit, is limited to 28 people per day; climbers must make arrangements with park authorities via email ahead of time, bring their own gear, arrive between 6am and 9am on the appointed day and be off the mountain by 5pm. Note that camping in the park is prohibited.

Fjordland Cavalgada Ecológica HORSE RIDING
(☎27 3248-0076; www.fjordland.com.br; Rota do Lagarto, Km 2.2; 20min/40min/1¾hr trail rides R$50/90/150; ⏲8am-4:30pm Fri-Sun) This outfit leads horseback excursions around the foot of Pedra Azul on beautiful Fjorde horses from Norway.

Sleeping & Eating

The area is dotted with pousadas and fancy resort hotels, many offering the option of full board.

Recanto da Pedra POUSADA $$

(☎27 99805-0639; www.recantodapedra-es.com.br; Rota do Lagarto, Iriri; d midweek/weekend R$250/300; 📶) Facilities are a bit faded at this older pousada, but the location directly adjacent to Pedra Azul and the state park entrance can't be beat. The best rooms have balconies with full-on views of the rock face.

★**Pousada Pedra Azul** POUSADA $$$

(☎27 3248-1101; www.ppazul.com; Rota do Lagarto, Km 1.5; d R$430-875, ste R$820-1065; 📶🏊) Set in lovely gardens only 500m from park headquarters, this high-end pousada is one of the region's oldest. The main brick-and-wood building with Alpine-style balconies and pagoda-like roofs was designed by Brazilian architect Zanine. Amenities include a pool, sauna, tennis courts, lake and waterfall. The spacious, renovated guest rooms have high ceilings, big tubs and armchairs.

Pousada Peterle POUSADA $$$

(☎27 3248-1171; www.pousadapeterle.com.br; Hwy BR-262, Km 88; d midweek/weekend from R$330/450; 📶🏊) Just off the busy main highway, directly opposite the Águia Branca bus stop and 2km below the park entrance, Pousada Peterle has attractive log cabins with fireplaces and balconies. On weekends, prices rise and a two-night minimum stay is often required.

★**Valsugana** ITALIAN $$

(☎27 3248-1126; www.restaurantevalsugana.com.br; off Hwy BR-262, Km 89.5; mains R$45-70; ⏲11:30am-3:30pm & 7-10:30pm Sat, 11:30am-3:30pm Sun year-round, plus 7-10:30pm Fri Apr-Sep) Hearty Italian fare and pretty perspectives on Pedra Azul make this one of the area's nicest restaurants. Dishes such as *saltimbocca* (prosciutto-and-sage-stuffed veal escalope), lemon and thyme-crusted lamb with golden gnocchi, and spinach ravioli with ricotta and walnuts all feature fresh local produce.

ℹ Information

Casa do Turista (☎27 3248-0035; Rota do Lagarto; ⏲8am-5pm Mon-Fri, to 4pm Sat & Sun) Pedra Azul's spiffy new tourist office is just off the main BR 262 highway, at the base of the road leading up to the state park.

ℹ Getting There & Away

Águia Branca (www.aguiabranca.com.br) buses pass within 2km of the park entrance. In Vitória, buy a ticket for Fazenda do Estado (R$27, two hours, roughly hourly from 5am to 6:20pm), and ask to be let off at Km 88. The Km 88 bus stop is directly opposite Peterle's pousada and restaurant. From here, it's a 2km uphill walk to the park entrance along a lovely winding cobblestone road, Rota do Lagarto.

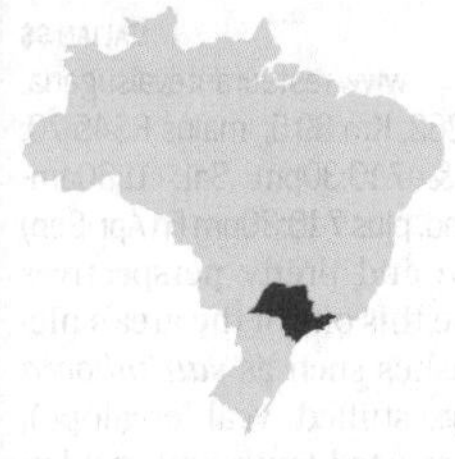

São Paulo State

☎11 / POP 41.2 MILLION

Includes ➡

São Paulo City............223
Paulista Coast............259
Ubatuba.....................259
São Sebastião...........262
Ilhabela......................263
Iguape & Around........267

Best Places to Eat

- Maní (p246)
- Patuá da Baiana (p246)
- Mocotó (p250)
- Cantinho da Lagoa (p261)
- Libertango (p258)

Best Places to Stay

- Pousada Picinguaba (p261)
- Hotel Emiliano (p238)
- We Hostel Design (p238)
- Na Mata Suites (p265)
- Guest Urban (p239)

Why Go?

Speaking of São Paulo state without using superlatives is difficult. The southern hemisphere's largest city! Its finest museums! Its best restaurants! Its worst traffic! (Well, you can't have everything.) São Paulo city – *Sampa* to locals – is Brazil's boomtown (commercially, financially, industrially and culturally), and an explosion of sophisticated travelers descending on the city's numerous arts and epicurean offerings has ensured the sprawling city remains a must-stop for nomad urbanites.

Inland from the cityscape, the Serra da Mantiqueira's 2500m peaks play the novel Alpine-esque getaway role, while Iporanga sits tucked away in the pristine Brazilian Atlantic Forest. Out to sea, some of southeastern Brazil's finest beaches cling both to the mountainous stretch of rainforest-backdropped coastline near Ubatuba, and to nearby Ilhabela, which relishes its position as São Paulo's cosmopolitan island escape.

When to Go

São Paulo

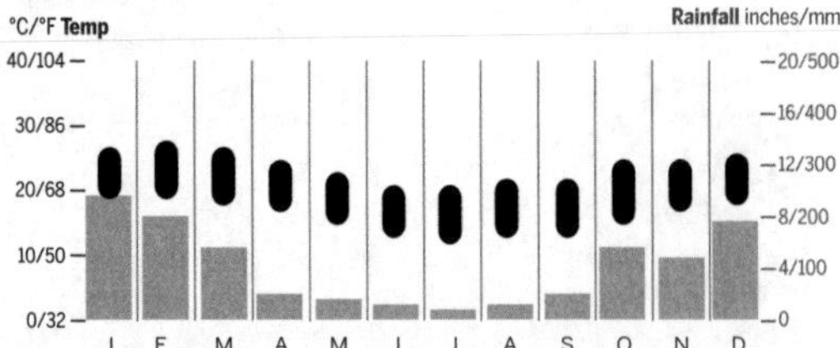

Dec–Feb Tropical downpours be damned, Sampa sizzles in summer nonetheless.

Mar & Sep Cooler temps, drier skies and São Paulo's best restaurants offering deals for Restaurant Week.

Jun & Jul Jackets required in the mountains, but therein lies the novelty.

Getting There & Around

The state's capital, São Paulo city, is Brazil's principal hub for international travel. Dozens of airlines from North America, Europe and Asia have direct international services to São Paulo's newish GRU Airport (p256). There are direct long-distance bus services from neighboring countries and destinations across Brazil from Terminal Rodoviária do Tietê (p256), Latin America's largest bus terminal. The city is also a major center for domestic air travel from Aeroporto de São Paulo-Congonhas (p256).

SÃO PAULO CITY

0XX11 / POP 11.3 MILLION (CITY), 19.9 MILLION (METRO) / ELEV 760M

São Paulo is home to 20 million fiercely proud *Paulistanos* (as residents are known), all of whom will happily rant and rave to you how they'd never live elsewhere. Spend time with them and the reasons will soon unfold. Maybe they will introduce you to the city's innumerable art-house cinemas and experimental theaters. If they're gourmands, they'll focus on the smart bistros and gourmet restaurants that make the city a world-renowned foodie haven. If they're scenesters, follow them on a raucous tour of underground bars and the 24/7 clubbing scene. Whatever pleasures you might covet, *Sampa* (the city's affectionate nickname) probably has them in spades.

Of course, it's also enormous, intimidating and, at first glance at least, no great beauty (to say nothing of the smog, the traffic, the crumbling sidewalks and the gaping divide between poor and rich).

A beautiful mess, if you will? And Brazil's city of dreams.

History

The history of the city of São Paulo largely mirrors that of the state. For the first three centuries after the arrival of Jesuits here in 1554, the city grew only gradually as a posting station for fortune hunters heading for the interior, and growers from nearby sugar plantations.

Upon Brazil's independence in 1822, São Paulo was declared a state capital, a decision that in turn led to the founding of the College of Law – arguably Brazil's first public institution of higher learning. An increasingly important political and intellectual center, the city was soon leading the fight both to end slavery and to found the republic.

The city's fortunes began to rise in the late 19th century when the region's planters began replacing sugar with the world's new, favorite cash crop: coffee. Some of the coffee barons' mansions still line Av Paulista today. The millions of descendants of immigrants who came to work those plantations – especially Italians and Japanese – are another legacy of the coffee boom.

When coffee prices plummeted at the beginning of the 20th century, there was enough capital left over to transform the city into an industrial powerhouse. Factory jobs attracted a new wave of immigrants from around the world, and the city's population practically doubled every decade between 1920 and 1980. In the 1980s, foreign immigration slowed, but laborers streamed in from the drought-stricken Northeast. Many found work building the city's new skyscrapers. Unfortunately, growth far outpaced investment in the city's infrastructure. Today, traffic, crime and pollution still flummox city leaders and remain serious problems, but the dynamism of its culture and economy is still attracting the best and brightest from all over Brazil.

In recent years, São Paulo's explosive population growth has slowed, though it is now firmly established as Brazil's banking, industrial and cultural capital. As such it enjoyed the lion's share of Brazil's recent economic boom, and still sees a continuing influx of foreign job seekers looking to tap into the action. Post-2014 FIFA World Cup, Sampa continues to make strides toward modernizing its infrastructure, including significant expansions of its metro, suburban train and highway systems (the long-anticipated express train to GRU Airport debuted in 2018). That said, a very serious water shortage in 2015 brought water rationing to many parts of the city, including tourist areas, leaving taps dry for all but a few hours per day; and 2018 was barely any wetter – devastating water shortages seem to be a constant threat to the city.

Sights

Praça da Sé & Around

The old heart of the city, **Praça da Sé** (Map p230; Praça da Sé, Sé) – literally, 'Cathedral Square' – has seen better days, but still draws animated crowds, from street hawkers and nose-down business types to, unfortunately, more than its fair share of pickpockets and homeless people. Crowning the square is the

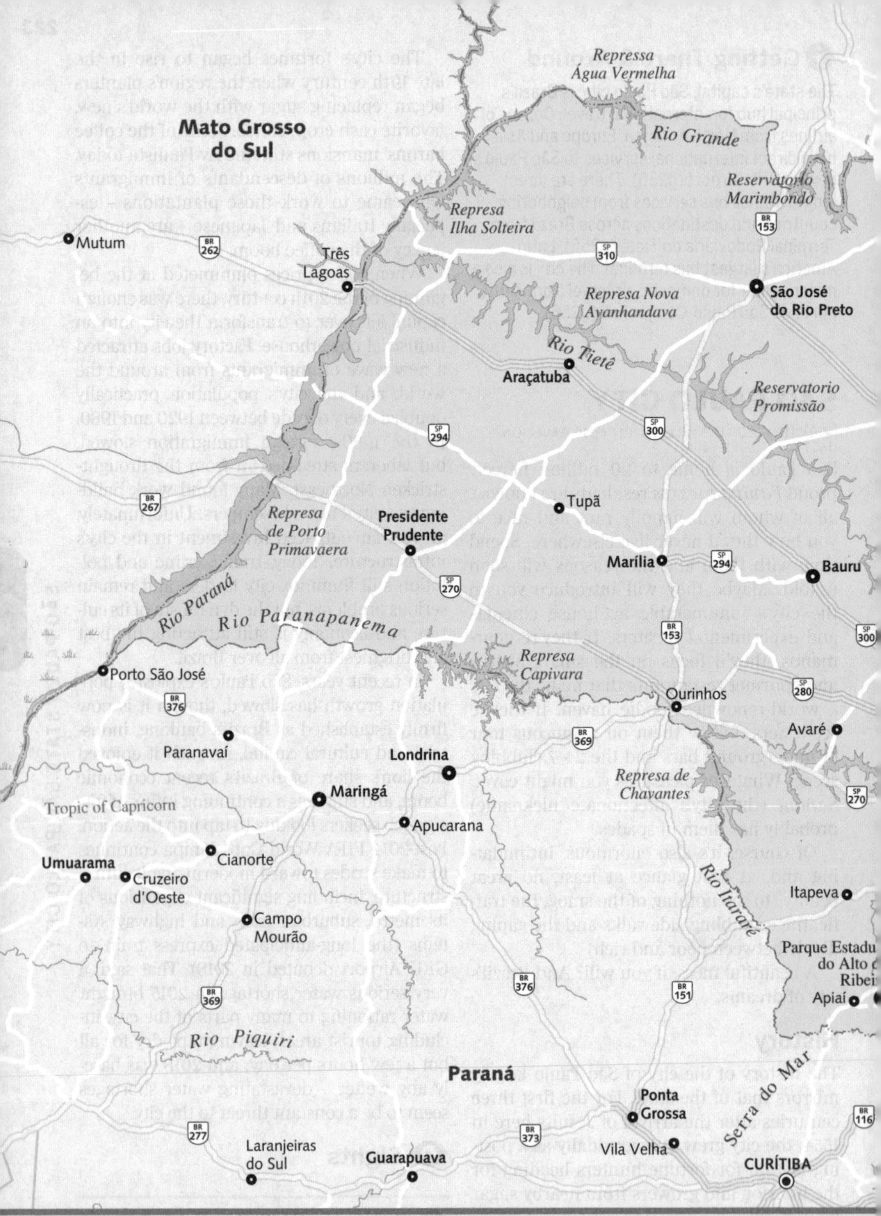

São Paulo State Highlights

❶ **Ubatuba** (p259) Seeking out deserted beaches where mountains meet the sea along the lush and lovely Litoral Norte.

❷ **São Paulo City** (p223) Overwhelming yourself with cuisine, culture, coffee and chaos in one of the world's largest cities.

❸ **Pousada Picinguaba** (p261) Hiding away amid lush rainforest and refined tropical luxury in an idyllic fishing village inside Parque Estadual Serra do Mar.

❹ **Farol Santander** (p228) Gawking at the sheer endlessness of São Paulo city's

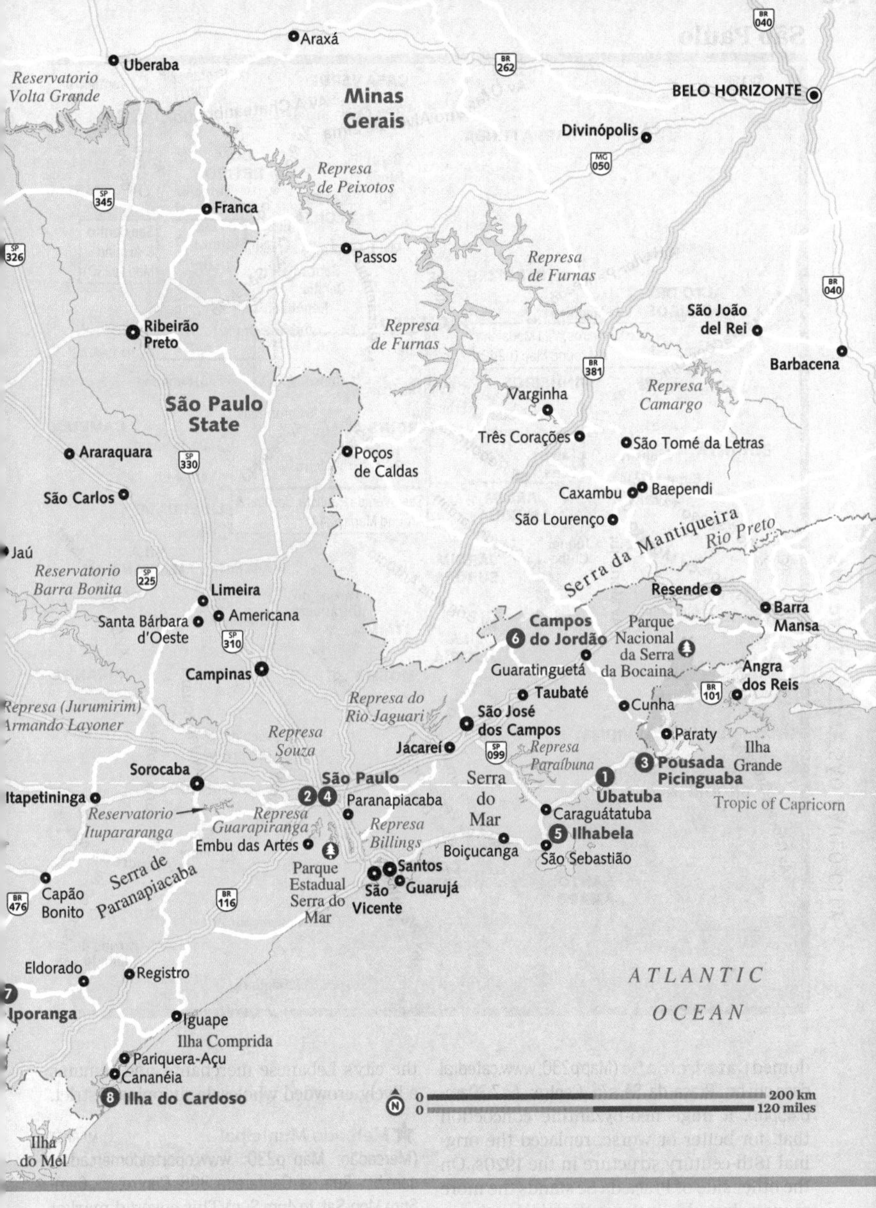

eye-popping skyline from the top of this former bank building.

❺ **Ilhabela** (p263) Escaping to São Paulo's idyllic island getaway for the rich and famous.

❻ **Campos do Jordão** (p258) Immersing yourself in the Alpine wonderland of Brazil's highest city.

❼ **Iporanga** (p266) Caving in the pristine Brazilian Atlantic Forest in Parque Estadual do Alto do Ribeira.

❽ **Ilha do Cardoso** (p264) Going wet and wild in this seldom-visited, off-the-grid island.

São Paulo

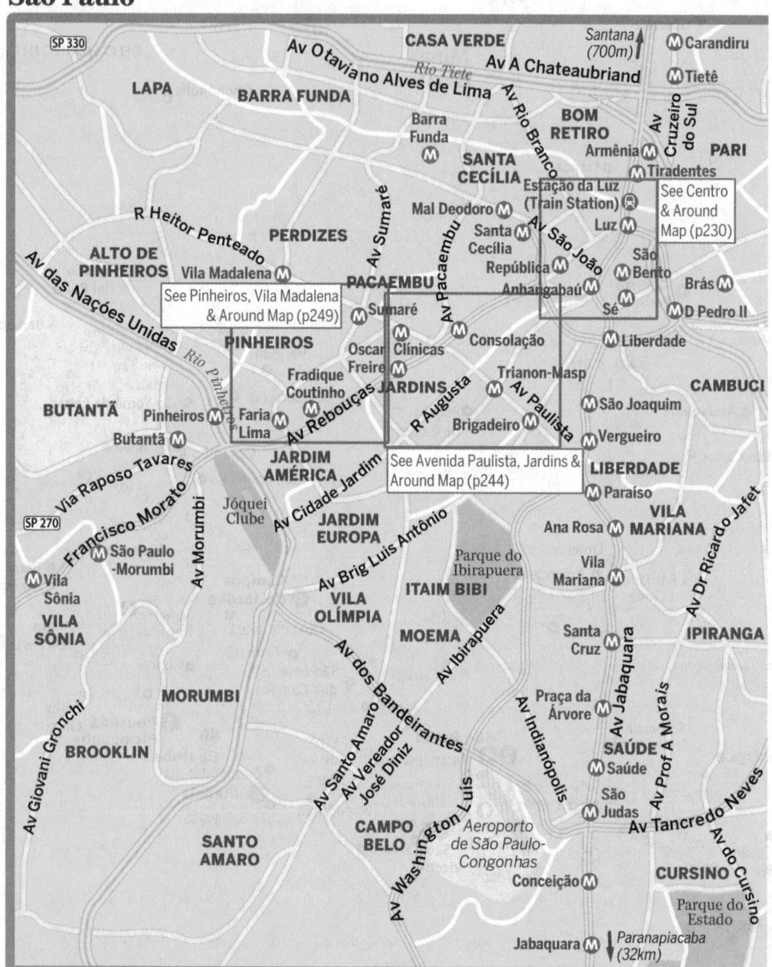

domed **Catedral da Sé** (Map p230; www.catedraldase.org.br; Praça da Sé s/n, Centro; ⏲7:30am-6:45pm), a huge neo-Byzantine concoction that, for better or worse, replaced the original 18th-century structure in the 1920s. On the other side of Praça da Sé stands the more modest, but also more authentic, **Igreja do Carmo** (Map p230; www.arquisp.org.br; Av Rangel Pestana 230, Centro; ⏲8am-5pm Mon-Fri, to noon Sat & Sun), which dates to the 1630s and still preserves its original high altar.

About 700m north of the cathedral, **Rua 25 de Março** is the traditional preserve of the city's Lebanese merchants, and remains a lively, crowded wholesale shopping district.

★ **Mercado Municipal** MARKET

(Mercadão; Map p230; www.oportaldomercadao.com.br; Rua da Cantareira 306, Centro; ⏲6am-6pm Mon-Sat, to 4pm Sun) This covered market is a belle epoque confection of stained glass and a series of vast domes. Inside, a fabulous urban market specializes in all things edible. It's also a great place to sample a couple of classic Sampa delights: mortadella sandwiches at **Bar do Mané** or **Hocca Bar**, and *pasteis* (fried, stuffed pastries).

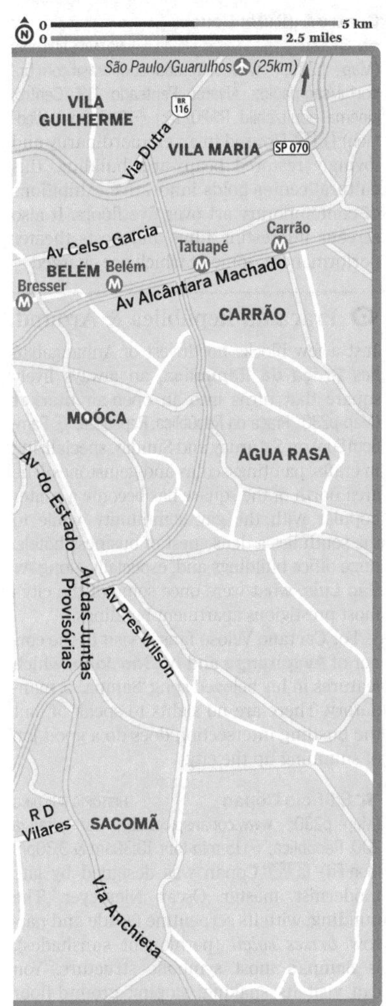

Wandering the various stalls here, sampling as you go and taking in the sights and sounds of everyday Paulistano moving and shaking, is one of Sampa's great joys.

Páteo do Collégio LANDMARK
(Map p230; www.pateodocollegio.com.br; Praça Páteo do Colégio; adult/student R$8/4; ⌚9am-5pm Tue-Sun) Occupying the exact spot where São Paulo was founded in 1554 by Jesuit brothers José de Anchieta and Manoel da Nóbregra, this mission is actually a 1950s replica of the monastery that once stood here.

Caixa Cultural CULTURAL CENTER
(Map p230; ☎11 3321-4400; www.caixacultural.com.br; Praça da Sé 111, Sé; ⌚9am-7pm Tue-Sun) FREE This cultural center occupies a grand neoclassical-style building with an imperious facade of black marble that served as Caixa Econômica Federal's regional headquarters. Temporary exhibits of major Brazilian artists are shown, and the executive office suite on the 6th floor is an oddly fascinating museum of the bank's history.

Casa da Imagem MUSEUM
(Map p230; www.casadaimagem.sp.gov.br; Roberto Simonsen 136-B, Centro; ⌚9am-5pm Tue-Sun) FREE Beautifully curated from some 84,000 historical photographs, this museum inside a restored colonial downtown mansion is a must for those interested in the São Paulo of days gone by (original frescoes from the 1880s were uncovered in the building's restoration). Themed exhibitions are changed every three months.

It's part of the multilocation Museu da Cidade de São Paulo.

Triângulo & Anhangabaú

Just north of Praça da Sé lies the **Triângulo**, a triangle bounded roughly by Praça da Sé, Mosteiro São Bento and the Prefeitura (city hall). It has narrow, pedestrian-only streets and towering office buildings that in the late 19th and early 20th centuries served as the city's commercial heart.

Heading west from Praça do Patriarca, you'll cross the 1892 **Viaduto de Chá**, which crosses the **Vale do Anhangabaú** (aka Parque do Anhangabaú), along with the **Viaduto Santa Efigênia** a little to the north and dating from the same era. Both of these elaborate cast-iron bridges were long synonymous with São Paulo's cultural and economic ascendancy. In the Tupi-Guarani language, Anhangabaú means Demon's Valley, and indigenous peoples believed evil spirits dwelled there. The area is dicey after dark.

★**Theatro Municipal** THEATER
(Map p230; ☎11 3397-0300; www.theatromunicipal.org.br; Praça Ramos de Azevedo; ⌚box office 10am-7pm Mon-Fri, to 5pm Sat & Sun) São Paulo's most splendid construction, this theater was begun in 1903 in the style of Paris' Palais Garnier. Its heavily ornamented facade seems to combine every architectural style imaginable, from baroque to art nouveau, and its interior is clad in gold and marble. Free English tours run

twice daily Wednesday to Friday at 11am and 5pm, and Saturday at 11am (additional tours are available in Portuguese).

★Mosteiro São Bento CHURCH
(Map p230; www.mosteiro.org.br; Largo de São Bento s/n, São Bento; ⏲6am-6pm Mon-Wed & Fri, 6-8:30am & 11:30am-6pm Thu, 6am-noon & 4-6pm Sat, 7am-noon & 4-8pm Sun) FREE Among the city's oldest and most important churches, São Bento dates to 1598, though its neo-Gothic facade dates only to the early 20th century. Step inside the church to view its impressive stained glass. Mass (7am weekdays, 6am on Saturday and 10am Sunday) includes Gregorian chanting.

There's a legendary, culturally rich brunch of monk and top chef delicacies – including prosecco! – on the second and last Sunday of each month; booking required well in advance (R$220 per person; reservations at brunchnomosteiro@multiplaeventos.com.br). The in-house bakery (7am to 6pm Monday to Friday; items R$7 to R$35) is also a real treat, with highly sought after breads, cakes, pastries, biscuits and jams made by the monks from centuries-old recipes.

★Farol Santander VIEWPOINT
(Edifício Altino Arantes/Banespa; Map p230; www.farolsantander.com.br; João Brícola 24, Centro; adult/child R$20/10; ⏲9am-8pm Tue-Sat, to 4pm Sun) For one of Sampa's best panoramas, head to the top of this 161m-high skyscraper, Brazil's version of the Empire State Building – completed in 1939 and most famously known as the Banespa (Banco do Estado de São Paulo) building. Book tickets online in advance.

The observation deck on the top floor offers spectacular views of the city and renovations have added cafes, a 21st floor skate park and exhibitions – highlights include a panorama of São Paulo's skyline made up of junk by Vik Muniz and a three-minute historical film screened in a mirrored cinema room. There's also a trendy R$4000 per night loft bookable on Airbnb.

Edifício Martinelli HISTORIC BUILDING
(Map p230; www.prediomartinelli.com.br; São Bento 405, Centro) FREE São Paulo's first skyscraper, in a gorgeous 1929 beaux-arts building, features a mansion built on top of its 26th-floor viewing terrace. However, the terrace and its incredible views are indefinitely closed to the public since 2017.

Centro Cultural Banco do Brasil NOTABLE BUILDING
(Map p230; www.culturabancodobrasil.com.br/portal/sao-paulo; Álvares Penteado 112, Centro; cinema adult/child R$20/10; ⏲9am-9pm Wed-Mon) FREE Housed in an extraordinarily and lovingly restored beaux-arts building, this cultural center holds innovative exhibitions of contemporary art over five floors. It also screens interesting films and hosts theater performances, some of which are charged

Praça da República & Around

Just a few blocks northwest of Anhangabaú lies **Praça da República**, an always lively square that turns into an open-air **market** (Map p230; Praça da República, República; ⏲8am-6pm Sun) on Saturday and Sunday, specializing in crafts, paintings, coins and gemstones. The area north of the square has become a center popular with the gay community, while to the south lies a dense nest of business hotels, huge office buildings and, especially along **Av São Luís**, what were once some of the city's most prestigious apartment buildings.

For Caetano Veloso fans, a visit to the corner of **Av Ipiranga** and **Av São João**, which features in his beloved song 'Sampa,' is mandatory. There are no sights to speak of, but the bustling intersection does do a good job of summing up the city.

★Edifício Copan HISTORIC BUILDING
(Map p230; www.copansp.com.br; Av Ipiranga 200, República; ⏲15-min tour 10:30am & 3:30pm Mon-Fri) FREE Copan was designed by late modernist master Oscar Niemeyer. The building, with its serpentine facade and narrow *brises soleil* (permanent sunshades), is Sampa's most symbolic structure. You can visit its snaking, sloping ground-floor shopping arcade anytime; its spectacular rooftop opens only on weekdays at 10:30am or 3:30pm, however. The 15-minute visit is no frills – there's barely a railing! – and feels wonderfully unrushed. Check-in at Bloco F (space limited – arrive at least 30 minutes in advance).

★Edifício Itália HISTORIC BUILDING
(Map p230; ☎11 2189-2997; www.edificioitalia.com.br; cnr Avs São Luís & Ipiranga, República; from R$30; ⏲3-7pm Mon-Fri) With 46 stories, this skyscraper just south of the Praça da República is the tallest in the city center. You have three options to see the view: weekdays from 3pm to 7pm, the building charges a R$30 fee

for top access (includes a welcome drink); after 7pm daily for R$35 you can visit the bar at Terraço Italia – which offers some of São Paulo's mightiest views; or book lunch or dinner at Terraço Italia's restaurant (the priciest option).

Luz

Located in a tough area just north of the city center, Luz has become an unlikely cultural hub thanks to major restoration of a series of grand turn-of-the-century buildings around the **Parque da Luz**.

Across the street from the park sits **Estação da Luz** (Map p230; Praça da Luz, Luz; ⌚24hr), a restored late-Victorian train station constructed with materials entirely shipped in from Britain and completed in 1901. It services São Paulo's extensive suburban lines, with a long tunnel linking it to Metrô Luz.

★Pina_Luz MUSEUM
(Map p230; www.pinacoteca.org.br; Praça da Luz 2, Luz; adult/student R$6/3, Sat free; ⌚10am-6pm Wed-Mon) This elegant neoclassical museum, formerly known as Pinacoteca do Estado but modernly rebranded 'Pina_Luz' (*with* the underline!) in 2017, houses an excellent collection of Brazilian – and especially Paulista – art from the 19th century to the present. Works include big names such as Portinari and Di Cavalcanti, and it has an excellent permanent collection of modernist Brazilian art. There is a lovely cafe that faces adjacent Parque da Luz.

Pina_Estacão (Map p230; www.pinacoteca.org.br; Praça da Luz 2, Luz; adult/student incl admission to Pinacoteca do Estado R$6/3; ⌚10am-6pm Tue-Sun), its temporary exhibition annex, is housed in nearby Estação Júlio Prestes.

Museu da Língua Portuguesa MUSEUM
(Map p230; www.museulinguaportuguesa.org.br; Praça da Luz, Luz; adult/student R$6/3; ⌚10am-6pm Tue-Sun) Half of Estação da Luz has been given over to this museum, with fascinating permanent exhibits documenting the rise of the Brazilian language as distinct from European Portuguese, as well as creative temporary installations celebrating Brazilian literature.

Estação Júlio Prestes HISTORIC BUILDING
(Map p230; Largo General Osório 66, Centro; ⌚24hr) This grand turn-of-the-century beaux arts–style working railway station (actually completed in the 1930s) houses the Pina_Estacão (p229), an annex of the Pina_Luz hosting Sampa's three best contemporary art halls. Also here is the powerful **Memorial da Resistência** (Map p230; www.memorialdaresistenciasp.org.br; Largo General Osório 66, Estação Júlio Prestes, Luz; ⌚10am-6pm Tue-Sun) FREE, occupying cells where dissidents were tortured during Brazil's military dictatorship, and the state-of-the-art Sala São Paulo (p254).

Museu de Arte Sacra MUSEUM
(Museum of Sacred Art; www.museuartesacra.org.br; Tiradentes 676; adult/student R$6/3, Sat free; ⌚9am-5pm Wed-Fri, 10am-6pm Sat & Sun) The best of its kind in Brazil, this museum includes works by renowned 18th-century sculptor Antônio Aleijadinho, along with some 1000 other ecclesiastical pieces from the 17th to the 20th centuries curated from an 18,000-strong archive. The museum is housed in the 18th-century Luz monastery, which is one of São Paulo's best-preserved buildings of the period.

Liberdade

Liberdade – a short walk south of Praça da Sé – has long been the traditional center of Sampa's massive Japanese community. Though most new Asian immigrants these days come from China and Korea, the gritty neighborhood is still lined with traditional Japanese shops and eateries, and is full of hidden gems of Asian culture.

Praça da Liberdade is the neighborhood's main square and also the location of its metro stop. It hosts an open-air **market** (www.feiraliberdade.com.br; Praça da Liberdade, Liberdade; ⌚9am-6pm Sun) on Sunday. A short walk south on Galvão Bueno takes you past many Asian shops and restaurants as well as some rather neglected Japanese-style gardens.

Museu Histórico da Imigração Japonesa MUSEUM
(Museum of Japanese Immigration; www.museubunkyo.org.br; São Joaquim 381, Liberdade; adult/student R$12/6; ⌚1:30-5:30pm Tue-Sun) This modest but fascinating museum, on the 7th floor of a Liberdade office building, documents the arrival and integration of the Japanese community. Photos, period objects and a full-scale reconstruction of a typical immigrant's farm lodging tell a poignant story: from the arrival in Santos of the first 781 settlers aboard the *Kasato-Maru* in 1908, through to today. Bring ID.

Centro & Around

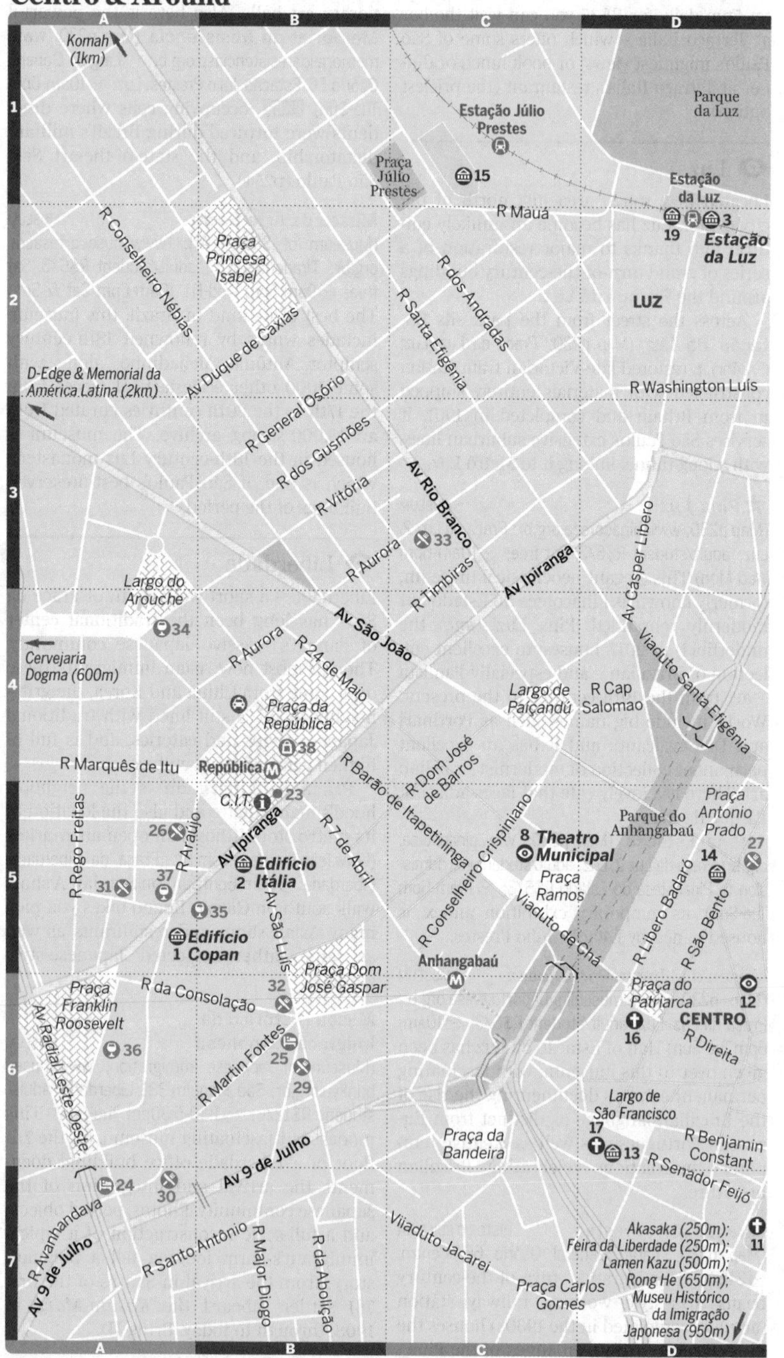

0 400 m
0 0.2 miles
E F
Museu de Arte Sacra (200m)
28
Pina_Luz
7
R São Caetano
Terminal Tietê Bus Station (5km)
Luz
R Paula Souza
Av Prestes Maia
Av Senador Queiroz
R da Cantareira
R Carlos de Souza
Mercado Municipal
5
R Florenciode Abreu
R 25 de Março
R Barão de Duprat
Rio Tamanduateí
6 Mosteiro São Bento
São Bento
Parque Dom Pedro II
Praça Ragueb Chohfi
Av do Estado
Farol 4 Santander
R Boa Vista
R Gen Carneiro
Praça Fernando Costa
Parque Dom Pedro II
R Dr Rodriguez
R 15 de Novembro
20
10
22
9
Av Angel Pestana
Memorial do Imigrante (2km)
18
21
Sé
Praça da Sé
R Anita Garibaldi
R de Carmo
R Tabatingüera
E F

Centro & Around

Top Sights

1 Edifício Copan ... A5
2 Edifício Itália ... B5
3 Estação da Luz ... D2
4 Farol Santander ... E5
5 Mercado Municipal ... F4
6 Mosteiro São Bento ... E4
7 Pina_Luz ... E1
8 Theatro Municipal ... C5

Sights

9 Caixa Cultural ... E6
10 Casa da Imagem ... E6
11 Catedral da Sé ... D7
12 Centro Cultural Banco do Brasil ... D6
13 College of Law ... D6
14 Edifício Martinelli ... D5
15 Estação Júlio Prestes ... C1
16 Igreja de Santo Antônio ... D6
17 Igreja de São Francisco de Assis ... D6
18 Igreja Nossa Senhora do Carmo ... E6
Memorial da Resistência ... (see 15)
19 Museu da Língua Portuguesa ... D2
20 Páteo do Collégio ... E6
Pina_Estacão ... (see 15)
21 Praça da Sé ... E7
22 Solar da Marquesa ... E6

Activities, Courses & Tours

23 SP Free Walking Tour ... B5

Sleeping

24 155 Hotel ... A7
25 Novotel SP Jaraguá ... B6

Eating

26 A Casa do Porco ... A5
27 Casa Mathilde ... D5
28 Esfiharia Effendi ... E1
29 Estadão ... B6
30 Famiglia Mancini ... A7
31 Hot Pork ... A5
32 Ramona ... B6
33 Rinconcito Peruano ... C3

Drinking & Nightlife

Bar da Dona Onça ... (see 1)
34 Barouche ... A4
35 Fel ... B5
36 Lekitsch ... A6
37 Love Story ... A5

Entertainment

Sala São Paulo ... (see 15)
Theatro Municipal ... (see 8)

Shopping

38 Feira da Praça da República ... B4

Higienópolis, Pacaembu & Barra Funda

Northwest of Av Paulista lies the leafy neighborhood of **Higienópolis**, one of the most traditional of the city's upscale neighborhoods and a good spot for a stroll. Praça Buenos Aires, a tree-filled, European-style square, serves as the neighborhood's lungs and playground. As you continue northwest, you pass through **Pacaembu**, a low-rise neighborhood of ramblingly luxurious homes reminiscent of upscale Los Angeles and home to the excellent Museu do Futebol (p232). Finally, you reach **Barra Funda**, a more workaday neighborhood that at night comes alive with some of the city's trendiest nightclubs.

Museu do Futebol MUSEUM

(Map p244; www.museudofutebol.org.br; Praça Charles Miller s/n, Pacaembu; adult/student R$12/6, Tue free; 9am-6pm Tue-Sun;) Tucked under the bleachers of colorfully art deco Pacaembu Stadium, this fantastic museum is devoted to Brazil's greatest passion – football (soccer). Its multimedia displays over two floors manage to evoke the thrill of watching a championship game, even for nonfans.

Avenida Paulista, Jardins & Around

There are several worthwhile museums and cultural centers of note on and around Av Paulista, including Latin's America's most important Western art museum, Museu de Arte de São Paulo. Largely residential Jardins isn't long on points of interest but does harbor the excellent Museu Xingu, a fascinating collection of Amazon tribal artifacts.

FREE SP!

There's no sugarcoating it: Brazil can be expensive depending on its currency fluctuation, and São Paulo is the beast of the bunch. But that doesn't mean you can't have fun on a shoestring budget. In addition to free admission on Saturdays at Museu Afro-Brasil and Museu de Arte Moderna, our favorite freebies include:

- Mosteiro São Bento (p228)
- Instituto Moreira Salles
- Casa da Imagem (p227)
- Japan House
- SP Free Walking Tour (p236)
- SESC Paulista

★ **Museu de Arte de São Paulo** MUSEUM

(MASP; Map p244; www.masp.art.br; Av Paulista 1578, Bela Vista; adult/student R$35/17, free Tue; 10am-6pm 10am-8pm Tue, to 6pm Wed-Sun) Sampa's pride, this museum possesses Latin America's most comprehensive collection of Western art. Hovering above a concrete plaza that turns into an antiques fair on Sunday (and acts as a protest gathering point almost always!), the museum, designed by architect Lina Bo Bardi and completed in 1968, is considered a classic of modernism by many and an abomination by a vocal few.

The collection, though, is unimpeachable, and ranges from Goya to El Greco to Manet. The impressionist collection is particularly noteworthy. There are also a few great Brazilian paintings, including three fine works by Cândido Portinari. The permanent collection is housed in glass panels wedged in concrete bases, an original Bo Bardi design that was taken away in 1996 but returned in 2015. Regrettably, the museum seems rather neglected by its guardians, with public areas looking shabby in places. More shocking was the theft in 2007 of paintings by Portinari and Picasso, which revealed that a museum with a billion-dollar collection lacked motion detectors or cameras with infrared capabilities. Fortunately, the two paintings were eventually recovered.

Parque Siqueira Campos PARK

(Map p244; Peixoto Gomide 949, Jardins; 6am-6pm) Just off Paulista across from the Museu de Arte de São Paulo (MASP) lies Parque Siqueira Campos, a beautifully designed and maintained park that re-creates the Atlantic rainforest that was leveled to build São Paulo. It's a remarkably tranquil refuge just off the city's busiest street.

★ **Museu Xingu** MUSEUM

(Map p244; www.casaamarela.art.br/espacos/museu-xingu; José Maria Lisboa 838, Jardins; 10am-4pm Mon-Fri) FREE Relatively unknown and blissfully uncrowded, the unassuming Casa Amarela is part NGO handicraft shop (p255), part two-table romantic cafe and part tiny Museu Xingu. The last of these has one the world's best collections of artifacts from Irmãos Villas-Bôas, a three-brother Brazilian activist team who were the first white men to ever come in contact with upper Xingu river indigenous communities of the Amazon.

★**Rua Oscar Freire** STREET
(Map p244; www.oscarfreiresp.com.br; Rua Oscar Freire, Jardins) Take a stroll down Brazil's 'Rodeo Drive', a leafy, tree-lined thoroughfare brimming with cafes, concept stores and flagship boutiques, top-end restaurants, beautiful people and usually a celebrity or two. It is said to be the eighth most luxurious street in the world, and clocks in as some of the most expensive real-estate per sq meter in Latin America.

The people-watching is ace!

Japan House CULTURAL CENTRE
(Map p244; www.japanhouse.jp/saopaulo; Av Paulista 52, Bela Vista; ⏲10am-10pm Mon-Sat, to 6pm Sun) FREE You can't miss the stunning facade of this Av Paulista newcomer. Its sliding vertical plank entrance sits in stark contrast to the surrounding concrete and steel, under the nose of a massive mural by local street-artist Kobra, depicting architect Oscar Niemeyer – who would no doubt approve – on the building behind. A Japanese government initiative, this contemporary art, gastronomy and technology cultural center houses stunning temporary exhibitions, a cafe and a top-end sushi restaurant by acclaimed chef Jun Sakamoto.

Instituto Moreira Salles CULTURAL CENTER
(IMS; Map p244; www.ims.com.br; Av Paulista 2424, Consolação; ⏲10am-8pm Tue-Sun, to 10pm Thu) FREE A 2017 artistic addition to Av Paulista, this striking, R$150 million, vertical museum and cultural center is a real treat for photography fans – three floors of galleries are home to oft-changing exhibitions from some of the world's most renowned shutterbugs.

The building itself, with its plexi-like see-through facade, took home an award for best architecture work in São Paulo from the Paulista Association of Art Critics. It also houses an art cinema, viewing terrace and the excellent new Balaio IMS (p243).

SESC Paulista CULTURAL CENTER
(Map p244; www.sescsp.org.br; Av Paulista 119, Bela Vista; ⏲9am-10pm Tue-Sat, 10am-7pm Sun) FREE This 2018 cultural addition to Av Paulista offers the best free view you're going to get of the country's most important avenue: the 17th floor terrace boasts panoramic 360° vistas straight down the belly of the beast.

Elsewhere on various floors, rotating cutting-edge audiovisual and tech-leaning art exhibitions are also worth a gander, but it's really all about the view.

Parque Ibirapuera

Designed by renowned landscape architect Roberto Burle Marx, Parque Ibirapuera was inaugurated in 1954 to commemorate the city's 400th anniversary. A series of landmark buildings in the park are the work of Oscar Niemeyer; most of them are linked by a long and distinctively serpentine covered walkway. At the north entrance stands Victor Brecheret's huge Monumento Bandeiras, erected in 1953 in memory of the city's early pioneers.

★**Museu Afro-Brasil** MUSEUM
(www.museuafrobrasil.org.br; Av Pedro Alvares Cabral s/n, Parque Ibirapuera, Gate 10; adult/student R$6/3, Sat free; ⏲10am-5pm Tue-Sun) This hugely important, absolutely fascinating Parque Ibirapuera museum features a permanent 3rd-floor collection chronicling five centuries of African immigration (and a nod to the 10 million African lives lost in the construction of Brazil) and hosts a rotating array of contemporary Afro-centric exhibitions on its bottom two floors.

Museu de Arte Contemporânea da Universidade de São Paulo MUSEUM
(MAC-USP; www.mac.usp.br; Av Pedro Álvares Cabral 1301, Parque Ibirapuera; ⏲10am-7pm Tue-Sun) FREE This fine museum, the best of three belonging to Universidade de São Paulo's Museu de Arte Contemporânea, is housed in the Oscar Niemeyer–designed former motor vehicle department building (Detran) and possesses what is arguably the country's best collection of Brazilian art since 1960. It includes an extensive sculpture collection, paintings, prints, photographs and objets d'art.

The new rooftop restaurant, Vista (p247), offers flabbergasting panoramic views.

Museu de Arte Moderna MUSEUM
(MAM; www.mam.org.br; Av Pedro Alvares Cabral s/n, Parque Ibirapuera, Gate 3; adult/student R$7/free, Sat free; ⏲10am-6pm Tue-Sun) Brazil's oldest modern-art museum possesses a fine permanent collection of Brazilian modernists such as Anita Malfatti and Di Cavalcanti, as well as works by Miró, Chagall, Picasso and Dufy. However, the public spaces are devoted exclusively to temporary exhibits. Check the museum's website for current offerings.

Pinheiros, Vila Madalena & Around

Pinheiros, west of Jardins, is a sprawling, mostly residential neighborhood of identikit high-rise apartments with bonafide restaurant, nightlife and arts scenes, but few sights. Bohemian **Vila Madelena** is the city's creative hub; home to artists, designers and other art-focused warriors. There are no big ticket sights in these parts, but Vila Madelena is a destination in itself, home to trendy bars and cafes, independent boutiques and galleries, and is a nerve center for the city's vibrant street-art scene.

★**Beco do Batman** PUBLIC ART
(Map p249; Gonçalo Afonso s/n, Vila Madalena; ⏲24hr) One of São Paulo's premiere street-art locations, 'Batman's Alley' has slowly risen from secret location for band promotional shots and Brazilian films to a bonafide tourist attraction - even school kids visit nowadays! The open gallery, tucked away in artsy Vila Madalena, is covered head-to-toe in cutting-edge street art by local and international artists.

Mercado Municipal de Pinheiros MARKET
(Map p249; www.mercadomunicipaldepinheiros.com; Pedro Cristi 89, Pinheiros; ⏲8am-6pm) A smaller, cleaner and more manageable version of São Paulo's far larger and more chaotic Mercado Municipal, Mercado Municipal de Pinheiros has served Pinheiros' produce needs since 1910, though the current building was built in 1971 and completely transformed in 2014.

Today, vendors sling fresh fruits, vegetables, meat and fish, but it's even more visit-worthy for its fantastic food stalls: Comedoria Gonzales' South American cuisine; Chef Rodrigo Oliveira's Mocotó Café; C6 Burger; and Alex Atala's cultural emporium, Instituto Ata (p254).

South & East of Jardins

Extra-wide Av Brigadeiro Faria Lima (called just 'Faria Lima') marks the southwestern edge of the Jardins neighborhoods. Faria Lima is also the main corridor connecting Pinheiros with the ritzy residential neighborhoods of **Morumbi**, **Vila Olímpia** and **Moema**. These districts are the domain of luxury high-rise condominiums and mostly banking and technology headquarters.

City Walk
Centro São Paulo

START PRAÇA DA REPÚBLICA
END PRAÇA DA REPÚBLICA
LENGTH 3.5KM; TWO HOURS

Downtown São Paulo is a vibrant living museum of architectural gems and glory days gone by. Head out on a weekday (weekends and nights are a little too dicey) on this pleasant Centro stroll.

Start at ❶ **Praça da República**, head down Av Ipiranga and then turn left onto Av São Luís to get a look at what's still one of the tallest buildings in town – the 46-story ❷ **Edifício Itália** (p228). Continuing down Av São Luís, check out the rather squat, gray building at the end of the small park on the left. It looks like a prison, but it's the ❸ **Mario de Andrade Municipal Library**, housing the largest book collection in the city.

Turning left onto Rua Xavier de Toledo, keeping the library on your left, follow the road downhill toward the Anhangabaú metro station a few blocks away. Follow Toledo until the ❹ **Theatro Municipal** (p227) appears – this baroque building, with its art nouveau features, is the pride of the city. Opposite the theater, on the right, is the ❺ **Viaduto de Chá**, a metal bridge built in 1892 and named after an old tea plantation that used to be in the area. Pedestrian traffic became too heavy for the old bridge and a new one was inaugurated in 1938.

Crossing the bridge, look out over the ❻ **Parque Anhangabaú** on the left. At the other side of the bridge, enter ❼ **Praça do Patriarca** straight ahead. Here you'll find the ❽ **Igreja de Santo Antônio**, which retains many of its original 18th-century contours, including its rococo altar dating to 1780..

Turn right some 20 paces beyond on Rua São Bento, leading to ❾ **Largo de São Francisco**, a triangular plaza that is home to twin churches, both known as ❿ **Igreja de São Francisco de Assis**, and the well-respected ⓫ **College of Law**. Just beyond the controversial statue of a Frenchman kissing an indigenous woman in front of the College of Law is Senador Feijó, leading to the famous

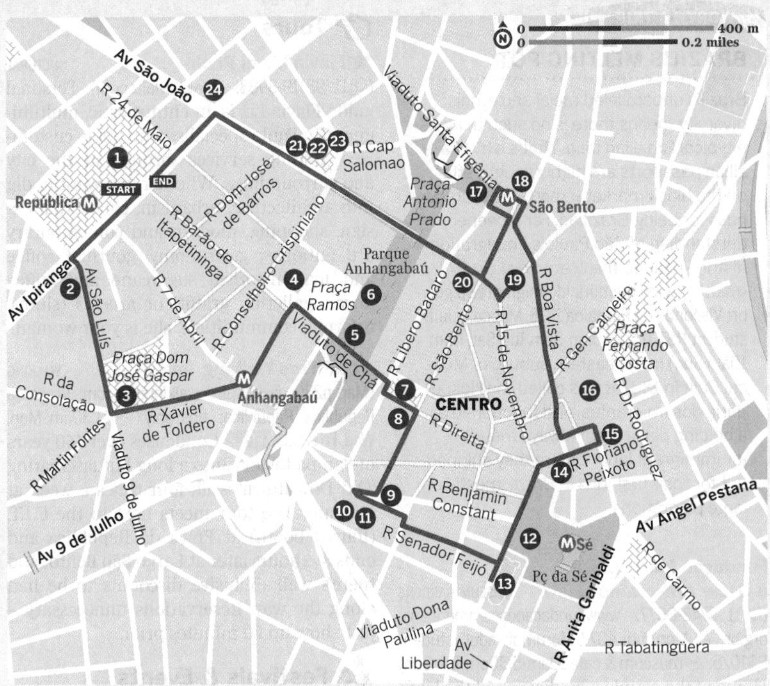

⑫ Praça da Sé (p223). Soak up the joyous vibe in the square, but watch your pockets. Step inside the enormous **⑬ Catedral da Sé** (p223).

As you exit the cathedral, head down the plaza and continue toward the **⑭ Caixa Economica Federal**, home to the city's coffers and also a great cultural center (Caixa Cultural) that features Brazilian artists. Turning right onto Rua Floriano Peixoto, walk to the end and feast your eyes upon the pinkish-colored **⑮ Solar da Marquesa**. Follow the street around to the left to **⑯ Páteo do Colégio** (p227), the actual site where São Paulo was founded in 1554.

Directly in front of this plaza is Boa Vista. Follow it away from Praça da Sé to the end, where you'll find **⑰ Largo de São Bento**, home to the **⑱ Mosteiro São Bento** (p228), a monastery and basilica built in an eclectic style with monks still putting on Gregorian-chant concerts, knocking out coveted baked goods and – in grand Belgium style – offering red- and golden-ales brewed from their own recipe.

Leaving the square, walk up the pedestrianized Rua São Bento to Av São João. Turn left at São João and another quick left at the next street, where on the right stands the art deco **⑲ Farol Santander** (p228) building. Head to the top floor for a sweeping view of São Paulo. Backtrack to São Bento and then keep heading straight down Av São João. On the left just past São Bento stands **⑳ Edifício Martinelli** (p228). You are now crossing the Vale do Anhangabaú that you saw earlier from the Viaduto de Chá.

Head up São João as far as **㉑ Largo de Paiçandú**. Behind the pretty **㉒ NS do Rosário dos Homens Pretos** is the magnificent **㉓ Monumento á Mãe Preta** (Monument to the Black Mother). This heart-wrenching statue depicts an African slave woman suckling a white child, and the poem underneath gives voice to her lament for her own children who must go hungry.

To wrap up a long day, continue forward and you will end up at the **㉔ intersection of Av São João and Av Ipiranga**, a corner that is considered the most famous in all of São Paulo and was immortalized in Caetano Veloso's beautiful ode to the city, 'Sampa.' Turn left and you will be back where you started at Praça da República.

WORTH A TRIP

BRAZIL'S MELTING POT

Brazil's unparalleled racial and ethnic diversity means there is no such thing as a typical Brazilian face. That's why Brazilian passports are highly sought after on the black market – many faces could pass for being Brazilian. For a deeper understanding of São Paulo's immigration history, head to the **Memorial do Imigrante** (www.memorialdoimigrante.sp.gov.br; Visconde de Parnaíba 1316, Moóca; adult/student R$10/5; ⏲9am-5pm Tue-Sat, from 10am Sun) in the eastern suburb of Moóca. Built in 1887, it was called the Hospedaria dos Imigrantes, and functioned as a holding place – not always friendly – for immigrant labor before they shipped out for their first jobs in Brazil, mostly on large plantations.

Fundação Maria Luisa e Oscar Americano MUSEUM, GARDENS
(☎11 3742-0077; www.fundacaooscaramericano.org.br; Av Morumbi 4077, Morumbi; adult/student R$10/5; ⏲museum & cafe 10am-5:30pm Tue-Sun) Home of the couple who developed the leafy, upscale suburb of Morumbi, this fine retreat hosts impressive gardens and a lovely collection of painting, sculpture and objets d'art from the 18th- to the 20th-centuries. The 1950s house-turned-museum is a small masterpiece of Brazilian modernism, and there's also a lovely cafe that serves traditional high tea for R$68.

Courses

Polyglot LANGUAGE
(☎11 3744-4397; www.polyglot.com.br; Av Luiz Carlos Berrini 96, Brooklyn) One of the most respected language schools for Portuguese. Prices start at R$170 per hour, with packages of four to eight hours of daily intensive instruction also available.

Receitaria Escola Gourmet COOKING
(Map p249; ☎11 2892-0031; www.receitaria.com; Fradique Coutinho 600, Pinheiros; class for 1/2/3/4 people R$415/519/739/975) Ever wonder how they get the chicken inside a *coxinha* (chicken-stuffed cornmeal ball), or why your caipirinhas at home never taste as good as in Brazil? Book a 3½-hour cooking course at this highly recommended cooking school and woo friends back home with your contemporary Brazilian kitchen feats.

Tours

★ **Flavia Liz di Paolo** CULTURAL
(☎11 98119-3903; www.flavializ.com) Personal guide Flavia Liz is an enthusiastic, multilingual São Paulo specialist who offers customized guiding services throughout the city and surroundings. Whether you want to dig into architecture, urbanism, conceptual design, shopping, modern and contemporary art, antiques, gastronomy, gourmet coffee and tea, historical sugarcane and coffee farms, galleries, graffiti or *favelas* (slums, informal communities), she is your woman.

★ **SP Free Walking Tour** WALKING
(Map p230; www.spfreewalkingtour.com; Praça da República, República; tips only; ⏲11:30am Mon, Wed, Fri & Sat) FREE Condenses over 450 years of Sampa history into a long but fascinating 'Old Downtown' walk four times a week at 11:30am. The tour meets next to the C.I.T. (tourist booth) at Praça da República and ends 3½ hours later at Largo São Bento; and there's walk-exclusive discounts to be had along the way. Reservations unnecessary – just show up 20 minutes prior.

Festivals & Events

SP-Arte – São Paulo International Art Festival ART
(☎11 3077-2880; www.sp-arte.com/en/the-fair; Parque Ibirapuera, Pavilhão da Bienal, Vila Mariana; ⏲Apr) This national and international art fair is one of the world's largest.

São Paulo Restaurant Week FOOD & DRINK
(www.sp-jpr.maitredigital.com.br; lunch/dinner from R$46.90/58.90; ⏲Apr/May & Aug/Sep) More than 200 restaurants offer special menus and promotional prices for two weeks, twice a year.

Virada Cultural MUSIC
(www.viradacultural.prefeitura.sp.gov.br; ⏲May) FREE A nonstop, free, 24-hour party of cultural – especially musical – events around the city in strategic locations such as Itaquerão, Praça do Campo Limpo, Parque da Juventude, Centro Esportivo Tietê and Chácara do Jockey.

São Paulo Gay Pride Parade LGBT
(www.paradasp.org.br; Av Paulista; ⏲Jun) Av Paulista morphs into a come-all, free-for-all for São Paulo's annual gay pride parade, often considered the biggest in the world (both the 2016 and 2017 events drew three million people!).

Bienal de São Paulo ART
(☎11 5576-7600; www.bienal.org.br; Parque Ibirapuera, Pavilhão Ciccillo Matarazzo, Vila Mariana; ⌚Sep-Dec) Modeled on the Venice Biennale, the Bienal de São Paulo, founded in 1951, has grown into one of the world's most important arts events. Many of the participants are working artists who have been nominated by their home country.

The event is held during even-numbered years, generally from September or October to December, in a sprawling pavilion designed by modernist master Oscar Niemeyer in the leafy **Parque Ibirapuera** (www.parqueibirapuera.org; Av Pedro Álvares Cabral, Vila Mariana; ⌚5am-midnight). In recent years, admission has been free, though this is subject to funding.

Mostra Internacional de Cinema FILM
(☎11 4118-2291; www.mostra.org; ⌚Oct) The country's largest film festival, with screenings throughout the city.

Reveillon NEW YEAR
(Av Paulista, Bela Vista; ⌚31 Dec) Av Paulista turns into a big outdoor party to ring in the new year.

Sleeping

Vila Madelena is the most traveller-friendly neighborhood for leisure visitors and is home to the majority of hostels (there's also a solid concentration around the residential neighborhoods of Paraíso and Vila Mariana off the southeastern end of Av Paulista). The city's top boutique hotels sit in the leafy, upscale district of Jardins, while many top-end business hotels line Av Paulista, Av Faria Lima, Av das Nações Unidas and Parque Ibirapuera.

Centro & Around

Akasaka HOTEL $$
(☎11 3207-1500; www.akasakahotel.com.br; Praça da Liberdade 149, Liberdade; s/d/tr/q with fan R$140/170/210/260, with air-con R$160/190/230/280; ❄📶) Conveniently located across from the metro on Praça Liberdade, this triumphantly no-frills budget option offers 40 simple but clean rooms. It's a handy choice for those especially interested in the city's Japanese and Korean subcultures.

155 Hotel BOUTIQUE HOTEL $$
(Map p230; ☎11 3150-1555; www.155hotel.com.br; Martinho Prado 173, Consolacão; d/tr/ste R$160/240/270; ❄@📶) This gay-friendly, 76-room affordable boutique hotel is located between Centro and the alterna-hipster bars of Baixo Augusta. Ultrasleek suites are steeped in minimalist blacks and grays; regular rooms aren't quite as hip but are still top-value all things considered, with tight bathrooms but hardwood floors and writing desks.

Novotel SP Jaraguá BUSINESS HOTEL $$
(Map p230; ☎11 2802-7000; www.accorhotels.com.br; Martins Fontes 71, Centro; d from R$250; ❄@📶) The Accor chain has refurbished the old Hotel Jaraguá, which had long been central São Paulo's most chic hotel. Digs are spacious, plush and cheerfully done up in soothing cafe tones. Rooms above the 20th floor have breathtaking city views and there's a free shuttle every 30 minutes (7:30am to 7:30pm) to anywhere within 2km of the hotel.

Avenida Paulista, Jardins & Around

Lobo Urban Stay GUESTHOUSE $
(Map p244; ☎11 3085-9888; www.lobourbanstay.com; Haddock Lobo 893, Jardins; dm/s/d R$54/150/200; 📶) This quiet, design-forward Jardins choice easily offers the best location for money in the city, situated smack dab in the middle of São Paulo's toniest environs. Run by two Paulista cousins, there's one eight-bed mixed dorm with its own private bath; one female-only four-bed dorm with a desk; and one spacious private (especially good value for solo travelers). No breakfast.

Augusta Park Hotel HOTEL $$
(Map p244; ☎11 3124-4400; www.augustapark.com.br; Augasta 922, Consolação; s/d R$230/280; ❄📶🏊) Set amid the action of Baixo Augusta, the 66-room Augusta Park has a convenient location and offers some of Sampa's best-value (if slightly dated) rooms – especially if you managed to snag the promotional rates.

Pousada Dona Ziláh POUSADA $$$
(Map p244; ☎11 3062-1444; www.zilah.com; Minas Gerais 112, Higienópolis; d/tr R$365/430; @📶) 🌿 This Av Paulista–adjacent 1932 mansion in Higienópolis has a long, steeped history in São Paulo comfort. The six rooms aren't flash but offer upgraded comforts, especially where the exquisitely tiled bathrooms are concerned, and extensive, fountain-drenched gardens that are watered with filtered shower and sink water.

★**Hotel Emiliano** BOUTIQUE HOTEL $$$
(Map p244; ☎11 3068-4399; www.emiliano.com.br; Oscar Freire 384, Jardins; d from R$2500; ❄@☎🏊) Sleek, bright and minimalist, Emiliano is the city's best hotel. It's steeped in refined luxury, with local touches such as the lobby's lush suspended orchid garden, along with impeccable service and a sun-drenched rooftop pool, all without taking itself too seriously. It nails the combo of cool (not too in your face) and opulent (but not too stuffy).

★**Hotel Unique** DESIGN HOTEL $$$
(☎11 3055-4710; www.hotelunique.com.br; Av Brigadeiro Luis Antônio 4700, Jardim Paulista; d from R$1500; ❄@🏊) Designed by Ruy Ohtake, the slice of watermelon–reminiscent Unique is certainly the city's most architecturally ambitious hotel, as well as a favorite of rock stars and fashionistas. Rooms, with their porthole-like windows, are elegantly minimalist, and the rooftop bar (p251) and pool offer some of the city's most stupendous views.

Hotel Fasano BOUTIQUE HOTEL $$$
(Map p244; ☎11 3896-4000; www.fasano.com.br; Vittorio Fasano 88, Jardins; d from R$1650; ❄@🏊) This ultrarefined 60-room hotel behind an English red-brick facade evokes a bygone era of modernist glamour, with muted gray travertine marble set off with exquisite 1930s-era antiques in rooms and common areas; and a reserve, formality and discreetness rare in Brazil (only four rooms per floor). The entrance frames the gorgeous lobby bar – you may not make it past!

The Zen-like rooftop pool area and intimate jazz bar Barretto (p254) alone are worth the price to stay here.

Parque Ibirapuera & Around

★**We Hostel Design** HOSTEL $
(☎11 2615-2262; www.wehostel.com.br; Morgado de Mateus 567, Vila Mariana; dm R$60-77, d without bathroom R$145-205; ❄@☎) Simply gorgeous, São Paulo's best hostel sits inside a beautiful historic 1926 white mansion on a quiet Vila Mariana residential corner. From the guest kitchen to the hammock-strewn, quasi-wraparound porch to the kitschy living room, everything here has been designed with expert connoisseurship of retro furniture and coveted antiques.

São Paulo Lodge HOSTEL $
(☎11 5084-5967; www.saopaulolodge.com; Sena Madureira 42, Vila Mariana; dm R$65-75, d with/without bathroom from R$165/110; ❄@☎) This well-loved newcomer, which bills itself as a 'business hostel,' sits just 400m from Metrô Vila Mariana and within a few kilometers of Parque Ibirapuera. Segregated dorms are better than the lobby suggests, with artsy bookshelves, outlet-equipped lockers and air-conditioning; and a big communal kitchen faces a welcoming open-air indoor garden.

Pinheiros, Vila Madalena & Around

Hostel SP011 HOSTEL $
(☎11 3673-0132; www.facebook.com/hostelsp011; Agostinho Mendicute 85, Sumaré; dm R$69, d with/without bathroom R$179/169; ☎) Just across from Vila Madelena in far more tranquil Sumaré, but still close enough to stumble home, this well-loved hostel is identified via an iconic *orelhão* (big ear – slang for phone booth cover) that houses its call button. Two six-bed mixed dorms and inviting, design-forward common areas – especially the glass-encased retro lounge and front patio – are highlights.

Ô de Casa HOSTEL $
(Map p249; ☎11 3063-5216; www.odecasahostel.com; Inácio Pereira da Rocha 385, Vila Madalena; dm R$45-60, r R$150-200, r without bathroom R$120-150; ❄☎) This artsy and colorful hostel is one of the neighborhood's oldest, with a sociable bar and rooftop terrace that gives way to shotgun-style lodging in four-, six- and eight-bed mixed dorm configurations and well-kept bathrooms. A newer annex houses spiffier private rooms with lofts and private bathrooms, but you won't escape the noise from the imbibing nighttime crowds.

California Hostel POUSADA $
(Map p249; ☎11 2619-6007; www.hostelcalifornia.com.br; João Moura 607, Pinheiros; dm R$45-55, s/d/tr from R$140/170/190, without bathroom from R$110/127/170; ❄☎) This colorful Pinheiros guesthouse turned a two-story town house into a design-forward spot to rest your weary head. Rooms are smallish, but the whole place is packed with personality and there are pleasant patios in both the main house and the less atmospheric annex across the street.

Sampa Hostel HOSTEL $
(Map p249; ☎11 3031-6779; www.hostelsampa.com.br; Girassol 519, Vila Madalena; dm from R$40, s/d/tr/q R$90/140/210/280; @☎) This newly remodeled veteran of Vila Madalena's hostel scene is one of its best, offering four-,

six- and eight-bed dorms (the last of these a bit cramped), a few sparse privates, kitchen facilities and a sun deck.

★Guest Urban BOUTIQUE HOTEL **$$**
(Map p249; ☎11 3081-5030; www.guesturbansp.com.br; Lisboa 493, Pinheiros; d R$259-309; ❄📶) This 1930s mansion, opened in late 2015, holds 14 suites reeking of industrial-chic (exposed brick and beams, unfinished steel and concrete) offset by a sunny open patio and cutting-edge art (reprints for sale in the lobby). It's one block from Praca Benedito Calixto in the heart of hip Pinheiros.

South & East of Jardins

Four Seasons Hotel São Paulo BOUTIQUE HOTEL **$$$**
(☎11 2526-0100; www.fourseasons.com/br/saopaulo; Av das Nacoẽs Unidas 14401, Chácara Santo Antônio; d weekday/weekend from R$1260/1400; ❄@📶≋) Opening in late 2018, Brazil's first Four Seasons sits inside the wellness-focused Parque da Cidade in tony Chácara Santo Antônio. A glistening stone-cladding facade greets guests, who hide away from the Sampa hustle inside rooms with yellow, retro-inspired love seats that both have sexy curves (a theme extending to the wavy lobby bar) and Nani Chinellato banana-fiber wall covering.

Eating

Centro & Around

★Estadão FAST FOOD **$**
(Map p230; www.estadaolanches.com.br; Viaduto 9 de Julho 193, Centro; specialty sandwiches R$7-33; ⏲24hr) This classic Centro *lanchonete* (snack bar) serves working folk's meals at all hours, but its signature *pernil* (pork loin) sandwich, smothered in the cheese of your choice (provolone!) and sautéed onions, is one of Sampa's gastronomic musts.

Hot Pork HOT DOGS **$**
(Map p230; http://acasadoporco.com.br; Bento Freitas 454, República; hot dogs R$15; ⏲11am-10pm) Superstar Sampa chef Jefferson Rueda's kids wanted hot dogs at their parties, so what was a gourmet chef to do? Make the best one ever! The 100% pork option (Hot Pork) has no additives or preservatives and is dressed with everything made in-house: a milk bread bun, tomato and apple ketchup, fermented mustard with *tucupi* (a manioc broth), mayo and onion and cucumber pickles.

Esfiharia Effendi FAST FOOD **$**
(Map p230; www.effendi.com.br; Dom Antônio de Melo, Luz; snack R$4.60-10; ⏲8am-late Tue-Sat, from 9am Sun) Started by refugees fleeing the Armenian genocide in 1973, this downright divey classic slings some of the city's best *esfihas* – open-faced or triangular meat pies hailing from the Levant. Go for beef, *za'atar* or cheese with *basturma* (air-dried cured beef) – São Paulo is rarely this tasty for so cheap.

Casa Mathilde SWEETS **$**
(Map p230; www.casamathilde.com.br; Praça Antônio Prado 76, Centro; sweets R$4.50-12; ⏲9am-7:30pm Mon-Fri, 9:30am-4:30pm Sat; 📶) Induce a sugar coma with the traditional sweets of Portugal, laid out here in a dizzying and mouthwatering 15m-long display case.

Rong He CHINESE **$**
(www.ronghe.com.br; Rua da Glória 622, Liberdade; mains for 2 people R$20-63; ⏲11:30am-3pm & 6:30-10:30pm Mon-Fri, 11:30am-10:30pm Sat & Sun) A Liberdade institution and the city's best Chinese. First and foremost, expect surly service; second to that, the *gyoza* (pan-fried Japanese dumplings) and the house-made Chinese noodle dishes are served in great-value portions *yakisoba*-style or in soupy, piping hot caldrons (*ensopada*) to out-the-door lines of devoted patrons. You can watch the dough masters at work through the show kitchen window.

★A Casa do Porco BRAZILIAN **$$**
(Map p230; ☎11 3258-2578; www.acasadoporco.com.br; Araújo 124, República; mains R$48-72; ⏲noon-midnight Mon-Sat, to 5pm Sun; 📶) Chef Jefferson Rueda's casual temple of swine is a wonderful descent into all things pork. Delicious and decadent specialties such as *porco san zé* (R$48 per person) offer the full treatment, carved from an eight-hour whole slow-roasted hog and served in perfectly crispy/decadently succulent squares with side dishes such as *tutu de feljão* (beans thickened with cassava flour). Heart-stoppingly satisfying.

But there's so much more! Pork belly with crispy guava, pork croquettes, pork bolognese pasta, all manner of smoked sausages, pork sushi with black *tucupi;* if it comes from a pig, it's done up here and done up oh so right! There's craft beer, good wines and creative cocktails to wash down all that pig. Reserve ahead. Hot Pork (p239), an offshoot gourmet hot dog takeaway, has opened two blocks away.

JABOTICABA FOTOS/SHUTTERSTOCK ©

1. Margherita pizza 2. Bráz Pizzaria
3. *Chope* (draft beer)

Pizza Paulistana

Swarms of Italian immigrants settled in São Paulo in the late 19th century, giving the city one of the largest Italian populations in the world outside Italy and one of South America's best-kept culinary secrets. Locals say the pizza is so good, even the Italians are jealous!

Bráz Pizzaria

The experience at **Bráz** (Map p249; ☎11 3037-7975; www.brazpizzaria.com.br; Vupabussu 271, Pinheiros; pizza R$43-88; ⏲6:30pm-12:30am Sun-Tue, noon-3pm & 6:30pm-midnight Wed-Thu, to 1am Fri & Sat;) will leave you thinking, 'Italy, schmataly.' Do as Brazilians do and order a Brahma draft beer *(chope)* followed by an appetizer of warm sausage bread (*pão de calabresa*) dipped in spiced olive oil, then let the feast commence. Bráz has a number of locations in both São Paulo and Rio de Janeiro; visit the website for details.

Speranza

One of the oldest and most traditional pizzerias, **Speranza** (Map p244; ☎11 3288-3512; www.pizzaria.com.br; Rua 13 de Maio 1004, Bixiga; pizza R$57-100; ⏲6:30pm-12:30am Sun-Thu, to 1am Fri & Sat;) is in the Italian neighborhood of Bixiga, where the Famiglia Tarallo has been serving serious pizza since 1958. Perfect meal: the life-changing bruschetta appetizer followed by a fiercely traditional margarita pizza. No, wait: those calzones are insanely good, too.

Leggera Pizza Napoletana

At **Leggera Pizza Napoletana** (☎11 3862-2581; www.pizzerialeggera.com.br; Diana 80, Vila Pompeia; pizza R$34-42; ⏲7-11pm Tue-Thu, to 11:30pm Fri & Sat, to 10pm Sun;) Brazilian-Italian-American *pizzaiolo* Andre Guidon imports everything humanly possible from Italy – and this small, family-run affair epitomizes the Brazilian-Italian diaspora. The 12 individual-sized, uncut pies here (plus a few calzones) are easily Sampa's best. They emerge from one of just 500 or so Neapolitan pizzeria ovens in the world certified by the Associação Verace Pizza Napoletana. Reservations prudent.

★ **Lamen Kazu** JAPANESE $$

(www.lamenkazu.com.br; Tomás Gonzaga 51, Liberdade; mains $29-47; 11am-3pm & 6-10:30pm Mon-Sat, 11am-3pm & 6-9pm Sun;) It's not as famous (or cheap) as its nearby rival Aska, but take the hint: the 99% Japanese clientele should tell you something. The fiery Kara Misso Lamen (spicy broth and spiced pork in addition to the usual condiments; R$42), doused with the house-made chili sauce, is a revelation; as is everything on the menu. Veg options as well. Get slurpin!

Famiglia Mancini ITALIAN $$

(Map p230; 11 3256-4320; www.famigliamancini.com.br; Avanhandava 81, Centro; mains for 2 people R$102-283; 11:30am-1am Mon-Wed, to 1:30am Thu, to 2:30am Fri & Sat, to midnight Sun;) On charming and romantic Rua Avanhandava – a leafy, almost European-feeling side street in Centro – this traditional trattoria is one of the city's most atmospheric, with throngs of Chianti fiascos hanging from the ceiling and an old-school family-style Italian ambience.

In reality portions serve three, which is how many you'll need to divvy up the perusing of the gigantic menu of pasta, meat and seafood dishes.

Rinconcito Peruano PERUVIAN $$

(Map p230; www.rinconcitoperuano.com.br; Aurora 451, Centro; mains R$24-58; noon-5pm Mon, to 10pm Tue-Sat, to 9pm Sun) Success has been good to the little Peruvian restaurant that could. Expanded, remodeled and borderline too classy for the dicey neighborhood, this is a wonderful spot for great-value Peruvian classics such as ceviche and *lomo saltado* (stir-fried sirloin with onions, tomatoes, and french fries).

You'll need to keep your guard up arriving here (it's fine during the day, but keep in mind that this area is rife with drug users), but Peruvian cooks, waitstaff and clientele mean it's the real deal.

Ramona BRAZILIAN, FUSION $$

(Map p230; www.casaramona.com.br; Av São Luís 282, República; mains R$40-69; noon-midnight Mon & Tue, to 2am Wed-Fri, 12:30pm-2am Sat, 12:30-6:30pm Sun;) This República hot spot was one of the first to give Paulistanos a reason to venture into Centro at night. The legitimately retro space, fueled by a holier-than-thou indie soundtrack, excels at burgers (especially the spicy bacon-jalapeño 'Rocks Off') and a long list of more sophisticated creative Brazilian grub. Also has great cocktails, including the elusive Bloody Mary, and delicious desserts.

Avenida Paulista, Jardins & Around

Jardins is your place to splurge. It offers an incredibly dense collection of some of Brazil's most illustrious restaurants, plus some surprisingly reasonable choices to boot, as does Itaím Bibi to the southeast.

★ **Bacio di Latte** GELATO $

(Map p244; www.baciodilatte.com.br; Oscar Freire 136, Jardins; gelato from R$12; 10am-11pm Sun-Fri, to 1am Sat;) A Scotsman and two Italians were the first to do what nobody outside Buenos Aires could previously do: produce amazing Italian gelato in South America. Often voted the city's best, it's one of Brazil's best as well, and this charming Oscar Freire location started it all.

Casa do Sabor AMMA SWEETS $

(Map p244; www.ammachocolate.com.br; Alameda Rocha Azevedo 1052, Jardins; chocolate R$1-17; 11am-8pm Tue-Sat) AMMA's sustainably-sourced, organic and milk-free chocolate is probably Brazil's best. Sample popular flavors such as sea salt, coffee and Gula Merah (made with coconut sugar) in to-go bars (R$17) or settle in with a portion of cake or *brigadeiro* (chocolate bonbon) baked in-house, accompanied by an espresso or hot chocolate.

★ **Shin-Zushi** JAPANESE $$

(11 3889-8700; Afonso de Freitas 169, Paraíso; tasting menu R$300, sushi combos R$65-120; 11:30am-2pm & 6-10:30pm Tue-Sun) Barely a blip from Paraíso metro station is this outrageously good and authentic sushi hotspot where brothers Robinson and Ken Mizumoto execute an exquisite, daily fresh menu of motherland-worthy raw fish that will leave you rubbing your eyes to verify you haven't traveled to Japan.

The fiercely traditional *omakase* (tasting menu) nets an extraordinary array of the day's best at the hands of an *itamae* (a step above sushiman in sushi hierarchy) who will wow you with the delicate and incredibly fresh flavors; while sushi combos – there's one entirely devoted to tuna! – are still pricey but extraordinary value compared with what you'd pay at this quality level in Japan.

★Tordesilhas BRAZILIAN $$

(Map p244; ☎11 3107-7444; www.tordesilhas.com; Alameda Tietê 489, Jardins; mains R$63-87; ⏰6pm-1am Tue-Fri, noon-5pm & 7pm-1am Sat, noon-5pm Sun; 📶) Chef Mara Salles creates some of the very best contemporary Brazilian cuisine in the city at dependable Tordesilhas. There is a palpable lean on specialties from the Amazon such as *pato no tucupí* (roasted duck flavored with juice of the manioc plant and *jambu,* a mouth-numbing indigenous herb) and grilled Amazonian fish, as well as Brazil-wide regional dishes.

★Kan Suke SUSHI $$

(Map p244; ☎11 3266-3819; Manoel da Nóbrega 76, Jardins; tasting menu R$120-300; ⏰11:30am-1pm & 6-8:30pm Mon-Sat) Sushi superman Keisuke Egashira speaks broken Portuguese, arriving a few years back after 23 years at Tokyo's Sushi-Kan. This uneventfully simple, raw-fish powerhouse hidden away in a nondescript shopping plaza off Av Paulista evokes *Jiro Dreams of Sushi*–level authenticity. It's generally pricy but the eight-piece set lunches are a steal (R$65). Japanese menu only.

★Capim Santo BRAZILIAN $$

(Map p244; ☎11 3089-9500; www.capimsanto.com.br; Alameda Ministro Rocha Azevedo 471, Jardins; dinner mains R$56-123, lunch buffet weekday/weekends R$63/96; ⏰noon-3pm & 7-11pm Tue-Fri, 12:30-4:30pm & 8pm-midnight Sat, 12:30-4:30pm Sun; 📶) 🍃 Top chef Morena Leite turns out excellent regional Brazilian fare, with an emphasis on local and organic ingredients, served in a relaxed, beautifully Brazilian indoor-outdoor space. The excellent weekday buffet is the affordable way into this higher-end spot.

Balaio IMS BRAZILIAN $$

(Map p244; ☎11 2842-9123; www.balaioims.com.br; Av Paulista 2424, Instituto Moreira Salles; mains R$49-59; ⏰noon-11pm Tue-Sat, to 5pm Sun, limited menu 4-7pm; 📶) In what can only be considered a gift to Paulistanos, one no longer needs to schlep all the way out to Mocotó (p250) to try upstart chef Rodrigo Oliveira's excellent contemporary Brazilian cuisine. Here at Instituto Moreira Salles, highlights are many: cashew fruit-infused G&Ts, *linguiça* rice with okra, a vegan *moqueca* (Bahian stew) with cashew fruit, hearts of palm and plantains and so on.

★Jiquitaia BRAZILIAN $$

(Map p244; ☎11 3262-2366; www.jiquitaia.com.br; Antônio Carlos 268, Consolação; mains R$55-62; ⏰noon-3pm Mon, 7-11:30pm Tue-Fri, noon-6pm & 7-11:30pm Sat, bar until 2am Tue-Sat) Accolades abound for upstart Brazilian chef Marcelo Bastos and his affordable entry-level into contemporary Brazilian cuisine. Pick any three courses at this cute and cozy bistro-style restaurant to create-your-own set menu (lunch R$55, dinner R$88), including – drum roll, please! – the elusive *moqueca* (seafood stew) for one person! Sister Nina admirably handles the excellent fresh fruit caipirinhas.

Zena Caffé ITALIAN $$

(Map p244; ☎11 3081-2158; www.zenacaffe.com.br; Peixoto Gomide 1901, Jardins; mains R$38-73; ⏰noon-midnight Sun-Wed, to 1am Thu-Sat; 📶) Despite his mug everywhere, including TV (Brazil's version of *Hell's Kitchen*), chef Carlos Bertolazzi remains a humble, immediately likable dude's dude. His menu, focused largely on the cuisine from his Ligurian bloodline, is homey and fiercely authentic Italian comfort food at prices that won't infuriate you. His gnocchi, focaccia and ragù (lamb or duck) are all outstanding, but you can't go wrong.

Veggie Raw Burger N Bar VEGETARIAN $$

(Map p244; www.rawburger.com.br; Augusta 2052, Jardins; burgers R$28-35; ⏰noon-11:30pm Wed-Thu, 1-11:30pm Fri & Sat, 1-10pm Sun; 📶🖊) Tucked away in a deep lane off Rua Augusta, this hipster veg burger delight was spawned from the opposite: a highly successful traditional burger joint in Vila Madelena. But you won't even think about beef here – the meatless offerings (toasted mushrooms, potatoes and mozzarella; pumpkin with tapioca; beet with avocado) excel in both taste and consistency. Sweet potato fries, too!

Town Sandwich Co SANDWICHES $$

(Map p244; www.townsandwichco.com; Melo Alves 445, Jardins; sandwiches R$22-50; ⏰noon-midnight Tue-Sun) This hotshot *sandwicheria* has been scooping up awards for the city's best sandwich joint since opening in 2015. These juicy concoctions tend towards an international pedigree, the most popular of which is the ambitious calamari (squid sautéed with bacon, purple onion, cherry tomatoes, grapes, paprika and Sicilian lime served hot dog style) but there's lamb, ribs ragout, barbecued pork and more.

Tenda do Nilo MIDDLE EASTERN $$

(Oscar Porto 638, Paraíso; dishes R$32-69.50; ⏰noon-3pm Mon-Sat) This criminally small, sidewalk-simple joint epitomizes the city's indelible Lebanese and Syrian links; two huge

Avenida Paulista, Jardins & Around

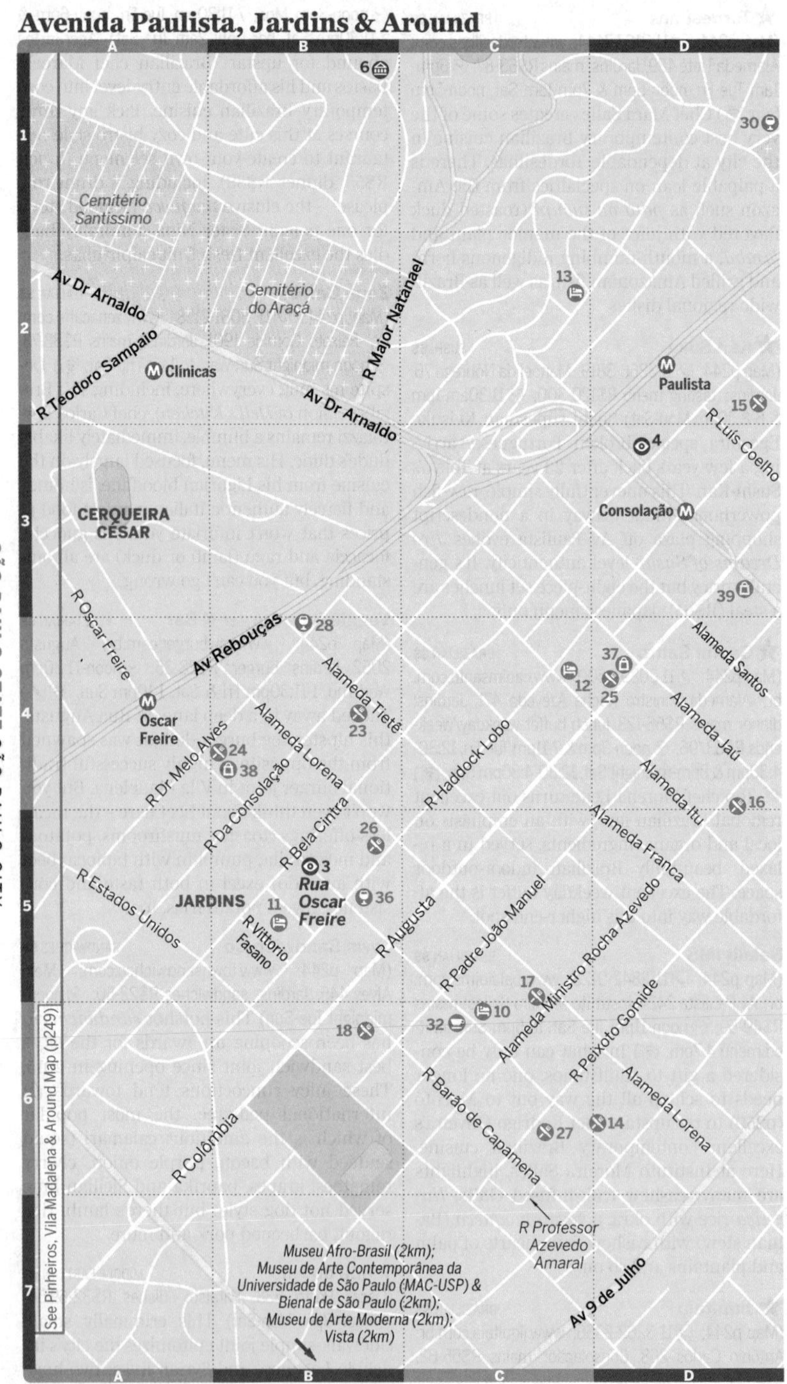

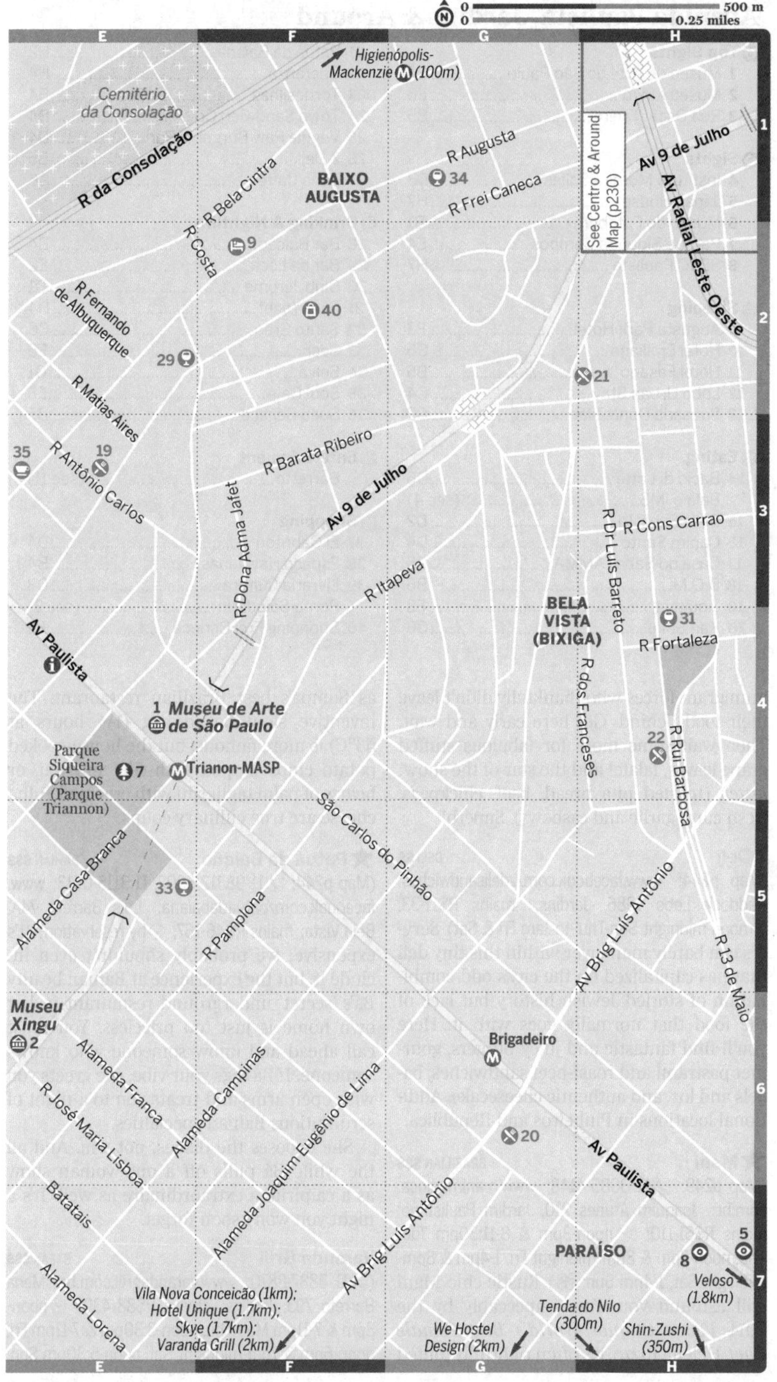

0 500 m
0 0.25 miles
Higienópolis-Mackenzie (100m)
Cemitério da Consolação
R da Consolação
R Bela Cintra
BAIXO AUGUSTA
R Augusta
34
R Frei Caneca
See Centro & Around Map (p230)
Av 9 de Julho
Av Radial Leste Oeste
R Costa
9
40
R Fernando de Albuquerque
29
21
R Matias Aires
35
19
R Antônio Carlos
R Barata Ribeiro
R Dona Adma Jafet
Av 9 de Julho
R Dr Luís Barreto
R Cons Carrao
R Itapeva
BELA VISTA (BIXIGA)
31
R Fortaleza
Av Paulista
R dos Franceses
1 Museu de Arte de São Paulo
Parque Siqueira Campos (Parque Triannon)
7
Trianon-MASP
22
R Rui Barbosa
São Carlos do Pinhão
Alameda Casa Branca
33
R Pamplona
Av Brig Luís Antônio
R 13 de Maio
Museu Xingu
2
Brigadeiro
Alameda Franca
Alameda Campinas
Alameda Joaquim Eugênio de Lima
R José Maria Lisboa
20
Av Paulista
Batatais
Av Brig Luís Antônio
PARAÍSO
5
8
Veloso (1.8km)
Alameda Lorena
Vila Nova Conceicão (1km); Hotel Unique (1.7km); Skye (1.7km); Varanda Grill (2km)
We Hostel Design (2km)
Tenda do Nilo (300m)
Shin-Zushi (350m)

Avenida Paulista, Jardins & Around

Top Sights
1 Museu de Arte de São Paulo ... E4
2 Museu Xingu ... E6
3 Rua Oscar Freire ... B5

Sights
4 Instituto Moreira Salles ... D3
5 Japan House ... H7
6 Museu do Futebol ... B1
7 Parque Siqueira Campos ... E4
8 SESC Paulista ... H7

Sleeping
9 Augusta Park Hotel ... F2
10 Hotel Emiliano ... C6
11 Hotel Fasano ... B5
12 Lobo Urban Stay ... C4
13 Pousada Dona Ziláh ... C2

Eating
14 Bacio di Latte ... D6
Balaio IMS ... (see 4)
15 Bella Paulista ... D2
16 Capim Santo ... D4
17 Casa do Sabor AMMA ... C5
18 D.O.M. ... B6
19 Jiquitaia ... E3
20 Kan Suke ... G6
21 Patuá da Baiana ... H2
22 Speranza ... H4
23 Tordesilhas ... B4
24 Town Sandwich Co ... B4
25 Veggie Raw Burger N Bar ... D4
26 Z Deli ... B5
27 Zena Caffé ... C6

Drinking & Nightlife
28 Bar Balcão ... B4
29 Bar da Lôca ... E2
30 Club Jerome ... D1
31 Club Yacht ... H4
32 Santo Grão ... C6
33 Seen ... E5
34 Selva ... G1
35 Soul Café ... E3
36 Suco Begaço ... B5

Entertainment
Barretto ... (see 11)

Shopping
37 El Cabriton ... D4
38 Espaço Havaianas ... B4
39 Livraria Cultura ... D3
Ponto Solodário ... (see 2)
40 Shopping Frei Caneca ... F2

immigrant forces who thankfully didn't leave their food behind. Get here early and wait. Then wait some more for fabulous stuffed grape leaves, falafel and the star of the show: *fatteh* (toasted pita bread, beef, chickpeas, fresh curd, garlic and cashews). Superb!

Z Deli DELI $$
(Map p244; www.facebook.com/zdelisandwiches; Haddock Lobo 1386, Jardins; mains R$11-33; noon-midnight Sun-Thu, to 1am Fri & Sat) Servers can barely maneuver within this tiny deli that has capitalized on the city's odd combination of storied Jewish history but lack of the food that normally goes with it. Here you'll find fantastic and juicy burgers, gourmet pastrami and roast-beef sandwiches, bagels and lox, and authentic cheesecake. Additional locations in Pinheiros and República.

★ Maní BRAZILIAN $$$
(Map p249; 11 3085-4148; www.manimanioca.com.br; Joaquim Atunes 210, Jardim Paulistano; mains R$51-110; noon-3pm & 8-11:30pm Tue-Thu, noon-3pm & 8pm-midnight Fri, 1-4pm & 8pm-midnight Sat, 1-4pm Sun;) Rustic-chic Maní will astound you. Run impeccably by the 2014 *Veuve Cliquot World's Best Female Chef*, Helena Rizzo, it's often rightfully touted as Sampa's best Brazilian restaurant. The inventive slow-cooked egg (1½ hours at 63°C) is more famous, but the house-cooked potato chips topped with filet mignon, or hearts of palm taglierini with creamed Tulha cheese are true culinary coups.

★ Patuá da Baiana BAHIAN $$$
(Map p244; 11 98312-5302, 11 3115-0513; www.facebook.com/patuadabaiana; Luis Barreto 74A, Bela Vista; mains R$46-167; by reservation) It's expensive; we probably shouldn't even include it, but the experience at Bahian beauty Bá's 'secret' underground restaurant in her own home is just too priceless. You must call ahead and know someone who knows someone. If Bá digs your vibe, she greets you with open arms and treats you to a night of scrumptious Bahian specialties.

She chooses the dishes, not you. And all the while Bá pulls off a one-woman show as a caipirinha extraordinaire as well. It's a night you won't soon forget.

Varanda Grill STEAK $$$
(11 3887-8870; www.varandagrill.com.br; Mena Barreto 793, Jardins; steaks R$88-430; noon-3pm & 7-11pm Mon-Thu, noon-3:30pm & 7-11pm Fri, noon-6pm & 7pm-midnight Sat, noon-5:30pm Sun;

) This top-quality casual grill (there's a more formal location at gastronomy-heavy Shopping JK (p255)) serves the city's best steak – don't let anyone tell you otherwise. Argentine and American cuts feature heavily in the exceptional beef (from Brazil and Argentina on over to Kobe), and one of Brazil's most extraordinary wine list follows suit.

D.O.M. BRAZILIAN **$$$**

(Map p244; 11 3088-0761; www.domrestaurante.com.br; Barão de Capamena 549, Jardins; tasting menus R$375-645, with wine R$485-1030; noon-3pm & 7pm-midnight Mon-Fri, 7pm-midnight Sat) Brazilian celebrity chef Alex Atala's small and deceptively casual contemporary Brazilian restaurant serves up some of the finest food in Sampa, which is saying a lot. Atala is nearly personally responsible for putting Brazilian haute cuisine on the international radar: it placed 30th on the 2018 *World's 50 Best Restaurants* list, which foodies fawn over relentlessly.

Obviously, it will put a serious dent in your wallet, but the R$98 set Brazilian lunch is a great option for more frugal foodies. Reservations mandatory.

Parque Ibirapuera & Around

Vista BRAZILIAN **$$**

(11 97382-7261; www.vistasaopaulo.com.br; Av Pedro Álvares Cabral 1301, 8th Fl, Museu de Arte Contemporânea, Parque Ibirapuera; mains R$62-99; 10am-7pm Mon-Fri, noon-4pm Sat;) Opened on the rooftop of Museu de Arte Contemporânea (p233) near Parque Ibirapuera in 2018, Vista is true to its name: the outstanding panoramic view on offer of the park and the city in all directions is nothing short of miraculous.

Chef Marcelo Bastos of Jiquitaia (p243) fame does commendable contemporary Brazilian cuisine, but you won't stop thinking about the view – until the gooey caramel tart arrives, that is; it's a revelation! Cocktails and apps are allowed on the terrace – main courses inside only.

Bráz Pizzaria PIZZA **$$**

(11 5561-1736; www.brazpizzaria.com.br; Graúna 125, Moema; pizza R$49-75; 6:30pm-12:30am Sun-Thu, to 1am Fri & Sat;) The Moema location of this classic *pizza Paulistana* chain follows suit from its more lively Pinheiros (p241) location, churning out wood-oven baked pies (try Fosca with smoked ham, *catupiry* cheese, mozzarella and tomato sauce) and fantastic *pão de calabresa* (sausage bread). It's popular with families.

Pinheiros, Vila Madalena & Around

★ **Bacio di Latte** GELATO **$**

(Map p249; www.baciodilatte.com.br; Harmonia 337, Vila Madalena; gelato from R$12; 11am-11pm Sun-Fri, to midnight Sat;) Most folks crave burgers and fries after a late night of being overserved in Vila Madelana, but if your sweet tooth is calling, the neighborhood outlet of Sampa's best gelato has you covered. In addition to the usual suspects, Brazilian fruits, such as *maracujá* (passion fruit) make their way into refreshing sorbets.

Vila Butantan FOOD HALL **$**

(www.vilabutantan.com.br; Agostinho Cantu 47, Butantã; 11am-8pm Mon-Tue, to 9pm Tue & Sun, to 10pm Wed-Sat;) What started out as a food truck parking lot in 2015 has exploded into a full-on gastronomy- and design-focused shipping container city. The food trucks are still here, but Vila Butantan is now home to stacked shipping containers housing restaurants, retail and bars, creating a one-stop alterna-destination of food, craft beer and lifestyle shops modeled after London's Boxpark.

It's 650m from Metrô Butantã on the yellow line.

Congolinária AFRICAN **$**

(www.facebook.com/congolinaria; Av Alfonso Bovero 382, Sumaré; mains R$26-30; noon-3pm & 7-10pm Tue-Sat, to 3pm Sun;) One of São Paulo's more interesting vegan choices, this simple Sumaré shack – which shares space with in-the-know vinyl record shop and bar Fatiado Discos – is the domain of Congolese refugee and renaissance man, Pitchou Luambo. Choose from three or so African-leaning options per day, including a lovely *feijoada* (bean-and-meat stew) with mushrooms and kale sautéed with peanut sauce. Everything is good!

Underdog Meat & Beers BURGERS **$**

(Map p249; João Moura 541, Pinheiros; burgers from R$22; noon-4pm & 6:30-11pm Tue-Thu, noon-1:30am Fri, 9am-midnight Sat, 9am-6pm Sun) A humble Argentine is behind the grilled perfection that emerges from this rapidly expanding den of carnivorism, where the perfectly charred meat – add cheese, grilled jalapeños and bacon to experience what is easily the city's most outstanding burger – will overwhelm you with decadent goodness.

A standing room–only crowd often spills onto the street despite an expansion into spaces on both sides. The soundtrack leans indie rock, the beer IPAs. With all due respect to vegetarians, our mouth waters just writing this review – the whole place smells like charred love.

★Carlos Pizza PIZZA $$

(Map p249; ☎11 3813-2017; www.carlospizza.com.br; Harmonia 501, Vila Madalena; pizzas R$36-56; ⏰6pm-midnight; 📶) This intimate Vila Madalena pizzeria has been scooping up citywide pizza awards and its novel concept makes for a quick explanation: Neapolitan-style tradition and sensibility but forged with farm-to-table Brazilian ingredients from small producers, such as cheeses matured in former post-harvest coffee compartments, and artisanal hams from the Serra da Mantiqueira. Portions are individual.

★Futuro Refeitório FUSION $$

(Map p249; ☎11 3085-5885; www.futurorefeitorio.com.br; Cônego Eugênio Leite 808, Pinheiros; small plates R$11-43, mains R$32-41; ⏰8am-10:30pm Mon-Thu, to 11pm Fri, 9am-4pm & 7-11pm Sat, 9am-4pm Sun; 📶📝) 🌿 A former Pinheiros parking lot has been transformed into this unapologetically trendy canteen that bills itself as the future of eating. Indeed, low-key Chef Gabriela Barretto has a vision: scale back on meat-derived and processed foods, and muck about less with things. Vegans flip over the plant-based lunch menu (R$34), while dinner mostly focuses on small plates and sandwiches.

Coffee is also taken very seriously, as espresso from the La Marzocco machine and gourmet *café coado* (Brazilian-style pour-over) can attest. With a hip and hot clientele (and out-of-the-box, Asian-leaning fusion keeping them satiated), the future looks bright.

★Feijoada da Lana BRAZILIAN $$

(Map p249; ☎11 3814-9191; Aspicuelta 421, Vila Madalena; feijoada weekday/weekend R$49/89; ⏰noon-3pm Mon-Fri, 12:30-7pm Sat & Sun Apr-Feb) Lana, a journalist by trade, and daughter Luísa, offer their hugely popular version of *feijoada,* Brazil's national dish, inside a smallish Vila Madalena house. Production here isn't as elaborate as at more expensive options or fancy hotels, but it's long on smiling service, hearty goodness and (included on weekends!) *batidinhas de limão,* a sort of shaken caipirinha.

In our humble opinion – and the late Anthony Bourdain's! – it's the best *feijoada* for the buck in town, and you don't have to wait until Saturday to enjoy it.

Izakaya Matsu JAPANESE $$

(Map p249; www.facebook.com/izakayamatsu; Av Pedroso de Morais 403, Pinheiros; small plates R$25-42, mains R$32-68; ⏰11:30am-2:30pm & 6-11pm) Foodies in the know consider this São Paulo's best traditional *izakaya* (Japanese pub), where Sergio Ouba, Toshi Akuta and Adriano Silva slice, dice, boil and fry up a divine list of tavern-style Japanese small plates. Spiced *karaaguê karê* (fried chicken curry), perfectly breaded *tonkatsu* (fried pork ribs) and oodles of noodles delight sake-swilling patrons at the long balcony.

Get there early to avoid the less atmospheric, open-air seating upstairs – this area is cramped and has views of a typically Paulistano 'spaghettied' utility pole (maze of electrical wires).

Banana Verde VEGETARIAN $$

(Map p249; www.bananaverde.com.br; Harmonia 278, Vila Madalena; meals R$38.20-49.50; ⏰noon-3:30pm & 7-10:30pm Tue-Fri, noon-4pm & 7-10:30pm Sat, noon-4pm Sun; 📶📝) 🌿 One of Sampa's most popular and best vegetarian restaurants. A daily-changing salad buffet is offered (okra with vinaigrette is perennially popular) along with a chef-driven main course or two that can be taken separately from each other, or combined with dessert for the *menu executivo* (R$49.50).

★Tuju BRAZILIAN $$$

(Map p249; ☎11 2691-5548; www.tuju.com.br; Fradique Coutinho 1248, Vila Madalena; tasting menus R$160-350, with wine R$250-495; ⏰7.30-11pm Tue-Fri, 1-4pm & 7.30-11pm Sat; 📶) Delicate flavors and unconventional Brazilian ingredients inventively spun to delight your taste buds are hallmarks of top chef Ivan Ralston, who still greets and chats to foodies despite his recent fame as the 45th entry on the coveted *Latin Americas's 50 Best Restaurants* list in 2018.

Watch him work his magic in the open kitchen, where seasonal, farmers market and vegetarian tasting menus (à la carte is officially discouraged) draw from the in-house organic gardens to reinvent contemporary Brazilian cuisine. The menu changes often, but dishes such as red snapper with hearts of palm, turmeric and algae, or the wagyu short rib with manioc and Brazil nuts showcase the evolution of Brazilian

Pinheiros, Vila Madalena & Around

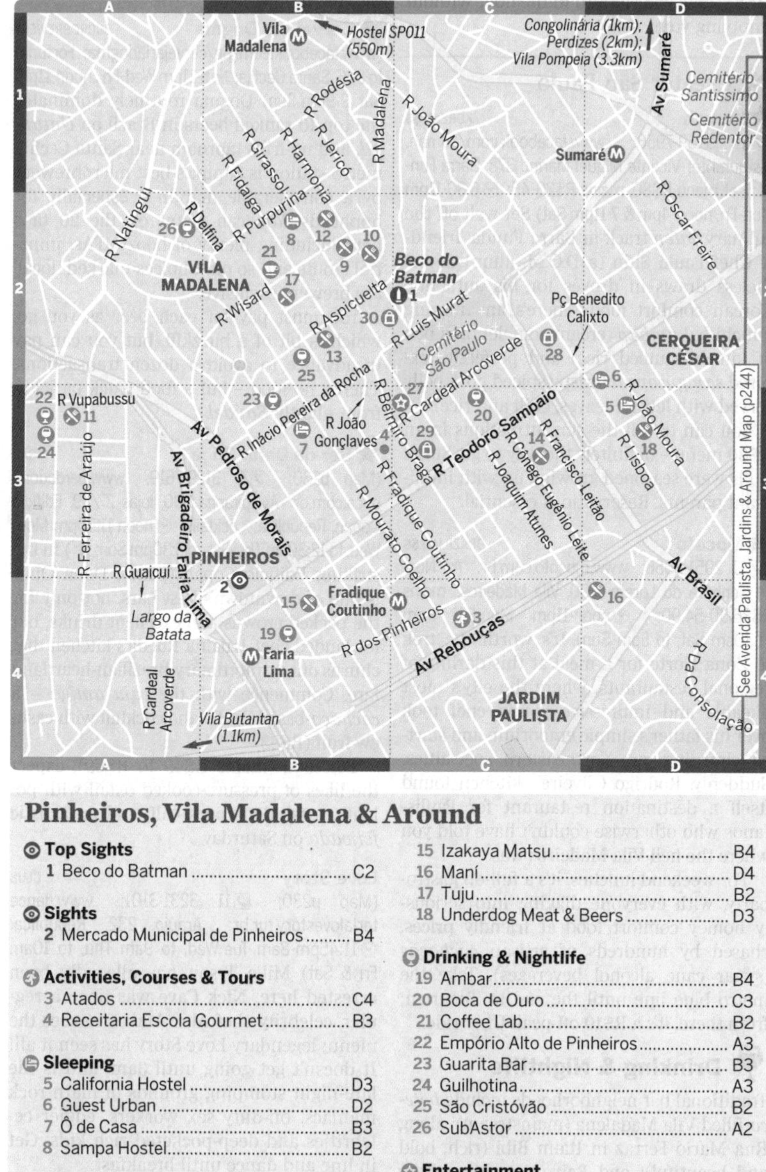

Pinheiros, Vila Madalena & Around

Top Sights
1 Beco do Batman C2

Sights
2 Mercado Municipal de Pinheiros B4

Activities, Courses & Tours
3 Atados C4
4 Receitaria Escola Gourmet B3

Sleeping
5 California Hostel D3
6 Guest Urban D2
7 Ô de Casa B3
8 Sampa Hostel B2

Eating
9 Bacio di Latte B2
10 Banana Verde B2
11 Bráz Pizzaria A3
12 Carlos Pizza B2
13 Feijoada da Lana B2
14 Futuro Refeitório C3
15 Izakaya Matsu B4
16 Maní D4
17 Tuju B2
18 Underdog Meat & Beers D3

Drinking & Nightlife
19 Ambar B4
20 Boca de Ouro C3
21 Coffee Lab B2
22 Empório Alto de Pinheiros A3
23 Guarita Bar B3
24 Guilhotina A3
25 São Cristóvão B2
26 SubAstor A2

Entertainment
27 Ó do Borogodó C3

Shopping
28 Feira Benedito Calixto C2
29 Galeria Nacional C3
Instituto Ata .... (see 2)
30 Retro 63 .... B2

gastronomy. The set three-course lunch (R$85) gets your mouth in the door without emptying your wallet.

Greater São Paulo

★Komah KOREAN $$

(☎11 3569-7956; www.facebook.com/komah.restaurante; Vicente Miguel Marino 378, Barra Funda; set menu R$80, mains R$20-45; ⏰6:30-11pm Mon-Fri, noon-4pm & 7-11pm Sat) Set well off the culinary *eaten* track in Barra Funda, friendly Chef Paulo Shin (a D.O.M. alum) nevertheless draws in droves for his authentic Korean comfort food. There's an amazing kimchi *bokumbap* (creamy omelet on a bed of kimchi-sautéed rice) and perfectly textured *samgyeopsal* (crispy spiced pork belly served with lettuce leaves, chili and rice).

You can try all the star attractions in an R$80 menu – definitely the way to go. Shin's skills were seasoned growing up with immigrant parents. Reservations essential.

★Mocotó BRAZILIAN $$

(☎11 2951-3056; www.mocoto.com.br; Av Nossa Senhora do Loreto 1100, Vila Madeiros; mains R$36.90-54.90; ⏰noon-11pm Mon-Fri, from 11:30am Sat, to 5pm Sun) It's worth the trek to Zona Norte for a meal at this darling of regional restaurants, where the city's most likeable and impressive young chef took over his father's simple emporium and started churning out Northeastern specialties. Suddenly, Rodrigo Oliveira's kitchen found itself a destination restaurant for Paulistanos who otherwise couldn't have told you where the hell Vila Madeiros was.

For weekend lunches, it's a full-on gastroparty, with everyone digging into seriously homey comfort food at friendly prices, chased by hundreds of artisan *cachaças* (sugar cane alcohol beverages). Take the metro blue line until the end at Tucuruvi; from there, it's a R$10 off-peak Uber ride.

Drinking & Nightlife

Traditional bar neighborhoods include *boteco*-filled Vila Madalena (mainstream); along Rua Mario Ferraz in Itaim Bibi (rich, bold and beautiful); and Baixo Augusta, where the GLS scene (Portuguese slang for Gay, Lesbian and Sympathetics) mingles with artsy hipsters in the city's edgiest-nightlife district. Artists, journalists and upper middle-class bohemians have claimed Pinheiros, immediately southeast of Vila Madalena. Current rage: rooftop bars!

Centro & Around

★Cervejaria Dogma MICROBREWERY

(www.facebook.com/pg/cervejariadogma; Fortunato 236, Santa Cecília; ⏰5-11pm Wed-Fri , noon-11pm Sat, 2-9pm Sun) Dogma routinely dominates the top 10 ranked beers in Brazil on *Untappd*, and no-frills taproom near Santa Cecília metro station is Sampa's best microbrewery by a considerable margin – especially for hopheads. You can count on the 20 taps here including plenty of boozy IPAs, imperial stouts and so on. Choices marked 'local' are brewery exclusive.

You must pay for each beer as you go, which is bit of a buzzkill, but you can pay in advance to avoid a dozen transactions. There's no food – but a food truck parks in front nightly. *Saúde!*

★Bar da Dona Onça BAR

(Map p230; ☎11 3129-7619; www.bardadonaonca.com.br; Av Ipiranga 200, lojas 27/29, Edifício Copan, República; cocktails; ⏰noon-11:30pm Mon-Wed, to 12:30am Thu-Sat, to 5:30pm Sun; 📶) In the striking Edifício Copan (p228), Dona Onça is one of downtown's best bars, not only for the packed crowds and excellent drinks, but for lauded chef Janaina Rueda's kitchen that churns out extraordinary Brazilian-heartland fare. Commence with the *caju amigo* – a *cachaça*-based Paulistano cocktail with cashew fruit (R$33).

For food (mains R$49 to R$69), expect the likes of pressure-cooked oxtail with polenta, a fabulous pork calf, and an artistic *feijoada* on Saturday.

Love Story CLUB

(Map p230; ☎11 3231-3101; www.danceterialovestory.tur.br; Araújo 232, República; ⏰11:45pm-8am Tue-Wed, to 9am Thu, to 10am Fri & Sat) Mike Tyson has allegedly been arrested here, Nick Cave was once a regular, celebrity chef Alex Atala oversees the menu; legendary Love Story has seen it all! It doesn't get going until 3am, and is the late-night stomping grounds of math rock maniacs, off-duty sex workers, edgier celebrities and deep-pocketed rich kids. Get in line and dance until breakfast.

Fel COCKTAIL BAR

(Map p230; Avenida Ipiranga 200, loja 69, Edifício Copan, República; cocktails R$35; ⏰7pm-1am Mon-Sat) Unsigned and built around a massive concrete support pillar of Edifício Copan (p228), this 13-seat cocktail bar has brought a new level of mixology to downtown. Resurrected drinks date as far back as 1862 and are served with proper ice. Art deco lighting and heavyweight metallic coasters demonstrate a hipsterized attention to detail. Prepare to stand!

Avenida Paulista, Jardins & Around

★Santo Grão CAFE

(Map p244; ☎11 3062-9294; www.santograo.com.br; Oscar Freire 413, Jardins; coffee R$7-19; ⏱7:30am-midnight Mon-Thu, to 1am Fri, 8am-1am Sat, 8am-11pm Sun; 📶) This Kiwi-run, top-end coffee haunt serves cappuccinos that are as good as those in Italy. Beans are roasted out back while the little terrace reverberates with caffeine-fueled conversation. There's a fab bistro menu (breakfast R$22 to R$34), insane people-watching and every prep – V60, Chemex, Aeropress, Bulletproof, cold brew – you could want.

Soul Café COFFEE

(Map p244; www.facebook.com/soulcafesp; Augusta 1524, Loja 6, Baixa Augusta; ⏱9am-7pm Mon-Wed, to 8pm Thu-Fri; 📶) This little-cafe-that-could brews some of the city's most sought-after 'third wave' coffee from a bright blue La Marzocco espresso machine that barely fits inside the cramped space. Patrons spill out into a small retail alley you'd most likely wander right past had we not told you. It does all the methods, hot or cold, including espresso (R$6).

Selva CLUB

(Map p244; ☎11 3120-4140; www.selva.club; Augusta 501, Baixa Augusta; ⏱11pm-5am Wed & Thu, from 10pm Fri & Sat) Rua Augusta's hottest club, and one of the city's newest, Selva makes no commitment to any one genre – you get funk, electronica, pop, reggaeton – and the cool kids wouldn't have it any other way. The architecturally savvy space creates a cozy atmosphere that plays up the rainforest contrasted with concrete and steel – welcome to the urban jungle, baby!

Seen COCKTAIL BAR

(Map p244; ☎11 3146-5923; www.seensp.com; Alameda Santos 1437, 23rd Fl, Hotel Tivoli Mofarrej, Jardins; ⏱7pm-1am Sun-Thu, to 2am Fri & Sat; 📶) Hobnob with a high-brow crowd at this trendy cocktail bar on the rooftop of the five-star Hotel Tivoli Mofarrej. The rectangular bar with hovering retro-inspired starburst lighting is prime people-watching real-estate; and you can groove to top-end sushi and DJs (from Tuesdays to Saturdays).

Cocktails (R$31 to R459) often give a wink and a nod to home as with the *Brasileiro,* a G&T made with Brazilian gin (Amázzoni) and cashew fruit. It's a bummer there is no outside terrace, however.

Suco Begaço JUICE BAR

(Map p244; www.sucobagaco.com.br; Haddock Lobo 1483, Jardins; juice R$9.50-17.90; ⏱9am-9pm Mon-Sat, noon-8pm Sun; 👪) The flagship of this rapidly expanding juice-chain burns through 600 glasses daily, mixed with water, orange juice, milk or coconut water. Also offers awesome-value, build-your-own salads and sandwiches.

Skye BAR

(www.unique.com.br; Av Brigadeiro Luis Antônio 4700, Jardim Paulista; cocktails R$35-42; ⏱bar 6pm-12:30am; 📶) Dress up a little for the rooftop bar on the top floor of the Hotel Unique (p238), whose sleek design and unparalleled views make it the perennially perfect place for a sundowner.

It's open for all three meals, but morphs into a cocktail bar as the night progresses.

Bar Balcão BAR

(Map p244; ☎11 3063-6091; Doutor Melo Alves 150, Jardins; ⏱6pm-2am) Good wine, light meals and a simple but elegant design built around a cleverly serpentine bar, this Jardins delight is especially popular with well-heeled designers, foreign correspondents and artists.

Parque Ibirapuera & Around

★Veloso BOTECO

(www.velosobar.com.br; Conceição Veloso 56, Vila Mariana; ⏱5:30pm-12:30am Tue-Fri, from 12:30pm Sat, 4-10:30pm Sun) Arrive early to this outstanding *boteco,* a quick walk from Vila Mariana's metro station, where crowds fight over tables for some of the city's best caipirinhas in exotic flavors (*jabuticaba,* starfruit with basil, or tangerine with *dedo-de-moça* pepper; R$20 to R$26), and shockingly good *coxinhas* (battered and fried shredded chicken, *catupiry* cheese and spices; R$33).

The house-made hot sauce is the best we've found in the country. Put your name on the list, but you'll be drunk and full before you get a table, though an expansion next door has relieved some of the long wait times.

LGBT+ SÃO PAULO

Latin America's largest and most visible gay community supports a dizzying array of options, day and night. There are not only gay bars and discos but also restaurants, cafes and even a shopping center – **Shopping Frei Caneca** (Map p244; www.freicanecashopping.com; Frei Caneca 569, Baixo Auga; ⌚10am-10pm Mon-Sat, 2-8pm Sun), known as 'Shopping Gay Caneca,' which has a largely gay clientele.

For nights out, don't miss the bars surrounding Feira Benedito Calixto in Pinheiros on Saturday afternoons after the street fair; the corner of Frei Caneca and Peixoto Gomide in Baixo Augusta, where the early-evening pre-party at the otherwise nondescript *lanchonete* (snack bar) **Bar da Lôca** (Map p244; cnr Frei Caneca & Peixoto Gomide, Baixo Auga; ⌚6am-1am) spills into the streets; and **Bella Paulista** (Map p244; www.bellapaulista.com; Haddock Lobo 354, Jardins; sandwiches R$12.20-51; ⌚24hr; 📶), the 24-hour restaurant where everyone ends up after the clubs close. Hot bars and clubs include **Club Jerome** (Map p244; ☎11 2614-6526; www.facebook.com/clubjerome; Mato Grosso 398, Higienópolis; ⌚11pm-5am Wed, 11.30pm-6am Thu-Sat), **Barouche** (Map p230; www.barouche.com.br; Largo do Arouche 103, República; ⌚noon-midnight Thu & Fri, 5pm-midnght Sat, 5-11pm Sun) and the perennial mixed superclub, D-Edge (p253). For roaming parties, try **Lunatica** (www.facebook.com/festalunatica).

Maritime-themed gay/straight nightclub **Club Yacht** (Map p244; ☎11 3111-6330; www.facebook.com/clubyacht; 13 de Maio 703, Bela Vista; ⌚11:30pm-5am Wed & Thu, from midnight Fri, midnight-9am Sat) mixes mirror balls and blue walls with nautical overload. Two large mezzanines stand sentinel above the large dance floor – for those that like to watch – and the whole space is bedazzled with encrusted shells throughout. It's no longer the glamorous choice *du moment*, but remains a solid bet.

Eclectic and funky, **Lekitsch** (Map p230; Praça Franklin Roosevelt 142, Consolação; ⌚6pm-2am Tue-Thu, to 3am Fri, 1pm-3am Sat, 1pm-midnight Sun) is part of the creative cradle of Praça Roosevelt, which is an established weekend gay-gathering point. Walls peppered in kitsch (doll heads, retro Simon Says games) surround a wildly mixed crowd of alterna-hipsters and creative types.

Bardega WINE BAR
(www.bardega.com.br; Alceu de Campos Rodrigues 218, Itaim Bibi; ⌚6:30pm-1am Tue-Sat; 📶) It's no secret Brazil is a beer country, so what's an oenophile to do? Bardega is one of the few wine bars in the city, where a wine-curious crowd sips from a dominating wall of self-serve interconnected Enomatic wine dispensing machines. Over 100 wines by the glass are dispensed, divided into three sizes (30ml, 60ml and 120ml; R$5 to R$282).

Highlights include excellent domestic wines such as Cave Geisse and Lidio Carraro, international heavyweights like Catena Zapata and Barolo Gaja, as well as boutique choices from Slovenia, Lebanon, Israel and Hungary, among the usual suspects.

🍷 Pinheiros, Vila Madalena & Around

★Guilhotina COCKTAIL BAR
(Map p249; www.guilhotinabar.com.br; Costa Carvalho 84, Baixa Pinheiros; ⌚6pm-1am Wed-Sat) Pages of in-house created cocktails are the calling at this hip den of mixology. At the helm, *Veja* magazine's 2017 bartender of the year, Márcio Silva, a SubAstor (p253) alum. Silva shakes and stirs 15 years of European experience into his fine concoctions, which actually come out cheaper (R$29) than classic preparations (R$31). Try Vitriol, a boozy and refreshing bourbon bombshell.

★Ambar CRAFT BEER
(Map p249; www.barambar.com.br; Cunha Gago 129, Pinheiros; ⌚noon-3pm Mon, to midnight Tue & Wed, to 1am Thu-Sat, 1-7pm Sun; 📶) Cozy and convivial, Ambar's long, welcoming bar is probably the single best spot in town to sip on juicy IPAs or a humidity-retreating pilsner or weiss. The craft beer on the 15 taps here is impossibly fresh, and good relationships with Rio de Janeiro, Rio Grande do Sul and Santa Catarina breweries mean you see suds here you don't easily find elsewhere.

★Coffee Lab CAFE
(Map p249; www.raposeiras.com.br; Fradique Coutinho 1340, Vila Madalena; coffee from R$6.50; ⌚10am-8pm; 📶) Both caffeine junkie and in-

ternational connoisseur, there are few *Brasileiras* as crazy about coffee as the adorable Isabela Raposeiras, who runs this part-cafe, part-barista school. This is the spot to go for single-origin varieties as well as outside-the-box preparations (Clever, for example, a type of drip coffee).

★SubAstor COCKTAIL BAR

(Map p249; ☎11 3815-1364; www.subastor.com.br; Delfina 163, Vila Madalena; ⏲8pm-3am Tue-Sat) This dark and speakeasy-sexy bar sits below a *boteco* called Astor (extraordinarily great as well for food and caipirinhas), hence the name: SubAstor. Sincere mixology goes down here, from creative takes on classics such as *caju amigo* (*cachaça* and cashew juice) to far-more cutting-edge liquid art.

★Empório Alto de Pinheiros BAR

(Map p249; www.altodospinheiros.com.br; Vupabussu 305, Alto de Pinheiros; ⏲noon-midnight Sun-Wed, to 1am Thu-Sat; 📶) This neighborhood beer emporium – one of the city's first – has evolved into a full-on gourmet craft-beer refuge as the brew scene in Brazil continues to explode. *Cerveza artesanal* geeks fret nervously over more than 400 bottled or 45 choices on draft, including the city's widest global selection. You'll need a few drinks to tolerate the service.

Beers come in numerous sizes (150ml, 200ml, 300ml, 400ml and 500ml) so prices vary wildly. Its in-house bottle shop is hands down the city's best for variety.

São Cristóvão BOTECO

(Map p249; www.facebook.com/barsaocristovao; Aspicuelta 533, Vila Madalena; mains R$30-53; ⏲noon-1:30am Mon-Sat, to 7:30pm Sun; 📶) This wildly atmospheric *boteco* is spilling over with football memorabilia from the owner's collection: more than 3500 pieces in all.

The Oswaldo Aranha steak – filet mignon topped with crispy garlic chips – for two (R$92) is a great way to go here, chased with ice-cold *chope* (draft beer; R$8.60).

Guarita Bar COCKTAIL BAR

(Map p249; www.guaritabar.com.br; Simão Álvares 952, Pinheiros; ⏲6pm-2am Tue-Fri, from 5pm Sat, 5pm-midnight Sun; 📶) Named after a common São Paulo sight (neighborhood security watch huts that pepper fancier residential districts), Guarita ('Guardhouse') is the unpretentious cocktail domain of ex-D.O.M. mixologist Jean Ponce, one of the city's best. The dark and industrial space doesn't inspire confidence, but his unbeatably priced caipirinha (R$18), made with aged *cachaça*, has been voted the city's best.

Boca de Ouro COCKTAIL BAR

(Map p249; www.bocadeouro.com.br; Eugênio Leite 1121, Pinheiros; cocktails R$16-30; ⏲6pm-midnight Mon-Wed, to 2am Thu-Sat; 📶) Classic and forgotten cocktails mixed with the methodicalness of art restoration in a distinctly un-Brazilian setup. It's a novel, actual belly-up-to type bar behind a Brownstone-like facade that passes for Brooklyn with a little imagination and attracts an artistic crowd.

Good bottled craft beer (and two on draft) and excellent bar grub like *bolovo* – a Brazilianized Scotch egg – round out this neighborhood-y watering hole nicely.

Barra Funda

★D-Edge CLUB

(☎11 3665-9500; www.d-edge.com.br; Av Auro Soares de Moura Andrade 141, Barra Funda; ⏲11pm-late Mon & Wed-Sat) With one of the city's most remarkable sound systems and a roster of world-famous DJs, this mixed gay-straight club is a well-established venue for the club scene but remains a 'don't miss' for fans of electronica; one of South America's best.

Clube VU CLUB

(www.facebook.com/clube.vu; Lavradio 559, Barra Funda; entry R$10-$50; ⏲8pm-2am Mon, 10pm-5am Fri & Sat) A homage to the Velvet Underground started by well-pedigreed alternative nightlife empresarios in Sampa, this 2017 newcomer on the club scene skews retro, rock and garage. Monday is cocktail night, with guest bartenders rocking an emphasis on mixology over tunes, while other nights cater to indie scenesters and alterna-hipsters. A R$10 to R$50 consumption is charged.

Greater São Paulo

★Bar do Luiz Fernandes BAR

(www.bardoluizfernandes.com.br; Augusto Tolle 610, Santana; ⏲4pm-1am Tue-Fri, 11am-8pm Sat & Sun) Friendly, supremely local and quintessentially São Paulo, it's worth traipsing into the North Zone for this authentic *boteco* to chase Doña Idalina's house-specialty *bolinhos* (croquettes; try the beef version, splashed with spicy vinaigrette and fiery *malagueta* pepper sauce) with ice-cold Original and Serramalte beers – something locals have adored for over 50 years.

Entertainment

★Vila do Samba SAMBA

(☎11 3858-6641; www.viladosamba.com.br; João Rudge 340, Casa Verde; ⊙8pm-3am Tue, 9-11pm Fri, 2-11pm Sat, 5pm-midnight Sun) A 'can't miss' stalwart in São Paulo's live samba scene, Vila do Samba – named as such due to its location inside a charming set of town-house villas – is worth a trip to the northern district of Casa Verde, which is said to be from where samba's origins lie. It swarms with connoisseurs at least four nights a week.

Ó do Borogodó SAMBA

(Map p249; ☎11 3814-4087; www.facebook.com/odoborogodobar; Horácio Lane 21, Vila Madelena; ⊙8:15pm-midnight Mon, from 6:30pm Tue & Wed, 10pm-3am Thu-Sat, 8pm-12:30am Sun) One of the best spots in town for live samba, *chorinho* (informal instrumental music) and *pagode* (popular samba music).

★Barretto LIVE MUSIC

(Map p244; ☎11 3896-4000; www.fasano.com.br; Vittorio Fasano 88, Jardins; cover R$60; ⊙7pm-3am Mon-Fri, from 8pm Sat) Hands down one of the best places to see live music in the world, this intimate bar inside the Hotel Fasano recalls prewar Milan and attracts top jazz and popular Brazilian musicians who normally play far larger venues.

Bourbon Street Music Club JAZZ

(☎11 5095-6100; www.bourbonstreet.com.br; Rua dos Chanés 127, Moema; ⊙8pm-late Tue & Wed, from 8:30pm Thu, from 9pm Fri & Sat, from 7:30pm Sun) One of the top spots for live jazz and blues in Sampa, Bourbon Street has hosted the likes of BB King and Ray Charles. There's also occasional Sunday night salsa.

Theatro Municipal THEATER, OPERA

(Map p230; ☎11 3223-3022; www.theatromunicipal.org.br; Praça Ramos de Azevedo, Centro; ⊙box office 10am-7pm Mon-Fri, to 5pm Sat & Sun) Operas, classical ballets and symphonic music are held in São Paulo's most ornate theater (p227).

Sala São Paulo CLASSICAL MUSIC

(Map p230; ☎11 3223-3966; www.salasaopaulo.art.br; Praça Júlio Prestes 16, Centro; ⊙box office 10am-6pm Mon-Fri, to 4:30pm Sat) Excellent classical-music venue in a refurbished 1925, neoclassical train station Estação Júlio Prestes. A suspended adjustable ceiling ensures maximum acoustics that can be tailored to the performance.

Sports

São Paulo's three biggest football teams are **Corinthians** (www.corinthians.com.br), who play at the **Arena Corinthians** (☎11 3152-4099; www.arenacorinthians.com.br; Av Miguel Ignácio Curi 111, Artur Alvim), 24km east of Centro (a 2014 FIFA World Cup venue); **Palmeiras** (www.palmeiras.com.br), who play in the modern 43,600-capacity **Allianz Parque** (☎11 4800-6670; www.allianzparque.com.br; Francisco Matarazzo 1705, Água Branca) near Barra Funda; and **São Paulo FC** (www.saopaulofc.net), who play at the 67,428-capacity **Estádio do Morumbi** (Estádio Cícero Pompeu de Toledo; Praça Roberto Gomes Pedrosa 1, Morumbi; a 2016 Olympic Games venue).

Shopping

★El Cabriton CLOTHING

(Map p244; www.elcabriton.com; Augusta 2008, Jardins; ⊙10am-6pm Mon-Sat) This uber-hip shop features hundreds of unique and clever T-shirts (R$68 to R$88) for men, women and babies from independent Brazilian designers arranged by category (browse the catalog for the entire inventory). They are printed on the spot, so don't fret if you need a different size (or even a different color!). Pelé kissing Salvador Dalí (or Mona Lisa) is the top seller!

★Espaço Havaianas SHOES

(Map p244; www.havaianas.com; Oscar Freire 1116, Jardins; ⊙10am-8pm Mon-Sat, noon-6pm Sun; 👪) You will find flip-flops in every imaginable design and hue – and at quite reasonable prices – at the flagship store for Brazil's favorite beach footwear, boldly designed by Isay Weinfeld. Flip-flops start at R$15.90.

★Retro 63 ANTIQUES

(Map p249; www.retro63.com.br; Harmonia 63, Vila Madalena; ⊙10:30am-6:30pm Mon-Sat) This supremely cool collection of original knick-knacks, objets d'art and other decorative items from the 1950s, '60s and '70s is like a gourmet graveyard for decades gone by. Pieces are one-of-a-kind, so if you're into something, snatch it up – it may be gone tomorrow!

★Instituto Ata FOOD & DRINKS

(Map p249; www.institutoata.org.br; Pedro Cristi 89, Mercado Municipal de Pinheiros, Pinheiros; ⊙8am-6pm) Brazil's most famous gourmet chef, Alex Atala of D.O.M. (p247) fame, is behind this expansive gourmet emporium featuring provisions from small farms and producers from the country's five ecoregions: caatinga, cerrado,

Mata Atlântica, Amazônia and Pampas, which are spread about various spaces on the bottom floor of hip Mercado Municipal de Pinheiros (p234).

Feira Benedito Calixto ANTIQUES
(Map p249; www.pracabeneditocalixto.com.br; Praça Benedito Calixto, Pinheiros; ⌚9am-7pm Sat) Open-air market for handicrafts, antiques and food stalls Saturday, plus live *chorinho* in the afternoon between 2:30pm and 6:30pm.

Galeria Nacional ARTS & CRAFTS
(Map p249; www.facebook.com/galerianacionalsp; Mateus Grou 540, Pinheiros; ⌚10am-7pm Mon-Fri, 11am-5pm Sat) This two-story design stop on Rua Mateus Grou – the neighborhood's design street – only sells works from Brazilian artists. It's worth a browse for leather clutches, art prints, jewelry, ceramic vases, watches, wood-framed glasses and other homegrown designs you won't find elsewhere.

Shopping JK Iguatemi MALL
(www.jkiguatemi.com.br; Av Juscelino Kubitschek 2041, Vila Olímpia; ⌚10am-10pm Mon-Sat, 2-8pm Sun) South America's most luxurious high-end shopping mall is worth a stroll for the sheer opulence of it all and some very good restaurants.

Ponto Solodário ARTS & CRAFTS
(Map p244; www.pontosolidario.org.br; José Maria Lisboa, Jardins; ⌚10am-7pm Mon-Fri, to 4pm Sat) This excellent handicraft shop, one of the few of quality in São Paulo, shares Casa Amarela space with Museu Xingu but is a separate business. It bills itself as 'socio-cultural art' and works with various Fair Trade businesses and NGOs all around Brazil. It's a great spot to pick up unique and sustainable handicrafts.

Livraria Cultura BOOKS
(Map p244; ☎11 3170-4033; www.livrariacultura.com.br; Av Paulista 2073, Bela Vista; ⌚9am-10pm Mon-Sat, 11am-8pm Sun; 👪) Spread out over three stores on the ground floor of the Conjunto Nacional building, this is hands-down the city's best bookstore. There is a large selection of both English-language books and travel guides, plus a pleasant cafe.

ℹ Information

DANGERS & ANNOYANCES

Crime is an issue in São Paulo, though the majority is limited to the city's periphery and tourists aren't often targeted unless they're the unlucky victim of an *arrastão*, when armed bandits rob an entire restaurant of patrons in the blink of an eye.

EMBU DAS ARTES

Founded in 1554, Embu das Artes spent most of its life as a quiet colonial village until, in the 20th century, it was swallowed up by São Paulo, whose center sits about 30km to the northeast. Yet Embu has managed to retain much of its colonial core, thanks largely to the hippies, artists and intellectuals who made the town their refuge from São Paulo's concrete jungle, starting in the 1970s. Today the town makes a popular weekend retreat for Paulistanos, when local artisans offer their wares at the outdoor *feira* (market). The area around the *feira* is full of antique and crafts shops that make good browsing on other days of the week.

EMTU bus 033 (www.emtu.sp.gov.br; M.M.D.C, Metrô Butantá, Butantá) heads to Embu (R$5.05, 1¼ hours, 4:50am to 12:20am), leaving regularly from Metrô Butantã in São Paulo.

General rules of thumb include being especially careful in the center and elsewhere at night (use taxis and ride-shares) and on weekends (when fewer people are about) and watching out for pickpockets on buses, around Praça da Sé and on Linhas 1 (blue) and 3 (red) of the metro. Otherwise, maintain the same common-sense vigilance you would in any developing-world metropolis.

MEDICAL SERVICES

Einstein Hospital (☎11 2151-1233; www.einstein.com.br; Av Albert Einstein 627, Morumbi)

MONEY

ATMs are widely available throughout the city. Bradesco and Banco do Brasil are feeless and the most foreign-friendly. Note that most are closed from 10pm to 6am for security reasons. Always use ATMs inside banks to avoid cloning.

TOURIST INFORMATION

São Paulo Turismo (aka SPTuris**)** is the official São Paulo tourist board, which offers a trilingual website (in Portuguese, Spanish and English; www.cidadedesaopaulo.com) in coordination with city hall. It also runs several tourist information booths known as *Central de Informação Turística* (C.I.Ts) strategically placed around the city. Also look out for its mobile vans and Segways, known as *C.I.T.s Móveis*, which park at Parque Trianon on Av Paulista, and near Portão 10 at Parque Ibirapuera, among other locations, on various days and hours.

In Portuguese, you can pick up a **Guia da Folha** at any newsstand for reviews of the city's dining, entertainment and nightlife options (also available at www1.folha.uol.com.br/guia). The weekly magazine **Veja São Paulo** (www.vejasp.abril.com.br) also has listings in Portuguese and is the best for up-to-date restaurant reviews. **Time Out** no longer publishes but does have a bilingual website with past databased listings (www.timeout.com.br/sao-paulo/en).

Useful C.I.T. offices include **Av Paulista** (Central de Informação Turística; Map p244; www.cidadedesaopaulo.com; Av Paulista 1853; ⌚9am-6pm), **Praça da República** (Central de Informação Turística; Map p230; ☎11 3331-7786; www.cidadedesaopaulo.com; Praça da República, República; ⌚9am-6pm), **Rodoviário Tietê** (Central de Informação Turística; www.cidadedesaopaulo.com; Av Cruzeiro do Sul 1800, Rodoviário Tietê, Santana; ⌚6am-10pm) and **Congonhas Airport** (Central de Informação Turística; www.cidadedesaopaulo.com; Av Washington Luis s/n, Congonhas Airport, Vila Congonhas; ⌚7am-10pm).

Getting There & Away

AIR

São Paulo is the Brazilian hub for many international airlines and thus the first stop for many travelers. Before buying a domestic ticket, check which of the city's airports the flight departs from, as the international airport also serves many domestic flights.

GRU Airport

GRU Airport (Aeroporto Guarulhos; ☎11 2445-2945; www.gru.com.br; Rod Hélio Smidt s/n), the international airport, is 25km northeast of the center.

Most domestic flights depart from Terminal 2 East or West; but Azul and Passaredo operate out of the newer Terminal 1 located 2km to the southwest, among others.

Most international flights operate out of the newer Terminal 3 (connected to T2 by corridor and people-mover), an impressive world-class terminal that opened in 2014. Exceptions include mid-haul flights from Central and South America and the Caribbean (Aerolíneas Argentinas/Austral, Aeromexico, Avianca/Taca, Copa, Tame etc), and a few stragglers from Africa (Ethiopian, Royal Air Maroc, TAAG) and Europe (Air Europa) – but check ahead.

Frequent free shuttles connect the terminals 24 hours a day.

Congonhas Airport

The domestic-only airport, **Congonhas** (Aeroporto de São Paulo-Congonhas; www.aeroportocongonhas.net; Av Washington Luís s/n) (CGH; Aeroporto de São Paulo-Congonhas), 14km south of the center, services many domestic destinations, including the majority of flights to Rio (Santos Dumont Airport), which depart every half-hour (or less).

BUS

São Paulo has three long-distance bus stations, all accessible by metro. Each terminal tends to specialize in a certain set of destinations, but there are no hard-and-fast rules, unfortunately. The handy app **Socicam** (www.socicam.com.br) details which terminal services which destinations, among other pertinent info.

The main terminal and South America's largest, **Terminal Tietê** (☎11 3866-1100; www.terminalrodoviariodotiete.com.br; Av Cruzeiro do Sul 1800, Santana), 4.5km north of Centro, offers buses to destinations throughout the continent. Avoid bus arrivals during early morning or late afternoon – traffic jams are enormous. You'll find left luggage (*Guarda-Volumes*) on the ground floor near the west entrance. Rates run between R$13 to R$25 per 24 hours depending on bag size.

Buses to Santos leave about every half hour from a separate bus station – the **Terminal Rodoviário do Jabaquara** (☎11 3866-1100; www.rodoviariadojabaquara.com.br; Rua dos Jequitibás s/n, Jabaquara), which is at the end of the southern metro line (Metrô Jabaquara). **Terminal Rodoviário da Barra Funda** (☎11 3866-1100; www.rodoviariadabarrafunda.com; Av Auro Soares de Moura Andrade 664, Barra Funda), in the west zone, near the Memorial da Ámerica Latina, services destinations in São Paulo state, including Iguape and Cananéia, Paraná and all buses to the Pantanal.

ClickBus (www.clickbus.com.br) is a good app for consulting departures times, fares and purchases (with foreign cards!) and there's a dedicated pickup booth on the eastern side of Tietê bus terminal in front of Bradesco bank. **BuscaOnibus** (www.buscaonibus.com.br) is another good resource.

Getting Around

TO/FROM THE AIRPORT

Bus

Passaro Marron (www.passaromarron.com.br) operates two airport bus options: the flashier **Airport Bus Service** (☎0800-770-2287; www.airportbusservice.com.br; btwn Terminal 2 East & West, GRU Airport; one-way from R$50), which is one of the most efficient ways to/from GRU Airport, making stops at Aeroporto Congonhas, Barra Funda, Tiête, Praça da República and various hotels around Av Paulista and Rua Augusta; and the cheaper and more crowded suburban Airport Service line 257 to/from Metrô Tatuapé (R$6.15, 30 to 45 minutes; every 15 minutes between 5am and 12:10am). It's easy to confuse the two from the airport – they depart right next to each other outside the terminals. To the airport, Airport Service line

257 is reached by exiting Metrô Tatuapé to the left toward Shopping Metrô Boulevard Tatuapé and the buses are on the street below to the left as you cross the pedestrian bridge.

For Congonhas, catch bus 875A-10 'Perdizes-Aeroporto' from Metrô São Judas or catch an Uber (R$45 to R$65) to/from most neighborhoods of interest (or get there for under R$20 if you catch an Uber from Metrô Jabaquara).

Bus 257 to Metrô Tatuapé – Terminal 2 (Terminal 2 East, GRU Airport)

Bus 257 to Metrô Tatuapé – Terminal 3 (Terminal 3, Platform 4, GRU Airport)

Airport Bus Service – Terminal 2 (☎0800-770-2287; www.airportbusservice.com.br; btwn Terminal 2 East & West, GRU Airport)

Airport Bus Service – Terminal 3 (☎0800-770-2287; www.airportbusservice.com.br; Terminal 3, Platform 5, GRU Airport)

Taxi & Ride Share

Guarucoop (☎11 2440-7070; www.guarucoop.com.br; GRU Airport) is the only taxi service allowed to operate from the international airport and charges vacation-spoiling prices to the city (R$150 to Jardins, R$150 to Vila Madalena, R$157 to Vila Mariana). There are Guarucoop booths outside of the terminals.

Uber and other ride-share apps are generally 50% cheaper than Guarucoop. They cannot pick you up on the near curve, however; you must meet the driver on the departures level near established Uber pickup/drop-off totems.

To GRU Airport, São Paulo taxis charge a 50% surcharge for crossing municipalities – one more reason to bypass them. You can get a good deal, however, with a family of taxi drivers, **Paulo, Marco and Stefan** (Map p230; ☎11 99236-2670; Praça da República, República), who hang around outside the Praça da República Airport Bus Service stop – they'll take you faster in a shared taxi for the same price as the bus.

An Uber from Congonhas Airport to Av Paulista runs around R$21 or so off-peak.

Train

The brand new CPTM Linha 13 (Jade) became operational in 2018 and connects GRU Airport with Engenheiro Goulart station on Linha 12 (Safira) in northeast São Paulo. The 15-minute ride (R$4) leaves from Estacão Aeroporto station

BUSES FROM SÃO PAULO

While there are plenty of options in addition to what's listed below, the following companies generally offer some of the most comfortable/reliable services:

DESTINATION	STARTING FARE (R$)	DURATION (HR)	BUS COMPANY
Angra dos Reis	84	7½	Reunidas Paulista (www.reunidaspaulista.com.br)
Asunción (PY)	250	20	Pluma (www.pluma.com.br)
Belo Horizonte	121	8	Cometa (www.viacaocometa.com.br)
Brasília	189	15	Real Expresso (www.realexpresso.com.br)
Buenos Aires (AR)	467	44	JBL (www.jblturismo.com.br)
Curitiba	89	6¾	Cometa (www.viacaocometa.com.br)
Florianópolis	149	11	Catatrinense (www.catarinense.net)
Foz do Iguaçu	220	17½	Catatrinense
Montevideo (UY)	490	32	JBL
Pantanal (Cuiabá)	395	27½	Andorinha (www.andorinha.com)
Pantanal (Campo Grande)	261	14	Andorinha
Paraty	65	6	Reunidas Paulista
Recife	379	45	Itapemirim (www.itapemirim.com.br)
Rio de Janeiro	96	6	1001 (www.autoviacao1001.com.br)
Santos	27	1¼	Cometa
Santiago (CH)	465	57	JBL
Salvador	375	26½	Gontijo (www.gontijo.com.br)

For international services, **JBL** heads to Montevideo (Uruguay) and Santiago (Chile) at 1:30pm on Sunday and Monday and to Buenos Aires (Argentina) at 9pm on Monday, Tuesday, Wednesday and Friday. For Asunción (Paraguay), **Pluma** heads out at 6:30pm on Monday, Wednesday and Friday and Sunday.

WORTH A TRIP

SERRA DA MANTIQUEIRA

About 180km northeast of São Paulo, the beautiful green peaks of the Serra da Mantiqueira are a hot spot for mountain biking and trekking for Paulistanos, and are a hugely popular winter weekend getaway for Paulistas desperate for a winter wonderland experience. **Campos do Jordão**, Brazil's highest city, is a kitschy and comfortable base from which to explore the nearby peaks, which are rife with virgin *araucária* (Paraná pine) forests and postcard-perfect views of the Paraíba valley.

Popular attractions in the area are **Parque Estadual de Campos do Jordão** (Horto Florestal; ☎12 3663-3762; www.saopaulo.sp.gov.br/conhecasp/parques-e-reservas-naturais/parque-estadual-campos-do-jordao; Av Pedro Paulo s/n; admission per vehicle R$14; ⏲9am-4pm), 14km east from Campos and home to the largest *araucária* reserve in the state, but don't miss **Parque Amantikir** (www.parqueamantikir.com.br; Rodovia Campos do Jordão 215; adult/child R$40/20; ⏲8:30am-5pm) either, a maze-filled garden clinging to a mountainside 10km south of town. One of the most popular climbs in the surrounding mountains is up to **Pedra do Baú** (1950m). **Altus** (☎12 3663-4122; www.altus.tur.br; Roberto Simonsen 1724, Vila Inglesa) is the go-to agency for outdoor adventure activities.

Campos itself is a well-heeled getaway. The peak tourist period is July, when the town receives up to a million tourists (expect a minimum one-week stay at this time; there are steep discounts on weekdays and outside winter months). The town is second only to São Paulo city in culinary supremacy, though many restaurants are overpriced; **Libertango** (☎12 3663-6218; www.libertango.com.br; Av José Manoel Gonçalves 160, Capivari; steak R$86.90-98.90; ⏲noon-4pm & 8-11pm daily Jul, noon-4pm & 8-11pm Wed-Sun Aug-Jun; 📶) is a notable exception. Don't miss the award-winning sausages from **Harry Pisek** (☎12 3663-4030; www.salsichariaharrypisek.blogspot.com.br; Av Pedro Paulo 857; mains R$41.60-82.80; ⏲10am-5:30pm Mon-Fri, to 11pm Sat, to 6:30pm Sun; 📶), either.

Campos is served by bus companies **Pássaro Marron** (www.passaromarron.com.br), which goes to São Paulo (R$52.55, three hours, six daily); and **Viacão Sampaio** (www.viacaosampaio.com.br), which heads once daily to Rio de Janeiro (R$74, four hours, 3:45pm).

across the highway from Terminal 1 between 4am and midnight. If you're lugging wheelless luggage that isn't a backpack, you might complain about the walking involved.

Additional services planned at the time of writing include **Connect**, which will run between Estação Brás and GRU Airport during peak hours (5am to 9am and 4pm to 8pm) for R$4; and **Airport Express** – the most convenient and easiest for travelers – which will link Estacão da Luz and GRU Airport (R$5 to R$10, 35 minutes, four times per day). Check ahead to be sure these services are up and running on arrival.

BUS

São Paulo's immense public-transport system, run by **SPTrans** (☎toll-free 156; www.sptrans.com.br; fare R$4), is arguably the world's most complex, with over 14,500 buses, 1300 lines and 500km worth of exclusive bus lanes. Buses (R$4) are crowded during rush hours and can be prone to pickpockets. Watch your valuables, especially phones in pockets or backpack side pockets. The city tourist-information booths are excellent sources of information about buses.

BIKE

The city has made considerable efforts to make São Paulo more hospitable to two-wheeled travel and now counts a bike lane network that clocks in around 468km, including along Av Paulista and Av Faria Lima. Weekends on the Minhocão (an elevated highway officially called Via Elevado Presidente João Goulart) and Av Paulista also offer great cycling opportunities, as does Parque Ibirapuera (p237). Itaú-sponsored **Bike Sampa** (☎11 4003-6055; www.bikeitau.com.br/bikesampa; 1st hour free, per following hour R$5), the city's bike-sharing scheme, has a fleet of 2600 bicycles spread over 260 stations.

CET (Companhia de Engenharia de Tráfego), the city's traffic management company, offers an updated city map of bike infrastructure at www.cetsp.com.br/consultas/bicicleta/mapa-de-infraestrutura-cicloviaria.aspx. **São Paulo Turismo** also maintains a very informative bicycle infrastructure website at www.cidadedesaopaulo.com/spdebike/index-desktop, in Portuguese only.

Proceed with caution, however – biking in Sampa remains a dicey proposition - and don't even think about not wearing a helmet.

METRO & TRAIN

You can reach many places on the excellent **Metrô São Paulo** (☎0800-770-7722; www.metro.sp.gov.br; fare R$4), the city's rapidly expanding subway system, which is integrated with its commuter rail counterpart, **CPTM** (Companhia Paulista de Trens Metropolitanos; www.cptm.sp.gov.br; fare R$4). The metro is cheap, safe and fast, and runs from 4:40am to midnight on most lines. A single ride costs R$4. A daily *Bilhete Diário Comum* pass costs R$15.30 (a R$20.50 *Bilhete Diário Comum Integração* pass includes buses as well). Refillable *Bilhete Único* (R$4) smart cards are worthwhile for discounts transferring between bus, metro and CPTM (up to four trips in three hours) and can be recharged at station booths, station machines and various apps. Passes are available at any *Bilhete Único* station booth.

TAXI & RIDE-SHARE

São Paulo's taxis are plentiful and generally honest – you don't see the same sort of gringo pricing as in some parts of Brazil and South America. Drivers generally always use the meter – if your driver doesn't turn the meter on, be sure to mention it. Do not continue with a driver who refuses to use the meter.

The conventional taxi flagfall (*bandeirada*) is R$5.50, with prices per kilometer clocking in at R$2.50 between 6am and 9pm Monday to Saturday (*Bandeira 1*), and R$3 from 9pm to 6am Monday to Saturday, and all day Sunday (*Bandeira 2*). Luggage charges run R$2.50 per bag, but this is at the discretion of the driver (some charge it, some don't – the inconsistency is maddening!). Wait time is R$31.50 per hour. Radio taxis are slightly more expensive.

99Taxis (www.99app.com) is the preferred app for local taxi drivers, and is far and away more convenient and always safer than calling for a taxi or hailing one in the street. Other taxi apps in operation include **Easy Taxi** (www.easytaxi.com), **Wappa** (www.wappa.com.br) and the newer **SPTaxi** (https://sptaxi.prefeitura.sp.gov.br).

Ride-share apps operating in the city include **Uber** (www.uber.com) and **Cabify** (www.cabify.com).

Bear in mind, only taxis can use São Paulo's exclusive bus lanes, so in rush hour or during an Uber price surge, a taxi may be cheaper *and* faster.

PAULISTA COAST

São Paulo's coast, known in Portuguese as the *Litoral Paulista,* is most spectacular in its northern reaches, especially around Ubatuba, thanks to the jungle-covered peaks of the Serra do Mar that reach all the way down to the Atlantic.

Ubatuba

☎0XX12 / POP 79,000

The fact that it sits in a privileged position on the Tropic of Capricorn ensuring it's the southern hemisphere's first spot to receive the summer sun tells you all you need to know about Ubatuba. Draped with the rich flora of the Mata Atlântica, the peaks of the Serra do Mar provide a dramatic, emerald-green backdrop to the winding, sun-kissed Ubatuba coastline – São Paulo state's most magical. This region has become a preeminent resort for well-heeled Paulistanos, with its elegant beach homes, stylish accommodations and an absolutely stunning arsenal of idyllic beaches – every one of which could possibly be the best you have ever seen. The area is especially agreeable in winter, when temps remain high enough, less rain bucks the town nickname (Uba*chuva* meaning Uba*rain*) and crowds dwindle.

⊙ Sights

★Ilha das Couves ISLAND

Ubatuba's most coveted beach destination is this tiny, 58-hectare island that is paradise in every sense of the word. Golden sands, lush rainforest and calm, boulder-strewn translucent waters combine forces to create the postcard-perfect beach of your dreams. But its popularity is its downfall – in December and January, boat after boat unloads passengers with no environmental controls in place, and the crowd taints the experience. The rest of the year, you've reached travel Nirvana, but give it a miss in high season.

Let's Go Ubatuba (p260) runs a fantastic trip to here and other isolated sands; or catch a boat on your own from Picinguaba beach (per person R$40, 12 minutes).

Ilha Anchieta ISLAND

This protected nature reserve was once home to a notorious penal colony and prison, which laid claim to hosting one of the biggest prison riots in the world when hundreds of inmates rebelled and escaped in 1952. While 129 prisoners were recaptured, many others were eaten by sharks whilst trying to flee in shoddy canoes. The island offers rare glimpses of fish and birds undisturbed in their natural habitats, and enviable views of the coast and its beautiful, deep-green waters.

To get here you can make reservations at the tourist office (p262) or many hotels

WORTH A TRIP

LONDON IN THE RAINFOREST

Founded by the British-owned São Paulo Railway Company, the pretty town of Paranapiacaba may sit amid the Atlantic rainforest of the Serra do Mar, about 40km southeast of São Paulo, but it still retains distinctly English traits, right down to a rough replica of Big Ben. Because of its remoteness, the town has been remarkably well preserved, with a neat grid of streets populated by English-style buildings of wood and brick wrapped in maroon picket fences, and vaguely feels like a future ghost town still clinging to life.

The home of the railway's chief engineer, dating to 1897, this classically Victorian wood building known as 'Castelinho' has been converted into the **Museu do Castelo** (11 4439-1318; Caminho do Mendes s/n; admission R$2; 10am-4pm Sat & Sun, by apt Mon-Fri) FREE, a small museum with period furnishings and fine views.

Paranapiacaba makes a good base for day hikes into the Parque Estadual da Serra do Mar – get in touch with **Paranapiacaba Ecotur** (11 99633-4062, 11 96570-0553; www.paranapiacabaecotur.com/trilha-poco-formoso).

The best way to arrive in Paranapiacaba is on the 1950s-era **Expresso Turístico Paranapiacaba** (0800-055-0121; www.cptm.sp.gov.br; fare 1/2/3 people R$50/82/115;) tourist train, which runs from São Paulo's Estação da Luz (p229) at 8:30am on Sunday to **Estação Paranapiacaba** (Santo André). Definitely buy tickets in advance – trains are a novelty in Brazil and this one, the country's second-oldest locomotive in operation, is very popular, especially in summer. Trains do not always run every Sunday – check the website for schedules.

and guesthouses. **Sol e Mar** (12 3832-5263; www.solemarubatuba.com.br; Av Leovigildo Dias Vieira 75, loja 2, Itaguá) is the most highly recommended agency. Cruise operators also leave from the Enseada and Saco da Ribeira neighborhoods in Ubatuba.

Tours

★Let's Go Ubatuba ADVENTURE
(12 98253-5456; www.letsgoubatuba.com; Av Governador Abreu Sodré 1245, Perequê-Açu; 9am-6pm) This upstart ecotourism agency run by Tulio and English-speaking Pedro out of Green Haven Hostel offers supreme boat trips to Ilha dos Couves (per person R$220) and can arrange all manner of hiking, surfing, wakeboarding, SUP and bird-watching experiences in the region.

Sleeping

★Green Haven Hostel HOSTEL $
(12 99600-8942; www.greenhavenhostel.com; Av Governador Abreu Sodré 1245, Perequê-Açu; dm R$55-65, d R$200-230, apt R$250;) Vini, both an ex-lawyer and former semi-pro rugby player in Malta, and his brother, Tulio, an eco-architect, are the personalities behind this good-time hostel on one of Ubatuba's best beaches for novice surfers. Sustainable touches abound (solar-heated showers, mud-fashioned front desk, Nespresso capsule fairy lighting, reclaimed railroad trestle support beams) and there's an excellent wraparound balcony where the magic happens.

Ecotrip Hostel HOSTEL $
(12 98122-6435; www.ecotriphostel.com.br; Dom Joao III 573, Centro; dm/s/d from R$55/165/198;) The friendly English-speaking Malu runs this welcoming, centrally located hostel. Situated just five blocks from the water, it's a simple but well-managed spot, with a nice outdoor kitchen, a small pool and, in season, breakfast fruits and preserves directly from Malu's secret fruit garden (though the morning sustenance carries an extra R$12 charge).

Pousada Todas As Luas POUSADA $$
(12 3845-3129; www.todasasluas.com.br; Rua C 115, Itamambuca; s/d from R$250/300;) This excellent pousada at Itamambuca beach sits 600m back from the sands surrounded by lush rainforest and immersed in Asian accents. The 26 rooms aren't flashy but are well appointed, many with hammock-strewn patios and, in the highest category, outdoor showers. Food is taken seriously (try the nut-crusted fish) and there's a jungly outdoor hot tub (book ahead!).

Hotel Solar das Águas Cantantes HOTEL $$
(12 3842-0178; www.solardasaguascantantes.com.br; Estrada Saco da Ribereira 951, Lázaro;

s/d from R$250/320; ❄📶🏊) With quarters ranged around a lush courtyard, this grand, whitewashed colonial affair – run by the son of the original Austrian owner – sits a short walk from the stunning (if crowded) Praia do Lázaro. The high-ceilinged rooms have an austere elegance. The hotel's critically-heralded restaurant is renowned for its travel-worthy *moquecas* (seafood stews; R$129 to R$198).

★ Pousada Picinguaba POUSADA **$$$**
(☎12 3836-9105; www.picinguaba.com; Rua G 130, Picinguaba; r incl dinner R$1493, ste R$2185; ❄📶🏊) 🍃 Tucked away in a small fishing village north of Ubatuba is one of the region's most charming pousadas; a 10-room, sustainably run gem owned by a discerning Frenchman. Everything here, from the original artworks and furniture to the outdoor poolside tables overlooking the calm bay, is subtle, meticulously curated and designed to instill a sense of place without going overboard.

It also offers horseback rides across the Parque Estadual da Serra do Mar to its countryside sister property, Fazenda Catuçaba. Brazil at its finest!

Eating

Don't miss *azul-marinho* (a delicious local stew of fish and green bananas) that gets its purplish-blue color from a chemical reaction between the latter and the iron cauldrons they're cooked in, and Ubatuba's own *bananinhas* (gooey sweets) at **Tachão de Ubatuba** (www.tachaodeubatuba.com.br; Javaés 20, Itaguá; sweets 250g R$5.90-8.80; ⏲10am-8pm Sun-Thu, to 11pm Fri & Sat).

O Limoeiro BRAZILIAN **$**
(www.facebook.com/olimoeiroubatuba; Praça Theoforico de Oliveira 08, Ilha dos Pescadores; mains R$21-68; ⏲5pm-1am Tue-Fri, from 11am Sat, 11am-7pm Sun; 📶) New owners have rejuvenated this laid-back riverside spot walking distance from Centro. Simple but well-prepared Brazilian food at good-value prices is their thing, along with excellent caipirinhas. The house-specialty *lemandarin* (honey, ginger and aged *cachaça*) goes down a treat. Live music Thursday to Sunday ensures a festive, local crowd.

Integrale BAKERY **$**
(www.padariaintegrale.com.br; Esteves da Silva 360, Centro; sandwiches R$10.25-23.60; ⏲7:30am-8:30pm Mon-Sat, to 7pm Sun; 📶📝) 🍃 This beautiful natural bakery is definitely a rare breed along this coast. Choose from a very long list of wholegrain, chemical- and preservative-free breads, salads, sandwiches, quiches, snacks and strong 100% arabica coffee from Minas Gerais, then tuck into it all on the lovely and lush patio.

★ Cantinho da Lagoa BRAZILIAN, SEAFOOD **$$**
(www.cantinhodalagoa-ubatuba.blogspot.com.br; Seis s/n, Praia de Prumirim; mains for 2 people R$69-210; ⏲9am-6pm Wed-Mon) The sophisticated dishes emerging from this excellent beach shack, perched on top of the rocks at one of the region's prettiest beaches (Prumirim), are the result of the owner's stint in London kitchens. Fabio, who's from the village, invented one of the best dishes on this coast, the *cajutapu* (palm-heart pasta with grilled shrimp and *juçara* fruit sauce; R$69).

Nós Gastronomia ASIAN **$$**
(☎12 99710-8512; www.nosgastronomia.com.br; Av Plínio França 335, Saco da Ribeira; mains R$63-70; ⏲6-11pm Thu-Sun; 📶) Chef Fabio Eustaquio of Cantinho da Lagoa (p261) fame brought his famed *cajutapu* (palm-heart pasta with grilled shrimp and *juçara* fruit sauce) to his classy newcomer, but similarities end there. With a marina and yacht club backdrop, his focus here is on Asian cuisines (Thai, Korean, Chinese) with recipes well-honed by years in London kitchens.

Jundu Praia Bar SEAFOOD **$$**
(☎12 3845-3027; www.jundupraiabar.com; Vereda 10, Prumirim; mains for 2 people R$139-157; ⏲9am-7pm) On the sands at pretty Prumirim, this is one of Ubatuba's best destination beach bars. The seafood – a wealth of fried and grilled fish dishes, shrimp and seafood stews – is higher-than-average quality and there's live music to accompany meals. With lounges on the sand, it's the kind of place well-heeled beachcombers book ahead and plant themselves for the entire day.

Terra Papagalli SEAFOOD **$$$**
(Xavantes 537, Itaguá; mains for 2 people R$194-198; ⏲10am-10pm Mon-Thu, to midnight Fri & Sat) This intimate restaurant along the waterfront manages to be both the least touristy and the most creative along this string of mostly carbon-copy options. A few dishes each night are served, depending on the local catch (expect the likes of perfectly seared *cambucu* fish with a lovely lime and turmeric sauce), and it all goes down very romantically among the candlelit tables.

Drinking & Nightlife

★Doca 390 CRAFT BEER
(www.doca390.com.br; Esteves da Silva 390, Centro; ⏲5pm-midnight Mon-Thu, 4pm-1am Fri, 2pm-1am Sat, 2-10pm Sun; 📶) This clearly unsuperstitious bar's 13 taps flow with a mix of local, regional and international craft beers, finally giving *Ubatubense* a hip spot to guzzle proper pints (R$13 to R$32), along with a wealth of elevated pub grub (rum-flambéed octopus, seafood stew-stuffed *pasteis,* awesome burgers).

Entertainment

Blues on the Rocks LIVE MUSIC
(☎12 3832-2810; www.bluesontherocks.com.br; Chico Santos 17, Av Itaguá; ⏲7pm-late) This wildly popular rock, blues and jazz venue is consistently voted the best live-music spot on the Paulista coast.

Information

Ubatuba's **tourist information** (Centro de Informações Turisticas; ☎12 3833-9123; www.turismo.ubatuba.sp.gov.br; cnr Conceição & Av Iperoig, Centro; ⏲8am-5:30pm Mon-Fri, 9am-4pm Sat & Sun) is housed inside the colonial blue-and-white Paço da Nóbrega building along the main road in Centro. There's useful maps of surrounding beaches and good local info.

Banco do Brasil (www.bb.com.br; Conceição 138, Centro)

Getting There & Away

Ubatuba has two intercity bus stations. For São Paulo (R$72.60, four hours, eight daily) and other destinations within the state, head to **Litorânea bus station** (☎12 3832-3622; www.litoranea.com.br; Maria Vitória Jean 381, Centro), located at the edge of the town center, about 1.5km from the tourist office and beach. For São Sebastião, head first to Caraguátatuba (R$18.80, 1½ hours, 5:30am or 12:10pm) to catch the one 4:50pm bus per day on to São Sebastião (R$9.90, one hour).

Rodoviário Oceano (www.rodoviariooceano.com.br) goes to Paraty (R$16.25, 1½ hours, 9:50am and 8:40pm) and **Viação Util** (www.util.com.br) goes to Rio de Janeiro (from R$18.20, five hours, 11am and 11:59pm) from the recently spruced up and renamed **Rodoviária Naim Elias Abdalla** (Rodoviária São José; ☎12 3832-5361; Thomaz Galhardo 513, Centro) – better known as São Jose bus station – on the main street a few blocks from the beach.

Getting Around

A car is optimal, but local **Verdebus** (☎12 3833-4002; www.verdebus.com.br; Hans Staden 474, Centro) buses (R$3.80, about hourly from 7am to 8pm) head up and down the coastal highway from their Centro terminal (between the two long-distance stations) and come at least within hiking distance of most beaches.

São Sebastião

☎0XX12 / POP 65,000

One of the only towns on the Paulista coast that has preserved a portion of its colonial charms, São Sebastião sits on a dramatic channel dividing the mainland from Ilha de São Sebastião (popularly known as 'Ilhabela'), a 15-minute ferry trip away. Prices in town are moderate by local standards, but for good reason. There are no beaches at hand, and the town is also a major oil depot, with huge tankers somewhat diminishing the natural beauty. Still, it makes a fine stopover if you're traveling to Ilhabela.

Sleeping & Eating

★Pousada da Ana Doce POUSADA $$
(☎12 3892-1615; www.pousadaanadoce.com.br; Expedicionários Brasileiros 196; s/d from R$230/260; ❄📶🏊) It's so hard to choose at this colonial center gem, São Sebastião's most charming inn. One of the 16 neat, cheerful little rooms arranged around a charming, plant-filled courtyard in the main structure? Or one of 10 that surround a pool in a newly built annex next door (two of which offer French doors opening right into the water)? Book ahead.

Pousada Ipé POUSADA $$
(☎12 3893-1698; www.pousadaipesaosebastiao.com.br; Três Bandeirantes 125; s/d/tr R$220/250/300; @📶) A charming 2016 newcomer, this 15 room *pousada* offers clean and simple rooms that are fine. On the other hand, the common areas – from the leafy open-air atrium to its loft breakfast area flanking the same ivy-draped centerpiece from above – are thick with local Brazilian character.

Família Restaurante BRAZILIAN $$
(www.familiarestaurante.com.br; Av Altino Arantes 58; mains for 2 people R$57-147; ⏲11am-midnight) Easily the most popular of the row of waterfront restaurants in São Sebastião. Pile in with festive Brazilians from far and wide for distinctly average grilled fish, shrimp nu-

merous ways, *moquecas* (seafood stews) and plenty of meat dishes as well.

★**Pimenta de Cheiro Toque Toque** BRAZILIAN $$$

(☎12 3864-9700; www.facebook.com/pimentadecheirotoquetoque; Yojiro Takaoka 790, Praia Toque-Toque Pequeno; mains for 2 people R$82-255; ⊙noon-11pm Thu-Mon; 📶) It's worth the 25km drive west from São Sebastião's cultural center to pretty Praia Toque-Toque Pequeno, where this open-air seafooder excels at both hospitality and gastronomy. First of all, half-portions are offered for 50% of the price – a Brazil first! – and choices like anything from the five-deep *moqueca* (seafood stew) menu or pesto risotto with basil and shrimp are full of wow.

Getting There & Away

The **bus station** (☎12 3893-4340; Praça Vereador Venino Fernandes Moreira 10) is located just off the main coastal highway and a short walk from the colonial center. **Litorânea** (☎12 3893-2475; www.litoranea.com.br; Praça Vereador Venino Fernandes Moreira 10, Rodoviária de São Sebastião) has frequent services to São Paulo (R$76.45, 3½ hours, seven daily), as well as a direct service to GRU Airport (R$56.10, four hours, four daily), Boiçucanga (R$14, 40 minutes, 7:45am, 1:45pm and 7:45pm) and other stops along the coast to Santos. **Util** (☎12 3892-6233; www.util.com.br; Praça Vereador Venino Fernandes Moreira 10, Rodoviária de São Sebastião) offers a service to Rio (R$112, seven hours, 9:30am and 10pm), with a stop in Paraty (R$41.75, 3½ hours).

Ilhabela

☎0XX12 / POP 28,000 IN WINTER, 120,000 IN SUMMER

Rising steeply from the narrow strait that divides it from the continent, the 350-sq-km Ilhabela (Beautiful Island) earns its name from its volcanic peaks, beautiful beaches, dense tropical jungle and some 360 waterfalls. Almost 85% of the island has been turned into Parque Estadual de Ilhabela, a state park and Unesco-protected biosphere, which shelters a remarkable profusion of plant and animal life, including toucans and capuchin monkeys. A haunt of pirates in the 16th and 17th centuries, its waters are scattered with shipwrecks, many of which make for excellent diving. The island also offers jungle hiking, windsurfing and beach-lazing.

Sights

Vila Ilhabela, on the northwestern part of the island, has quite a few well-preserved colonial buildings, including the slave-built **Igreja NS da Ajuda** (founded 1532); the **Fazenda Engenho d'Agua** in Itaquanduba (founded 1582); and **Fazenda Santa Carmen** at Feiticeira beach. Two kilometers inland from Perequê beach (near the ferry terminal), **Cachoeira das Tocas** has various small waterfalls with accompanying deep pools and waterslides.

Beaches

Over 40 beaches are found along Ilhabela's considerable coastline. Of the sheltered beaches on the north side of the island, **Praia Jabaquara** is recommended. It can be reached by car via a dirt road. On the eastern side of the island, where the surf is stronger, try beautiful **Praia de Castelhanos** (good for camping and surfing), which is backed by the steeply rising jungle. From the town of Borrifos at the southern end of the island, you can take a four-hour walk to **Praia Bonete**, a windy surf beach that you will share mostly with a local community of fisherfolk. Other worthwhile beaches you can drive to include **Praia da Ilha das Cabras** and **Praia do Curral**, 1.8km and 8km south of Barra Velha, respectively.

Activities

The most popular activities on Ilhabela involve boating/trekking to far-flung beaches and waterfalls. However there is also diving (two-tank outing R$260 to R$420; try **Narwhal** (☎12 98886-7268; www.narwhal.com.br/ilhabela; Av Princesa Isabel 171, Perequê; ⊙9am-6pm Mon-Fri, to 6pm Sat & Sun)), wakeboarding (per hour R$100) and treks to the island's prominent peak, the 1048m-high **Pico do Baepi** – a 14km return trek that can be done without a guide. Sea kayaking and stand-up paddle (SUP) boarding can also be arranged.

Maremar Aventura Turismo OUTDOORS

(☎12 3896-3679; www.maremar.tur.br; Praça Elvira Storace 12, Perequê; ⊙8:30am-6pm May-Nov, to 8pm Dec-Apr) Near the ferry, this recommended agency organizes all kinds of outdoor activities, including schooner trips around the island (from R$80 per person); full-day trips to the idyllic fishing village and beach of Bonete (R$170; which includes the private but spectacular Praia de Indaiaúba);

OFF THE BEATEN TRACK

SÃO PAULO SEASHORE ESCAPES

There's a lot more beach on São Paulo's coast than we could possible cover. In addition to the beach towns we feature, consider escaping the city and digging your toes into these alternative sands, several of which won't be quite so crowded.

Santos Though it never receives a star for cleanliness, Santos is the closest beach to the city of São Paulo, just over an hour away on a good traffic day. Due to oil money, it's a fun town in its own right, with lots of great bars and restaurants. Locals consider Boqueirão, between canals 3 and 4, to be the city's best beach. Santos' beachfront garden, clocking in at 5335m, is in the record books for the largest in the world. **Expresso Luxo** (www.expressoluxo.com.br) buses to Santos leave frequently from Terminal Rodoviário do Jabaquara in São Paulo (R$26.65, 1¼ hours).

Guarujá With its fine beaches along the stretch of coast closest to São Paulo, once-glamorous Guarujá has suffered from overdevelopment. Still, if you can't get further afield, it retains some charm as a quick getaway – even if concrete towers line the beaches, which get packed with weekend day-trippers. Surfers should note that there are good waves along Praia do Tombo and Praia do Éden (reached by a downhill trail from the road to Pernambuco or Iporanga beaches) that are a good bet for beating the crowds. Ultra (www.viacaoultra.com.br) buses to Guarujá (R$35.10, 1¼ hours) leave throughout the day from Terminal Rodoviário do Jabaquara in São Paulo.

Boiçucanga & Around The laid-back surfer town of Boiçucanga makes a good base to explore the stretch of coast that runs almost due west from São Sebastião. The variety of beaches, many backed by the steeply rising Serra do Mar, is remarkable, and there's good surf at nearby Camburi and Maresias, which have also developed into major party towns. Juqueí is popular with families. Boiçucanga is reached by bus from São Paulo Tietê (R$55.50, four hours, five daily), Guarujá (R$34.30, two hours, 7:45am, 1:45pm and 7:45pm) and São Sebastião (R$140, 40 minutes, 7am, 1:30pm and 7:45pm) with Litorânea (www.litoranea.com.br).

Ilha do Cardoso As wild as it gets in São Paulo state, this ecological reserve near the state's southern border with Paraná offers gorgeous natural pools, waterfalls and untouched beaches, and is home to only 400 residents and no cars. Dark sands and brownish-gray sea don't sway the nouveau hippies, who love these beaches due to their isolation. One Valle Sul (www.vallesulservicos.com.br) bus per day leaves São Paulo's Barra Funda bus station for Cananéia (R$86.33, five hours, 2:30pm), from where a number of private operators offer a boat service to the island along the waterfront. Prices vary according to group size, but expect to pay around R$20 to R$30 per person (four-person minimum). You can also take a Dersa (www.dersa.sp.gov.br) ferry at least three times a week (R$55.30, 1½ to two hours). You can also reach Cananéia from Iguape (R$27.90, 1¾ hours) via Pariquera-Açu.

and 4WD/boat tours to Praia de Castelhanos (R$110 to R$160 per person).

It also runs a **kiosk** (☎12 3896-1418; www.maremar.tur.br; Av Princesa Islabel 90, Perequê; ⏲9am-6pm May-Nov, to 10pm Dec-Apr) near the Perequê pier.

Sleeping

Making a reservation is a good idea on weekends – mandatory on summer weekends. Prices are high, so some travelers choose to stay in São Sebastião, where rates are more reasonable.

★ **Hostel da Vila** HOSTEL $
(☎12 3896-2096; www.hosteldavilailhabela.com.br; São Benedito 202; dm without breakfast R$40-65, d/tr from R$110/250;) Up a dramatic driveway from Vila, this relative newcomer sits tucked away in jungly surrounds. Dorms come in four- to 12-bed configurations (the latter almost Japanese pod-like); or opt for sleeping in a tent, a VW Kombi or even a boat. The banana-yellow colonial house is splashed with artistic doses of color from *Paulistana* artists and the pool is paradise.

Green Hostel HOSTEL $

(☎12 99149-6412; www.greenhostelilhabela.com; Luiz Ameixeiro 181, Perequê; dm/d/tr R$60/160/240;) Friendly, English-speaking owner Gabriel runs one of Ilhabela's coziest hostels. Renovated dorms with nice bathrooms and ample hammock-strung terraces (including the rooftop, which also features an outdoor shower) are pluses. The in-house agency can get you out and about while Mel, Menina and Crispim, the three cats, will keep you company on a rainy day.

★**Na Mata Suites** POUSADA $$

(☎11 99985-2042; www.namatasuites.com.br; Benedicto Mariano Leite 690, Barra Velha; d R$296;) Cradled in a small thatch of lush neighborhood rainforest, here you'll find an absolutely lovely four-bungalow trove of hospitality. Originally converted from private jungle into a discerning getaway by the English-Brazilian owners, it's now leased to an equally hospitable, creatively-engulfed Argentine-Brazilian duo (he's an actor, she's a photographer) who are carrying on the consummate traveler vibe.

Pousada Canto Brava POUSADA $$

(☎12 3896-5111; www.pousadacantobravo.com.br; Praia do Bonete; d R$220-560;) Unplugged and mostly candlelit, this sustainably slanted 12-room pousada hidden away on Bonete beach is Ilhabela's most romantic escape. It's a haul to arrive on foot – a 12km hiking trail from Sepituba – but you'll share sand with nobody beyond local fisherfolk (sweating for your dinner, which will be spruced up by their organic gardens!) and undaunted surfers.

Pousada Mariola POUSADA $$$

(☎12 3896-4141; www.pousadamariola.com.br; Chico Reis 304, Saco da Capela; s/d from R$445/460;) An engineer owns this fabulous choice implanted into giant granite stones perched high on a view-riffic hillside and reached via a charming street with upright palms shooting straight from the cobblestones. The 20-room boutique inn offers spacious rooms with Asian aesthetics and patios that take full advantage of the expansive vistas of the sailboat-strewn sea below.

DPNY Beach BOUTIQUE HOTEL $$$

(☎12 3894-3000; www.dpnybeach.com.br; Av José Pacheco do Nascimento 7668, Curral; d weekday/weekend from R$1200/1500;) Set right on the sands of Praia do Curral, this uber-trendy getaway for São Paulo fashionistas isn't subtle: the Mediterranean-on-overdrive aesthetic would be jarring if the crowd here didn't subscribe to the more-is-more line of trendsetting decorating.

Eating

Cura BUFFET $

(www.restaurantedocura.com; Av Princesa Isabel 337, Perequê; per kg R$60; ⌚11:30am-4pm;) The island's best *por-kilo* restaurant, set in a large and homey space across from the sands of Perequê.

Cheiro Verde BRAZILIAN $$

(☎12 3896-3245; www.facebook.com/cheiro.verdeilhabela; Rua da Padroeira 109, Vila; meals R$31.50; ⌚11:30am-4:30pm Mon, Wed & Thu, to 10:30pm Fri-Sun;) The best place in Vila for a generous *prato feito* (plate of the day) with grilled meat or fish, plus rice, beans and salad. It's a simple but clean and airy place that attracts tourists and locals alike. Each day's menu awaits on an electronic monitor by the door.

★**Prainha do Julião** SEAFOOD $$

(☎12 3894-1867; www.prainhadojuliao.com.br; Av Riachuelo 5370, Praia do Juliao; mains R$49-94; ⌚10am-6pm Mon-Thu, to 6:30pm Fri-Sun;) Hidden from the main road along the island's southside is this upscale beach shack, firmly planted into the sands of one of Ilhabela's best and most easily-accessed beaches, Julião. Creative seafood with actual vegetables are served on a pristine stretch of beach dug into only by those in the know, who imbibe in the all-day bar scene as well.

Capitano ITALIAN $$

(☎12 99770-9581; www.pastadelcapitano.com.br; Pedro Paula de Moraes 703, Saco de Capela; mains R$48-82; ⌚7pm-1am;) Chef Fabio Piscioto hails from São Paulo's most traditional Italian neighborhood and was destined to return to his pasta-making roots after 30 years as a graphic designer, part of which was in Milan. The simple, clean pasta dishes here are very satisfying (the squid-ink tagliatelle with shrimp grew better and better as it steamed on our plate).

★**Restaurante Ilha Sul** BRAZILIAN $$$

(☎12 3894-9426; www.restauranteilhasul.com.br; Av Riachuelo 287, Portinho; mains for 2 people R$98-298; ⌚1-11pm daily Jan, 1-11pm Fri-Sun Feb-Dec;) On the island's south end, this award-winning seafooder is most

WORTH A TRIP

PARQUE ESTADUAL DO ALTO DO RIBEIRA

Nestled in the Vale do Ribeira in the hills near the São Paulo–Paraná border, the town of Iporanga was founded in 1576 after gold was discovered here. Today, the surrounding region remains one of the least-disturbed stretches of the Brazilian Atlantic Forest and is of international importance for its biodiversity. It also makes a good base for visiting the Parque Estadual do Alto do Ribeira (PETAR), Brazil's premier cave destination.

The park's Núcleos de Visitação (Visitor Centers) are well set up with information on cave trips, guides and campgrounds. There are four Núcleos: **Núcleo Santana** (www.petaronline.com.br; per person R$12, plus per vehicle R$6), 18km northwest of town, is the park's main entry point and has good facilities for visitors and campers, including an exhibition hall and five caves and a 3.5km-long trek to a beautiful waterfall; Núcleo Ouro Grosso (13km northwest of town) has basic accommodations for groups and offers cooking facilities, two caves and a walking trail; Núcleo Casa de Pedra (9km by road plus 3km by walking trail, northwest from town) is the base for visiting the Casa de Pedra, famous for its 215m-high entrance (a Guinness world record) and pristine Atlantic forest; and **Núcleo Caboclos** (www.petaronline.com.br; entrance/camping R$12/18), the park's most isolated and pristine sector, which is 86km by road from town and has good camping facilities, basic visitors' lodgings and several caves.

For information as well as camping and caving reservations, contact **PETAR** (PETAR; ☎15 3552-1875; www.petaronline.com.br; SP165, Km156). **Parque Aventuras** (☎15 99745-8656, 15 3556-1485; www.parqueaventuras.com.br; SP165, Km13; ⏲7am-11pm) organizes expeditions to the caves, as well as hiking, bird-watching and inner-tubing.

From São Paulo's Barra Funda bus station, Transpen (www.transpen.com.br) offers service to Apiaí (R$97, five hours, 7:30am, 12:30pm and 7:30pm), where you can catch a Princesa dos Campos (www.princesadoscampos.com.br) 3pm bus to Iporanga (R$6.75, 1¾ hours).

famous for its top-end shrimp dishes, but you can't go wrong with anything you encounter on its pleasant, bamboo-strewn patio.

★ **Marukuthai** THAI $$$
(☎12 3896-5874; www.marakuthai.com.br; Av Força Expedicionária Brasileira 495, Indaiá; mains R$49-119; ⏲8pm-12:30am Wed-Fri, 11am-5pm & 8pm-12:30am Sat, 11am-5pm Sun; 📶) Dine on the sands overlooking romantic, yacht-filled seas at Ilhabela's best gourmet restaurant, the domain of darling local chef Renata Vanzetto and her tropical take on Brazilianized Thai. Her best acts pilfer from both cuisines, such as a seared tuna with a goat cheese and apricot sauce over cashew jasmine rice; or sautéed shrimp with grilled pumpkin, *catupiry* cheese and crunchy *mandioquinha* (starchy taproot) sticks.

Drinking & Nightlife

Ponto das Letras CAFE
(Dr Carvalho 146, Vila; coffee R$5-12; ⏲10am-8pm Mon, Wed, Thu, to 10pm Fri & Sun, to 11pm Sat; 📶) Extremely pleasant cafe and bookshop in the historic district; easily the island's best.

DPNY Beach Club/Bistrô LOUNGE
(www.dpnybeach.com.br; DPNY beach, Av José Pacheco do Nascimento 7668, Curral; ⏲beach club 10am-7pm, bistro 10pm-midnight; 📶) With bass-heavy lounge music at tolerable volumes, hip-tropical decor and table service on the sand, the island's fanciest beach club/bar attracts rich *Paulistas* eager to show off this season's designer gear. Specialty cocktails are R$30 to R$56. The beach club runs a day-use fee of R$160 for nonguests.

Entertainment

★ **Teatro de Vermelhos** THEATER
(☎12 3512-7107; www.vermelhos.org.br; Governador Mário Covas Júnior 11474, Ponta da Sela) This extraordinary 1100-seat theater in the jungle was inaugurated in 2016 as part of Ilhabela's new Centro Cultural Baía dos Vermelhos. It hosts the annual Festival de Vermelhos in September: a two-day music, performing arts and visual arts event. The complex is also home to a smaller amphitheater in jungly surrounds.

Shopping

★ **Teiú** ARTS & CRAFTS

(www.facebook.com/teiuarte; Av Força Expedicionária Brasileira 32; ⏲10am-8pm) A standout option on an island that disappoints from a shopping perspective, local artist Fred Teiu not only presents his own tropical-themed paintings that range in theme from Frida Kalho to jungle macaws, but also a vibrant and colorful collection of ceramics, and arts and crafts from Brazil, Turkey, Mexico, India, Indonesia and beyond. Well worth a browse.

Getting There & Away

The 15-minute **ferry** (Dersa; ☎0800-726-6300; www.dersa.sp.gov.br; Av Princesa Isabel s/n) trip between São Sebastião and Ilhabela runs around the clock every 30 minutes from 5:30am to 10:30pm, and more or less hourly after that. Cars/motorbikes cost R$18.50/$9.20 weekdays and R$27.70/R$13.80 on weekends; pedestrians ride free. Returning to the mainland, you pay an environmental tax only (R$3.50 for motorbikes, R$7.50 for cars).

Getting Around

It's best to have your own vehicle for exploring Ilhabela, but **Expresso Fênix** (www.ilhabela.fenixfacil.com.br) has local buses (R$4, every 30 minutes, 5am to 1:30am) that run the length of the island, including a stop at the ferry. Reduced fares of R$2.50 are available if you take the time to get a *Bilhete Único* rechargeable card.

Taxi Ilhabela (☎12 3895-8587) is a reliable taxi service and is usually waiting at the ferry.

Good roads run along the western coast of the island; however, the south and east coasts are reachable only by boat or on foot except for a rough road accessible by 4WD that extends to Praia de Castelhanos on the west coast.

Iguape & Around

☎0XX13 / POP 29,000

Founded by the Portuguese in 1538 to defend Brazil from the Spanish, Iguape is one of Brazil's oldest colonial settlement towns and one of the few along São Paulo's coast to retain its colonial contours. An ongoing federal initiative is helping to restore the old city center, which has long been neglected. While beaches are a bit of a hoof, the town makes a tranquil base from which to explore the region.

Sights

With impressive buildings and few foreign tourists, Iguape is good for those who appreciate their colonial architecture in various shades of preservation and decay. These buildings are clustered around the whitewashed main plaza, **Largo da Basílica**, and the 18th-century **basilica** (open 8am to 8pm). About 1.5km along the road to Barra do Ribeira is a turnoff to the **Mirante do Morro do Espia**, a lookout with a good view of the port and region.

Iguape looks across a narrow strait to **Ilha Comprida**, a long, skinny island (86km by 3km) that shelters Iguape from the open ocean. The island is covered with a combination of mangrove and Atlantic rainforest, and has an uninterrupted beach that stretches the entire Atlantic-facing length of the island. A toll bridge connects Iguape with the island.

Sleeping & Eating

Iguape is small and sleepy. There are but a few hotels and pousadas, of which **Pousada Solar Colonial** (☎13 3841-1591; solarcolonial@terra.com.br; Praça da Basílica 30; s/d R$110/160, with air-con R$120/180; ❄📶) and **Silvi Hotel** (☎13 3841-1421; www.silvihotel.com.br; Sandoval Trigo 515; s/d/tr from R$95/280/320; ❄@📶) are standouts.

There are a number of inexpensive pizzerias and other eateries on Largo da Basílica.

Getting There & Away

From Iguape's **bus station** (☎13 3841-1209; Bento Pereira da Rocha 102), **Valle Sul** (www.vallesulservicos.com.br) offers four daily buses to São Paulo (R$66, 3½ hours, 5:30am, 11am, 3:30pm and 8:15pm). For Cananéia (R$21.80, 1¾ hours), switch in Pariquera-Açu.

Local buses cross the bridge to Ilha Comprida. If you have a 4WD, it is possible to drive along the long, flat beach on Ilha Comprida and take the **Dersa** (www.dersa.sp.gov.br) ferry across to Cananéia (per vehicle weekday/weekend R$11.90/17.90, passengers free), which leaves every 30 minutes during peak hours; or hourly otherwise from 6am to 11:30pm.

Paraná

Includes ➡

Curitiba 269
Morretes 274
Paranaguá 275
Ilha do Mel 277
Iguaçu Falls & Around 282
Foz do Iguaçu 282
Parque Nacional do Iguaçu (Brazil) 289
Parque Nacional Iguazú (Argentina) 291

Best Places to Eat

- Manu (p272)
- Barolo (p272)
- Mar e Sol (p280)
- Fim da Trilha (p281)
- Casa do Barreado (p276)

Best Places to Stay

- Belmond Hotel das Cataratas (p291)
- Tetris Container Hostel (p283)
- Motter Home (p271)
- Hostel Nature (p284)
- Astral da Ilha (p280)

Why Go?

Since its 1853 secession from São Paulo state, Paraná has been endlessly compared with its larger neighbor to the north. Indeed, the two share a slew of superlatives, rating among Brazil's highest standards of living and best-educated populations.

With its efficient public transportation, innovative architecture and outstanding urban parks, the capital, Curitiba, exemplifies the state's successes. Though no tourism magnet, the city's air of European culture and excellent restaurants make for a nice dose of Brazil at its most developed. Sunbathers and surfers sigh for Ilha do Mel and Parque Nacional do Superagüi, where large swaths of unspoiled rainforest and pristine coastline make for some of the least developed and most idyllic beaches in southern Brazil.

But it's Iguaçu Falls that has always earned the wonder and admiration of travelers, from indigenous tribes to Jesuit missionaries to modern-day tourists. The awe it inspires cannot be overstated.

When to Go

Foz do Iguaçu

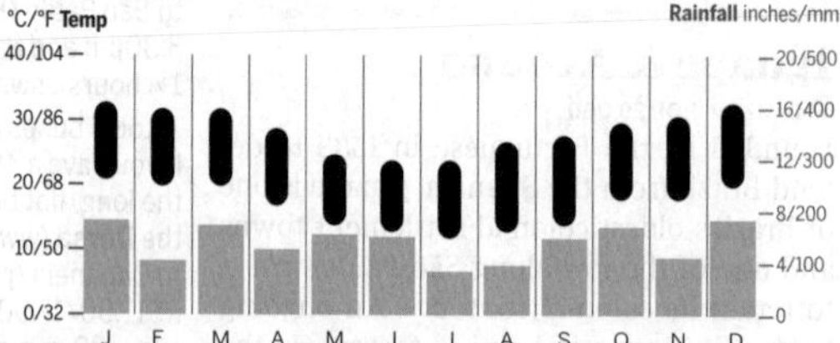

May & Sep Off-peak prices and crowds paired with tolerable weather at Iguaçu Falls.

Dec–Feb Peak season brings the sunshine at Iguaçu Falls and Ilha do Mel.

Aug Retreating cold and mugginess in Curitiba makes for comfortable days.

History

Like much of southern Brazil, Paraná was neglected by the Portuguese colonists; even a brief gold rush in the 17th century withered when bigger finds were discovered in Minas Gerais. When Paraná seceded from São Paulo in 1853, the economy was based on cattle and *erva maté* (tea), and the government encouraged Italian immigration to spur development. Waves of Germans, Ukrainians and Poles followed. Following immigration and railroad construction, Curitiba developed into one of the country's richest cities.

Getting There & Around

Curitiba is the state's transportation hub, with bus and air services to every major city in Brazil from Rodoferroviária de Curitiba (p274) and Aeroporto Internacional Afonso Pena (p273), respectively. Foz do Iguaçu also has a small international airport (p288) and direct bus services to Argentina and Paraguay as well as São Paulo, Rio de Janeiro and most large southern Brazilian cities.

CURITIBA

0XX41 / POP 1.75 MILLION

While not necessarily sexy, Curitiba has long garnered praise for being one of the world's best models of urban planning, mainly due to the bold initiatives of its three-term mayor, Jaime Lerner, whose daring moves in the early 1970s transformed a six-block length of downtown into a pedestrian zone (done in secret under the cover of darkness), created

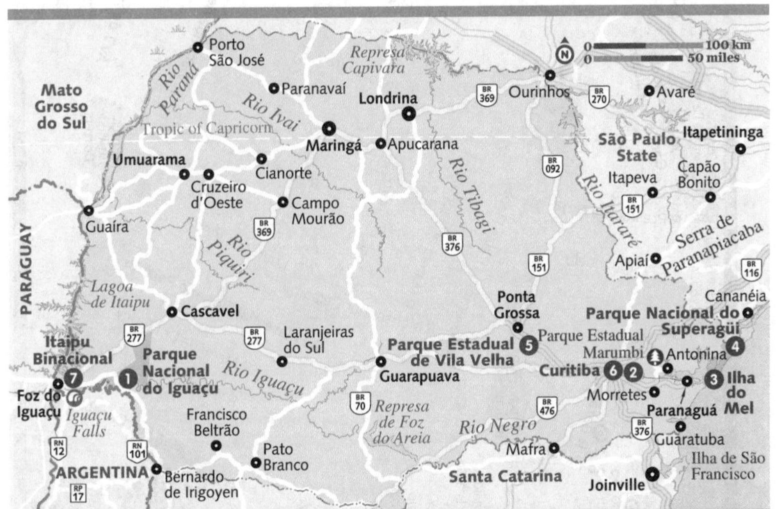

Paraná Highlights

1. **Parque Nacional do Iguaçu** (p289) Experiencing Mother Nature's heart-stopping, thunderous roar at Garganta do Diablo, Iguaçu Falls' most tumultuously glorious moment.
2. **Serra Verde Express** (p275) Riding the rails on this cinematic locomotive trip to Morretes, one of Brazil's last great train rides.
3. **Ilha do Mel** (p277) Lazing about the wild beaches and sandy trails in Paraná's car-free paradise.
4. **Parque Nacional do Superagüi** (p281) Witnessing the barrage of coupled-up red-tailed parrots on their afternoon return to Ilha dos Pinheiros.
5. **Vila Velha** (p272) Marveling at this ancient 'stone city' of massive, mysterious red-toned sandstone formations outside Curitiba.
6. **Museu Oscar Niemeyer** (p271) Appreciating art and architecture at this museum designed by and dedicated to Brazil's most famous modern architect.
7. **Itaipu Binacional** (p282) Admiring the engineering behind the world's second-largest hydroelectric power station.

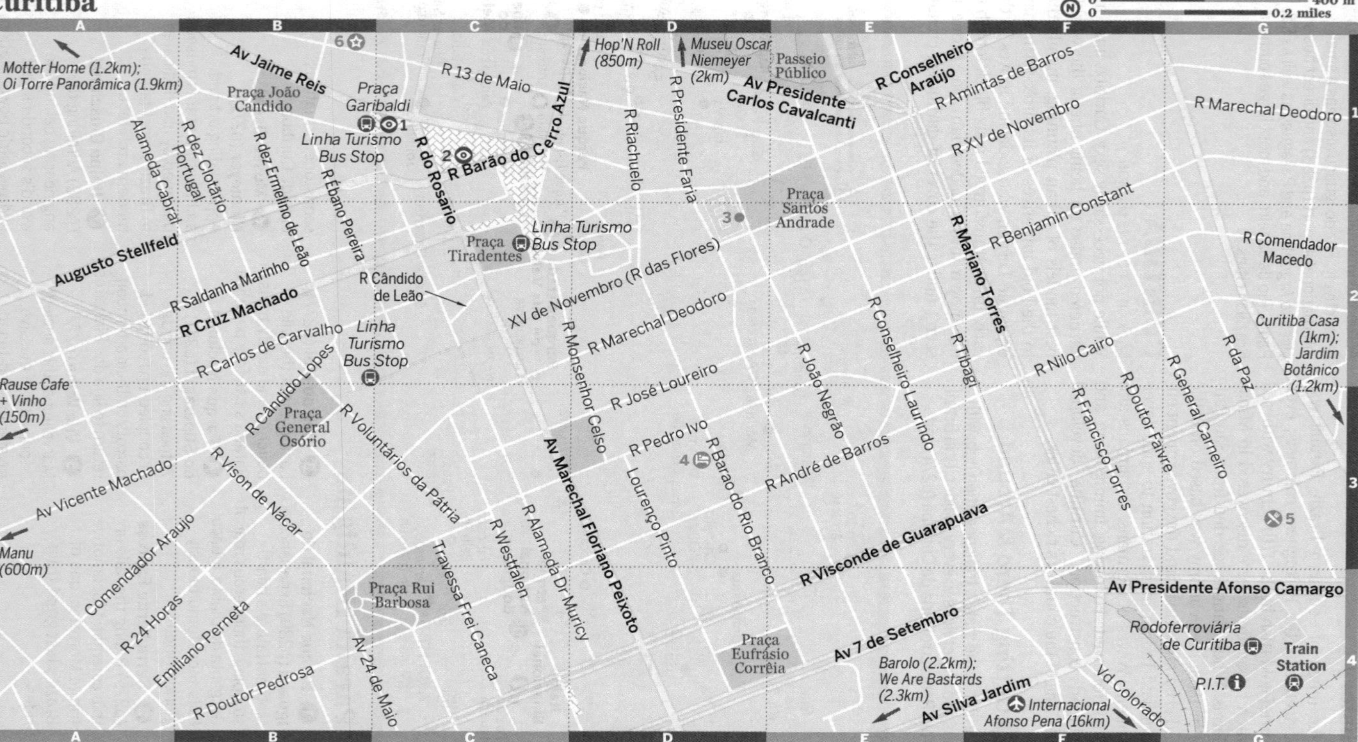

Curitiba
400 m
0.2 miles
Motter Home (1.2km); Oi Torre Panorâmica (1.9km)
Av Jaime Reis
Praça João Cândido
Praça Garibaldi
Linha Turismo Bus Stop
R 13 de Maio
Hop'N Roll (850m)
Museu Oscar Niemeyer (2km)
Passeio Público
Av Presidente Carlos Cavalcanti
R Conselheiro Araújo
R Amintas de Barros
R Marechal Deodoro
R XV de Novembro
Alameda Cabral
R dez Clotário Portugal
R dez Ermelino de Leão
R Ébano Pereira
R do Rosario
R Barão do Cerro Azul
R Riachuelo
R Presidente Faria
Praça Santos Andrade
R Mariano Torres
R Benjamin Constant
R Comendador Macedo
Praça Tiradentes
Augusto Stellfeld
R Saldanha Marinho
R Cruz Machado
R Cândido de Leão
XV de Novembro (R das Flores)
R Marechal Deodoro
R Carlos de Carvalho
R Monsenhor Celso
R Conselheiro Laurindo
R João Negrão
R Tibagi
R Nilo Cairo
R Doutor Faivre
R General Carneiro
R da Paz
Curitiba Casa (1km); Jardim Botânico (1.2km)
Rause Cafe + Vinho (150m)
R Cândido Lopes
Praça General Osório
R Voluntários da Pátria
R José Loureiro
R Pedro Ivo
R Barao do Rio Branco
R André de Barros
R Francisco Torres
Av Vicente Machado
R Vison de Nácar
Av Marechal Floriano Peixoto
Lourenço Pinto
R Alameda Dr Muricy
R Westfalen
Travessa Frei Caneca
Praça Rui Barbosa
R Visconde de Guarapuava
Manu (600m)
Comendador Araujo
R 24 Horas
Emiliano Perneta
R Doutor Pedrosa
Av 24 de Maio
Praça Eufrásio Corrêia
Av 7 de Setembro
Barolo (2.2km); We Are Bastards (2.3km)
Av Silva Jardim
Internacional Afonso Pena (16km)
Vd Colorado
Av Presidente Afonso Camargo
Rodoferroviária de Curitiba
Train Station
P.I.T.

Curitiba

Sights
1 Feira do Largo C1
2 Largo da Ordem C1

Activities, Courses & Tours
3 Curitiba Free Walking Tour D2

Sleeping
4 San Juan Johnscher D3

Eating
5 Mercado Municipal G3

Entertainment
6 Dizzy Café Concerto B1

five express-bus avenues with futuristic tubular boarding platforms, encouraged recycling and sustainable design long before it was fashionable, and planted trees and created parks on an enormous scale.

Curitiba has also taken innovative approaches to urban ills such as homelessness, pollution and poverty, and it's now the envy of urban planners the world over and the country's most efficient city. With its abundant green spaces, sophisticated population and well-heeled infrastructure, this is a good spot to recharge your batteries and enjoy Brazil at its functioning best.

Sights

★Museu Oscar Niemeyer MUSEUM
(MON; 41 3350-4400; www.museuoscarniemeyer.org.br; Marechal Hermes 999; adult/child R$20/10, free Wed 10am-6pm & 1st Weds of the month until 8pm; 10am-6pm Tue-Sun) Designed by and named for the architect responsible for much of Brasília, this striking museum features an iconic eye-shaped tower painted with whimsical dancing figures in shadowy black. Rotating exhibits highlight Brazilian and international artists of the 20th and 21st centuries. Permanent exhibitions include a photographic time capsule of the museum's construction (housed in the tower) and an excellent presentation on Niemeyer himself, the highlight of the space.

Largo da Ordem PLAZA
(Largo da Ordem) Curitiba's colonial heart. Here, the pedestrian-only cobblestone streets are lined with beautifully restored buildings, many of which now house trendy art galleries, pubs and cafes. On Sunday, it fills up along with adjacent Praça Garibaldi for a lively **art and artisan market** (Praça Garibaldi; 9am-2pm Sun) with more than 1000 stalls.

Oi Torre Panorâmica VIEWPOINT
(Castro Vellozo 191; adult/child R$5/2.50; 10am-7pm Tue-Sun) For an overview of Curitiba, head to the 109m-high Torre Panorâmica, offering 360-degree views from the observation deck.

Tours

Curitiba Free Walking Tour WALKING
(41 98875-7721; www.curitibafreewalking.com; 11am Sat) FREE This recommended walking tour meets on the steps of the Federal University of Paraná every Saturday at 11am for a 2½-hour jaunt through the historic *centro*. Tipping is encouraged (R$10 to R$15 is fine).

Sleeping

★Motter Home HOSTEL $
(41 3209-5649; www.motterhome.com.br; Desembargador Motta 3574; dm R$40-54, d/tr R$150/200;) In leafy Mercês, Curitiba's top hostel inhabits a canary-yellow, turret-style mansion from the '50s, with striking art, retro-sophisticated common areas, original hardwood floors and funky door handles. It's a 15-minute walk from Largo da Ordem.

Curitiba Casa HOSTEL $
(41 3044-7313; www.curitibacasahostel.com; Brasílio Itiberê 73; dm R$46-52, r R$135;) Despite its odd location 15 minutes east of the *rodoferroviária* (bus and train station), this hostel has more fans than *futebol*. Clean, colorful and classy.

San Juan Johnscher BOUTIQUE HOTEL $$
(41 3302-9600; www.sanjuanhoteis.com.br; Barão do Rio Branco 354; s/d from R$200/250, ste R$280-310;) Behind a beautiful neoclassical facade, this renovated hotel retains much of its original architectural detail, but does not skimp on modern amenities. Stained-wood floors, painted moldings and black-and-white photos give the 24 rooms an aura of understated elegance. The lobby, designed with a Jenga-like aesthetic of stacked Brazilian-walnut support beams and fireplace, is a sight to see.

Nomaa Hotel BOUTIQUE HOTEL $$$
(41 3087-9595; www.nomaa.com.br; Gutemberg 168; s/d from R$400/480;) This 41-room hot spot in hip Batel is steeped in local art and culture. From the owner's photographs

WORTH A TRIP

VILA VELHA

Located in Campos Gerais, 93km west of Curitiba, **Parque Estadual de Vila Velha** (☎42 3213-3832; www.pontagrossa.pr.gov.br/parque-estadual-vila-velha; Rodovia BR-376, Km 515; Arenito, Furnas & Lagoa Dourada R$18, Furnas & Lagoa Dourada R$8, guide R$10; ⏲8:30am-3:30pm Wed-Mon) is known as the 'stone city.' The park's centerpieces are the 23 *aretinhas* (sandstone pillars), created over millions of years. The mysterious red-toned sandstone – some taking recognizable shapes such as boots and bottles – create striking silhouettes against the blue sky and green foliage. A guide is compulsory and must be booked in advance on Mondays, Wednesdays and Thursdays (or park security can call one for you).

Within the boundaries of the same park, visitors can witness another geological marvel: a series of *furnas* (craters) that are the result of underground erosion.

From Curitiba, catch a **Princesa dos Campos** (www.princesadoscampos.com.br) bus to Vila Velha (R$33.91, 1½ hours, 7:45am, 2:30pm or 5:30pm). Any bus to Ponta Grossa will also stop here; the prevailing wisdom is that you should take the earliest buses at 6:30am, 7:45am, 8:15am or 9:45am to arrive early enough to see the whole park. Stop first at the park center, where you can watch an introductory video and buy tickets for the various tours, and catch buses to Furnas and Lagoa Dourada on weekends (9:30am, 11am, 1:30pm, and 3:30pm).

of local points of interest to Paraná marble and Holaria ceramic amenity containers in the bathrooms, nearly everything that could come from Paraná did come from Paraná.

Lênin Palhano, Curitiba's 2018/2019 chef of the year, helms the hotel's restaurant, Nomade. Eat local, drink local…sleep local!

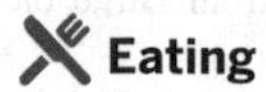

Eating

Mercado Municipal MARKET $
(www.mercadomunicipaldecuritiba.com.br; 7 de Setembro 1865; ⏲7am-2pm Mon, to 6pm Tue-Sat, to 1pm Sun) Curitiba's excellent urban market, full of food stalls, cafes, gourmet emporiums and Brazil's first organic food court.

★**Barolo** ITALIAN $$
(☎41 3243-3430; www.barolotrattoria.com.br; Av Silva Jardim 2487; pasta for 2 people R$91.80-179.80; ⏲11am-2:30pm & 7pm-12:10am Mon-Fri, 11am-2:30pm & 6pm-12:40am Sat & Sun; 📶) It's not located in Curitiba's touristy Italian neighborhood, yet this upscale trattoria is the real deal. The pasta – pick your type, then pick your sauce (priced separately) – is served in cast-iron pans and is an absolute treat. Reservations are recommended for dinner.

Swadisht INDIAN $$
(☎41 3015-1056; www.swadisht.com.br; Av Vicente Machado 2036; mains for two R$82-104; ⏲7-11:30pm Mon-Thu, to midnight Fri & Sat; 📶) Hankering for a fiery curry? This upscale Indian restaurant in Batel is easily Brazil's (and maybe South America's) best. The kitchen staff are not afraid to light you up if you ask for 'Indian spicy' (well off the five-level heat chart for locals); our curries packed a wallop of spice and authentic flavor.

★**Manu** BRAZILIAN $$$
(☎41 3044-4395; www.restaurantemanu.com.br; Dom Pedro II 317; tasting menu R$220, with wine pairing R$400; ⏲8-11:30pm Tue-Sat; 📶) Manoella Buffara is one of Curitiba's hottest chefs and her pedigree backs up her impressive creations, which appear on a nightly-changing tasting menu that relies heavily on regional farm cooperatives and the restaurant's own organic garden.

'Manu' – short for Manoella – counts stints in two of the world's most famous kitchens, Noma (Copenhagen) and Alinea (Chicago), as the inspiration behind her ever-evolving dishes, which often get unorthodox pairings with outside-the-box wines, organic juices and craft beer. This is the south's only spot where gourmands can gather over subtle culinary feats – it's the equivalent of a Michelin-starred meal for a lot less than you would pay elsewhere. Reservations essential.

Drinking & Nightlife

★**Rause Cafe + Vinho** CAFE
(www.rausecafe.com.br; Carlos de Carvalho 696; coffee from R$6.50; ⏲9am-11pm Mon-Fri, 9am-7pm Sat; 📶) At its heart, this is a retro coffeehouse (choose from specialty Bahia and Minas coffees, brewed in a variety of pour-over methods), but there's a great selection of eats as well (wild boar and gorgonzola risotto, fig confit and brie crepes), plus wine.

★ Hop'N Roll BAR

(☎41 3408-4486; www.hopnroll.com.br; Mateus Leme 950; ⊙5:30pm-1am Mon-Thu, to 2am Fri & Sat;) The hophead assault on this excellent craft beer bar's 32 draft options – served in proper pints – is relentless. Aficionados will find the lion's share of local and southern Brazil's artisanal beers either on draft or on the 120+ bottle menu – and Hop'N Roll brews its own, too. Book ahead if you want a seat.

We Are Bastards CRAFT BEER

(☎41 3557-2207; www.bastardsbrewery.com.br; Av Iguaçu 2300; ⊙6-11:45pm Tue-Thu, to 1am Fri, 4pm-1am Sat,;) There's no better way to introduce yourself, or your beer, than shooting straight from the hip: we are bastards! One of Curitiba's best breweries, the bar occupies a whitewashed historic mansion in Água Verde. You'll find 31 taps (beers R$12 to R$33) and lots of cheeky merchandise and mottoes.

☆ Entertainment

Dizzy Café Concerto LIVE MUSIC

(☎41 3527-5060; www.facebook.com/DizzyCuritiba; 13 de Maio 894; ⊙7pm-2am Tue-Sat) Curitiba's best live music venue, focused on jazz, blues and MPB (Música Popular Brasileira), inside an acoustically friendly old home. Shows get going around 9pm. Cover is R$15 to R$25.

Information

Curitiba's tourist information offices are stocked with glossy brochures and maps and staffed with helpful employees who speak a little English.

Helpful locations include:

C.A.T. Jardim Botânico (Centro de Atendimento ao Turista; ☎41 3362-3831; www.turismo.curitiba.pr.gov.br; Ostoja Roguski 690, Jardim Botânico; ⊙9am-6pm)

P.I.T. Aeroporto Internacional Afonso Pena (Posto de Informações Turísticas; ☎41 3381-1153; www.turismo.curitiba.pr.gov.br; Av Rocha Pombo, Aeroporto Internacional Afonso Pena, Arrivals Hall; ⊙7am-11pm Mon-Fri, to 6pm Sat & Sun)

P.I.T. Oi Torre Panorâmica (Posto de Informações Turísticas; ☎41 3339-7613; www.turismo.curitiba.pr.gov.br; Castro Vellozo 191, Oi Torre Panorâmica; ⊙10am-7pm Tue-Sun)

P.I.T. Rodoferroviária (☎41 3225-4336; Av Affonso Camargo 330, Rodoferroviária; ⊙9am-6pm)

Getting There & Away

AIR

There are direct flights from **Aeroporto Internacional Afonso Pena** (CWB; ☎41 3381-1515; www.aeroportocuritiba.net; Av Rocha Pombo s/n, São José dos Pinhais), 18km southeast of Centro, to cities throughout Brazil.

BUS

Curitiba's long-distance bus and train stations form a single three-block complex called the

BUSES FROM CURITIBA

DESTINATION	STARTING FARE (R$)	DURATION (HR)	COMPANY
Buenos Aires* (AR)	385	32	JBL (www.jblturismo.com.br)
Florianópolis	56	5	Catarinense (www.catarinense.net)
Foz do Iguaçu	193	10	Catarinense
Joinville	31	2	Catarinense
Montevideo (UY)**	415	25	TTL (www.ttl.com.br)
Morretes	27	1½	Graciosa (www.viacaograciosa.com.br)
Paranaguá	33.50	1¾	Graciosa
Rio de Janeiro	172	14	Penha (www.nspenha.com.br), Kaissara (www.kaissara.com.br)
Santiago (CL)***	455	50	JBL
São Paulo	65	7	Kaissara (www.kaissara.com.br), Cometa (www.viacaocometa.com.br)

* Departs Tuesday, Thursday and Saturday at 4am.

** Departs Tuesday at 5:30am.

*** Departs 8pm on Sunday.

rodoferroviária (☎41 3320-3000; www.urbs.curitiba.pr.gov.br/comunidade/rodoferroviaria; Av Pres Affonso Camargo 330), which sits 2km southeast of downtown. Ticket counters for interstate bus travel (*interestadual*) are on the 2nd floor of the first block; bus companies for destinations within Paraná (*estadual*) are located on the 2nd floor of the second block. The train station block is behind the two bus station blocks.

The ticket booths for international destinations are not well marked – look for **Roderotas**, the company representing the international bus companies, on the northeast end of the *interstadual* block. Buses to Asunción leave from Foz de Iguaçu only.

Getting Around

TO/FROM THE AIRPORT

The classy, wi-fi-enabled **Aeroporto Executivo** (☎41 99817-9666; www.aeroportoexecutivo.com.br; one way R$15) runs direct every 15 minutes from 5:25am to midnight (from 6am Sunday) between the airport and well-marked Centro stops.

A taxi from the airport to Centro runs between R$60 to R$70. Uber fares are about 50% less – meet your driver outside Exit 3 (Saída 3) of the arrivals terminal.

BUS

URBS (www.urbs.curitiba.pr.gov.br) runs Curitiba's space-age bus system, made up of integrated station pods, known as *tubos*. City buses, several of which are electric/biodiesel (Hibribuses), cost R$4.25.

MORRETES

☎0XX41 / POP 16,000

Founded in 1721 on the banks of the Rio Nhundiaquara, this calm and collected colonial town rests on an emerald-green plain at the foot of the Serra do Mar. The loveliest buildings are clustered around Praça Lamenha Lins and along Rua das Flores, the cobblestone walkway that runs along the river.

The region's culinary gift to the world is *barreado*, a rib-sticking meat stew cooked in a clay pot. Originally, it served to keep revelers nourished over the course of several days of Carnaval (February/March), but you can test its sustaining qualities any time of year.

Tours

Calango Expedições ADVENTURE

(☎41 3462-2600; www.calangoexpedicoes.com.br; Gabriela de Souza Nogueira 350; ⏲9am-10pm) These eco-minded adventure-tour specialists will get you out and about. Options include kayaking (R$90, 1½ hours), mountain biking (R$90, three hours) and tubing (R$120) in the stunning surrounds, plus hiking and mountaineering in **Parque Estadual Pico do Marumbi** (☎41 3462-3598; Estrada das Prainhas; ⏲8am-6pm Thu-Sun) FREE.

Sleeping & Eating

Hotel Nhundiaquara POUSADA $

(☎41 3462-1228; www.nundiaquara.com.br; General Carreiro 13; s/d R$125/200, s/d without bathroom R$70/140;) The spotlight no longer shines on the oldest building in town, which, from the outside, sits in pristine blue-and-white glory on the riverfront. Its days as an award-winning hotel are rearview mirror material, and there's an antiquated air about the place among the warped flooring and cramped bathrooms with low water pressure.

Nevertheless, the on-site restaurant is famous for its *barreado* (R$49.90), served on the breezy, colonial-style terrace overlooking a lovely bend in the Rio Nhundiaquara. And you're sleeping in the town's most storybook setting.

★**Villa Morretes** BRAZILIAN $$

(☎41 3462-2140; www.barreado.com.br; Frederico de Oliveria 155; mains for two R$72-163; ⏲11:30am-3pm Wed, Thu & Mon, to 4pm Sat & Sun;) Amid lush gardens and bubbling fountains on the more tranquil side of the river sits this scenic restaurant, a great and friendly option for regional specialties, including *barreado* (from R$54.70), fish with *maracujá* (passion fruit) sauce and several fantastic value seafood/*barreado* all-you-can-eat combos.

Sit on the riverside and don't miss its version of *bolinho de chuva* on Saturdays, a sort of banana-flavored funnel cake. It's 100m on the left after you cross the bridge from the more touristy options.

Information

The **tourist office** (☎41 3462-1024; Praça dos Imigrantes; ⏲Sat & Sun) occupies a small kiosk just beside the riverbank near Pousada Nhundiaquara, but it seems to be perpetually abandoned. During the week, the **Secretary of Tourism** (☎41 3462-1266; turismo@morretes.pr.gov.br; Largo Andrade s/n, Casa Rocha Pombo; ⏲8am-noon & 1:30-6pm Mon-Fri) is open and can help. The **Morretes Convention & Visitor's Bureau** (☎41 3462-1902; Praça Rocha Pombo, Estacao Ferroviária; ⏲10am-3pm Tue-Sun) is a better option – at least there's a map up for grabs!

DON'T MISS

ALL ABOARD!

The **Serra Verde Express** (☎41 3888-3488; www.serraverdeexpress.com.br; Estação Ferroviária) between Curitiba and Morretes offers sublime views of threatening mountain canyons, tropical green lowlands and the vast, blue Atlantic. As you descend, watch as the climate and environment change – the weather becoming hotter and muggier, the vegetation lusher and greener.

The train leaves Curitiba at 8:30am daily (9:30am on weekends December to January), descending 900m through the lush Serra do Mar to the historic town of Morretes, arriving at noon and returning at 3pm (arriving back in Curitiba at 6:30pm). There are three classes of service. One-way economy/tourist/cabin or imperial class tickets cost R$85/119/235. The last of these includes a bilingual guide (and beer!) for up to four people (in a private cabin or *camorote*) or in an car decked out in '30s-era decor (imperial). Additional services are sometimes available.

Views are most spectacular from the left side of the train (right side on the return trip), but the democratic computer ticketing system prevents requests – it takes turns between left and right (good luck!). Reservations are highly recommended during summer. Prices and times change frequently, so be sure to stop by the train station or check the website in advance.

If you want to make the ride a little more interesting (and start drinking at 7am!), **Cervejaria Bodebrown** (☎41 3082-6354; www.bodebrown.com.br; Carlos de Laet 1015), one of Brazil's leading craft beer breweries, runs the Beer Train on the same route three or four times per year. The trip isn't cheap, but includes unlimited tastings of five beers (usually unique or new offerings paired with bread and cheese), lunch and transport. Trust us – it's a good time!

Getting There & Away

The Morretes **train station** (Padre Saviniano 768) is on a pretty square in the center of town. The Serra Verde Express runs to Curitiba daily at 3pm.

The **bus station** (Mário Marcondes Lobo 61) is about 1km from the center of town. **Viação Graciosa** (☎41 3462-1115; www.viacaograciosa.com.br) has seven daily buses to Curitiba (R$22.07, 1½ hours, 5:30am to 8:15pm) and frequent departures on a bus that circulates between Morretes, Antonina and Paranaguá (R$6.45, one hour).

PARANAGUÁ

☎0XX41 / POP 140,500

This colorful old port, sitting serenely on the banks of the Rio Itiberê, has an appealing atmosphere of tropical decadence. Commercially important since the late 18th century, the city has some impressive churches and other public buildings, many of which are being carefully restored. For travelers, Paranaguá serves primarily as a point of departure to Ilha do Mel and Parque Nacional do Superagüi.

Sights

The city's colonial churches are simple but striking. Several churches were constructed during the 18th century, including **Igreja São Francisco das Chagas** (XV Novembro s/n; ⊙8:30am-12:30pm & 1-5:30pm Mon-Sat, 9am-1pm & 3-6pm Sun) and **Igreja São Benedito** (Conselheiro Sinimbu s/n; ⊙8am-6pm), built specifically for the town's slaves.

Museu de Arqueologia e Etnologia MUSEUM

(Archeology & Ethnology Museum; www.facebook.com/maeufpr; XV de Novembro 575; ⊙8am-8pm Tue-Sun) FREE Housed in an 18th-century Jesuit college, this surprisingly great museum displays indigenous artifacts, primitive and folk art, and old tools and machines.

Tours

Paranaguá Tours OUTDOORS

(☎41 98409-5191; www.paranaguatours.com.br; General Carneiro s/n, Mercado de Artesanato, box 3; ⊙9am-5pm Mon-Fri, 10am-3pm Sat) Friendly and helpful, English- and Dutch-speaking Renato is a great one-stop resource for the region, working with tours and transport to Ilha do Mel, Parque Nacional do Superagüi, Guaraqueçaba, Sebuí and beyond.

Paranaguá

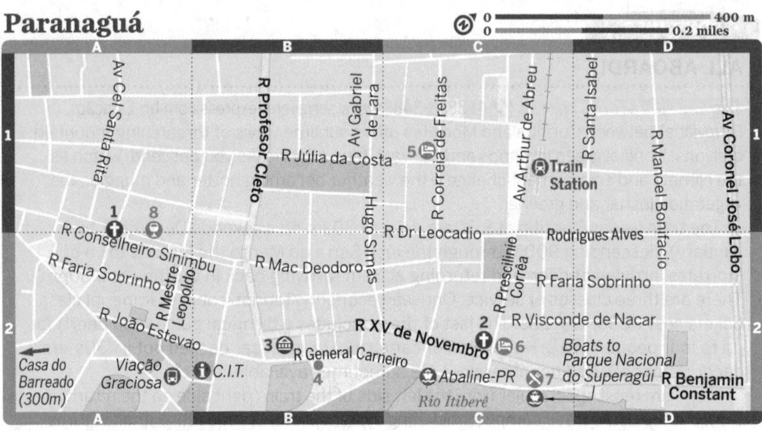

Paranaguá

Sights
1 Igreja São Benedito A1
2 Igreja São Francisco das Chagas C2
3 Museu de Arqueologia e Etnologia B2

Activities, Courses & Tours
4 Paranaguá Tours B2

Sleeping
5 Hotel Monte Libano C1
6 Hotel Ponderosa C2

Eating
7 Danubio Azul C2

Drinking & Nightlife
8 Toca do Barril A1

Sleeping

Hotel Ponderosa HOTEL $

(41 3423-2464; Prescilinio Corrêa 68; s/d R$80/100, d with view R$120;) Occupying a restored colonial building on a prominent corner, the simple Ponderosa evokes a grand past, with its high ceilings and wide-plank wood floors. The rooms facing the port are particularly pleasing, with lots of light and lovely views of the waterfront.

Hotel Monte Libano HOTEL $$

(41 3422-2933; Júlia da Costa 152; s/d/tr R$150/210/300;) If you're not fussed about being on the waterfront, this simple but friendly hotel is a step up in professionalism by Paranaguá's standards. Modern, no-frills rooms with Sky TV, decent wi-fi, Lorenzetti Jet Turbo electrical showers and semitrained reception staff are highlights.

Eating & Drinking

★ **Casa do Barreado** BRAZILIAN $$

(41 3423-1830; José Antônio da Cruz 78; per person incl dessert R$40; noon-3pm Sat & Sun) In her own home a few blocks behind the historic district, Norma cooks up real-deal *barreado* true to its original recipe (simmered for 24 hours in an earthen clay pot), a less commercialized version than you'll find in Morretes. This weekend-only affair has earned a culinary star 15 years running. A true local experience.

Danubio Azul BRAZILIAN, SEAFOOD $$

(www.restaurantedanubioazul.com.br; XV de Novembro 95; mains for two R$25-190, per kg R$79.90; 11am-3pm & 7-11:30pm Mon-Sat, to 3pm Sun;) The *centro histórico*'s best restaurant does excellent fish preparations and a tasty filet mignon among bland decor but stretching water views. At lunch it's a high-quality *por-kilo* buffet.

Toca do Barril BAR

(www.facebook.com/tocadobarril; Conselheiro Sinimbu 210; 7pm-1am Mon-Thu, to 2:30am Fri & Sat;) This cozy cantina is Paranaguá's best, serving up a good mix of bottled craft beers from Curitiba and Santa Catarina (plus a few Belgian stragglers), good burgers (from R$23) and live rock and MPB (Thursday to Saturday).

Information

Paranaguá's most convenient and helpful **tourist information booth** (Centro de Informações Turística; 41 3420-9863; www.fumtur.com.br; Praça dos Povos Arabes; 8am-6pm) is just outside the bus station.

Getting There & Away

BOAT

Abaline-PR (41 3455-6325; www.abaline.com.br; General Carneiro 258) runs boats to Ilha do Mel throughout the day (R$53 return). Three boats – **Megatron** (41 99806-0119, César 41 3482-7131; General Carneiro s/n), **Superagüi** (Rone 41 3482-7152; General Carneiro s/n) and **Silvano Sena** (Jaco 41 3482-7150; General Carneiro s/n) – alternate runs to Parque Nacional do Superagüi (R$50 return, one hour) at 3pm Monday to Saturday, from four **docks** (General Carneiro s/n) northeast of Ilha do Mel's dock, returning from Superagüi at 7am.

BUS

From the **bus station** (41 3420-2925; Ponta do Caju) on the waterfront, **Viação Graciosa** (41 3423-1215; www.viacaograciosa.com.br; Ponta do Caju, Rodoviária de Paranaguá) has 13 buses per day to Curitiba (R$30.87, 1½ hours) and frequent departures on a bus that circulates between Paranaguá, Antonina and Morretes (R$6.45, one hour). You can also continue south without heading back to Curitiba – two buses per day leave for Joinville (R$30.45, two hours, 6am & 4pm).

ILHA DO MEL

0XX41 / POP 1100

This hourglass-shaped island at the mouth of the Baía de Paranaguá is the most pristine and picturesque beach resort in all of southern Brazil, offering mostly wild beaches, good surfing waves and scenic coastal walks. Accessible only by boat, Ilha do Mel is traversed by sandy paths and has not a single car, so traffic jams throughout the island's scenic sandy lanes consist of surfboard-toting Brazilians on bicycles and bedazzled foreigners in their new Havaianas (flip-flops). Rowdy summer holidaying aside, Ilha do Mel, or 'honey island,' is the territory of surfers, campers, beachcombers and other escapists in search of simplicity, serenity and isolation.

Sights

The fatter, northern half of the island is a no-go ecological preserve. The hillier southern portion is the locale of three small villages: Nova Brasília and Praia do Farol near the isthmus, and Encantadas at the far southern tip. Ilha do Mel's easternmost point is marked by its landmark lighthouse sitting atop a *morro* (hill) 2km and 750m east of Nova Brasília and Praia do Farol, respectively. Another smaller settlement, Encantadas, at the southern end of the island, is the closest point to the mainland. A 6km trail on the east coast links the two towns, traversing a series of undeveloped beaches including Praia da Fora, Praia do Miguel and Praia Grande.

Farol das Conchas LIGHTHOUSE

(Conchas Lighthouse) Built in 1872 on orders from Dom Pedro II, this lighthouse stands picturesquely atop a hill at the island's most easterly point. From here you have panoramic views of the island, the bay and the Serra do Mar. It's a popular spot to watch the sun drop below the horizon – don't miss it.

Grutas das Encantadas CAVE

Legend has it that these small caves at the island's southern tip are inhabited by beautiful mermaids who enchant all who come near. Signs clearly mark the way to the caves, accessible at low tide (usually between 8am and 1pm), from Encantadas and Praia da Fora.

Fortaleza de NS dos Prazeres FORT

(Fort of Our Lady of the Pleasures) This picturesque fort, which dates to the 1760s, is a 3km hike from Nova Brasília via Praia da Fortaleza. Inspect the deserted fortress before climbing up to the lookout for an incredible vista of the bay.

Activities

Beaches

Ilha do Mel has no shortage of beaches. Those facing the bay enjoy warm waters gently lapping at the white sand, while those facing the ocean boast the big surf. But almost all of them are unspoiled, marked only by windswept dunes, forested hills and rocky outposts. **Praia da Fora** and **Praia Grande** are a 20-minute walk (2km) from Nova Brasília and a 40-minute walk (4km) from Encantadas. According to local surfers, in winter these beaches have the best waves in Paraná.

The **Praia do Farol** is the long stretch of sand between the Nova Brasília dock and the Farol das Conchas. It is backed by the swampy, grassy, protected area of the *restinga* (a tropical and subtropical moist broadleaf forest unique to Brazil), which also preserves the natural beauty of the beach. Surfers congregate at the base of the hill and ride the legendary **Ondas das Paralelas**.

If you didn't bring your surfboard, you might prefer the calmer, warmer waters of the beaches that face the shallow bay. In the north, **Praia da Fortaleza**, often nearly deserted, allows you to bathe in the shadow of

Ilha do Mel

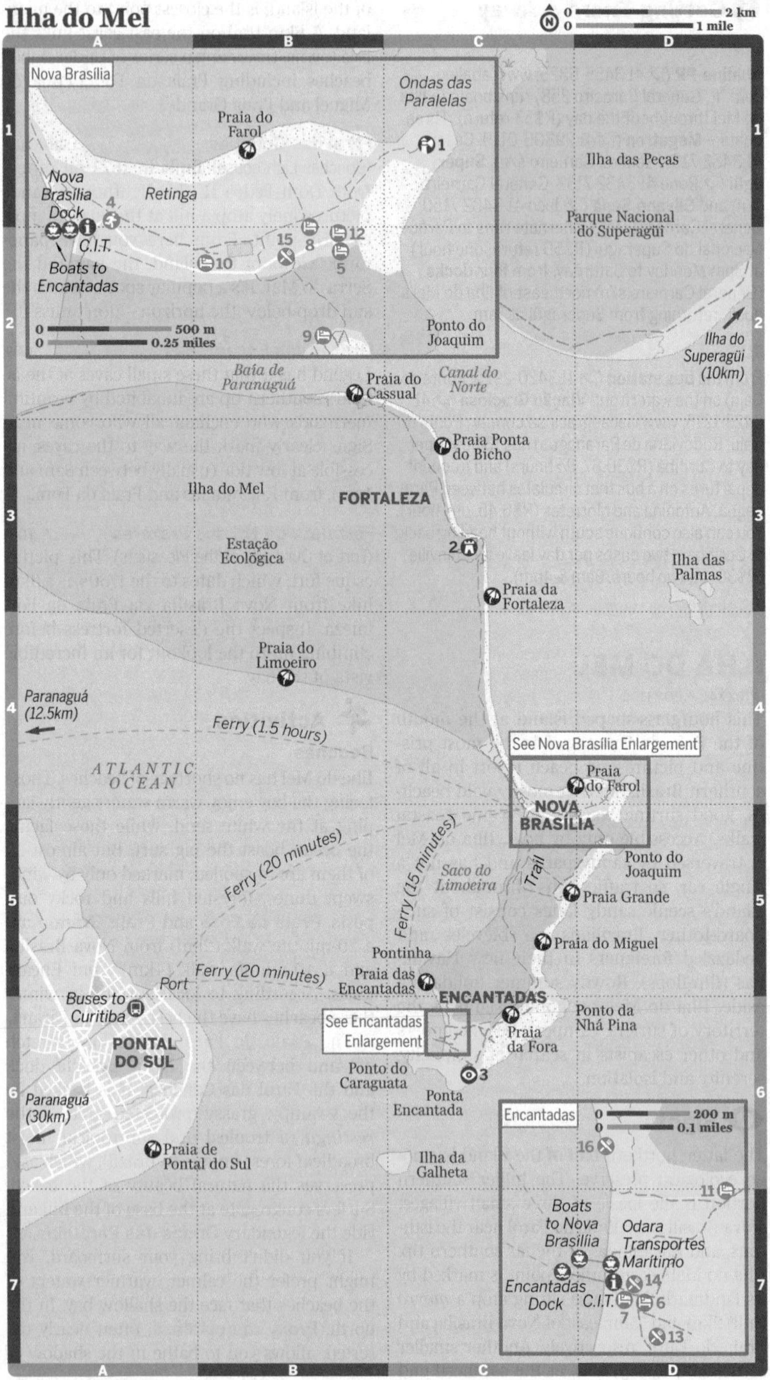

0 2 km
0 1 mile
A B C D
1 2 3 4 5 6 7
Nova Brasília
Ondas das Paralelas
Praia do Farol
1
Nova Brasília Dock
Retinga
4
C.I.T.
Boats to Encantadas
15
8
12
5
10
9
0 500 m
0 0.25 miles
Ponto do Joaquim
Ilha das Peças
Parque Nacional do Superagüi
Ilha do Superagüi (10km)
Baía de Paranaguá
Praia do Cassual
Canal do Norte
Praia Ponta do Bicho
Ilha do Mel
FORTALEZA
Estação Ecológica
2
Ilha das Palmas
Praia da Fortaleza
Praia do Limoeiro
Paranaguá (12.5km)
Ferry (1.5 hours)
See Nova Brasília Enlargement
Praia do Farol
NOVA BRASÍLIA
ATLANTIC OCEAN
Ferry (20 minutes)
Ferry (15 minutes)
Saco do Limoeira
Trail
Ponto do Joaquim
Praia Grande
Praia do Miguel
Pontinha
Ferry (20 minutes)
Port
Praia das Encantadas
ENCANTADAS
Buses to Curitiba
Ponto da Nhá Pina
See Encantadas Enlargement
Praia da Fora
PONTAL DO SUL
Ponto do Caraguata
3
Ponta Encantada
Paranaguá (30km)
Encantadas
0 200 m
0 0.1 miles
16
11
Praia de Pontal do Sul
Ilha da Galheta
Boats to Nova Brasília
Odara Transportes Marítimo
14
Encantadas Dock
C.I.T.
6
7
13

Ilha do Mel

Sights
1 Farol das Conchas ... C1
2 Fortaleza de NS dos Prazeres ... C3
3 Grutas das Encantadas ... C6

Activities, Courses & Tours
Astral da Ilha Surf Club ... (see 5)
4 Pura Vida ... A1

Sleeping
5 Astral da Ilha ... B2
6 Bob Pai e Bob Filho ... D7
7 Caraguatá ... D7
8 Enseada das Conchas ... B2
9 Grajagan Surf Resort ... B2
10 Pousada das Meninas ... B2
11 Recanto Francês ... D7
12 Treze Luas ... B2

Eating
13 Fim da Trilha ... D7
14 Lumo ... D7
15 Mar e Sol ... B2
16 Shams ... D6

the 18th-century Portuguese fort. The best beach near the settlement of Encantadas is **Praia da Fora**, which has big waves and a few stalls selling *cervejas* (beers) and *sucos* (fruit juices).

Boating

You can hire boats to explore Ilha do Mel and nearby islands. Reliable boatman **Isael Pereira** (☎41 99921-8160) leaves from Praia do Farol; he charges R$350 for Ilha do Superagüi, R$300 for Ilha das Peças, R$250 for Ilha das Palmas and R$150 for Fortaleza and Baía dos Golfinhos. **Odara Transportes Marítimo** (☎41 99979-3545, 41 3426-3545; Praia das Encantadas) is another dependable option.

Cycling

Biking is a great way to beat the heat and land on the sand faster. Note that you cannot take bikes to Encantadas due to large rocks in the path.

Pura Vida CYCLING
(☎41 3426-8138; Caminho do Farol s/n, Nova Brasília; per hour/day R$15/70; ⏲9am-8pm) Tony and his English-speaking partner rent the best single-gear beach cruisers on the island. It's on your left just past the ferry dock.

Water Sports

Astral da Ilha Surf Club WATER SPORTS
(☎41 3426-8196; www.astraldailha.com.br; Praia de Fora; ⏲8am-8pm) This well-organized outfit based out of Pousada Astral da Ilha in Vila do Farol is the spot to come for surf lessons and stand-up paddle instruction (per hour R$50) and surfboard (per hour/day R$40/60) and SUP (per hour/day R$50/70) rentals.

Sleeping

Most of the hotels are clustered in the village of Nova Brasilía, which occupies the isthmus linking the two ends of the island, and Vila do Farol, just east of Nova Brasília.

Encantadas is less charming than Nova Brasília, though it has more of a village ambience. There is a party scene on the beach itself which has more infrastructure than other beaches, and the contrasting atmosphere is otherwise a quieter mash-up of simpler residential abodes with vaguely hippie-dippie transients, campers and backpackers.

To escape the summer crowds, head to the few pousadas around Fortaleza, though you are a good one-hour, 3km hike from the Nova Brasília pier.

Prices are for the summer high season – book ahead for holidays and any November to March weekend. Expect discounts of 20% to 50% between April and October. Camping is available.

★**Bob Pai e Bob Filho** POUSADA $$
(☎41 3426-9006; joelsonbobpai@yahoo.com.br; Praia de Encantadas s/n; r R$270; ❄@🛜) 'Father Bob and Son Bob' easily wins the island's personality contest with eight unadorned but well-equipped rooms (flatscreen TVs, minibars, beach kits – some with hammock-strewn patios) surrounding the atmospheric Captain's Bar and knickknack-peppered gardens.

★**Pousada das Meninas** POUSADA $$
(☎41 3426-8023; www.pousadadasmeninas.com.br; Vila do Farol s/n, Nova Brasília; s/d without bathroom from R$180/360, with bathroom from R$280/400, chalets R$210-550; ❄🛜) Built from driftwood and recycled material, this pousada has the charm of a guesthouse and a family welcome. Hung with hammocks and chock-full of cutesy kitsch, the simple but tasteful rooms are set around a cozy garden.

Recanto Francês POUSADA $$

(☎41 99673-7856; www.recantofrances.com.br; Praia de Encantadas s/n; d with fan R$200; 📶) Charming Luciane runs this pousada steps from Mar do Fora beach. The rustic but colorful clapboard rooms surrounding a pleasant garden offer good hospitality for the money. Her *crepiocas* (a mix between a crepe and tapioca) at breakfast are a nice touch, and afternoon coffee (from 4pm) draws locals.

★**Astral da Ilha** POUSADA $$$

(☎41 3426-8196; www.astraldailha.com.br; Praia de Fora; r from R$600, with meals from R$850; ❄📶) 🍃 Its own craft beer? Hibiscus caipirinhas? In-house masseuse? Surf/SUP school? Jazz festival every August? Things are done a little differently at this internationally themed (Bali, Africa, Hawaii) and sustainable top-end choice, easily the island's best. Bungalows, fashioned from 100% recycled woods, feature fireplaces and sinks made from giant seashells and tree trunks.

We prefer the more jungly and discreet Suites da Figueira flanked by a 100-year-old ficus tree.

Grajagan Surf Resort POUSADA $$$

(☎41 3426-8043; www.grajagan.com.br; Praia Grande; r R$690-1080; ❄📶) 🍃 Catering to wealthy surfers who like their creature comforts, the Indonesian-inspired Grajagan's rooms are easily the Ilha's most luxurious: each has a private veranda and hammock facing the sea. Though it's the island's largest resort at 26 rooms, you wouldn't know it as you douse yourself under the clandestine outdoor showers or wander the lush, eco-friendly property.

The whimsical surfers' bar and upscale restaurant (great wholewheat pizzas; R$64 to R$79) is awash in intricately carved wood and an astonishing mosaic floor (two years of meticulous work). It's open to nonguests.

Enseada das Conchas POUSADA $$$

(☎41 3426-8040; www.pousadaenseada.com.br; Praia do Farol 9; s/d/tr R$320/420/520; ❄📶) This quaint pousada has four well-appointed guest rooms painted in striking colors and decorated by theme ('Sunrise,' 'Sea Blue'). A wide deck is shaded by a thatch roof and scattered with lounge chairs and 13 cats. It's steps from the lighthouse and the island's best surf beach; homespun hospitality comes courtesy of veteran innkeepers Carlos and Sueli.

Treze Luas POUSADA $$$

(☎41 3426-8067; www.pousadatrezeluas.com.br; Povoado do Farol s/n; s/d from R$307.50/615; ❄📶) Brightened by whimsical artwork and bold-colored linens, this charming pousada has shiny stained-wood walls and cool tile floors (some have private verandas). A common porch overlooks a makeshift Zen garden flocked by striking-red Brazilian tanagers.

The restaurant serves rarer dishes for these parts: fish tacos, rösti, pad thai and vegan options.

Caraguatá POUSADA $$$

(☎41 3426-9097; www.caraguata-ilhadomel.com.br; Praia de Encantadas s/n; r from R$370; ❄📶) 🍃 Just a few steps from the pier, Caraguatá's pretty chalets are adorned with flower boxes and greenery. Intimate rooms vary in size but they all have stained-wood ceilings, whitewashed walls and crisp linens. Run by an amicable Argentine Brazilian couple, it's a rare top-end choice.

Eating

Shams MIDDLE EASTERN $

(www.facebook.com/shams.ilhadomel; Praia das Encantadas; mains R$16-25; ⏰11am-11:30pm late Dec–Feb, 6-11:30pm Mon, Thu & Fri, noon-11:30pm Sat & Sun Apr-Dec) Yassir, a first generation Lebanese descendant, has moved his plastic-tables-in-the-sand operation to the beach – he churns out great shawarma, falafel, homemade burgers, pizzas and – drum roll, please – banoffee pie! At night it's more bar-like, with live music on weekends.

★**Mar e Sol** SEAFOOD $$

(www.restaurantemaresol.com.br; Praça Felipe Valentim, Farol dos Conchas; meals R$29-38; ⏰11am-10pm; 📶) En route to the lighthouse, Mar e Sol serves spectacular fish, shrimp and crab *moquecas* (seafood stews; R$109 to R$255 for two), seafood risottos, and cheaper daily specials in individual portions. Junior, the local pet parrot, gives recommendations.

★**Lumo** BRAZILIAN $$

(☎41 3426-9010; www.facebook.com/chefluizmoura; Caminho da Gruta s/n, Pousada Lua Cheia; mains R$43.90-56.90; ⏰11:30am-3pm & 7:30-11pm; 📶) At Ilha do Mel's most interesting newcomer, chef Luiz Moura is shaking up the culinary scene armed with kitchen experience at both London's Meantime Brewing and Vinícola Araucária, a winery outside Curitiba. The results (Angus rib eyes with mushroom risotto, net-caught local fish,

OFF THE BEATEN TRACK

PARQUE NACIONAL DO SUPERAGÜI

Composed of the Superagüi and Peças islands, this national park in the Baía de Paranaguá is covered by mangroves and salt marshes, which support an amazing variety of bird and plant life.

The park is famous for its array of orchids. Hummingbirds and toucans live here, not to mention the roseate spoonbill and the stunning Brazilian tanager. Every evening at sunset, hundreds – sometimes thousands – of red-tailed parrots return to roost in the canopy on nearby **Ilha dos Pinheiros**, also part of the national park. Bottleneck dolphins are often sighted in the waters between Ilha do Superagüi and Ilha do Mel. Other mammals are more elusive, but include agoutis, pacas, deer, howler monkeys and pumas. The park is also home to the endangered black-faced lion tamarin, though it is rarely sighted.

The tiny village, Barra do Superagüi, is a rustic collage of colorful wooden homes connected by cement walkways traversing swampy mangroves. It's the kind of place where Simba, the local yellow lab, greets boats on arrival and local restaurants sometimes only open with enough advance notice to fish for your meal. It's not for everybody, but disappearing here for a day or two carries a certain type of off-the-grid appeal.

Boats run to Parque Nacional do Superagüi (R$50 return, one hour) at 3pm Monday to Saturday from Paranaguá, returning from Superagüi at 7am – but always check ahead as transportation here is iffy and fluid. You can also make private transportation arrangements with tour agents and pousadas in Paranaguá or Ilha do Mel.

excellent prawn cakes) are a delight that thoroughly outshine the simple ambience.

Moura also does simpler but well-executed *prato feitos* (meals of the day; R$24.90 to R$32.90).

★**Fim da Trilha** BRAZILIAN, SPANISH **$$**
(☎41 3426-9017; www.fimdatrilha.com.br; Povoado do Farol, s/n, Pousada Treze Luas; mains R$45-85; ⏲noon-3pm & 7-11:30pm; 📶) One of the island's best restaurants, Fim da Trilha has spicy, Spain-indistinguishable *paella* served – stop the presses! – in individual portions (R$50 to R$60), including a vegetarian option. Occasional craft beers are available, but the most interesting chaser is the *caipikult,* a caipirinha made with Yakult, a milky probiotic drink. Try it!

Drinking & Nightlife

Encantadas draws a beach party scene fueled by acoustic guitar–wielding wanderers, especially in summer, and Shams caters to a bar crowd with live music. Guesthouses in Vila do Farol such as Treze Luas and Astral da Ilha draw drinking crowds as well, as do Grajagan Surf Resort and **Mahalo Hostel Bar** in Praia Grande.

Information

There are no banks, ATMs or pharmacies on the island, so plan ahead. Most services are clustered near the ferry dock in Nova Brasília.

Ilha do Mel's tourist information booths are handily located at each arrival dock.

C.I.T. (Centro de Informaçãos Turística; ☎41 3426-9112; Arrival Dock, Nova Brasília; ⏲8am-7pm, to 8pm Nov-Mar)

C.I.T. (Centro de Informaçãos Turística; Encantadas; ⏲8am-noon & 2-6pm Wed-Sun)

Getting There & Away

Abaline-PR (p277) runs boats (R$53 return) at 8:30am, 9:30am, 11am, 1pm, 3pm, 4:30pm and 6pm in summer (these dwindle to 9:30am and 3:30pm in low season) from the jetty opposite Paranaguá's tourist office, stopping first in Nova Brasília (p277; 1½ hours), and then in **Encantadas** (Praia das Encantadas) (two hours). Returning to the mainland, boats depart Nova Brasília for Paranaguá in summer at 8am, 10am, 1:30pm, 3:30pm, 4:30pm, 6:30pm and 7pm. In low season, departures are 8am and 5pm during the week and 10:30am and 5pm on weekends. All boats leave a half hour earlier from Encantadas.

Alternatively, **Viação Graciosa** (www.viacaograciosa.com.br) runs four to six daily buses to/from Curitiba to Pontal do Sul (p277; R$42.74, 2½ hours), on the mainland opposite Encantadas, where you can embark for the 30-minute crossing to Nova Brasília or Encantadas (R$35 return). In high season, boats leave every half hour from 8am to 8pm from Pontal and from Ilha do Mel; in low season, every hour until 6pm.

If you arrive with clunky wheeled luggage, a battalion of wooden cart-wielding sand porters have your back: from Nova Brasília, it's R$40 as far as Farol and R$60 to Praia Grande.

Getting Around

It's a 4.5km tide-dependent walk from Nova Brasília to Encantadas – do not set out without checking with tide charts and/or locals; otherwise, grab the island ferry from one village to the other (R$15, 20 minutes, hourly, 8am to 7:30pm).

IGUAÇU FALLS & AROUND

Rising in the coastal mountains of Paraná and Santa Catarina, and running along the border between Brazil and Argentina, the Rio Iguaçu snakes west for 600km, picking up a few dozen tributaries along the way. It widens majestically and sweeps through a magnificent forest stage before a dramatic plunge in the tiered cascades known as Iguaçu Falls. Thousands of years before they were 'discovered' by Europeans, the falls were a holy burial place for the Tupi-Guarani and Paraguas tribes. Spaniard Don Alvar Nuñes happened upon the falls in 1541, dubbing them 'Saltos de Santa María.' But this name didn't stick, and the falls retained their Tupi-Guarani name, Iguaçu (Great Waters).

Foz do Iguaçu

0XX45 / POP 263,500

The Brazilian city of Foz do Iguaçu went through a period of frenzied growth during the 18 years that Itaipu Dam was under construction (completed in 1982), when the population increased more than fivefold. It was an edgy place then, but it has since settled down and is relatively pleasant as far as border towns go. There is little about the town to get excited about, but it works perfectly fine as a base for exploring Iguaçu Falls in both Brazil and Argentina as well other attractions in the area such as Itaipu Binacional and Parque das Aves.

Sights

★Itaipu Binacional DAM

(45 3576-7000; www.turismoitaipu.com.br; Tancredo Neves 6702; panoramic/special tour R$38/82; tours 8:30am-4:45pm) With a capacity of 14 million kilowatts, this binational dam is the world's second-largest hydroelectric power station, and the one that produces the most electricity per year. The impressive structure, at some 8km long and 200m high, is a memorable sight, especially when the river is high and a vast torrent of overflow water cascades down the spillway.

The **visitors center** (8am-6pm Sun-Thu, to 9pm Fri & Sat) is 12km north of Foz. From here, regular tours (*visita panorâmica*) depart every 20 minutes between 8:30am to 4:45pm. The more detailed option (*circuito especial;* minimum age 14), which takes you into the power plant itself, leaves eight times daily Sunday to Thursday, and 12 times daily on Friday and Saturday. A variety of other attractions within the complex include a museum, wildlife park and river beaches, and a sunset catamaran tour.

The project was controversial: it plunged Brazil into debt and necessitated the large-scale destruction of rainforest and the displacement of 10,000 people. But it cleanly supplies 75% of Paraguay's energy needs, and 17% of Brazil's.

To get to the Itaipu Dam, catch bus 101 (Vila C Norte-Sohab) or 102 (Vila C Sul-Profilurb), among others (R$3.45, 30 minutes), which leave every 20 to 30 minutes from Foz do Iguaçu's Urban Bus Terminal (TTU; p289).

★Parque das Aves BIRD SANCTUARY

(Bird Park; 45 3529-8282; www.parquedasaves.com.br; Av das Cataratas, Km 17.1; R$45; 8:30am-5pm) This 5-hectare bird park, located 300m from the entrance to Parque Nacional do Iguaçu (p289), is home to 800-plus species of birds, including red ibis, bare-throated bellbird, and flamingos galore. They live in 8m-high aviaries that are constructed right in the forest, some of which you can walk through. Kids and adults freak out alike. Well worth it!

Marco das Três Fronteiras VIEWPOINT

(45 3132-4100; www.marcodastresfronteiras.com.br; Av Gen Meira s/n; 2-11pm; adult/child R$22/12) Once little more than an uneventful obelisk, the Parque Nacional do Iguaçu concession folks have now built a small tourist complex around the viewpoint of all three tri-border countries that includes a children's park, a light and water show, cultural shows and a memorial to Álvar Núñez Cabeza de Vaca – the first European to have recorded the existence of the falls around 1540.

Tours

There are no tours offering both sides in the same day, but it can be done. Be on the Brazilian side bang at opening at 9am, get out of there on a Rio Uruguay (www.riouruguaybus.com.ar) or Crucero del Norte (www.crucerodelnorte.com.ar) bus from outside the Brazilian park entrance to Puerto Iguazú's bus station (eight departures per day,

Iguaçu Falls

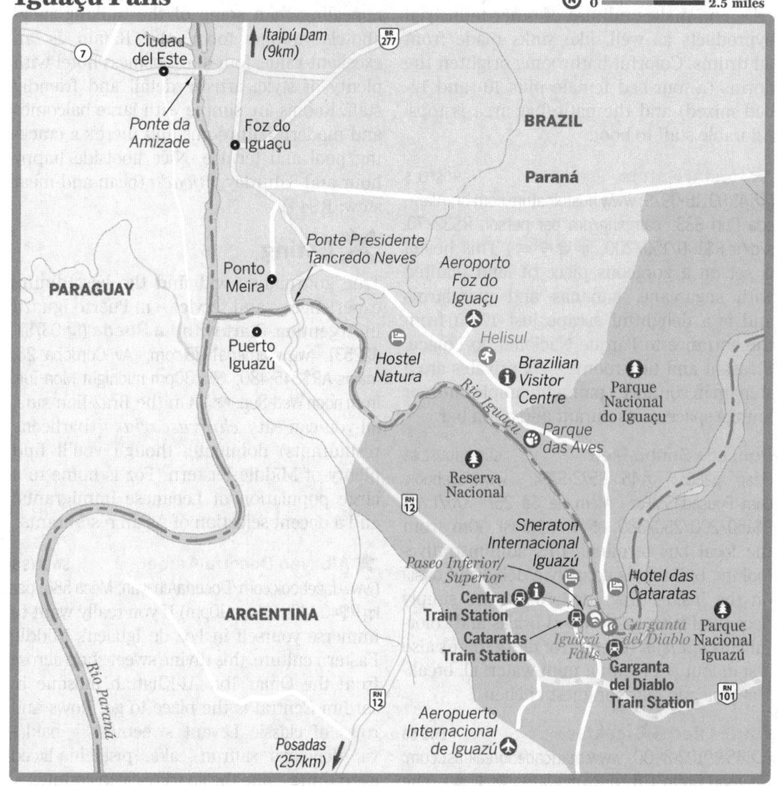

you'll want the 10am, 11am, noon or 1pm to make it happen) and transfer to the local bus to the falls. Be sure to be on a bus back to Brazil by 6pm.

Hotels and agencies in Foz do Iguaçu offer tours to the Argentine park for around R$50 to R$120 (transport only). You'll save a bit of cash and a few hours if you opt to go independently.

Aguaray Eco Esportes OUTDOORS
(☎45 99158-8826; www.aguaray.com.br; Alameda Caete s/n; R$150) Arranges a recommended three-hour excursion on the Rio Iguaçu that involves a nature hike, kayak or stand-up paddleboard, and visits to waterfalls.

Helisul HELICOPTER TOURS
(☎45 3529-7327; www.helisulfoz.com.br; Rodovia das Cataratas, Km 16.5; 10min flights R$430; ⏲9am-5pm) Not far from the Parque Nacional do Iguaçu entrance, this helicopter-tour specialist has been running chopper flights at 450m over the Brazilian side of the falls for 40 years now. The 10-minute flights carry four or seven people depending on the bird; longer 30-minute flights are priced per helicopter (R$3913 for four people).

Sleeping

Foz is a rather dull city as far as hotel options go, though it's jam-packed with run-of-the-mill midrange chains and certainly has its fair share of hostels. Av das Cataratas on the way to the falls is lined with convention-style hotels. Don't be shy about trying to negotiate a lower price if the hotel is not full. Foz hotels charge a R$2.50 per person per night optional tourism tax.

★**Tetris Container Hostel** HOSTEL $
(Map p285; ☎45 3132-0019; www.tetrishostel.com.br; Av das Cataratas 639; dm R$50-65, d from R$140;) Brazil's coolest hostel is crafted from 15 shipping containers – even

the pool is a water-filled shipping container! – and makes full use of other industrial byproducts as well, like sinks made from oil drums. Colorful bathrooms brighten the dorms (a four-bed female plus 10- and 12-bed mixed) and the patio/bar area is tops. Adorable staff to boot.

★ **Hostel Nature** HOSTEL $
(☎ 45 99116-0979; www.hostelnature.com.br; Alameda Buri 333; camping/dm per person R$32/70, s/d/tr R$100/150/200;) This hostel is set on a gorgeous piece of land planted with sugarcane, bananas and mandarins and is a delightful escape just 12km from the entrance to Parque Nacional do Iguaçu. Pleasant and tidy rooms – six privates are a step up in comfort – pair with ample outdoor lounge space, a restaurant and a fun bar.

Pousada Sonho Meu GUESTHOUSE $$
(Map p285; ☎ 45 3573-5764; www.facebook.com/PousadaSMFoz; Mem de Sá 267; s/d/tr/qd R$150/200/250/380;) Just 50m from the local bus terminal, this administrative-looking building is actually a delightful oasis on the inside. Upgraded rooms are simply decorated with rustic wood bricks and colorful faux *azulejos* (decorative tiles); there's also a standout pool with a mini waterfall, breakfast area and outdoor guest kitchen.

Maricá Bed & Breakfast B&B $$
(☎ 45 99102-8900; www.maricabedbreakfast.com; Gregório Dotto 118; d R$153-309;) The friendly innkeeper at this intimate guesthouse runs a one-woman show to the tune of all sorts of traveler accolades. There are four-themed rooms, all colorful and classic, and a spiffy little pool and walled garden. It's a 3.3km walk to the property from Av Jorge Schimmelpfeng. Reservations necessary.

Hotel Del Rey HOTEL $$
(Map p285; ☎ 45 2105-7500; www.hoteldelreyfoz.com.br; Tarobá 1020; s/d R$280/315;) Friendly, spotless and convenient hotel, more intimate than most of the big guns around. The completely modernized rooms are spacious and comfortable, facilities are excellent and the breakfast solid (served from 3am if you give them a head's up). The English-speaking front desk makes up for the skimpy towels. A 10% service tax is added to bills here.

Hotel Rafain Centro HOTEL $$
(Map p285; ☎ 45 3521-3500; www.rafaincentro.com.br; Marechal Deodoro da Fonseca 984; s/d/tr from R$272/320/399;) Much more appealing than some of the hulking megahotels around town, the Rafain is an excellent-value, four-star business hotel with plenty of style, artistic detail and friendly staff. Rooms are simple with large balconies and modern bathrooms and there's a cracking pool and terrace. Nice poolside happy hour and Saturday *feijoada* (bean-and-meat stew; R$44).

Eating

True gourmands will find the best dining experiences – and service – in Puerto Iguazú in Argentina. Start with **La Rueda** (☎ 03757-422531; www.larueda1975.com; Av Córdoba 28; mains AR$245-480; ⏰ 5:30pm-midnight Mon-Tue, from noon Wed-Sun;). On the Brazilian side, all-you-can-eat *churrascarias* (barbecue restaurants) dominate, though you'll find plenty of Middle Eastern (Foz is home to a large population of Lebanese immigrants) and a decent selection of Asian restaurants.

★ **Albayan Doceria Arabe** SWEETS $
(www.facebook.com/DoceriaAlbayan; Meca 586; per kg R$40-140; ⏰ 8am-10pm) If you really want to immerse yourself in Foz de Iguaçu's Middle Eastern culture, this divine sweet shop across from the Omar Ibn Al-Khattab mosque in Jardim Central is the place to go. Rows and rows of classic Levant sweetness – baklava, delicious saffron cake, pistachio-laced everything – line the sparkly-clean counter.

Castelo Libanês MIDDLE EASTERN $
(☎ 45 3526-1218; Vinícius de Moraes 520; mains R$16-60; ⏰ noon-10pm) Foz's Lebanese community is second in size only to São Paulo's; come here to sample the Middle Eastern cuisine. The bakery does great *esfihas* (open-faced or triangular meat pies); other well-done staples include roast chicken, Lebanese *kafta* (beef kebabs), shawarma and hummus.

It's about 2.5km north of TTU to Jardim Central, the city's middle-class Muslim area.

Tropicana CHURRASCARIA $
(Map p285; www.facebook.com/tropicanafoz; Av Juscelino Kubitschek 228; buffet R$35; ⏰ 11am-11pm;) This all-you-can-eat shoestring savior offers absolutely ridiculous taste for money. Expect a madhouse.

★ **Empório com Arte** CAFE $$
(Map p285; Av das Cataratas 569; mains $30-62; ⏰ 3-11pm Tue-Fri, 2-11pm Sat, 2-10pm Sun;) This *mineiro* (from Minas Gerais state)-run highlight of the Foz scene ('scene' used loose-

Foz do Iguaçu

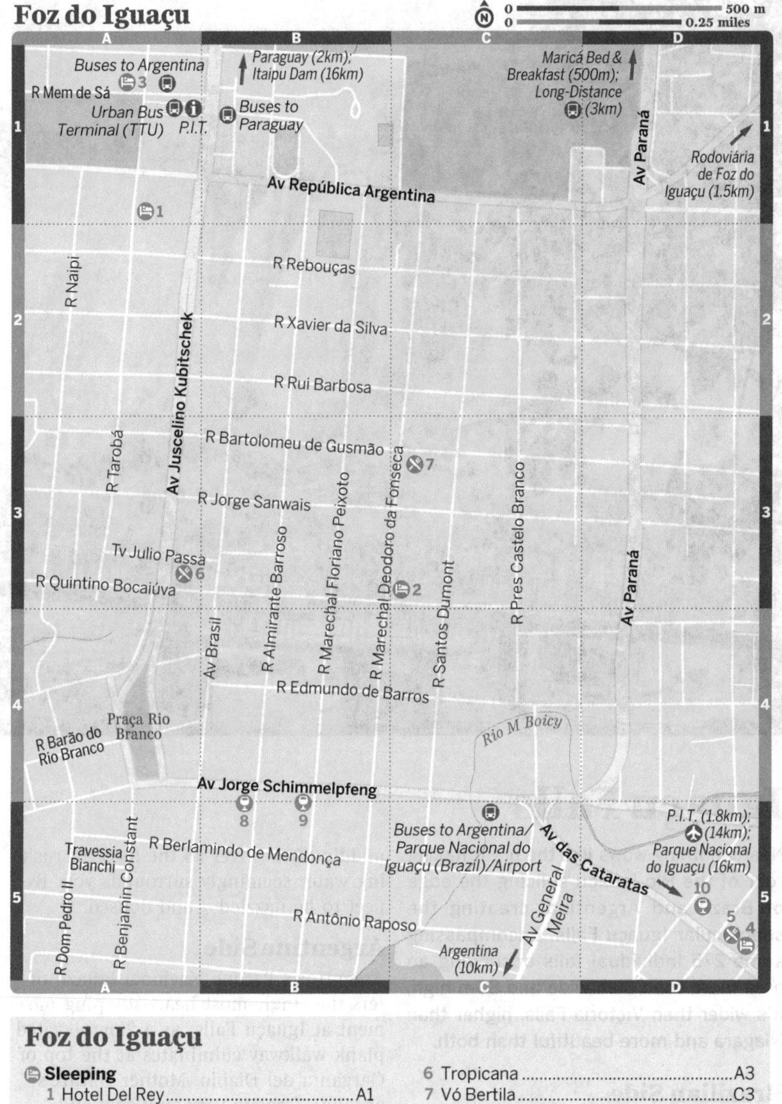

Foz do Iguaçu

Sleeping
1 Hotel Del Rey A1
2 Hotel Rafain Centro C3
3 Pousada Sonho Meu A1
4 Tetris Container Hostel D5

Eating
5 Empório com Arte D5
6 Tropicana A3
7 Vó Bertila C3

Drinking & Nightlife
8 Capitão Bar B5
9 Rafain Chopp B5
10 Zeppelin Old Bar D5

ly) is full of country charm and swarming with town sophisticates gossiping among a potpourri of mostly Minas Gerais art and handicrafts (all for sale). Decent espresso, elaborate mixed-fruit caipirinhas made with local *cachaça,* and a few elaborate main courses (eg duck confit in dark beer reduction) make for rustic-romantic encounters.

Iguaçu Falls

Nearly nothing wows like the breathtaking roar of the Rio Iguaçu splicing the edge of Brazil and Argentina, creating the spectacular Iguaçu Falls. Encompassing some 275 individual falls occupying an area more than 3km wide and 80m high, it's wider than Victoria Falls, higher than Niagara and more beautiful than both.

Brazilian Side

The main event of Parque Nacional do Iguaçu in Brazil is the Trilha das Cataratas, or 'Waterfall Trail.' This 1200m trail follows the shore of the Iguaçu river, providing innumerable photo ops and a grand overview of the falls along the way. It terminates at the bottom of Garganta do Diabo, or 'Devil's Throat,' the most spectacular part of the falls. A walkway allows you to go out to the middle of the river so the force of rushing water seemingly surrounds you. Expect to be dazzled – and doused.

Argentine Side

Argentina's Parque Nacional Iguazú offers the single-most heart-stopping moment at Iguaçu Falls: as a 2km elevated plank walkway culminates at the top of Garganta del Diablo, Mother Nature's absolute ferocity very suddenly and shockingly leaps from the stuff of legend to very real indeed. The sound and the fury is nothing short of electrifying.

Boat Trips

While admiring the falls from above, you will surely spot fearless adventurers experiencing the falls from below. You can get closer to Garganta do Diabo on boat tours on the Argentine side, but

1. Iguaçu Falls (p289), Brazilian side
2. Boat trip under the Falls
3. Toucan, Parque das Aves (p282)

the Brazilian version is more elaborate. Plus Brazilian boats have a backup motor and are Navy-inspected. See Macuco Safari (p290) and Iguazú Jungle Explorer (p291).

Outdoor Adventures

Parque Nacional do Iguaçu covers 550 sq km of rainforest, most of which is inaccessible to anybody but the wildlife. Hiking is more rewarding in the morning, when the weather is cooler and birds and animals are more active. Look for butterflies, parrots, parakeets, woodpeckers, hummingbirds, toucans, lizards and spiders, among more elusive creatures such as monkeys, deer, sloths and anteaters. A worthwhile activity to tack on to your day is a visit to the 5-hectare Parque das Aves, home to 800-plus species of birds, living in 8m-high aviaries that are constructed right in the forest, some of which you can walk through.

Aerial Views

While the Brazilian side gives the grand overview of the falls and Argentina the up-close-and-personal look, no view is quite as memorable as fitting the entire motherlode into one panoramic camera frame. Helisul (p283), next to the entrance to Parque Nacional do Iguaçu, offers 10-minute helicopter tours of the falls for up to four or seven people at a time.

★Vó Bertila PIZZA **$$**
(Map p285; www.facebook.com/vobertila; Bartolomeu de Gusmão 1116; pizza R$27-82, pasta for 2 people R$58-86; ⊙6:30-11:30pm Tue-Sun) This informal, family-run cantina churns out wood-fired pizza – even in personal sizes – and reasonably authentic pasta in heaping portions. This is the kind of down-home Italian spot Brazil does so very well. Don't expect Bologna or Napoli, but expect it to be packed.

Cheff Lopes BRAZILIAN **$$$**
(www.facebook.com/restaurantechefflopes; Av das Cataratas 3570, Shopping Catuaí Palladium; per kg week/weekend R$59.90/76.90; ⊙11am-11pm; 📶) Cheff – two f's! – Lopes churns out the town's best *por-kilo* lunch buffet (weekday/weekend R$46.90/56.90) and, for dinner, a top-end menu loaded with Argentine-cut steak options like *bife do chorizo* and non-farmed local fish like *congrio* and *surubi.* It's somewhat inconveniently located in Foz's shiny new Shopping Catuaí Palladium in Vila Yolanda.

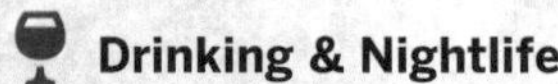

Drinking & Nightlife

Nightlife is hopping along Av Jorge Schimmelpfeng, where you'll find breezy beer gardens, lively outdoor patio bars and hot-to-trot nightclubs that stay open late. Good outdoor drinking dens include **Rafain Chopp** (Map p285; www.facebook.com/rafainchopp; Av Jorge Schimmelpfeng 450; ⊙4pm-2am Mon-Thu, from 2pm Fri-Sun; 📶) and **Capitão Bar** (Map p285; www.capitao.bar; Av Jorge Schimmelpfeng 288; ⊙11:30am-2am; 📶).

★Zeppelin Old Bar LIVE MUSIC
(Map p285; www.facebook.com/ZeppelinFoz; Raul Mattos 222; ⊙7pm-midnight Tue, 9pm-2am Wed-Sat; 📶) Outstanding bar serving up excellent cocktails and live music that spans the gamut from grunge to reggae. The beautiful people congregate from Thursday onwards.

ℹ Information

The region's tourist board has an excellent website, a toll-free English-speaking information line, maps and detailed info about the area. The main office is in **Vila Yolanda** (☎45 3521-8128; www.pmfi.pr.gov.br/turismo; Av das Cataratas 2330, Vila Yolanda; ⊙8am-8pm), out of town on Av das Cataratas toward the falls, reachable on bus 120. Other branches are at the **airport** (☎45 3521-4276; www.pmfi.pr.gov.br/turismo; Hwy BR-469, Km 16.5, Aeroporto Internacional de Foz do Iguaçu/Cataratas; ⊙9am-8:30pm), **long-distance bus station** (☎45 3522-1027; www.pmfi.pr.gov.br/turismo; Av Costa e Silva 1601, Rodoviária Internacional de Foz do Iguaçu; ⊙7am-6pm) and **local bus station** (Map p285; ☎45 3523-7901; www.pmfi.pr.gov.br/turismo; Juscelino Kubitschek 1385, TTU; ⊙7:30am-6pm).

ℹ Getting There & Away

AIR

Daily flights link **Foz do Iguaçu/Cataratas International Airport** (IGU; ☎45 3521-4200; Hwy BR-469, Km 16.5) to Lima and several major Brazilian cities. Sit on the left-hand side of the plane on arrival for good views of the falls.

BUS

The **long-distance bus station** (☎45 3522-2590; Av Costa e Silva 1601) is 4.5km northeast of the center of town. **Central de Passagens** (☎45 99819-0303; www.centraldepassagens.

BUSES FROM FOZ DO IGUAÇU

DESTINATION	STARTING FARE (R$)	DURATION (HR)	COMPANY
Asunción*	59	6½	NSA (www.nsa.com.py)
Buenos Aires**	286	18	Crucero del Norte (www.crucerodelnorte.com.ar)
Campo Grande	114	13	Eucatur (www.eucatur.com.br)
Curitiba	192	10	Catarinense (www.catarinense.net)
Florianópolis	179	16	Catarinense, Nordeste (www.expnordeste.com.br)
Rio de Janeiro	299	24	Catarinense, Nordeste
São Paulo	213	16	Catarinense, Pluma (www.pluma.com.br)

* Departs at 6:30pm (*convencional*) and midnight (*leito*).
** Departs at 10:30am

com; Av Juscelino Kubitschek 526; ⌚8am-7pm Mon-Fri, to 3pm Sat) sells tickets downtown for the same price as the bus companies.

Getting Around

Local bus fare is R$3.55. The local transport terminal, the **Urban Bus Terminal** (TTU; Terminal de Transporte Urbano; Map p285; ☎2105-1385; Av Juscelino Kubitschek 1385), is referred to colloquially as '*terminal*.'

TO/FROM THE AIRPORT

Bus 120 'Aeroporto/Parque Nacional' runs to the airport (R$3.55, 30 minutes) and the Brazilian side of the waterfalls (40 minutes) every 22 to 30 minutes from 5:25am to 12:10am (from 5:10am Sunday). Catch it at the local bus terminal or any stop along Av Juscelino Kubitschek south of Barbosa. Bus 120 'Centro/TTU' goes from the airport to Centro (exit to the far left end and look for the multilingual 'Parada de Ônibus' sign).

Taxis run around R$20 to R$25 to the falls and R$50 to R$60 to Centro (Uber runs around R$7 to R$8 to the falls and R$20 to R$25 to Centro). If you want to dump your bags, there's a self-service luggage deposit at the airport (R$30 for 24 hours).

TO/FROM THE BUS STATION

City buses 105 and 115 (R$3.55) cover the 6km between the long-distance bus station and the local terminal downtown. Taxis cost R$60 to the Brazilian side of the falls, R$50 to the Argentine border and R$20 to the Paraguayan border (though taxis don't like to go any further than Brazilian customs as lines are often too long).

TO/FROM THE FALLS

For the Brazilian side of the falls, catch the 'Aeroporto/P Nacional' bus (R$3.55) to the park entrance. You can catch it in the local bus terminal, or at stops along Av Juscelino Kubitschek and Av Jorge Schimmelpfeng.

To get to the Argentina side, catch a Puerto Iguazú bus (R$5/AR$25, one hour) on **Mem de Sá** across from the local bus terminal or along Av das Cataratas, closer to most hostels. They pass every 30 minutes or so between 7am and 7:15pm (fewer on Sunday). At Puerto Iguazú bus station, **Río Uruguay** (www.riouruguaybus.com.ar) services the falls (A$170 return, 30 minutes) frequently between 7am and 7:40pm.

Alternatively, Río Uruguay (www.riouruguaybus.com.ar) and **Crucero del Norte** (www.crucerodelnorte.com.ar) buses also leave for Puerto Iguazú directly from outside Parque Nacional do Iguaçu between 9am and 5pm (R$10/AR$40, 30 minutes).

> **BE PREPARED**
>
> Remember, it's always wet at the falls, and water attracts sunlight. Pack rain gear and sunblock. Bug repellent is a must on the walking trails. Also note that lighting for photography is best in the morning on the Brazilian side.

Parque Nacional do Iguaçu (Brazil)

Brazil's second-oldest national park, created in 1939, protects one of South America's most magical and majestic sights, Iguaçu Falls, part of the largest waterfall system in the world. The 1200m-long Trilha das Cataratas ('Waterfall Trail') is one of Brazil's best moments – a series of islands cut the river into numerous waterfalls along the path, each sparking one 'wow' moment after another until it all culminates in a magnificent display of Mother Nature's raw power at Garganta do Diabo ('Devil's Throat').

You can't miss the shiny entrance to the **Parque Nacional do Iguaçu** (☎45 3521-4400; www.cataratasdoiguacu.com.br; Hwy BR-469, Km 18; adult foreigners/Mercosur/Brazilians R$62/49/36, child R$10; ⌚9am-5pm), which houses bathrooms, ATMs, lockers, souvenir shops, left-luggage facilities and a vast parking lot (R$22). You can purchase your ticket in advance on the website and pick it up in the preferential line at the ticket windows, or buy from on-site machines (if you have a chip-and-pin card). Once ticketed, you will be directed to board a free double-decker bus, which departs every 10 minutes.

In addition to the main event, the park and its environs offers trails, boat trips, whitewater rafting and other nature-focused adventures – as well as coati galore (devious but adorable food-begging mammals related to raccoons – don't feed them!).

Sights

★Cataratas do Iguaçu WATERFALL
(www.cataratasdoiguacu.com.br; Parque Nacional do Iguaçu) Once you're in the park and ready to visit the falls, take the Parque Nacional do Iguaçu bus to the third stop at Belmond Hotel das Cataratas. Here you can pick up the main waterfall observation trail, Trilha das Cataratas ('Waterfall Trail'), a 1200m trail following the shore of the Iguaçu River, terminating at the Garganta do Diabo.

It's a 1.5km walk down a paved trail with brilliant views of the falls on the Argentine side, the jungle and the river below. Every twist of the path reveals a more splendid view until the trail ends right under the majestic Salto Floriano, which will give you a healthy sprinkling of water via the wind it generates. A catwalk leads out to a platform with majestic vistas, with the Garganta do Diabo close at hand, and a perspective down the river in the other direction. If the water's high, it's unforgettable; a rainbow is visible in the spray on clear afternoons.

An elevator heads up to a viewing platform at the top of the falls at Porto Canoas, the last stop of the double-decker buses. Porto Canoas has a gift shop, a couple of snack bars and an excellent buffet restaurant.

Activities & Tours

Boat Trips

Boats from both sides of the border take adventurous passengers under the falls.

Macuco Safari (☎45 3529-6262; www.macucosafari.com.br; Av das Cataratas, Km 25, Parque Nacional do Iguaçu; boat trip R$215, excursions R$61-515) offers the Brazilian side's spectacular opportunity to get up close, personal and wet at the base of the falls. The excursion starts with a 3km ride through the jungle, with an English-speaking guide pointing out the park's flora and fauna. The second phase is a short hike (600m) to a small waterfall called Salto de Macuco (no swimming allowed). Finally, climb aboard a Zodiac for a 4km journey over flat water and rapids, culminating with a trip under the falls known as the Three Musketeers. You *will* get soaked (unless you opt for the dry boat). The boat ride is 30 minutes, but the whole excursion takes about two hours. Buy a protective camera/phone sleeve if you want your own photos! To reach Macuco, get off the double-decker bus at the second stop.

CROSSING TO ARGENTINA AND PARAGUAY

Many nationalities can enter Argentina without a visa, but double-check before you arrive or at the **Argentine Consulate** (☎45 3574-2969; http://cfdig.cancilleria.gov.ar; Travessia Bianchi 26, Foz do Iguaçu; ⏲10am-3pm Mon-Fri). Argentina had suspended the reciprocity fee that previously saddled Americans, Australians and Canadians with a hefty bill to cross into the country at time of writing, but it's always best to check ahead.

For Paraguay, Americans ($160), Australians ($135) and Canadians ($150) need a visa – though not unless you go beyond Ciudad del Este. Get this in advance at home or from the **Paraguayan Consulate** (☎45 3523-2898; fozconsulpar@mre.gov.py; Marechal Deodoro da Fonseca 901; ⏲9am-1pm Mon-Fri) in Foz.

To Puerto Iguazú, Argentina If traveling by bus, at Brazilian immigration in either direction, most bus drivers won't wait around while you finish formalities. Officially, you should get a pass from the driver, get your passport stamped, then wait and reboard the next bus *from the same bus company*. The reality is that some wait, some don't; some give you a pass, some don't (most folks just pay again, rather than wait out the hour for the same company to come through again).

It's important you pay attention as drivers may or may not ask if anyone needs to stop at immigration on the Brazilian side – but in Portuguese (or Spanish). Many travelers miss it and end up with serious immigration hassles later (ie hefty fines).

At Argentine immigration, the bus always stops and usually waits for everyone to be processed. Both borders are open 24 hours but bus service ends around 7:15pm. The last bus you can catch is the second-to-last bus back to Brazil (around 6:45pm); if you don't, there will be no bus coming after yours to scoop you up after you finish with border formalities.

To Ciudad del Este, Paraguay To get to the border, take a bus (R$5.50/10,000G, 30 minutes, 6am to 6pm) from Av Juscelino Kubitschek across from TTU (p289), or any bus inside TTU signed 'Ponte da Amizade' (101, 102, 103 etc), which pass by Ponte da Amizade ('Friendship Bridge'), or a taxi – buses also leave regularly from the bus station (p288). At the border, get your passport stamped, then catch the next bus or taxi to Ciudad del Este, or walk across the Ponte da Amizade. If traveling further into Paraguay, you'll need to complete formalities with Brazil's **Polícia Federal** (www.pf.gov.br; Hwy BR-277; ⏲24hr) and the Paraguayan immigration authorities at the consulate.

Hiking

Trilha do Poço Preto HIKING, BOAT

(☎45 3574-4244; www.macucosafari.com.br; Av das Cataratas, Km 25, Parque Nacional do Iguaçu; R$150) A 9km guided hike (get off the bus at the first stop) through the jungle on foot, by bike or on an electric cart. The trail ends at Taquara Island, where you can kayak or take a boat cruise to Porto Canoas. You can also return via the Bananeiras Trail.

Trilha das Bananeiras WALKING

(☎45 3574-4244; www.macucosafari.com.br; Av das Cataratas, Km 25, Parque Nacional do Iguaçu; incl boat ride R$216) The Bananeiras Trail is a 1.5km walk passing lagoons and observing aquatic wildlife, ending at a jetty where you can take boat rides or silent floating excursions in kayaks down to Porto Canoas. If you plan to do any of these, chat with one of the agents touting them around the park visitor center; they can get you a discount.

Sleeping & Eating

★Belmond Hotel das Cataratas HOTEL $$$

(☎45 2102-7000; www.belmond.com; Hwy BR-469, Km 32; r with/without view from R$1679/1079, ste with view from R$2279;) You'll find spectacular views from the Sheraton on the Argentine side, but nowhere on either side of the falls is as delightful, delicious and deluxe as this 193-room, pink-as-peppercorns Belmond luxury hotel. The edifice is located within Parque Nacional do Iguaçu, just across from the main trail to the falls.

The coup of staying here is access to the park after hours, which includes the Trilha das Cataratas – the waterfall is your oyster! There's a spa, fitness center and the classiest restaurant in the region by an incalculable margin. The dinner-only Itaipu (mains R$71 to R$126) serves fine-dining rarities in these parts like rabbit, lobster tail and *pirarucu*, a farm-controlled Amazonian fish; nonguests are welcome for dinner with reservations. There's a classic bar with American-style jazz and, if you're not tired of getting wet, the pool ain't too shabby either.

Restaurante Porto Canoas BUFFET $$

(www.cataratasdoiguacu.com.br; Parque Nacional do Iguaçu; buffet R$59.90; ⊙noon-4pm) After the falls, you (and your camera-trigger finger) deserve a break. This spot has a long pleasant terrace overlooking the river just before it descends into the maelstrom – a great spot for a beer – and a good buffet lunch with plenty of salads and hot dishes.

Parque Nacional Iguazú (Argentina)

Parque Nacional Iguazú (☎03757-491469; www.iguazuargentina.com; adult foreigners/Mercosur/Argentines AR$600/480/310, child AR$150/120/100; ⊙8am-6pm) has plenty to offer, and involves a fair amount of walking. The spread-out complex at the entrance has various amenities, including lockers, a couple of ATMs and a restaurant. The complex ends at a train station, where a train runs every half hour to the Cataratas train station, where the Circuito Inferior and Circuito Superior waterfall walks begin; the last stop is for the elevated walkway to the spectacular **Garganta del Diablo**.

Activities

Boating

Iguazú Jungle Explorer (☎03757-421696; www.iguazujungle.com) offers three adventure tours for those 12 years of age and up. Most popular is the short boat trip leaving from the Paseo Inferior that takes you right under one of the waterfalls for a high-adrenalin soaking (AR$550). The Gran Aventura (AR$950) combines this with a jungle drive, while the Paseo Ecológico (AR$300) is a wildlife-oriented tour in inflatable boats upstream from the falls.

Protective bags are provided for cameras and other gear; anything not contained therein – including you – will get wet.

Hiking

Sendero Macuco WALKING

This 3.5km jungle trail leads through dense forest to a nearly hidden waterfall. It's a rare opportunity to explore the park independently. Six interpretive stations explain the flora, including bamboo, palmitos and pioneer plants. The white-bearded manakin and toco toucan live in these parts, as does a troupe of brown capuchin monkeys.

The trail ends at the **Arrechea waterfall**, a 20m cascade that has gouged out a lovely natural pool below. The first 3km to the top of the waterfall is almost completely level, but there is a steep, muddy drop to the base of the falls and beyond to the Río Iguazú, about 650m in all. Figure on about 1¼ hours each way from the trailhead.

You can swim at the base of the waterfall but take care and don't head out into the river. Early morning is best, with better opportunities to see wildlife. Last entry is at 3pm. There's a map-guide available at the information desks.

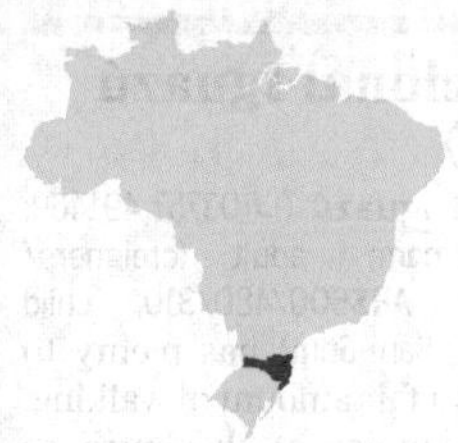

Santa Catarina

Includes ➡

Ilha de Santa Catarina 293
Florianópolis 295
North Island 298
East Coast 300
South Island 302
The Mainland 304
Joinville 304
Blumenau 306
North of Florianópolis 310
South of Florianópolis 312

Best Places to Eat

- ➡ Ostradamus (p303)
- ➡ Urucum (p313)
- ➡ Restaurante Lagoa Azul (p302)
- ➡ Dolce Vita (p302)

Best Places to Stay

- ➡ Janela de Márcia (p301)
- ➡ Pousada Naturezas de Floripa (p303)
- ➡ Pousada Verde Natur (p303)
- ➡ Quinta do Bucanero (p313)

Why Go?

Life's a beach – at least in sunny Santa Catarina, which has 560km of spectacular coastline. If you like your beach deserted, there is a spot of sand for you in the south of Ilha de Santa Catarina. If you prefer a party scene, head further north on that same island. If you're all about big surf, it's up in Guarda do Embaú and Praia do Rosa, two absolutely stunning surf villages south of Florianópolis.

Sun and sand aside, the inland regions are also where Santa Catarina exhibits the profound influence of its German ancestry, most evident during Oktoberfest, Blumenau's huge festival for folk dancing, accordion playing and beer drinking – well, mostly beer drinking. But the Alpine architecture and fresh-brewed beer are here to enjoy year-round.

When to Go

Florianópolis

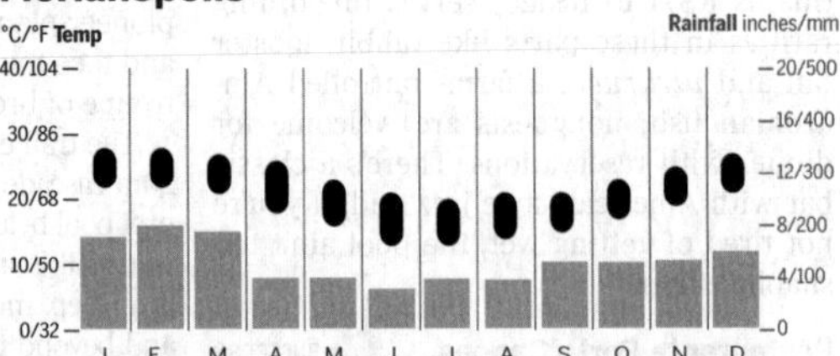

Jan, Feb & Oct Whether Sommerfest or Oktoberfest, Blumenau is awash in beer and brats.

Mar & Apr Post-Carnaval, the sun still shines in Florianópolis.

Jun & Jul Join the Brazilian celebration of winter kitsch in Santa Catarina's Serra Geral.

History

In the 1820s, a newly independent Brazil realized the strategic importance of this region on the frontier between the Spanish and Portuguese Americas. The emperor invited German-speaking immigrants to develop the land and serve as a buffer against Spanish insurgency. The German immigrants – and the Italians who followed – never adopted the plantation culture of the Northeast. Instead, the economy was based on small family-owned farms, a legacy that lives on in the region's egalitarian politics and equitable distribution of income.

Getting There & Around

Florianópolis is the state's transportation hub, with direct bus and air services to every major city in Brazil from **Terminal Rodoviário Rita Maria** (48 3212-3508; Av Paulo Fontes 1101) and Floripa Airport (p297), respectively. Joinville also has direct air services from Joinville-Lauro Carneiro de Loyola Airport (p305) to São Paulo, with connections to other major cities. Most destinations within Santa Catarina are accessible from Florianópolis by bus; services are extensive and dependable.

ILHA DE SANTA CATARINA

Ilha de Santa Catarina has a vibrant and varied coastline, from the calm, crowded bays of the north, to the wild, cliff-hugging beaches south. But it's not just the beaches that make this island so enchanting. A forest of protected pines shelters the east coast, while the dunes near Praia da Joaquina create a lunar landscape. The spine of mountains,

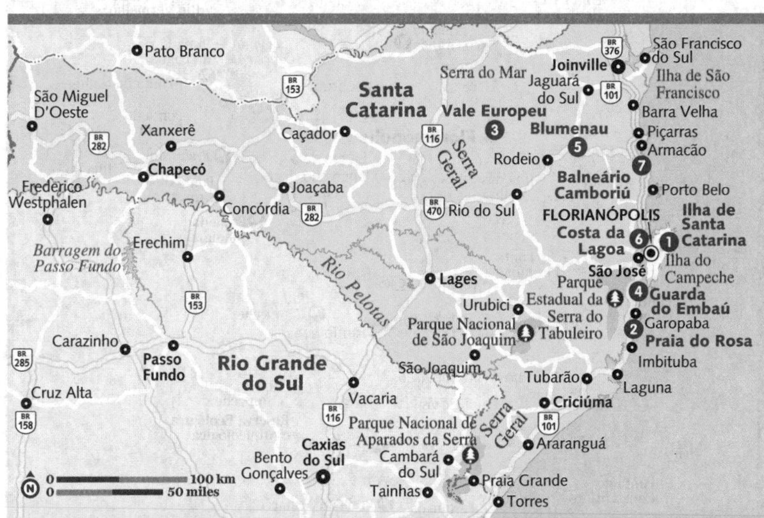

Santa Catarina Highlights

1. **Ilha de Santa Catarina** (p293) Sunning, surfing and beach-hopping around the wild sands of beautiful Florianópolis.
2. **Praia do Rosa** (p312) Sucking up the sophisticated surfer atmosphere at southern Brazil's most stunning beach.
3. **Vale Europeu** (p310) Drinking your way through the rich beer culture in the Vale Europeu.
4. **Guarda do Embaú** (p312) Joining the parade of surfers and sun worshippers wading through the Rio da Madre.
5. **Blumenau** (p306) Saying *Prost!* to the world's second-largest Oktoberfest in this German-spun city.
6. **Costa da Lagoa** (p302) Losing a day gorging on fresh seafood at the waterfront in Ilha de Santa Catarina.
7. **Balneário Camboriú** (p310) Beach-hopping via the fun-packed Parque Unipraias in Santa Catarina's mini-Rio.

Ilha de Santa Catarina

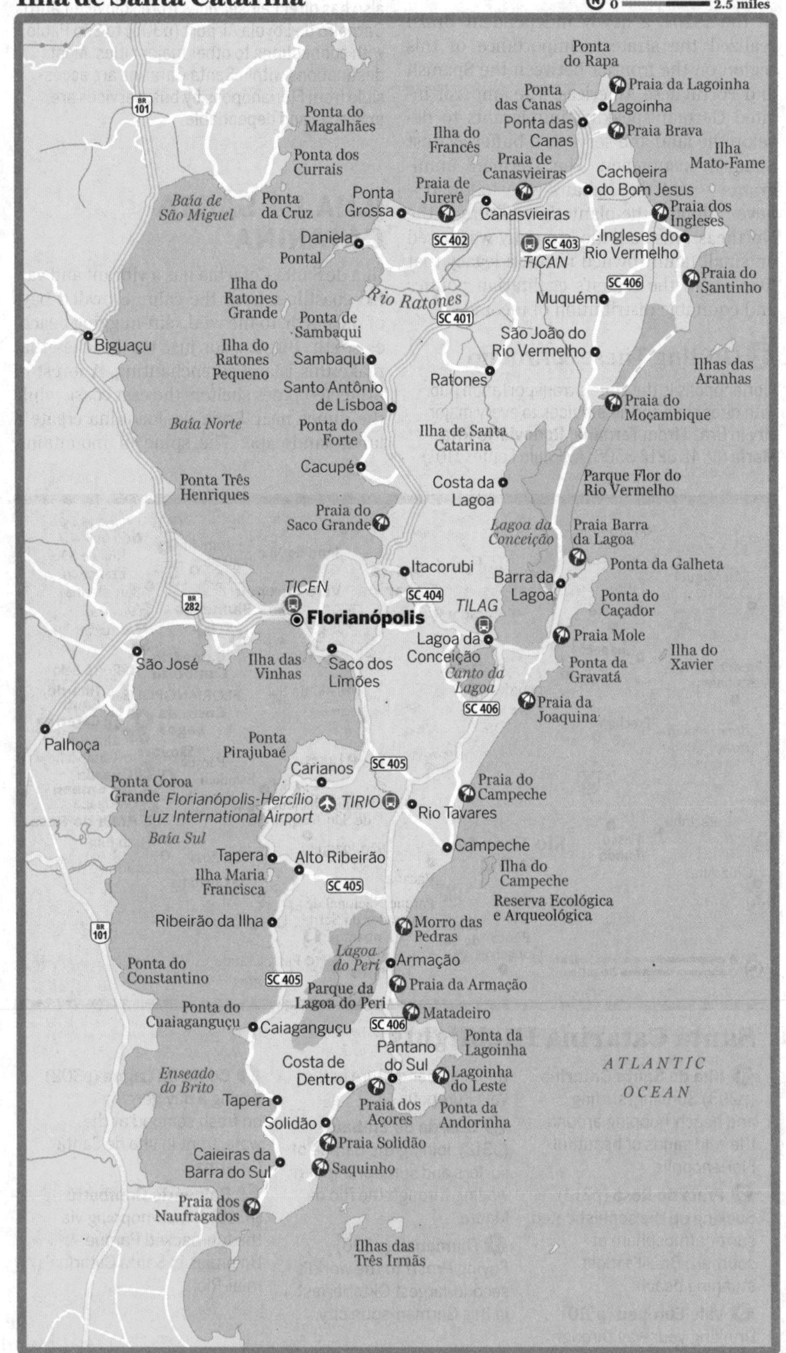

luxuriant with the Mata Atlântica (Atlantic rainforest), drops precipitously down to the lovely Lagoa da Conceição.

Though technically speaking, the whole island is Florianópolis, it's downtown Floripa, known as Centro, that is both the political capital of Santa Catarina, the cultural capital of southern Brazil and the gateway to the rest of the island. The island's *bairros* (districts) can feel like completely different towns, with their own distinct personalities and infrastructure.

Florianópolis

0XX48 / POP 421,000

There are two faces to Florianópolis (Floripa). On the mainland, the industrial zone occupies the districts of Estreito and Coqueiros. Across the bay, the island holds the historic center (Centro) and the chic district of Beira-Mar Norte. Two picturesque bridges link these halves. The old suspension bridge, the Ponte Hercílio Luz, is no longer open to traffic, but it still lights the night sky, acting as the defining feature of Floripa's spectacular skyline.

Sights

The center of town is the inviting **Praça XV de Novembro** (Praça XV de Novembro), with its shady walks and nearly 150-year-old fig tree.

★Museu Histórico de Santa Catarina MUSEUM
(Palácio Cruz e Sousa; 48 3028-8091; www.mhsc.sc.gov.br; Praça XV de Novembro 227; R$5; 10am-6pm Tue-Fri, to 4pm Sat & Sun) Formerly the colonial governor's palace, this gorgeous must-see building has ornate parquet floors and extravagant 19th-century ceilings. The entrance is off Rua Trajano.

Mercado Público MARKET
(www.mercadopublicofloripa.com.br; Jerônimo Coelho 60; restaurants 10am-1pm Mon-Fri, to 5pm Sat & Sun) Floripa's historic public market bolted out of a huge refurbishment in 2015 with an improved look. It houses numerous bars and restaurants in addition to a wealth of shops; the festive food court is a superb spot for a drink and meal – try **Vai Quem Quer** (www.facebook.com/botecovaiquemquer; Jerônimo Coelho 60, box 2; mains R$26-55; 11am-10pm Mon-Fri, to 6pm Sat;).

Sleeping & Eating

Le Flâneur Hostel HOSTEL $
(48 3733-7551; www.leflaneur.com.br; Delminda Silveira 815; dm R$60-80;) Don't let the Agronômica location between a Petrobras gas station and a prison deter you, this cycling-themed hostel is well run, well appointed and well positioned for quick access to Lagoa de Conceicão and the North Island. Dorms come in two-, four- and eight-bed configurations, some with living rooms, huge bathrooms and a hammock (mixed) or bathtubs (female). Hangout spaces are artsy and spacious.

★Central BUFFET $
(www.centralrestaurante.com.br; Vidal Ramos 174; per kg weekday R$59.90; 10:50am-3pm Mon-Fri;) This outstanding, award-winning *por-kilo* buffet concentrates on a more subtle selection of daily dishes, all focused on high-quality, home-cooked goodness. Lines out the door are not uncommon. The **Esteves Junior** (Esteves Junior 242; per kg weekday/weekend R$59.90/69.90; 11am-3pm Mon-Sat) branch is open on Saturday.

O Padeiro de Sevilha BAKERY $
(www.opadeirodesevilha.com.br; Esteves Júnior 2144; items R$1.50-6.50, bread per kg R$12.65-36; 6:50am-8:30pm Mon-Fri, 7am-2pm Sat;) Considered one of the top 30 bakeries in Brazil, this social magnet features an 11m-long communal table flanked by a self-serve cornucopia of fresh-baked artisanal breads and both savory and sweet treats selected from some 200 recipes.

★Rita Maria Lagosteria SEAFOOD $$$
(48 4009-2442; Henrique Valgas 318; mains R$80-121; 11:30am-11:30pm;) Occupying one of Florianópolis' first colonial homes and the former abode of the faith healer Rita Maria, this crotchety old maritime-themed restaurant specializes in crustaceans, *moquecas* (seafood stews) and seafood rices. Local chef Narbal Corrêa does wonders with fat, juicy shrimp, lobster and octopus, despite the overeager historical promotion.

★Black Sheep JAPANESE $$$
(48 99189-9015; www.theroof.com.br; Majestic Palace Hotel, Av Beira Mar 2746; omakase R$149, rolls R$17-49; 7:30pm-midnight Wed-Sat;) Korean-Japazilian chef Emerson Kim and his Latvian wife honed their skills at Nobu

Florianópolis

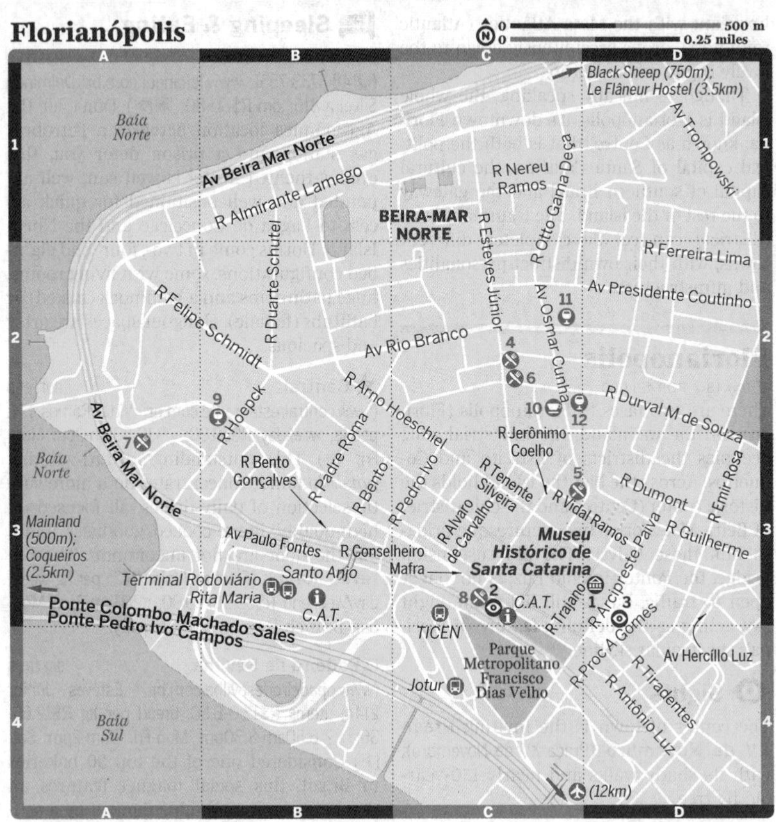

Florianópolis

Top Sights
1 Museu Histórico de Santa Catarina D3

Sights
2 Mercado Público C3
3 Praça XV de Novembro D3

Eating
4 Central C2
5 Central C3
6 O Padeiro de Sevilha C2
7 Rita Maria Lagosteria A3
8 Vai Quem Quer C3

Drinking & Nightlife
9 1007 Floripa B2
10 Arbor Café C2
11 Concorde Club C2
12 Jivago Social Club C2

(yes, *that* Nobu). You will find a grand total of zero items with cream cheese, but perhaps more surprising are the shockingly fair prices. The R$125 *omakase* (chef's menu) is not only extraordinary, it's extraordinary value.

It's tucked away on the Roof, a sleek nightclub atop one of Floripa's most upscale hotels. Reservations essential.

Drinking & Nightlife

★Cervejaria Cozalinda MICROBREWERY
(www.facebook.com/cozabar; Pedro Silva 2406, Coqueiros; 7-11.30pm Mon-Thu, to 1am Fri & Sat;) True to its name, Cozalinda (a play on *coisa linda,* a beautiful thing) is a cozy and colorful Coqueiros brewery. You'll find 20 taps, most of which are dedicated to experimental sours and lambics, some of which have been barrel aged in Brazilian woods like *ipê* and sassafras.

★ Arbor Café COFFEE

(www.arbor.cafe; Av Osmar Cunha 251; ⏲8am-7pm Mon-Fri; 📶) If any evidence was needed that the Brazilian coffee scene has changed (outside of São Paulo, that is), look no further than the adorable to-go espresso cups at this fair-trade cafe in Centro. Plenty of pour-over options are available, in addition to serious espresso (R$5) pulled from top producers like Pereira Villela (Minas Gerais) and Fazenda Vargem Grande (São Paulo).

Boteco Zé Mané BOTECO

(www.facebook.com/botecozemane; Desembargador Pedro Silva 2360, Coqueiros; ⏲6pm-midnight Sun-Thu, to 1:30am Fri & Sat; 📶) It's worth the trek to the mainland for this fantastic *boteco* (bar) along the Via Gastrônomica in Coqueiros. Jazzed-up caipirinhas (R$21) – like bergamot with passion fruit or *jabuticaba* (a grape-like fruit) with basil – fuel the raging scene here in a revamped colonial house overlooking the waterfront. It's especially great when they have a *feijoada* (bean and meat stew) with samba (R$50).

Information

C.A.T (Centro de Atendimento ao Turista; ☎48 3228-1095; www.vivendofloripa.com.br; Rodoviária; ⏲8am-6pm); **Airport** (Centro de Atendimento ao Turista; ☎48 3337-5040; www.santur.sc.gov.br; Florianópolis-Hercílio Luz International Airport; ⏲7am-midnight); **Mercado Público** (Centro de Atendimento ao Turista; ☎48 3240-4407; www.vivendofloripa.com.br; Conselheiro Mafra 255, Mercado Público; ⏲9am-6pm Mon-Fri, to noon Sat)

Getting There & Away

AIR

Daily flights from the rebranded **Floripa Airport** (Florianópolis-Hercílio Luz International Airport; ☎48 3331-4000; www.floripa-airport.com/contato.html; Rod Deputado Diomício Freitas 3393, Bairro Carianos), 12km south of Centro, serve Buenos Aires, Brasília, Campinas, Porto Alegre, Rio de Janeiro and São Paulo, among other cities, depending on the season. A remodeled airport and new terminal is expected to be operational by the end of 2019.

To reach the airport, bus 183 'Corredor Sudoeste' (35 minutes) and 186 'Corredor Sudoeste Semi-Direto' (25 minutes) leave from TICEN (p298) terminal frequently between 5am and 12:30am. Uber fares are around R$18 or so to Centro, R$26 or so to Lagoa da Conceicão and R$36 or so to Barra da Lagoa.

BUS

The long-distance bus station (p293) lies a few blocks west of the Praça XV de Novembro. Buses link Florianópolis with every major city in southern Brazil. There are buses to Asuncion daily at 4pm, Buenos Aires daily at 10:30am and Santiago Monday at 12:30pm. For Montevideo, buses depart at 11am on Saturday.

Getting Around

The city is a convenient transportation hub, with all of the island's 42 beaches within an hour's drive.

TO/FROM THE AIRPORT

To reach the airport, bus 183 'Corredor Sudoeste' (35 minutes) and 186 'Corredor Sudoeste Semi-Direto' (25 minutes) leave from TICEN terminal frequently between 5am and 12:30am. Uber fares are around R$18 or so to

BUSES FROM FLORIANÓPOLIS

DESTINATION	STARTING FARE (R$)	TIME (HR)	BUS COMPANY
Asunción (Paraguay)	104	22	Nordeste (www.expnordeste.com.br)
Blumenau	53	3	Catarinense (www.catarinense.net)
Buenos Aires (Argentina)	458	25	JBL (www.jblturismo.com.br)
Curitiba	51	5	Catarinense
Foz do Iguaçu	179	14	Catarinense
Garopaba	27	2	Santo Anjo (www.santoanjo.com.br)
Joinville	63	2½	Catarinense
Montevideo (Uruguay)	350	18	EGA (www.ega.com.uy)
Porto Alegre	115	6	Eucatur (www.eucatur.com.br)
Rio de Janeiro	214	17	Itapemirim (www.itapemirim.com.br)
Santiago (Chile)	440	44	BL (www.jblturismo.com.br)
São Paulo	122	12	Catarinense

GAY FLORIPA

Floripa is Brazil's second gay capital – everything is gay-friendly. As one local put it, 'The whole island is very, very gay – even the country bars draw big numbers of gays!' Its Pride celebration, **Parada da Diversidade** (www.facebook.com/floripadiversidade; Av Beira-Mar Continental; ⏲Sep), has grown into one of Brazil's biggest and draws over 100,000 revelers annually. Check out Guia Gay Floripa (www.guiagayfloripa.com.br). Popular GLS (Gays, Lesbians and Sympathetics) hot spots of the moment include **Jivago Social Club** (☎48 3028-0788; www.jivagosocialclub.com; Leoberto Leal 4; ⏲11pm-5am Fri & Sat) and, skewing younger, **1007 Floripa** (☎48 3204-6175; www.1007brasil.com; Alameda Adolfo Konder 1007). And, of course, the trashier **Concorde Club** (☎48 3024-4969; www.conca.com.br; Av Rio Branco 729; ⏲midnight-8am Sat) remains a hardcore standby. In summer, **Bar do Deca** (www.bardodeca.com.br; Praia Mole; ⏲9am-midnight Dec-Feb, 10am-8pm Thu-Tue Mar-Nov; 📶) at Praia Mole is teeming with beautiful people.

For LGBTQ travel adventures (surfing, trekking etc) around Florianópolis and the Santa Catarina coast, **Brazil Ecojourneys** (☎48 99111-6366; www.brazilecojourneys.com) runs highly recommended trips and an annual surf camp.

Centro, R$26 or so to Lagoa da Conceicão and R$36 or so to Barra da Lagoa.

BUS

Local buses run on an integrated scheme called SIM – *Sistema Integrado de Mobilidade*. Buses leave from the **TICEN** (Terminal de Integração Centro; www.consorciofenix.com.br; Av Paulo Fontes s/n) terminal, one block east of Florianópolis' long-distance bus station. Connections to the island's beaches are made via three outlying terminals: **TIRIO** (Terminal Rio Tavares; www.consorciofenix.com.br; SC-405 630; Rio Tavares Terminal), **TILAG** (Terminal Lagoa da Conceição; www.consorciofenix.com.br; Av Afonso Delambert Neto 51) (Lagoa da Conceição Terminal) and **TICAN** (Terminal Canasvieiras; www.consorciofenix.com.br; Francisco Faustino Martins 877; Canasvieiras Terminal).

A single fare of R$4.20 (paid at the TICEN ticket booth) covers your initial ride plus one transfer. **Floripanoponto** (www.floripanoponto.com.br) is a handy trip planner. It's available both online and as an app (Android/iOS).

CAR

You won't regret renting a car for easier exploration of the island's beaches. **Inova** (☎48 3225-7779; www.alugueinova.com.br; Silva Jardim 495; ⏲7:30am-7pm) is a dependable local option. Beware that traffic can be exasperating on weekends.

North Island

Ilha de Santa Catarina's northern outposts are far more developed than other parts of the island – this is the land of midrise condominiums and apart-hotels, with many of the neighborhoods feeling like small cities in direct contrast to the village atmosphere that mostly prevails elsewhere. That's not to say there are no redeeming qualities here – beautiful beaches like Praia do Santinho and Praia dos Ingleses maintain a slow and easy quality, while those looking to get their groove on should head to tony Jurerê Internacional, home to world-renowned nightclubs that cater to the rich and famous until sunrise. Santo Antônio de Lisboa is the odd one out, maintaining an atmosphere painted with an Azorean brush, and is a wonderful spot for a meal and a wander.

ℹ Getting There & Away

For Canasvieiras and northern beaches, catch bus 210 'Canasvieiras Direto' (Platform B) from TICEN to TICAN. Also from TICAN, bus 266 serves Praia da Lagoinha, Praia Brava, Praia dos Ingleses and Praia do Santinho; bus 271 serves Jurerê and Jurerê Internacional.

Santo Antônio de Lisboa

On the west coast, Santo Antônio de Lisboa is among the oldest communities on the island. An old-fashioned, fishing-village atmosphere is complemented by cobblestone streets and Azorean architecture. The most prominent edifice is the Igreja da NS da Necessidade, dating from 1750. The district has become an island reference for fresh seafood; the Centro skyline views between the masts of moored sailboats certainly makes for a pretty setting for a bite.

Eating

Marisqueira Sintra SEAFOOD $$

(☎48 3234-4219; www.marisqueirasintra.com.br; XV de Novembro 147; mains R$54-84; ⏰noon-3pm & 7:30-11:30pm Mon & Wed-Fri, noon-4pm & 7:30-11:30pm Sun) The favored Marisqueira Sintra does wonderful things with octopus and *bacalhau* (salted cod) in a postcard waterfront setting.

Canasvieiras, Jurerê & Jurerê Internacional

The island's northwest corner is home to *Pleasantville*-esque Jurerê Internacional, one of the most privileged residential neighborhoods in all of southern Brazil. More subdued Jurerê (Traditional) sits just west, with one long 3.2km strand of sand flanking the two.

Canasvieiras, 4km east of Jurerê, is not the most attractive place on the island, but it has easy access to water-sport hub Praia de Canasvieiras; you'll likely change buses here at some point.

Sleeping & Eating

Pousada dos Sonhos POUSADA $$$

(☎48 3282-1002; www.pousadadossonhos.com.br; Haroldo Calado 25, Jurerê; d R$519-719, ste R$1099; ❄📶🏊) Teetering between the charm of a small pousada and the services of a beach hotel, this 22-room choice has an English-speaking reception and spacious rooms, all with kitchenettes, indoor BBQs and at least a partial sea view.

Toca de Jurerê SEAFOOD $$$

(☎48 3282-0795; www.tocadejurere.com.br; Acácio Melo 78, Jurerê; mains R$84-251; ⏰11am-4pm & 7-11pm Tue-Sat, 11am-4pm Sun; 📶) Tucked down a dead-end lane behind the beach, Toca de Jurerê is a dependable seafood stop that appears expensive at first glance; that is, until you realize even the half-portion sizes feed two! There's an exhaustive list of fish preparations, *moquecas* and *caldeiradas* (seafood stews, with a vegan option), plus shrimp, lobster, *bacalhau* (salted cod) and squid dishes.

Praia da Lagoinha & Praia Brava

The northeastern tip of the island is a slender peninsula, accessed by slow-moving roads that wind around the hills to the beach. These towns are ritzier than their neighbors, though the beaches are still overbuilt. Praia da Lagoinha is a crescent-shaped patch of sand, surrounded on three sides by rocky cliffs that keep the water calm. Here you'll still find a traditional fishing colony slinging nets into the sea and a colorful armada of simple fishing boats moored on the beach's eastern end near the mouth of the small river.

Praia Brava, 3km southeast of Lagoinha, attracts surfers and a privileged, easy-on-the-eyes crowd in summer, many of whom tumble out of the upscale condominiums that face the sands some 400m back from the beach.

Sleeping & Eating

Villabella Villaggio POUSADA $$$

(☎48 3284-2017; www.villabellavillaggio.com.br; Av Epitácio Bittencourt 470, Praia Brava; d/chalet from R$350; ⏰closed Jun-Sep; ❄@📶🏊) Santa Catarina's Italian heritage is lovingly showcased in the design and decor at the luxurious Villabella Villaggio. Every guest room has an expansive view toward either Praia da Lagoinha or Praia Brava, and the dark hardwood chalets (some fashioned from reforested eucalyptus) are dressed up in sophisticated country decor.

Pousada da Vigia POUSADA $$$

(☎48 3284-1789; www.pousadadavigia.com.br; Cônego Walmor Castro 291, Lagoinha; d from R$400; ❄📶🏊) The pink Pousada da Vigia overlooks Praia da Lagoinha – and what a miraculous view! With only 10 guest rooms scattered around lovely gardens, service is attentive and reaches to the beach, which is accessible by a 200m footpath. Room 4 knocked us out.

Lo Stivale ITALIAN $$

(☎48 3284-2079; www.lostivale.com.br; Av Luiz Boiteux Piazza 483, Ponta das Canas; mains R$62-75; ⏰7pm-midnight daily, midday-4pm Sat & Sun Jan & Feb, 7pm-midnight Thu-Sat, noon-4pm Sun Mar-Dec; 📶) One of the classiest options within easy reach of Praia dos Ingleses and Praia do Santinho. Chef Paolo hails from Bologna, and while he isn't playing by all the rules of the homeland (*tortellini al ragù* would certainly raise Emilia-Romagnan eyebrows), his pappardelle with lamb ragù and seafood spaghettini are definitely palette pleasers.

Find it in Ponta das Canas, 3.5km south of Praia Brava.

Praia dos Ingleses & Praia do Santinho

Praia dos Ingleses and Praia do Santinho sit at a right angle to each other, separated by the protected rocky promontory Ponta dos

Inglêses. Praia dos Ingleses is one of the busiest beaches in the north and is elbow-to-elbow in the summer. Far more ideal is Praia do Santinho, a 2km stretch of protected beach backed by vegetation-draped dunes and pounded by surfer-alluring swells.

Sleeping

Solar do Santinho POUSADA $$
(48 3269-4168; www.pousadasolardosantinho.com.br; Estrada Vereador Onildo Lemos 2197; s/d R$280/320;) This 16-room pousada is tucked away in leafy surrounds 100m from the beach. Bi- and trilevel rooms are spacious, with kitchenettes, balconies and tasteful art. Buddha statues dot the property, which treats its own waste water and runs solar-heated showers.

Pousada do Atobá POUSADA $$
(48 3269-2560; www.pousadadoatoba.com.br; Servidão Ipê do Costão 146; d R$320-400;) Superb value awaits at this gem of a guesthouse with airy, bright rooms looking onto well-kept gardens. It's worth splashing out an extra R$80 for bigger rooms with small lounges and kitchenettes. Aline has lived in Canada and speaks English; the family takes exceptionally good care of guests (but was looking to sell when we came through).

Bus 264 'Ingleses' from TICAN stops just 30m away.

East Coast

Ilha de Santa Catarina's East Coast is home to traveler-friendly enclaves like Lagoa da Conceição, the epicenter of dining and nightlife outside Centro, and the picturesque fishing village of Barra da Lagoa. Both hug the island's lagoon, a 19 sq km pool of blue bisected by a narrow 2km-long strip of land along Av das Rendeiras.

Barra da Lagoa & Around

The fishing village of Barra da Lagoa sits about 8km north of Lagoa da Conceição along the eastern side of the lake. It's a backpacker-friendly enclave made all the more picturesque by the Canal da Barra, with colorful fishing boats and pretty rock formations dotting the snaking route to the sea. Praia Barra da Lagoa merges here with Santa Catarina's longest beach, the 8.5km Praia do Moçambique, to form a stunning, 14km strand, the latter hidden from the road by a thriving pine forest. Praia do Moçambique is protected as part of the Parque Florestal do Rio Vermelho, so the only construction is around the town of Barra da Lagoa.

Sleeping & Eating

★**Barra Beach Club** HOSTEL $$
(48 3232-3336; www.barrabeachclub.com; Servidão da Prainha 122; dm R$80-90, d with/without bathroom R$250/220; closed May-Aug;) This American-run hostel earns top honors across the pedestrian bridge. Three-, four- and 10-bed dorm facilities are spread across several buildings, all with spectacular seaview terraces. It's popular with surfers (wetsuits, short and longboards, and bodyboards all available for free) who are content to kick back here with Asian and Italian meals, veranda massages and post-wave beers at the bar.

Pousada Oceanomare CHALET $$
(48 4052-9013; www.pousadaoceanomare.com.br; Rodovia João Gualberto Soares 5158; s/d R$300/350, lofts R$400-500;) A great family option north of Praia do Moçambique. The island's best pool and sun deck, plus numerous distractions for the kiddos, means parents can enjoy the contemporary hardwood chalets that climb up the forested hillside worry-free.

Isadora Duncan POUSADA $$$
(48 3232-7210; www.bistroisadoraduncan.com.br; Manoel de Menezes 2658; d R$880;) A trickling fountain beckons guests up the stone staircase to this gay-friendly, two-room guesthouse and bistro, which sits right on the lagoon before Barra da Lagoa. Stunningly spacious rooms feature antique accents and sea-view whirlpool bathtubs that are bigger than some rooms altogether! Terraces and in-room breakfast service complement the beautiful views.

Ponta das Caranhas SEAFOOD $$$
(48 3232-3076; www.pontadascaranhas.com.br; Manoel de Menezes 2377; mains for 2 people R$75-245;) This classy, white-tablecloth seafooder is popular with locals for top-end preparations that often lean on the heavier side due to the generous use of béchamel sauce and *catupiry* and Parmesan cheeses. Shrimp-stuffed pumpkin and breaded fish options are popular. There's a pretty outdoor patio for summer waterfront dining.

Information

You'll need to go back to Lagoa da Conceição for a foreign-friendly ATM.

Getting There & Away

Bus 360 (R$4.20) from TILAG (p298) heads to Barra da Lagoa. In summer, traffic can be maddening – it's faster, easier and prettier to take a Cooperbarco (p302) boat from Lagoa da Conceição. Boats ply the scenic waters hourly between 7am and 10pm in summer only (R$22 return, Christmas to Easter).

For Praia do Moçambique, take bus 267 'Rio Vermelho Direto' from TILAG and ask to be let off at the trail to the beach.

Praia Mole & Praia da Joaquina

Praia Mole is famous for its world-class waves and internationally heralded party scene, especially among the LGBT+ community. The beach is absolutely beautiful; it does get crowded, but that's part of the appeal. If you want less people, Praia da Galheta, the next beach north, is gorgeous as well (and clothing optional).

About 3km south of Praia Mole, the huge white dunes of 'Joaca' are visible for miles. These massive sandy mounds at Praia da Joaquina have inspired a new sport: sand surfing. But ideal wave conditions nearly year-round ensure surfing remains the beach's main draw. Several competitions are held here annually.

Sleeping & Eating

Bangalôs da Mole CHALET $$

(☎48 3232-0723; www.facebook.com/bagalosdamole; Rodovia Jornalista Manoel de Menezes 1007; bungalows R$280-360; ❄📶) Directly across from the beach, this place has 22 spacious suites and bilevel bungalows, all with cool tile floors and high ceilings.

Pedra Careca SEAFOOD $$

(☎48 3232-5075; www.facebook.com/restaurantepedracareca; Praia da Joaquina 2500; mains for 2 people R$88-150; ⏱9:30am-7pm; 📶) A local favorite on the sands at Praia da Joaquina, where fresh grilled *anchova* (bluefish) with capers and anything with shrimp goes down a treat. It's just steps from the crashing waves; an Eisenbahn beer fridge means you don't have to chase it all down with tasteless suds.

Getting There & Away

Praia Mole sits about 4.2km east of Lagoa da Conceição in a secluded location just a few hundred meters from the main road, though largely out of sight. From TILAG (p298), bus 363 (R$4.20) practically drops you on the sand at Praia da Joaquina. For Mole, buses 360, 840 and 850 pass by from TILAG.

Lagoa da Conceição

For spectacular scenery, exhilarating water sports or all-night parties, Lagoa da Conceição is a popular alternative to the beaches. Forested hills form a fabulous backdrop for the pretty lagoon. The town of Lagoa, often packed with tourists, sits on a sandbar that divides the two halves of the lagoon and is the island's action-packed center.

Sights & Activities

★Mirante da Lagoa da Conceição VIEWPOINT

(SC-404 s/n; ⏱24hr) FREE The postcard view of Lagoa da Conceição awaits at this must-stop lookout, which frames both sides of the lagoon, the dunes of Joaquina and beyond.

Rebel Store SURFING

(Henrique Veras do Nascimento 150; ⏱10am-10pm) A nice surf shop renting boards (per day R$100). It can also arrange surf lessons.

Sleeping

★Tucano House HOSTEL $

(☎48 3207-8287; www.tucanohouse.com; Rua das Araras 229; dm R$55-75, d with/without bathroom from R$260/240; ⏱closed Mar 15-Nov; ❄@📶🏊) 🌿 Siblings Lila and Caio are your hospitality wizard hosts at this eco-forward hostel in the heart of Lagoa. Their childhood home now features solar-heated showers, a recycled rainwater cistern and amenities like bike and surfboard rentals. Dorms have personal USB ports and the revamped outdoor bar is killer for a cold one. Island adventures are in a decked-out VW van.

★Janela de Márcia B&B $$$

(☎48 99958-1782; www.janelademarcia.com; Rua do Beija Flor 112; d R$425; ❄@📶) Brazilian returnee Márcia and her big, hospitable personality run the show at this intimate B&B – don't call it a pousada – hidden away in an upscale residential neighborhood five minutes from TILAG. Márcia's keen eye for art and design triumphs in her five cozy guest rooms; the marvelous breakfast comes in part from her own gardens.

Eating

★Café Cultura CAFE $$

(www.cafeculturafloripa.com.br; Severino de Oliveira 635; mains R$9-46.50; ⏱8:30am-11:30pm Mon-Sat, to 10pm Sun; 📶) Breakfast until 1pm, waffles, salads, panini (really bruschetta, but who's paying attention?), sophisticated mains and specialty java served by various methods. Floripa's best cafe is brought to you by a Californian ex-Starbucks barista and his Brazilian coffee-heiress wife. The expanded location is gorgeous, with coffee sacks as lampshades and cushy couch seating.

★**Restaurante Lagoa Azul** SEAFOOD $$

(www.restaurantelagoaazul.com.br; Servidão Caminho Costa da Lagoa 177, Pier 17; mains for 2 people R$69-157; ⏲10:30am-6:30pm; 📶) 🍃 Our favorite of the atmospheric seafood restaurants that line the western coast of Lagoa de Conceicão in the village of Costa da Lagoa. A wealth of just-caught seafood is on offer at this sustainably leaning waterfront hot spot, but the *carapava* is the way to go, available only in this village.

To reach Pier 17, catch a frequent boat from Lagoa de Conceicão and stay on board past the far more crowded first stop (you will also catch the boat back more easily from here as it passes by first on its way back to town).

O Barba Negra SEAFOOD $$

(☎48 3232-5098; www.obarbanegra.com.br; Av das Rendeiras 1628; mains for 2 people R$71-178; ⏲noon-11pm Wed-Mon, to 5pm Sun Mar-Nov; 📶) The best of a battery of seafood restaurants along 2km-long Av das Rendeiras, the 'Black Beard' does a fantastic *pastel de camarão* (fried pastry stuffed with shrimp), and follows with excellent seafood creations like *A Moda da Pirata* (fish with a shellfish and tomato reduction sauce) or *Dueto Barba Negra* (crispy octopus and shrimp with anchovy tapenade and mint vinaigrette).

★**Dolce Vita** MEDITERRANEAN $$$

(☎48 98427-6643; www.facebook.com/dolcevitafloripa; Laurindo Januário da Silveira 1233; mains R$62-98; ⏲7-11pm Wed-Fri, noon-4pm & 7-11pm Sat, noon-3pm Sun; 📶) From a charming candlelit porch in Canto da Lagoa, a small but delectable daily-changing menu of Med-inspired contemporary dishes makes for one of Floripa's most memorable meals. Housemade pappardelle with tender, three-day marinated lamb ragù and *calamarata* pasta with lemon sauce and grilled octopus are standouts. The enthusiastic English-speaking server Luís makes service exceptional.

Drinking & Nightlife

★**Books & Beers** BAR

(www.booksbeers.com; Ivo D'Aquino 103; ⏲5pm-midnight Tue-Fri, from 12:30pm Sat, 12:30-10:30pm Sun; 📶) The once outrageous bottled craft beer list at this cultured bar has been trimmed to 25 or so, but 14 taps means the draft selections – mostly southern and regional Brazilian brews – has been expanded. Drink it all down with an *Old Man and the Sea*–inspired library-vibe with sunset views.

Layback Park CRAFT BEER

(www.laybackbeer.com.br; Henrique Veras do Nascimento 190; ⏲8am-midnight; 📶) Lagoa da Conceição's former Food Truck Parking Lot got a swift makeover in 2018 by local craft beer empire Layback Beer with Brazilian skateboarding legend Pedro Barros providing a bit of the monetary might. Nine shipping containers house a pizzeria, burger joint, Back Joy Coffee and Layback Tap and Cheese (craft beer and gamey bar snacks).

☆ Entertainment

John Bull Pub LIVE MUSIC

(www.facebook.com/johnbullfloripa; Rua das Rendeiras 1046; ⏲9:30pm-4am Wed-Fri, from 10pm Sat) Famous for live rock, with bonus views over the lagoon.

Getting There & Away

From TICEN (p298) in Centro, catch bus 330 'Lagoa da Conceição' (Platform A) to TILAG (p298) for R$4.20.

Getting Around

Cooperbarco (☎48 3232-1266; www.cooperbarco.wordpress.com; Ivo D'Aqunio 14; return R$15) runs the local transport boats to the restaurants at Costa da Lagoa as well as Barra da Lagoa (a massive and scenic timesaver to beat the brutal summer traffic). To Costa da Lagoa (R$25 return), boats launch every 45 to 60 minutes between 7:10am and 11:30pm weekdays, and Saturday and Sunday between 8am and 10pm. To Barra da Lagoa (R$22 return), boats run hourly between 7am and 10pm in summer only (Christmas to Easter).

Boats leave from next to the bridge across the lagoon in Lagoa de Conceicâo.

South Island

With white-sand beaches and mountains that drop into the sea, the south is the most pristine and picturesque part of the island. But south-island residents are engaged in the inevitable struggle between developers and preservers: the former see the potential for more tourists and big bucks; the latter fear that their piece of paradise will soon resemble the north. The balance is delicate and ever shifting – gorgeous Campeche is constantly teetering between these two extremes. For now, these towns retain their idyllic appeal. The beaches are less crowded (hot surf spots excepted) and the vibe is more laid-back than other island destinations.

Getting There & Away

For southern beaches, including Armação, Pântano do Sul and Costa de Dentro, catch bus 410 'Rio Tavares' (Platform B) from TICEN (p298), then transfer at TIRIO (p298) to bus 563. For Campeche and Ribeirão da Ilha, hop on bus 463 and bus 561, respectively, from TIRIO instead.

Ribeirão da Ilha

More than any other town, the tiny village of Ribeirão da Ilha has preserved its Azorean heritage, evident in its cobblestone streets and colorful roof tiles. The main square centers on the lovely Igreja NS da Lapa do Riberão, which dates to 1806. The town is known for its oyster harvesting and has developed into a gastronomic destination throughout the years. Today, its waterfront is lined with lovely seafood restaurants.

Sights

Igreja NS da Lapa do Riberão CHURCH
(www.nossasenhoradalapa.org.br; Alberto Cavalheiro 238; hours vary) Dating back to 1806, this intimate baroque-inspired church was restored on order from Emperor Dom Pedro II himself, who visited in 1845 and coughed up R$400,000 to get the job done. The ceiling is adorned with paintings, including notable depictions of the Holy Family and the crucifixion.

Eating

★Ostradamus SEAFOOD $$$
(48 3337-5711; www.ostradamus.com.br; Rod Baldicero Filomeno 7640; oysters R$35-45, mains for 2 people R$135-195; noon-11pm Tue-Sat, to 5pm Sun;) Atmospheric tables line the glass-enclosed deck at this incredibly cinematic seafood restaurant. You can slurp oysters served over a dozen ways, but don't fill up on those – the outstanding and incredibly presented seafood dishes here are a vacation highlight.

Campeche

Campeche is a bohemian outpost, home to artists, massage therapists, surfing hippies and other free thinkers seeking to escape the crowds. The beach is protected, so the sand is completely undeveloped, yet those condo complexes – especially in up and coming Nova Campeche – have managed to creep in as close as the law allows. The beach faces Ilha do Campeche, home to a single beach and summer-only restaurant, as well as over 100 petroglyphs distributed around 10 archaeological sites. Only 400 people per day are allowed to visit.

Sights

★Praia do Campeche BEACH
(Campeche) The 3.5km Praia do Campeche is one of Floripa's five-star beaches, an absolute stunner of sun-kissed perfection with wind conditions lending themselves to fantastic surfing and kitesurfing. Desolate dunes and pounding surf – stretching for miles in either direction – offer relative solitude for swimmers and sunbathers.

Bus 463 (R$4.20) from TIRIO (p298) drops you 350m from the beach.

Sleeping

★Pousada Naturezas de Floripa POUSADA $$
(48 99190-9674; www.naturezasdefloripa.com.br; Servidão Família Nunes 59A; s/d from R$240/300;) The pousada formerly known as Campeche Natur has been split into three inns – Naturezas de Floripa, Verde Natur and Old Beach – all looked after by the same family. At this one, the bulk of the rooms – seven spacious nation-themed retreats flanked by hammocks, lush gardens and artistically fed common areas – await travelers just 100m from Campeche beach.

★Pousada Verde Natur POUSADA $$$
(48 99171-9997; www.naturcampeche.com.br; Servidão Família Nunes 59C; s/d from R$368/459;) Talmir, the English-speaking and world-traveling owner, has built an endlessly charming empire on Servidão Família Nunes that includes neighbors Naturezas de Floripa (p303) and Old Beach. He now oversees the five rooms here decorated with foraged international treasures. Rooms feature small gardens and carbon-neutral touches like solar-heated showers.

Armação

The little district of Armação dates to the 18th century, when it served as a whaling center. The impressive Igreja Santa Ana still stands from those days. While whaling is no longer practiced, the fishing industry still thrives here. Inland from Armação, the Lagoa do Peri is a pretty lagoon surrounded by parkland.

Sights

Parque Municipal Lagoa da Peri NATURE RESERVE
(Francisco Thomaz dos Santos 3150) Lesser known and less visited than Lagoa da Conceição, Parque Municipal Lagoa da Peri has wonderful opportunities for swimming and hiking (as well as kayaking and stand-up paddleboarding (SUP) in summer) and picnic and child playground facilities.

The jumping-off point for the lake is about 1km south of Praia de Armação on the main road approaching the town – you can't miss the large park entrance.

Sleeping

Pousada Pénareia POUSADA $$
(48 3338-1616; www.pousadapenareia.com.br; Hermes Guedes da Fonseca 207; d R$320-440;) The 13 rooms at this simple but very popular Armação choice have direct access to the beach. Friendly Klaus speaks multiple languages and is an excellent source of island knowledge. There's a tranquil backyard with a shaded hammock nook and a welcoming common area with pool table and fireplace. Visiting Sagui monkeys pop in at breakfast.

Information

C.A.T. (48 3237-5660; Francisco Thomaz dos Santos 3150, Lagoa da Peri; 9am-5pm Dec-Mar) Seasonal tourist information at Lagoa da Peri.

Pântano do Sul & Costa de Dentro

Pântano do Sul is both the figurative and literal end of the road, and it feels like it. Fishers of Azorean descent still inhabit the village, and the beach is dotted with fishing boats and seafood shacks. Ringed by mountains, the protected cove contains calm, cool waters that are ideal for sunning and swimming.

Costa de Dentro, 3.5km west, has access to the lovely, calm waters of the Praia dos Açores – making this a good escape from the surfing scene – or you can continue all the way to Praia Solidão or Saquinho.

Sleeping & Eating

★ **Pousada Sítio dos Tucanos** INN $$
(48 3237-5084; www.pousadasitiodostucanos.com; Estrada Rozália Ferreira 2776; s/d from R$190/330, chalet R$400;) About 1.5km past Costa de Dentro, this multilingual German-run pousada sits high up in peaceful farm country, the domain of animal lovers and bird-watchers. Extremely cozy, it has rustic but comfortable rooms, most with balconies; common areas are flooded with light.

★ **Bar do Arante** SEAFOOD $$
(48 3237-7022; www.facebook.com/arantebarerestaurante; Abelardo Otácilio Gomes 254; mains for 2 people R$59-179, weekend buffet per person R$69; 11:30am-midnight;) The rustic seafood shack Arante has become an island institution, its walls covered with poetry and artwork that patrons have added over the years. Massive servings of fish and shrimp dishes often are coming straight off the boat; it all goes down right on Pântano do Sul beach.

THE MAINLAND

North and south of Florianópolis, fine sand and big surf attract beachcombers, sunbathers and surfers. Inland, the Serra Geral runs parallel to the coast, protecting some of southern Brazil's most remote destinations. This is where Santa Catarina's German and Italian heritage endures most tenaciously.

Joinville

0XX47 / POP 515,000

While Joinville does not have the historic center (or the beer festival) of Blumenau, it does have its own claims to fame. It's the only city outside Moscow with a school of the Bolshoi Ballet, a coup that goes hand in hand with its annual dance festival, one of the largest and most renowned in South America, and it relishes its own decidedly German roots. They are evident in the city's nouveau-Alpine architecture and well-manicured parks.

Sights & Activities

★ **Mirante de Joinville** VIEWPOINT
(Pastor Guilherme Ráu s/n; 6am-8pm) FREE To get a stupendous 360-degree panorama of Joinville and the Baía da Babitonga, head to the city's 250m-high viewpoint. The lookout, at the top of Morro de Boa Vista, is closed to private cars and accessible only by foot, bike, public bus or taxi (Uber is not authorized).

Bus 2015 (www.gidion.com.br; Saguaçu s/n) 'Mirante' leaves from Terminal Central, stopping at the base of the hill every 30 minutes between 7:50am and 6:20pm during the week and every 20 minutes between 8am and 7pm on weekends (R$4.65).

Barco Príncipe III BOATING
(☎47 3455-4444; www.barcoprincipe.com.br; Baltazar Buschle 3870; adult/child incl lunch from R$158/79; ⏲tours 10:30am) This famous boat cruise runs tours around the Baía da Babitonga, stopping in São Francisco do Sul for 1½ hours. It departs from the Espinheiros neighborhood, 10km from the center, but only when it has 100 people or more on board. Pricey, but everyone raves about it.

Festivals & Events

Festival de Dança DANCE
(www.festivaldedancadejoinville.com.br; Av José Vieira 315, Centreventos Cau Hansen; ⏲Jul) Holding a Guinness World Record for the largest dance event in the world by number of participants, Joinville's annual two-week dance festival is one of the continent's most important competitions and attracts the best of the best of South American companies in a variety of schools, including ballet, hip-hop, jazz, tap, contemporary and folk, among others.

Sleeping & Eating

★**Joinville Hostel & Pousada** HOSTEL $
(☎47 99954-3434; www.joinvillehostel.com.br; Dona Francisca 1376; dm from R$55, s/d R$99/135, without bathroom R$89/125; @📶) If you like your hostel to feel like home, this one, run by the immediately likable Kely, is for you. Boasting large green spaces, a little garden and a good bit more attention to detail and decor than the norm, Kely has created a homespun vibe – with deeply snuggly beds – just a 10-minute walk from Centro.

★**Restaurante Hübener** GERMAN $$
(☎47 3428-0275; SC-418, Km 83; buffet weekdays/Sat R$38/52; ⏲11:30am-2pm Mon-Fri, to 2:30pm Sat) This high-quality buffet of Brazilian-interpreted German specialties is not the kind of place you want to go more than once, but once is worth the waistline expansion. Joinville's best *marreco* (stuffed duck), pork shanks, a gaggle of *wursts* (German sausages) – it's all here. And don't forget the duck-fat fried bananas!

The downside, besides the excess of calories, is the location 23km northwest of central Joinville.

Biergarten BRAZILIAN $$
(www.biergarten.com.br; Visconde de Taunay 1183; mains R$16-76; ⏲11am-midnight Mon-Thu, to 1am Fri & Sat, to 5pm Sun; 📶) The most agreeable restaurant in Joinville is a convivial spot to sample regional specialties like *marreco* (stuffed garganey, a kind of small duck; R$119 for two). Wash it down with Zeit, the house *chope* (draft beer), of which there are numerous staples (try the Munich Helles) and seasonal options ranging from a chocolate dunkel to pumpkin ale.

Drinking & Nightlife

★**Mad Dwarf** CRAFT BEER
(www.maddwarf.com.br; Ottokar Doerffel 1112; ⏲5-11pm Tue & Wed, to midnight Thu-Sat; 📶) *Joinvilense* take their suds very seriously and Mad Dwarf is the best of several brewpubs. There's 40 rotating taps, 10 of which are reserved for guest brews (available in pints) while the remaining 30 are devoted to its own concoctions (available up to 300ml). It's just outside of Centro in Atiradores, a quick hop and skip from the bus station.

Information

Joinville's tourist information booths are helpful, but most unhelpfully located around

BUSES FROM JOINVILLE

DESTINATION	STARTING FARE (R$)	TIME (HR)	COMPANY
Blumenau	39	2½	Catarinense (www.catarinense.net)
Curitiba	31	2	Catarinense
Florianópolis	64	2½	Catarinense
Foz do Iguaçu	170	13	Catarinense, Expresso Nordeste (www.expnordeste.com.br)
Porto Alegre	163	9	Catarinense
Rio de Janeiro	219	17	Penha (www.nspenha.com.br)
São Paulo	96	9	Catarinense

the town's outskirts, though the **branch** (☎47 3433-5007; www.joinville.sc.gov.br; XV de Novembro, Pórtico; ⏲9am-6pm) at the town Pórtico is adjacent to Opa's great beer bar. There are other branches at the **airport** (☎47 3427-4409; www.joinville.sc.gov.br; Santos Dumont 9000; ⏲10am-7pm Mon, 7:30am-1:30pm & 2-8pm Tue-Fri, 8am-5pm Sat), **Casa Krüger** (☎47 3427-5623; www.joinville.sc.gov.br; SC-418, Km 0, Casa Krüger; ⏲9am-6pm) and near the base of **Mirante de Joinville** (☎47 3453-0177; www.joinville.sc.gov.br; Pastor Guilherme Rau s/n; ⏲9am-6pm).

Getting There & Away

AIR

Joinville-Lauro Carneiro de Loyola Airport (JOI; ☎47 3481-4000; www4.infraero.gov.br/aeroportos/aeroporto-de-joinville-lauro-carneiro-de-loyola; Av Santos Dumont 9000) is 13km north from the city; regular flights go to Campinas and São Paulo.

BUS

Viacão Verdes Mares (www.vmares.com.br) runs regular buses to Ilha de São Francisco, both from the bus station (R$17.30), and, more conveniently and cheaply, from Centro (R$14.10).

Getting Around

TO/FROM THE AIRPORT

To reach the airport, catch bus 800/Iririú (R$4.30) from Box 3 at the Terminal Central and switch at Terminal Iririú for the 0240 'Aeroporto via Emilio Landmann' to the airport (plan on an hour ride to be safe).

BUS

The bus station is 2km southwest of the city center. Local buses go every 15 minutes to the city center from a stop just outside the station on Rua Parnaíba (R$4.65).

Blumenau

☎0XX47 / POP 309,000

Blumenau isn't the only city in Santa Catarina that was founded by German immigrants who transplanted their beer-brewing expertise and their taste for Alpine architecture to South America. But it is the best known, thanks in part to its uninhibited, over-the-top Oktoberfest. The annual beer-drinking extravaganza is among Brazil's largest street parties, second only to Carnaval in Rio.

Oktoberfest is what makes Blumenau famous, but it is not what makes the city German. Throughout the historic city center, the architecture is dominated by Germanic themes. Local restaurants specialize in *eisbein* (cured ham hock) and *kassler* (smoked pork chop), and numerous beer brands are brewed locally. Most telling, perhaps, is the tall, fair population, many of whom still speak German in their homes.

Sights

Parque Vila Germânica AREA

(www.parquevilagermanica.com.br; Alberto Stein 199; ⏲8am-11pm Mon-Fri, from 10am Sat, from 11am Sun) Blumenau's festivals are held at Parque Vila Germânica, part convention hall, part kitschy Alpine village. There are several good bar/restaurants (Bier Vila (p310)), gourmet shops and a whole lot of lederhosen. To get there, catch buses 30, 31 or 32 from Estação Dr Blumenau (p310).

Rua XV Novembro AREA

Rua XV Novembro is home to the city's best examples of Germanic architecture, including the **Castelinho da XV** (XV de Novembro 1050), a replica of the city hall of Michelstadt, Germany, and now a Havan department store.

Festivals & Events

★**Oktoberfest** BEER

(☎47 3381-7700; www.oktoberfestblumenau.com.br; Alberto Stein 199, Parque Vila Germânica; per day R$30-40) A festive parade kicks off nearly 20 days of folk music, dancing and beer drinking that ranks as the world's second-biggest German party after Munich. A smaller Sommerfest takes place in January.

Sleeping & Eating

★**Hotel Glória** HOTEL $$

(☎47 3326-1988; www.hotelgloria.com.br; 7 de Setembro 954; d/tr/q from R$219/309/359; ❄@📶) With its wood-paneled entrance, stained glass and traditional German *kaffeehaus* (coffeehouse), this Blumenau classic has modernized its entire fleet of rooms but maintains its Old World flair. Upgraded rooms have restrained style and explosive showers. Breakfast at **Cafehaus Glória** (www.cafehaus.com.br; buffet from R$29-38; ⏲6am-9pm Mon-Fri, 7am-8pm Sat, 6am-10am Sun; 📶) is extraordinary.

Moinho do Vale BUFFET

(☎47 3322-3440; www.restaurantemoinhodovale.com.br; Porto Rico 66; buffet weekdays/weekends

Blumenau

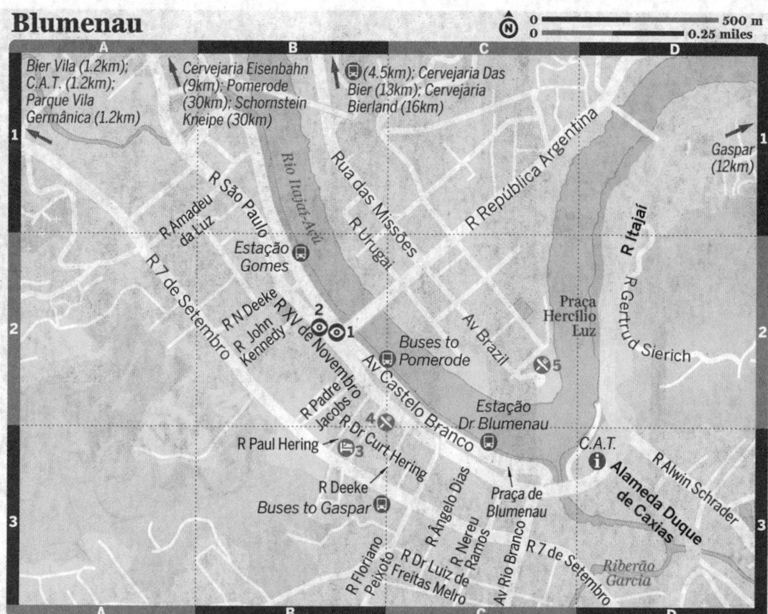

R$58.90/69, mains R$39-135; ⏲11:30am-3pm & 7pm-midnight Tue-Sat, 11:30am-3pm Sun; 📶) One of Blumenau's classiest choices, this is a high-quality buffet lunch stop with excellent service, great regional and Brazilian choices (stuffed duck, trout ceviche, *tambaqui* fish ribs, pork knuckle) and even better desserts (walnut stroganoff with *doce de leite*, banoffee pie) – included in the price. Dig in while ogling city and river views and the epic Santa Catarina beer list.

★ **Basement English Pub** PUB FOOD **$$**
(www.basementpub.com.br; Paul Hering 35; mains R$26.50-50.50; ⏲6pm-midnight Mon-Sat; 📶) Easily one of Brazil's best bars in a gorgeous authentic English pub atmosphere. It does a good job with homesick-remedy pub grub like fish and chips, steaks and pastrami that hit the spot among a blitzkrieg of brats. There's often live music.

★ **Abendbrothaus** GERMAN **$$$**
(☎47 3378-1157; www.abendbrothaus.blogspot.com; Henrique Conrad 1194, Vila Itoupava; meals R$76; ⏲11:30am-4pm Sun; 📶) This Sunday-only feast is the most coveted table in Santa Catarina for *marreco* (stuffed Garganey, a kind of small duck); in fact, the menu's only item begins its journey to your stomach at 6am, when Josefa Jensen begins a sunrise recipe ritual handed down from her grandmother. Cooked in banana leaves for 2½ hours, the bird emerges crispy, golden brown and perfect.

It's served alongside sauerkraut, purple cabbage, fried manioc with bacon, mashed potatoes. macaroni salad, beef tongue and a family-secret apple sauce. The restaurant is 30km north of centro in Vila Itoupava. Reserve.

Blumenau

Sights

1	Castelinho da XV	B2
2	Rua XV Novembro	B2

Sleeping

3	Hotel Glória	B3

Eating

4	Basement English Pub	B2
	Cafehaus Glória	(see 3)
5	Moinho do Vale	C2

ℹ Information

You'll find tourist information about Blumenau and the Vale Europeu at the **C.A.T.** (Centro de Atendimento ao Turista; ☎47 3331-7726; www.turismoblumenau.com.br; Albero Stein 199; ⏲10am-7pm Mon-Fri, to 4pm Sat & Sun) located inside Parque Vila Germânica. Additional locations operate on **Rua Itajaí** (Centro de Atendimento ao Turista; ☎47 3222-3176; www.turismoblumenau.com.br; Praça Johan Peter Wagner 3435; ⏲10am-2pm

Vale Europeu

The collection of towns and villages around Blumenau that were populated by Italian and German immigrants is called the Vale Europeu. Their descendants still preserve their European culture, and during the 17 days of Oktoberfest many towns host their own unique festivals. All year long, the area has bucolic views dotted by traditional German timber-framed (*Fachwerk*) houses, characterized by high-pitched roofs and brick facades.

Towns & Villages

For a profound insight into the region's Germanic roots, head about 30km north of Blumenau to Pomerode, where an estimated 70% of the population still speaks German. The Festa Pomerana celebrates its northern German heritage every January, and the **Museo Pomerano** (☎48 3387-0408; Harmann Weege 111, Pomerode; R$6; ⊙10-11:30am & 1-5pm Tue-Fri, 10am-4pm Sat & Sun) explores the town's history in loving detail.

The region's Italian heritage is alive in Nova Trento, 61km south of Blumenau, which celebrates local gastronomy during the Grape Festival in January and is home to the important pilgrimage site Santuário Santa Paulina, an imposing modern church with a dramatic slalom-like sloping ceiling. Some 40,000 pilgrims and tourists visit this church per month. Timbó, founded by both Germans and Italians, is brimming with verdant gardens and is considered by the UN to be one of the best places to live in Brazil.

MARCELO RUDINI/ALAMY STOCK PHOTO ©

RICARDO RIBAS/ALAMY STOCK PHOTO ©

VIAGENS E CAMINHOS/SHUTTERSTOCK ©

1. Cycling in Vale Europeu
2. Roasted duck and side dishes, Abendbrothaus (p307)
3. Santuário Santa Paulina

Festivals

Blumenau's massive Oktoberfest (p306) is nearly 20 days of folk music, dancing and beer drinking – lots of beer drinking. This is the 'biggest German party in the Americas' (well, second biggest after Ontario, but who's counting?).

Outdoor Adventures

The Vale Europeu – like Europe itself – lends itself to beautiful countryside pedaling. See the Circuito Vale Europeu website (www.circuitovaleeuropeu.com.br) for an excellent self-guided bike tour. The helpful website www.valeeuropeu.com.br, and the comprehensive booklet *Vale Europeu*, which can be picked up at the tourist office in Blumenau, both cover ecotourism opportunities in the valley.

Best Place to Stay

A pleasant place to lay your head in Pomerode is **Hotel Bergblick** (47 3387-0952; www.bergblick.com.br; Georg Zeplin 120, Pomerode; s/d from R$198/328;), which has gigantic rooms with mountain views and an Alpine feel.

Best Restaurant

The feast at Abendbrothaus (p307) in Vila Itoupava, 25km north of Blumenau, is the most coveted table in Santa Catarina for *marreco* (stuffed garganey, a kind of small duck).

Best Microbrewery

Schornstein Kneipe's (p310) pilsners, India pale ale, weiss, bock and imperial stout all cure 'homebeersickness'; and it has the best tasting room of the bunch, as well. It's a must on the artisanal beer trail.

EIN BIER, POR FAVOR!

Brazil's mainstream brews – Skol, Brahma and Antarctica – are fine for staving off the tropical heat, but let's face it: taste is not their strong suit. Luckily, the craft beer revolution is in full swing throughout Brazil, but German immigrants from the Vale Europeu have had a handle on suds for decades! There is a true beer culture here dating back to the mid-19th century. The following are some of the region's best breweries, all with tasting rooms in and around Blumenau (start off at **Bier Vila** (www.biervila.com.br; Alberto Stein 199, Parque Vila Germânica; 11am-midnight;) and pick your favorites, then head to the breweries themselves!). Check out www.valedacerveja.com for more information on local breweries.

Cervejaria Eisenbahn (47 3488-7307; www.eisenbahn.com.br; Bahia 5181, Blumenau; 5-11pm Mon & Tue, to midnight Wed, to 1am Thu-Sat)

Schornstein Kneipe (47 3333-2759; www.schornstein.com.br; Hermann Weege 60, Pomerode; 5-11pm Mon-Thu, to midnight Fri, 11am-midnight Sat, 11am-9pm Sun; W)

Cervejaria Bierland (47 3323-6588; www.bierland.com.br; Gustavo Zimmermann 5361, Blumenau; 8am-noon & 1-6pm Mon-Fri)

Cervejaria Das Bier (47 3397-8600; www.dasbier.com.br; Bonifácio Haendchen 5311, Gaspar; 5pm-midnight Wed-Fri, from 11am Sat, 11am-7pm Sun)

Cervejaria Blumenau (www.cervejablumenau.com.br; Arno Delling 388, Blumenau; 10am-6pm Mon-Sat;).

Mon-Fri) at the eastern entrance to town and at the **Museu da Cerveja** (Centro de Atendimento ao Turista; 47 3326-6791; www.turismoblumenau.com.br; XV de Novembro 160, Museu da Cerveja).

Getting There & Away

The **bus station** (47 3323-2155; 2 de Setembro 1222) is 6km west of the center. To get into the center of town, take bus 11 or 17 (R$4.05) from the far side of **Rua 2 de Setembro** (2 de Setembro) – a bit of a schlep – to **Estação Gomes**, or order an Uber for around R$13 off-peak. Heading back, the same buses leave from **Estação Dr Blumenau** (Av Castelo Branco).

For the Vale Europeu, half-hourly to hourly **Volkmann** (47 3395-1400; www.turismovolkmann.com.br) buses head from **Av Castelo Branco** to Pomerode (R$6.20, 3:55am to 10:10pm, less on weekends). From the bus station, **Expresso Presidente** (47 3352-1093; www.expressopresidente.com.br; 2 de Setembro 1222, Rodoviária de Blumenau) has three or so daily buses (less on weekends) making the 30km jaunt from Blumenau to Timbó (R$11.35, one hour, 12:10pm, 4pm and 6:45pm). **Reunidas** (47 3323-3207; www.reunidas.com.br; 2 de Setembro 1222, Rodoviária de Blumenau) has two buses from Blumenau to Nova Trento (R$25.30, two hours, 6:40am and 2:45pm).

North of Florianópolis

Varied and inviting, the beaches along the coast north of Florianópolis are both its blessing and its curse. The blessing is the crystalline waters and fine sand, not to mention the endless days of sun. The curse is the high-rise hotels and condominiums that are more prominent than the forested hillsides and rocky outposts.

Balneário Camboriú

0XX47 / POP 108,000

Balneário Camboriú is considered a pauper's Rio. Indeed, it has a giant Christ statue, beautiful beaches, hopping nightlife and a long stretch of skyscraper-lined sand that suspiciously mirrors Copacabana right down to its name – Av Atlântica – all for a fraction of Copacabana prices. But the vibe is forced and unsophisticated at times, and can often feel like one big cliché. Camboriú is known for being as gay-friendly as Rio, and also for its *teleférico* (cable car) connecting a large central *morro* (hill) with two beaches.

Sights

★ **Parque Unipraias** NATURE RESERVE

(47 3404-7600; www.unipraias.com.br; Av Atlântica 6006; combo ticket adult/child R$121/100; 9am-8pm Dec-Feb, 9:30am-6pm Mar-Nov) Camboriú's pride and joy is this six-hectare urban reserve. In addition to 500m of walking trails, the real coup is the amusements, which are sold separately or as a combo ticket: the **bondinho** (Cable Car; 47 3404-7600; www.unipraias.com.br; Av Atlântica 6006, Parque Unipraias; adult/child R$42/21; 9am-8pm Dec-Feb, 9:30am-6pm Mar-Nov), said to be the only *teleférico* (cable car) in the world connecting a large

central *morro* (hill) with two beaches; the absolutely thrilling **Yoohooo!** (R$34; ⌚9am-8pm Dec-Feb, 9:30am-6pm Mar-Nov), a low-riding mountain sled that barrels through the Atlantic rainforest at speeds of 60km per hour; and **ZipRider** (R$45; ⌚9am-8pm Dec-Feb, 9:30am-6pm Mar-Nov), a 750m-high zipline.

The park is mostly weekends only in June and August, so check ahead.

Cristo Luz Statue LANDMARK
(www.cristoluz.com.br; Indonésia 800; adult before/after 7pm R$20/35, child R$5/10; ⌚4pm-midnight Mon-Sat, from 10am Sun) The 33m Cristo Luz statue holds a sombrero from which a spotlight illuminates the city at night, sometimes in streaming colors. During summer, live music is often staged from 7pm.

It's roughly R$7 to R$12 for an Uber ride from Avenida Atlântica.

Beto Carrero World AMUSEMENT PARK
(☎47 3261-2222; www.betocarrero.com.br; Inácio Francisco de Souza 1597, Penha; adult/child R$135/120; ⌚9am-6pm) Latin America's biggest amusement park. Attractions are divided among nine themed areas and include plenty of high-adrenaline roller coasters (such as the FireWhip, reaching speeds of nearly 100km per hour) and other rides spread over 14 sq km.

The park is located in Penha and is most easily and often visited from Balneário Camboriú, 35km to the south.

Sleeping & Eating

Bonabrigo Hostel HOSTEL $$
(☎47 3056-0446; www.bonabrigohostel.com; Rua 500, 501; dm R$80-130, d R$400; ❄📶) You can't miss the blinding yellow-and-blue-trimmed facade of this newer hostel occupying a residential home 1km back from the breach. Dorms come in four- to 10-bed configurations and are indeed top-end – privacy curtains, personal outlets, modern bathrooms – and there is a large shared kitchen and pool table. But high-season prices here teeter outside reality.

Felissimo Exclusive Hotel BOUTIQUE HOTEL $$$
(☎47 3360-6291; www.felissimoexclusivehotel.com.br; Alles Blaun 201, Praia dos Amores; r R$810-1460; ❄📶🏊) This refined, 12-room pousada is a worthwhile spot to break the bank in Balneário. Classic white dominates the interior, all designed by the discerning, hands-on owner. Nespresso machines and Bose SoundDocks are standard, and some of the tuck-away-forever rooms feature outdoor bathtubs.

Bistrô Palatare FRENCH $$
(☎47 3366-3699; www.palatare.com.br; Rua 2550, 699; mains R$48-82; ⌚7:30pm-midnight Fri & Sat; 📶) A hands-on couple runs the best contemporary restaurant in town, specializing in Franco-Italian dishes that only grace their eight tables on Friday and Saturday nights. Zé Eduardo handles the kitchen, where mains like duck confit with soft polenta and mustard sauce or Uruguayan beef are made; his wife, Margaret, runs the dining room. Reserve.

Drinking & Nightlife

★**Green Valley** CLUB
(☎47 99903-4303; www.greenvalleybr.com; Antônio Lopes Gonçalves Bastos 1083; R$15-220; ⌚9am-8am Thu-Sun) One of the two world-renowned mega dance clubs in Balneário Camboriú, whose name is often tossed about in the 'World's Best Club' conversations among internationally famous DJs.

Explosive sets focus on big room, deep house, electro house, house, progressive house, tech house and techno. No shorts, sleeveless T-shirts, flip-flops or caps. Buy tickets online at www.ingressonacional.com.br.

Warung Beach Club CLUB
(☎47 3348-7643; www.warungclub.com.br; Av José Medeiros Viêira 350, Praia Brava, Itajaí; R$88-132) Surrounded by virgin Atlantic forest and Indonesian-inspired architecture, Warung Beach Club marries a world-renowned mega dance club with lush surroundings.

BUSES FROM BLUMENAU

DESTINATION	STARTING FARE (R$)	TIME (HR)	BUS COMPANY
Balneário Camboriú	23	1½	Catarinense (www.catarinense.net)
Curitiba	48	4	Catarinense
Florianópolis	50	3	Catarinense
Joinville	36.50	2	Catarinense
Piçarras	28	2	Catarinense

Information

P.I.T. (Posto de Informações Turísticas; 47 3367-8005; www.secturbc.com.br; Av do Estado 5041; 6am-midnight) Balneário Camboriú's tourist information is helpful though inconveniently located at the entrance to town, 2km southwest of Av Atlântica.

Getting There & Away

From the **bus station** (47 3367-2901; Av Santa Catarina 81), Catarinense (www.catarinense.net) runs frequent buses to Florianópolis (from R$32, 1½ hours), Joinville (from R$36, 1½ hours) and Blumenau (from R$26, 1½ hours).

For Bombinhas, **Praiana** (47 3367-1224; www.praiana.com.br; Av Santa Catarina) buses between Itajaí and Porto Belo pass the intermunicipal bus stop on Rua Santa Catarina next to the bus station between 14 and 25 times per day around 30 to 40 minutes after departing Itajaí (R$5.85, one hour). Once in Porto Belo, you must switch to a Bombinhas-bound bus (R$4, 20 minutes).

It's a R$10 or less off-peak Uber ride from the bus station to Av Atlântica.

South of Florianópolis

The waves have put this stretch of coastline on the map. While the local population is still largely descended from Azorean fisherfolk, you'll be hard-pressed to find them amid the suntanned surfers and bikini-clad beauties.

Guarda do Embaú

0XX48

Famous for its excellent left that breaks at the mouth of the river, Guarda do Embaú often makes the list of Brazil's best surfing beaches. This laid-back, bohemian surf village is one of southern Brazil's most postcard-perfect settings, and is an excellent destination for wave riders and other bohemian types.

Sleeping & Eating

Guarda is home to plenty of charming pousadas and other budget-friendly accommodations. In winter, many shut down completely.

Zululand CHALET $$

(48 3283-2706; www.zululand.com.br; Servidão Emerenciana s/n; d without air-con R$290, bungalows with air-con from R$350;) Owned by model/actor/surfer Paulo Zulu, Zululand is a collection of funky-shaped bilevel bungalows well equipped with tasteful art and flat-screen TVs, all set about a property flush with lush tropical foliage.

Big Bamboo SEAFOOD $$$

(www.bigbamboo.com.br; Beira do Rio da Madre; mains for 2 people R$74.90-187.50; 11:30am-midnight Dec-Mar, 11:30am-4pm & 7-11pm Thu-Fri, to 5pm Sat & Sun Apr-Nov) A solid choice for seafood with organic leanings and good microbrews in a seaside setting with views of the river and beach. It's owned by the father of Brazilian footballer Fernando Prass, whose memorabilia decorates the bar.

Shopping

Made in Guarda CLOTHING

(www.madeinguarda.com.br; Geral da Guarda do Embaú s/n; 9am-midday, 1-8pm Wed-Mon Mar-Nov) This ecologically minded clothing brand now has stores in hip surf spots all over southern Brazil, but it hails from here.

Getting There & Away

From Platform C at TICEN in Florianópolis, catch **Jotur** (48 3279-3200; www.jotur.com.br; Av Paulo Fontes s/n, TICEN) bus 2050 to Estacão Palhoça (R$6, 45 minutes, every 20 minutes, 6am to 11:15pm). From the station, Jotur bus 06 'Pinheira/Guarda da Embaú' leaves for Guarda do Embaú every 30 or 45 minutes (R$6.75, 1¼ hour, 6:20am to 11:35pm).

To continue south to Praia do Rosa, catch a **Jotur bus** in the village back to Hwy BR-101 (R$3.60, 10 minutes), flag down a Santo Anjo Garopaba-bound bus (R$11, 30 minutes) from the **southbound bus stop** (Hwy BR-101) near the underpass, and get off at the Praia do Rosa turnoff on the road to Garopaba and catch a Praia do Rosa-bound **Expreso Garopaba** bus (R$3.50, every 30 to 45 minutes, 6:55am to 11pm) on **Rua Laudelino Antônio Teixara** in front of Maresia Launches (there's no official bus stop) or order an Uber (R$6 to R$10). However, buses will only go as far as RodOil gas station, 850m north of Centrinho.

Praia do Rosa

0XX48 / POP 900

Santa Catarina's swankiest seaside destination, Praia do Rosa, is about 15km south of Garopaba. The beach here, all 3km of it, is the stuff of models and photo shoots. It's one of Brazil's storybook destinations, backed by small sand dunes and flanked by outcrops of lush Mata Atlântica. Besides the stunning beach, Rosa has two things going for it: a cultured, ecoconscious population and waves. It was the latter that propelled the town, which sits high on a bluff above the beach, from a modest fishing hamlet in the '70s to one of Brazil's most sophisticated surf villages.

In winter, the bay becomes a breeding ground for southern right whales, and mothers and calves can be seen from the beach.

Activities

Rosa Norte SURFING

(48 99938-8635; www.facebook.com/escoladesurfrosanorte; Estrada Geral do Rosa Norte s/n; 3/5 classes R$308/460, rental per hour/day R$25/90) This recommended outfitter has year-round surf classes and surfboard rentals. In summer, it also operates direct from the sand on the north end of the Praia do Rosa.

Pousada Vida, Sol e Mar WHALE WATCHING

(48 99981-0592; www.vidasolemar.com.br; Estrada Geral da Praia do Rosa; tours R$50-140; tours 8am & 11am) Every winter, between July and November, hundreds of southern right whales return to the Santa Catarina coast. English-speaking Argentine whale enthusiast Rodrigo Litman has been running ecologically sound whale-watching tours with IBF (Instituto Baleia Franca) scientists on board for over a decade. At time of writing boat tours were suspended, but ground tours were leaving whenever whales were spotted.

Sleeping

Paraíso Hostel HOSTEL $

(48 99147-4456; www.paraisohostelpraiadorosa.com.br; Rua 41803 s/n; dm R$80-90, d with fan R$280;) This laid-back hostel is run by Argentine escapees and sits 700m from the beach and 200m from Centrinho, the center of the village. It's a well-built house with expansive views, though none of the ocean. It sometimes closes from June to August.

★**Quinta do Bucanero** POUSADA $$$

(48 3355-6056; www.bucanero.com.br; Estrada Geral da Praia do Rosa; r R$861-1268, ste R$1984;) Built bedrock-style literally in and around the rocky cliffside, Rosa's most charming option is a 12-room gem of hospitality in jungly surrounds. Rooms are dressed in light colors and feature five-star comforts and view-riffic patios (suites take that mantra to stupendous levels).

Eating & Drinking

★**Urucum** SEAFOOD $$

(48 4141-9141; www.facebook.com/restaurante.urucum; Av Central Praia do Rosa 100; mains for 2 people R$101-156; 1pm-midnight;) Chef Rafael Miralha hails from Espírito Santo and trained in Southern California before landing in Rosa, hometown recipes in hand. In stylish new Centrinho digs, his scrumptious *moquecas* are healthier and lighter than the Bahian version and served in clay cookware.

★**Lua Marinha** SEAFOOD $$$

(48 3354-0613; www.facebook.com/luamarinha; Rua 41251; mains for 2 people R$139-264; 6pm-midnight Thu & Fri, from noon Sat & Sun Apr-Nov;) Hidden down a pothole-ridden track that will surely have you believing you are marching to your demise, you'll find Tais running the show at this artistically driven seafood shack, the kind of find that postcards are written about. Octopus is the specialty (seven-pepper, with raisins and mushrooms) along with *butiá* caipirinhas made with artisanal *cachaça*. It sits on Lagoa de Ibirapuera, 1.4km northwest of Centrinho.

Beleza Pura - Cosmic Bar BAR

(48 3355-7490; www.belezapurabar.com.br; Estrada Geral da Praia do Rosa s/n; 8:30pm-3am Fri & Sat) A top see-and-be-seen refuge in Praia do Rosa, with DJs, live music and miles and miles of beautiful people. The owners have lived in Rio de Janeiro, Buenos Aires and Europe and have incorporated upscale lounge elements into the experience here. They also have a bar at the beach, Beleza Pura.

Information

There are no banks in Praia do Rosa: Garopaba and Imbituba have the nearest ATMs. Try to find a map – it's a complicated labyrinth of dirt roads layered over various hillsides, most of which eludes Google.

Getting There & Away

The bus situation in Praia do Rosa is complicated due to stifling traffic and intermunicipality transit spats (Praia do Rosa belongs to Imbituba, not Garopaba, but it sits right on the border between the two). In low season, local buses head to Imbituba every 30 to 45 minutes (R$4.10, 1¼ hours, 5:50am to 10pm) from a **bus stop** (48 3255-0439; www.santoanjo.com.br) in Centrinho catercorner to Tigre Asiático. In summer, they leave from a **bus stop** (48 3255-0439; www.santoanjo.com.br) two blocks southwest near Supermercado Bem Perto. From Imbituba, Santo Anjo and **Eucatur** (www.eucatur.com.br) go to Porto Alegre (from R$76, six hours) up to eight times per day.

Buses to Garopaba (R$4.50, 20 minutes), from where you can continue on to Florianópolis (R$27.50, two hours) with **Santo Anjo** (www.santoanjo.com.br; Av Paulo Fontes 1101, Terminal Rodoviário Rita Maria), leave from the **RodOil** (Rua 41251 s/n) gas station, 850m north of Centrinho.

Or you could take an Uber. Off-peak fares run R$25 or so to Garopaba and R$33 to Imbituba.

Rio Grande do Sul

Includes ➡

Porto Alegre 316
Serra Gaúcha 320
Bento Gonçalves 320
Vale dos Vinhedos 321
Pinto Bandeira 326
Gramado 326
Cambará do Sul 328
Litoral Gaúcho 331
Torres 331
Rio Grande 333

Best Places to Eat

- ➡ Valle Rustico (p325)
- ➡ Belle du Valais (p328)
- ➡ Mamma Gema (p324)
- ➡ Atelier das Massas (p318)
- ➡ Agridoce Café (p318)

Best Places to Stay

- ➡ Parador Casa da Montanha (p330)
- ➡ Pousada Borghetto Sant'Anna (p324)
- ➡ Jardim Secreto Pousada (p327)
- ➡ Vila Ecológica (p330)
- ➡ Hostel Britanico (p327)

Why Go?

From the forest-covered canyons of the national parks near Cambará do Sul, and cascading river valleys near cozy Brazilian Alpine villages like Gramado, to the stunning Vale dos Vinhedos, where Italian-descended vintners produce emerging New World wines, Rio Grande do Sul defies stereotypical notions of Brazil.

Brazil's southernmost state is its most culturally distinct, home to an independently minded population steeped in cattle herding and cowboy culture. *Gaúchos,* as residents of Rio Grande do Sul are known, are a fiercely proud and traditional lot. In the countryside, it is not unusual to see old-timers sporting wide-brimmed hats and other traditional dress. And everywhere – even in the cosmopolitan capital of Porto Alegre – locals suck down *chimarrão,* the distinctive, traditional tea made from the maté plant.

When to Go

Porto Alegre

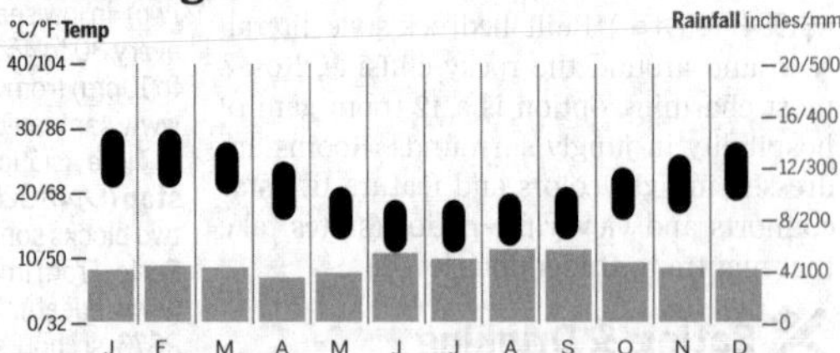

Jan–Mar Hot days and cool nights during harvest season in the Vale dos Vinhedos.

May–Oct Prices are higher, but you *might* see Brazilian snow in Cambará do Sul.

Dec, Jun & Jul Gramado is in Alpine wonderland mode for Christmas, then again in winter.

History

Living on land long disputed by the Spanish and Portuguese, the people of Rio Grande do Sul used the conflict to create an identity distinct from the rest of Brazil. The region even declared its independence during the ill-fated Guerra dos Farrapos, a decade-long civil war ending in 1845. A wave of immigrants, mostly German, Italian and Swiss, began arriving in the late 19th century, reinforcing the region's cultural differences.

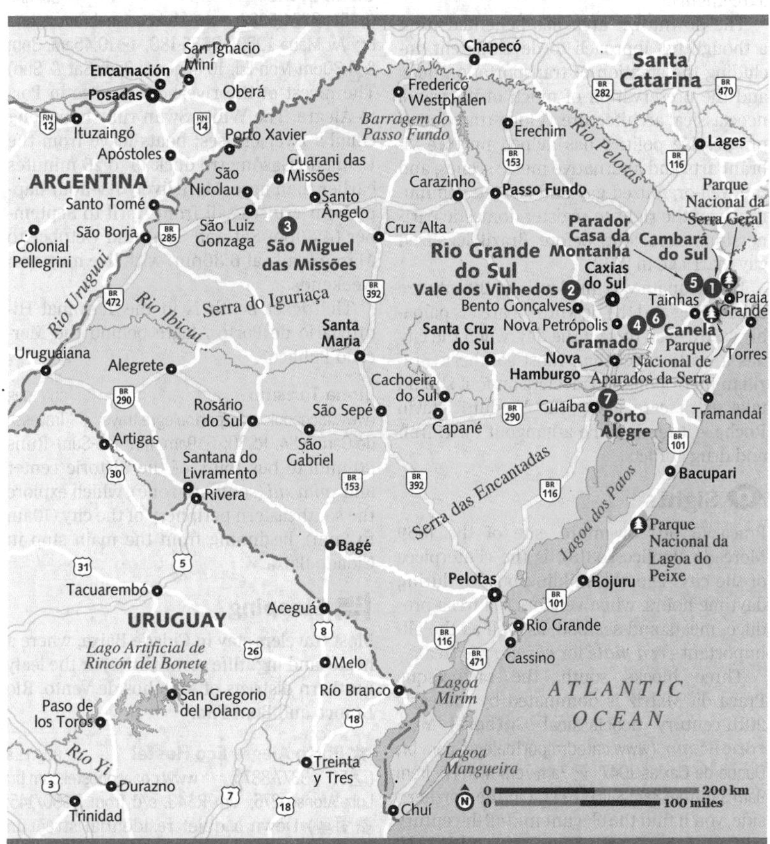

Rio Grande do Sul Highlights

❶ **Cambará do Sul** (p328) Peering over the edges and wandering through canyons at Parque Nacional da Serra Geral and Parque Nacional de Aparados da Serra.

❷ **Vale dos Vinhedos** (p321) Tasting your way through this gorgeous emerging wine region.

❸ **São Miguel das Missões** (p325) Exploring the stunning grounds of a ruined Unesco-listed Jesuit mission along the Rota Missões.

❹ **Gramado** (p326) Overindulging in fondue and chocolate while exploring the Swiss-style mountain village that rates as Brazil's most cinematic winterscape.

❺ **Parador Casa da Montanha** (p330) Holing up in tented luxury surrounded by bucolic countryside near Parque Nacional de Aparados da Serra.

❻ **Canela** (p329) Gawking at a postcard-perfect 131m free-falling waterfall at Parque Estadual do Caracol.

❼ **Porto Alegre** (p316) Drinking your way through Brazil's microbrewery-crazed capital.

PORTO ALEGRE

0XX51 / POP 1.4 MILLION

On the banks of the huge freshwater Lagoa dos Patos, Porto Alegre is southern Brazil's most important port city and a key player in Mercosul (the South American free-trade agreement).

The downtown area has benefited from a thoughtful approach to development, including the creation of transportation hubs and the preservation of much of its grand, neoclassical architecture. A long tradition of progressive politics has helped nurture vibrant arts and alternative music scenes, and the well-organized gay and lesbian community won the right to register domestic partnerships here long before Brazil legalized gay marriage in 2013.

Unfortunately, crime levels in the city are concerning and the downtown area is palpably seedy, even during the day, when the city has a grittier feel than most southern Brazilian metropolises. Travelers on foot should take extra care along the Viaduto Otávio Rocha – it tends to be a hangout for riffraff and drug addicts.

Sights

Praça 15 de Novembro, site of the 1869 Mercado Público (p318), is the centerpiece of the city. The old building bustles during daytime hours, when vendors sell fresh produce, meats and seafood, as well as the all-important *erva maté* for *chimarrão* (tea).

Three blocks south, the picturesque Praça da Matriz is dominated by the early 20th-century neoclassical **Catedral Metropolitana** (www.catedralportoalegre.com.br; Duque de Caxias 1047; 7am-7pm Mon-Fri, from 9am Sat, from 8am Sun) FREE. On the northern side, you'll find the elegant mid-19th-century edifice of the **Teatro São Pedro** (51 3227-5100; www.teatrosaopedro.com.br; Praça Mal Deodoro s/n; box office 1-6:30pm Mon-Fri, to 3pm Sat & Sun) and the sculpted facade of the **Biblioteca Público** (51 3224-5045; www.bibliotecapublica.rs.gov.br; cnr Riachuelo & General Câmara; 9am-7pm Mon-Fri, 2-6pm Sat).

Museu de Arte do Rio Grande do Sul MUSEUM
(MARGS; www.margs.rs.gov.br; Praça da Alfândega; 10am-7pm Tue-Sun) FREE A pedestrian promenade runs into Praça da Alfândega, the leafy square that is home to the Museu de Arte do Rio Grande do Sul. The neoclassical building is an impressive venue for regional artists. On the ground floor, the inviting **Bistrot de MARGS** takes advantage of the leafy environment, which is a lovely setting for lunch (R$37.50 to R$76.90).

Activities & Tours

Cisne Branco BOATING
(51 3224-5222; www.barcocisnebranco.com.br; Av Mauá 1050; R$35-180; 10:45am, 3pm & 4:30pm Mon-Fri, 10:45am & 3pm Sat & Sun) The nicest of the riverboat cruises in Porto Alegre. The White Swan runs hour-long Guaíba river cruises; boats leave from the Usina do Gasômetro dock 15 to 20 minutes earlier than here. More lively 1½-hour happy hour cruises sail from April to September (4:30pm Sat and Sun) and October to March (daily at 6:30pm) with live music on weekends.

The ticket booth is in the Terminal Hidroviário de Porto Alegre behind the Mercado Publico.

Linha Turismo CITY TOUR
(www.facebook.com/portoalegre.travel; Travessa do Carmo 84; R$30; 9am-4pm Tue-Sun) Runs 90-minute bus tours of the historic center and *zona sul* (southern zone), which explore the southeastern periphery of the city (10am to 3pm), beginning from the main stop in Cidade Baixa.

Sleeping

Most travelers stay in Cidade Baixa, where a hostel and nightlife scene thrive, or the leafy northern districts of Moinhos de Vento, Rio Branco and Bom Fim.

★ **Porto Alegre Eco Hostel** HOSTEL $
(51 3377-8876; www.poaecohostel.com.br; Luiz Afonso 276; dm R$43, s/d from R$80/145; @) Down a quiet residential street in the heart of Cidade Baixa, this excellent hostel, chock-full of demolition wood furniture and eco-awareness, has a lovely backyard garden in a pristine '30s-era home.

Eko Residence Hotel HOTEL $
(51 3215-7600; www.facebook.com/ekoresidence; Av Des André da Rocha 131; s R$139-159, d R$149-164; @) This 97-apartment hotel near Parque Farroupilha has solar-heated showers, a vertical garden and rainwater toilets. Rooms are criminally cheap, especially the Plus options, which are far bigger and better than the slightly cheaper studios. Design touches run from house-made lighting to headboards from reclaimed wood.

Porto Alegre

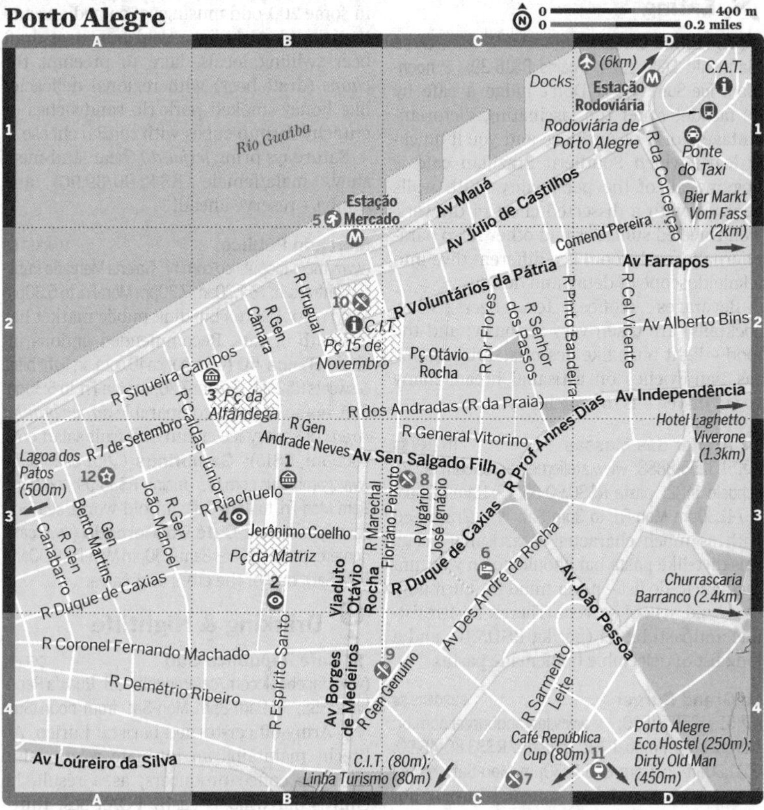

Porto Alegre

Sights
1 Biblioteca Público B3
2 Catedral Metropolitana B3
3 Museu de Arte do Rio Grande do Sul B2
4 Teatro São Pedro B3

Activities, Courses & Tours
5 Cisne Branco B1

Sleeping
6 Eko Residence Hotel C3

Eating
7 Agridoce Café C4
8 Atelier das Massas C3
Banca 40 .... (see 10)
Bar Gambrinus .... (see 10)
9 Boteco Natalicio C4
10 Mercado Público B2

Drinking & Nightlife
11 Bahamas D4
Café do Mercado .... (see 10)

Entertainment
12 Casa da Cultura Mario Quintana A3

Shopping
ArteLoja CCMQ .... (see 12)

Hotel Laghetto Viverone BOUTIQUE HOTEL $$
(☎51 2102-7272; www.hotellaghettomoinhos.com.br; Dr Vale 579; s/d from R$289/319, ste from R$700; ❄@🛜🏊) Porto Alegre's best boutique hotel is built off an exquisite 1937 mansion (housing the lobby, bar and restaurant) with a glass atrium connecting the 132-guest-room tower to the historic property. Muted gray rooms are modern, minimalist and comfortable, while the three themed suites feature huge mirrors, sink-in bathtubs and unique design (we dig Nuptials and NYC).

Eating

★ Agridoce Café CAFE $
(Sarmento Leite 1024; mains R$16-29; noon-10pm Tue-Sun;) Don't judge a cafe by its facade! Enter the fascinating Victorian-vintage world of Agridoce and you'll quickly learn which Southern Brazilian cafe is hogging all of the personality. With walls adorned with a dissected chest of drawers, well-traveled suitcases and other retro paraphernalia, each room is a different dive into a kaleidoscope of detail and design.

Beverages (coffee, tea, beer, wine, cocktails) are taken very seriously; and the food – light bites like desserts, quiches, pizzas, sandwiches on artisanal bread, many vegan or veg – is topnotch.

★ Atelier das Massas ITALIAN $$
(51 3255-8888; www.atelierdemassas.com.br; Riachuelo 1482; pasta R$30.90-65; 11am-2:30pm & 7-11:30pm Mon-Fri, to 3pm Sat;) Crammed with as much character as artisanal pasta, this dive-like pasta bar should go on your immediate to-do list – never mind the curmudgeonly old school servers. There's an irresistible antipasti buffet (per kg R$115.40) and a long list of delectable homemade pastas.

Le Grand Burger BURGERS $$
(51 3395-1520; www.legrandburger.com.br; Marquês do Pombal 191; burgers R$33.80-46.90; 11:30am-2:30pm & 6-11:30pm Mon-Sat;) It pains us to think a gourmet burger hot spot in the middle of Brazilian beef country needs to import its main ingredient from the UK, but such is life. This whimsical, French-inspired *hamburgueria* consistently takes the city's best burger honors.

The long list of creative burgers (all of which can be made vegetarian, with five vegan choices as well) satiates a beautiful Moinhos de Vento crowd. Reservations recommended.

Churrascaria Barranco STEAK $$
(51 3331-6172; www.churrascariabarranco.com.br; Av Protásio Alves 1578; steaks for 2 people R$56-74; 11am-2am;) Established in 1969, this always-crowded temple of beef has no cowboy shows or skewers of speared meat, but it is where locals go for their *carne* fix.

Boteco Natalicio BOTECO $$
(51 3026-5539; www.facebook.com/botecon atalicio; Genuíno 217; mains R$18.90-79.90; 5pm-1am Mon-Sat;) The walls of this lively, bilevel *boteco* (neighborhood bar) straddling Centro and Cidade Baixa are covered in some 200-odd musings of comedians and locals, and packs in a wild bunch of draft beer-swilling locals, here to preempt the *chope* (draft beer) with regional delicacies like honey-smoked pork rib sandwiches or crunchy shrimp cubes with *coalho* cheese.

Saturdays bring *feijoada* (bean-and-meat stew; male/female R$42.90/39.90) and samba – reserve ahead!

Mercado Público MARKET $$
(www.mercadopublico.com.br; Galeria Mercado Público Central s/n; 7:30am-7:30pm Mon-Fri, to 6:30pm Sat) Porto Alegre's bustling public market has a wealth of eats. Recommended options include **Banca 40** (www.banca40.com.br; light bites & sweets R$2-24; 8am-7:30pm Mon-Fri, to 6:30pm Sat), home of the incomparable *super bomba royal* (a showy ice cream and fruit salad concoction; R$15); **Gambrinus** (51 3226-6914; www.gambrinus.com.br;; mains R$38-99; 11am-9pm Mon-Fri, to 4pm Sat), an old-world seafood restaurant; and **Café Do Mercado** (www.cafedomercado.com.br; 8am-7:30pm Mon-Fri, 9:30am-5pm Sat), one of the city's best cafes.

Drinking & Nightlife

★ Café República Cup COFFEE
(www.facebook.com/caferepublica38; Rua da República 358; 9am-8pm Mon-Sat, from noon Sun;) Army-officer-turned-barista Eurico Albrecht maintains an intimate relationship with his coffee producers; as a result, he churns out what is easily POA's best third-wave coffee (R$5 to R$24).

★ Dirty Old Man BAR
(www.dirtyoldman.com.br; Lima e Silva 956; 6pm-midnight Sun-Thu, to 1am Fri & Sat;) This awesomely named bar (a nod to Bukowski) is Cidade Baixa's best. Draft ales (Baldhead, Malvadez, Bardos) and cool cocktails (R$15 to R$28) fuel the good time, while the crowd swilling it down is as eclectic as the environment itself.

★ Bier Markt Vom Fass BAR
(www.biermarkt.com.br; Barão de Santo Ângelo 497; 6-11:30pm Mon-Sat;) With its 38 taps and 100 international labels by the bottle, this Moinhos de Vento drinking den has won the city's Best Beer List honors every year since 2010. There's is a strong emphasis on local breweries — including Seasons, Tupiniquim and Irmãos Ferraro — and the music supervisor unearths some real toe-tapping gems from the '80s you may have forgotten about.

CHEERS TO CHIMARRÃO

It was the indigenous Guarani who taught the Spanish the pleasures of *chimarrão* (tea from the maté plant) and how to sip it – not from a cup but through a *bomba* (straw) stuck into a hollowed-out *cuia* (gourd). Also known as *erva maté*, this tea-like beverage is made from the leaves of the maté tree, which is native to the *Pampas* (grassy plains) that extend from Argentina and Uruguay through southern Brazil.

The original *gaúchos*, the men who tended the region's vast cattle herds, quickly became addicted to maté's pleasurable effects, which are at once energizing and calming. *Chimarrão* is an acquired taste and a serious addiction, but these days this ancient tradition is getting a boost from scientists and pseudoscientists alike, who make claims about maté's health benefits, from lower blood pressure to increased intelligence. Hard data has yet to come. Anyone you meet with a gourd (that's nearly everyone!) will offer you some.

Perro Libre Tap Room CRAFT BEER
(www.perrolibre.com.br/tap-room; Praça Dr Maurício Cardoso 71; ⌚5pm-midnight Tue-Sat, 2-10pm Sun; 📶) Perro Libre, one of the South's top breweries, doesn't actually brew here, but this modern, industrial-chic bar inside Casa Prado pumps its fresh *cerveja artesanal* (craft brew) from an inventive self-serve pay-by-the-milliliter system. Register for a card, load it with credit, and fill up from 10 taps of hoppy IPAs, Gose (a top-fermented beer that originated in Goslar, Germany) with exotic Amazonian fruits and tonka bean stouts.

Bahamas GAY
(www.facebook.com/barcidadebaixa; Rua da República 198; ⌚6pm-midnight Tue & Wed, to late Thu-Sat, 5pm-midnight Sun; 📶) This down-to-earth, almost divey *boteco* (neighborhood bar) is the epicenter of Rua da República's GLS (Gays, Lesbians and Sympathetics) scene, a great spot to knock back ice-cold beer or excellent caipirinhas. The party spills well beyond the sidewalk seating, especially on Sundays.

☆ Entertainment

Casa da Cultura Mario Quintana CINEMA
(☎51 3221-7147; www.ccmq.rs.gov.br; Rua dos Andradas 736; ⌚9am-9pm Tue-Fri, from noon Sat) The cultural center in this pink baroque building has a cinema (Cinemateca Paulo Amorim; films R$12 to R$14), a busy cafe, and a great arts and crafts shop, **ArteLoja CCMQ**. The 7th-floor Café Santo de Casa is a lovely place to listen to live music and watch the sunset over Lagoa dos Patos.

ℹ Information

Both the municipality and the state have tourist information booths in Porto Alegre, the former at the **Mercado Público** (Centro de Informações Turísticas; ☎51 3211-5705; www2.portoalegre.rs.gov.br/turismo; Mercado Público; ⌚8am-6pm Mon-Sat) and the main **Linha Turismo bus stop** (Centro de Informações Turísticas; ☎51 3289-6765; www2.portoalegre.rs.gov.br/turismo; Travessa do Carmo 84; ⌚8am-6pm); the latter at the **airport** (Centros de Atenção ao Turista; ☎51 3374-0294; www.turismo.rs.gov.br; Arrivals Hall, Terminal 1, Porto Alegre Airport; ⌚8am-10pm) and the **bus station** (Centro de Atencão ao Turista; ☎51 3225-0677; www.turismo.rs.gov.br; Rodoviária; ⌚8am-6pm).

ℹ Getting There & Away

AIR

The city's airport – privatized and renamed **Porto Alegre Airport** (POA; ☎51 3358-2000; www.portoalegre-airport.com.br; Av Severo Dulius 90.010) in 2017 – is 6km northeast of downtown, with two terminals connected by a free shuttle. The majority of airlines operate out of Terminal 1, but Azul departs from the older Terminal 2. In addition to major destinations throughout Brazil, international destinations include Buenos Aires, Lima, Montevideo and Panama City.

Prepaid **Cootaero** (☎51 3358-2500; www.cootaero.com.br; Arrivals Hall, Porto Alegre Airport) taxis from the arrivals hall run R$33 or so to Centro and R$38 or so to Cidade Baixa. An Uber is considerably less.

BUS

The busy **long-distance bus station** (☎51 3210-0101; www.rodoviaria-poa.com.br; Largo Vespasiano Julioveppo 70), 1.5km northeast of Centro, is accessible by metro; alternatively, a taxi downtown costs R$10 to R$20 or so from the prepaid **Ponte do Taxi** (☎51 3221-9371; Estação Rodoviária de Porto Alegre).

Two day and two overnight buses go to Chuí (R$124 to R$175, eight hours) on the Uruguayan border during the week (two less on weekends) with **Planalto** (www.planalto.com.br); otherwise, you can connect in Pelotas with **Expresso Embaixador** (www.expressoembaixador.com.br).

Buses to Buenos Aires depart at 5pm and 6pm daily; to Montevideo at 10pm daily as well as 8pm on Monday, Wednesday, Thursday, Saturday and Sunday, 7pm on Tuesday and 9pm and 9:15pm on Friday and Sunday, respectively; to Santiago, buses depart on Monday at 7:30am. **Citral** (☎51 3358-2960; www.citral.tur.br; Arrivals Hall, Porto Alegre Airport) also runs buses to some provincial destinations direct from Porto Alegre Airport.

Getting Around

Porto Alegre's metro, **Trensurb** (www.trensurb.gov.br; one-way R$3.30; 5am-11:25pm), has convenient stations at Estação Mercado (by the port), Estação Rodoviária (the next stop) and the airport (three stops beyond). For Cidade Baixa, catch bus T5/T51/T52 from the airport or 282, 282.1, 244, 255, 272 or 343 from the bus station (R$4.30).

SERRA GAÚCHA

The scenic stretch of mountains north of Porto Alegre is known as the Serra Gaúcha. The landscape – particularly beautiful between Nova Petrópolis and Gramado – is characterized by forested hillsides and unexpected rocky cliffs, often sparkling with waterfalls. The region was first populated by Germans (beginning in 1824) and later by Italians (beginning in the 1870s), and this heritage is still a source of pride. Although the mountains don't reach much higher than 1000m, the architecture and atmosphere of Gramado and parts of Canela resemble Swiss villages. In Bento Gonçalves and the nearby wine regions of Vale dos Vinhedos and Pinto Bandeira, descendants of Italian immigrants continue fostering momentum within the wine industry.

Bento Gonçalves

☎0XX54 / POP 107,200

Considering the region's Italian heritage and its dry, mountainous landscape, it makes sense that Rio Grande do Sul would be Brazil's wine epicenter. The command post for this burgeoning wine industry is

BUSES FROM PORTO ALEGRE

DESTINATION	STARTING FARE (R$)	DURATION (HR)	BUS COMPANY
Buenos Aires (Argentina)	335	21	Flecha Bus (www.flechabus.com.ar), JBL (www.jblturismo.com.br)
Cambará do Sul	46.75	6	Citral (www.citral.tur.br)
Canela	37.60	3	Citral
Chuí	124	8	Planalto (www.planalto.com.br)
Curitiba	192	13	Penha (www.passagempenha.com.br), Catarinense (www.catarinense.net)
Florianópolis	89	6	Santo Anjo (www.santoanjo.com.br), Eucatur (www.eucatur.com.br)
Gramado	35	3	Citral
Montevideo (Uruguay)	267	12	TTL (www.ttl.com.br), EGA (www.ega.com.uy)
Pelotas	61	3½	Expresso Embaixador (www.expressoembaixador.com.br)
Rio de Janeiro	358.50	26	Penha
Rio Grande	77.50	5	Planalto
Santiago (Chile)	486	40	JBL
Sânto Angelo	127	7	Ouro e Prata (www.ouroeprata.com)
São Francisco de Paula	28	3	Citral
São Paulo	180	19	Penha, Eucatur
Torres	49	3	Unesul (www.unesul.com.br)

Bento Gonçalves, 124km north of Porto Alegre, a distinctly indistinct middle-class Brazilian city that does not offer much beyond convenient access to the region's vineyards. The entrance to town leaves no doubt about its allegiances: a gigantic 'wine barrel' known as Pórtico da Pipa straddles the street.

Tours

Vale das Vinhas Tur WINE

(☎54 3451-4216; www.valedasvinhastur.com.br; Barão do Rio Branco 245, Hotel Vinocap; half-/full-day tour per person R$110/230) Vale das Vinhas runs three-hour tours that visit three wineries in the Vale dos Vinhedos (8:30am and 1:30pm; minimum two people) as well as a full-day option that hits up five. It's located in the lobby of Hotel Vinocap.

An English interpreter can be arranged (for a higher cost, of course).

Sleeping & Eating

There is little reason to stay in Bento proper, with beautiful countryside inns just steps away in Vale dos Vinhedos. It's more convenient, however, if you're dependent on public transportation.

Hotel Vinocap BUSINESS HOTEL $$

(☎54 3455-7100; www.vinocap.com.br; Barão do Rio Branco 245; s/d from R$189/288; ❄@📶) This agreeable, centrally located business hotel is well equipped for wine tourism.

★**Canta Maria Gastronomia** ITALIAN $$

(☎54 3702-3099; www.facebook.com/pg/cantamariagastronomia; Parnaíba 777; buffet R$53.80-87; ⏲11:30am-3pm & 7-11pm Tue-Sun; 📶) Occupying a lovely residential home in Planato near Igreja São Bento, this is the best of the restaurants specializing in the *comida típica italiana* buffet: *capeletti* (meat-filled pasta) soup, salad, pasta, *galeto* (rotisserie spring chicken), *linguiça* (garlicky pork sausage), pork ribs, polenta and fried cheese. Shhhh...just don't tell the owner's brother, who owns the *other* good one!

Information

Pick up a must-have Vale dos Vinhedos map at one of two tourist information booths in Bento Gonçalves. **Caminhos de Pedra** (Centro de Atendmiento ao Turista; ☎54 3455-6333; www.caminhosdepedra.org.br; Estrada Barracão 600, Barracão; ⏲9am-5pm Mon-Fri, to 3pm Sat & Sun) also runs a tourist info booth.

C.A.T. (Centro de Atendmiento ao Turista; ☎54 3453-6699, 0800-603-6060; www.bentogoncalves.rs.gov.br; Marechal Deodoro 70; ⏲8am-5:30pm Mon-Fri)

C.A.T. (Centro de Atendmiento ao Turista; ☎0800-603-606, 3453-2555; www.bentogoncalves.rs.gov.br; Travessa Carazinho s/n, Pórtico da Pipa; ⏲8am-5:30pm Mon-Fri, 9am-5pm Sat & Sun)

Getting There & Away

The **long-distance bus station** (☎54 3452-1311; www.rodoviariabento.com.br; Gomes Carneiro 19) is about 1km north of the center. **Bento** (☎54 3452-1311; www.bentotransportes.com.br; Gomes Carneiro 19, Estação Rodoviária de Bento Goncalves) has hourly service to Porto Alegre (from R$34, 2½ hours); for Caxias do Sul (R$9.70, 1¼ hours), **Ozelame** (☎54 3452-3777; www.ozelame.com.br; Gomes Carneiro 19, Estação Rodoviária de Bento Goncalves) departs hourly as well. For Canela, Gramado or Cambará do Sul, connect in Caxias. **Unesul** (☎54 3452-2977; www.unesul.com.br; Gomes Carneiro 19, Estação Rodoviária de Bento Goncalves) has at least two daily buses to Santo Ângelo (R$121.60, 7½ hours, 2pm and 8pm).

For Vale dos Vinhedos, **Transportes Monte Bello** (☎54 3457-1100; http://montebelotur.wixsite.com/montebeloturismo) can get you onto Via Trento four times a day (R$4.50, 30 minutes, 6:30am, 10:25am, 4:25pm and 6:10pm) from a stop along Av Osvaldo Aranha in front of Salini Veículos, 100m or so from the bus station. But renting your own vehicle, a local tour or an Uber (R$20 or so to Almaúnica, R$25 or so to Miolo) are best.

Vale dos Vinhedos

When connoisseurs debate world-class wine production, Brazil isn't usually the first country that comes to mind. Discerning palates, however, are starting to rave about the outstanding vintages of southern Brazil. The award-winning sparkling wines, cabernets and chardonnays fermented in the Vale dos Vinhedos are the result of generations of hard work and innovation – particularly by Italian families that immigrated to the region starting in the 1870s – as well as excellent soil and growing conditions. Now, nearly 150 years later, the awards have finally started to roll in. In 2013, the Vale dos Vinhedos was even named one of the year's 10 Best Wine Travel Destinations by *Wine Enthusiast* magazine. Brazilian wine has arrived.

KLEYTON KAMOGAWA/SHUTTERSTOCK ©

1. Entrance to Bento Gonçalves (p320) **2.** Vinícola Almaúnica **3.** Vinícola Miolo **4.** Vineyards in Vale dos Vinhedos

WOLFGANG DIEDERICH/ALAMY STOCK PHOTO ©

Vale dos Vinhedos

Today, Brazil ranks 14th in the world in vinifera wine production (falling between Romania and Hungary), the lion's share coming from Rio Grande do Sul. The Vale dos Vinhedos welcomes hundreds of thousands of visitors to more than 30 wineries, rural inns and restaurants along the Estrada do Vinho and Via Trento, a picturesque loop that stretches west of Bento Gonçalves. Visually speaking, the whole valley will leave you rubbing your eyes to triple-confirm you have not been suddenly teleported to France, Italy or northern California.

Vinícola Almaúnica

Almaúnica (☎54 3459-1384; www.almaunica.com.br; RS-444, Km 17.35; tastings 6/12 wines R$50/90; ⏲8am-5:30pm Mon-Fri, from 10am Sat, 10am-1pm Sun) FREE is one of the region's most awarded vineyards, and the syrahs and Quatro Castas blends are topnotch. The friendly owner is often in the tasting room, happily serving glasses over gorgeous vineyard views.

Casa Valduga

One of Brazilian wine's big guns, **Valduga** (☎54 2105-3154; www.casavalduga.com.br; Via Trento 2355; tasting & tour R$40; ⏲9:30am-6pm Mon-Sat, to 5pm Sun) has R$20 tastings (five wines) in its wine shop or tasting-and-tour combos almost hourly from 9:30am to 4:30pm (to 3:30pm Sunday have the most impressive vineyard views.

Vinícola Miolo

Sparkling wines, cabernet sauvignon and merlot are the specialties at **Vinícola Miolo** (☎54 2102-1540; www.miolo.com.br; Estrada do Vinho, Km 21; tour & tastings standard/premium R$30/R$90; ⏲9am-4:30pm). The huge complex spreads out from an artificial lake and guided tours are run hourly. If you want to taste without doing the tour, your only option is the R$60 premium tasting (five wines).

PARADISE LOST

In 1608, the governor of the Spanish province of Paraguay ordered the local Jesuit leader, Fray Diego de Torres, to convert the local Tupi and Guarani people. The Jesuits established missions across a vast region that encompassed much of southern Brazil, as well as portions of southern Paraguay and northern Argentina.

Unlike their brethren elsewhere in the Americas, the Jesuits made a concerted effort to convert the indigenous people without destroying their culture or language. The missions became centers of culture and intellect, as well as religion. The arts flourished, combining elements of European and Guarani music and painting. Scholars created a written form of the Tupi-Guarani language and, beginning in 1704, published several works, using one of South America's earliest printing presses. The missions produced sophisticated sculpture, metallurgy, ceramics and musical instruments. In an age of monarchies and institutionalized slavery, the missions were an island of idealism, where wealth was divided equitably, and religion, intellect and arts were cultivated in tandem.

From the beginning, the missions faced threats from the outside world. In the 1620s they were harassed by Portuguese *bandeirantes,* bands of Paulistas who raided the interior in search of gold and indigenous people to enslave. Thousands of people were captured, and the 13 missions of Guayra (present-day Paraná) were eventually abandoned. Beginning in the 1630s, the Jesuits consolidated their position in 30 sites across the northwest corner of present-day Rio Grande do Sul, as well as in Argentina and Paraguay.

To a large part, it was the success of the missions that brought about their downfall. The independent-minded Jesuits became an embarrassment to Rome and to the Spanish and Portuguese kings. In 1750, the Treaty of Madrid dictated that the sites be handed over to Portuguese rule, which would not protect the local population from enslavement. The Guarani were commanded to evacuate in 1754, but they refused to abandon their settlements and thus incited the Guarani War. In 1756, a combined Spanish-Portuguese army attacked the missions, killing more than 1500 Guaranis and selling many more into slavery, thus decimating the Guarani population. It was a tragic, bloody end to an amazing social experiment.

The missions were lauded by great thinkers from Voltaire to Montesquieu as a real incarnation of Christian utopia, which was destroyed by the very forces that created it. Robert De Niro and Jeremy Irons relive this story in the 1986 film *The Mission,* a moving, fictional account of these events.

Today, all 30 missions are in ruins. Together, they form the **Rota Missões** (www.rotamissoes.com.br), or 'Missions Route,' a network of pilgrimage sites for the faithful and the curious. Seven are in Brazil (in the northwestern part of Rio Grande do Sul), eight are in southern Paraguay and 15 are in northeastern Argentina.

Sleeping & Eating

★Pousada Borghetto Sant'Anna POUSADA $$$
(☎54 3453-2355; www.borghettosantanna.com.br; Linha Leopoldina 868; ste R$480, cottages R$550-600; ❄📶) Perched above the Vale dos Vinhedos, this cluster of romantic stone houses gives a fantastic view of the valley below. The lodgings mix rustic charm with sumptuous comfort and unobtrusive construction, right down to large portions of sedentary rock in the showers. Breakfast is simple, but the views make up for it. It's about 4km west of Bento.

Hotel Spa do Vinho HOTEL $$$
(☎54 2102-7200; www.marriott.com.br; RS-444, Km 21; r/ste from R$390/667; ❄@📶🏊) The region's largest hotel takes top honors for its explosive, unobstructed views of the surrounding vineyards. Perched on a hill in front of Vinícola Miolo, you can't miss the living postcard, from the pool and wine-barrel hot tub to the upscale restaurant.

★Mamma Gema ITALIAN $$
(☎54 3459-1392; www.mammagema.com.br; Estrada RS-444, Km 18.9; mains for 2 people R$92-135; ⏲11am-4pm Tue-Sun) Unlike many of the trattorias in the region, Mamma focuses on quality, not quantity, and is a mainstay in Vale dos Vinhedos. The owner, a former professional footballer, harvests his own wild mushrooms for use in perfectly executed pasta and risotto dishes.

At night, all eyes turn to the downstairs pizzeria, **Pizza Entre Vinhos** (pizzas R$82-87;

The small, pleasant city of **Santo Ângelo** is the regional transportation hub and jumping off point for exploring the Brazilian missions. The impressive **cathedral** (www.diocesedesantoangelo.org; Praça da Catedral; hours vary) is a 1929 replica of the church at São Miguel das Missões and casts a gorgeous rust-orange glow over the center of town at sunrise. From here you can organize tours with **Caminho das Missões** (55 3312-9632; www.caminhodasmissoes.com.br; Antunes Ribas 984; 8am-noon & 1-6pm Mon-Fri, 8am-noon Sat) or **Marino Theobald** (55 99961-3826; marino_theobald@yahoo.com.br; per site R$60-80) or, ideally, rent your own vehicle – try **Pontual** (55 3313-6000; www.pontualautolocadora.com.br; Marquês do Herval 1845; per day from R$95; 8:30am-noon & 2-6pm Mon-Fri, 9am-noon Sat).

The most striking of the missions is **Sítio Arqueológico São Miguel Arcanjo** (adult/child R$14/7, incl Museu das Missões; 9am-noon & 2-8pm Oct-Mar, 9am-noon & 2-6pm Tue-Sun, 1:30-6pm Mon Apr-Sep) in **São Miguel das Missões**, 53km southwest of Santo Ângelo. The elegant church, designed by an Italian architect who was also a Jesuit frivale ar, earned Unesco World Heritage status in 1984. It is surrounded by the mystical ruins of the Jesuit settlement, which evokes the feeling of 'paradise lost.' On a beautiful day, snapping pics will drain your iPhone battery. The archaeological site also includes the excellent little **Museu das Missões** (www.museudasmissoes.blogspot.com; Sítio Arqueológico São Miguel Arcanjo; adult/child R$14/7, incl São Miguel Arcanjo; 9am-noon & 2-8pm Oct-Mar, 9am-noon & 2-6pm Tue-Sun, 1:30-6pm Mon Apr-Sep). Designed by Lúcio Costa, of Brasília fame, the museum contains an impressive collection of religious artifacts that were rescued from the ruins. A spectacular, if campy, sound-and-light show illustrates the history of the missions. Additional ruined missions in the region worth visiting include **São João Batista** (Map p74 Entre-Ijuís; 9am-5pm) FREE, **Santuário de Caaró** (55 99681-4506; Caibaté; 8-11:30am & 1:30-6pm Mon-Fri, or by appt) FREE, **São Lourenço Mártir** (São Luiz Gonzaga; 7am-noon & 1:30-7pm) FREE and **São Nicolau** (São Nicolau; 24hr) FREE.

From Santo Ângelo, **Unesul** (55 3313-2618; www.unesul.com.br; Sete Povos das Missões s/n, Rodoviária de Santo Ângelo) has two buses to Bento Gonçalves (R$132, 7½ hours, 2pm and 8pm; 2pm only on Saturday). **Ouro e Prata** (0800-51-8666; www.viacaoouroeprata.com.br; Sete Povos das Missões s/n, Rodoviária de Santo Ângelo) buses run frequently between Santo Ângelo and Porto Alegre (from R$149, seven hours, up to 10 per day).

Antonello Turismo (55 99632-3075; Sete Povos das Missões s/n, Rodoviária de Santo Ângelo) has four daily buses to São Miguel das Missões (R$13.25, 1½ hours, 8am, 11am, 3:30pm and 6:20pm) Monday to Friday, two on Saturday (10am, 3:30pm) and two on Sunday (9:30am, 6:20pm).

7-10:30pm Tue-Sat;), where the best pizza in the region is served alongside the best selection of Vale dos Vinhedos wines.

★Valle Rustico BRAZILIAN **$$$**
(54 98123-0080; www.vallerustico.com.br; Linha Marcílio Dias, 15 da Graciema; prix-fixe 7/10 courses R$130/210; 7:30-10pm Thu-Sat, noon-3:30pm Sun;) Wine country's best restaurant sits down a lonely and dark Vale dos Vinhedos dirt road – don't worry, it's open – where you'll find a wood-beamed dining room in the basement of a house and a lovely patio. Local chef Rodrigo Bellora has a seasonal surprise menu (organic where possible) that changes weekly, plus an impressive local wine list.

Information

C.A.T. - Aprovale (Associação dos Produtores de Vinhos Finos do Vale dos Vinhedos; 54 3451-9601; www.valedosvinhedos.com.br; Dávile Sandrin 525; 9am-noon & 1-5pm Mon-Fri, 9am-12:30pm & 1:30-4pm Sat & Sun) At the main gateway to Vale dos Vinhedos, the valley's member-only wine-growers association runs a helpful tourist info office. Many of the best wineries, including Miolo (p323), Valduga (p323) and Almaúnica (p323), are members. They sell wine as well.

Getting There & Away

For information on getting to and around Vale Dos Vinhedos, see the Bento Gonçalves Getting There & Away section (p321).

Pinto Bandeira

Sleepy Pinto Bandeira, just 15km northeast of Bento Gonçalves, is a separate wine appellation from the more established Vale dos Vinhedos and has soil more suited for sparkling wines. It has its own share of charming places to sleep and taste.

For more information on Pinto Bandeira, see www.asprovinho.com.br.

Sights

Don Giovanni WINERY

(54 3455-6293; www.dongiovanni.com.br; Linha Amadeu, Km 12; tastings R$25; 9-11:30am & 1-5pm Mon-Fri, 9am-5:30pm Sat, 9am-1pm Sun) Both a winery and a homey **pousada** (Linha Amadeu, Km 12; r R$450-700; P), Don Giovanni is a one-stop shop in Pinto Bandeira. It's most famous for sparkling wines (the tasting fee works as a credit toward purchases).

Vinícola Geisse WINERY

(54 3455-7461; www.vinicolageisse.com.br; Linha Jansen s/n; tastings R$30-80; 9-11:30am & 1-5pm Mon-Fri, 10am-5pm Sat, 10am-4pm Sun) Founded by famed Chilean winemaker Mario Geisse, Cave Geisse produces Brazil's most internationally heralded sparkling wines and is a cult favorite abroad. Reservations are best.

Eating

Casa Vanni ITALIAN $$

(54 3455-6383; www.casavanni.com.br; Linha Palmero 44; mains R$41-76; noon-3:30pm Thu-Tue;) Around 6km southeast of the Pinto Bandeira turnoff along the Caminho das Pedras, this historic, cinematic wooden house dates to 1935 and is considered one of the top dining destinations near Pinto.

The chef trained for three years in Italy's Piedmont region and does a fine job fusing her skills with homespun recipes, like *carne de panela* (stewed beef) risotto, in a cinematic stone cellar.

Getting There & Away

Bento (p321) services Pinto Bandeira four times a day (R$10, one hour, 10:30am, noon, 4:30pm and 5:45pm), passing the turnoffs for many of the wineries. An Uber to Vinícola Geisse from central Bento Gonçalves is around R$35 off-peak.

Gramado

0XX54 / POP 32,200

Gramado isn't as sexy as Ipanema or as alluring as the Amazon, but this tiny mountain resort, which bills itself as 'naturally European,' is one of Brazil's nicest. It does indeed feel like a Swiss mountain village – boutiques sell avant-garde glasswork and gourmet chocolate, local restaurants specialize in fondue, hotels are decked out like Swiss chalets – while the infrastructure, safety and scenery all meet the standards of similar-sized towns in North America or Europe (pedestrian crosswalks are respected!). At times the Alpine vibe crosses over into kitsch, but this chocolate fantasyland is pleasant, and the standard of living in this little piece of paradise is unparalleled in Brazil.

Sights & Activities

Lago Negro LAKE

(Renner s/n) About 1.5km southwest of the center, Lago Negro is an attractive artificial lake surrounded by hydrangeas and crowded with swan boats.

Snowland SNOW SPORTS

(54 3295-6000; www.snowland.com.br; RS-235 9009; adult/child R$169/139; 10am-5pm) Latin America's first snow park, opened in 2013, is an artificial winter wonderland with skiing, snowboarding, tubing and ice skating, as well as bars and restaurants. It's 6km west of Centro.

Festivals & Events

Festival de Gramado FILM

(www.festivaldegramado.net; Av Borges de Medeiros 2697, Palácio dos Festivais; tickets R$40-140) In August, Gramado hosts the eight-day Festival de Gramado, Brazil's most prestigious film festival.

Natal Luz CHRISTMAS

(www.natalluzdegramado.com.br; late Oct–mid-Jan) Gramado goes Christmas crazy for this annual holiday festival, the largest in Brazil and one of the longest such events in the world (it goes for for nearly three months). It draws 1.5 million people to the city annually. Expect floating light shows, circus acts, Christmas-tree lighting competitions, parades and classical music concerts, among other St Nick–related celebrations.

Gramado

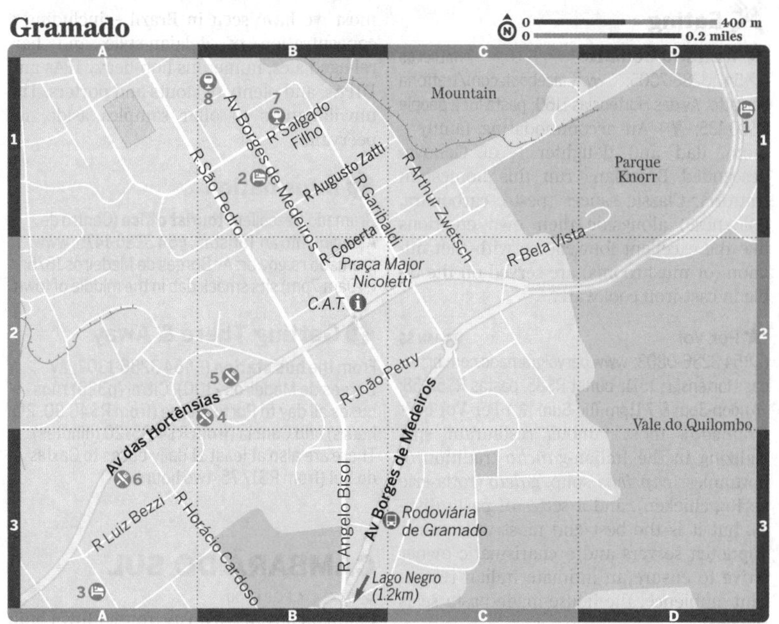

Gramado

Sleeping

1 Hostel Britanico D1
2 Hostel Chocolatchê B1
3 Jardim Secreto Pousada A3

Eating

4 Belle du Valais B2
5 Per Voi B2
6 Trattoria Boniatto A3

Drinking & Nightlife

7 Taberna MF B1
8 White Fly Pub B1

Sleeping

★ **Hostel Britanico** HOSTEL $
(☎54 3286-6250; www.britanico.com; Arthur Reimann 1; dm R$59, d/q R$199/399; ❄📶) This outstanding choice – call it a 'poshtel' – is an eight-minute stroll from central Gramado on the road to Canela. Dorms are of a craftsmanship previously unseen in Brazil, with reading lights, electricity outlets and privacy curtains (there are even a few double-bed dorms for you and yours); private rooms and common areas are better than many hotels. English-spoken.

Hostel Chocolatchê HOSTEL $
(☎54 99633-1795; www.hostelchocolatche.com; Av Borges de Medeiros 2889; dm from R$65, s/d without bathroom R$181/198, with bathroom R$182/260; ❄📶) A once stale, institutionalized choice behind the hallowed halls of the town's Methodist church has been given a major makeover by snazzy new owner Raquel, whose cleverness extends right down to the name – the phonetic spelling of how Brazilians pronounce 'chocolate.' Big, industrial-style bathrooms remain, but new beds and a jazzy lounge and kitchen with a wood-burning stove equal backpacker salvation.

★ **Jardim Secreto Pousada** POUSADA $$$
(☎54 3286-2023; www.pousadajardimsecreto.com.br; F G Bier 110; r from R$512; ❄📶) A mostly English-speaking sibling threesome runs this triumphantly lovely pousada just 800m from the main square. Extensive gardens surround the property, which is dotted with gnomes, birdhouses and other rustic-chic knickknacks. If there's a downside, it's the four- to five-night minimums in high season (and two-night weekend minimums otherwise).

Eating

★Trattoria Boniatto ITALIAN $$
(☎54 3286-7005; www.facebook.com/trattoriaboniatto; Av das Hortênsias 1160; pasta for 2 people R$80-135; 📶) An accommodating family – mom, dad and daughter – of Genova-descended Brazilians run this homespun trattoria. Classic sauces (pesto, carbonara, bolognese) alongside their own creations like the excellent four-cheese with filet mignon (or mushrooms) are served on the table in cast-iron cookware.

★Per Voi ITALIAN $$
(☎54 3286-0803; www.pervoigramado.com.br; Av das Hortênsias 1511; buffet R$85, pastas R$52-58; ⏰noon-3pm & 7-11pm Tue-Sun; 📶) Per Voi isn't Gramado's most famous restaurant specializing in the Italian-*gaúcho* tradition of bottomless *capeletti* soup, *galeto* (rotisserie spring chicken), and a series of pasta dishes, but it is the best and most welcoming. Topnotch servers and a charismatic owner strive to ensure an intimate Italian restaurant ambience; the house-made pasta seals the deal.

Belle du Valais SWISS $$$
(☎54 3286-1744; www.belleduvalais.com.br; Av das Hortênsias 1432; mains R$94-156, fondue for 2 people R$198-230; ⏰7pm-midnight; 📶) Fondue is as common as the cold in Gramado, but this old school–elegant hot spot is considered one of Brazil's best. The menu is rounded out by filets cooked on volcanic rocks and a wealth of impressive meat and fish preparations. Pair your meal with one of the local wines, including Lidio Carraro, Pizzato and Almaúnica. Reserve.

Drinking & Nightlife

★White Fly Pub CRAFT BEER
(www.whitefly.beer; Borges de Medeiros 3143; ⏰5pm-12:45am Tue-Sat; 📶) This 15-tap newcomer is run by a couple of welcoming young brewers who are often behind the bar. Their own brews, made in Porto Alegre, are great, and they put in a valiant effort to ring in craft beers from all over Brazil. The modern bar atmosphere is Gramado's best.

★Taberna MF MICROBREWERY
(www.facebook.com/legadoMF; Salgado Filho 170; ⏰6-11:30pm Sun-Fri, from 5pm Sat; 📶) Yes, the 'MF' stands for 'Motherfucker' (we asked!). As if that's not reason enough to pop in, you'll find 50 taps of craft beer here – the most we have seen in Brazil – including a concentration of Belgian-style and barrel-aged ales, numerous hop-heavy IPAs and DIPAs, and plenty of stouts and porters. The unwillingness to offer samples aside, it's beervana.

Information

Gramado's excellent **tourist office** (Centro de Atendimento ao Turista; ☎54 3286-1475; www.gramado.rs.gov.br; Av Borges de Medeiros 1675; ⏰9am-7pm) sits smack dab in the middle of town.

Getting There & Away

From the **bus station** (☎54 3286-1302; Av Borges de Medeiros 2100), Citral (p329) runs buses all day to Porto Alegre (from R$46.90, 2½ hours) and Canela (from R$4.05, 20 minutes). There are also at least 11 daily buses to Caxias do Sul (from R$17.75, two hours).

CAMBARÁ DO SUL

☎0XX54 / POP 6500

Cambará do Sul is a dusty frontier town built on cattle ranching with an authentic *gaúcho* aura. Located 186km northeast of Porto Alegre, it serves as a base for both Parque Nacional de Aparados da Serra and Parque Nacional da Serra Geral, the national parks that are somewhat ambitiously described as the 'Brazilian Grand Canyon.'

At an altitude of 1000m, Cambará receives more snowfall than any other destination in Rio Grande do Sul, making it a popular destination during winter months (May to October), when prices are higher.

Cambará do Sul claims to be the 'capital of honey,' and you can sample this local delicacy all over town.

Sights

★Parque Nacional de Aparados da Serra CANYON
(☎543251-1227; www.icmbio.gov.br/parnaaparadosdaserra/guia-do-visitante.html; RS-429, Km 18; Brazilian/foreigner R$25/45; ⏰8am-6pm Tue-Sun) Located 18km southeast of Cambará do Sul, this magnificent park occupies 102.5 sq km on the border between Rio Grande do Sul and Santa Catarina. It's here that vast, uninspired pasturelands give way to a series of stunning canyons, where the earth opens up and drops to depths of 720m.

The park preserves one of the country's last *araucária* (Paraná pine) forests, earn-

WORTH A TRIP

CANELA & PARQUE ESTADUAL DO CARACOL

While lacking Gramado's sophistication, neighboring Canela has a small-town charm of its own. Around a leafy green square, the village center is lined with shops and cafes and is anchored at one end by the impressive Gothic **Catedral de Pedra** (Catedral Nossa Senhora de Lourdes; Praça da Matriz 69; ⌚8:30-11:30am & 1:30-5:30pm). Canela offers cheaper accommodations and more convenient access to the state parks, which are popular hiking spots. The major attraction near town is the **Parque Estadual do Caracol** (☎54 3278-3035; www.canela.com.br/parque-do-caracol; RS-466, Km 0; adult/child R$20/10; ⌚9am-5:30pm), 7km northeast of Canela, and its spectacular **Cascata do Caracol**, a 131m waterfall. For tourist information, stop by **C.I.T.** (Central de Informações Turísticas; ☎54 3282-2200; www.canela.com.br; Largo da Fama 77; ⌚8am-7pm) in central Canela.

Citral (☎54 3282-1185; www.citral.tur.br; Danton Corrêa da Silva 630, Estação Rodoviária de Canela) runs buses to/from Gramado every 20 minutes (from R$4.05, 20 minutes, 5am to 11:30pm). **Ozelame** (☎54 3228-4088; www.ozelame.com.br; Danton Corrêa da Silva 630, Estação Rodoviária de Canela) buses go to São Francisco de Paula every two hours or so (from R$10.25, one hour, 8am to 7:30pm), where you can connect to Cambará do Sul (R$19.45, one hour); and nine buses per day to Caxias do Sul (from R$19.45, two hours), where you can connect to Bento Gonçalves (R$9.70, 1½ hours, hourly). Frequent buses go to Porto Alegre (from R$35.45, 2½ hours). **Viação Canelense** (☎54 3282-2326; Danton Corrêa da Silva 630, Estação Rodoviária de Canela) operates three buses a day from outside the bus station to and from Parque Estadual do Caracol (R$3.50, 20 minutes).

ing it its protected status. But the main attraction is the **Cânion do Itaimbezinho**, a narrow, 5800m-long canyon with sheer parallel escarpments, ranging from 600m to 720m. Two waterfalls drop into this incision in the earth, which was formed by the Rio Perdiz's rush to the sea.

Three trails wind through the park. **Trilha do Vértice** runs for 2km to an observation point for the canyon and the Cascata do Andorinhas. **Trilha Cotovelo** is a 3km trail (2½ hours round-trip) passing by the Véu de Noiva waterfall, with wonderful vistas of the canyon.

For a completely different perspective, **Trilha do Rio do Boi** follows the base of the canyon for 7km, from the Posto Rio do Boi entrance. This last route is most easily accessed from the town of Praia Grande in Santa Catarina. A professional guide is required for the challenging, loose, rocky trail. During rainy season it is closed because of the danger of flooding.

There is a **visitors' center** (⌚8am-6pm Tue-Sun) at Itaimbezinho with information on flora, fauna and topography in Portuguese only.

★**Parque Nacional da Serra Geral** CANYON
(☎54 3251-1277; www.icmbio.gov.br/portal/visitacao1/unidades-abertas-a-visitacao/730-parque-nacional-da-serra-geral.html; RS-429, Km 18; ⌚8am-6pm) FREE Parque Nacional da Serra Geral, 23km east of Cambará do Sul, contains canyons that rival Itaimbezinho. The **Cânion da Fortaleza** is an 8km stretch of escarpment with 900m drops. A gently inclining **Trilha do Mirante** leads about 7km to the edge of the canyon, yielding incredible views of the **Cachoeira do Tigre Preto** waterfall.

The **Pedra do Segredo** is a tower of rocks that balances precariously on this precipice. **Cânion Malacara** is formed by the river of the same name; the **Trilha Piscina do Malacara** leads to a natural pool with cool, crystal waters and wonderful views.

Tours

★**Cânion Turismo** HIKING, ADVENTURE TOUR
(☎54 3251-1027; www.canionturismo.com.br; Getúlio Vargas 876; ⌚8am-7pm) Pop into this excellent agency and check out the scale model of the canyons for a much-needed perspective of the area (R$7). Guided treks like Trilha do Rio do Boi are around R$511 for one person, dropping to R$179 per person for a group of 10 people.

It also arranges recommended one- or three-hour horseback riding excursions on surrounding *fazendas* (ranches) for R$92 to R$203.

★**Aparados da Serra Adventure** HIKING, OUTDOORS
(☎54 99984-5766; www.aparadosdaserraadventure.com.br; Rua da Tradição 53; ⌚8am-8pm) The former mastermind of Cânion Turismo (Cambará's other great ecotourism agency),

friendly Josemar has branched out on his own and arranges a wealth of recommended ecominded excursions in the surrounding canyons, including four-hour horseback trips to Cânion Pedra do Segredo (R$190), half-day mountain-bike jaunts (R$130) and three-day, 62km treks to Cânion Josafaz (R$1200 all-inclusive for up to four people).

Sleeping

Pousada Oliveira POUSADA $

(54 3251-1544; www.pousadaoliveira.tur.br; RS-020 148; s R$90-110, d R$150-180;) A good deal for budget travelers, these bright-green A-frame cabins (two with fireplaces) evoke a more local feel than elsewhere and are as welcoming as can be for the price, featuring traditional wooden accents (we prefer the back ones facing the *araucária* forest). There's a rustic communal kitchen with wagon-wheel tables, too. It's 800m or so southwest of town.

★ **Vila Ecológica** POUSADA $$

(54 98121-1175; www.vilaecologica.blogspot.com.br; João Pazza 1166; r R$200-250;) Vila Ecológica sits colorfully but most ordinarily on a hill behind Casa do Turista. You wouldn't look twice. But closer inspection reveals Cambará's great-value hospitality option. Rooms are equipped with heaters/air-con and cable TV and were constructed from ecologically savvy materials. Eco-touches abound – like old tennis shoes as planters – and friendly, English-speaking Erica handles everything.

Pousada Corucacas POUSADA $$

(54 99618-6806; www.corucacas.com.br; RS-020, Km 1; camping per person R$20, r per person incl breakfast & dinner R$150, s/d cabanã R$190/350;) About 1km north of town on the road to Ouro Verde, this working farm has rustic rooms and a big-sky setting, flush with duck-filled lakes and sheep-grazed farmland with *araucária* trees. Endless opportunities for horseback riding and hiking are just out the back door, and a fireplace heats up the common room in the evening.

Two newly constructed cabanãs face bucolic pasturelands.

★ **Parador Casa da Montanha** LODGE $$$

(54 3295-7575; www.paradorcasadamontanha.com.br; Estrada do Faxinal, RS-429; d incl afternoon tea R$450-2500;) Midway between Cambará and Itaimbezinho, the poshest place in the region is modeled after luxurious African safari camps. Overlooking *araucária* forest and a rushing waterfall, Brazil's only heated, elevated tents are perched amid postcard-envy scenery and combine creature comforts with rusticity to supremely tranquil effects.

The cheapest option features luxurious shared shower facilities while the most expensive has outdoor fireplaces and patio whirlpool bathtubs. There's a lovely gourmet restaurant dishing up lamb, duck and trout-heavy mains (R$40 to R$80). It's one of Brazil's most unique accommodations.

Eating

Galpão Costaneira BUFFET $

(Dona Úrsula 1069; buffet R$29-48; 11:30am-3pm & 7:20-10:30pm Mon-Sat, to 3pm Sun;) A hearty local buffet served in a rustic farmhouse setting. It's best when you choose tabletop-cooked *picanha* (beef), spicy linguiça and colonial cheese – that is, if you've got any room left over after sampling the various specialties warmed over an open flame.

★ **Restaurante do Lago** SEAFOOD $$

(5499975-5553; www.facebook.com/RestauranteDoLagoCambara; Estrada do Faxinal, RS-427; meals R$51; 11am-3pm & 7-11pm;) Chef Marcos Barberi pumps a ton of personality into his restaurant with a rustic, fireplace-warmed space full of antique furniture, colorful knickknacks and friendly demeanor. The speciality is fresh trout, prepared traditionally (*meunière,* passion fruit sauce) or in the house style (with mushrooms, cream cheese, capers, raisins and nuts), and served alongside aligot (a fondu-like cheese and potato dish) or rösti (grated fried potatoes).

★ **Galeteria O Casarão** BUFFET $$

(54 3251-1711; www.galeteriaocasarao.com.br; João Francisco Ritter 969; buffet R$43.50-71.50; 11:30am-3pm & 6:30-10pm Tue-Sat) Set among homey hardwoods, this excellent restaurant serves the comfort food of Brazil's Italian immigrants. A buffet of organic salads, house-made pastas and soups accompanies house-specialty *galeto* (rotisserie spring chicken) or 12 types of farmed trout. Local wines and *grappas* are served as well.

Drinking & Nightlife

Máchina da Tempo BAR

(www.facebook.com/maquinadotempopub; Doná Úrsula 574; 7-10pm Sun-Fri, to midnight Sat;) Folks of a certain age will love this

'80s-themed bar with cassette-tape napkin holders, floppy-disc coasters and a very young 'Steven' Jobs on the TV explaining the Apple IIe computer (younger folks will just gawk in amusement). 'Tchê' and Patricia heard up to 30 types of bottled regional craft beer and there's local Grota Bier on tap.

There's live rock on Saturday nights and no wi-fi – just like the '80s!

Information

The **Casa do Turista** (www.cambaradosul.rs.gov.br; Av Getúlio Vargas 1720; 8am-6pm) is at the far end of town on the road to Fortaleza.

Getting There & Away

The tiny **bus station** (54 3251-1567; Dona Úrsula s/n) is right in town, though rarely staffed. **Citral** (www.citral.tur.br; Dona Úrsula s/n, Estação Rodoviária) offers one bus from Porto Alegre for Cambará do Sul (R$47.15, 5½ hours) at 6am Monday to Saturday. Returning, you must catch a 7am or 1:30pm bus to São Francisco de Paula (R$19.45, one hour) and switch there for Porto Alegre (from R$29.80, three hours), Canela (from R$10.45, one hour) or Gramado (from R$11.85, one hour).

Expresso São Marcos (www.expressosaomarcos.com.br; Dona Úrsula s/n, Estação Rodoviária) has two buses going to Caxias do Sul (from R$32.55, three hours, 7:30am and 10:45am) on Monday, Tuesday, Wednesday and Friday (10:45am only on Thursday, 7:30am only on Saturday, 5:30pm only on Sunday), where you can connect hourly to Bento Gonçalves (R$9.70, 1¼ hours) with **Ozelame** (54 3228-4088; www.ozelame.com.br; Andrade Neves 999, Rodoviária de Caxias do Sul, Caxias do Sul). If you are coming from the north, you can connect from Torres via Tainhas or via Criciúma.

Getting Around

The parks are not serviced by public buses. A taxi to PN Aparados da Serra costs R$100 for two people (R$200 for four) round-trip. Local tour companies are a reasonable alternative, especially if they can hook you up with a small group.

LITORAL GAÚCHO

On paper, it sounds amazing: a 500km strip of Brazilian coastline that forms one seemingly endless beach, stretching from Torres on the Santa Catarina border, all the way to Chuí at the Uruguayan border. Unfortunately, the reality is less enticing. The water tends to be murky and the beaches are undistinguished, but there's good surf and alluring culture.

WORTH A TRIP

PRAIA GRANDE

The oddly named Praia Grande (it's not big and there's no beach!) sits just across the border in Santa Catarina at the bottom of the canyons that make up Parque Nacional de Aparados da Serra and Parque Nacional da Serra Geral; it offers an alternative perspective to Cambará do Sul. In this blossoming ecotourism destination, a wealth of waterfalls and natural swimming pools are at your disposal, as are hiking, tree climbing, rappelling and ziplines. Bed down at the wonderful **Refúgio Ecológico Pedra Afiada** (48 3532-1059; www.pedraafiada.com.br; Estrada Geral Vila Rosa s/n, Praia Grande; d incl meals R$350-1100;).

There is one daily bus from Cambará do Sul to Praia Grande (R$13.72, 1½ hours, 9:45am Monday to Saturday); as well as service from Araranguá in Santa Catarina. For more info, see www.praiagrande.sc.gov.br/turismo.

Torres

0XX51 / POP 34,600

On the border with Santa Catarina, Torres is the exception to the state's uninviting coastline. It's not thrilling, but the pleasant town, 205km north of Porto Alegre, has attractive (if crowded) beaches punctuated by basalt rock formations, vegetative dunes and a lively boardwalk bursting with crepes and churros (fried dough pastries) – the *gaúchos*-digging-their-toes-in-the-sand culture is unique in Brazil.

In winter, Antarctic currents bring cold, hard winds to the coast, dispersing the crowds and causing some hotels to shut down from May to November.

Sights

Praia Grande, the town's main beach, is quite calm and is bookended by the smaller **Prainha** to the south and Praia dos Molhes to the north, a famous surf spot where the Rio Mampituba dramatically enters the sea. **Praia da Cal**, 2km south of Praia Grande, also draws serious surfers.

Parque Estadual da Guarita NATURE RESERVE
(https://torres.rs.gov.br/parque-da-guarita; Benjamin Constant 154; 2 hr car access R$8, unlimited R$20; ⏲8am-8pm Dec-Feb, to 6pm Mar-Nov) The gardens of the 350-hectare Parque Guarita, 2km south of Av Beira Mar, make for a gorgeous natural setting, while the nearby beach of the same name is considered the most beautiful in Torres.

Activities & Tours

Felipe Raupp Escola de Surf SURFING
(☎51 99991-4049; www.frsurf.com.br; Praia Grande) Internationally renowned surfer Felipe Raupp is the man to get you up in Torres, offering serious multiday surf courses on the north end of Praia Grande.

Marina BOATING
(☎51 3626-2933; www.barcosmarina.com.br; Ponte Pênsil, Passo de Torres; adult/child R$70/45; ⏲10am & 2pm Jan-Apr) Marina runs boat trips to Ilha dos Lobos, an ecological reserve that is home to a colony of sea lions between January and April. In season there is a booth at the beginning of Av Beira Mar.

Festivals & Events

★**Festival Internacional de Balonismo** HOT AIR BALLOONING
(International Hot-Air Balloon Festival; ☎51 3028-2200; www.torres.rs.gov.br/balonismo; Estrada do Faxinal, Parque Balonismo) Every April Torres hosts a hot-air balloon festival, a spectacular sight.

Sleeping

Expect discounts of 20% to 40% between March and November and a 25% hike during the hot-air-balloon festival.

★**Pousada Solar Inn** POUSADA $$$
(☎51 3626-3731; www.solarinn.com.br; Av Beira Mar 1713; s/d from R$350/400, with seaview R$450/500; ❄📶🏊) Excellent beachfront location, German-style architecture and welcoming owners who speak some English – you can't beat this spartan inn perched across from Prainha beach.

Eating

Monsieur Café CAFE $
(www.facebook.com/monsieurcafetorres; Av Benjamin Constant 23; light meals R$3.50-18; ⏲12:30-8pm Mon-Fri, to 8:30pm Sat, 1:30-8pm Sun; 📶) Full of Torres charm, the welcoming patio of this cafe sits just off the lagoon a few blocks back from Prainha. There's fine espresso, tea and *pão de queijo* (tapioca cheese bread) pressed panini – and an absolutely unrelenting choice of sweets and cakes.

Cantinho do Pescador SEAFOOD $$
(www.cantinhodopescador.com.br; Av Cristóvão Colombo 210; mains for 2 people R$44-156; ⏲10am-midnight; 📶) This always-packed, partly open-air seafood stop does a commendable job with local fish at the Praia dos Molhes end of town, with panoramic Rio Mampituba views. The crab in its own shell (*siri na casca;* R$19.50) is wildly popular and the pineapple stabbed with skewers of shrimp (*camarão à Grega;* R$135) is just wild.

Drinking & Nightlife

★**The Nicolas Pub** BAR
(www.thenicolaspub.com; José Picoral 51, Loja 2; ⏲6pm-1am Tue-Sun; 📶) If you've just crossed the border into Rio Grande do Sul, this upscale pub is the perfect spot to dive into the *gaúcho* craft beer scene. Twelve taps await, along with an inviting patio with Prainha views and sheepskin seat covers in winter. Pub grub, too.

Information

Casa do Turista (☎51 3664-1411; www.torres.rs.gov.br; Av Barão do Rio Branco 315; ⏲9am-7pm)

Getting There & Away

The town is small and all conveniences are accessible by foot, including the **bus station** (☎51 3664-1787; www.rodoviariatorres.com.br; Av José Bonifácio 524). Destinations include Porto Alegre (from R$50, three hours) and Florianópolis (from R$52, five hours, one to two daily).

For Cambará do Sul, **Expresso São Marcos** (www.expressosaomarcos.com.br) goes to the dusty one-horse town of Tainhas (R$26.60, two hours, 9am and 3pm Monday to Saturday, 9:30am and 3pm Sunday) where you can connect with **Citral** (☎54 3244-1315; www.citral.tur.br; Frederico Tedesco 602, São Francisco de Paula) buses leaving São Francisco de Paula at 9:15am and 5pm Monday to Saturday (11am on Sunday), passing through **Tainhas** (Tainhas) for Cambará (R$7.65, ¾ hour) around 30 to 45 minutes later. However, do not get the timing wrong – if you miss the bus, Tainhas has no accommodations whatsoever.

GETTING TO URUGUAY

Located 245km south of Rio Grande, the border town of Chuí/Chuy is the end of the Brazilian line. The city is both Brazilian and Uruguayan, respectively. The main drag acts as the border: on the northern (Brazilian) side it is Av Uruguaí, while on the southern (Uruguayan) side it is Av Brasil. The Uruguayan side has grown over the last decade to be synonymous with duty-free shops, which are flooded with Brazilians from open to close. It's not interesting (unless you are a Brazilian in need of some electronics or reasonably priced Malbecs), but increased security in recent years means it's relatively safe as far as border towns go. Those who linger usually only do so to take advantage of cheaper accommodations when visiting Uruguayan attractions further afield. If you stay, the best value for money is at **Etnico Hostel** (4474-2281; www.facebook.com/etnicohostelchuy; Liber Seregni 299; dm/s/d US$16/28/46;), three blocks into Uruguay, where trilingual host Rodrigo is eager to help, and bakery-fresh breakfast pastries are a nice touch.

Brazilian **immigration** (53 3265-2523; www.dpf.gov.br; Hwy BR-471, Km 650; 24hr) is on the main highway, several kilometers north of town. You do not need a visa or entry or exit stamp to visit the town; however, if you are continuing further into Uruguay, you will need to tell the driver to stop at the border post for an exit stamp. In Uruguay, **immigration** (4474-2072; https://migracion.minterior.gub.uy; Ruta 9; 24hr) is 2.5km south of town. The bus will stop again for the Uruguayan officials to check your Brazilian exit stamp. **Uruguay** (53 3265-1151; cdchui@mrree.gub.uy; Venezuela 311; 9am-3pm Mon-Fri) maintains a consulate in Chuí, though most nationalities do not need a visa for Uruguay.

Pop into Chuy's **Centro de Informes** (4474-3627; www.turismorocha.gub.uy; cnr Av Artigas & Arachanes; 10am-6pm Tue-Sat Mar-Dec, 9am-7pm Jan-Feb) for helpful Uruguayan tourist info.

Rio Grande

0XX53 / POP 197,200

Located at the mouth of Lagoa dos Patos, Rio Grande was founded in 1737 to guard the disputed southern border of the Portuguese empire. The region's oldest city, it blossomed during the 19th century, when its port became a vital link in the profitable beef trade. Rio Grande has a charming historic center that is home to some interesting colonial and neoclassical buildings.

Sights

Museu Oceanográfico MUSEUM

(53 3231-3496; www.museu.furg.br/museus/museu-oceanografico; Capitão Heitor Perdigão 10; R$5; 9-11:30am & 2-6pm Tue-Sun) The excellent Museu Oceanográfico is one of the best in Latin America and is home to the continent's most important collection of mollusks.

Sleeping & Eating

Paris Hotel HISTORIC HOTEL $

(53 3231-3866; www.hotelvillamoura.com.br; Marechal Floriano Peixoto 112; s/d R$60/80, without bathroom R$40/60;) This hotel was built in 1826 and is the oldest in Rio Grande do Sul, exhibiting a bygone grandeur in its high ceilings, antique furnishings and leafy courtyard. At this price, it would be silly not to sleep in an antique bed that once hosted Dom Pedro II.

Casa Europa Gastrobar BISTRO $$

(53 3035-6257; www.casaeuropa.com.br; Benjamin Constant 460; mains R$30-57; 6:30-11pm Mon-Sat;) A sophisticated little surprise for Rio Grande, this Euro-style bistro does a small but great selection of Italian and French dishes, complemented by sweet service.

Getting There & Away

From the **bus station** (53 3232-8444; www.rodoviariariogrande.com.br; Vice Almirante Abreu 737), buses connect Rio Grande with all major cities in southern Brazil. **Embaixador** (www.expressoembaixador.com.br) has two departures for Chuí (R$66.40, four hours, 7am and 4:30pm) on the Uruguayan border as well as Pelotas (from R$14.85, one hour, every 30 minutes), which is the major transportation hub. **Planalto** (www.planalto.com.br) has at least seven buses most days to Porto Alegre (from R$98.55, five hours).

Brasília & Goiás

Includes ➡

Brasília 335
Goiás 349
Goiânia 350
Cidade de Goiás 352
Pirenópolis 354
Parque Nacional da Chapada Dos Veadeiros 358
Alto Paraíso de Goiás ... 359
São Jorge 361

Best Places to Eat

- ➡ Taypá (p347)
- ➡ Botequim Mercatto (p351)
- ➡ Olivae (p347)
- ➡ Mangai (p347)
- ➡ Bloco C (p347)
- ➡ Jambalaya (p360)

Best Places to Stay

- ➡ Brasília Palace Hotel (p345)
- ➡ Pouso, Café e Cultura (p356)
- ➡ Cullinan Hplus Premium (p345)
- ➡ Buddy's Hostel (p359)
- ➡ Taiuá Ambiental (p361)

Why Go?

The national capital Brasília was conceived as a workable, utopian answer to modern urban chaos. The purpose-built city is lauded by many for its futuristic architecture and avant-garde design but knocked by detractors who bemoan the impracticality of the uberorganized, themed city blocks. As Brazil's seat of government, bureaucrats rule, but a thriving city is there, the first in the world constructed in the 20th century to achieve World Cultural Heritage designation by Unesco.

Enveloping the Distrito Federal (DF), Goiás is Brazil's 'road less traveled,' though not for good reason: fiery red sunsets over the lush, rolling hills of the dramatic cerrado (savanna) landscape set the stage for unparalleled postcard-perfect views.

When to Go

Brasília

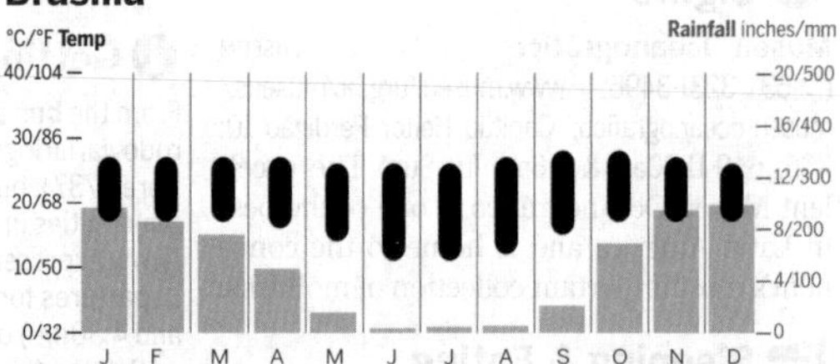

May The wet season ends and the warm dry period starts.

Jul Hotel prices are down during the holidays and there are family-friendly events and activities.

Aug Sunny days and zero rain make this another prime month.

BRASÍLIA

☎ 0XX61 / POP 3.1 MILLION / ELEV 1172M

Brasília, carved out of untouched cerrado vegetation from scratch, replaced Rio as capital in 1960 and remains an impressive monument to national initiative. The original design (*plano piloto*) was inspired by the crucifix but is often referred to as an airplane, with each of its architectural marvels strategically laid out

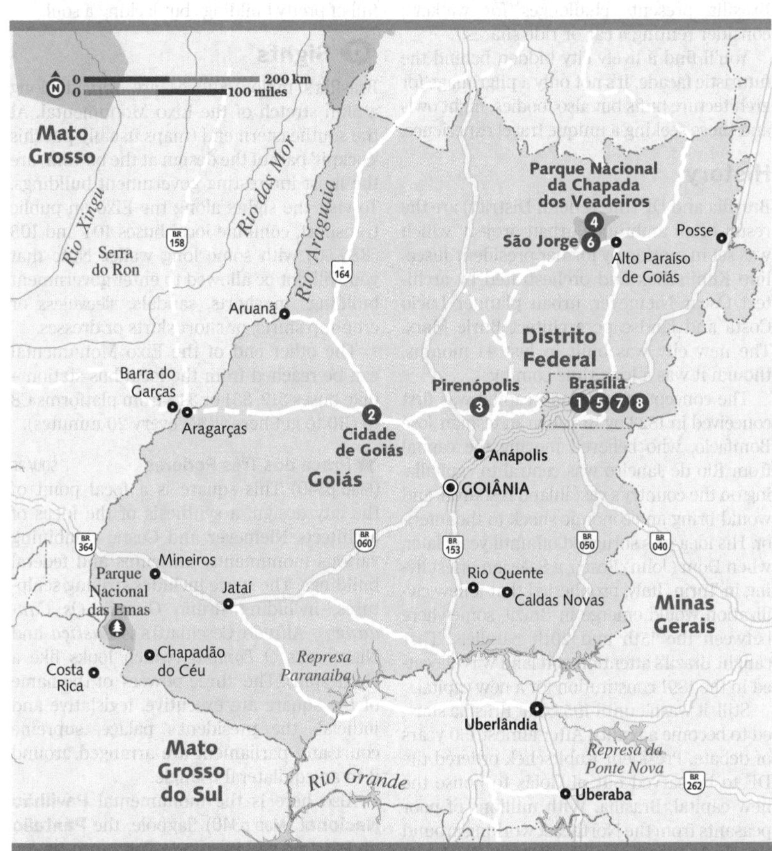

Brasília & Goiás Highlights

1. **Eixo Monumental** (p336) Admiring the series of Niemeyer's architectural marvels down Brasília's principal axis.
2. **Cidade de Goiás** (p352) Wandering the picturesque cobblestone streets of this historic town and investigating its restored 18th-century buildings.
3. **Pirenópolis** (p354) Beating the heat amid a barrage of waterfalls and enjoying the hip cafes and boutiques of the center.
4. **Parque Nacional da Chapada dos Veadeiros** (p358) Hiking through the unique high-cerrado landscapes in this picturesque national park and its surrounding attractions.
5. **Santuário Dom Bosco** (p343) Stepping inside this ethereal blue building in Brasília and watching your 'seen one church, seen them all' attitude disappear.
6. **São Jorge** (p361) Kicking back in your hammock in this chilled-out dirt-road village.
7. **Outro Calaf** (p348) Dancing the night away to live samba, *pagode*, *choro* or *sertanejo* in this lively central spot in Brasília.
8. **Superquadra Dining** (p347) Losing yourself in the excellent bars and restaurants of Brasília's *superquadras*. Bloco C makes a fine stop.

along the Eixo Monumental (which forms the fuselage), and its residential and commercial blocks along its two outspread wings (*asas*).

With long distances and six-lane highways connected by spaghetti junctions, Brasília presents challenges for walkers; consider renting a car or ride shares.

You'll find a lively city hidden behind the futuristic facade. It's not only a pilgrimage for architecture buffs but also foodies, night owls and those seeking a unique travel experience.

History

Brasília and DF (the Federal District) are the result of an ambitious urban project, which was set in motion by former president Juscelino Kubitschek and orchestrated by architect Oscar Niemeyer, urban planner Lúcio Costa and landscape architect Burle Marx. The new city was built in just 41 months, though it was a long time coming.

The concept of an inland capital was first conceived in 1823 by Brazilian statesman José Bonifácio, who believed moving the capital from Rio de Janeiro was central to capitalizing on the country's vast inland resources and would bring an economic shock to the interior. His idea was shrugged off until years later, when Dom (John) Bosco, a Salesian priest living in Turin, Italy, prophesied that a new civilization would emerge in Brazil, somewhere between the 15th and 20th parallels. That caught Brazil's attention and land was allocated in the 1891 constitution for a new capital.

Still, it wasn't until 1955 that Brasília started to become a reality. After almost 150 years of debate, President Kubitschek ordered the DF to be carved out of Goiás to house the new capital, Brasília. With millions of poor peasants from the Northeast working around the clock, Brasília was built from absolutely nothing in just three years (Niemeyer later admitted that it was all done too quickly). It wasn't exactly finished, but it was ready to be the capital. The capital was officially moved from Rio to Brasília on April 21, 1960.

Kubitschek made the building of Brasília a symbol of the country's determination and ability to become a great economic power. He successfully appealed to all Brazilians to put aside their differences and rally to the cause. In doing so, he distracted attention from the country's social and economic problems, gained enormous popularity and borrowed heavily from the international banks.

Today, Kubitschek is heralded as a national hero (he died in a suspicious automobile accident in 1976) but the jury is still out on Brasília. For some, the city represents the outstanding capabilities of this great and vast nation, and a world model for urban development, architecture and society. Others, meanwhile, consider the city a wasted opportunity, full of pretty buildings but lacking a soul.

Sights

Brasília's major edifices are spread along a 5km stretch of the Eixo Monumental. At the southeastern end (maps usually put this 'cockpit' part of the design at the bottom) are the most interesting government buildings. To visit the sights along the Eixo on public transport, combine local buses 104 and 108 (R$2.50) with some long walks. Note that you will not be allowed to enter government buildings in shorts, sandals, sleeveless or crop-top shirts, or short skirts or dresses.

The other end of the Eixo Monumental can be reached from the local bus station – take buses 312, 331 or 343 from platforms C8 to C10 to get here (R$5, every 20 minutes).

★Praça dos Trés Poderes SQUARE

(Map p340) This square is a focal point of the city design, a synthesis of the ideas of architects Niemeyer and Costa, combining various monuments, museums and federal buildings. The space includes striking sculptures, including Bruno Giorgi's *Os Candangos,* Alfredo Ceschiatti's *A Justiça* and Niemeyer's *O Pombal* (which looks like a clothespin). The 'three powers' of the name of the square are executive, legislative and judicial; the president's palace, supreme court and parliament are arranged around it in an equilateral triangle.

Also here is the monumental **Pavilhão Nacional** (Map p340) flagpole, the **Panteão da Pátria e da Liberdade Tancredo Neves** (Map p340; 61 3325-6244; www.cultura.df.gov.br; 9am-6pm Tue-Sun) FREE, a cenotaph commemorating Brazilian national heroes, and two museums detailing the history of Brasília's planning: the **Espaço Lúcio Costa** (Map p340; 9am-6pm Tue-Sun) FREE and the **Museu da Cidade** (Museu Histórico de Brasília; Map p340; 61 3325-6244; 9am-6pm Tue-Sun) FREE.

It's worth visiting the plaza during the day and again at night for two very different experiences. After dark, surreal lighting casts an eerie glow across the futuristic buildings, as though they are being lit up by the landing lights of an alien spacecraft. Robberies have been reported here at night, though, so have a taxi wait for you while you visit.

BRASÍLIA – CAPITAL OF THE THIRD MILLENNIUM

In 1883 an Italian priest, Dom Bosco, prophesied that a new civilization would arise between parallels 15 and 20, and that its capital would be built between parallels 15 and 16, on the edge of an artificial lake. Many consider Brasília to be that city, and a number of cults have sprung up in the area. If you tire of Brasília's architectural monuments, a visit to one of the cults may be part of your destiny.

Templo da Boa Vontade (Temple of Goodwill; Map p340; ☎61 3114 1070; www.tbv.com.br; SGAS, Quadra 915, Lotes 75/76; 24hr) FREE The striking Templo da Boa Vontade was created by the Legion of Goodwill in 1989 as a symbol of universal solidarity. It incorporates seven pyramids, joined to form a cone that is topped with the biggest raw crystal you will ever see (it weighs in at 21kg). In the main chamber, you are encouraged to take off your shoes and walk along the spiraling inner circle via the black path, returning via the white path.

There is also an interesting Egyptian room for meditation, an art gallery, a fountain and a restaurant. There are a few mixed messages, with ideas of interfaith harmony combined with Christ-the-King propaganda and crystals for sale. Get there on bus 105 or 107 from the city bus station.

Vale do Amanhecer (Valley of the Dawn; ☎61 3389-8754; www.valedoamanhecer.org; DF-130, Planaltina; 10am-midnight) About 45km east of Brasília, near the satellite city of Planaltina, this religious community was founded in 1959 by a clairvoyant, Tia Neiva. It's really a small town where mediums dressed in elaborate robes and capes conduct rituals for the wider community of believers (over 10,000 across Brazil), who hold that a new civilization will come during the third millennium. The town's main temple is the focus of the community. Get there by bus 617 from the center of Brasília.

The belief system is complex: based on Catholicism, it also includes elements from Egyptian, Greek, Aztec, Indian, Romany, Inca, Trojan and Afro-Brazilian beliefs and iconography. Near the temple, a lake, a star-shaped outdoor area and a pyramid are also the focus of rituals.

★Congresso Nacional NOTABLE BUILDING
(Parliament; Map p340; ☎61 3216-1771; www.congressonacional.leg.br; Praça dos Três Poderes; 9am-5:30pm Thu-Mon) FREE Featuring photogenic roof 'dishes' and twin towers, the Congresso Nacional has one of the more interesting interiors in the city. In addition to the color-coded chambers of the Senate (blue) and House of Representatives (green), there is an architecturally interesting 'Tunnel of Time' and an exhibit of antique Senate benches and microphones from 1867.

The convex dome on the roof of the House of Representatives is supposed to signify that membership is open to all ideologies. Visits on Thursday (or for non-Portuguese guides) must be booked online or by phone. Otherwise, tours leave about every half hour, lasting an hour. No flip-flops, sleeveless tops, shorts or miniskirts are allowed.

★Palácio do Planalto PALACE
(Map p340; ☎61 3411-2317; www2.planalto.gov.br; Praça dos Três Poderes; 9am-1:30pm Sun) FREE The Palácio do Planalto, where Brazil's president works, is another Niemeyer design that's worth seeing inside and out. From the curved lines of the exterior to the lustrous columns and sweeping curved ramp inside, it's one of the best examples of architectural modernism in the world. The tour even lets you peek into the president's office.

There is a ceremonial changing of the guard outside the gates every hour on weekends and every two hours during the week.

★Catedral Metropolitana CATHEDRAL
(Nossa Senhora Aparecida; Map p340; ☎61 3224-4073; www.catedral.org.br; Esplanada dos Ministérios; 8am-4:30pm Wed, Thu & Sat-Mon, 10:30am-4pm Tue & Fri) FREE The 16 curved ribs rising to the crown of the iconic exterior coupled with the light-filled circular interior, which sits under a dome of wavy stained-glass, make this cathedral a heavenly sight. At the entrance are Ceschiatti's haunting *Four Disciples* statues; he also created the aluminum angels hanging inside. Wearing shorts and visiting during Mass are not encouraged.

Niemeyer's Brasília

Oscar Ribeiro de Almeida Niemeyer Soares Filho passed away just 10 days short of his 105th birthday on 5 December 2012, but his legacy lives on in Brazil's futuristic capital. As the creative genius behind the 'free-flowing, sensually curved' designs of the DF's (Federal District's) civic buildings, as well as some of Brazil's most eye-catching edifices elsewhere, the great architect had a unique gift for turning reinforced concrete into artistic masterpieces.

Niemeyer was visited in September 1956 by Brazilian president Juscelino Kubitschek, who was an admirer of his work. Tasked with the job of building a brand new capital, a legendary partnership began, and, with the addition of Lúcio Costa as the landscaper, the dream soon became a reality. The readying of the city took place remarkably quickly and Brasília was ready for business on 21 April 1960, though many of the major buildings were completed later; some are still being worked on. Niemeyer later lamented the rush, but to the nonperfectionist, the results were still outstanding.

Though an atheist himself, the 'crown of thorns' form of the Catedral Metropolitana (p337) is widely recognized as one of his most cutting-edge designs, with a heavenly dome of long stained-glass panels. The heavens theme contin-

MAREKORSZEWSKI/SHUTTERSTOCK ©

ESB PROFESSIONAL/SHUTTERSTOCK ©

1. Palácio da Alvorada (p342)
2. Museu Nacional (p342)
3. Catedral Metropolitana (p337)

R.M. NUNES/SHUTTERSTOCK ©

ues nearby at the simple but stunning Museu Nacional (p342), a white dome with a circumnavigating ramp leading to the entrance that recalls Saturn and its rings. Less visually striking, the design of the domes on the roof of the Congresso Nacional (p337) represents an openness of government to all political ideologies and reflected the optimistic future that Brasília would embody. Inspired by the words of Kubitschek 'What is Brasília, if not the dawn of a new day for Brazil?', Niemeyer created the modernist Palácio da Alvorada (p342) as the official residence of the president, its simplistic layout turning its nose up at the excesses of previous incumbents of Brazil's top job.

Niemeyer was politically leftist and designed Brasília along socialist principles, with similar apartment blocks to prevent the emergence of wealthy neighborhoods. He was a friend of Fidel Castro, who once described himself and Niemeyer as the last communists on earth. Niemeyer's political beliefs led to persecution under the military dictatorship of the 1960s and he was driven into exile, returning only when the country returned to democratic principles in the mid 1980s. Niemeyer continued to work right up to his death and lived to see Brazil finally beginning to fulfill the promises it pledged with the building of Brasília.

Brasília

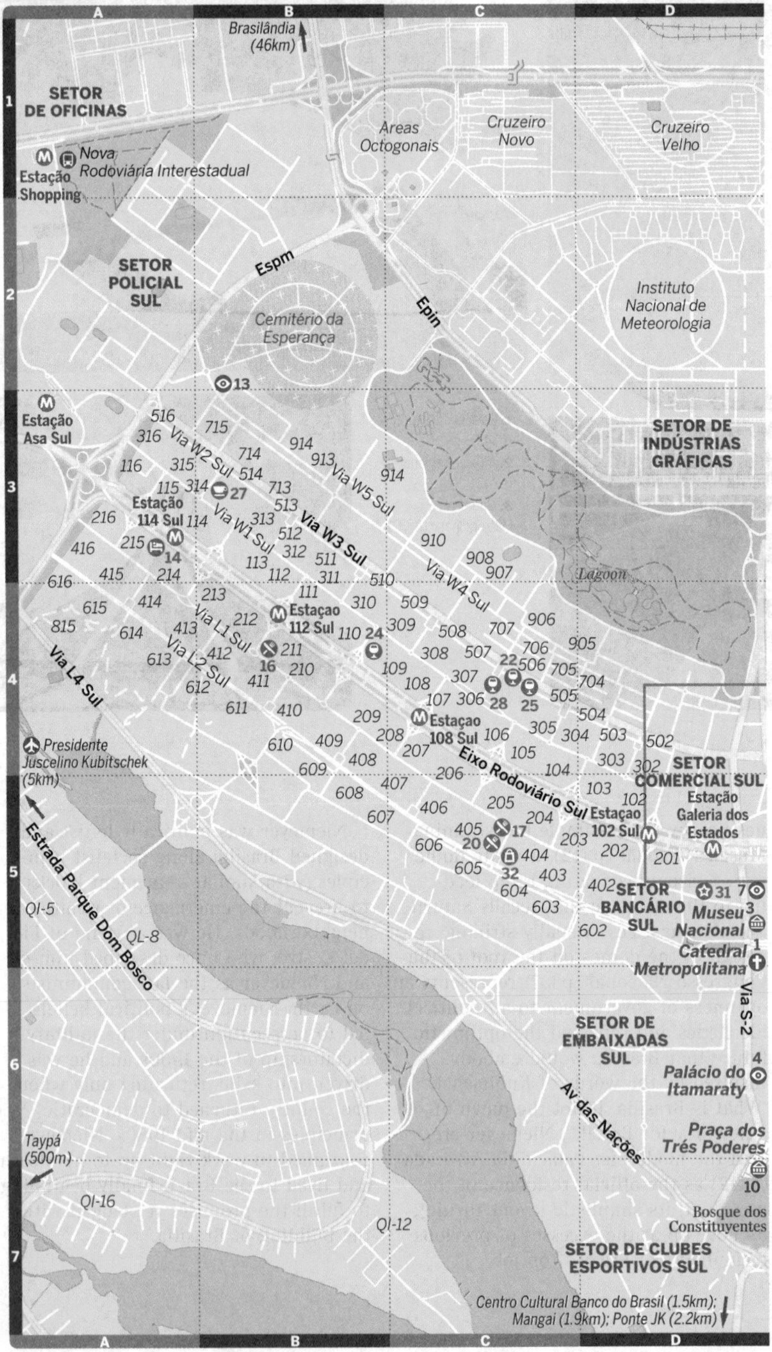

SETOR DE OFICINAS
Estação Shopping
Nova Rodoviária Interestadual
Brasilândia (46km)
Areas Octogonais
Cruzeiro Novo
Cruzeiro Velho
SETOR POLICIAL SUL
Espm
Epin
Cemitério da Esperança
Instituto Nacional de Meteorologia
13
Estação Asa Sul
SETOR DE INDÚSTRIAS GRÁFICAS
Via W2 Sul
Via W5 Sul
Via W3 Sul
Via W1 Sul
Via W4 Sul
Estação 114 Sul
27
14
Lagoon
Estaçao 112 Sul
Via L1 Sul
Via L2 Sul
Via L4 Sul
16
24
22
28
25
Estaçao 108 Sul
Eixo Rodoviário Sul
Presidente Juscelino Kubitschek (5km)
SETOR COMERCIAL SUL
Estação Galeria dos Estados
Estaçao 102 Sul
17
20
32
Estrada Parque Dom Bosco
QI-5
QL-8
SETOR BANCÁRIO SUL
31
7
3
Museu Nacional
1
Catedral Metropolitana
Via S-2
SETOR DE EMBAIXADAS SUL
4
Palácio do Itamaraty
Av das Nações
Praça dos Três Poderes
10
Bosque dos Constituyentes
Taypá (500m)
QI-16
QI-12
SETOR DE CLUBES ESPORTIVOS SUL
Centro Cultural Banco do Brasil (1.5km); Mangai (1.9km); Ponte JK (2.2km)

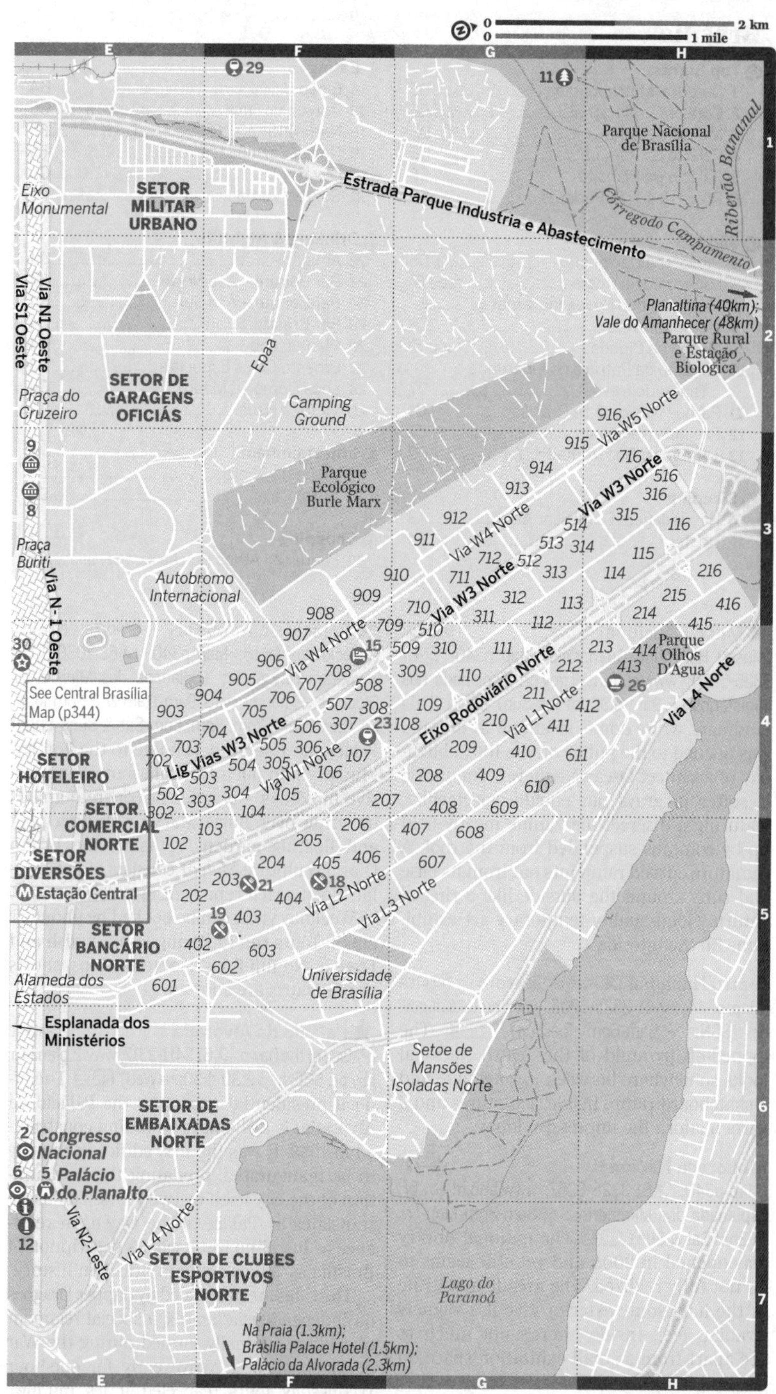
0 2 km
0 1 mile
Parque Nacional de Brasília
Estrada Parque Industria e Abastecimento
Corregodo Campamento
Riberão Bananal
Eixo Monumental
SETOR MILITAR URBANO
Via N1 Oeste
Via S1 Oeste
Planaltina (40km); Vale do Amanhecer (48km)
Parque Rural e Estação Biologica
Epaa
SETOR DE GARAGENS OFICIÁS
Praça do Cruzeiro
Camping Ground
Parque Ecológico Burle Marx
Praça Buriti
Via N-1 Oeste
Autobromo Internacional
Via W5 Norte
Via W4 Norte
Via W3 Norte
Eixo Rodoviário Norte
Via L1 Norte
Via L4 Norte
Parque Olhos D'Agua
See Central Brasília Map (p344)
Lig Vias W3 Norte
Via W1 Norte
SETOR HOTELEIRO
SETOR COMERCIAL NORTE
SETOR DIVERSÕES
Estação Central
Via L2 Norte
Via L3 Norte
SETOR BANCÁRIO NORTE
Universidade de Brasília
Alameda dos Estados
Esplanada dos Ministérios
Setoe de Mansões Isoladas Norte
SETOR DE EMBAIXADAS NORTE
Congresso Nacional
Palácio do Planalto
Via N2-Leste
SETOR DE CLUBES ESPORTIVOS NORTE
Lago do Paranoá
Na Praia (1.3km); Brasília Palace Hotel (1.5km); Palácio da Alvorada (2.3km)

Brasília

Top Sights
1 Catedral Metropolitana ... D5
2 Congresso Nacional ... E6
3 Museu Nacional ... D5
4 Palácio do Itamaraty ... D6
5 Palácio do Planalto ... E6
6 Praça dos Trés Poderes ... E6

Sights
7 Biblioteca Nacional ... D5
Espaço Lúcio Costa ... (see 6)
8 Memorial dos Povos Indígenas ... E3
9 Memorial JK ... E3
Museu da Cidade ... (see 6)
10 Panteão da Pátria e da Liberdade Tancredo Neves ... D7
11 Parque Nacional de Brasília ... G1
12 Pavilhão Nacional ... E7
13 Templo da Boa Vontade ... B2

Sleeping
14 Hospedagem Domiciliar Asa Sul ... A3
15 Hostel 7 ... F4

Eating
16 Bloco C ... B4
17 Boteco do Juca ... C5
18 Naturetto ... F5
19 Nossa Cozinha Bistrô ... F5
20 Olivae ... C5
21 Supren Verda ... F5

Drinking & Nightlife
22 Amigão ... C4
23 Bar Beirute – Asa Norte ... F4
24 Bar Beirute – Asa Sul ... B4
25 Bar Brasília ... C4
26 Clandestino ... H4
27 Ernesto Cafés Especiais ... B3
28 Loca Como Tu Madre ... C4
29 Victoria Haus ... F1

Entertainment
30 Clube do Choro ... E4
31 Outro Calaf ... D5

Shopping
32 Fundacão Athos Bulcão ... C5

★Museu Nacional MUSEUM
(Museu Honestino Guimarães; Map p340; ☎61 3325-5220; www.cultura.df.gov.br; Esplanada dos Ministérios; ⏰9am-6:30pm Tue-Sun) FREE This landmark white dome, gleaming in the sun, was opened to the public on the 100th birthday of architect Oscar Niemeyer. The inside is softer in grays but equally spectacular, featuring a discreet mezzanine mostly held up by columns suspended from the roof. A signature curved ramp juts out from its base and runs around the outside like a ring of Saturn. Good-quality temporary art exhibitions fill the interior.

Teatro Nacional Cláudio Santoro THEATER
(Map p344; ☎61 3325-6205; www.cultura.df.gov.br; SCN; ⏰9am-6pm Tue-Sun) FREE The lopped-off pyramid of the Teatro Nacional looks somewhere between a waterslide and a skateboard ramp. Inside, sculptures and a garden adorn the impressive lobby.

Biblioteca Nacional LIBRARY
(Map p340; ☎61 3325-6257; www.bnb.df.gov.br; Esplanada dos Ministérios; ⏰8am-8pm Mon-Fri, to 2pm Sat & Sun) FREE The national library was opened in 2008 and yet still seems to be not fully realized. The arcade and grille of the handsome exterior give it a vaguely Arabian feel. Inside, there's not much to see apart from a small exhibition space on the 2nd floor.

★Palácio do Itamaraty NOTABLE BUILDING
(Palácio dos Arcos; Map p340; ☎61 2030-8051; www.itamaraty.gov.br; Esplanada dos Ministérios, Bloco H; ⏰hourly visits 9am-11am & 2-5pm Mon-Fri, 9am, 11am, 2pm, 3pm, 5pm Sat & Sun) FREE Palácio do Itamaraty is home to the Foreign Ministry and one of Brasília's most impressive buildings – a series of concrete arches towering over Burle Marx's reflecting pool and floating gardens. Outside, the Bruno Giorgi sculpture *Meteor* consists of five marble blocks, each representing a continent.

Weekday visits can be booked by phone or email. Tours run in Portuguese, English and French. No flip-flops, sleeveless tops, shorts or miniskirts are allowed.

★Palácio da Alvorada PALACE
(Palace of the Dawn; ☎61 3411-2317; www2.planalto.gov.br; SCEN; ⏰2:30-4:50pm Wed) FREE The official presidential residence, the Palácio da Alvorada, is a Niemeyer building constructed in 1958. It was the first edifice in the city to be inaugurated, predating the inauguration of the city itself by two years. The name translates as 'Palace of the Dawn,' in reference to Juscelino Kubitschek's description of Brasília as 'a new dawn in Brazilian history.'

The gates are marshaled by dapper Dragões da Independência guards, a special regiment of soldiers originally formed during the War of Independence. Arrive early for one-hour Wednesday tours (canceled if it's raining).

Take bus 0.104 (R$2.50; every 30 minutes) from platform A16 in the local bus station.

★ **Santuário Dom Bosco** CHURCH

(Map p344; ☎61 3223-6542; www.santuariodombosco.org.br; SEPS 702, Bloco B; ⌚7am-8pm) FREE Santuário Dom Bosco is made of 80 concrete columns that support 7400 pieces of illuminated Murano glass, symbolizing a starry sky, which cast a blue submarine glow over the pews. The central chandelier weighs 2.5 tons and adds an amazing 435 light bulbs' worth of energy to the monthly electricity bill.

Bus 0.107 (R$3.50; platform E10 in the local bus station) passes here every eight minutes.

★ **Centro Cultural Banco do Brasil** ARTS CENTER

(CCBB; ☎61 3108-7600; www.culturabancodobrasil.com.br; SCES, Trecho 2, Conjunto 22; ⌚9am-9pm Tue-Sun) FREE Brasília's most important contemporary museum houses temporary exhibitions in two galleries, an indie cinema, a cafe and a bookstore. Buses 0.103 and 103.2 run here from the center.

Torre de TV TOWER

(Map p344; Eixo Monumental; ⌚9am-7pm Tue-Sun) FREE The 75m-high observation deck of the TV Tower gives a decent overview of the city, but it's still not quite tall enough to really get a sense of the city's airplane design. The mezzanine level sometimes has exhibitions; there is also a tourist information point and cafe here, both closed for refurbishment on our last visit.

Caixa Cultural MUSEUM

(Map p344; ☎61 3206-9448; www.caixacultural.com.br; SBS Q4, Lote 3/4; ⌚9am-9pm Tue-Sun) FREE This bank-run center has several galleries for temporary exhibitions, a sculpture garden, a cafe and theater. The lobby of the main bank building across the car park, the Átrio dos Vitrais, is a feast for the eyes: a series of gorgeous stained-glass panels represent each Brazilian state. Watching them shimmer over pools of water is a spectacular sight.

Museu de Valores MUSEUM

(Map p344; ☎61 3414-2093; www.bcb.gov.br/?museu; SBS Quadra 3, Bloco B; ⌚10am-6pm Tue-Fri, 2-6pm 1st Sat of month) FREE Numismatists will be interested in visiting this museum in the central bank HQ. A detailed history of Brazilian coins and banknotes – try keeping track of the cruzeiro-cruzado-cruzeiro shenanigans in the '70s and '80s – is complemented by foreign notes. In the gold section, an enormous 60kg nugget is striking, as are photos of the mining in the Serra de Pelada where it was found. You get a commemorative coin on entry, but you'll need to show your passport.

Parque Nacional de Brasília PARK

(Map p340; ☎61 3233-4553; www.icmbio.gov.br; Brazilian/foreigner R$13/26; ⌚8am-4pm, last exit 5pm) In the northern reaches of the city limits, some 10km from the center, the 30-sq-km Parque Nacional de Brasília is a good place to relax. It has natural swimming pools and is home to a number of threatened animals, including deer, anteaters, giant armadillos and maned wolves. Two trails (1300m and 5km) explore the park, and there is also a mountain-biking route. Bus 128 from box E12 in the city bus station goes past the front gate.

Memorial JK MUSEUM

(Map p340; ☎61 3226-7860; www.memorialjk.com.br; Praça do Cruzeiro; adult/child R$10/5; ⌚9am-6pm Tue-Sun) Inside this enormous memorial is the tomb of former president Juscelino Kubitschek (JK), which lies underneath eerily beautiful stained glass by French artist Marianne Peretti. The museum houses JK's 3000-book personal library as well as a pictorial history of Brasília. Don't miss his 1973 Ford Galaxie!

Memorial dos Povos Indígenas MUSEUM

(Map p340; www.cultura.df.gov.br; Praça Buriti; ⌚9am-5pm Tue-Fri, 10am-5pm Sat & Sun) FREE Opposite the Memorial JK, in a Niemeyer building inspired by the circular form of the indigenous Yanomani hut, is a small but colorful display of indigenous artifacts put together by anthropologists Darcy and Berta Ribeiro and Eduardo Galvão. It's complemented by temporary exhibitions on aspects of indigenous culture.

Tours

★ **Experimente Brasília** TOURS

(www.experimentebrasilia.com.br) Go local with this excellent agency, determined to show you a side of Brasília that will surprise you, whether that be on foot or two wheels. The most fascinating of the tours goes deep into *superquadra* life (R$95).

Billy Deeter TOURS

(☎61 3037-1823; www.mrbrasilia.com) Charismatic Billy Deeter, otherwise known as Mr Brasília, organizes custom group and private multilingual tours, which include some off-the-beaten-track points of interest.

Central Brasília

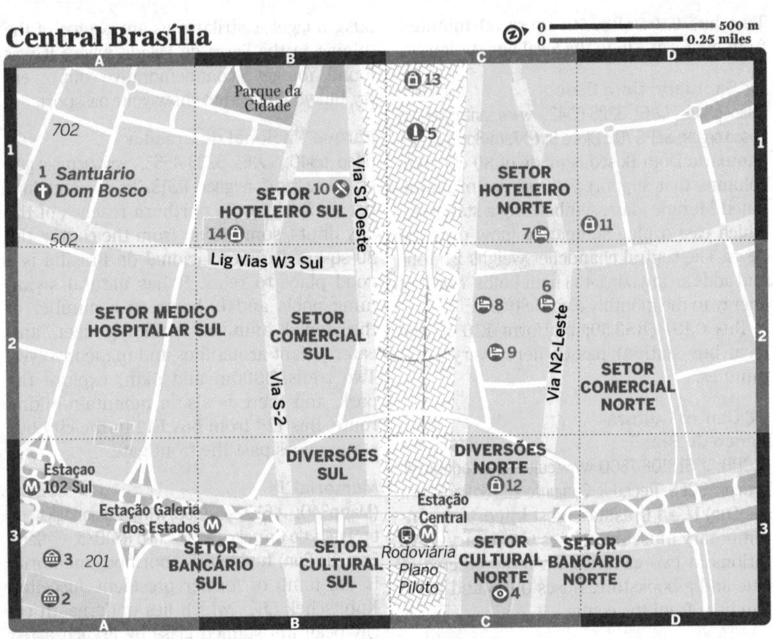

Central Brasília

Top Sights
1 Santuário Dom Bosco A1

Sights
2 Caixa Cultural A3
3 Museu de Valores A3
4 Teatro Nacional Cláudio Santoro C3
5 Torre de TV C1

Sleeping
6 Aristus Hotel C2
7 Cullinan Hplus Premium C1
8 Hotel Diplomat C2
9 Kubitschek Plaza C2

Eating
10 Fogo de Chão B1

Shopping
11 Brasília Shopping D1
12 Conjunto Nacional C3
13 Feira de Artesanato C1
14 Pátio Brasil B1

Sleeping

Bank on spending more than you'd like to in Brasília, especially during the business week. Characterless high-rise chain hotels, crammed into the central Setor Hoteleiro, are the norm. Those in the SHN (Setor Hoteleiro Norte) are more conveniently located for shopping centers, but those in the SHS (Setor Hoteleiro Sul) are better value.

Rates listed are for weekdays; they can drop as much as 75% on weekends.

Hostel 7 HOSTEL $
(Map p340; ☎61 3033-7707; www.hostel7.com.br; SCLRN 708, Bloco I, Loja 20; dm R$50-80; ❄@📶) This excellent hostel has tightly packed but decent dorms with lockers, air-con and bathrooms, plus a couple of private rooms sleeping up to four. Common spaces are limited, but there's a nice covered courtyard and bar in the back. Rooms named after Brasília's key founders and historic photos add a local touch; you've gotta love the Kombi-van reception and car couch.

Take bus 116 from the central bus station.

Hospedagem Domiciliar Asa Sul HOMESTAY $
(Map p340; ☎61 99932-9021; marcus.senise@hotmail.com; SQS 215, Bloco H, 107; s/d R$120/160; ❄@📶) You couldn't feel more at home in this apartment, where a comfortable twin room comes with Netflix and a bathroom across the hall. The family and their cat are very welcoming and prepare an excellent breakfast. This is a spot to get a feel for real Brasília *super-*

SUPERQUADRA LIFE

Although the sprawl of rapidly growing Brasília now extends far beyond the original design, with mushrooming satellite cities all around, it is worth taking the time to investigate the two wings of the *plano piloto* to gain an appreciation of life in the *superquadras*.

These ordered rows and blocks of apartments encapsulate the optimism and democratic ideals of the era. Each *superquadra* consists of a square block roughly 300m long with various apartment buildings, typically supported on columns. You'll see no power lines or fences but plenty of parkland and trees. Each *superquadra* shares a street of shops and restaurants with its neighbor, preserving a strong community feel. These little hubs are what Brasília life is all about, and it's worth visiting a few of them, for it's here that the city's best bars, cafes and restaurants are located.

Like the *superquadra* vibe? Hospedagem Domiciliar Asa Sul is a welcoming homestay in a typical apartment.

quadra life, and it also has great transport connections to the center from the doorstep.

No website, but you can find it on various online booking sites.

Hotel Diplomat HOTEL **$**

(Map p344; ☎61 3204-2010; www.diplomathotelbrasilia.com; SHN, Quadra 2, Bloco L; s/d/tr R$139/179/249; ❄📶) A solid cheapie in the northern hotel zone. You can tell that Niemeyer didn't do this one, but it's a well-run, good-value spot that wins votes for its ample breakfast, free soup on weekday evenings and substantial weekend discounts (basement rooms are the cheapest). There's also train compartment–sized cabins for solo travelers (R$89 to R$109).

★Brasília Palace Hotel HOTEL **$$**

(☎61 3306-9000; www.brasiliapalace.com.br; SHTN, Trecho 1, Lote 1; d R$320-650; ❄@📶🏊) Near the presidential palace, this emblematic hotel is a marvelous spot for architecture fans. Designed by Oscar Niemeyer in 1957, common spaces are a living midcentury modern treasury, with furniture and art by Niemeyer, Athos Bulcão and others around every turn, all shaded by an exterior blanketed with massive movable shutters. The whole experience screams: this is Brasília!

Rooms, set along astonishingly long and wide corridors, have light-wood furnishings and balconies. There's only a small difference between the superior and luxe categories, but the latter give you a better chance of lake views. Prices vary widely according to demand but it's often great value.

Cullinan Hplus Premium HOTEL **$$**

(Map p344; ☎61 3426-5000; www.hplus.com.br; SHN, Quadra 4, Bloco E; r R$230-500; ❄📶🏊) A modern choice in the northern hotel agglomeration, this high-rise often has significant value for spacious rooms that are bland but pleasant, with big windows framing interesting cityscapes. The array of breakfast choices is pretty impressive, and there's a gym, pool and sauna on the 1st floor. It's directly opposite two shopping centers with decent eating options. Free parking.

Kubitschek Plaza HOTEL **$$**

(Map p344; ☎61 3329-3333; www.kubitschek.com.br; SHN, Quadra 2, Bloco E; r R$230-400, luxo R$450-600; P❄@📶🏊) The halls and lobby of this classic choice feature wonderful local art and famous photographs of Juscelino Kubitschek's administration, giving it a leg up when it comes to character. Rooms include gorgeous hardwood floors and earth-toned headboards. Standard rooms are spacious, while 'luxo' rooms are huge, with balconies and lots of added extras.

Aristus Hotel HOTEL **$$**

(Map p344; ☎61 3328-8675; www.aristushotel.com.br; SHN, Quadra 2, Bloco O; s/d from R$150/200; ❄📶) If you spend any time in Brasília, you'll eventually get sick of elevators. The affable Aristus is comfortably squat with only two floors, so you won't need one. Rooms are spacious, modernized and simple, a proper window being the only difference in the more expensive rooms. Prices are much lower on weekends.

Eating

Brazilians may say that Brasília is boring, but foodies still flock here – the capital has one of the highest concentrations of starred restaurants in the country. Rather than there being a concentrated central food strip, restaurants are found out in the *superquadras*, in the commercial streets between blocks. Shopping centers are other eating hubs.

ADDRESSES FOR THE LOGICAL MIND

Believe it or not, Brasília's addresses – a series of numbers and letters that pinpoint an exact location – are designed to make your life easier (once you know what the acronyms mean!).

For example, take the address SQS 704, Bloco Q, Casa 29. That means it's in Super Quadra Sul (South) 704, *bloco* (building) Q, *casa* (house) 29. The first digit in the address (7) shows the position east or west of the Eixo Rodoviário (the main north–south arterial road) – odd numbers (1, 3, 5, 7) are to the west and even are to the east, increasing as they move away from the center. The last two digits (04) show the distance north or south of the Eixo Monumental. So the place you are looking for is four blocks to the south of the Eixo Monumental and four blocks east of the Eixo Rodoviário. The higher the number of the *superquadra*, the further it is from the center.

Get to know these acronyms:

Asa Norte/Asa Sul The two 'wings' of the city, connected by main roads. The N (Norte) or S (Sul) after an acronym indicates on which side of the Eixo Monumental it's located.

SBN/SBS (Setor Bancário Norte/Sul) The banking areas either side of the Eixo Monumental.

SCEN/SCES (Setor de Clubes Esportivos Norte/Sul) The main recreational zone on the shores of Lago do Paranoá.

SCLN/SCLS (Setor Comércio Local Norte/Sul) The main shopping blocks between the *superquadras*.

SCN/SCS (Setor Comercial Norte/Sul) The commercial office block areas next to the main shopping centers.

SDN/SDS (Setor de Diversões Norte/Sul) The main *conjuntos* (shopping centers) either side of the Eixo Monumental.

SEN/SES (Setor de Embaixadas Norte/Sul) The embassy sectors.

SHIN/SHIS (Setor de Habitações Individuaís Norte/Sul) The residential areas around the lake. SHIN is reached on the Eixo Norte. SHIS is accessed via the bridges off Av das Nações.

SHN/SHS (Setor Hoteleiro Norte/Sul) The hotel sectors each side of the Eixo Monumental.

SMHN/SMHS (Setor Médico Hospitalar Norte/Sul) The hospital sectors each side of the Eixo Monumental, next to the SCN and SCS, respectively.

SQN/SQS (Super Quadras Norte/Sul) The individual *superquadras* in the main residential wings of the *plano piloto*.

The best restaurant selections are in the Asa Sul, around SCLS 209/210, 409/410 and 411/412, which forms a sort of 'gourmet triangle' (it is also home to some of the city's most lively nightlife). Another good selection of restaurants is clustered in SCLS 405 and SCLN 412/413.

Elsewhere, Brazilians in need of sustenance head to the shopping malls. Three centrally located oases – **Brasília Shopping** (Map p344; www.brasiliashopping.com.br; Quadra 5, Asa Norte SCN; ⏲10am-10pm Mon-Sat, 1-7pm (shops), noon-10pm (food court) Sun; 📶), **Pátio Brasil** (Map p344; ☎61 2107-7400; www.patiobrasil.com.br; Asa Sul, W3 SCS; ⏲10am-10pm Mon-Sat, 2-8pm Sun) and **Conjunto Nacional** (Map p344; www.conjuntonacional.com.br; SDN CNB, Conjunto A; ⏲9am-10pm Mon-Sat, food only noon-8pm Sun) – all have food courts with enough variety to cater to most tastes.

Boteco do Juca BOTECO $

(Map p340; ☎61 3242-9415; www.botecodojuca.com.br; CLS 405, Bloco A; petiscos R$17-55; ⏲11:30am-midnight; 📶) Deservedly popular, this sprawling Rio-style outdoor bar has icy draft beer and on-the-ball service. All-you-can-eat evening pizza (R$26 to R$28) draws crowds, but there's also a nice range of skewers, grilled meats and shared finger-food plates that are great value.

Supren Verda VEGAN $

(Map p340; www.facebook.com/restaurantesuprenverda; CLN 203, Bloco D; per kg R$58; ⏲11:30am-3pm & 7-10pm Mon-Sat, 11:30am-3pm Sun; 🌿) A family that has eschewed meat for five generations runs this cute tucked-away corner buffet. The food is all vegan and of high quality and inventiveness: try cold zucchini spaghetti with avocado sauce or a shiitake risotto. The buffet takes up all the indoor space; shady outdoor seating makes this a very pleasurable experience.

Naturetto BRAZILIAN **$**

(Map p340; ☎61 3201-6223; CLN 405, Block C; per kg R$62; ⏰11:30am-3pm & 6:30-9:30pm Mon-Fri, 11:30am-4pm Sat & Sun; 📶🌱) This excellent pescatarian (fish but no meat) *por-quilo* (per kilo) restaurant is worth seeking out for creative dishes and the rustic, inner-city environment in which to enjoy it all. Nutritionists are on hand, overseeing the food and answering questions; it's packed at lunch.

★Olivae BRAZILIAN **$$**

(Map p340; ☎61 3443-8775; www.facebook.com/olivaerestaurante; SCLS 405, Bloco B, Loja 6; mains R$62-73; ⏰noon-3pm & 7-11pm Tue-Sat; 📶) With a disciple of Brazilian super chef Alex Atala running the show, this classy spot has everyone's taste buds doing a happy dance. The three-course lunch special for R$64 is an astonishing deal; there's prix-fixe dinners (R$92) and weekend grills as well. Presentation is exquisite.

Nossa Cozinha Bistrô FUSION **$$**

(Map p340; ☎61 3326-5207; www.nossacozinhabsb.blogspot.com.br; SCLN 402, Bloco C; mains R$36-65; ⏰11:30am-3pm & 7:30-11pm Mon-Thu, to midnight Fri & Sat; 📶) At this sweet, welcoming bistro tucked away on Bloco C's backside, superb value awaits. The US-trained chef excels at gourmet treats like the signature pork ribs (velvety! chocolatey!). For Brazil, the check is a pleasant surprise.

Mangai BRAZILIAN **$$**

(☎61 3252-0156; www.mangai.com.br; SCES, Trecho 2, Conjunto 41; per kilo R$79; ⏰noon-3pm & 6-10pm Mon-Fri, noon-10pm Sat, 11am-9pm Sun; 📶) This northeastern *por-quilo* restaurant is a culinary experience like no other. An assembly line of tempting creative dishes will totally overwhelm you – and that's just the salad section. The space itself is gargantuan and full of Brazilian character. It's down by the Ponte JK and gets very busy at lunch.

★Taypá PERUVIAN **$$$**

(☎61 3248-0403; www.taypa.com.br; SHIS QI 17, Bloco G, Loja 208; mains R$60-110; ⏰noon-3pm & 7pm-midnight Mon-Fri, noon-4pm & 7pm-1am Sat, noon-5pm Sun; 📶) It's worth a trip to the edges of Lago Sul – a R$40 or so taxi fare – for Marco Espinoza's authentic upscale Peruvian fare. His whole team hails from Peru and it shows: the fabulous ceviche *criollo,* drowning in creamy *leche de tigre* (citrus marinade), and decadent *suspiro de limeño* (milk caramel and meringue) were the best we've had outside Peru. Great *pisco* cocktails.

Bloco C FUSION **$$$**

(Map p340; ☎61 3363-3062; www.facebook.com/blocoCrestaurante; CLS 211, Bloco C; mains R$80-100; ⏰noon-3:30pm & 7:30pm-midnight Mon-Sat) Smart but not pretentious, this restaurant has an elegant two-level interior and lovely back deck. The cuisine shows off its French and Italian roots with dishes like house carpaccio with truffled honey and a hits-the-spot cassoulet that replaces beans with *fregola* pasta.

Fogo de Chão CHURRASCARIA **$$$**

(Map p344; ☎61 3322-4666; www.fogodechao.com.br; SHS, Quadra 5, Bloco E; rodízio R$139; ⏰noon-4pm & 6-11:30pm Mon-Fri, to 1:30pm Sat, to 10:30pm Sun; 📶) In the southern hotel district, Fogo de Chão is of imposing dimensions. The *rodízio* (all-you-can-eat grilled meat) certainly isn't cheap, but service is very attentive – almost too much at times – and the meat is of excellent quality. The salad bar has a huge range.

🍷 Drinking & Nightlife

Bars are found scattered around on the commercial streets between *superquadra* blocks. In general, the Asa Sul has more options than the Asa Norte, but there are good bars in both. Most nightclubs are on the edges of town.

For cheap drinks with the university crowd, head to SCLN 408/9 for a collection of options.

★Ernesto Cafés Especiais CAFE

(Map p340; ☎61 3345-4182; SCLS 115, Bloco C, Loja 14; ⏰7am-10pm; 📶) Easily Brasília's best coffee experience, this serious java joint has specialty microlot coffees from Minas Gerais and is hopping with locals day or night, whether over breakfast (fresh baked bread, good tapiocas) or simply losing an afternoon entrenched in conversation on the pleasant back patio. Non-dairy milks are available; there's also a bakery.

★Clandestino CAFE

(Map p340; ☎61 3340-4919; www.facebook.com/clandestinocafeemusica; CLN 413, Bloco D; ⏰9am-9pm Mon & Wed-Sat, 9am-3pm Sun; 📶) Clandestino has a very pleasant setting next to a park with typical cerrado vegetation. The balcony seats are a great spot to sip on well-prepared coffee, munch on tapioca or chill out to well-curated music; there are also regular DJs and live sessions.

Amigão BAR
(Map p340; 61 3244-1109; www.facebook.com/amigaobaroficial; SCLS, Quadra 506, Bloco B, Loja 46; 11am-10pm Mon-Fri, 11am-5pm Sat) Amiable and no-frills, this neighborhood bar occupies twin garage-like spaces and is a prime spot for a casual beer or three. There's a menu of steaks, but go for the daily specials (R$48 to R$70 for two), which rotate through *feijoada* (bean and meat stew), pork knuckle etc.

Victoria Haus GAY & LESBIAN
(Map p340; 61 99552-2891; www.victoriahaus.com; SAA, Quadra 1, Lote 930; cover R$20-60; 10:30pm-6am Fri & Sat) This warehouse venue is Brasília's iconic LGBT+ venue, with shows, DJs and a very late license.

Na Praia BAR
(www.tevejonapraia.com.br; SCEN 19; Jul–early Sep) It's quite a way to the coast, so they made a beach of sorts in Brasília. This seasonal affair by the lake combines outdoor drinking with plenty of events and a series of weekly big-name concerts; check the website to see what's on offer, as the setup changes quite a bit each year.

Bar Beirute – Asa Sul BOTECO
(Map p340; 61 3244-1717; www.barbeirute.com.br; SCLS 109, Bloco A; 11am-1am Sun-Wed, to 2am Thu-Sat) This Brasília institution has a massive outdoor patio packed with an edgy crowd. It's a GLS point (the clever Brazilian acronym for gays, lesbians and sympathetics) but it's really a free-for-all and a great spot for a mug of cold Beira – Beirute's own brand of beer! There's Lebanese food to soak it up.

There's another branch in the **Asa Norte** (Map p340; 61 3272-0123; SCLN 107, Bloco B; 11am-1am Sun-Wed, to 2am Thu-Sat;).

Bar Brasília BAR
(Map p340; 61 3443-4323; www.barbrasilia.com.br; SCLS, Quadra 506, Bloco A, Loja 15A; 11:30am-midnight Mon-Sat, to 4pm Sun) This bar is in the same vein as classics from Rio and São Paulo, complete with a hardwood bar relocated from a pharmacy in 1928 and antique tiled floors. It's great for excellent draft beer and Friday-Saturday *feijoada* (R$48).

Loca Como Tu Madre PUB
(Map p340; 61 3244-5828; www.facebook.com/locacomotumadregastropub; SCLS 306 Bloco C, Loja 36; noon-3pm & 6-11pm Mon, to midnight Tue-Thu, to 1am Fri, noon-1am Sat;) 'Crazy Like Your Mama' has a great outdoor space that caters to well-heeled *brasiliense* imbibing to the sounds of nightly DJs spinning pop and MPB at pleasant sound levels. They take their cocktails seriously here and there's even a little shop flogging designer threads. It's also a popular lunch spot.

☆ Entertainment

★Outro Calaf LIVE MUSIC
(Map p340; 61 3322-9581; www.outrocalaf.com; SBS, Quadra 2, Bloco Q; cover R$20-40; 11am-3pm Mon, to 2am Tue, 1:30pm-4am Wed-Sat, 5pm-midnight Sun) The city's top dance floor is everybody's favorite; the excellent live samba, *pagode* (popular samba), *sertanejo* and *choro* (improvised samba) keep things pumping. Owner Venceslau Calaf has long been a driving force in the live music scene, and Tuesday night samba is a favorite. Entry varies but is usually half price or free before 11pm.

There's also a Spanish-influenced restaurant turning out paella and tortillas, as well as *feijoada* on the weekends.

Clube do Choro LIVE MUSIC
(Map p340; 61 3224-0599; www.clubedochoro.com.br; Setor de Divulgação Cultural, Bloco G; cover R$30-40; 9pm-midnight Tue-Sat) A wildly mixed crowd of serious music aficionados – No talking! No standing! – descends on this locals' secret. You can walk here from the hotel sectors, and it's a showcase for some of the country's most magnificent *choro*. Reserve the best seats online. Food and drinks are (quietly) served.

Shopping

The **crafts fair** (Map p344; Eixo Monumental; most stalls 9am-6pm Fri-Sun) at the base of the TV Tower is a good place to pick up leather goods, ceramics and art.

You should be able to satisfy your other shopping needs in one of Brasília's many shopping malls.

Fundacão Athos Bulcão DESIGN
(Map p340; www.fundathos.org.br; SCLS 404, Bloco D, Loja 1; 9am-6pm or 7pm Mon-Fri, 10am-5pm Sat) Painter/sculptor Athos Bulcão was the only artist allowed to colorfully spruce up Niemeyer and Costa's grand plan and his iconic designs are as much a part of Brasília history as his more well-known counterparts. Pick up art, coffee mugs, beach towels and the like.

Information

DANGERS & ANNOYANCES

➡ Brasília is much safer than Brazil's large coastal cities, but it's still wise to not walk far at night.

- Crossing the central Eixo Monumental at night is a particularly bad idea.
- Be wary of pickpockets at the crowded local bus station.

MEDICAL SERVICES

De Base do Distrito Federal (☎61 3315-1280; www.saude.df.gov.br; SMHS 101) Central public hospital.

Santa Luzia (☎61 3445-6000; www.hsl.com.br; SHLS, Quadra 716, Conjunto E) Hospital in the Asa Sul.

TOURIST INFORMATION

The city's two most helpful tourist information booths are on the Praça de Três Poderes and at the airport:

CAT (Centro de Atendimento ao Turista; Map p340; ☎61 3226 0153; www.turismo.df.gov.br; Praça dos Três Poderes; ⏲9am-noon & 1-6pm)

CAT Aeroporto (Centro de Atendimento ao Turista; www.turismo.df.gov.br; Presidente Juscelino Kubitschek International Airport; ⏲9am-noon & 1-6pm)

Getting There & Away

AIR

Brasília has a large daily influx of sightseers and lobbyists, so the international airport connects with all major Brazilian cities. There are also some direct international connections.

Brasília's shiny **Aeroporto Presidente Juscelino Kubitschek** (BSB; ☎61 3364-9000; www.bsb.aero) is 12km south of the center.

BUS

From the flashy long-distance bus station **Rodoviária Interestadual** (Map p340; ☎61 3234-2185; www.rodoviariabrasilia.com; SMAS, Trecho 4, Conjunto 5/6), 3km southwest off the edge of Asa Sul, buses go almost everywhere in Brazil.

Getting Around

Brasília has a bus network and a metro line. The Bilhete Único (www.bilheteunicobrasilia.df.gov.br) covers all forms of public transport but the standard version is only for residents. The +Turista version of the card, available for set numbers of journeys, was experiencing teething problems at the time of research.

From the intercity bus station, catch the metro or local bus 108.8 (R$3.50, 20 minutes) into the center.

TO/FROM THE AIRPORT

The easiest way to and from the airport is **Ônibus Executivo Aeroporto** (Bus 113; ☎61 3344-2769; www.tcb.df.gov.br; fare R$12; ⏲6:30am-11:55pm), which runs from the far right of the arrivals hall (as you arrive) into the center (20 to 40 minutes). It's a good introduction to the city, as it takes you right past most of the iconic buildings before dropping off in the hotel districts. It departs just outside the arrivals hall to the far right as you leave.

Bus 0.102/102.1 runs between the local bus station and the airport for R$3.50 (40 minutes).

Taxis to the airport cost around R$60.

BUSES FROM BRASÍLIA

DESTINATION	STARTING FARE (R$)	DURATION (HR)	COMPANY
Belém	255	35	Satélite Norte (www.satelitenorte.com.br), Rápido Marajó (www.rapidomarajo.com.br)
Campo Grande	238-261	23-25	Motta (www.motta.com.br), Viação São Luiz (www.viacaosaoluiz.com.br)
Cuiabá	208-232	23	Expresso São Luiz (www.expressosaoluiz.com.br), Eucatur (www.eucatur.com.br), Andorinha (www.andorinha.com)
Goiânia	40-62	3-4	Araguarina (www.araguarina.com.br), Viação Goiânia (www.viacaogoiania.com.br), Expresso São Luiz, Catedral Turismo (www.catedralturismo.com.br)
Porto Velho	512	43	Andorinha, Eucatur
Rio de Janeiro	220	18	Viação Util (www.util.com.br), Kaissara (www.kaissara.com.br)
Salvador	270-310	25	Catedral Turismo, Real Expresso (www.realexpresso.com.br)
São Paulo	228	17	Catedral Turismo, Real Expresso, Emtram (www.emtram.com.br)

BUS

The key point for the city's complex series of bus routes, run by DFTrans (www.dftrans.df.gov.br), is the central local bus station, **Rodoviária Plano Piloto** (Map p344; ☎61 3327-4631).

Bus journeys in the city cost R$2.50, R$3.50 or R$5 for longer routes.

CAR & MOTORCYCLE

Driving in Brasília is relatively easy and can be a good way to get around. There are several car rental companies at the airport, and some in town. Localiza has an **office** (☎61 3326-9925; www.localizahertz.com; SCN Quadra 1 Edificio 1; ⏲8am-8pm Mon-Sat, 8am-2pm Sun) close to the northern hotel hub. Parking around town is mostly free.

METRO

The **Metrô DF** (www.metro.df.gov.br; R$5; ⏲6am-11:30pm Mon-Sat, 7am-7pm Sun) is clean and comfortable. It only covers the south side of the city but is useful for access to restaurants and bars in the Asa Sul as well as to the intercity bus station (stop: Shopping). It runs from the city bus station to the huge suburbs of Ceilândia and Samambaia, with a predictably named station (102 Sul, 104 Sul etc) every two blocks or so from the central station.

TAXI

You'll need Uber or a taxi number with you in Brasília. Street cabs are as scarce as snow in the *superquadras*.

Uber works well, with lots of vehicles and low fares. Taxi companies include **Unitaxi** (☎61 3325-3030; www.unitaxidf.com.br), which offers a 30% discount for phone bookings.

GOIÁS

POP 6.8 MILLION

Goiás is generally undervisited by international travelers and well worth some of your time. Agriculture is big business here, with soya, biodiesel and ethanol industries making this one of the wealthiest states in the country, albeit at the expense of the landscape in some parts. Fortunately, its unrelenting natural beauty is preserved in sensational highland areas, while handsome colonial towns are perfect places to try the much-lauded regional cuisine.

Major attractions include picturesque Cidade de Goiás and Pirenópolis, and the rivers, waterfalls and forest trails of Parque Nacional da Chapada dos Veadeiros.

Goiânia

☎0XX62 / POP 1.5 MILLION / ELEV 749M

The capital of Goiás, Goiânia is the region's other planned city, predating Brasília by almost 30 years. Designed by urbanist Armando de Godói and founded in 1933, it's a pleasant enough combination of parks, leafy avenues and high-rise buildings laid out around circular streets. There's not much to see here, but it's a major transport nexus and if you're touring the state, you'll inevitably find yourself passing through more than once.

Sleeping

There are numerous places to stay for all budgets close to the gigantic bus station, as well as good options in the center. Midrange and top-end hotels drop as much as 50% off rack rates when business is slow.

Hostel 7 HOSTEL $

(☎62 3877-6077; www.hostel7.com.br; Av T2, Quadra 107, Lote 4, Setor Bueno; dm R$55-85, r R$98-120; ❄@🛜🏊) Goiâna's best hostel, an HI-affiliate, has a minimalist aesthetic in a well-to-do residential neighborhood southwest of Centro, with striking accents like carved-out Volkswagen buses, hip common spaces and a good pool. But charging for bath towels and leaving bed dressing to guests in cramped private rooms is a definite overreach.

Pousada Zé do Alamin POUSADA $$

(☎62 3252-1098; www.facebook.com/pousadazedoalamin; Rua T-35, Quadra 98, Lote 20, Setor Bueno; dm/s/d R$75/130/180; ❄🛜) Attractive and relaxed, this modern pousada in an appealing zone southwest of the center is comfort at a fair price. Spacious common areas include a garden, while rooms are pared back with firm mattresses, desk and well-stocked minibar. One room with five beds serves as a dorm.

Goiânia Palace HOTEL $$

(☎62 3224-4874; www.goianiapalace.com; Av Anhanguera 5195, Setor Central; s/d R$145/190; ❄🛜) This magenta main-road hotel has art deco brick-and-wood *apartamentos* with wardrobes, full-length mirrors and made-to-order eggs for breakfast. Very welcoming and centrally located, with attractive, spacious public areas. English and French are sometimes spoken and there are usually heavy discounts.

Eating

There is some great regional food to try here. For the best options, head to the adjacent Setor Marista and Setor Bueno zones on the south-

GOIÁS CUISINE

The long isolation of remote inland Goiás led to the development of a distinctive local cuisine that is one of Brazil's most interesting and shares some similarities with neighboring Minas Gerais. Trying some of the characteristic dishes that feature unusual cerrado products is an intriguing element of any visit here.

Pequi This orange fruit has a curious, almost cheesy taste and you'll likely either love it or hate it. It features in many dishes, particularly stews and rice. Don't bite into it, as concealed spines can give you a painful shock; just scrape the flesh away carefully with a knife.

Empadão goiano Savory baked pie that is a local highlight. It comes with a variety of fillings that include pork, chicken, sausage, cheese, fruit, eggs and olives.

Pamonha You'll find this across several states but nowhere is it more common than here. It's a sweet or savory corn paste tied up in a maize leaf and boiled. A leaf-free fried version is also popular.

Guariroba This species of palm produces a palm heart that is more bitter than usual. It's used extensively in local cooking, particularly around Pirenópolis.

Galinhada Though usually considered a *mineiro* dish, this much-loved chicken rice is also typical of Goiás, with the addition of cerrado fruits like *pequi*.

Cerrado fruits Numerous unusual fruits like *bacupari, buriti, mangaba* and *araticum* crop up in juices, desserts, ice cream and the region's famous crystallized fruits and pastries.

western side of the center. Shopping centers around the bus station provide other options.

★Botequim Mercatto BRAZILIAN $$
(62 3541-7129; www.botequimmercatto.com; Rua T-36 2775, Setor Bueno; mains for 2 people R$50-75; 11am-1am) They had a good idea here: take the traditional Brazilian bar-restaurant, focus on upmarket food, but keep quantities big and the *chope* (draft beer) abundant and cold. Must-tries include the *pastel de feijoada* (pie filled with meat and bean stew) and the slow-roasted *cupim* (the hump on the back of Brazilian cattle). It does half-portions, which are enormous in themselves.

It works brilliantly – so well, in fact, that there's an affiliate at the end of the block.

Chão Nativo I BRAZILIAN $$
(62 3241-2266; www.restaurantechaonativo.com.br; Av República do Líbano 1809, Setor Oeste; fixed-price meals from R$36, per kg R$62; 11am-3pm Mon-Fri, to 3:30pm Sat & Sun) Break out the calculator to help you choose between pay-by-weight or all-you-can-eat at this smorgasbord of bubbling Goiânian cauldrons, often voted the city's best for local cuisine.

Drinking & Nightlife

The Setor Marista and Setor Bueno zones are the best spots for bars. Rua 137 and around is a major drinking hub.

Celsin & Cia BOTECO
(www.celsinecia.com.br; Rua 22, 475, Setor Oeste; 5pm-2am Mon-Fri, 11am-2am Sat, 11am-6pm Sun;) *Goianienses* drink in droves at this traditional *boteco,* filling the dozens of outdoor tables under illuminated almond trees. The food's pretty good – try the homemade sausage – and there's a play area for kids.

Mönch Bier BAR
(www.facebook.com/monchbierpub; Rua 144, 665, Sector Marista; 6pm-2am Tue, Wed & Sun, to 3am Thu, to 4am Fri & Sat;) Look for the eagle sign to find this worthwhile bar with an unparalleled domestic craft beer list, including 11 taps that rotate brews rarely seen outside the bottle. Tack on a great crowd and cool music: this wins the top spot for hopheads.

Information

If you're just passing through, pretty much everything you are likely to need – from food to ATMs to a post office – is in the monster-size bus station–mall (p354). If you're traveling on to the national parks or colonial towns, get cash here.

CAT (Centro de Atendimento ao Turista; www.goiania.go.gov.br; Rodoviária de Goiânia; 8:30am-8:30pm) This desk right in the middle of the bus station building (by the play area and escalator) can provide you with a map

Getting There & Away

Aeroporto de Goiânia (GYN; 62 3265-1500; www.aeroportogoiania.net; Praça Capitão Frazão 913) is 6km northeast of the city center. You can fly to Rio, São Paulo and other major Brazilian cities, but flights from nearby Brasília are often cheaper.

Getting Around

Goiânia buses do not accept cash. Buy paper tickets at numerous newsstands and other locations around town.

From the airport, sporadic bus service 313 connects to the city bus terminal at Praça da Bíblia, but it's not especially handy. It's around a R$20 Uber ride to the center.

Cidade de Goiás

☎0XX62 / POP 24,100

Straddling the Rio Vermelho and surrounded by the rugged Serra Dourada, Cidade de Goiás is a sleepy and charming town of lamplit cobblestone streets and whitewashed colonial homes. The former state capital, once known as Vila Boa (and briefly Goiás Velho and sometimes today only as Goiás or Goyaz), features gorgeous baroque churches, interesting museums and a laid-back character that make it a real highlight. The population of the Unesco-listed town swells during its notable Semana Santa (Holy Week). Every July 25, the anniversary of the town's 1727 founding, the state governor visits Cidade de Goiás, which becomes the state capital for three days.

Sights

★Palácio Conde dos Arcos PALACE

(☎62 3371-1200; Praça do Coreto; R$4; ⏲8am-5pm Tue-Sat, to 1pm Sun) The restored colonial governor's residence is a very handsome piece of work. The guided tour (English usually spoken) takes in antique furniture, a curious triangular courtyard and lots of information about the history of the town and the building. It still gets to be a seat of power when the state capital transfers back here every July.

Museu das Bandeiras MUSEUM

(☎62 3371-1087; Praça Brasil Caiado; ⏲9am-noon & 1-6pm Tue-Sat, 9am-1pm Sun) FREE The fascinating Museu das Bandeiras is an old jail (1766–1950) that's full of antiques and original furniture – the 1.5m-thick cell walls, originally made of weak *taipa de pilão* wood and reinforced with much stronger *aroeira* (pepper-tree) wood, are a museum piece in themselves. Upstairs is the former court; it is not open to the public. Outside in the square, the 1778 **Chafariz de Cauda fountain** is perfectly preserved, except no water flows.

Museu de Arte Sacra MUSEUM

(Praça do Coreto; R$4; ⏲9am-5pm Tue-Sat, 9am-1pm Sun) In the old baroque Igreja da Boa Morte, this appealing museum has a good selection of 19th-century religious sculptures by renowned local artist José Joaquim da Veiga Valle (1806–74), whose mortal remains are also here. The lovely *ipê*-wood floor is another highlight.

Casa de Cora Coralina MUSEUM

(☎62 3371-1990; www.museucoracoralina.com.br; Dom Cândido Penso 20; R$10; ⏲9am-4:45pm Tue-Sat, 9am-1pm Sun) This handsome house is the birthplace of the area's renowned poet, Cora Coralina (1889–1985). It contains period furniture and a small display on her life and work; largely inspired by Goiás and rural Brazil.

Igreja São Francisco de Paula CHURCH

(Praça Zaqueu Alves de Castro; R$4; ⏲1-5pm) FREE The most impressive of the town's seven churches is the oldest, built in 1761. It's worth visiting for its beautiful painted ceiling as well as original features like the altar and pulpit. There's also a small museum of religious art.

Festivals & Events

Semana Santa RELIGIOUS

(⏲Mar or Apr) The highlight of the week before Easter is the Wednesday-night procession re-enacting the arrest of Christ. The streetlights are turned off and thousands march through the streets carrying torches, led by 40 eerie, pointy-hooded figures – the *farricocos* – whose colorful dress harks back to the days of the Inquisition.

Sleeping

Pousada do Ipê POUSADA $$

(☎62 3371-2065; www.pousadadoipe.com; Colonial Luiz Guedes de Amorim 22; s/d R$206/227, chalet s/d R$230/269; ❄📶🏊) At one end of the central area, this pousada is a tranquil, venerable property set around a huge courtyard that's quite a surprise after the small street frontage. White rooms are very simple but preserve historic character; the chalets near the large pool are more modern but lack the same ambience. Enjoy the sugar-laden breakfast of local jams and jellies.

Chácara da Dinda POUSADA $$

(☎62 3371-4327; www.chacaradadinda.com.br; Praça do Asilo 10; s/d R$130/230; ❄📶🏊) A pleasant 10-minute stroll southwest from the central area, you'll find this relaxing spot with simple concrete-floored rooms set around a large courtyard with trees and a pool. No frills and no fuss.

Casa da Ponte HOTEL $$

(☎62 3371-4467; casadapontehotel_@hotmail.com; Moretti Foggia s/n; s/d R$150/250; ❄📶) The downstairs public areas are handsome

Cidade de Goiás

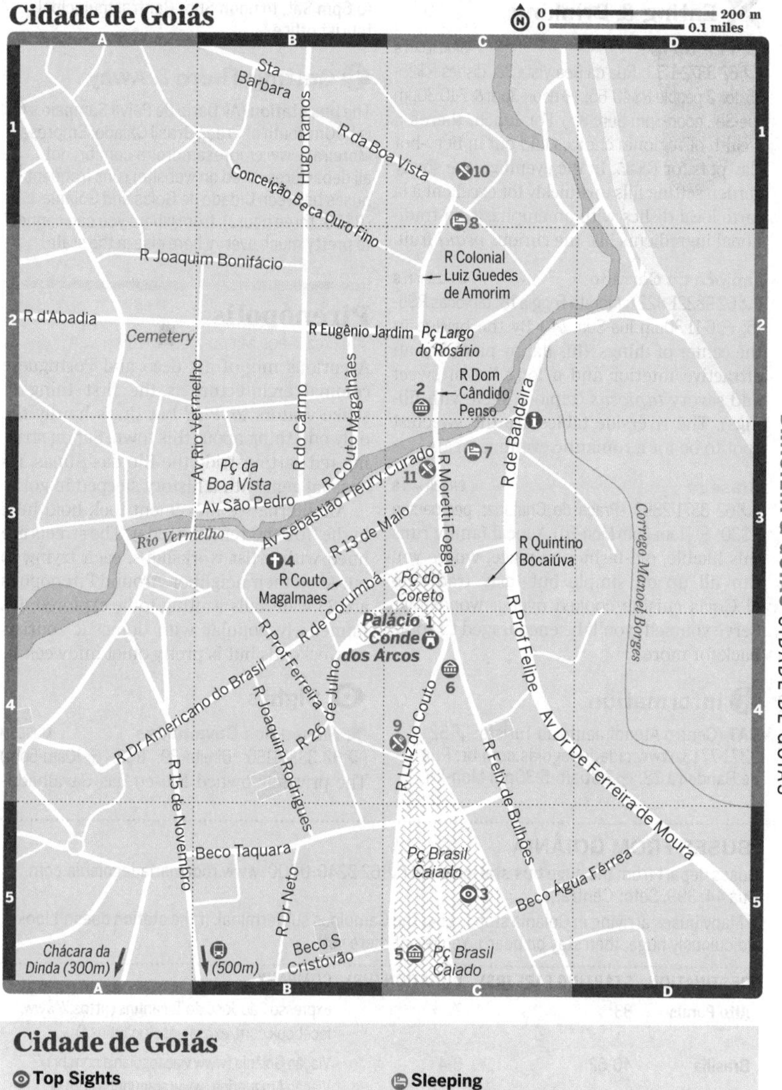

Cidade de Goiás

Top Sights
1 Palácio Conde dos Arcos C4

Sights
2 Casa de Cora Coralina C2
3 Chafariz de Cauda C5
4 Igreja São Francisco de Paula B3
5 Museu das Bandeiras C5
6 Museu de Arte Sacra C4

Sleeping
7 Casa da Ponte C3
8 Pousada do Ipê C1

Eating
9 Braseiro C4
10 Flor do Ipê C1
11 Tapioca do Cerrado C3

enough in this salmon-colored hotel in a superb location by the Rio Vermelho. Upstairs is more of a throwback, with rickety parquet and photocopied room numbers. Rooms are compact but OK for the price; there's a nice common balcony overlooking the river.

Eating & Drinking

★Flor do Ipê BRAZILIAN $

(☎62 3372-1133; Rua da Boa Vista 32; dishes R$25-35, for 2 people R$40-65; ⊙noon-3pm & 7-10:30pm Tue-Sat, noon-3pm Sun;) For lunch, there's a wealth of regional choices laid out in fiery-hot clay pots for R$35. In the evenings, the shady garden setting fills up quickly for excellent à la carte local dishes with an emphasis on traditional ingredients like the curious *pequi* fruit.

Tapioca do Cerrado BRAZILIAN $

(☎62 98221-4227; Moretti Foggia 18; tapiocas R$5-15; ⊙6-11:30pm Tue-Sun;) By the bridge in the center of things, this happy place has an attractive interior and a long list of sweet and savory *tapiocas* (tapioca shell with fillings). The riverside tables are the sweetest spot to be for a romantic evening meal.

Braseiro BRAZILIAN $

(☎62 3371-2892; Praça do Chafariz; per person R$30; ⊙11am-2pm Mon-Fri) A local family runs this likable, old-fashioned place, where you can fill up on simple but tasty traditional Goiás cuisine cooked over a woodstove. Serve yourself; you'll be encouraged to come back for more.

Information

CAT (Centro Atendimento ao Turista; ☎62 3371-7713; www.cidadedegoias.com.br; Rua de Bandeira 28; ⊙7:30am-5:30pm Mon-Fri, to 6pm Sat, to noon Sun) Central municipal tourist office.

Getting There & Away

The **bus station** (Av Dario de Paiva Sampaio s/n) is 500m south of Praça Brasil Caiado. Empresa Moreira (www.empresamoreira.com.br; not all departures listed on website) runs frequent buses between Cidade de Goiás and Goiânia (R$38, three hours), from where you can connect to pretty much everywhere else in the state.

Pirenópolis

☎0XX62 / POP 24,600 / ELEV 770M

A curious mix of art deco and Portuguese colonial architecture is the first thing to strike visitors to 'Piri,' but that's hardly the only odd thing about this town. Set on striking red earth astride the Rio das Almas, it's a visual gem with a history steeped in gold.

An alternative movement took hold here in the '70s and remains today. The streets are lined with artist workshops, each trying to out-kook their neighbor. Around Pirenópolis are 73 waterfalls waiting to be explored. It's immensely popular with domestic tourists on weekends but is pretty quiet midweek.

Sights

★Museu das Cavalhadas MUSEUM

(☎62 3331-1166; Direita 39; R$2; ⊙10am-5pm) The privately owned Museu das Cavalhadas

BUSES FROM GOIÂNIA

Buses depart from the huge **bus station-mall** (☎62 3240-0000; www.rodoviariadegoiania.com; Rua 44, 399, Setor Central).

Many buses arriving in Goiânia stop first at the Campinas subterminal. If the station doesn't look ridiculously huge, then stay on board. You're not there yet!

DESTINATION	STARTING FARE (R$)	DURATION (HR)	COMPANY
Alto Paraíso	83	7	Expresso São José do Tocantins (https://www.facebook.com/expsaojosetocantins/)
Brasília	40-62	3-4	Viação Goiânia (www.viacaogoiania.com.br), Viação Araguarina (www.araguarina.com.br), Expresso São Luiz (www.expressosaoluiz.com.br), Catedral Turismo (www.catedralturismo.com.br)
Caldas Novas	43	3	Viação Estrela (www.viacaoestrela.com), Viação Paraúna (www.viacaoparauna.com.br), Roderotas (www.roderotas.com)
Cidade de Goiás	38	3	Empresa Moreira (www.empresamoreira.com.br; not all departures listed on website)
Cuiabá	160-175	14-17	Expresso São Luiz, Satélite Norte (www.satelitenorte.com.br), Eucatur (www.eucatur.com.br)
Pirenópolis	36	2	Viação Goiânia

is cluttered with bright and colorful artifacts associated with the town's major festival, Festa do Divino Espírito Santo, brought to life in a guided tour from the owner. Ring the bell.

★**Museu do Divino** MUSEUM
(☎62 3331-3763; Bernardo Sayão; R$2; ⌚8am-5pm Mon-Fri, from 9am Sat, 9am-2pm Sun) The municipal Museu do Divino exhibits the masks and costumes used during the Festa do Divino Espírito Santo. These masks were made by local craftspeople using methods passed down from generation to generation.

Igreja NS do Bonfim CHURCH
(Bonfim; R$2; ⌚8am-noon & 2:30-5pm Thu-Sun) Full of charisma, the Portuguese-built Igreja NS do Bonfim (1750) is a simple adobe church with wooden floor and ceiling, flanked by two lateral chapels. The restored gilded turquoise altar and wooden pulpit are worth a look.

Igreja NS do Carmo & Museu de Arte Sacra CHURCH, MUSEUM
(☎62 3331-1012; Rua do Carmo; R$2.50; ⌚11am-5pm Wed-Sun) The town's most famous church, Igreja NS do Carmo (1750), has attractive colonial features. It houses a museum of religious art.

Igreja NS do Rosário Matriz & Museu da Matriz CHURCH, MUSEUM
(Praça de Matriz; R$2; ⌚8am-noon & 2-6pm Tue-Sun) The oldest church in Goiás, the 1728 Igreja NS do Rosário Matriz was tragically gutted by fire in 2002. Inside, the Museu da Matriz explains the history and ongoing renovation. The new altar was restored and brought in from the former slave church, a necessary house of worship since slaves were banned from this one.

Parque Estadual da Serra dos Pirineus PARK
(☎62 3265-1320; www.secima.go.gov.br; ⌚8am-5pm, 9am-8pm summer) Pireneus, 18km northeast of town, is the Brazilian form of the word 'Pyrenees' and the top spot in the state for bouldering and mountain climbing. There are waterfalls and interesting rock formations to see along the way, some dating back to Gondwanaland. You'll need an accredited guide to enter; ask at a local agency. The tourist office displays a list of guides.

Santuário de Vida Silvestre Vagafogo WILDLIFE RESERVE
(Vagafogo Farm Wildlife Sanctuary; ☎62 99115-0376; www.vagafogo.com.br; Estrada O Morro do Frota; guided walk R$20; ⌚9am-5pm) This 44-hectare private nature reserve is a great place to spot wildlife. Even if you don't see much, the light hike is a welcome retreat from the heat, and there are two natural pools for swimming. It's 6km northwest of town; to walk here from town, head north along Rua do Carmo and follow the signs.

The cafe at the visitors center does a ridiculously good brunch (R$55; 9am to 4pm), with a rainbow coalition of homemade wild cerrado fruit preserves. Try them all. There's also rappelling and ziplines available.

Reserva Ecológica Vargem Grande WATERFALL
(☎62 99652-6857; www.vargemgrande.pirenopolis.tur.br; Estrada Parque dos Pirineus, Km 9; R$35; ⌚9am-4:30pm) This 360-hectare park on private land contains two impressive waterfalls: **Cachoeira Santa Maria** and **Cachoeira do Lázaro**. There are small river beaches and natural pools for swimming. If you're here for waterfalls, these are the ones to see. The reserve is 11km east of town on the road to Serra dos Pireneus.

You don't need a guide to enter, but unless you have a car, you'll need a ride from one.

Festivals & Events

★**Festa do Divino Espírito Santo** CULTURAL
(As Cavalhadas; ⌚May or Jun) Pirenópolis is famous for performing the story of Festa do Divino Espírito Santo, a tradition begun in 1818 and more popularly known as As Cavalhadas. Starting 50 days after Easter, for three days the town looks like a scene from the Middle Ages as it celebrates Charlemagne's victory over the Moors. The festival is a happy one, and more folkloric than religious. If you're in the neighborhood, make a point of seeing this stunning and curious spectacle, one of Brazil's most fascinating.

Sleeping

You can't walk more than 100m without finding a pousada in Pirénopolis, but book ahead on weekends and during festivals (when prices can triple!). Two-night weekend stays are usually much better value than single nights.

Jardim Secreto HOSTEL $
(☎62 96629-3517; www.jardimsecretohostel.com.br; Matutina 4; dm R$35-45; 📶) Laid-back and daubed with the graffiti of satisfied customers, this casual hostel offers tight-packed dorms, some of which are triple-deckers. Upgrade to a four-berth room if you don't fancy that. Hammocks and a kitchen are on offer; you can pitch a tent here, too.

Pirenópolis

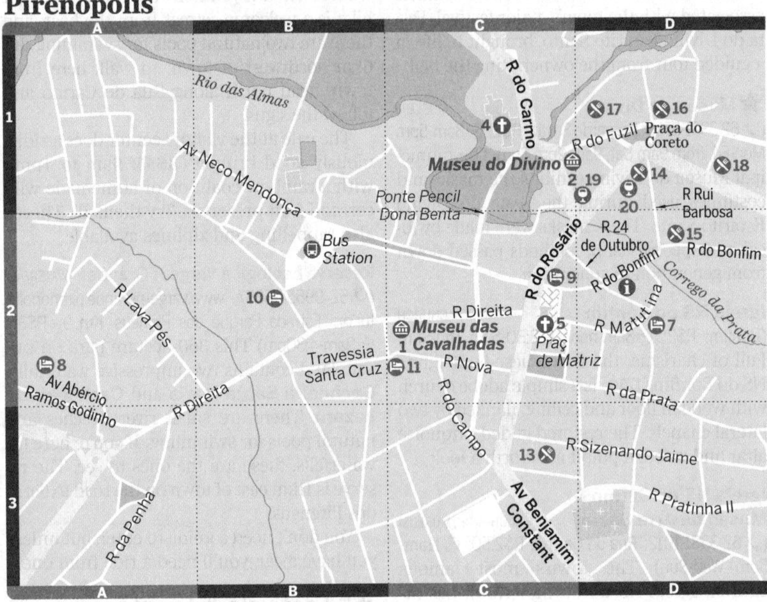

Casamatta Hostel HOSTEL $

(☎62 99962-6559; www.casamattahostel.com; Luiz Gonzaga Jaime 109; dm R$60, d without bathroom R$150;) This sweet hostel is home to a supreme hammock patio, high-pressure showers and a small pool for a refreshing dip to ward off the cerrado heat. There's liberal use of stone throughout, from tables to flooring, which also helps keep temperatures manageable. Rubens, the amiable owner, runs transport to surrounding waterfalls in his Volkswagen van.

Pousada Arvoredo POUSADA $$

(☎62 3331-3479; www.pousadaarvoredo.com.br; Av Abercio Ramos Qd 17 Lt 15; weekend r R$330-430, weekday r R$190-220;) This excellent-value pousada is steeped in sustainable tourism (all the bricks were recycled from old homes in Goiânia) and has lovely verandas and large rooms full of natural handicrafts.

Pousada das Cavalhadas POUSADA $$

(☎62 3331-1261; www.pousadacavalhadas.com.br; Praça do Matriz 1; s/d/tr/q R$130/250/290/370;) In a great central location, this pousada has a smart lobby but dated rooms. Still, it's a well-run, cheery budget choice with options for families and groups.

★**Pouso, Café e Cultura** POUSADA $$$

(☎62 3331-3647; www.pousocafeecultura.com; Santa Cruz 32; chalet weekday/weekend R$290/580;) This enormous, venerable complex once belonged to a Brazilian ambassador – his collection of antiques and knickknacks from around the world adds a sense of character to the lush property. The 12 chalets are draped by floral paths through a well-kept garden and feature beautiful hardwood flooring and vintage Brastemp minibars.

★**Taman Baru** BUNGALOW $$$

(☎62 3331-3880; www.tamanbaru.com.br; Estrada dos Pireneus, Km 2; r R$740, bungalows R$959-1159;) Taman Baru is a romantic retreat with the occasional Balinese touch set inside a forest, located just east of town. The colorful bungalows and gorgeous infinity pool both have outstanding views across the cerrado. It's worth springing for the bungalows, which don't share walls with other rooms. It's better for couples than families.

Pousada Tajupá POUSADA $$$

(☎62 3331-1305; www.pousadatajupa.com.br; Rua 4, 33; r weekday R$294-407, weekend R$613-1025;) Just opposite the bus station, this modern but charming pousada has large contemporary rooms with attractive decorative features. They open onto a central gar-

Pirenópolis

Top Sights
1 Museu das Cavalhadas C2
2 Museu do Divino C1

Sights
3 Igreja NS do Bonfim E2
4 Igreja NS do Carmo & Museu de Arte Sacra C1
5 Igreja NS do Rosário Matriz & Museu da Matriz C2

Sleeping
6 Casamatta Hostel F2
7 Jardim Secreto D2
8 Pousada Arvoredo A2
9 Pousada das Cavalhadas C2
10 Pousada Tajupá B2
11 Pouso, Café e Cultura C2

Eating
12 Armazém da Gabi E2
13 As Flôr C3
14 Bacalhau da Bibba D1
15 Bistrô Maria Docéu D2
16 Forneria e Café Pireneus D1
17 Montserrat Gastronomia D1
18 Pé di Café D1

Drinking & Nightlife
19 Cachaçaria do Dill D1
20 Rosário 26 .... D1

den with pool, bar and sauna. Facilities and breakfast are great. It feels slightly overpriced on weekends, but it's a bargain midweek.

Eating

Rua do Rosário, aka Rua do Lazer, is the main restaurant-cafe strip and turns into a pedestrianized free-for-all of outdoor tables and lively city dwellers on weekends. Most restaurants close on Monday, and some only open on weekends.

★**Forneria e Café Pireneus** CAFE $
(62 3331-3047; https://forneria-pireneus-cafe.business.site; Pireneus 41; sandwiches R$24-36; 3-11pm Mon-Thu, 4pm-midnight Fri, 9am-1am Sat & Sun) This sophisticated spot overlooking Praça do Coreto serves life-changing grilled focaccia sandwiches, wraps and ciabatta, first-rate coffee, and the town's best craft beer selection. Try the local standout IPA, Bica.

Armazém da Gabi BRAZILIAN $
(62 99389-8413; www.facebook.com/armazemecomedoriadagabi; Av Luiz Gonzaga Jaime 57; mains R$25-50; 2-8pm Tue, to 11pm Fri, 11am-11pm Sat, 11am-8pm Sun) Both bar and restaurant, this simple spot by the Igreja do Bonfim has seriously cold beer and delicious home cooking, including fresh pasta. There's a nice atmosphere here on warm evenings, with outdoor seating and weekend music.

Bistrô Maria Docéu VEGETARIAN $
(62 99357-9022; www.facebook.com/mariadoceu27; Bonfim 27; dishes R$20-30; noon-5pm Thu & Sun, noon-5pm & 7-11pm Fri & Sat;) This central vegetarian lunch spot has good-quality home cooking. There are quite a few vegan options available, too. A hot lunch plus salad buffet is R$28.

Pé di Café CAFE $
(62 3331-2183; www.facebook.com/pedicafe; Aurora 21; items R$5-30; 1-9pm Mon & Wed-Fri, 9:30am-11pm Sat, 9:30am-9pm Sun;) The most adorable and best coffeehouse in town, but don't discount the sweet treats that could accompany your espresso or tea, with *brigadeiro* (*doce de leite* covered with chocolate) in traditional farmers' cups and the guava cake topping the list.

As Flôr BRAZILIAN $$
(62 3331-1276; Sizenando Jaime 16; per person R$35; 11:30am-3:30pm Tue-Sun) Come with an empty stomach to this simple lunch spot for regional delights, an outrageous amount of

which are slapped in front of you for a ridiculously cheap price. The chicken and pork are especially tasty and there's a plethora of interesting vegetables and local side dishes like *jiló* (green eggplant) and *feijão tropeiro* (a hearty bean and pork dish).

Montserrat Gastronomia FUSION $$
(☎62 99688-2628; Ramalhuda 11; mains R$50-90; ⊙noon-4pm & 7pm-midnight Fri & Sat, noon-4pm Sun; 📶) This small Catalan-run choice serves a cautiously creative menu with plenty of nods to the Iberian Peninsula. The food is tasty, with well-prepared *bacalhau* (salt cod) among other offerings. There's also a decent wine selection.

Bacalhau da Bibba SEAFOOD $$$
(☎62 3331-2103; Rua do Rosário 42; mains for 2 people R$215-245; ⊙noon-4pm & 7-11pm Thu-Sun) This elegant and slightly surreal place doubles as an antique shop, so you'll dine surrounded by lovely paintings, ceramics and other objets d'art. The restaurant serves only *bacalhau* (salt cod) in a variety of styles. It is also open Monday to Wednesday if you prebook.

Drinking & Nightlife

Rosário 26 BAR
(☎62 3331-1216; www.facebook.com/rosario26pub; Rosário 26; ⊙5pm-midnight Mon, Wed & Thu, to 2am Fri, 2pm-2am Sat, 2pm-1am Sun; 📶) One of the few actual bars along action-packed Rua do Rosário. There's a small craft beer selection, including local brews.

Cachaçaria do Dill BAR
(☎62 3331-2046; Rua do Rosário 17; ⊙11am-1am) In the tourist-trappy Pirenopolis strip, this bar serves decent, but not spectacular food. More interesting is the stupendous *cachaça* selection, with hundreds to select from. Try one of the tasting flights (R$32 to R$52 for six).

Information

CAT (Centro de Atendimento ao Turista; ☎62 3331-2633; www.pirenopolis.go.gov.br; Rua do Bonfim 14; ⊙8am-6pm Mon-Sat, 8am-3pm Sun) Tourist info.

Getting There & Away

The **bus station** (☎62 3331-1080; Av Neco Mendonça s/n) is 500m northwest of Igreja Matriz. Goianésia (www.viacaogoianesia.com.br) has four daily services to Brasília (R$48, three hours) and a morning departure to Goiânia (R$36, two hours) with further connections via Anápolis (R$16, six daily, 1½ hours).

Getting Around

Pirénopolis is foot-friendly. To explore the surrounding area and its waterfalls, grab a bike from **JC Bikes** (☎62 99126-4576; Bonfim 730; rental per 1/multiple day R$80/60; ⊙10am-noon & 2-7pm).

Parque Nacional da Chapada Dos Veadeiros

This fabulous ecotourism destination has stunning cerrado scenery with its big skies, enchanting flora and dramatic hills rising up like waves breaking across the plains. The rivers have left their mark on the underlying sandstone, creating a web of canyons, cliffs and waterfalls that make for great hiking, usually with a cool dip at the end of the trail.

The sublime landscape has also attracted New Agers who have established alternative communities and a burgeoning *esoturismo* (alternative tourism) industry in the area. It is also noticeably well maintained.

The national park itself is just part of the story, with other waterfalls and attractions on privately owned land around the area. The best time to visit is between April and October, before the rivers flood and access becomes very slippery. You'll need two days to see the main attractions.

Sights

★Parque Nacional da Chapada dos Veadeiros NATIONAL PARK
(☎62 3455-1116; www.icmbio.gov.br; ⊙7am-5pm, last entry noon Tue-Sun, also Mon in Jul) FREE This spectacular national park in the highest area of the Central West showcases the unique landscape and flora of high-altitude cerrado across 650 sq km of pristine beauty. With high waterfalls, raging canyons, natural swimming pools and oasis-like stands of wine palms, the park is a popular destination. The visitor center at the park entrance is 1km from São Jorge. You must enter by noon, and it's wise to get started early: there's a maximum capacity, plus the sun gets hot.

Vale da Lua AREA
(Moon Valley; R$20; ⊙7am-5pm) Over millions of years, the rushing waters of the Rio São Miguel have sculpted rock formations in the landscape of Vale da Lua, a gorgeous valley whose blackish stone outcrops contrast with the green cerrado vegetation. In the river, a metaconglomerate of rocks containing quartz, sand and clay reflect a rainbow of

colors; pools of chilly emerald waters give relief from the baking heat.

Vale da Lua is outside the national park and subject to flash floods during the rainy season. There's a signed turnoff 5km from São Jorge on the way to Alto Paraiso, then it's 3.5km down a dirt road to the car park. From here, it's an easy stroll of under 1km to the river, but take sunscreen and water with you.

Activities

Hiking in the Parque Nacional da Chapada dos Veadeiros is a major attraction, with three principal trails. It gets very hot and there is little shade, so come prepared.

Visitors need to watch a short video before being let loose on the trails.

Guides are no longer required, but they are recommended if you want to learn more about the ecosystem. Private guides can be organized at the visitors' center, through the local guide association (ACV-CV), or via tourist information points or hotels in São Jorge and Alto Paraíso.

Guides run half- and full-day tours to the park's two principal trails. The price of the guide (R$150 to R$300) can be divided by up to 10 people.

★Travessia das Sete Quedas HIKING
(www.ecobooking.com.br; 7am-noon Tue-Sun mid-Jun–mid-Sep, also Mon in Jul) This 23km traverse of the park runs in the dry season only and takes in the spectacular Cânion I, then the Rio Preto, which you cross twice (the optional campsite at the second crossing is a magical spot with seven small waterfalls). The trail ends 12km from São Jorge on the road to Alto Paraíso, so you'll need to organize transport or hitch.

You must book ahead. If you aren't overnighting, you can book up to the day before at the park entrance. If you are camping, booking must be three days in advance online and the site fee (R$18 per person) paid in a Banco do Brasil. At time of research, you needed to input a Brazilian identity number to complete the online reservation; ask a local to help out.

Trilha dos Saltos e Corredeiras HIKING
(www.icmbio.gov.br; park 7am-5pm, last entry noon Tue-Sun, also Mon in Jul) Follow the yellow arrows for the 'waterfalls and rapids' trail, which is about 10.5km in length. The falls are set in a picturesque valley at the end of a trail that weaves through a classic cerrado landscape of meadows and gallery forests. Take loads of water and sunscreen; it's a long uphill return under often-brutal sun.

A spectacular viewpoint over the first Rio Preto fall (120m) is followed by a small lake for swimming under the second (80m), where the sun creates a dazzling celestial effect under the water. You continue the walk to the rapids upstream, where you can also swim.

Trilha dos Cânions e Cariocas HIKING
(www.icmbio.gov.br; park 7am-5pm, last entry noon Tue-Sun, also Mon in Jul) Red arrows mark this 12km return trail that weaves along the Rio Preto through the middle of the park. After a fairly flat, scenic stroll, the trail branches, one path heading into the spectacular Cânion II, cut by the river through sandstone with sheer 20m-high walls on either side. The other leads to rock formations and a huge waterfall.

You can swim at both the canyon and the waterfall, which is named Cachoeira das Cariocas for two girls from Rio who went missing here in the 1980s.

Getting There & Away

The park is close to the town of São Jorge, which can be accessed by road (and infrequent buses) from Alto Paraíso de Goiás, connected by bus to the rest of the state.

Alto Paraíso de Goiás

0XX62 / POP 7700 / ELEV 1273M

Crystal shops, dreadlocks and dirty feet are ubiquitous in Alto Paraíso, 38km from Chapada dos Veadeiros national park and one of the state's highest settlements. It's one of Brazil's kookiest towns; besides unleashing your inner hippie it makes a good base for tours or exploration of the region's natural attractions.

Tours

★Travessia Ecoturismo ADVENTURE
(62 3446-1595; www.travessia.tur.br; Av Ari Valadão Filho 979; 9am-6pm Mon-Fri, 9am-noon Sat & Sun) An excellent eco-agency on the main road in Alto Paraíso that can arrange everything in the Chapada region, including ziplining and more adventurous canyoning and rappelling trips. Prices include transportation and English-speaking guides.

Sleeping

★Buddy's Hostel HOSTEL $
(62 3446-1232; www.buddysalto.com; Lt 01 Qd 01, Av João Bernardes Rabelo; dm R$48-55, s/d R$110/135;) Our favorite hostel is owned by a Brazilian-French-American Cirque du Soleil acrobat and run by his sweet mother, who lived in France for two decades. Two

FOOD OF THE TROPEIROS

After the *bandeirantes* swept Goiás clean of its gold, the *tropeiros* (the Brazilian muleteers) followed in their path, conquering the region and bringing slaves from Brazil's coast. Food was scarce en route, so the *tropeiros* adapted various foods from Afro-Brazilian, Portuguese and indigenous cultures to complete the lengthy journey without refrigeration.

This long-lost subculture of Brazilian cuisine has been resurrected at **Fazenda Babilônia** (62 99294-1805; www.fazendababilonia.com.br; GO-431, Km 3; banquet R$78; 9am-3:30pm Sat & Sun), a sugar plantation established in 1800 and *fazenda* (farm) on the Patrimonial Nacional (National Heritage) register since 1965. Every weekend, this restored *fazenda*, 24km southwest of Pirenópolis, breaks out the historical gastronomy for a fascinating breakfast called **Café Sertanejo**. Hearty meats, cheeses and pastries highlight the near-endless options. *Carne de porco* (a succulent pork dish stored in its own fat for conservation), *mané pelado* (a sweet cake of grated manioc, eggs, cheese and coconut milk) and *matula galinha* (chicken with saffron, eggs, aromatic peppers and toasted corn wrapped in a corn husk) highlight a banquet that includes nearly 30 dishes that you're likely to have never seen before. The whole thing costs R$78, and includes a tour of the *fazenda* itself. If you just want to visit, it's R$22.

six-bed dorms and a few privates open out onto a small garden with a *palapa* (thatched hut). It's just a few steps from the main street, on the opposite end from the bus station.

The included breakfast is coffee only; a more substantial meal is extra. Cash only.

Pousada Veadeiros POUSADA **$$**
(62 3446-2060; www.pousadaveadeiros.com.br; Rua das Nascentes 129; s/d/tr R$170/230/260;) Hard-to-beat value is the calling at this sweet pousada not far from the bus station. Each fan-cooled room is named and decorated after a native bird and nearly all of the breakfast comes from the property or is made in-house. Prices drop substantially outside of peak periods (s/d R$120/180).

Recanto da Grande Paz POUSADA **$$$**
(62 3446-1452; www.recantodagrandepaz.com.br; Rua 2, 322; r R$350-505;) Secluded and utterly relaxing, this luxurious but understated pousada features inviting rooms with hammock deck surrounding a large, tranquil palm-filled garden. Breakfast is a real treat and service is helpful. There are also spacious apartments and family rooms available, plus spa and massage treatments. It's just a short stroll to the center.

Eating

Cravo e Canela VEGETARIAN **$**
(62 3446-1376; Av Ari Valadão Filho 1363; mains R$18-35; noon-9pm Thu-Mon) With a garden setting, this cute bamboo-faced restaurant is a fine destination for vegetarian and vegan snacks, sandwiches, pizzas on chapati bread and daily specials. There are also great juices and açaí options.

Alquimia do Sabor VEGETARIAN **$**
(62 3446-1634; www.facebook.com/alquimiadosaboraltoparaiso; Av Ari Valadão Filho s/n; per kg R$54; noon-4pm Wed-Mon;) Alto Paraiso has good options for noncarnivores and this great vegetarian pay-by-weight restaurant is one of the favorites, started by the same kitchen team as Alto Paraiso's former best restaurant, Oca Lila. Prepare to queue on weekends.

★ **Jambalaya** INTERNATIONAL **$$**
(62 3446-1775; Rua dos Colibris s/n; mains R$38-62; 7-11:30pm Wed-Sat, 6-10:30pm Sun;) Tables at this contemporary gem – tucked away in a residential neighborhood a short walk from the main road – are shrouded in candle-lit romanticism and surround a pleasant garden. This kitchen churns out excellent risotto, fish and chicken dishes, along with international specials – look for Arab, Thai and Cajun theme nights. It opens for lunch during holiday periods in July and January.

Information

CAT (Centro Atendimento ao Turista; 62 3446-1159; Av Ari Valadão Filho s/n; 8am-8pm) On the main street, 200m from the bus station.

Banco do Brasil (www.bb.com.br; Av Ari Valadão Filho 690; 10am-3pm Mon-Fri) Visa/MasterCard ATM.

Getting There & Away

Real Expresso (www.realexpresso.com.br) has three daily buses between Brasília and Alto Paraíso (R$52, four hours).

From Goiânia, **São José do Tocantins** (62 3224-8330) heads to Alto Paraiso (R$83, seven hours, 8:20pm daily and 12:10pm Tuesday,

Thursday and Saturday), with one daily bus doing the reverse leg at 11pm and another at 1:30pm Monday, Wednesday and Friday. The buses go on into the state of Tocantins to the north.

A daily bus leaves for São Jorge at 6pm (R$12, 45 minutes); the return leaves São Jorge at 6am. Pay on board.

Getting Around

Paraíso das Bicicletas (62 99652-4092; 12 de Dezembro; rental from R$50 per day; 7am-7pm Mon-Sat) Rents mountain bikes good for exploring the region.

São Jorge

0XX62 / POP 500 / ELEV 1010M

With sandy streets (for now) and a laid-back vibe, the former crystal-mining hamlet of São Jorge (1km from the national-park entrance) has the feel of a beach town, despite its inland location. Though Alto Paraíso has more going on and better options for organizing excursions beyond the national park itself, many travelers prefer to stay in São Jorge because it is prettier, closer to the park and has more of a village atmosphere.

Sleeping

★Taiuá Ambiental CAMPGROUND $
(62 99822-9666; Rua 6; prepitched tent weekend/weekday per person $80/50;) This rather extraordinary compound has an elaborate structure of bamboo platforms furnished with comfortable mattresses to relax on: it's easy to not make it back to your tent. As well as pitching your own (R$35 per person), there are comfortable tents for rent, as well as a series of rooms. No alcohol allowed.

Savana Hostel HOSTEL $
(62 3455-1151; www.savanahostel.com.br; Rua 10 (Mangaba); dm Sun-Thu R$75, Fri & Sat R$85;) Efficiently run and well kept, this hostel is based around a patio, where there's a small kitchen space and room to lounge. The triple-deck dorms have lockers, air-conditioning and bunks with mini-safes for valuables.

Flor do Cerrado POUSADA $$
(62 99998-5384; www.pousadaflordocerrado.com.br; cnr Ruas 5 & 10; s/d/tr R$160/190/250;) Small, cozy and the best of the cheaper options in town, with wooden furniture, earthy decor and hammocks for lounging in.

Baguá POUSADA $$$
(61 98172-8886; www.baguapousada.com.br; Block 16, Rua 1; bungalows weekday R$320-450, weekend R$630-700;) Classy bungalows at this designer pousada are the most sophisticated in town. Safari-chic lounge furnishings in the common area and a sizable pool add value. It's closest to the park's entrance as well, but no meals are available beyond breakfast.

Eating

Santo Cerrado BRAZILIAN $$
(62 99974-1150; www.santocerradorisoteria.blogspot.com; Block 8, Viela C; risotto for 2 people R$68-111; 5pm-1am Wed-Sun;) Follow the paper lantern trail to the edge of the village for an open two-floor timber restaurant with a tree-house feel and loads of character. The specialty is pan-cooked risotto, which comes in intriguing combinations, including lactose-free and vegan options. Book ahead or expect a long, long wait on weekends.

Paladar Bistrô BRAZILIAN $$
(62 99648-0795; Block 10, Rua 12; portions for 1 person R$31-36, portions for 2 people R$54-70; 6-11pm Wed-Fri, noon-11pm Sat & Sun) Run by local folk and more down to earth than some of the flashy out-of-town places, this pleasant outdoors spot does nice omelettes, *moqueca* (Bahian fish stew; there's also a veggie version), *picanha* (rump steak) and *carne de sol* (sun-cured beef). Single portions are available, making this handy for solo diners.

Information

CAT (Centro Atendimento ao Turista; 62 3455-1090; cnr Rua 6 & Av A; 8am-6pm) On the main street through town, this laid-back tourist info point can furnish you with a map and arrange guides. It theoretically stays open until 8pm on weekends, but you are advised to turn up before 6pm – just in case.

Getting There & Away

A daily bus leaves Alto Paraíso for São Jorge at 6pm (R$12, 45 minutes); the return leaves São Jorge at 6am. Pay on board.

Otherwise, book a transfer with a tour operator or grab a taxi driver, who charge R$80 to R$100 depending on your negotiation skills. Mototaxis charge half that if you're traveling light. The trip takes about 30 minutes.

Getting Around

Loca'l Bike (61 98299-0716; www.facebook.com/localbike1; Lot 5, Block 14, Rua 12; per hour/day R$7/50; 8am-6pm) This enthusiastic agency rents mountain bikes and also runs guided bike tours to the area's attractions.

Mato Grosso & Mato Grosso do Sul

Includes ➡

Cuiabá....................... 365
Parque Nacional da Chapada dos Guimarães.................. 371
Bom Jardim............... 372
Poconé....................... 373
Alta Floresta.............. 373
The Pantanal............... 375
Campo Grande........... 384
Corumbá..................... 389
Bonito & Around........ 393
Ponta Porã.................. 398

Best Places to Eat

- Mahalo (p368)
- Casa do Peixe (p387)
- Gaucho Gastão (p387)
- Morro dos Ventos (p370)
- Juanita (p396)

Best Places to Stay

- Refúgio Ecológico Caiman (p384)
- Cristalino Lodge (p374)
- Araras Eco Lodge (p380)
- Casa da Quineira (p370)
- Deville Prime (p386)
- Hostel Roadriders (p391)

Why Go?

Mato Grosso was once Brazil's wild west, a land known only to indigenous hunters, poachers, gold seekers and naturalists. Today, some of Brazil's most photogenic wildlife and incredible scenery make it a prime destination for ecotourists and anglers.

The Pantanal, one of the most important and fragile ecosystems on the planet, truly shines as Brazil's top destination for animal-spotting and bird-watching. The attractions don't stop there: the crystal-clear rivers and cave lakes around Bonito and Bom Jardim allow you to explore a remarkable underwater world by donning a scuba tank or snorkeling mask.

In the far-north town of Alta Floresta, the cerrado (savanna) morphs into the Amazon; in the south near Bonito, the Serra da Bodoquena is a breathtakingly beautiful, watery wonderland. In between the two, the Parque Nacional da Chapada dos Guimarães has some of the most commanding plateau views in Brazil.

When to Go

The Pantanal

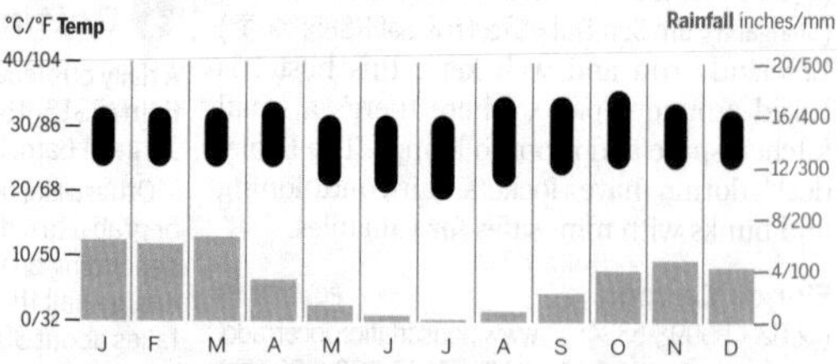

Feb Carnaval time in Corumbá; the biggest in the region.

Jun–Aug Top time for jaguar tours in the Pantanal.

Nov Bonito's many watery attractions without the holiday crowds.

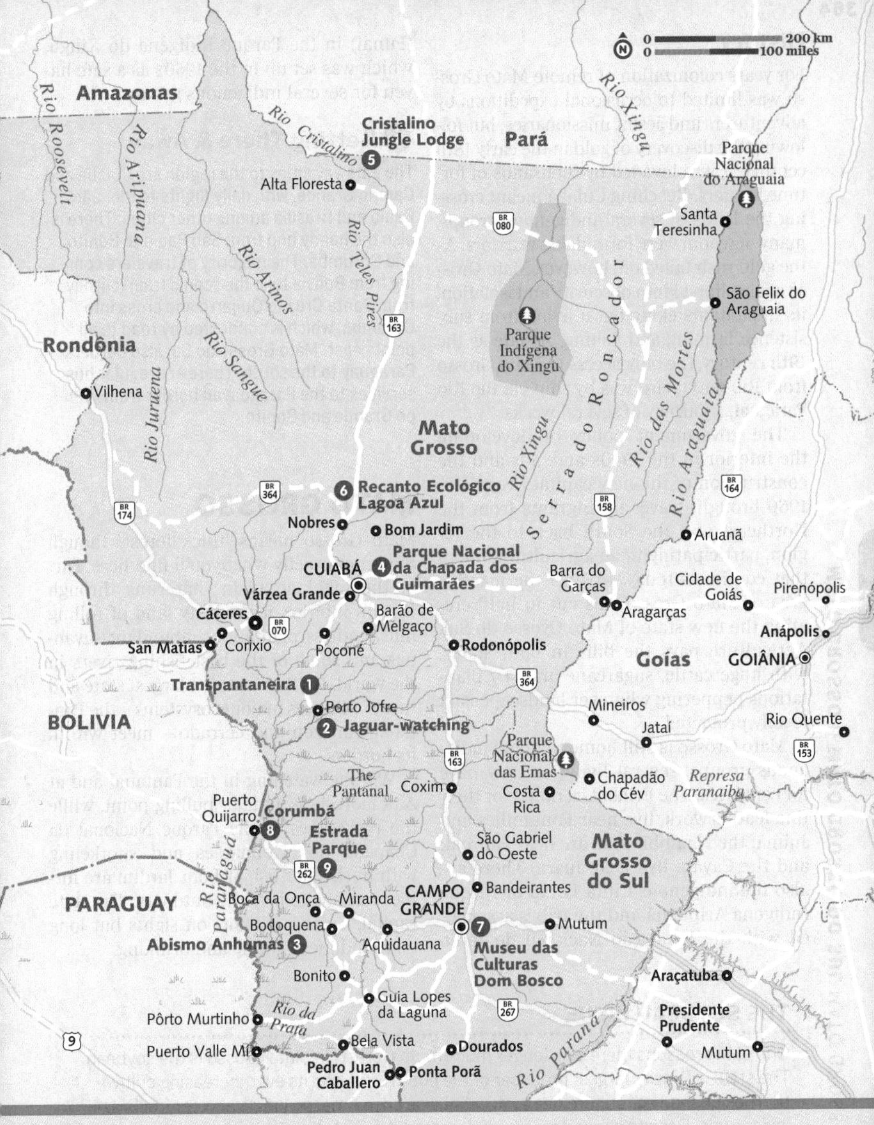

Mato Grosso & Mato Grosso do Sul Highlights

1. **Transpantaneira** (p376) Gawking at incredible wildlife along this 145km Pantanal 'highway'.
2. **Jaguar-watching** (p382) Seeing this magnificent feline on boat trips from Porto Jofre.
3. **Abismo Anhumas** (p393) Journeying to the center of the earth at this cave and lake near Bonito.
4. **Parque Nacional da Chapada dos Guimarães** (p371) Watching the sun set over dramatic landscapes.
5. **Cristalino Lodge** (p374) Going bird bonkers in the southern Amazon rainforest.
6. **Recanto Ecológico Lagoa Azul** (p372) Snorkeling with exotic fish in this crystal-clear water world near Bom Jardim.
7. **Museu das Culturas Dom Bosco** (p385) Delving into indigenous culture at this superb museum in Campo Grande.
8. **Carnaval** (p391) Dancing in the streets Mato Grosso style in Corumbá's big knees-up.
9. **Estrada Parque** (p375) Fishing for piranhas, canoeing and caiman-spotting in the southern Pantanal.

History

For years colonization of remote Mato Grosso was limited to occasional expeditions by adventurers and Jesuit missionaries, but following the discovery of gold in the early 18th century, it was invaded by thousands of fortune hunters. Reaching Cuiabá meant crossing the lands of several indigenous groups, many of whom were formidable warriors. As the gold rush tailed off, however, Mato Grosso again slipped into obscurity and isolation, its inhabitants eking out a living from subsistence farming and fishing. As late as the 19th century, the only access to Mato Grosso from Rio de Janeiro was by ship via the Rio Paraguai, a journey of several weeks.

The government policy of developing the interior in the 1940s and '50s and the construction of the new capital Brasília in 1960 brought waves of migrants from the Northeast and the South back to the region, participating in an agricultural boom that continues today. In 1979 the massive area of Mato Grosso was cut in half, creating the new state of Mato Grosso do Sul. Agriculture pays the bills in both states, with huge cattle, sugarcane and soy plantations peppering whatever landscape isn't legally protected.

Mato Grosso is still home to many indigenous groups, several living as they have for centuries. The Erikbatsa, noted for their fine featherwork, live near Fontanilles and Juima; the Nhambikuraa are near Padroal; and the Cayabi live near Juara. There are also the indigenous Cinta Larga of Parque Indígena Aripuanã and the tribes associated with the Fundação Nacional do Indio (Funai) in the Parque Indígena do Xingu, which was set up in the 1950s as a safe haven for several indigenous groups.

ℹ Getting There & Away

The gateway cities to the region are Cuiabá and Campo Grande, with daily flights to Rio, São Paulo and Brasília among other cities. There is also the handy hop from São Paulo to Bonito and Corumbá. The majority of travelers coming from Bolivia take the scenic train journey from Santa Cruz to Quijarro and cross into Corumbá, which is connected by road to all points east. Mato Grosso do Sul also borders Paraguay to the south. There are regular bus services to the Paraguayan border from Campo Grande and Bonito.

MATO GROSSO

Mato Grosso means 'thick forest,' though that's not exactly what you'll find here. Part of the highland plain that runs through Brazil's interior, it's a dusty land of rolling hills, endless plantations, abundant savannas and some of the best fishing rivers in the world. It's Brazil's third-largest state and three of Brazil's major ecosystems – the Pantanal, Amazon and cerrado – meet within its borders.

Wildlife-watching in the Pantanal and at Alta Floresta is a major pulling point, while the rockscapes of the Parque Nacional da Chapada dos Guimarães and snorkeling with freshwater fish at Bom Jardim are further reasons to love the outdoors. The state capital, Cuiabá, is short on sights but long on friendliness, eating and drinking.

THE SOYBEAN ISSUE

One of the reasons there's no longer much *mato* (forest) in Mato Grosso is the soybean. The state is Brazil's largest producer of the boom crop, and its ever-increasing cultivation has pushed agriculture deep into what was once Amazon jungle and central Brazilian cerrado. Despite a moratorium on increased deforestation, it continues to happen, with Mato Grosso the worst offender.

The industry in Mato Grosso began as an experiment in the 1970s when the cerrado, formerly seen as unproductive for farming, was cleared and soybeans were planted with the help of Japanese technology. It was a wild success and the state soon became one of the world's key producers.

Brazil's soy industry boomed again in the early 2000s when the currency crashed, making exports cheaper and resulting in more tracts of land being cleared for the crop. Soy is a key export industry for Brazil, but it has worrying ecological implications. The reduction of habitat combined with the heavy use of pesticides and fertilizers have resulted in a significant decline of biological diversity, turning vast swaths of the state into a monoculture desert.

Cuiabá

☎0XX65 / POP 590,100

Cuiabá is a boomtown basking in the relentless Mato Grosso sun. It's actually two sister cities separated by the Rio Cuiabá: Old Cuiabá and Várzea Grande (where the airport is located).

The town's name is an indigenous Bororo word meaning 'arrow-fishing,' though it was first gold and later agriculture that led to the city becoming one of the fastest-growing capitals in Brazil over the last 30 years. A lively place with a vibrant dining scene and some beautiful colonial architecture around its main square, Cuiabá is an excellent starting point for excursions to the Pantanal, Chapada dos Guimarães and Bom Jardim.

Sights

Museu Rondon de Etnologia e Arqueologia MUSEUM

(MUSEAR; ☎65 3313-7391; www.museurondonufmt.blogspot.com; Av Fernando Corrêa da Costa 2367; 7:30-11am & 1-5pm Mon-Fri) FREE The small Museu Rondon has exhibits on indigenous culture and is well worth a visit to check out the ornate headdresses and weaponry. The museum is located on the grounds of the Federal University of Mato Grosso (UFMT), behind the swimming pool. To get here, catch a C01 Universitária bus (R$3.85) from Praça Alencastro. Ring ahead to check it's open.

Parque Mãe Bonifácia PARK

(Av Miguel Sutil; 6am-6pm or 7pm) This sizable forested park northwest of the city center makes a fine escape from Cuiabá's relentless sun. Pleasant shaded trails and a playground make it worth a visit.

Centro Geodésico da America do Sul MONUMENT

(Barão de Melgaço) An underwhelming obelisk here allegedly marks the center of the continent, calculated before the invention of satellite mapping. Tell residents that the actual geographical center of South America lies 67km away near Chapada dos Guimarães and it's unlikely you'll win any popularity contests.

Tours

Cuiabá is the major gateway to the northern Pantanal – in particular the Transpantaneira road – as well as Parque Nacional Chapada dos Guimarães and the aquatic attractions around Bom Jardim. City tour operators (p379) run trips to all these places.

Festivals & Events

Festa de São Benedito CULTURAL

(www.facebook.com/festadesaobeneditocuiaba; early Jul) The Festa de São Benedito takes place during the first week of July at the Igreja Nossa Senhora do Rosário e São Benedito. The holiday has a more Umbanda (white magic) than Catholic flavor; it's celebrated with colorful, traditional dances and regional foods such as *bolos de queijo* (cheese balls) and *bolos de arroz* (rice balls).

Sleeping

★ **Hostel Pousada Ecoverde** POUSADA $

(☎65 99638-1614; www.ecoverdetours.com.br; Celestino 391; s/d without bathroom R$50/100;) This rustic pousada occupies a 100-year-old house with a tranquil, hammock-hung mini-jungle out back and a notable collection of antique radios, record players and telephones. Affable owner, music lover and local wildlife expert Joel Souza is a founder of ecotourism in the area; the accommodation consists of five fan-cooled rooms that share four external bathrooms.

You can camp in the garden here for R$30 per person.

Dom Bosco Hostel HOSTEL $

(☎65 99245-1007; www.domboscohostel.com.br; Cândido Mariano 1390; dm R$62, breakfast R$8;) Very handy for restaurants and nightlife, Dom Bosco occupies an unmarked purple house on a quiet street. Dorms are tight but have an excellent lockable wardrobe space and en-suite bathrooms. Air-con is nighttime only. Attractive common areas include a proper kitchen, and it is run in a calm, welcoming fashion.

Hotel Mato Grosso HOTEL $

(☎65 3614-7777; www.hotelmt.com.br; Comandante Costa 643; s/d R$120/150;) For basic comfort in a central location, the simple but clean rooms here are good value. It's a curious design, with rooms reached by fire-escape-style walkways.

Mato Grosso Palace Hotel HOTEL $$

(☎65 3614-7000; www.hotelmt.com.br; Joaquim Murtinho 170; d R$180-210) This aging business hotel sits in a you-couldn't-be-more-central-if-you-tried location. Expect helpful staff (some English spoken), cable TV and an ample breakfast buffet. Room price varies slightly by whether you want an old- or new-model air-conditioner. Our one quibble is that the hot water occasionally runs out.

Central Cuiabá

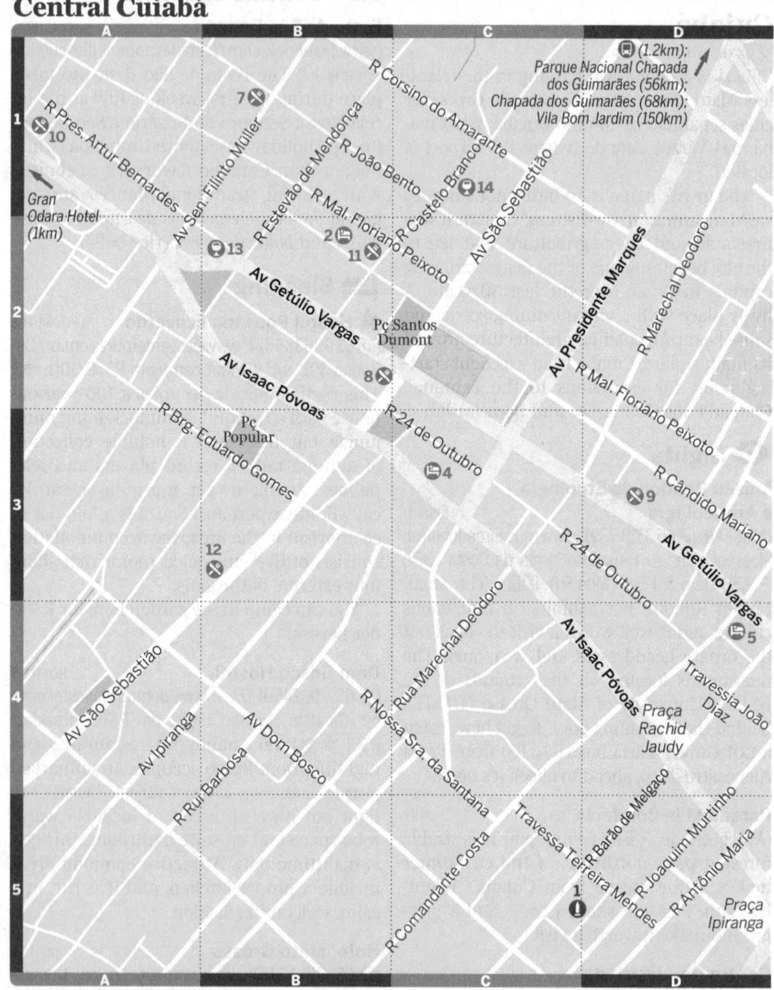

Hotel Deville Prime Cuiabá HOTEL **$$$**
(☎65 3319-3000; www.deville.com.br; Av Isaac Póvoas 1000; r R$350-550;) This smart hotel tower fills the 'luxury digs within a five-minute walk of Cuiabá's best nightlife' niche very nicely. Post-Pantanal pampering beckons, in the form of spa, pool, elegant surroundings, spacious rooms bursting with mod cons, varied dining and on-the-ball service.

Gran Odara Hotel BUSINESS HOTEL **$$$**
(☎65 3616-2014; www.hotelgranodara.com.br; Av Miguel Sutil 8344, Ribeirão da Ponte; r R$340-500;) With its exquisite reception area, the Gran Odara makes an impact as soon as you enter, and tasteful rooms are along the same lines – all dark wood and creams. It's a little removed from the center but worth it to enjoy the spa, rooftop pool and good restaurant. It's usually a small upgrade to luxo rooms, which are much larger with better views.

Eating

The center is where locals work during the day, making it almost deserted at night. The biggest concentration of decent restaurants is around Praça Popular and along and north of Av Getúlio Vargas.

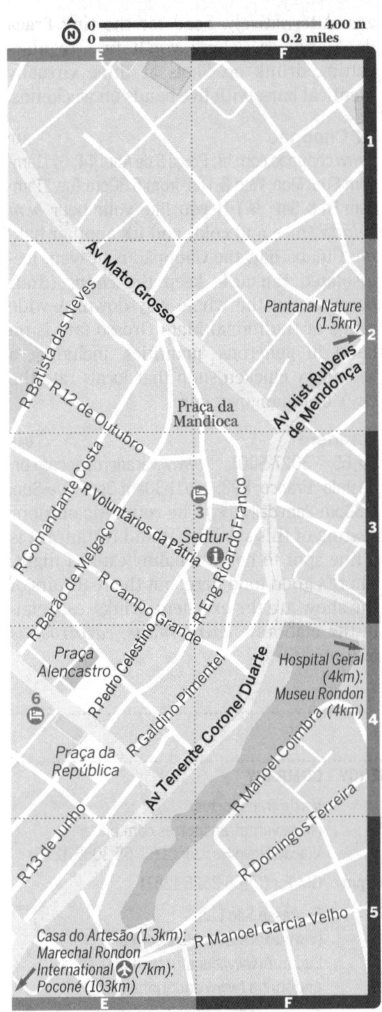

Central Cuiabá

Sights
1 Centro Geodésico da America do Sul C5

Activities, Courses & Tours
Ecoverde Tours .... (see 3)

Sleeping
2 Dom Bosco Hostel B2
3 Hostel Pousada Ecoverde F3
4 Hotel Deville Prime Cuiabá C3
5 Hotel Mato Grosso D4
6 Mato Grosso Palace Hotel E4

Eating
7 Galeto Cuiabano B1
8 Getúlio B2
9 Ki-Nutre D3
10 Lélis Peixaria A1
11 Mahalo B2
12 Sabor Mil B3

Drinking & Nightlife
13 Choppão B2
14 Varadero C1

Sabor Mil GRILL $
(www.facebook.com/sabormilgrelhados; Av São Sebastião 2175; skewers R$25-40; 6-11pm Mon-Sat) There are a few grill places around the nightlife areas, catering to locals who want to fill up fast and cheaply before tearing up the town. This casual spot is the same idea but more of a restaurant, serving succulent skewers as well as some more elaborate *picanha* (rump steak) and river fish options. Beer and good caipirinhas are on hand.

Ki-Nutre VEGETARIAN $
(www.facebook.com/kinutre.vegetariano; Av Getúlio Vargas 714; per kg R$47; 11am-2pm Sun-Fri;) Mato Grosso being one of the biggest cattle-producing regions in Brazil does nothing to diminish this cheerful lunch spot's popularity. The loyalty of fans has been won with excellent fruit juices, a fully stocked veggie buffet and the ability to work wonders with tofu and pulses.

Lélis Peixaria SEAFOOD $$
(65 3322-9195; www.lelispeixaria.com.br; Marechal Mascarenhas de Moraes 36; rodízio lunch/dinner R$60/90; 11:30am-3pm & 6:30-11pm Mon-Sat, 11:30am-3pm Sun) You'll be gobbling up river fish like a caiman at this quality *rodízio* (all-you-can-eat), which features several dozen preparations of pintado, *pacu* and other denizens of the local waterways, including caiman itself. À la carte options include great stews for two.

Galeto Cuiabano BRAZILIAN $$
(www.galetocuiabano.com.br; João Bento 817; mains R$31-38; 11am-2:30pm Mon-Fri, to 3pm Sat & Sun) *Galeto* is a small chargrilled chicken, and it is delicious, coming in a variety of ways (which, in the end, aren't very different). It's a deservedly popular lunch stop.

Getúlio INTERNATIONAL $$
(65 3624-9992; www.getuliogrill.com.br; Av Getúlio Vargas 1147; mains R$39-75; 11am-3pm & 5:30pm-midnight Sun-Thu, to 1am Fri & Sat;)

At this en vogue restaurant (or is it a sports bar?), you can sample from the respectable wine list, eat your fill at the lunchtime buffet or take your date for a romantic Italian/Brazilian/Japanese dinner. The desserts are worth lingering over and DJs feature on the outdoor patio every night.

★Mahalo FUSION **$$**
(☎65 3028-7700; www.mahalocozinhacriativa.com.br; Presidente Castelo Branco 359; mains from R$45; ⏰11am-2:30pm & 7:30pm-midnight Mon-Sat) Inside a converted mansion, the city's big splurge is one of Brazil's top restaurants, thanks to the efforts of Parisian-trained chef Ariani Malouf. Go for the set weekday lunch (R$55 for two courses) or else choose from the likes of pintado (giant catfish) encrusted with Brazil nuts or a perfectly-seared rack of lamb with sweet potato puree. Dress nicely and book ahead.

Drinking & Nightlife

There are two main nightlife clusters in town: the buzzy sports bars with ample outdoor seating around the lovely Praça Popular (aka Praça Eurico Gaspar Dutra) and more establishments along Av Getúlio Vargas. Alternatively, head for the tiny Praça da Mandioca, where you'll find regulars getting drunk on Skols at three virtually identical bars, with live bands on weekends.

★Choppão BAR
(www.choppao.com.br; Praça 8 de Abril 44; ⏰11am-2am Sun, Mon, Wed & Thu, from 5:30pm Tue, 11am-5am Fri & Sat; 📶) If you like your beer *bem gelada* (nice and cold) and it's another baking Cuiabá day, the Choppão is heaven. Ice-insulated tankards keep the *chope* (draft beer) glacial the whole way down. A wide range of traditional Mato Grosso fare is on hand in generous quantities, including a legendary chicken soup that locals rate the city's best hangover cure.

Varadero BAR
(☎65 3027-5001; www.varaderobar.com.br; Castelo Branco 898; ⏰11:30am-3pm Tue-Sun, 6:30pm-2am daily; 📶) The romantic outdoor seating of this sizable bar and restaurant is a fine spot to be on a balmy Cuiabá night. There's good food here, but the real stars of the show are the excellent drinks, especially the elaborate *caipirinhas, caipiroskas* and *mojitos*.

BUSES FROM CUIABÁ

DESTINATION	COST (R$)	TIME (HR)	FREQUENCY	COMPANY
Alta Floresta	223	14	6 daily	Verde Transportes (www.verdetransportes.com.br), Viação Novo Horizonte (☎65 3056-1256)
Bom Jardim	41	4	daily at 2pm	GM Tur (☎65 3625-1287)
Brasília	208-232	23	7 daily	Expresso São Luiz (www.expressosaoluiz.com.br), Eucatur (www.eucatur.com.br), Andorinha (www.andorinha.com)
Campo Grande	147-170	11-14	20 daily	Andorinha, Eucatur, Motta (www.motta.com.br), Nova Integração (www.eucatur.com.br), Viação São Luiz (www.viacaosaoluiz.com.br)
Chapada dos Guimarães	17	1¼	10 daily	CMT (☎65 3046-6151)
Goiânia	160-200	18	9 daily	Expresso São Luiz, Eucatur, Satélite Norte (www.satelitenorte.com.br)
Poconé	29	2¾	5 daily	CMT
Porto Velho	206-324	23-26	15 daily	Eucatur, Gontijo (www.gontijo.com.br), Expresso Itamarati (www.expressoitamarati.com.br), Roderotas (www.roderotas.com)
São Paulo	220-350	28-30	12 daily	Andorinha, Roderotas, Eucatur, Gontijo, Viação Util (www.util.com.br)

Bar do Edgare BAR
(www.facebook.com/bardoedgare; Traçaia 280; 5pm-2am Tue-Fri, 11am-11pm Sat;) West of downtown, this is worth the cab ride for its relaxed good cheer, regular live rock (Fridays) and popular Saturday *feijoada* (bean-and-meat stew; R$30). It's an old favorite and most of the crowd are 30-plus.

Shopping

Casa do Artesão ARTS & CRAFTS
(65 3611-0500; www.sescmatogrosso.com.br; Av Tenente Coronel Duarte 2140; 8:30am-5:30pm Mon-Fri, 7:45am-1pm Sat) This warehouse spot south of the center has a wide range of Mato Grosso handicrafts and sweets, including ceramics, wood carvings, straw baskets and *pequi* créme liqueur.

Information

MEDICAL SERVICES

Hospital Geral (65 3363-7000; www.hg.cuiaba.br; cnr 13 de Junho & Thogo da Silva Pereira) University hospital with 24-hour emergency services.

TOURIST INFORMATION

Sedtur (65 3613-9300; www.cultura.mt.gov.br; Voluntários da Pátria 118; 1-7pm Mon-Fri) Has some helpful maps and brochures in Portuguese.

Getting There & Away

AIR

Cuiabá's **international airport** (CGB; 65 3614-2511; Av João Ponce de Arruda, Várzea Grande) is in Várzea Grande, 7km from central Cuiabá. There are flights all over Brazil, principally operated by Azul. Gol, LATAM and Avianca also have some routes, principally to São Paulo and Brasília.

BUS

Cuiabá's **bus station** (Jules Rimet) is 3km north of the center.

Getting Around

From the airport, bus 7 (R$3.85) runs to town and on to the bus station. A taxi costs around R$40. Buses back to the airport run along Av Isaac Póvoas and Rua Barão de Melgaço.

From inside the bus terminal, you can get a Centro bus to Praça Alencastro (R$3.85). More frequent buses marked 'Centro' leave from outside the bus station and drop you along Av Isaac Póvoas. A taxi from inside the bus station costs around R$35.

Referência (65 3682-6689; www.referencia.com.br; Av Governador João Ponce de Arruda 1034, Várzea Grande; 7am-11pm) and **Localiza Hertz** (65 3925-9250; www.localizahertz.com; Av Governador João Ponce de Arruda 820, Várzea Grande) are a couple of reliable car rental companies with offices at the airport. The best car for the Pantanal is one with high clearance, though any car can make it during dry season. In the wet season (November to March) you'll need a 4x4 and off-road driving experience, and some sections may be impassable anyway.

Chapada dos Guimarães

0XX65 / POP 19,100 / ELEV 798M

The Chapada dos Guimarães region is a spectacular plateau with dramatic red sandstone escarpments and is surprisingly different from the typical Mato Grosso terrain. The town is much higher than state capital Cuiabá and provides a cool and convenient base for exploring the surrounding areas. It is also home to a lush central square. Very quiet midweek, it packs out with weekend visitors from Cuiabá.

The area surrounding the national park has numerous attractions. On the way from Cuiabá to Chapada town, you pass **Rio dos Peixes**, **Rio Mutaca** and **Rio Claro**, which are popular weekend bathing spots for *cuiabános,* and three commanding valleys, **Vale do Salgadeira**, **Vale do Paciência** and **Vale do Rio Claro**. The sheer 80m drop called **Portão do Inferno** (Hell's Gate) is also unforgettable – it was the town 'prison' in the early 20th century (use your imagination!).

Sights & Tours

Mirante da Chapada VIEWPOINT
(Centro Geodésico) The *mirante* (lookout), marked with a modest concrete square, is the geographic center of South America. While the monument is underwhelming, the views are magnificent! Off to your right you can see the Cuiabá skyline, and, beyond that, the flatlands that eventually become the Pantanal. To get here, follow Route 251 through Chapada and head east for 7km; a cycle path connects the viewpoint to the town. The rim of the canyon is a couple of hundred meters away.

Chapada Explorer ECOTOUR
(65 3301-1290; www.chapadaexplorer.com.br; Praça Dom Wunibaldo 57; 8-11am Mon-Sat) An excellent Chapada-based agency run by local operators who have grown up around

ecotourism and are actively involved in teaching the benefits of low-impact tourism to locals. It runs excursions to all of the area's attractions in groups (max 10 people), as well as multiday excursions to the Pantanal or Bom Jardim.

Sleeping

There are numerous sleeping choices in Chapada, ranging from cheap digs to romantic luxury pousadas.

Pousada Bom Jardim POUSADA $

(☎65 3301-2668; www.pousadabomjardim.com.br; Praça Dom Wunibaldo 461; s/d/q with fan R$100/149/250, s/d/tr with air-con R$120/185/230;) There's little reason to spring for air-con at this cheapie right in the main square – the fans are high-octane. A favorite with backpackers, the rooms are a bit dingy but spotless. There's a surcharge if you only stay one night on a weekend.

Pousada Villa Guimaraes POUSADA $$

(☎65 3301-1366; www.pousadavillaguimaraes.com.br; Neco Siqueira 41; s/d R$254/350;) Ideally located near the main square, this cheerful yellow pousada is all heavy wooden furniture and colorful accents. The breakfast is one of the best in town. There's an in-house tour agency, too.

★**Casa da Quineira** LODGE $$$

(☎65 3301-3301; www.casadaquineira.com.br; Frei Osvaldo 191; d standard/superior/deluxe R$510/650/870;) Tucked away down a quiet street, this classy and welcoming spot abuts the forest, with abundant birdlife. Contemporary art merges seamlessly with extensive sculpted grounds, hammocks and pool. On cooler nights, you can sit around the firepit or fireplace. All rooms have good beds; standards are quite compact but luxo rooms are huge, with hydromassage tub. Breakfast is brilliant.

Pousada do Parque Eco Lodge LODGE $$$

(☎65 99671-6876; www.pousadadoparque.com.br; Estrada do Parque Ecológico, Km 52; r R$435;) This intimate eco-choice borders 150 hectares of national park. Delicious, home-cooked food and a knowledgeable wildlife guide enhance your stay here, miles away from the nearest neighbor. It's down a fairly rough road that leads to the Waterfall Circuit; book in advance and communicate your arrival time as the park gate is otherwise locked.

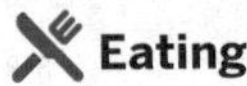

Eating

Restaurants with dramatic outlooks are a couple of kilometers southeast of the center, while cheap budget buffets cluster in town. There's a good lunchtime restaurant on the premises of Parque Nacional da Chapada dos Guimarães. A couple of places have homemade ice cream in tempting local fruit flavors on the town's main square.

★**Morro dos Ventos** BRAZILIAN $$

(☎65 3301-1030; www.morrodosventos.com.br; Estrada do Mirante, Km 1; mains R$36-86; 11am-4pm;) Head past the pride of wooden lions to find fantastic takes on regional cuisine: perfectly grilled *picanha* with a full entourage of sides, rice slow-cooked with chunks of pork, great slabs of grilled pintado and fantastic fruit juices. The restaurant is by a viewpoint with dizzying glimpses of the valley below and has great perspectives itself.

Entrance to this compound, 2.5 km southeast of central Chapada, costs R$5 per pedestrian or R$20 per car.

Pomodori ITALIAN $$

(☎65 3301-3061; www.facebook.com/Pomodoritratoria; Caldas 60; mains R$35-60; 4-10pm Mon-Thu, to midnight Fri, noon-midnight Sat & Sun) The cutest restaurant in the center is decked out with checkered tablecloths and serves a handful of select Italian dishes nightly as well as excellent fish, like pintado with passion-fruit sauce. It is also renowned for its *empadas* (stuffed pastries) with savory fillings.

Bistrô da Mata FUSION $$$

(☎65 3301-3483; www.facebook.com/bistrodamatamt; Av Morro dos Ventos; dishes R$60-100; 7pm-midnight Fri, from 11am Sat, 11am-4:30pm Sun) A romantic bistro with stupendous views, rough-hewn stone walls and an appealing outdoor terrace. The creative daily menu incorporates the likes of bacon-wrapped veal medallions with wild mushroom risotto and grilled pintado (catfish) with olive pesto; on Sundays there's a buffet of homemade pasta (R$60). It feels totally rural but is only a couple of kilometers south of central Chapada.

Getting There & Away

CMT buses (☎65 3301-2679) leave Cuiabá's bus station for Chapada town (R$17, 1¼ hours, nine daily) between 6am and 7:40pm. The miraculous views are on the right-hand side from Cuiabá.

In the other direction, the first bus leaves Chapada town at 5:30am and the last at 7:40pm. Chapada's **bus station** (Fernando Correa) is two blocks from the main plaza.

Getting Around

You can rent hybrid bikes from **Bike's** (65 3301-2637; www.bikescia.com.br; Tiradentes 104; half/full day R$50/70; 8-11:30am & 1-6pm Tue-Sat).

Parque Nacional da Chapada dos Guimarães

0XX65

Only receiving national park status in 1989, the outstanding 33 sq km Parque Nacional da Chapada dos Guimarães remains under the mass tourism radar, though it's hard to see why. Picture the scene: red rock buttresses soaring up from a green valley; lines of palm trees marking the location of clear rivers and pools for snorkeling; waterfalls ranging from immense to petite and swimmable; dusty hikes through parched land, observed only by yellow-eyed burrowing desert owls; mysterious caves to explore... The park sits high on a plateau, meaning that evening and morning temperatures are mercifully cooler than elsewhere in Mato Grosso.

The Véu de Noiva area is the only part of the park you can visit independently. Otherwise a certified guide is required.

Sights

Véu de Noiva — WATERFALL

(Bridal Veil; 9am-5pm, last entry 4pm) FREE The impressive Véu de Noiva, an 86m free-falling waterfall, provides the park's characteristic postcard moment. A small trail leads to the lookout, perched on top of rocks with the canyon below. This is one of Chapada's most dazzling spots; no guide necessary.

It is around 9km west of Chapada town. You can get off the bus from Cuiabá at the park turnoff, spend a couple of hours, then flag down the next bus to Chapada. The **visitors center** (65 3301-1133; www.icmbio.gov.br; 8am-5pm) here has a restaurant.

Cachoeirinha & Cachoeira dos Namorados — WATERFALL

(9am-4:30pm, last entry noon) These two gentle, pretty waterfalls are reached via a 1km trail from the carpark at Véu de Noiva. They are very popular with local families as they have safe bathing for children and the closest beach is a thousand miles away.

Tours

Entrance to the national park attractions was free at time of research, but most could only be entered with a registered guide or driver. The website www.ecobooking.com.br has a list of guides for each attraction, together with contact details and languages spoken. It's also easy to arrange guides at your lodgings in Chapada dos Guimarães.

Prices vary according to your itinerary, whether you have your own transport or not, group size and negotiating skills. Figure on around R$150 to R$250 per person for a half- to full-day excursion.

★Cidade de Pedra — MOUNTAIN

(Stone City; www.icmbio.gov.br/parnaguimaraes/guia-do-visitante.html; entry only with authorized guide; 9am-5pm Sun-Fri, from 3pm Sat) FREE Cidade de Pedra provides the region's most transcendent moment. Jagged red sandstone rock formations jut up into the sky from the tops of enormous cliffs that drop down into the vast green valley beneath. You follow the short footpath that skirts the edge of the cliff through scrubland, peering at the abyss below. Morning is the best time to visit, when the sunlight illuminates most of the cliffs. It's 25km northwest of Chapada.

Morro São Jerônimo — HIKING

(www.icmbio.gov.br; entry only with authorized guide; 8:30am-5pm, last entry noon) The flat, table-like summit of Morro São Jerônimo rises above the southern edge of the national park, affording spectacular 360° views of Chapada's rock formations, the Pantanal and the valleys below. It's an excellent and not particularly difficult day hike, though it is an 18km round-trip. Bring plenty of water and appropriate shoes.

Circuito das Cachoeiras — WATERFALL

(Waterfall Circuit; www.icmbio.gov.br; entry only with authorized guide; 8:30am-5pm, last entry noon) FREE The Waterfall Circuit involves a gentle 6.5km hike through a parched red landscape, covered with scrubland and low trees, with six waterfall stops en route; the whole thing takes four to six hours, depending on how easy you want to take it. The first waterfall is the highest, while the others are better for swimming, with deep pools and cascades forming natural Jacuzzis. Access to some involves negotiating steep steps. Entry is free, but you must go with a registered guide.

Vale do Rio Claro SNORKELING
(Rio Claro Valley; www.icmbio.gov.br; ⏲8am-5pm, last entry 1pm) A steep scramble takes you to a viewpoint overlooking the lush valley and the razor-thin rock formations of the Crista do Galo (rooster's crest). Then you swim and snorkel in clear, deep, rapid-fed pools in the forest before embarking on a 500m float, following your guide along the twists and turns of the narrow river, the somber underwater world revealing itself beneath you.

You need to go with a registered guide. If you don't have a 4x4, you'd better contract a guide that does.

Roteiro da Caverna Aroe Jari e Lagoa Azul CAVING
(Aroe Jari Cave Circuit; from R$250 per person) This tour focuses on Brazil's largest sandstone cave, reachable via a hiking trail through scrubland and featuring unusual rock formations and a startling, mirror-like cave lake. It's not part of the national park.

Getting There & Away

Buses run regularly between Cuiabá and Chapada dos Guimarães town (R$17, 1¼ hours, 10 daily). They will drop off and pick up at the entrance to Véu de Noiva.

Bom Jardim

☎0XX65 / POP 800

The watery attractions around Bom Jardim – a hot one-street town 150km north of Cuiabá – are similar to those of Bonito in Mato Grosso do Sul, albeit on a smaller scale and minus the crowds. Crystalline rivers overloaded with tropical fish, caves, waterfalls and macaws make this an extremely rewarding place to spend some time, whether you take a tour from Cuiabá or overnight in the town proper.

Activities

You'll need to be accompanied by a guide to visit some attractions, while others have guides on-site. Book visits ahead of time with tour agencies in town, though they don't provide transport. Tour companies in Cuiabá also run these excursions. If staying the night in Bom Jardim, it can be cheaper to book both accommodation and tour together.

★Recanto Ecológico Lagoa Azul SNORKELING
(☎65 99238-5090; R$75; ⏲7:30am-4:30pm) The underground-spring-fed Aquário Encantado here has incredible visibility down to its maximum depth of 6m and schools of fish that mill about as you explore the underwater world. 'Aquarium' aside, you can snorkel-float 850m along the Rio Salobra on the same *fazenda* (farm). It's 10km from town. Guides are on-site but you'll usually need to book your time slot ahead.

Rio Triste SNORKELING
(Fazenda Água Branca; snorkeling R$75; ⏲7:30am-4:30pm) At Rio Triste, 17km from Bom Jardim, you're delivered to the start of a forest trail by tractor. With any luck, you may spot some monkeys before floating face to face with red-finned piraputanga fish in a deep, clear pool. Then float downriver behind your guide, dodging submerged tree trunks and trying to spot sand-colored freshwater stingrays. You can rent an underwater camera (R$50).

Lagoa das Araras BIRDWATCHING
(R$20) A 15-minute walk signposted from Bom Jardim's main street leads south to Lagoa das Araras, a tranquil sunken palm forest. Sunset is the best time to observe dozens of cawing blue and yellow macaws coming noisily to roost; you'll see a handful during the day too. Pay the fee at the yellow shop by the main road and take insect repellent.

Cachoeira da Serra Azul WATERFALL, SNORKELING
(SESC Serra Azul; snorkeling R$70; ⏲8am-5pm) This is the most impressive of the area's numerous waterfalls. The 50m-high cascade plunges into an 8m-deep vivid-blue pool, and excellent *flutuação* (snorkeling/flotation) can be done here; there's also a speedy zipline descent. You can only enter with a guide. It's 20km east of town, followed by a 1.5km walk from the parking lot.

Sleeping

Pousada Rota das Águas POUSADA **$$**
(☎65 3102-2019; www.rotadasaguas.tur.br; Rodovia MT-241, Km 65; s/d/tr R$130/250/350; ❄📶) Right in town, the colorful rooms at this appealing pousada face a green courtyard with slat hammocks and attractive timber features. The windows could use screens. The owner is happy to share his knowledge of the area and there's an on-site **agency** (☎65 3102-2019; www.rotadasaguas.tur.br; Rodovia MT-241, Km 65). Rates are often discounted.

Pousada Bom Jardim POUSADA **$$**
(☎65 3102-2018; www.pousadabomjardim.com; Rodovia MT-241, Km 65; s/d/tr R$160/250/340;

) In the heart of Vila Bom Jardim, this amiable pousada doubles as a tour agency. Rooms have crimson accents and hammocks surround a tranquil green space and pond out back.

Eating

Bom Jardim has a handful of simple eating places along the main drag.

Rancho do Chapolín BRAZILIAN **$**
(65 99930-2104; all-you-can-eat R$30; roughly noon-3pm Tue-Sun, 7-11pm daily) Head up the side of the Serra Azul pousada to find this convivial open shed where long communal tables and an open kitchen set the scene for rustic, very tasty traditional farmhouse-style cooking served in deep metal pots. Unusually, your chef and host is dressed as an ant (actually a satirical anti-superhero from 1970s Mexican TV) but couldn't be more welcoming.

It's very casual; help yourself to drinks from the freezer, eat as much as you want and work out your own bill. Opening hours are not set in stone, so ring ahead if you're relying on it.

Balneario Estivado BUFFET **$**
(65 3102-2021; www.facebook.com/balnearioestivadooficial; buffet R$25; 9am-5pm) This thatched restaurant comes with an additional attraction that's good for small children: a shallow pool filled with fish (R$15). The buffet is simple but showcases regional dishes. It's a couple of kilometers east of town.

Getting There & Away

One **GM Tur bus** (65 3625-1287) a day runs from Cuiabá to Bom Jardim at 2pm (R$41, four hours) with the return leaving at 6am. Transport is included in guided tours from Cuiabá.

Poconé

0XX65 / POP 32,200

This dusty frontier town is a place travelers invariably have to pass through on their way to the Transpantaneira 'highway.' It's so sleepy that, as one local put it, 'In Poconé, even the restaurants close for lunch!' This place is unlikely to detain you for longer than a meal stop, though those driving themselves to a lodge along the Transpantaneira might consider overnighting here to get an early start and catch the wildlife in action on the way.

Tours

Transpantanal TOURS
(65 3345-2343; www.transpantanal.com.br; Av Aníbal de Toledo 1895; 7:30am-5:30pm Mon-Fri, to noon Sat) The only agency in town that caters to serious fishers, Transpantanal offers six-night fishing packages for groups along the Cuiabá, São Lourenço, Piquiri and Paraguai rivers, with accommodations in the floating lodge that in the dry season is Flotel/Jaguar Suites (p381). The fishing season is March to June.

Eating

Pousada Pantaneira CHURRASCARIA **$**
(65 3345-3357; www.pousadapantaneira.com.br; Rodovia Transpantaneira, Km 0; rodizio R$40, per kg R$40;) This justifiably popular *churrascaria* (barbecue restaurant) sits at the top of the Transpantaneira and it's where most travelers stop for a meal. The different cuts of meat are gut-bustingly good, as is the extensive buffet of Pantaneiro sides. There are also some simple rooms, if you need to stay the night (s/d/tr R$75/130/170).

Information

Two banks with ATM in town represent your last chance to withdraw cash if heading along the Transpantaneira.

Getting There & Away

There are five daily CMT buses between Cuiabá and Poconé (R$29, 2¾ hours). Arriving in Poconé, they first stop at the **bus station** (Justino Francisco), about 10 blocks from the center of town, then continue on to Praça da Matriz; behind the Matriz church is the road that leads to the beginning of the Transpantaneira.

Alternatively, shared taxis leaving from the Ponto de Taxi at Praça da Matriz will drop you at your final destination in Cuiabá for a mere R$40 per person if full.

Alta Floresta

0XX66 / POP 50,200

The bustling agricultural service town of Alta Floresta, 873km north of Cuiabá, is a staging post for trips into the vast expanse of the Amazon jungle that lies beyond. There is one excellent reason to head here, and that is to visit the Cristalino Private Natural Heritage Preserve, considered one of Amazonia's best for spotting rare birds and mammals, including the endangered

WORTH A TRIP

CRISTALINO LODGE

On the banks of the Rio Cristalino (39km north of Alta Floresta), in an area rich in flora and fauna, the luxurious **Cristalino Lodge** (☎66 3521-1396; www.cristalinolodge.com.br; s US$600-960, d per person US$510-750, plus one-time US$90 per person conservation fee; 📶) has two 50m-high observation towers and over 20km of bird- and animal-watching trails that pass through nine different ecosystems. The rooms and VIP bungalows flash creature-comfort luxe. Rates include transfers, gourmet meals, expert multilingual guides, excursions and insurance.

The reserve, reached by an hour's drive and a half-hour boat trip from Alta Floresta, is considered one of the top spots in the world for birding and the lodge now produces its own coffee-table books on the hundreds of bird species found here. The reserve hosts ornithologists and other researchers and the Cristalino Foundation (an NGO) is petitioning the Brazilian government to surround the existing private land with a national park, thus extending the protected area by 20km.

Facilities are topnotch, with a library, screening room, outdoor bar and varied buffet meals prepared by a skilled chef. In keeping with the sustainability ethos, the complex uses extensive solar energy.

Activities are not limited to bird-watching: canoeing, seasonal caiman-spotting evening tours on the river, and swimming off the pontoon dock are all part of the fun.

white-nosed bearded saki monkey, lowland tapir, giant otter and five species of macaw. Another highlight is a dedicated trip to see harpy eagles in the wild.

Soy, beef and maize are the major products of the nearby large ranches. On the edges of town you'll easily spot macaws.

Tours

Southwild BIRDWATCHING

(www.southwild.com; 4-day trips/d US$1590/2600) This professional, innovative outfit runs four- and five-day trips to harpy eagle nesting sites, with a guarantee of seeing them or your money back. You can sleep in a camp near the birds or in hotel accommodation. Southwild is also developing other intriguing ecotourism options in this far-northern part of the state.

Sleeping & Eating

Caleche Park Hotel HOTEL $$

(☎66 3521-4008; www.calechehotel.com.br; Av Perimetral Deputado Rogério Silva 1850; s R$189-199, d R$239-259; ❄@📶) This modern business hotel was doing things right when we last passed by, with well-equipped rooms, a spacious lobby with bar and dinner restaurant, and helpful staff. It's easily the best hotel in town. There's a bit of noise and the edge-of-center location isn't perfect if you don't have wheels, but head out back and you'll probably see macaws. Prices are very reasonable.

Floresta Amazônica Hotel HOTEL $$

(☎66 3512-7100; www.fah.com.br; Av Teles Pires 2001; s R$149-249, d R$199-299; ❄📶🏊) Set in jungly surroundings near the airport, this hotel is in need of a touch-up but still has appeal, particularly with the numerous bird species flitting around the property. There are three grades of room, all rather basic, but the luxo class gets you a king-sized bed and slightly better bathroom. The complex is set around a pool; there's also a guests' only restaurant.

Higher-grade rooms come with a little private terrace; some of the luxo ones face the forest and are best for birders. The hotel is associated with the Cristalino Lodge, which has an office here that can organize seasonal **day trips** (☎66 3521-2221; US$130 per person; ⏲8am-5pm Mon-Fri, to noon Sat).

Hangar CAFE $

(www.facebook.com/restaurantehangaraf; Aeroporto de Alta Floresta; dishes R$20-35; ⏲10am-5pm Mon-Fri, to 4pm Sat & Sun; 📶) At the airport, this is a popular hangout with bright, affable service, good-value meals, decent coffee and local craft beer. Grab a table outdoors.

Churrascaria Cambalacho BRAZILIAN $$

(☎66 3521-3376; www.facebook.com/churrascariacambalacho; Av Jaime Veríssimo Campos 520; half-portions R$21-55; ⏲11am-2:30pm daily, 6-11pm Tue-Sun) A huge range of food is available at this cheerful local favorite, with lunchtime per-kilo buffets (R$37 without the grill, R$60 mixed, R$90 meat-only) and numerous beefy options in the evening, as well as pizzas, fish dishes and more. Most half-portions feed two. They keep the *chope* (draft beer) flowing.

Getting There & Away

From Cuiabá, Verde Transportes (www.verdetransportes.com.br) and **Viação Novo Horizonte** (65 3056-1256) run bus services north to Alta Floresta (R$223, 14 hours, six daily). Azul (www.voeazul.com.br) has one to two daily flights.

Getting Around

Car rental is available at the airport. Taxis will shuttle you around town for R$25 to R$30. Motorbike taxis are also available.

THE PANTANAL

Located in the heart of South America, the world's largest wetland covers some 210,000 sq km. The majority is in Brazil, split between the states of Mato Grosso and Mato Grosso do Sul. These open marshes are home to an immense variety of life – if you like to see animals in their natural environment, the Pantanal is an unmissable destination.

The Pantanal has few people and no towns. Distances are so great and ground transport so poor that people get around in small airplanes and motorboats; car travel is restricted by the seasons.

You can either penetrate the Pantanal from the north, where the **Transpantaneira** runs deep into the region, or from the south, where **Estrada Parque** cuts across the wetlands. The much-mooted road right across the Pantanal has long been shelved due to concerns about the general absurdity of having a road that's underwater for half the year.

Geography & Climate

Although *pantano* means 'swamp' in both Spanish and Portuguese, the Pantanal is not a swamp but a vast alluvial plain. From the surrounding highlands the rains flow into the Pantanal, forming the Rio Paraguai and its tributaries (which flow south and then east, draining into the Atlantic Ocean). During the wet season (November to March), the rivers flood their banks, inundating much of the low-lying Pantanal and creating *cordilheiras* (vegetation islands above the high-water level), where the animals cluster together. The waters reach their high mark – up to 3m – in January or February, then start to recede in March. This seasonal flooding has made systematic farming impossible and has severely limited human incursions into the area. However, it does provide an enormously rich feeding ground for wildlife.

The floodwaters replenish the soil's nutrients, which would otherwise be very poor, due to the excessive drainage. The waters teem with fish, and the ponds provide protective niches for many animals and plants. Enormous flocks of wading birds gather in rookeries several square kilometers in area.

Later in the dry season, the water recedes, the lagoons and marshes dry out and fresh grasses emerge on the savanna (the Pantanal's vegetation includes savanna and forest that blend together, often with no clear divisions). The hawks, storks and caiman *(jacaré)* compete for fish in the remaining ponds. As the ponds shrink and dry up, the caiman crawl around for water, sweating it out until the rains return.

Planning

It's possible to visit the Pantanal year-round, but it's best to go during the dry season (May to September) as the wildlife concentrates around the reduced water. This is peak jaguar-spotting time. The best time to watch birds is from July to September, when the waters have receded and the bright-green grasses pop up from the muck.

Flooding, incessant rains and heat make travel difficult during the wet season (November to April), though this time is not without its special rewards – this is when the cattle and wildlife of the Pantanal clump together on the *cordilheiras*. However, these islands are covered with dense vegetation that can make spotting wildlife difficult.

The heat peaks from December to February, when temperatures higher than 40°C (104°F) are common, roads turn to mush, and the mosquitoes are out in force. Many hotels close at this time and in the northern Pantanal tour companies effectively take a break.

Sleeping

Pantanal accommodations are divided into roughly three types: pousadas, which range from simple to top-end; *fazendas,* which are ranch-style hotels that usually have horses and often boats for use; and *pesqueiros,* which cater for anglers and usually have boats and fishing gear for rent. All accommodations in the Pantanal offer meals; rates are mostly full board.

Driving the Transpantaneira

In 1973 the government decided to push a road through the Pantanal from Cuiabá to Corumbá. After they had arrived at Porto Jofre, 145km from Poconé, they then made the wise choice of stopping and questioning the wisdom of putting a road through an area that was underwater for six months a year. The result, or remnant, is the Transpantaneira, a raised dirt road that extends deep into the wetlands.

Wildlife is plentiful along the roadside and you'll typically see *jacarés* (caimans), capybaras and lots of birds. Once you get off the road and onto some of the farms, the impressive display of wildlife becomes even more varied. There are several places to stay along the Transpantaneira, all with horseback riding, walking and boating expeditions.

If you are driving from Cuiabá, head out around 4am to reach the Transpantaneira by sunrise, when the animals come to life. Though the road officially starts in Poconé, most folks mark the wooden sign and guard station 17km south of the city as the beginning of the journey. Don't forget to fill up your fuel tank in Poconé. There is a gas station at Hotel Porto Jofre for client use only, but you'll pay twice the going rate.

Heading south, it won't take long for a caiman or a macaw to cross your path as you navigate the 125 little wooden bridges and meter-wide potholes. Notice the interesting carved statue of Sào

PARALAXIS/SHUTTERSTOCK ©

GTW/GETTY IMAGES ©

ELLEON/SHUTTERSTOCK ©

1. Aerial view of the Transpantaneira
2. Gateway to the Transpantaneira
3. Capybara

Francisco, Protector of Ecology, around Km 18. He was installed by a priest in Poconé a few years back. Barara is a small bar at Km 32, where you can stop for a beer and *galinhada* (boneless chicken and rice) or fried fish.

At Km 65 you leave the grid – everything for the next 40km is run on solar energy or generators (though cabling is on the way...slowly). After Km 105, the landscape changes, with denser vegetation and an altogether wilder feel. You are now in jaguar country, where the deep Pantanal begins. Even if you don't spot a jaguar, you are rewarded for your intrepid efforts once you hit the beautiful wide-open spaces of Campo do Jofre, just north of Porto Jofre. Here the wildlife is so plentiful, you'll wind up draining your camera or phone battery in just a few kilometers.

Weekdays are better for driving, as there's less traffic kicking up dust. At the end of the road, check out the gigantic water lilies you always see in photos from the Amazon: there are hundreds in the pond at the back of Hotel Porto Jofre, out on the small wooden pier beyond the swimming pool.

In Cuiabá there are car-rental agencies just outside the airport grounds. In the dry season, and providing it hasn't recently rained, a normal car is all you need to drive the Transpantaneira, but double-check vehicle requirements with your accommodations. Don't even think about driving at other times of the year.

The Pantanal

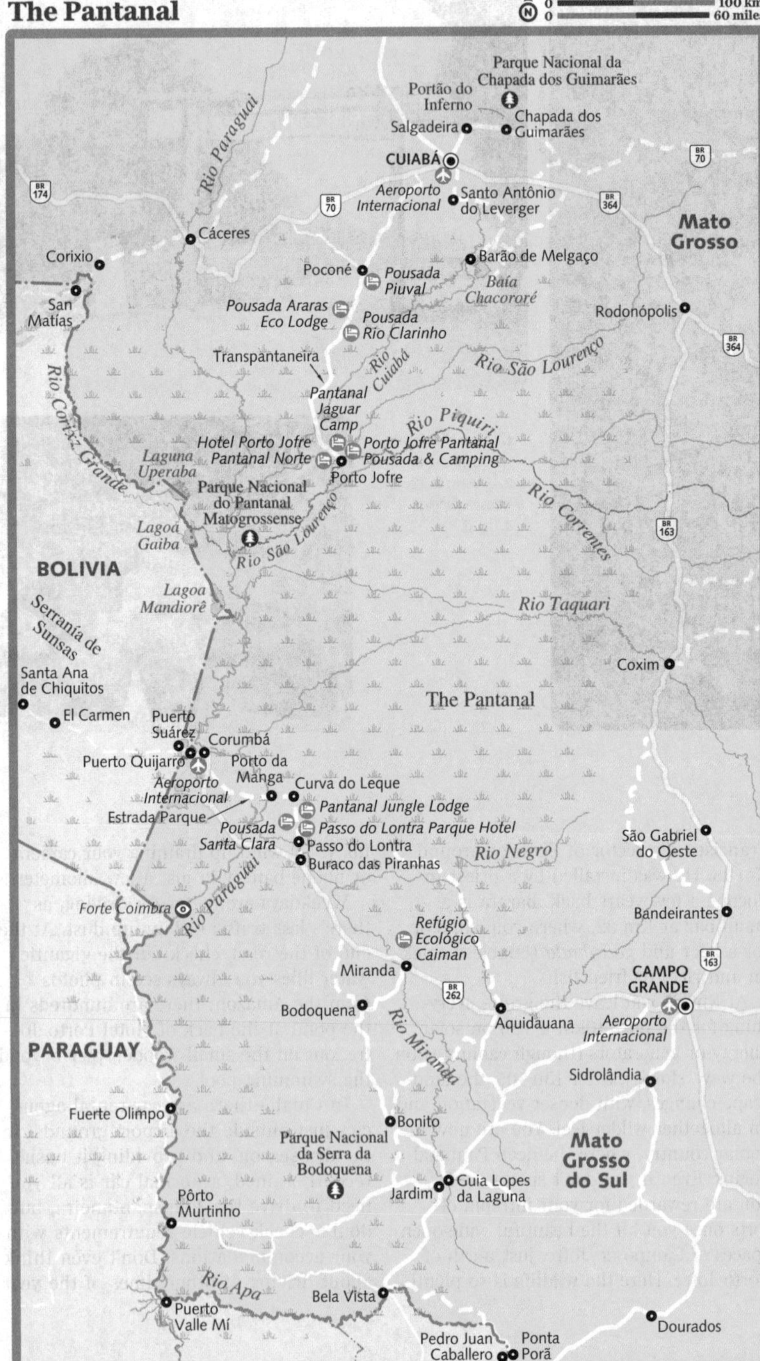

If you have doubts about roughing it on the budget tours, it is better to spend a bit more money for basic comforts – a bed, running water and some hope of avoiding a million mosquito bites. It rarely costs much more and the investment is worth it for a good night's sleep.

If you travel independently, you can rent a car in season. Transportation is almost never included in the room rates and can take a sizable chunk out of your budget if you don't have your own wheels. From Cuiabá, transfers in and out may require any combination of 4WD, boat, horseback and plane, depending on the season.

For this reason, many travelers go in under the services of a tour operator. Transportation in and out is then included and they often have access to more remote lodges.

Tours

The principal access towns where you can arrange tours are Cuiabá in the north (for the Transpantaneira) and Campo Grande in the south (for the Estrada Parque). Tours from Cuiabá tend to be slightly more expensive, but more professional with smaller groups and better-trained guides; they also go deeper into the Pantanal.

Northern Pantanal

Famed for its wonderful animal and birdlife, including the gruff prowling jaguar, the wetlands of the northern part of the Pantanal are a superb highlight for wildlife lovers.

The region has a few access points, notably the iconic Transpantaneira. This raised dirt road sectioned by small wooden bridges begins at Poconé and ends 145km south at Porto Jofre. It's a spectacular drive, with plentiful wildlife the whole way. At Porto Jofre, jaguar-spotting boat trips are a major drawcard in the dry season, while great fishing is also a possibility.

Beyond Cáceres, west of Cuiabá, there are also jaguar-watching opportunities with tour operators that run trips on the Rio Paraguai.

Tours

From Cuiabá, the capital of Mato Grosso, small tour operators arrange safaris along the Transpantaneira that include transportation, ranch accommodations on farms, and guides. Guides speak English and are well trained on the whole, and the smaller groups increase your chances of seeing the shyer animals. Fortunately, while there is healthy competition between tour operators in Cuiabá, it's not as intense as in Mato Grosso do Sul and some operators share the same Pantanal camps.

Tours here are well organized and quite comfortable, starting from around R$600 per day – if you are serious about seeing animals they are worth the extra money. Some companies also run pricier 'jaguar tours' with an excellent chance of seeing this magnificent feline in the Porto Jofre area from June to November.

★ Pantanal Nature WILDLIFE

(☎65 99925-2265, 65 3322-0203; www.pantanalnature.com.br; Av Historiador Rubens de Mendonça 1856, Cuiabá; 4-day nature tour per person R$4150, jaguar tour R$5800; ⊙office hours 7-11:30am & 1:30-5pm Mon-Thu, 8am-noon Fri & Sat) Superb agency run by Ailton Lara that has a sterling reputation for its professional tours and expert guides. It runs Pantanal nature tours and, in season, jaguar tours from the Pantanal Jaguar Camp (p381) in Porto Jofre. You can also go for a five- or six-day combination. Tours are cheaper off-season and if you opt to camp. Single supplement is 20%.

You are best to book several months ahead. Tours run in English and Portuguese, with other languages available by prior arrangement.

★ Southwild WILDLIFE

(www.southwild.com; 7-day jaguar-spotting packages per person US$5000-7000) This innovative high-end operator has been a pioneer in Pantanal wildlife tourism. It has upmarket packages involving stays at Southwild Pantanal Lodge and Flotel/Jaguar Suites (p381) and have also developed other jaguar-spotting bases removed from the increasingly busy Porto Jofre scene. Tours cater for serious nature-watchers with on-site biologists and wildlife databases. Many trips offer money back if certain animals aren't spotted.

Pantanal Explorer WILDLIFE

(☎65 3682-2800; www.pantanalexplorer.com.br; Av Governador João Ponce de Arruda 670, Várzea Grande) Owner André has been working with sustainable Pantanal tourism for decades and fights harmful government interference. He is actively involved in saving the hyacinth macaw and giant otter. As well as Transpantaneira-area excursions, this outfit has a jaguar-spotting base in a more remote location on the Paraguay river, as well as other lodges in different ecosystems in Mato Grosso.

It is affiliated with Pousada Araras Eco Lodge (p380).

PANTANAL PACKING LIST

You can't buy much in the Pantanal, so come prepared. The dry season is also the cooler season, though it can still get pretty hot. Don't forget the following:

- ☐ Quick-dry, light-colored long-sleeved shirts; leave behind red (it scares animals), yellow (mosquitoes love it) and black clothing (it's too hot and mosquitoes love it, too)
- ☐ Neutral-colored long pants
- ☐ Sneakers or hiking boots
- ☐ Rain poncho
- ☐ Flip-flops or water sandals
- ☐ Sun hat
- ☐ Swimwear
- ☐ Fleece or sweater
- ☐ Day pack
- ☐ Mosquito repellent with plenty of DEET
- ☐ Sunscreeen
- ☐ Sunglasses
- ☐ Binoculars
- ☐ Strong flashlight or headlamp
- ☐ Camera with good zoom lens
- ☐ Flask or reusable water bottle

Ecoverde Tours WILDLIFE

(☎65 99638-1614; www.ecoverdetours.com.br; Pedro Celestino 391, Cuiabá; 4-day nature tour s/d R$2400/4000, jaguar tour R$3000/5000) This relaxed budget company has decades of service and experienced guides. Working with local pousadas toward an ecofriendly approach, Joel Souza can guide you in several languages. You can find him at Hostel Pousada Ecoverde. He runs Pantanal nature tours year-round and jaguar-spotting tours from June to October.

Focus Tours WILDLIFE

(☎Brazil 31 9134-3833, USA +1 505-216-7780; www.focustours.com) In operation for nearly four decades, this trailblazing ecotourism operator was founded by ecologist Douglas Trent. As well as customizable birdwatching and nature-watching trips, it runs jaguar-watching excursions on the Rio Paraguai and operates a major conservation project.

Sleeping

Accommodations along the Transpantaneira are plentiful and there is a good variety of choices, from fairly rustic to high end.

Pousada Rio Clarinho POUSADA $

(☎65 99637-0516; www.pousadarioclarinho.com.br; Transpantaneira, Km 40; s/d/tr incl full board & excursions R$290/460/690; ❄) An avian symphony is your wake-up call at this rustic *fazenda* right on the Rio Clarinho (there's a river platform for swimming). There is an extensive area of forested trails, and more than 260 species of birds on the property, as well as capybaras and giant otters. The food is authentic *pantaneiro* and the owners' warmth transcends the language barrier.

Prices are very reasonable. It's 3.5km off the Transpantaneira; you might struggle if you don't have a 4WD vehicle.

Porto Jofre Pantanal Pousada & Camping POUSADA, CAMPING $$

(Pousada de Neco; ☎65 99971-3699; www.portojofrepantanal.com.br; Transpantaneira, Km 145, Porto Jofre; s/d incl full board R$350/660, camping R$40; ❄📶) Turn left at the end of the Transpantaneira to reach this budget favorite that is better known hereabouts as Pousada de Neco. It's a genuinely welcoming place with a wonderful riverfront location – ideal for wildlife-spotting boat tours, as well as tasty food, spartan but air-conditioned rooms, and clean showers for campers. Meals are included in the room price (campers pay extra).

Boat excursions cost R$750 to R$950 per day (R$500 to R$650 half day) depending on engine capacity. It's worth going for the bigger engine if you're jaguar-spotting. Do not confuse with the Pousada Porto Jofre Pantanal Norte.

★Araras Eco Lodge LODGE $$$

(☎65 3682-2800; www.araraslodge.com.br; Transpantaneira, Km 32; s/d incl full board & excursions R$1591/2482; ❄📶) This pioneering ranch offers great comfort and luxury in a peaceful setting. Rooms have lovely artisanal bedspreads and patios with hammocks. There is a treetop tower for bird-watching (hyacinth macaws) and super welcoming owners André and Akhila make an immense effort to be sustainable (water recycling, solar panels and much more). The food is really good, with vegetarian choices and home-grown produce.

You can also book a Jaguar Express day tour (US$550) that whisks you down to Porto Jofre in the morning and heads out feline-spotting before returning here in the evening. There's a minimum stay of three nights and a conservation fee of R$130 per person per stay.

Flotel and Jaguar Suites HOUSEBOAT **$$$**
(www.southwild.com; Rio Piquirí; 6-night packages per person US$5000-6700; Jun-Nov;) Moored on the Piquirí in the heart of jaguar territory, these twin houseboats are the accommodations for wildlife-viewing packages run by Southwild (p379). The Flotel has small cabin-like en-suite rooms; the adjacent Jaguar Suites are a newer construction with very roomy wood-fitted chambers with mosquito-netted beds, large windows and balconies. Tasty meals, a jaguar database and wildlife talks make this tops for serious nature-watchers.

Packages include transfers from Cuiabá, meals and two daily excursions. From March to May, it functions as a base for fishing excursions with Transpantanal (p373).

Pantanal Jaguar Camp LODGE **$$$**
(65 99925-2265; www.pantanaljaguarcamp.com.br; Transpantaneira, Km 145, Porto Jofre; d with meals & excursion R$1035, camping per person R$60, with own tent R$45;) Intimate, solar-powered wilderness lodge with seven comfortable rooms, camping and an on site restaurant. This is a great Porto Jofre base for jaguar-seeking boat trips (R$410 per person) that is affiliated with Pantanal Nature (p379). Other activities include night safaris on the Transpantaneira and bird-watching.

Pousada Piuval POUSADA **$$$**
(65 3345-1338; www.pousadapiuval.com.br; Transpantaneira, Km 10; full board s/d standard R$500/713, luxo R$604/857;) Popular, genuinely welcoming and family-run, this sizable working ranch is just 10km from Poconé. Rooms are comfortable with hammocks, but it's worth the upgrade to the much newer luxo ones that come with a private balcony and lots of space. It's one of the better pousadas for parents with children. The pool is wonderful, as are sunset boat rides.

SouthWild Pantanal Lodge LODGE **$$$**
(Fazenda Santa Tereza; www.southwild.com; Transpantaneira, Km 68; d incl full board R$820;) This laid-back and low-slung reddish ranch house right on the banks of the Rio Pixaim is 2.5km off the Transpantaneira. Fifteen impeccable large rooms with comfy exec-style chairs and beds with mosquito nets make commodious bases for wildlife-spotting (good giant otter chances) and

CHOOSING A GUIDE

Pantanal tourism is big business and in the past some companies have been guilty of employing underhand tactics in the race to hook clients. Though measures have finally been taken to clamp down on the worst offenders, it is still worth bearing a few suggestions in mind to have a safe and enjoyable trip.

- Resist making a snap decision, especially if you've just climbed off an overnight bus.
- Do not make your decision based on cost. Cheaper very rarely means better, but even expensive tours can be a letdown.
- Go on forums. Read online reviews. Speak to other travelers. What was their experience like? Be aware that operators often run each other down both by mouth and in online reviews.
- Remember that the owner or salesperson is not always your guide, and it's the guide you're going to be with in the wilderness for several days. Ask to meet your guide if possible. Ascertain your guide's linguistic abilities.
- Don't hand over your cash to any go-betweens.
- If you are even remotely concerned about sustainable tourism, do not use operators and lodges that harm this fragile environment. That means no picking up the animals for photographs or touching them whatsoever.
- Group budget tours focus squarely on the spectacular and easy-to-see species. Serious wildlife-watchers should be prepared to pay more for a private guide.

DON'T MISS

JAGUAR-WATCHING FROM PORTO JOFRE

One of the world's great wildlife experiences is a visit to the Pantanal, and the crowning moment of a trip here just might be spotting a jaguar.

The largest big cat in the Americas, and the third-largest in the world (behind only lions and tigers), jaguars have become habituated to humans in boats and haughtily ignore them, going about their daily business on the shore or in the water as if the observers weren't there.

Jaguar-watching trips run from Porto Jofre in the dry season, from May to November. All the boats communicate with each other by radio; when a jaguar is spotted, everyone races toward it. The upside is that your chance of seeing one is dramatically increased; the downside is that you'll likely see it as part of a jostling crowd of 10 to 20 boats. Nevertheless, they are a majestic sight.

While jaguars are the main focus, there is plentiful other wildlife on these tours. Caimans and capybaras are numerous and you may well spot giant river otters, howler monkeys or even tapirs. The birdlife is simply extraordinary. If you are interested in birds, it's worth bringing the *Birds of the Pantanal* field guide, which is on sale at most lodges (R$150).

It's worth letting your guide know of your specific wildlife interests, as otherwise they may assume that you are only there for the jaguars and that birds are a sideshow.

Other things to take along on the boat trip include sunglasses, binoculars, insect repellent, a hat, sunscreen and maybe even a jacket for the early morning chill. It's hot, so drink water but don't overdo it: you may be out there four hours without a toilet break.

Most visitors book jaguar-watching trips as part of a multiday package that includes accommodation (these should be booked up to a year in advance), but you can also book single excursions via Porto Jofre Pantanal Pousada (p380), Hotel Porto Jofre Pantanal Norte and Pantanal Jaguar Camp (p381) among others. Some tour operators such as Southwild (p379) and Pantanal Explorer (p379) are establishing further-flung jaguar-spotting bases to escape the crowds, while in the southern Pantanal Refúgio Ecológico Caiman (p384) is another prime spot.

horseback riding; there's also a plunge pool and a tower where ocelots come to feed at night.

Hotel Porto Jofre Pantanal Norte LODGE **$$$**
(☎65 3637-1593; www.portojofre.com.br; Transpantaneira, Km 145, Porto Jofre; s/d incl full board R$560/942; ⏲Mar-Nov; ❄@📶🏊) This sprawling complex sits where the Transpantaneira meets the river at Porto Jofre. Catering for anglers and wildlife enthusiasts, it has wide river frontage, excellent birdlife (regular hyacinth macaws) and extensive facilities, from pool tables to an airstrip. Rooms are simple and a little dated in avocado green but decent. The hotel has a fleet of boats for fishing and jaguar-spotting trips.

Do not confuse with nearby Pousada Porto Jofre Pantanal Norte.

Eating

In the northern Pantanal, the cuisine is often fish-based. *Pacu, dourado* and *pintado* are the most consumed fish, and they come *frito* (fried), *grelhado* (grilled), *assado* (baked) or *defumado* (smoked). Both *dourado* and *pacu* have lots of small bones, but they separate easily when baked slowly. *Pacu* is often baked and served with an *escabeche* sauce consisting of onions, tomatoes and peppers. Another favorite fish is *pintado,* excellent when spiced with rough salt and pepper and grilled. One specialty is *peixe à urucum,* where the chosen fish is served topped with spices, condensed milk, coconut milk and melted mozzarella. Piranha soup is also popular and considered an aphrodisiac by the *pantaneiros*.

ℹ Getting There & Away

Cuiabá is the main access point for the northern Pantanal and easily accessed by air or bus from other Brazilian cities.

From Cuiabá, buses go as far as Poconé, at the beginning of the Transpantaneira road. If you're not driving or on a tour, your only options to go further are taxis or hitching.

Southern Pantanal

The Mato Grosso do Sul part of the Brazilian Pantanal has a panoply of wildlife and a fine choice of lodges from backpacker favorites to exclusive eco-havens. All accommodations arrange nature-watching trips on both land and water, as well as horseback riding and other Brazilian countryside experiences. There is easier access to the wetlands here than in the north, although you can't penetrate as far into the region. Southern gateways to the Pantanal are the cities of Campo Grande, Corumbá, Aquidauana and Miranda. Most travelers head to Campo Grande. Corumbá, Aquidauana and Miranda are popular with Brazilian anglers.

Tours

Budget tour operators working in Mato Grosso do Sul arrange packages at camps along Estrada Parque, a 117km stretch of dirt road through the region known as Nhecolândia. Estrada Parque is actually closer to Corumbá than to Campo Grande, but the vast majority of companies have long relocated to Campo Grande, a travel hub convenient for onward travel to other parts of Brazil. The city has made a big effort to clean up its act, with the local government closing down lodges that didn't comply with ecological legislation and tightening the screws on dodgy operators. Problems persist, but things are definitely moving in the right direction. The cheapest tours are rough-and-tumble affairs and groups are often large, but with prices starting at around R$500 per day, it is an economical way to see the Pantanal and its wildlife.

Pantanal Discovery WILDLIFE
(☎6&7 99163-3518; www.gilspantanaldiscovery.com.br; Hotel Mohave, Afonso Pena 602, Campo Grande; 3-day, 2-night package hammock/dm/s/d R$1000/1200/1550/2800) Owner Gil is a perennial operator with a polished sales pitch. He's assertive, very helpful and the pick of budget operators in town. He's used to dealing with short notice or tight schedules and has his own transportation.

Pantanal Viagens WILDLIFE
(☎67 3321-3143; www.pantanalviagens.com.br; Room 9, Old Bus Terminal, Joaquim Nabuco 200, Campo Grande) A nice agency working with Pousada Passo do Lontra and other Pantanal lodgings that has worked hard to maintain its excellent reputation. Caters to mid- to high-end budgets and has professional and reliable packages.

Sleeping

Much of the accommodation in this part of the Pantanal is along the road called Estrada Parque, while there are also high-end hotel-*fazendas* around Aquidauana and Miranda.

Estrada Parque runs off the main Campo Grande–Corumbá road (Hwy BR-262) at Buraco das Piranhas, 72km from Corumbá and 324km from Campo Grande. Parts of this road can be flooded even during the dry season.

To get to the Estrada Parque you can take the Campo Grande–Corumbá bus and arrange for your lodge to pick you up (for a small fee) at the Buraco das Piranhas intersection.

Pantanal Jungle Lodge LODGE $$
(☎67 3242-1488; www.pantanal-jungle-lodge.com; Estrada Parque, Km 8; 3-day, 2-night package dm/s/d R$910/1380/2310;) This boardwalk lodge is a backpacker favorite, thanks to its enviable riverside location and well-organized activities – from canoeing and piranha fishing to night safaris on the river and wildlife-spotting treks. Lodge either in one of the breezy dorms or in a private room with air-conditioning. All have an insect-screened porch to relax in.

Pousada & Camping Santa Clara POUSADA, CAMPGROUND $$
(☎67 99939-3570; www.pantanalsantaclara.com.br; Estrada Parque, Km 22; 3-day, 2-night package incl full board & excursions camping/dm/s/d R$580/860/1220/1980;) This working ranch is enthusiastically run and has a host of activities (hikes, piranha fishing, night safaris, horseback riding), accommodations to suit all budgets and hearty *pantaneiro* cooking. It is deservedly popular; expect large groups. Rooms are compact but OK, dorms have decent spacing, there's a plunge pool and games, and macaws and peccaries are about.

The campsite is 500m from the accommodations block by the river. It's a lovely spot in itself with tents, a simple screened dormitory (no sheets) and hammocks.

Passo do Lontra Parque Hotel LODGE $$
(☎67 99987-2569; www.passodolontra.com.br; Estrada Parque, Km 8; chalet/apt incl full board R$500/630;) Rickety boardwalks,

basking caimans and buildings on stilts give this riverside place authentic Pantanal character. It's worth the upgrade to the *apartamento* rooms, which are larger than the chalets and have a terrace. It's in an accessible location near the beginning of the Estrada Parque. Canoeing, boat safaris and nocturnal excursions along Rio Miranda (activities R$65 to R$140) are the focus.

★ **Refúgio Ecológico Caiman** LODGE **$$$**
(67 3242-1450, reservations 11 3706-1800; www.caiman.com.br; r incl full board, transfers & excursions R$11,490-13,138;) This eco-pioneering lodge is a private Pantanal for a privileged few. There's a main building and two luxurious lodges; forest-side Cordilheiro is the most remote with sumptuous suites and a great lookout tower, while lakeside Baiazinha has prime position for spotting jaguars. Both have pool decks, lounge areas and superb comfort. Tours are led by on-site multilingual guides. It's 36km north of Miranda.

There are dozens of jaguars and hundreds of macaws on the property, which is the location of the standout Onçafari jaguar project (all-day jaguar excursions in season have an extra cost of R$700). Prices include meals and numerous activities; there is a three-night minimum in high season with fixed entry and exit days. There's an additional one-off environmental charge of R$320 per person.

Eating

In the southern Pantanal, the dishes are strongly influenced by the cattle and grains produced in the area. Specialties include *carne seca com abobora* (sun-dried beef with pumpkin) and *paçoca-de-pilã* (sun-dried beef with manioc flour), the latter eaten with bananas and unsalted rice. There's also *arroz de carreteiro* (rice with sun-dried beef served with fried manioc and banana) and *galinha caipira* – chicken served with white rice.

Getting There & Away

Campo Grande and Corumbá are the main access points for the southern Pantanal, and buses running between the two can drop you at Miranda, Aquidauana or the Buraco das Piranhas intersection for Estrada Parque.

There are shared and private transfers available from both Campo Grande and Bonito to the southern Pantanal.

If driving, go slow along the Campo Grande–Corumbá highway as wildlife often ventures onto it. Numerous cameras enforce the speed limits.

MATO GROSSO DO SUL

Mato Grosso do Sul was created in 1977 when the military government decided it would be the best way to administer and develop such a large region (cynics claimed it was to provide more high-paying bureaucratic jobs for cronies). But even before the split, the area had a different economic and social makeup from the northern Mato Grosso.

In the late 19th century, many migrants from southeastern Brazil arrived in the area, so Mato Grosso do Sul has a greater number of smaller farms and much more intensive agriculture compared to the large ranches in the north. All this is thanks to the rich red earth, known as *terra roxa,* which has generated wealth and a modern agricultural sector. The main crop is soy, but there's also corn, rice, cotton and cattle. The region also encompasses two-thirds of the Pantanal and the Serra da Bocaina, two wonderful natural areas.

Campo Grande

0XX67 / POP 874,200 / ELEV 592M

Known as the Cidade Morena (dark-complexioned city) for its red earth, Campo Grande is the capital of Mato Grosso do Sul and the main gateway to the southern Pantanal. It's a vast, modern metropolis, where high-rises tower above the shopping malls and streets are lined with restaurants – contrasting with the source of its wealth, which mainly lies in cattle and farming. Home to no fewer than four universities, Campo Grande is young at heart, its large student population producing an almost insatiable demand for nocturnal entertainment.

Orientation

The downtown area of Campo Grande is compact and easily navigated on foot. Av Afonso Pena, the main boulevard, runs east-west. Going west, it becomes Av Duque de Caxias and then Hwy BR-262 before passing the airport (7km) and heading on to Corumbá. To the east, it runs past the Shopping Campo Grande and the Parque das Nações Indígenas. The center of the city is a grid, with the main commercial area concentrated around Afonso Pena and cross streets Av Calógeras and Rua 14 de Julho.

Sights

Most of the city's attractions are found inside the immense **Parque das Nações Indígenas** (Av Afonso Pena; 6am-9:30pm), an ecological reserve with a lake, cycling and jogging tracks, and a scattering of monuments and museums.

★Museu das Culturas Dom Bosco — MUSEUM

(☎67 3326-9788; www.mcdb.org.br; Parque das Nações Indígenas, Av Afonso Pena; R$10; 8am-4:30pm Tue-Sat) Built on the site of a Bororo burial ground, this superb museum is divided into two parts. One is a collection of over 10,000 insects and stuffed flora and fauna, while the other is a visually striking, unmissable introduction to the indigenous people of the Mato Grosso region, with subtly lit underfloor and suspended-glass displays showcasing shaman paraphernalia, weaponry, everyday tools, splendid adornments made of feathers and funerary objects. The enlarged black-and-white photos are almost equally striking.

Museu de Arte Contemporânea de Mato Grosso do Sul — MUSEUM

(MARCO; ☎67 3326-7449; www.marcovirtual.wordpress.com; Antônio Maria Coelho 6000; 7:30am-5:30pm Tue-Fri, 2-6pm Sat & Sun) FREE Just outside the northern gate of Parque das Nações Indígenas, this compact but well-presented modern art museum showcases a permanent collection of works both by local talent and temporary exhibits by other Brazilian artists.

Aquário do Pantanal — AQUARIUM

(Parque das Nações Indígenas) Originally slated for completion in 2014, this ambitious aquarium and research center was still in development in 2018. You will either find a hugely impressive freshwater aquarium, a mediocre finish-at-all-costs half-measure or a weed-choked building site.

Feira Central — MARKET

(www.feiracentralcg.com.br; Av Calógeras & 14 de Julho; 4pm-late Wed-Fri, from noon Sat & Sun) A great market worth a stroll, this massive open-air food and shopping court is lined with Japanese soba-noodle joints and other stalls, as well as some indigenous crafts and leatherwork. It's packed with revelers on weekends.

Sleeping

The area immediately around the old bus station, where there are several popular budget choices, is seedy, so choose wisely.

More upmarket sleeping options are at the eastern end of town, around the Parque das Nações Indígenas.

Turis Hotel — HOTEL $

(☎67 3382-2461; www.turishotel.com.br; Allan Kardec 200; s R$90-112, d R$155-180;) Modern and minimalist, this excellent option is entirely too hip for its location and is very good value. Great breakfast, and the staff go out of their way to be helpful in spite of limited English.

Hauzz Hostel — HOSTEL $

(☎67 98118-7270; www.hauzzhostel.wixsite.com/hostel; Piratininga 1527; dm R$50-60, s/d R$80/150;) A quiet, secure hostel with snug, fan-cooled rooms that share several bathrooms, in a pretty bungalow with floorboards underfoot. There's also an air-conditioned private room. Towels are R$10 extra. It's a short walk to Shopping Campo Grande and handy for visiting Parque das Nações.

Hotel Internacional — HOTEL $

(☎67 3384-4677; www.hotelinternacionalms.com.br; Allan Kardec 223; s/d R$140/160; @) Good-value downtown hotel with fetching blue-tiled floors and snug rooms that are decent and clean, with mattresses that have seen better days. Some rooms have a fridge. The breakfast spread is impressive.

Hotel Nacional — HOTEL $

(☎67 3383-2461; www.hotelnacionalms.com.br; Dom Aquino 610; s/d with air-con R$80/140, with fan R$70/120, with shared bathroom R$50/90; @) A basic budget choice hugely popular with international backpackers and Brazilian student groups. Choose between simple digs with clean shared facilities and plusher ones with air-con, bathrooms and TV. Good value.

Bahamas Suite Hotel — HOTEL $$

(☎67 3303-9393; www.bahamassuitehotel.com.br; José Antônio 1117; r R$287-380;) Sleep in spacious split-level apartments in this decent-value high-rise with aquamarine window panes. Upstairs is a pleasant sleeping area; downstairs is the living room with a basic kitchenette and – bonus ! – a bowl of plastic fruit. The higher up you go, the better the views, and some rooms even have balconies. The plumbing, however, can be temperamental.

Campo Grande

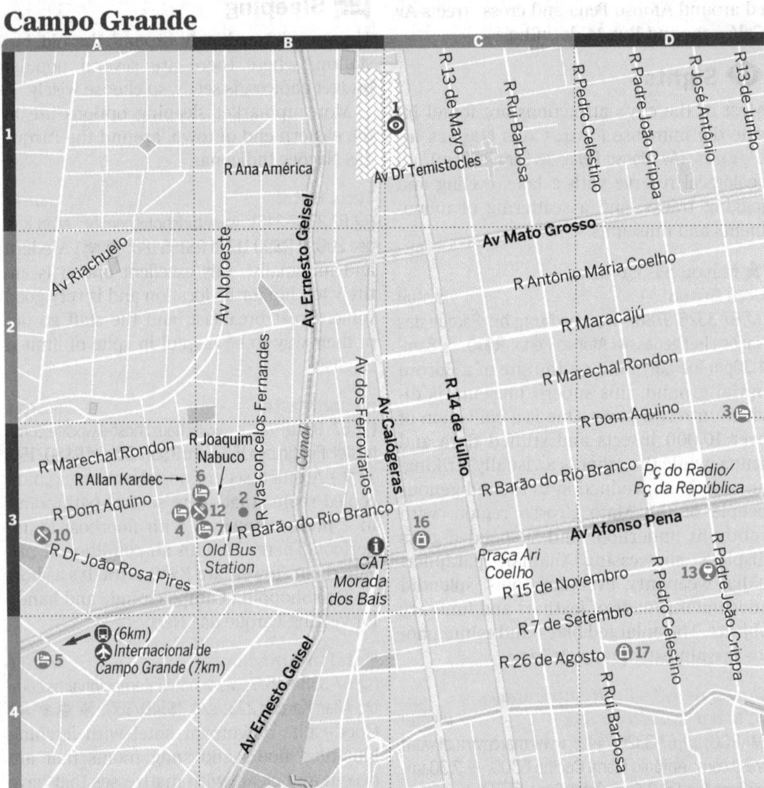

Hotel Mohave HOTEL $$
(☎67 3306-7743; www.hotelmohave.com.br; Av Afonso Pena 602; s R$170-250, d R$185-280; ❄📶) Handily close to the airport but still central, the minimalist modern lines of the Mohave are backed up by professional multilingual service and a good breakfast spread. For a little bit extra, you get a balcony; premium rooms come with a kitchenette. Rates are usually reasonable.

★**Deville Prime** BUSINESS HOTEL $$$
(☎67 2106-4600; www.deville.com.br; Av Mato Grosso 4250; r R$350-550; ❄@📶🏊) Raising the bar in Campo Grande, the Deville is excellent in many ways. Large rooms with king beds have exemplary comfort, staff are helpful and the breakfast spread is impressive. The only downsides are the pool, which is stuck in a corner of the building, and the ad hoc bar area.

✕ Eating

There's a wide range of excellent places to eat in Campo Grande for all budgets. The city boasts the third-highest Japanese population in Brazil and soba noodles feature prominently on some menus, as well as at the Feira Central.

Restaurante da Gaúcha BUFFET $
(Allan Kardec 238; buffet R$15; ⏲11:30am-11pm) This handy cheapie is central and a backpacker favorite due to its rock-bottom prices and all-you-can-gobble buffet dishes.

Cantina Romana ITALIAN $$
(☎67 3324-9777; www.cantinaromana.com.br; Rua da Paz 237; mains for 2 people R$45-80; ⏲11am-2pm & 6:30-11pm Mon-Fri, 11am-2:30pm & 6:30-11:30pm Sat & Sun) An old-school Italian cantina and pizzeria that has been going strong since 1978. Expect attentive service, authentic surroundings and mega portions – we're big fans

Campo Grande

Sights
1 Feira Central C1

Activities, Courses & Tours
Pantanal Discovery .... (see 5)
2 Pantanal Viagens B3

Sleeping
3 Bahamas Suite Hotel D2
4 Hotel Internacional A3
5 Hotel Mohave A4
6 Hotel Nacional B3
7 Turis Hotel B3

Eating
8 Cantina Romana F2
9 Casa Colonial F3
10 Casa do Peixe A3
11 Fogo Caipira E4
12 Restaurante da Gaúcha B3

Drinking & Nightlife
13 Bar Mercearia D3
14 Cachaçaria Brasil E4
15 Território do Vinho F2

Shopping
16 Casa do Artesão C3
17 Feira dos Artesãos D4

of its *gnocchi alla siciliana*. If you graze at the weekday lunchtime buffet, you won't need dinner.

Vermelho Grill STEAK **$$**
(☎67 3326-7813; www.vermelhogrill.com.br; Av Afonso Pena 6078; steaks for 1 person R$39-78; ⏰11:30am-2:30pm & 6-11pm Mon-Fri, 11:30am-11:30pm Sat, 11:30am-4pm Sun; 📶) It's quite a relief to be served a normal-sized steak in Brazil. This log-cabin-style place opposite the park has an excellent range of cuts of beef, with provenance information. The wine list looks impressive, but many are often out of stock. Service is helpful and personable.

★**Casa do Peixe** SEAFOOD **$$$**
(☎67 3382-7121; www.casadopeixe.com.br; Av João Rosa Pires 1030; mains for 2 people R$95, rodízio R$86; ⏰11am-2pm daily, 6-11pm Mon-Sat) This place rightfully deserves its reputation as the best *peixaria* (fish restaurant) in town, with a superior buffet accompanying the hearty mains. The *rodízio* is an awesome way to acquaint yourself with *pintado, pacu* and other fish of the Pantanal, prepared in many sublime ways, while the inclusion of sushi and sashimi pays homage to the city's large Japanese population.

★**Gaúcho Gastão** CHURRASCARIA **$$$**
(☎67 3029-4325; www.facebook.com/gauchogastao; Dr Zerbini 38; rodízio weekday/weekend R$45/79; ⏰11am-2:30pm & 6-10:30pm Mon-Sat, 11am-3pm Sun) On weekends in particular, this family-run *churrascaria* heaves with local families and skewers featuring succulent cuts of beef and pork, chicken hearts, grilled pineapple and all the other ingredients that add up to the perfect *rodízio*. Its signature melt-in-the-mouth *costela* (boneless beef rib) alone is worth the trip. *Por quilo* (per kilo; price by weight) available upstairs.

Fogo Caipira BRAZILIAN **$$$**
(☎67 3382-0731; www.fogocaipira.com.br; José Antônio 145; dishes R$34-85; ⏰11am-2pm & 7-11pm Tue-Thu, 11am-3pm & 7pm-midnight Fri, 11am-midnight Sat, 11am-4pm Sun) The best dishes at this regional institution require an advance order, such as the *pacu recheado* (fish stuffed with manioc and spices; three-hour

preparation). It's pricey, but as the only restaurant in the city with culinary stars, it's worth it.

Casa Colonial BRAZILIAN $$$

(☎67 3383-3207; www.casacolonial.com.br; Av Afonso Pena 3997; mains R$60-105; ⊙11am-2:30pm Wed-Sun, 6:30pm-midnight Tue-Sun) The walk-in wine cellar is the first thing that catches your eye when you enter this sophisticated bar-restaurant. There are two dining areas, the romantic brick-vaulted dining room and a more summery space in a handsome wooden house on the Afonso Pena strip. It serves delicious Italian-influenced Brazilian dishes like *galeto* (chargrilled chicken served with sides).

Drinking & Nightlife

Campo Grande's nightlife knows no evening off, especially beyond the 3900 block of Av Afonso Pena, east of downtown, where there is a cluster of happening bars.

★Território do Vinho WINE BAR

(☎67 3029-8464; www.territoriodovinho.com.br; Euclides da Cunha 485; ⊙11:30am-2:30pm & 7pm-midnight Mon-Sat, 11:30am-3:30pm Sun; 📶) A stylish, jazz-tinged wine bar by night and equally classy lunch spot on weekends, Territorio do Vinho is the place to acquaint yourself with Brazilian and international wines. The food? Gourmet Italian-Brazilian. Opposite, the Território Lab (5pm to midnight Monday to Saturday) does delicious tapas-style fare, weekend *feijoada* and DJs.

Bar Mercearia BOTECO

(☎67 3384-9622; www.merceariabar.com.br; 15 de Novembro 1064; ⊙5pm-midnight Mon-Fri, from noon Sat & Sun; 📶) A handsome corner bar decked out in historic style to resemble São Paulo botecos of the 1930s. Football shirts and beer posters reflect the main two obsessions here, but it's the wraparound exterior seating under the awning that's the real charmer.

Cachaçaria Brasil BAR

(☎67 3313-6731; www.cachacariabrasilms.com.br; Av Fernando Corrêa da Costa 1618; ⊙5:30pm-12:30am Mon-Wed, to 1:30am Thu-Sat) Samba, over 100 kinds of *cachaça* (sugarcane alcohol), an extensive food and drink menu, pool tables, nightly live music and live *futebol* make this Campo Grande's in place for a crowd of all ages.

Shopping

Casa do Artesão ARTS & CRAFTS

(☎67 3383-2633; www.fundacaodecultura.ms.gov.br; cnr Avs Calogeras & Afonso Pena; ⊙8am-6pm Mon-Fri, to 4pm Sat) An excellent selection of indigenous arts, including colorful Terena ceramics and Kadiwéu wooden carvings depicting mythical figures. There's also 'jungle jewelry' that makes use of seeds, and locally brewed liquor.

BUSES FROM CAMPO GRANDE

DESTINATION	COST (R$)	TIME (HR)	FREQUENCY	COMPANY
Bonito	63	6	3 daily	Cruzeiro do Sul (www.cruzeirodosulms.com.br)
Brasília	238-261	23-25	4 daily	Motta (www.motta.com.br), Viação São Luiz (www.viacaosaoluiz.com.br)
Corumbá	124	7	8 daily	Andorinha (www.andorinha.com)
Cuiabá	147-170	11-14	20 daily	Andorinha, Eucatur (www.eucatur.com.br), Motta, Nova Integração (www.eucatur.com.br), Viação São Luiz
Foz do Iguaçu	235-290	16-20	No direct buses, change in Cascavel or Toledo, several daily options.	Nova Integração, Eucatur, UneSul (www.unesul.com.br), Ouro e Prata (www.viacaoouroeprata.com.br)
Ponta Porã	85-97	6	7 daily	Expresso Queiroz (www.expresso-queiroz.com.br), Cruzeiro do Sul
Rio de Janeiro	427	24	2 daily	Andorinha (www.andorinha.com)
São Paulo	249-304	15½	7 daily	Andorinha, Motta

Feira dos Artesãos ARTS & CRAFTS
(67 3325-9251; www.campogrande.ms.gov.br; Praça Dos Imigrantes, cnr Rui Barbosa & Joaquim Murtinho; 9am-6pm Tue-Fri, 8am-noon Sat) High-quality leatherwork and embroidery by local craftspeople in a couple dozen booths.

Information

MEDICAL SERVICES

Hospital Regional de Mato Grosso do Sul (67 3378-2500; www.hospitalregional.ms.gov.br; Av Lutero Lopes 36) Main city hospital with 24-hour emergency.

TOURIST INFORMATION

There are small tourist kiosks at the **bus station** (67 3314-4448; www.campogrande.ms.gov.br; Rodoviária; 8am-10pm) and **airport** (67 3363-3116; www.campogrande.ms.gov.br; 7:30-11:30am, 1-5pm & 6-10pm Mon-Fri) and a larger one at the central **Morada dos Bais** (67 3314-9968; www.campogrande.ms.gov.br; Av Noroeste 5140; 2-8pm Mon-Fri, noon-6pm Sat & Sun).

Getting There & Away

AIR

Aeroporto Internacional de Campo Grande (CGR; 67 3368-6000; Av Duque de Caxias) is 7km west of town.

Azul, Avianca Brasil, Gol and Latam all serve Campo Grande, with daily flights to Brasília, São Paulo, Cuiabá, Curitiba and others. Amaszonas serves Asunción in Paraguay twice weekly.

BUS

Campo Grande's **bus station** (67 3026-6789; Av Gury Marques 1215) is inconveniently located 6km south of the center on the road to São Paulo. Buses coming from the north may make a stop in the center first.

For the Pantanal, nondirect intercity buses to Corumbá can drop you at the intersection with Estrada Parque. Otherwise, accommodation providers can arrange shared (R$80 to R$100) or private transfers.

Vanzella (p397) and **Terra Transportes** (67 3255-1001; www.terratransportes.com.br) run door-to-door bus and van services between Campo Grande and Bonito, with several daily departures for R$80.

For Foz do Iguaçu, change in Toledo or Cascavel. Companies will sell through tickets. The evening Unesul service is one of the quickest. From Foz, the 6pm Eucatur service is a good route.

Getting Around

Local buses 61 and 87 (R$3.75) connect the long-distance bus station to the city center. To use city buses you need to buy a *passe de ônibus* (bus pass) from newsstands, pharmacies or bus stop kiosks. They come as one-time use (*unitário*) or rechargeable (*recarregável*). A taxi to the center will cost around R$30.

To get a bus to the center from the airport, walk out of the airport to the bus stop on the main road and catch the 409 (R$3.75, buy ticket from the airport). A taxi costs around R$30 to R$40.

Corumbá

0XX67 / POP 109,900

'Corumbaly' (old Corumbá) is a gracefully aging river-port city close to the Bolivian border. Known as Cidade Branca (White City), it is 403km northwest of Campo Grande by road. The city sits atop a steep hill overlooking the Rio Paraguai; on the far side of the river, a huge expanse of the Pantanal stretches out on the horizon.

Founded in 1776 by Captain Luis de Albuquerque, by 1840 it had become the biggest river port in the world. The impressive, brightly painted buildings along the waterfront reflect the wealth that passed through the town in the 19th century before Corumbá went into decline with the coming of the railway.

Sights

Corumbá's star attraction is the Pantanal; you can get a preview of it from the highest point in the area, **Morro Urucum** (1100m), 20km south of the city. The Christ statue that overlooks the bus station on the hillside is the **Cristo Rei do Pantanal** (7am-9pm), also a good lookout.

★**Museu de História do Pantanal** MUSEUM
(MUHPAN; 67 3232-0303; Manoel Cavassa 275; 1-5:30pm Tue-Sat) FREE On the waterfront, this partially interactive museum tells the story of the formation of the Pantanal and 10,000 years of human habitation in the region. Exhibits range from presentations on the flora and fauna in different parts of the great wetlands to the history of European exploration of this hard land and the founding of Corumbá. Look out for a splendid Bororo headdress of macaw feathers, and some wonderful vintage photos of indigenous people and Pantaneiro gauchos herding cattle.

Corumbá

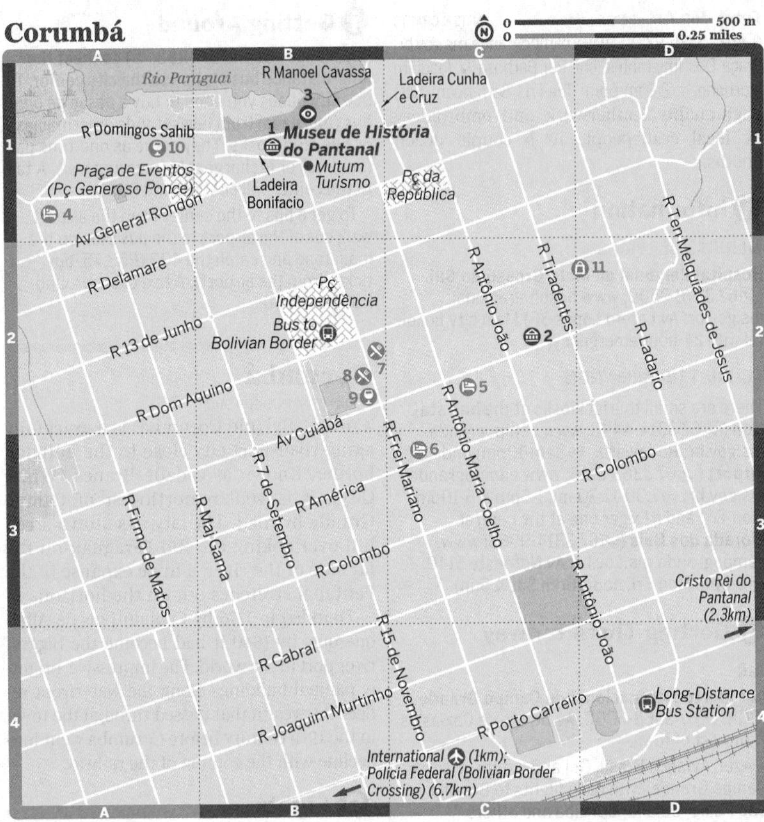

Corumbá

Top Sights
1 Museu de História do Pantanal ... B1

Sights
2 Art Izu ... C2
3 Porto Geral ... B1

Sleeping
4 Hostel Roadriders ... A1
5 Hotel Laura Vicuña ... C2
6 Hotel Nacional Palace ... C3

Eating
7 Avalom Bistrô ... B2
8 Laço do Ouro ... B2

Drinking & Nightlife
9 Dolce Cafe ... B2
10 Viva Bella ... A1

Shopping
11 Casa do Artesão ... D2

Porto Geral PORT

(Manoel Cavassa) Corumbá's riverside is a charming locale with colorful historic facades opposite bobbing boats, some of which are waiting to take you out on a boisterous pleasure cruise on the Paraguai or a fishing trip. You'll find several agencies that book Pantanal excursions, Bolivian traders selling colorful handicrafts and people gathering to watch the spectacular sunsets silhouetting the distinctive cargo pier.

Forte de Coimbra FORT

(☎67 3282-1001; www.eb.mil.br) FREE Located some 80km downriver from Corumbá along Rio Paraguai, this large fort was built in 1775 to repel invaders from Paraguay, which it failed to do quite spectacularly in 1864, when

GETTING TO & FROM BOLIVIA

Bus 102 (R$3.25, 15 minutes) goes from Corumbá's Praça Independência to the Bolivian border hourly (at minimum) from 6am to 7pm. A taxi from the center to the border is around R$45; groups of two or less traveling light are better off using a moto-taxi (R$25).

All Brazilian exit formalities must be completed with the **Polícia Federal** (☎67 3234-7822; www.pf.gov.br; ⏰8am-6pm) at the border. There are often lengthy queues. There's also a tourist information booth (7:30am to 1:30pm Monday to Friday) here. Bolivian immigration is open the same hours as Brazilian immigration. To enter Bolivia, most countries do not need a visa, but citizens of the United States must obtain a visa (US$160) from abroad, via online application or at the **Bolivian Consulate** (☎67 3231-5605; www.cancilleria.gob.bo; 7 de Setembro 47; ⏰visas 8:30-9:30am Mon-Fri) in Corumbá.

In Bolivia *colectivos* (B$5) and taxis (around B$15 to B$25) run the 3km between the border and Quijarro train station for onward travel to Santa Cruz. There are two train options (www.fo.com.bo): the faster and more comfortable *Ferrobus* that departs at 6pm on Monday, Wednesday and Friday (B$235, 13 hours), arriving at 7am, and the cheaper *Expreso Oriental* that leaves at 1pm on Tuesday, Thursday and Sunday (B$100, 16¾ hours), arriving at 5:40am. Buy tickets in advance if you can. The *Ferrobus* makes the return journey from Santa Cruz on Tuesday, Thursday and Sunday at 6pm, arriving at 7am, while the *Expreso Oriental* departs on Monday, Wednesday and Friday at 1:20pm, arriving at 6am.

The road from Puerto Quijarro to Santa Cruz is in decent condition and bus journeys take about half the time as train journeys.

Travelers arriving in Corumbá are often assailed by dodgy characters selling Pantanal tours; hold off and book with a proper operator.

it was overrun by the Paraguayan army. As the fort is on Brazilian army territory, tour agencies have to obtain permission to visit. Tours are done either by boat – a spectacular journey that passes by two impressive caves – or by driving to Porto Morrinho and then continuing by boat.

Expect to pay around R$400 including lunch for a tour. The military base in Corumbá can give you further information on visiting the fort.

Art Izu GALLERY

(Av Cuiabá 558; ⏰1-5pm Mon-Fri) FREE Art Izu is home to one of Corumbá's premier artists, Izulina Xavier. You can't miss it – the giant bird sculptures and bronze statue of São Francisco in the front are stunning and the crazy paving is, well, crazy. You can purchase some handicrafts inside. Ring the well-disguised bell if the doors aren't open.

Tours

Boat and fishing tours around Corumbá, as well as tours of the Pantanal, are available from all travel agencies or in the boat offices along the port road, Manoel Cassava.

The cruises from the old port run in large pleasure boats with lunch, music, caipirinhas and maybe a pool. Most are trips of three hours or so.

Mutum Turismo TOURS

(☎67 3231-1818; www.mutumturismo.com.br; Frei Mariano 17; ⏰8am-6pm Mon-Fri, to 1pm Sat) A reliable and long-established travel agency for Pantanal river cruises. Can recommend reputable guides.

Festivals & Events

★**Carnaval** CARNAVAL

(www.corumba.ms.gov.br; ⏰Feb or Mar) One of Brazil's biggest and best Carnaval celebrations really makes this hot, sleepy backwater come to life. The tradition was imported by naval officers, many from Rio, who found themselves stationed here and felt the need to liven things up.

Sleeping

★**Hostel Roadriders** HOSTEL $

(☎67 3232-8143; www.hostelroadriders.com.br; Firmo de Matos 1; dm/d R$50/130; ❄📶) This super hostel makes a great base. Sturdy, well-spaced bunks in air-conditioned dorms with pretty traditional floor tiles are comfortable, as is a private en-suite room. All upstairs rooms have great views over the river from the balcony. There's a kitchen, bar, barbecue, laundry and secure parking.

Hotel Laura Vicuña HOTEL $
(☎67 3231-5874; www.hotellauravicuna.com.br; Av Cuiabá 775; s/d/tr R$100/150/200; ❄📶) Very central, this budget option has everything you are likely to need (clean rooms, decent mattresses, hot showers) and is well run. It's the best of the many hotels in this price category around town.

Hotel Nacional Palace HOTEL $$
(☎67 3234-6000; www.hnacional.com.br; América 936; s/d R$257/348; ❄@📶🏊) The top hotel in town, the Nacional Palace is popular with visiting fisherfolk. Amenities include a gym and pool, and breakfast is generous. Rooms are comfortable, but not luxurious. By day, Bolivian traders set up colorful handicraft displays out front; by night, you're likely to see ladies of negotiable affection haunting the lobby.

Eating

The best eating options cluster in the center of town. Expect big portions of meat as well as some local river fish.

Laço do Ouro CHURRASCARIA $$
(☎67 3232-5555; www.facebook.com/restaurantelacodeouro; Frei Mariano 556; rodízio R$55, 1 person mains R$35-65; ⏰11am-midnight; 📶) *Corumbaenses* flock to this unpretentious, family-run *churrascaria* for the best meat *rodízio* in town at lunchtimes; dinner is à la carte. Portions are predictably generous, service is attentive and quality is very solid.

Avalom Bistrô INTERNATIONAL $$
(☎67 99841-3005; Frei Mariano 499; mains R$25-70; ⏰6pm-midnight Thu-Tue, 11:30am-3:45pm Sun; 🖉) Avalom's menu pays homage to the diverse groups of Corumbá's residents, with indigenous, Portuguese, French, Spanish and Italian dishes, some of which are executed better than others. Fig salad with gorgonzola and homemade pizza are excellent.

Drinking & Nightlife

Dolce Cafe BAR
(☎67 3232-7333; www.facebook.com/dolcecafecorumba; Frei Mariano 572; ⏰5:30am-11pm; 📶) Locals with huge tankards of beer pack the outdoor tables at this hugely popular cafe in the evenings. The food – fried chicken, burgers and more – is the ideal accompaniment to watching soccer on the big screen.

Viva Bella BAR
(☎67 3232-3396; www.facebook.com/restaurantevivabella; Arthur Mangabeira 1; ⏰11am-1pm Mon, 11am-1pm & 5pm-late Tue-Sat) Viva Bella is perched precariously on a hillside over the Rio Paraguai. From the outdoor deck, watch the sunsets over the Pantanal while sipping beer or caipirinhas, or turn up later for live music (Thursday to Saturday).

Shopping

★**Casa do Artesão** ARTS & CRAFTS
(☎67 3231-2715; www.facebook.com/groups/1759750764321612; Dom Aquino 405; ⏰8:30-11am & 1-5pm Mon-Fri) 🌿 The old prison has swapped inmates for artists; each cell holds a different workshop. There's a strong sustainable focus, with lots of impressive creations from recycled materials. An extraordinary women's social collective, Amor Peixe, produces beautiful things from fish skin, while others weave wickerwork from water plants and fashion fascinating objects from discarded towels and socks.

You'll often find somebody here on the weekends, too.

Getting There & Away

Corumbá is a major transit point for travel to and from Bolivia. To get to Paraguay by river you'll need to strike a private deal with a boat operator down in the port area. It won't be cheap!

BUSES FROM CORUMBÁ

DESTINATION	COST (R$)	TIME (HR)	FREQUENCY	COMPANY
Bonito (bus)	100	6	1 Mon-Sat	Cruzeiro do Sul (www.cruzeirodosulms.com.br)
Bonito (minibus)	102	5	1 daily	Call ☎67 99809-2397
Campo Grande	124	7	8 daily	Andorinha (www.andorinha.com)
Ponta Porã	176	12½	1 Mon-Sat	Cruzeiro do Sul

AIR

Corumbá **international airport** (CMG; 67 3231-3322; Santos Dumont) is 3km west of the town center. The only regular service is an Azul flight that links the city with São Paulo twice a week, once via Bonito.

BUS

From the **long-distance bus station** (Porto Carreiro), regular buses run to Campo Grande. It pays to buy your ticket in advance as services fill up with those crossing the border.

The center can be easily reached on foot from the bus station, or take a moto-taxi for R$5.

Bonito & Around

0XX67 / POP 21,000

This small but thronged town in the southwestern corner of Mato Grosso do Sul has few attractions of its own, but the natural resources of the surrounding area are spectacular, and local authorities have taken the high road in their regulation and maintenance. There are caves with lakes and amazing stalactite formations, beautiful waterfalls and incredibly clear rivers surrounded by lush forest where it's possible to swim eyeball to eyeball with hundreds of fish.

Bonito's long main street, Coronel Pilad Rebuá, is a 3km stretch that is home to everything you are likely to need during your stay.

Activities & Tours

The local government has strict regulations in place for visiting the area's natural attractions, partly because many are on private land and partly to minimize the impact of tourism on pristine areas. Most attractions have a daily limit on the number of visitors they will accept, and an authorized, locally registered guide must accompany visitors at all sites. Not all guides speak English.

Prices of attractions are regulated by their owners, so it makes no difference who you book your tour with. However, transportation is usually only included in the cost when you book through a hotel, not an agency, but it sometimes depends on group size; you should ask in advance.

Snorkeling and *flutuação* (flotation) in Bonito's incredibly clear waters are the main attractions, but remember that sunscreen and insect repellent are not allowed. Many of the best tours take a full day and will include lunch.

In the high season, the most popular tours must be booked in advance, preferably months in advance in the case of small-capacity attractions like Abismo Anhumas. You'll need several days to take in the best of Bonito.

★Abismo Anhumas ADVENTURE

(www.abismoanhumas.com.br; rappelling plus floating R$910, with scuba diving R$1270) Rappel into a gigantic, beautiful cave that culminates in an underground lake. After you make it down the 72m, it's time for a spin around the lake to admire the beautiful rock formations. Then you dive (license required) or snorkel in the frigid underwater world (visibility 30m), with phallic pinnacles rising from the depths, before climbing back out. A heart-stopping experience.

The whole thing is otherworldly – it's Bonito's most unforgettable attraction by a landslide, and limited to 20 visitors per day. You'll usually need to book weeks or months in advance, though cancellations do occur so you may be lucky. You'll need to do a rappel practice session at its **training center** (67 3255-3313; General Osório 681; 8:30-11:30am & 1:30-6pm) the afternoon before your tour.

★Rio da Prata SNORKELING

(www.riodaprata.com.br; 5-hour trip incl lunch R$280; 7:30am-5pm) The marvelous Rio da Prata, 50km south of Bonito, includes a hike through rainforest and some great snorkeling. The latter involves a 3km float downstream along the Rio Olha d'Agua, amazingly crystal clear and full of fish, and Rio da Prata, a little foggier but still fantastic for viewing massive *pacu* and big, scary *dourado*.

Nascente Azul SNORKELING

(67 3255-4505; www.nascenteazul.com.br; adult/child R$220/185; 8am-4pm Wed-Mon) This fabulous *flutuação* attraction, 29km from town, begins with a 1900m forest trek that culminates in your arrival at the breathtakingly beautiful *nascente* (spring), an indigo-colored gateway to the center of the earth. From here you leisurely float your way back to base along a crystal-clear forest stream teeming with fish.

Boca da Onça Ecotour ADVENTURE

(67 3268-1711; www.bocadaonca.com.br; Rodovia Bodoquena, Km 26; hike incl lunch adult/child R$270/216, incl rappelling R$575; 9:30am-6pm) The Boca da Onça Ecotour, 59km northwest of Bonito, is a manicured 4km trail through the forest to a series of eight waterfalls, a

Bonito

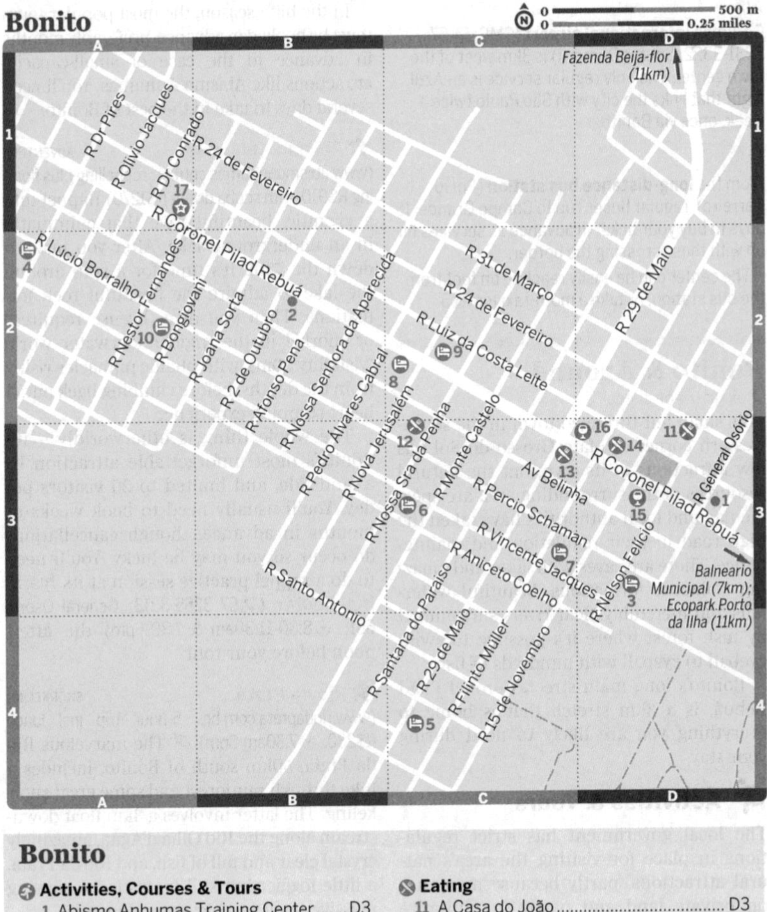

Bonito

Activities, Courses & Tours
1 Abismo Anhumas Training Center D3
2 Boca da Onça Training Center B2

Sleeping
3 Bonito Ecotel D3
4 Bonito HI Hostel A2
5 Hotel Pousada Águas de Bonito C4
6 Papaya Hostel C3
7 Pousada Gira Sol C3
8 Pousada Muito Bonito C2
9 Pousada Remanso C2
10 Pousada Surucuá A2

Eating
11 A Casa do João D3
12 Juanita C3
13 Vício da Gula C3
14 Zapi Zen D3

Drinking & Nightlife
15 Bonito Beer D3
16 Taboa Bar D3

Entertainment
17 Project Jibóia A1

few of which you can take a chilly dip in. It all culminates with the 156m Boca da Onça waterfall, an impressive cascade that takes the state's highest honors.

Rappelling is possible from reportedly the highest platform in Brazil, and there is an excellent lunch and hang time by a fantastic river pool. If you want to rappel, you'll need to complete a course at this outfit's in-town **training center** (☎67 99974-8191; Coronel Pilad Rebuá 1180; ⊙4-9pm) the day before.

DON'T MISS

IT'S CLEAR TO SEE: BONITO IS BEAUTIFUL

If you've never tried freshwater snorkeling in Bonito (or Bom Jardim) before, it's a remarkable experience. You peer at the curious fish surrounding you, the tiny fish nibbling on your skin, marvel at how you can make out the detail of every dead leaf lining the bottom of the river in HD clarity, or suck in your belly as the current carries you over the obstacle course of dead tree trunks. But how did this happy accident of nature happen? The river waters spring from subterranean sources in a limestone base (almost entirely free of clay), which releases calcium carbonate into the water. The calcium carbonate calcifies all impurities in the water, which then sink to the riverbed (this is the reason you're asked to stay afloat and not touch the bottom during river tours). The result is an area filled with natural aquariums surrounded by lush forest – a beautiful environment in which to study the abundant and fascinating fish of the rivers and streams.

Gruta do Lago Azul CAVING
(half-day excursion R$65; ⏲7am-5pm) The centerpiece of this large, vaulted cave is a luminous underground lake with incredibly clear water and seemingly immeasurable depths (actually over 70m by current estimates). Twenty kilometers west of Bonito, it is worth visiting for the strange stalactite formations alone. Wear sturdy footwear.

Buraco das Araras BIRDWATCHING
(☎67 3255-4344; www.buracodasararas.com.br; R$75) A sunset visit to Buraco das Araras, one of the world's largest sinkholes, is usually tagged on to a day out at Rio da Prata and Laguna Misteriosa. It's a 1km walk, complete with two viewpoints, that allows you to watch dozens of scarlet macaws flying home to roost, their metallic cries piercing the air. An impressive spectacle.

Lagoa Misteriosa DIVING, SNORKELING
(☎67 98403-5204; www.lagoamisteriosa.com.br; snorkeling/diving R$158/380; ⏲7:30am-5:30pm mid-Apr–mid-Oct) No one knows the true depth of this crystal-clear *cenote* (natural pool); researchers have only reached a depth of 200m and that's not even the cave lake's deepest part. You can snorkel and marvel at the seemingly infinite blue, interspersed with drowned tree trunks, but it's scuba divers and cave divers (appropriate certification mandatory) who get the best of this watery world.

Lagoa Misteriosa can get rather crowded. From mid-October to mid-April, algae make the visibility poor so it only opens for deeper (25m) diving excursions.

Balneário Municipal SWIMMING
(R$36; ⏲8am-6pm) One of the few natural attractions that doesn't need a guide is the Balneário Municipal, a natural swimming pool on the Rio Formoso with clear water, nice beach and lots of fish, 7km southeast of town. It was closed on our last visit following flood damage; check before heading out there.

You can spend the whole day here and have lunch at the kiosks. Get there by cycling or else moto-taxi (around R$15 one-way).

Sleeping

Bonito's stupendous popularity during peak season (December to March) means that you should book ahead to get the lodgings you want. Out of season, higher-end options may slash their prices by as much as 50%.

Bonito HI Hostel HOSTEL $
(☎67 3255-1022; www.bonitohostel.com.br; Dr Pires 850; dm R$45, d with/without air-con R$150/100;) One of Brazil's top HI hostels, this well-oiled backpacker haunt is a bit far from the action, but perks include hammocks, a pool, large lockers, kitchen, laundry and multilingual staff. Dorms come with private bathrooms, and the private en-suite rooms with air-con (a must in summer!) are hotel quality. The hostel runs tours to all local attractions.

Papaya Hostel HOSTEL $
(☎67 3255-4690; www.papayahostelbonito.com; Vicente Jacques 1868; dm R$35-55, d R$120-160;) This papaya-colored hostel, handily located near the bus station, is the kind of place where backpackers find themselves delaying their departure, seduced by the poolside chill-out area, communal barbecues, fellow travelers to chat with and a plethora of tours organized by the English-speaking owner.

GETTING TO & FROM PARAGUAY

Brazilian formalities take place at a **booth at the airport** (67 3437-0512; www.pf.gov.br; Airport, Rua Batista de Azevedo 770; 8am-6pm Mon-Fri, 10am-1pm & 3-6pm Sat & Sun). Outside of working hours, if you can prove your need to travel is urgent, try the **Federal Police** (67 3437-0500; Av Presidente Vargas 70; 9am-noon & 1-4pm Mon-Fri) in town.

The **Paraguayan immigration office** (+595 336 272 195; www.migraciones.gov.py; Av Internacional 4642, Pedro Juan Caballero, Paraguay; 7am-10pm Mon-Fri, 8am-10pm Sat & Sun) is by Shopping China, a 10-minute walk from the Brazilian office. If you need a visa, head to the **Paraguayan consulate** (67 3431-6312; www.mre.gov.py; Av Presidente Vargas 277; 8am-4pm Mon-Fri) in the center of town.

To change money, go to Calle Mariscal Francisco Solano López near General Díaz, just across the border in Pedro Juan Caballero.

From the bus station on Alberdi in Pedro Juan Caballero, there are hourly buses to Asunción (R$70/G90,000, eight to 10 hours) and Concepción (R$30/G35,000, five hours). There are also flights to Asunción with Sol (www.viajaconsol.com).

Pousada Gira Sol POUSADA **$$**
(67 3255-2677; www.pousadagirasol.com.br; Filinto Müller 813; d R$258-340;) Large and professional, this pousada can feel more like a resort but is a pleasant spot handily close to the center of the action. Rooms are spacious and modern, with tiled floors, hammocks and attractive headboards and furniture from repurposed wood. There's an in-house tour agency but staff aren't at all pushy. The complex surrounds a garden with pool and Jacuzzi.

Bonito Ecotel POUSADA **$$**
(67 3255-3804; www.bonitoecotel.com.br; Nelson Felício dos Santos 1035; r R$280-380;) Very central but still enjoying a peaceful edge-of-town location, with sheep grazing in the garden and trees beyond, the Ecotel is designed along sustainable lines. Helpful staff and comfortable modern rooms with furniture and art from recycled wood make this a very appealing option.

Pousada Muito Bonito POUSADA **$$**
(67 3255-1645; www.pousadamuitobonito.com.br; Coronel Pilad Rebuá 1444; d/tr R$280/340;) On the main street, a flashy facade fronts a simple but pleasing pousada with well-appointed inexpensive rooms in brick around a small courtyard with plunge pool. These folk also run one of the most popular tour agencies in town and are happy to provide plenty of information on the area.

Pousada Remanso POUSADA **$$**
(67 3255-3469; www.pousadaremanso.com.br; Coronel Pilad Rebuá 1515; s/d/tr R$263/329/440, superior d R$421;) Good-value, mid-range hotel right in the heart of town, with hammocks, nicely maintained landscaping and a pool and hot tub. Upstairs rooms may be slightly quieter. There's a large, secure parking area.

Pousada Surucuá POUSADA **$$$**
(67 3255-2337; www.pousadasurucua.com.br; Bongiovani 860; s/d/q R$397/467/672;) This well-kept modern pousada makes for a peaceful base, with a tranquil location a few blocks from the center. Rooms are commodious and contemporary, surrounding a handsome garden with decent-sized pool. Breakfast is an impressive spread, and tea and cake is offered in the afternoon.

Hotel Pousada Águas de Bonito HOTEL **$$$**
(67 3255-2330; www.aguasdebonito.com.br; 29 de Maio 1679; s/d R$488/530, superior s/d R$561/608;) A little out of the center, this two-story retreat comes with a recommended restaurant, peaceful surroundings and helpful staff. A series of chalets house rooms that are modern and spacious; the superior ones on the second level have pleasant patios. There's an in-house tour agency.

Eating

Bonito has a cosmopolitan selection of quality restaurants. Local freshwater fish is the highlight and served everywhere; farmed caiman meat is also common, including in snack-sized portions if you just want to sample it.

Vício da Gula BURGERS $

(☎67 3255-2041; www.facebook.com/viciodagulacafe; Coronel Pilad Rebuá 1852; burgers R$13-24; ⌚3-11:30pm Thu-Mon, from 9am Tue, 9am-5pm Wed) Popular corner spot for great burgers, fries and *açaí na tigela* (a berry-like fruit, in a bowl). There's also all-you-can-eat soups for R$20. The cake display may delay your exit.

★**Juanita** SEAFOOD $$

(☎67 3255-1924; www.facebook.com/juanitarestaurante; Nossa Senhora da Penha 854; portions for 2 people R$65-95; ⌚11:30am-2:30pm & 6:30-10:30pm Wed-Mon) There are a few fish dishes at this likable rustic restaurant, but the star of the show is the chargrilled boneless *pacu* served with plump capers and sides. It's really delicious. Half-portions are available if you ask, which would still serve two. Tables on the sunny front deck are at a premium on warm days; inside, a harpist accompanies your meal.

Ribs and steaks are also available. It opens Tuesdays, too, at busy times.

Zapi Zen PIZZA $$

(☎67 3255-2455; www.facebook.com/zapizenbonitoms; Filinto Müller 573; wraps R$23-27, pizzas R$28-64; ⌚6-11:30pm; ✎) Just off the main drag, this warm-hearted spot serves topnotch pizzas with mostly – but not exclusively – vegetarian toppings. All are brimming with goodness and you can choose between white or wholewheat crusts. There are also wraps: pick from the menu or create your own.

A Casa do João SEAFOOD $$$

(☎67 3255-1212; www.casadojoao.com.br; Nelson Felicio 664a; 1 person mains R$44-80; ⌚11:30am-2:30pm & 6-11:30pm; 📶) 🍃 A famous spot in town for fish, especially renowned for *traíra* (a predatory fish), which comes fried whole. There are also soups, ceviches and several other dishes on offer, many smothered by heavy sauces. It's a big operation but runs very efficiently with solicitous service. All the furniture here is made from reclaimed wood from fallen trees in the area.

Drinking & Nightlife

Bonito Beer MICROBREWERY

(www.facebook.com/bonitobeer; Coronel Pilad Rebuá 2052; ⌚5-11pm Mon-Sat) This tiny microbrewery is in the heart of things. You buy a refillable token, grab a glass and pour your own from the selection of taps out front (our favorite was the American pale ale). Minimum charge is R$30, which gets you just under a liter, but you can always come back if you don't spend it all. There's also G&T on tap.

Taboa Bar BAR

(☎67 3255-1862; www.taboa.com.br; Coronel Pilad Rebuá 1837; ⌚5pm-midnight) A graffiti-clad institution on the main drag where locals and travelers converge over the house special: *pinga (cachaça)* with honey, cinnamon and guaraná. The food ain't bad, either, but the service is lacking. Live music at weekends.

Entertainment

Project Jibóia LIVE PERFORMANCE

(☎67 8419-0313; www.projetojiboia.com.br; Nestor Fernandes 610; R$50; ⌚7pm) Project Jibóia is a one-man crusade to change the world's opinion of snakes by showing that they're not necessarily dangerous and can be lovable. You're treated to a 90-minute stand-up show in Portuguese, complete with audience participation and boa constrictors. You'll practically be swapping spit with the latter by the end of the night.

BUSES FROM BONITO

DESTINATION	COST (R$)	TIME (HR)	FREQUENCY
Campo Grande (bus)	63	6	three daily
Campo Grande (minibus)	80	5	four daily (Vanzella); three daily (Terra)
Corumbá (bus)	102	6	one Mon-Sat
Corumbá (minibus; call ☎67 99809-2397)	100	5	one daily
Foz do Iguaçu (via Dourados or Campo Grande)	210-250	21-24	three daily
Ponta Porã (bus)	78	5½	one daily

Information

Lodgings have all the tourist information you need and will waste no time in telling you what your options are.

Some travel agencies are more helpful than others and can organize English-speaking guides.

Getting There & Away

AIR

There are two weekly flight with **Azul** (www.voeazul.com.br) between Bonito and São Paulo (Campinas) airport on Sundays and Wednesdays (1½ hours); more operate during high season. Some services go via Corumbá.

BUS

Cruzeiro do Sul (www.cruzeirodosulms.com.br) is the principal bus company. **Vanzella** (☎67 3255-3005; www.vanzellatransportes.com.br) and Terra Transportes (p388) run door-to-door services from Campo Grande that are faster and not much more expensive than the regular bus.

For Estrada Parque, catch the 5am Corumbá bus (R$75 to Passo do Lontra, from where your pousada can pick you up). Minibus transfers are also available for R$80 to R$100 per person.

For Foz do Iguaçu you can either head to Campo Grande or Dourados and catch a direct bus from there. There are also various two-stop options. Operators sell through-tickets.

Getting Around

Most of Bonito's attractions are a fair hike from town, and there's no public transport. Some guesthouses lend their guests bicycles, or you can rent a decent mountain bike along the main street for around R$30 per day. Hotels and agencies can arrange transport for an extra R$40 to R$80 per excursion. Vanzella also runs some scheduled departures to popular excursion points and can be chartered.

If you are part of a group, it might end up being more economical to hire a taxi for the full day (R$80 to R$180 depending on the distance). Moto-taxis can also be a good option for solo travelers.

Ponta Porã

☎0XX67 / POP 89,600

It's a strange feeling to cross the street and change countries, but you can do just that in Ponta Porã, a bustling little border town joined at the hip with the Paraguayan town of Pedro Juan Caballero. The beer changes from Skol to Pilsen, you see flasks of *tereré* (iced *maté*) and prices on electronics are slashed – other than that, it's hard to even notice there is a border here (Portunhol vernacular is rampant). There are only two reasons to come: either because you are a member of the hordes of Brazilian bargain hunters, or because you are crossing the border to Paraguay. Extra caution is a good idea at night, but it's not a seedy place despite well-documented drug-trafficking issues.

Sleeping & Eating

Hotel Internacional HOTEL **$**

(☎67 3431-1243; Av Marechal Floriano Peixoto 2604; s/d R$70/140; ❄📶) Popular, central but by no means luxurious, the budget Internacional is a dignified old place with aging – no, aged – rooms and mattresses. All have an air-con system of sorts.

It still uses the old street name in its address, so online maps have it in the wrong place.

Prime Hotel HOTEL **$$**

(☎67 3431-7404; www.phpp.com.br; Av Marechal Floriano Peixoto 3130; r R$195-285; ❄📶) The modern rooms in shades of gray here are some of the best in town. Luxo category rooms are bigger, but all are appealing and comfortable. This hotel was only two months old when we checked it out, so it was bound to look good, but they seemed to be doing things right.

BUSES FROM PONTA PORÃ

DESTINATION	COST (R$)	DURATION (HR)	FREQUENCY	COMPANY
Bonito	78	5½	daily at 6am	Cruzeiro do Sul (www.cruzeirodosulms.com.br)
Campo Grande	85-97	6	7 daily	Cruzeiro do Sul, Expresso Queiroz (www.expressoqueiroz.com.br)
Corumbá	176	12½	daily at 6am	Cruzeiro do Sul
São Paulo	292-358	21	3 daily	Motta (www.motta.com.br)

Hotel Barcelona HOTEL $$

(☎67 3437-2500; www.hotelbarcelona.com.br; Guia Lopes 50; r R$196; ❄@📶🏊) This aging, centrally located high-rise has big rooms that could do with better maintenance, plus a nice pool. Puzzlingly, the hotel logo is the symbol of Madrid.

Lo de Pepe PARAGUAYAN $$

(☎+595 981 169 853; Mariscal Francisco Solano López 1418, Pedro Juan Caballero, Paraguay; mains R$20-60; ⏰11am-2pm & 6-11:30pm Thu-Tue) Warmly decorated and welcoming, this restaurant a street into Paraguay has a long and wide-ranging menu of *picadas* (antipasto plates), pasta, steaks and surubí river fish, as well as cold draft beer. The outdoor seats are the place to watch border town life go by.

Shopping

Shopping China SHOPPING CENTER

(☎+595 986 850002; www.shoppingchina.com.py; Ruta V c/Callejón Internacional, Pedro Juan Caballero; ⏰8am-7pm, food court to 8pm) Go see what all the fuss is about! This megastore has...well, *everything* and is teeming with wide-eyed Brazilians throwing down real after real for substantial discounts on everything from Johnny Walker to Canon.

Getting There & Away

The **bus station** (Água Azul 99) is 4km from the center of Ponta Porã. A local bus (R$3.50) runs between the main bus station and the central local bus station every 45 minutes until 10pm.

As well as buses, there are minibus transfers from Campo Grande to Ponta Porã (R$65) but the schedule is only decided on a weekly basis. Contact 67 98472-1594 by phone or Whatsapp to get the latest.

Ponta Porã's airport had no scheduled flights at time of research, but there was talk of Azul adding it to its network.

Getting Around

Local buses (R$3.50) run the length of Ponta Porã. Taxis charge a hefty R$20 to R$40 for trips around the joint towns.

Bahia

POP 15.2 MILLION

Includes ➡

Salvador....................402
Recôncavo................427
Cachoeira & São Felix....................427
Praia do Forte............430
Morro de São Paulo.... 434
Itacaré........................ 441
Ilhéus..........................443
Porto Seguro............. 447
Lençóis....................... 457
Parque Nacional da Chapada Diamantina...............462

Best Places to Eat

- ➡ Rabanete (p454)
- ➡ Lampião (p461)
- ➡ Restaurante do Senac (p418)
- ➡ Paraíso Tropical (p419)

Best Places to Stay

- ➡ O Céu de Boipeba (p438)
- ➡ Casa do Amarelindo (p415)
- ➡ Pousada Erva Doce (p451)
- ➡ Open House Barra (p416)

Why Go?

Brazil's African heritage comes alive in the staggeringly beautiful Northeastern state of Bahia. The heady blend of two seemingly disparate cultures – classic Portuguese architecture and African drumbeats, Catholic churches and Candomblé (Afro-Brazilian religion) – is unique and, for most travelers, truly intoxicating. Bahia's centerpiece is Salvador, a sprawling colonial city with gilded churches, cobblestone streets, lively festivals, powerful percussion reverberating off old stone walls and capoeiristas (practitioners of capoeira) battling against the backdrops of 16th-century buildings. Beyond the city limits, Bahia awaits with more than 900km of coastline, World Heritage–listed sites, deserted beaches and paradisaical islands. In the south, idyllic coastal villages attract vacationers and divers, while inland, the spectacular Parque Nacional da Chapada Diamantina features waterfalls and quiet hiking paths waiting to be explored.

When to Go

Salvador

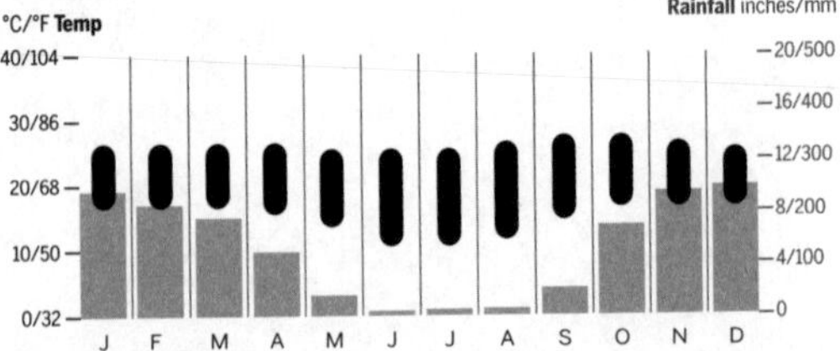

Dec–Mar Crowds during February's Carnaval, meaning packed pousadas and higher prices in Salvador.

Apr–Sep Warm weather, occasional rainy days. *Festas juninas* bring lively events in June.

Oct & Nov Minimal crowds and summery weather.

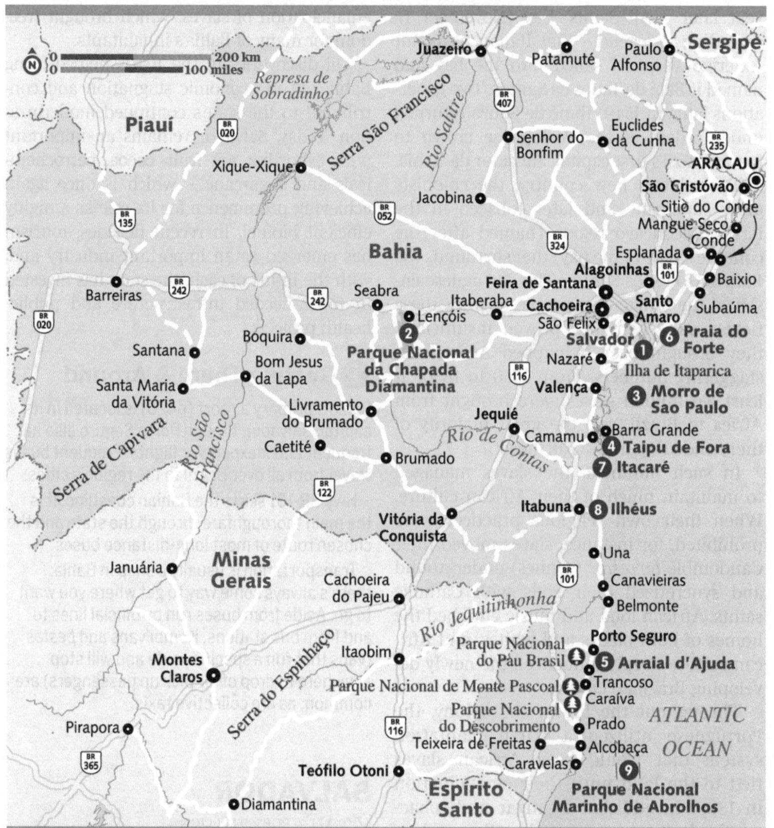

Bahia Highlights

1 Salvador (p402) Following the sounds of the famous Olodum drum corps in Latin America's inspiring Afro-Brazilian capital.

2 Parque Nacional da Chapada Diamantina (p462) Hiking to natural waterslides.

3 Morro de São Paulo (p434) Zooming around the island village on a speedboat tour.

4 Taipu de Fora (p439) Traveling over dirt roads to this beautiful beach on the Peninsula de Maraú.

5 Arraial d'Ajuda (p450) Lingering over alfresco meals and coastal strolls.

6 Praia do Forte (p430) Watching tiny sea turtles hatch on the sand.

7 Itacaré (p441) Catching a wave or taking a capoeira lesson on the sand.

8 Ilhéus (p443) Tracing the footsteps of Brazil's literary great, Jorge Amado.

9 Parque Nacional Marinho de Abrolhos (p457) Diving beneath the deep.

History

Prior to the Portuguese arrival, the region known today as Bahia had a wide variety of ethnic groups scattered inland and along the coast, speaking dozens of languages. Many of the tribes were completely killed off during the brutal colonial era, though some – like the Pataxó – have surviving members alive today. The original Bahians practiced some form of agriculture, raising manioc, sweet potatoes and maize, and hunted, fished and gathered fruits from the forest

Portuguese sailors first made landfall near Porto Seguro in 1500, but it wasn't until one year later – All Saints' Day (November 1), according to legend – that Italian navigator Amerigo Vespucci sailed into the bay and named it Baía de Todos os Santos. Two generations later, in 1549, Tomé de Souza returned under orders of the Portuguese crown to found Brazil's first capital, Salvador da Bahia.

To fuel this new country, the colonists grew sugarcane and later tobacco in the fertile Recôncavo region (named after the concave shape of the bay) that surrounds the Baía de Todos os Santos. The Portuguese enslaved the indigenous people to work these fields, and when they proved insufficient, they brought over kidnapped Africans in staggering numbers. From 1550 to 1850, at least 3.6 million slaves were brought from Africa to Brazil, and the great majority of them ended up in the Northeast.

In such numbers, the slaves managed to maintain much of their African culture. When their own religious practices were prohibited, for instance, slaves moved their Candomblé *terreiros* (venues) underground and syncretized their gods with Catholic saints. African food and music enriched the homes of both blacks and whites, and African culture deeply influenced the newly developing Brazilian culture.

Throughout the life of the colony, the Portuguese utilized a harsh plantation system that would keep African slaves tied to the land until their emancipation in 1888. In addition to sugar and tobacco, the Portuguese created cattle ranches, which spread inland, radiating west into the *sertão* (backlands) and Minas Gerais, then northwest into Piauí.

Primary products were shipped out, while slaves and European luxury goods were shipped in. Bahia was colonial Brazil's economic heartland, with Salvador da Bahia the capital of colonial Brazil between 1549 and 1763. The city was the center of the sugar industry, which sustained the prosperity of the country until the collapse in international sugar prices in the 1820s. During the gold and coffee booms in the south, Salvador continued its decline.

Industrialization in Bahia began in the mid-19th century and continued slowly, with developments in banking and industry, as new rail lines brought goods from the interior to Salvador's large port. Factories appeared and the economy, once a monoculture of the sugarcane industry, diversified. The most important event of the late 19th century was the emancipation of slaves, which brought freedom for many of Bahia's inhabitants.

Oil discoveries in the 1940s helped bring Bahia out of economic stagnation and contributed to the state's continued modernization. Today, Salvador remains an important port, exporting soy, fruit, cocoa, petrochemicals and sugarcane – which is once again achieving prominence for its role as a highly efficient biofuel. In recent decades, tourism has emerged as an important industry and, with the influx of cash, the state has invested in much-needed infrastructure and public-health projects.

Getting There & Around

Bahia's primary airport (p425) is located in its capital, Salvador, though Porto Seguro also has frequent and inexpensive flights. Frequent buses travel from all over Brazil to the region's cities.

Hwy BR-101 skirts the Bahian coastline. It is the main thoroughfare through the state and the chosen route of most long-distance buses.

Transportation is usually a snap in Bahia: there's always some way to get where you want to go. Aside from buses run by official lines to and from bus stations, Kombi vans and *bestas* (vans that run a specific route and will stop anywhere to drop off or pick up passengers) are common, as are collective taxis.

SALVADOR

0XX71 / POP 2.9 MILLION

Salvador da Bahia has an energy and unadorned beauty that few cities can match. Once the magnificent capital of Portugal's New World colony, today Salvador is the pulsating heart of the country's Afro-Brazilian community. Its brilliantly hued center is a living museum of 17th- and 18th-century architecture and gold-laden churches. Wild festivals happen frequently, with drum corps pounding out rhythms against the backdrop of colonial buildings almost daily. Elsewhere in town, a different spirit flows as crowds of religious adherents celebrate and reconnect with African gods at Candomblé ceremonies. In fact, there's no other place in the world where the culture of those brought as slaves from Africa has been preserved as it has been in Salvador – from music and religion to food, dance and martial-arts traditions. Aside from the many attractions within Salvador, a gorgeous coastline lies right outside the city – a suitable introduction to the tropical splendor of Bahia.

History

In 1549 Tomé de Souza landed on Praia Porto da Barra under Portuguese royal orders to found Brazil's first capital, bringing city plans, a statue, 400 soldiers and 400 settlers, including priests and prostitutes. He founded the city in a defensive location: on a cliff top facing the sea. After the first year a city of mud and straw had been erected, and by 1550 the surrounding walls were in place to protect against attacks from the indigenous people that lived in the area prior to the Europeans' arrival. Salvador da Bahia remained Brazil's most important city for the next three centuries.

During its early years, the city depended upon the export of sugarcane and later tobacco from the fertile Recôncavo region at the northern end of Baía de Todos os Santos. Later, cattle ranching was introduced, which, coupled with gold and diamonds from the Bahian interior, provided Salvador with immense wealth, as is visible in the city's opulent baroque architecture.

African slaves were first brought to Salvador in the mid-1500s, and in 1587 historian Gabriel Soares tallied an estimated 12,000 whites, 8000 converted indigenous people and 4000 black slaves. The number of blacks eventually increased to constitute half of the city's population, and uprisings of blacks almost upended Salvador's slavery-reliant economy multiple times.

After Lisbon, Salvador was the most important city in the Portuguese empire. It was the glory of colonial Brazil, famed for its many gold-filled churches, beautiful mansions and numerous festivals. It was also renowned as early as the 17th century for its bawdy public life, sensuality and decadence – so much so that its bay won the nickname Baía de Todos os Santos e de Quase Todos os Pecados (Bay of All Saints and of Nearly All Sins)!

Salvador remained Brazil's seat of colonial government until 1763, when with the decline of the sugarcane industry, the capital was moved to Rio.

In 1798, the city was the stage for the Conjuração dos Alfaiates (Conspiracy of the Tailors), the beginning of a wave of battles between Portuguese loyalists and those wanting independence. It was only on July 2, 1823, with the defeat of Portuguese troops in Cabrito and Pirajá, that the city found peace. At that time, Salvador numbered 45,000 inhabitants and was the commercial center of a vast territory.

For most of the 19th and 20th centuries the city stagnated as the agricultural economy foundered on its disorganized labor and production. Today, Salvador is Brazil's third-largest city, and it has only begun moving forward in the last few decades. New industries such as petroleum, chemicals and tourism have brought wealth to the city's coffers, but the rapidly increasing population is still faced with major economic and social problems.

Sights

The Cidade Alta (the Pelourinho and Carmo) is packed with the city's most impressive sights, though you'll also find worthwhile museums in Vitória, a wonderfully scenic lighthouse in Barra and other fascinating attractions scattered about the city.

Pelourinho

★Pelourinho AREA

(Map p408) The centerpiece of the Cidade Alta is the Pelourinho, a Unesco-declared World Heritage site of colorful colonial buildings and magnificent churches. As you wander the cobblestone streets, gazing up at the city's oldest architecture, you'll realize that the Pelô is not just for tourists. Cultural centers and schools of music, dance and capoeira pack these pastel-colored 17th- and 18th-century buildings.

Largo do Pelourinho SQUARE

(Map p408; Pelourinho) Picture-perfect Largo do Pelourinho is a sloping, triangle-shaped square, once the site of the *pelourinho* (whipping post) – one of several nearby locations where slaves were exposed and punished. After slavery was outlawed in 1835, the neighborhood fell into disrepair; in the 1990s major restoration efforts were initiated to preserve the cobblestone square's colonial houses and churches. Today, the square is the heart of Salvador's historic center.

Casa do Carnaval da Bahia MUSEUM

(Map p408; ☎71 3324-6760; Praça Ramos de Queirós; R$30; ⏲11am-7pm Tue-Sun) The story of Salvador's world-famous Carnaval is told through wonderfully evocative archival video and photographs at this museum which opened in 2018. Even just walking through the museum with its explosions of color and displays of musical instruments and folk-art statues is worth the trip. Downstairs you'll find an excellent gift shop.

Salvador

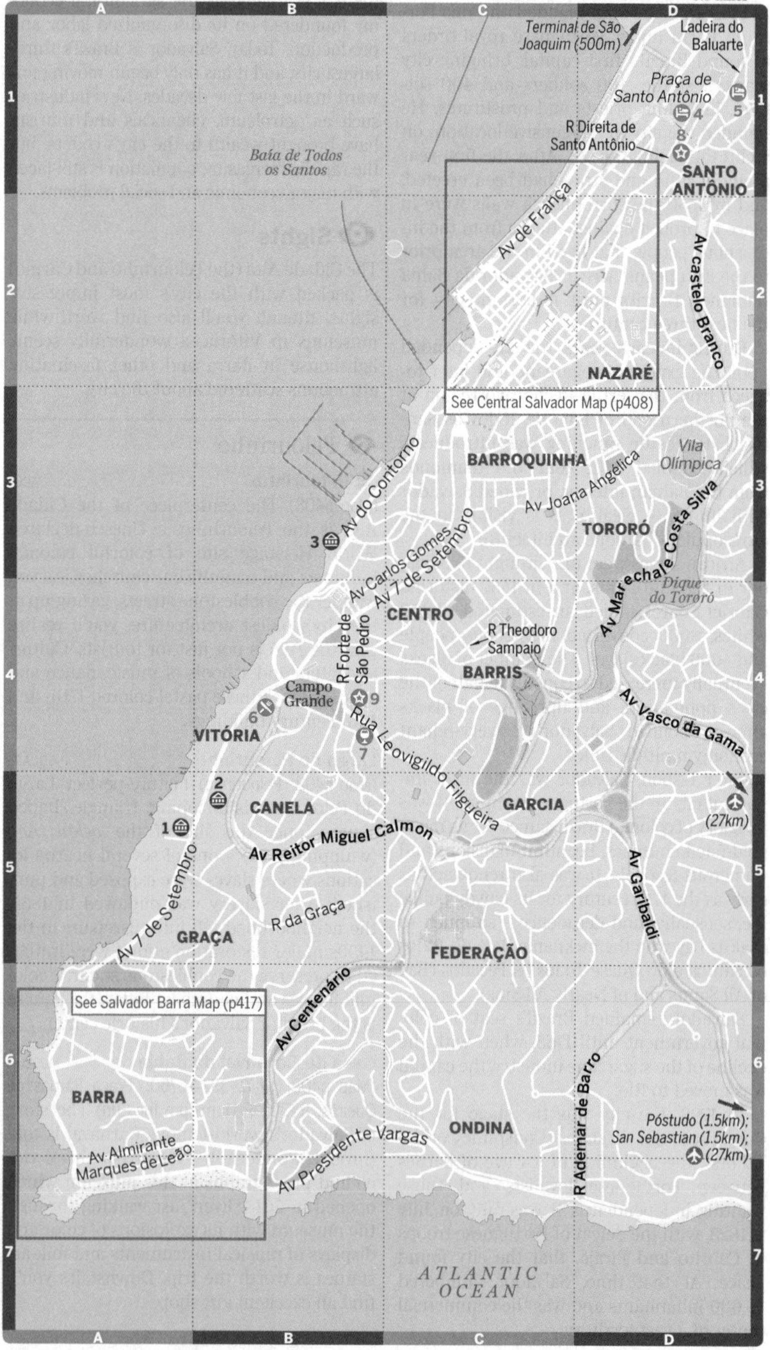

0 — 1 km
0 — 0.5 miles

A B C D
1 2 3 4 5 6 7

Terminal de São Joaquim (500m)
Ladeira do Baluarte
Praça de Santo Antônio
R Direita de Santo Antônio
4 5 8
SANTO ANTÔNIO
Baía de Todos os Santos
Av de França
Av castelo Branco
NAZARÉ
See Central Salvador Map (p408)
Vila Olímpica
BARROQUINHA
Av do Contorno
Av Joana Angélica
TORORÓ
Av Marechale Costa Silva
3
Av Carlos Gomes
Av 7 de Setembro
Dique do Tororó
CENTRO
R Theodoro Sampaio
R Forte de São Pedro
BARRIS
Campo Grande
6 9 7
Av Vasco da Gama
VITÓRIA
Rua Leovigildo Filgueira
2
CANELA
GARCIA
(27km)
1
Av Reitor Miguel Calmon
Av Garibaldi
Av 7 de Setembro
R da Graça
GRAÇA
FEDERAÇÃO
See Salvador Barra Map (p417)
Av Centenário
R Ademar de Barro
BARRA
ONDINA
Póstudo (1.5km); San Sebastian (1.5km); (27km)
Av Presidente Vargas
Av Almirante Marques de Leão
ATLANTIC OCEAN

Salvador

Sights

1 Museu Carlos Costa Pinto A5
2 Museu de Arte da Bahia B5
3 Museu de Arte Moderna B3
Solar do Unhão ....(see 3)

Sleeping

4 Aram Yami Hotel D1
5 Pousada Baluarte D1

Eating

6 Coffeetown Salvador B4

Drinking & Nightlife

7 Beco dos Artistas B4

Entertainment

8 Espaço D'Venetta D1
Jam no MAM ....(see 3)
9 Teatro Castro Alves B4

Fundação Casa de Jorge Amado MUSEUM
(Map p408; ☎71 3321-0070; www.jorgeamado.org.br; Largo do Pelourinho 51; R$5, Wed free; ⏰10am-6pm Mon-Fri, to 4pm Sat) Literary types shouldn't miss a quick visit to the Fundação Casa de Jorge Amado, offering an overview of the life of one of Brazil's best-known writers. A wall of Amado's book covers in every major language demonstrates his widespread popularity, while the museum cafe is a good place to grab a coffee and pastry. Most of the exhibits are in Portuguese, but you will find a few English and French translations here and there.

Igreja e Convento São Francisco CHURCH
(Map p408; Cruzeiro de São Francisco; R$5; ⏰10am-5pm) One of Brazil's most magnificent churches, the baroque Igreja e Convento São Francisco is filled with displays of wealth and splendor. An 80kg silver chandelier dangles over ornate wood carvings smothered in gold leaf, and the convent courtyard is paneled with hand-painted *azulejos* (Portuguese tiles). The complex was finished in 1723.

Elevador Lacerda HISTORIC BUILDING
(Map p408; ☎71 3322-7049; fare R$0.15; ⏰6am-11pm) The beautifully restored, art deco Elevador Lacerda connects the Cidade Alta with Comércio via four elevators traveling 72m in 30 seconds. The Jesuits installed the first manual rope-and-pulley elevator around 1610 to transport goods and passengers from the port to the settlement. In 1868 an iron structure with clanking steam elevators was inaugurated, replaced by an electric system in 1928.

Terreiro de Jesus SQUARE
(Map p408; Praça 15 de Novembro) A colorful intersection of vendors, tourists, capoeiristas and colorful locals, the Terreiro de Jesus is a historic site of religious celebrations, and is ringed by four churches, as well as the 19th-century Faculdade de Medicina Building. The plaza feeds into the Cruzeiro de São Francisco, named for the cross in the square's center.

Praça da Sé SQUARE
(Map p408) The history of Praça da Sé reveals intriguing details about Salvador's development. From 1552 to 1933, the square was the site of the grand Sé Primacial cathedral, overlooking the bay. Sadly, the cathedral and its cemetery were razed in the '30s (roped-off remnants remain today) part of a plan to make wider avenues where streetcars could travel. By the 1950s, Praça da Sé was the home of Salvador's main bus terminal. Today, the plaza sees mostly tourist traffic.

Museu Afro-Brasileiro MUSEUM
(Map p408; ☎71 3283-5540; www.facebook.com/museuafro2; Terreiro de Jesus; adult/child R$6/3; ⏰9am-5pm Mon-Fri, 10am-5pm Sat) Holding one of Bahia's most important collections, the Museu Afro-Brasileiro exhibits wood carvings, baskets, pottery and other artwork and crafts linking Brazilian and African artistic traditions. The highlight of the museum is a room lined with 27 huge, breathtaking carved wooden panels depicting *orishas* (spirits common in Afro-Brazilian spirituality) by Argentine-born Carybé, who is perhaps Salvador's most renowned 20th-century fine artist.

Catedral Basílica CHURCH
(Map p408; Terreiro de Jesus; admission by donation; ⏰9am-5pm Mon-Sat, from 1pm Sun) The Catedral Basílica dates from 1672 and is a marvelous example of Jesuit architecture. The interior is elegant and simple, with marble-covered walls and towering pillars. The sacristy has a beautiful carved jacaranda archway and a painted dome and floor.

Igreja NS do Rosário dos Pretos CHURCH
(Map p408; Largo do Pelourinho; admission by donation; ⏰8am-5pm Mon-Fri, to 7pm Sat) The king of Portugal gave the Irmanidade dos Homens Pretos (Brotherhood of Black Men) the land for the periwinkle-blue Igreja NS do Rosário dos Pretos in 1704. Building in their free time, it took these slaves and freed slaves almost 100 years to complete it.

WORTH A TRIP

IGREJA NOSSA SENHORA DO BONFIM

This famous 18th-century **church** (☎71 3316-2196; www.santuariosenhordobonfim.com; Praça Senhor do Bonfim; ⏲6:30am-6.30pm Mon-Thu & Sat, from 5:30am Fri & Sun), located a few kilometers north of Comércio on the Itapagipe Peninsula, is the source of the *fitas* (colored ribbons) you see everywhere in Salvador, a souvenir of the church and a symbol of Bahia Bonfim's fame derives from its power to effect miraculous cures, making it a popular shrine.

In the Sala dos Milagres (Room of Miracles) on the right side of the church, devotees leave photos, letters and ex votos – wax replicas of body parts representing those that were cured or need curing.

Due to Candomblistas' syncretization of Jesus Christ (Nosso Senhor do Bonfim) with Oxalá (their highest deity), Bonfim is their most important church. Huge services are held here on Friday, Oxalá's favorite day of the week.

If you tie a *fita* around your wrist, you are making a commitment that lasts for months. With each of the three knots a wish is made, which will come true by the time the *fita* falls off. Cutting it off is inviting doom.

Check its website for a full schedule of various services and events held daily.

Plano Inclinado Gonçalves CABLE CAR
(Map p408; Praça da Sé & Guindaste dos Padres, Comércio; R$0.15; ⏲7am-7pm Mon-Fri, to 1pm Sat) After sitting, unused, for almost three years, the 1874 funicular railway Plano Inclinado Gonçalves reopened in 2014. The restored line connects Comércio and Cidade Alta on steep tracks, a scenic alternative to the nearby Elevador Lacerda.

Museu de Arqueologia e Etnologia MUSEUM
(Archaeology & Ethnology Museum; Map p408; ☎71 3283-5533; www.mae.ufba.br; Faculdade de Medicina, Terreiro de Jesus; adult/child R$6/3; ⏲9am-5pm Mon-Fri) Below the Museu Afro-Brasileiro (p405) (one admission ticket gets you into both), the Museu de Arqueologia e Etnologia exhibits indigenous Brazilian pottery, bows and arrows, masks and feather headpieces. Also tucked between the building's arching stone foundations is 19th-century glass and porcelain found during the excavations for the metro.

⊙ Carmo

Igreja da Ordem Terceira do Carmo CHURCH
(Map p408; Largo do Carmo; R$5) The original church, founded in 1636, burnt to the ground; the present neoclassical structure dates from 1828. The nave has a French organ and a baroque altar with a scandalous statue of NS Senhora do Carmo. Church historians claim the statue was modeled on the likeness of Isabel II, daughter of Garcia d'Ávila, the largest landholder in the Northeast.

Escadas do Carmo LANDMARK
(Map p408; btwn R do Passo & Ladeira do Carmo) Leading away from the Pelourinho, the steep Ladeira do Carmo provides access to the Escadas do Carmo, a wide set of steps that were the setting of *O Pagador de Promessas* (1962). This was the first Brazilian film to win a Cannes film-festival award. They lead to the eternally 'closed for renovation' Igreja do Santíssimo Sacramento do Passo (1737).

⊙ Cidade Baixa (Lower City)

Interspersed between the Comércio's modern skyscrapers is some fantastic 19th century architecture in various stages of decay.

Mercado Modelo MARKET
(Map p408; www.mercadomodelobahia.com.br; Praça Visconde de Cayru; ⏲9am-6pm Mon-Sat, to 2pm Sun) The original 1861 Customs House, where slaves were housed when they arrived in Salvador, was partly destroyed in a fire in 1986. After reconstruction, it was transformed into the **Mercado Modelo**. The market is a great spot to pick up tourist trinkets, and a couple of cafes out back provide seating with great views of the bay.

Perhaps owing to the building's grisly history, night guards report ghostly activities after closing hours.

Solar do Unhão HISTORIC BUILDING
(Map p404; ☎71 3117-6139; Av Contorno s/n; ⏲1-6pm Tue-Sun) FREE This well-preserved, 18th-century complex served as a transfer point for sugar shipments: legend says it's haunted by the ghosts of murdered slaves. Today, the building houses the **Museu de Arte Moderna** (MAM; www.jamnomam.com.br/mam) FREE, with a changing display of avant-garde exhibits, a hillside sculpture garden, and popular Saturday-evening jazz

and bossa nova concerts (JAM no MAM; p421) with stunning views over the bay. Take a taxi – the area is known for tourist muggings.

Vitória

The main artery of this leafy suburb is a well-traveled boulevard between Barra and the Pelourinho. You'll find several museums and a few restaurants to enjoy.

Museu Carlos Costa Pinto MUSEUM

(Map p404; ☎71 3336-6081; Av Sete de Setembro 2490; R$10; ⏰2:30-7pm Mon & Wed-Fri, to 6pm Sat) This lovely two-story mansion houses some of Salvador's finest decorative art, from the collection of the patrician couple Carlos de Aguiar Costa Pinto and his wife Margarida, both born in Bahia in the late-19th century. Displays highlight gold, crystal, porcelain and silver pieces, as well as beautifully carved coral jewelry and tortoiseshell fans.

Museu de Arte da Bahia MUSEUM

(Map p404; ☎71 3117-6902; Av Sete de Setembro 2340; ⏰1-7pm Tue-Fri, 2-7pm Sat & Sun) FREE Museu de Arte da Bahia showcases works from Bahian artists, with paintings by José Teófilo de Jesus (1758–1817) and drawings by Argentine artist Carybé. There are also rotating exhibits of contemporary artists. Admission is free unless there is a special program on.

Barra

Barra's busy waterfront has three jutting points of land, occupied by the colonial forts of **Forte São Diogo** (Map p417; Praça Azevedo Fernandes), **Forte Santa Maria** (Map p417; Porto da Barra) and the most impressive of the bunch, Forte de Santo Antônio da Barra.

Forte de Santo Antônio da Barra HISTORIC BUILDING

(Map p417; Largo do Farol da Barra s/n) Built in 1698, Bahia's oldest fort is more commonly called the Farol da Barra for the lighthouse (South America's oldest) within its walls. In addition to having superb views, the fort houses an excellent nautical museum, with relics and displays from the days of Portuguese seafaring, plus exhibits on the slave trade.

★**Museu Náutico da Bahia** MUSEUM

(Nautical Museum of Bahia; Map p417; ☎71 3264-3296; www.museunauticodabahia.org.br; Largo do Farol da Barra s/n, Forte de Santo Antônio da Barra; adult/student & senior R$15/7.50; ⏰9am-6pm Tue-Sun, daily Jan & Jul) This excellent nautical museum in Forte de Santo Antônio da Barra contains relics and displays from the days of Portuguese seafaring, plus exhibits on the slave trade. It also offers superb views on the surrounds. All information is offered in both Portuguese and English – a rarity in Bahia. If you only have time for one museum in Salvador, this is the one.

WORTH A TRIP

ILHA DE ITAPARICA

The Baía de Todos os Santos, occupying 1000 sq km, is Brazil's largest bay, containing 56 islands rich with lush vegetation and historic architecture. The most popular escape for residents of Salvador is the island of Itaparica. The shores are lined with vacation homes, and while the beaches are only average, many travelers enjoy taking a day trip to the bars, restaurants and relaxed atmosphere of the likable island town of **Mar Grande**, 9km south of the transport hub of **Bom Despacho**.

Guarding the northern tip of the island, the **Forte de São Lourenço** (1711) was built by Dutch invaders and figured prominently in Bahia's battle for independence in 1823. In the center of the island, a huge tree wraps its roots around and grows through the ruins of the **Igreja Baiacu** church. **Praia Barra Grande** is Itaparica's finest public beach. It has clear water and weekend homes, and lies in front of its namesake village. Plenty of casual restaurants, clustered near the ferry dock, serve Bahian-style seafood with bay views.

The boat journey from Salvador is half the fun. Passenger ferries (Monday to Saturday/Sunday and holidays R$7/8.50, 40 minutes, every 30 minutes, 6:30am–8pm) run between Salvador's Terminal Marítimo Turístico (p426) and Terminal Maritimo De Mar Grande in Vera Cruz on the island (R$5.60/7.40, 5am–6:30pm). Taxis and shared vans wait just outside to whisk you off to Barra Grande (taxi/van R$40/5, 30 minutes) and other parts of the island. You can try to negotiate with the taxis for a better rate. The vans are cheap but uncomfortable and don't stop right on the beach.

Central Salvador

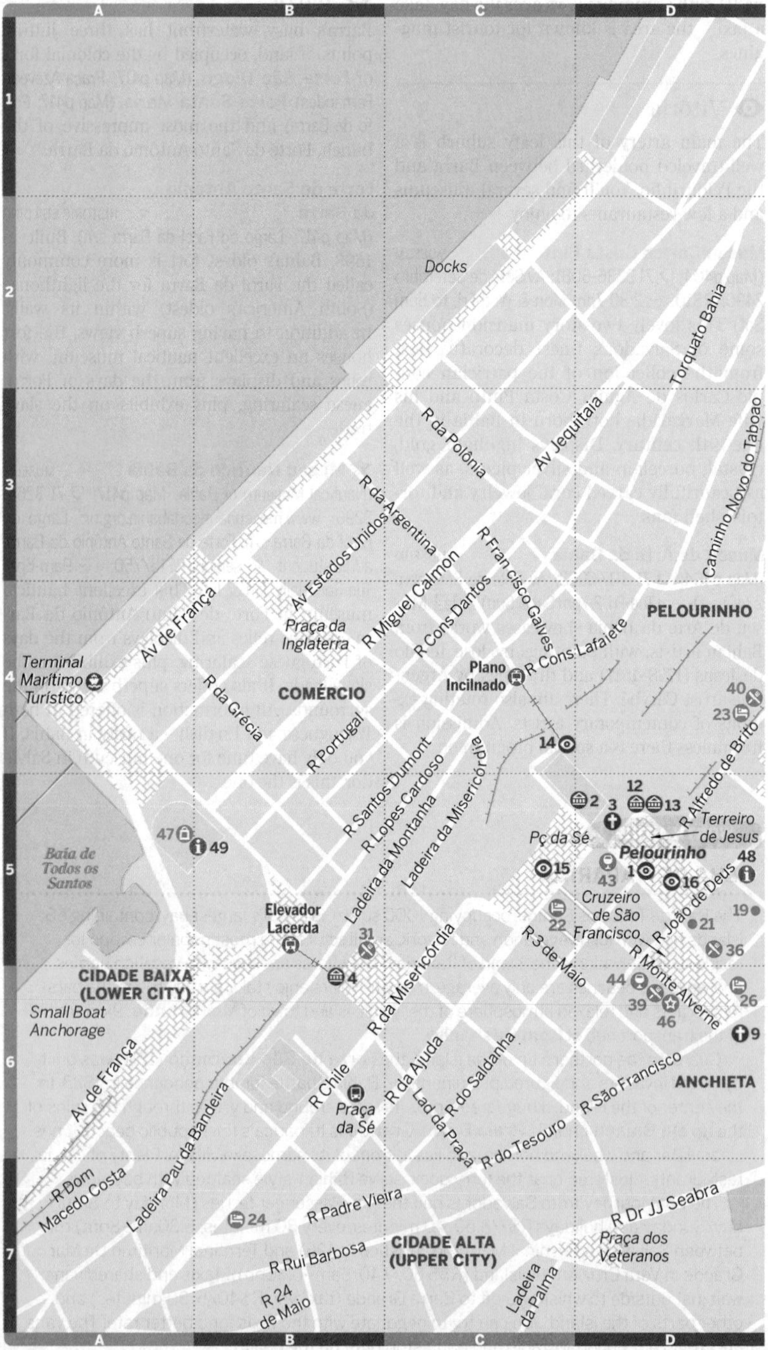

A B C D
1 2 3 4 5 6 7

Docks
Torquato Bahia
R da Polônia
Av Jequitaia
Caminho Novo do Taboao
R da Argentina
Av Estados Unidos
R Miguel Calmon
R Francisco Galves
R Cons Dantos
Praça da Inglaterra
Av de França
PELOURINHO
R Cons Lafaiete
Plano Incilnado
Terminal Marítimo Turístico
COMÉRCIO
R da Grécia
R Portugal
R Santos Dumont
R Lopes Cardoso
Ladeira da Montanha
Ladeira da Misericórdia
R Alfredo de Brito
Terreiro de Jesus
Pç da Sé
Pelourinho
Baía de Todos os Santos
Cruzeiro de São Francisco
R João de Deus
Elevador Lacerda
R 3 de Maio
R Monte Alverne
CIDADE BAIXA (LOWER CITY)
Small Boat Anchorage
R da Misericórdia
R Chile
R da Ajuda
R do Saldanha
Lad da Praça
R São Francisco
ANCHIETA
Praça da Sé
Ladeira Pau da Bandeira
R do Tesouro
R Dom Macedo Costa
R Padre Vieira
R Dr JJ Seabra
CIDADE ALTA (UPPER CITY)
Praça dos Veteranos
R Rui Barbosa
R 24 de Maio
Ladeira da Palma

1 2 3 4 9 12 13 14 15 16 19 21 22 23 24 26 31 36 39 40 43 44 46 47 48 49

Beaches

When locals talk about going to a city beach, they're usually referring to Barra. **Praia Porto da Barra**, on a horseshoe-shaped stretch of coast, is small, picturesque, usually crowded, loaded with vendors selling everything imaginable, and a great place to be at sunset. The bay's waters are clear and calm, and the people-watching is fantastic. To the left of the lighthouse, **Praia do Farol da Barra** has a beach break popular with surfers at high tide, and tidal pools popular with children and families at low tide.

Smaller crowds and an unpolluted Atlantic are about 40 minutes' bus travel east from the center (or more with traffic). Calm seas lap on flat, white sands with *barracas* (stalls) and swaying palms at popular beaches **Piatã** (25km) and **Itapuã** (27km). As you reach the beaches of **Stella Maris** (31km) and **Flamengo** (33km), the waves get progressively stronger, *barracas* begin to space out, and sand dunes and more greenery create a more natural setting. Catch an Itapuã, Aeroporto or Praia do Flamengo bus, making sure it goes up the coast *(via orla)* and as far as you are going.

Courses

Capoeira, Dance & Percussion

Classes in capoeira, African dance and percussion are easily arranged through hostels and pousadas (guesthouses) in the Pelourinho. Course prices vary depending on season, availability and the number of people in your party, but generally you can expect to pay anywhere from R$55 to R$120 per hour for a class.

Associação Brasileira de Capoeira Angola CAPOEIRA

(Map p408; ☎71 8824-7869; www.facebook.com/abcangola; Maciel de Baixo 38; prices vary; ⊙classes 6pm Mon & Wed; 👪) This friendly capoeira association (known as ABCA) runs classes open to all ages, including children five and older. Be sure to wear comfortable, loose-fitting pants you can move around in.

Associação Artística e Cultural Diaspora DANCING

(Diáspora Art Center; Map p408; ☎71 3323-0016; Rua das Laranjeiras 44; prices vary; ⊙10am-6pm Mon-Fri) Stop in to inquire about the latest schedule of classes in traditional and contemporary Afro-Brazilian dance, capoeira and percussion.

Central Salvador

Top Sights
1 Pelourinho D5

Sights
2 Casa do Carnaval da Bahia D5
3 Catedral Basílica D5
4 Elevador Lacerda B6
5 Escadas do Carmo E3
6 Escola Olodum E6
7 Fundação Casa de Jorge Amado E4
8 Igreja da Ordem Terceira do Carmo F2
9 Igreja e Convento São Francisco D6
10 Igreja NS do Rosário dos Pretos E4
11 Largo do Pelourinho E4
Mercado Modelo .... (see 47)
12 Museu Afro-Brasileiro D5
13 Museu de Arqueologia e Etnologia D5
14 Plano Inclinado Gonçalves C4
15 Praça da Sé C5
16 Terreiro de Jesus D5

Activities, Courses & Tours
17 Associação Artística e Cultural Diaspora E6
18 Associação Brasileira de Capoeira Angola E4
19 Fundação Mestre Bimba D5
20 SENAC E4
21 Toursbahia D5

Sleeping
22 Bahiacafé Hotel C5
23 Casa do Amarelindo D4
24 Fera Palace Hotel B7
25 Hostel Galeria 13 .... E5
26 Hotel Villa Bahia D6
27 Laranjeiras Hostel E6
28 Pestana Convento do Carmo E2
29 Pousada do Boqueirão F1
30 Studio do Carmo E3

Eating
31 A Cubana B5
32 A Cubana E4
33 Bar Zulu E6
34 Cafélier E2
35 Casa da Roça E3
36 Cuco Bistrô D5
37 Dona Chika-ka E5
38 Maria Mata Mouro E6
39 O Coliseu D6
40 Pelô Bistrô D4
41 Pysco F2
42 Restaurante do Senac E4

Drinking & Nightlife
Casa do Amarelindo Bar .... (see 23)
43 O Cravinho D5
44 Odoyá D6

Entertainment
45 Balé Folclórico da Bahia E4
Bar Fundo do Cravinho .... (see 43)
46 Topázio D6

Shopping
47 Mercado Modelo A5

Information
48 Bahiatursa D5
49 Bahiatursa Mercado Modelo B5
50 Grupo Gay da Bahia E5
51 Salvador Central E4

Fundação Mestre Bimba CAPOEIRA
(Map p408; ☎71 3322-0639; www.capoeiramestrebimba.com.br; Rua das Laranjeiras 01) A school run by the son of the founder of Capoeira Regional, Mestre Bimba.

Cooking

SENAC COOKING
(Map p408; ☎71 3186-4000; www.ba.senac.br; Largo do Pelourinho 13-19; from R$180; ⏲9-11am & noon-4:30 Mon-Fri) A must-see for foodies, SENAC is a Bahian culinary school where both locals and tourists take cooking classes – one course focuses solely on the preparation of popular street foods like *acarajé* (Bahian fritters made of brown beans and dried shrimp fried in palm oil).

Language

Hostels and pousadas (guesthouses) in Salvador can recommend language courses – a minimum one-week commitment is common – and private teachers. Prices start around R$530 a week for a spot in a group class. Check the schools' websites for the latest details and promotions.

Idioma Escola de Português LANGUAGE
(Map p417; ☎71 98107-3825; www.portugueseinbrazil.com; Florianópolis 96, Barra; 1 week for up to 5 people R$458; ⏲8am-6pm Mon-Fri) Convenient if you're staying in Barra, this language school offers group classes and private sessions in addition to cultural excursions like Bahian cooking workshops and scuba-diving classes.

Diálogo LANGUAGE
(Map p417; ☎71 3264-0053; www.dialogo-brazilstudy.com; Dr João Pondé 240, Barra; 1 week of classes from R$526; ⏲9am-6pm Mon-Sat) Language classes here get mixed reviews from travelers, though some teachers are reportedly

excellent. Benefits include language exchange with Brazilian students, city excursions and samba classes. Diálogo also specializes in arranging homestays with local families.

Tours

Toursbahia TOURS

(Map p408; ☎71 3320-3280; www.toursbahia.com.br; Cruzeiro de São Francisco 4, Pelourinho; prices vary; ⏰9am-6pm Mon-Sat) Toursbahia is a multilingual agency offering local and national tours.

Salvador Bus TOURS

(Map p417; ☎71 3356-6425; www.salvadorbus.com.br; Av Sete de Setembro s/n; adult/child R$65/50; ⏰9:30am-6:45pm Mon-Sat) If you're short on time, climb aboard the open-air Salvador Bus at Farol da Barra, the Mercado Modelo or a number of other downtown destinations; the hop-on, hop-off sightseeing bus offers multilingual tours.

Festivals & Events

Procissão do Senhor Bom Jesus dos Navegantes RELIGIOUS

(⏰Jan 1) A maritime procession transports the image of Bom Jesus from Igreja NS da Conceição in Cidade Baixa north along the bay to Igreja de NS da Boa Viagem. A festival ensues on Praia da Boa Viagem.

Festas de Reis RELIGIOUS

(⏰Jan 6) On the Dia de Reis, a procession of the *reis magos* (wise men) statues travels to a *crèche* (nursery) in the Igreja da Lapinha.

Lavagem do Bonfim RELIGIOUS

(⏰2nd Thu Jan) Salvador's biggest festival outside of Carnaval honors the saint with

SALVADOR'S CARNAVAL

Carnaval in Salvador is billed as 'the world's largest party'. It's a debatable distinction, but as the organizers explain, while Rio de Janeiro's Carnaval may draw more people, Salvador's Carnaval occupies more physical space (several kilometers at a time) than its sister party in A Cidade Maravilhosa. Either way, it's a huge party, attracting upwards of two million revelers for six straight days of revelry before Ash Wednesday. Each day, the festivities kick off around 5pm every afternoon and wind down around 5am.

The focus is on music, namely nationally famous city bands playing *axé* and *pagode* (Bahia's pop music) atop creeping *trios elétricos* (long trucks loaded with huge speakers). Between them march a few *blocos afros* (groups with powerful drum corps promoting Afro-Brazilian culture) and *afoxés* (groups tied to Candomblé traditions). A *trio* (drum corps), together with its followers grouped in a roped-off area around it, form a *bloco*. People pay big bucks for the *abadá* (outfit) for their favorite band, mostly for prestige and the safety of those ropes. Choosing to *fazer pipoca* (be popcorn) in the street is still a fine way to spend Carnaval, as you'll see a variety of music and be spared the hassle involved with picking up the *abadá*.

There are three major parade circuits: Dodô, between Barra and Ondina along Av Oceânica; Osmar or 'the Avenidas', between Campo Grande and Praça Castro Alves along Av Sete de Setembro; and Batatinha in the Pelourinho.

Crowds pose the greatest threat during Carnaval, so be aware of your surroundings. A large police presence helps to keep violence to a minimum. On the Barra–Rio Vermelho circuit, avoid the section where the coastal road narrows near the Morro do Cristo – the tension heats up there.

Otherwise, if you're planning on spending Carnaval in Salvador, the best thing to do is to plan ahead: many hostels and pousadas (guesthouses) offer packages, but they tend to fill up quickly. It's advisable to look closely at a city map before committing to anything: some city neighborhoods can be so noisy during Carnaval that you wouldn't be able to sleep if you wanted to. Many locals living in the Barra neighborhood clear out completely for Carnaval, renting out their apartments and houses to tourists, which is another accommodation option if you're up for the adventure.

For more information and details on specific events and schedules, log onto the official online portal for Salvador's Carnaval at www.carnaval.salvador.ba.gov.br. For English-language background on the music at the center of the event, check out the helpful page at www.bahia-online.net/Carnival.htm.

Candomblé

Candomblé religion is deeply rooted in Bahian culture and connects countless Afro-Brazilians to a long line of West African ancestry.

African Origins

Candomblé is the most orthodox of the religions brought from Africa by the Nago, Yoruba and Jeje peoples. Candomblé is an African word denoting a dance in honor of the gods. Afro-Brazilian rituals are directed by a *pai de santo* or *mãe de santo* (literally 'saint's mother or father' – the Candomblé priests) and practiced in a *casa de santo* or *terreiro* (house of worship). The ceremonies are conducted in the Yoruba language.

Orixás

The religion centers around *orixás* (deities). Like the gods in Greek mythology, each *orixá* has a unique personality and history. Candomblé followers believe that every person has a particular deity watching over them – from birth until death. A person's *orixá* can be identified when a *pai* or *mãe de santo* makes successive throws with a handful of *búzios* (shells), in a divination ritual known as Jogo dos Búzios (Casting of Shells). The position of the shells is used to interpret one's luck, one's future and one's past relationship with the gods. Although *orixás* are divided into male and female types, there are some that can switch from one sex to the other, such as Logunedé, son of two male gods, Ogun and Oxoss.

1. Festa de Iemanjá, Salvador (p414)
2. Food offerings to *orixás* in a *terreiro*
3. Candomblé priestess, Salvador (p411)

Candomblé in Practice

To keep themselves strong and healthy, followers of Candomblé give food or other offerings to please their respective *orixás*. For example, to Iemanjá, the goddess or queen of the sea, one should give perfumes, flowers, combs and mirrors. Oxúm, god of fresh waters and waterfalls, is famous for his vanity, and is honored with earrings, necklaces, champagne and honey. In Bahia and Rio, followers of the Afro-Brazilian religion turn out in huge numbers for the festival held during the night of December 31 and on New Year's Day – and in Salvador, on February 2. Millions of Brazilians go to the beach at this time to pay homage to Iemanjá. Flowers, perfumes, fruits and even jewelry are tossed into the sea to please the mother of the waters, or to gain protection and good luck in the new year.

Attending a Candomblé Ceremony

Ceremonies take place in richly decorated halls called *terreiros*. Drummers pound out powerful rhythms while the mostly female dancers, chanting in Yoruba, glide in a counterclockwise circle, representing the rolling back of the centuries, as they reach out to their ancestors. A festive, celebratory atmosphere prevails, with the *mãe de santo* or *pai de santo* presiding. The chiming of bells conjures the spirits: when a spirit arrives, those dancing may take on the attributes of the *orixá* in question. A good list of *terreiros* can be found at www.salvadorcentral.com.

Bahia's largest following – Senhor do Bonfim, associated with Candomblé. A procession of *baianas* (women dressed as Bahian 'aunts') in ritual dress carrying buckets of flowers walk 6km from Cidade Baixa to Igreja NS do Bonfim.

Festa de Iemanjá RELIGIOUS
(Feb 2) Perhaps Candomblé's most important festival, the event pays homage to the *orixá* (deity) Iemanjá, goddess of the sea and fertility. Devotees descend on Praia Rio Vermelho in the morning, where ceremonies are held to bless offerings of flowers, cakes, effigies and perfume bottles. The ensuing street festival goes until night and is packed with people and some of Salvador's best bands.

Festa de São João da Bahia RELIGIOUS
(www.saojoaobahia.com.br; late Jun) Pyrotechnics, street parties and *forró* (popular music of the Northeast) performances spring up all over town for a week near the end of June. Bahia's so-called *festas juninas* (June celebrations) take place in Salvador and throughout the state.

Festa de NS da Conceição RELIGIOUS
(Dec 8) Candomblistas honor the saint's *orixá* alter ego, Iemanjá, with a procession and ceremonies in Cidade Baixa.

Passagem do Ano Novo NEW YEAR
(Dec 31) New Year's Eve is celebrated with all the zest of Carnaval, especially on the beaches.

Sleeping

Pelourinho

Staying in the Pelourinho means being close to the action, but the beach suburbs are mellower (and just a short bus or taxi ride away). Santo Antônio is a peaceful neighborhood with classy pousadas in renovated old buildings just a short walk from the Pelourinho. Reservations during Carnaval are essential.

★**Hostel Galeria 13** HOSTEL $
(Map p408; 71 3266-5609; www.hostelgaleria13.com; Inacio Acciole 23, Historic Center; dm/d from R$40/135;) Located in an old colonial house complete with a swimming pool and a Moroccan-style lounge (rarities at any hostel), but especially in one at such a great location in the middle of the historic center – Galeria 13 is a huge hit with backpackers. Breakfast is served till noon, and nonguests are welcome to hang out.

Laranjeiras Hostel HOSTEL $
(Map p408; 71 3321-1366; www.laranjeirashostel.com.br; Rua da Ordem Terceira 13; dm/d R$44/98;) This cheerful colonial mansion-

turned-hostel is one of the best budget options in the Pelô. High-ceilinged rooms range from dorms to comfortable suites – save cash by choosing a room with a fan instead of air-conditioning. Perks include kitchen access, laundry facilities and an on-site crêperie.

Bahiacafé Hotel BOUTIQUE HOTEL **$$**
(Map p408; ☎71 3322-1266; www.bahiacafehotelsalvador.com; Praça da Sé 22; s/d/tr from R$179/233/287;) This chic but low-key boutique hotel has fashionably outfitted rooms and an excellent location close to the center of the action in the Pelourinho. The lobby cafe, filled with locally produced artwork and open to the public, is the perfect spot for a quick cappuccino during an afternoon of sightseeing.

★**Casa do Amarelindo** BOUTIQUE HOTEL **$$$**
(Map p408; ☎71 3266-8550; www.casadoamarelindo.com; Portas do Carmo 6; d from R$509, with view from R$594;) Inside a 19th-century colonial mansion on a historic block, this charming boutique hotel is truly a gem. Ten impeccably outfitted guest rooms have first-class bedding, hot tubs or rainfall showers, and huge windows; there's an adorably petite rooftop swimming pool, a popular bistro (p418) and a small fitness center. No children under age 14 are permitted.

Hotel Villa Bahia BOUTIQUE HOTEL **$$$**
(Map p408; ☎71 3322-4271; www.lavillabahia.com; Largo do Cruzeiro de São Francisco 16; d R$708-982;) Occupying a pair of restored Portuguese-style colonial houses, this sustainably run boutique hotel (practices include recycling and employment of local craftspeople) has 17 rooms with hardwood floors, shuttered windows and antique furnishings from heavy armoires to twinkling chandeliers. There's a panoramic terrace and plunge pool, plus a good organic restaurant that's open to the public.

Fera Palace Hotel HISTORIC HOTEL **$$$**
(Map p408; ☎71 3266-0487; www.ferapalacehotel.com.br; Chile 20; r/ste from $670/1396;) Sleep inside a living piece of Salvador's history at this newly restored boutique hotel. The facade of the building still retains its 1930s art deco charm, but inside everything has been given a luxurious modern makeover with amenities including a rooftop pool and spa.

Carmo & Santo Antônio

Many of the city's most charming (and best-value) pousadas are located in this neighborhood. It pays to look around online before booking a room.

Pousada Baluarte POUSADA **$$**
(Map p404; ☎71 3327-0367; Ladeira do Baluarte 13; d with/without bathroom R$155/200;) Run by a friendly French-Brazilian couple, Baluarte feels like a B&B, with a welcoming, homelike ambience and just five rooms with hardwood floors and beautiful block prints by a local artist. A delicious breakfast is served on the veranda. It's right off the trendy Praça de Santo Antonio and a 10-minute walk from the Pelourinho.

Pousada do Boqueirão POUSADA **$$**
(Map p408; ☎71 3241-2262; www.pousadaboqueirao.com.br; Direita de Santo Antônio 48; d/ste from R$150/230;) Two early-20th-century houses have been joined together to form this elegant guesthouse, tastefully decorated with antiques and artwork. Spacious common rooms back onto a porch with a fantastic bay view, where breakfast is served.

Studio do Carmo BOUTIQUE HOTEL **$$**
(Map p408; ☎71 3326-2426; www.studiodocarmo.com; Ladeira do Carmo 17; d/tr from R$218/272;) The location of this historic boutique hotel is iconic: directly across from the Escadas do Carmo (p406). Try to snag the triple room which has a balcony overlooking them. The rooms are large and

REVIVING A LANDMARK: THE PALACE HOTEL

An art deco landmark immortalized in literature, the Palace Hotel had been closed for more than a decade. But it was the pinnacle of glamour in its heyday. The hotel opened in 1934 and hosted famous guests from Orson Welles to Carmen Miranda; Jorge Amado chose its ballroom as the setting for a memorable scene in his novel *Dona Flor e Seus Dois Maridos (Dona Flor and Her Two Husbands)*.

Now, the newly crowned Fera Palace Hotel has reopened after a multi-milllion-dollar restoration overseen by the Brazilian entrepreneur Antonio Mazzafera and the noted Scandinavian architect Adam Kurdahl. The hotel has around 100 guest rooms and suites, two restaurants, and a swimming pool with views over the bay. It's part of a larger effort to revive the neighborhood – keep your eye on this pocket of the old city that's being called the 'Bahia Design Destrict.'

AFRICAN SLAVE ARTISANS

African slaves played a key role in building the culture of the Pelourinho. Forced to work on their masters' churches, and prohibited from practicing their own religion, these enslaved artisans expressed themselves through their work. At Igreja e Convento São Francisco (p405), the faces of the cherubs are distorted, and some angels given noticeably large genitals, while others appear pregnant. Most of these creative touches were chastely covered by 20th-century sacristans. The polychrome figure of São Pedro da Alcântara by Manoel Inácio da Costa shows a figure suffering from tuberculosis – just like the artist himself. One side of the saint's face is more ashen than the other, so he appears to become more ill as you walk past him. José Joaquim da Rocha painted the entry hall's ceiling using perspective technique, a novelty during the baroque period.

Meanwhile, over at Igreja da Ordem Terceira do Carmo (p406), the artist known as O Cabra (Half-Caste) was hard at work on his infamous statue of Nossa Senhora do Carmo. O Cabra was a slave with no artistic training, and he was reportedly besotted with Isabel II, daughter of the rich landholder Garcia d'Ávila. He supposedly modeled the Virgin on Isabel II's likeness, and gave African facial features to the Christ child cradled in the statue's arms. Could this be what O Cabra imagined their love child would look like? O Cabra took eight years to finish the life-size image of Christ (1630), with blood made from 2000 rubies. It's on display in the church's small museum.

a bit outdated, but the hotel has more than enough charm (all of the art on the walls is for sale!) to make up for it.

Pestana Convento do Carmo HOTEL **$$$**
(Map p408; 71 3327-8400; www.pestana.com/en/pestana-convento-do-carmo; Rua do Carmo 1; ste from R$485;) Set in a restored 17th-century convent, this magnificent hotel has elegantly furnished rooms with old-world details and modern comforts, and even more impressive common areas. There's a stone chapel and arched walkways around the cloister.

Aram Yami Hotel BOUTIQUE HOTEL **$$$**
(Map p404; 71 3242-9412; www.aramyamihotel.com; Direita de Santo Antonio 132; ste from R$495;) How about taking in the sunset from an infinity pool overlooking the bay? The dream is a reality at the exclusive Aram Yami Hotel, a chic urban getaway that's practically a vacation in itself. The terraces offer spectacular views, six suites are spacious and plush, and the staff is particularly helpful with planning cultural excursions.

Barra & Coastal Suburbs

Of all the beachside suburbs, happening Barra attracts the majority of visitors due to its proximity to the Pelourinho.

★Open House Barra POUSADA **$**
(Map p417; 71 99142-1285; www.openhousebarra.com; Bernardo Catarino 137, Barra; dm from R$44, r with/without bathroom from R$118/69;) This fantastically colorful and homey place is run by professional artists with deep connections to the local music, dance and film community. Musicians and capoeira demonstrations periodically take place at the hostel, especially during Carnaval, when the guesthouse offers one of Salvador's most memorable party experiences. Special packages and classes, including Portuguese language, can be booked through the hostel.

Pousada Estrela do Mar POUSADA **$$**
(Map p417; 71 3022-4882; www.estreladomarsalvador.com; Afonso Celso 119, Barra; d from R$220;) This white stucco house with dark-blue shutters – very Portugal-meets-the-tropics – is surrounded by greenery, while inside plain white walls set off bright Bahian paintings and vibrant blue tilework. The location is close to the beach on a mellow, tree-shaded street.

Pousada Bamboo da Barra POUSADA **$$**
(Map p417; 71 3033-4448; https://pousadabamboodabarra.com.br; Afonso Celso 485; d/tr R$153/180;) The rooms at this guesthouse (formerly a popular hostel) are small and simple, but the location is fantastic and the price is right. Travelers appreciate the friendly staff and ample outdoor space. Note that the doubles are small and that some of the private bathrooms are only separated by a partition, not a door.

Pousada Noa Noa POUSADA **$$**
(Map p417; 71 3264-1148; www.pousadanoanoa.com; Av Sete de Setembro 4295, Barra; s/d

Salvador Barra

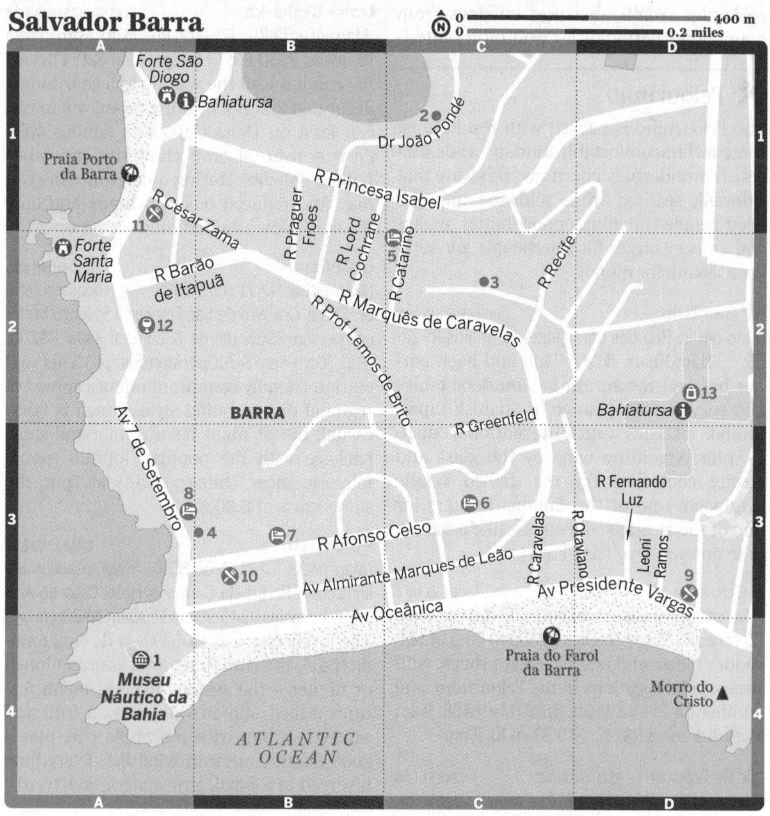

Salvador Barra

Top Sights
1 Museu Náutico da Bahia A4

Sights
Forte de Santo Antônio da Barra .... (see 1)

Activities, Courses & Tours
2 Diálogo C1
3 Idioma Escola de Português C2
4 Salvador Bus B3

Sleeping
5 Open House Barra C2
6 Pousada Bamboo da Barra C3
7 Pousada Estrela do Mar B3
8 Pousada Noa Noa A3

Eating
9 Caranguejo do Porto D3
10 Du Chef Arte e Gastronomia B3
11 Portal do Mar A1

Drinking & Nightlife
12 Pereira A2

Shopping
13 Shopping Barra D2

from R$140/160; ❄☎) The buzzy oceanfront terrace and bar – an ideal spot from which to watch the sunset with a cocktail in hand – is the key selling point of this welcoming guesthouse. Of 15 simply furnished guest rooms, only a few have ocean views, and the others are on the dark side.

Eating

Dining out is a delight in Salvador. Traditional Bahian cuisine has a heavy African influence, featuring ingredients like coconut cream, tomato, seafood, bell pepper and spices of ginger, hot peppers and coriander. You'll also find cuisines from many other nationalities well represented.

Pelourinho

The Pelourinho is packed with restaurants; some feel uncomfortably touristy, while others are wonderfully charming. Be aware that sidewalk seating, while allowing unparalleled people-watching opportunities, makes you an easy target for salespeople and children asking for money.

★Bar Zulu INTERNATIONAL $

(Map p408; Rua das Laranjeiras 15; mains R$22-56; 11am-10pm;) This laid-back corner bar and restaurant has outdoor tables and serves a wide range of Spanish tapas, Bahian classics and international dishes, plus Argentine wine by the glass and strong cocktails. Try the grilled veggie sandwich, one of the famous burgers, or one of the rice-based dishes – like a lighter take on *moqueca* (fish stew).

A Cubana ICE CREAM $

(Map p408; www.acubana.com.br; Portas do Carmo 12; cones R$7-13; 9:30am-10:30pm) One of Salvador's oldest and best ice-cream shops, with two popular locations in the Pelourinho, and another on **Praça Municipal** (Map p408; Praça Municipal; cones R$7-13; 9:30am-10:30pm).

★Restaurante do Senac BUFFET $$

(Map p408; 71 3324-8101; www.ba.senac.br; Largo do Pelourinho 13; buffet per kg R$50, típico per kg R$51.90; buffet a quilo 11:30am-3:30pm Mon-Fri, buffet típico 11:30am-3:30pm Mon-Sat;) The best Bahian buffet in town. The cooking school SENAC (p410) spreads a tempting array of regional dishes, including several varieties of seafood, *moqueca* (fish stew), and traditional desserts. The impressive *buffet tipico* (traditional Bahian food) is on the top floor, not to be confused with the more general street-level *buffet a quilo*, which is also good for a quick lunch.

Cuco Bistrô INTERNATIONAL $$

(Map p408; 71 3321-8722; www.cucobistro.com.br; Largo do Cruzeiro de São Francisco 6; mains R$48-78; 11am-11pm Mon-Sat, to 5pm Sun) This charming cafe is a favorite among locals and tourists alike for its Mediterranean-influenced cuisine and modern takes on Bahian dishes. At lunchtime, try the frequently changing set menu (R$50), including an appetizer and dessert.

Dona Chika-ka AFRO-BRAZILIAN $$

(Map p408; 71 3321-1712; Rua João Castro Rabelo 10; mains R$30-80; 6-10pm Mon-Sat) Flickering candles lead the way up to a charmingly decorated 2nd-floor dining room, where you can feast on Dona Chika-ka's famous *bobó de camarão* (shrimp chowder) and other Bahian delights. During quieter months you may find reduced business hours and only the small downstairs dining area is open.

O Coliseu BAHIAN $$$

(Map p408; 71 3321-5585; www.ocoliseu.com.br; 2nd fl, Cruzeiro de São Francisco 9; lunch buffet per person R$65, dinner & cultural show R$200; 11:30am-4pm & 7-10pm Mon-Sat;) This vegetarian-friendly restaurant offers a spread of regional dishes, buffet-style. Lunch is fairly casual, but at night it's a dinner-and-show package with the popular Topázio (p424) folkloric show. Dinner begins at 7pm, the show starts at 8:30pm.

Pelô Bistrô BRAZILIAN $$$

(Map p408; 71 3266-8550; www.casadoamarelindo.com; Portas do Carmo 6, Hotel Casa do Amarelindo; mains R$45-90; 11:30am-10:30pm;) The lovely bistro at Hotel Casa do Amarelindo (p415) is a sure thing for a gourmet lunch or dinner – the seafood-focused menu features grilled salmon with passion fruit and sauteed shrimp with pineapple rice, plus a good South American wine list. Everything is served in a small, atmospheric courtyard.

Maria Mata Mouro BRAZILIAN $$$

(Map p408; 71 3321-3929; www.mariamatamouro.com.br; Rua da Ordem Terceira 8; mains R$40-80; noon-11pm) The picture-perfect garden patio and elegant dining room are fine settings to enjoy one of Pelô's top menus. You'll find Bahian classics, fresh seafood and Portuguese dishes prepared with a gourmet twist, plus a varied wine list and a talented bartender shaking up unique cocktails.

Carmo

★Cafélier CAFE $

(Map p408; 71 3241-5095; www.cafelier.com.br; Rua do Carmo 50; mains R$15-40; 2-9pm Mon, Tue & Thu-Sat, to 8pm Sun) This quaint hideaway cafe, located inside an antique house that's positioned dramatically on a cliff top over the ocean, is one of a kind. Come for the views, plus beautifully prepared cappuccino, rich chocolate cake, delicious sandwiches and wines by the glass.

Pysco PERUVIAN $$
(Map p408; ☎71 3241-7962; www.facebook.com/Pyscorestaurantebar; Rua do Carmo 42; mains R$45-69; ⊙noon-11pm Tue-Sat, to 10pm Sun) Dig into some crispy grilled octopus and a potent pisco sour at this Peruvian restaurant with impressive harbor views. If you want to dine at sunset make a reservation or arrive early.

Casa da Roça PIZZA $$
(Map p408; ☎71 3241-8580; Ladeira do Carmo 27; mains R$35-60; ⊙6pm-late) Come to this nondescript pizzeria in the Carmo area for hearty, homemade Italian staples and strong drinks. The owners are friendly and fun and the portions are massive.

Cidade Baixa

In the Comércio, cheap *lanchonetes* (snack bars) and self-service restaurants abound. For something more memorable, head south along the bay, where there are several fine (if expensive) restaurants with views over the water.

Vitória

Coffeetown Salvador CAFE $
(Map p404; ☎71 3565-1325; www.facebook.com/coffeetownsalvador; Av Sete de Setembro 1755; dishes R$10-48; ⊙9am-9pm Mon-Thu, to 10pm Fri-Sun; 📶) If you find yourself craving pancakes or other American-style breakfast staples try this ultramodern coffee shop just up the street from the museums in Vitória.

Barra & Coastal Suburbs

Budget-minded travelers will find plenty of self-serve restaurants, sandwich shops, tapioca stands and supermarkets in Barra.

Du Chef Arte e Gastronomia SEAFOOD $$
(Map p417; ☎71 3042-4433; www.facebook.com/duchefartegastronomia; Afonso Celso 70, Barra; mains R$45-90; ⊙noon-11pm Tue-Thu, to 1am Fri & Sat, to 5pm Sun; 🅥) Fresh seafood and upscale plating make the dishes at this swish Barra restaurant pop. You're likely to make the acquaintance of the chef, Lucius Gaudenzi, while you dine on tender shrimp or one of the vegan dishes on the menu.

Portal do Mar BRAZILIAN $$
(Map p417; ☎71 3267-6250; Sete de Setembro 510, Barra; mains R$27-50; ⊙10am-midnight) Open all day, with outdoor tables just across the street from the beach, this is an appealing spot for a sunset caipirinha (cocktail made from limes, sugar, ice and high-proof sugarcane alcohol) or an easygoing dinner – the staff boldly call themselves the *moqueca* (fish stew) experts, but they also serve pasta, steak and grilled fish.

Caranguejo do Porto SEAFOOD $$
(Map p417; ☎71 3245-9197; Av Oceânica 819, Barra; mains R$34-80; ⊙11am-midnight Mon-Sat, 10am-10pm Sun) Another of Barra's seaside hot spots for traditional Bahian food (think *moqueca*, fresh crabs, empanada-like pasteles, cold beer and caipirinhas), this lively restaurant transitions into a casual bar scene as the night rolls on and sometimes stays open quite late on the weekends.

★**Paraíso Tropical** BAHIAN $$$
(☎71 3384-7464; www.restauranteparaisotropical.com.br; Edgar Loureiro 98B, Cabula; mains R$53-98; ⊙noon-10pm Tue-Sat, to 5pm Sun) Far off the beaten path in the residential neighborhood of Cabula, but foodies don't mind the detour to Paraíso Tropical: the classic Brazilian restaurant has long been considered one of Salvador's top choices for beautifully prepared Bahian cuisine with a gourmet twist. Come for a leisurely lunch; expect long waits on weekends.

LGBT+ SALVADOR

Salvador's gay nightlife scene may be subdued compared to those of other Brazilian capitals, but these off-the-beaten-path venues are worth seeking out.

A young, gay-friendly crowd flocks to **Beco dos Artistas** (Artist's Alley; Map p404; Av Cerqueira Lima 4, Garcia; ⊙hours vary), a lively alley with several bars popular for preclubbing drinks. Take a taxi and enter from Rua Leovigildo Filgueira. After midnight In Rio Vermelho, good-looking **San Sebastian** (☎71 3012-5013; www.sansebastianoficial.com.br; Rua da Paciência 88, Rio Vermelho; ⊙midnight-5am Fri & Sat) draws the LGBT crowd with three floors, four bars and two dance floors.

Grupo Gay da Bahia (p425) is a cultural center for the LGBT+ community.

Check www.guiagaysalvador.com.br for the latest listings and events.

A NIGHT OUT IN RIO VERMELHO

The coastal neighborhood of Rio Vermelho has always been culturally significant to the city of Salvador: Portuguese sailors wrecked their ship offshore in 1510, famed writer Jorge Amado lived here and the important Candomblé (Afro-Brazilian) festival Festa da Iemanjá (p414), honoring the goddess of motherhood and fertility, takes place on its shores. But in recent years, the neighborhood has also emerged as a hub of nightlife.

Arrive around sunset and take your pick from the sea of plastic tables and chairs set up on the lively plaza of **Largo de Santana**. Several casual bars serve cold beer to these outdoor tables, but the real attraction is the traditional street food prepared by colorfully dressed Bahian women at stands around the square. Particularly legendary are the *acarajé* (balls of dough fried in *dendê* oil and served with spicy sauces and shrimp.)

On any given evening, there are cultural events and free concerts in the square, at the cultural center **Casa de Lemanjá** (71 3334-3041; Guedes Cabral 81, Rio Vermelho; hours vary), and around the waterfront market **Mercado do Peixe**. Afterwards, go for drinks at nearby Póstudo, then catch some live music at Commons Studio Bar. After midnight, hit the dance floor at San Sebastian (p419).

Rio Vermelho is about a 30-minute walk along the coast – or a short bus ride from Barra on any bus marked 'Orla' (waterfront).

Drinking & Nightlife

The Pelourinho is Salvador's nightlife capital: bars with outdoor tables and live music spill onto the cobbled streets.

In Barra, find relaxed ambience and music along Av Almirante Marques de Leão and the waterfront around the Farol da Barra. Bohemian Rio Vermelho has one of the more interesting nightlife scenes in the region.

Pelourinho & Carmo

O Cravinho BAR
(Map p408; 71 99314-6022; www.ocravinho.com.br; Terreiro de Jesus 3; 11am-11:30pm) This friendly neighborhood bar specializes in flavored shots of *cachaça* (sugarcane alcohol), including its trademark clove-infused variety. Decorated with barrels and packed with a vibrant mix of locals and tourists and featuring live music many evenings of the week, it's an atmospheric place to stop in for a quick drink while sightseeing in the Pelourinho.

Casa do Amarelindo Bar COCKTAIL BAR
(Map p408; 71 3266-8550; www.casadoamarelindo.com; Rua das Portas do Carmo 6, Hotel Casa do Amarelindo; noon-late) The chic tropical-style bar at the lovely Pelô Bistrô (p418) at Casa do Amarelindo is the ideal spot for a nightcap; better still is the panoramic terrace where a skilled bartender shows up after dark to mix classic cocktails.

Odoyá BAR
(Map p408; 71 3322-7892; Praça Anchieta 1; 11am-11pm) Drinks are standard, and you'll have to deal with an endless stream of panhandlers sitting at these outdoor tables, but the views at night - several gorgeously illuminated churches surround you - are memorable as you relax with a caipirinha or two.

Barra & Coastal Suburbs

★**Pereira** BAR
(Map p417; 71 3264-6464; www.pereirarestaurante.com.br; Sete de Setembro 3959, Barra; noon-4pm & 5pm-midnight Tue-Fri & Sun, noon-4pm & 5:30pm-1am Sat) Up a staircase from the seaside road that curves around the tip of Barra, Pereira is a stylish restaurant and wine bar. Excellent *chop* (draft beer) is on tap and the sunset views over the ocean are beautiful.

Póstudo BAR
(71 3015-8800; João Gomes 87, Rio Vermelho; noon-2am) This perpetually cool bar and restaurant, right in the middle of the Rio Vermelho nightlife action, has ocean views and a long drink menu.

Entertainment

Bars and clubs tend to come and go in Salvador, so ask around to see what's hot at the moment, or log onto the agenda of parties, concerts and performances at Festa da Semana (www.festadasemana.com.br/salvador).

Live Music

Salvador is the pulsing center of an incredible music scene, where a blend of African and Brazilian traditions has produced mind-blowing forms of percussion that *salvadorenos* mix into their reggae, pop and rock, *pagode* and *axé*. The city has also produced unique styles such as *afoxé* and samba reggae. Almost every bar or restaurant in the city has live music at least one night of the week, so catching some of Salvador's talented artists isn't hard.

During the high season, there are almost nightly concerts in the inner courtyards of the Pelourinho, with cover charges ranging from free to R$50. Take a stroll by the following places and find out what's on for the evening: Largo de Tereza Batista, Largo do Pedro Arcanjo and Praça Quincas Berro d'Água (all usually free). There are also occasional concerts on the Terreiro de Jesus (p405) and you can frequently hear drum corps, which rehearse by walking through the Pelourinho, blocking traffic and gathering a following as they go.

Traditional groups (characterized by strong Afro drum corps) to look out for include Ilê Aiyê (the first exclusively black Carnaval group), the all-female Dida, Muzenza and Male Debalê. More pop, and with strong percussion sections, is world-famous Olodum (a Tuesday-night Pelourinho institution) Araketu and Timbalada, brainchild of master composer and musician Carlinhos Brown. The queens of Salvador pop music – Margareth Menezes, Ivete Sangalo and Daniela Mercury – also often 'rehearse' publicly.

For the biggest acts, keep your eye on Salvador's finest venue, the **Teatro Castro Alves** (Map p404; www.tca.ba.gov.br; Praça 2 de Julho, Campo Grande); its amphitheater has weekly concerts throughout summer.

★ Jam no MAM LIVE MUSIC

(Map p404; www.jamnomam.com.br; Av Contorno s/n, Museu de Arte Moderna; adult/child R$8/4; ⏲6-9pm Sat) Saturday-evening jazz and bossa nova at MAM (p406) is a must for music lovers. Go early to see the museum first and catch the views at sunset. Though the venue is located within walking distance of the Pelourinho, muggings are common along this quiet stretch; taking a taxi is recommended.

Commons Studio Bar LIVE MUSIC

(☎71 3022-5620; www.facebook.com/commonsstudiobar; Doutor Odilon Santos 224, Rio Vermelho; from R$20; ⏲10pm-5am Thu-Sat) Rustic-chic, with state-of-the-art equipment, this cool venue is a relatively modern addition to Salvador's nightlife scene. Commons hosts up-and-coming Brazilian musical acts and runs community-focused programming, from workshops to special events.

Bar Fundo do Cravinho LIVE MUSIC

(Map p408; www.clubedosamba.com.br; Terreiro de Jesus 5, Pelourinho; from R$10; ⏲4-11:30pm Tue, to 1am Fri, to 1:30am Sat, 2-11:30pm Sun) You can find samba parties throughout the week down an alley behind the eponymous bar here. The weekly schedule changes periodically, so check the website for up-to-date listings.

Espaço D'Venetta LIVE MUSIC

(Map p404; www.dvenetta.com.br; Rua dos Abodes 12, Santo Antônio; cover varies; ⏲6pm-midnight Wed-Fri, noon-midnight Sat, noon-6pm Sun) This buzzed-about cultural center, bar and art space in Santo Antônio features live samba, *samba de roda* and jazz. Some events are free.

OLODUM

Walking around in Salvador, the bold symbol of a red, yellow and green peace sign is everywhere: it's the iconic symbol of Olodum, an Afro-Brazilian cultural group founded in 1979 by percussionist Neguinho do Samba. Originally, the objective was to curb racism and create opportunities for Bahia's marginalized youth. The organization still works towards these aims, primarily through music: the Olodum school is famous for developing its leader's signature style of *afro bloco,* also known as samba reggae, which takes inspiration from the musical styles of Caribbean reggae, salsa and Brazilian samba.

Today, Olodum runs a school, and the official band records music with big-time Brazilian musicians; during Carnaval, Olodum features prominently on the musical lineup. The colorful band of percussionists has also made waves in the international pop-culture scene: Michael Jackson filmed his 1996 music video for the single 'They Don't Care About Us' with the Olodum troupe in the streets of the Pelourinho. Log onto www.olodum.com.br for more on the organization, or take a peek into the **Escola Olodum** (Map p408; ☎71 3321-4154; www.olodum.com.br; Gregório de Mattos 22; tours by donation, workshops free; ⏲9am-6pm Mon-Fri, to 1pm Sat) in the Pelourinho.

Capoeira

Combining elements of the fight, the game and the dance, capoeira was developed by Afro-Brazilian slaves more than 400 years ago as a means of maintaining a ready self-defense against their masters. Today it remains a uniquely Bahian art form.

Origins

Capoeira is said to have originated from a ritualistic African dance. It was prohibited by slave owners and banished from the *senzalas* (slave barracks), forcing slaves to practice clandestinely in the forest. Later, in an attempt to disguise this act of defiance from the authorities, capoeira was developed into a kind of acrobatic dance. The clapping of hands and striking of the *berimbau*, a one-string musical instrument that looks like a fishing rod, originally served to alert fighters to the approach of the boss and subsequently became incorporated into the dance to maintain the rhythm.

As recently as the 1920s, capoeira was still prohibited. In the 1930s, Mestre Bimba changed the emphasis of capoeira from a tool of insurrection to a form of artistic expression that's become an institution in Bahia.

Traditions & Variations

Today there are two schools of capoeira: the slow and low Capoeira de Angola, originally led by Mestre Pastinha, and the more aggressive Capoeira Regional, initiated by Mestre Bimba. The former school believes capoeira came from Angola; the latter maintains it was born in the plantations of Cachoeira and other cities of the Recôncavo region (named after the concave shape of the bay).

GOLERO/GETTY IMAGES ©

JABOTICABA FOTOS/SHUTTERSTOCK ©

1. Capoeira fighters, Salvador (p409) **2.** *Berimbau* instrument

The movements are always fluid and circular, the fighters always playful and respectful as they exchange mock blows. Capoeira is typically practiced by two fighters at a time inside a *roda* (circle) of spectators/fighters who clap and sing. In addition to the *berimbau,* other instruments such as the *pandeiro* (tambourine), *agogô* (bell) and *atabaque* (drum) provide musical accompaniment. Capoeira gains more followers by the year, both nationally and abroad. Throughout Brazil – particularly in Bahia – you will see people practicing their moves on the beach and street *rodas* popping up in touristy areas.

Watching Capoeira

At night in the Pelourinho, you'll hear music spilling out of capoeira studios clustered in the area of Teatro San Miguel Santana. Take a peek inside and don't be surprised if you're asked to pay a small fee to observe – you're supporting the studio. It's more authentic than the capoeira you'll see in touristy areas: linger to watch the performers in the Terreiro de Jesus and the ground level of the Mercado Modelo, and you'll be hustled for cash within moments. More professional capoeira is on proud display in folkloric shows like Salvador's famous Balé Folclórico da Bahia (p424).

Capoeira Classes

In Salvador, capoeira classes (p409) are held in the Pelourinho. Elsewhere in Bahia, capoeiristas often advertise lessons at youth hostels. Expect to pay anywhere from R$55 to R$120 for a one-hour class; wear comfortable, loose-fitting pants you can move around in.

Folkloric Shows & Capoeira

The chance to see a folkloric performance that showcases the unique range of Bahian music and dance – including live percussion and vocals, the dances of the *orixás*, *maculêlê* (stick dance), samba and capoeira – shouldn't be missed. You can also catch some authentic capoeira in the Pelourinho, where studios charge a few reais for watching a class (often called a 'show') and for taking pictures.

★**Balé Folclórico da Bahia** PERFORMING ARTS
(Map p408; ☎71 3322-1962; www.balefolclorico dabahia.com.br; Gregório de Mattos 49, Teatro Miguel Santana; R$60; ⊙shows 8pm) The most astounding professional show is put on by this world-renowned folkloric ballet company.

Topázio PERFORMING ARTS
(Map p408; ☎71 3033-3366; www.capoeira topazio.com.br; 2nd fl, Cruzeiro de São Francisco 9; show incl buffet dinner R$200; ⊙8:30pm Mon-Sat) The popular show that used to be staged at the Solar do Unhão, featuring 18 dancers, musicians and capoeiristas, now happens here after dinner at O Coliseu (p418). Dinner starts at 7pm and the show begins around 8:30pm. Reserve ahead.

Shopping

For most visitors, shopping opportunities in Salvador fall into one of two camps: the artisan crafts and traditional Bahian souvenirs of the Pelourinho and the Mercado Modelo (p406), and large shopping centers like **Shopping Barra** (Map p417; ☎71 2108-8288; http://shoppingbarra.com; Av Centenário 2992, Barra; ⊙9am-10pm Mon-Sat, noon-9pm Sun) and **Shopping da Bahia** (www.shopping dabahia.com.br; Av Tancredo Neves s/n, Iguatemi; ⊙9am-10pm Mon-Sat, noon-9pm Sun) (which is across from the bus station, and previously known as Shopping Iguatemi). Both shopping centers are busy with Brazilian fashionistas and bustling food courts.

Orientation

Salvador sits at the southern tip of a V-shaped peninsula at the mouth of the Baía de Todos os Santos. The city can be difficult to navigate as there are many one-way, no-left-turn streets that wind through Salvador's hills and valleys. The center of the city is on the bay side of the peninsula and is divided by a steep bluff into two parts: Cidade Alta (Upper City) and Cidade Baixa (Lower City).

The heart of historic Cidade Alta is the Pelourinho (or Pelô), which is also the heart of Salvador's tourism and nightlife. This roughly refers to the area from Praça da Sé (p405) to Largo do Pelourinho (p403).

From Praça Castro Alves, Av 7 de Setembro runs through the Centro to the wide Praça Campo Grande, then continues southwest through the well-to-do Vitória neighborhood, and down to the mouth of the bay. Here, at the tip of the peninsula, is the affluent Barra district, with its lighthouse, forts and popular beach.

A main thoroughfare, which constantly changes names (one being Av Presidente Vargas), snakes east from Barra along the Atlantic coast. It cuts inland briefly around Forte de Santo Antonio (where pedestrian-only promenades have been built), then passes through the coastal neighborhoods of Ondina and Rio Vermelho, continuing through a chain of middle-class beachfront suburbs all the way to Itapuã.

Cidade Baixa contains the Comércio (the city's commercial and financial center), the ferry terminals and port. North, the land curves around the bay to create the Itapagipe Peninsula, including the Bonfim and Boa Viagem neighborhoods. The suburbs along the bay are poverty stricken, and the level of poverty generally increases with the distance from the center.

Information

DANGERS & ANNOYANCES

In the center, tourist police maintain a visible presence, particularly in the Pelourinho. Crime in the Pelô increases during the high season (especially around Carnaval) and on crowded Tuesday nights, and pickpocketing is common on buses and in congested places where tourists are easily singled out. To minimize risks, dress down, keep jewelry to a minimum, carry just enough cash for your outing and only a photocopy of your passport, and try to be roughly oriented before you set out.

If you must carry a bank card, take only one – and use ATMs inside banks instead of freestanding machines that are more susceptible to hackers.

The Pelourinho shifts quickly into sketchy areas, so avoid wandering out of the way. Cidade Baixa is deserted and unsafe at night and on weekends, and the *ladeiras* (steep roads) should be used with caution. They are both off the beaten path and prone to reckless drivers, so think twice before traversing them on foot and keep aware of your surroundings.

On the beaches, keep a close eye on juvenile thieves – or *capitães d'areia* (captains of the sand) – who are quick to make off with unguarded possessions.

WORTH A TRIP

SANTO AMARO

Santo Amaro is a friendly town that sees very few tourists and has an unpretentious charm. It is most well known for being the hometown of the brother–sister pair Caetano Veloso and Maria Betânia, two of Brazil's most popular singers (who often put in an appearance during Carnaval). The center bustles with people, especially around the small outdoor market. Paper production has replaced sugar as the major industry, visible in the invasion of bamboo on the hillsides where sugarcane once flourished, and a large paper mill outside of town.

The decrepit sugar-baron mansions along the old commercial street, Rua General Câmara, and the numerous churches are reminders of Santo Amaro's prosperous days. The ornate **Matriz de NS da Purificação** (1668) is the largest church, with *azulejos* (handmade tiles imported from Portugal) and a painted ceiling. Unfortunately, a gang of thieves stole most of the church's holy images and exported them to France.

The **Lavagem da Purificação** (January 23 to February 2) is celebrated by a procession and ritual washing of the church steps by *baianas* (Bahian 'aunts' in traditional dress), before bands and *trios elétricos* (long trucks loaded with huge speakers) take over the streets.

Buses leave Salvador for Santo Amaro (R$20, one hour) almost every 30 minutes from 5:30am to 7pm. Most continue on to Cachoeira/São Félix (R$9, one hour).

Don't hesitate to use taxis after dark or in areas where you feel apprehensive, though taking buses in the evening is not necessarily unsafe.

EMERGENCY

Any crime involving a tourist must be handled by the city's **tourist police** (Tourist Police; ☎71 3116-6817; Cruzeiro de São Francisco 14, Pelourinho). A few speak English or French.

Pronto Socorro (Ambulance) ☎192

MEDICAL SERVICES

Hospital Espanhol (☎71 3644-0136; https://hospitalespanhol.com.br; Av Sete de Setembro 4161, Barra) One of the city's main hospitals (and a lovely architectural landmark, too).

MONEY

There are plenty of banks with ATMs that can be used all over Salvador. Banco do Brasil and Brandesco are typically the most reliable for use with foreign cards. You can usually count on the banks at the bus station and airport to be well stocked and safe. Most places – even many of the street vendors – accept credit and debit cards.

TOURIST INFORMATION

You can find plenty of tourist information at the many travel agencies spread throughout the city. **Salvador Central** (Map p408; ☎71 99924-6522; João de Deus 22, Pelourinho; ⏰10am-7pm Mon-Sat) , located in the Pelourinho, is a good place to start.

Bahiatursa The tourism authority is friendly if not terribly organized. The **Pelourinho office** (Map p408; ☎71 3321-2463; www.bahiatursa.ba.gov.br; Rua Francisco Muniz Barreto 12, Pelourinho; ⏰8:30am-9pm Mon-Thu, to 10pm Fri-Sun), which has maps and listings of what's happening around town, is your best bet. There are also desks at the **bus station** (☎71 3450-3871; www.bahiatursa.ba.gov.br; Av Antônio Carlos Magalhães, Iguatemi; ⏰9am-6pm Mon-Sat) and the **airport** (☎71 3204-1244; www.bahiatursa.ba.gov.br; Praça Gago Coutinho s/n; ⏰7:30am-11pm), at **Shopping Barra** (Map p417; ☎71 3264-4566; www.bahiatursa.ba.gov.br; Av Centenário 2992, Barra, SAC, Shopping Barra; ⏰9am-6pm Mon-Sat), **Mercado Modelo** (Map p408; ☎71 3241-0242; www.bahiatursa.ba.gov.br; Praça Cayru, Mercado Modelo; ⏰9am-6pm Mon-Sat) and a **Barra office** (Map p417; ☎71 3264-5440; www.bahiatursa.ba.gov.br; Av 7 de Setembro, Instituto Mauá, Porto da Barra; ⏰9am-6pm Mon-Sat). Also see www.bahia.com.br.

Grupo Gay da Bahia (Map p408; ☎71 3322-2552; www.ggb.org.br; Frei Vicente 24, Pelourinho; ⏰9am-6pm Mon-Fri) A cultural center for the LGBT+ community.

Quatro Cantos Turismo (☎71 3264-2000; www.4cantosturismo.com.br; Marquês de Caravelas 154, Barra; ⏰9am-6pm Mon-Fri) This travel agency is a helpful stop for maps, tourist information and trip planning; the agents can also help you buy plane tickets.

ℹ Getting There & Away

AIR

Aeroporto Deputado Luis Eduardo do Magalhães (SSA; ☎71 3204-1010; Praça Gago Coutinho s/n, São Cristóvão) is served by domestic airlines like **GOL** (☎0300 115-2121; www.voegol.com.br; airport), **LATAM** (☎1-866-435-9526; www.latam.com), and **Azul** (☎1-888-587-2985; www.voeazul.com.br). There are several direct flights to/from foreign cities such as Miami or Lisbon via **TAP** (Air Portugal; ☎1-800-221-7370; www.flytap.com), and Buenos Aires via **Aerolíneas Argentinas** (☎1-800-333-0276; www.aerolineas.com.ar), but generally speaking, flights to international destinations go via São Paulo or Rio.

BOAT

Boats to Morro de São Paulo and points on Baía de Todos os Santos leave from the **Terminal Marítimo Turístico** (Map p408; Av da França s/n, Comércio), behind the Mercado Modelo, and the **Terminal de São Joaquim** (Av Oscar Pontes 1051), a 10-minute taxi ride north. Note that at the airport or bus station, these boats are often referred to by the English phrase 'ferry boat'.

BUS

For shorter trips, you can buy bus tickets at the time of travel. For longer journeys, especially during peak travel times, you'll want to book ahead to make sure you have a spot. The easiest way to purchase bus tickets is at the main station – but Salvador's Rodoviario bus station is a long haul from the center. So it's best to plan your strategy and buy tickets when you're passing through; unlike with plane tickets, most travel agencies in town don't sell bus tickets.

Brazilians often reserve online, a privilege not extended to foreigners, with a few exceptions. A few bus lines are starting to offer the option to use a foreign credit card, and you might have luck through new websites like www.clickbus.com.br or www.busbud.com. When in doubt, ask the staff at your hotel or hostel: they're often willing to help make travel arrangements, or at least give advice.

Note that, in addition to the fares, for many bus tickets out of Salvador, you are also required to buy an Interestadual card (R$6) at the time of ticket purchase. Swipe it at the departure gates for access to the bus platforms.

ℹ Getting Around

TO/FROM THE AIRPORT

The airport is located about 30km east of the center. For a taxi going to Barra or the Pelourinho, you'll pay around R$140 in advance at the airport; the official Taxi COMTAS and Taxi COOMETAS stands inside the arrivals hall accept credit cards, which is convenient if you're not carrying local currency. The trip takes 40 to 60 minutes. You'll pay slightly less if you hail a taxi outside, though you might not see any available cars. Follow the signs for 'taxi comum'.

A new executive bus called First Class (www.firstclassbus.com.br) travels between the airport and key tourist points, including Praca da Sé (in the Pelourinho) and a handful of large beach hotels in Barra. The flat fee is R$25 per person and buses leave from the airport, roughly every 40 minutes, all day and into the evening. Look for the First Class desks: there's one in the baggage-claim area, and another in the arrivals hall. The same service takes you back to the airport: check the First Class website for information on pick-up times and places.

There are also public buses (R$3.70, running 5:30am to 10pm, with fewer departures on weekends) that provide access to the center. For Barra or the Pelourinho (or Terminal Marítimo Turístico for the ferry to Morro de São Paulo, accessible from the Cidade Alta via Elevador Lacerda), take the bus marked 'Praça da Sé-Aeroporto'. For the ferry to Bom Despacho, take the Aeroporto–São Joaquim bus, which also stops at the Rodoviario bus station. The ride to the center takes anywhere between 90 minutes and two hours, depending on traffic.

The same buses make the return journey. Buses to the airport depart regularly from the so-called **Praça da Sé bus stop** (Bus Stop; Map p408), a block southeast of Praça Municipal. Supposedly they leave every 30 minutes, but the

BUSES FROM SALVADOR

DESTINATION	DURATION (HR)	COST (R$)	FREQUENCY (DAILY)	BUS COMPANY
Aracaju	4-6	72-105	8	various
Ilhéus	8	108-231	4	Águia Branca
Lençóis	7-8	86	3	Real Expresso
Maceió	11	93-145	6	various
Natal	25	250-262	2	Gontijo
Penedo	10	104	1	Águia Branca
Porto Seguro	11	144	1	Águia Branca
Recife	16	130-171	2	various
Rio de Janeiro	30	330-410	2	Águia Branca & Kaissara
São Paulo	32	199-462	2	Kaissara & Catedral Turismo
Vitória	21	281	1	Águia Branca

schedule isn't fixed, so leave plenty of time. You can pick up the same bus in Barra.

TO/FROM THE BUS STATION

Salvador's **bus station** (Bus Station; ☎71 3616-8300; www.rodoviariadesalvador.com.br) is 8km east of the city center. A taxi to Cidade Alta or Barra runs R$25 to R$55, depending on traffic.

Buses (R$0.70) marked 'Praça da Sé' go to the center from in front of Shopping Bahia (previously known as Shopping Iguatemi), just across the footbridge in front of the bus station. Going to the bus station, any bus that's labeled 'Shopping Bahia' or 'Iguatemi' will get you to the vicinity.

PUBLIC TRANSPORTATION

Linking Cidade Alta (the Pelourinho) and Cidade Baixa (Comércio and the ferry terminals) are the Elevador Lacerda (p405) and the Plano Inclinado Gonçalves (p406).

Public buses crisscross the city; particularly useful to tourists are those that run between Barra and Praça da Sé (R$3.70).The destinations are clearly labeled on the front of the bus.

Note that passengers board the bus through the rear door (and pay the attendant seated there), then disembark from the front door of the bus (near the driver). There are two main city bus terminals in the center that can serve as destinations or transfer points: Terminal da França in the Comércio, and Lapa, behind Shopping Lapa and Shopping Piedade. If heading north to the Igreja NS do Bonfim, catch a bus from the stop at the base of the Elevador Lacerda.

TAXI & RIDE-SHARE

Taxis can be taken at meter price (legal) or negotiated, but you might not get to choose which. Uber is also available.

RECÔNCAVO

A region of green, fertile lands surrounding the Baía de Todos os Santos, the Recôncavo brought riches to Salvador (and the Portuguese crown) with its sugar and tobacco crops. The profits reaped off these lands also spurred the growth of once-rich towns like Cachoeira, which is full of colorful, mostly preserved colonial architecture.

Cachoeira & São Felix

☎0XX75 / POP 35,000

Cachoeira, affectionately known as the jewel of the Recôncavo, is a sleepy place, full of colorful, mostly preserved colonial architecture uncompromised by the presence of modern buildings. The town sits below a series of hills, strung along the banks of the Rio Paraguaçu across from its twin, São Félix – the two towns are connected by a striking British-built bridge divided for cars and pedestrians. A steady trickle of tourism flows through the area, attracted by Brazil's best tobacco, its reputation as a renowned center of Candomblé (a Bahian religious tradition) and a strong wood-sculpting tradition.

History

Diego Álvares, the father of Cachoeira's founders, was the sole survivor of a ship bound for the West Indies that was wrecked in 1510 on a reef near Salvador. This Portuguese Robinson Crusoe was saved by the indigenous Tupinambá of Rio Vermelho, who dubbed the strange white sea creature Caramuru, or 'Fish-Man.' Álvares lived 20 years with the indigenous group and married Catarina do Paraguaçu, the daughter of the most powerful Tupinambá chief. Their sons João Gaspar Aderno Álvares and Rodrigues Martins Álvares killed off the local indigenous people, set up the first sugarcane *fazendas* (ranches) and founded Cachoeira.

By the 18th century, tobacco from Cachoeira was considered the world's finest, sought by rulers in China and Africa. The 'holy herb' also became popular in Brazil, taken as snuff, chewed or smoked in a pipe.

Sights

Cachoeira is one of Candomblé's strongest and perhaps purest spiritual and religious centers. On Friday and Saturday nights, ceremonies are often held in small homes and shacks in the hills. Travelers who are especially interested in learning more should contact the tourist office (p430) for information about local guides who specialize in this particular scene.

The town also maintains a strong tradition of African-influenced wood carving. Stop in on the ateliers (studios) of two of the best sculptors in town, **Doidão** (cnr Ruas 25 de Junho & 7 de Setembro, Cachoeira; 10am-4pm Mon-Fri) and **Louco** (Rua 13 de Maio, Cachoeira; 10am-4pm Mon-Fri), to get a sense of the local style.

Note that, as elsewhere in Bahia, churches are sometimes closed even when their posted opening hours indicate otherwise. Admission is by donation.

Cachoeira & São Felix

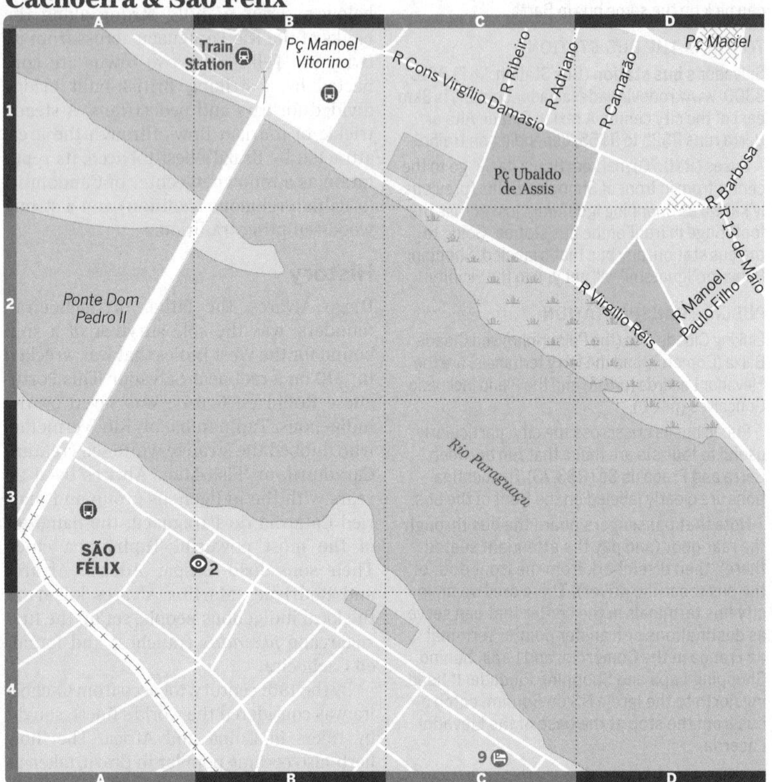

Centro Dannemann CULTURAL CENTRE

(☎75 3438-2500; www.terradannemann.com; Salvador Pinto 29, São Félix; ⏲8:15-11:45am & 1-4:45pm Mon-Fri) In its boom times the area was known for tobacco production, the history of which is memorialized at this interpretive center where you can even buy a few cigars to take home. Dannemann has been in operation since the late 1800s and remains one of the most well respected cigar manufacturers in Bahia. From here you can also arrange tours to the company's nearby tobacco farm (per person from R$50).

Museu Hansen Bahia MUSEUM

(☎75 3425-1453; www.hansenbahia.com.br; Rua 13 de Maio, Cachoeira; ⏲9am-5pm Mon-Fri, to 1pm Sat) FREE Karl Heinz Hansen (1915–76) was a German artist who emigrated to Brazil in 1949. He felt such an affinity with his new home that he had his surname changed to 'Hansen Bahia'. Today, this museum displays his powerful block prints and paintings, many showing the influence of Cachoeira's wood-carving tradition. The striking building is the birthplace and former home of Brazilian heroine Ana Nery, who organized the nursing corps during the Paraguay War.

Igreja Matriz NS do Rosário CHURCH

(Nery s/n, Cachoeira; ⏲8am-noon & 2-5pm Mon-Fri, 8am-noon Sat) This church dates to between 1693 and 1754. It has beautiful *azulejos* (handmade tiles imported from Portugal) and a ceiling painted by Teófilo de Jesus. On the 2nd floor, the Museu das Alfaias contains remnants from the abandoned 17th-century Convento de São Francisco do Paraguaçu.

Casa da Câmara e Cadeia HISTORIC BUILDING

(Prefecture & Jail; Praça da Aclamação, Cachoeira; ⏲8am-noon & 2-5pm) FREE At the Casa da Câmara e Cadeia, organized criminals ran the show upstairs and disorganized criminals were kept behind bars downstairs. The building dates to 1698 and served as the seat of the Bahian government in 1822.

Cachoeira & São Felix

Sights

1 Casa da Câmara e Cadeia F3
2 Centro Dannemann B3
3 Doidão E3
4 Igreja da Ordem Terceira do Carmo F3
5 Igreja Matriz NS do Rosário E2
6 Louco E2
7 Museu Hansen Bahia E2

Sleeping

8 Pousada do Convento do Carmo F3
9 Pousada Paraguassú C4

Eating

10 Aclamação Restaurante E3
11 Pai Thomaz E3
12 Restaurante Rabbuni E3

Drinking & Nightlife

13 Baiana's Point E3
14 Bar do Reggae E3

Festivals & Events

Festa de São João FOLKLORIC
(3rd week Jun) The largest popular festival of Bahia's interior, celebrated with folklore, music, dancing and a generous amount of food and drink.

Festa de NS do Rosário RELIGIOUS
(mid-Oct) A religious festival featuring great music and food.

Festa de NS D'Ajuda RELIGIOUS
(mid-Nov) Features a ritual *lavagem* (washing) of the church and a street festival.

Sleeping

Pousada do Convento do Carmo POUSADA $
(75 3425-1716; www.pousadadoconvento.com.br; Praça da Aclamação, Cachoeira; s/d from R$85/120;) The 18th-century convent attached to the **Igreja da Ordem Terceira do Carmo** (Praça da Aclamação; 8am-noon & 2-5pm Mon-Fri, 8am-noon Sat) FREE has been converted into a comfortable guesthouse, with no loss of atmosphere. Rooms are spacious, with tall ceilings and heavy wood floors. The classy on-site restaurant, **A Confraria** (11am-10pm), is open to the public.

Pousada Paraguassú POUSADA $
(75 3438-3369; www.pousadaparaguassu.com.br; Salvador Pinto 3, São Félix; s/d from R$110/150;) Located on the riverfront in São Félix, Paraguassú has basic, cozy rooms surrounding a small garden. The riverside terrace is a breezy place to enjoy the ample breakfast buffet, or, at night, Bahian food or pizza in its restaurant.

Eating

Aclamação Restaurante BRAZILIAN $
(75 3425-3428; Praça da Aclamação 2, Cachoeira; sandwiches R$7-13, mains R$20-35; 11am-10pm) This busy corner eatery offers a range of great-value sandwiches, acai and traditional Bahian dishes. Try the sandwich named after the nearby river, Rio Paraguaçu, piled high with bacon, cheese, grilled chicken, beef, tomatoes and lettuce.

Restaurante Rabbuni BRAZILIAN $
(Praca da Aclamação, Cachoeira; per kg R$32.90; 11:30am-3pm Mon-Fri) A cheerful and popular buffet lunch spot on the square.

Pai Thomaz BAHIAN $$

(☎75 3425-3182; www.pousadapaithomaz.com.br; Vinte e Cinco de Junho 12, Cachoeira; mains R$47-69; ⏰11am-11pm; 📶) Pai Thomaz (the nickname of the original owner) opened in 1981 and was famous for its superbly spiced Bahian cuisine. The restaurant closed in 2005 and was reopened in 2015 under new management, but with the same popularity. You can get excellent *moquecas* (seafood stew) and admire wood carvings from local artists Doidão (p427) and Louco (p427) which decorate the walls.

Although the name of the restaurant is the same as the titular character in the Portuguese translation of *Uncle Tom's Cabin*, the theme of the restaurant bears no relation.

Drinking & Nightlife

Bar do Reggae BAR

(Virgilio Réis s/n; ⏰5pm-late) On warm evenings, everyone and his brother is sitting at these sidewalk tables, drinking beer and enjoying a starlit view of the river.

Baiana's Point RESTAURANT BAR

(☎75 3425-4967; Virgílio Reis, Cachoeira; ⏰9am-10pm) Perched on scenic stilts over the river, this restaurant makes a great setting for an early-evening drink – if you can get anyone to serve you (service is painfully slow).

Information

Both São Félix and Cachoeira have banks with ATMs, including a reliable **Bradesco Bank** (Praça Dr Milton, Cachoeira) branch in Cachoeira.

For more information on the towns' history, river excursions or church visits, stop into the helpful **tourist office** (Tourist Information; Ana Nery 4, Cachoeira; ⏰8am-noon & 2-5pm Mon-Fri) in Cachoeira.

Getting There & Away

These twin towns are served by nearly identical bus stations, positioned directly across the river from each other at each base of the bridge: most trips commence on the **São Félix** (Av Salvador Pinto, São Felix) side, stopping to pick up passengers in **Cachoeira** (Virgílio Réis 482-612, Cachoeira) before continuing out of town.

Numerous daily buses run to Salvador (R$27, two hours, 5:30am to 7pm), stopping in Santo Amaro along the way.

To make connections north, south or west, you can also catch one of Transporte Santana's various daily services to Feira de Santana (R$11, 1½ hours, six daily Monday to Saturday, five on Sunday).

NORTH OF SALVADOR

Bahia's northern coast is not as startling as its southern, but the beaches here are still lovely, boasting tall bluffs with rustling palms and white sands (that grow finer the further north you go), which front a mix of calm inlets and wild surfable breaks. Keep in mind that when *salvadorenos* want a day at the beach, they naturally head for Bahia's northern coast. As a result, the sands close to the city get packed on weekends. To escape the crowds, head further north, where there are many kilometers of deserted pristine shoreline.

The Estrada do Coco (Coconut Hwy) runs as far north as Praia do Forte, where the Linha Verde (Green Line) picks up, continuing all the way to the Sergipe border. You may feel that you are going against the grain if you are trying to access this coast heading north to south. Grassy medians in the highways require buses to pass town entrances and then double back, so few do. Instead, they drop passengers on the highway, leaving you to walk or pick up other transportation into the small towns and fishing communities along this stretch of coast. Traveling from south to north is a much smoother process.

Praia do Forte

☎0XX71 / POP 1800

Beloved by tourists, upmarket Praia do Forte is an attractive and somewhat ecologically sensitive beach village overflowing with stylish restaurants and shops. The main drag, Alameda do Sol, is a pedestrian walkway that leads to an incredibly picturesque and pint-sized church, a sea-turtle reserve and fantastic, palm-lined beaches with sparkling white sands that fill up on weekends. Surrounding the village are castle ruins, a lagoon for canoeing and the Sapiranga forest reserve, which has hiking and biking trails and a zip line. If you can, time your visit for the full moon and walk along the beach past the resort at sunset, when the sun turns the waters of the Rio Timeantube red as the moon rises over the sea.

Sights & Activities

Parque Klaus Peters PARK

(⏰6am-6pm) FREE Just outside of town you'll find the dramatic entrance for this charming coastal park – a long wooden bridge over a buzzing lagoon. Inside the park is a 3.4km trail that takes you across a small island and then back to the mainland, ending at some

DON'T MISS

THE SEA TURTLES OF TAMAR

There are only five remaining species of sea turtle left in the world – and all of them live on the Bahian coast. A true highlight of any trip through the region is a visit to the sea-turtle reserve that's dedicated to protecting loggerhead, hawksbill, olive ridley and green turtles – and their adorably tiny babies.

Of the 18 stations in Bahia run by the nonprofit organization Projeto Tamar (the name is an abbreviation for the Portuguese word for sea turtle, *tartaruga marinha)*, the Praia do Forte station (p432) is perhaps the most impressive, exhibiting pools with marine turtles of various sizes and species, as well as urchins, eels and other sea life.

Outside the station itself, the most important action happens on the shoreline during the turtles' nesting season (September to March). Tamar researchers protect around 550 nests a year along 50km of coast close to Praia do Forte. The moist, leathery, ping-pong-ball-size eggs are buried in the sand when laid and either left on the beach or brought to the hatcheries for incubation. When they hatch, the baby turtles are immediately released into the sea. Though this system allows some 500,000 baby turtles to hatch each year in Bahia, only several hundred will reach adulthood.

A trip to the reserve, located just behind the church on Praia do Forte's main square, is interactive and family friendly; take your time and have an outdoor lunch beside the ocean at Souza Bar (p432), located inside the project station.

natural pools on the beach. Along the way are signs identifying flora and fauna.

Castelo do Garcia d'Ávila RUINS
(71 3676-1133; www.fgd.org.br; Avenida do Farol 1540; R$10; 8am-noon & 2-6pm Mon-Fri) Dating from 1552, the Castelo was the first great Portuguese edifice in Brazil. Desperate to colonize, the king of Portugal granted lands to merchants, soldiers and aristocrats; a farmer named Garcia d'Ávila, endowed with this tract of land, chose this ocean-view plot for his home. Today, it's an impressive ruin with sweeping views. It's 7km outside of town – take a taxi.

Reserva da Sapiranga HIKING
(71 9985-3349; www.fgd.org.br; R$10, guided tours R$15-100; 9am-5pm) About 2.5km outside of Praia do Forte just off of the Linha Verde is the Reserva da Sapiranga, where guides take visitors along trails skirting through 600 hectares of secondary Atlantic rainforest. Hikes range from 30 minutes to five hours, with one of the more popular hikes leading down to the Rio Pojuca (bring your swimsuit).

There have been recent reports of armed robberies happening within the reserve, so it's prudent to ask around town about the current safety warnings before going.

Tours

Worthwhile tours in the area include hiking and bird-watching treks, canopy tours, kayaking and whale-watching (in season). A handful of professional outfitters such as **Portomar** (71 3676-0101; www.portomar.com.br; Rua da Aurora 1; tours per person from R$70; 8am-6pm) handle these trips and run popular excursions at low tide to nearby *piscinas naturais* (natural pools), where you can snorkel or scuba dive around a colorful coral reef.

Sleeping

Praia do Forte has an abundance of attractive midrange guesthouses that fill to capacity on summer weekends. Prices here are more expensive than many other destinations in Bahia, though you'll save by visiting during the week. Rua da Aurora, parallel to Alameda do Sol, has a handful of more affordable pousadas.

★ **Casa Verde Apart** APARTMENT $$
(71 3676-1531; www.casaverdeapart.com; Rua do Peixe Espada 100; apt for 2/4 people from R$266/409;) In a leafy setting near the beach, these six attractive and spacious apartments are complete with well-equipped kitchens and balconies with hammocks. The place is managed by a gracious couple; breakfast is available on request, for an extra fee.

Shanti House Apart APARTMENT $$
(71 99959-0442; www.shantihouseapart.com; Rua da Maria Mole 14; studio for 2 with/without balcony R$282/262, duplex for 4 R$353;) If you're traveling in a group this is one of the better deals in town. Each apartment has a kitchen and, with the exception of the most standard studio, all apartments also feature a private balcony with hammock. All include

access to the central swimming pool and are close to the beach.

Praia do Forte Hostel HOSTEL $$
(☎71 3676-1094; www.albergue.com.br; Rua da Aurora 155; dm/d R$80/245; ❄📶) This popular hostel has a convenient location, clean rooms facing onto a grassy courtyard, and a good breakfast spread. Rental bikes and surfboards are available too. Air-con is available in some rooms, but not others: read the fine print if it's the middle of summer.

Pousada dos Artistas POUSADA $$$
(☎71 3676-1147; www.pousadadosartistas.tur.br; Praça dos Artistas s/n; d/tr R$414/539; ❄📶) This friendly guesthouse – run by a dancer and a painter-sculptor, as the name suggests – offers lovely colonial-style rooms (each with a private balcony and hammock) looking out over a lush tropical garden.

Pousada Ogum Marinho POUSADA $$$
(☎71 3676-1165; www.ogummarinho.com.br; Alameda do Sol s/n; s from R$439; ❄📶) One block from the beach, Ogum Marinho has attractive rooms with stone-slab floors, comfortable furnishings and private decks strung with hammocks.

Tivoli Ecoresort RESORT $$$
(☎71 3676-4000; www.tivolihotels.com; Av do Farol 39; d from R$1458; ❄📶🏊) It's all luxury at this lavish beachfront resort, where walkways wind through groomed gardens past eight swimming pools to the beach. Rooms all have verandas, the cuisine is top-notch and the spa offers a wide range of treatments. Although there's nothing particularly 'eco' about the design, the hotel does contribute to social and educational programs.

Eating

Countless attractive restaurants line the town's pedestrian walkways, but prices are high and the food, generally speaking, is nothing special. If you're in the market for a quick lunch or a beach picnic, grab a deli sandwich or stock up on snacks at the supermarket.

★ **Souza Bar** BAHIAN $
(Alameda do Sol s/n, Tamar Project Station; small plates R$15-35; ⏰8am-6pm Tue-Sun) Festive and popular Souza Bar, inside the **Tamar Project Station** (☎71 3676-0321; www.tamar.org.br; R$24; ⏰8:30am-5:30pm), has a dramatic setting along the rocky coastline. It's a sure bet for fresh clams, crispy *bolinho de peixe* (fried fish balls) and caipirinhas.

Cafe do Forte BISTRO $$
(☎71 3676-1725; www.cafedoforte.com.br; Alameda do Sol 180; mains R$35-78; ⏰11:30am-5:30pm Mon-Wed, to 11pm Thu, to 1am Fri & Sat, to 8pm Sun) Elegantly plated seafood dishes and an extensive menu of fresh juice and coffee drinks can be found at this nondescript spot on Praia do Forte's main drag. The menu is extensive (albeit a little overpriced) and there's a pleasant shady patio to dine on.

Vila Gourmet BRAZILIAN $$$
(☎71 3676-1156; www.sobradodavila.com.br; Alameda do Sol; mains for 2 R$90-180; ⏰noon-10pm) This tropical-style eatery (connected to the centrally located Pousada Sobrado da Vila) serves regional cuisine that's a cut above the rest – thanks to organic vegetables and eggs sourced from a private farm.

Orientation

Buses stop at the northern end of the main pedestrian thoroughfare, Alameda do Sol (also called Av ACM). Though beaches are often crowded in front of the plaza and church, you can find a peaceful spot under the palm trees by walking south along the coast for five to 10 minutes.

Information

Several ATMs are located near the bus stop.

Travel agencies scattered around town can help you arrange area excursions or book onward travel.

Getting There & Away

Praia do Forte is 3km off the highway. **Linha Verde** (☎71 3460-3636) has regular departures to Praia do Forte from Salvador's bus station (R$10, 1¾ hours.) Three daily departures go directly to Praia do Forte (at 9am, 10am and 2pm at the time of writing) though other buses can typically get you there too: just ask at the Linha Verde desk. Buses make the return journey regularly between 7am and 6:30pm. Informal Kombi vans make the same trip to Salvador for the same price; wait near the bus stop for pickup.

Mangue Seco

☎0XX75 / POP 200

Mangue Seco is a tiny, beautifully rustic riverfront village at the tip of a peninsula formed by the Rio Real, which delineates the Bahia–Sergipe border. The town itself is just a scattering of simple dwellings along sandy paths, a tiny church and plaza, a modern lighthouse (yielding lovely views

NORTH OF PRAIA DO FORTE

For many Praia do Forte is as far north as they get on Bahia's coast, but there's still a few places worth checking out further up. **Imbassaí** is a rustic beach town 16km north of Praia do Forte. A tall sand dune and the peaceful Rio Barroso, which runs parallel to the coast, separate the village from a pretty beach with rough surf. Most guesthouses in town are midrange and top-end options. Even the HI option, **Imbassaí Eco Hostel Lujimba** (☎71 3677-1056; www.imbassaihostel.com.br; Rua P, Quadra 21, Imbassai; dm/d from R$50/150; 🛜), is on the pricier side for a hostel, but is well liked for its pleasant wooden-floor rooms in a rustic, thatched-roof guesthouse amid greenery. Hammocks, fruit trees and excursions add to the allure.

A few kilometers north of Imbassaí, along the river, lies the more rustic town of **Diogo**, which sees fewer visitors and retains the charm of village life. For those looking to unwind, the relaxing **Pousada Too Cool** (☎71 99952-2190; www.toocoolnabahia.com; Mata de São João, Diogo; bungalows for 2 from R$325; ❄) is a destination in itself with colorfully designed chalets with verandas overlooking the lush surroundings. The friendly owner can arrange kitesurfing, kayaking, horseback riding and other activities.

About 100km north you'll find **Sítio do Conde**. Wet lowlands full of cattle surround this quiet, working-class beach retreat. While there's little to the town itself (just a few main streets and a sleepy central plaza) Sítio has a lovely beach with pounding surf (located 1km from the plaza). North or south along the coast quickly leads to a deserted shore with churning seas and flat sands backed by bluffs topped with coconut trees. **B&B Bela Bahia** (☎75 99927-6633; www.bela-bahia.com; Principal 346, Poças; d from R$190; 🏊) has simple rooms right off of the beach, and you can get an authentic Bahian seafood feast at **Zecas & Zecas** (☎75 99815-5856; Praça Arsênio Mendes 51, Sítio do Conde; mains for 2 R$60-90; ⏰11:30am-9pm) in the main square.

You can head north on the Expresso Linha Verde bus which departs from the downstairs of Salvador's bus station regularly (alert the driver of your destination when you get on), but to get to Sítio do Conde you'll need to have your own car or arrange private transportation. Area pousadas like B&B Bela Bahia also offer private transportation from the Salvador airport (R$640 round-trip per carload).

for intrepid climbers) and a few friendly guesthouses and restaurants. The town ends at the edge of an enormous expanse of tall white sand dunes, beyond which the wide, flat sands of the Bahian coast stretch to the south. Mangue Seco's remote location prompts most visitors to come on guided day tours, preventing rapid growth and leaving nights decidedly quiet. It's about a 1.5km walk to the ocean, which has a handful of simple *barracas* (food stalls) strung with hammocks.

Mangue Seco's culinary specialty is *aratu*, a tiny red shellfish sometimes prepared in *moquecas* (fish stews).

Activities

Buggy Ride DUNE BUGGY
(buggy ride R$130; ⏰8am-3pm) Up to four people can be taken on a tour of the dunes behind the village of Mangue Seco that ends at a secluded beach that's perfect for swimming. Look for the stand south of the ferry dock.

Sleeping & Eating

There are only a few options in and around the village, but they are all fairly solid choices for anyone looking to stay on the peninsula and have some real peace and quiet.

Resort Recanto da Natureza HOTEL $$$
(☎79 99881-8761; www.resortrecantodanatureza.com.br; Sítio Angelin; ste from R$380; ❄🛜🏊) Don't let the word 'resort' fool you: travelers from far and wide sing the praises of the laid-back atmosphere at Resort Recanto da Natureza. It's more like a rustic-chic country hotel with a great swimming pool and attentive staff.

Pousada O Forte POUSADA $$$
(☎75 3445-9039; www.pousadaoforte.com; Praia da Costa s/n; d from R$390; ❄🛜🏊) 🌿 Located just outside the village center on the riverfront, on the way to the beach, this ecofriendly French–Brazilian–owned guesthouse occupies an isolated spot overlooking the river. With pretty bungalows

and a lovely swimming pool, it's family friendly, too.

Recanto de Dona Sula CAFE $
(☎79 98843-0590; pastries R$10; ⏲8:30am-7pm) At this local favorite, homemade candies, ice creams and liqueurs are made from regional fruits; the coffee is excellent too. The specialty of the house are *pastéis de forno,* savory filled pastries that are baked instead of fried. It's located on the main town square near the church.

Getting There & Away

Mangue Seco is remote; unless you're hiring private transportation or coming on a day trip from Salvador or Aracaju (usually around R$95 per person), getting here requires a combination of bus, taxi and boat.

Most travelers arrive in Mangue Seco as follows: from the south, a Rota (p443) bus from Salvador (R$75 to R$81, five daily) to Estância; or from the north, a Coopertalse (www.coopertalse.com.br) bus from Aracaju to Estancia (R$12.50, several daily). A taxi from Estância to Pontal (R$65) takes you to the speedboat between Pontal and Mangue Seco (around R$100 for five people).

Especially if you're traveling with others, it's worthwhile asking your accommodation in Mangue Seco if they offer more direct transportation. Pousada O Forte, for example, offers service from Salvador (R$450 to R$500 for up to four people) and Aracaju (R$270 for up to four people).

SOUTH OF SALVADOR

Morro de São Paulo

☎0XX75 / POP 4000

Boasting postcard-pretty beaches and a lively town set amongst lush coastal jungle, Morro de São Paulo has long been a favorite weekend getaway for travelers and Salvador locals alike. Though Morro is overtly touristy, many visitors don't care, since it's also a fabulous tropical paradise with sandy lanes, calm waters and a candlelit nightlife scene.

Remotely perched at the northern tip of the Ilha de Tinharé, Morro's appeal stems from its relaxed pace – no cars are allowed on the island – and unique geography: three jungle-topped hills on a point at the meeting of the mangrove-lined Canal de Taperoá and a clear, shallow Atlantic.

During the high season the village booms, dozens of vendors mix fresh-fruit caipirinhas on the sand, and lighthearted dancing and music enliven the beaches every night.

Sights

The town's icon is a 17th-century carved-stone fortress gate, which welcomes each arrival from its position above the dock.

Around the corner at the point are the fort ruins (1630). Catching the rare sight of the sun setting over the river and mangroves from the fort is a visitor ritual. The lighthouse (1835) above the fort affords a fantastic view over Morro's beaches.

Down a sandy lane from the main square, the **Fonte Grande** (Great Fountain), in operation since the 17th century, is a good example of an old urban water-supply system in Bahia.

Beaches

The waters of Morro's four conveniently named main beaches are mostly calm, shallow and warm, and their sands are narrow and swallowed by the high tides. Tiny **Primeira Praia** is lined with pousadas, occasionally hosts lively football matches on the sand, and has a decent surf break. Deep **Segunda Praia** (500m) is the 'action' beach, with pousadas, restaurants, nightclubs and a sea of tables and chairs. Pousadas and anchored boats dominate one end of **Terceira Praia** (1km). Once you pass a pair of restaurants, **Quarta Praia** (2km) is a long, lovely stretch of sand graced by tall, swaying palms. For even more isolated peace, continue on at low tide to **Praia do Encanto** (5km) or further down the island to **Garapuá**.

Activities

Tiroleza ADVENTURE SPORTS
(☎75 99814-9478; tirolezamsp@hotmail.com; R$50; ⏲8am-4pm) Adrenaline junkies should hike to the top of the hill with the lighthouse near the boat dock. There you will find a zip line that takes you flying in front of the coastline and into the water. If you want pictures of your ride it's an extra R$40. Note that the hours of operation aren't always consistent.

Tours

A daylong boat trip around the island (around R$140), with stops at the Garapuá and Moreré offshore reefs and the villages of Boipeba and historical Cairu, is obligatory. You'll fly over waves in a speedboat, past gorgeous beach and mangrove scenery, jump off the boat for swimming and snorkeling, stop at a floating oyster bar, and walk around historic island villages. Many agencies in town, like **Zulu Turismo** (☎75 3652-1358; www.morrodesaopaulobahiabrasil.com; Rua da Mangaba 98; ⏲8am-6pm Mon-Fri, to noon Sat) and **Viva Bahia Turismo** (Centro de Informações ao Turista; ☎75 3652-1083; Praça Aureliano Lima; ⏲8am-10pm), run the trip. It doesn't matter which agency you book with: they all redirect travelers to the same boats.

Another popular daylong excursion (around R$80) takes travelers to Garapuá via 4WD vehicle. It's a good way to enjoy the natural pools at a more leisurely pace.

Scuba enthusiasts can log onto the website or stop into the local office of **Companhia do Mergulho** (☎75 3652-1200; www.facebook.com/ciamergulhomsp; Prainha s/n, Primeira Praia; ⏲8am-6pm), located on the path to the beach.

Sleeping

Since Morro is a popular getaway from Salvador, prices vary wildly: during peak Brazilian vacation times, prices skyrocket and pousadas book up well ahead of time. Be forewarned that staying on Segunda Praia during summer means sleeping to the nightclubs' pounding beats; the least expensive pousadas are in town.

Che Lagarto Hostel HOSTEL $
(☎75 3652-1018; www.chelagarto.com; Rua da Fonte Grande 11; dm/d from R$75/226; ❄📶) Convenient to the ferry dock and local nightlife, yet with a middle-of-the-jungle feel thanks to its forest-shrouded wooden sundeck, this chain hostel is geared to those looking for a youthful party vibe.

★**Porto de Chima Surf Hostel** POUSADA $$
(☎75 99810-3242; www.portodecimahostel.com; Porto de Cima 56; dm/d from R$69/279; ❄📶) This former pousada, now a chill hostel catering to surfers, sits along the path to Porto de Cima Beach. Watching electric-blue hummingbirds and the occasional monkey from the vantage point of one of the porch hammocks is about as relaxing as it gets, and the breakfast is downright picturesque.

Le Terrace Beach Hotel HOTEL $$
(☎75 3652-1308; www.leterrace.com.br; Segunda Praia; r R$280-475; ❄📶) Tucked into the trees on the far end of Segunda Praia, Le Terrace has, well, plenty of terraces: one for breakfast with an ocean view, another off your guest room. These spacious apartments are well equipped and stylish. The only downside is that it can be noisy at night: those earplugs are provided for a reason.

Villa dos Graffitis POUSADA $$
(☎75 3652-1803; www.villadosgraffitis.com.br; Segunda Praia; d R$290; ❄📶🏊) As the name suggests, modern art is the focus at this cool, sustainably built guesthouse with more personality than any other on Morro's beachfront. The owners commissioned Brazilian street artists to paint murals in guest rooms and public spaces, including around the stylish swimming pool, hot tub and solarium, and the cool billiards room.

Pousada Bahia Bacana POUSADA $$
(☎75 99191-3477; www.pousadabahiabacana.com.br; Prainha 35, Primera Praia; d R$304-490; ❄📶🏊) Bahia Bacana is located on the main road in town and features a small but extremely memorable swimming pool perched high over the beach. Guest rooms are bright and welcoming, with hardwood floors; many have private balconies with hammocks and views of the ocean.

Pousada O Casarão POUSADA $$
(☎75 3652-1022; www.pousadaocasarao.com; Praça Aureliano Lima 190; d/bungalow from R$135/158; ❄📶🏊) Reigning over the main plaza, this beautifully renovated colonial mansion – dating from 1906 – has lovely rooms with classic furnishings and large windows, plus hillside bungalows with private balconies. Amenities include two swimming pools: one, with a bar, for adults, and another for children. Note that the rooms overlooking the square have great views, but can be noisy at night.

Pousada Colibri POUSADA $$
(☎75 3652-1056; www.pousada-colibri.com; Porto de Cima 7; d/ste from R$195/235; ⏲Jul-Apr; ❄📶🏊) In a marvelous hilltop position, the lushly landscaped Colibri has pretty cabins and suites with verandas and hammocks. Surrounding jungle assures quiet, but it's a bit of a hike from the beach – luckily, rates include round-trip baggage transfer from the harbor. To reach it, take the path to the spring, then turn right up a quiet forested lane.

Villa das Pedras POUSADA $$$
(☎75 3652-1075; www.villadaspedras.com.br; Segunda Praia; d from R$420; ❄📶🏊) This eye-catching guesthouse, with vibrant hues and clean, modern lines, wins the most style points on busy Segunda Praia. The lavish breakfast spread, swimming pool and bar, and location directly across from the beach make it a

worthy stay; the downside to the central location is that the area can be loud at night.

Eating

Casual dining options abound on the island. You'll find the best variety in town along the main road down to the beach, as well as around the Fonte Grande. At night, Segunda Praia is alive with restaurants competing for your business – it's a prime opportunity to dine with the sand between your toes.

Bar Dos BURGERS $

(www.facebook.com/bardosmorrodesaopaulo; Rua da Praia, Segunda Praia; burgers R$26-39; ⊙11am-11pm) If you need a break from seafood you can grab a gourmet burger at Bar Dos. The burger menu is varied and relatively inexpensive given the prime location right on the beach. In addition to red meat there are also chicken and tuna options and a small menu of creative salads.

Café das Artes BRAZILIAN $$

(☎75 3652-1057; www.solardasartes.net; Praça Aureliano Lima; mains R$30-53; ⊙noon-11pm) This pretty cafe-restaurant doubles as an art space; the patio overlooking the square is a sweet spot for a little night music. House specialties include seafood risotto and shrimp cooked in green coconut sauce. It's located at a popular pousada, Solar das Artes.

Jony Milanesa Club ITALIAN $$

(☎75 99879-4834; Porto de Cima; mains R$25-35; ⊙4pm-midnight) If the name wasn't enough of a giveaway, at Jony Milanesa Club you'll find a slew of different varieties of chicken milanesa, as well as burgers and salads. The food is great and the atmosphere is fun, especially at night, when you can reliably get a good cocktail with the island's younger crowd.

Andina LATIN AMERICAN $$

(☎75 98326-7555; www.facebook.com/andinacozinhalatina; Porto de Cima 44; mains R$36-65; ⊙7:30pm-midnight Tue-Sun) Creative Latin American cuisine and cocktails in a lovely treehouse-like setting. Andina is a bit of a hidden gem: to get there from the main square, step through the archway closest to the O Casarãao mansion. When you reach the historic fountain, hang a right and walk uphill to the restaurant. It's worth finding.

Minha Louca Paixão BRAZILIAN $$

(☎75 3652-1318; www.minhaloucapaixao.com.br; Terceira Praia; mains R$32-68; ⊙5-11pm; ✎) Well-prepared seafood dishes served at elegant (and quiet) waterfront tables make this sophisticated eatery, located at an upscale pousada of the same name, one of the more romantic dining options along the beaches. It's a great spot for a special occasion.

Sabor da Terra SEAFOOD $$

(☎75 3652-1490; Caminho da Praia; mains R$24-42; ⊙noon-11pm) Excellent seafood is prepared simply or with Bahian spice; fish *moqueca* and *casquinha de siri* (shredded crab meat) are excellent. Part of the appeal is people-watching and hearing live music from nearby restaurants at these tables lining the pedestrian walkway.

Bianco e Nero PIZZA $$

(☎75 3652-1097; Caminho da Praia; mains R$30-65; ⊙5:30pm-late) This fashionable Italian pizzeria and eatery is hugely popular for its fresh seafood pastas, oven-fired pizzas, rich Italian desserts and wines by the glass, all served on a large terrace above the main pedestrian thoroughfare. Service can be lax; you're paying for the stylish atmosphere.

Drinking & Nightlife

For such a small town there is plenty of nightlife to be enjoyed in Morro de São Paulo, especially in peak tourist seasons. You'll find several bars and even a few nightclubs where you can drink and dance until morning. Don't miss the dexterous vendors on the beach at night mixing delicious fruity cocktails.

★**Portaló Bar & Restaurante** COCKTAIL BAR

(☎75 3652-1375; www.hotelportalo.com; Hotel Portaló; ⊙noon-10pm) This hotel's terrace is the place to be at sunset for glorious views over the harbor, a DJ-spun soundtrack and festive drinks served with the flourish of tropical flowers. There's a full dinner menu, too, if you want to make an evening of it (mains R$24–R$46). Look for it when you're stepping off the boat upon arrival on the island.

Café Espresso Cappuccino COFFEE

(☎75 99102-6152; http://espresso-capuccino.negocio.site; Rua da Prainha 175; ⊙8am-11:30pm Mon-Sat, to 11pm Sun) Keep your eyes peeled for this modern coffee shop on the bend right before the main road turns down to the beach. It serves strong espresso drinks and a fun array of pastries that can be enjoyed on tables overlooking the street.

Orientation

At the dock, wheelbarrow valets wait to help you transport your luggage and lead you to your accommodations, which is especially useful for travelers with rolling luggage (be sure to negotiate the price beforehand).

Uphill lies the main square (Praça Aureliano Lima) in the Vila, with an information office and a few restaurants. To reach the beaches, take a left at the square; this passes along the main street, Rua Caminho da Praia, and is lined with restaurants and shops. Continue downhill to access the shores, reaching Primeira Praia (First Beach), then Segunda Praia, and so on. Heading right from the main plaza, you'll go through an archway down Rua da Fonte and pass the spring-fed fountain that was once the village's freshwater source.

Information

There are a few ATMs on the island, at **Banco do Brasil** (Praça Aureliano Lima) and **Brandesco** (Caminho da Praia), but it's wise to bring necessary funds with you from the mainland, especially during high season, when tourists deplete the ATMs' cash supplies. Most establishments also accept credit cards, but some essential services, such as the boat service, require cash.

Most pousadas and restaurants around the island have complimentary wi-fi.

At the top of the hill up from the dock and along the path to the beach, several travel agencies sell boat and domestic airline tickets, organize excursions and distribute maps.

Getting There & Away

A handful of operators run catamarans and small ferries (around R$100) between Morro and the Terminal Marítimo Turístico in Salvador. There are five to seven daily departures each way. For reservations, contact **Biotur** (☎75 3641-3327; www.biotur.com.br), **Farol do Morro** (☎71 3319-4570; www.faroldomorrotour.com), **IlhaBela** (☎in Salvador 71 3326-7158; www.ilhabelatm.com.br) or **Lancha Lulalu** (☎75 9917-1975), or stop into a travel agency on the island. Note that the ride can be rough, even if you aren't prone to seasickness. Come with travel-sickness medication. Also keep in mind it's common for passengers to get wet on smaller boats.

There are also daily boats to Valença (R$25–R$27, 40 minutes), convenient if you're heading to Boipeba, the Peninsula Marau or points south.

If you're heading directly to Salvador's airport from Morro, contact **Cassi Turismo** (☎71 99121-1111; www.cassiturismo.com.br). The agency sells a transfer package (R$95 to R$125, five daily) involving a short boat ride from Morro to Ponto do Curral, then a 1½-hour van ride to Mar Grande on Ilha Itaparica, a 40-minute ferry to Salvador, and, finally, a ride to the airport.

Two small airlines have daily flights between Salvador and Morro (R$478, 25 minutes). Contact **Aerostar** (☎in Salvador 71-3612-8600; www.aerostar.com.br), **Addey Taxi Aéreo** (☎in Salvador 71-3377-1993; www.addey.com.br) or a travel agency.

Boipeba

☎0XX75 / POP 2500

South of the Ilha da Tinharé, across the narrow Rio do Inferno, sits the Ilha de Boipeba. The village of Boipeba, on the northeastern tip of the island, is quiet, rustic and said to be what Morro was 20 years ago – though this is slowly changing as more travelers hear about this little paradise. The island's coastline is pristine, with more than 20km of beautiful, deserted beaches, including **Ponta de Castelhanos**, known for its diving.

Sights

Praia da Cueira BEACH

Located about 1.5km outside of the village, Praia da Cueira has a nice stretch of palm-tree-lined beach facing the Atlantic that you'll likely find less crowded than the beaches in town. It's a popular spot for surfers and at the northern end of the beach you'll find **Guido's Restaurante** (☎75 3653-6049; Praia da Cueira; mains R$50-160; ⏲11am-6pm), an island institution.

Sleeping & Eating

There are a fair number of pousadas in and around the village, several of which boast front doors that open directly onto the beach. Most pousadas have charming tropical-themed bars and restaurants that are open to the public.

Abaquar Hostel HOSTEL $

(☎75 3653-6263; www.abaquarhostel.com; Rua do Areal s/n; dm/d with fan R$45/125, with air-con R$55/150; ❄📶) Paradise for the backpacker set. Abaquar has four- and six-bed dorms, each with its own bathroom and balcony, plus tidy doubles with views of the gardens. There are plenty of hammocks to choose

> **ARRIVING ON THE ISLAND**
>
> No matter how you arrive on the island, you'll pay a fee (R$15) to enter. Most visitors arrive by boat and are ushered directly to the payment kiosks before leaving the dock.

from in this quiet, palm-tree-shaded setting. Children age 12 and up are welcome.

★O Céu de Boipeba BOUTIQUE HOTEL **$$**
(75 99908-8995; www.oceudeboipeba.com; Outeiro dos Namorados s/n; ste from R$295;) The appeal of this boutique hotel is in its name, which translates as 'the sky of Boipeba.' It's located on a hill just outside of the village which provides panoramic views of the island and its famous beaches. The glass walls of the suites make it possible to enjoy the scenery from bed.

Pousada Pérola do Atlântico POUSADA **$$**
(75 3653-6096; peroladoatlanticoboipeba@hotmail.com; Rua da Praia s/n; d/tr from R$260/360;) On the beach, this welcoming guesthouse has lush gardens with winding pathways leading through the tranquil setting. Rooms offer private patios with hammocks, and breakfast is served on a patio right next to the ocean.

Pousada Santa Clara POUSADA **$$$**
(75 3653-6085; www.santaclaraboipeba.com; Travessa da Praia 5; d from R$330;) A 10-minute walk from the town center, this restful guesthouse truly feels like a getaway. Santa Clara has lush foliage and large, cheerful rooms; the wonderful breakfast and onsite restaurant (open to the public Tuesday to Sunday), both using local produce, are particularly beloved by repeat guests.

Restaurante Familia SEAFOOD **$**
(75 3653-6211; Rua da Praia; mains R$30-90; 11am-6pm) Stop by this popular spot on Boipeba's main beach drag for a hearty seafood lunch or to just enjoy a cold beer with your feet in the sand.

Information

Stop by or email the reputable **Bahia Terra** (75 3653-6017; www.boipebatur.com.br; Rua da Praia; 8am-noon & 2-6pm) to organize transfers and tours.

Getting There & Away

The easiest way to arrive is by speedboat from Valença (accessible from Salvador by a combination of ferry and bus via Bom Despacho.) From Valença's ferry dock, catch a speedboat (R$44, one hour, five departures between 10am and 4pm on weekdays, reduced service on weekends) to Boipeba. There are other options between Valença and Boipeba, including a bus-boat combination via Torrinha, but the direct speedboat is easier to plan. Accommodations owners in Boipeba are helpful resources as you're planning your travel strategy to or from the island.

If you're arriving from Morro de São Paulo you can ask the travel agencies there about hitching a ride on one of their tours of the island and you may even be able to negotiate a lower price for a one-way trip if their tour is light on people. Keep in mind that in the off season the tours may be more sporadic. Some companies also offer a 4x4 tour to Boipeba, but they are more expensive (R$95–R$110).

Check www.boipebatur.com.br for more details on these and other transportation options.

Valença

0XX75 / POP 99,000

Valença is a colonial fishing town on the banks of the Rio Una, historically the site of Portuguese encounters with both indigenous tribes and the Dutch. Locals know it as a center of shipbuilding: 15th-century techniques have been so well maintained that the town was chosen to produce a replica of the Spanish galleon *La Niña* for the American epic film *1492* (1992) about Christopher Columbus' journey. Tourists mostly know it as one of the gateways to the Arquipelago de Cairu, home to popular destinations Morro de São Paulo and Boipeba. If you're on your way to either location it's possible you'll end up staying overnight in Valença due to bus and boat schedules.

Sleeping & Eating

Hotel Portal Rio Una HOTEL **$$**
(75 3641-5050; www.portalhoteis.tur.br; Maestro Barrinha s/n; d from R$209;) This large, attractive hotel has Valença's finest restaurant and rooms, each with verandas overlooking the river. It's 1km from the river, on the opposite side of the port.

Mega Chic BRAZILIAN **$**
(75 3641-4704; www.facebook.com/RestauranteMegaChic; Maçônica 11; mains R$25-75; 7am-10pm Mon-Sat, to 6pm Sun) Across the bridge from the center, Mega Chic offers a self-serve buffet and an à la carte menu of pastas, salads, sandwiches and cocktails.

Getting There & Away

If they're not coming straight from Salvador, travelers generally reach Morro de São Paulo and Boipeba via Valença. Regular boats depart to both towns. Valença is directly linked by bus from Feira de Santana (R$43, four hours) and Bom Despacho (R$22, two hours) in the north and Camamu in the south (R$15–R$18, two hours). The **bus station** (☎75 3641-4894; Abel Aguiar Queiroz 78) is about 1km from the boat dock.

Boats leave regularly for Morro de São Paulo (R$25–R$27, 40 minutes). There are also five boats daily on weekdays to Boipeba, as well as less frequent weekend service (R$44, one hour). The **boat dock** (Comendador Madureira) is right on the river next to the entrance to the bridge.

Barra Grande

☎0XX73 / POP 21,000 (PENINSULA MARAÚ)

Once a remote fishing village on the northern tip of the Peninsula de Maraú, Barra Grande has transformed over the years into a popular vacation getaway for Brazilian families. Dozens of pousadas and restaurants now line the town's sandy streets and although the quaint center is bustling with tourists, once you venture out to the rest of the peninsula you'll find plenty of palm-tree-lined roads and quiet beaches to explore.

Beaches

At the base of the village, where the boats arrive from Camamu, is the 2km-long **Barra Grande beach**, where the calm waters are fine for swimming and those traveling with children. A short walk along the beach leads to the **Ponta da Mutá**, the northeastern point of the peninsula, with a lighthouse marking the bay's entrance. Around the rocky point, you access a long stretch of coast, with **Praia da Bombaça** the next notable beach (3.5km from Barra Grande). Further south you'll find **Taipu de Fora** (7km from town), which has a reputation for being one of Brazil's top beaches.

Visitors should note that, although the town center is small, the surrounding area is not: many beaches are a hike from the pousadas. It's easy to arrange private or shared transportation to the beaches, as well as quad-bike rentals, which are a popular option for navigating the sandy roads.

Sleeping

There's a wide range of accommodations in town, from homey pousadas to luxurious beach hotels and apartment-style rentals with kitchens for those interested in self-catering.

Taipabas Hotel POUSADA **$$**
(☎73 3258-6177; www.taipabashotel.web2007.uni5.net; Vivaldo Monteiro 20; d/tr R$190/228;) This charming family-run hotel offers treehouse-like guest rooms with private hardwood balconies that overlook a central swimming pool, plus one of the best breakfasts in town.

Flat Barra APARTMENT **$$**
(☎73 3258-6124; www.flatbarra.com.br; Jose Melo Pirajá s/n; apt for 2/3 people R$290/368;) Staying at this lovely property is like renting your own beach apartment. The place looks like a pousada – complete with tropical foliage, a lavish breakfast spread and

PASSING THROUGH CAMAMU

Most people arrive in Barra Grande on a boat from Camamu, which is on the mainland, shielded from the open ocean by the Peninsula de Maraú. The town is the port of call for the many tiny fishing villages in the region and overlooks a maze of mangrove-filled islets and narrow channels. Buses pass through frequently enough that it's unlikely you'd need to spend the night, but if you do there are a few inexpensive, family-run pousadas (guesthouses) and simple cafes around the boat dock.

Although it is a mini transportation hub there is no real bus station here. Instead you'll just see the offices of a few bus companies near the ports. From the south buses arrive from Itacaré (R$12–R$17, one hour) and from the north from Valença (R$16, two hours), Bom Despacho (R$37, four hours) and Feira de Santana (R$60, 5½ hours). Frequent buses travel to those destinations from Camamu as well. Aguia Branca, Cidade Sol and Empresa Santana all provide service to the town.

If you're continuing on to Barra Grande you can't miss the port from where you get off the bus. There are actually two, each launching boats for rival companies that basically offer the same service for the same price to Barra Grande. One is directly across the street from the buses, the other a little to the right if you're facing the river. However, you're likely to be intercepted right off the bus by a representative from one of the aforementioned companies to lead you to buy a ticket from their employer. This 'service' is free, so disregard if they try to ask for money.

a swimming pool – but instead of regular guest rooms, these accommodations have full kitchens, private balconies and separate sleeping and living areas.

Pousada Barrabella POUSADA $$
(☎73 3258-6285; www.pousadabarrabella.com.br; Vasco Neto 3; d from R$369;) This pretty guesthouse, decorated with furnishings made by local craftspeople, offers tranquil rooms with sea or bay views and private balconies, an excellent restaurant, an inviting swimming pool with a waterfall, and a cocktail bar that overlooks the ocean.

Ponta do Mutá POUSADA $$
(☎73 3258-6028; www.pousadapontadomuta.com.br; Anjo s/n; d with/without sea view from R$390/385;) This welcoming guesthouse's primary selling point is its location right on the beach, near the boat dock, and its grassy lawn dotted with chaise lounges facing the water. Pleasantly decorated rooms each feature a veranda and hammock; many have sea views.

Pousada Porto da Barra POUSADA $$$
(☎73 3258-6349; http://pousadaportodabarra.wixsite.com/pousada; Vasco Neto 13; d/tr R$360/460;) Near the dock, Porto da Barra offers standard rooms with tile floors and hammocks strung outside the doors. The sea breezes and leafy, palm-tree-dotted grounds, just steps from the beach, are the main draw.

Eating

The village center has a decent number of restaurants, although most are only open for dinner, and opening hours can be unpredictable in the off season. On the beaches you'll find plenty of *barracas* (food stalls) and seafood restaurants.

A Tapera BAHIAN $$
(☎73 3258-6119; Doutora Lili 95; mains for 2 R$100-130; noon-10pm) Just off the plaza, this traditional Bahian restaurant – considered by many to be the best on the peninsula – serves fresh seafood, including a fine *moqueca* (fish stew). Dine outside under the trees for the best atmosphere.

Praça da Taínha BRAZILIAN $$
(Jose Melo Piraja; mains R$20-50; 5pm-late) This grassy open-air plaza is home to several casual, budget-friendly eateries – look for crepes, pizzas, sandwiches, tapioca, *moqueca* (fish stew), ice cream and cocktails – and a stage where live musicians often perform. The pretty lights and festive atmosphere make the place extremely appealing at night.

Drinking & Nightlife

In the town center you'll find plenty of places to grab a beer or cocktail, including stalls in the Praça da Taínha that throw together cheap fruity mixed drinks.

Barra Beer Conveniências CRAFT BEER
(☎73 99933-2648; Maraú; 5pm-late) Barra Beer offers a nice reprieve from the beachy cocktail-soaked nightlife in Barra Grande. It has an exciting selection of craft beers – everything from IPAs to wheat brews – including many from local breweries. You can get yours to go or drink it in the small storefront where you'll often find the town's hipper residents and visitors congregating.

Information

Get funds before going to Barra Grande, as there are no banks or ATMs. Most restaurants and hotels take cards but it's good to have cash on hand for beach vendors and transport.

You'll find plenty of tourist information next to the dock – keep your eyes peeled for people in blue or green shirts. You can also check www.barragrande.net for the complete lowdown on the area.

Getting There & Away

The most common way tourists arrive in Barra Grande is via speedboat from Camamu (R$30, 30 minutes). Boats run hourly between 6am and 5pm. Two companies make the trip, Camamu Adventure (www.camamuadventure.com.br) and Camamu Lanches Rapidas, and you're likely to get approached by representatives from each company as you near the dock, trying to sway you to choose their service. Both are nearly identical, with the boats used by Camamu Adventure being slightly more upscale. It's possible to arrive overland from nearby towns like Itacaré (around R$250, 2½ hours) and Ilhéus (around R$350, 3½ hours) but it's much more expensive and the roads can be difficult if it's been raining.

Getting Around

Four-wheel-drive *jardineiras* (pickup trucks with bench seating in the back) park on the road between the main plaza in town and the dock. They leave for the beaches as soon as they have a full load. The most common destination is Taipu de Fora (R$12.50 one way, 40 minutes). Look for the 'Ponto das Jardineiras' sign and the drivers in yellow T-shirts. From the same spot, you can also arrange travel to the beaches by taxi (R$50 to Taipu de Fora).

One of the more popular ways to explore the peninsula is renting your own quad bike. There are several operations around town, but **Locadora Ribeiro** (73 3258-6433, WhatsApp 73 99963-3030; locadoraribeiro@hotmail.com; quad-bike rentals per day R$100-200) is the most popular. You can arrange the rental the day before and the operator will meet you at your hotel with the bike.

Itacaré

0XX73 / POP 13,100

Beautiful Itacaré has long been sought out by hippies and surfers mesmerized by wide stretches of virgin Atlantic rainforest, picturesque beaches and reliable surf breaks. Countless pousadas (guesthouses) and restaurants now pack the streets; still, a mellow, youthful vibe prevails, surf culture reigns supreme, and many establishments in the area are committed to environmentally friendly practices (look for the Carbon Free Tourism sign proudly posted around town).

Sights & Activities

The closest beach to town is **Praia da Concha**. Though not overly remarkable, it features the most services – beach cabanas serve drinks and food and rent lounge chairs – and calm waters ideal for those traveling with children.

The lovely coast south of Itacaré is characterized by rough surf, better for surfing than for swimming. **Resende**, **Tiririca** and **Ribeira** beaches are set in coves separated by rainforest-covered hills. Offering palm-tree shade and basic services, they're located within 1.5km of town – just follow the signs (and the parade of surfers.)

Slightly beyond these is the idyllic **Prainha**, reachable by trail from Praia do Ribeira, and further, the paradise-like **Engenhoca**, **Havaizinho** and **Itacarezinho** beaches, located 12km south of town.

Easy Drop SURFING

(73 3251-3065; www.easydrop.com; João Coutinho 140; 1-day class R$213, 1-week package from R$1926) This well-established surf camp, offering a weeklong surfing experience with classes and accommodations, gets great reviews from travelers.

Brazil Trip Tour ADVENTURE

(73 9996-3331; www.braziltriptour.com; Pedro Longo 235) One of several reliable agencies offering excursions, surf lessons, transfers and tours, Brazil Trip Tour specializes in English-speaking guides and eco-minded tours.

Sleeping

The majority of guesthouses are scattered along Rua Pedro Longo/Pituba. For a quieter stay that's still close to the action, try a pousada on a side street or in the Condomínio Conchas do Mar area instead of one that's located right on the main drag.

Concha Tropical Flat APARTMENT $

(73 3251-3426; www.conchatropical.com.br; Rua B, Praia da Concha; apt for 2/4 people R$150/235;) Ideal for self-caterers, these modern apartments are equipped with kitchens, flat-screen televisions and private balconies with ocean views. The hosts are known for their attention to their guests' needs. There's no breakfast included; communal facilities include a barbecue area.

Pousada Casa Tiki POUSADA $

(73 99804-8901; www.pousadacasatiki.com.br; Rua C, Praia da Concha; d with/without bathroom from R$150/120;) The home-away-from-home vibe is what makes this small guesthouse special: there are only four rooms, leisurely breakfasts happen around a communal table, and the owners, a young English-speaking couple, mix potent cocktails and offer travel advice.

Casarão Verde Hostel HOSTEL $

(73 3251-2037; http://casaraoverdehostel.com.br; Castro Alves s/n; dm from R$35, d without bathroom from R$80;) Budget travelers rave about the friendly reception and pristine, spacious rooms at this lovely colonial house – painted pale green, as the name suggests – that's been smartly converted into a hostel.

Albergue O Pharol HOSTEL $

(73 99825-4455; www.alberguepharol.com.br; Praça Santos Dumont 7; dm/d from R$45/125, apt for 4 from R$250; @) A favorite among backpackers, this centrally located and low-key hostel has tidy rooms, some with private balconies. There's a shared kitchen and a guest laundry area; the only downside is that there's no breakfast.

★ **Pousada Ilha Verde** POUSADA $$

(73 3251-2056; www.ilhaverde.com.br; Ataíde Setúbal 234; s/d from R$210/240, chalet for 4 R$439;) In a lush setting, Ilha Verde has uniquely decorated rooms inspired by the owners' world travels. Features include private

WORTH A TRIP

LITTLE HAWAII

Hawaizinho means 'Little Hawaii' in Portuguese – and it's just one of the paradise-like beaches south of Itacaré, which are popular destinations for intrepid surfers and sunbathers alike. Some of the following beaches are located within easy walking distance of the highway, while others require a hike through the woods.

You can reach the access points on any of the buses that make the regular trip between the bus stations of Itacaré and Ilhéus. Drivers are used to dropping people off: just make sure to advise the driver where you'd like to disembark, and be sure to bring your own food and water, as there's little infrastructure along this stretch.

The beaches listed below are ordered from north to south, starting after Itacaré and the beaches of **Prainha** and **São José**, located immediately to Itacaré's south.

Jeribucaçu Strong waves, plenty of shade and a few places to eat.

Engenhoca Popular with surfers. Has coconut-water and tapioca vendors.

Hawaizinho and Camboinha Reefs, strong waves. Accessible from the highway by the same path as Engenhoca.

Itacarezinho The longest beach in the area; sea-turtle mating ground. There's a bar-restaurant on the sand.

patios, an inviting swimming pool, abundant outdoor lounge space for luxuriating in the greenery, and a fair-trade shop with handicrafts made from Brazilian straw and shells.

Pousada Casa Zazá POUSADA $$
(☎73 3251-3022; www.pousadazaza.com.br; Bromélia 12; d/tr from R$160/180; ❄📶🏊) There's a lot of personal charm on display at this otherwise fairly standard guesthouse. The staff is friendly and eager to help guests make the most of their time in town. Accommodations are clean and comfortable and there's a large garden with a pool.

Pousada Maresia POUSADA $$
(☎73 3251-2338; www.maresiapousada.com.br; Pedro Longo 388; d/tr from R$160/215; ❄📶) 🍃 Simple rooms and a leafy garden courtyard – a memorable setting for breakfast – are part of the charm of this budget-friendly guesthouse that's focused on sustainable tourism. It's well positioned between the beach path and the heart of the action in the village.

Eating & Drinking

A browse up and down Itacaré's main thoroughfare is the best way to get the gastronomic lay of the land – look for pop-up food stands and makeshift caipirinha stands at night.

★ **Agua** BISTRO $
(☎73 99950-9548; Pedro Longo 147; mains R$25-28; ⏲4-11pm Tue-Sun; 🌱) Agua is a blast of modern cool in Itacare's beach-bum-centric dining scene. The regular menu features exquisitely cooked dishes inspired by Brazilian and Asian cuisine (including some good vegan and vegetarian options), but you'll want to make sure to go on Wednesday evening when the restaurant features a menu of various curries.

Bastante Elefante BURGERS $
(☎73 99968-8229; www.bastanteelefante.com.br; Pedro Longo 354; mains R$25-27; ⏲7-10:30pm Thu-Tue; 🌱) One of the more popular spots on Itacaré's main thoroughfare is this stylish burger joint that (surprise!) also specializes in vegetarian and vegan options. It's both hip and kid friendly, with a few outdoor tables, and a full cocktail list too.

Alamaim MIDDLE EASTERN $
(☎73 3251-3462; www.restaurantealamaim.com.br; Pedro Longo 204; mains R$24-39; ⏲2:30-10pm Mon-Sat; 🌱) Get your hummus fix here: this cool but casual eatery specializes in vegetarian Arabic food, from falafel to couscous, and has a relaxing lounge space where you can kick back after a day of surfing or swimming.

Estrela do Mar SEAFOOD $$
(☎73 3251-2230; Praia da Concha; mains R$30-50; ⏲5-9pm Mon-Sat, from noon summer; 👪) Overlooking the beach, elegant Estrela do Mar serves expertly prepared seafood, pasta and salads. There's a children's menu and a decent wine list too.

Mar e Mel BAR
(☎73 3251-2358; www.maremel.com.br; Alpínia s/n; mains R$28-60; ⏲5pm-midnight) This is the place to hear (and dance to) live *forró* three nights a week (Tuesday, Thursday and Saturday

at 9pm). There's a spacious wooden deck and abundant seafood and drink choices.

Orientation

Itacaré lies at the mouth of Rio de Contas, where the river meets the sea. A short walk east of the working-class neighborhoods around the fishing port leads to the area known as Pituba, which is essentially one long street, Rua Pedro Longo, lined with pousadas, restaurants and shops. Follow this road east out of town to access Itacaré's prettiest beaches. North of the Pituba strip is known as Condomínio Conchas do Mar, and has higher-end restaurants and pousadas in a more verdant setting. The neighborhood ends at the small beach of Praia da Concha.

Information

There are several exchange offices and banks with ATMs in town. Visit www.itacare.com.br for an overview.

Getting There & Around

Itacaré's **bus station** (☎73 3251-2181; Rua da Rodoviário) is just out of the center, but it's a bit of a hike from many of the pousadas. A taxi will cost around R$15–R$20 depending on where your pousada is.

Many travelers arrive in Itacaré from points north: from Salvador, taking the ferry to Bom Despacho and then connecting to a bus; or from Camamu, the jumping-off point for Barra Grande and the Peninsula Maraú. From Camamu, Águia Branca has buses at 12:50pm and 5:05pm (R$12, one hour.) Santana (www.empresasantana.com.br) also makes the trip at 9:39pm (R14). Buses depart from the bus companies' offices, around the corner from the port where boats depart for Barra Grande.

Coming or going from the south, **Rota** (☎73 3251-2181; http://rotatransportes.com.br) has around 15 daily departures to Ilhéus (R$15, 1¾ hours, from 5:15am to 8pm). The same buses will drop you at the access points to the beaches between Itacaré and Ilheús – make sure to tell the driver where you'd like to be let off. Rota also has one 7am bus to Porto Seguro (R$87, eight hours). You'll have more options for the same trip if you're willing to switch buses in Ilheús.

Rental cars and private taxi services advertised around town are useful for transfers to Ilheús (R$220 to R$280) and Camamu (R$250).

WORTH A TRIP

BAHIA FOR CHOCOLATE LOVERS

Take a break from the beach and head into the forest to **Vila Rosa** (www.vilarosaitacare.wix.com/vilarosaitacare; tour with transportation adult/child R$85/60, without transportation R$50/25; ⏲9am-4pm), a beautifully restored cocoa farm. Guided tours take visitors around the plantation to see the collection, fermentation and drying of cocoa beans, then into the chocolate factory to taste the final product. The farm is located 20km from Itacaré: the best way to arrive is to make a reservation on Vila Rosa's shuttle, which leaves Itacaré between 9am and 10am.

Have a coffee in the charming cafe, go for a dip in the stone pools, or take a kayak out on the reservoir. You can even stay the night in one of five guest rooms in the old colonial manor (rooms from R$225).

Ilhéus

☎0XX73 / POP 142,210

Bright, early-20th-century architecture and oddly angled streets lend a vibrant and rather whimsical air to slightly rough-around-the-edges Ilhéus. The town's fame comes from its history as a prosperous cocoa port, as well as being the hometown of Jorge Amado, the famous Brazilian novelist, who used it as the setting for one of his best novels, *Gabriela, Cravo e Canela (Gabriela, Clove and Cinnamon)*. The city's reputation as a tourist destination has been rising in the past few years, with plenty of visitors from elsewhere in Brazil stopping through to tour the historic center and lounge on the beaches south of the city.

History

Ilhéus was a sleepy place until cacao was introduced into the region from Belém in 1881. With the sugar plantations in the doldrums, impoverished agricultural workers and freed or escaped slaves flocked from all over the Northeast to the hills surrounding Ilhéus to participate in the new boom: cacao, known as the *ouro branco* (white gold) of Brazil.

Sudden, lawless and violent, the scramble to plant cacao displayed all the characteristics of a gold rush. When the dust settled, the land and power belonged to a few ruthless *coroneis* (so-called 'colonels') and their hired guns. The landless were left to work, and usually live, on the *fazendas* (plantations), where they were subjected to a harsh and paternalistic labor system. This history is graphically told by Amado, who grew up on a cacao plantation, in his book *Terras do Sem Fim* (published in English as *The Violent Land*).

In the early 1990s the *vassoura de bruxa* (witch's broom) disease left cacao trees shriveled and unable to bear fruit, hurting the area's economy dramatically. Though the disease persists to this day, you can still see cacao *fazendas* and rural workers like those Amado described throughout the lush, tropical hills.

Sights

The best thing to do in Ilhéus is explore the old streets. The center has several quaint antique buildings, a few small museums and some pedestrian-only thoroughfares, an ideal setting for photographers to wander.

Catedral de São Sebastião CHURCH
(Praça Dom Eduardo; 10am-8pm) The Catedral de São Sebastião is the city's towering icon – construction began in 1931 – and is a unique, eclectic mix of architectural styles. For an unforgettable view of the fairy-tale-like spires, walk out onto the beach at sunset and look back at the cathedral silhouetted against the clouds.

Casa de Jorge Amado MUSEUM
(71 99168-0571; Jorge Amado 20; R$5; 9am-12:30pm & 2-6pm Mon-Fri, 9am-1pm Sat) The Casa de Jorge Amado, where the eponymous writer lived with his parents while working on his first novel, has been restored and turned into a lovely and informative museum honoring Amado's life. Not many writers can boast this sort of recognition while still alive, but he became a national treasure well before his death in 2001.

Beaches

City beaches aren't the cleanest (though that doesn't stop local surfers taking to the waves). Your best bet is to head south, but even then you'll find that the area's broad, flat beaches are best for soccer games, and it takes kilometers for the water to lose the muddy color of the river outflow. **Praia dos Milionários** (7km) has some *barracas* and is popular with locals.

Tours

Trips to a tree-sloth recuperation center, Primavera Fazenda (where you'll be taken through the process of cacao production) and Lagoa Encantada, a state-protected area of Atlantic rainforest with waterfalls and wildlife, can all be arranged through local travel agencies like **Órbita Turismo e Expedições** (73 3231-3704; www.orbitaexpedicoes.com.br; Leite Mendes 71).

BAHIA'S FAVORITE SON

Nobody is more responsible for bringing Bahian culture to the rest of the world than Jorge Amado, Brazil's most famous modernist author. Amado's tales have been translated into 49 languages and read the world over.

Born in 1912, Jorge spent his youth in Ilhéus, the scene of many of his later novels. After secondary studies in Salvador, Amado studied law in Rio, but instead of going into practice he decided to become a writer. He surprised critics and the public by publishing his first novel, *O País do Carnaval*, when he was only 19 years old.

An avowed communist, Amado participated in the rebel literary movement of the time, launching two romances set in the cacao zone around Ilhéus: *Cacau* and *Suor*. The first novel was banned by the fascist-leaning Vargas government, which only increased Amado's popularity. Sent to prison several times for his beliefs, Amado was elected a federal deputy for the Brazilian communist party (PCB) in 1945, but he lost his seat after a disagreement with the party several years later. He left Brazil and lived for more than five years in Europe and Asia, finally breaking ties with the communist party after the crimes of Stalin were revealed to the world.

With *Gabriela, Cravo e Canela (Gabriela, Clove and Cinnamon)*, published in 1958, he entered a new writing phase, marked by a romantic and playful style that intimately described the colorful escapades of his Bahian heroes and heroines. This and his later novel *Dona Flor e Seus Dois Maridos (Dona Flor and Her Two Husbands)*, set in Salvador, were both adapted into popular films.

Amado died in Salvador in August 2001, just short of his 89th birthday.

Ilhéus

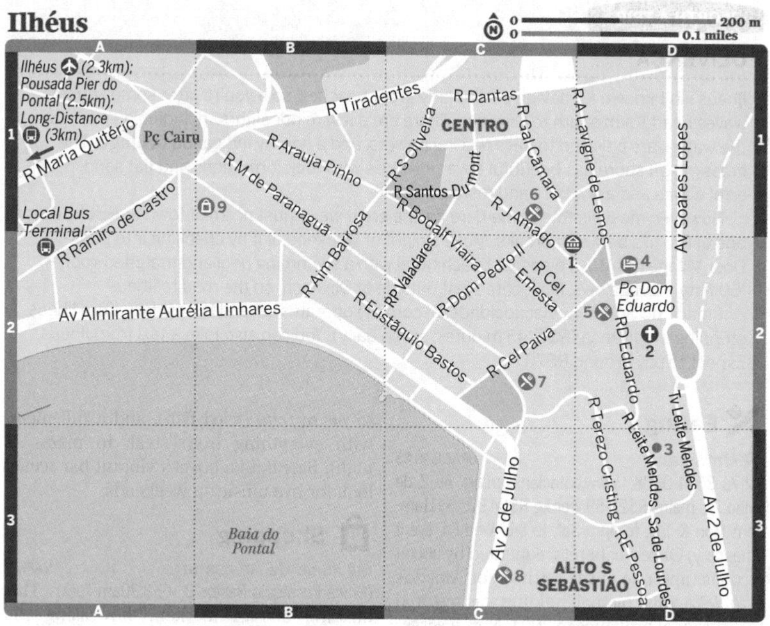

Ilhéus

Sights

1 Casa de Jorge Amado C2
2 Catedral de São Sebastião D2

Activities, Courses & Tours

3 Órbita Turismo e Expedições D3

Sleeping

4 Ilhéus Praia Hotel D2

Eating

5 Bar Vesúvio D2
6 Barrakítika C1
7 Bataclan C2
8 Restaurante Maria Machadão C3

Shopping

9 Mercado de Artesanato B1

Festivals & Events

Festa de São Sebastião CULTURAL
(11-20 Jan) As any Amado fan would guess, Ilhéus has highly spirited festivals, and this is one of the best.

Sleeping

There are a few hotels in Ilheus that boast historic charm, but not much in the way of modern comfort. Note that the city's best hotels, located south of the historic center and the Pontal neighborhood, are convenient only for those traveling by car.

Back Door Village HOTEL $$
(73 3269-1141; www.villagebackdoor.com.br; Rodovia Ilhéus–Olivença Km 13.5, Olivença; d/tr from R$247/346;) A pleasant beach hotel with a swimming pool and thatched-roof, '60s-style bungalows. On the road between Ilhéus and Olivença.

Pousada Pier do Pontal POUSADA $$
(73 3221-4000; www.pierdopontal.com.br; Lomanto Junior 1650, Pontal; s/d from R$206/222;) Despite needing some upgrades to the decor, this pleasant guesthouse is on the waterfront and has a swimming pool. From here you can head north to check out Ilheus' historic center, or south for the beaches.

Ilhéus Praia Hotel HOTEL $$
(73 2101-2533; www.ilheuspraia.com.br; Praça Dom Eduardo, Centro; s/d from R$140/172;) This high-rise hotel is fraying around the edges, but many rooms have fine views of the cathedral across the plaza. The prices don't seem in line with these average rooms, but it's extremely convenient for a few nights if you're hoping to sightsee in the historic center.

WORTH A TRIP

OLIVENÇA

Ilhéus isn't known for having particularly great beaches, so if you're after some serious waves head 16km south to Olivença. There are a few minor sights, including a **spa**, where the waters are believed to have healing powers, and a nearby indigenous **village**. The grassy town shore has beautiful cove **beaches** with rock formations and flat sand, powerful waves and a few bars and restaurants.

However, most visitors come here for the great waves just north of town at **Backdoor**, one of Brazil's best surf breaks. Make a night or weekend of it by checking into Back Door Village (p445), a pleasant beach hotel with a swimming pool and thatched-roof, '60s-style bungalows. It's located just outside of Olivença, on the road to Ilhéus.

Cidade do Sol (www.viacaocidadesol.com.br) operates several buses daily from Ilhéus stopping in Olivença (R$5, 45 minutes, seven daily). You can also take a taxi from Ilhéus. Expect to pay around R$70.

Eating

★ Bataclan BRAZILIAN $$

(☎73 3634-0088; www.bataclan.com.br; Av 2 de Julho 77; mains R$22-59, per kg R$54.90; ⏰11am-5pm Mon & Tue, to 4pm Sat, to late Wed-Fri, event times vary) Once a cabaret frequented by cocoa tycoons (and one of the settings for Amado's *Gabriela*), this colonial building was restored to its original brilliance in 2004. Now it serves as a restaurant and cultural center. There's a lunch buffet from 11:30am to 2:30pm. You can tour the house while you wait for your food or visit without eating for R$5.

★ Bar Vesúvio BAHIAN $$

(☎73 3634-2164; Praça Dom Eduardo 190; mains R$30-58; ⏰10am-midnight Mon-Sat) This landmark bar and restaurant attracts Amado fans (two of the novelist's fictional protagonists met here) for *moquecas* (fish stews) and cold beer served at the outdoor tables facing the cathedral, which is beautifully illuminated at night. Start with a few *pasteles arabes* (Arabic-style pastries stuffed with spicy meat).

Restaurante Maria Machadão ITALIAN $$

(☎73 3634-1001; Av 2 de Julho 955; mains R$39-50; ⏰6pm-midnight) Pizzas, Italian and Brazilian dishes and sushi can all be found at this charming restaurant just south of Ilhéus' center on the river. The menu is varied and there is ample seating, making it a great choice for families.

Barrakítika BRAZILIAN $$

(☎73 3231-8300; www.facebook.com/barrakitika; Jorge Amado 39; mains R$30-60; ⏰10am-2am Mon-Sat) This casual and hugely popular restaurant has outdoor tables, inexpensive set lunches from *feijoada* (bean-and-meat stew) to *peixe frito* (fried fish), and a full menu with everything from steak to pizza. At night, Barrakítika hosts a vibrant bar scene; look for live music on weekends.

Shopping

Mercado de Artesanato MARKET

(Praça Eustáquio Bastos 2; ⏰8:30am-7pm) This bustling artisan market, showcasing the lovely white dresses, crocheted textiles and beaded jewelry typical of the region, is a great place to pick up a few Bahian souvenirs.

Orientation

The city center is located on a beach-lined point that reaches into the mouth of the Rio Cachoeira, and is sandwiched between two hills. On the southern side of the S-curving river mouth is the modern neighborhood of Pontal – catch a taxi over the bridge to reach it.

Information

The downtown pedestrian streets near the cathedral are lined with ATMs.

Getting There & Away

AIR

LATAM (☎0300 570-5700; www.tam.com.br) and **GOL** (☎0800-704-0465; www.voegol.com.br) can fly or connect you to anywhere in Brazil from Ilhéus' **Aeroporto Jorge Amado** (IOS; ☎73 3234-4000; Brigadier Eduardo Gomes s/n, Pontal).

BUS

The **long-distance bus station** (Rodoviaria Ilheus; ☎73 2102-5335; Av Roberto Santos 15) is located east of the center.

Rota (www.rotatransportes.com.br) buses go to Porto Seguro (R$63 to R$85, six hours, four daily), and Aguia Branca (www.aguiabranca.com.br) has buses to Salvador (R$95 to R$231, eight hours, seven daily) making a long sweep around the Baía de Todos os Santos, recommended if you are stopping in the Recôncavo on the way.

Getting Around

The airport is in Pontal, 3.5km from the center. A taxi from the center costs around R$25. Also running along the waterfront between Pontal and the center are bright yellow Via Metro buses (R$3.50).

A taxi between the bus station and the center takes about 10 minutes and costs around R$20 to R$25. From the center, buses labeled 'Teotônio Vilela' pass the bus station.

City buses can be flagged down along their routes or caught at the **local bus terminal** (Ramiro de Castro 164) .

Porto Seguro

0XX73 / POP 145,531

Historically, Porto Seguro is significant: it's the point where Portuguese sailors first landed in the land now known as Brazil. But apart from its small historic center and colorful colonial houses, the city is more a popular destination for hordes of Brazilian and Argentinian package tourists, here for beach action and nightlife. It's also a popular place for high schoolers to get into trouble on school-break holidays. Many travelers linger in town only long enough to catch the ferry toward the lovely coastline and mellow village of nearby Arraial d'Ajuda.

History

Pedro Cabral's landing 16km north of Porto Seguro (Safe Port) at Coroa Vermelha is officially considered the first Portuguese landfall in Brazil. The sailors stayed just long enough to stock up on supplies. Three years later Gonçalvo Coelho's expedition arrived and planted a marker in what is now Porto Seguro's Cidade Histórica (Historic City). Jesuits on the same expedition built a church, now in ruins, in Outeiro da Glória. In 1526 a naval outpost, convent and chapel (Igreja NS da Misericórdia) were built in the present-day Cidade Histórica.

The Tupininquin, not the Pataxó, were the indigenous tribe around the site of Porto Seguro when the Portuguese landed. They were rapidly conquered and enslaved by the colonists, but the Aimoré, Pataxó, Cataxó and other inland tribes resisted Portuguese colonization and constantly threatened Porto Seguro. Military outposts were built along the coast in Belmonte, Vila Viçosa, Prado and Alcobaça to defend against both European attacks by sea and attacks from indigenous groups by land.

Sights

Motivation is required to climb the stairs to the **Cidade Histórica**; sweeping views over the coastline make the hike worthwhile. The historic center features remnants of Brazil's early settlement, the colonial era, and indigenous life. Opposite the museum is **Gonçalo Coelho's marker stone** (Cidade Historica), now encased in glass and ringed with a fence. Other reminders of the past are old stone churches such as the **Igreja NS da Misericórdia** (1526), the **Igreja NS da Pena** (1772) and the **Capela de São Benedito** (Frei Calixto 127), dating from the 16th century. Note that while the area is beautifully illuminated at night, the steps are not safe after dark – it's best to take a taxi.

Memorial da Epopéia do Descobrimento MEMORIAL
(73 3268-2586; www.memorialdodescobrimento.com.br; Av Beira-Mar 800; R$30; 8:30am-12:30pm & 1:30-5pm Mon-Sat) Down by the beach, just north of town, the Memorial da Epopéia do Descobrimento is a worthwhile stop. The park features a replica of the Portuguese ship that first landed on Brazilian shores. The surrounding botanical gardens also feature a replica of an indigenous village; the guides are descendants of the Pataxó.

Museu de Porto Seguro MUSEUM
(Museum of Discovery; 73 3012-2782; Praça Pero Campos Tourinho; R$10; 9am-5pm) Housed in the former Câmara Municipal (Town Council), the Museu de Porto Seguro contains exhibits on Brazil's early settlement, with rooms dedicated to exploration and colonial life; even more interesting are the museum's exhibits on indigenous life, including films covering important rites and celebrations.

Beaches

North of town is one long bay dotted with *barracas* (food stalls) and clubs creating the Orla Norte (North Coast): **Praia Curuípe** (3km), **Praia Itacimirim** (4km), **Praia Mundaí** (6km), **Praia de Taperapua** (7km) and **Praia do Mutá** (10km.) The sands are white and fluffy, backed by green vegetation

Porto Seguro

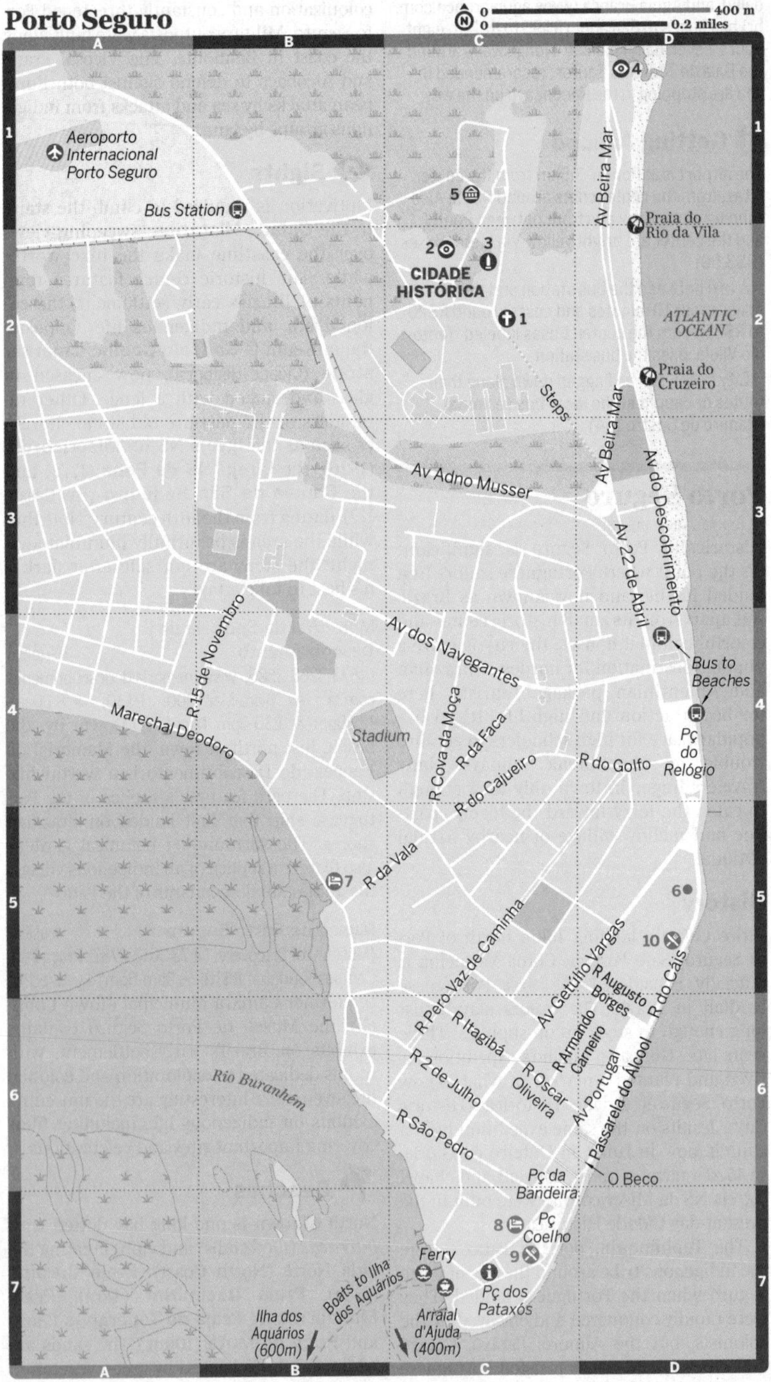

0 — 400 m
0 — 0.2 miles

Aeroporto Internacional Porto Seguro
Bus Station
5
2
3
CIDADE HISTÓRICA
1
4
Av Beira Mar
Praia do Rio da Vila
ATLANTIC OCEAN
Praia do Cruzeiro
Steps
Av Beira Mar
Av Adno Musser
Av do Descobrimento
Av 22 de Abril
R 15 de Novembro
Av dos Navegantes
Bus to Beaches
Marechal Deodoro
Stadium
R Cova da Moça
R da Faca
R do Cajueiro
R do Golfo
Pç do Relógio
R da Vala
7
6
10
R Pero Vaz de Caminha
Av Getúlio Vargas
R Augusto Borges
R do Cáis
R Itagibá
R Armando Carneiro
R 2 de Julho
R Oscar Oliveira
Av Portugal
Passarela do Álcool
Rio Buranhém
R São Pedro
Pç da Bandeira
O Beco
8
Pç Coelho
9
Ferry
Pç dos Pataxós
Boats to Ilha dos Aquários
Ilha dos Aquários (600m)
Arraial d'Ajuda (400m)

Porto Seguro

Sights
1 Capela de São Benedito C2
2 Cidade Histórica C2
3 Gonçalo Coelho's Marker Stone C2
4 Memorial da Epopéia do Descobrimento D1
5 Museu de Porto Seguro C1

Activities, Courses & Tours
6 Pataxó Turismo D5

Sleeping
7 Hotel Estalagem B5
8 Pousada Brisa do Mar C7

Eating
9 Rabanete C7
10 Tia Nenzinha D5

lapped by a tranquil sea, dotted with big beach clubs like Tôa-Tôa, where MCs and dancers lead Brazilian crowds through popular dances.

Tours

Pataxó Turismo TOURS
(☎73 3288-1256; www.pataxoturismo.com.br; Shopping Rio Mar loja 3; day tours per person R$85-160) Tour agency specializing in cultural exchanges with the Pataxó community, who are indigenous to the area.

Festivals & Events

Carnaporto CULTURAL
(www.carnaporto-axemoi.com.br; ⏲Feb/Mar) Porto Seguro's Carnaval, Bahia's most famous after Salvador's, is relatively small and safe, consisting of a few *trios electricos* (long trucks loaded with huge speakers) cruising the main drag blasting *axé* music. These days, just as many tourists come for the parties across the way in Arraial d'Ajuda.

Sleeping

Hotel Estalagem BOUTIQUE HOTEL $
(☎73 3288-2095; www.hotelestalagem.com.br; Marechal Deodoro 66; r R$90-150; ❄📶🏊) One of the more stylish options in Porto Seguro, this affordable boutique hotel is housed inside a colonial building dating from 1801 – check out the antique stones, sourced from the coral reef and originally joined together with whale oil, in the entryway. Today, renovated guest rooms are understated and comfortable, with private balconies overlooking the swimming pool below.

Pousada Brisa do Mar POUSADA $
(☎73 3288-1444; Praça Coelho 180; s/d/tr R$55/75/95; ❄📶) This basic guesthouse, in a long, narrow house near the waterfront, is nothing fancy. But as Porto Seguro accommodations go, the location is good: it's close to restaurants, the Passarela do Álcool (Alcohol Walkway) and the ferry to Arraial.

Eating

Most dining and drinking options are found around the Passarela do Álcool. At night, the *passarela* has craft stalls and street performers, with live music spilling onto the plazas. Look for fresh-fruit cocktail stands making *capeta* (guaraná, cocoa powder, cinnamon, sweetened condensed milk and vodka) – just the thing to kick off the evening.

★**Rabanete** BUFFET $$
(☎73 3288-2743; www.restauranterabanete.com.br; Saldanha Marinho 33; per kg R$61; ⏲noon-4:30pm) One of the classiest per-kilo eateries around, Rabanete puts out a mouthwatering buffet of gourmet dishes, from pasta with sun-dried tomatoes and basil to fresh fish fillets. Both the leafy patio tables and the stylish rustic interior offer plenty of atmosphere. Look out for its locations in Arraial d'Ajuda and Trancoso too.

Tia Nenzinha BAHIAN $$
(☎73 3288-1846; Av Portugal 170; mains for 2 R$70-110) A classic in Porto since 1976, no-frills Tia Nenzinha serves an assortment of Bahian dishes.

Drinking & Nightlife

Porto Seguro is not a quiet city at night. Young partiers selling club and party tickets (R$30 to R$80) around the *passarela* let you know what's happening on any given night. The major beach clubs all put on weekly nighttime luaus (parties).

Tôa-Tôa CLUB
(☎73 3679-1714; www.portaltoatoa.com.br; Av Beira Mar, Km 5, Praia de Taperapuã; ⏲8am-6pm) If you're really looking to chill out try this 'leisure complex' on the beach north of Porto Seguro.

Barramares CLUB
(☎73 3679-2980; Av Beira Mar, Km 6, Praia de Taperapuã) The major beach clubs all put on weekly nighttime luaus (parties); the one at Barramares is the most stunning. It's about 6km north of town.

FRIDAY NIGHT ON ILHA DOS AQUÁRIOS

Everywhere you go in Porto Seguro, you'll see ads and promotions for **Ilha dos Aquários** (☎73 3268-2828; www.ilhadosaquarios.com.br; Ilha Pacuio; adult/child under 10 R$75/free; ⏱8pm-late Fri) – and down by the water, a dedicated boat dock next to the Arraial d'Ajuda ferry. But what *is* Ilha dos Aquários (travelers often wonder, staring down at the brochure)? Is it an aquarium or a nightclub? Both, in fact. It's one of those quintessentially Brazilian entertainment complexes that wears a few hats, catering to the stroller-set earlier in the evening and the up-all-night party crowd after midnight.

As the name indicates (*ilha* means 'island'), you can't walk or drive here: all guests arrive by a quick boat ride, included with the entrance fee. The illuminated shark aquariums and family-oriented shows are fun for all ages; there's also a food court and a number of different dining and drinking venues. There's a certain novelty to the fact that it's only open on Friday evenings after dark. After the families head out, the party kids start coming in, and the island morphs into a huge party with live *forró,* house music, specially invited DJs and Bahian music.

Information

There are plenty of banks and ATMs around town.

Banco do Brasil (Av 22 de Abril)

Bradesco (Praça do Relógio)

Bradesco (Av dos Navegantes)

Tourist Information Kiosk (Praça dos Pataxós; ⏱10am-6pm Mon-Sat) You can usually find someone here during the day for info or a map.

Getting There & Away

AIR

GOL (☎73 3162-1031; www.voegol.com.br), Azul (www.voeazul.com.br) and **LATAM** (☎73 3288-5014; www.latam.com) can connect you to just about anywhere in Brazil from **Aeroporto Internacional Porto Seguro** (BPS; ☎73 3288-1880; Primeiro de Maio 68), a short drive outside of town.

BUS

The **bus station** (☎73 3288-1914) is 1.5km outside town; taxis cost around R$20 to the ferry or the center.

Rota (www.rotatransportes.com.br) buses go to Ilhéus (R$63 to R$75, six hours, four daily). Rota also has one daily bus to Itacaré (R$87, eight hours). You'll have more options for the same trip if you're willing to switch buses in Ilheús. **Águia Branca** (☎73 3288-1039) offers one daily departure to Salvador (R$146, 11 hours) – an overnight bus at the time of writing. Águia Branca also runs the long haul to Rio de Janeiro (R$306, 22 hours, including a connection in Vitória.)

For more frequent connections, three companies run buses to Eunápolis (R$15, one hour, every 30 minutes from 5:30am to 10pm).

FERRY

The *balsa,* a quick car and passenger ferry, connects Porto Seguro to Arraial d'Ajuda (R$4.50, 10 to 15 minutes). From Arraial's port, you can catch buses into town, or to points further south like Trancoso.

Getting Around

Taxis cost around R$35 to the port or the city center.

If you're heading to beaches north of Porto Seguro, look for Riacho Doce, Alto do Mundaí, Campinho–Barramares or Cabrália buses (R$3.25) that pick up passengers at a **bus stop** (Praça do Relógio) on the main square or another bus stop a little north, among other places. Taxis are widely available throughout the city: a cab from the bus station to the ferry costs around R$20.

Arraial d'Ajuda

☎0XX73 / POP 17,000

Atop a bluff overlooking an enchanting stretch of coastline, Arraial d'Ajuda is a peaceful tourist village with an indisputable appeal. Its narrow paved roads and dusty lanes wind beneath large, shady trees, with lovely pousadas (guesthouses) and open-air restaurants hidden among the greenery. Solid, brightly painted facades surround its plazas, and the air remains tinged with the scent of tropical vegetation. In the past, Arraial was the playground of the wealthy, which isn't far removed from the upmarket tourists the town tends to attract: the place is an extremely popular vacation spot for well-off Argentinians. More recently, however, a new wave of international backpackers and nouveau hippies have brought a little diversity to the idyllic surroundings.

Sights & Activities

Arraial's beaches are sheltered by offshore reefs, making the clear water particularly appealing (and family friendly) at low tide. **Praia Mucugê** is Arraial's main beach and is crowded with *barracas*. Head north past Eco Parque entrance for less crowds. Heading south, **Praia do Parracho** is also built up, but with beach clubs and a few condominium complexes. Around the point, beautiful **Praia Pitinga** has red-striped sandstone cliffs, pretty, calm waters and a few *barracas*. South of Pitinga, **Praia da Lagoa Azul** and **Praia Taípe** are backed by tall cliffs, and face stronger waves.

Eco Parque WATER PARK
(☎73 3575-8600; www.arraialecoparque.com.br; Estrada da Balsa; adult/child R$120/90; ⏰10am-5pm; 👪) Occupying a huge piece of land on the coast, this family-friendly water park has long, twisting waterslides, a wave pool and a 'lazy river' you can float down on rafts. There's also a *tiroleza* (zip line), kayaks for rent and a host of other outdoor activities, plus live music and entertainment.

Tours

Several travel agencies organize day trips to beautiful beach villages south of Arraial. Popular excursions include the trip to **Praias Espelho and Curuípe**, including a stop in **Trancoso**; a long day's outing to **Caraíva**; and a snorkeling trip to the offshore reef of **Recife de Fora**. If you're visiting between July and October, ask about humpback-whale-watching tours.

Arraial Trip Tur TOURS
(☎73 3575-2805; www.arraialtriptur.com.br; Rua do Mucugê 150) Offers excursions to Praia do Espelho (R$70), Trancoso (R$60), Caraíva (R$85), plus whale-watching (R$230) and scuba tours (prices vary). Check the website for details to help you plan your time: many trips are scheduled for specific days of the week.

Sleeping

Arraial is home to a large number of lovely pousadas. You'll see plenty of options on the road from the ferry dock to the center. They offer access to more secluded beaches, but aren't near most of the dining and nightlife options. Frequent buses run up the hill into town, but if you want easy access to restaurants, staying in the center is your best bet.

Arraial d'Ajuda Hostel HOSTEL $
(☎73 3575-1192; www.arraialdajudahostel.com.br; Manoel Crescêncio Santiago 94; dm/d from R$60/140; ❄@📶🏊) This colorful HI hostel offers well-equipped private rooms as well as dorm-style accommodations in a funky Greco Bahian–style building with a courtyard swimming pool. Travelers like the communal outdoor kitchen and the location near the beach.

Prices rise significantly during the post-Christmas season, January and for Carnival.

★**Pousada Erva Doce** POUSADA $$
(☎73 3575-1113; www.ervadoce.com.br; Rua do Mucugê 200; d from R$240; ❄📶🏊) Squarely in the center of the village on a cobblestone plaza lined with boutiques and cafes, this peaceful guesthouse has spacious, thoughtfully designed rooms with roomy showers and mosquito-net canopies. Surrounding the small swimming pool is a leafy tropical garden with an open-air bar and hammocks, ideal for lazing away the afternoon.

★**Pousada Catamarã** POUSADA $$
(☎73 3575-1556; www.pousadacatamara.com.br; Alameda dos Oitis 90; s/d from R$310/350; ❄📶🏊) The inviting outdoor pool, festive thatched-roof pool bar, comfortable guest rooms with private verandas, and proximity to the beach make this guesthouse a top choice. It's located downhill from the village on a side street just before you reach Praia Mucugê.

Art Hotel Aos Sinos Dos Anjos POUSADA $$
(☎73 3575-1176; www.aossinosdosanjos.com; Rua do Ipê 71; s/d from R$200/220; 📶🏊) A unique gem in Arraial d'Ajuda, this guesthouse is entirely decorated with the works of local artists and filled with colorful mosaics, healing crystals, seashells and sculptures. Two levels of suites, each with its own patio and hammock, face the pretty swimming pool. It's tucked away on a side street that runs parallel to Rua do Mucugê.

Atmosphera Pousada POUSADA $$
(☎73 3575-1954; www.atmospherapousada.com.br; Rua do Mucugê 735; d from R$320, bungalows R$980; ❄📶🏊) 🌿 This smart and sustainably built guesthouse is set in a pretty tropical garden just steps from Praia Mucugê. Each guest room features a private balcony with hammock, and a solar-powered shower.

Vila do Beco POUSADA $$
(☎73 3575-1230; www.viladobeco.com.br; Beco dos Jegues 173; d from R$290; ❄📶🏊) This tranquil property spreads toward the edge

of the bluff – white buildings are sprinkled through lush grounds, ending at a pool with jaw-dropping ocean views. Many guest rooms, outfitted with rustic wood furnishings and romantic mosquito nets, offer two levels and a terrace.

Eating

Arraial has no shortage of excellent restaurants, many offering atmospheric outdoor seating. For something more casual, head to the main square at night for inexpensive crepes, tapioca, caipirinhas and traditional Bahian plates of rice, beans and grilled steak, or stop at one of the gourmet ice-cream stands along Rua do Mucugê.

★ Portinha BUFFET $
(☎73 3575-1882; www.portinha.com.br; Shopping d'Ajuda, Rua do Mucugê 333; per kg R$59.50; ⏰11am-4:30pm Tue-Sun; ✎) Portinha is several steps up from most per-kilo restaurants you'll find. There is a plethora of meat and seafood dishes on offer, most of which are inspired by traditional Bahian cuisine and taste like they were made-to-order in an upscale bistro. It's located on a pleasant patio in the Shopping d'Ajuda complex.

Café da Santa CAFE $
(☎73 3575-1078; www.facebook.com/CafeDaSanta; Praça Brigadeiro Eduardo Gomes 134; pastries R$4-7, mains R$17-50; ⏰7am-10pm Tue-Sun, closed last Sun of the month) Fresh pastries, strong coffee, and well-made sandwiches and salads are on the menu at this airy coffee shop in the historic center. It's also one of the few restaurants in town open for breakfast.

Beco das Cores BRAZILIAN $
(Rua do Mucugê 201; mains R$20-50; ⏰6pm-late) This lively galleria is a big draw for its atmosphere and variety: you'll find good sushi, crepes, pizza and more gourmet fare; there's live music on summer weekend nights, and even on slower evenings it's a great place to grab a beer or cocktail.

Egadi BISTRO $$
(☎73 99183-6627; www.egadi.com.br; Praça da Igreja 86; mains R$30-48, small plates R$10-18; ⏰5:30-11:30pm Mon-Sat) This sleek bistro opened in 2018 and specializes in fresh, artful Mediterranean inspired cuisine that utilizes the region's bountiful seafood. There are main dishes, such as shrimp with Sicilian lemon, and an exciting small-plates menu that features everything from bruschetta and Caprese salad to tender squid sautéed in olive oil.

Rosa dos Ventos BRAZILIAN $$
(☎73 3575-1271; Alameda dos Flamboyants 24; mains R$55-75; ⏰4pm-midnight Mon-Tue & Thu-Sat, 1-10pm Sun) Considered one of Arraial's finest restaurants, Rosa dos Ventos offers a short menu of exquisite grilled seafood, perfect cocktails and decadent desserts; the candlelit front patio is the ideal place to linger over a bottle of wine. It's located on a road that runs parallel to Rua do Mucugê.

Manguti ITALIAN $$
(☎73 3575-2270; www.manguti.com.br; Rua do Mucugê 99; mains R$36-80; ⏰noon-11:30pm) This Italian classic, housed in a sweet, old-fashioned house on the main drag, is known for its hearty portions of homemade gnocchi. Also on the menu: excellent grilled fish and wines by the glass.

Aipim BRAZILIAN $$
(☎73 3575-3222; www.arraialdajuda.tur.br/aipim; Beco do Jegues 131; mains R$50-107; ⏰6pm-midnight Thu-Tue Jun-Apr, closed 1st Sun of month) A first-rate locale for a romantic evening out in Arraial: this stylish eatery exudes tropical chic with its old-world decor, new-world music, superb grilled seafood and an impressive wine list.

Drinking & Nightlife

Arraial has lively nightlife options throughout the summer, when beach clubs host huge parties (cover R$25 to R$50); you'll see promoters everywhere, and local travel agencies can also provide the latest details. Another popular option for night owls is the Ilha dos Aquarios (p450) nightclub complex on an island between Porto Arraial and Porto Seguro.

Morocha Club CLUB
(☎73 3575-2611; www.morochaclub.com; Rua do Mucugê 260; cover generally free; ⏰5pm-late, event times vary) In town, Morocha is ground zero for nightlife, particularly in summer and around Carnaval. This popular local hangout and restaurant serving pizza, steaks, sandwiches and Tex-Mex (mains R$22–R$55) has a lounge-like vibe earlier in the evening. Things get rowdy late at night with concerts, dancing, DJs and theme parties.

Information

There are several ATMs around town.

There is a tourist kiosk in the main plaza at the top of Rua do Mucugê – although it's no longer well staffed. You can get maps and information for excursions in the area at the various tourism agencies.

WORTH A TRIP

PRAIA DO ESPELHO

Rated among Brazil's top-10 beaches,Praia do Espelho (Beach of the Mirror; so named for the reflections on the still surface of the water) is 27km south of Trancoso and 14km north of Caraíva. Protective offshore reefs create calm, warm, transparent waters, while reefs closer to shore create natural pools at low tide. White and orange cliffs divide Espelho from **Praia do Curuípe**, its neighboring beach, which has a collection of top-end pousadas.

Tour agencies in Arraial d'Ajuda and Trancoso offer day trips (around R$70) to these beaches (recommended, as the roads are bumpy and arriving on your own is a challenge) or you can catch one of Aguia Azul's two to three daily buses (around R$15, depending on where you get on) that run from Arraial d'Ajuda, stopping in Trancoso and continuing on to Caraíva and vice versa. Let the driver know where you'd like to get off. Visit www.praiadoespelho.net.br for the latest departure times and additional information about this remote and beautiful destination.

Getting There & Away

If arriving by plane or bus you'll first land in Porto Seguro. Car and passenger ferries (p450) travel almost constantly between Porto Seguro and Arraial d'Ajuda between 7am and midnight, with half-hourly boats running from midnight through the early morning. Prices for the *balsa* (ferry) vary slightly depending on which way you're going, and which ferry you happen to get on: typically you will travel for free going from Arraial to Porto Seguro and pay R$4.50 the other way around. Cars cost between R$10 and R$12. The ride takes 10 to 15 minutes. From the boat dock, jump on a bus or Kombi van to the center of Arraial d'Ajuda (R$3.25). Depending on where you're staying, you can also ask the driver to drop you off at one of the many pousadas (guesthouses) located along the road into town.

From Arraial's ferry port, you can also catch a van or **Aguia Azul** (73 3575-1170; www.viacaoaguiaazul.com.br) bus to Trancoso (R$11, one hour). Return buses from Trancoso pick up in the square a few minutes' walk inland from the Quadrado area along the main road (Estrada de Trancoso). Aguia Azul buses also make the bumpy journey to Caraíva (R$20, three hours) at 7am and 3pm daily, and from Caraíva to Arraial at 6:20am and 4pm.

Getting Around

Bicycles, motorbikes, cars and beach buggies are all available for rental from agencies in Arraial. Just be sure to have a good map and ask for advice before you set out for an excursion, as many dirt roads heading south aren't marked and can be difficult to pass if it has been raining.

Trancoso

0XX73 / POP 9860

Sitting atop a grassy bluff overlooking fantastic beaches, Trancoso embodies a certain rustic sophistication that captivates style-minded travelers. It's a favorite destination for jetsetters, who want to get away from it all while still having access to a few fashionable venues for dining and shopping. You'll also find beachy bohemians, yoga enthusiasts and some families among the crowds.

Trancoso is smaller in scale than Arraial, with a relaxed air, an assortment of pretty guesthouses, a postcard-worthy church overlooking the ocean, and irresistible open-air bars and restaurants surrounding the pedestrian only Quadrado (the main square). The sight of the square bathed in moonlight and candlelight is quite magical.

Sleeping

Accommodations are on the pricier side and reservations are a must during January and major holidays. There has been an influx of new options and if you're willing to stay a bit further inland you can find a better deal.

Baianeiro Hostel HOSTEL $

(73 99160-3065; Carlos Chagas 851; dm R$70;) Things are simple at Baianeiro Hostel: three dorm-style rooms, two shared bathrooms, a kitchen and ample indoor and outdoor communal space. What makes it special is the familial atmosphere cultivated by hosts Maria Luiza and Adriano. It is a 15-minute walk from the Quadrado, making it a better choice for those who value affordability and tranquility over convenience.

★ **Pousada Jacarandá** POUSADA $$

(73 3668-1950; www.pousadajacaranda.com.br; Jovelino Rodrigues Vieira 91; bungalows for 2 from R$279;) This ecofriendly guesthouse features six freestanding bungalows built with natural, locally sourced materials, plus a lovely swimming pool and art-filled interiors. It's a short walk from both the

Quadrado and the beach, but the quiet location is a benefit if you're looking to relax.

Pousada Samambaia POUSADA $$
(☎73 3668-1774; www.samambaiatrancoso.com; Viera s/n; ste/chalets from R$250/275; P ❄ ☎ ≋) Space and tranquility are major selling points at this lovely guesthouse, consisting of 10 pretty chalets with kitchens, patios and hammocks. The central swimming pool, fringed with palm trees, is the perfect place to take a break from the beach.

Pousada Mundo Verde POUSADA $$
(☎73 3668-1279; www.pousadamundoverde.com.br; Telégrafo 43; d from R$320; ❄ ☎ ≋) A swimming pool with a spectacular view is the crowning glory of this peaceful guesthouse, set on a quiet bluff overlooking the ocean, not far from the Quadrado. Stylish Mundo Verde has spacious, airy rooms with mosquito nets; each has a private balcony or patio with hammock, table and chairs.

Pousada Quarto Crescente POUSADA $$
(☎73 98866-2904; www.quartocrescente.net; Rua das Mangabeiras 30; ste from R$415; P ❄ ☎ ≋) At this popular guesthouse, just a short walk from the Quadrado, gardens surround a picturesque wooden deck and swimming pool. Guest rooms have private patios with hammocks; pricier options include kitchenettes and Jacuzzis. There's also a well-stocked library with helpful travel books and maps, and an excellent breakfast spread.

★ **Pousada Hibisco** POUSADA $$$
(☎73 3668-1117; www.pousadahibisco.com.br; Bom Jesus s/n; chalet from R$342; P ❄ ☎ ≋) A few blocks off of Trancoso's main drag and set among lush foliage is Pousada Hibisco, which offers chalets for rent and a fun pool and bar area decorated in a 1950s tiki theme. The chalets range in size with the larger options featuring family-friendly amenities such as kitchens, bathtubs and private yards.

Eating

In the evening, the colorful glowing lanterns that illuminate the restaurants around the Quadrado are quite stunning. However, the dining scene here is known for high prices and hit-or-miss quality and service. In this town, you're paying first and foremost for the atmosphere. You can find more casual snacks, ice cream and tapioca pastries in the small plaza behind the main square, where taxis and buses drop off.

Bem Te Vi BRAZILIAN $
(☎73 3668-1314; Estrada de Trancoso 12; mains R$26-50; ⏲11am-midnight) At Bem Te Vi traditional Brazilian staples (lots of grilled meat and ample accompaniments) are served up in an airy outdoor dining space that has the feel of a hip Los Angeles taqueria. Make sure to try one of the several barbecue chicken options, which are all juicy and well seasoned.

★ **Rabanete** BUFFET $$
(☎73 3668-1835; Quadrado s/n; per kg R$69.99; ⏲noon-5:30pm) This Trancoso classic, formally known as Portinha, woos diners with a sumptuous buffet (don't miss the dessert spread) and atmospheric seating at tree-shaded picnic tables on the Quadrado. It's one of only a few places open for lunch in town.

Maritaca ITALIAN $$
(☎73 3668-1702; Telégrafo 388; mains R$40-80; ⏲6pm-midnight Tue-Sun, to 2am Jan & Feb) Elegant and airy Maritaca does delicious thin-crust pizzas – the carpaccio is a standout – as well as Italian pastas and rich desserts made with top-end imported ingredients. The prices are lofty for a pizzeria; but this is Trancoso.

O Cacau BAHIAN $$$
(☎73 3668-1266; Quadrado; mains R$60-100; ⏲5pm-midnight Tue-Sun, daily Jan & Feb) This beautifully appointed restaurant is a haven for foodies interested in Bahian cuisine. Look for light, modern takes on classic dishes from *acarajés* (fritters of brown beans and dried shrimp) to *moqueca* (fish stew) and grilled lobster. O Cacau has a great wine list (especially for Brazil) and to-die-for desserts, with prices to match.

Capim Santo BRAZILIAN $$$
(☎73 3668-1122; www.capimsanto.com.br; Quadrado; mains R$65-92; ⏲7-11pm Mon-Sat) Dining on the impossibly quaint porch of this old house – or in the beautifully illuminated garden beside it – makes for a memorable evening. Part of the pousada of the same name, Capim Santo specializes in fresh, innovative juice infusions and traditional Bahian seafood dishes with an international twist.

Information

At the small plaza inland from the Quadrado you'll find a taxi stand and a tourist office offering maps and information (at least when it's open, which it often isn't outside of the peak summer months). Walks inland to find ATMs (most located in grocery stores and open-air malls), pharmacies, supermarkets and less expensive beachwear shops.

Getting There & Away

Hourly Aguia Azul buses connect Trancoso with Arraial d'Ajuda and the ferry dock – some continue to Porto Seguro – and run from 6am to 8:30pm (R$11, one hour). Some buses leave from the Quadrado area, but to catch most of the departures, walk inland from the Quadrado on the main road that runs in and out of town. You'll see a sign for a bus stop on a small square. From here you can also catch the twice-daily bus to Caraíva that originates in Arraial d'Ajuda (R$17, two hours). It usually arrives in Trancoso at around 8am and 4pm.

Kombi vans run the same route between Trancoso and Arraial d'Ajuda for the same price. They can be caught at the bus stop, or by flagging one down as it goes down Estrada de Trancoso.

Caraíva

0XX73 / POP 1000

Time moves slowly in the remote and beautiful village of Caraíva, flanked by the mangrove-lined Rio Caraíva and warm waves of the Atlantic ocean, where roads and cars don't exist (neither did electricity before 2007). The easygoing atmosphere has long attracted hippies and those looking for a quiet pace of life. Today, there's cell-phone reception, internet access and a stronger infrastructure to support tourism (although you still expect power outages). Surfers, yogis and hipsters have flocked to the tiny town, giving it a nice mix of traditional village and progressive commune.

The village also makes for the optimal jumping off point to explore the Parque Nacional de Monte Pascoal, as well as the remote beaches of Corumbau..

Sights

Parque Nacional de Monte Pascoal PARK
(73 3294-1870; www.icmbio.gov.br; hikes R$40-50, guides R$5) Experience wild flora and fauna and the culture of the Paxato, one of the largest indiginous communities in Brazil, at this stunning park. It's free to enter, but you pay by the hike.

Sleeping

Aruanda Hostel HOSTEL $
(73 99937-1801; www.facebook.com/AruandaHostelCaraiva; Rua dos Navegantes 175; dm R$40; wifi) If a lack of privacy doesn't bother you then Aruanda Hostel is a great way to experience the nouveau-beach-bum delights of Caraíva first hand. In the dorm rooms luxury stops at mosquito netting, but the charms of this place exist elsewhere. The location (near the main drag of restaurants), lush grounds and a friendly, community-oriented vibe have guests raving.

Pousada Caraiva Guest House POUSADA $$
(73 99967-3848; www.caraivaguesthouse.squarespace.com; Rua Doze de Outubro 1300; d from R$300; air-con wifi) Set in a beautifully landscaped garden near the beach, this guesthouse is a traveler favorite, thanks in part to the friendly service. Even the most standard rooms are spacious, with private patios, and the alfresco breakfast is a delight.

Pousada Lagoa POUSADA $$
(73 99985-6862; www.lagoacaraiva.com.br; Rua da Lagoa 1900; d/bungalows from R$315/396; wifi) At this eco-minded place (they recycle, compost, and employ local workers), choose between simple but stylish cottages with small verandas, or slightly cheaper suites. The restaurant-bar is a popular nighttime hangout, and open to the public: in addition to fresh fish and homemade bread, the restaurant serves produce sourced from the guesthouse's own garden.

★ **Pousada Cores do Mar** POUSADA $$$
(11 94011-0527; www.pousadacoresdomarcaraiva.com.br; Rua da Praia 850; 2-/4-person cottages from R$500/800; air-con wifi) At this heavenly oceanfront getaway, palm trees tower over freestanding cottages and inviting chaise lounges facing the water. Travelers love the peaceful interiors, complete with top-end bed linens and private terraces with sea views, and the ample breakfast spread.

Eating

Tapioca Caraíva CAFE $
(31 98466-9940; www.instagram.com/tapiocacaraiva; Rua dos Navegantes; mains R$20-25; 5-11pm Tue-Sun; vegetarian) Classic Brazilian tapioca dishes spiced up with ingredients like hummus and grilled banana are served in a hip, beachy setting at this popular restaurant on Caraíva's main drag. Also on the menu are plenty of vegan and vegetarian options and freshly made juices. Hours can fluctuate a lot, check their Instagram for up-to-date opening times.

Mangue Sereno ITALIAN $$
(31 99974-1711; Rua Sete de Setembro s/n; mains R$45-84; 7-11:30pm Dec-Mar) Homemade pastas and creative seafood dishes are locally famous at this lovely restaurant at the pousada of the same name; the romantic, low-key setting is a great spot for a leisurely dinner.

Casinha Gourmet BUFFET $$
(☎73 99906-3724; Rua Sete de Setembro; per kg R$65; ⏰noon-7pm; 📶) Located close to the beach, this lovely per-kilo restaurant offers a small but delicious selection of salads and seafood-oriented dishes to be enjoyed in its shady courtyard dining area.

Getting There & Away

Two daily buses run by **Aguia Azul** (☎73 3575-1170; www.viacaoaguiaazul.com.br) travel between Caraiva and the ferry in Arraial d'Ajuda (R$20, two hours) stopping in Trancoso along the way. Buses leave Arraial for Caraíva at 7am and 3pm, leaving Caraíva for the return journey at 6:20am and 4pm. Visit the Aguia Azul website for schedule and fare information.

Getting Around

On arrival in Caraíva, hop on a canoe (R$5) to cross the river into the village. You can also opt to buy a R$10 'eco-ticket' which supports maintaining the unique local environment.

Caravelas

☎0XX73 / POP 21,500

Caravelas is a calm fishing town on the banks of the mangrove-lined Rio Caravelas; the primary reason visitors come here is to visit the Parque Nacional Marinho de Abrolhos and other offshore reefs.

Sights

To get a feel for the town's thriving fishing industry, wander along the riverfront where the fishers return with the day's catch. When the locals go to the beach, most head north for **Praia Grauçá** (7km) or the more isolated **Praia Iemanjá** (20km). Both have calm water colored brown with river silt. Reachable by boat are **Praia Pontal do Sul** (across Rio Caravelas) and the island beach **Coroa da Barra** (30 minutes offshore).

Tours

Horizonte Aberto TOURS
(☎73 3297-1474; www.horizonteaberto.com.br; Av das Palmeiras 313; tours from R$400) This popular tour operation runs everything from day trips to overnight excursions to the Parque Nacional Marinho de Abrolhos. If you are looking to scuba dive in the park it has packages for those with their own gear, as well as rental equipment. Check the website for the tour schedule.

Sleeping & Eating

Pousada Liberdade POUSADA $$
(☎73 3297-2415; www.pousadaliberdade.com.br; Nogueira 1551; s/d from R$120/220; ❄🏊) This conveniently located guesthouse offers accommodations in small cottages with a few creature comforts like televisions and minibars; there's also a pool and trundle beds, making it suitable for families. It's a good place to base yourself while you figure out your plans for heading into the park.

Carenagem BRAZILIAN $$
(☎73 3297-1280; Av das Palmeiras 210; mains R$37-65; ⏰11am-midnight) Basic but good value, this popular meeting spot has an extensive menu of seafood and meat dishes, as well as a sushi menu. Come by on the weekends for live music and strong cocktails.

Information

There are several banks with ATMs around town, including **Banco do Brasil** (Praça Dr Imbassaí; ⏰10am-3pm Mon-Fri).

Getting There & Away

Caravelas isn't easy to get to. Buses to the town are infrequent, sometimes only coming and going once or twice a week in the winter low season. Aguia Branca (www.aguiabranca.com.br) goes to Salvador (R$172, 16 hours) and Eunapolis (R$42, 4¾ hours), convenient if you're trying to come or go from the Porto Seguro area. More frequent buses run to Teixeira de Freitas, 74km west. The **bus station** (☎73 3297-1422; Praça Teófilo Otoní 1) is located in the center of town.

If you're planning to pass through on your way to Abrolhos, planning an organized excursion that includes a transfer is probably the best option. You can also rent a car in the Porto Seguro area and drive down. Make sure to confirm that this is OK with the rental company, as some do have limits on which municipalities you're allowed to take their cars.

Getting Around

Local buses do a round trip between Caravelas and the neighboring village of Barra (providing access to Praia Grauçá), leaving every roughly every 30 minutes from 6:30am until 10:30pm.

WEST OF SALVADOR

The great attraction in Bahia's interior is the Parque Nacional da Chapada Diamantina, a verdant area of scenic plateaus, grassy valleys, waterfalls and rushing rivers. Opportunities

DON'T MISS

PARQUE NACIONAL MARINHO DE ABROLHOS

It is thought that the name of Brazil's first marine park comes from a sailor's warning: when approaching land, open your eyes *(abre os olhos)*. **Abrolhos** (☎73 3297-2258; www.icmbio.gov.br/parnaabrolhos; tickets R$86) covers an area of 913 sq km, including reefs noted for the variety of colors and a five-island archipelago that Charles Darwin, aboard the HMS *Beagle*, visited in 1832. These days the primary residents of the archipelago are migrating birds and humpback whales (June to October), which come here to rest and give birth. Only the Ilha de Santa Bárbara has a handful of buildings, including a lighthouse built in 1861. In these crystal-clear waters, visibility can reach 20m in the dry season (May to September).

Abrolhos is located 80km offshore from Caravelas, the primary gateway, where travel agencies offer one- to four-day trips to the park. Day trips start around R$370 per person, depending on availability and what onboard amenities are included. Schooner tours lasting from two to four days, with overnight stays and meals onboard, are offered by small outfitters like **Sanuk Turismo** (☎73 98871-6634; http://sanukturismo.com.br; Travessa das Estrelas 80) or Horizonte Aberto. Prices start around R$1200 per person for scuba/snorkeling trips; you can also rent equipment here.

for trekking and outdoor adventures abound. In contrast to this verdant area, the rest of this region comprises the bizarre moonscapes of the *sertão* (backlands of the Northeast), a vast and parched land on which a struggling people eke out a living raising cattle and tilling the earth

Lençóis

☎0XX75 / POP 11,400

If you want to see a flip side to surf-and-sand Bahia, or have time for only one excursion into the Northeastern interior, this is it. Lençóis is the prettiest of the old diamond-mining towns in the Chapada Diamantina, a mountainous wooded oasis in the dusty *sertão* (backlands of the Northeast). While the town itself has charming cobbled streets, brightly painted 19th-century buildings, and appealing outdoor cafes and restaurants, the surrounding areas are the real attractions. Caves, waterfalls, idyllic rivers and panoramic plateaus set the stage for some fantastic adventures, with the town of Lençóis serving as a base for treks into the Parque Nacional da Chapada Diamantina and for sights outside the park.

History

The history of Lençóis epitomizes the story of the diamond boom and subsequent bust. After earlier expeditions by *bandeirantes* (Paulista explorers and hired guns) proved fruitless, the first diamonds were found in Chapada Velha in 1822. After large strikes in the Rio Mucujê in 1844, a motley collection of prospectors from across Brazil arrived seeking their fortunes.

Miners began searching for diamonds in alluvial deposits. They settled in makeshift tents, which, from the hills above, looked like bedsheets drying in the wind – hence the town's name: Lençóis (Sheets). The tents of these diamond prospectors grew into villages: Vila Velha de Palmeiras, Andaraí, Piatã, Igatu and Lençóis. Exaggerated stories of riches in the Diamantina mines precipitated mass migrations, but the area proved rich in clouded industrial stones, not display-quality gems.

At the height of the diamond boom, the French – who purchased diamonds and used them to drill the Panama Canal (1881–89), St Gothard Tunnel and London Underground – built a vice-consulate in Lençóis. French fashions and *bons mots* made their way into town, but with the depletion of diamonds, the falloff in French demand and the newly discovered South African mines, the boom went bust at the beginning of the 20th century.

Despite these developments, mining held on. Powerful and destructive water pumps were introduced in the 1980s, which increased production until they were finally banned in 1995. The few remaining miners have returned to traditional methods to extract diamonds from the riverbeds. With the establishment of the national park in 1985, the town's economy turned to tourism, which continues to be the major industry here.

Sights

Casa de Cultura Afrânio Peixoto MUSEUM

(☎75 3334-1728; Afrânio Peixoto s/n; 8am-8pm) FREE It's worth stopping in this small museum dedicated to the life and career of Julio Afrânio Peixoto, considered one of Lençóis'

THE PATAXÓ

Bahia's largest indigenous group, the Pataxó (pa-ta-*sho*), who number roughly 3000, are among Brazil's many indigenous groups facing an uncertain future. Historically, the Pataxó are survivors. They were a strong tribe who held out against the Portuguese, and up until the 1800s were one of the most feared indigenous groups of the interior. Their resistance hindered frontier expansion, though by the early 19th century their power had waned.

Today, the Pataxó practice subsistence agriculture in the south of Bahia, supplemented by hunting, fishing and gathering. Similar to Amazonian indigenous groups, the Pataxó utilize local plants as their pharmacy, with the rainforests of southern Bahia providing a vital source for traditional medicine. The region boasts incredible biodiversity, with many of its plants and animals found nowhere else on earth. In all, the Pataxó use more than 90 different plant species to treat colds, asthma, fever, toothaches, rheumatism, anemia and dozens of other illnesses.

As with many indigenous groups, the slow creep of modernity into Pataxó communities, coupled with economic hardship, has put the future of their traditions at risk. In Barra Velha, the largest Pataxó community (numbering some 1800), all of the traditional healers *(curandeiros)* are over 60, and it's possible that their knowledge will be lost within two decades. Today's *curandeiros* may be the final generation of traditional healers in Pataxó culture.

In addition to struggles within their own communities, the Pataxó face severe threats from outside. As Bahia's population grows, farmers have pushed them off their lands, leading to violent skirmishes. In 2007, 15 indigenous Pataxó went to Brasília to settle the matter of their land rights. In 2012 the family of a gravely ill indigenous child fought for treatment in the hospital in Porto Seguro, and then Salvador. Though the child survived, the treatment was delayed due to bureaucratic struggles over who should pay for her healthcare, and the case caught the attention of a large number of Bahians. These tensions between indigenous Brazilians and the government are not unique to the Pataxó, and many other tribes in the country are facing similar issues.

most accomplished citizens. There are two rooms of exhibits for which you'll get a tour from one of the friendly docents.

Igreja Senhor dos Passos CHURCH
(Av Senhor dos Passos 220) Honors the patron saint of miners – and was built by slaves. The church is open occasionally to visitors during festivals and other special events.

Mercado Cultural MARKET
(Praça Aureliano Sá; ⌚8am-8pm Mon-Sat) For handicrafts made of local wood and stone, clay soaps, and semiprecious jewelry, stop by the beautiful old Mercado Cultural. Perched above the river on the main square, the market's construction began construction in the 19th century.

Activities

Numerous local agencies offer a wide range of outdoor activities, including hiking, rappelling, climbing, kayaking, mountain biking and horseback riding, in Parque Nacional da Chapada Diamantina (p462). There are also great hikes leaving from town that the adventurous can undertake without a guide.

Rio Lençóis Hike

One lovely hike is a 3km walk out of town, following the Rio Lençóis upstream. You first pass a series of rapids known as **Cachoeira Serrano**; off to the right is the **Salão de Coloridas Areias** (Room of Colored Sands), where artisans gather material for bottled-sand paintings. You then pass **Poço Halley** (Swimming Hole), before seeing **Cachoeirinha** (Little Waterfall) on a tributary to your left. Continuing upriver, **Cachoeira da Primavera** (Spring Waterfall) is on another tributary on your left. (When the water is low, you can start this hike by climbing up the rocky slope on the right side of the stream. When the water is higher, you'll have to cut through the woods – the 'trail,' if you can call it that, should start at the traffic turnaround and run parallel to the river.)

Ribeirão do Meio Hike

A relaxing 4km hike is to Ribeirão do Meio, a series of swimming holes with a natural waterslide. It's not a long journey from town, but the path is hardly marked, so it can be a little tricky to access. To begin, follow Rua São Benedito (known as Rua dos Negros) from Pousada & Camping Lumiar (p460). Continue past the pousada's entrance and keep walking

Lençóis

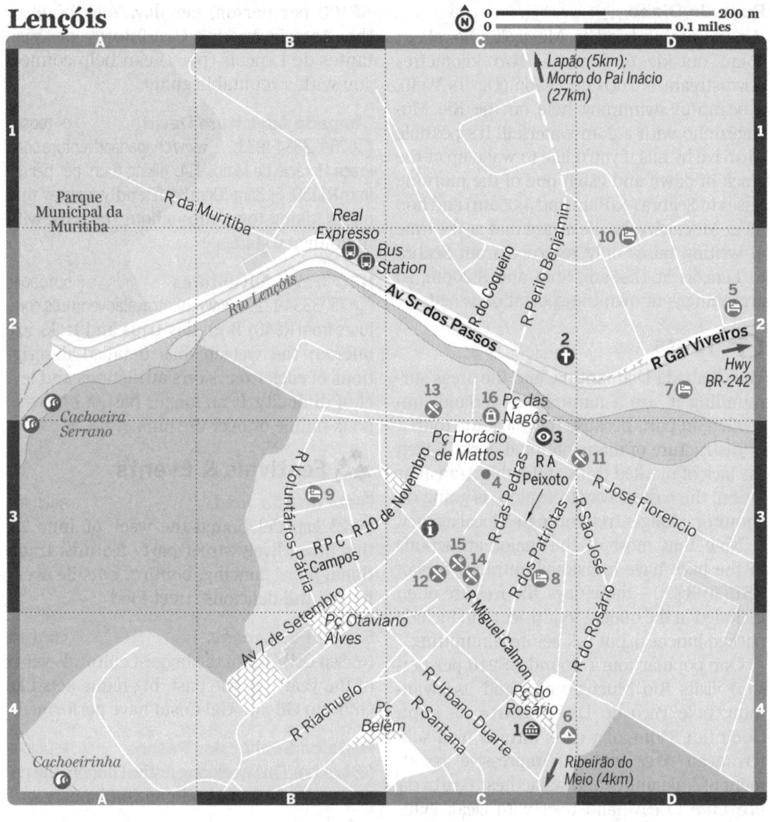

Lençóis

Sights
1 Casa de Cultura Afrânio Peixoto C4
2 Igreja Senhor dos Passos C2
3 Mercado Cultural C3

Activities, Courses & Tours
4 Chapada Adventure David C3

Sleeping
5 Alcino Estalagem & Atelier D2
6 Pousada & Camping Lumiar C4
7 Pousada Canto das Águas D2
8 Pousada Lua de Cristal C3
9 Pouso Da Trilha B3
10 Vila Serrano D2

Eating
11 Burritos y Taquitos D3
12 Café do Mato C3
13 Cozinha Aberta C2
14 Lampião C3
15 Os Artistas da Massa C3

Shopping
16 Dos Irmãos C2

out of town. Continue onto the red stone and dirt path that leads uphill. Five to 10 minutes later, the trail levels off and you'll see a sign for Ribeirão do Meio. Keep going along the dirt road until you see the archway entrance for Pousada Luar do Sertão. The trail to Ribeirão do Meio really starts here, to the left of the pousada entrance, on a stone staircase that leads down through the woods. Keep following the trail until you reach a ridge overlooking Rio Ribeirão. There's no 'right way' to scramble down to a series of swimming holes and the natural waterslide, but there are easier ways and harder ways – just use common sense. Avoid injury by climbing the dry rocks (not the slide's wet ones) before launching off.

Poço do Diabo

For swimming head to Mucugêzinho, about 25km outside of Lençóis. Two kilometres downstream is Poço do Diabo (Devil's Well), a beautiful swimming hole on the Rio Mucugêzinho with a 25m waterfall. It's possible to arrive by bus if you'd like to wake up at the crack of dawn and catch one of the morning buses to Seabra (4:01am and 5:05am) and hop off at Mucugêzinho. Be aware that at the time of writing buses only returned from Seabra to Lençóis at 11:45am, 8pm and 8:20pm, so arranging your own transportation is better.

Tours

The Chapada Diamantina, and the areas surrounding it, are a natural wonderland; unspoiled, in part, because they lack the tourist infrastructure of many national parks. Given the lack of marked trails and public transportation, the easiest way to explore is going on a tour or a longer trek through a local agency.

Note that most of the major attractions in the park have individual entrance fees of R$15 to R$20 – these days, the fees are often included in the quoted tour price (and include packed lunches), but ask before committing.

One popular tour (around R$240 per person) visits Rio Mucugêzinho and its swimming hole Poço do Diabo, **Gruta da Lapa Doce** (an 850m-long cave, formed by a subterranean river, with an impressive assortment of stalagmites and stalactites), **Gruta da Pratinha** (a cave and river with clear, light-blue waters), and **Morro do Pai Inácio** (an 1120m peak affording an awesome view over a plateau-filled valley).

Tours to **Poço Encantado** (the Lençóis poster child: a cave filled with stunningly beautiful blue water) and **Poço Azul** (another rainwater-filled cave you can swim in) are also offered (around R$280 per person). Before planning this one, ask the agency about the expected quality of the light; after rains, the water remains murky.

Another popular outing is the trip to **Cachoeira da Fumaça** (around R$190 per person).

If you're not interested in going on a formal tour, consider going into the park with a guide: they're affordable (plan on around R$200–R$300 per day for groups of up to six people), they're incredibly knowledgeable about local flora and fauna, and they can find the best swimming holes – all priceless in a park with few signs or official trails. For multiday treks, guides also arrange basic lodging and meals in local homes for the bargain price of around R$100 per person, per day. Your hotel or the Associação dos Condutores de Visitantes de Lençóis (p462) can help connect you with a reputable guide.

Chapada Adventure David OUTDOORS
(☎75 3334-1933; www.chapadaadventure.com; Praça Horácio de Matos 114; hiking tours per person from R$150; ⊙8am-10pm) A friendly agency that offers hiking tours throughout the park with multilingual staff.

H2O Travel Adventures OUTDOORS
(☎75 3334-1229; www.h2otraveladventures.com; tours from R$40) Both day trips and treks are offered; the website has detailed descriptions of each excursion's attractions and level of difficulty. It no longer has an office, so book online or over the phone.

Festivals & Events

Festa de São João CULTURAL
(⊙23 Jun) Celebrated the week of June 23, this huge, lively street party features traditional *forró* dancing, bonfires outside every house, and delicious street food.

Festival de Lençóis CULTURAL
(⊙Sep-Oct) One of the biggest cultural events of the year – in the past, big-name acts like Gilberto Gil and Gal Costa have performed.

Festa de Senhor dos Passos RELIGIOUS
(⊙late Jan) This weeklong festival honors the patron saint of miners, beginning on January 23.

Sleeping

Lençóis' best pousadas are famous for their fantastic breakfast spreads. Note that many of the accommodations located on the same side of the river as the bus station – ie, not in the so-called 'center' of Lençóis – are only accessible by a fairly steep uphill hike, and most streets aren't labeled. Ask your pousada ahead of time for directions or for a guide to meet you at the bus station.

★ **Pousada Lua de Cristal** POUSADA $
(☎75 3334-1658; Rua dos Patriotas 27; r R$140-375; 📶) Run by an exceptionally kind owner, this charming guesthouse offers sweet, simple rooms with antique stained-glass windows, many opening to views over the town. Outdoor breakfast tables are an added bonus.

Pousada & Camping Lumiar CAMPGROUND $
(☎75 3334-1241; lumiar.camping@gmail.com; Praça do Rosário 70; campsites with/without breakfast R$35/25, d from R$100; 📶) Grassy campsites

shaded by flowering trees in a gorgeous garden beside a church. Bar, restaurant and guest-use kitchen.

★Pouso Da Trilha POUSADA $$
(☎75 3334-1192; www.pousodatrilha.com.br; Rua dos Mineiros 60; d with/without air-con R$170/280; ❄📶) Conveniently located on the edge of the historic center, this guesthouse has simple rooms with homey design flourishes and a tranquil patio area with hammocks and a small garden. A great breakfast spread and friendly staff give it an edge over some of the other accomodations in town.

Alcino Estalagem & Atelier INN $$
(☎75 3334-1171; www.alcinoestalagem.com; General Viveiros139; d R$390; ❄📶) This lovely yellow mansion, filled with antiques and hand-painted tiles, was designed and built by a local artist. Staying here is like being a guest in a private home. Peruse the library or relax in the charming interior patio; the extensive breakfast is rightfully famous.

Vila Serrano POUSADA $$
(☎75 3334-1486; www.vilaserrano.com.br; Alto do Bonfim 8; d/q from R$350/460; 📶) 🍃 In a lush setting, the classy, environmentally conscious Vila Serrano comprises spacious apartments, designed according to the principles of feng shui with romantic drapery, rustic wooden accents and private verandas with hammocks.

Pousada Canto das Águas POUSADA $$$
(☎75 3334-1154; www.lencois.com.br; Av Senhor dos Passos 1; d from R$364; ❄📶🏊) 🍃 At the river's edge, this family-friendly, sustainably designed hotel has a sophisticated but earthy look – think stone, hard wood, and large windows facing the trees. There's a swimming pool; the sound of the river's flowing water fills guest rooms at night. The hotel's coffee shop and restaurant, São Benedito Cafeteria and Azul, respectively, are open to the public.

Eating

At night Lençóis' atmosphere is wonderfully charming as many restaurants on Praća Horácio de Matos and Rua das Pedras put candlelit tables out on the cobblestone walkways. The town also has a number of bakeries and basic minimarkets catering to hikers.

Burritos y Taquitos MEXICAN $
(☎75 99288-1437; José Florencio 3; mains R$15-42; ⏲6-10pm Tue-Sun) A rare chance to get your Mexican fix in rural Bahia: this casual restaurant does burritos, tacos and guacamole, and has a back patio overlooking the river.

★Lampião BRAZILIAN $$
(☎75 3334-1157; www.facebook.com/lampiaofood; Rua da Baderna 51; mains R$34-53; ⏲4-11pm Tue-Sun; 📶) This popular eatery specializes in cuisine from Brazil's Northwest – grilled meats, fish and chicken, served at cute alfresco tables for two. It's also a popular drinking spot.

★Os Artistas da Massa ITALIAN $$
(☎75 99935-4758; Rua da Baderna 49; mains R$38-48; ⏲11:30am-midnight) Fantastically fresh, hearty portions of handmade pastas and jazz music are on the menu at this gourmet restaurant. Opening days can vary during the off seasons, so check before you go.

Café do Mato CAFE $$
(☎75 99926-7151; Miguel Calmon 38-50; mains R$30-34; ⏲4-10pm Wed-Mon; 📶) Lençóis' burgeoning bohemian population can be found congregating at this cafe that specializes in tasty crepes, pastas and craft beer, some of which is produced locally.

Cozinha Aberta FUSION $$
(☎75 3334-1321; www.cozinhaaberta.com.br; Barbosa 42; mains R$42-50; ⏲noon-4pm & 6-10:30pm; 📶) This gourmet bistro serves fusion dishes from Thai noodles to Indian curries and Italian pastas, all of which emphasize simple presentation and thoughtful flavors. The setting is charming and homelike.

Shopping

Lençóis has several small boutiques and shops where you can pick up locally produced artwork, crafts and artisanal liqueurs.

Dos Irmãos SPORTS & OUTDOORS
(☎75 3334-1405; www.doisirmaos.com.br; Praça Horácio de Matos 3; ⏲8am-10pm) This outdoor outfitter sells backpacks, water bottles, camping equipment and hiking boots.

Information

MONEY

Banco do Brasil (Praça Horácio de Matos 56), located on the main square once you cross the bridge into the old town, has ATMs.

USEFUL WEBSITES

The online portal of Guia Lençóis (www.guialencois.com.br) is a great resource for tourist information. Another excellent resource – especially for those heading into the park for a few days – is the English-language Guia Turistico Chapada Diamantina (R$49), an excellent information booklet with color photos, maps and detailed descriptions of area hikes. It's for sale at the tourist office and

> **NAVIGATING LENÇÓIS**
>
> In the past few years, almost all of the Lençóis' streets have been officially renamed but locals continue to use the original names, causing confusion for tourists. Note that while some businesses have embraced using their new addresses, many have not: you might have trouble when you're asking for directions. Luckily, Lençóis is small and easy to navigate, but if you're arriving at night, you should look at the map so you know where you're going when you arrive at the bus station. It's also common for staff from pousadas and hostels to meet the buses arriving from Salvador: ask ahead if you'd like some help getting from the station to your destination.

at businesses around town (more information at www.guiachapadadiamantina.com.br).

TOURIST INFORMATION

Associação dos Condutores de Visitantes de Lençóis (75 3334-1425; www.acvlencois.com.br; cnr Miguel Calmon & Antiga das Pedras; 8am-noon & 2-8pm) has information about tour guides. Guides may also be hired through the town's various outfitters and travel agencies.

Getting There & Away

BUS

The **bus station** (Av Sr dos Passos s/n) is north of the center. If coming from the south, the journey, though indirect, will be a lot quicker if you route through Salvador or Feira de Santana. **Real Expresso** (75 3334-1112; www.realexpresso.com.br) runs a few buses daily from Salvador (R$85, seven to eight hours). The same buses can be caught in Feira de Santana (R$63). Be sure to bring a sweater for the journey: these buses are notorious for blasting the air-conditioning.

CAR

Lençóis is 13km off Hwy BR-242, the main Salvador–Brasília route. There's a gas station 22km east of Lençóis on Hwy BR-242, in Tanquinho. The drive from Salvador to Lencois takes about five to six hours.

Parque Nacional da Chapada Diamantina

Within the 1520 sq km of the **Parque Nacional da Chapada Diamantina** (www.guiachapadadiamantina.com.br) FREE, waterfalls cascade over the Sincora Range's mountains and plateaus, dropping into rivers and streams that wind their way through grassy valleys and clean swimming holes. The region's unique natural beauty and the tranquility of its small colonial towns have attracted a steady trickle of Brazilian and foreign travelers and hiking and nature enthusiasts, for several decades; some have never left. These introduced residents, moved by the degradation of the environment and depletion of the wild-animal population, spearheaded an active ecological movement in direct opposition to the extractive mentality of diamond miners and many locals. After six years of bureaucratic battles, biologist Roy Funch helped convince the government to create the park in 1985.

Day Trips & Hikes

The most popular day trip into the park is to the top of Brazil's tallest waterfall, **Cachoeira da Fumaça** (Smoke Waterfall), so named because before it has plummeted the entire 420m, the water evaporates into mist. This 6km hike requires a guide, so contact an agency in Lençóis. Alternatively, start from the closest village, **Capão** (80km west of Lençóis by road), which has a number of pousadas and a few travel agencies. The nearby mystical **Vale do Capão**, or **Caeté-Açu**, has attracted an international community of folks interested in an alternative, back-to-the-land lifestyle.

Hikers may want to take the trail along Barro Branco between Lençóis and **Morro do Pai Inácio**, an 1120m peak affording a brilliant view over a plateau-filled valley. Allow four or five hours one way for the hike.

Just southwest of Lençóis, upstream from Ribeirão do Meio, is the lovely **Cachoeira do Sossêgo** waterfall, with a deep pool at its base and rock ledges for diving. The 7km hike involves a great deal of stone-hopping along the riverbed and should not be attempted without a guide, or when rain or high water has made the lichen-covered rocks slippery.

Gruta do Lapão is one of the largest sandstone caves in South America and is just a 5km hike north of Lençóis. A guide is required.

'Chapada's Pantanal', or **Marimbus**, is a marshy microregion 94km south of Lençóis where you can canoe or kayak while fishing for *tucunaré* (peacock bass) and keeping a lookout for capybaras and *jacarés* (caimans).

Longer Hikes

Navigating the correct routes for the longer treks in the park can be very difficult, so going on a guided tour (p460) is strongly recommended. Treks organized with a guide can last anywhere from two to eight days, and can be custom fitted to the group. They usually involve a combination of camping and staying in local homes and pousadas.

Some popular hikes are the **Base of Fumaça**, an extremely beautiful yet tiring 36km trek that traverses the park from Lençóis to Capão in three days. Detours to other waterfalls are taken along the way, in addition to reaching the base of **Cachoeira da Fumaça**. An extra day can be added walking back to Lençóis or you can continue with the Grand Circuit. Be forewarned that the area around Fumaça's base gets extremely crowded at times, so you may find yourself sharing your sleeping cave with unexpected companions.

Another popular option is the **Vale do Patí** hike. This recommended hike starts and ends in Vale do Capão, and can last from four to six days depending on detours. You are likely to have the trails to yourself here, and the views over the plains and Chapada's table mountains are spectacular. Stopping in at a local home for a meal or a night is a possibility; it's much easier to negotiate if you're traveling with a local guide.

Grand Circuit

The Grand Circuit of the park covers about 100km, best done in a counterclockwise direction. It takes about five days, but at least eight days are required to include side trips. Especially if you're not carrying all of your own camping equipment and food, go with a guide, who can arrange overnight stays and meals in locals' homes along the way.

On the first day, make the hike from Lençóis to **Vale do Capão** (25km, about seven hours); on the way, you can take a side trip to the top of **Cachoeira da Fumaça**. In the visitor-friendly Vale do Capão, you can camp or stay at a pousada such as the eco-minded Pousada Pé no Mato, offering peaceful and affordable dorms, private rooms and freestanding cabins, plus an on-site tour agency that can help you plan almost any adventure in the park.

From the Bomba neighborhood of Vale do Capão, continue on to cross the plains region of **Gerais do Vieira** and the **Rio Preto** highlands to the **Vale do Patí**. You can camp overnight on the plains; if you're with a guide, you'll probably stay overnight in a local home.

You can power on in one day to **Andaraí**, or take a recommended day or two to explore the Vale do Patí, checking out the gorgeous waterfall **Cachoeirão** and the **Morro do Castelo** mountain before moving on.

Once in Andaraí, side trips to **Poço Encantado** (56km from Andaraí) and the intriguing diamond-era stone ruins in **Igatú** (12km from Andaraí) are highly recommended. In Andaraí, either camp or check into cozy Pousada Sincorá. You can go for a dip at the nearby river beaches along the Rio Paraguacu or take the short hike to **Cachoeira do Ramalho**, a 90m waterfall.

In Igatú, take the two-hour hike along the **Rampa do Caim** for sweeping views over the Vale do Patí. You can spend the night at the charming Flor de Açucena, offering campsites, guest rooms built into the rocky hillside, abundant greenery and striking views, with a trail leading down to the river.

Most choose to drive from Andaraí to Lençóis as the walk is on an uninteresting dirt road. If you decide to walk, allow two days, camping the first night near **Rio Roncador**.

Sleeping

There are many guesthouses in the region, while camping or sleeping in the park's small caves is free and can be done without a permit. If you are planning a longer hike with a guide, you may also be able to arrange homestays.

Pousada Pé no Mato POUSADA $

(75 3344-1105; www.penomato.com.br; Rua da Vila 2, Caeté-Açú; dm/d from R$65/140) Eco-minded Pousada Pé no Mato offers peaceful and affordable dorms, private rooms and freestanding cabins, plus an on-site tour agency that can help you plan almost any adventure.

Flor de Açucena POUSADA $$

(75 98274-0408; www.pousadaflordeacucena.com; 7 de Setembro 48-126, Igatú; d from R$210;) In Igatu, the charming Hospedagem Flor de Açucena has wildly natural rooms built into the rocky hillside, abundant greenery and striking views, with a trail to the river.

Pousada Sincorá POUSADA $$

(75 3335-2210; www.sincora.com.br; Paraguaçu 120, Andaraí; d/tr from R$175/220;) Cozy guesthouse renowned for its delicious breakfast and friendly owners who speak English. It also has guides who run a river inner-tubing operation just out of town (two-hour innertube ride R$30).

Getting There & Around

Local bus service for the region is infrequent and can be tricky to navigate, so if you do plan on exploring the park a car rental is worth considering. Guides can often provide transportation and there are taxis available in most of the towns, including Lençóis. If you have a specific destination in mind it's a good idea to ask your hotel for recommendations on how to get there.

Sergipe & Alagoas

POP 3.3M

Includes ➡

Sergipe......466
Aracaju......466
Alagoas......470
Maceió......470
Praia do Francês......477
Penedo......478
Maragogi......480

Best Places to Eat

➡ Cariri (p469)
➡ Sushi Bowl (p473)
➡ Janga (p474)
➡ Wanchako (p475)
➡ Odoiá (p481)

Best Places to Stay

➡ Maceió Mar Hotel (p472)
➡ Pousada Olho D'água (p481)
➡ Hotel São Francisco (p479)
➡ Pousada Ricardinho do Frances (p477)
➡ Pousada do Sol (p468)

Why Go?

Overshadowed by big Bahia to the south, the tiny states of Sergipe and Alagoas have long been overlooked by travelers. But it's a tendency that's changing – in the past few years, the thoroughly likable coastal city of Maceió has emerged as a buzzing vacation destination for Brazil. Still, despite the influx of ecofriendly pousadas (guesthouses) and stylish restaurants, there remain plenty of isolated, paradise-like stretches of white sand, emerald waters, swaying palms and quaint villages along Alagoas' coast.

Inland travel appeals to history-minded travelers: Penedo is a charming riverfront town with picturesque colonial churches and hilly cobblestone streets. Further south, Sergipe's provincial capital has fewer attractions of its own, but Aracaju serves as a gateway to more sleepy colonial towns. In these off-the-beaten-path hamlets, historic 17th-century churches attest to the region's prominence in the early days of European settlement in Brazil.

When to Go

Maceio

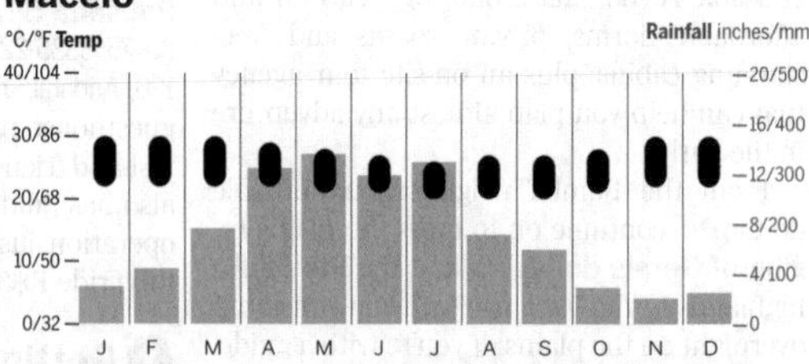

Dec–Feb High season brings crowds of domestic tourists to Maceió and Aracaju.

Mar–Aug Temperatures remain high and periods of rain are likely; hotel prices drop.

Sep–Nov Near-perfect weather and few tourists: an ideal time to visit.

History

During the invasion by the Dutch in 1630, many slaves took advantage of the confusion and escaped to the mountains behind the coasts of northern Alagoas and southern Pernambuco. Where the Alagoan towns of Atalaia, Capela, Viçosa, União dos Palmares and Porto Calvo stand today, virgin forests with fruit and wildlife once provided for colonies of runaway slaves. Palmares, the mightiest republic of escaped slaves, led by the former African king Zumbi, covered present-day Alagoas and Pernambuco. In the 18th and 19th centuries,

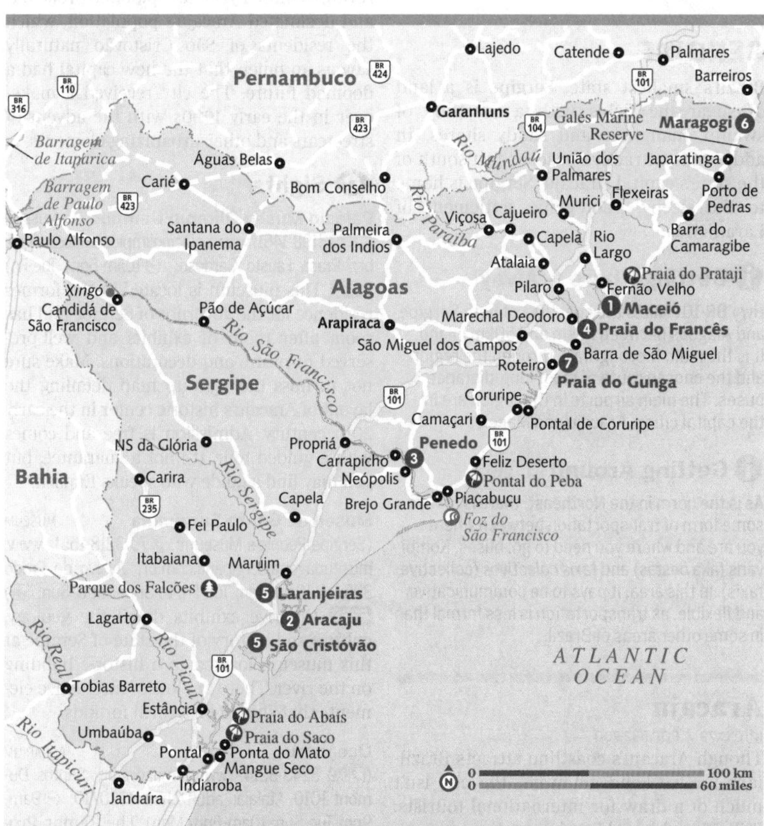

Sergipe & Alagoas Highlights

1 Maceió (p470) Pedaling a bike along friendly beach paths, or taking a *jangada* (boat) into the ocean to explore natural pools created by offshore reefs.

2 Aracaju (p466)Feasting on fresh crabs and listening to traditional *forró* music in the open-air eateries.

3 Penedo (p478) Exploring the colonial churches and cobblestone streets of the historic city.

4 Praia do Francês (p478) Enjoying a *moqueca* after a morning of exploring tidal pools.

5 Laranjeiras & São Cristóvão (p467) Walking down winding streets to discover stunning examples of colonial-era architecture.

6 Maragogi (p480) Snorkeling the colorful coral reefs miles offshore.

7 Praia do Gunga (p471) Boarding a dune buggy for a joyride along the smooth white sands of Praia do Gunga.

sugarcane and cotton brought the region prominence; today, sugarcane is still an important crop in the area, alongside oranges and cassava, though tourism is making inroads in Maceió. Unfortunately, the states are also known for extreme poverty in the interior and rampant corruption.

SERGIPE

Brazil's smallest state, Sergipe is a land of sugarcane fields with a coastline of swamp, mangrove and sandy shores. In addition to attractive beaches just south of the state's capital Aracaju, Sergipe is home to the sleepy, photogenic settlement of Laranjeiras.

Getting There & Away

Hwy BR-101 skirts the coastline of both Sergipe and Alagoas between 25km and 50km inland. It is the main thoroughfare through the region and the chosen route of most long-distance buses. The main airports in the region are in the capital cities, Aracaju and Maceió.

Getting Around

As is the norm in the Northeast, there is always some form of transportation between where you are and where you need to go: buses, Kombi vans (aka *bestas*) and *taxis colectivos* (collective taxis). In this area, it pays to be communicative and flexible, as transportation is less formal than in some other areas of Brazil.

Aracaju

0XX79 / POP 632,700

Though Aracaju's coastline attracts Brazilians for weekend getaways, the city isn't much of a draw for international tourists. Still, if you're looking for a relaxing beach vacation in a city environment, it's worth considering. You'll find a few points of interest in the historic center, including the picturesque main square with its towering cathedral. But most of the historic center is a utilitarian business district. The beaches are the real attraction in Aracaju. In the city there are several miles of lovely coastline, and, especially in the off-season, you won't find it as hectic as other large cities. Along the beach you'll find a growing number of restaurants and hotels popping up to meet tourism demands.

History

The seat of state government was moved from São Cristóvão to Aracaju in 1855, in part because of its good, deep harbor – badly needed to handle large ships transporting sugar to Europe – and because residents of the old capital were on the verge of armed revolt. Within a year, an epidemic broke out and decimated Aracaju's population, which the residents of São Cristóvão naturally saw as an omen that the new capital had a doomed future. The city received a makeover in the early 1900s with the advent of streetcars and other urbanizing elements.

Sights

Palácio Museu Olímpio Campos MUSEUM
(79 3198-1461; www.palacioolimpiocampos.se.gov.br; Praça Fausto Cardoso; 10am-5pm Tue-Fri) FREE This museum is located in the former residence for the governor of Sergipe and has room after room of exhibits and well-preserved furniture and decorations. Make sure not to miss the light-up map detailing the layout of Aracaju's historic center in the early 20th century. Admission is free and comes with a guided tour. It's not a guarantee, but you may find a guide who speaks English.

Museu de Gente Sergipana MUSEUM
(Sergipe People's Museum; 79 3218-1551; www.museudagentesergipana.com.br; Av Ivo do Prado 398; 10am-4pm Tue-Fri, to 3pm Sat & Sun;) FREE Creative exhibits detail the geology, culture and history of the state of Sergipe at this museum located in a historic building on the river. There are lots of interactive elements that should be a thrill for kids.

Oceanário AQUARIUM
(79 3243-3214; www.tamar.org.br; Santos Dumont 1010, Atalaia; adult/child R$20/10; 9am-9pm Tue-Sun, 10am-6pm Mon) The Tamar Project's small, interesting Oceanário has tanks with sea turtles, rays and eels as well as examples of specific local freshwater environments and their species.

Centro Cultural de Aracaju CULTURAL CENTRE
(79 3214-5387; Av Rio Branco, Historic Center; 8am-5pm Mon-Fri, 8:30am-1pm Sat) FREE Here you'll find several fun exhibits on Sergipe's culture, including puppet art and the reconstruction of a formerly long-lost early 20th-century carousel that used to operate in the city. Few of the exhibits have English translations, but you may find an English-speaking guide working the day you visit.

WORTH A TRIP

LARANJEIRAS

Positioned between three grassy, church-topped hills, Laranjeiras is the colonial gem of Sergipe and, together with São Cristóvão, it makes a short and sweet side trip from Aracaju for travelers interested in Sergipe's history. It's short on significant tourist attractions but long on visual interest – ideal for travelers interested in photography.

First settled in 1605, Laranjeiras became the commercial center for its surrounding verdant sugar and cotton fields during the 18th and 19th centuries. At one point there were more than 60 sugar mills in and around Laranjeiras sending sugar down the Rio Cotinguiba to Aracaju for export to Europe.

With a quiet grandeur, Laranjeiras has picturesque cobblestone roads, colonial buildings with intricate wood-carved doorways and terracotta roofs. From the higher points in town, there are lovely views over the meandering Rio Cotinguiba. The whole town seems unblemished by modern development; the surrounding countryside hides crumbling ruins of old sugar mills and estates.

Facing the bus station, the **Trapiche** is an imposing 19th-century structure that historically held cargo waiting to be shipped downriver. At the top of **Alto do Bonfim** (Bonfim Heights) is the picturesque 19th-century **Igreja NS do Bonfim**. Although the church is often closed, the fine views make it worth the climb.

In town you'll find two small museums well worth a visit. The **Museu de Arte Sacra** (Museum of Sacred Art; ☎79 3281-2486; Praça Dr Heráclito Diniz Gonçalves 39, Laranjeiras; R$6; ⏰10am-2pm Tue-Fri) contains several rooms filled with historic religious art from the Catholic church and the **Museu Afro-Brasileiro** (☎79 3281-2418; José do Prado Franco 70, Laranjeiras; R$6; ⏰10am-5pm Tue-Fri, 1-5pm Sat & Sun) details the history of African transplants to Brazil, including the country's brutal history of slavery.

Upriver 4km from town is the baroque **Igreja de Comandaroba**, constructed by Jesuits in 1734. Unfortunately, the church hasn't been well-maintained, and you're unlikely to see inside. A 1km tunnel leads from the church to the **Gruta da Pedra Furada**, a large cave built by the Jesuits to escape their persecutors.

If you happen to be in the area in January during the last week of the month, Laranjeiras hosts the **Festa de Reis** (also called Encontro Cultural), a religious and folklore festival of traditional music and dance. More folklore revelry occurs during **Semana Folclórico** (Folklore Week), usually the second week of August. You can also catch colorful religious processions during **Semana Santa** (Holy Week; the week preceding Easter).

To get here from Aracaju head to the Rodoviaria Velha and look for the Coopertalse bus headed for Laranjeiras (R$3.70, 35 minutes). They leave frequently.

Mercado Municipal MARKET
(José do Prado Franco s/n, Centro; ⏰6am-6pm Mon-Sat, to noon Sun) At the colorful Mercado Municipal, locals sell and barter a wide range of goods; if you're passing through downtown around lunchtime, stop in for a casual meal and people-watching.

Beaches

With rustling palms and a relative lack of buildings, **Praia Atalaia Nova** (6km across the Rio Sergipe, southeast of the center), is generally calmer than the city beaches to the south, namely **Praia dos Artistas** (7km), **Praia Atalaia** (9km) and **Praia Aruana** (11km). These beaches are heavily developed but are popular with locals; they are also good sources of inexpensive seafood. Further south, **Praia do Refúgio** (18km) is the prettiest and most secluded beach nearby.

Tours

Local travel agencies offer a variety of day tours, including catamaran trips on the **Rio São Francisco** to the green waters of the canyon of **Xingó**, or to the **Foz do São Francisco**, where the river meets the sea. A tour is also a pretty good way to check out difficult-to-reach Mangue Seco (p432), on the border with Bahia. Bird enthusiasts will enjoy a visit to the **Parque dos Falcões** (☎79 99962-8396; www.parquedosfalcoes.com.br; BR 235 s/n, Itabaiana; adult/children R$25/15), a reserve located 45km from Aracaju. Most tours are R$75–130 per person and you will be pooled with other people who purchased from different companies. **Nozes Tur** (☎79 3243-7177;

www.nozestur.com.br; Santos Dumont 340, Atalaia; tours from R$130; ⏲9am-midnight) is a solid bet if you are looking for a place to book.

Festivals & Events

Festa de São João CULTURAL
(⏲Jun) The largest festival in Aracaju runs for the entire month of June and includes live *forró* (a music and dance style of the Northeast) bands and *quadrilha* (a type of square dancing) presentations.

Bom Jesus dos Navegantes CULTURAL
(⏲1 Jan) On New Year's Day a huge fleet of fishing boats sails along the Rio Sergipe following the image of their patron saint to celebrate Bom Jesus dos Navegantes.'

Sleeping

The majority of Aracaju's hotels are along the beachfront in the Atalaia neighborhood. If you're staying on the beach, remember that the coastline is several miles long. Most visitors are happiest staying on the far northern end in the district of Coroa de Meio, or on the far southern side near the Passarela do Caranguejo, though there are plenty of pousadas (guesthouses) in between.

Hotel Jangadeiro HOTEL $
(☎79 3211-1350; www.jangadeirose.com.br; Santa Luzia 269, Centro; s/d from R$137/167; ❄📶🏊) Located a few blocks south of the historic center's main plaza, this business-style hotel is dated but serviceable, good for a quick overnight stay in Aracaju. In-room perks include new bed linens, fluffy pillows and flat-screen TVs.

Mercure Aracaju del Mar HOTEL $$
(☎79 2106-9100; www.delmarhotel.com.br; Santos Dumont 1500, Atalaia; d from R$220; ❄📶🏊) This contemporary high-rise, featuring minimalist interior design, several bars and restaurants, and a large swimming pool complete with waterfalls and a bar, is a slick addition to Atalaia's waterfront; it's usually occupied by business travelers, but it's also family-friendly.

Pousada do Sol POUSADA $$
(☎79 3226-5500; www.hotelpousadadosol.com.br; Eng Francisco Manoel de Costa 43, Atalaia; r/chalet from R$214/231; ❄📶🏊) This well-located guesthouse, a stone's throw from many of Atalaia's waterfront attractions, is a travelers' favorite. Expect simple, spotless and bright guest rooms, a pleasant swimming pool and terrace, and a children's play area.

Pousada Encantare POUSADA $$
(☎79 3243-7045; www.facebook.com/Pousada.Ola; Niceu Dantas 618, Atalaia; d from R$202; ❄📶🏊) This simple, efficiently run guesthouse is one of several located near the Passarela do Caranguejo (Crab Lane), offering easy access to the beach and some of Aracaju's best dining and drinking options.

Pousada Mirante Das Águas POUSADA $$
(☎79 3255-2610; www.mirantedasaguas.com.br; Delmiro Gouveia 711, Coroa do Meio; d R$161; ❄@📶) Two blocks from the waterfront, the Pousada Mirante das Águas has standard rooms and family-friendly amenities, including a games room. The location in Coroa do Meio is about midway between downtown and the Passarela do Caranguejo – access either by a long walk or short bus or taxi ride.

Eating

Although its restaurant scene is not as big a draw as Salvador or Maceió, you'll find a number of great places to east in Aracaju. Make sure to head down the waterfront south of Atalaia where you'll find the popular Passarela do Caranguejo (Crab Lane), a row of open-sided restaurants facing the waterfront that serve the respected local dish – the locals' favorite is Cariri.

Burgeria BURGERS $
(www.facebook.com/goburgeria; Travessa Benjamin Constant 98, Centro; burgers R$10-24; ⏲11am-8pm Mon-Fri, 10am-3pm Sat) Burgeria is a new addition to the dull restaurant scene in the historic center. This small spot pretty much only does burgers, but they are juicy with perfectly melted cheese and thick buns. It's a great pick for lunch if you're in the area sightseeing.

Los Palitos ICE CREAM $
(☎79 3025-2005; www.facebook.com/lospalitosbrasil; Av Santos Dumont 1329; desserts R$8-24; ⏲1-10pm Tue-Thu & Sun, to 11pm Fri & Sat) Carefully constructed sundaes overloaded with ingredients and topped with a signature Mexican-style popsicle are on offer at this beachfront ice-cream shop. The sundaes are big enough for two. If you just want a taste you can buy the popsicles separately.

il Sordo GELATO $
(☎79 3027-1258; www.facebook.com/ilsordose; Store 3, José Ramos da Silva 303; medium gelato R$13; ⏲10am-8pm Sun-Thu, to 9pm Fri, to 10pm Sat) This cheery shop is well known in

Aracaju for its delicious, creamy gelato and the fact that it's entirely staffed by deaf individuals. It's a 20-minute walk or short cab ride from the historic center.

Madre Deli Café CAFE $
(☎79 98827-7355; www.facebook.com/madredelicafe; Av Santos Dumont 641; dishes $15-25; ⊙7am-10pm Tue-Sun) Check out this hip 2nd-floor cafe that specializes in Mexican-inspired sandwiches and desserts. They have a small breakfast menu and daily specials.

República dos Camarões SEAFOOD $$
(☎79 3255-3361; Av Santos Dumont 10, Coroa do Meio; mains R$32-55; ⊙11am-4pm & 6-11pm Mon-Fri, 11:30am-11:30pm Sat, 11:30am-9pm Sun) Fresh, creatively prepared shrimp are the specialty at this popular waterfront restaurant, located within easy walking distance of many beachfront pousadas; it's a safe bet for a good seafood dinner.

★**Cariri** SEAFOOD $$$
(☎79 3243-1379; www.cariri-se.com.br; Santos Dumont 530, Atalaia; mains R$60-92; ⊙11:30am-late) If you have only one night in Aracaju, Cariri is the place to be for a taste of local culture. This famed Northeastern restaurant on the Passarela do Caranguejo features live *forró* music in the traditional style of *pé de serra* (Luis Gonzaga's signature 'foothills' *forró*). The show begins at 8pm.

Bada Grill BRAZILIAN $$$
(☎79 3223-3664; Santos Dumont 526, Atalaia; mains R$60-90; ⊙11:30am-1:30am Tue-Thu, to 2am Fri & Sat, to midnight Sun) Located just north of the Passarela do Caranguejo and across the street from the beach, this casually elegant eatery has a breezy open terrace that's inviting for happy hour drinks and *petiscos* (snacks) such as the popular *lambretas gratinadas* (clams baked in cheese).

ℹ Orientation

Aracaju's Centro sits on the Rio Sergipe, guarded from the ocean by a sandy barrier island, the Ilha de Santa Luzia. To the south, past the river mouth, are the city beach neighborhoods of Coroa do Meio, Jardim Atlantico (Praia dos Artistas) and Atalaia, collectively referred to as the *orla* (waterfront). Most of the action and nightlife is concentrated in these suburban neighborhoods.

ℹ Getting There & Away

AIR

GOL (☎0800-280-0465; www.voegol.com.br) and **LATAM** (☎1-866-435-9526; www.latam.com) can fly or connect you to other Brazilian cities from Aracaju's **airport** (AJU; ☎79 3212-8500), 11km south of the center.

A taxi to the airport from the center will cost about R$60. From the Rodoviária Velha, take the Aeroporto city bus.

BUS

Most long-distance buses leave from the **Rodoviária Nova** (Terminal Rodoviário Govanador José Rollemberg Leite; ☎79 3238-3900; Av President Tancredo Neves, Capucho), 6km east of the center.

Águia Branca (p450) and Rota (www.rotatransportes.com.br) each offer 11 daily departures to Salvador (R$72 to R$105, four to six hours). Rota buses also go to Maceió (R$52, four to five hours, four daily), as do **Real Alagoas** (☎79 3259-2832; www.realalagoas.com.br) buses (R$62, four hours, three daily). Aguia Branca goes to Penedo (R$20, three hours, one daily.)

ℹ Getting Around

BUS & TAXI

There are two main bus stations: Rodoviária Nova, where buses come and go from other cities, and **Rodoviária Velha** (Terminal Rodoviário Governador Luiz Garcia; ☎79 3238-2900; Av 7 de Setembro), located downtown, where you can catch buses and minibuses to smaller towns and destinations near Aracaju.

From Rodoviária Nova, catch a bus into the city from a large shelter with a series of triangular roofs beside the station. Buses marked 'Centro' take you downtown. Alternatively, catch a taxi to downtown for around R$30, or to the beaches for around R$40–50.

The city buses (R$3.25) are sometimes infrequent, but safe and good options for traveling from the beaches to the historic center. If going from the beach to the historic center, walk inland to Av Mario Jorge Menezes Viêira. If you're in the *centro* head over to Av Ivo do Prado along the river and look for line No 51, marked 'Atalaia/Centro.' When in doubt, simply look for buses that advertise either 'Centro' or 'Atalaia.' Most buses have the highlights of their route printed on the side by the door.

CAR

Find a range of car-rental agencies along Atalaia's waterfront: these agencies do steady business, as many destinations in the region are much easier to visit with your own car than by public transportation.

ALAGOAS

POP 3.3M

Despite its diminutive size there's much to recommend the small state of Alagoas. Its star attraction is the city of Maceió with lovely shoreline and a burgeoning dining and drinking scene. Further afield, there remain plenty of isolated, paradise-like stretches of white sand, emerald waters, swaying palms and quaint villages along Alagoas' coast. In towns like Praia do Francês and Maragogi you'll find natural pools created by expansive offshore reefs to explore. Inland, the state is home to architectural treasures like Penedo.

Maceió

☎0XX82 / POP 1M

Maceió is a modern city set on a truly beautiful beachfront. Though not well known to international tourists – at least not yet – Brazilians have rediscovered Maceió as a vacation getaway, and the past few years have seen a boom in domestic tourism. The city has a small but buzzing dining and drinking scene and a much less hectic attitude than other larger cities; it's also the gateway to wonderfully idyllic shorelines to the north and south. On the city's beaches, vivid, emerald-hued water laps the powdery sands that are lined with palms and brightly painted *jangadas* (traditional sailboats). By night, locals follow the meandering beachfront path as it weaves past thatched-roof restaurants and palm-shaded football pitches. Maceió's sights are relatively few, leaving you plenty of time to catch some rays and soak up the relaxed atmosphere.

Sights

Mercado do Artesanato MARKET

(☎82 3315-4774; Melo Morais 617, Levada; ⏲7am-5pm Mon-Fri, to 2pm Sat, to noon Sun) If you want a better variety of goods and a better deal than what's on offer at the markets on the beach, head to the Mercado do Artesanato in the city center. To get there, catch a bus that stops in front of the *antigo* (old) Cine Ideal.

Beaches

Protected by an offshore coral reef, Maceió's ocean waters are calm and a deep emerald color. City beaches include the popular **Praia de Ponta Verde**, **Praia de Pajuçara**, **Praia dos Sete Coqueiros** and **Jatiúca** – a pair of lounge chairs and a rental umbrella will run you about R$20 to R$30 for the afternoon. Be forewarned that Praia do Sobral and Praia da Avenida, closer to the city center, are polluted.

The nicest beaches north of the city are thought to be **Garça Torta** (14km) and **Pratagi** (17km), but **Jacarecica** (9km), **Guaxuma** (12km) and **Riacho Doce** (17km) are also tropical paradises. The Riacho Doce bus, which you can pick up in several spots along the coastal road, runs up the coast to these northern beaches.

Tours

From Praia de Pajuçara, **jangadas** (Sailboats; trips R$30) travel 2km offshore at low tide to natural pools formed by the reef (R$30). After a short journey aboard one of the delightfully old-fashioned, colorfully painted *jangadas*, you're free to float in the clear water; snorkel-mask rental (R$18) is optional. On weekends, floating bars serve beer and *agua de coco* (coconut water), making the whole experience more festive. You can arrange trips with any boat captain – stop in early to find out when the boats are sailing or just stroll down the beach and wait for someone to approach you first. The whole trip lasts about two hours.

A plethora of organized day trips are possible from Maceió, including a **beach tour** (R$35, taking in Praia do Francês, Barra de São Miguel and Praia do Gunga), an excursion to **Foz do São Francisco** (R$120), a trip to Porto de Galinahs (R$80) and a trip to the **natural pools** (from R$125) off the coast of Maragogi. Another popular excursion is the **Nove Ilhas** (Nine Islands) tour (R$85) – in addition to cruising the Lagoa Mundaú, you'll stop at the outlet of the lake into the ocean.

Such excursions are extremely easy to plan for much of the year: a large number of travel agencies' representatives camp out around Pajuçara's artisan market, advertising their services to passersby. For the most part companies combine passengers to make sure the numbers are filled out, but in the low season consider planning further ahead, contacting a few travel agencies through their web forms – a minimum number of passengers is required for most tours. Try contacting **Marcão Turismo** (☎82 3231-0843; www.turismomaceio.com.br; 2nd fl, Hotel Expresso R1, Avenida João Davino 386) or **Edvantur Turismo** (☎82 3327-9993;

WORTH A TRIP

PRAIA DO GUNGA

Praia do Gunga, near the village of Barra de São Miguel, is considered one of the finest beaches in Alagoas and is a popular day trip destination from nearby Maceió. The shores are protected by a huge offshore reef, leaving the waters calm for bathing or kayaking. Especially compared to the nice, but hectic, city beaches it's a true paradise. If you'd like to stay longer Brisamar Pousada (p472) is one of the better options in the area.

During high season on Praia do Gunga, dune buggies (R$50 per person) take tourists on an hour-long adventure: you'll speed along the sands, stop to photograph the rocky dune-lined landscape, and go for a dip in a natural pool. You can also hike to a lookout (R$3) for stunning views of the surrounding areas.

Note that in Praia do Gunga, dining options are infamously overpriced: be aware that most of the *barracas* (food stalls) insist on a minimum consumption of at least R$80–100 per person. Many beachgoers prefer to bring their own picnic from Maceió, or buy simple snacks and sandwiches from the stands set up around the gigantic parking lot. There is also an entry fee (R$5 per person), or a parking fee (R$15 per vehicle) which covers your entrance if you are arriving in your own car.

Barra de São Miguel and Praia do Gunga are located 35km from Maceió. Brazilian tourists usually arrive in their own cars, while most foreigners visit Praia do Gunga on a day trip with a travel agency in Maceió (R$35).

To arrive independently from Maceió, you can get one of the municipal buses (p476) from the main bus station (R$5.20, 40 minutes). There are many departures, with a slightly reduced schedule on Sundays.

www.edvanqueeuvoualagoas.com.br; Store 4, Jangadeiros Alagoanos 1206; tours per person from R$35; ⏲6am-10pm Mon-Fri, 6am-10am & 4-10pm Sat & Sun).

Festivals & Events

Festa Junina RELIGIOUS

(⏲late Jun) Fifteen days of folk dancing, fireworks, street food, bonfires, costumed revelry and free-flowing beer take over Maceió during Brazil's winter solstice; it's a Portuguese tradition beginning on St Anthony's day in mid-June and lasting through St Peter's day at the end of the month.

Carnaval CARNAVAL

(⏲mid-Feb) Maceió hosts a small but lively Carnaval with all of the usual trappings: music, food and dancing. The bigger parties happen at beaches outside the city, especially Barra de São Miguel.

Sleeping

Many high-rise chain hotels have opened along the waterfront in the past decade. In general, Maceió's lodging options are expensive, but you can still find some solid budget options. Few hotels and pousadas (guesthouses) offer much in the way of style or character. Luckily, you're not going to spend much time in your room in this lively coastal city.

Gogó da Ema POUSADA $

(☎82 3231-2117; www.hotelgogodaema.com.br; Francisco Laranjeiras 97, Ponta Verde; s/d/tr from R$100/120/160; ❄📶) On a quiet street near two lovely beaches, reliable budget pick Gogó da Ema (named for a famous old palm tree that fell in the city in 1955 and has come to symbolize Maceió itself) is a five-story guesthouse with a tropical theme. The 24-hour front desk is particularly helpful if you're arriving late or catching an early plane.

Pousada Hotel Maceio POUSADA $

(☎82 3316-8645; www.pousadahotelmaceio.com.br; Pompeu Sarmento 455, Ponta Verde; s/d from R$100/115; ❄📶) This simple eight-room guesthouse is nothing fancy, but the place is clean, well managed and conveniently located a half-block from the beach action, making it one of the better-value sleeping options in the area.

Maceió Hostel e Pousada HOSTEL $

(☎82 3231-7762; www.maceiohostel.com.br; Jangadeiros Alagoanos 1528, Pajuçara; dm/d from R$55/129; ❄📶) A budget option a few blocks from the beach, this HI hostel is small – shared quads don't leave much room for your backpack – but the staff are friendly and the place is efficiently run. Doubles are basic with good showers and large lockers.

Maceió

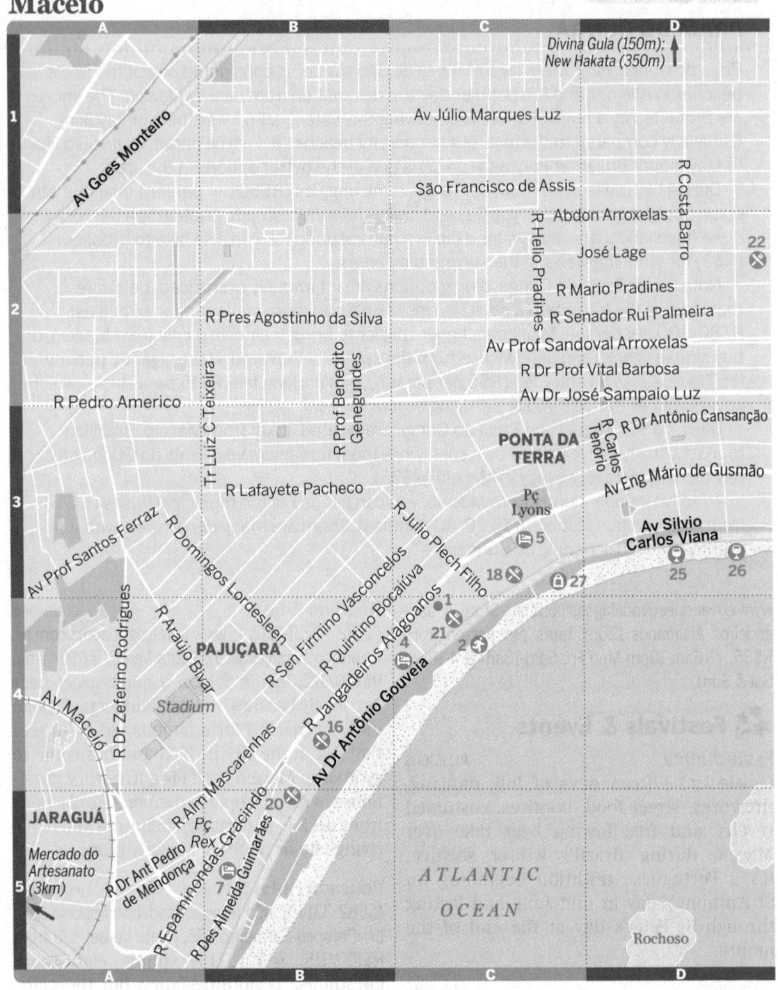

★ Maceió Mar Hotel HOTEL $$
(☎82 3142-0001; www.maceiomarhotel.com.br; Álvaro Otacílio 2991, Ponta Verde; r from R$347;) This popular high-rise, beachfront hotel has spacious, brightly lit rooms with floor-to-ceiling windows, all with sea views. Recently renovated, with upscale amenities and a swimming pool, it's suited to both business travelers and families.

Soft Inn HOTEL $$
(☎82 3131-1600; www.bhghoteis.com.br; Eng Mario de Gusmão 988, Ponta Verde; d from R$236;) If you're looking for simple comfort and a great location, the shiny newness of this hotel (which opened in 2018) makes it a cut above the other high-rise beachfront options. It has spotless, well serviced rooms and is located just a few blocks from the water.

Brisamar Pousada POUSADA $$
(☎82 3272-2030; www.brisamarpousada.com.br; Margarida Oiticica Lima 38, Barra de São Miguel; d from R$260;) The lovely Brisamar Pousada is one of the better options for staying close to Praia do Gunga. Rooms are clean and there's a great breakfast spread.

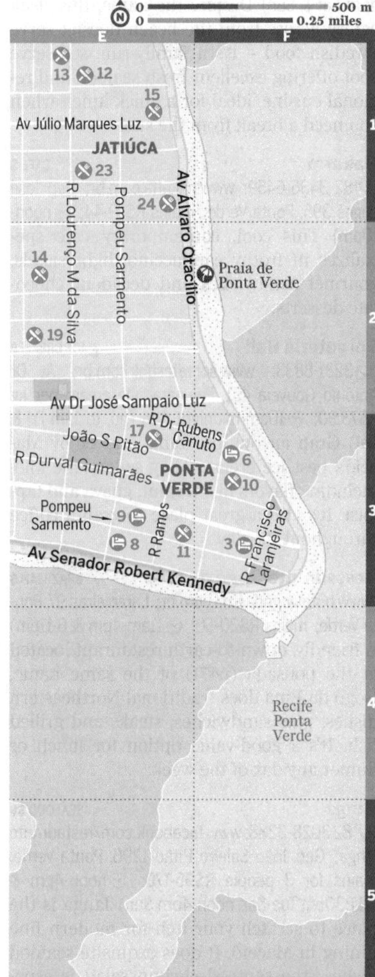

Maceió

Activities, Courses & Tours

1	Edvantur Turismo	C4
2	Jangadas	C4

Sleeping

3	Gogó da Ema	F3
4	Hotel Praia Bonita	C4
5	Maceió Hostel e Pousada	C3
6	Maceió Mar Hotel	F3
7	Pousada Aquarela do Brasil	B5
8	Pousada Hotel Maceio	E3
9	Soft Inn	E3

Eating

10	Janga	F3
11	Le Corbu	E3
12	Maria Antoineta	E1
13	Massarella	E1
14	Nakaffa	E2
15	O Peixarão	E1
16	Panificação Alteza	B4
17	Panificação Alteza	E3
18	Parmegianno	C3
19	Patrick's Wine Bar	E2
	Restaurante Gogó da Ema	(see 3)
20	Sorveteria Bali	B5
21	Sueca Comedoria	C4
22	Sushi Bowl	D2
23	Villa Maceio Food Park	E1
24	Wanchako	E1

Drinking & Nightlife

25	Kanoa Beach Bar	D3
26	Lopana	D3

Shopping

27	Mercado Praia de Pajuçara	C3

Hotel Praia Bonita HOTEL $$

(☎82 2121-3700; www.praiabonita.com.br; Dr Antônio Gouveia 943, Pajuçara; s/d from R$219/229;) This small and friendly waterfront hotel, dwarfed by the high-rise buildings around it, has an attractive, modern design and a breakfast room that faces the *jangada* launch across the street.

Pousada Aquarela do Brasil POUSADA $$

(☎82 3231-0113; www.pousadaaquareladobrasil.com; Desembargador Almeida Guimarães 367, Pajuçara; d from R$180;) Just off the waterfront, this pretty guesthouse offers simple but (relatively) sophisticated rooms with flat-screen TVs and modern artwork. Ground-level rooms have tiny private patios.

Eating

There's a wide selection of casual open-air eateries along the beachfront promenades. On weekend evenings and more frequently in high season, look for food trucks at the bend on the promenade where Ponta Verde turns into Pajuçara: you'll find gourmet burgers, craft beer, even Greek food. Heading inland a bit to the neighborhoods of Ponta Verde and Jatiúca will yield more options.

Pajuçara & Ponte Verde

★ **Sushi Bowl** SUSHI $

(☎82 3432-3637; www.facebook.com/amosushibowl; Dep José Lage 405, Ponta Verde; bowls R$26-41; 11:30am-3pm & 6-10:30pm) It may look like a hole-in-the-wall but you'll find

SAILING INTO THE PAST

Maceió's colorful wooden *jangadas* (sailboats) – lined up on the beach of Pajuçara, waiting to carry passengers to the natural pools around the coral reef offshore – are products of a long tradition in Northeast Brazil. *Jangadas* are made of native wood. No nails or other metal elements are used in their construction: the logs are held together with ropes. The slightly curved mast is mounted with a simple triangular sail. Though the origins of the *jangada* aren't entirely known, historians believe that this style of sailboat has its roots in India and Mozambique – influences that would have made their way to the shipping capitals of Northeast Brazil after the arrival of Portuguese explorers.

some of the most inventive seafood in Maceió at Sushi Bowl. Each one of their bowls is thoughtfully constructed with fresh ingredients, but if you can only choose one, go with the impressive-looking dragon bowl, which features salmon prepared via blowtorch.

Villa Maceio Food Park FOOD TRUCK $
(☎82 99937-7174; www.facebook.com/villamaceiofoodpark; Lourenço Moreira da Silva 203-245, Ponta Verde; mains R$20-40; ⏲6-11pm Tue & Wed, to midnight Fri & Sat, 5-11pm Sun; 🖉) You'll find both post-beach tourists and post-work locals flocking to this collection of food trucks at night. Everything from Brazilian favorites to gourmet hamburgers are represented and there is (of course) a beer-keg cart that dispenses several varieties of craft brew.

Panificação Alteza BAKERY $
(☎82 3231-0447; João Pitão 1181, Ponta Verde; snacks & sandwiches R$5-17; ⏲6am-8pm Mon-Sat) This gourmet mini-market, complete with a coffee bar and bakery, is the perfect place to get your caffeine fix while stocking up on fresh bread, tropical fruits, cold cuts, Argentinian wine and chocolate cake for your picnic or hotel room. There's also a small cafe open for breakfast. There's a **second outlet** (☎82 3231-0447; Jangadeiros Alagoanos 732, Pajuçara; snacks & sandwiches R$5-17; ⏲6am-8pm Mon-Sat).

Sueca Comedoria BUFFET $
(☎82 3327-0359; Dr Antônio Gouveia 1103, Pajuçara; per kg R$59.90; ⏲11:30am-3pm Mon-Fri, to 4pm Sat & Sun) Despite the name, this sleek eatery across from the beach doesn't serve Swedish food – it's a family-run, self-serve spot offering excellent fresh seafood and regional cuisine, ideal for a quick lunch when you need a break from the sun.

Nakaffa CAFE $
(☎82 3436-6459; www.nakaffa.com.br; Dep José Lages 395, Ponta Verde; mains R$19-44; ⏲noon-10pm) This cool, contemporary cafe specializes in frothy cappuccino, light salads, gourmet sandwiches and decadent chocolate desserts.

Sorveteria Bali ICE CREAM $
(☎3231-8833; www.sorvetesbali.com.br; Av Dr Antônio Gouveia 451, Pajuçara; ice cream per kg R$73.90; ⏲10am-midnight Sun-Thu, to 1am Fri & Sat) Grab an outdoor table and enjoy Maceió's best ice cream. They sell by the kilo, including flavors like walnut, guava and tapioca. It's also a great place to grab a coffee throughout the day.

Restaurante Gogó da Ema BRAZILIAN $
(www.hotelgogodaema.com.br; Laranjeiras 97, Ponta Verde; mains R$20-50; ⏲11am-4pm & 6-11pm) A friendly, down-to-earth restaurant located at the pousada (p471) of the same name, Gogó da Ema does traditional Northeastern dishes, plus sandwiches, steaks and grilled fish. It's a good-value option for lunch or dinner any day of the week.

Janga SEAFOOD $$
(☎82 3028-3288; www.facebook.com/restaurantejanga; Gen João Saleiro Pitão 1296, Ponta Verde; mains for 3 people R$95-170; ⏲noon-4pm & 6-11:30pm Tue-Sat, noon-4pm Sun) Janga is the place to scratch your itch for modern fine dining in Maceió. It does exquisite seafood dishes (the sauteed shrimp salad is especially tasty and can easily feed two) in an ultra-chic dining room. Most dishes are for two to three people, so make sure to bring friends.

Patrick's Wine Bar BISTRO $$
(☎82 3028-9916; https://patrickwinebar.business.site; Dr Odilon Vasconcelos 517, Ponta Verde; mains R$29-52; ⏲6pm-midnight Tue-Thu & Sun, plus noon-3pm Sat) As the name suggests, you'll find a staggering array of wines from South America and around the world available at this small, but lovely, restaurant. The food is classic French fare with some Brazilian touches, and the servers are more than ready to help you with a pairing.

Le Corbu FRENCH $$
(☎82 3327-4326; Guimarães 877, Ponta Verde; mains R$70-94; ⏰noon-4pm & 7-11pm Wed-Fri, 7pm-midnight Sat, noon-4pm Sun) A step up, style-wise, from many of the restaurants near the beach, Le Corbu specializes in French cuisine. Come on Wednesdays and Thursdays for an elegant lunch, or in the evening to peruse the wine list.

Parmegianno BRAZILIAN $$
(☎82 3313-9555; Dr Antônio Gouveia 1259, Pajuçara; mains R$44-90; ⏰11am-midnight Sun-Wed, to 1:30am Thu-Sat) Brazilian families flock to this popular chain restaurant, just across from the beach, for gourmet pizzas and hearty portions of shrimp, steak, fish, and chicken – accompanied with beans, rice and salad.

Jatiúca

★**Divina Gula** BRAZILIAN $$
(☎82 3235-1016; www.divinagula.com.br; Nogueira 85, Jatiúca; mains R$35-84; ⏰noon-midnight Tue-Thu & Sun, to 2am Fri & Sat;) A Maceió institution, Divina Gula specializes in the hearty cuisine of Minas Gerais and the Northeast. The *picanha* (steak) is excellent as is the *carne de sol* (grilled salted meat) with plantains, corn and zucchini. It has a children's menu, vegetarian options and a full cocktail list.

★**Wanchako** PERUVIAN $$
(☎82 3235-2151; www.wanchako.com.br; São Francisco de Assis 93, Jatiúca; mains R$70-93; ⏰6-11pm Mon-Thu, to midnight Fri & Sat) Worth a detour, this highly acclaimed Peruvian restaurant serves excellent seafood, including a dozen different varieties of ceviche and *tiradito* (a Peruvian version of sashimi). The sleek, art-filled setting makes for a memorable night out.

Maria Antoineta ITALIAN $$
(☎82 3202-8828; www.mariaantonieta-al.com.br; Dr Antônio Gomes de Barros 150, Jatiúca; mains R$42-85; ⏰noon-4pm & 6pm-midnight Sun-Fri, to 1am Sat) Hand-rolled pastas, classic seafood dishes, a good wine list and live piano music make Maria Antoineta a top pick for a leisurely dinner. Try the *risotto di baccalá* (risotto with salt cod) and the gourmet pepperoni pizza.

New Hakata JAPANESE $$
(☎82 3325-6160; www.newhakata.com.br; Paulo B Nogueira 95, Jatiúca; mains R$38-70; ⏰11:30am-1am) With a spacious outdoor seating area, Maceió's ultra-popular Japanese restaurant offers a long menu of sushi and sashimi, tempura, noodles and calamari; in the evenings, there is live music, free-flowing caipirinhas and sake cocktails.

Massarella ITALIAN $$
(☎82 3325 6000; www.massarella.com.br; José Pontes Magalhães 271, Jatiúca; mains R$30-85; ⏰noon-midnight Tue-Thu & Sun, to 1am Fri & Sat; ❄) This festive cantina is the place for homemade pastas and brick-oven pizzas; Italian pastas are traditionally prepared, and each plate is big enough for two to share. It's especially popular in summer.

O Peixarão SEAFOOD $$
(☎82 3325-7011; Av Dr Júlio Marques Luz 50, Jatiúca; mains R$64-81; ⏰11am-11pm) This casual restaurant is a longtime local favorite for its filling (if a bit overpriced) seafood dishes. Grilled fish with shrimp sauce and *caldeirada* (Portuguese seafood stew) are top picks.

Drinking & Nightlife

For a laid-back caipirinha with an ocean view, just pick any place along the waterfront in Ponta Verde or Pajuçara. It's not hard to find a nightclub or theme party to attend at night.

★**Lopana** BAR
(☎82 3231-7484; www.lopana.com.br; Av Silvio Carlos Viana 27, Ponta Verde; ⏰10am-midnight Tue-Fri, 9am-1am Sat & Sun) Maceió's best beachfront bar is always buzzing: when an acoustic guitarist is playing and a good-looking crowd is drinking beer and caipirinhas under the sky-high palm trees, the place looks straight out of a movie.

Kanoa Beach Bar BAR
(Av Silvio Carlos Viana 25, Ponta Verde; ⏰9am-midnight) This busy beach bar offers live music and free-flowing cocktails in a prime location on the oceanfront promenade.

Shopping

Mercado Praia de Pajuçara MARKET
(Pajuçara waterfront; ⏰10am-10pm) The Mercado Praia de Pajuçara is an enclosed craft market on Pajuçara's waterfront selling lacework, hammocks, baskets and ceramics.

Orientation

Maceió sits on a jagged peninsula between the Lagoa Mundaú and the ocean. The peninsula features two main headlands: one is the site of the city's port, and the other divides Praia de Pajuçara and Praia dos Sete Coqueiros from the more northern Praia de Ponta Verde and the long Praia de Jatiúca. The Centro is located near the oceanfront, 2km from Pajuçara and 4km from Ponta Verde.

Information

ATMs can be found all over the place in the neighborhoods close to the beach, and credit and debit cards are accepted almost everywhere.

Hospital Vida (ambulance/first aid; ☎82 3214-9700; Dep Elizeu Teixeira 488, Ponta Verde)

SAFE TRAVEL

Maceió is surrounded by favelas (slums) and, away from the beaches, it is plagued with crime. But with basic precautions you're unlikely to become the victim of crime in the city's tourist areas.

Should you run into any problems while in the city make sure to contact the **police** (☎190) and report the incident. You'll see officers on patrol all over the oceanfront tourist areas.

Getting There & Away

AIR

GOL (☎0300 115 2121; www.voegol.com.br) and **LATAM** (☎1866-435-9526; www.latam.com) can fly you or connect you to just about anywhere in Brazil from **Aeroporto Zumbi dos Palmares** (MCZ; ☎82 3036-5200; Rodovia BR 104, Rio Largo).

BUS

Real Alagoas (www.realalagoas.com.br) and Rota (www.rotatransportes.com.br) buses go to Aracaju (R$53–63, four to five hours, seven daily). Real Alagoas also goes north to Recife (R$50–78, five to six hours, seven daily). Rota buses go to Salvador (R$140–145, 11 hours, four daily).

Municipal buses (www.arsal.al.gov.br) – some look more like vans – make regular runs all over Alagoas. They can be caught at the main bus station in Maceió, or flagged down along the road if you know the route. Keep your eyes peeled for white vehicles with either blue or green signage on the sides. They can take you to destinations as close as Praia do Francês and Marechal Deodoro (R$5.20, 35 minutes), to further afield towns like Penedo (R$30, two hours) and Maragogi (R$22, three hours).

NORTHERN BEACH TOWNS

Many travelers zip up the coastline from Maceió with one destination in mind: Maragogi, and its spectacular offshore coral reef and snorkeling site. But if you have more than a day or two, it's worthwhile to slow down and explore some of the rustic beach villages along this stretch of Alagoas' northernmost shoreline with its fluffy white sands, green waters and tall coconut palms. These easygoing towns barely have the basics to support tourism – save for a few luxury pousadas – but they offer an authentic look at the local lifestyle, and a chance to truly unplug. Wherever you go, it's advisable to get cash before heading out, as you won't find a bank until you reach Maragogi.

Heading north from Maceió, the first town you'll pass through is **Barra de Santo Antônio**, a mellow fishing village built along the mouth of the Rio Jirituba. The main attraction of the area is the deserted **Praia de Carro Quebrado**, an exotic white-sand beach backed by thick palms. It is a 7km walk or beach-buggy ride (R$100) to/from the beach across the bridge from Barra de Santo Antônio. Note that it's not advisable to visit Praia de Carro Quebrado by driving further north and through the sugarcane field adjacent to the beach as there have been reports of robberies. **Praia Tabuba** is a pretty, tranquil bay with a few bars and a couple of pousadas 4km south of Barra de Santo Antônio. There are reef tidal pools off the beach – ask at the bars about a ride there by *jangada* (R$50).

Next you'll find **Barra Do Camaragibe**. This idyllic fishing village is strung along the road, on the edge of a small, reef-laden bay. *Jangadas* make trips south to **Praia do Morro**, a deserted beach with cliffs and clear waters. A little further north are **São Miguel Dos Milagres** and **Porto de Pedras**, both of which have fine beaches with warm, shallow seas protected by offshore reefs. You can stay a night or two at the opulent ecoresort **Pousada da Amendoeira** (☎82 3295-1213; www.amendoeira.com.br; Praia do Toque 7, São Miguel dos Milagres; r with half board from R$800; ❄📶) 🌿.

To get the full experience of meandering through these villages it's best to rent a car in Maceió and drive up. If you're traveling without a car you can reach any of these towns using the white and blue or green municipal buses from Maceió's main bus station. You can also flag them down along the main road, which is helpful if you're planning to go town-to-town.

Getting Around

TO/FROM THE AIRPORT

Maceió's airport is 20km north of the center. To reach the center, hop in one of the spiffy taxis operated by the local taxi collective (R$70) – you pay inside the airport and take your ticket to a driver waiting curbside. It's a 30-minute drive to the city if there's no traffic. Buses also run between Ponta Verde and the airport (labeled Aeroporto–Ponta Verde) every 45 minutes or so (R$4.40). The same bus can be picked up in Pajuçara heading north along Rua Jangadeiros Alagoanos – there are several stops along this stretch – look for a bus with 'Aeroporto' on the front.

TO/FROM THE BUS STATION

The **bus station** (☎82 3221-4615; Rodovia João Paulo II s/n, Feitosa) is about 7km north of the beaches.

Many of the city buses pass the bus station and most lines have their major stops listed on the side of the bus or will have their major destination (ie 'Centro' or 'Ponta Verde') as the name of the route. If getting a bus from the bus station to elsewhere in the city make sure to ask your bus driver which direction the bus is heading as there is only one stop for all buses. A taxi to the center costs R$15 to R$20, and around R$25–30 to the beaches.

WORTH A TRIP

MARECHAL DEODORO

On the banks of the tranquil Lagoa Manguaba, Marechal Deodoro is a small, peaceful town with pretty churches and a few streets of colonial architecture dating back to early settlement days. Marechal served as capital of Alagoas between 1823 and 1839, and although there's not a lot to see, it's an easy jaunt from Praia do Francês – if you have a few minutes, check out the pretty white-and-yellow facade of the **Igreja de NS da Conceição**, located on top of the hill above the lagoon. If you're around on a weekend, the Saturday market, held until noon along the waterfront, is particularly lively. Arrive in the morning to see fisherfolk working their nets out along the water.

Catch one of the white and blue or green municipal buses as it goes down the main road in Praia do Francês. Most will pass by Marechal Deodoro, but make sure to ask before getting on.

Praia do Francês

☎0XX82

Francês is a surfer's paradise. Given its proximity to Maceió (22km), Praia do Francês has long functioned as a day trip destination: cars and buses roll in on weekend days and clear out by sunset. But this is changing quickly as more travelers fall in love with the beach town, and pousadas (guesthouses) have popped up left and right to accommodate the influx of visitors.

The action is concentrated on one end of Francês' fine, white sands, where just-offshore reefs create calm green waters, and a string of restaurants serve beer and fried shrimp. Alagoas' best waves are at the southern end – don't despair if you're not traveling with your own equipment: bodyboards and longboards are available for rent right on the sand. Swimmers opt for the protected reef at the beach's northern end. Walk a few minutes in either direction to escape the crowds.

Sleeping & Eating

There are quite a few pousadas, hotels and apartment rentals around town. Avoid eating on the beach if possible, as the restaurants are absurdly overpriced. You'll find a small, but growing, restaurant district a few blocks inland along Avenida dos Corais and Rua Carapeba.

★ Hostel Ciganos HOSTEL $
(☎82 98717-1857; Av Verdes Mares 27; dm/d R$52/137;) To fully appreciate this budget jewel on the beach keep expectations managed: the rooms are clean but in need of updating. However, the private doubles with oceanfront balconies are large, cheap and give you the opportunity to fall asleep with the sound of waves crashing outside. Bonus: the hosts could not be friendlier.

★ Pousada Ricardinho do Frances POUSADA $$
(☎82 3260-1488; www.pousadaricardinhodofrances.com.br; Arrecifes 10; d/tr from R$150/170;) An ideal location close to the beach, plus fantastic breakfasts and tidy guest rooms with private balconies and hammocks, make this guesthouse one of the favorites in town.

Rústico Burger Gourmet BURGERS $
(☎82 99927-2384; www.facebook.com/rusticoburguergourmet; Carapeba 48; burgers R$20; 5:30-11:30pm Tue-Sun) Big, juicy burgers and cold beer are served on a popular patio

at this spot a few blocks from the ocean. You can also get an excellent Argentinian-style steak and *batatas rustica* (thick-cut french fries) smothered *chimichurri* sauce.

Dona Madalena BRAZILIAN $$
(☎82 3260-1369; Av dos Corais 284; mains R$24-44; ⏰noon-midnight Thu-Tue) Praia do Francês' most popular restaurant serves succulent meat and grilled fish dishes in a charming historic house.

Information

The closest **ATM** (Loteamento Santa Rita) to the beach is about a mile inland in a gas station by the freeway on-ramps.

Getting There & Away

From the bus station in Maceió, white and blue municipal buses (www.arsal.al.gov.br) run regularly to Praia do Francês, often on the Marechal Deodoro line (R$5.20, 35 minutes). You can catch the same buses back to Maceió along Rua Caravelas and Avenida dos Corais. Just make sure to confirm that they are returning to Maceió before hopping on.

Penedo

☎0XX82 / POP 64,450

Note the elegant sculpture of Christ, standing tall in a riverboat, at the entrance to town: it's a hint at the significance of Penedo's position on the Rio São Francisco. The city is the architectural masterpiece of the state, known for its many baroque churches and decorative colonial-style buildings. It's not much to look at from the dusty (or muddy) riverfront square – to experience Penedo's charms, you'll have to wander up into the hilly cobblestoned streets. It's busy by day, when the downtown bustles with a daily market as people from surrounding villages pour in to do their shopping, and quiet at night. Apart from a few hotels and organized excursions on the river, Penedo is almost unaltered by tourism.

History

Since its founding, Penedo has been a commercial center, owing to its prime position on the Rio São Francisco. The town was founded sometime between 1535 and 1560 by Duarte Coelho Pereira, who descended the Rio São Francisco in pursuit of the indigenous Caetés who were responsible for killing a bishop. Penedo is claimed to be the river's first colonial settlement. It was also the scene of a fierce 17th-century battle between the Dutch and the Portuguese for control of the Northeast. In the 19th century, Penedo was one of the focal points of the abolitionist movement in Alagoas. In the 20th century, the city lost its prominence as a commercial center, which probably saved its colonial buildings from destruction.

Sights

Penedo has a rich collection of 17th- and 18th-century colonial buildings, including many churches. Unfortunately, regardless of the posted opening hours, these churches are not reliably open to visitors – your best bet is to walk around and see what's open.

Igreja de São Gonçalo Garcia CHURCH
(Floriano Peixoto) The Igreja de São Gonçalo Garcia was built at the end of the 18th century. The small *oratório* (Praça Barão de Penedo) is where the condemned spent their last night praying before being hanged.

Convento de São Francisco e Igreja NS dos Anjos CHURCH
(Praça Rui Barbosa; R$3; ⏰7am-noon & 2-5pm) The Convento de São Francisco e Igreja NS dos Anjos was under construction for nearly 100 years before its completion in 1759, and is considered the finest church in the state. Even Dom Pedro II (Brazil's second and last emperor) paid a visit. Of particular note are the richly colored ceiling, the gold rococo altar and the statue of St Francis to the left of it that was carved by Aleijadinho.

Igreja de NS da Corrente CHURCH
(Praça 12 de Abril) The Igreja de NS da Corrente, completed in 1765, has some fine Portuguese *azulejos* (tiles), painted in green, purple and gold – colors rarely seen in Brazil, or Portugal for that matter. The Lemos family were big benefactors of the church (their family seal is marked on the floor) and abolitionists; slaves fled to the church for protection – some were even hidden behind panels of the church walls.

Museu do Paço Imperial MUSEUM
(Praça 12 de Abril 9; R$4; ⏰11am-5pm Tue-Sat, 8am-noon Sun) Occupying the top floor of a house Dom Pedro II once slept in, the Museu do Paço Imperial displays lamps, portraits, furniture and elegant finery from the imperial period (17th and 18th centuries); it's tiny but nicely presented. It's free to visit the exhibit downstairs, but you pay to go upstairs.

OFF THE BEATEN TRACK

PONTAL DE CORURIPE

If you plan to head from Penedo to Maceió or other points north, considering sparing a night or two for sleepy Pontal de Coruripe, a village about 58km to the north.

A traditional fishing village that sees few visitors, Pontal de Coruripe lies in an area of verdant coconut plantations, on the edge of a long, deserted beach with beautiful emerald waters. On the peaceful streets of town, women sit in front of their homes gossiping and weaving palm baskets, placemats and handbags, while out at the cove just opposite the lighthouse, fisherfolk guide their boats across the sunlit sea. Stay at **Pousada Canto de Yemanjá** (82 3273-7316; www.pousadacantodeyemanja.com; Rua da Praia 244, Pontal de Coruripe; d from R$140;), which is right on the water, making it the perfect place to have a sunset cocktail, as well.

From Penedo's bus station you catch a municipal bus (www.arsal.al.gov.br) to the town of Coruripe (R$5, two hours), which is adjacent to Pontal de Coruripe. From town you can easily find a taxi to the point. Buses also come and go between Coruripe and Maceió (R$17, two hours).

Igreja NS do Rosário dos Pretos CHURCH
(Catedral do Penedo; Praça Marechal Deodoro) The Igreja NS do Rosário dos Pretos is a beautiful cathedral uphill from the river built by slaves.

Activities

Regular ferries (R$3.50) depart from the center for **Neópolis**, a hilltop colonial town with historic buildings and fine crafts for sale. The **ferry dock** (Avenida Beira Rio) is on the river near the restaurant Oratório. During high season, it may be possible to get on an organized tour to the **Foz do São Francisco** (around R$70 per person), where the river meets the sea at a beach with dunes and natural pools. Try **Farol da Foz Ecoturismo** (82 3552-1298; www.faroldafozecoturismo.com; Av Conselheiro Ulisses Guedes 228, Piaçabuçu; tours per person from R$70), located about a 30-minute drive south, for these and other trips in the area.

Festivals & Events

Festa do Senhor Bom Jesus dos Navegantes RELIGIOUS
(mid-Jan) This festival is held over four days from the second Sunday in January, and features an elaborate procession of boats and a sailboat race.

Sleeping

Options are limited, but the city is rarely totally overrun with tourists so you shouldn't have trouble getting a room most times of year. Make sure you book in Penedo, Alagoas and not Penedo, Rio de Janeiro state.

Pousada Colonial POUSADA $
(82 3551-2355; Praça 12 de Abril 21; d/tr/q R$140/180/220;) To fully soak up the atmosphere of Penedo, book a room at this charming historic house on the waterfront. Dating from 1734, the building has stained-wood floors, dramatic high ceilings, antique furniture and old-fashioned wooden shutters, some of which open to fabulous views over the river. It could use some updates, but the place is memorable.

Hotel São Francisco HOTEL $$
(82 3551-2275; www.hotelsaofrancisco.tur.br; Floriano Peixoto 237; d from R$190;) Don't let the boxy exterior fool you: this 1960s-style hotel (considered an eyesore on the town's scenic skyline by some) has some of the nicest rooms around, with a smooth '80s parquet charm, large glass-encased showers, flat-screen TVs, minibars and private balconies. Thanks to its slight elevation over the river, most rooms also have lovely water views.

Eating

Several supermarkets, sandwich kiosks and self-service eateries are on the main waterfront plaza. There are a few good places to eat in town, but it's hardly a culinary capital.

Yspeto's Grill GRILL $$
(82 3551-5799; www.facebook.com/yspetos.penedo; Praça Jácome Calheiros 79; dishes $20-59; 10am-11pm Wed-Sun, to 2pm Mon & Tue) Yspeto's is the type of place where if the restaurant gets crowded, more tables are brought from the back, and where you might be asked to shift over so that the local firefighters

can have lunch. They are known for their high-quality cuts of meat that they cook into exquisitely rustic dishes.

Forte da Rocheira BRAZILIAN $$
(☎82 3551-2486; Rocheira 2; mains R$46-64; ⏰11am-4pm) This former Dutch fortification has a splendid view out over the water. The location is slightly out of the way – just follow the signs, as the restaurant is well advertised in town, and try to time your visit with sunset.

Oratório BRAZILIAN $$
(Beira Rio 301; mains R$35-78; ⏰10am-midnight Sun-Thu, to 2am Fri & Sat) This casually elegant riverfront spot is popular throughout the day: come for a juice in the morning, lunch, or a dinner of grilled fish and marinated shrimp.

Information

You'll find a **Bradesco bank** (Av Duque de Caixas 71) with an ATM on the riverfront. Other ATMs are located nearby, around the central square.

You may find staff handing out tourist maps of the city in the **municipal offices** (Praça Barão de Penedo; ⏰9am-6pm) in Casa da Aposentadoria. The service is irregular at best.

Getting There & Away

For transportation to Maceió and Aracaju, head to Penedo's small **bus station**, located a few blocks away along the river, behind the large supermarket.

For Maceió, bus options are either one daily Real Alagoas (www.realalagoas .com.br) bus at noon (R$31, 4¼ hours) or the municipal buses (R$30, 2½ hours), which are less comfortable but much more frequent. If you're not sure, just head down to the bus station and you'll likely hear someone calling passengers for Maceió.

Aguia Branca (www.aguiabranca.com.br) runs one daily bus leaving for Salvador at 6am (R$104, 10 hours). The same bus stops in Aracaju (R$20, four hours). You can usually find informal Kombi vans running to Aracaju for the same price at the bus station as well.

Maragogi

☎0XX82 / POP 32,000

Maragogi is a beach town with the typical cluster of pousadas and restaurants along its waterfront, old-fashioned sailboats bobbing in the sea, and wide, flat beaches where local kids play soccer every evening at sunset. Though these beaches aren't particularly special, Maragogi is one of the most visited destinations in the state, thanks to its major draw: the sandbars and reefs that make up the **Galés marine reserve**, 6km offshore, where the underwater scene is rich with colorful sea life. The town itself has been developing rapidly into a tourist destination in its own right, with new hotels and restaurants opening periodically.

Activities

Many travelers visit the natural pools of the marine reserve on day trips from Maceió, but Maragogi is also a friendly destination to spend a night or two. Trips to the reserve (around R$70) at low tide are easily organized through beachfront restaurants or hotels – the excursion is heavily advertised

MIRACLE MAKERS

In many shrines and churches in the Northeast, visitors come face-to-face with carved wooden heads, arms, feet and other body parts, hung from ceilings or piled in baskets in a special room. A unique mixture of faith and folk art, these ex-votos are called *milagres* (miracles) and are left by supplicants seeking a cure for a specific ailment such as an injured limb or a congenital deformity. In exchange, the petitioner makes a vow (usually to a particular saint) promising to give up their wicked ways or perhaps make a long pilgrimage – which may even be performed on the knees.

The makers of these ex-votos are often self-taught artisans and their work has an almost cubist quality. If the artisans are particularly skilled they may model their work – made of either wood or clay – on the sufferer. No one knows exactly how this custom originated, but the *milagre* probably has links to old Iberian traditions, mingled with African and indigenous customs. In some communities, there is an element of mysticism to these carved objects, as if they could absorb the ills of the sufferer.

Many churches and shrines in the *sertãos* (backlands) have a *casa dos milagres* (miracle house), where such objects are displayed. During religious festivals, *milagre* artisans make the rounds, offering their services for a small fee.

left and right. You can also ask directly at the boats, but be prepared to negotiate your price as some operators are known to overcharge tourists.

Maragogi Dive Sub DIVING
(☎82 99416-0010; www.maragogidivesub.com.br; Av Senador Rui Palmeira 208) A one-stop shop for scuba-related activities in the Maragogi area. This operation has a storefront on the beach and offers courses, equipment rental and excursions.

Sleeping

There are a handful of decent hotels and guesthouses. Most are fairly bland, but offer good amenities and, of course, a great location.

Pousada Maragolfinho POUSADA $
(☎82 3296-1513; www.pousadamaragolfinho.com.br; Escritor Graciliano Ramos 14; d/tr from R$134/170;) If you're willing to stay away from the beach you'll find Pousada Maragolfinho to be a great deal. It takes up several buildings on a dirt road and has an enviable pool and large rooms, including a family room with a queen and two twin beds (from R$200).

★**Pousada Olho D'água** POUSADA $$
(☎82 3296-1263; www.pousadaolhodagua.com; Senador Rui Palmeira 94; d from R$336;) Smart-looking Pousada Olho D'água offers a terrace overlooking the ocean, comfortable rooms with private balconies (some have views) and a lovely swimming pool.

Pousada Mariluz POUSADA $$
(☎82 3296-1511; www.pousadamariluz.com.br; Senador Rui Palmeira 885; d with/without veranda from R$250/215;) On the waterfront, Pousada Mariluz is fair value (for the area), offering small but cheerfully painted rooms, some with verandas facing the ocean.

Eating

Several seafood restaurants on the waterfront offer Bahian food, pizza, fresh juices and cocktails, plus relaxed outdoor seating on the beach. For better deals head a few blocks inland.

Restaurante Casa do Turista BUFFET $
(☎82 3296-2294; www.facebook.com/restaurantecasadoturista; Av Senador Rui Palmeira s/n; per kg R$42.90; ⊙11am-10pm) Conveniently located right across the street from the beach, this solid buffet restaurant is one of the best lunch deals in town. They are also famous for their desserts that use tropical ingredients such as coconut and passionfruit.

★**Odoiá** SEAFOOD $$
(☎82 3296-2214; http://odoiamaragogi.com.br; Senador Rui Palmeira 956; mains R$28-52; ⊙11am-10pm) The exquisitely prepared seafood dishes at Odoiá are a cut above other restaurants in Maragogi. Most recipes are simple, such as pesto pasta with shrimp or grilled fish with roasted vegetables, but the preparations and flavors are divine.

Restaurante Frutas do Mar SEAFOOD $$
(☎82 3296-1329; Senador Rui Palmeira 876; mains R$35-60; ⊙8am-4pm) If you find yourself on the far southern stretch of Maragogi's coast, or on a tour to the *piscinas naturais* (natural pools), you'll likely end up at this restaurant right off the beach. The food is overpriced, but the sprawling outdoor dining area complete with hammocks and umbrellas makes for a great place to hang for a few hours.

Drinking & Nightlife

Pallet Bar BAR
(☎82 99975-9662; www.facebook.com/palletbarmaragogi; José Carvalho Raposo 230-286; ⊙7pm-2am Wed-Sun) If you need an escape from the family-oriented atmosphere of Maragogi you can mingle with the town's younger, hipper set over a few happy hour drinks (two cocktails for R$10, check website for daily specials) at this fun bar a few blocks from the beach.

Information

The helpful and well respected travel agency **Costazul** (☎82 3296-2087; Av Candido Portinari 370; ⊙7am-7pm) can arrange transfers and excursions.

Getting There & Away

Daily municipal buses run between Maceió to Maragogi (R$22, three hours, six daily), but they are not very large, lack air-con and generally are not ideal if you're traveling with a lot of luggage. Catch them at the bus **stop** (José Buarque Sampaio 176-252) on the west side of town. Most hotels in town will offer transfers from Maceió or Recife, which are quite a bit more expensive.

Pernambuco, Paraíba & Rio Grande do Norte

Includes ➡

Pernambuco 483
Recife 483
Olinda 497
Fernando de Noronha 502
Paraíba 513
João Pessoa 513
Rio Grande do Norte ... 517
Natal 517
Praia da Pipa 526
São Miguel do Gostoso 530

Best Places to Eat

- ➡ Mangai (p515)
- ➡ Pão com Gergelim (p515)
- ➡ Peixada do Amor (p515)
- ➡ Turek (p520)
- ➡ Casa do Bacalhau (p515)

Best Places to Stay

- ➡ Slow Hostel (p515)
- ➡ Pousada Bemtevi (p520)
- ➡ Verdegreen Hotel (p515)
- ➡ Fazenda Pai Mateus (p518)

Why Go?

The nearly 1000km-long coastline edging the three states at Brazil's northeastern corner consists of one sandy, sun-kissed beach after another, backed by dunes, palms or cliffs. It's dotted with villages and small towns that are just perfect for tasty meals, sunset drinks and chilling out in a homey pousada (guesthouse) – that's when you're not dipping, snorkeling, surfing, kitesurfing, windsurfing or diving in the enticing tropical waters. Or racing around the beaches and dunes with the wind in your hair on a buggy ride.

The coast is home to four very different cities: gutsy, historic, cultural Recife; cute, artsy Olinda; appealingly revived João Pessoa; and the holiday playground of Natal. You'll never lack for urban vibes to spice up your beach idylls. What is arguably the continent's greatest aquatic treasure also lies 350km offshore: Fernando de Noronha, a tropical-island getaway unrivaled in South America for its world-class beaches, diving and scenery.

When to Go

Recife

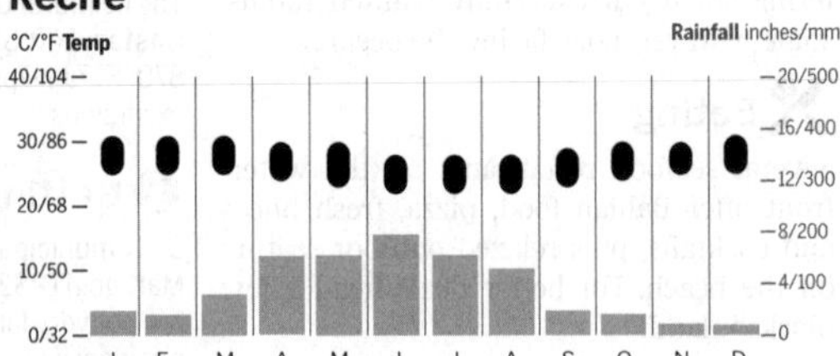

Apr–Jul Rainy season and lower temperatures keep crowds at bay and prices drop dramatically.

Aug–Nov Winds blow and skies brighten, attracting water-sports enthusiasts to all corners of the region.

Dec–Feb High season; dry, sunny days mean prime beach weather, plus more people and higher prices.

ℹ Getting There & Around

Recife and Natal are the region's main gateways. Both receive direct flights from Europe, including Lisbon, and in Recife's case also from Miami. Recife, Natal and João Pessoa all have plenty of daily flights from other significant Brazilian cities.

Decent bus services link all major cities and towns along the coasts, both within the region and to places beyond such as Fortaleza and Salvador. Main cities have direct bus services to Rio de Janeiro and São Paulo. Smaller, more remote towns and villages may be reached by only a few bus or van services a day, or even less frequently in cases such as Galinhos.

Fernando de Noronha is reachable only by flights from Recife or Natal.

Rental cars are widely available and worth considering if you plan to cover a lot of kilometers.

History

This corner of Brazil was a hotly contested colonial property, with both the French and Dutch vying for control against the Portuguese. French *pau brazil* (brazilwood) traders were already in the region when Portugal founded Olinda in 1535 as the capital of its new Pernambuco captaincy. Recife began life as Olinda's port. With the indigenous population brutally subdued, coastal Pernambuco quickly became one of Brazil's most important sugarcane producers, using the labor of African slaves. The region's other major cities, Natal and João Pessoa, started out as Portuguese river-mouth forts built to stake out territory against their colonial rivals and their indigenous allies.

Dutch invaders sacked Olinda in 1631 but, doubtless feeling more at home among the waterways of Recife, developed it as the capital of (ambitiously named) New Holland. In 1637 they shipped in Prince Maurice of Nassau to govern the colony. Maurice's enlightened freedom-of-worship policy helped keep things calm while the Dutch extended their control along the coast as far as São Luís (Maranhão). After the prince was ordered home in 1644, uprisings against Protestant Dutch rule eventually led to their expulsion in 1654. Olinda was rebuilt, but Recife outgrew it to become South America's biggest city in the late 17th century.

As the Northeast's sugar economy floundered with the abolition of slavery in the 19th century, Brazil's balance of population, power and money tipped to the Southeast, and the Northeast declined to backwater status. For most of the 20th century the region – and especially its arid interior, the *sertão* – was a Brazilian byword for grinding poverty. Many Northeasterners migrated to the Southeast in search of a better life.

PERNAMBUCO

POP 9.3 MILLION

Pernambuco is one of the most exhilarating destinations in the Northeast. Among the earliest centers of Portuguese settlement in Brazil, it has developed rich cultural traditions melding European, African and indigenous influences, especially in music and dance.

Recife, Pernambuco's capital, is one of Brazil's biggest cities; it's a very urban place with a rich entertainment scene. By contrast its much smaller and calmer neighbor, Olinda, is a charming, historical town, full of picturesque churches and talented artisans. North and south of these centers stretches a short but glorious coast with dozens of palm-fringed sandy beaches, great waves and crystal-clear reef pools.

But Pernambuco's most glittering gem sits more than 350km out in the Atlantic. The archipelago of Fernando de Noronha is a tropical-island getaway to dream about, a fervently protected aquatic Eden with near-empty, postcard-perfect beaches, surrounded by warm, brilliantly clear waters. It is one of Brazil's most awed destinations.

Recife

☎0XX81 / POP 1.63 MILLION

Recife ('heh-*see*-fee'), capital of Pernambuco, is one of the Northeast's most exciting cities. It has a vibrant cultural, entertainment and restaurant scene, an intriguing historic center (Recife Antigo), an impressive coastal setting and a fabulous Carnaval. It's a sprawling, urban place of glassy high-rises, crowded commercial areas, thundering traffic and extensive suburbs; if you like your cities gutsy, gritty and proud, Recife is for you. It takes its name from the offshore *recifes* (reefs) that calm the waters of its ports and shoreline.

The charming and far more tranquil historic town of Olinda lies on Recife's northern edge, just 6km from the city center, and many visitors opt to stay in Olinda and visit Recife during the day, or venture into Recife for its animated nightlife.

Pernambuco, Paraíba & Rio Grande do Norte Highlights

1. **Fernando de Noronha** (p502) Beach-hopping Brazil's most stunning – and gloriously empty – beaches.
2. **Olinda** (p497) Dancing in the streets of the Unesco-betrothed historic center during euphoric Carnaval.
3. **Praia da Pipa** (p526) Soaking up the dramatic coastline, chilled beach vibes and party scene among laid-back locals and travelers.
4. **Recife** (p483) Getting a crash course in Northeastern culture at the city's impressive museums.
5. **São Miguel do Gostoso** (p530) Digging your toes into sands less traveled.
6. **Praia de Tambaba** (p520) Skinny dipping at the Northeast's original nudist beach.
7. **Porto de Galinhas** (p495) Swimming in tidal pools chock-full of tropical fish.
8. **Natal** (p517) Sipping a coconut while observing a classic Brazilian beach scene at lovely Ponta Negra.

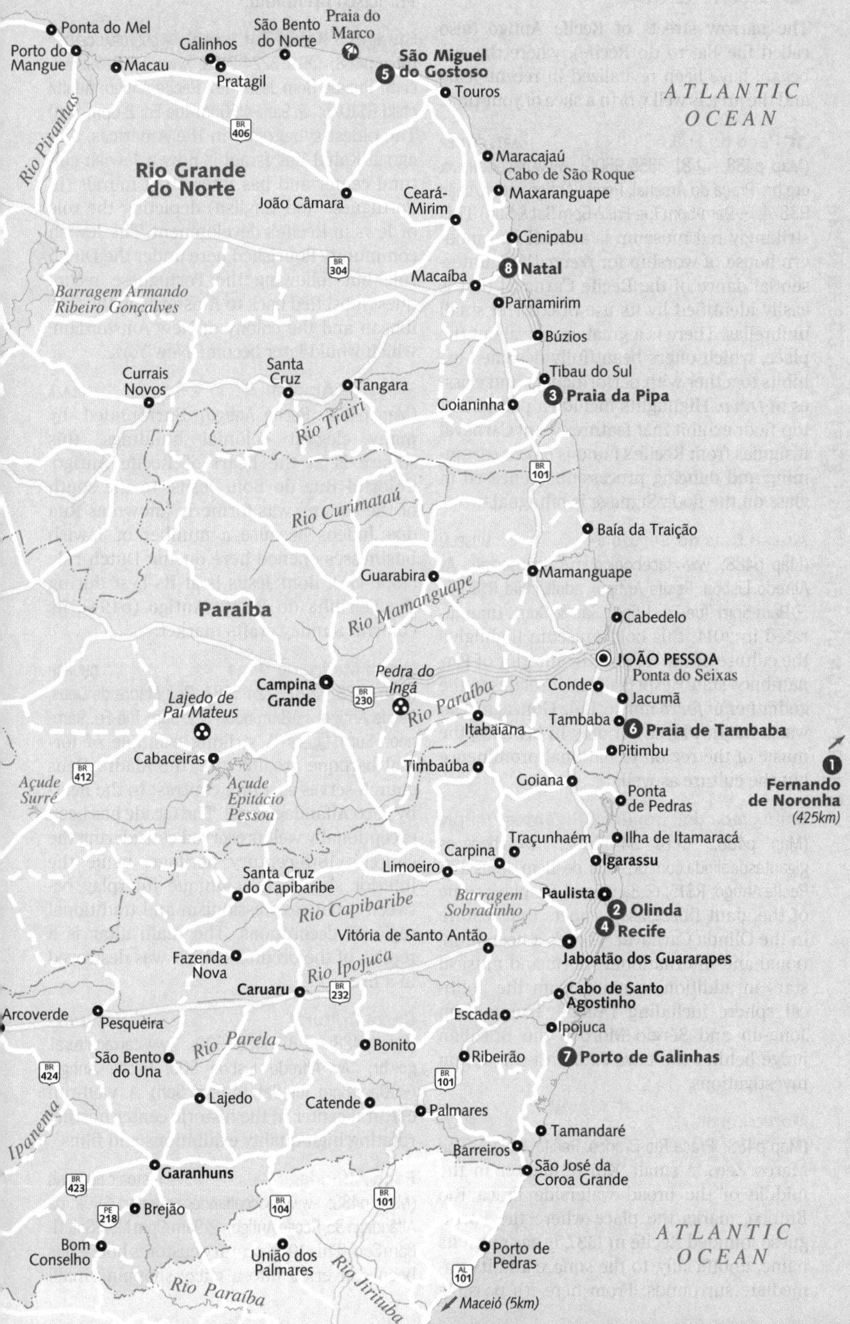

0 100 km
0 60 miles
ATLANTIC OCEAN
Ponta do Mel
Porto do Mangue
Macau
Galinhos
Pratagil
São Bento do Norte
Praia do Marco
5 São Miguel do Gostoso
Touros
BR 406
Rio Piranhas
Rio Grande do Norte
Maracajaú
Cabo de São Roque
Maxaranguape
João Câmara
Ceará-Mirim
Genipabu
BR 304
8 Natal
Macaíba
Parnamirim
Barragem Armando Ribeiro Gonçalves
Búzios
Tibau do Sul
3 Praia da Pipa
Goianinha
Currais Novos
Santa Cruz
Tangara
Rio Trairi
BR 101
Rio Curimataú
Baía da Traição
Mamanguape
Guarabira
Rio Mamanguape
Paraíba
Cabedelo
JOÃO PESSOA
Ponta do Seixas
Conde
Jacumã
Tambaba
6 Praia de Tambaba
Pitimbu
1 Fernando de Noronha (425km)
Campina Grande
BR 230
Pedra do Ingá
Rio Paraíba
Lajedo de Pai Mateus
Itabaiana
Timbaúba
Cabaceiras
BR 412
Açude Surré
Açude Epitácio Pessoa
Goiana
Ponta de Pedras
Traçunhaém
Ilha de Itamaracá
Carpina
Igarassu
Limoeiro
Santa Cruz do Capibaribe
Barragem Sobradinho
Paulista
2 Olinda
4 Recife
Rio Capibaribe
Vitória de Santo Antão
Jaboatão dos Guararapes
Fazenda Nova
Rio Ipojuca
Caruaru
BR 232
Cabo de Santo Agostinho
Arcoverde
Pesqueira
Escada
Ipojuca
Rio Parela
Bonito
São Bento do Una
Ribeirão
7 Porto de Galinhas
BR 424
BR 101
Lajedo
Catende
Palmares
Ipanema
Tamandaré
Barreiros
São José da Coroa Grande
Garanhuns
BR 423
PE 218
Brejão
BR 104
BR 101
ATLANTIC OCEAN
Bom Conselho
União dos Palmares
Porto de Pedras
AL 101
Rio Paraíba
Rio Jiritub
Maceió (5km)

Sights

Recife Antigo

The narrow streets of Recife Antigo (also called the Bairro do Recife), where the city began, have been revitalized in recent years and the area is well worth a slice of your time.

★**Paço do Frevo** ARTS CENTER
(Map p488; ☎81 3355-9500; www.pacodofrevo.org.br; Praça do Arsenal, Recife Antigo; adult/child R$8/4; ⏲9am-5pm Tue-Fri, 2-6pm Sat & Sun) This strikingly red museum is a small and modern house of worship for *frevo,* the quintessential dance of the Recife Carnaval that is easily identified by its use of colorful small umbrellas. There is a great energy about the place, which offers beautifully designed exhibits together with performances and classes of *frevo.* Highlights include a permanent top-floor exhibit that features giant Carnaval insignias from Recife's famous *blocos* (drumming and dancing processions), encased in glass on the floor. Signage is bilingual.

Museu Cais do Sertão MUSEUM
(Map p488; www.facebook.com/caisdosertao; Av Alfredo Lisboa, Recife Antigo; adult/child R$10/5; ⏲9am-5pm Tue-Fri, 1-5pm Sat & Sun) Inaugurated in 2014, this bold museum highlights the culture of the *sertão* (the interior of Pernambuco state), especially as it relates to the godfather of *forró* music, Luiz Gonzaga, who was a major player not only in bringing the music of the region to national prominence but the culture as well.

Embaixada dos Bonecos Gigantes MUSEUM
(Map p488; ☎81 3441-5102; www.bonecosgigantesdeolinda.com.br; Rua do Bom Jesus 183, Recife Antigo; R$15; ⏲8am-6pm) Displays some of the giant fibreglass puppets that feature in the Olinda Carnaval. There's a host of national and international sports and musical stars in addition to many from the political sphere including Donald Trump, Kim Jong-un and Sérgio Moro – the Brazilian judge behind the Lava Jato anti-corruption investigations.

Marco Zero PLAZA
(Map p488; Praça Rio Branco, Recife Antigo) The Marco Zero, a small 'Km 0' marker in the middle of the broad waterside Praça Rio Branco, marks the place where the Portuguese founded Recife in 1537. It has given its name, unofficially, to the square and its immediate surrounds. From here it's possible to take a boat (R$2.50 each way, 7am to 5pm) across the channel to the sculpture park on the breakwater featuring works by Francisco Brennand.

Sinagoga Kahal Zur Israel CULTURAL CENTER
(Map p488; ☎81 3224-2128; www.kahalzurisrael.com; Rua do Bom Jesus 197, Recife Antigo; adult/child R$10/5; ⏲9am-4:50pm Tue-Fri, 2-6pm Sun) The oldest synagogue in the Americas, Sinagoga Kahal Zur Israel is now a Jewish cultural center and has interesting murals (in Portuguese and English) depicting the role of Jews in Recife's development. The Jewish community flourished here under the Dutch rule but following the Portuguese reconquest most fled back to Amsterdam, the Caribbean and the colony of New Amsterdam, which would later become New York.

Praça do Arsenal PLAZA
(Map p488; Recife Antigo) Surrounded by many elegant colonial buildings, this square is at the heart of Recife Antigo. Colorful Rua do Bom Jesus, to the south of the square, was formerly known as Rua dos Judeos because a number of Jewish businesses opened here during Dutch rule (1630–54). Bom Jesus is at its best during the Feirinha do Recife Antigo (p494), its colorful Sunday crafts market.

Igreja Madre de Deus CHURCH
(Map p488; ☎81 3224-5587; Rua Madre de Deus, Recife Antigo; ⏲8am-noon & 2-5pm Tue-Fri, 9am-noon Sun) FREE A striking example of formal baroque architecture, the Madre Deus church serves as a nice contrast to the nearby Paço Alfândega mall. The facade has been exceptionally well preserved considering the church's 18th-century heritage, while the interior showcases a unique interplay between ornate expressionism and traditional regional decorations. The main altar is a replica of the original, which was destroyed in a fire.

Caixa Cultural ARTS CENTER
(Map p488; ☎81 3425-1900; www.caixacultural.gov.br; Av Alfredo Lisboa 505, Recife Antigo; ⏲10am-8pm Tue-Sat, to 5pm Sun) A well-run cultural center in the historic center hosting rotating high-quality exhibitions and films.

Paço Alfândega HISTORIC BUILDING
(Map p488; www.pacoalfandega.com.br; Rua da Alfândega 35, Recife Antigo; ⏲9am-9pm Mon-Sat, 11-8pm Sun) This 19th-century customs house has been converted into a glitzy shopping mall;

it's worth dropping in for a coffee or a bite in its food court to check out the architecture.

Santo Antônio

This district encompasses both the formal **Praça da República** (Map p488; Santo Antônio), surrounded by imposing 19th-century governmental buildings, at its northern end and a bustling commercial area further south, where the streets are lined with shops, stalls, ornate facades and colonial churches in assorted states of preservation.

The area is fine when the shops and businesses are open but can be sketchy after dark and on weekends, so plan your visit accordingly.

Capela Dourada CHAPEL
(Golden Chapel; Map p488; ☎81 3224-0530; www.capeladourada.com.br; Rua do Imperador s/n, Santo Antônio; R$5; ⌚8-11:30am & 2-5pm Mon-Fri, 8-11:30am Sat) Built between 1696 and 1724, this gem of Brazilian baroque, part of the Convento de Santo Antônio, owes its name to the huge quantities of gold (said to total more than 120kg!) covering its elaborately sculpted walls, altars and ceiling. Admission also includes access to the attached Museu de Arte Sacra (Museum of Sacred Art).

Pátio de São Pedro SQUARE
(Map p488; Santo Antônio) This traffic-free square, lined with bars, restaurants and colorful 19th-century houses, is one of Santo Antônio's more peaceful spots and a good place to stop for a drink.

The magnificent 18th-century baroque **Concatedral de São Pedro dos Clérigos** (R$5; ⌚8am-5pm Mon-Fri, to 1pm Sat) contains incredibly fine stonework and wood carvings throughout, while the **Memorial Chico Science** (☎81-3355-3158; www.recife.pe.gov.br/chicoscience; ⌚9am-5pm Mon-Fri) FREE highlights the revered founder of the *mangue beat* musical movement, who died tragically in a Recife car accident in 1997.

Museu de Arte Moderna Aloisio Magalhães MUSEUM
(MAMAM; Map p488; ☎81 3355-6871; Rua da Aurora 265, Boa Vista; ⌚noon-6pm Tue-Fri, 1-5pm Sat & Sun) FREE In a lovely historical house, this museum was the first gallery in Pernambuco and has three floors of changing exhibitions of interesting contemporary art with a focus on local artists from the Northeast of the country.

Museu da Cidade do Recife MUSEUM, FORT
(Map p488; www.recife.pe.gov.br/cultura/museucidade.php; Praça das Cinco Pontas, São José; ⌚9am-5pm Tue-Sat) FREE Recife's City Museum is housed in the Forte das Cinco Pontas (Five-Pointed Fort), originally built by the Dutch in 1630 and later reconstructed by the Portuguese. It exhibits old maps and historic photos, but could be so much more interesting given Recife's fascinating history.

Oficina Cerâmica Francisco Brennand & Instituto Ricardo Brennand

The ceramics 'workshop' of Francisco Brennand and the art institute of his cousin Ricardo constitute a regional highlight; it's well worth setting aside half a day for the trip out to Várzea, on Recife's western edge, to see them. The only times both places are open simultaneously are Tuesday to Sunday afternoons.

★ **Oficina Cerâmica Francisco Brennand** MUSEUM
(☎81 3271-2466; www.brennand.com.br; Várzea; R$20; ⌚8am-5pm Mon-Thu, to 4pm Fri, 10am-4pm Sat & Sun) Francisco Brennand, born in 1927 into an Irish immigrant family and now considered Brazil's greatest ceramicist, revitalized his family's abandoned tile factory to create his own line of decorative ceramic tiles. The expansive indoor and outdoor space in Várzea, 11km west of central Recife, is now mostly dedicated to his enormous and fascinating oeuvre, which ranges across painting, tile work and hundreds of highly original sculptures. It's best reached by taxi from Boa Viagem and visited in combination with Instituto Ricardo Brennand.

Instituto Ricardo Brennand MUSEUM
(☎81 2121-0352; www.institutoricardobrennand.org.br; Alameda Antônio Brennand, Várzea; adult/child R$30/15; ⌚1-5pm Tue-Sun) This scenic museum in Várzea, 11km west of central Recife, contains a huge collection of European and Brazilian art, swords, armor and historical artifacts, all set in fake medieval castles on lovely grounds. While there are some worthwhile pieces here, especially the collection of art from the Dutch occupation of Recife, there's limited written information (audio guides cost an additional R$10) and the best pieces often get lost among the sheer quantity of works covering the walls and corridors.

Central Recife

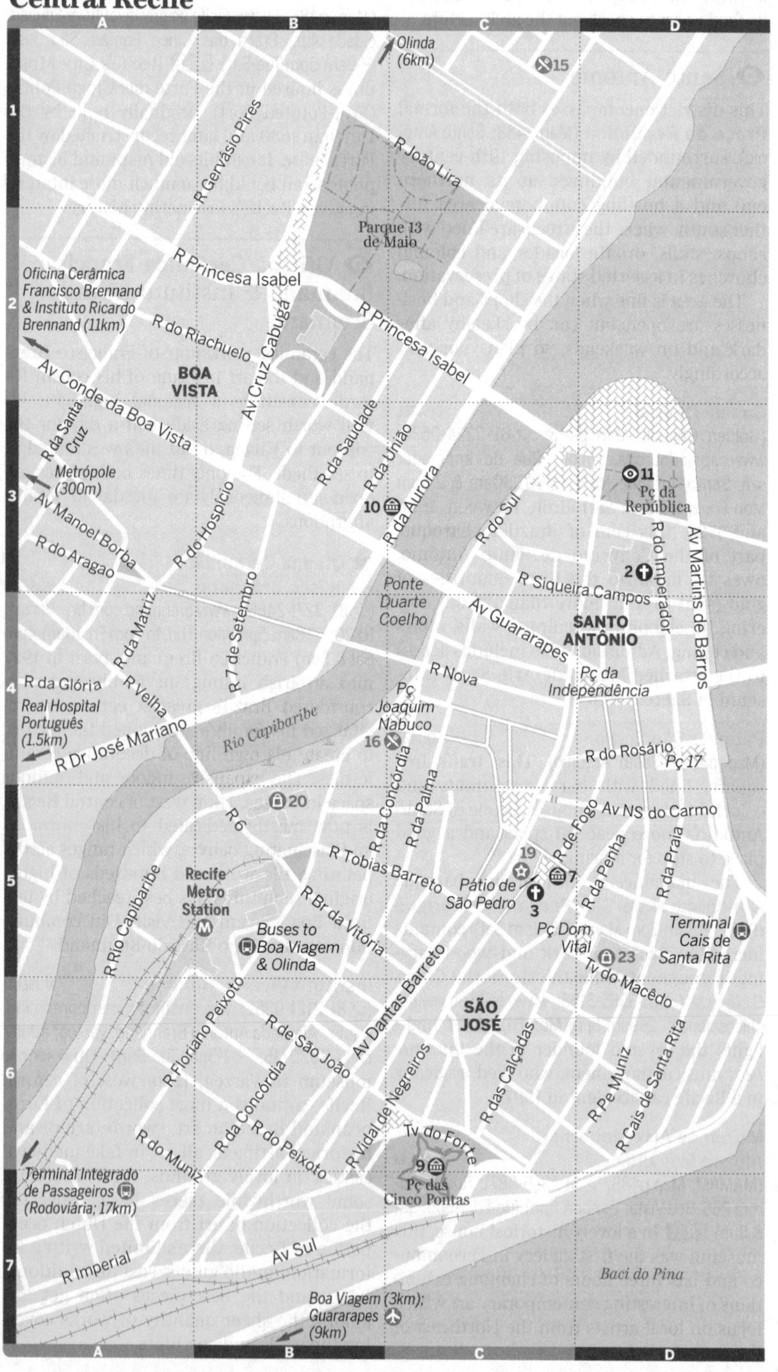

Central Recife

Top Sights
1 Paço do Frevo....F3

Sights
2 Capela Dourada....D3
3 Concatedral de São Pedro dos Clérigos....C5
4 Embaixada dos Bonecos Gigantes....F3
5 Igreja Madre de Deus....E4
6 Marco Zero....F4
7 Memorial Chico Science....C5
8 Museu Cais do Sertão....F3
9 Museu da Cidade do Recife....C6
10 Museu de Arte Moderna Aloisio Magalhães....C3
Pátio de São Pedro....(see 7)
11 Praça da República....D3
12 Sinagoga Kahal Zur Israel....F3

Sleeping
13 Azul Fusca Hostel....E4

Eating
14 Bodega de Véio....E3
15 Restaurante do Geraldo....C1
16 Restaurante Leite....C4

Drinking & Nightlife
17 Armazéns do Porto....F4
18 Burburinho....E4

Entertainment
19 Terça Negra....C5

Shopping
20 Casa da Cultura....B5
21 Centro de Artesanato de Pernambuco....F3
22 Feirinha do Recife Antigo....F3
23 Mercado de São José....D5

Activities

Several of Recife's main thoroughfares are closed to traffic on Sundays to form a *ciclovia* bicycle route that runs to all corners of the city. The most interesting route runs along Avenida Boa Viagem up to Recife Antiguo. You can rent bicycles (one-/three-day pass R$8/15) with a credit card from the orange public cycle stations dotted throughout the city center.

Olha Recife OUTDOORS

(www.olharecife.com.br) A wonderful initiative of the forward-thinking local government, Olha Recife organizes free outings around town with a cultural slant. Activities change regularly but include boat trips up the Rio

Capibaribe to get to know the city from the water, and walking tours through the historic center. Check the website for the program; some tours require advanced registration.

Festivals & Events

The Recife **Carnaval** (www.carnavalrecife.com) is a hard-to-believe explosion of color, costume, crowds, alcohol, fabulous music and dancing, and infectious happiness that adds up to one of Brazil's most euphoric and folkloric festivals. It has claims to being the best Carnaval in the country, despite attracting far fewer tourists than Salvador's or Rio's. While there are many hundreds of music and dance events held on stages around the city, Carnaval is essentially a participatory event: people don't just sit and watch; they don elaborate costumes and dance for days to Brazilian rhythms, and especially to Recife's very own, frenetic *frevo*.

Galo da Madrugada (Cock of the Morning), which is claimed, probably correctly, to be the largest Carnaval *bloco* (parade group) in the world, erects a giant rooster on the Ponte Duarte Coelho and pulls more than a million people into central Recife for its parade on Carnaval Saturday morning, starting around 8am. Carnaval activity focuses around a number of *polos* (poles) dotted about the city. Recife Antigo (especially Marco Zero, Praça do Arsenal and the Paço Alfândega) and the Pátio de São Pedro are among the best areas to head for.

Carnaval in Olinda is so close that you could participate in both on the same day, and there is a lot of crossover in the events. Accommodations in both cities hike prices mercilessly and may demand three- to five-night minimum stays; some get booked up months, even a year, in advance.

MUSIC OF RECIFE & OLINDA

In Recife and Olinda you'll hear plenty of that very popular, typically Northeastern country music known as *forró*. You'll also come across music from further south in Brazil, such as samba, *pagode* and *choro*. But Pernambuco state, and these two cities in particular, is an exciting music-and-dance world of its own; it's home to some wonderful original genres, mostly bound up with Carnaval, featuring fabulous costumes and fast-paced, mostly percussion-heavy music.

Top of the list has to be *frevo*, a feverishly fast brass-and-percussion music that inspires frenetically energetic dancing. Dancers sport super-colorful shiny costumes and twirl equally colorful mini-umbrellas. *Frevo's* origins are thought to lie in the marching-band music of Carnaval in 19th-century Recife and the capoeira movements of those who cleared the way for the bands. The umbrellas are today's equivalent of the capoeiristas' sticks or knives.

Maracatu nação (also called *maracatu de baque virado*) involves large African-style drum ensembles with dancers dressed as baroque-era Portuguese courtiers – an odd juxtaposition that derives from investiture ceremonies for leaders of the African slave community. *Maracatu rural* (or *maracatu de baque solto*) is rooted in similarly heavy drum rhythms, with dancers representing a mélange of characters from animals to *baianas* (women dressed as Bahian 'aunts' in full skirts and turbans) and spectacular *caboclos de lança* (spear-carrying guards with enormous beehive-like headdresses of brilliantly colored tassels).

Then there's *caboclinho*, which has roots in the rituals of Brazil's indigenous groups. A set of characters, from kings and queens to witch doctors and the *caboclinhos* themselves (indigenous–European mixed-race characters wearing fantastic feathered headdresses), dance energetically to the *pífano* flute, maracas and big drums.

Pernambuco is also one of the homes of *afoxé*, an Afro-Brazilian music-and-dance genre based on the rhythms and spirit of Candomblé.

A more recent Recife contribution to Brazilian music is *mangue beat*, which emerged in the 1990s among young bands who combined traditional forms such as *maracatu* with electrified instruments and rhythms of rap, hip-hop and electronica. They did a lot to connect the younger generation with the traditions of their ancestors. Leader of the genre was singer Chico Science and his group Nação Zumbi, whose iconic 1996 album *Afrociberdelia* summed up the *mangue* movement as neatly as one word can. Science died in a car crash in 1997 and is still much mourned; Nação Zumbi plays on.

Sleeping

Travelers have traditionally gravitated towards the high-rise, middle-class beach suburb of Boa Viagem, which has the best range of accommodations and restaurants. It begins 3km south of the center and extends about 5km along the coast. The city center has limited and poor options, but a couple of new hostels are making that choice more interesting these days.

Recife Antigo

Azul Fusca Hostel HOSTEL $
(Map p488; 81 97906-6338; www.azulfuscahostel.com; Mariz e Barros 328, Recife Antigo; dm R$45;) The 'Blue Beetle' (as in Volkswagen Beetle) is an intriguing hostel mere steps from Marco Zero. All spartan chic and minimalist steel, it offers two sparse 12-bed dorms and a design-forward common area with mid-century furniture and quality kitchen appliances. If you have just one day to take in Recife Antigo's cultural attractions, stay here.

Boa Viagem & Pina

Pousada Casuarinas POUSADA $
(Map p492; 81-3325-4708; www.pousadacasuarinas.com.br; Antônio Pedro Figueiredo 151, Boa Viagem; s/d/tr R$110/140/170, with veranda R$120/150/180;) A tranquil former family home run by two sisters (who speak English, Italian and German), Casuarinas is a marvelous retreat from the heat and bustle outside. Spotless rooms are set around a shady courtyard, where regional folk art and knickknacks spice up the decor. Recife's best-value stay, bar none!

Cosmopolitan Hostel HOSTEL $
(Map p492; 81 3204-0321; www.cosmopolitanhostel.com; Paulo Setúbal 53, Boa Viagem; dm/s/d/tr from R$45/119/129/160;) This bright, welcoming hostel in a converted family home on a quiet residential street is the best budget bet for ambience, space and location. Private rooms and six- or seven-bed dorms (one is women-only) are set around a courtyard with mango and *acerola* (acidic, cherry-like fruit) trees. Amiable bilingual owner Filipe is a fount of local information.

Albergue Piratas da Praia HOSTEL $
(Map p492; 81 99776-4949, 81 3326-1281; www.piratasdapraia.com; Av Conselheiro Aguiar 2034, Boa Viagem; dm with air-con R$40-50, r R$140;) You'd never know it was here, but this friendly hostel occupies the 3rd floor of a building named Edificio Barão de Camaçari (entered from Rua Osias Ribeiro). It's a bit like staying in a friend's apartment, as it has a good clean kitchen and wonderfully colorful common areas. One of the two private rooms comes with a hammock.

Vitória Praia Hotel POUSADA $$
(81 3462-6446; www.vitoriapraiahotel.com.br; Capitão Zuzinha 234, Boa Viagem; s/d from R$185/190;) Aside from having more color and character than any other place in this price range, this cute 30-room pousada is a mere 1.5km from the airport, perfectly located for those just passing through. A good breakfast is served in the top-floor dining room.

Vivaz Boutique Hotel BOUTIQUE HOTEL $$
(81-3097-7332; www.vivazboutiquehotel.com; Capitão Rebelinho 374, Pina; s/d from R$149/160;) On a restaurant-heavy street one block from the beach in Pina, Recife's first boutique hotel (call it economic-boutique, anyway) offers a marriage of modern rooms with vaguely Victorian-chic design motifs. Some of the themed rooms look onto small urban gardens while others are a bit poky, so ask to look around. There's a nice relaxing deck with a pool.

Eating

Recife has great places to eat, ranging from cheerful and bustling to refined establishments comparable with the country's finest. Armazéns do Porto (p493), a modern drinking and dining complex next to Marco Zero, houses several bars and restaurants that come alive at night and is part of a larger, ongoing port revival complex.

For cheap bites, head to the nightly food and artisan fair at Praça de Boa Viagem.

Central Recife

Bodega de Véio BRAZILIAN $
(Map p488; 81 3432-9581; Rio Branco 328, Recife Antigo; meals R$15; 11am-10pm) The Recife branch of this Olinda classic, Bodega de Véio is part corner store, part bistro and is one of the few restaurants in the historic center that opens on Sunday when festivities in the area are in full swing. It's a fun place for a meal, a drink or to pick up some nail clippers.

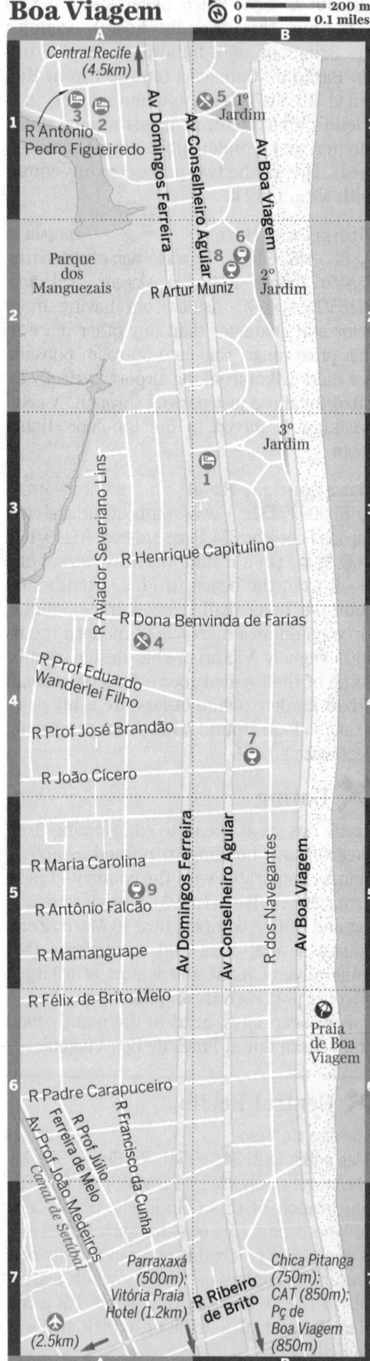

Boa Viagem

Sleeping

1 Albergue Piratas da Praia B3
2 Cosmopolitan Hostel A1
3 Pousada Casuarinas A1

Eating

4 Bercy Village A4
5 Camarada Camarão B1

Drinking & Nightlife

6 Alphaiate B2
7 Companhia do Chope B4
8 Guaiamum Gigante B2
9 UK Pub A5

Restaurante Leite BRAZILIAN $$$
(Map p488; ☎81 3224-7977; www.restaurante leite.com.br; Praça Joaquim Nabuco 147, Santo Antônio; mains R$53-98; ⏰11am-4pm Mon-Fri; 📶) One of the oldest restaurants in Brazil, this traditional lunch place was opened in 1882. Though modernized these days and void of much historical air, it remains a power-lunch favorite of *politicos* and businesspeople. If you're feeling spendy, this is old-school refined dining at its most classic: tables and waiters draped in white, accompanied by piano music. Reservations? Probably.

Santo Amaro

Restaurante do Geraldo BRAZILIAN $
(Map p488; ☎81 3231-4177; www.restaurante dogeraldo.com.br; Rua da Piedade 107, Santo Amaro; mains R$17-40; ⏰11am-5pm Mon-Sat) A classic corner diner, Geraldo is known as *o rei do omelete* (the king of the omelet) but also serves up a variety of flavorful homestyle dishes including a great *galinha cabidela* (chicken in spiced brown sauce) in addition to some fine desserts. Try the *banana rica* – caramelized banana with sweet cream and meringue.

Boa Viagem & Pina

Chapéu do Couro BRAZILIAN $
(☎81 3325-3426; Av Conselheiro Aguiar 524, Pina; mains for 2 R$40-86; ⏰11am-midnight) For huge portions of traditional grilled meats and seafood at great prices, it's hard to go past this expansive restaurant a couple of blocks back from the beach in Pina. The menu mains can easily feed three, so unless you're famished, go for one of the executive plates (R$19), which are also very generous.

Bercy Village CRÊPES $
(Map p492; www.bercyvillage.com.br; Rui Batista 120, Boa Viagem; crepes R$26-33; ⏲6pm-midnight Mon-Thu, to 12:30am Fri & Sat, 5:30-11:30pm Sun;) Atmospheric Bercy Village serves up good-value savory and sweet crepes, and fab salads and sandwiches in a cool, semi-outdoor ambience that's pretty classy for a creperie. Perpignan (with filet mignon, gorgonzola and raisins) and Champagne (with shrimp and Gruyère cheese) are big hits.

★**Chica Pitanga** BUFFET $$
(www.chicapitanga.com.br; Petrolina 19, Boa Viagem; per kg lunch weekday/weekend R$77.40/82.10, dinner R$65.50; ⏲11:30am-3:30pm & 6-10pm Mon-Fri, 11:30am-4pm & 6-10pm Sat & Sun;) As near as *por kilos* restaurants can get to a gourmet experience, Chica Pitanga offers a changing array of diverse dishes every day. The dozen or so salad options might, for example, include tabbouleh or mango salad, while duck rice or shrimp in spinach sauce might appear among the hot dishes. Most dangerous pay-by-weight restaurant in Brazil!

Camarada Camarão SEAFOOD $$
(Map p492; ☎81 3325-1786; www.ocamarada.com.br; Baltazar Pereira 130, Boa Viagem; mains for 2 people R$73-165; ⏲noon-11pm Mon-Thu, to midnight Fri & Sat, to 10pm Sun;) Airy, bustling Camarada does shrimp in endlessly creative ways – think shrimp fondue, salads, marinated in beer and served in *moquecas* (stews) – but it's also wildly popular for happy hour, when patrons flood the front deck with ice-cold draft beers in hand. The shrimp and lobster *moqueca* and *bobó de camarão* (shrimp in manioc sauce) are extraordinary.

Parraxaxá BUFFET $$
(www.parraxaxa.com.br; Av Fernando Simões Barbosa 1200, Boa Viagem; per kg lunch weekday/weekend R$63.90/68.90, dinner R$56.90; ⏲11:30am-11pm;) Festive decor and staff dressed in *cangaceiro* (outlaws from the interior) outfits spice up your meal at this fun Northeast-themed restaurant. The self-serve food is a cornucopia of tasty Northeastern dishes: *carne de sol* (salted, grilled meat), *macaxeira* (cassava root), *baião de dois* (a spicy rice, beans and cheese dish) and grilled meats. There are good salads, too.

Drinking & Nightlife

Recife is justly proud of its nightlife and the variety of music that can be found in the city. You can discover somewhere exciting to go every night of the week. Many venues are in Boa Viagem, but the streets behind Recife Antigo's Paço Alfândega also have lively bars. Tourist offices hand out useful entertainment guides, and several websites provide good listings, including Agenda Cultural do Recife (http://agendaculturaldorecife.blogspot.com.br; in Portuguese).

Central Recife

Metrópole GAY
(☎81 3423-0123; www.clubemetropole.com.br; Rua das Nínfas 125, Boa Vista; ⏲10pm-6am Fri & Sat) Recife's best gay (and GLS – Gay, Lesbian and Sympathetics) club has multiple spaces, from its main DJ-ruled 'NY Street' dance area to an outdoor area with a swimming pool. There are frequent theme parties and live shows by big-name artists. There are several good gay-orientated bars in the surrounding blocks if you want to get an early start.

Burburinho BOTECO
(Map p488; www.burburinhobar.com.br; Tomazina 106, Recife Antigo; ⏲11:30am-late) Frequented by students, journalists and a generally bohemian crowd, Burburinho is nicer inside than it appears and usually has regular live music – mainly blues/jazz, soul and rock sessions. They prepare good hot sandwiches and *pastéis* (fried pastries).

Armazéns do Porto BAR
(Map p488; www.armazensdoporto.com.br; Av Alfredo Lisboa, Recife Antigo; ⏲10am-late) This modern dining and harborside entertainment complex next to Marco Zero houses a series of bright and inviting cafes, restaurants and bars that come alive in the evening.

Boa Viagem & Pina

Alphaiate BAR
(Map p492; 2nd Jardim Boa Viagem, Boa Viagem; ⏲11:30am-midnight) The most happening of several bistros in this middle section of Boa Viagem, Alphaiate is a bit hectic for a meal but is a good place for a drink. It has an expansive air-conditioned interior but the best crowd-watching action goes on at the wooden tables packed onto the sidewalk. Stocks a decent selection of Portuguese, Argentine and Chilean wines.

Companhia do Chope BOTECO

(Map p492; www.chopperiacompanhia.com.br; Av Conselheiro Aguiar 2775, Boa Viagem; bar food R$8.50-105, chope R$5.40-12; ⏲5-11:30pm Mon-Thu, 10am-midnight Fri-Sun; 📶) Swarming with interesting people since 1984, this rambunctious *boteco* (small open-air bar) fills a breezy open-air shopping plaza in Boa Viagem. Some of Recife's best shared bar food (just try to resist those *coxinhas* – cornmeal balls filled with chicken – and *empadas* – little meat-filled pies) and coldest draft beer is delivered by nimble waiters as the easy-on-the-eye crowd flirts its way through the evening.

Haus Lajetop & Beergarden BAR

(☎81 3039-6304; Galeria Joana D'Arc, Av Herculano Bandeira 513, Pina; cocktails R$15-30; ⏲6pm-midnight Sun-Wed, to 2am Thu-Sat; 📶) Tucked away in the back of the artsy Galeria Joana D'Arc, this boxy bar and beer garden gets the balance right: a smart, industrial-chic atmosphere marrying unfinished concrete walls with reclaimed wooden doors and shutters on the ceiling; cool tunes; and an extensive cocktail, beer and wine list that is perfect for washing down the range of bar eats.

UK Pub LOUNGE

(Map p492; ☎81 3465-1088; www.ukpub.com.br; Francisco da Cunha 165, Boa Viagem; door entry R$40-50; ⏲11pm-6am Fri-Sun) UK Pub is a fairly posh lounge that draws a sexy crowd for imported beers plus varied live bands and DJs. Despite the name it's mostly Brazilian music – *brega*, *forró* and MPB (Música Popular Brasileira). Take ID or you won't get in.

Guaiamum Gigante BAR

(Map p492; ☎81 3327-1413; Artur Muniz 82, Boa Viagem; ⏲11:30am-midnight Mon-Wed, to 2am Thu-Sat, to 11pm Sun) An upscale, beach-facing *boteco* (small open-air bar) that pulls a crowd on most nights. The breezy dining area serves as a decadent drinking den, and you can also sample tasty seafood (dishes for two cost from R$85 to R$140).

☆ Entertainment

Recifenses are passionate about their football, even though their most successful teams, Sport (www.sportrecife.com.br) and Náutico (www.nautico-pe.com.br), both have a history of yo-yo-ing between the national Série A and Série B. Náutico plays at the large **Arena de Pernambuco** (☎81 3319-1919; www.arenadepernambuco.com.br; Av Deus É Fiel, Cidade de Copa; tours R$2), which sometimes also hosts Sport's home fixtures that are too big for their smaller private ground.

Terça Negra LIVE MUSIC

(Black Tuesday; Map p488; www.facebook.com/tercanegrarecife; Pátio de São Pedro, Santo Antônio; ⏲8pm-1am Tue) This great free night of Afro-Brazilian rhythms takes place in the picturesque Pátio de São Pedro two Tuesdays a month. The crowd in the plaza is alternative and laid-back but the surrounding area is sketchy, so don't wander off. Check with one of the CAT info centres or the Terça Negra Facebook page for scheduling.

Terça do Vinil LIVE MUSIC

(Av Herculano Bandeira 513, Pina; ⏲7pm-midnight Tue) DJs spin MPB (Música Popular Brasileira) on vinyl at this popular outdoor concert event held every Tuesday night in the courtyard at the Galeria Joana D'Arc. It attracts a well-heeled and flirty crowd.

Shopping

Casa da Cultura ARTS & CRAFTS

(Map p488; Floriano Peixoto, Santo Antônio; ⏲9am-6pm Mon-Fri, to 5pm Sat, to 2pm Sun) An excellent source of Pernambuco crafts, plus it stocks a lot of T-shirts. The Casa da Cultura occupies a creepy colonial-era jail where prisoners languished until 1973.

Centro de Artesanato de Pernambuco ARTS & CRAFTS

(Map p488; www.artesanatodepernambuco.pe.gov.br; Praça Rio Branco, Recife Antigo; ⏲8am-7pm Mon-Sat, to 4pm Sun) Displays and sells high-end Pernambuco crafts in wood, ceramics, lace, lithographs and other media.

Feirinha do Recife Antigo ARTS & CRAFTS

(Map p488; Rua do Bom Jesus, Recife Antigo; ⏲2-10pm Sun) This interesting street market specializing in local artisanry, such as dresses, jewelry and ceramics, brings Recife Antigo to life on Sunday afternoons. Nearby bars open and there's often live music. On the last Sunday of the month, there are extras such as performances and kids' activities.

Mercado de São José MARKET

(Map p488; Praça Dom Vital, São José; ⏲7:30am-5:30pm Mon-Fri, to 3:30pm Sat, to noon Sun) As well as traditional Pernambuco handicrafts, such as lace and leather goods, palm baskets and clay figurines, this bustling city-center market sells all manner of food, and stocks shelves of medicinal herbs. On Sundays just a few of the stalls open and the surrounding area is a bit sketchy.

Information

DANGERS & ANNOYANCES

Surfing is prohibited at Praia Boa Viagem due to the danger of shark attacks. Swimmers there are advised to stay out of the water at high tide and not to go beyond the reef at any time. Since 1990 more than 30 shark attacks have been recorded along Recife's shores, most of them at Boa Viagem or the next beach south, Piedade.

Although crime levels have fallen significantly in recent years, Recife still has one of Brazil's highest murder rates. Tourists are more at risk from pickpockets and bag snatchers: stay alert to your surroundings and the people around you, and don't walk down unlit streets at night. Boa Viagem is arguably safer than the city center, though crime can be an issue there, too.

MEDICAL SERVICES

Real Hospital Português (☎81 3416-1122; www.rhp.com.br; Av Agamenon Magalhães 4760; ⏱24hr) Modern 24-hour private hospital; its smaller **clinic** (☎81 3416-1800; www.rhp.com.br; Av Conselheiro Aguiar 2502, Boa Viagem) in Boa Viagem also offers 24-hour emergency service.

MONEY

The airport has numerous ATMs and exchange offices. There are plenty of banks with ATMs in Boa Viagem.

Banco do Brasil (Av Dantas Barreto 541, Santo Antônio; ⏱branch 10am-4pm Mon-Fri, ATMs 6am-10pm daily)

Bradesco (Av Conselheiro Aguíar 3256, Boa Viagem)

Bradesco (Av Marquês de Olinda 136, Recife Antigo)

TOURIST INFORMATION

Most Recife tourist offices, known as Centro de Atendimento ao Turista (CAT), have helpful, professional English-speaking staff and can provide good city maps and other pertinent travel information.

BEACHES SOUTH OF RECIFE

Twenty years ago, **Porto de Galinhas** (Port of Chickens) was just another fishing village at the end of a dirt road, with a palm-fringed beach and a few recifenses' holiday homes. Today it's one of Brazil's booming beach destinations, with several large resort hotels strung along Praia Muro Alto and Praia do Cupe, north of the center, and dense festive crowds flocking here at holiday times. Pedestrianizing the few streets that make up the town center, where the odd restaurant opens right on to the beach, has preserved some village ambience. Beautiful beaches with light-colored sands stretch several kilometers in both directions from the town.

Veracruz runs buses from Recife's Terminal Cais de Santa Rita every half-hour from 4:50am to 8:30pm, heading to Porto de Galinhas via Boa Viagem (Av Domingos Ferreira) and Recife Guararapes International Airport (outside the arrivals hall). Departures alternate between Line 195 (R$15.60, two hours) which is air-conditioned and line 191 (R$10.70, two hours) which is not.

Tamandaré, 30km south of Porto de Galinhas (57km by road), is a small beach town that is far less hyper than its northern neighbor. It boasts a big stretch of coastline – 16km of lovely palm-fringed beaches.

Eight kilometers north of Tamandaré, fashionable and ultra-relaxed Praia dos Carneiros is one of Northeast Brazil's loveliest strands. It has wonderful calm, clear, shallow waters, fine sand shaded by coconut palms, and tidal pools formed by a rocky bar stretching across the wide mouth of the Rio Formoso. Unfortunately word of its appeal has spread and it now hosts busloads of package tours from Recife and Porto Galinhas during the day; after they leave it is wonderfully empty.

Viação Cruzeiro runs buses to Tamandaré (R$15.50, three hours) from southern Av Dantas Barreto in central Recife at 7am, 10am, 2pm and 5:40pm Monday to Saturday, and 7:30am Sunday.

Moto-taxis cost R$7 to R$10 and taxis R$30 between Tamandaré and Praia dos Carneiros.

Appealing lodging options in the area include **Pousada Flor de Maraca** (☎81 3552-2963; www.flordemaraca.com; Av Sertânia 39, Praia de Maracaípe; r R$225-250) in Porto de Galinhas, **Hotel Coral Beach** (☎81 3676-1310; São José 450; r R$510; ❄📶🏊) in Tamandaré and **Bangalôs do Gameleiro** (☎81 3676-1421; www.praiadoscarneiros.com.br; Praia dos Carneiros; apt R$480, bungalows R$560-720; P❄📶) in Praia dos Carneiros.

Airport (Centro de Atendimento ao Turista; 81 3182-8299; www.turismonorecife.com.br; Arrivals Hall, Guararapes International Airport; 24hr)

Bus Station (Centro de Atendimento ao Turista; 81 3182-8298; Terminal Integrado de Passageiros; 7am-7pm)

Praça do Arsenal (Centro de Atendimento ao Turista; Map p488; 81 3355-3402; www.turismonorecife.com.br; Praça do Arsenal, Rua da Guia s/n, Recife Antigo; 8am-6pm)

Praça do Boa Viagem (Centro de Atendimento ao Turista; 81 3182-8297; www.turismonorecife.com.br; Praça de Boa Viagem, Boa Viagem; 8am-8pm)

Getting There & Away

AIR

Recife's **Guararapes International Airport** (REC; 81 3322-4188) is at the south end of Boa Viagem, 2km inland, and offers direct flights to/from some 20 Brazilian cities. International destinations served include Buenos Aires, Frankfurt, Lisbon, Madrid, Miami, Milan, Munich and Panama City.

BUS

Recife's bus station is the large **Terminal Integrado de Passageiros** (TIP/Rodoviária; 81 3207-1088; Av Prefeito Antônio Pereira s/n, Várzea), generally known as the Rodoviária, 17km west of the center. TIP handles all interstate buses and many destinations within Pernambuco.

CAR

Recommended car-rental agencies with airport offices include **Avis** (81 3322-4016, 0800-725-2847; www.avis.com.br; Guararapes International Airport; 6am-midnight) and **Localiza Hertz** (81 3092-7750; www.localizahertz.com; Guararapes International Airport; 24hr). **Foco** (81 4007-2109; www.aluguefoco.com.br; Mascarenhas de Morais 6133, Boa Viagem; 24hr), across the road just outside, is local and sometimes cheaper.

Getting Around

Recife is spread out and some of the buses (R$3.20; R$1.60 on Sundays) take circuitous, confusing routes. Taxis will save you time and stress, while Uber has a big presence here and is often significantly cheaper.

Bus routes and schedules are online at www.granderecife.pe.gov.br (click Serviços then Atendimento ao Usuário then Itinerário). The city is also served by a two-line metro (R$3) that is handy for the bus station, airport and football matches at Arena Pernambuco.

There are convenient public bicycle stations throughout Boa Viagem, Pina and Recife Antigo; visitors need a credit card to rent one but the process is fairly straightforward.

TO/FROM THE AIRPORT

Coopseta (81 3322-4153; Arrivals, Guararapes International Airport) prepaid taxis from the airport cost between R$23 and R$39 to Boa Viagem, and R$87 to Olinda or the bus station. During high traffic times prepaid taxis can be a better-value option then metered taxis; at other times it's cheaper to go with metered rivals **Coopstar** (81 3072-4433; Arrivals, Guararapes International Airport). Booths for both taxi companies are located just outside the baggage-claim area. Prices increase between 10pm and 6am with both operators.

Air-conditioned bus 042 leaves from outside the arrivals hall and heads to Boa Viagem and the city center (R$4) but you need a transit card to board and it takes a convoluted route, which slows it considerably. At busy times, a better option for Boa Viagem is to walk to the right outside the arrivals hall and catch bus 040 CDU/Boa Viagem/Caxangá (which initially heads south) from the stop on busy Av Mascarenhas de Morais.

Going to the airport from Boa Viagem, catch any Aeroporto bus on Av Domingos Ferreira; from the center, take a 033 Aeroporto bus from **Terminal Cais de Santa Rita** (Map p488; Cais de Santa Rita s/n, São José).

BUSES FROM RECIFE

DESTINATION	COST FROM (R$)	TIME (HR)	COMPANY
Caruaru	26-28	2	Progresso (www.progressoonline.com.br)
Fortaleza	165	13	Expresso Guanabara (www.expressoguanabara.com.br)
João Pessoa	41	2	Progresso
Maceió	58	4-5	Real Alagoas (www.realalagoas.com.br)
Natal	83	4½	Progresso
Rio de Janeiro	490-600	38	Gontijo (www.gontijo.com.br), Itapemirim (www.itapemirim.com.br)
Salvador	182	18	Catedral Turismo (www.catedralturismo.com.br), Kaissara (www.kaissara.com.br)

TO/FROM THE BUS STATION

To get to Boa Viagem from the Terminal Integrado de Passageiros (p496) (TIP), take the metro to Joana Bezerra station, then follow the signs to 'SEI – Integraçao' for Boa Viagem–bound bus 080 (it leaves from embarkation point 2). The R$1.60 metro ticket from the Rodoviária metro station in the TIP covers both rides.

From Boa Viagem to the TIP, take a TI Aeroporto/Joana Bezerra bus from Av Conselheiro Aguiar to Joana Bezerra metro station, then a Camaragibe-bound metro train to the Rodoviária stop.

If you arrive outside metro hours (5am to 11pm), taxis run R$60 to Boa Viagem and R$70 to Olinda.

TO/FROM BOA VIAGEM

In Boa Viagem, southbound buses run along Av Domingos Ferreira; northbound buses run along Av Conselheiro Aguiar. The 032 Setúbal/Conde da Boa Vista bus runs north to Recife Antigo, Av Guararapes and Av Conde da Boa Vista (westbound) in the center, and back to Boa Viagem. Bus 033 runs north from Boa Viagem to Terminal Cais de Santa Rita and back.

From the center to Boa Viagem, you can also take a Setúbal/Príncipe bus from the **stop** (Map p488) outside Recife metro station but it takes a somewhat long way round.

A taxi between central Recife and Boa Viagem costs around R$35 to R$40.

Olinda

☎0XX81 / POP 390,770

Picturesque Olinda, set around a tree-covered hill 6km north of Recife, is the artsy, colonial counterpart to the big city's hubbub. It's an artist colony full of creative types and brimming with galleries, artisans' workshops, museums, lovely churches and music in the streets. With twisting streets of colorful old houses and gorgeous vistas over tree tops, church towers and red-tile roofs, this is one of the best-preserved and prettiest colonial towns in Brazil.

The picturesque historic center, declared a Unesco World Heritage site in 1982, has some delightful pousadas and good restaurants and bars, and makes a much more tranquil base than its bigger neighbor that stands towering in the distance.

Sights

Olinda's sights are easy and enjoyable to visit on foot, although highly random opening hours make it impossible to look in on everything in one day. There are *a lot* of churches! A good place to start is Praça do Carmo, where most buses arrive. The square is overlooked by the restored **Igreja NS do Carmo** (Praça do Carmo; entry by donation; ⏲9am-noon & 1-5pm Tue-Sat, 9am-12:45pm Sun), built in 1580. Climb up to Alto da Sé, which affords superb views of both Olinda and Recife. The area is peppered with food, drink and craft stalls.

Museu do Mamulengo MUSEUM
(São Bento 344; R$4; ⏲10am-5pm Tue-Sat) The Museu do Mamulengo has a unique and surprisingly interesting collection of more than 1000 pieces devoted to the traveling puppet shows called Mamulengos, an authentic popular tradition of the Northeast.

Casa dos Bonecos Gigantes MUSEUM
(Prudente de Morais 440; R$5; ⏲1-9pm Tue-Thu, to 9:30pm Fri & Sat, to 8:30pm Sun) This small upstairs gallery displays a collection of the giant puppets used in Olinda's Carnaval (p499). Unlike some more commercial galleries in Recife, almost all of the puppets here, which weigh between 15kg and 50kg, are representations of notable locals including patrons of Carnaval and folkloric heroes.

Convento de São Francisco MONASTERY
(Rua de São Francisco 280; R$2; ⏲9am-11:30pm & 2-5:30pm Mon-Sat) This is a large structure containing the 16th-century Igreja NS das Neves and two later chapels, with rich baroque detailing and lovely *azulejos* (Portuguese ceramic tiles).

Igreja da Sé CATHEDRAL
(Alto da Sé; ⏲9am-5pm) The imposing Igreja da Sé was originally built in 1537. Burnt in 1631, it has been reconstructed four times since, most recently from 1974 to 1984 in a Mannerist style that attempts to recreate the original 16th-century look. Pass through the door to the right of the main altar and continue past the original Portuguese tiles to reach the patio, which offers great views over the town to the brilliant blue sea and Recife in the distance.

Mosteiro de São Bento MONASTERY
(São Bento; ⏲8-11:30am & 2:15-5:30pm Mon-Sat, 8-9:30am & 2:30-5pm Sun) The huge Mosteiro de São Bento, originally built in 1582, has some exceptional woodcarving in its impressive church. Sunday morning Mass (10am) is celebrated, complete with Gregorian chants.

Olinda

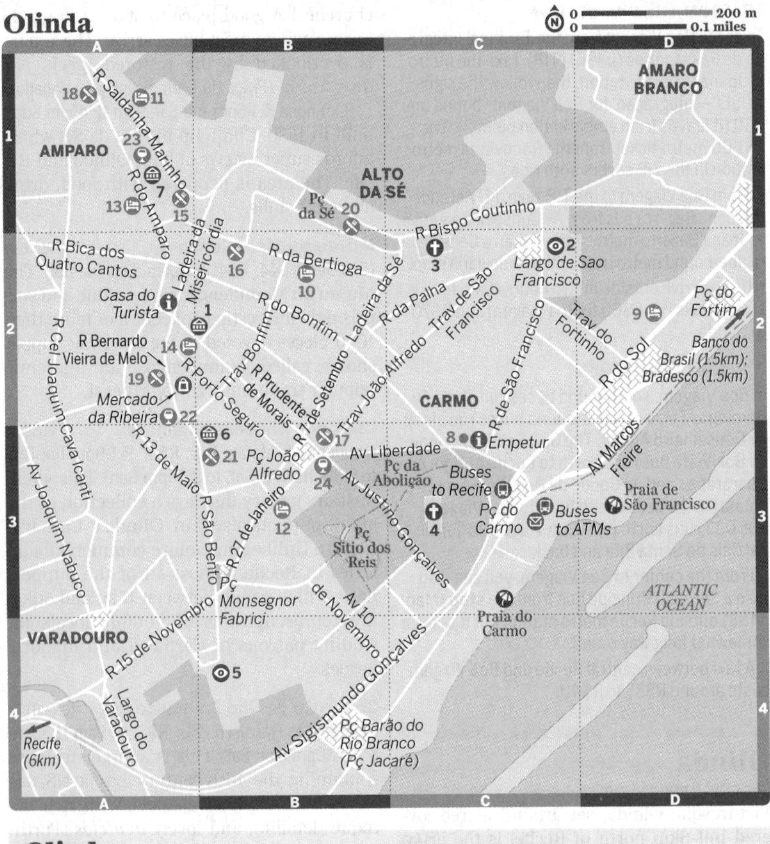

Olinda

Sights

1 Casa dos Bonecos Gigantes B2
2 Convento de São Francisco C2
3 Igreja da Sé C2
4 Igreja NS do Carmo C3
5 Mosteiro de São Bento B4
6 Museu do Mamulengo B3
7 Museu Regional de Olinda A1

Activities, Courses & Tours

8 Associação dos Condutores Nativos de Olinda C3

Sleeping

9 Albergue de Olinda D2
10 Cama e Cafe Olinda B2
11 Mameluco Hostel A1
12 Pousada de São Pedro B3
13 Pousada do Amparo A1
14 Pousada dos Quatro Cantos A2

Eating

15 Beijupirá A1
16 Casa de Noca B2
17 Creperia B3
Estação Café .... (see 1)
18 Oficina do Sabor A1
19 Patuá A2
20 Tapioca Stands B1
21 Tribuna Sabores Ibéricos B3

Drinking & Nightlife

22 Bento Ferreiro A2
23 Bodega de Véio A1
24 Casbah B3

Museu Regional de Olinda MUSEUM
(Rua do Amparo; R$2; ⏲9am-5pm) Located in a classic house that was formerly inhabited by the local clergy, this museum houses a small collection of colonial-period furniture and porcelain with descriptions in English and Portuguese.

Tours

Associação dos Condutores Nativos de Olinda TOURS
(ACNO; 81 98511-0292; www.acno.com.br; Av da Liberdade 68) While in Olinda you'll no doubt hear the offer *'Guia!'* ('Guide!'). The best guides are those accredited by this local guides association. Based in the Praça do Carmo, they wear blue shirts bearing their name, and an ACNO tag, though the colors change regularly to reflect who remains credentialed. The official charge for a two-hour tour is R$80 for two to four people.

Festivals & Events

Olinda's **Carnaval** (www.carnaval.olinda.pe.gov.br) celebrations last a full 11 days and have a spontaneity, inclusiveness and great irreverence that you don't get in big-city Carnavals. 'Pre-Carnaval' events get going the Sunday before Carnaval weekend, with the parade of the Virgens do Bairro Novo, a *bloco* of more than 400 'virgins' (men in drag) who are joined by up to 900,000 revelers. They start out at noon from Praça 12 de Março.

There are organized Carnaval events, including balls and gatherings of *maracatu* (Afro-Brazilian music with a slow, heavy beat) and *afoxé* (based on the rhythms and spirit of Candomblé) dance and music groups, but everything else happens in impromptu fashion on the streets, where endless groups of fabulously costumed musicians and dancers work their way through packed throngs of revelers, who often dance along to the rhythms of *frevo,* samba, *maracatu, caboclinho* or *afoxé.* The euphoric atmosphere and the sheer fun have to be experienced to be believed. Another famous feature of Olinda's Carnaval is the *bonecos gigantes,* huge puppets representing historical, cultural and other figures. A Carnaval high point is the parade of the top-hatted Homem da Meia-Noite (Man of Midnight) *boneco,* who emerges on Largo do Bonsucesso at midnight on Carnaval Saturday night.

Sleeping

★ **Cama e Cafe Olinda** B&B $
(81 98822-9083; www.camaecafeolinda.com; Rua da Bertioga 93; r R$165;) Austrian Sebastian and his Brazilian wife, Yolanda, are the hospitality gatekeepers at this signless B&B with just two rooms. It's chock-full of local art, lazy-day hammocks and views of both the sea and Recife. You'll encounter extraordinary care and character here; breakfast on the terrace, with fresh juices and fruits picked straight from the property, is just one of many highlights.

Mameluco Hostel HOSTEL $
(81 3493-6864; Saldanha Marinho 206, Amparo; dm/r R$40/100;) The best budget bet in the center of the old town, this arty hostel has spacious air-conditioned private rooms with polished concrete floors and a large dorm with windows overlooking a lush garden.

Albergue de Olinda HOSTEL $
(81 3439-1913; www.alberguedeolinda.com.br; Rua do Sol 233; dm/s/d R$55/105/120;) Olinda's excellent HI hostel isn't on a colorful street, but offers modern amenities; spotless no-frills rooms; sex-separate fan-cooled dorms; and a sizable garden with a lovely pool, loungers, outdoor kitchen, barbecue and plenty of hammocks. Some private rooms have air-con.

Pousada dos Quatro Cantos POUSADA $$
(81 3429-0220; www.pousada4cantos.com.br; Prudente de Morais 441; s/d from R$269/333;) High ceilings, tall windows, hardwood floors, lots of attractive art and a nice pool make this 19th-century house a delightful place to stay. While the cheapest (standard) rooms are quite acceptable, a small amount extra will get you a much brighter, more characterful luxury abode. Rooms 119 and 115 frame Olinda's postcard-perfect view. English spoken.

Pousada de São Pedro POUSADA $$
(81 3439-9546; www.pousadapedro.com; 27 de Janeiro 95; s/d/tr from R$170/200/240;) The charming São Pedro occupies a 19th-century house full of art, crafts and antiques, and it has a lovely pool in the leafy, shady garden, plus a pretty special breakfast. But it also has its share of complaints about upkeep and service is a bit unconventional, so pick your druthers.

Pousada do Amparo POUSADA $$$
(81 3439-1749; www.pousadadoamparo.com.br; Rua do Amparo 199; s/d from R$344/430;) The refined Amparo occupies two 18th-century houses (though it may be reduced to one) with lovely gardens and views back toward Recife. It's full of character, very comfortable and is one of the loveliest spots to rest your weary head

WORTH A TRIP

ILHA DE ITAMARACÁ

Less than 40km north of Olinda, Ilha de Itamaracá (separated from the mainland by a wide channel) is a peaceful island retreat with some interesting historical buildings and a pleasant weekend beach scene that feels a world apart from the urban sprawl that surrounds Recife just a short drive away.

Immense **Forte Orange** (1631) on the southern tip of the island is Itamaracá's star attraction. There are several bars and restaurants here, and locals offer boat trips across to **Ihla Coroa do Avião**, a tiny island surrounded by inviting waters.

Three kilometers west of Forte Orange is **Vila Velha**, a small port founded in 1540, one of the earliest Portuguese settlements in Brazil. Overlooking the grassy main plaza is **Nossa Senhora da Conceição**, one of the oldest churches in Brazil. Behind the church there are fantastic views across the river to tiny **Ilha Coroa do Avião**. Walk down the hill towards the water to check out the urns used by the Portuguese to fire the bricks used to build the first structures on the island.

A walking trail, the **Trilha dos Holandeses**, leads to Vila Velha from behind the chapel about 500m back up the road from the Eco-Parque Peixe-Boi near Fort Orange. It takes about 45-minutes each way and it's fairly remote, so it's best to go in a group.

Itamaracá island has plenty more beaches, strung out along its 15km ocean shore. The quietest and prettiest are north of the central, most built-up part of the coast around Pilar and Jaguaribe. If you don't have a vehicle, take a Kombi (R$2) to the end of the line north of Jaguaribe where a small boat (R$2) carries passengers across the river to wide and wild **Praia do Sossego.** From there it's possible to hike 3km north to palm-lined **Praia do Fortinho**, the nicest beach on the island. If you're driving, a dirt road leads to the beaches from a turnoff on PE-035 in the interior of the island.

Itamaracá is an easy day trip from Recife but if you want to stay, the best accommodations are found around the southeast tip of the island, where you'll find several mid-range hotels and guesthouses.

To reach Itamaracá, take the 1946 Igarassu bus (R$4.40, one hour), with departures every few minutes from Av Martins de Barros in central Recife. It passes through Olinda in both directions. At Igarassu's Terminal Integração bus station, change to one of the frequent 968 Itamaracá buses (free). A few of these go to Forte Orange; most of the others head to Jaguaribe, but you can get off at the Forte Orange turnoff *(entrada do forte)* and catch a frequent Kombi van or *colectivo* (shared taxi; R$1.50) for the remaining 5km.

in the Northeast. Try to get room 'Fortim', which has a Jacuzzi with fine panoramas. English is spoken.

Eating

A variety of good restaurants are tucked away among the old town's cobblestone streets. A great way to start an evening is with a tasty tapioca snack and a beer or caipirinha from the myriad **tapioca stands** (Praça da Sé; snacks R$3-11; ⏲approx 6-11pm) and food stalls overlooking Recife from Alto da Sé.

Casa de Noca BRAZILIAN $

(☎81 3439-1040; Rua da Bertioga 243; meals for 2/3/4/5 people R$60/80/100/120; ⏲11am-4pm & 6-11pm) For simple Northeastern food at its best, you can't beat this backyard restaurant that offers just one dish: chunks of grilled *queijo coalho* (a salty white cheese that's grillable) and slabs of surprisingly tender *carne de sol* (salted, grilled meat) atop a mountain of steamed cassava. If you're still hungry, they offer more *queijo coalho* for dessert – this time covered in honey.

Creperia CRÊPES $

(☎81 99774-4825; www.facebook.com/creperiaolinda; Praça João Alfredo 168; crepes R$9-39, pizzas R$29.50-44; ⏲11am-11pm; ✎) A nice spot for crepes, pizza and salads, which you can enjoy on a pleasant outdoor patio under tall bamboo trees. You'll find most of the standards here as well some some interesting options like a chicken curry pizza with raisins.

Estação Café CAFE $

(Prudente de Morais 440; dishes R$7-30; ⏲1-9pm Tue-Thu, to 9:30pm Fri & Sat, to 8:30pm Sun; 📶) This artsy cafe is a perfect little pit stop for a coffee hit and light bites such as salad, soup, gourmet sandwiches and pasta. There's free bossa nova and *chorinho* (samba-related instrumental music) at 8pm on Fridays and Saturdays.

Tribuna Sabores Ibéricos EUROPEAN $$
(☎81 3439-1577; São Bento 210; mains R$23-60, seafood for 2 R$50-160; ⏰noon-11pm Mon-Sat, to 9pm Sun) This popular down-to-earth bistro in the historic center is good for carefully prepared Portuguese and Spanish seafood plates, alongside steaks and some pasta dishes. The *bacalhau* (salted cod) is tasty and succulent, though the portion for two could be a little more generous. Enthusiastic waitstaff create a pleasant dining ambience.

Patuá BRAZILIAN $$
(☎81 3055-0833; www.restaurantepatua.com.br; Rua da Ribeira 79; mains R$39-75; ⏰11am-3pm Tue, Wed & Sun, 11am-3pm & 6-10pm Thu-Sat; 📶) Humble, local and a kitchen magician, chef Alcindo Queiroz has produced a creative menu of regional *moquecas* and seafood at this Olinda sleeper. While the flavor combinations are interesting, dishes can be hit and miss in the execution. Start with the Taperoá appetizer – flambéed shrimp over a fried banana drizzled with a pink-peppercorn and star-anise sauce.

★**Oficina do Sabor** BRAZILIAN $$$
(☎81 3429-3331; www.oficinadosabor.com; Rua do Amparo 335; mains for 2 people R$62-192; ⏰11:30am-4pm & 6pm-midnight Tue-Thu, 11:30am-1am Fri-Sat, to 5pm Sun; 📶) With a specialty in baked pumpkin stuffed with assorted fillings – the shrimp, lobster and passion-fruit sauce variety is fantastic – this is one of the Northeast's best restaurants, and worth every centavo. It's also great on seafood in general (go for the crab in coconut and parsley appetizer), and offers an extensive Brazilian wine list, if you're curious.

Beijupirá SEAFOOD $$$
(☎81 3439-6691; www.beijupiraolinda.com.br; Saldanha Marinho s/n; mains R$62-144; ⏰noon-midnight Mon & Wed-Sat, to 5pm Sun) This romantic spot with views over Olinda's roofs is one of the region's best places for creative seafood. Try the shrimp in whisky and béchamel sauce with pineapple chunks, or the *beijucastanha* – a filet of the eponymous fish (cobia in English) in a chopped-cashew crust, served with spinach rice.

Drinking & Nightlife

Alto da Sé bustles in the evenings as locals and visitors buy drinks and snacks from the street vendors, watch capoeira and savor the view and the breeze. There's usually live samba, *chorinho* or other Brazilian rhythms somewhere in Olinda Wednesday to Saturday nights and Sunday afternoons – tourist offices have information. On Friday nights from 9pm, strolling musicians circuit through town, joined in song by onlookers, in what's known as the *serenata* or *seresta*.

★**Bodega de Véio** BAR
(www.facebook.com/bodegadoveio; Rua do Amparo 212; ⏰10am-11:30pm Mon-Sat) Also a small and very eclectic general store, this wonderful little bar serves ice-cold bottled beer, shots of *cachaça* (potent sugarcane liquor) and great charcuterie plates (R$10 per 100g), while doing its best to manage the crowds of locals and tourists congregating on the street.

Casbah BAR
(Praça João Alfredo 7; ⏰7-11pm Wed-Thu, to 1am Fri-Sat, 4-10pm Sun) If drinking in historic places is your thing, head down to this bar on Praça João Alfredo, set in a lovely old building that is one of the best examples of Moorish architectural influences remaining in Olinda. It's said the Empreror Dom Pedro II stayed here when visiting the town. It hosts exhibitions and frequent concerts.

Bento Ferreiro BAR
(São Bento 225; ⏰noon-3pm Mon-Thu, to 2am Fri-Sat) During the week this bar/restaurant in an elegant older building with dark wood ceilings and a large balcony out the back just opens for lunch but the best time to visit is on weekends when it gets packed for live music – usually *forró*. On Sunday they host a *roda de pagode* (samba concert).

Shopping

Olinda is full of small shops and galleries selling a plethora of art and artisanry such as ceramics, textiles, and wood and stone carvings. Much of the work is incredibly colorful, and browsing these places is one of Olinda's great pleasures. The hub of the creative scene is Rua do Amparo, where many of the best artists and artisans have their homes, workshops and galleries.

Mercado da Ribeira ARTS & CRAFTS
(Bernardo Vieria de Melo s/n; ⏰8am-6pm) Friendly little outdoor market for handicrafts. Out the back there is a large terrace with fine views.

Information

DANGERS & ANNOYANCES

Crime (mostly petty) exists, especially during Carnaval. Don't walk alone along deserted streets at night.

EMERGENCY

Ciatur (Companhia de Apoio ao Turista; ☎81 3181-3703; www.ciaturpmpe.blogspot.com.br; Av Justino Gonçalves; ⏲24hr) Main office of Pernambuco's friendly tourism police.

Ciatur (☎81 3181-1718; Bernardo Vieria de Melo s/n; ⏲24hr) Branch office of tourism police.

MONEY

There are no ATMs in the historic center. The nearest ATMs are Banco do Brasil and Bradesco, close to each other on Av Getúlio Vargas about 2km north, reachable on any of several northbound **buses** (1983, 1973, 910, 881) from the **post office** (www.correios.com.br; Rua do Farol; ⏲9am-5pm Mon-Fri), opposite Praça do Carmo.

TOURIST INFORMATION

Casa do Turista (☎81 3305-1060; Prudente de Morais 472; ⏲8am-6pm Mon-Fri, from 9am Sat & Sun) The municipal tourist-information office has helpful staff, but little English.

Empetur (Empresa de Turismo de Pernambuco; ☎81 3182-8294; www.pe.gov.br/orgaos/empetur-empresa-de-turismo-de-pernambuco; Av Liberdade s/n; ⏲8am-6pm) The state tourist info office has lovely English-speaking staff.

Getting There & Away

Bus 910 Piedade/Rio Doce runs about every half-hour from Boa Viagem (any stop on Av Conselheiro Aguiar) in Recife to Olinda and back. The 1983 Rio Doce/Princesa Isabel and 1992 Pau Amarelo buses run from Terminal Cais de Santa Rita (p496) in central Recife to Olinda and back. All cost R$3.20. Olinda's main bus stop is on Praça do Carmo.

From Recife airport, you can take bus 042 from outside Arrivals to Terminal Cais de Santa Rita, then the 1983 or 1992 from there to Olinda. Usually the quicker option, however, is to make the five-minute walk to Aeroporto metro station on Rua 10 de Julho, taking a 20-minute metro ride to the central Recife station (also called Estação Central; R$3), and then a 1992 Pau Amarelo bus to Olinda, departing about every 15 minutes from Rua Floriano Peixoto outside the station.

From Recife bus station (Terminal Integrado de Passageiros) to Olinda, take the metro to the central Recife station and then a 1992 Pau Amarelo bus.

Taxis to Olinda cost around R$60 from Boa Viagem, R$70 from Recife bus station and R$75 from the airport.

Fernando de Noronha

☎0XX81 / POP 3015

While religion, science and philosophy continue to battle out what happens when we die, in Brazil there is little discourse on the subject: heaven plays second fiddle to the 21-island Fernando de Noronha archipelago. Located in the Atlantic, 525km from Recife and 350km from Natal, Noronha's natural beauty holds its own against any tropical locale in the world.

With crystal-clear waters, rich marine life – including the highest known concentration of resident dolphins in the world – and spectacular tropical landscapes, it's in a Brazilian class all of its own. The country's 'beach bible,' *Guia Quatro Rodas Praias,* awards five stars to just five beaches in the whole country – and three are right here.

It's the perfect place to get away from the crowds and do very little at all. Not that there's a shortage of activities; hikes along deserted beaches, snorkeling with turtles and sailing cruises await those visitors who manage to get up off their towels.

Planning Your Visit

When planning your visit to the archipelago, give yourself plenty of time because Noronha is addictive. It's a wonderful place for doing things both on water (diving, surfing and snorkeling) and on land (hiking and touring), and the average stay is four or five nights. Thanks in large part to the **Parque Nacional Marinho de Fernando de Noronha** (Fernando de Noronha National Marine Park; www.parnanoronha.com.br; Brazilian/foreigner R$97/195; ⏲8am-6:30pm) and conservation projects based here, the marine and coastal environment is tightly regulated: locals joke that it's the island of 'No' – no, you can't do this; no, you can't do that, etc.

With only between 270 and 400 plane seats normally available per day to Noronha, tourism doesn't overwhelm the islands, and it's rarely a problem to find an isolated patch of sand on a dreamy beach, even in high season. However, it's advisable to reserve accommodations and flights well ahead for December, January, February, July and August. The week or so either side of New Year can get booked up six months or more in advance.

Paradise comes at a premium: due to the cost of transporting goods from the mainland, prices are surreal and rooms cost about double what you'd pay on the mainland. But as a guaranteed highlight of any trip to South America, Fernando de Noronha is well worth the expense.

The largest and only inhabited island, Ilha de Fernando de Noronha is 10km long, with its population concentrated in the village of **Vila dos Remédios** and the adjoining, spread-out neighborhoods of **Vila do Trinta**, **Floresta Velha** and **Floresta Nova**. A single paved road, the BR-363, runs 7km from the port near the island's northeast tip, through the populated area, to the airport and down to Baía do Sueste on the south coast. Unpaved side roads lead to several other beaches. The spectacular extinct volcanic cone **Morro do Pico** is the highest point, 323m above sea level – and more than 4300m above the ocean floor. No, you cannot climb it.

The showery season is from February to June and the islands are blessed by fresh breezes year round. The time zone here is one hour ahead of Brasília time.

Sights

Forte dos Remédios FORT

(24hr) FREE Easily the best preserved of the island's Portuguese forts, Forte dos Remédios is well worth a visit and has great views from its hilltop above Vila dos Remédios. At the time of writing, the fort was in the middle of a slow restoration process; it's likely a small admission fee will be charged once it's complete.

Beaches

There are 16 or 17 beaches on Noronha (depending on who you ask); all are clean, postcard-ready and almost deserted. The 'five-star' **Baía do Sancho**, **Praia do Leão** and **Baía dos Porcos** are all impossibly gorgeous, but there is a lot of competition.

Note that access to some of the beaches is difficult. Porcos is only accessible on foot from neighboring Praia da Cacimba do Padre during low tide, while Baía do Sancho requires climbing down two ladders and steep stairs cut into the side of a cliff. Those with mobility issues or traveling with young children may prefer to visit on a boat tour.

The sandy beaches facing the Mar de Dentro (Inner Sea) on the northwest side of the island – **Cachorro** (at Vila dos Remédios), **Conceição**, **Boldró**, **Americano**, **Quixaba** and **Cacimba do Padre** – are also good for surfing. On the opposite side of the island, **Praia do Atalaia**, which has shallow tide pools great for snorkeling, can only be accessed with reservations.

Access to beaches in the national park is closed off from 6:30pm to 8am.

Baía dos Golfinhos is strictly off-limits to swimmers and all watercraft.

Activities

Boat Tours

A number of boats make enjoyable daily three- to five-hour tours from the Port, along the main island's northwest coast and back, which are highly recommended for admiring the island from a distance. Spinner dolphins like to swim and perform acrobatics near the boats, and a 40-minute snorkeling stop at Baía do Sancho is normally part of the trip. Prices include pickup and drop-off at your accommodation.

Most operators offer 'planasub' or 'prancha-sub' – snorkeling while being slowly towed along by the boat – as an optional extra at the end of the trip.

Trovão dos Mares II BOATING

(81 3619-1228; www.trovaodosmares.com.br; adult/child R$280/140) Recommended trips of about five hours that include a buffet lunch overlooking Praia do Sancho. Planasub – snorkeling while being towed behind the vessel – costs R$50 extra.

PRICE OF PARADISE

Visitors to Fernando de Noronha have to pay two special charges. The first is the fees for visiting the Parque Nacional Marinho de Fernando de Noronha – you're almost certain to enter the national park while here. In addition to this, the state government environmental preservation tax, known as the TPA, is R$70.66 per day for the first four days, then progressively discounts per day for days five to 10 and then increases progressively by varying amounts for each extra day after that: a one-week/two-week/four-week stay costs, in total, R$449/1026/4291, at 2018 rates. You pay by cash or credit card on arrival at the airport (at the time of writing the site was *still* not set up to receive payments from foreigners in advance). If you decide to stay longer than planned, go to the airport between 11am and 5pm at least one day before your original departure date and pay for your extra days – otherwise you'll pay double.

1

2

I LOVE NATURE! - I LOVE BRAZIL!/GETTY IMAGES ©

Conceição beach (p503) **2.** Diving (p506) **3.** Fernando de ronha cove (p502)

Fernando de Noronha

For many Brazilians a trip to the archipelago of Fernando de Noronha, 350km out into the Atlantic from Natal, is the holiday of a lifetime. What is it that makes this former penal colony and military base, comprising one medium-sized and 20 small islands, so magnetic?

Scenery

Small-scale but majestic, the combination of long sandy strands, lush vegetation, towering rock pinnacles and ocean rollers breaking on dramatic rocky cliffs and islets has few parallels on the planet.

Conservation

Much of the archipelago's land and sea areas are a strictly regulated national park, so fauna, flora, landscape and the marine environment are protected from the effects of overdevelopment. Visitor numbers are restricted so there is always plenty of space, and active conservation organizations zealously protect its dolphin and turtle populations.

Beaches

The main island's 17 or so sandy bays are some of Brazil's most beautiful, mostly backed by thickly vegetated slopes or cliffs, and all fronted by wonderfully warm, clear waters. Some are protected by promontories or picturesque offshore islands, and ideal for swimming and snorkeling; others have sets of ocean breakers rolling in and are a dream for surfers.

Diving & Snorkeling

With 30m-plus visibility, beautifully warm seas and abundant marine life including big creatures such as turtles, dolphins and (harmless) sharks, the diving around Noronha is Brazil's best. For the same reasons, snorkeling is fantastic too.

Fernando de Noronha

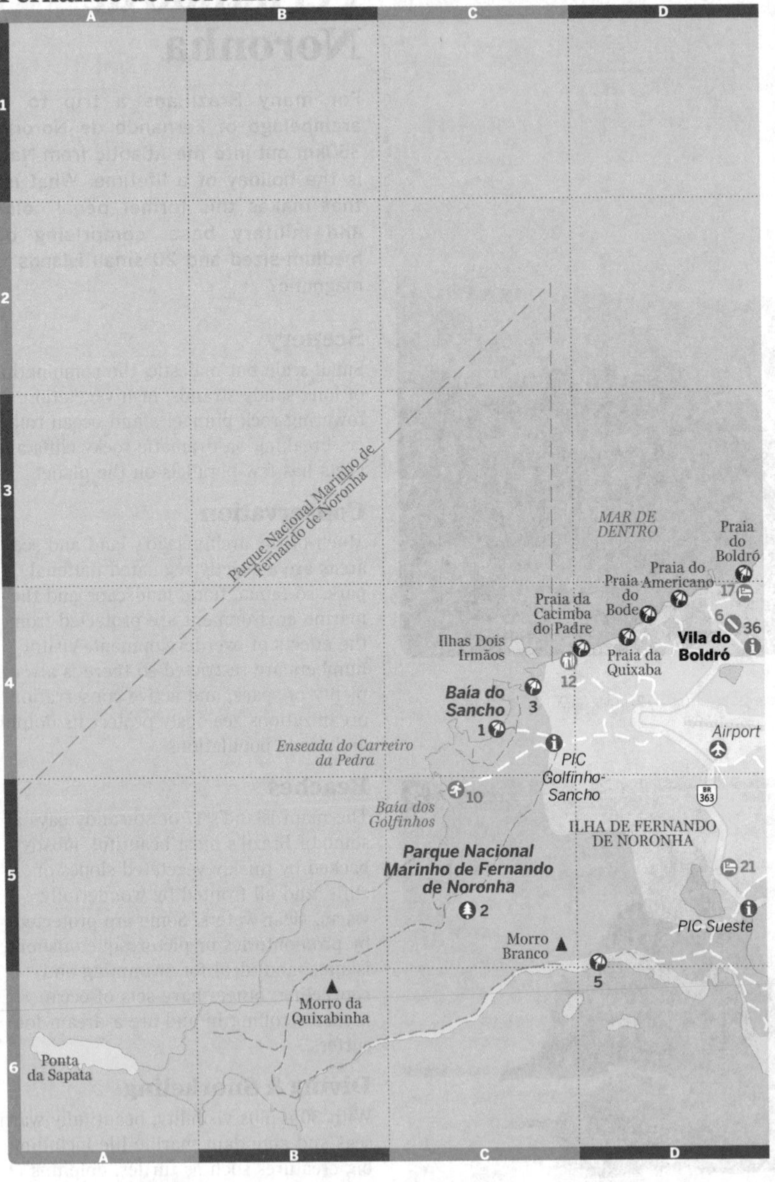

Naonda BOATING
(☎81-3619-1307; www.barconaonda.com; adult/child R$180/90) A recommended boat tour, and one of the least expensive; for R$100 more you can add Planasub.

Diving

With 30m to 40m of visibility (at its very best in October), beautifully warm seas, a well-preserved underwater environment and abundant marine life – from iridescent

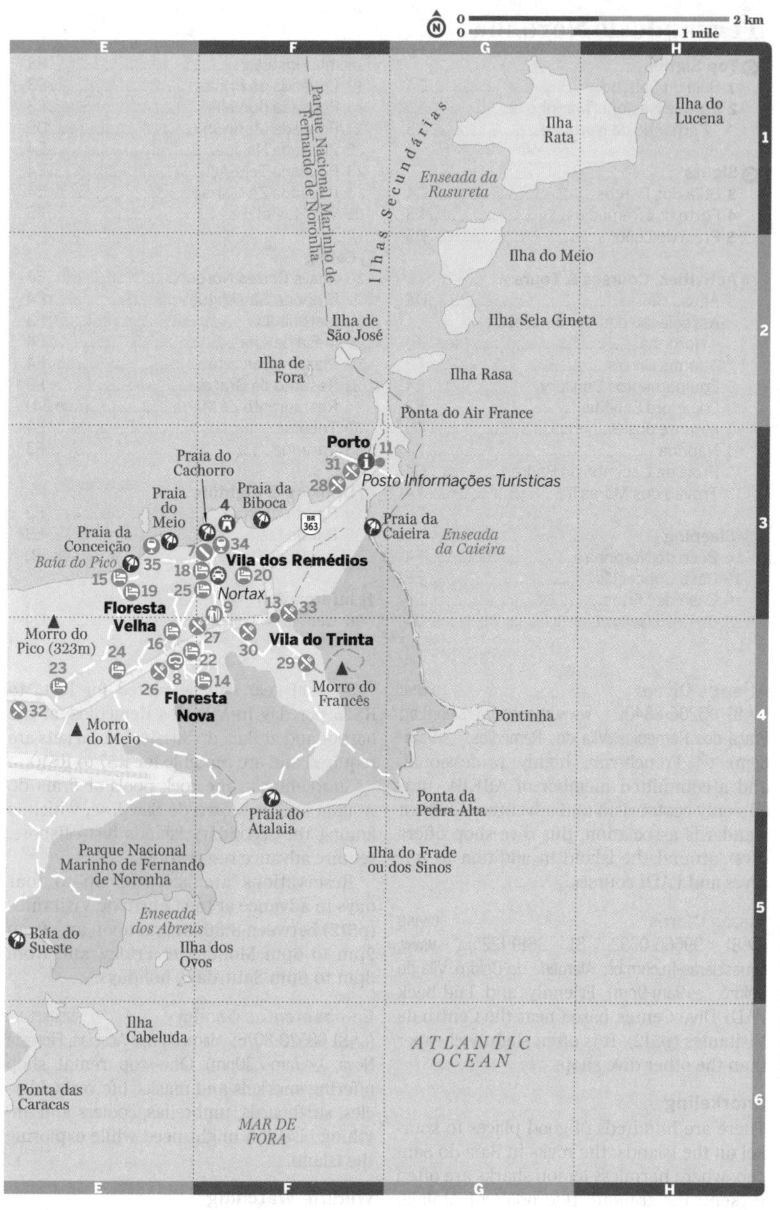

fish to spinner dolphins and giant sea turtles – diving around Noronha is world class. There are 230 fish species, including five types of (harmless) shark and 15 coral varieties. For certified divers, a two-tank dive including transfers and all equipment normally costs around R$680. Open Water courses cost around R$3800 and *batismo* (baptism) dives for first-timers are around R$200.

Fernando de Noronha

Top Sights

1 Baía do Sancho C4
2 Parque Nacional Marinho de Fernando de Noronha C5

Sights

3 Baía dos Porcos C4
4 Forte dos Remédios F3
5 Praia do Leão D5

Activities, Courses & Tours

6 Águas Claras D4
Associacão dos Condutores de Noronha .... (see 36)
7 Atlantis Divers F3
8 Equipamentos Danilory E4
9 Locadora SolyMar F3
10 Mirante dos Golfinhos C5
11 Naonda F3
12 Praia da Cacimba do Padre C4
13 Trovão dos Mares II F4

Sleeping

14 Beco de Noronha F4
15 Casa Conceção E3
16 Casa de Mirtes E4
17 Casa do Gerson D4
18 Ihla Hostel F3
19 Pousada da Praia E3
20 Pousada do Vale F3
21 Pousada Maravilha D5
22 Pousada Naiepe E4
23 Pousada Teju-Açu E4
24 Pousada Zé Maria E4
25 Vila Hostel F3

Eating

26 Açaí e Raízes Noronha E4
27 Empório São Miguel F4
28 Mergulhão F3
29 Mesa da Ana F4
30 Pizzaria Namoita F4
31 Recanto da Graça F3
Restaurante Zé Maria .... (see 24)
32 Tricolor E4
33 Varanda F3

Drinking & Nightlife

34 Bar do Cachorro F3
35 Bar do Meio E3
Bar Duda Rei .... (see 19)

Information

36 Centro de Visitantes D4

Atlantis Divers DIVING

(☎81 3206-8840; www.atlantisdivers.com.br; Praça dos Remedios, Vila dos Remédios; ⊙9am-8pm) French-run, highly professional, and a committed member of ABETA, Brazil's only ecotourism and adventure-tourism standards association, this dive shop offers dives around the island in addition to try-dives and PADI courses.

Águas Claras DIVING

(☎81 99666-0692, 81 3619-1225; www.aguasclaras-fn.com.br; Alameda do Boldró, Vila do Boldró; ⊙9am-9pm) Friendly and laid-back PADI Dive Center, based near the Centro de Visitantes (p512). It is often slightly cheaper than the other dive shops.

Snorkeling

There are hundreds of good places to snorkel on the islands: the rocks in Baía do Sancho, where harmless lemon sharks are often present; the tranquil tide pools of Atalaia; or Baía do Sueste, where you can swim with turtles at high tide. It's worth taking a local guide (R$60 for one snorkeler, R$40 per participant for two or more) in Baía do Sueste as they know where to find the greatest array of marine life.

Snorkel gear can be rented for R$15 to R$25 per day in Vila dos Remédios, at the harbor and at Baía do Sueste. Life jackets are required and are rentable for R$7 to R$10.

Snorkeling in the rock pools at Praia do Atalaia and at Morro de São José, which is among the secondary islands just offshore, require advance reservations.

Reservations are accepted up to four days in advance at the Centro de Visitantes (p512) between 8:30am and noon and from 2pm to 6pm Monday to Friday, and from 3pm to 6pm Saturdays/holidays.

Equipamentos Danilory SNORKELING

(☎81 98520-8076; Alameda das Acacias, Floresta Nova; ⊙7am-7:30pm) One-stop rental shop offering snorkels and masks, life vests, bicycles, surfboards, umbrellas, coolers and anything else you might need while exploring the island.

Wildlife Watching

From the clifftop lookout **Mirante dos Golfinhos** you can watch an average of more than 300 spinner dolphins cavorting in Baía dos Golfinhos from 6:30am. Trainee biologists provide Portuguese commentary from Monday to Saturday.

Several times a week, staff from the turtle-conservation NGO Tamar Project (www.tamar.org.br) head into the waters of Praia do Boldró and bring turtles back to the sand for tagging. Sometimes they emerge with a small juvenile turtle, while on other occasions they struggle out of the water with a large adult.

A biologist on hand gives commentary while visitors wait for the turtles to appear. The event is especially popular with younger visitors. Look for the timetable posted around town or at the visitors center.

Hiking

A few trails within the national park can only be walked with a local guide or with prior reservations. A popular trail runs from **Vila do Trinta** to **Praia do Atalaia**, where there's good snorkeling in tidal pools (no flippers or sunscreen allowed). It's possible to combine this trail with the **Trilha Pontinha Pedra Alta** which continues on to **Praia da Caieira**, where there are more tidal pools; note that the last 2km is on tough volcanic rock and a guide is obligatory for this part. It's about three to four hours return. Reservations for both trails are accepted up to four days in advance at the Centro de Visitantes (p512) between 8:30am and noon and from 2pm to 6pm Monday to Friday, and from 3pm to 6pm Saturdays/holidays. There are 96 spots per day allowed.

Other hikes, such as **Abreus** and **Morro São José**, must also be booked in advance. Morro São José also requires a guide and is only possible at low tide when a path appears. The longest trail on the island, the 5.2km **Trilha Capim Açu**, which runs from the Bahía do Sancho gate and ends at Praia do Leão, does not require advanced booking but does need a guide in order to cross some treacherous sections.

Portuguese-language guides (there are about 200 on the island) charge R$150 per person, usually with a two-person minimum, to guide a hike to Praia do Atalaia and Praia da Caiera, with prices increasing for longer hikes.

You can find a list of recommended guides and their contact details at the Centro de Visitantes or call in at the **Associacão dos Condutores de Noronha** (Acitur-FN; ☎81 99120-8280; condutoresdenoronha@gmail.com; Centro de Visitantes, Alameda do Boldró s/n, Vila do Boldró; ⏲8am-5pm) office in the same complex.

Surfing

Praia da Cacimba do Padre is the most famous surfing beach on Noronha and it hosts surf festivals and championships during the December to March season. Waves can reach 5m in height. Other surfing beaches on the Mar de Dentro, including Boldró and Bode, are also good, and in a big swell there are some thrilling waves among the Ilhas Secundárias.

Locadora SolyMar SURFING
(São Miguel, Vila dos Remédios; snorkel gear/boards per day R$10/R$70; ⏲7am-8pm) Rents surfboards and snorkel gear.

Sleeping

Noronha has around 150 pousadas, ranging from very basic to luxurious. Most are in the area of Vila dos Remédios, Vila do Trinta and Floresta Velha and only a handful have sea views. It's highly advisable to book ahead, and essential for the dozen or so most luxurious places (which charge R$1000-plus) except perhaps in May and June.

Note that some accommodations require 100% credit-card prepayment and a scan or photo of your passport. Most rates include airport transfers. High season runs from June to February.

Vila Hostel HOSTEL $$
(☎81 99687-1017, 81 3619-0091; www.vilahostelnoronha.com.br; Mestre Gouveia 399, Vila dos Remédios; dm/s/d/tr R$160/220/320/450) In an historic 18th-century building, Noronha's first hostel is comfortable and homey but the main reason to stay here is the energetic owners, who go above and beyond to ensure their guests get a full island experience. Graciela is a historian who will get you up to speed with local culture, while triathlete Pedro loves to guide guests outdoors.

Ihla Hostel HOSTEL $$
(☎81 3619-0132; São Miguel 333, Vila dos Remédios; dm R$150; ❄📶) With a privileged position right across from the church and close to Praia do Cachorro in the heart of Vila de Remedios, this well-run all-dorm hostel is a great budget choice. Facilities are bright and clean, including the spacious kitchen and social area, and there are free bicycles for guest use.

Casa do Gerson POUSADA $$
(☎81 3619-0216, 81 99540-8221; Praia da Boldró; r R$400; ❄) One of only two pousadas right on the sand on Noronha, this basic three-room

place is excellent value considering its sought-after location. Rooms are simple but comfortable with split-system air-conditioning and glass sliding doors out to the water. If hearing the waves crashing at night is more important to you than luxury or attentive service, this is your place.

Casa de Mirtes HOMESTAY **$$**
(☎81 99750-5211; www.facebook.com/casa.demirtes; Antônio Alves Cordeiro 457, Floresta Velha; s/d from R$150/210) Simple, clean accommodation in a welcoming private home decorated with quirky local art; though it is without services (breakfast and room cleaning), you can use the kitchen and garden barbecue. No English is spoken but the welcoming hosts go out of their way to make guests feel at home.

★ **Pousada Maravilha** BOUTIQUE HOTEL **$$$**
(☎81 3619-0028; www.pousadamaravilha.com.br; Bahia Sueste; r from R$2850;) The top pousada on a top-end island, Maravilha is a luxurious retreat with just a handful of bungalows perched on a hillside overlooking Bahia Sueste. There is a full-service restaurant and the panoramas from the infinity pool are first class. It's pricey but you won't find this level of comfort nor these views anywhere else on the island.

Casa Conceçião POUSADA **$$$**
(☎84 98807-3781; Praia Conceição; s/d R$1152/1280;) One of the island's only pousadas right on the sand, this cozy three-room place feels like an exclusive private residence in one of Noronha's best locations. Comfortable rooms open out onto a great wide veranda where breakfast is served. In front is an inviting garden area with a BBQ for guest use.

Pousada Naiepe POUSADA **$$$**
(☎81 3619-0001; www.pousadanaiepe.com.br; Alameda das Acácias 555, Floresta Nova; r R$680-735;) With just five solidly constructed rooms on the corner of the main road, this cute pousada wins over travelers with its value for money and attention to detail. It features a gorgeous, hammock-strung patio and garden and there's a good kitchen for guest use. When they're in, Duda, who speaks English, and Edilene are pillars of hospitality.

Beco de Noronha POUSADA **$$$**
(☎81 3619-1568; www.becodenoronha.com.br; Alameda das Acácias 3, Floresta Nova; s/d/t R$769/1082/1255;) With quaint eco-artisanal touches (such as short pathways made of upturned bottles) and charmingly helpful staff, wood-built Beco is a good choice for a comfortable stay in a central location on the island. Bonus: there's a Japanese bath in the garden!

Pousada do Vale POUSADA **$$$**
(☎81 3619-1293; www.pousadadovale.com; Pescador Sérgio Lino 18, Vila dos Remédios; s R$1170-1550, d R$1400-1850;) Intimate Vale is one of the most service-oriented pousadas on the island. Rooms aren't as high-end as the prices suggest, but are bright and well appointed with design-forward touches including *mantas nordestinas* (colorful throws). It is in a peaceful tree-filled valley just a short walk from Villa dos Remédios and the water.

Pousada da Praia POUSADA **$$$**
(☎81-3224-4476, 81 98829-9749; www.pousadadapraianoronha.com.br; Praia da Conceição; s R$787-1150, d R$847-1210, t R$1162-1452;) Just steps away from dramatic Praia da Conceicão, this small five-room pousada in the historic former Italian cable company building offers some of the best-value seaside rooms on the island. Historical protections prevent the alteration of some unfortunately small or odd window details, but otherwise you'll find plenty of comfort.

Pousada Zé Maria POUSADA **$$$**
(☎81 3619-1258; www.pousadazemaria.com.br; Nice Cordeiro 1, Floresta Velha; s R$918-2758, d R$1158-3458;) Luxurious Zé Maria boasts spacious hardwood rooms and a stunning view of the Morro do Pico from its pool. While it's hard to fault the rooms, lovely grounds or friendly and professional staff, it's important to note that it's a large and popular hotel which doesn't really offer the splendid isolation that many seek on the island.

Pousada Teju-Açu POUSADA **$$$**
(☎81 3040-0299; www.pousadateju.com.br; Estrada da Alamoa, Vila do Boldró; s R$2135-2542, d R$2317-2719;) Located almost underneath Morro do Pico, Pousada Teju-Açu is a well managed, quirkily designed pousada with a good restaurant. Rooms are spacious and quite stylish, with tiny bathrooms but huge beds, and there's a pleasant wood-decked pool area.

Eating

Most larger hotels have restaurants, and Noronha has a solid selection of independent eateries that are well worth a visit. But note that dining on Noronha is expensive, so if you're on a limited budget, consider finding self-catering accommodations. There are a couple of minimally stocked supermarkets around Vila dos Remedios and Vila do Trinta.

Recanto da Graça SOUP $

(Praia do Porto; soup R$20, mains for 2 R$100-120; ⏲7am-5pm) This simple blue *barraca* (stall) right on the sands of Praia do Porto serves up good-value fried fish plates, great soups and cold beers. The star of the show is the chunky *caldo de polvo* (octopus soup) – add a few drops of hot sauce and its hangover-busting properties are phenomenal.

Açaí e Raízes Noronha CAFE $

(BR-363, Floresta Nova; dishes R$12-60; ⏲9am-11:30pm; 📶) Locals and tourists alike people-watch from the veranda of this store that's good for *açaí,* tapioca and fresh sandwiches. They also offer a more substantial daily set meal, breakfasts and soup in the evenings and there are baked goods to go. Good wi-fi.

Empório São Miguel BUFFET $$

(☎81 3619-1859; Bosque Flamboyant, Vila dos Remédios; per kg R$84, mains R$48-88; ⏲11:30am-11:30pm Mon-Sat, 5-11:30pm Sun) The best of a few *por kilo* lunch places in Remédios, open-air Empório São Miguel has a good selection of dishes that change daily and usually include chicken, fish, pasta, sushi and salads. It also has some quality à la carte fare together with pizzas at night.

Pizzaria Namoita PIZZA $$

(BR-363, Vila do Trinta; pizza R$51-90; ⏲7-11pm Fri-Wed, closed last Wed of month) São Paulo émigré Mauricio Vilela does his best to recreate *pizza paulistana,* and does a fine job considering Noronha logistics. Favorites such as *cearense* (spicy ground sausage with chillis and mozzarella) are served in an atmospheric setting beneath the trees in his front yard.

★ **Mesa da Ana** BRAZILIAN $$$

(☎81 3619-0178; Estrada do Atalaia 230, Vila do Trinta; dinner per person R$250; ⏲seating 8:30pm) Husband-and-wife team Ana (a Cordon Bleu grad) and Rock (pronounced 'hockey;' Noronha's resident artist eccentric) serve only eight to 10 people per night at this rustic island gem. The four-course fish-heavy meals are served in a wonderful island setting. Make sure to arrive on time to avoid missing the first course and note that it's cash only.

Varanda BRAZILIAN $$$

(☎81 3619-1546; www.restaurantevarandanoronha.com.br; Major Costa 130, Vila do Trinta; mains R$60-98, mains for 2 people R$120-230; 📶) One of the best-value upscale choices, within walking distance of most pousadas, Varanda is an unpretentious place with a varied menu that includes a good selection of steak and seafood mains along with pasta, salad and risotto. The *moqueca* and shrimp with okra are outstanding.

Restaurante Zé Maria SEAFOOD $$$

(☎81 3619-1258; www.pousadazemaria.com.br; buffet R$230; ⏲7am-10pm Wed & Sat) Located inside the hotel (p510) of the same name, this high-end restaurant is famed Brazil-wide for its over-the-top, all-you-can-eat R$230 seafood buffet spectacle on Wednesday and Saturday evenings (reservations essential). Owner Zé Maria catches a good amount of the fish himself.

Most of the vegetables on the plates here – and indeed served in other restaurants around the island – come from the hotel's impressive hydroponic farm.

Tricolor BRAZILIAN $$$

(☎81 3619-1286; www.restaurantetricolor.com; BR 363, Vila do Boldró; mains for 2 R$120-220; ⏲noon-9:30pm) Run by a hardworking husband-and-wife team, this simple open-air place on the main road in Boldró offers tasty Bahian home cooking at reasonable prices. The menu is small and mostly seafood, with *moquecas* (fish cooked in a clay pot) and rice dishes specialties. Solo diners can order half plates of any of the mains.

Mergulhão MEDITERRANEAN $$$

(☎81 3619-0215; www.mergulhaonoronha.com.br; Av Joaquim Ferreira Gomes 40, Porto; mains R$94-198; ⏲noon-10pm Mon-Sat; 🖉) Mergulhão makes full use of its breezy site offering stupendous views over the port, while its Mediterranean menu with a Brazilian twist is one of Noronha's most innovative. Try the signature *peixe crocante* (crispy fish stuffed with shrimp, cheese and palm hearts) or the *arroz do amado* (grilled octopus rice with *coalho* cheese, cashews and fresh tomatoes).

Drinking & Nightlife

Bar Duda Rei BAR

(Praia da Conceição; ⏲10am-sunset) Noronha's only real beach *barraca* has a fabulous setting beneath a couple of palms, with Morro do Pico towering behind. It serves good food, too.

LAMPIÃO & THE CANGACEIROS

Apart from *forró* music, perhaps the biggest contribution of the Northeast to popular Brazilian culture is the cult of the *cangaceiros*, the legendary nomadic outlaws of the *sertão* (backlands of the Northeast) who held the nation to ransom from the late 19th century until the 1930s.

Born out of the desperate conditions in the interior at the time, the *cangaceiros* robbed ranch owners and government offices and kidnapped members of the upper classes for ransom. Upon entering towns, the outlaws would appeal for assistance and supplies from the local residents; those who collaborated were often richly rewarded and thus they began to develop a following among some sectors of the society.

From afar this soon developed into a Robin Hood–like mythology and despite the fact that in reality many were little more than brutal criminals out for personal gain, their resistance to authority made them heroes to ordinary downtrodden Brazilians.

The most famous *cangaceiro* of all was Virgulino Ferreira da Silva, known as Lampião, who together with his outlaw wife, Maria Bonita, controlled vast swathes of the interior in the 1920s and '30s. With his Gandhi-style glasses and free-flowing locks, Lampião looked more like an intellectual than a gunslinger, but the charismatic leader built a mystical cult of personality that reached far beyond his region of activity.

This fame infuriated the authorities and he was eventually ambushed and beheaded alongside Maria and most of his gang in 1938. But his legend lives on; you can still see his portrait in his signature leather hat proudly hanging on the walls of homes, bars and restaurants throughout the Northeast.

Bar do Meio BAR
(www.bardomeionoronha.com; Praia do Meio; ⏲noon-9pm) The fanciest of Noronha's bars, Bar do Meio is set on the headland that divides Praia do Meio and Praia da Conceição. It adds a touch of Ibiza to the Northeast vibe and is a good place for a drink with a view of Morro do Pico during the day or to check out the live music in the evening.

Bar do Cachorro BAR
(Vila dos Remédios; cover R$30-40; ⏲noon-midnight) The famous open-air 'Dog Bar' is the hub – in fact the only locale – of Noronha nightlife. It's busy every night but really packed from Thursdays through Sundays. There's music to dance to from around 10:30pm, including live *forró* on Fridays and *sertanejo* on Saturdays, and a saxophonist at sunset during the week.

Information

MEDICAL SERVICES

Hospital São Lucas (☎81 3619-1377; Bosque Flamboyant, Vila dos Remédios; 24hr) The island's hospital offers basic medical services.

MONEY

The ATM at the airport and the Bradesco bank branch at Vila do Trinta, across from Poty Supermarket, accept international cards, but they can run out of cash at weekends, so do bring some with you.

TOURIST INFORMATION

National park information is available from the **Centro de Visitantes** (Alameda do Boldró s/n, Vila do Boldró; ⏲8am-10pm), the **Kiosk** (Bosque Flamboyant, Vila dos Remédios; ⏲8am-10pm) in Bosque Flamboyant, **PIC Golfinho-Sancho** (Posto de Informações e Controle; ⏲8am-6:30pm) and **PIC Sueste** (Posto de Informações e Controle; Baiha Sueste; ⏲8am-6:30pm).

You can pick up a map at the **tourist info booth** (PIT; Porto; ⏲8am-6pm) above the port. There's another branch in the airport.

The island government site Fernando de Noronha (www.noronha.pe.gov.br) has every detail on the archipelago imaginable.

TRAVEL AGENCIES

Your Way (☎81 99949-1087; www.yourway.com.br) An indispensable contact on the island, this veteran ecotourism organizes accommodations and activities for independent travelers.

Getting There & Away

The **airport** (FEN; ☎81 3619-0950) sits in the middle of the main island. Azul (www.voeazul.com.br) and Gol (www.voegol.com.br) both fly Recife–Noronha–Recife daily; Azul also flies Natal–Noronha–Natal daily. Round-trip fares from either city normally range from R$700 to R$1200. Buy your ticket as early as you can.

GOL seats are available to Brazil and South America airpass holders, but availability is scarce.

Getting Around

A good bus service (R$5) runs the length of the BR-363 between the port, Vila dos Remédios, the airport and Baía do Sueste, about every 30 to 40 minutes from 7am to 11pm. You'll see bus-stop signs along the road. Hitchhiking, though we don't generally recommend it, is safe here and commonplace.

Taxis (☎81 3619-1314; Vila dos Remédios) (a few of which are buggies) have fixed rates from R$20 to R$45 depending on distance – drivers have a card showing the prices. The trip from the airport to Vila dos Remédios costs R$30, while from the port it's R$25.

A popular way to get around is to rent your own buggy. Rates for reliable vehicles range from R$250 to R$400 (on national holidays) per 24 hours, plus fuel. Be aware: vehicle owners on the island do not have insurance so you'll be expected to pay for any accidental damage.

Pousadas will usually organize a buggy for you, and all renters will deliver it to you, although many buggies on the island are not in good shape, so it's worth going to the rental places and checking out a few before making the choice. You can also rent motorcycles, if you are licensed for one back home.

PARAÍBA

Sandwiched between Pernambuco and Rio Grande do Norte, the small, sunny state of Paraíba contains the easternmost point of the continent, Ponta do Seixas, where you are closer to Senegal than to southern Brazil. The tranquil and orderly João Pessoa is a fine counterbalance to the crowded metropolises elsewhere in the region, with quality city beaches, good restaurants and plenty of parks. Just a short drive to the south there are many spectacular beaches backed by pink cliffs and lined with coconut palms, free from crowds.

João Pessoa

☎0XX83 / POP 811,600

The coastal city of João Pessoa – known as Jampa, a play on São Paulo's nickname of Sampa – is the capital of Paraíba and the third-oldest city in Brazil. It claims to have more trees than any other capital city, including an Atlantic rainforest preserve, and has a reputation for being friendly and safe. It's an increasingly popular holiday destination for Brazilian families.

The 20km-long beachfront, stretching north and south of the central coastal hub of Tambaú, is agreeably clean, low-key and low-rise (no buildings above four stories allowed) while the historic center, 7km inland, is being slowly spruced up after attaining National Heritage site status in 2007, and makes for an interesting wander. All in all, João Pessoa, or 'John Person', is a very nice spot to break up a journey.

History

Founded in 1585, the city was formerly known as Vila de Filipéia de NS das Neves. It was renamed in the 20th century for João Pessoa, a governor of Paraíba who formed an alliance with Getúlio Vargas to run for the Brazilian presidency in 1930. When courted by opposing political parties, João Pessoa uttered a pithy '*nego*' (I refuse), which is now given prominence in all Brazilian history books and emblazoned in bold letters on the Paraíba state flag. The Vargas–Pessoa ticket lost the election, and Pessoa was assassinated a few months later – an event which sparked a revolutionary backlash that swept Vargas to power later in 1930.

Sights & Activities

Every morning the Avenida Beira Mar along the length of the city beaches is closed to traffic from 5am to 8am to make space for runners and cyclists who come down in droves to exercise.

Centro Histórico

Under the guidance of IPHAN (Brazil's national cultural heritage institute), some parts of João Pessoa's historic center have been attractively renovated, with architectural styles ranging from baroque to art deco. The area makes for an enjoyable wander, although don't stray too far from the main attractions as it can get sketchy pretty fast. Tourist offices have a useful walking-tour map available, and there are many important churches dotted around town.

★Centro Cultural São Francisco MONASTERY

(Map p514; ☎83 3218-4505; www.igrejadesaofranciscopb.org; Praça São Francisco; admission with guided tour R$6; ⏲8:30am-5pm Mon-Fri, 9am-2pm Sat & Sun) This is one of Brazil's most beautiful monasteries. São Francisco's construction was interrupted by battles

Central João Pessoa

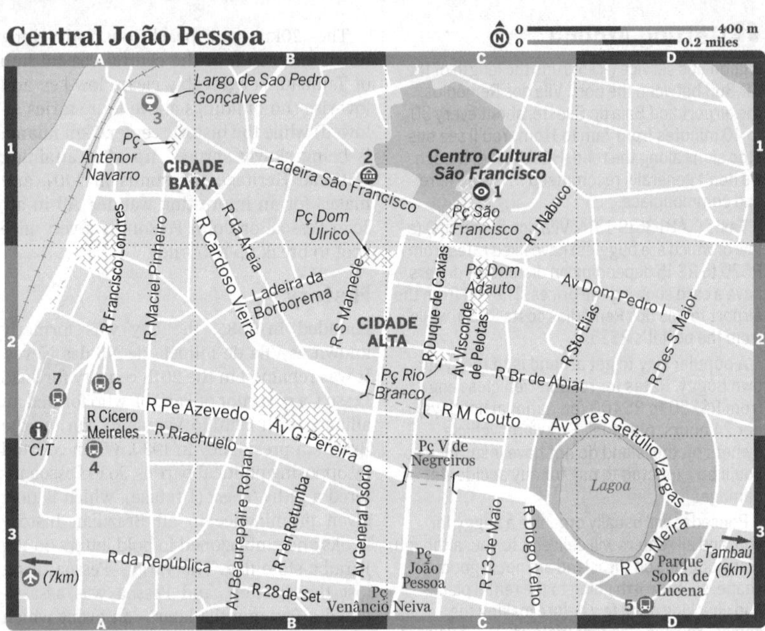

Central João Pessoa

Top Sights
1 Centro Cultural São Francisco............C1

Sights
2 Casa de Polvora...............................B1

Drinking & Nightlife
3 Vila do Porto....................................A1

Transport
4 Buses to Airport..............................A3
5 Buses to Tambaú & Manaíra...............D3
6 Terminal de Integração......................A2
7 Terminal Rodoviário Severino Camelo – Varadouro........A2

with the Dutch and French, resulting in an impressive but architecturally confused complex built over two centuries (1589–1779), with the facade, the church towers and the adjoining Santo Antônio monastery displaying a hodgepodge of styles.

Casa de Polvora HISTORIC BUILDING
(Map p514; Ladeira São Francisco; ⌚8am-6pm) On the side of the hill halfway between the Cidade Alta and Cidade Baixa, this arched brick building was erected in 1710 to store the city's gunpowder reserves. It now serves as a mini-cultural center hosting temporary art and photographic exhibitions and offers fine views over the river.

Tambaú & the Coast

Praia de Tambaú BEACH
(Map p516) Praia de Tambaú, 7km east of the center, is an urban beach but nevertheless an enjoyable area to spend time. Bars, restaurants, coconut palms, fig trees and a broad promenade are strung along the seafront. Southward, Praia Cabo Branco, a beautiful stretch of sand, cliffs and palms, curves 5km round to Cabo Branco and Ponta do Seixas.

Ilha de Areia Vermelha BEACH
Ilha de Areia Vermelha is an island of red sand that emerges off the northern beaches at low tide for roughly half the days in each month. Boats park around the island and the party lasts until the tide comes in. You can catch a boat out there for R$30 to R$35 from Praia de Camboinha, 15km north of Tambaú. Organize the trips in one of the beachside bars. Some boats have rowdy bars while others are more relaxed affairs.

Check in at the tourism office the day before to find out if a trip is going.

Festivals & Events

Folia da Rua STREET CARNIVAL

João Pessoa cuts loose in the Folia da Rua (Party in the Streets), held the week before Carnaval proper (Friday to Friday); *blocos* (music and dancing groups) parade through parts of the city, some attracting up to a million revelers.

Sleeping

The central beach neighborhoods of Tambaú, Manaíra and Cabo Branco are the best areas to base yourself.

Slow Hostel HOSTEL $

(Map p516; 83 3021-7218; www.slowhostel.net; Av Cajazeiras 108, Manaíra; dm with/without air-con R$55/50, s/d from R$95/150;) This excellent hostel has a friendly atmosphere and is set in a spacious house one short block from the beach. It's run by the charmingly helpful Marina and her family. Most of the rooms (single-sex and mixed dorms and one extreme-value private) have private bathrooms, and common areas are attractive and spacious.

Varandas Hostel HOSTEL $

(Map p516; 83 98164-3138; Av Bananeiras 251, Manaíra; dm R$40, r with/without bathroom R$130/90, r with air-con R$150;) A great-value family-run option a few blocks back from the beach in Manaíra, ultra-friendly Varandas has bright and impeccably clean rooms set over two stories surrounding a good pool. Breakfast is better than your average hostel offering.

Verdegreen Hotel HOTEL $$$

(Map p516; 83 3044-0000; www.verdegreen.com.br; Av João Maurício 255, Manaíra; s/d R$674/746;) Verdegreen is the eco-conscious choice on the main beach strip, with solar-heated showers, reforested wood, half-flush toilets, and LED TVs and lighting throughout. It's all very hip and stylish, too, decked out in soothing greens and beiges with tasteful art scattered around. If there's one downside, it's that the rooms can feel a tad small.

Eating

Most of João Pessoa's best restaurants are located in Tambaú and Manaíra. In the evening it can be difficult to find places to eat in the center.

Peixada do Amor SEAFOOD $

(Rua dos Cajueiros, Ponta do Seixas; mains for 2-3 R$33-40; 11am-5pm) For a cheap meal with a local flavor, head to this huge open-air restaurant south of the city. Pull up a plastic chair alongside the hordes of local families and take your pick from three types of fish – fried or with coconut or shrimp sauce, all served with rice and *pirão* (yuca flour with fish stock). Cash only.

Pão com Gergelim BURGERS $

(www.facebook.com/paocgergelim; Artur Enedino dos Anjos 78, Altiplano; burgers R$19-26; 6-11pm Tue-Sun;) These rockstar-themed gourmet burgers are worth the 3km haul up to Altiplano, where the owners' former home has been transformed into a trendy gathering point for beautiful carnivores. Hand-cut fries and local craft beers round out this hidden residential hot spot. A taxi from Tambaú is around R$15.

It's a great concept and the BB King with sweet pickles is a real winner, but where's the Hendrix?

Empório Café CAFE $

(Map p516; www.facebook.com/emporiocafe; Coração de Jesus 145, Tambaú; mains R$10-40; 4pm-1am Mon, to 2am Tue-Thu, to 4am Fri & Sat, to midnight Sun;) This alternative-indie cafe-bar dishes up great-value salads, sandwiches, quiches, hummus and cheese-and-meat platters to a beautiful crowd. As the evening wears on, Empório packs in more trend and beauty for cocktails and indie tunes and is the town's GLS (gays, lesbians and sympathetics) gathering point.

The entrance is behind the craft market on the Beira Mar.

★Mangai BRAZILIAN $$

(www.mangai.com.br; Av General Édson Ramalho 696, Manaíra; per kg R$66.90; 11am-10pm;) Mangai's spectacular regional buffet is available in other cities, but it hails from João Pessoa. Most items are labeled in English, and there's plenty for vegetarians, as well as great meat and seafood dishes. Save room for some of the decadent desserts!

Casa do Bacalhau PORTUGUESE $$

(Map p516; 83 3247-8511; Av Franca Filho 52, Manaíra; mains R$40-65; noon-3pm & 6:30-11pm, closed Mon) With tiled walls and waitstaff in traditional garb, this busy restaurant goes out of its way to recreate a piece of Portugal and the food is no letdown. Authentic

Tambaú

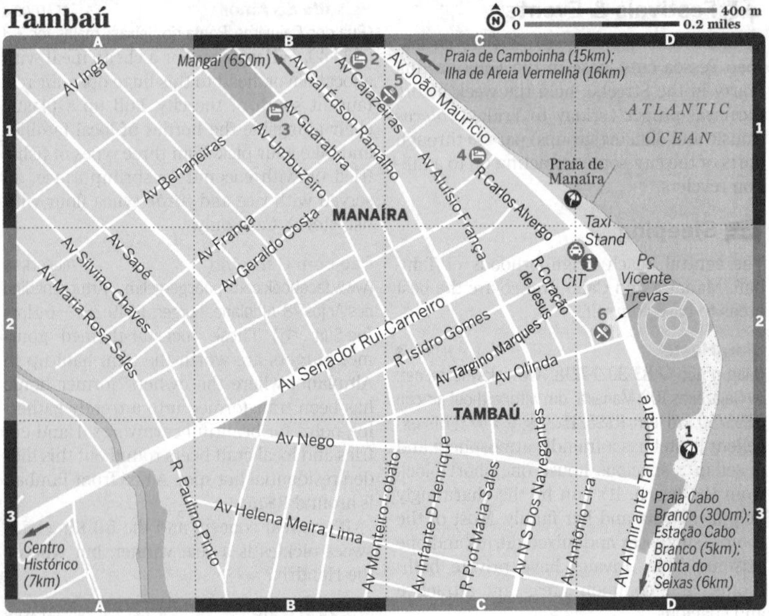

Tambaú

Sights
1 Praia de Tambaú D3

Sleeping
2 Slow Hostel B1
3 Varandas Hostel B1
4 Verdegreen Hotel C1

Eating
5 Casa do Bacalhau C1
6 Empório Café D2

seafood dishes, including *bacalhau* (salted cod) prepared in a dozen different ways, are delicious and generously proportioned. Wash it down with a bottle from the imported wine list.

Drinking & Nightlife

Nightlife in Tambaú is centered in the area near the Mercado de Artesanato on and around Rua Coração de Jesus as well as in the seafront kiosks, some of which offer live music.

The historic center has a lively nocturnal scene, with some good bars and music venues attracting students, their teachers and an informal, arty crowd. It's safe to travel to the historic center by bus till late afternoon, but best to taxi back later.

Vila do Porto BAR
(Map p514; ☎83 3222-6900; www.facebook.com/restauranteviladoporto; Largo de São Pedro Gonçalves 8; ⊙11am-2am Mon, to 8pm Tue-Thu, 10pm-5am Fri-Sat, 3-9pm Sun) A popular late-night spot in the historic center, Vila do Porto often has live music and has a pleasant courtyard overlooking the river. Generally Saturday is electronic music while on Sunday there is rock and on Monday it's samba.

☆ Entertainment

Bolero at Sunset LIVE MUSIC
(Praia do Jacaré; ⊙sunset) Almost every Brazilian tourist in João Pessoa heads to the north of the city to Cabodelo (10km from Tambaú) for sunset to see saxophonist Jurandy play Ravel's *Bolero* while being paddled up and down the Rio Paraíba in a canoe. The daily event is a supremely kitschy, classically Brazilian phenomenon; some people come from Natal and Recife just for this!

People can buy a ticket to watch from the water on catamarans (R$40), which also travel down the river for some sightseeing, or watch for free from the riverside where a loudspeaker amplifies Jurandy's notes.

Taxis from Tambaú are about R$30 each way; or ride bus 513 from Tambaú to the end of the line and transfer free to a Jacaré bus which is marked 'Cabedelo Intermares'. Don't linger afterwards – the area can get dicey once the crowds clear out.

Information

Deatur (☎83 3214-8022; Centro Turístico, Av Almirante Tamandaré 100, Tambaú; ⏰8am-10pm) Tourism Police office.

Banco do Brasil (Av Senador Rui Carneiro 166, Tambaú) ATMs in Tambaú.

The Paraíba tourism department (PBTUR) runs helpful, well-informed information offices. Some convenient locations:

Airport (Centro de Informações Turísticas; ☎83 98828-9769; www.destinoparaiba.pb.gov.br; Presidente Castro Pinto International Airport; ⏰11am-5pm & 10pm-4am)

Bus Station (Centro de Informações Turísticas; Map p514; ☎83 3218-6655; www.destinoparaiba.pb.gov.br; Bus Station, Rua Francisco Londres; ⏰8am-5pm Mon-Fri, 1-6pm Sat & Sun)

Tambaú (Centro de Informações Turísticas; Map p516; ☎83 3214-8185; www.destinoparaiba.pb.gov.br; Centro Turístico, Av Almirante Tamandaré 100, Tambaú; ⏰8am-7pm)

Getting There & Away

AIR

Presidente Castro Pinto Airport (JPA; ☎83 3041-4200), 8km west of the center, has flights to Rio, São Paulo, Brasília and the major cities of the Northeast.

BUS

João Pessoa's bus station, **Terminal Rodoviário Severino Camelo – Varadouro** (Map p514; ☎83 3221-9611; Francisco Londres), is located 8km west of Tambaú in central João Pessoa. The area around the terminal is not particularly safe, so don't wander around with bags.

Getting Around

A taxi from the airport to Tambaú costs around R$60 to R$85. Airport **buses** (Map p514; Cícero Meireles) (R$3.25) from central João Pessoa leave from the first of the four bus stops along Rua Cícero Meireles, coming from the bus station nearby.

A taxi from the bus station to Tambaú is around R$30 to R$40. For taxis from Tambaú, there's a **stand** (Map p516) near the corner of Av João Maurício and Av Senador Rui Carneiro.

Local buses run from the **Terminal de Integração** (Map p514; Padre Azevedo), across the street from the bus station. **Buses** (Map p514) 510, 511 and 513 run frequently to Tambaú (R$3.55, 25 minutes) via Parque Solon de Lucena. The 513 continues up the coast to Praia do Bessa.

Returning from Tambaú, catch them southbound on Av General Édson Ramalho or Rua Maria Sales.

RIO GRANDE DO NORTE

Pure air, sun, fine beaches and sand dunes symbolize this small state in Brazil's northeast corner. Rio Grande do Norte has one of the country's most spectacular coastlines, some 500km of beautiful beach after beautiful beach, many of them fronted by reefs with natural pools and backed by tall dunes or cliffs. The locals are generally very friendly and welcoming.

Natal

☎0XX84 / POP 885,180

Rio Grande do Norte's capital is a clean, bright and rather bland city that has swelled as a hub for coastal package tourism, much of it catering to Brazilian families. Its main attractions are touristic beaches, buggy rides and other organized excursions, restaurants and nightlife – it won't appeal too much if you seek museums, theater or wild empty strands.

BUSES FROM JOÃO PESSOA

DESTINATION	COST FROM (R$)	DURATION (HR)	COMPANY
Fortaleza	94	10	Viação Nordeste (www.viacaonordeste.com.br)
Maceió	85	7½	Catedral Turismo (www.catedralturismo.com.br), Gontijo (www.gontijo.com.br)
Natal	40	3	Viação Nordeste
Recife	40	2	Progresso (www.progressoonline.com.br)
Salvador	155	16	Catedral Turismo, Rota Transportes (www.rotatransportes.com.br)

THE TIMELESS SERTÃO

The interior of the Northeast, known as the *sertão,* is not all drought-stricken countryside and dirt-poor towns, as its stereotype might have us believe. The *sertanejos* (residents of the *sertão*) are a proud people with a rich popular culture evident in their music, festivals and artisanship. There is also amazing natural beauty out there in the rocky backlands, and fascinating evidence of a history stretching right back to the dinosaurs. The towns of the *sertão* are equipped with adequate hotels and pousadas and are served well enough by buses. The ideal (greenest and coolest) months to venture there are June and July. Natal-based Cariri Ecotours (p520) specializes in tours to these areas. These are a few highlight destinations to launch your explorations:

Ingá, Paraíba The **Pedra do Ingá** (www.pedradoinga.blogspot.com; R$5; ⏲9am-noon & 1-4pm Tue-Fri, 9am-1pm Sat & Sun) is a single rock 23m long and nearly 4m high in the middle of the Rio Ingá. It's covered in beautiful carvings that are possibly up to 5000 years old. It's 95km west of João Pessoa and 46km short of Campina Grande, a city famed for its huge **Festa Junina**, a party lasting all June.

Lajedo de Soledade, Rio Grande do Norte Rock paintings up to 10,000 years old (including the world's oldest macaw pictures), ancient ceremonial sites and ice-age animal fossils are all found here. Guided visits are run from the **Museu do Lajedo** (☎84 3333-1017; www.lajedodesoledade.org.br; Soledade; R$7; ⏲8am-5pm Tue-Sun), 75km southwest of Mossoró, near Apodi.

Lajedo de Pai Mateus, Cariri, Paraíba A bizarre, otherworldly, rocky landscape of round boulders, granite blocks, caves and ancient petroglyphs, some 70km west of Campina Grande; several Brazilian films have been shot here. Excellent accommodations are available at **Fazenda Pai Mateus** (☎83 3356-1250; www.paimateus.com.br; Cabaceiras; s/d R$230/275; ❄☕🏊).

Serra da Capivara, Piauí The earliest evidence of humanity in the Americas and a vast 30,000 rock paintings can be found in a dramatic rocky landscape near São Raimundo Nonato.

Most visitors stay in the beach neighborhood of Ponta Negra; it's a striking location, overlooked by fantastic dunes, with steady surf and some lively nightlife. The older part of Natal, including the unexciting city center, Cidade Alta, about 12km northwest of Ponta Negra, is on a peninsula flanked to the west by the Rio Potengi and to the east by Atlantic beaches and reefs.

History

An early Portuguese attempt to settle the Natal area in 1535 failed due to resistance of the *potiguares* (the local indigenous people) and French brazilwood traders. The Portuguese didn't return until December 25, 1597, when a fleet arrived at the mouth of the Rio Potengi with orders to build a fort to keep the French and *potiguares* at bay; the name Natal is Portuguese for Christmas. On January 6, 1598, the day of the Reis Magos (Three Wise Men), the Portuguese began building their fortress, the Forte dos Reis Magos.

Apart from a period of Dutch occupation (1630–54), Natal remained under Portuguese control thereafter. During WWII its strategic location close to Brazil's northeastern tip prompted Presidents Getúlio Vargas and Franklin D Roosevelt to turn the sleepy city into a supply base for Allied operations in North Africa. Thousands of US military were stationed here and the city became known as the 'Trampoline to Victory.' These days, it's marketed as the Cidade do Sol (Sun City), and with good reason.

Sights & Activities

Forte dos Reis Magos FORT

(⏲8am-4pm Tue-Sun) FREE The fort that got Natal started in 1598 still stands in its original five-pointed star shape on the reef at the tip of the peninsula at the north end of town. The views of the city, the Ponte Nova and the dunes across the Rio Potengi are fantastic.

The fort contains a chapel, a well, cannons and soldiers' quarters. It also boasts the Marco de Touros, a marker stone placed by the Portuguese in 1501 at Praia do Marco, near São Miguel do Gostoso, which is considered Brazil's oldest historical document. A taxi to

Central Natal

the fort from Praia da Areia Preta (reached by bus 56 from Ponta Negra) costs around R$15.

Dunas de Genipabu

Feeling adventurous? Try a popular and exciting outing to the spectacularly high and steep dunes about 10km north of the city near Genipabu, where you can be driven up and down the sand mountains for an hour or so in a beach buggy. A number of operators are recommended: **Natal Vans** (☎84-3642-1883; www.natalvans.com.br; Av Praia de Ponta Negra 8822, Ponta Negra; ⏱7am-10pm Mon-Fri, to 9pm Sun) and Marazul (p524) offer several fairly standardized out-of-town trips, easily booked through your accommodation.

You'll be asked if you want the trip *com ou sem emoção* (with or without excitement), and if you choose *com*, you'll be treated to thrills such as the Wall of Death and the Vertical Descent.

Operators generally include Genipabu as part of longer day trips (R$440 to R$680 per buggy depending on season) that may involve a 15km beach drive north from Genipabu to Jacumã – with a river crossing by raft – and several other stops for zip lining, dune surfing into lakes and other thrills. Buggies hold up to four passengers; operators can usually put separate individuals together to share the total cost.

Top Buggy ADVENTURE
(☎84 99996-8184; www.topbuggy.com.br; Av Moema Tinoco 1559) A pioneer in beach-buggy expeditions, Marcos offers trips far and wide, including multi-day adventures to Fortaleza. The office is way out of town on the way to Genipabu, so it's best to call to arrange trips.

Beaches

Natal's northern city beaches, **Praia do Meio** (Map p519), **Praia dos Artistas** (Map p519) and **Praia da Areia Preta**, stretching 5km south from the Forte dos Reis Magos to Farol de Mãe Luiza lighthouse, are lackluster urban beaches that get crowded at weekends and holidays. South of the lighthouse, the coast road Via Costeira continues 8km south to Ponta Negra, passing the calm **Praia da Barreira d'Água** and its resort hotels.

The nearly 400km of coastline between Natal and the Ceará state border (along which the coast veers from east-facing to north-facing) is a growing playground for weekenders and day-trippers from Natal, but there are still dozens of lovely beaches to enjoy. The further from Natal you go, the more isolated and empty the beaches become.

WORTH A TRIP

JACUMÃ & AROUND

The string of good beaches and small, spread-out villages from Jacumã to Tambaba, south of João Pessoa, make a relaxed and inexpensive stop on the way to or from Recife, or a day out from João Pessoa.

Jacumã, the biggest of the villages, has *forró* (popular music of the Northeast) bars by night and a thin 3km-long beach featuring colored sandbars, natural pools and pink cliffs (although other beaches in the area are more enticing). Praia de Carapibus, divided from Praia de Jacumã by a small bush-covered headland, is just 500m long, with low cliffs and pools, and merges into the broader Praia da Tabatinga, which curves nearly 2km south. The most beautiful beach is Praia dos Coqueirinhos, round the headland at the south end of Praia Tabatinga; it has coconut palms, high red cliffs, freshwater springs and a dozen *barracas* (stalls), but it can get overly crowded on weekends.

Turek (PB-008, Carapibus; mains for 2 R$64-120; 5-10pm Mon, Tue & Thu, noon-10pm Fri-Sat, to 5pm Sun, closed Wed), on the main road out of Jacumã, is the best choice for an evening meal, with its small but varied menu of steaks, ribs, pastas and traditional dishes, served at colorful tables under a large mango tree. **Pousada Bemtevi** (83-3290-1334; www.bemtevipousada.com; PB-008, Tabatinga; s/d from R$190/220;), beside the road 1km back from Tabatinga beach, offers 12-lovely, clean-lined rooms with queen-sized beds, solar-heated water and private sea-view terraces overlooking the attractive garden and pool, which is romantically lit at night.

Praia de Tambaba, 4km further south, is famed as the only official nudist beach in the region. Men may only enter the nude section if they are gay couples or accompanied by a woman. The clothing-optional part of Tambaba is also stunning, with a broad swathe of petrified sandstone forming natural tidal pools along the shoreline. Tambaba hosts the one-of-a-kind Open de Surf Naturista (Nude Surfing Festival) in August. Unless the tide is very high, it's possible to walk this entire coast along the beach.

Transportes Santa Maria runs buses about every hour from João Pessoa to Jacumã (R$7.50, one hour) from 5am to 10pm. They depart from the third of the four bus stops along Rua Cícero Meireles coming from the João Pessoa bus station. The 5:30am departure (only) continues to Tambaba, and there's one daily bus back at 5:20pm from Tambaba.

Shared taxis also run between João Pessoa and Jacumã, charging R$9 per person (or R$36 for the whole car); in João Pessoa you can find them near the Lagoa dos Irerês and near the bus station: ask for 'Jacumã' outside the Terminal de Integração or in Rua Cícero Meireles. Regular taxis charge around R$80 to R$100 to Jacumã.

Praia de Ponta Negra BEACH

Praia de Ponta Negra, at the far south end of town, is the nicest stretch of sand in Natal and one of the most appealing big-city beaches in the Northeast. Framed by tall dunes at both ends, it's 3km long and lined with beach bars, with the city's best selection of hotels, pousadas and restaurants in the streets behind. The surf here is consistent, if small.

Tours

Cariri Ecotours ADVENTURE

(84 99993-0027; www.caririecotours.com.br; Travessa Joaquim Fagundes 719, Tirol; 9am-5pm Mon-Fri) A very experienced agency, recommended for adventurous coastal and inland tours from Natal specializing in excursions with a nature or cultural focus. It can, for example, take you to Fortaleza along the beach via Galinhos, São Miguel do Gostoso and Canoa Quebrada using Land Rovers for transport, or to inland destinations such as Lajedo de Pai Mateus.

Festivals & Events

Carnatal PARADE, MUSIC

(www.carnatal.com.br; Dec) Natal's out-of-season Carnaval, Carnatal, takes to the streets of the Lagoa Nova district over four days in early December, with Salvador-style *trios elétricos* (bands playing atop huge trucks) and *blocos* (parade groups) sporting names such as Burro Elétrico (Electric Donkey) and Cerveja & Coco (Beer & Coconut). It's the wildest out-of-season Carnaval in Brazil.

Ponta Negra

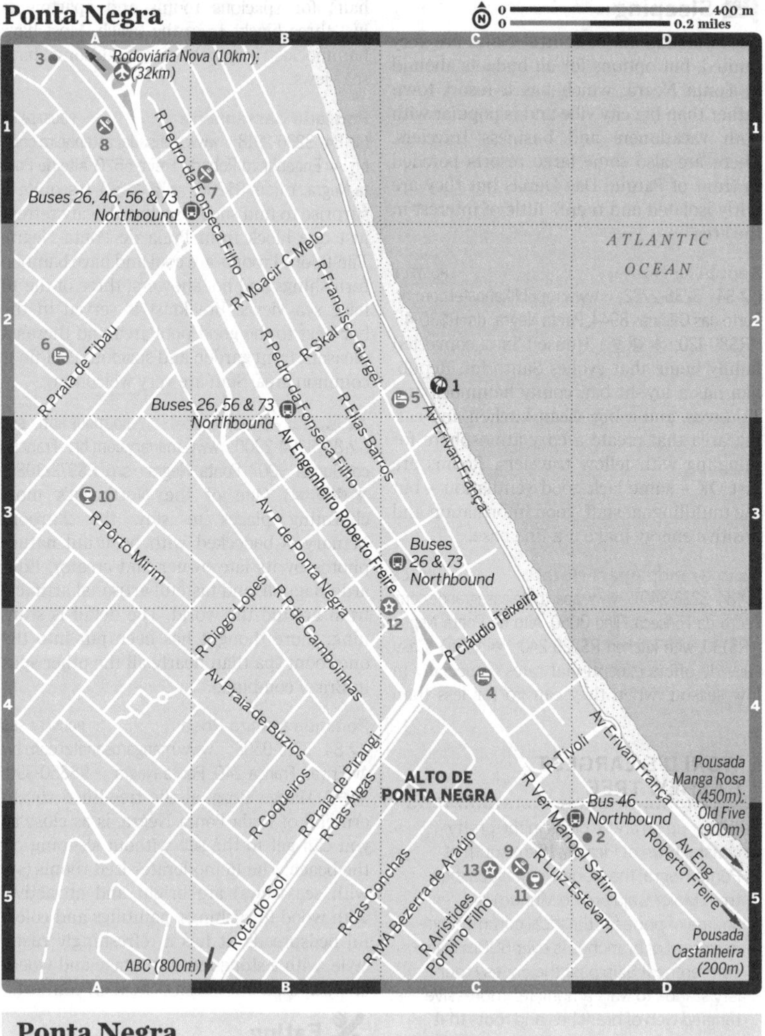

Ponta Negra

Sights
1 Praia de Ponta Negra ... C2

Activities, Courses & Tours
2 Marazul ... D5
3 Natal Vans ... A1

Sleeping
4 Casa Grande Apart-Hotel ... C4
5 Manary Praia Hotel ... C2
6 Republika Hostel ... A2

Eating
7 Camarões Potiguar ... B1
8 Casa de Taipa ... A1
9 Cipó Brasil ... C5
Manary Gastronomia & Arte ... (see 5)

Drinking & Nightlife
10 Bar 54 ... A3
11 Estacão do Malte ... C5

Entertainment
12 Decky ... C3
13 Rastapé Casa de Forro ... C5

Sleeping

Accommodations in central Natal are very limited, but options for all budgets abound in Ponta Negra, which has a resort town rather than big city vibe and is popular with both vacationers and business travelers. There are also some large resorts perched in front of Parque Das Dunas but they are fairly isolated and there's little of interest in the area.

Republika Hostel HOSTEL $
(84 3236-2782; www.republikahostel.com.br; Porto das Oficinas 8944, Ponta Negra; dm R$30-45, r R$80-120;) Housed in a converted family home that evokes Santorini, Republika has a low-lit bar, comfy hammock and TV areas, and a big, clean kitchen and eating area that create a cozy atmosphere for mingling with fellow travelers. Rooms are just OK – some lack good ventilation – but the multilingual staff, good information and positive energy make it a fine base.

Casa Grande Apart-Hotel HOTEL $
(84 3236-3401; www.aparthotelcasagrande.com; Pedro da Fonseca Filho 3050, Alto de Ponta Negra; r R$130, with kitchen R$220-240;) Casa Grande offers exceptional rates (especially in low season, when they can go for less than half) for spacious rooms and apartments just three blocks from the beach. Most have hammock-strung balconies and some have sea views.

Pousada Castanheira POUSADA $$
(84 3236-2918; www.pousadacastanheira.com.br; Av Engenheiro Roberto Freire 5620, Alto de Ponta Negra; r from R$206;) It's quite a surprise to find such a secluded, leafy retreat just one block from Praia de Ponta Negra. Tile-floored rooms are cool and have bamboo furnishings and hot showers; three of the 10 have sea views. Breakfast is served in the bar next to the good pool area and there's a pleasant front garden and spacious 2nd-floor common area. Staff are very welcoming.

★ **Manary Praia Hotel** BOUTIQUE HOTEL $$$
(84 3204-2900; www.manary.com.br; Francisco Gurgel 9067, Ponta Negra; s/d R$972/1080;) One of the Northeast's most charming places to stay, the 23-room Manary is bedecked with beautiful nature photos by its late owner and creator, Eduardo Bagnoli, and tasteful artisanal artifacts from around the world. The detail is stunning: more thought has been put into the one-room spa than nearly all the other spas in Brazil combined.

Pousada Manga Rosa POUSADA $$$
(84 3219-0508; www.mangarosanatal.com.br; Av Erivan França 240, Ponta Negra; r R$350-390;) Manga Rosa, at the tree-lined southern end of Praia Ponta Negra, is as close as you can get to the sea without sleeping on the beach. The 15 moderate-sized rooms (six with sea views) are bright and attractive, with wood furnishings, paintings and colorful bedspreads. It has a refreshingly rustic style, with a stone-faced frontage and wooden balconies, but doesn't cheat on comfort.

WORLD'S LARGEST CASHEW TREE

Taking up an entire block in the pretty coastal town of Pirangi, 15km south of Ponta Negra, the world's largest cashew tree (Maior Cajuiero do Mundo) is a source of pride for the local community: its sprawl of branches is over 500m in circumference! Skip past the cheesy touristy stands to walk among its impressive tangled web of branches and roots that spiral out from the main trunk to form an interwoven enchanted forest. Climb the lookout to appreciate the scale.

While it's already the undisputed champion, the tree is still growing and sprawling out of its fenced-in lot onto the roads outside, forcing the local government to seek a way to reshape the urban environment to free up more land.

Buses to Pirangi (R$3, one hour) leave from the side of the BR gas station on Av Cel Estevam next to the Rodoviária Nova (p525) every 30 minutes between 6am and 7:30pm.

Eating

During the day it's possible to find a good meal in downtown Natal but in the evening the area shuts down. Most of the city's best restaurants are found around Ponta Negra, where fresh seafood and ocean breezes make for a relaxed meal.

Casa de Taipa BRAZILIAN $
(www.facebook.com/casadetaipatapiocariaecuscuzeria; Av Praia de Ponte Negra 8868, Ponta Negra; dishes R$12-36; 6-11pm, closed Wed;) What is probably Brazil's most famous *tapiocaria* flips the script on a traditional street food and turns it into a gourmet treat fit for

OFF THE BEATEN TRACK

GALOS & GALINHOS

On a narrow sandbar between a brilliant blue inlet and the ocean, 160km northwest of Natal, these two isolated fishing villages are still only emerging as beach destinations and are fantastic places to unwind surrounded by some magnificent nature. The peninsula is in many ways the quintessential Northeast fantasy – tiny colorful villages, backed by dunes with marvelous beaches and phenomenal sunsets, and inhabited by friendly locals who prepare delicious seafood meals. It's a slice of paradise, but the oil rigs just offshore show that development is never far away, and tour vans have already started rolling in, so make space in your itinerary to visit before it all changes.

The breezes here can be good for kitesurfing, and boat, buggy, horseback and horse-cart excursions are easily arranged. There are numerous accommodations in Galinhos with a mix of simple hotels and pousadas both on the beachfront and facing the lagoon; in Galos there aren't many options apart from the recommended **Pousada Peixe-Galo** (84 3206-8841; www.pousadapeixegalo.com.br; Rua da Candelária 30, Galos; r R$390;).

Access to Galos and Galinhos is not particularly easy, which is also part of the charm. The most exciting approach is by beach buggy from São Miguel do Gostoso. Private buggy hire for up to four people costs R$400/500 per one-way/round-trip transfer.

Expresso Cabral (www.expressocabral.com.br) runs one bus a week from Natal to Pratagil (R$32, three hours) just across the inlet from Galinhos. The bus leaves the Rodoviária Nova at 6am on Sunday and returns from Pratagil at 5:15pm.

Alternatively, take a Macau-bound Cabral bus (departing Natal every three hours from 6am to 6pm) as far as the Galinhos turnoff *(trevo de Galinhos)* on Hwy BR-406 (R$35, 2½ hours), and then a taxi to Pratagil (organized through Galinhos/Galos accommodations).

Public boats run every half an hour between Pratagil and Galinhos (10 minutes, 24 hours); the service is free, although it's customary for visitors to give the captain a small tip. There are three or four free public boats a day between Galinhos and Galos (15 minutes); otherwise you can hire a buggy or private boat for R$40 to R$60. If you don't have too much luggage, it's a fairly easy walk along the beach between the villages.

If you have a vehicle, you can leave it safely parked under lights at the Pratagil car park for free.

Taxis between Natal's airport to Pratagil should cost around R$350; an Uber will cost significantly less.

foodies. Droves of visitors and locals alike swarm this colorful and festive place for lightly pan-grilled tapioca 'pancakes' stuffed with sweet and savory goodies (vegetables, cheeses, grilled salted meats, prawns – even a *moqueca* version).

★Camarões Potiguar SEAFOOD **$$**
(www.camaroes.com.br; Pedro da Fonseca Filho 8887, Ponta Negra; mains for 2-3 diners R$81-131; 11:30am-3:30pm & 6:30pm-midnight, to 11pm Sun) This bright, stylish and creative homage to the shrimp is arguably Natal's best dining experience, and it's permanently packed. Start with a traditional shrimp-and-Catupiry *pastel* (thin square of dough stuffed with shrimp and cheese then fried) then follow up with anything from shrimp in a pumpkin to our fav: the Bonfim (sauteed with cashews, *coalho* cheese and fragrant *biquinho* peppers with *vatapá* risotto).

Old Five SEAFOOD **$$**
(84 3025-7005; www.oldfive.com.br; Av Erivan França 230, Ponta Negra; mains R$25-85; 9am-6pm Mon-Tue, to midnight Wed-Sat, to 10pm Sun;) Voted Natal's best beach bar, this American-owned Ponta Negra hot spot completely transformed the forgotten far end of the beach. During the day, dig your toes in the sand with a cocktail in hand and order from all manner of dishes including plenty of fresh seafood, risottos, burgers and salads. At night, candles and lamps move the atmosphere into more romantic territory.

Cipó Brasil PIZZA **$$**
(www.cipobrasil.com.br; Aristides Porpino Filho 3111, Alto de Ponta Negra; pizzas R$29-78; 6pm-midnight;) A unanimous favorite, this fun jungle-themed place is great for sesame-crusted pizza (more than 30 types, from shrimp and four cheese, to banana and chocolate) and both savory and sweet crepes. It's

BUGGYING THE NORTHEAST: THE GOOD, THE BAD & THE UGLY

With broad, sandy beaches that stretch along much of the 1800km-long coastline from Tamandaré (Pernambuco) to São Luís (Maranhão), the Northeast is Brazil's true beach-buggy paradise. These four-wheel, five-seat contraptions – usually built on a VW Beetle chassis – roar along beaches and up and down dunes the length of the region, with cargoes of happy tourists enjoying off-road trips amid fabulous scenery with the ocean wind in their hair.

If you can cope with the fact that buggies guzzle a liter of gasoline every 5km or 6km, and make an unholy racket, a buggy trip is invariably a lot of fun. One passenger sits in front with the driver; up to three sit in the back, although with bags it can be a tight fit. Trips can be as short or long as you like, and you can stop wherever you please. The Dunas de Genipabu (p519) make a fun half-day outing from Natal, while the 180km round-trip from São Miguel do Gostoso to **Galinhos** and back is a fabulous day trip.

Even longer trips such as Natal to **Fortaleza** (in Ceará; 700km), Fortaleza to **Jericoacoara** (nearly 300km), or Jericoacoara to the **Lençóis Maranhenses** (in Maranhão; 300km) are quite feasible.

The Natal to Fortaleza stretch is one of the most beautiful and least-developed coastlines in Brazil, strung with colored cliffs, rolling dunes, salt flats, reefs, palm-lined beaches, freshwater lagoons, tiny traditional fishing villages and some larger settlements popular with local weekenders. The trip takes four to five days and passes approximately 92 beaches; at the economic end prices begin from R$4800 per buggy, including transport, guide, and fees but excluding accommodations and meals, and increase up to R$4300 per passenger for more complete packets including comfortable pousadas, transport and an English-speaking guide.

Make sure you go with an authorized driver. Marcos from Top Buggy (p519) is a pioneer in the field and knows the area inside out, while **Marazul** (☎84-3219-6480, 84-99608-8000; www.marazulreceptivo.com.br; Vereador Manoel Sátiro 75, Ponta Negra; ⏰8am-noon & 3-7pm) also organizes long-distance expeditions. It's also possible to do these trips more comfortably in 4WD with agencies such as Natal's Cariri Ecotours (p520). Coming from Jericoacoara try Jeri Off Road (p542).

For good environmental reasons and/or consideration for other beach users, local regulations prohibit vehicle traffic on certain beaches and dunes on some or all days, and sometimes you have to duck inland around river mouths, mangrove areas and so on, but there is still plenty of beach to roar along.

a starting point for evenings out. Get there early to avoid waiting. On Saturday there is an all-you-can-eat pizza *rodízio* for R$35.

Manary Gastronomia & Arte BRAZILIAN **$$$**
(☎84 3204-2900; www.manary.com.br; Francisco Gurgel 9067; mains R$59-89; ⏰noon-4pm & 7-11pm; 🖉) The Manary Praia Hotel's (p522) poolside restaurant serves creative salads and superb seafood and is one of Natal's very best restaurants. During the day it's a fairly laid-back affair but in the evening they turn up the romance a couple of notches. It has one of the best vegetarian menus in town and is famed for its rich desserts and cocktails.

Drinking & Nightlife

The Alto de Ponta Negra neighborhood in the upper part of Ponta Negra, around Rua MA Bezerra de Araújo and Rua Aristides Porpino Filho, is dense with a variety of bars, and packed from Wednesday to Saturday nights. Sex tourism is an unfortunate part of this scene but has been reduced significantly. Petrópolis, in the city center, is the best neighborhood for hip local bars and *botecos* (open-air bars).

Bar 54 BAR
(www.facebook.com/54bar; Pôrto Mirim 8995, Ponta Negra; ⏰6pm-2am; 📶) One of Ponta Negra's best bars, especially if you want to mingle with the cool kids away from the rowdier, tourist-geared places. A breezy patio flush with vintage furniture and tables of reclaimed wooden cable spools sets the vibe.

Estacão do Malte BAR
(www.estacaodomalte.com; Poeta Jorge Fernandes 146, Alto de Ponta Negra; ⏰6pm-midnight Tue-Sat) Tucked away a couple of blocks from the beach, this corner bar has a rock soundtrack

and a decent selection of Brazilian craft beers on tap; most are from the south of the country but there are a couple produced right in Natal. It attracts a youngish, slightly alternative crowd.

Entertainment

Rastapé Casa de Forró LIVE MUSIC
(☎84-3219-0181; www.rastapecasadeforro.com.br; Aristides Porpino Filho 2198; cover R$20; ⏰10pm-4am Thu-Sat) Hugely popular with locals and visitors alike, this massive *forró* club has a faux abode facade that represents the humble houses of the interior of the region. Inside there's three separate sections – two with live music and a more relaxed bar area that's good for taking a breather or striking up a conversation. It's a welcoming place where it's easy to socialize.

Arena das Dunas FOOTBALL
(☎84 3673-6800; www.arenadunas.com.br; Av Prudente de Morais 5121; tours R$30; ⏰9am-4pm Tue-Sat) Natal gained the futuristic and intimate 31,375-seat Arena das Dunas, located about halfway between the city center and Ponta Negra, for its four group-stage matches in the 2014 World Cup. Today it's the home of **America** (www.americadenatal.com.br; Arena das Dunas, Av Prudente de Morais 5121), which along with **ABC** (www.abcfc.com.br; Estadio Maria Lamas Farache, Rota do Sol), represent the city in the professional leagues of Brazilian football (both are usually found in national Série B).

Decky LIVE MUSIC
(www.facebook.com/deckybaroficial; Av Engenheiro Roberto Freire 9100, Ponta Negra; ⏰6pm-5am Tue-Sat) While it's a bit too polished to be much of a cultural experience, this popular spot in Ponta Negra pulls a crowd across several age brackets with live rock, blues, jazz or MPB every night from 8:30pm. Plop down on the massive, breezy patio or inside the spacious main room with air-con. Expect a cover charge.

Shopping

Centro de Turismo ARTS & CRAFTS
(Map p519; ☎84 3211-6149; Aderbal Figueiredo 980, Petrópolis; ⏰8am-6pm) Set in a restored neo-classical building that once served as the city jail, the Centro de Turismo houses a lot of craft and souvenir stalls and offers fine views over the city. Downstairs it's mostly clothes, hammocks and other textiles but the 2nd-floor gallery sells more diverse crafts.

Information

There's a central **Banco do Brasil** (www.bb.com.br; Av Engenheiro Roberto Freire & JM Vasconcelos) ATM to the north of Ponta Negra, plus the airport, **Praia Shopping** (www.praiashopping.com.br; Av Engenheiro Roberto Freire 8790, Ponta Negra; ⏰10am-10pm; 📶) and **Natal Shopping** (Av das Brancas Dunas, Candelária; ⏰10am-10pm) malls all have ATMs that should accept non-Brazilian cards.

Hospital Walfredo Gurgel (☎84 3232-7500; www.walfredogurgel.rn.gov.br; Av Salgado Filho, Tirol) The main public hospital, with emergency service.

Tourist Police (Delegacia Especializada Assistência Ao Turista; ☎84 3232-7402; Praia Shopping, Av Engenheiro Roberto Freire 8790, Ponta Negra; ⏰8am-6pm Mon-Fri) can be found at Praia Shopping.

Getting There & Away

AIR

Natal's **Aeroporto de Natal** (Aeroporto Internacional Governador Aluízio Alves; ☎84 3343-6060; www.natal.aero; Av Ruy Pereira dos Santos 3100, São Gonçalo do Amarante) is in São Gonçalo do Amarante, around 35km west of Ponta Negra. It has scheduled flights to many international cities in addition to services to all over Brazil.

BUS

Long-distance buses go from the **Rodoviária Nova** (☎84 3205-2931; Av Capitão Mor Gouveia 1237), northwest of Ponta Negra, which received a facelift for the 2014 World Cup.

CAR

Recommended car-rental companies with airport desks include **Avis** (☎84 3343-6277; www.avis.com.br; Aeroporto de Natal; ⏰6am-midnight) and **Localiza Hertz** (☎84 3343-6395; www.localizahertz.com; Aeroporto de Natal; ⏰24hr). Located outside of Natal's airport, **Foco** (☎84 99969-9978; www.aluguefoco.com.br; Nazireu Samuel 100, São Gonçalo do Amarante; ⏰24hr) sometimes offers slightly better rates than the in-airport competition and has a shuttle van from the arrivals area.

Getting Around

TO/FROM THE AIRPORT

Natal's airport at São Gonçalo do Amarante is quite a haul, 35km west of Ponta Negra. **Trampolím da Vitória** (☎84-3343-5151; www.trampolimdavitoria.com; R$4.20; ⏰5:10am-11:10pm) runs a public bus that's hardly worth the hassle from Ponta Negra. You need to catch bus 46, 54 or 73 along Av Engenheiro Roberto Freire to **Midway Mall** (Av Bernardo

Vieira 3775, Tirol) (R$3.35, 45 minutes), then switch for the 'R' bus, which hems and haws its way to the airport (R$4.20, 1½ hrs, every 30 to 45 minutes from 5:10am to 11:30pm), passing the bus stop directly in front of the bus station exit along the way. From the airport, catch the 'R' just outside Arrivals. Most travelers opt for the far more convenient shared van services such as **24 Horas Turismo** (☎84 3343-6430, 84 3086-1349; www.24horasturismo.com.br; R$30) and **Van Service** (☎84-3278-3013, 84-4141-2848; www.vanservice.com.br; airport transfer R$40; ⏲8am-10pm), which run shared vans to Natal ($40) and Praia da Pipa (R$60) usually leaving after each flight; to the airport; make a reservation in advance for pickup three hours before departure.

A **taxi** (☎84 3343-6429; www.coopcon.com.br; Aeroporto de Natal, Av Ruy Pereira dos Santos 3100) from the airport costs about R$100 to Ponta Negra, R$226 to São Miguel do Gostoso and R$240 or so to Praia da Pipa.

TO/FROM THE BUS STATION

For Ponta Negra (Av Engenheiro Roberto Freire), catch bus 66 (R$3.35) from the stop opposite the Petrobras gas station next to the Rodoviária Nova; a taxi costs R$35 to R$50 depending on time of day and location in Ponta Negra.

From the city center take buses 19, 38 or 23–69 from the **Rodoviária Velha** (Map p519; Praça Augo Severo) local bus terminal.

BUS

From stops north of Rota do Sol on Av Engenheiro Roberto Freire in Ponta Negra, **buses 26**, **46** and **73** run north to the Praia Shopping and Via Direta malls; 56 goes along the Via Costeira to Areia Preta then heads inland towards the city center.

Most city center buses leave from the Rodoviária Velha local bus terminal.

City bus fares are R$3.35.

Praia da Pipa

☎0XX84 / POP 6500

Pipa is one of Brazil's magical destinations: pristine beaches backed by tall cliffs, dreamy lagoons, decent surfing, dolphin- and turtle-filled waters, a great selection of pousadas, hostels, global restaurants and good nightlife. It was just another small, roadless fishing village when discovered by surfers in the 1970s; today Pipa rivals Jericoacoara (Ceará) as the Northeast's hippest beach town, and attracts partiers from Natal, João Pessoa, Recife and beyond at holidays and weekends, and a slew of international travelers year-round. Its laid-back, ecological and independent-traveler vibe still reigns and, with luck, Pipa may be just too small for that to change, despite the ranks of umbrella'ed tables along the main beaches catering to van loads of day-trippers from Natal.

Sights

Pipa boasts some of the best beaches in the Northeast, with many framed by towering cliffs that protect the wilderness by limiting access and keeping development at bay.

The main beach, **Praia da Pipa** (Praia do Centro), about 1.5km long, has fishing boats, numerous bars and restaurants, and rock pools at low tide.

Praia do Madeiro curves northward from the headland at the far end of Baía dos Golfinhos and is perhaps Pipa's most enchanting stretch of sand. It has a few upmarket hotels on the cliffs above but the sands below are free of buildings. It's good for beginner surfers (individual classes/three day courses cost around R$80/210).

BUSES FROM NATAL

DESTINATION	COST FROM (R$)	DURATION (HR)	COMPANY
Aracati (Canoa Quebrada)	70	6	Expresso Guanabara (www.expressoguanabara.com.br), Viação Nordeste (www.viacaonordeste.com.br)
Belém	522	36	Expresso Guanabara
Fortaleza	98	8	Viação Nordeste, Expresso Guanabara
João Pessoa	44	3	Viação Nordeste, Autoviação Progresso (www.progressoonline.com.br)
Recife	96	4½	Autoviação Progresso
Salvador	250	21	Gontijo (www.gontijo.com.br)
São Miguel de Gostoso	18	2½	Expresso Cabral (www.expressocabral.com.br),

Praia do Amor, the advanced surf beach, is accessed off the eastern part of Av Baía dos Golfinhos. You can rent surfboards here and in town for around R$30 per hour (or R$50 for the day); swimming can be dangerous. For a fantastic view of Praia do Amor and beyond head to the **Chapadão**, a fantastic viewpoint at the cliff's edge on the southern side of town.

Lagoa de Guaraíras, behind the river mouth at Tibau do Sul, 8km northwest of Pipa, is one of the area's most stunning landscapes, a massive, dune- and mangrove-bound lagoon, particularly spectacular at sunset. The dockside Creperia Marinas (p528) is a brilliant sunset-viewing spot.

Santuário Ecológico de Pipa NATURE RESERVE
(☎84 99982-8044; Baia dos Golfinhos s/n; R$15; ⏲7am-5pm) This small, privately owned reserve, 2km west along the main road from the town center, does a valuable job of protecting at least some of the Pipa coast from development. Well-marked trails lead through secondary forest to impressive lookouts over Baía dos Golfinhos and Praia do Madeiro, from which you can often see large green turtles at high tide.

Tours

Bicho do Mangue KAYAKING
(☎84 98176-5736; www.bichodomangue.blogspot.com.br; per person R$35) Does excellent 2½-hour guided kayak excursions starting about an hour before high tide. The tour leaves from the Bicho do Mangue *barraca* on the beach in Tibau do Sul and goes through the Lagoa de Guarairas and then into the mangroves. You can book through accommodations in Pipa.

Sleeping

Pipa has dozens of pousadas, hostels and hotels, ranging from dumpy to five-star gorgeous. Many accommodations offer good discounts in low season.

Pipa Hostel HOSTEL $
(☎84 3246-2151; www.pipahostel.com.br; Arara 105; dm/d R$40/120; ❄@🛜🏊) More sedate than some hostels, this HI hostel has good air-conditioned facilities with tidy private bathrooms. Separate-sex, six- or eight-bed dorms and private rooms overlook a large grassy garden with a pool. The pleasant and well-traveled staff speak English and are a good source of information for further adventures around Brazil. Rents bicycles for getting around town.

DOLPHIN VIEWING IN PIPA

Baía dos Golfinhos, immediately to the west of Praia da Pipa, is where you can get up close and personal with dolphins within about 2½ hours either side of low tide. The area is backed by cliffs and accessible on foot only from the main beach – during which time you can get cold beer, coconuts and caipirinhas from enterprising locals. Try to avoid viewing dolphins from the boat tours; they do not all have a reputation for properly respecting the marine life or the environmental rules in place.

Hostel do Céu HOSTEL $
(☎84 3246-2235; www.hosteldoceu.jimdo.com; Rua do Céu 153; dm/d/tr R$45/160/190; P@🛜🏊) It's no party hostel, but this Argentine family-run spot offers some of the best budget infrastructure in Pipa, with top-notch separate and mixed dorms and, if you can manage to snag it, the best-value private room in town: a colorful top-floor space complete with large, breeze-blown windows, and both sea *and* sunset views!

Media Veronica Hostel HOSTEL $
(☎84 3246-2607; www.mediaveronicahostel.com; Rua da Albacora 267; dm R$33-38, r with/without bathroom from R$133/95, all excl breakfast; ❄🛜) This relaxed hostel is a labor of love for Argentine Juan Pablo, who impresses with reasonable prices and an emphasis on cleanliness, security and information for guests. Dorms come in four-, six- and eight-bed configurations (the latter is cramped) and a few private rooms have sea and floral garden views.

Paraíso das Tartarugas POUSADA $$
(☎84 99455-5183; www.paraisodastartarugas.net; Praia do Amor; r from R$200; 🛜) If you've dreamt of staying in a wooden shack inches from the ocean, 'Turtle Paradise' is your place. The seven rooms and apartments are rustic but clean and pleasant, and four have decks almost on top of the waves. While it's just a short walk from town, here there is nothing but nature.

The pousada is 200m along the shore from the east end of the main beach; at times it can involve scrambling over rocks – take care when the tide's up. If you're coming with bags, it's easier to access it from the marked path leading from the Praia do Amor carpark.

Morada dos Ventos POUSADA $$
(☎84 3246-2284; www.moradadosventos.com; Rua dos Colibris 3; 1-/2-bedroom apt R$300/500; ❄📶🏊) Large one- and two-bedroom hexagonal apartments in a breezy location; a good restaurant with a well-stocked bar; and a large garden and excellent pool make this welcoming Dutch-Brazilian operation a dependable choice.

Pousada Tamanduá POUSADA $$
(☎84 3246-2734; www.pousadatamanduapipa.com.br; Tamanduá 3; r R$200-250; ❄📶🏊) This cute and intimate 12-room place, run by an amiable young couple, has pretty rooms adorned with framed Peruvian patchwork cushion covers and appealing stone-and-wood stairs and walkways.

Pousada Xamã POUSADA $$
(☎84 3246-2267; www.pousadaxama.com.br; Rua dos Cajueiros 12; r R$220; ❄@📶🏊) Hidden up a side street near Pipa's southeastern edge is one of the Northeast's best-value pousadas. Spacious, pleasantly decorated rooms with good modern bathrooms have glass doors opening onto a leafy, flower-fringed pool and garden area, with hammocks and hummingbirds. The breakfast is good and there's a gym and sauna, as well as a social area with pool table.

Pousada Alto da Pipa POUSADA $$
(☎84 3246-2281; www.pousadaaltodapipa.com.br; Rua da Gameleira 555; r R$220; ❄@📶🏊) This cute and colorful pousada uphill from the main street has small, clean and pretty pastel-hued rooms, but it's the setting along a lush courtyard-garden, with palm trees and small footbridges over tiny ponds inhabited by lazy turtles, that makes it a special find.

★**Toca da Coruja** POUSADA $$$
(☎84 3246-2226; www.tocadacoruja.com.br; Av Baía dos Golfinhos; r R$995-1605; ❄@📶🏊) 🌿 One of Brazil's most charming luxury pousadas, Toca da Coruja is an eco- and community-conscious place wrapped in sprawling tropical gardens with sagui monkeys, birds and two gorgeous pools. All rooms are huge, but the deluxe bungalows are gigantic, with breezy wraparound verandas in the style of old Northeast ranch houses.

Spa da Alma POUSADA $$$
(☎84 3246-2357; www.spadaalma.tur.br; Rua do Spa 9; s/d from R$330/360; ❄@📶🏊) 🌿 On lush, sprawling hilltop grounds, 1.5km beyond the southeast edge of town, this great-value place boasts luxury at reasonable prices. The scattered bungalows offer wide bay windows and verandas with incredible views towards the beaches below; there's a gorgeous pool overrun with peacocks beside the restaurant, and a lovely multiservice garden spa down below.

Eating

Pipa is a wonderful place to eat out, but prices are generally higher than in other places in the region.

Gelateria Preciosa ICE CREAM $
(Av Baia dos Golfinhos 1074; scoops R$9-17; ⏲noon-11pm Tue-Sun; 📶) Beat the heat at this Italian-owned gelateria. The 16 flavors change daily, but stalwarts include the namesake Preciosa (with Belgian chocolate) and Variegato Amarena (cream-based with Italian cherries). They also serve good coffee and iced drinks.

Creperia Marinas CRÊPES $
(☎84 3246-4111; www.hotelmarinas.com.br; Av Governador Aluizio Alves 301; crepes R$16-45; ⏲11am-8pm) The dockside Creperia Marinas is a brilliant sunset-viewing spot over Lagoa de Guaraíras (p527). Take your pick from sweet or savory crepes or a salad and enjoy the panorama.

★**Cruzeiro do Pescador** SEAFOOD $$
(☎84 3246-2026; www.cruzeirodopescador.com.br; cnr Av Baía dos Golfinhos & Concris; mains R$65-85, for 2 people R$125-230; ⏲1-4pm & 7-10:30pm; 📶) On the southeast edge of town, about 1.5km from the center, what looks like a typical mess of a house hides a don't-miss culinary experience. Chef Daniel does everything with homemade and home-grown finesse, from the poetically hand-written menus and the romantic candlelit setting to the products from his own garden. The flavors of his cooking – some pinched from India and Bahia – are delicious.

Tapas FUSION $$
(☎84 99465-4468; Bem-Te-Vis 8; dishes R$11-73; ⏲6:30-11pm Tue-Sat; 🖉) Tapas is a culinary godsend, a labor of love of a well-traveled *paulista* couple who dish out large Brazilian tapas peppered with Thai, Indian, French and Italian influences in a casual and artsy space. Sesame-crusted fresh tuna is one specialty, but it's all tasty, including the shrimp with honey and ginger, and the arugula, lettuce, mango and Gorgonzola salad.

El Farolito ARGENTINE $$
(☎84 3246-2643; Rua da Albacora; mains R$40-63) There's a large Argentine community in Pipa and this simple place pleases homesick travelers with good-sized portions of imported Argentine beef served with great chimichurri and a selection of wines. There's also *milanesas* (breaded meats) and a couple of pasta dishes.

Aprecíe INTERNATIONAL $$
(☎84 99422-8604; www.facebook.com/aprecierestaurante; Bem-Te-Vis 34; mains R$39-72; ⊙6:30-11:30pm) One of Pipa's few *potiguar* chefs runs this notable and intimate little place with just seven tables. A small but well-rounded menu awaits; whichever of the substantially portioned mains you choose – our favorite is the sesame-crusted tuna – you'll find yourself with order envy when you see the others go by!

Pan'e Vino ITALIAN $$
(Rua da Albacora; mains R$23-55; ⊙6:30-10:30pm Tue-Sun) Real Italian food from well-traveled Roman-born chef Michele, whose passion for fresh ingredients can be seen in his ever-changing menus: lamb with rosemary; Messina-style fish with capers, olives and white wine; plus homemade pasta, risottos and pots of real Italian basil (seeds brought over direct from Italy!).

Garagem SEAFOOD $$
(Praia do Centro; plates R$28-38, mains R$38-65; ⊙10:30am-sunset; 📶) With superb views of Pipa's cliffs, Garagem got its start as a famous bar, and is still good for sundowners; but it's also the best spot in Pipa proper for a beach lunch, such as excellent Argentine *picanha* (rump steak), fresh fish, sandwiches and salads and a Bohemia to wash it down. It's the westernmost bar on the main beach.

Drinking & Nightlife

Nightlife focuses on Av Baía dos Golfinhos between Rua do Céu and Rua Bem-Te-Vis, which is lined with bars that are usually pretty full by mid-evening. There's often live music in at least one bar.

Orishas BAR
(☎84 9815-26547; Rua da Praia 9; cocktails R$8-20; ⊙9am-10pm) All by itself at the far end of the main beach away from the crowds, this colorful bar set on wooden decks right above the sea is easily Pipa's best place to drink. Come early for the fantastic views across the bay to the cliffs and stick around in the evening for the live music.

Nativos Bar BAR
(Av Baía dos Golfinhos 748; cocktails R$12-39; ⊙6pm-1am) The classiest and certainly the most beautiful option along a bar-heavy stretch of Av Baía dos Golfinhos.

Boate dos Calangos CLUB
(☎84 3246-2429; www.facebook.com/calangos; Av Baía dos Golfinhos; ⊙from 1am Fri-Sun) A big dance hall at the far end of Av Baía dos Golfinhos that fills for live *forró* on Sunday and Euro-style DJs the other nights.

Shopping

Bookshop BOOKS
(☎84 98882-7172; Rua da Gameleira; ⊙7:30pm-10:30pm Thu-Sat) A cute wooden house with a good selection of books in 18 languages, for rent or trade, and a chill spot for an evening coffee. Portuguese owner Sandra runs a free library for local residents and gladly receives book donations.

Orientation

Pipa is small but it can be a little hard to get your bearings on arrival. The main, central beach faces north. At its east end the coastline curves southeast to Praia do Amor. To its west, Baía dos Golfinhos and then Praia do Madeiro curve northwest. The narrow main street, Av Baía dos Golfinhos, runs about 2km through town parallel to the main beach and Praia do Amor, with small streets and lanes running off it down to the beach or uphill inland. The inland streets in central Pipa are, from west to east, Céu, Bem-Te-Vis, Gameleira, Mata and Albacora (with Arara branching off Albacora).

Information

DANGERS & ANNOYANCES

Crime does occur in Pipa, doubtless exacerbated by the use of crack-cocaine in some areas here. Don't leave belongings unattended on beaches and don't leave valuables lying around in your room.

MONEY

Cash is king in Pipa – many places do not accept cards at all or only accept debit cards. At the time of writing, options for foreign cards were limited to high-fee-charging Banco 24-horas, which has six fairly reliable ATMs around town, including near the **bus stop, the central plaza** (Av Baía dos Golfinhos 234; ⊙8am-10pm), and the town **center** (Vila Pipa Shopping, Av Baía dos Golfinhos 647). For branches of other banks, it's necessary to travel to Tibau do Sul or Goianinha.

TOURIST INFORMATION

There's a new tourism **information office** (84 99608-9999; Av Baía dos Golfinhos; 8am-6pm) at the beginning of Av Baía dos Golfinhos at the entrance to town.

Pipa is also extraordinarily well endowed with helpful, informative websites. Take your pick from www.pipa.com.br or www.pipa.tur.br.

TRAVEL AGENCIES

Mandacaru Expedições (84 99988-5892; www.mandacaruexpedicoes.com.br) This excellent small Pipa-based agency can arrange any Brazilian travel experience or itinerary based on its widely traveled owner's personal knowledge. There's an emphasis on high ecotouristic and safety standards. Highlights include buggy tours both north and south, tips for dolphin sightings and excursions further afield.

Pipatour (84 3246-2234; www.pipatour.com; 3-8pm) Helpful agency for flight, bus and tour bookings.

Getting There & Away

Full-size public buses and tour vans stop at the west end of Av Baía dos Golfinhos; public minibuses and microbuses terminate on Rua dos Cajueiros close to the corner with Av Baía dos Golfinhos near the southeast edge of town.

Riograndense (84 3205-4388; Rodoviária Nova; R$19) has 10 daily buses (six on Sundays) from Natal's Rodoviária Nova (p525) to Pipa (R$19, 1½ hours) and back. Last departure from Natal is 6pm and from Pipa is 6:30pm except on Sundays when it's 5pm and 5:30pm respectively. Going to Pipa from Natal, you can also catch the bus at the stop on Av Salgado Filho in front of Carrefour in Lagoa Nova (reached from Ponta Negra by bus 26, 46 or 73), about 10 minutes after they leave the Rodoviária Nova.

Alternatively, **Opcional** (84 3205-6868; Rua dos Cajueiros) runs microbuses from the Rodoviária Nova to Pipa at 5:30am, 9:10am and 1:55pm, returning from Pipa to Natal at 7:30am, 11:30am and 4:30pm (R$18, 2½ hours).

Schedules on all these services change frequently, so check in advance.

If you're coming by bus from the south, get out at Goianinha (1½ hours from João Pessoa), where minibuses – nicknamed 'Dolphin van' – run every 10 to 15 minutes to Pipa (R$4.50, 50 minutes, from 5am to 11:40pm) from behind the faded pale-blue church, 250m off the main road. In Pipa they leave from the van stop at the Av Baía dos Golfinhos near the southeast edge of town from 5:45am to just after midnight.

Pipatour can reserve bus seats from Goianinha to Recife or Salvador for a R$20 fee.

Getting Around

A private taxi between Aeroporto de Natal (p525) and Pipa should cost R$240. **Pipa Aventura** (84 3246-2024; www.pipaaventura.com.br; Av Baía dos Golfinhos 654; R$80-90; 8am-10pm) offers airport transfers by reservation for R$80 per person (minimum four people) between 6am and 10pm, and R$100 between 10pm and 6am. Book in advance.

São Miguel do Gostoso

0XX84 / POP 9605

'Gostoso,' 110km northwest from Natal, is an increasingly popular weekend and holiday getaway, with an excellent wide beach and a fine selection of pousadas, restaurants and bars. It also has several gorgeous little-known beaches nearby that are mostly empty. If you want to go somewhere still undiscovered by package tourism and still be awed by the scenery, go here, now.

Sights & Activities

The main beaches in town – **Praia do Maceió**, **Praia da Xêpa** and **Praia do Cardeiro** – make up a wide, continuous 2km stretch of relaxing sands; but the true gem is **Praia de Tourinhos**, 8km west at the end of a gravel road. It's a beautiful semicircular bay with just a few kiosks, and nothing more. During the week you won't share it with more than a few others. You can walk there along the coast, or take a round-trip by moto-taxi (R$25 per person) or buggy (R$120 for up to four).

Dr Wind KITESURFING

(84 99981-0583; www.drwind.com.br; Ponta do Santo Cristo; 9:30am-5:30pm) A recommended kitesurfing school that offers six-hour beginner courses for R$1080 and individual classes (per hour with/without equipment R$200/160). Also rents equipment for R$215 per day with discounts for longer-term rentals. Surfboards (R$25 per hour) and SUP boards (R$50 per hour) are also available.

Clube Kauli Seadi KITESURFING, WINDSURFING

(84 99197-1297; www.clubekauliseadi.com; Praia do Cardeiro; 9am-5:20pm) Run by a champion multi-discipline sportsman, Clube Kauli Seadi offers six-hour kite courses (R$900) in English, Spanish and Portuguese and rents equipment.

Buggy Trips to Galinhos

About three hours each way, the sand-traversing adventure from São Miguel do Gostoso to Galinhos is an unforgettable wind-blown expedition along a spectacular 90km sequence of long, empty beaches, dunes and lagoons. The trip can be organized through your accommodations (R$400/500 one way/round-trip for up to four people).

Sleeping & Eating

Pousada Ilha do Vento POUSADA, HOSTEL **$$**
(84 3263-4048; www.ilhadovento.com.br; Caraúnas 70; r R$180-290;) A superb option on a sizable garden property at the east end of town. Rooms are spotless, comfy, well designed and pleasingly decorated, with sofas molded into the walls. There's a pool and kitchen for guest use, the breakfast is top quality and the well-traveled Italo-Brazilian owners are super-helpful and welcoming.

Pousada Casa de Taipa POUSADA **$$**
(84-3263-4227; www.pousadacasadetaipa.com.br; Bagre Caia Coco 99; r R$230;) The owners of this spot, 300m from the beach, are English-speaking and lovely to the core. The property has a Northeastern cultural theme and is especially memorable for the artsy endeavors of one of the owners, who has painted beautiful murals in each room and decorated the common spaces with wonderful features.

Pousada Chantilly POUSADA **$$**
(84 3263-4216; www.pousadachantilly.com; Av Enseada das Baleias 1403, Praia da Xepa; r R$170-220;) A discerning choice right next to the main beach, this small eight-room hotel has eight elegantly finished rooms with top-quality bedding and high-end bathrooms set around a nice pool in a lush garden.

★ **Pousada dos Ponteiros** HOTEL **$$$**
(86 3263-4007; www.pousadadosponteiros.com.br; Enseada das Baleias 1000, Praia do Maceió; s/d/t from R$286/372/458;) One of the first hotels in town and still one of the best, this place is set on a hectare of tropical gardens that run down to the beach. It features a variety of elegant and spacious rooms that are big on privacy, and charming social areas, including an elegant 'sand-pool' and a lookout offering views over the dunes.

Bar do Tico SEAFOOD **$**
(Praia do Cardeiro; mains for 2 R$32-50; 10am-8:30pm;) Just across from wide Praia do Cardeiro, this simple beach bar does simple fare very well: the *posta de cavala* (mackerel), served with salad, fried potato or *macaxeira* chips and *farofa* (seasoned tapioca flour), is a treat along with a couple of beers.

★ **Genesis Resto Bar** BRAZILIAN **$$**
(Praia da Xêpa 86; mains R$30-58; 6-10:30pm) What comes off as a tad ramshackle at first glance reveals itself as Gostoso's most adorable bistro, serving up a choice few gussied-up dishes – curried shrimp fettuccine, sesame-crusted tuna, a gourmet burger – in a whimsical space donned with rustic furniture and Frida Kahlo kitsch. If the mains were just a bit more generous, it would be pretty close to perfect.

Information

There's a Bradesco ATM on Av dos Arrecifes that accepts foreign cards, but it can be temperamental.

Getting There & Away

Expresso Cabral (84 3205-4572; www.expressocabral.com.br) runs six daily buses from Monday to Saturday from Natal's Rodoviária Nova (p525) to Gostoso (R$18, two to three hours, 6:15am, 9:45am, 11:30am, 2:30pm, 3:15pm and 4:45pm); the 6:15am and 2:30pm departures go express via BR-101, which is a significantly shorter trip. On Sundays, departures from Natal are at 7:15am, 2:15pm and 4:45pm.

Taxis from Aeroporto de Natal (p525) should cost around R$230, while a buggy along the beach costs R$1000.

Westbound public transportation is nonexistent, so if you are heading on to Galos and Galinhos, you'll either need to fork out for a buggy (p531) along the beach or head back through Natal.

Ceará, Piauí & Maranhão

Includes ➡

Ceará.......................... 533
Fortaleza.................. 533
Canoa Quebrada........ 543
Icaraí de Amontada ... 549
Jericoacoara 550
Maranhão................ 556
São Luís 556
Parque Nacional dos Lençóis Maranhenses............ 564

Best Places to Eat

- ➡ Bistro Caiçara (p553)
- ➡ Pimenta Verde (p553)
- ➡ Tamarindo (p553)
- ➡ 50 Sabores (p540)
- ➡ Espaço Gourmet (p549)

Best Places to Stay

- ➡ Casa Zulu (p549)
- ➡ Oh! Linda Pousada (p548)
- ➡ Vila Kalango (p552)
- ➡ Villa Chic (p552)
- ➡ Refugio Hostel Fortaleza (p538)

Why Go?

These three Northeastern states stretch along Brazil's only north-facing coast and back deep into the arid interior. The main draw for visitors is the beaches of Ceará, arrayed for hundreds of glorious kilometers either side of Fortaleza, the state's fun-loving biggest city. These are some of the very best beaches in Brazil, some supporting growing resort towns, others at most a small, traditional fishing village. The hip travelers' hangout Jericoacoara, uniquely located inside a dune-swept national park, is the jewel in Ceará's gorgeous coastline.

An adventurous coastal route leads west from Jericoacoara to the scenic, wildlife-rich Delta do Parnaíba and the vast expanse of high dunes and clear lagoons known as the Lençóis Maranhenses, one of Brazil's highlights. The beauty of the Lençóis will floor you. Further west still lie two of Brazil's most picturesque, intriguing colonial gems: half-decayed, half-restored São Luís, with its markedly Afro-Brazilian culture, and its perfect sleepy neighbor Alcântara.

When to Go

Fortaleza

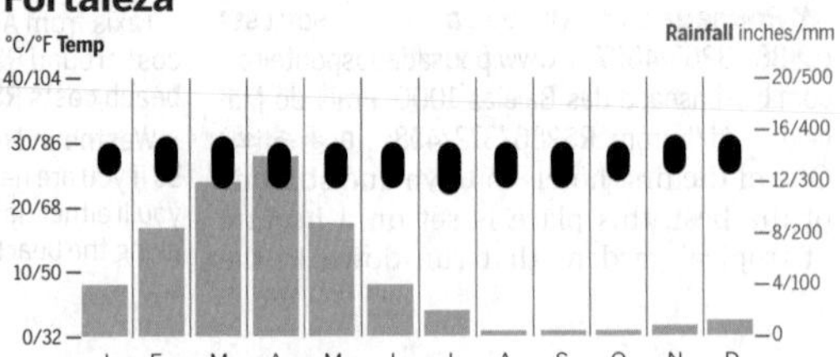

Mar–May Best waves for surfing in many places, including Jericoacoara.

Jul Fortaleza's Carnaval fills the streets with color and music.

Aug–Jan Constant strong breezes make the coast one of the world's premier kitesurfing destinations.

History

The Portuguese were slow off the mark in occupying these distant northern lands; it was the French who founded São Luís, the capital of Maranhão, in 1612. But the raising of the French flag – along with the founding of the fort at Fortaleza by the Dutch – spurred the Portuguese into action and they soon exerted their authority on the ground.

Until 1774 Maranhão was governed together with Pará as a separate entity from the rest of Brazil, with the capital at São Luís. Piauí was first settled inland by poor cattle herders moving westwards from Ceará and north from São Paulo in the 17th and 18th centuries.

Despite fierce resistance, the indigenous population in the state was defeated by the 18th century. Once the wars ended, the colonists in the interior were faced with serious droughts. As many as two million people died in droughts in Ceará in the 1870s, with survivors streaming into Fortaleza. Neighboring Piauí was initially landlocked but eventually a land swap was arranged with Ceará in the 19th century so that it could enjoy the benefits of a coastline. Piauí still has the lowest population density of any Brazilian state.

Fortaleza, with its commerce and tourism, is the region's economic powerhouse. Some large industrial projects have been sited near São Luís in recent decades, but all three states are still among Brazil's poorest.

Getting There & Around

Fortaleza has an international airport with flights from Europe as well as from many Brazilian cities. São Luís and Teresina are served by domestic flights. Fortaleza, Teresina and São Luís have bus connections with Natal and Recife to the east, and cities to the south such as Brasília, Rio and São Paulo. There are also buses from the main cities to Belém at the mouth of the Amazon, but the stretch between São Luís and Belém has a history of bus robberies, so it's an idea to consider flying that journey. In general, flying into or out of the region is often cheaper than a long bus trip.

Buses link pretty much every town and village in this region. Road quality has improved a lot, though access to a few coastal villages, including Jericoacoara, is unpaved. Beach buggies and 4WDs with drivers provide trips along the coasts and dunes. A hire car is useful if you plan to visit some smaller places with limited bus service, but you should research road conditions first as some less-traveled routes require 4WD – notably the stretch between Paulino Neves and Barreirinhas on the route between Parnaíba and the Lençóis Maranhenses. Fortaleza is the easiest place to organize a rental vehicle.

CEARÁ

In a country of glorious coastlines, Ceará has one of the most glorious of all: almost 600km of beautiful and varied beaches, from idyllic little palm-fringed bays to 20km strips washed by ocean breakers. From the busy urban beaches of Fortaleza, to hip Jericoacoara, to the smallest of fishing villages where people still sail *jangadas* (triangular-sailed fishing boats), Ceará has everything you could wish for in terms of beach ambience.

Much of the coast is backed by large expanses of high white dunes, lending a starkly elemental touch to the landscape, while the waves and winds provide some of the world's best conditions for kitesurfing, surfing and windsurfing.

But Ceará is not all about chilling on soft sands. Fortaleza is one of Brazil's biggest cities and boasts one of the country's most happening nightlife scenes, while the interior is home to the giant caves of Parque Nacional de Ubajara (p544).

Fortaleza

0XX85 / POP 2.6 MILLION (METROPOLITAN AREA 3.6 MILLION)

Considering its isolation, Fortaleza is a surprisingly large and sprawling place. It's one of Brazil's biggest cities, and an economic magnet for people from Ceará and beyond. It's also a draw for tourists from Brazil and overseas, who come for its beaches, party atmosphere and the spectacular smaller beach spots, rolling dunes and fishing villages accessible from here.

History

According to many historians, the Spanish navigator Vicente Yáñez Pinzón landed on Praia Mucuripe on February 2, 1500, more than two months before Pedro Álvares Cabral first sighted Monte Pascoal in Bahia (the officially recognized European discovery of Brazil). The first Portuguese attempts to settle here, in the early 17th century, were short-lived, and it was the Dutch who built Fort Schoonenborch in 1637. When the Dutch abandoned their Brazilian possessions in 1654, the Portuguese renamed this fort the Fortaleza de NS da Assunção (Fortress of Our Lady of the Assumption). Around it grew a village, then a town, then a city that came to be called Fortaleza.

Ceará, Piauí & Maranhão Highlights

❶ **Jericoacoara** (p550) Surfing, chilling, partying and staring at spectacular sunsets in this magical village.

❷ **Parque Nacional dos Lençóis Maranhenses** (p564) Dipping into pristine lagoons between endless dunes in this surreal national park.

❸ **São Luís** (p556) Getting your party on to the beat of Afro-Brazilian drums.

❹ **Alcântara** (p564) Stepping back in time in the region's most atmospheric historical town.

❺ **Fortaleza** (p533) Discovering the restaurants, museums, nightlife and beach scene of the sprawling state capital.

❻ **Beaches Northwest of Fortaleza** (p567) Kitesurfing or windsurfing some of the world's best breezes.

❼ **Parque Nacional da Serra da Capivara** (p555) Getting up close to thousands of cave paintings at one of the continent's most important archaeological sites.

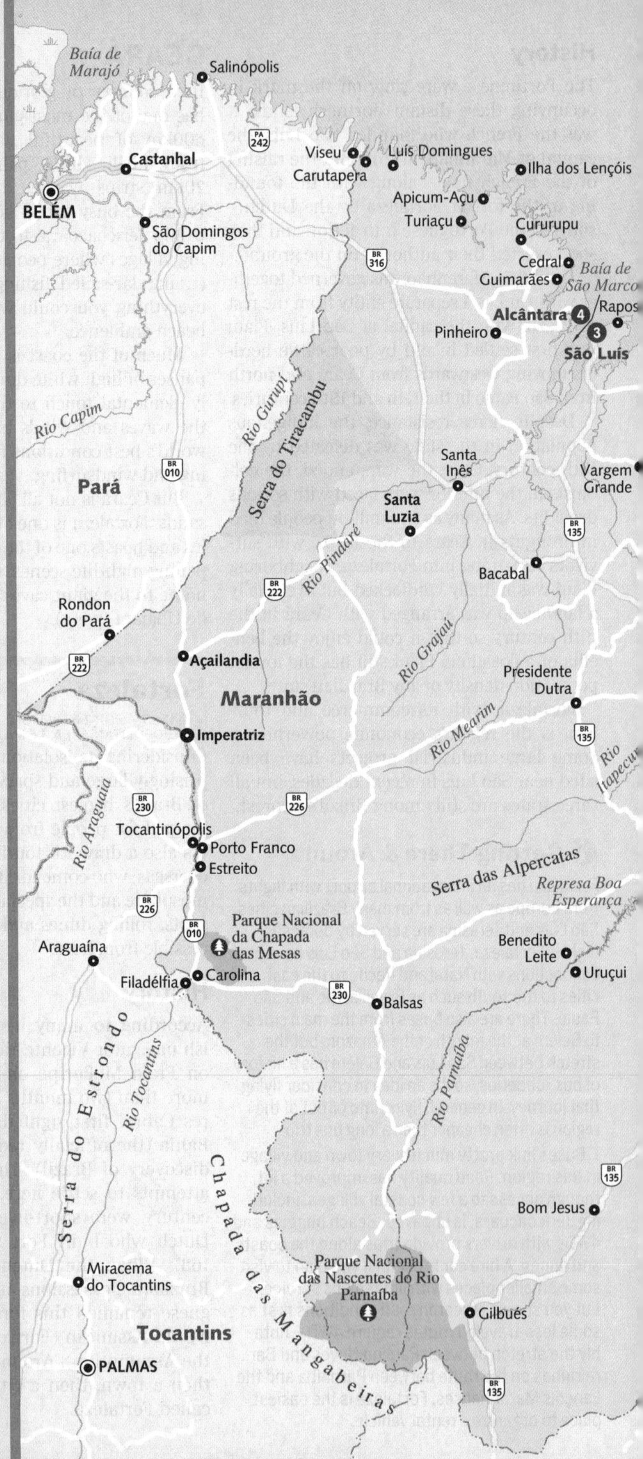

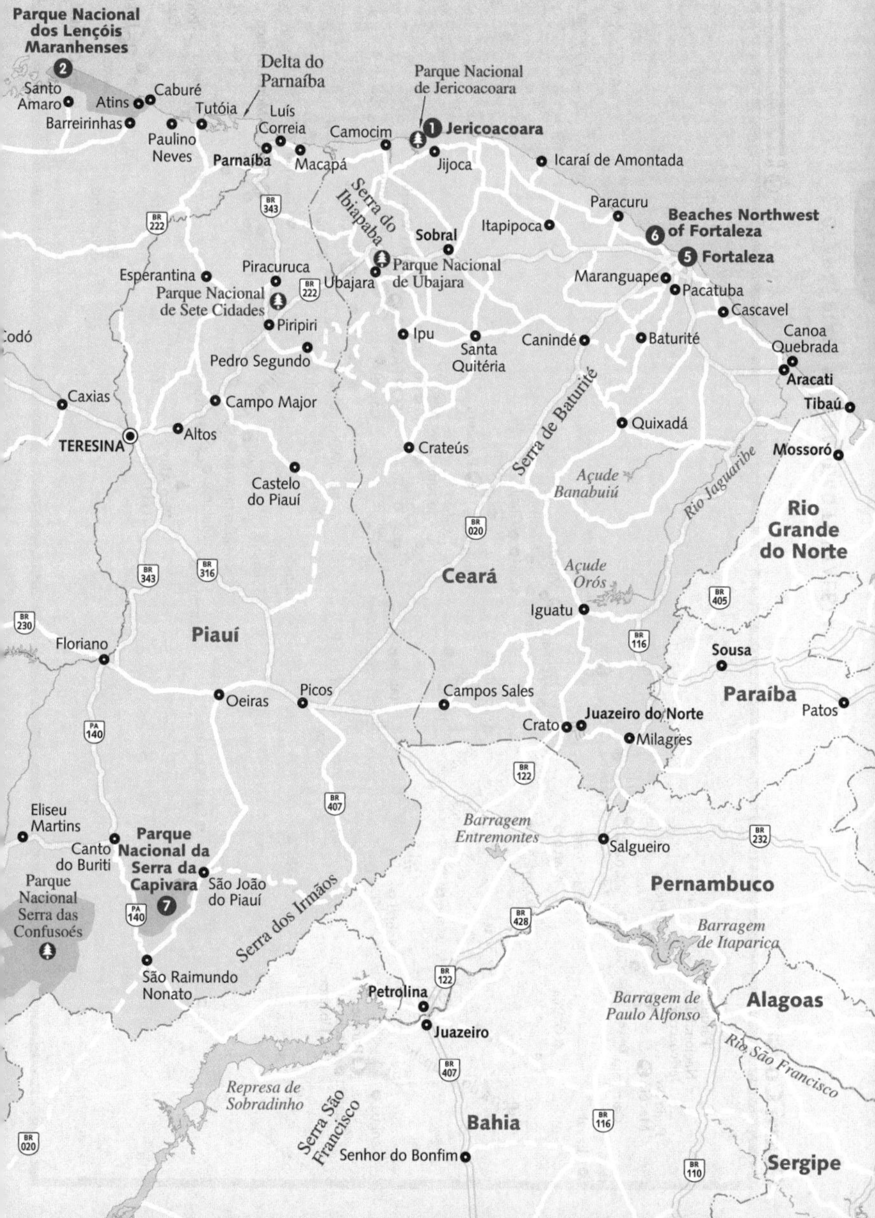

0 200 km
0 120 miles
ATLANTIC OCEAN
Parque Nacional dos Lençóis Maranhenses
2
Santo Amaro
Atins
Caburé
Barreirinhas
Paulino Neves
Tutóia
Delta do Parnaíba
Luís Correia
Parnaíba
Macapá
Camocim
Parque Nacional de Jericoacoara
1 Jericoacoara
Jijoca
Icaraí de Amontada
Serra do Ibiapaba
Sobral
Itapipoca
Paracuru
6 Beaches Northwest of Fortaleza
5 Fortaleza
Parque Nacional de Ubajara
Ubajara
Piracuruca
Esperantina
Parque Nacional de Sete Cidades
Piripiri
Pedro Segundo
Maranguape
Pacatuba
Cascavel
Codó
Ipu
Santa Quitéria
Canindé
Baturité
Canoa Quebrada
Aracati
Tibaú
Caxias
Campo Major
TERESINA
Altos
Crateús
Serra de Baturité
Quixadá
Mossoró
Castelo do Piauí
Açude Banabuiú
Rio Jaguaribe
Rio Grande do Norte
Ceará
Açude Orós
Iguatu
Piauí
Floriano
Sousa
Paraíba
Patos
Oeiras
Picos
Campos Sales
Juazeiro do Norte
Crato
Milagres
Eliseu Martins
Canto do Buriti
Parque Nacional da Serra da Capivara
7
São João do Piauí
Parque Nacional Serra das Confusoés
Barragem Entremontes
Salgueiro
Pernambuco
Serra dos Irmãos
Barragem de Itaparica
São Raimundo Nonato
Petrolina
Juazeiro
Barragem de Paulo Alfonso
Alagoas
Rio São Francisco
Represa de Sobradinho
Serra São Francisco
Bahia
Senhor do Bonfim
Sergipe

Ceará Coast

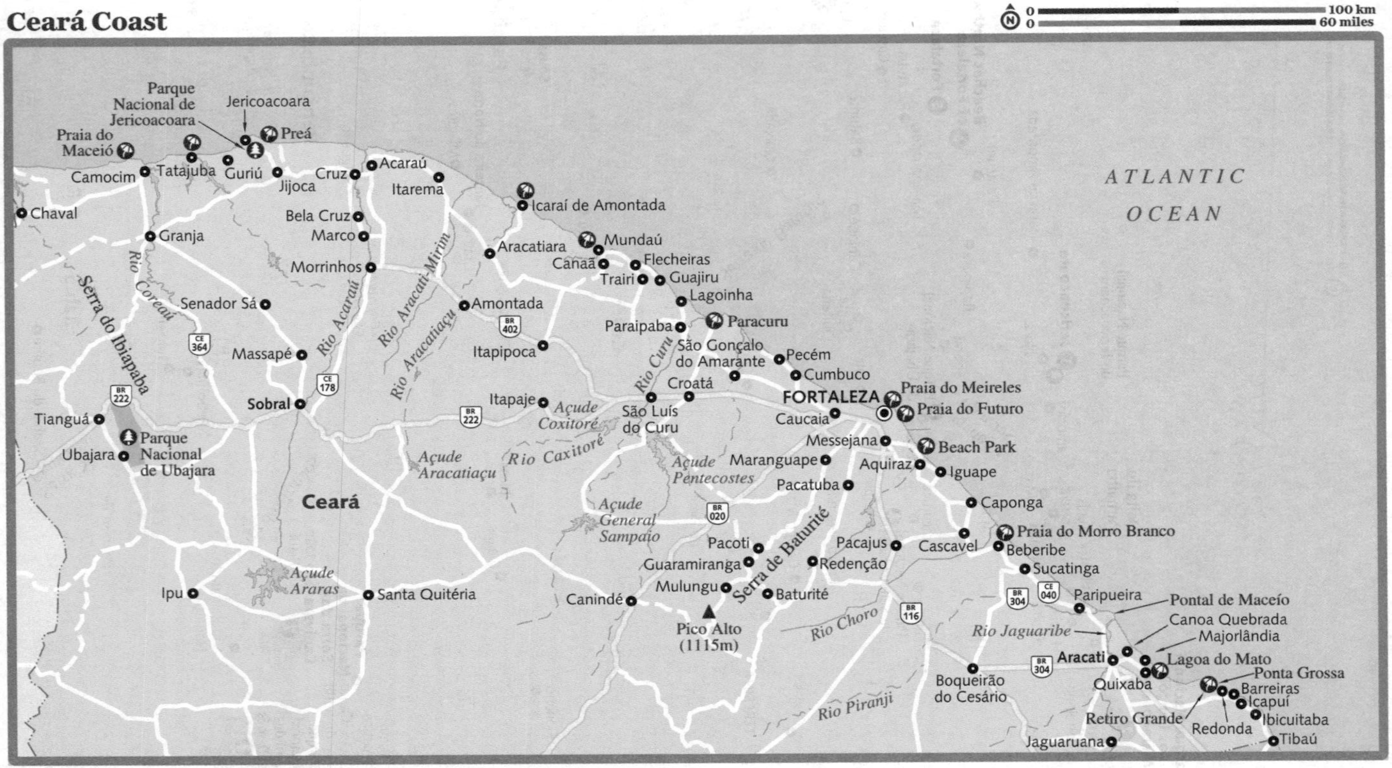

0 100 km
0 60 miles
N
ATLANTIC
OCEAN
Parque Nacional de Jericoacoara
Jericoacoara
Preá
Praia do Maceió
Camocim
Tatajuba
Guriú
Jijoca
Cruz
Acaraú
Itarema
Chaval
Granja
Bela Cruz
Marco
Morrinhos
Icaraí de Amontada
Aracatiara
Mundaú
Canaã
Flecheiras
Trairi
Guajiru
Lagoinha
Rio Coreaú
Serra do Ibiapaba
Senador Sá
CE 364
Massapé
Rio Acaraú
Rio Aracati-Mirim
Rio Aracatiaçu
Amontada
BR 402
Itapipoca
Paraipaba
Paracuru
São Gonçalo do Amarante
Pecém
Cumbuco
Rio Curu
Croatá
BR 222
CE 178
Sobral
Tianguá
Parque Nacional de Ubajara
Ubajara
Itapaje
Açude Coxitoré
Rio Caxitoré
São Luís do Curu
FORTALEZA
Praia do Meireles
Praia do Futuro
Caucaia
Messejana
Beach Park
Açude Aracatiaçu
Ceará
Açude Pentecostes
Maranguape
Aquiraz
Iguape
Pacatuba
Caponga
Açude General Sampaio
BR 020
Serra de Baturité
Pacoti
Guaramiranga
Mulungu
Baturité
Pacajus
Redenção
Cascavel
Praia do Morro Branco
Beberibe
Sucatinga
Açude Araras
Ipu
Santa Quitéria
Canindé
Pico Alto (1115m)
Rio Choro
BR 116
BR 304
CE 040
Paripueira
Pontal de Maceío
Canoa Quebrada
Majorlândia
Rio Jaguaribe
Aracati
Lagoa do Mato
Quixaba
Ponta Grossa
Barreiras
Icapuí
Ibicuitaba
Boqueirão do Cesário
Rio Piranji
Retiro Grande
Redonda
Jaguaruana
Tibaú

Indigenous resistance slowed Portuguese colonization of interior Ceará until the 18th century, but cattle ranchers, and later cotton growers, occupied land. It was cotton exports in the 19th century that made Fortaleza an important town (it had previously played second fiddle to Aracati). Growing commerce and industry in Fortaleza, and droughts in the interior, have since pulled ever more migrants to the city. Since the early 1990s tourism has joined textiles and food among its leading industries.

Sights

Centro Dragão do Mar de Arte e Cultura ARTS CENTER

(☎85 3488-8600; www.dragaodomar.org.br; Dragão do Mar 81; ⊙8am-10pm Mon-Thu, to 11pm Sat & Sun) FREE This excellent, extensive complex includes cinemas, performance spaces, a good cafe, a planetarium and two good museums: the **Museu de Arte Contemporânea** (MAC; www.dragaodomar.org.br; Dragão do Mar 81, Centro Cultural Dragão do Mar; ⊙9am-7pm Tue-Fri, 2-9pm Sat & Sun) FREE and the **Memorial da Cultura Cearense** (MCC; www.dragaodomar.org.br; Dragão do Mar 81, Centro Cultural Dragão do Mar; ⊙9am-7pm Tue-Fri, 2-9pm Sat & Sun) FREE, which features exhibits on Ceará's traditional life and culture. Elevated walkways join blocks on different streets; it all blends well with the surrounding older buildings, many of which have been restored to house bars, restaurants and artisans' workshops. It's a successful social focus for the city, and is very popular with locals.

Centro de Turismo MUSEUM

(☎85-3101-5508; Senador Pompeu 350; ⊙8am-6pm Mon-Fri, to 4pm Sat, to noon Sun) FREE The Centro de Turismo, a converted 19th-century jail, houses a lot of craft stalls and a tourist information office. Upstairs, the Museu de Arte e Cultura Popular, which has an impressive collection of Ceará crafts, is currently closed for renovations. You can often see lacemakers at work here.

Beaches

For most tourists, Fortaleza's greatest attractions are its beaches. Its north-facing beach, nearer the areas you're likely to be staying in, is lined by a broad and hugely popular pedestrian promenade running 4km from the Ponte dos Ingleses pier to Praia do Mucuripe. The nicest part is the central **Praia do Meireles** which, with all its high-rise hotels, resembles a northeastern Copacabana but also has numerous beach bars beneath leafy trees, popular places to hang out by day or evening. The water here is less clean than at Praia do Futuro, although that doesn't deter surfers.

Praia do Futuro BEACH

A clean length of soft sand stretching 5km along Fortaleza's east-facing coast, this is easily the best city beach, though it's far from most accommodations. It's lined by huge restaurants known as *barracas*, which serve seafood, beer and cocktails at tables on the sand, and attracts enormous crowds at weekends; fortunately the beach is long enough to accommodate everyone without being overcrowded.

The nicest part starts a couple of kilometers down from the industrial port at the north end. Unless you are a strong swimmer, beware of rough waves.

You can reach Praia do Futuro on the 49 Caça e Pesca bus running east on Av Monsenhor Tabosa, Av Historiador Raimundo Girão and Av Beira Mar. Or get a bus to Terminal Papicu then a Papicu/Praia do Futuro or Papicu/Caça e Pesca bus from there.

Tours

Day trips from Fortaleza to beaches along the coast to the east and west are very popular. Dozens of travel agencies, hotels and pousadas (guesthouses) will arrange these for you. Operators will normally come and pick you up from your accommodations. The main destinations (with transport-only prices per person) are to Brazil's best water park, Beach Park (R$35); **Cumbuco** (R$35); Canoa Quebrada (R$55); Lagoinha (R$50); and Mundaú (R$55). The tours are easier than taking public buses, and you can take them just one way if you want to stay over. Many agencies also offer 'Jericoacoara in one day' packages but visitors spend more time traveling than in the town – give them a miss.

Some agencies also offer longer-distance 4WD or beach-buggy tours along Ceará's glorious beaches wherever possible, as far afield as Jericoacoara or even the Lençóis Maranhenses (p564) or Natal.

Festivals & Events

Réveillon (New Year's Eve) sees a huge party with live bands at Praia de Iracema. Carnaval is also at its liveliest in the Praia de Iracema district, which additionally sees four Saturdays of pre-Carnaval revelry in preceding weeks.

Fortaleza

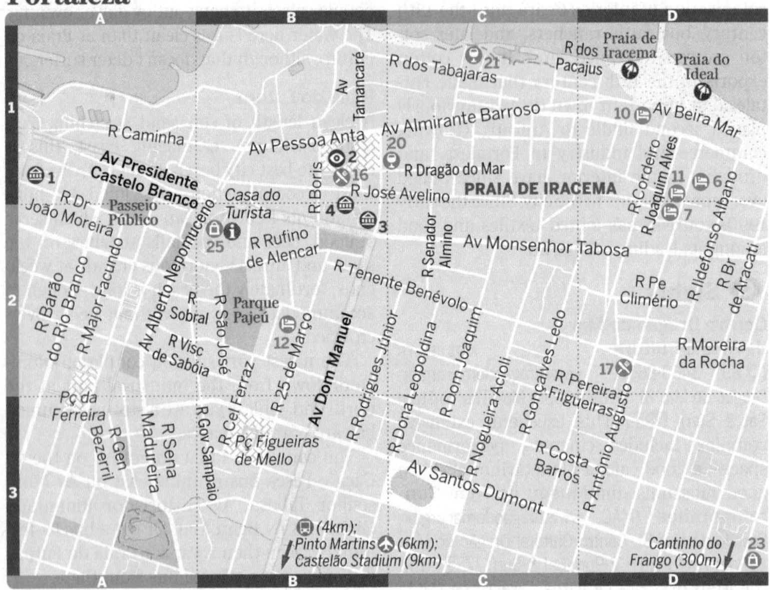

Maloca Dragão PERFORMING ARTS
(www.dragaodomar.org.br; Apr) The Northeast's premier arts festival takes place in late April at the Centro Cultural Dragão do Mar (p537) with free concerts, theater, street performances and film.

Fortal PARADE, MUSIC
(www.fortal.com.br; Jul) Fortaleza's lively out-of-season Carnaval is held for four days over the last weekend of July and is attended by half a million people.

Parada pela Diversidade Sexual PARADE
(Jun) Fortaleza's Parada pela Diversidade Sexual (Sexual Diversity Parade) takes place on Av Beira Mar on the last Sunday of June; it's one of Brazil's biggest gay pride events.

Sleeping

★ **Refugio Hostel Fortaleza** HOSTEL $
(85 3393-4349; www.refugiohostelfortaleza.com; Deputado João Lopes 31, Centro; dm from R$30, r R$120-130;) Easily Fortaleza's best hostel. German owner Karl has whipped an old mansion into shape, following an eco-ethos with breezy natural ventilation and solar-heated showers. The bathrooms and kitchen are astonishing for a hostel, while other design-forward common spaces of note include a sunny patio/BBQ area and various terraces. Dorms feature colorful lockers, original tiling and hardwood floors.

Albergaria Hostel HOSTEL $
(85 3032-9005; www.albergariahostel.com.br; Antônio Augusto 111, Praia de Iracema; dm with fan/air-con R$40/45, d/tr/q R$140/180/270;) This cheerful, well-located, well-run hostel has very good facilities, including a backyard with a pool, plus a sociable atmosphere helped along by the friendly English-speaking owner. There are separate-sex and mixed four-bed dorms (with privacy curtains and lockers with electrical outlets) and four good private rooms with bathroom, although some are cold water only. Breakfast is plentiful. Reservations only.

Hotel La Maison HOTEL $
(85 3048-4200; www.hotellamaison.com.br; Av Desembargador Moreira 201, Meireles; r R$159;) This excellent-value place in Meireles is just a couple of blocks from the beach, and has 27 spotless rooms (those upstairs are generally the brightest) and bright, colorful common areas. The French owner knows the city very well, speaks English and can point you in the right direction – whatever your needs. The fruit-heavy breakfast is substantial, but where's the Brie?

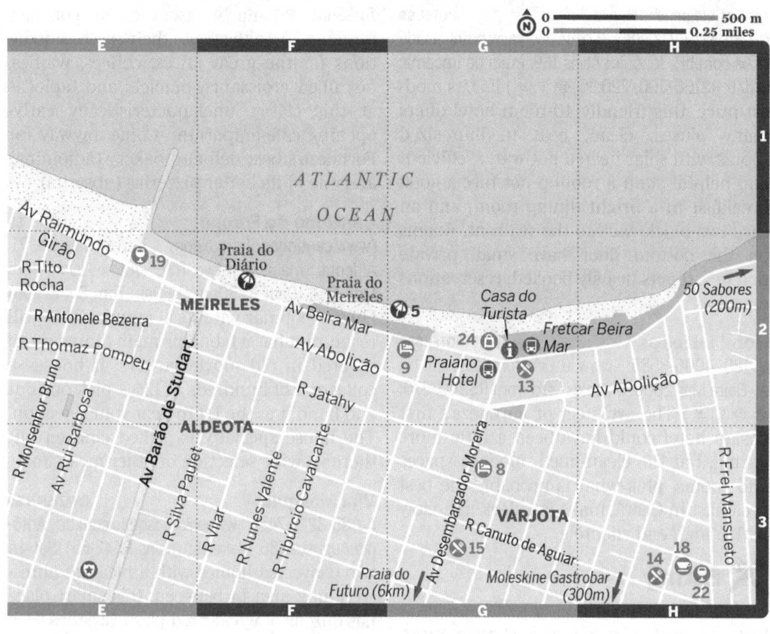

Fortaleza

Sights

1 Centro de Turismo ... A1
2 Centro Dragão do Mar de Arte e Cultura ... B1
3 Memorial da Cultura Cearense ... B2
4 Museu de Arte Contemporânea ... B2
5 Praia do Meireles ... G2

Sleeping

6 Albergaria Hostel ... D1
7 Hotel Casa de Praia ... D2
8 Hotel La Maison ... G3
9 Hotel Luzeiros ... G2
10 Hotel Sonata de Iracema ... D1
11 Pousada Três Caravelas ... D1
12 Refugio Hostel Fortaleza ... B2

Eating

13 50 Sabores ... G2
14 Coco Bambu ... H3
15 Empório Delitalia ... G3
16 Santa Clara Café Orgânico ... B1
17 Vila Mosquito ... D2

Drinking & Nightlife

18 Amika ... H3
19 Boteco Praia ... E2
20 Órbita ... C1
21 Pirata Bar ... C1
22 Turatti ... H3

Shopping

23 Ceart ... D3
24 Feira de Artesanato ... G2
25 Mercado Central ... B2

Hotel Sonata de Iracema HOTEL **$$**
(☎85-4006-1600; www.sonatadeiracema.com.br; Av Beira Mar 848, Praia de Iracema; s/d R$290/320; ❄@📶🏊) The cute two-story street frontage is slightly misleading, as most of the hotel is contained in the 13-story block behind, but that means all the tasteful, bright and modern rooms have sea views. One of Fortaleza's nicest larger hotels, it has an outdoor pool deck and very pleasant staff.

Pousada Três Caravelas POUSADA **$$**
(☎85 3219-0722; www.trescaravelas.com; Antônio Augusto 182, Praia de Iracema; s/d/tr R$180/210/260; ❄@📶) A little more personal than the larger hotels, this pousada in Iracema is run by friendly English-speaking owner Vera and offers the right amount of cozy for the price. Rooms are clean and simple, with new air-conditioners, hot water and the odd piece of colorful local art. There's a restaurant on the premises.

Hotel Casa de Praia HOTEL $$
(☎85 3219-1022, 85-3129-1609; www.hotelcasadepraia.com.br; Joaquim Alves 169, Praia de Iracema; s/d/tr R$160/190/220;) For its modest price, this friendly 40-room hotel offers many pluses: clean, neat medium-sized rooms with solar-heated hot water; efficient and helpful staff; a rooftop hot tub; a good breakfast in a bright dining room; and an easy two-block walk to the seafront. Rooms on the bottom floor have small private porches. It gets heavily booked; reservations essential.

Hotel Luzeiros HOTEL $$$
(☎85 4006-8585; www.luzeirosfortaleza.com.br; Av Beira Mar 2600, Meireles; s/d from R$340/370;) The architect of Fortaleza's first design hotel could have been a little more daring, but the clean-lined, modern spaces and rooms, plus what is probably the best breakfast in Ceará, make it a sleek mainstay with a high-end clientele.

Eating

Varjota, a short taxi ride south of Meireles, is home to most of Fortaleza's best restaurants.

★ **50 Sabores** ICE CREAM $
(☎85 3023-0050; www.50sabores.com.br; Av Beira Mar 2982, Meireles; 1/2 flavors R$14/20; 10am-11:45pm) One of Brazil's most famous ice cream shops, though with a terribly misleading name: there are actually *150* flavors here, including caipirinha (made with *cachaça* sugarcane liquor – you must be 18 to purchase!) and beer, plus loads of Brazilian fruits and more classic options. There's another a branch in **Mucuripe** (www.50sabores.com.br; Av Beira Mar 3958, Mucuripe; 1/2 flavors R$14/20; 7am-midnight).

Santa Clara Café Orgânico CAFE $
(Centro Dragão do Mar, Praia de Iracema; items R$8-23; 3-10pm Tue-Sun;) Santa Clara is one of the city's happening *pontos de encontros*; loosely translated, this means where hot people go to mingle (and cool down in the icy air-con). It's a wonderful little cafe on an upper level of Dragão do Mar (p537), and serves organic coffee, sandwiches, crepes, omelets, waffles, tapiocas and a plethora of fancier coffee drinks.

Empório Delitalia CAFE, PIZZERIA $
(Av Desembargador Moreira 533; breakfast items R$5.80-14.90, pizza R$28-72; 6:30am-10pm Mon-Sat, 7:30am-10pm Sun; pizzeria 6pm-midnight Tue-Sun;) Early risers could consider forgoing breakfast at their accommodations for the great juices, coffees, waffles, hot filled croissants, omelets and tapiocas at this classy, uncharacteristically early-opening cafe-emporium. Come anyway for Fortaleza's best deli and bakery (adjoining) and one of its better pizzerias (upstairs).

Cantinho do Frango GRILL $$
(www.cantinhodofrango.com; Torres Câmara 71, Aldeota; mains for two R$65-70; 10am-4pm Mon-Thu, 10am-10:30pm Fri, 9am-7pm Sat & Sun) Hugely popular with local families, this grill restaurant has a fabulous main dining room covered in old movie posters; it houses a collection of hundreds of LPs – pick one out and hand it to the DJ to hear your selection. The house specialty is grilled chicken but there's a wide selection of other meats too.

Vila Mosquito BRAZILIAN $$
(☎85 3226-7422; www.vilamosquito.com.br; Antônio Augusto 786, Meireles; mains R$42-65) Set in two converted homes with a pleasant alfresco dining area in between, this smart place has dozens of wood-fired pizza varieties with gourmet toppings, plus an interesting selection of mains, with many seafood options and some great desserts. Relaxed ambience, quality service and fair prices make it a winner.

Moleskine Gastrobar BRAZILIAN $$
(www.moleskinegastrobar.com.br; Professor Dias da Rocha 578, Meireles; mains R$39-75; noon-2am Tue-Sat, to midnight Sun & Mon;) One of Fortaleza's trendiest restaurants, this gastrobar draws the young, hot and restless as much for its striking design – denim-covered banquets and rope-hung lighting wrapped around suspended rail beams – as for its grill-heavy menu. Start with the *bobó de camarão* (shrimp with manioc) croquettes before choosing a slab of meat from the impressive barbecue.

Crocobeach SEAFOOD $$
(☎85 3521-9600; www.crocobeach.com.br; Av Clóvis Arrais Maia 3125, Praia do Futuro; buffet per kg R$69; 8am-6pm Sun-Wed & Fri, to 2am Thu, to 7pm Sat;) For the full Praia do Futuro experience, head to *megabarraca* (megastall) Crocobeach, which is shaded by scores of coconut palms and has swimming pools and a variety of comfortable seating options. It's a hyper-complex of fun and sun, and the buffet is excellent. There's usually live music on Saturdays and Sundays.

Coco Bambu BRAZILIAN $$

(www.restaurantecocobambu.com.br; Canuto de Aguiar 1317, Varjota; mains for two R$70-228, pizzas R$39-119; ⌚11am-midnight Sun-Thu, to 2am Fri & Sat; 📶) This massive, iconic eatery does a whole lot of everything, with a 26-page menu covering pizza, tapiocas, crepes, pasta and regional mains (seafood is the specialty) – and it's all pretty good. The casual dining areas with tropical plants are pleasant, although you might object to paying the cover charge for the cheesy rock ballads.

 Drinking & Nightlife

Fortaleza is famed for its nightlife. The Dragão do Mar area is one of the best places to go out.

Turatti MICROBREWERY

(☎85 3099-2829; www.cervejariaturatti.com.br; Rua Ana Bilhar 1178; small beer R$8-14; ⌚5pm-midnight) Locals descend on this enormous open-air microbrewery in hordes to beat the heat with artisanal draft beer brewed right on the premises. There are six varieties on tap; you can buy it by the glass but pretty much everyone goes for the 3.5-liter towers (R$69 to R$120).

Amika CAFE

(Ana Bilhar 1136B, Varjota; coffee R$4.25-9; ⌚1-8pm Tue-Sun; 📶) When you tire of sickly presweetened bus-station coffee, head to this trendy coffeehouse, where its business is to know beans. Three weekly-changing espressos from single-origin Minas Gerais plantations are available daily, as are the usual caffeine junkie methods (Aeropress, Chemex etc). Serves light bites as well.

Boteco Praia BAR

(☎85 3248-4773; www.botecofortaleza.com.br; Av Beira Mar 1680, Meireles; ⌚5pm-midnight Mon-Fri, noon-3am Sat & Sun; 📶) The number-one spot for evening drinks and conversation, Boteco Praia attracts all ages to its long arcaded hall and its terrace facing the seafront promenade. Live music nightly. It's a fine place to knock back cold *chope* (draft beer).

Órbita BAR

(www.orbitabar.com.br; Dragão do Mar 207, Praia de Iracema; admission R$30; ⌚9pm-4am Thu-Sun; 📶) Reminiscent of a college-town rock club (but with way better-looking people than your college most likely, or ours), this large Dragão do Mar (p537) bar hosts live rock, surf and pop amid snooker tables and a legion of flirtatious upper-class clientele. Admission is cheaper or free if you come early.

Pirata Bar CLUB

(www.pirata.com.br; Rua dos Tabajaras 325; admission R$40-50; ⌚8pm-4am) The bar and club scene around the Praia de Iracema waterfront area is rather touristy, but the *'Segunda-feira Mais Louca do Mundo'* (Craziest Monday in the World) at Pirata is still legendary. Live bands play *forró* and other Brazilian dance rhythms to packed crowds through the night.

☆ Entertainment

Arena Castelão FOOTBALL

(☎85 3304-4501; Av Alberto Craveiro 2901) Fortaleza's Castelão stadium, 9km south of the center, was completely renovated to seat 67,000 fans for the 2014 World Cup. The city's two top clubs, Ceará (www.cearasc.com) and Fortaleza (www.fortalezaec.net), play their home games here.

Shopping

You can find handicrafts from all around Ceará in Fortaleza. Some of the finest work is in delicate lace, a tradition that came with the Portuguese. Artisans also work with *carnaúba*-palm fronds, bamboo, vines and leather.

Ceart ARTS & CRAFTS

(Av Santos Dumont 1589, Aldeota; ⌚9am-8pm Mon-Sat, 2:30-8:30pm Sun) The main showroom of this beautiful, state-run craft store, which sells lace, ceramics, wood carvings, textiles, and baskets and bags of sisal and *carnaúba* palm. There's another branch at Centro Dragão do Mar (p537).

Feira de Artesanato MARKET

(Praia do Meireles; ⌚5pm-midnight) A bustling beachside handicraft market on Praia do Meireles. The small stalls sell similar items to those found in the central market: leather goods, jewelry, bottles of *cachaça*, T-shirts, lacework and wood carvings.

Mercado Central MARKET

(www.mercadocentraldefortaleza.com.br; Av Alberto Nepomuceno 199; ⌚8am-6pm Mon-Fri, to 4pm Sat, to 1pm Sun) Mainly geared to a tourist clientele, the three-story central market has good prices at more than 500 stalls that sell everything from leather bags and colorful palm baskets to excellent local cashews and a huge variety of *cachaça* – some bottles have fruit salad or crabs pickled inside. You might find a desirable curio. There's an ATM on the top floor.

Information

DANGERS & ANNOYANCES

Beware of pickpockets in the city center and petty theft on the beaches; gaggles of adolescents specialize in snatch-and-grab robbery along Av Beira Mar (watch your necklaces and purses). Tourists waiting at bus stops to return from Praia do Futuro have been targeted. Empty streets in Centro and Praia de Iracema are best avoided after dark.

EMERGENCY

Deprotur (Delegacia de Proteção ao Turista; ☎85 3101-1344, 85 3101-2488; www.policia civil.ce.gov.br; Costa Barros 1971, Aldeota; ⏰8am-6pm Mon-Fri)

MONEY

Banco do Brasil (Av Beira Mar; ⏰8am-10pm) ATM on the waterfront.

Banco do Brasil (Av Abolição 2308, Meireles; ⏰8am-10pm) Convenient ATM.

Bradesco (www.bradesco.com.br; Av da Abolição 1810, Meireles; ⏰8am-10pm) Visa/Mastercard ATM.

Bradesco (www.bradesco.com.br; Av Pessoa Anta 274; ⏰8am-10pm) Visa/Mastercard ATM.

TOURIST INFORMATION

The city tourism department operates information booths around town; staff may or may not speak English but you'll find useful maps and guides.

Meireles (SETFOR; ☎85 3105-2670; https://turismo.fortaleza.ce.gov.br; Av Beira Mar, Meireles; ⏰9am-5pm)

Mercado Central (SETFOR; ☎85 3105-1475; https://turismo.fortaleza.ce.gov.br; Basement level, Mercado Central, Av Nepomuceno 199; ⏰9am-5pm Mon-Fri, 9am-noon Sat)

Aeroporto Pinto Martins (☎85 3488-5869; https://turismo.fortaleza.ce.gov.br; Av Carlos Jereissati 3000, Aeroporto Pinto Martins; ⏰8am-8pm)

Getting There & Away

AIR

Aeroporto Pinto Martins (☎85 3392-1030; Av Carlos Jereissati 3000) has direct flights to/from Amsterdam, Bogotá, Buenos Aires, Cabo Verde, Lisbon, Miami, Milan, Orlando and Paris as well as domestic flights through Brazil.

BUS

Fortaleza's **bus station** (☎85 3256-5786, 85 3256-2200; Av Borges de Melo 1630) is 5.5km south of Meireles.

To Jericoacoara, several companies, such as **Girafatur** (☎85 3219-3255; www.girafatur.com.br) and **Vitorino** (☎85 3047-1047; www.vitorinotur.com.br; office 503, Av Beira Mar & Oswaldo Cruz; ⏰8am-noon & 2-7pm), offer direct door-to-door van transfers from Fortaleza hotels (R$80 to R$100, five hours) – most accommodations can book these for you.

Another option is **Fretcar** (☎85 3402-2244; www.fretcar.com.br; Terminal Rodoviário), which runs up to five buses daily to Jericoacoara (from R$73, six to seven hours) departing at 4am, 7am, 2:45pm, 4pm and 6pm from Fortaleza's bus station. A 6:30am departure (year-round) and usually one afternoon bus (2:15pm, depending on season) begin from the airport before picking up at the bus station 30 minutes later, and then at the **Praiano Hotel** (www.praiano.com.br; Av Beira Mar 2800) on Praia do Meireles about 30 minutes after that. The last part of the Fretcar trip is a one-hour ride in a *jardineira* (open-sided 4WD truck) along sandy tracks and the beach and through dunes from Jijoca to Jericoacoara.

There are also additional services to Jijoca de Jericoacoara (R$35 to R$46, 11 daily) from where you can take a public pickup to Jericoacoara. You can check Fretcar schedules and buy tickets (advisably a day ahead) at the Fretcar office on the Beira Mar in **Meireles** (☎85 99675-9981; www.fretcar.com.br; Av Beira Mar 2985; ⏰7am-10pm) or at the Beach Point **office** (☎85 3086-7055; cnr Av Beira Mar & Oswaldo Cruz, No 1 Beira Mar Trade Center; ⏰9am-noon & 1-8pm).

The most exciting way of reaching Jericoacoara is by 4WD along the coast – an option offered by agencies such as **Jeri Off Road** (☎88 99971-3336, 88 99971-3330; www.jeri.tur.br; Pousada Bella Jeri, Travessa da Rua do Forró), which charges R$850 for up to four people.

CAR

Half-a-dozen rental agencies have airport desks, including the recommended **Avis** (☎85 3392-1369; www.avis.com.br; Aeroporto Pinto Martins; ⏰6am-midnight) and **Localiza Hertz** (☎85 3308-8351; www.localizahertz.com; Aeroporto Pinto Martins; ⏰24hr), which also has a convenient agency in **Meireles** (☎85 3248-2900; www.localizahertz.com; Av Abolição 2236; ⏰8am-8pm, to 2pm Sun). There's a slew of local rental firms on Av Monsenhor Tabosa in Praia de Iracema, including **Maresia** (☎85 3219-8000; www.maresiarentacar.com.br; Av Monsenhor Tabosa 1001; ⏰8am-6:30pm), where the owner speaks some English.

Getting Around

TO/FROM THE AIRPORT

A **Coopaero** (☎85 3105-1500; www.coopaero.com.br; Aeroporto Pinto Martins) fixed-rate taxi from the airport to Meireles or Praia de Iracema is R$47 during the day and R$70 at night. Metered **Coopertaxi** (☎85-3477-5549) common taxis run R$35 to R$50 to Meireles or Praia de Iracema and R$25 to R$30 to the bus station.

A special local bus, 917, runs between the airport and Beira Mar/Av Aboliçao and costs R$10 per trip.

Using the normal services, bus 027 Siqueira/Papicu/Aeroporto and 066 Parangaba/Papicu/Aeroporto both run to Terminal Papicu in the east of the city, where you can change to the 051 Grande Circular 1 for Meireles and Praia de Iracema. Alternatively, take the 066 to Terminal Parangaba, and change there to the 077 Parangaba/Mucuripe bus, which runs to the Centro Dragão do Mar, Praia de Iracema and Meireles.

The airport is 6km south of Centro.

TO/FROM THE BUS STATION

Bus 013 Aguanambi leaves from outside the bus station and runs north up Av Dom Manuel to the Centro Dragão do Mar. For Praia de Iracema and Meireles, walk left outside the bus station, turn right at the traffic signal along Av Borges de Melo and walk to a bus stop about 200m along on the far (south) side of the street. From here buses 073 Siqueira/Praia de Iracema and 078 Siqueira/Mucuripe will take you up Av Dom Manuel to the Centro Dragão do Mar, then to Praia de Iracema and (the 078 only) Meireles.

A taxi from the bus station to Meireles costs around R$25.

BUS

Fortaleza has a very extensive city bus system with good frequency on most routes. Fares are mostly R$3.40 (R$2.80 on Sundays and holidays) and if you have to transfer at a Terminal de Integração (Integration Terminal), such as Papicu or Parangaba, you don't have to pay a second fare.

BICYCLE

Bicicletar (☎85 4003-9594; www.bicicletar.com.br; Av Beira Mar, Mucuripe) Fortaleza's city bike-share scheme is free for the first hour (for 90 minutes on Sundays). After that, it's R$5 per hour. There are stations throughout the city including convenient locations on Av Beira Mar in **Meireles** (www.bicicletar.com.br; Av Beira Mar) and **Mucuripe** (☎85 4003-9594; www.bicicletar.com.br; Av Beira Mar, Mucuripe), **Rui Barbosa** (www.bicicletar.com.br; Rui Barbosa 1680, Praia da Iracema) close to Iracema and at **Dragão do Mar** (www.bicicletar.com.br; Dragão do Mar).

You'll need to register (R$5 per day) on the website or with the app. There are a few choice locations along the beach.

TAXI

Taxis are metered. A 4km trip across town from the Centro Dragão do Mar to Varjota, for example, costs about R$15 to R$18.

Canoa Quebrada

☎0XX88 / POP 4000

The coast southeast of Fortaleza has many fine beaches, many of them backed by dunes, but it's developed and built-up. It's not until you reach the red-hued windswept wonderland of Canoa Quebrada, 140km from Fortaleza, that the coast starts to regain its natural majesty. Once a tiny village cut off from the world by its huge pink sand dunes and beloved by early hippie travelers, Canoa Quebrada today has become a more family-oriented beach spot, and it's a favorite destination of daily van tours from Fortaleza. But the craggy, eroding sand cliffs and the large dune expanses still lend Canoa that elemental, otherworldly feel for which it's famous. With numerous good pousadas and restaurants, and varied outdoor activities easily available, it's an enjoyable spot to relax for a few days.

Activities

Southeast of Canoa a 30km stretch of beautiful uninterrupted beach, backed by colorful cliffs, sweeps round to the red-rock

BUSES FROM FORTALEZA

DESTINATION	COST FROM (R$)	DURATION (HR)	COMPANY
Belém	170	24	Guanabara (www.expressoguanabara.com.br) Itapemirim (www.itapemirim.com.br)
Natal	98	9	Viação Nordeste (www.viacaonordeste.com.br)
Parnaíba	75	9	Guanabara
Piripiri	54	8	Guanabara
Recife	100	14	Guanabara
Rio de Janeiro	565	48	Itapemirim
São Luís	160	19	Guanabara
Teresina	60	11	Guanabara
Ubajara	46	7	Guanabara

WORTH A TRIP

PARQUE NACIONAL DE UBAJARA

It's the smallest national park in the country, but **Parque Nacional de Ubajara** (☎88-99937-5544, 88-99942-3051; admission R$5; ⊙8am-5pm Tue-Sun) crams plenty of attractions into its boundaries. Atop a thickly forested escarpment 850m above sea level, Ubajara offers some spectacular vistas over the *sertão* (interior or backlands of the Northeast) below. The main attractions are giant caves (11 in total but only one is open to the public), a pair of impressive waterfalls and walks in the surrounding forest.

With the cable car out of service at the time of writing, to see the main cave you'll need to take a 14km, six-hour round-trip guided hike (R$30 per visitor) down to the entrance. Hikes leave at 8am, 9am and 10am from the visitors center. Wear sturdy footwear and take enough to drink. Last entry to the cave is at 2pm.

If you have your own vehicle you can also drive 64km along a large loop to the lower entrance of the park from where it's a just a two-hour hike to the cave entrance.

Inside the cave there are nine chambers with strange limestone formations extending more than 500m into the side of a mountain. The main formations seen inside the caves are Pedra do Sino (Bell Stone), Salas da Rosa (Rose Rooms), Sala do Cavalo (Horse Room) and Sala dos Retratos (Portrait Room).

Less strenuous hikes include a 2.5km walk to an elevated walkway and a lookout point (R$8); the 6km circuit to the Cachoeira do Cafundó waterfall (R$15); and the 8km trek to the park's most dramatic waterfall, Cachoeira do Gavilão (R$20).

All activities in the park apart from the lookout at the main entrance require a guide.

Guanabara (☎85 3233-6759; www.expressoguanabara.com.br; Terminal Rodoviário) has five daily buses between Ubajara and Fortaleza (R$46, six hours);

headland of **Ponta Grossa**. It's a great beach-buggy trip (R$250 to R$350 for three or four hours round-trip, up to four people) and you can stop for a good-value lobster lunch when the seafood is in season (from July to December). It's only possible to complete this trip when the tide is low.

North of Canoa a large area of high dunes stretches 12km to the mouth of the **Rio Jaguaribe**: a one-hour buggy trip with some exciting steep descents costs around R$200 to R$300 for up to four people. It's also possible to add a boat trip on the river onto this loop. Pousadas can recommend and organize authorized buggy drivers.

Kitesurfing is best around the mouth of the Rio Jaguaribe, 12km northwest, where there is reliable wind and calm waters; the season runs from July to December. It's reachable only by buggy.

Parapente Canoa Quebrada PARAGLIDING
(☎88 99911-9285, 88 99810-2433; Francisco Caraco; 10-15min flight R$158) Tandem paragliding is hugely popular and huge fun if you have a head for heights. You'll ride the breezes above Canoa's beaches from the takeoff point at the east end of Broadway. It's also possible to fly triple with two clients in the harness beneath the instructor.

Extreme KiteSchool Canoa Quebrada KITESURFING
(☎88 98819-3632, 88 99960-6070; extremekitedaniel@hotmail.com; Dragão do Mar) A recommended kitesurfing outfitter, IKO-certified instructor Daniel offers a three-day (nine-hour) beginners' course for R$1080. He also rents equipment (R$200 per day) and organizes transport to the best spots. Ask for him in the Art Canoa shop on the main drag.

Tours

Lua Estrela OUTDOORS
(☎88 99732-7212; Dragão de Mar 209) A well-organized local tour operator that offers the standard buggy and ATV tours both to the north and south of town, including a 60km adventure to the Rio Jaguaribe (R$600 for four visitors) that includes a 10km boat ride up the river.

Sleeping

Hostel Pousada Ibiza HOSTEL $
(☎88 3421-7262; www.hostelpousadaibiza.com; Dragão do Mar 360; dm R$55-65, d R$130-160; ❄📶) Dorms and rooms are smallish but brightened by colorful throws and flags, and each comes equipped with its own bathroom. But what's best about this hostel is the long, airy balcony-lounge-bar overlooking

the heart of the Broadway action. It shares premises with a pizzeria (downstairs) and has a small guest kitchen.

★ Pousada Dolce Vita POUSADA $$
(88 3421-7213; www.canoa-quebrada.it; Descida da Praia s/n; r from R$220;) The Dolce Vita is friendly and relaxed. Bungalows are arranged around a garden of palms, flowers and lawns with a beautiful pool at its center. Rooms are spotless and have more character than your average pousada; each is named for a Fellini film and decorated with movie memorabilia. The classic tiled bathrooms are fantastic for the price range.

Il Nuraghe POUSADA $$
(88 3421-7418; www.nuraghe-canoa.com; Descida da Praia s/n; r R$260-385;) Located at the entrance to town, Il Nuraghe is one of Canoa's nicest places to stay, with 26 stylish minimalist rooms colored with fresh local art; the nicest of the rooms look out onto the extraordinary pool (about 25m long). Features including a small spa with a welcoming sauna and bathrobes show the Italian owners are trying a bit harder.

Vila Canoa POUSADA $$
(88-3421-7183; www.vilacanoa.com; Av Beira Mar 35; r R$265-295;) Canoa's only beachfront pousada is welcoming and Dutch-run; it's an excellent choice. Cool, tasteful rooms are dotted around a garden of grass and flagstone pathways that slope down to the pool, a great sunbathing deck and the pousada's own *barraca* (beach bar-restaurant), which has cozy beach cushions.

Pousada California POUSADA $$
(88-3421-7039; www.californiacanoa.com; Nascer do Sol 135; r R$250-330;) This popular 33-room pousada has a variety of neat, comfortable rooms on two sides of the street, and an attractive courtyard with a sociable bar and pool. Free fruit and coffee are available all day in the breakfast-room-cum-TV-lounge, a chill hang spot. There's also a new gym, and many bathrooms have recently been done up.

Eating

Cabana BRAZILIAN $
(88 3421-7018; Dragão do Mar s/n; mains for two R$35-62; 4:30pm-midnight Tue-Fri, noon-midnight Sat & Sun Feb-Apr, Jun & Aug-Dec, 4:30pm-midnight Mon & noon-midnight Tue-Sun Jul & Jan, closed May) If you're not interested in the plethora of foreign-owned restaurants in town, give your money to this Brazilian spot, a solid bet for local foods such as *peixadas* and *caldeiradas* (both are types of local seafood stews), and a long list of shrimp, fish and filet mignon dishes. Food is consistent and good.

La Torinese BAKERY $
(Dragão do Mar s/n; items R$4-15; 7am-noon & 4-9pm;) Near the beginning of Broadway, this Italian-run bakery serves Canoa's best espresso and does a perfect little variety of early-rise, baked-in-house breakfast pastries (guava croissants!), along with decadent, profiterole-heavy sweets throughout the day. It's also a pleasant spot for a pre-dinner Aperol spritz.

Lazy Days SEAFOOD $
(Praia; mains R$25-40; 9am-5pm, closed Mon) At the eastern end of the beach, Lazy Days is the best of the beach *barracas* that rub up against Canoa's picturesque red cliffs. There are excellent fish plates, pastas and steaks alongside some lighter options including octopus salad.

Adega dos Portugueses PORTUGUESE $$
(88 99623-2649; Dragão do Mar s/n; mains R$25-55; 6-11pm Tue-Fri, noon-4pm & 6:30pm-midnight Sat & Sun) A popular new entry to the dining scene, this unassuming open-air Portuguese-owned place on the main strip serves top seafood dishes including seven types of *bacalhau* (dried salted cod) as well as some good squid dishes. Wash it all down with a bottle from their extensive wine collection which covers the walls.

Mezza Luna ITALIAN $$
(88 99697-3113; Nascer do Sol 138; mains R$35-48; 6pm-midnight) The most romantic dining option in Canoa, Mezza Luna is down a small alley off Broadway that opens out onto a lovely sand-floored garden with tables dotted among the plants; meals are accompanied by soft jazz and bossa nova. The menu is small but includes some excellent homemade pasta dishes and seafood in a variety of interesting sauces.

El Argentino ARGENTINE $$
(88 3421-7123; Dragão do Mar 15; steak R$38-69; 11:30am-11:30pm;) At the east end of Broadway with picture windows looking down to the beach, El Argentino is the best spot for grilled meats, all of which are served with the excellent house *chimichurri* (Argentine herb sauce). The grillman here claims to have 'the best steak in Ceará!' which is perhaps pushing it a bit, but carnivores will certainly leave content.

PHAELNOGUEIRA/GETTY IMAGES ©

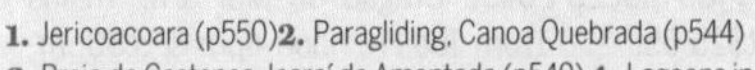

1. Jericoacoara (p550) **2.** Paragliding, Canoa Quebrada (p544) **3.** Praia de Caetanos, Icaraí de Amontada (p549) **4.** Lagoons in Parque Nacional dos Lençóis Maranhenses (p566)

3

LUCIA PITTER/SHUTTERSTOCK ©

Beach Beauties

In a country famed for its fabulous beaches, the shoreline of Ceará, Piauí and Maranhão has both hands on the supreme crown. The 1000km from Ceará's southeastern limits to São Luís is a rarely interrupted succession of long, sweeping, dune-backed strands and smaller palm-lined bays with a few fishing boats riding at anchor.

Jericoacoara

Set inside a national park with no paved roads (only sandy tracks), this hip, ultra-laid-back travelers' hangout (p550) just about has it all. Majestic dunescapes, world-class winds for kite- and windsurfers, a nightly party scene on the beach and in the music joints, good restaurants and dozens of good-value pousadas (guesthouses).

Atins

For that true end-of-the-road feeling, head down the jungle-clad Rio Preguiças to tiny Atins (p566), with a scattering of pousadas along its sandy streets, and the incredible expanse of high dunes and freshwater lagoons that is the Lençóis Maranhenses (p564) beginning a short walk away.

Icaraí de Amontada

Little Icaraí (p549), just far enough from Fortaleza to preserve its tranquility, spreads round a gorgeous curve of palm-lined sand with a few fishing boats bobbing in the surf and rarely more than a handful of people in sight. A few surprisingly good pousadas and restaurants cater to those in the know.

Canoa Quebrada

A budget backpackers' destination that is transitioning into a more family-friendly spot, Canoa (p543) sits on an endless beach lined by pink cliffs on one side and high dunes on the other, and is full of fun things to do, from tandem paragliding to beach reggae parties.

OFF THE BEATEN TRACK

REDONDA

The peaceful fishing village of Redonda, 35km southeast of Canoa Quebrada, beyond the headland of Ponta Grossa, is reminiscent of Canoa Quebrada before tourism set in – a fine place to forget the wider world for a few days amid authentic Cearense village life.

Like Canoa, the beach is backed by cliffs, with the town on the top of the plateau. One road leads down to the beach, which is always busy with fisherman getting ready to go to sea or bringing in their catch from their traditional sailing vessels.

The waterfront is lined with pleasant open-air restaurants that serve seafood straight off the boats and are good places to eat lobster at lower-than-usual prices.

While Redonda is an easy day trip from Canoa Quebrada, there are several good places to stay around town, including **Pousada O Pescador** (88 3432-3018; Rua Praia 496, Redonda; r R$120;), right on the beach, and the slightly fancier (but still relaxed) brick chalets of **Oh! Linda Pousada** (88 99307-3771; www.ohlindapousada.com.br; Rua da Serra 100, Saida a Peroba; s/d R$160/230;) up on the clifftop.

You can get to Redonda from Fortaleza by taking a bus to Aracati (R$21.50, three hours, 12 daily), then a van/shared taxi from Aracati's Igreja Matriz to Redonda (R$5/10, 45 minutes). A taxi from Canoa Quebrada costs around R$120 – for slightly more the driver will wait while you eat and bring you back. If you want to tour around the area consider hiring a private driver; Alexandre dos Santos offers transport all over the region in his tiny Fiat Uno.

Bar Evolução PIZZA **$$**

(Francisco Eliziário 1060; pizza R$20-46; 7-11pm Thu-Tue) Great little Italian-run place serving up thin-crust, wood-oven pizzas with farm-fresh mozzarella and quality pasta dishes in an atmospheric open-air eatery.

Drinking & Nightlife

There's no need to structure your evening; just walk along Broadway and you'll find what's going on. On weekends, the vibe is electric, fueled by live music nearly every 10 meters. Reggae parties take place at **Freedom Bar** (Praia; 9am-6pm Sun-Thu, 9am-6pm & 11pm-4am Fri & Sat) on the beach.

Regart Bar BAR

(Dragão do Mar s/n; 3pm-2am) Located at the entrance to Broadway, Regart is our favorite local bar for its pleasant sidewalk seating and second-floor balcony overlooking the action.

Information

The post office and a multi-card 24-hour ATM – which charges exorbitant fees – are both in a small shopping plaza near the west end of Dragão do Mar.

Getting There & Away

São Benedito (85 3444-9999; www.sbautovia.com.br; Terminal Rodoviário) runs six daily buses to/from Fortaleza bus station (p542) (R$25, 3¼ hours) departing 6am, 8:30am, 11am, 1:30pm, 4:30pm and 5:30pm. In Canoa you can buy tickets in advance at **SB Viagens** (85 3051-3939; Dragão do Mar s/n; 5:30-6am, 8am-12:30pm & 1:45-7:30pm Mon-Sat, 8am-12:30pm & 1:45-6pm Sun), the agency in town representing São Benedito.

Alternatively, you can travel by tour van (R$55, 2½ hours) with companies such as **Oceanview** (85-3219-1300; www.oceanviewturismo.com.br). The tour vans pick up and drop off at accommodations in Fortaleza, departing around 8am and returning from the west end of Canoa's Dragão do Mar around 4pm.

Coming from Rio Grande do Norte, get off the bus at Aracati, 13km southwest of Canoa. From there with any luck you can catch São Benedito's Fortaleza–Canoa bus (R$1.85, 20 minutes), departing around 9am, 11:20am, 2pm, 4:35pm, 7:20pm and 8:35pm. Otherwise, minibuses known colloquially as *topics* (R$3, about every half-hour) depart 6am to 7:30pm from the Igreja Matriz in Aracati's center, about 1km from the bus station.

Taxis charge R$35 to R$40 for the quick Aracati–Canoa run.

Commercial flights were approved in 2015 for the new airport at Aracati, but at time of writing its runways remained unused, although charter flights may be in the pipeline.

Getting Around

If you want to tour around the area consider hiring a private driver; **Alexandre dos Santos** (88 98868-8003; Dragão do Mar s/n) offers economic transport all over the region in his tiny Fiat Uno.

Icaraí de Amontada

☎0XX88

Icaraizinho, as it's affectionately known, is the loveliest of the small beach spots between Fortaleza and Jericoacoara. Its wide beach of fine sand sits on a beautiful palm-lined curve of the bay, with a few fishing boats on the water, high dunes rising to the west, and rarely more than a handful of people in sight. It's reminiscent, some say, of Jericoacoara as it was 25 years ago, although the surrounding scenery is not quite as spectacular.

The small town has a selection of excellent pousadas and some good restaurants. It's a top windsurfing and kitesurfing spot. Being located 190km from Fortaleza, Icaraí is mercifully beyond the reach of most day-tour buses and there's wonderfully little going on here. It's a fantastic place to chill and explore nature away from the crowds.

Activities

Club Ventos WINDSURFING, KITESURFING

(☎88 3636-3006; www.clubventos.com) At the east end of the beach, Club Ventos offers windsurfing and kitesurfing classes and rents quality equipment; also rents kayaks and stand-up paddle (SUP) boards. It's next to **Pousada Les Alizés** (☎88 3636-3006; www.lesalizes.com.br; Joaquim Alves Parente 219; d/tr R$239/298; ❄📶🏊).

Sleeping

★**Casa Zulu** POUSADA **$$**

(☎88 3636-3016; www.casazulu.com; Francisco Gonçalves de Sousa 194; r/bungalow from R$300/350; ❄📶🏊) A young French windsurfer and his South African wife have built their dream pousada where once nothing stood but coconut palms, nailing the perfect marriage of rustic vibe and stylish comfort along the way. Colorful rooms (four bungalows and four apartments) boast good mattresses and organic cotton mosquito nets and are decorated with artistic touches throughout.

It's all set around gorgeous leafy gardens with direct beach access. There's a patio that's great for breakfast and drinks, a pool area, a slew of friendly pets, and windsurfing and kitesurfing lessons for guests. Pretty perfect.

Pousada Malea POUSADA **$$**

(☎88-3636-3115; www.pousadamalea.com; Francisco Gonçalves de Sousa s/n; s/d R$120/170; P📶🏊) The best budget bet in Icaraizinho is set on expansive grounds with nice gardens and a pool a few blocks back from the sea. The fan-cooled wooden chalets are private and very spacious, while the service is laid-back and friendly. Hard to beat the value.

Villa Mango CHALET **$$$**

(☎88 3636-3089; www.villamango.com.br; Lagoa Verde s/n; apt/bungalow from R$550/680; ❄📶🏊) 🌿 Nine rustic but luxurious wooden stilt chalets (some two-level) stand in a garden that slopes down to the west end of the beach. Villa Mango also has a good restaurant, a bar, a pool and its own kitesurfing club. It does its best with sustainable initiatives, such as ecological drains and solar heating.

Eating

Espaço Gourmet JAPANESE, BRAZILIAN **$$**

(☎88 99473-5318; Noé Praciano Sampaio 194; mains R$20-50; ⏲6:30pm-11pm Mon-Sat) Who needs a menu? An honest-to-goodness Japazilian chef from São Paulo has slapped down just five tables and cooks up what's fresh. That means anything from an insanely portioned chicken yakisoba (feeds at least three) or cashew-nut pesto tagliatelle to fresh-caught tuna sushi and sashimi, which comes in twice a week. Options are limited; reservations prudent.

Sabor Minas BRAZILIAN **$$**

(☎88 98148-5712; Francisco Gonçalves de Sousa 17; mains R$35-65; ⏲11am-10pm) It doesn't look like much from outside, but this little family-run restaurant offers outstanding value, with massive plates of tasty typical food from both the Northeast and the owner's home region of Minas Gerais. Meals are served in the rear patio next to the garden that provides herbs and vegetables for many of the dishes.

Café Zapata BRAZILIAN **$$**

(www.cafezapata.com; Joaquim Alves Parente 94; mains R$26-47; ⏲6:30pm-11pm Tue-Sun; 📶) This pretty garden restaurant on a narrow street leading toward the far east end of the beach focuses on interesting pastas such as seafood puttanesca, and fish and lobster lasagna. It's all pretty good, and so are the prices.

Information

There's no ATM in town but most accommodations accept cards.

Getting There & Away

Icaraí is 190km from Fortaleza (beyond the reach of most day-tour buses). The 24km road linking it to Hwy CE-085 sees little traffic.

A daily Fretcar (p542) bus leaves Fortaleza bus station (p542) for Icaraí de Amontada (R$35, five hours) at 1:45pm (3pm on Sundays), returning at 5:40am (1:10pm Sundays).

You do not need to backtrack to Fortaleza to continue on to Jericoacoara from Icaraí; you can catch the **Fretcar** (☎88 98106-9797; www.fretcar.com.br; Av Couto Garces; ⏲5-11:30am & 2-10pm) bus (R$7, 45 minutes) at 5:40am (1:10pm on Sundays) or **Cooperita** (☎88 3631-1432) *topique* (minivan; R$10, one hour, hourly from 5:30am to 10:30am and 1pm Mon-Sat) from the gas station on the edge of town to Amontada, from where there are regular Fretcar buses departing to Jijoca.

Jericoacoara

☎0XX88 / POP 3000

Jericoacoara, known to its many friends simply as 'Jeri,' is one of Brazil's most cinematic destinations. Lodged between a magnificent national park and the sea, it magnetizes travelers with its perfect combination of hard-to-reach location (access is by unpaved tracks through the dunes), stunning coastal scenery, exciting activities, excellent pousadas and restaurants, and fun nightlife. During the day, its beaches, dunes and lagoons are postcard-worthy; at night, illuminated by moonlight and the lights of inviting boutiques and restaurants, it oozes atmosphere. While it's no longer a tranquil hippy haven, Jeri's allure remains undeniable and it's a must-visit on any Northeast itinerary.

Activities

Steady winds between late June and February make Jericoacoara a top destination for kitesurfing and windsurfing; there's also decent surfing waves.

Other activities include visiting the dunes and lakes outside town by buggy; yoga classes; and strolling along the beach or through the hills to Pedra Furada, an arched rock 3km east of town that's become an emblem of Jeri.

Buggy Rides

The most popular day trips head east (to Preá, Pedro Furada, Lagoa Azul and, the belle of the ball, Lagoa Paraíso) for R$300 per buggy; or west (to Guriú and Tatajuba, with an option to see seahorses) for R$350. Each vehicle seats four; buggy drivers, hotels and tour operators will help to fill the spots with other travelers.

While the trip east to the lagoons offers the chance to cool off in postcard-perfect, brilliant blue lagoons (one of the highlights of a trip to Jeri), the trip to the west packs in more adventure. It includes a visit to the fishing village of Tatajuba, 24km from Jericoacoara, where there's a beach at the mouth of a tidal river, and a large lagoon among the dunes behind the village. There are *barracas* (stalls) beside the lagoon. One of the dunes overlooks the site of old Tatajuba, which had to be moved to its present site brick by brick. You can still see evidence of where the church used to be.

Both trips can also be done by ATV (R$300 to R$350) with each vehicle able to carry two.

Capoeira

Classes (R$30, 1½ hours) are usually held from 7am to 8am and 4pm to 5pm every day on the beach, followed daily (except Sunday) by a sunset *roda de capoeira* (open capoeira performance), which always attracts a crowd.

Massage

Ashti Ma Parithosh MASSAGE

(☎88 99949-8299; www.ashti.com.br; Pousada Vila Bela Vista, Preá; 75min massage R$160; ⏲10am-7:30pm) Fed up with all the buggy noise and crowds, Jerís best masseuse has upped and left town; fortunately for those in need of relaxation she hasn't gone far and can be found by the more tranquil sands of Preá 12km east. English-speaking Ashti, who trained in Brazil and Italy, offers a 75-minute massage that will deal with what ails you.

Surfing

There are good waves for surfing (best from about March to May) right out in front of Praia de Jericoacoara. Neighboring Praia Malhada, round the bend to the east, has bigger waves for more advanced surfers. Board rental costs R$30 or so per hour but you can negotiate a better deal for longer rentals.

Windsurfing

The same winds that make Jeri a kitesurfing mecca work for windsurfing too. July to January are the best months, with fine conditions for experienced riders right in front of Jeri beach.

Club Ventos WINDSURFING

(☎88-3669-2288; www.clubventos.com; Praia de Jericoacoara; ⏲9:30am-6pm) Just east of the foot of Rua do Forró, Club Ventos is professional and well equipped, though more expensive than some similar outfits. It also rents kayaks, surfboards and stand-up paddle (SUP) boards.

KITESURFING JERI & THE NORTHEAST

Steady, strong trade winds blowing across the Atlantic from Africa during the second half of the year help put Brazil's northeast coast among the world's very best kitesurfing zones. Lovers of this exciting, physically demanding sport fly in from around the world and have spawned a whole infrastructure of kite schools, kite pousadas and kite safaris. There is a full range of conditions from flat water to waves, and the steady easterly breeze blowing along the whole coast makes for some epic downwinder voyages.

Equipment rentals are widely available, but with rates of R$300 to R$315 per day it makes more sense for experienced surfers to bring their own. A rental car is a huge help both for transporting your gear and for reaching the best spots. Beginners can learn the art at almost any kitesurfing destination on the coast: a course of nine or 10 hours, usually spread over three days, costs around R$1450 to R$1800 with IKO-certified instructors. For proper safety standards and quality teaching, choose a school with instructors certified by the International Kiteboarding Organization (www.ikointl.com).

Jericoacoara is one of the most popular kitesurfing locations, thanks to its combination of traveler facilities and winds that blow at an average 23 to 30 knots for eight months of the year. From late June to February the breeze springs up mid-morning and blows until sunset; it's strongest in September and October. The best spot for beginners is Preá (13km east of Jeri) at low tide, where there are idyllic side-on-shore wind conditions. Other good spots are the river-mouth waters at Guriú, 12km west of Jeri (though it's becoming more crowded) and along the shore for several kilometers back toward Jeri; and Tatajuba, 12km beyond Guriú, where there's a flat-water lagoon. For experienced kitesurfers, the 25km of downwind conditions from the Pôr do Sol (Sunset) dune all the way to Tatajuba is a popular route. It's also possible to kitesurf the entire journey from Fortaleza to Jericoacoara.

Jeri has numerous kite schools. Freelance teachers may charge less, but it's better to use a school with IKO instructors such as **MH Kiteschool** (☎88-99971-3330; www.mhkiteschool.com; Pousada Bella Jeri, Travessa da Rua do Forró) (IKO II Senior), **Kiteiscool** (☎88 99670-2330; www.kiteiscool.com; Praça Principal; ⏲8:30am-noon & 4:30-11pm) or Preá-based **Rancho do Kite** (☎88 3669-2080; www.ranchodokite.com.br; Principal; ⏲shop 10am-1pm & 3:30-11pm).

The whole coast around Jeri – from Barrinha, 6km east of Preá, to Camocim, 20km west of Tatajuba – is great for downwinders. It's easy to find a buggy for transport; for example, it's R$140 for four or five people from Jeri to Guriú. Much longer downwinders are equally possible on any stretch of the coast; adventures can be organized through local pousadas, agencies and kite schools. Jeri Off Road (p542), for example, offers 'kitesurfaris' of several days with 4WD from Canoa Quebrada to Fortaleza (140km), Fortaleza to Jeri (300km), or Jeri to Barra Grande (100km), running around R$1000 per day per vehicle.

Other Northeast kitesurfing locations include Natal, São Miguel do Gostoso, Galinhos, Canoa Quebrada, Fortaleza, Cumbuco (p537), Flecheiras and Icaraí de Amontada.

Ticowind WINDSURFING
(☎88 99662-9291; www.ticowindjeri.com; Vila Kalango, Rua das Dunas 30; ⏲8am-6pm) Ticowind is highly popular for its good quality/price combination (and it's thus sometimes necessary to book ahead for its services): it rents windsurfing boards and runs three-hour beginner courses for R$400. Also organizes specialized insurance.

Tours

In addition to buggy day trips, you can also take buggy or 4WD trips as far west as Parnaíba, the Lençóis Maranhenses and São Luís, a route known as the Rota das Emoções (Route of the Emotions). A tour is a lot easier, though more expensive, than taking public transportation: a three-day (or more) 4WD expedition to São Luís – including accommodations, transportation, a Delta do Parnaíba boat trip, a boat along the Rio Preguiças and a Lençóis Maranhenses dunes tour – costs around R$2000 per traveler with Jeri Off Road (p542).

The same company also offers one-and two-day trips to Fortaleza visiting villages and beaches along the way for R$850 to R$1500 for up to four travelers.

Sleeping

There are dozens of pousadas and small hotels in Jericoacoara. Some hotels close during May, the low point of Jeri's season. The high seasons are July and January.

Villa Chic HOSTEL $
(☎88 99968-5980; www.villachicjeri.com; Principal; dm R$65, r/t/q R$260/320/410; ❄@📶🏊) If you've outgrown the hostel party scene, the excellent dorms here are Jeri's best, but exist within the environment of a boutique pousada. Each eight-bed dorm (one mixed, one male, one female) boasts one-and-a-half bathrooms (the 'half' has no shower), which are some of the most fashionable you'll come across at these prices.

Jeri Central HOSTEL $
(☎88 99747-8070; www.jericentral.com.br; São Francisco 222; dm/r R$60/250; ❄📶🏊) This popular hostel in the center of town wins big points for its bright, neat facilities and welcoming atmosphere. The swimming pool and large thatch hammock space promote easy socializing, and trilingual manager Gaúcho is constantly assisting guests with travel advice, well-organized information boards and reasonably priced laundry service – and keeps a watchful, anti-shenanigans patrol.

It's conveniently located right in front of the Fretcar (p556) office.

Pousada Papaya POUSADA $$
(☎88 3669-2219, 88 99651-8015; www.jeripapaya.com.br; Dunas II 74; r R$260-380; ❄📶🏊) Tucked away inside this walled oasis are 11 neat, comfy rooms with colorful bedspreads, a pool in a flowery front garden, and attractive common areas inside and out. These features and a great breakfast make this a deservedly popular choice, although service could be better at times. Room 10 with its dune views is the pick of the bunch.

Bella Jeri POUSADA $$
(☎88 99971-3330; www.bellajeri.com.br; Travessa da Rua do Forró; s/d/t R$260/290/390; ❄📶🏊) Bella Jeri has seven cute, tasteful rooms with brick walls, solid wood furniture and hammocks, plus a pleasant garden, pool and breezy roof terrace with views to the dunes and the ocean. The breakfast is great, and the English-speaking owners also run Jeri Off Road (p542) and MH Kiteschool (p551), which makes it a one-stop shop for all you desire in Jeri.

★ **Vila Kalango** POUSADA, CHALET $$$
(☎88 3669-2290; www.vilakalango.com.br; Rua das Dunas 30; r R$830-1300; ❄@📶🏊) A longtime top-end favorite, Vila Kalango offers a variety of charming accommodations set in a lovely garden. The round brick bungalows are serene escape pods with beautiful canopy beds and native wood furniture. There are also breezy fan-cooled *palafitas* (stilt houses) with driftwood staircases and smaller but equally elegant *apartamentos* (rooms with private bathroom).

The staff is charming, and the pool deck and restaurant look out onto the beach.

Casa Fufi POUSADA $$$
(☎88 99773-0303; www.casafufi.com.br; Rua do Ibama; r R$390-510; ❄📶🏊) This newish intimate top-ender offers just five rooms within its white-stone-and-brick, thatched-roof construction, flanked by a healthy patch of grass (a rarity in Jeri) and a stylish pool deck. Breakfast is served privately on the expansive verandas, where there are hammocks and ample table space. The spacious rooms all come with modern kitchens. Top honors for privacy and price.

Pousada Jeribá POUSADA $$$
(☎88 99768-0007, 85 4062-9193; www.jeriba.com.br; Rua do Ibama; r R$775-1620; ❄@📶🏊) Spacious rooms with gorgeous hardwood verandas and hammock chairs are set in tasteful exposed-brick bungalows, amid colorful grounds draped in lush tropicalia. Rooms 5, 8 and 12 have the most panoramic views. Facilities are top-notch throughout – the wifi is turbo speed – and the oceanfront patio and lounge with views over Jeri's dunes is a near-perfect chill-out pad.

Eating

Jeri offers a great variety of excellent food for such a small place. Deciding on which charming spot to eat at can be painful. Cheap local eateries where simple meals start from R$10 cluster on the eastern end of Rua São Francisco.

Naturalmente BRAZILIAN $
(Praia de Jericoacoara; crepes R$16-39; ⏲noon-11pm) Tasty crepes, great *açaí* and fresh juices served with sea views in a breezy thatched hut right on the beach make this one of Jeri's best places to chill out after a long tour or a night of too many caipirinhas.

Gelato & Grano ICE CREAM $
(Praça Principal 1; 1/2/3 scoops R$10/12/16; ⏲noon-midnight) If there's one thing you'll eventually crave in this heat, it's ice cream. This wildly popular, farmhouse-chic gelato shop on the main square serves up 20 flavors and is constantly swarmed by sweet-toothed vacationers and locals. Belgian chocolate and pistachio are the most popular, but Brazilian staples such as *açaí* and tapioca are here as well.

There's a second, smaller location closer to the beach on Rua Principal (4pm to midnight).

Padaria Santo Antônio BAKERY $

(São Francisco; items R$1-9; ⏲2am-7pm) A Jericoacoara classic, this bakery opens in the wee hours of the morning to provide coffee and freshly baked goods to partygoers on their way home.

★Bistro Caiçara BRAZILIAN $$

(☎88 99916-0072; Principal 16; mains R$38-95; ⏲5-11pm Mon-Sat; 📶) Right in the center of town, this place is a real crowd-pleaser for Chef Apolinário's more-creative-than-most menu which includes plenty of seafood: *robalo* (sea bass) in soy, ginger and honey; fish in passion-fruit or cashew-fruit sauces; and sweet-and-spicy octopus are standouts. Service is top-notch and it all goes down very romantically on a candlelit 2nd-floor open-air patio overlooking Rua Principal.

Peixe Brasileiro SEAFOOD $$

(cnr São Francisco & Beco do Guaxêlo; fish/shrimp/lobster per kg R$50/90/150; ⏲7-11:30pm) Just a few plastic tables in the sand alley where local fisherfolk grill fresh catch nightly. Pick your dinner by size from the family's *peixaria* (fishmonger) next door: *pargo* (red snapper), *garoupa* (grouper), *robalo* (sea bass), shrimp and/or *langosta* (lobster). Weigh it, sit back and wait while they barbecue it, garnished with nothing but lime and salt.

Service is slow and somewhat surly. Unfortunately the fishmongers sometimes assume you have a bigger appetite than you do. Keep them honest: about 500g is a good fish portion per person. The entire experience is one to remember.

Tamarindo BRAZILIAN $$

(☎88 99937-9057; Travessa Ismael; medium pizza R$34-65, mains R$44-76; ⏲6-11pm) Jeri's most creative dining experience is romantically lit under the shadow of a giant tamarind tree. Nearly everything is cooked in the brick oven, which may be the norm for pizza, but not for exquisite gems such as the Brazil-nut-crusted filet mignon. From the cocktails (frozen *tangeroskas* made with tangerine and ginger) to the staff and service, it's a class act.

Pimenta Verde INTERNATIONAL, BRAZILIAN $$

(São Francisco; mains for two R$103-141; ⏲noon-11pm, closed two Sun per month; 📶) This delightful little corner restaurant with only a few tables pumps out memorable cuisine, from octopus Provençal (best dish in Jeri?) to a divine green-peppercorn filet and perfectly creamy seafood risotto. Cute artistic touches round out the culinary happiness.

Pizzaria Araxá PIZZA $$

(www.araxapousada.com; Rua das Dunas; pizza R$35-45; ⏲6:30-10:30pm) Intimate Italian-owned pizzeria inside a well-to-do pousada producing Jeri's best pies. All the classics are represented (margherita, marinara etc) as well as white pizzas and a few Brazilianized versions to appease the locals (chicken with Catupiry cheese etc). There are just a few tables, divided loft-style between those overlooking the pool and those in the sand below.

Club Ventos BUFFET $$

(☎88-3669-2288; www.clubventos.com; Praia de Jericoacoara; per kg R$90, mains for two R$70-120; ⏲noon-6pm; 📶) Soak up the spectacular views from the cashew-tree-shaded oceanfront terrace at Jericoacoara's best *por kilo* eatery, then settle into a lounge chair and catch some rays for the rest of the afternoon. An excellent selection of salads compensate for the limited – but tasty – array of main dishes. There are also à la carte dishes with plenty of inspired seafood choices.

🍷 Drinking & Nightlife

Everything starts at the cocktail *barracas* on the beach at the foot of Rua Principal. From early evening, caipirinhas and *caipifrutas* are mixed up with exotic fruits. Cocktails average R$7 to R$16. From here partiers move on to other entertainments around the village.

Places and events change frequently; ask around. For live music, expect covers between R$15 and R$20.

Cachaçaria Gourmet BAR

(www.facebook.com/cachacariagourmetjeri; Travessa Ismael; cachaça R$8-12; ⏲6pm-midnight) If you'd like a stiff drink without a soundtrack, this cute, tiny bar specializes in Brazil's national firewater, *cachaça*. There are around 90 labels, many of which come from Minas Gerais (as does the owner); around 30 labels are available at any given time. The liquor is even mixed into frozen caipirinhas (a rarity, despite the obviousness of the idea!).

Also sells microbrews made locally in Jeri.

Samba Rock Cafe BAR

(www.sambarockcafe.com; Principal; Cover R$8; ⏲6pm-1am) Sitting on prime corner real estate across from the main square, this is easily Jeri's most atmospheric drinking spot. Rustic wooden seating is arranged under a massive, illuminated acacia tree. There are often bands playing *sertanejo*, rock, samba, *forró* (popular music of the Northeast), or MPB (Música Popular Brasileira); at other times, DJs spin an eclectic mix.

☆ Entertainment

Pousada Solar de Malhada LIVE MUSIC
(www.solardamalhada.com; Rua da Matriz; cover R$20; ⏲10pm-late) Hosts Jeri's best samba night from 11pm on Fridays.

Maloca LIVE MUSIC
(☎88-99810-6347; Igreja) At the top end of Rua Igreja, Maloca is a cultural center that hosts live music, film nights and other events. Its *forró* nights are especially good.

Restaurante Dona Amélia LIVE MUSIC
(Rua do Forró; cover R$5; ⏲8pm-midnight Wed, Thu & Sat) Live band *forró* nights here have a distinct local flavor and are usually thronged with swaying couples on the dance floor.

ℹ Information

All visitors to Jericoacoara are required to pay a R$5 per day tourism tax. It can be paid in advance online but it's easier just to pay at the entrance to the village. If you decide to stay longer you'll need to go to the payment point again.

DANGERS & ANNOYANCES

Jeri's isolated position is a blessing and a curse: don't walk on the dunes alone in the wee hours or leave valuables unattended in restaurants or on the beach.

With the exception of the beach, don't go barefoot in Jeri: wear flip-flops in town and on the Pôr do Sol (Sunset) dune to avoid *bicho-de-pé* (chigoe flea), a parasite that can embed in your foot and reproduce, which – trust us – isn't fun.

It's not common but the waters around Jeri are occasionally plagued by *águas-vivas*, a stinging jellyfish. If there's noone else in the water ask before diving in.

PIAUÍ

Piauí is one of the largest states in the Northeast but is one of the least visited despite boasting several fantastic natural attractions. One reason that it remains off the tourism radar is that, unlike its neighbors, it has only a short stretch of coastline and its biggest city, Teresina, is far inland. **Eco Adventure Tour** (☎86 3323-9595; www.ecoadventure.tur.br; Av Presidente Vargas 26; ⏲8am-8pm Mon-Fri, 8am-noon & 4:30-8:30pm Sat) is an excellent, sustainably minded ecotourism agency for all adventures in Piauí.

Parque Nacional de Sete Cidade

Sete Cidades is a small 62-sq-km national park with bizarre rock formations that some have claimed are *sete cidades* (seven cities) left behind by some mysterious long-departed culture (aliens, Vikings etc). The place doesn't need such fantasies to make it worth visiting, as the rock formations are indeed fantastic – some look like giant turtle shells, others resemble a castle, an elephant, a map of Brazil or the head of emperor Dom Pedro II. The park offers superb vistas over *caatinga* (semi-arid land) and *cerrado* (savanna) vegetation. There are also some 1500 intriguing rock paintings between 3000 and 5000 years old; wildlife that includes marmosets, small rodents called *mocós* (cavies) that like to pose for photos, tarantulas and (we're told) rattlesnakes; and two delectable natural bathing pools.

The park entrance is 190km northeast of Teresina, 24km northeast of the small town of Piripiri and 8km north by paved road off Hwy BR-222. Buses run regularly to Piripiri from Fortaleza (R$70, nine hours), Parnaíba (R$59, four hours) and Teresina (R$38, three hours). A taxi from Piripiri costs R$80 to or from the park,

Delta do Parnaíba

The **Delta of the Rio Parnaíba** (sometimes called the Delta das Américas) is a 2700-sq-km expanse of islands, beaches, lagoons, channels, high sand dunes and dense mangrove forests full of wildlife. Around 65% of its area is in the state of Maranhão, but the easiest access is from Parnaíba in Piauí. Agencies around Parnaíba's Porto das Barcas offer several half-day and day tours into the delta (R$70 to R$80 per passenger) in fast motor launches or big party boats, starting from Porto dos Tatus, 11km north of Parnaíba. A better option if you're interested in peace, quiet and nature is boatman **José Ribamar** (☎83 99924-5598; Rua da Glória 900, Centro Ilha Grande), who uses traditional, quiet wooden boats; he can

EMERGENCIES

BPTur (Batalhão de Policiamento Turístico do Ceará; ☎88 99682-7500, 88 3669-2113; Principal; ⏰24hr)

MONEY

Many pousadas and restaurants will accept Visa or Mastercard, but Jeri has no international-friendly ATMs. Stock up with cash at **Banco do Brasil** (Av Manoel Teixeira 139, Jijoca; ⏰branch 9am-2pm Mon-Fri, ATMs 8am-10pm daily) in Jijoca, 23km southeast.

Tem de Tudo (Principal; ⏰7am-midnight) supermarket can usually give cash back, with a 10 per cent charge for debit cards and 15 per cent for credit cards, up to a R$500 limit.

TRAVEL AGENCIES

Global Connection (☎88 99900-2109; Rua do Forró; ⏰9am-10pm) Sells bus/van tickets for many regional routes, organizes transport from Jericoacoara to Lençóis Maranhenses (R$1050 for up to 4 passengers) and sells air tickets.

Getting There & Away

Jericoacoara is in an isolated position, inside a far-flung national park at the top edge of the country. However, the opening of the new Jericoacoara **airport** (☎85 2181-6277) – 30km away in Cruz municipality – has made it easier than ever to visit.

AIR

Jericoacoara's airport, some 30km southeast of town outside the boundaries of the national park, now receives direct flights from São Paulo and Recife.

Collective transport in pickups from the airport into town costs R$75 to R$80 per passenger; a private transfer costs R$250.

4WD TRUCK & BUGGY

The main form of transportation between Jeri and Jijoca is by 4WD passenger trucks (R$20 one way), known as D-20s, which leave whenever they fill with passengers – about every 30 minutes from 6am to 6pm. Departures are most frequent from 6am and 10am. In Jeri the departure point is in front of Padaria Jeripan on Rua São

pick you up in Parnaíba. José speaks Portuguese but a multilingual guide is available for an extra R$200. His most popular day trip (R$350 for up to five people), will take you to the Morro Branco dunes; Pontal, where you can swim at a meeting point of freshwater and ocean; a fishing village; and then by motorized canoe into mangrove channels where you can hope to see plenty of wildlife such as howler and capuchin monkeys, caimans, iguanas, snakes and birds. Other options include a six- to seven-hour one-way tour through the delta to Tutóia (R$700 for up to eight people), hikes and overnight trips.

Parnaíba is serviced by buses from Fortaleza (R$62 to R$81, nine hours, six daily), Camocim (R$24, 2¼ hours, 7:15am, 9:30am, 6:15pm and 10pm), São Luís (R$104, nine hours, 6:25am and 9pm) and Teresina (R$84 to R$88.50, six hours, 10 daily via Piripiri).

Parque Nacional da Serra da Capivara

One of Brazil's most important national parks, this 1300-sq-km reserve contains more than 40,000 rock paintings among spectacular panoramas of immense chiseled rock formations surrounded by dry forest. The scenery and wildlife here are themselves reason enough to visit, but the archaeological sites are a must-see for those with an interest in the field. The park has good facilities including wooden walkways, firm vehicle tracks and bilingual signs. There's disabled access to many sites.

More than 170 sites are open to the public, organized into five main driving circuits and several walking trails helping visitors appreciate the landscape, geology, vegetation and wildlife as well as the evidence of ancient humanity.

A local guide is obligatory for visiting the park, costing R$150 per day for up to eight people – best organized through your accommodations in São Raimundo Nonato.

The most common access point is the one at Boqueirão da Pedra Furada, which can be reached from a turnoff on Hwy BR-20 22km north of São Raimundo Nonato. From the turnoff it's 6km down a firm dirt road to the gate.

Three daily buses run by **Princesa do Sul/Viação Transpiaui** (Rodoviária; ☎89-3218-1761; Av Getúlio Vargas) make the 500km odyssey from Teresina to São Raimundo Nonato (R$80, nine to 10 hours) and back. Buses leave from Teresina's bus station at 2pm, 8:15pm and 8:30pm.

Francisco. In Jijoca D-20s meet your bus before scooping up more passengers around town.

Alternatively, a buggy costs around R$120 to R$150 for up to four people.

From Jijoca there are up to nine Fretcar buses to Fortaleza (R$35 to R$49, five to six hours) and up to five to Camocim (R$12 to R$15, 1½ to two hours).

BUS

Fretcar (☎88 99700-7373; www.fretcar.com.br; São Francisco; ⏰6-6:15am, 8-11am, noon-5pm & 6-10:30pm) runs a service to Fortaleza (R$74 to R$97, six to seven hours), leaving at 6:15am, 2:55pm, 4:55pm and, the most comfortable, at 10:30pm. You travel by *jardineira* (open-sided 4WD truck) as far as Jijoca, then by bus. The trip begins at Fretcar's office on Rua São Francisco, across from Jeri Central (p552) hostel. Buy tickets at least one day in advance.

You can also travel to Fortaleza in the tour vans of companies such as Girafatur (p542) and Vitorino (p542), which drop off at Fortaleza hotels (R$80 to R$100, five hours). Most accommodations can book these for you. The vans usually leave about 9am and some stop for 2½ hours at Lagoa Paraíso, near Jijoca, en route.

A private transfer to Fortaleza runs from R$500 to R$600.

CAR

If travelling to Jeri by car, it's best to leave your vehicle in Jijoca, where there are safe parking lots for R$20 per day; it's easy to damage vehicles on the trip to Jeri, and rental insurance is void in the sand. Even if you make it to Jeri, unauthorized vehicles are not permitted to circulate in the town. From Jijoca, get a D-20 or buggy on to Jeri.

TO/FROM THE LENÇÓIS MARANHENSES

Moving on westward toward the Parque Nacional dos Lençóis Maranhenses (p564), there are several routes and combinations of vehicles for making the trip.

To reach the Lençóis with local transport take a regular Fretcar bus from Jijoca to Camocim (R$12.15, 1½ to 2¼ hours) and then the daily 3pm Expresso Guanabara (www.expressoguanabara.com.br) bus from Camocim to Parnaíba (R$22, two hours).

It's necessary to spend the night in Parnaíba before taking the 5:30am bus to Tutóia (R$20, 2½ hours), from where there is a bus to Barreirinhas (R$16, two hours) at noon.

If you want to avoid the overnight stay it's also possible to take a night bus from Parnaíba to São Luís and then pick up a morning van or bus from to Barreirinhas, although it's a far longer trip.

It's far quicker to take a straight one-day transfer in a private vehicle from Jeri. Local tour operators get you there in seven to nine hours for around R$1000 to R$1200 per vehicle (up to four people) traveling to Camocim then along the highway to Barreirinhas.

Try Global Connection (p555) which offers regular shuttles and will fill unused seats with other travelers. They also sell a combination ticket from Jericoacoara to Barreirinhas using two local van services (R$260) but it requires an overnight stay in Parnaíba, which adds to the price.

Heading to Jeri from the Lençóis on local transport, it's usually necessary to spend the night in Camocim unless you fork out for a private transfer for the last leg to Jericoacoara.

MARANHÃO

The atmosphere-laden colonial city of São Luís, its tranquil but gorgeous neighbor Alcântara, and the wild natural beauty of the Parque Nacional dos Lençóis Maranhenses have put the Northeast's furthest-flung state firmly on the travel map. The coastal route from Jericoacoara (Ceará) to the Lençóis Maranhenses is an adventure in itself.

Southern and eastern Maranhão are characterized by vast expanses of *babaçu* (palms) and typical *sertão* (backlands of the Northeast) landscapes, but the state's western and northwestern regions merge into humid Amazon rainforests.

São Luís

☎0XX98 / POP 1,091,868

The World Heritage-listed historical center of São Luís is an enchanting neighborhood of steamy cobbled streets and pastel-colored colonial mansions, some handsomely restored, many crumbling. It's a charming area with a unique atmosphere and one of the Northeast's best concentrations of museums, galleries and craft stores. Unfortunately, a general sketchiness pervades some of its streets after dark.

The city as a whole has a markedly Afro-Brazilian tinge to its culture, from a lively reggae scene to the highly colorful Bumba Meu Boi (p561) festivities. The trip across Baía de São Marcos to Alcântara, an impressive historical town slumbering in regal decay, is an added reason to put São Luís on your itinerary.

São Luís sits at the northwest corner of the 50km-long Ilha de São Luís, which is separated from the mainland only by narrow channels.

São Luís

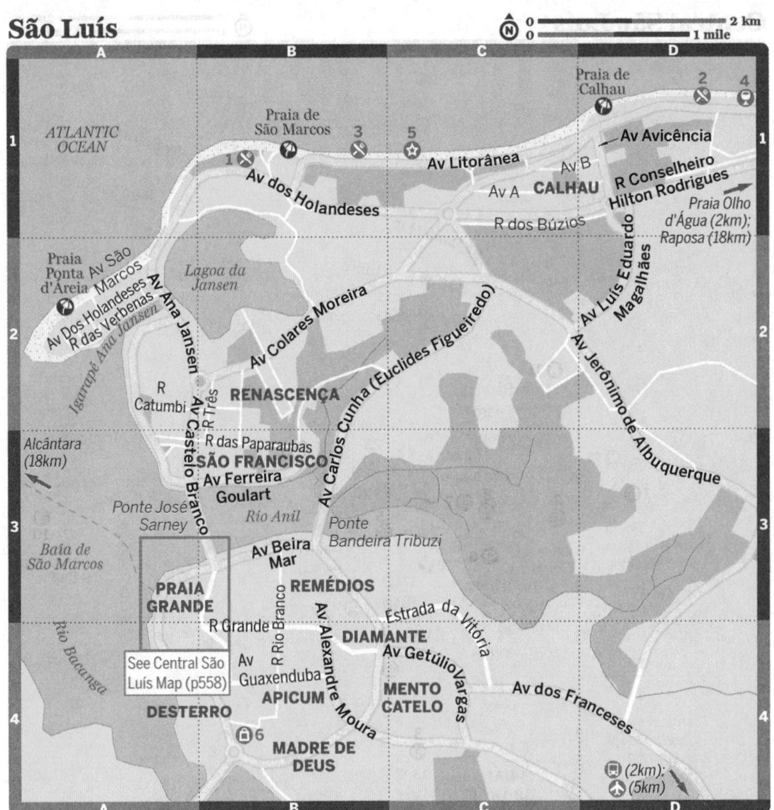

History

São Luís is the only city in Brazil that was founded by the French. In 1612 three French ships sailed for Maranhão to try to commandeer a piece of South America. Once established at São Luís the French formed an alliance with the local indigenous population, the Tupinambá, to assail tribes around the mouth of the Amazon in an effort to expand their foothold in the region. But when the inevitable Portuguese attack came in 1614, the French fled within a year.

After a brief Dutch occupation between 1641 and 1644, São Luís developed gradually as a port for exporting sugar, and later cotton. The plantation owners prospered, and by the early 19th century São Luís was one of the wealthiest cities in Brazil, built on the back of the labor of African slaves. Today the city has the third-highest Afro-Brazilian population in the country (after Rio and Salvador).

São Luís

Eating

1 Cabana do Sol B1
2 Cabana do Sol D1
3 L'Apero B1

Drinking & Nightlife

4 Bar do Nelson D1

Entertainment

5 Casa das Dunas C1

Shopping

6 Ceprama B4

When demand for São Luís' crops slackened later in the 19th century, the city went into a long decline, but the economy has been stimulated by several megaprojects in recent decades. In the 1980s a big port complex was constructed at Itaqui, just west of São Luís, to export the mineral riches of the

Central São Luís

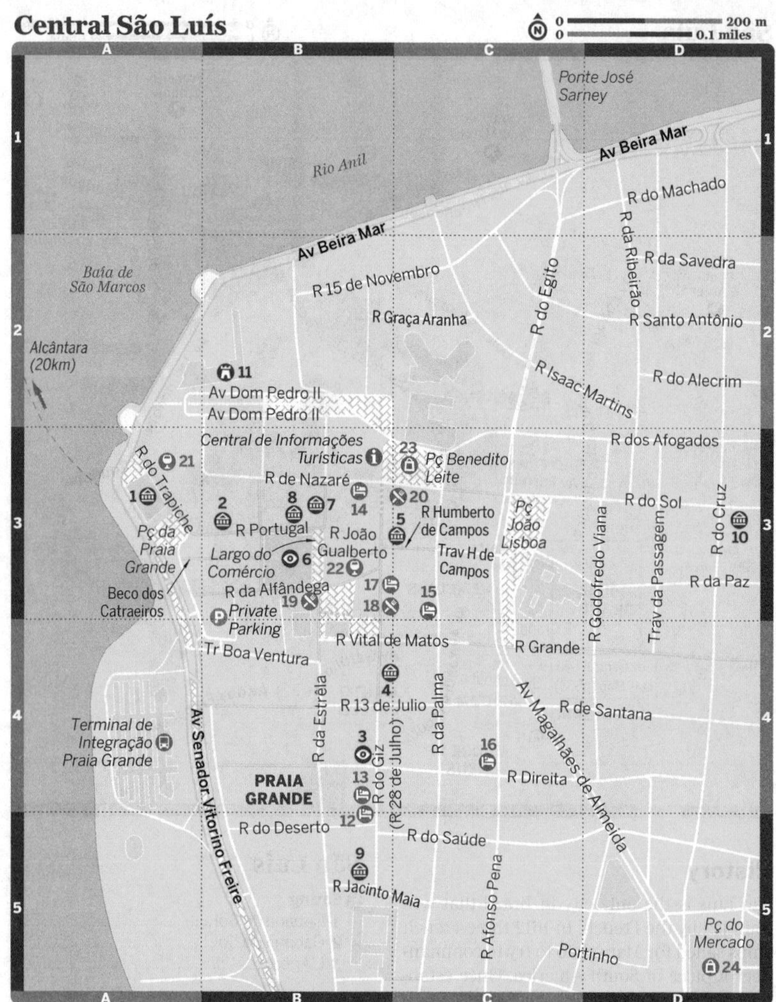

Carajás in neighboring Pará state, and Alcoa built an enormous aluminum-processing plant on the highway south of the city; both constructions remain key to the city's economy today. Thanks to the restoration of many of São Luís' beautiful old buildings and its proximity to the Lençóis Maranhenses, tourism has also become important.

Sights

The center of São Luís has the best-preserved colonial neighborhood in the Northeast; it's full of 18th- and 19th-century mansions covered in colorful 19th-century European *azulejos* (decorative ceramic tiles; often blue, or blue and white). The historical center has been under piecemeal restoration under Projeto Reviver (Project Revival) since the late 1980s, following many decades of neglect and decay. Many of the restored buildings house interesting museums, galleries, craft shops and restaurants. Many buildings still need to be restored and much work is stalled, but their state of interrupted repair is also part of the charm.

Casa do Maranhão MUSEUM

(Map p558; Rua do Trapiche; 10am-6pm Tue-Sun) **FREE** Set in the former customs house built right on the river mouth, this informative and

Central São Luís

Sights
1 Casa do Maranhão A3
2 Casa do Nhôzinho B3
3 Centro Cultural Vale Maranhão B4
4 Centro de Cultura Popular Domingos Vieira Filho B4
5 Centro de Pesquisa de História Natural e Arqueologia do Maranhão C3
6 Mercado das Tulhas B3
7 Museo do Reggae Maranhão B3
8 Museu de Artes Visuais B3
9 Museu do Negro B5
10 Museu Histórico e Artístico do Estado de Maranhão D3
11 Palácio dos Leões B2

Sleeping
12 Casa Frankie B5
13 Casa Lavinia B4
14 Hostel Reviver B3
15 Palma Hostel C3
16 Pousada Colonial C4
17 Pousada Portas da Amazônia B3

Eating
18 Dom Francisco B3
19 O Rei de Beiju Recheado B3
20 Restaurante Senac C3

Drinking & Nightlife
21 Bar do Nelson A3
22 Cafofinho da Tia Dica B3

Shopping
23 Feirinha São Luís C3
24 Mercado Central D5

colorful museum is dedicated to Maranhense culture and features a great collection of costumes and props from Carnaval and Bumba Meu Boi. There are also displays on river-going boats of the region and explanations of Maranhão's different kinds of drums. Some displays are accompanied by English text.

Casa do Nhôzinho MUSEUM
(Map p558; Portugal 185; ⏲9am-6pm Tue-Sun) FREE At the eclectic and fascinating Casa do Nhôzinho, you can see a collection of ingenious fish traps, rooms featuring Maranhão indigenous artisanry, and hosts of colorful, delicate Bumba Meu Boi figurines made by the 20th-century master artisan Mestre Nhôzinho. It was closed for electrical work when we visited but was due to reopen imminently.

Centro Cultural Vale Maranhão CULTURAL CENTRE
(Map p558; ☎98 3232-6363; www.ccv-ma.org.br; Av Henrique Leal 149; ⏲8am-8pm) This hip new cultural center in a stylishly renovated colonial mansion in the heart of the historical center features rotating exhibitions of high-quality local and national art. Also hosts performances and has a good cafe. It's funded by a multinational mining company, but the friendly staff and guides are anything but corporate.

Museo do Reggae Maranhão MUSEUM
(Map p558; ☎98 98137-2423; Rua da Estrela 124; ⏲10am-8pm Tue-Sat, 10am-1pm Sun) FREE A small, bright museum covering the history of reggae music in Maranhão. In addition to displays dedicated to the local artists and promoters who bought the Caribbean sounds to these shores, there are listening posts and a replica of the Voz do Ouro Canarinho – one of the city's most famous mobile sound systems. It's worth engaging one of the free guides as there's few explanatory notes. English and French speakers are available on request.

Museu do Negro MUSEUM
(Map p558; Jacinto Maia 43; admission R$2; ⏲9am-6pm Mon-Fri) In this building that once housed a slave market (notice the absence of windows), the Museu do Negro exhibits relics of slavery, including a replica whipping post and a striking collection of wood carvings and statuettes from West Africa. It was closed for restoration when we visited but is slated to reopen soon.

Centro de Pesquisa de História Natural e Arqueologia do Maranhão MUSEUM
(Map p558; www.cultura.ma.gov.br/portal/cphna; Rua do Giz 59; ⏲8am-noon & 2-6pm Mon-Fri) FREE Contains exhibits of artifacts – from ancient ax heads to contemporary feather adornments – from Maranhão's indigenous cultures past and present, plus models of megafauna that roamed Maranhão 95 million years ago.

Centro de Cultura Popular Domingos Vieira Filho MUSEUM
(Map p558; Rua do Giz 221; ⏲9am-6pm Tue-Sun) FREE An impressive 19th-century mansion housing four fascinating floors of exhibits on São Luís' festivals – Carnaval, Bumba Meu Boi and Divino Espírito Santo – and its Afro-Brazilian cults such as Umbanda and Tambor de Mina. The friendly staff will show you around and explain, but speakers of English or other non-Portuguese languages are rarely available.

Mercado das Tulhas MARKET
(Map p558; Largo do Comércio; ⊙7am-8pm Mon-Sat, to noon Sun) This 19th-century market building now trades in an interesting variety of typical Maranhão crafts and foods, from dried prawns and Brazil nuts to an artificially colored purple cassava liquor called *tiquira* and Maranhão's most hailed regional soda, Guaraná Jesus. It also has a couple of bars that get animated in late afternoon.

Museu Histórico e Artístico do Estado de Maranhão MUSEUM
(Map p558; www.cultura.ma.gov.br/portal/mham; Rua do Sol 302; admission R$5; ⊙9am-5:30pm Tue-Sun) In a restored 1836 mansion, the Museu Histórico e Artístico is set out as it might have been in days of yore, displaying all the furnishings, valuables and everyday belongings of an upper-class 19th-century family. It's very well done. Entry includes a guided tour in Portuguese.

Palácio dos Leões PALACE
(Map p558; Av Dom Pedro II; ⊙8am-noon & 2-5:30pm Thu & Fri, 3-5:30pm Sat & Sun) FREE The Palácio dos Leões is the state governor's palace, built in the 18th century on the site of the original French fort. It still houses state government offices and the governor's residence but some rooms are open to visitors; these contain a wealth of valuable antique furnishings and art, mostly French from the 18th and 19th centuries. Visits include an obligatory guided tour in Portuguese, English or French.

Beaches

The city's beaches are along the north-facing ocean coast, beginning about 4km north of the historical center. They can be busy and fun, but are far from Brazil's finest, and a distinct smell pervades most of the city's water. Beware of rough surf, tides and pollution.

Praia Ponta d'Areia is the closest beach to the center, and the busiest, with bars and restaurants for beach food. It can be polluted. Two kilometers further along, **Praia de São Marcos** is frequented by younger groups and surfers. The best local beach, **Praia de Calhau** is broad and attractive, with hard-packed sand perfect for football games. It is 9km from the center and popular on weekends. The large *barracas* lining the beach cater to late-night partiers throughout the week.

A short bus ride from São Luís, the little fishing village of **Raposa** is a fine place for a swim. Many local establishments offer good-value seafood meals, and the water here tends to be cleaner than at the city beaches.

You can reach Ponta d'Areia, São Marcos and Calhau on bus 403 Calhau/Litorânea (R$3.10) from the Terminal de Integração Praia Grande (p564). Regular buses to Raposa leave from the **central market** (Map p558; Av Guaxenduba; ⊙8am-4pm).

Festivals & Events

São Luís has one of Brazil's richest folkloric traditions, evident in its many festivals, including Carnaval. For two to three weeks between early May and early June the city celebrates the **Festa do Divino Espírito Santo**, which has a strong Afro-Brazilian influence. São Luís' famous festival Bumba Meu Boi lasts through the second half of June. The **Tambor de Mina** festivals in July are important events for followers of the Afro-Brazilian religions.

Sleeping

★**Palma Hostel** HOSTEL $
(Map p558; ☎98 3182-8787; Rua da Palma 142; dm/s/d R$50/80/110; ❄📶) Long overdue in the historical center, this bright and well-run hostel is the perfect base for budget travelers. It offers spotless colorful dorms with single beds – no bunks – and neat private rooms with good bathrooms. The fantastic common areas have plenty of comfy seating, and there are elegant decorative touches throughout. Breakfast is served in the courtyard.

Casa Frankie POUSADA $
(Map p558; ☎98 3222-8198; www.casafrankie.com; Rua do Giz 394; s/d/tr without bathroom R$80/100/120, ste R$140; ❄@📶🏊) The historical center's best deal is overseen by a low-key Dane, who has restored this colonial mansion – a former brothel – into simple but superb budget sleeps. Rooms are huge but it's the common spaces – including a breezy veranda with fine original shutters, a lovely pool and a patio that wraps around a very giving mango tree – that set it apart.

Pousada Portas da Amazônia POUSADA $
(Map p558; ☎98 3182-8787; www.portasdaamazonia.com.br; Rua do Giz 129; s/d/tr R$115/140/170, ste s/d/t R$145/185/225; ❄📶) Rambling, creaky old corridors in this restored mansion lead around two patio-gardens to attractive and comfortable rooms with good mattresses and modern air-con. The master suites are way roomier and have much more character than the rather poky regular rooms. Street-side rooms can be noisy. You can take the good buffet breakfast in one of the courtyards.

BUMBA MEU BOI

São Luís is famous for its **Bumba Meu Boi** a fascinating and wild folkloric festival. Derived from African, indigenous and Portuguese influences, it's a rich mixture of music, dance and theater, with fantastic and colorful costumes and masks. In a Carnavalesque atmosphere, participants dance, sing, act and tell the story of the death and resurrection of the bull – with plenty of room for improvisation. The festivities take place all over Maranhão, and in São Luís alone some 400 groups take to the streets every June. New songs, dances, costumes and poetry are created every year.

The story and its portrayal differ throughout the Northeast, but the general plot is as follows: Catrina, goddaughter of the local farm owner, is pregnant and feels a craving to eat the tongue of the best *boi* (bull) on the farm. She cajoles her husband, Chico, into killing the beast. When the dead bull is discovered, several characters (caricatures drawn from all levels of society) track down the perpetrator of the crime. Chico is brought to trial, but the bull is resuscitated by magic incantations and tunes. A pardon is granted, and the story reaches its happy ending when Chico is reunited with Catrina.

Groups traditionally start rehearsing on Easter Saturday in preparation for the 'baptism' of their *boi* on June 13, the feast of Santo Antônio, or June 23, the feast of São João. Many rehearsals are open to the public, and some groups begin months before Easter; check with tourist offices or your accommodations for schedules. During the festival, several groups perform in different places in the city every night from June 13 to 30. The more commercial performances may last only one hour, while local community celebrations can go on all night. Things get especially lively on the nights of June 23 to 24 and 29 to 30.

The Bumba Meu Boi period is also a good time to catch other Afro-Brazilian cultural manifestations, such as the Tambor de Crioula dance performed by women.

Hostel Reviver HOSTEL $

(Map p558; ☎98 3213-9955; Rua de Nazaré 200; s/d R$70/90, dm/s/d without bathroom R$35/50/70) A work in progress when we visited, this spacious new hostel in a huge renovated house has a good central location and plenty of potential. Rooms are large and airy but very basic. There are several good common areas and a decent kitchen overlooking the atmospheric statue-filled garden.

Pousada Colonial POUSADA $

(Map p558; ☎98 3232-1258; www.pousadacolonialslz.com; Afonso Pena 112; s/d/tr R$100/120/170; ❄@☜) A certain colonial charm pervades this refurbished old-town mansion, which features an interior patio and unusual raised *azulejos* (decorative ceramic tiles) inside and out. The rooms don't quite live up to the ambience; some have no natural light, but they do offer new mattresses with crisp sheets, split-system air-con and, in a few cases, views over the old-town rooftops.

★ **Casa Lavinia** B&B $$

(Map p558; ☎98-3232-9959; www.casalavinia.com; Rua do Giz 380; d/t/q R$240/280/320; ❄☜) The Italian owners have achieved a truly gorgeous conversion of this 19th-century mansion. The four big beautiful rooms boast four-poster beds, polished-wood floors and stylish, uncluttered decor and furnishings from Africa, Italy, Brazil and elsewhere. The Padronal suite's bathroom alone is as big as three rooms in your average pousada. An excellent breakfast is served in a cool courtyard.

Eating

São Luís's specialty is *arroz de cuxá* (rice with shrimp, toasted sesame and the slightly bitter herb *vinagreira*). Unfortunately the culinary scene in the historical center is rather sparse (and almost nonexistent on Sundays), and foodies must head out to the northern beaches for most of the best options.

O Rei de Beiju Recheado FAST FOOD $

(Map p558; Rua da Estrêla & Alfândega; beijus R$5-8; ⏲6-10pm, to 2am Fri & Sat) The best cheap eats in the historical center can be found at this friendly roadside stand on the Largo do Comércio that serves delicious savory and sweet filled *beijus* (cassava flour pancakes). They're all good, but the shrimp in coconut milk with cheese is outstanding. Also makes a mean hamburger.

★ **Restaurante Senac** BUFFET $$

(Map p558; Rua de Nazaré 242; lunch buffet R$42; ⏲noon-3pm Mon-Sat; ☜) Showpiece for the São Luís branch of Brazil's best-known cooking school, this place gets packed at lunchtime for its superb all-you-can-eat buffet, which includes a big salad bar and eight or 10

AZULEJOS OF SÃO LUÍS

Everywhere you walk in the historical center of São Luís you'll see buildings clad with fabulously detailed *azulejos* – Portuguese tin-glazed ceramic tiles that have become an integral part of the identity of the city and were a major factor in the awarding of Unesco World Heritage status to the area.

In São Luís the use of tiles adorning mansions was not purely decorative: the hot, humid climate plays havoc with masonry and the tiles serve to protect the walls from humidity damage. Many were added to the facades well after construction and not all are from Portugal; tiles made in Germany and France were also imported. In general French tiles tend to be slightly smaller than the others.

The best preserved *azulejos* are found along Rua Portugal, which is lined with three-story mansions with mostly intact tilework. The street is also home to the **Museu de Artes Visuais** (Map p558; Portugal 273; admission R$2; ⌚9am-6pm Tue-Fri, to 4pm Sat & Sun) which contains some fine original examples.

hot meat and seafood dishes, plus rice, vegetables, yummy desserts – and a piano man.

★Cabana do Sol BRAZILIAN **$$**
(Map p557; ☎98 3233-6628; www.cabanadosol.com.br; Av Litorânea 10, Calhau; mains for two R$90-103; ⌚11am-midnight) This huge two-story picture-windowed 'cabin' is a memorable spot for Maranhense cuisine. It's pricey, but the enormous standard portions can serve four, and there is a limited menu for two diners. The specialty is *carne de sol* (grilled salted meat) – the *picanha* (steak) version is superb – but there's also a wealth of chicken and seafood dishes.

Solo diners should ask for the special menu, which features six dishes in individual portions (R$37 to R$63). The older, more traditional location is slightly closer to town at **Praia de São Marcos** (Map p557; ☎98 3235-2585; www.cabanadosol.com.br; Jõao Damasceno 24A, Praia de São Marcos; mains for two R$90-103; ⌚11am-midnight; 📶).

L'Apero FRENCH, BRAZILIAN **$$**
(Map p557; ☎98-3227-8121; Av Litorânea, Modulo 4A; mains R$43-47; ⌚9am-11pm Tue-Thu, to 1am Fri & Sat, to midnight Sun; 📶) This megakiosk on São Marcos' sands has a more loungy vibe than its neighbors and is a great bet for good food, good music and good times, especially on Sundays, when there's a DJ playing and everyone knows it's the best gig in town!

Dom Francisco BRAZILIAN **$$**
(Map p558; Rua do Giz 155; lunch per kg R$38.90, mains R$35; ⌚11am-3:30pm & 6-11pm Mon-Sat) An excellent buffet that doesn't try to do every dish ever known to Maranhão, but rather a select repertoire of well-prepared meals. Sure the tablecloths might have the odd stain but all the dishes are delicious and English translations are thoughtfully written on the serving pans. It's open at night for à la carte dining.

🍷 Drinking & Entertainment

Evenings in the historical center, things get lively around Largo do Comércio; on Fridays, young locals turn it into one massive block party. Hot spots include the stairs in front of **Cafofinho da Tia Dica** (Map p558; Beco da Alfândega; ⌚11am-midnight), and along Rua da Trapiche near the water.

Ask locals or tourist offices about what's hot, and check www.kamaleao.com/saoluis. There's a vibrant LGBT scene here.

Bar do Nelson CLUB
(Map p557; ☎98 98840-3196; www.facebook.com/bardonelsonreggaeroots; Av Litorânea 135, Calhau; admission R$5-20; ⌚9pm-3am Thu-Sat) With its favela clubhouse feel, Bar do Nelson is the most famous reggae spot in town, and it's good for live music and dancing. A second **location** (Map p558; Rua da Trapiche 39; ⌚10pm-3am) has opened among the lively bars of Rua da Trapiche in the historical center.

Casa das Dunas LIVE MUSIC
(Map p557; ☎98 3227-8695; Av Litorânea s/n; ⌚7pm-2am Fri & Sat, to midnight Sun) The biggest thing to happen in São Luís since sliced *picanha*, this massive, architecturally stunning entertainment complex opened in 2015. Overlooking Praia do Calhau, it's equal parts bar and live-music venue, and a good bet for DJs, MPB (Música Popular Brasileira) and *forró*. Attracts national acts as well.

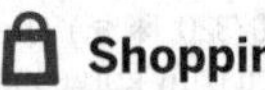

Shopping

Feirinha São Luís MARKET
(Map p558; Praça Benedito Leite; ⌚10am-3pm Sun) Every Sunday the Praça Benedito Leite

in the historical center hosts this market fair. Stalls selling traditional meals, cheese, fresh vegetables, dry goods and handicrafts set up on the plaza, while vans selling fast food and microbrews park around the perimeter. Live music and dance performances on the big stage create a party-like atmosphere.

Ceprama ARTS & CRAFTS
(Centro de Producão de Artesanato do Maranhão; Map p557; Rua de São Pantaleão 1232, Madre de Deus; ⌚9am-6pm Mon-Sat) The large Ceprama, 2km southeast of the center, functions as an exhibition hall and major sales outlet. It's neat and organized and well worth the trip.

Information

EMERGENCY

BPTur (Batalhã de Policiamento em Áreas Turísticas; Largo do Comércio; ⌚24hr)

DETUR (Delegacia Especial de Turismo; ☎98 3214-8682; Rua da Estrela 427; ⌚8am-6pm Mon-Fri)

MEDICAL SERVICES

UDI Hospital (☎98 3216-7979; Av Carlos Cunha 2000, Jacarati; ⌚24hr) Private hospital with emergency service.

MONEY

Banco do Brasil (www.bb.com.br; Travessa Boa Ventura; ⌚8am-10pm) Visa/Mastercard ATM.

Banco do Brasil (www.bb.com.br; Av Dom Pedro II 78; ⌚8am-10pm) Visa/Mastercard ATM.

Banco do Brasil (www.bb.com.br; Av Gomes de Castro 46; ⌚8am-10pm) This is the only Banco do Brasil branch offering currency exchange here.

TOURIST INFORMATION

Central de Informações Turísticas (SETUR; Map p558; ☎98 3212-6210; www.saoluis.ma.gov.br/setur; Praça Benedito Leite; ⌚8am-6pm Mon-Fri, to noon Sat & Sun) The main information office of Setur, the city tourism department, and also the most helpful; English and French were spoken when we visited.

Maranhão Tourist Information (☎98 3256-2585; www.turismo.ma.gov.br; São Luís airport; ⌚24hr) Maranhão's official state tourist information office, located in the Arrivals hall of the airport. English isn't a strong point, but the bilingual tourism site has helpful descriptions.

TRAVEL AGENCIES

Terra Nordeste (☎98 3221-1188; www.terra-nordeste.com; Miquerinos 1, Golden Tower, Sala 416, Renascença II; ⌚9am-6pm Mon-Fri) This excellent ecotourism-focused Northeast Brazil specialist is friendly, French-owned and multilingual. It can organize any trip for any budget, from two days to a month or more, including treks across the Lençóis Maranhenses.

Getting There & Away

AIR

From **Aeroporto Internacional de São Luís – Marechal Cunha Machado** (☎98 3217-6100; Av dos Libaneses, Tirirical), there are direct flights to main destinations in the Amazon and Northeast, as well as Rio de Janeiro and São Paulo.

BUS

The **bus station** (☎81 3275-9886; www.rodoviariasaoluis.com.br; Av dos Franceses 300, Santo Antônio), Terminal Rodoviário de São Luís, is located 8km southeast of the historical center and has departures to many destinations. Night buses to Belém have a history of being robbed, so consider flying, which can be cheaper in any case.

Getting Around

Coopertaxi (☎98 3245-4404; São Luís airport) operates taxis from the airport. Drivers are not likely to use a meter (or even to have one) but official prices are posted in the arrivals hall dispatch booth. A ride to the *centro histórico* costs R$53.

From the bus station, taxis run between R$40 to R$50. Traffic on the main roads in and out of São Luís is so heavy that this can take up to an hour.

BUSES FROM SÃO LUÍS

DESTINATION	COST FROM (R$)	DURATION (HR)	COMPANY
Barreirinhas	51	5	Cisne Branco (www.cisnebrancoturismo.com.br)
Belém	146	13	Boa Esperança (www.viajeboaesperanca.com.br), Rápido Marajó (www.rapidomarajo.com.br)
Brasília	330	33	Rápido Marajó
Fortaleza	197	19	Expresso Guanabara (www.expressoguanabara.com.br)
Parnaíba	105	10	Expresso Guanabara
Teresina	90	8	Expresso Guanabara

WORTH A TRIP

ALCÂNTARA

Across the Baía de São Marcos from São Luís is the colonial town of Alcântara. Built using slave labor between the 17th and 19th centuries, Alcântara was once the preferred residence of Maranhão's rich plantation owners. In decline since the latter half of the 19th century, Alcântara today is an atmospheric amalgam of ruined, maintained and restored mansions, houses and churches set along streets of artistic crisscrossed cobblestones. With a population little bigger today than 150 years ago, it is one of the country's most tranquil, authentic and beautiful historical sites. Keep an eye out for *guarás*, beautiful red ibises that are unusually plentiful around here and add another wonderful element to an Alcântara trip.

Since 1990 the Centro de Lançamento de Alcântara (CLA), the rocket-launching facility for the Brazilian space program, has operated nearby. It is an odd juxtaposition: rockets alongside a slumbering colonial town.

Don't miss the broad, hilltop Praça da Matriz, where the best-preserved *pelourinho* (whipping post) in Brazil stands beside the shell of the 17th-century Igreja de São Matias. Two 18th-century mansions on the square's west side have been turned into museums – **Museu Histórico de Alcântara** (Largo de São Matias; admission R$2; ⌚9am-3pm Tue-Fri, to 1pm Sat & Sun) and the Casa Histórica – exhibiting the lifestyle of Alcântara's privileged families of yore, including a wealth of period furnishings and memorabilia.

Moving north along Rua Grande, with its beautiful row of two-story houses, you can visit the intriguing Casa do Divino, the main center of activities during Alcântara's famous Festa do Divino in May, before reaching the two-towered Igreja de NS do Carmo. Built in 1665, it was restored, and there's a ruined convent beside it. In front of and opposite the church stand the ruined 1° and 2° Palácios do Imperador (First and Second Palaces of the Emperor), built for a visit by the 19th-century emperor Dom Pedro II that never actually happened.

Alcântara is a straightforward day trip from São Luís, but an overnight stay here is enjoyable and allows more time for exploring and for excursions to colonies of red ibis.

Two or three boats to Alcântara (R$15, 1¼ hours) leave daily from the Cais da Praia Grande in São Luís. Times vary with tides but there are usually two departures between 7am and 9am and one later.

Bus 901 (São Cristóvão Aeroporto) runs between the airport – just outside the terminal and to the left – and Praça Deodoro, which is about 1km east of most of the *centro histórico* accommodations; note this is not a safe option at night. Between the bus station and the **Terminal Praia Grande** (Map p558; Av Senador Vitorino Freire) take the Socarrão II–Rodoviária bus.

Local bus fares are R$2.70 or R$3.10 and can be paid in cash upon boarding.

Parque Nacional dos Lençóis Maranhenses

The name of this 1550 sq km **national park** FREE refers to its immense expanses of dunes, which look like *lençóis* (bedsheets) strewn across the landscape; they stretch 70km along the coast and up to 50km inland. Located halfway between São Luís and the Piauí border, it's a spectacular place, especially from about May to September when rain filtered through the sand forms thousands of crystal-clear pools and lakes between the dunes. The lagoons are at their best in June, July and August. The park also includes beaches, mangroves and some interesting fauna, especially turtles and migratory birds.

The main base for visiting the park is the not particularly charming town of Barreirinhas on the picturesque Rio Preguiças near the southeast corner of the park. Other access points – well worth the effort of getting to if you have at least two nights to spend in the area – are the remote villages of Atins and Santo Amaro.

Activities

Keep in mind that quad bikes are completely forbidden inside the dunes, but that won't stop unscrupulous guides from trying to sell you trips on them. Just say no.

Trekking

A wonderful way to experience the Lençóis is to trek across them. It takes three or four days to cross from west to east or vice versa, sleeping in hammocks or fishers' huts in the few tiny poor villages along the way. A locally arranged Portuguese-speaking guide should cost around R$250 per day (R$350 for an English speaker). If you go east to west, you'll have the prevailing wind behind you. The most magical way of all is to trek by night under the full moon.

São Luís-based Terra Nordeste (p563) arranges well-organized trans-Lençóis hikes: a four-day return trip from São Luís with three days of trekking costs R$5000 to R$6000 for two people including transfers, meals, nights and guide (English, Spanish, French, Italian and German are available).

Caetés Turismo ADVENTURE
(98 3349-0528; www.caetesturismo.com.br; Av Brasília 40B; 8am-6pm) Run by local man Roberdan Caldas, Caetés is a member of ABETA, Brazil's strict ecotourism organization, and can handle excursions both far and wide through Maranhão and Ceará.

São Paulo Ecoturismo TOURS
(98 3349-0079; www.saopauloecoturismo.com.br; Av Brasília 108; 7am-8pm) A recommended agency in Barreirinhas for organized tours in and around Parque Nacional dos Lençóis Maranhenses. They arrange private transfers between Caburé and Tutóia (R$450, three hours), Parnaíba (R$700, four hours) and (Jericoacoara R$1300, eight hours).

Sandwalkers WALKING
(98 98864-0526; sandwalkers.ma@gmail.com; Atins; 2/3-day treks per hiker R$600/800) Bernard de Laroche of Sandwalkers is one of the Lençóis' most experienced, knowledgeable and multilingual guides; he is getting older and doesn't guide that much anymore but runs the most established trekking agency in town. Prices are based on groups of four hikers and change according to group size.

Erick Tour OUTDOORS
(98 98742-6522, 98 99965-6798; werycksonmello@yahoo.com.br; Praça Nossa Senhora de Conceição, Santo Amaro; half-/full-day tour for up to 10 R$450/650) Reliable and straight-shooting guide offering all the standard itineraries into the national park. For smaller groups (ie just a couple of travelers) he has one pickup with just four seats in the back and is often willing to cut a deal.

Scenic Flights

The best way to truly get an idea of the scale of the dunes of the Lençóis – and get pictures to set your social media streams alight – is to take a **scenic flight** (98 98264-2945; www.voarfotografiaaerea.com.br; Av Brasília 100; per passenger R$350) over the park in a small plane from Barreirinhas. Flights typically costs R$300 to R$350 per passenger and fly in a loop heading out over the Pequeno Lençóis, Caburé, Atins and back over the national park.

Sleeping & Eating

Barreirinhas has plenty of good accommodations, many with river views. High season is July and August, but many places charge the same rates year-round, outside of holidays.

Casa do Professor Hostel HOSTEL $
(98 98808-2546; www.casadoprofessorhostel.com.br; Projetada 33; campsite/hammock/dm R$15/25/40; @) The street doesn't lend itself to high hopes, but this family-run affair, overseen by an English professor, is simply and surprisingly well done. Dorms are a bit crowded but there are good social areas, including an artsy sand-floored backyard lounge space that's a great spot to swap travel tales over beers. A good-sized kitchen is open to guests.

★**Pousada Sossego do Cantinho** POUSADA $$
(98 3349-0753; www.sossegodocantinho.com.br; Rua Principal 2, Povoado Cantinho; r R$310;) On the riverbank 1.5km north of town, the Swiss-owned Sossego is a perfect haven for resting for a couple of days, or as a relaxed base for excursions. The four large bungalows have elegant bathrooms and big beds with lots of pillows. There's a white-sand river beach at the foot of the gardens and free kayaks for guest use.

Pousada do Porto POUSADA $$
(98 3349-0654; Anacleto de Carvalho 20; s/d/tr R$100/200/250;) Just upriver from the Cisne Branco (p567) bus stop, Pousada do Porto's best-value rooms are its upstairs units with river views; there's a small social area out the back with views across to a forested area.

Encantes do Nordeste POUSADA $$$
(98 3349-0288; www.encantesdonordeste.com.br; Boa Vista s/n; s/d from R$292/391; @) This ecofriendly pousada is a gem of comfort 3.5km east of Barreirinhas' center. The sloping plot leads down past cozy chalets to a beautiful garden with a pool. There's also a Zen lounge, which makes use of reclaimed woods and has Asian touches, and a massage area.

It has a lovely riverside restaurant, Bambaê (mains R$67 to R$118), and in-house pizzeria.

The pousada's own travel agency can arrange all Parque Nacional dos Lençóis Maranhenses excursions.

Restaurante Bela Vista BRAZILIAN $$
(98 3349-1746; Anacleto de Carvalho 617; mains R$35-48; 10am-10pm) Pull up a table on the breezy wooden deck overlooking the river at this excellent local restaurant and choose from a variety of fantastic typical plates. It's all good but the fish dishes are especially tasty. Portions are generous and prices are reasonable for the quality involved. Also a fine choice for an evening drink.

O Jacaré INTERNATIONAL $$
(Av Beira Rio 109; mains R$30-50; 11am-2am;) The French owners of this riverfront pub-restaurant are trying to raise the bar in Barreirinhas. Several pages of the menu are devoted to cocktails and craft beer (Devassa on draft, Eisenbahn and Baden Baden in bottles – impressive for these parts!) and there's a variety previously unseen here.

Atins

Atins is a small but expanding village of sandy streets amid dune vegetation at the mouth of the Rio Preguiças. It has an ocean beach, a sizable foreign population and a surprising number of pousadas scattered among its dwellings. It's a good base for visiting some of the more isolated parts of Parque Nacional dos Lençóis Maranhenses – you can have many gorgeous dunes and lagoons to yourself.

Pousada da Tia Rita POUSADA $
(98 99993-7537; Principal, Atins; s/d with fan R$70/100, with air-con R$100/150;) One of the original places to stay in Atins, Tia Rita is still a popular budget option, offering simple and clean rooms in a spick-and-span family home. It's just a short walk from the boat dock.

Rancho do Buna POUSADA $$
(98 99190-9646; www.ranchodobuna.com; Atins; s/d/t R$250/280/310;) This is easily one of Atins' best pousadas, despite the large property's chickens, guinea fowl, peacocks, ducks, dogs and cats wailing a dawn chorus from 5am. The comfortable brick chalets (built using recycled materials), the appealing common area and the expansive grounds (with a pool and a duck pond), are all big on charm.

Chalet rooms are bigger and offer greater privacy than the apartments. The restaurant serves well-prepared meals and a good breakfast. It offers wonderful excursions to the dunes and lakes of Parque Nacional dos Lençóis Maranhenses, and can arrange transportation by boat or 4WD.

Pousada Irmão Atins POUSADA $$
(98-98864-4288; www.pousadairmaoatins.com.br; Principal, Atins; s/d/t R$190/230/310;) This attractive, locally owned place offers clean and colorful rooms set along a strip of grassy garden; rooms sport verandas strung with hammocks, and bathrooms walled with hundreds of seashells. Good fish, chicken and shrimp dishes (mains for two R$60 to R$80) are served in the shell-floored dining area under a big *palapa* palm roof. Top honors for midrange digs.

La Ferme de Georges POUSADA $$$
(98-99172-2935, 98 98725-1389; www.georges.life; Atins; r R$850-1500;) This boutique pousada is what people mean when they say, 'Atins is changing,' but this French–Belgian affair is a change for the better. The nine wonderful chalets, all bastions of style and comfort (including European art, 600-thread-count sheets, Thai mosquito nets) are richly constructed in quality *ipê* and *tatajuba* hardwoods and feature solar-powered showers.

Restaurante Ceu Aberto BRAZILIAN $$
(98 99168-0502; Nova 184, Atins; mains for two R$60-70; 9am-9pm;) Tucked away between the main road and the sea, this breezy open-air restaurant on an elevated deck hits the mark both in terms of ambience and meals. It's fairly elegant for Atins and the seafood plates are particularly good.

★ **Restaurante do Antônio** SEAFOOD $$
(Restaurante Canto dos Lençóis; 98 98881-3138; Canto de Atins; mains for two R$60-90; 7am-8pm) Get yourself here by foot, horseback, car, boat, on a tour or any way you can to experience the wonderful grilled shrimp at this rustic culinary destination 7km west of Atins. The location, isolated between the dunes (600m away) and the sea (1.5km at low tide), is travel-memory fodder at its finest.

A private transfer from Atins to the restaurant costs around R$200 for four to five visitors. Otherwise you can walk here after breakfast (it takes about two hours), enjoy a leisurely lunch, explore the dunes and walk back late afternoon.

There are a couple of tidy and comfortable rooms with private bathrooms (R$75 per visitor) on-site if you want to spend more time out here. It's also possible to sleep here in hammocks (R$35).

Caburé

On the far bank a 15-minute boat ride upriver from Atins, Caburé is little more than a handful of rustic pousadas and restaurants sitting on an isolated sand peninsula between the lower Rio Preguiças and the Atlantic. It's a nice place for lunch, but you're much better off sleeping in Atins.

Porto Caburé CHALET **$**

(☎98 98733-6377; Caburé; s/d R$80/150;) These colorful chalets are the nicest option in Caburé, but that's not saying a whole lot. The place feels more than a bit run-down but if creature comforts are not a huge priority, there's a rustic appeal here and you're surrounded by wild sands in all directions. Laze away a day or two in the hammock area.

Cabana do Peixe SEAFOOD **$$**

(☎98 98732-2213; Caburé; mains for two R$69-85; noon-4pm) The best and most atmospheric of Caburé's restaurants serving fresh fish and seafood stews to incoming day-trippers. We especially like the individual thatch-roofed tables that sit in the sands in front of the main dining area.

Santo Amaro

Let your van driver know where you're staying and you'll be dropped at the door. Hotels are quite spread out and it's difficult to hike around town with luggage in the heat.

★**Ciamat Camp** CHALET **$$**

(☎98 99604-5824; www.ciamatcamp.com; MA-320 s/n; r/tr/q R$306/374/436;) This Brazilian-Italian operation has half a dozen comfortable wooden chalets and some air-conditioned rooms scattered around its lovely and luxuriant riverside garden across the Rio Alegre from the village. They will ferry you back and forth across the river, and kayaks are free for guest use. Meals available.

Information

You'll find a **Banco do Brasil** (Av Joaquim Soeiro de Carvalho; 8am-10pm) ATM in Barreirinhas.

Getting There & Away

TO/FROM SÃO LUÍS

A good paved road, Hwy MA-402, runs east to Barreirinhas from Hwy BR-135 south of São Luís. **Cisne Branco** (☎98 3243-2847; www.cisnebrancoturismo.com.br; Anacleto de Carvalho 623) runs four daily comfortable buses from São Luís to Barreirinhas (R$53, five hours, departing 6am, 8:45am, 2pm and 7:30pm); in the other direction they depart Barreirinhas for São Luís at 6am, 9am, 2pm and 6:45pm. Buses start and finish at São Luís' bus station (p563), which is way out of the city center; you can be dropped at the São Luís airport (p563) turnoff, 800m from the terminals, if you are heading straight there.

More convenient are the door-to-door 'vans' (minibuses) of **BRTur** (☎98 98896-6610, 98 98114-3649; reservasbrtur@gmail.com); these take 4½ hours and will pick you up from your accommodation in São Luís around 7am, and start back from Barreirinhas at 5pm. **Coopcart** (☎98-3349-1511; Av Joaquim Soeiro de Carvalho; R$70) is the only door-to-door transfer service with morning departures from Barreirinhas. Your accommodations can book these for you.

Heading east from Barreirinhas toward Jericoacoara, the easiest way is to take a Cisne Branco bus at 11am or 7pm to Tutóia (R$16, two hours), from where there are bus connections to Parnaíba and beyond. A direct transfer from Barreirinhas costs around R$650 for up to five people to Parnaíba, or R$1250 all the way to Jericoacoara.

TO/FROM ATINS

To get to Atins from Barreirinhas, you can take a scheduled boat service (R$40, 1½ hours) down the Rio Preguiças leaving at around 11:30am from the Beira Rio dock. Alternatively take a boat tour (R$80 to R$90) to Caburé and transfer across to Atins after lunch on the peninsula.

Another option is to take a Toyota 4WD (R$25, two hours), leaving from the corner of Rua Major Galas and Monsenhor Gentil. There are usually departures around 9am, 11am and 1pm. The 4WDs head back from Atins to Barreirinhas at around 6am.

Local tour operators can organize private 4WD transfers from Caburé to Tutóia (R$450 to R$500, three hours), Parnaíba (R$700, four hours) and Jericoacoara (R$1300, eight hours). Otherwise ask around in Atins – occasionally local vehicles will take paying passengers.

TO/FROM SANTO AMARO

Air-conditioned door-to-door vans run from São Luís to Santo Amaro three or four times a day, with departures early in the morning and around noon although the drivers spend an hour or two driving around town picking up passengers. Among those making the trip are **Cito** (☎98 98784-4044, 98 99903-3282) and **Lisboa** (☎98 98702-0178).

TO/FROM PARNAÍBA AND JERICOACOARA

Heading east from Barreirinhas toward Jericoacoara, the easiest way is to take a Cisne Branco bus at 11am or 7pm to Tutóia (R$16, two hours) from where there are bus connections to Parnaíba and beyond. A direct transfer from Barreirinhas costs around R$650 for up to five people to Parnaíba, or R$1250 all the way to Jericoacoara.

The Amazon

POP 21 MILLION

Includes ➡

Pará 572
Belém 572
Ilha de Marajó 587
Santarém 590
Palmas 602
Amazonas 606
Manaus 606
Mamirauá Reserve 637
Boa Vista 646
Porto Velho 649
Rio Branco 653

Best Places to Eat

- ➡ Flor do Luar (p622)
- ➡ Quiosque da Praça (p593)
- ➡ Mirante do Gavião Amazon Lodge (p622)
- ➡ Coco Bambu Manaus (p614)

Best Places to Stay

- ➡ Mirante do Gavião Amazon Lodge (p621)
- ➡ Amazon Antonio's Lodge (p611)
- ➡ Juma Lodge (p618)
- ➡ Pousada Uacari (p638)

Why Go?

Named after female warriors of Greek mythology, the Amazon is itself a place of near-mythical status. What traveler drawn to the wild places of the planet hasn't imagined a trip to the Amazon, not only to admire the towering trees, secretive wildlife and awesome river, but to enter, in a real sense, the very life spring of the planet? Expecting a Discovery Channel–like experience (jaguars in every tree, anacondas on every shore) is a recipe for disappointment. In fact, the Amazon's quintessential experiences are more sublime than superlative: canoeing through a flooded forest, dozing in a hammock on a boat chugging upriver, waking to the otherworldly cry of howler monkeys. On a river whose size is legendary, it's actually the little things that make it special. Give it some time, and the Amazon is all this and more.

When to Go

Manaus

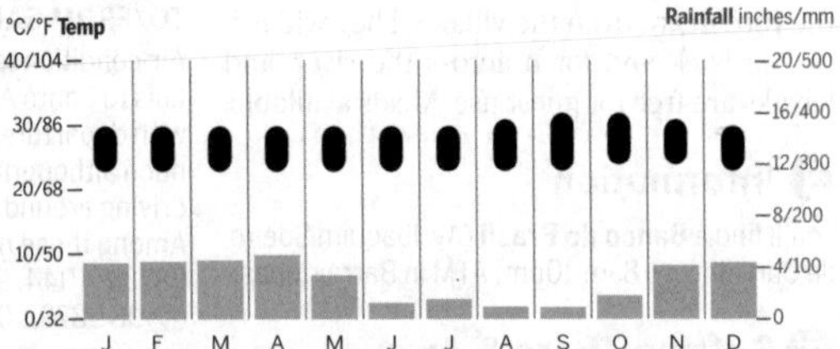

Dry Season (Jun–Dec) River levels fall, warm temperatures, good wildlife-spotting.

Wet Season (Jan–May) Rain possible although not all day every day; water levels rising.

Jun Manaus hosts the Festival Folclórico do Amazonas, a fabulous time to be in the city.

History

The Amazon Basin has been inhabited for 11,000 to 14,000 years. Its earliest inhabitants made up hundreds of far-flung tribes, some tiny, others numbering in the tens of thousands. Early researchers believed the rainforest was simply too inhospitable to support large populations, but recent studies have challenged that notion, suggesting up to five million people may have lived in the Amazon by the time of European contact. That occurred in 1541, when Francisco de Orellana and 60 men floated the length of the Amazon from present-day Peru to the Atlantic. The expedition was attacked by indigenous groups, including by what they thought were bands of women like the Amazons of Greek mythology. Thus the world's greatest river got its name. Still, it wasn't until 1616 that the Portuguese built their first fort on the river, and another 20 years before Pedro Teixeira explored upriver as far as Quito.

Amazonian indigenous groups had long used the sap from rubber trees to make waterproof bags and other items, but the material proved difficult to work with outside the warm, humid rainforest. But once American Charles Goodyear developed vulcanization (which made natural rubber durable) in 1842, there soon was an unquenchable demand for rubber in the recently industrialized US and Europe. As the price for Brazilian rubber soared, so did exploitation of the *seringueiros* (rubber-tappers) who were lured into the Amazon, mostly from the drought-stricken Northeast, by the promise of prosperity only to be locked into a cruel system of indentured labor. In 1876, a Briton named Henry Wickham smuggled 70,000 rubber-tree seeds from the Amazon to London, and before long, rubber trees were growing in neat and efficient groves in the British colonies of Ceylon and Malaya. The price of latex plummeted, and by the 1920s Brazil's rubber boom was over.

Fearful of foreign annexation of the Amazon, Brazil embarked on a development and settlement program embodied by the 1970s slogan '*Integrar para não entregar*' (essentially, 'Use it or lose it'). The effort proved disastrous for the rainforest. Roads meant to facilitate settlement of the interior became arteries from which rampant destruction of the Amazon rainforest was – and still is – fed. In Rondônia, the population leaped from 111,000 in 1970 to 1.13 million in 1991, and 20% of the state's primary forest was cut down. The rate of deforestation in the 1980s was equivalent to more than a football field a minute, for a whole decade.

In December 1988, Chico Mendes, an internationally recognized union and environmental leader from Acre state, was gunned down on his back porch by ranchers angry about his efforts to stop clear-cutting. The attack, by no means the first of its kind, but remarkable for its brazenness, focused worldwide attention on deforestation in the Amazon. Brazil has since introduced strict regulations, and even adopted satellite monitoring, with remarkable success – deforestation of the Amazon has dropped to its lowest recorded rates.

However, the effects of global climate change on the Amazon continue unabated. Since 2005, the Amazon has been whiplashed by a series of extreme droughts and floods, each breaking the record set by the previous one. There were severe droughts in 2010 and 2013, and record-breaking floods in 2012, 2014 and 2015, with water levels rising nearly 30m, more than double the 'normal' seasonal rise.

THE AMAZON BASIN

The Amazon Basin spans nine countries and three standard time zones. It has an area of more than seven million square kilometers, accounting for 40% of the entire South American continent. The Amazon Basin is nearly the size of the contiguous United States and more than twice that of India. The Amazon rainforest is the world's largest tropical rainforest, and despite rampant deforestation, remains 80% intact and untouched. (By contrast, many forests in Asia, Africa and Central America, and even the Brazilian Atlantic coast, are down to their last 5% to 10%.) The Amazon River is the world's second-longest river – the Nile beats it by a hair – but the biggest in volume by far: when it's at its fullest, the river dumps 300 million liters of water into the ocean every second, sending a plume of fresh water more than a hundred miles out to sea. The Amazon discharges more water than the next seven biggest rivers combined, and two of the Amazon's tributaries, the Rio Negro and Rio Madeira, are themselves among the 10 largest rivers in the world. There are places, when the water is high, where the Amazon River stretches fully 50km from bank to bank – a massive moving sea of creamy brown water too wide to see across.

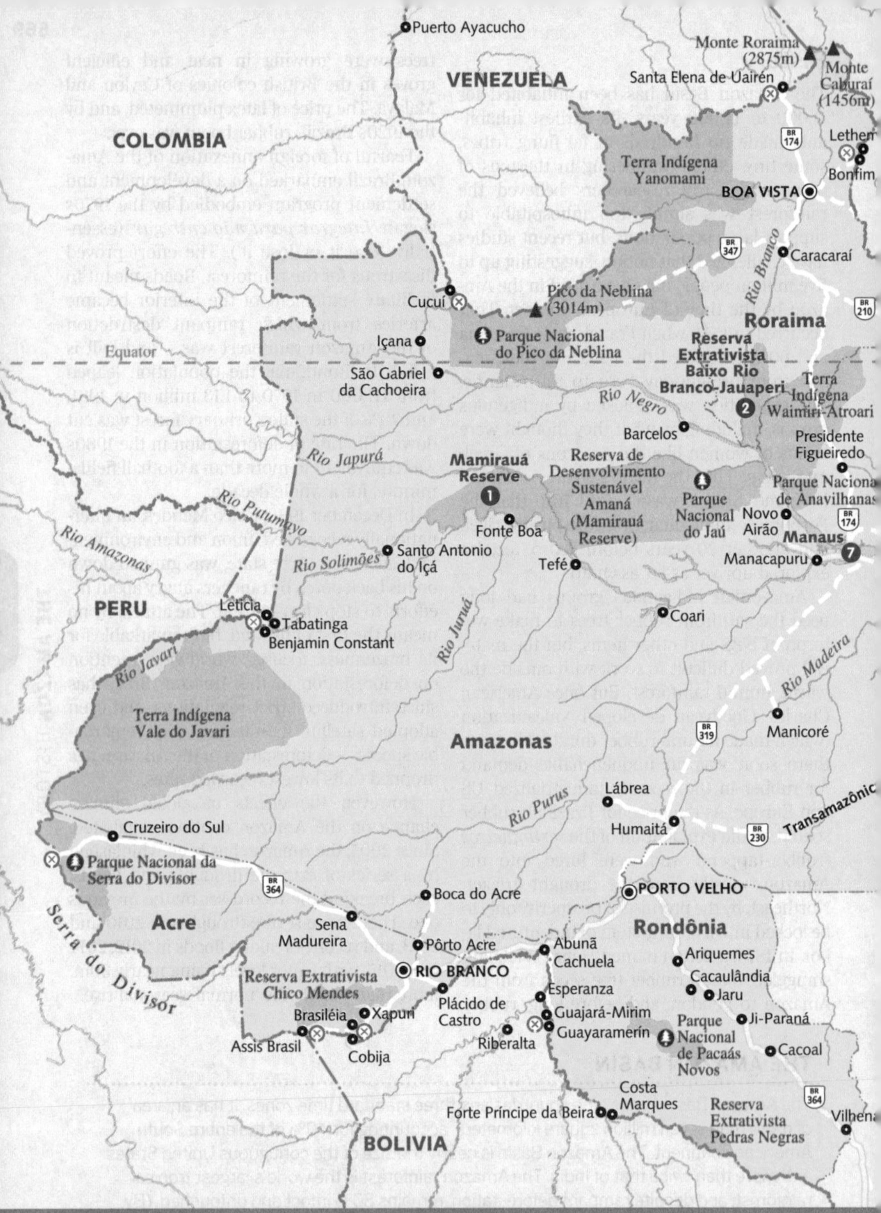

The Amazon Highlights

❶ **Mamirauá Reserve** (p637) Gliding through flooded forests in search of jaguars and the white uakari monkey.

❷ **Reserva Extrativista Baixo Rio Branco-Jauaperi** (p623) Exploring the Amazon as it once was, with endless forests, waterways and wildlife.

❸ **Floresta Nacional do Tapajós** (p596) Immersing yourself in the rainforest with massive trees and forest trails.

❹ **Lago Maicá** (p591) Taking a boat trip into wildlife-rich wetlands.

❺ **Alter do Chão** (p598) Chilling in one of Brazil's loveliest river-beach towns.

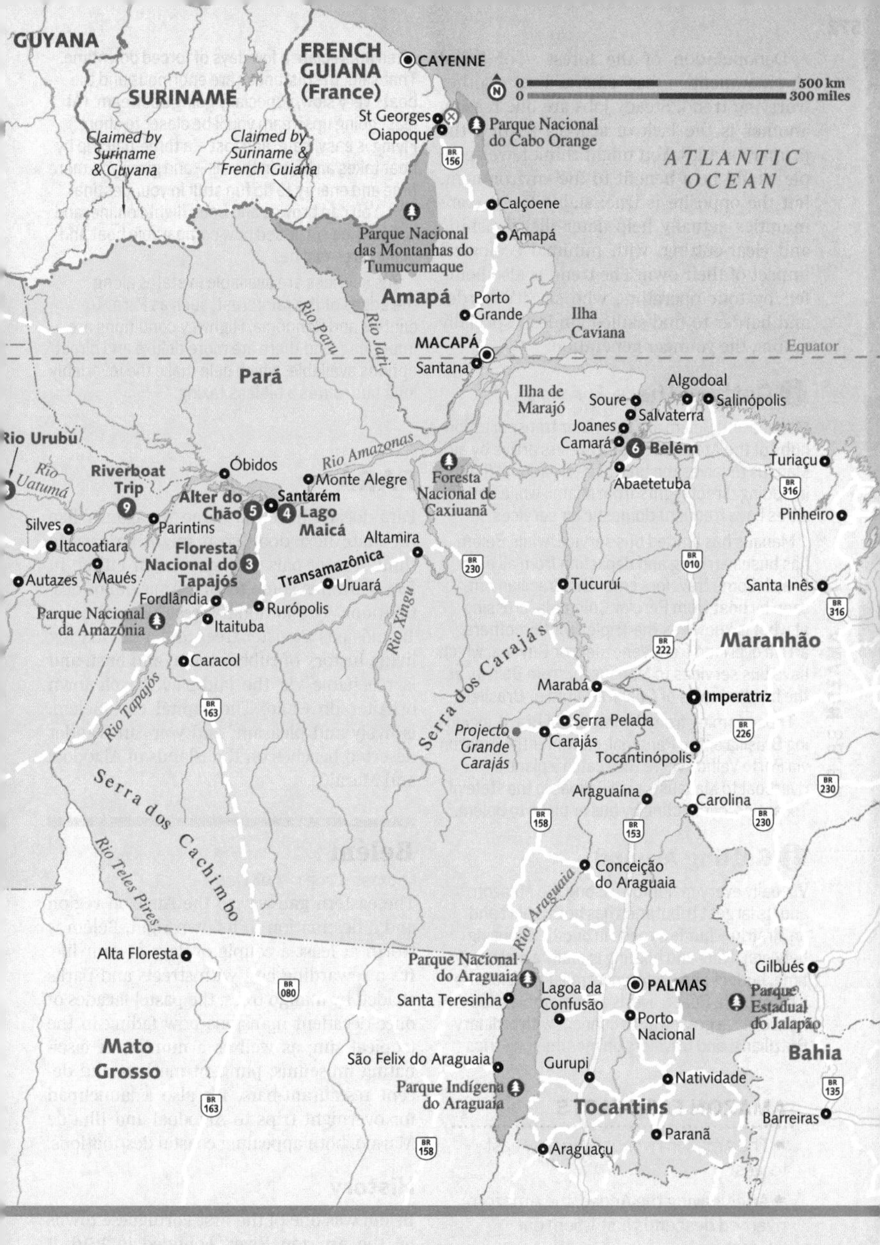

6 Belém (p572) Wandering cool city markets and dining in great restaurants near the Amazon's mouth.

7 Manaus (p606) Discovering the regional capital, where mighty rivers meet the world's most unlikely opera house.

8 Rio Urubu (p611) Experiencing the wild Amazon within a day's journey of Manaus.

9 Riverboat Trip (p582) Relaxing with regular folks in your hammock between Manaus and Santarém.

Depopulation of the forest – or 'rural abandonment' – has emerged as another worrying trend. Steady jobs are one reason, another is the lack of schools beyond the primary grades. You might think fewer people would be a benefit to the environment, but the opposite is true: stable forest communities actually help deter illegal fishing and clear-cutting, with minimal ecological impact of their own. The trend is also being felt by tour operators, who say it's harder and harder to find skilled guides, especially among the younger generation.

Getting There & Away

Manaus and Belém are the major transportation hubs of the Amazon. Most travelers arrive by air. Manaus receives the bulk of international flights, including direct flights from Miami, while both cities have frequent domestic air services.

Manaus has limited bus service, while Belém has buses arriving and departing from all over Brazil. Some travelers enter the Brazilian Amazon by boat from Peru or Colombia, crossing at what is known as the Triple Frontier; others arrive overland from Venezuela or Guyana, which have bus services to Manaus, or from Bolivia, at the border towns of Guajará-Mirim or Brasiléia.

Those coming from the interior of Brazil, including Brasília or the Pantanal, can enter the Amazon via Porto Velho, where they catch a plane or riverboat to Manaus, or via Palmas in the state of Tocantins, connecting by bus or plane to Belém.

Getting Around

Virtually every major town along the Amazon and its largest tributaries has both a port and an airstrip – but few roads in or out. Choosing between flying and boating is really a matter of time, budget and preference; most travelers do a bit of both. Boat travel is a memorable experience; it's a great way to connect with ordinary Brazilians, and travelers on months-long trips often appreciate a few days of forced downtime. That said, the distances are enormous and the boats very slow, especially going upstream. (At least going upstream you'll be closer to shore.) Flying is easy, safe, and fast – a three-day trip by boat takes an hour in the air – and gives you more time and energy to do fun stuff in your destination. You can browse and book flights online, and you may be surprised how comparable boat and plane fares can be.

Bus services are available in states along the edges of the rainforest, such as Pará, Tocantins and Rondônia. Highway conditions are improving, and there are more deluxe and direct options available, which help make the invariably long bus routes a bit less taxing.

AMAZON FAST FACTS

- The Amazon river used to flow east to west.
- After leaving the Andes, the Amazon riverbed descends just 1.5cm per kilometer.
- Pink river dolphins (*botos*) can bend their necks and shrug their shoulders.
- Up to 30% of the animal biomass in the Amazon is ants.
- Half the rainfall in the Amazon never reaches the ground.

PARÁ

Pará doesn't have the name 'Amazonas' like the state next door, so it might be easy to think it's not part of 'the Amazon' either. In fact, Pará has some terrific Amazonian destinations. The national forest along the Rio Tapajós has monster trees and a fascinating living history of rubber boom and bust, and is reachable via the laid-back beach town of Alter do Chão. The capital city, Belém, is lively and pleasant, and you can wander deserted beaches on the islands of Algodoal and Marajó.

Belém

0XX91 / POP 1.44 MILLION

The eastern gateway to the Amazon region and a destination in its own right, Belém is worth at least a couple of days of your life. It's a rewarding city, with streets and parks shaded by mango trees, the pastel facades of once-decadent mansions now fading in the tropical sun, as well as a number of fascinating museums, pungent markets and decent restaurant-bars. It's also a launchpad for overnight trips to Algodoal and Ilha de Marajó, both appealing coastal destinations.

History

Belém was one of the first Portuguese towns on the Amazon River. Founded in 1616, it prospered for over two centuries, relying on enslaved indigenous groups (and later enslaved Africans) to find and harvest Amazonian treasures such as cacao, indigo and animal skins, all for export to Europe. But it was a fragile success, and an economic downturn in the early 19th century helped spark a popular uprising and bloody civil war.

The rubber boom at the turn of the century sent Belém's population rocketing, from 40,000 in 1875 to more than 100,000 in 1900. The city suddenly had electricity, telephones, streetcars and a distinctly European feel. Officials erected a few grand monuments such as the Teatro da Paz, earning the city the nickname 'the tropical Paris.'

Rubber eventually crashed, but the ports built during the boom have remained active. Today, over a million tons of cargo pass through Belém, mostly timber, soy beans, aluminum and iron ore, as well as fish, Brazil nuts and black pepper.

Sights

Central Area

★Mercado Ver-o-Peso MARKET
(Blvd Castilhos França; 7:30am-6pm Mon-Sat, to 1pm Sun) The name of this waterfront market, with its iconic four-turreted structure at its southwestern end, comes from colonial times, when the Portuguese would *ver o peso* (check the weight) of merchandise in order to impose taxes. The display of fruit, animals, medicinal plants and more is fascinating; go early to see fishing boats unloading their catch.

Some stands sell souvenirs, but be alert for pickpockets and avoid going after 5pm.

★Estação das Docas MARKET
(91 3212-5525; www.estacaodasdocas.com.br; Blvd Castilho França; 9am-1am) An ambitious renovation project converted three down-at-heel riverfront warehouses into a popular gathering spot, with restaurants, bars, shops and even an art-house theater. There are river views and displays about Belém's history, plus a post office and numerous ATMs. Enjoy live music most nights, performed from a moving platform in the rafters, rolling slowly the length of the dining area.

Teatro da Paz HISTORIC BUILDING
(Praça da República; R$6, free Wed; guided visits 9am-noon & 2-6pm Tue-Fri, 9am-noon Sat & Sun) Overlooking Praça da República, the Teatro da Paz is one of Belém's finest buildings. Completed in 1874 and built in the neoclassical style, the architecture has all the sumptuous trappings of the rubber-boom era: columns, busts, crystal mirrors and an interior decorated in Italian theatrical style. Half-hour tours are a mildly interesting trip to the city's former glory years.

Cidade Velha

The 'Old City' has most of Belém's museums and galleries, fronting the river and four nearly adjoining plazas. The area is safe during the day, with plenty of people about, but is tucked below the Comercio neighborhood, which gets seedy at night. Take a taxi if you're there late.

Forte do Presépio FORTRESS
(Praça Fr Brandão; R$4, free Tue; 10am-6pm Tue-Fri, to 2pm Sat & Sun) The city of Belém was founded in 1616 with the construction of this imposing fort, which was intended to protect Portuguese interests upriver from incursions by the French and Dutch. Today it houses a small but excellent museum, primarily about Pará's indigenous communities (displays in Portuguese only), and has great river and city views from atop its thick stone walls.

Palácio Antonio Lemos & MABE MUSEUM
(MABE; 91 3283-4665; Praça Dom Pedro II; 10am-8pm Tue-Fri, 9am-1pm Sat & Sun) FREE This rubber-boom palace served as city hall in the late 1800s, and its 2nd floor now houses the Museu de Arte de Belém. The museum has gorgeous wood floors – cloth slippers are provided – and a fine collection of statuettes, antiques and Brazilian 20th-century paintings, such as Theodoro Braga's 1908 oil *Fundação da Cidade de Belém*. Two first-floor galleries hold rotating exhibits.

Museu do Estado do Pará MUSEUM
(Pará State Museum; 91 3225-2414; Praça Dom Pedro II; R$4, free Tue; 10am-6pm Tue-Fri, to 1pm Sat & Sun) The State Museum of Pará is housed in the grand Palácio Lauro Sodré, originally the residence of Portugal's royal representatives in Belém and later home to various state governors. One such governor, Ernesto Lobo, was killed on the staircase during the Cabanagem Rebellion in 1835. The museum today is less thrilling, with a vaguely interesting collection on the founding and growth of Belém and Pará.

Casa das Onze Janelas MUSEUM
(Praça Frei Brandão; R$3, free Tue; 10am-5pm Tue-Fri, 9am-1pm Sat & Sun) Once the home of a sugar baron, then a military hospital, the Casa das Onze Janelas now houses an excellent gallery of modern art. The first and second floors contain an intriguing mix of classical and modern paintings and drawings, and a smattering of sculpture and photography. Out back are views of the Rio Guamá.

Belém

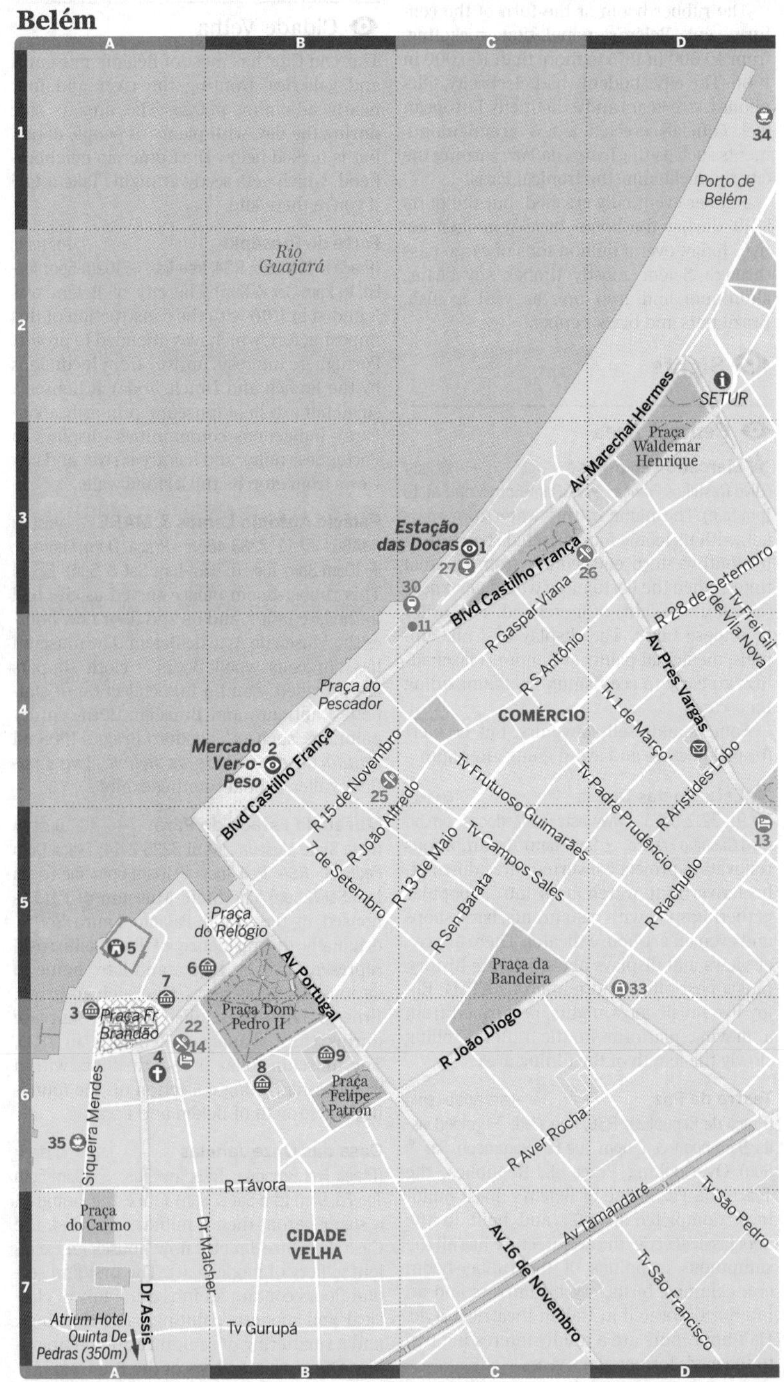

A
B
C
D
1
2
3
4
5
6
7
Rio Guajará
Porto de Belém
34
SETUR
Av Marechal Hermes
Praça Waldemar Henrique
Estação das Docas
1
27
26
30
11
Blvd Castilho França
R Gaspar Viana
R 28 de Setembro
Tv Frei Gil de Vila Nova
R S Antônio
Av Pres Vargas
Praça do Pescador
COMÉRCIO
Tv 1 de Março
Mercado Ver-o-Peso
2
R 15 de Novembro
25
R João Alfredo
Tv Frutuoso Guimarães
Tv Padre Prudêncio
R Aristides Lobo
13
7 de Setembro
R 13 de Maio
Tv Campos Sales
R Riachuelo
R Sen Barata
Praça do Relógio
5
6
Av Portugal
Praça da Bandeira
33
7
3
Praça Fr Brandão
Praça Dom Pedro II
22
14
4
8
9
R João Diogo
Praça Felipe Patron
Siqueira Mendes
35
R Aver Rocha
R Távora
Praça do Carmo
Dr Malcher
CIDADE VELHA
Av 16 de Novembro
Av Tamandaré
Tv São Pedro
Tv São Francisco
Dr Assis
Atrium Hotel Quinta De Pedras (350m)
Tv Gurupá

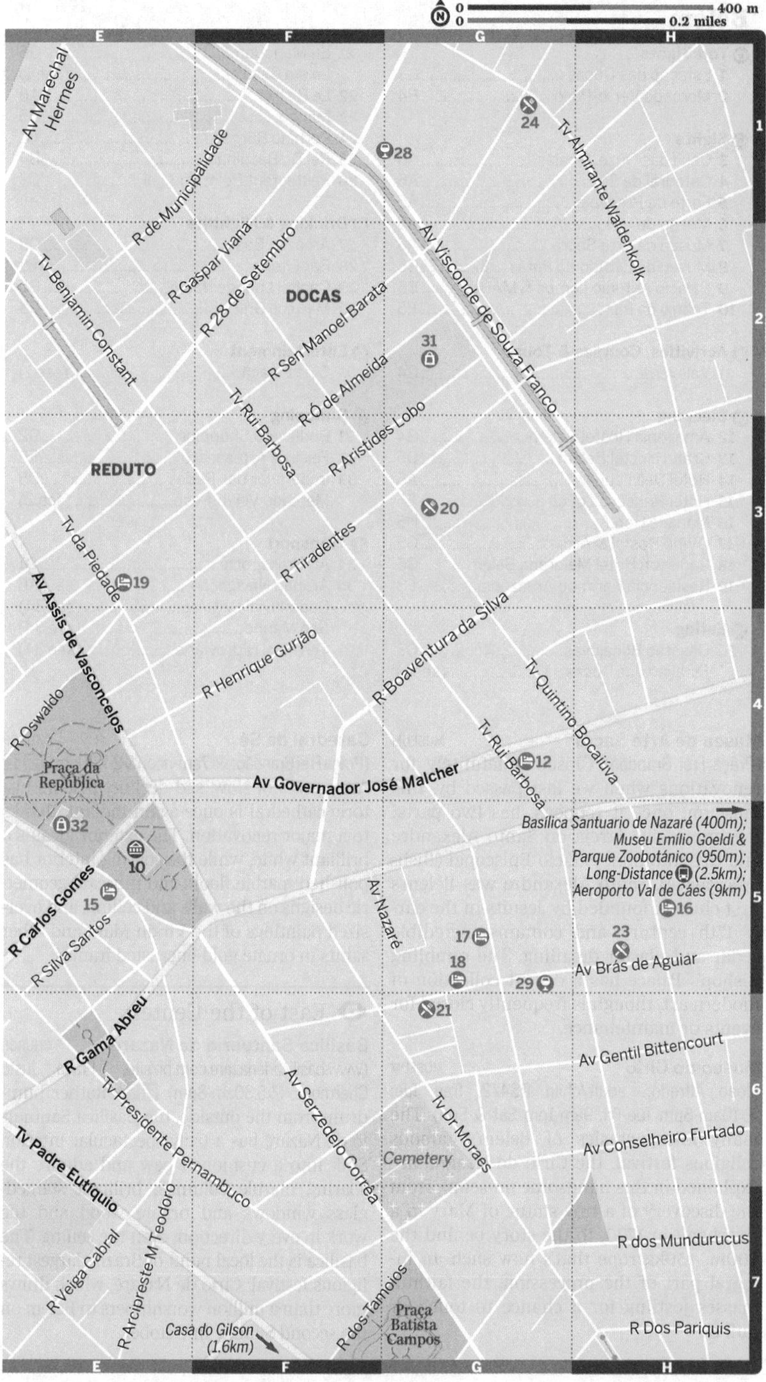
0 400 m
0 0.2 miles
E
F
G
H
1
2
3
4
5
6
7
Av Marechal Hermes
R de Municipalidade
28
24
Tv Almirante Waldenkolk
R Gaspar Viana
R 28 de Setembro
Av Visconde de Souza Franco
Tv Benjamin Constant
DOCAS
R Sen Manoel Barata
31
R Ó de Almeida
Tv Rui Barbosa
R Aristides Lobo
REDUTO
20
Tv da Piedade
R Tiradentes
19
Av Assis de Vasconcelos
R Henrique Gurjão
R Boaventura da Silva
Tv Quintino Bocaiúva
R Oswaldo
Tv Rui Barbosa
12
Praça da República
Av Governador José Malcher
32
Basílica Santuario de Nazaré (400m);
Museu Emílio Goeldi &
Parque Zoobotánico (950m);
Long-Distance (2.5km);
Aeroporto Val de Cáes (9km)
10
R Carlos Gomes
15
Av Nazaré
16
17
23
R Silva Santos
18
Av Brás de Aguiar
29
21
R Gama Abreu
Av Gentil Bittencourt
Av Serzedelo Corrêa
Tv Presidente Pernambuco
Tv Dr Moraes
Av Conselheiro Furtado
Cemetery
Tv Padre Eutíquio
R Arcipreste M Teodoro
R Veiga Cabral
R dos Mundurucus
R dos Tamoios
Praça Batista Campos
Casa do Gilson (1.6km)
R Dos Pariquis

Belém

Top Sights
1 Estação das Docas C3
2 Mercado Ver-o-Peso B4

Sights
3 Casa das Onze Janelas A6
4 Catedral da Sé A6
5 Forte do Presépio A5
6 Museo do Círio A5
7 Museu de Arte Sacra A6
8 Museu do Estado do Pará B6
9 Palácio Antonio Lemos & MABE B6
10 Teatro da Paz E5

Activities, Courses & Tours
11 Valeverde C4

Sleeping
12 Amazônia Hostel Belém G4
13 Grand Hostel Belém D5
14 Hotel Della Luna A6
15 Hotel Princesa Louçã E5
16 Manacá Hotel H5
17 OVibe Hostel & Arts G5
18 Radisson Hotel Maiorana Belém G5
19 Residencia Karimbo Amazônia E3

Eating
20 Casarão Bocaiúvas G3
Estação das Docas .... (see 1)
21 Eti Mariqueti G6
La em Casa .... (see 1)
22 Le Bistrot A6
23 Mango H5
24 Porpino Burger G1
25 Rei Do Bacalhau B4
26 Restaurant Point do Açaí C3

Drinking & Nightlife
27 Amazon Beer C3
28 Bar Fiteiro G1
29 Capital Lounge Bar G5
30 Marujos Grill C3

Entertainment
Cine Estação .... (see 1)

Shopping
31 Boulevard Shopping G2
32 Feira de Artesanato E5
33 Imperador das Redes D5
Mercado Ver-o-Peso .... (see 2)

Transport
34 AR Transporte D1
35 Arapari Navigação A6
Rodofluvial BANAV .... (see 34)
San Marino .... (see 34)
Terminal Hidroviária .... (see 34)

Museu de Arte Sacra MUSEUM
(Praça Frei Brandão) Closed indefinitely for renovations when we last passed by, this museum, once it reopens, has two parts: the impressive Igreja do Santo Alexandre and the adjoining Palâcio Episcopal (Bishop's Palace). Santo Alexandre was Belém's first church, founded by Jesuits in the early 17th century, and contains incredible cedar and plaster detailing. The rambling Bishop's Palace has a decent collection of modern art, though is frequently closed for events or maintenance.

Museo do Círio MUSEUM
(Jóao Alfredo; adult/child R$4/2, free Tue; 10am-6pm Tue-Fri, 9am-1pm Sat & Sun) The many idiosyncrasies of Belém's famous religious festival, the Círio de Nazaré, are explained in this handsome museum, from the discovery of a tiny statue of Mary in a riverbank in 1700, to the story behind the 400m, 450kg rope that's now such an integral part of the procession, the faithful masses jostling for a chance to touch or pull it.

Catedral da Sé CHURCH
(Praça Frei Brandão; 7am-noon & 2-7:30pm) FREE After years of slow, sad decline, Belém's historic cathedral is once again radiant, thanks to a major renovation. The exterior gleams a brilliant white, while the soaring interior has polished marble floors and intricate geometric designs on the walls and ceiling, and oversized paintings of the Virgin Mary and other saints in ornate gold-encrusted frames.

East of the Center

Basílica Santuario de Nazaré CHURCH
(www.basilicadenazare.com.br/site; Praça Justo Chermont; 5:30am-8pm) FREE Rather humdrum from the outside, the Basílica Santuario de Nazaré has a truly spectacular interior. Sink into a cushioned pew and admire the soaring marble columns, brilliant stained-glass windows and ornate wood and tile work in every direction, even the ceiling. The basilica is the focal point of Brazil's largest religious festival, Círio de Nazaré, which draws more than a million worshippers to Belém on the second Sunday in October.

Museu Emílio Goeldi & Parque Zoobotánico
ZOO

(☎91 3219-3300; www.museu-goeldi.br; Av Governador Magalhães Barata 376; adult/child R$3/1; ⏲9am-5pm Tue-Sun) This museum and zoo contains Amazonian species, from anacondas and white-whiskered squirrel monkeys to jaguars and giant river otters, plus an aviary, small aquarium and an exhibition hall with rotating exhibits on everything from an environmental history of the Amazon to cultural artifacts. The grounds are lovely with some towering trees, but most enclosures are pretty depressing – it remained unclear at the time of writing whether a planned overhaul will improve things. It gets very busy on weekends.

Bosque Rodrigues Alves
ZOO

(Jardim Zoo Botânico da Amazônia; ☎91 3277-1112; www.belem.pa.gov.br; Av Almirante Barroso 2305; adult/child R$2/1; ⏲8am-5pm Tue-Sun) Bosque Rodrigues Alves' aging but well-maintained animal enclosures (which harbor tapir, bird, feline and primate species) and wide, tree-shaded paths are especially nice for families, with huge, curious structures including a castle and replica grotto. From the center, take any 'Alm Borroso' bus, and get off when you see the park's long yellow exterior wall.

Tours

There are plenty of possibilities for getting out on the river. They include:

Amazon Star Turismo (☎91 3212-6244; www.amazonstar.com.br; Henrique Gurjão 56; ⏲8am-6pm Mon-Fri, to noon Sat) Organizes day trips around Belém, including birdwatching, nature walks and city tours (per person R$150 to R$300), plus overnight tours combining these options, and multiday packages to Ilha de Marajó.

Valeverde (☎91 3218-7333; www.valeverdeturismo.com.br; Estação das Docas) Runs a variety of short tours on the river (per person R$50 to R$175), including sunrise trips and pleasant evening cruises. Valeverde has an office and daily schedule at the pier at Estação das Docas; in most cases you can simply show up.

Festivals & Events

Every year on the morning of the second Sunday of October, Belém explodes with the sounds of hymns, bells and fireworks. Started in 1793, the **Círio de Nazaré** is Brazil's biggest religious festival. People from all over the country flock to Belém, and even camp in the streets, to participate in the grand event.

SURF THE POROROCA!

Every month or so, when alignment of the sun and moon makes tides their strongest, powerful waves can form at the mouth of certain rivers and barrel upstream with tremendous force. The phenomenon – which occurs when the tide briefly overpowers the force of the river – is technically a 'tidal bore' but in Brazil is better known as the *pororoca*, an indigenous word for 'mighty noise.' And no wonder: the waves can reach heights of 4m and speeds of 30km/h, and can rip full-sized trees off the bank with their force.

All of which is music to the ears of extreme surfers (and wave-surfing kayakers) in search of the mythic 'endless wave.' The record for the longest ride is 37 minutes, covering nearly 13km. Surfers generally report the *pororoca* to be stronger than a like-sized ocean wave, and it constantly changes size and speed according to the river's contours. What's more, the water is loaded with debris that's been swept off the shore and river bottom, including tree trunks and abandoned canoes. (At least the caimans tend to stay away.)

The National Pororoca Surfing Championship has been held at the town of São Domingos do Capim, 120km east of Belém on the Rio Guamá, since 1999. (A related competition is held on the Rio Araguari in Amapá.) The event usually takes place in March, on the full moon nearest the spring equinox, when the *pororoca* is strongest. The bash draws top-ranked surfers and includes street fairs, cultural performances, even a Miss Pororoca competition. A paved road makes getting there easier, though there still is no direct service; from Belém, go to Castanhal and transfer. Alternatively, Amazon Star Turismo, a travel agency in Belém, organizes *pororoca* packages.

The diminutive image of NS de Nazaré (Our Lady of Nazareth) is believed to have been sculpted in Nazareth (Galilee) and to have performed miracles in medieval Portugal before getting lost in Brazil. It was rediscovered in 1700 by a humble cattleman on the site of the basilica, to which it later returned of its own accord, apparently after being moved away several times.

The day before the main annual event, the little statue, having previously been taken 23km north to Icoaraci, is carried in a river procession back to the cathedral in Belém. On the Sunday itself, well over a million people fill the streets to accompany the image from the Catedral da Sé to the Basílica Santuario de Nazaré. The image is placed on a flower-bedecked carriage, and thousands squirm and jostle in an emotional frenzy to get a hand on the 400m rope pulling the carriage. Five hours and just 3.5km from the cathedral, the Virgin reaches the basilica, where she remains for the duration of the festivities.

Sleeping

Grand Hostel Belém HOSTEL $
(91 3355-8889; www.grandhostelbelem.com; Av Presidente Vargas 646; dm R$50, d with shared/private bathroom R$90/120;) This central hostel overlooks Praça da República and has brightly painted rooms with a mix of dorms and private rooms. It has a fun vibe and staff are clued in to travelers' needs. It gets a lot of repeat visitors, which is the best recommendation we can make.

Residencia Karimbo Amazônia GUESTHOUSE $
(91 3298-1373; www.rkamazoniabrasil.sitew.com; Travessa Piedade 391; d/tr R$145/185) A true guesthouse, the French-Brazilian owners live in the front part of the house, while visitors stay in five comfortable rooms, with bright artful decor, new bedding and well-appointed bathrooms. A VIP room (first come, first served) has a private balcony overlooking the hotel's garden area, with a small pool and attractive wood patio.

Hotel Della Luna HOTEL $
(Hotel Portas da Amazônia; 91 3222-9952; www.portasdaamazoniabelempara.com.br; Praça Frei Caetano Brandão; s R$100-145, d R$150-200;) A former mansion with a gorgeous tile facade, this attractive hotel has just nine rooms and a recommended pizzeria. Huge front rooms have large windows overlooking Praça Brandão, but they're also subject to the frequent tolling of nearby cathedral bells. Rear rooms have less light, but high ceilings and exposed brick. The area can get a bit dodgy late at night.

Amazônia Hostel Belém HOSTEL $
(91 3278-4355; www.amazoniahostel.com.br; Av Governador José Malcher 592; dm R$54, s/d R$81/111, s/d without bathroom R$71/103;) A century-old rubber-baron mansion in a safe area is the perfect home for Belém's longest-running youth hostel. Smallish dorms have solid bunks and large lockers, plus 4m ceilings and gorgeous wood floors. Internet, kitchen and laundry are welcome features. Prices are high for a hostel, and management is oddly stingy with breakfast and linens, but it's still a pleasant spot. HI discount available.

★ **OVibe Hostel & Arts** HOSTEL $$
(91 3349-0008; www.ovibe.com.br; Travessa Benjamin Constant 1374; dm/f R$75/450;) This snazzy hostel has wonderful decor and a real artsy vibe. The rooms feature lovely wrought-iron furnishings and daring artistic flourishes at every turn. The location is ideal, in a relatively quiet corner of town but within walking distance of just about everywhere.

★ **Manacá Hotel** HOTEL $$
(91 3222-9224; www.manacahotel.com.br; Travessa Quintino Bocaiúva 1645; s/d/tr R$160/195/225;) Rooms in this boutique hotel are cozy and up to date (though a bit dark), while the common areas have beautiful wood and stone floors, and creative artwork on the walls. The neighborhood is equally appealing, with stylish shops and restaurants nearby. Small swimming pool.

Atrium Hotel Quinta De Pedras HOTEL $$
(91 3199-1603; www.facebook.com/atriumquintadepedras; Doutor Assis 834; s/d/apt from R$170/230/315) One of Belém's best river-side choices, this place is a curious mix of a handsome old facade, contemporary design riffs in the public spaces, and tidy if unremarkable rooms with tiled floors. What you gain in proximity to the river you lose in convenience – it's a long walk to some areas of town.

Hotel Princesa Louçã HOTEL $$
(91 4006-7000; www.hotelprincesalouc.site; Av Presidente Vargas 882; r R$239-395;) Formerly the Hilton Belém, Princesa Louçã has fallen from grace somewhat but continues as one of Belém's largest downtown hotels, centrally located opposite Praça da República, offering business class comfort

with a midrange price tag. Amenities include business center, exercise room, lobby bar and swimming pool. Rooms are spacious and reasonably modern; those on the top floors have river views.

Radisson Hotel Maiorana Belém HOTEL $$$
(☎91 3205-1399; www.radisson.com; Av Bras de Aguiar 321; s/d R$250/390) In a city that lacks top-end hotels, the Radisson is a reliable choice. The rooms are modern and large, although some of the suites are oddly shaped. The breakfast buffet is one of the best in the city; the same can be said for the rooftop swimming pool. Ask for a room on the upper floors.

Eating

★Rei Do Bacalhau SEAFOOD $
(☎91 3241-5824; Travessa Campos Sales 216; mains from R$15; ⏰8am-6pm) The 'King of Cod' is a Belém classic, with cheap and cheerful service and fresh street-food staples straight from the nearby fish market. It's no-frills, which makes us love it all the more.

Porpino Burger BURGERS $
(☎91 3202-5900; www.facebook.com/porpinoburger; Jerônimo Pimentel 242; burgers from R$20; ⏰noon-midnight) The good people of Belém love their burgers, and this small chain is the pick of a rather plentiful bunch of hamburger grills. The recipe for success is simple: fast service, terrific sesame buns and high-quality meats. There are other outposts around town, including in the **Boulevard Shopping Mall** (☎91 3299-0500; www.boulevardbelem.com.br; Av Visconde de Souza Franco 776; ⏰10am-10pm).

Eti Mariqueti CAFE $
(☎91 3223-2714; www.etimariqueti.com.br; Av Brás de Aguiar 232; snacks from R$1; ⏰9am-8pm) This cool and contemporary cafe is popular with well-heeled locals looking for good coffee served up with an enticing range of sweet and salty treats.

★La em Casa BRAZILIAN $$
(☎91 3212-5588; www.laemcasa.com; Av Marechal Hermes, Estação das Docas; mains R$28-70, set menu for 1/2 people R$72/120) Around since 1972, La em Casa is an excellent choice for Pará specialties centered around Amazon fish and duck dishes, as well as Brazilian barbecued meats. Try the Pará tasting menu to sample the local flavors; if you snag a riverside table on a warm Amazonian night, you'll love being here even more.

★Estação das Docas FOOD HALL $$
(www.estacaodasdocas.com.br; Blvd Castilho França; ⏰noon-midnight Sun-Wed, noon-3am Thu-Sat) One of the best places in Belém to eat, no matter what you're hungry for. The bustling complex has almost a dozen restaurants, most with indoor and outdoor seating, open for lunch, dinner and late-night feasting. Favorites include Lá em Casa, serving pricey but outstanding regional food, and Amazon Beer, with delectable pub grub to accompany its artisanal beer.

Mango CAFE $$
(☎91 3199-2731; www.mangoalimentacaosaudavel.com.br; Av Brás de Aguiar 593; mains R$14-45; ⏰11:30am-4pm Tue-Sun & 6-10pm Tue-Sat; 🌶) Wildly popular with Belém's hip young crowd, Mango is devoted to the art of healthy eating with fab dishes such as duck burger and grilled mango for dessert. Terrific juices, salads, light quiches and sandwiches round off a fine choice, with plenty of options for vegetarians.

Restaurant Point do Açaí BRAZILIAN $$
(☎91 3212-2168; www.pointdoacai.net; Blvd Castilhos França 744; mains R$46-78; ⏰11am-4pm Sun-Tue, to 10:30pm Wed-Sat) This enduringly popular place a block back from the waterfront is named after the *açaí* berry, which has taken Brazil by storm with its antioxidant properties. They do excellent steaks, Amazon fish fillets (both fried and grilled), as well as drinks made from said berry.

Le Bistrot FRENCH $$
(☎91 98411-2660; Rua Dr Malcher 15; mains R$40-75; ⏰7pm-midnight Tue-Sat) This charming French bistro right by the cathedral serves French specialties from *croque monsieur* to *filet de bouef au Roquefort* in a gorgeous century-old mansion. The service rubs some travelers up the wrong way, although French visitors don't seem to mind.

Casarão Bocaiúvas SEAFOOD $$
(☎91 8112-6300; www.facebook.com/casaraobocaiuvas; Travessa Quintino Bocaiúva 945; mains R$25-50; ⏰11:30am-3:30pm & 6:30-11:45pm Thu & Sun, 11:30am-2:30am Fri & Sat) If you've visited a Pará beach town, you'll recognize some of the dishes at this popular restaurant. *Caranguejo* (crab feast) is an Algodoal staple and a crowd favorite, served with a hammer for cracking the shells. And then there's the buffalo fillet, a taste of Ilha Marajó. The pizza is great too.

Drinking & Nightlife

Belém has a busy evening scene, although there's little that rises above the pack. Av Visconde de Souza Franco has several bars and clubs, where you can simply follow the music to find the current hot spot.

★Amazon Beer BEER HALL
(☎91 3212-5400; www.amazonbeer.com.br; Av Marechal Hermes, Estação das Docas; ⊙5pm-1am) As much as Brazilians love beer, it's can be surprisingly tough to find anything heftier than a pilsner. This award-winning brewery is an exception, with an amber ale, a Dutch *witbier* (wheat beer), an IPA and even an *açaí* stout, all brewed on-site. Indoor and outdoor seating, a full menu and souvenir beer glasses for sale. Gets busy.

Marujos Grill BAR
(☎91 3242-4809; Av Marechal Heremes, Estação das Docas; ⊙11am-1am) Outdoor tables have river views at this lively but low-key bar-restaurant. There's the *Torre de Chope* (Tower of Beer), a 2.5-liter silo of suds for just R$55, plus a long list of beers and cocktails of the non-gargantuan variety. Occasional musical performances, for which a cover of R$8 may be added to your bill.

Bar Fiteiro BAR
(☎91 3224-0075; www.facebook.com/FiteiroBelem; Av Visconde de Souza Franco 555, at Senador Lemos; ⊙5pm-1am Sun-Fri, from noon Sat) This spacious, colorful bar has a fun, irreverent air and a commitment to not let its customers go hungry – in fact, the bar's tagline is 'We Have Food.' There's live music most nights, often paired with a dish or drink, like 'Feijoada com Samba' on Saturday afternoons.

Capital Lounge Bar BAR
(☎91 3249-0056; www.capitalloungebar.com.br; Av Brás de Aguiar 420; ⊙7pm-3am Wed-Sat) A huge Union Jack and other flags from around the world suggest an old-school English pub, but the sleek booths, creative cocktails and pulsing DJ-mixed music give this much more of a club vibe. There's restaurant service, but the real action gets started long after dinner time. Popular with Belém's jet set.

☆ Entertainment

Teatro da Paz (p573) holds a variety of theatrical events, from plays to symphonies to international dance performances. Most events have same-day tickets available. Otherwise, Casa do Gilson (p580) is a revered stage for live music, including samba and more.

★Casa do Gilson LIVE MUSIC
(☎91 3272-7306; www.facebook.com/casadogilson; Travessa Padre Eutíquio 3172; ⊙8pm-3am Fri, from noon Sat & Sun) Come here for Belém's best live music. Opened in 1987, Gilson's attracts crowds with first-rate samba, *choro* (improvised samba-like genre) and other music, and terrific food and atmosphere. It's between ruas Nova and Tambés.

Cine Estação CINEMA
(☎91 3212-5615; www.estacaodasdocas.com.br; Estação das Docas; R$15) Cine Estação has month-long runs of Brazilian and international art films, typically with screenings twice-nightly three or four days per week.

Shopping

Imperador das Redes SPORTS & OUTDOORS
(☎91 3241-4363; Padre Eutíquio, at Riachuelo; ⊙7:30am-5pm Mon-Fri, 8am-2pm Sat) Large hammock store, with everything from light, simple varieties to deluxe matrimonial ones with lace fringe and more (R$40 to $150).

Mercado Ver-o-Peso MARKET
(Av Castilho França; ⊙5am-6pm) This is Belém's best place to browse and shop, whether for long pants, lacquered piranha or anything in between. Pará has gained national attention with *technobrega* music, a defiantly from-the-streets genre whose best collections aren't sold in stores but on amateur CDs in Ver-o-Peso (and on YouTube). Be wary of pickpockets in the early and late hours.

Feira de Artesanato MARKET
(Praça da República; ⊙7am-3pm Fri-Sun) A large crafts fair that has the city's biggest range of attractive artwork, a lot of which is homemade. It's especially busy on Sundays.

Information

DANGERS & ANNOYANCES

Pickpocketing is a problem in Mercado Ver-o-Peso and the Comercio districts, although a recently increased police presence in the former has improved things a little. Take care during the day and avoid both at night. Take a cab if you're returning late from bars or the movies.

Police (☎91 3222-2602, 190; Av Marechal Heremes, Estação das Docas; ⊙24hr) In the Estação das Docas complex by the river.

Tourist Police (CIPTUR) (☎91 3222-2602; 28 de Setembro) City-center police station.

Tourist Police (CIPTUR) (☎91 3212-0948; Praça Waldemar Henrique s/n, Paratur Office) Another riverside police station.

LAUNDRY

Laundromat (☎ 91 3224-0529; Av Serzedelo Correia, at Av Bittencourt; R$30 per basket; ⏲ 8am-8pm Mon-Fri, to 6pm Sat) Next-day service.

Lav & Lev (☎ 91 3223-7247; Travessa Dr Moraes 576, at Av Conselheiro Furtado; ⏲ 8am-6pm Mon-Sat) Drop-off service costs R$15 per wash cycle (7kg max), R$15 per dry cycle (some loads may require more than one) plus a R$15 service charge. For R$25 more, they'll pick up and drop off at your hotel.

MEDICAL SERVICES

Hospital Adventista de Belém (☎ 91 3084-8686; www.hab.org.br; Av Almirante Barroso 1758) One of the better private hospitals.

MONEY

Bradesco (Av Presidente Vargas 988, at Rua Silva Santos; ⏲ 10am-1pm & 2-4pm Mon-Fri) Bank with foreign exchange services.

Estação das Docas (Blvd Castilhos França) Numerous ATMs in a secure setting.

Turvicam (☎ 91 3201-5465; www.turvicam.com.br; Av Presidente Vargas 636; ⏲ 8am-6:30pm Mon-Fri, to 1pm Sat) There's a foreign exchange desk out the back of this travel agency.

POST

Main Post Office (☎ 91 3211-3147; Av Presidente Vargas 498; ⏲ 9am-5pm Mon-Fri)

TOURIST INFORMATION

SETUR (☎ 91 3212-0575; www.paraturismo.pa.gov.br; Praça Waldemar Henrique; ⏲ 8am-2pm Mon-Fri) A reasonably helpful branch office of the state tourism department.

ℹ Getting There & Away

AIR

Airport

Belém's **Aeroporto Internacional Val-de-Cans** (☎ 91 3210-6000; www.infraero.gov.br) is a hub for international, domestic and regional flights.

Around Belém

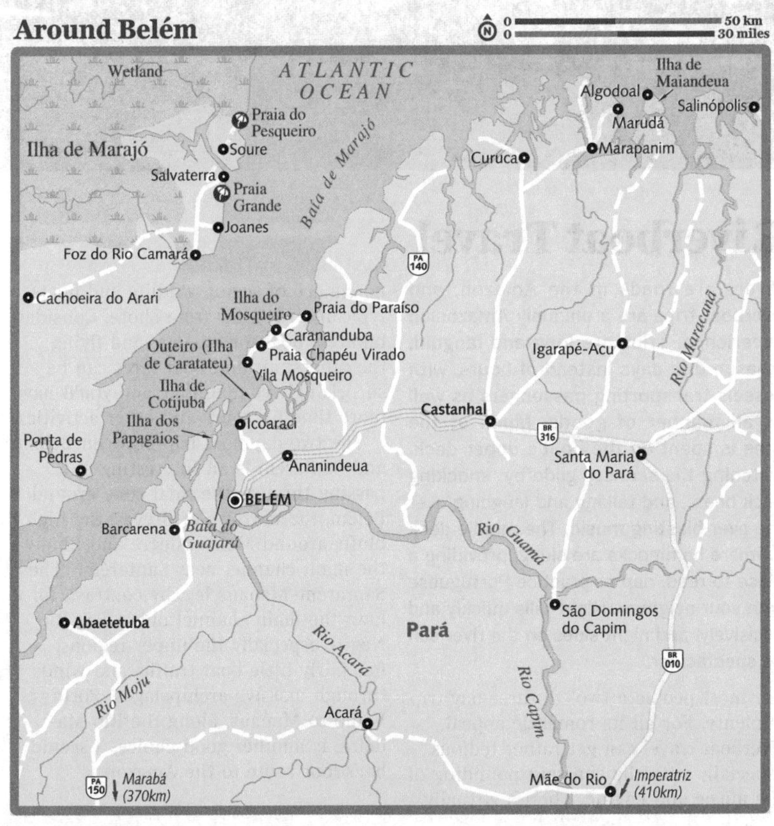

Riverboat Travel

Rivers are roads in the Amazon, and riverboat trips are a uniquely Amazonian experience. Trips are long and languid, measured in days instead of hours, with vessels transporting passengers as well as all manner of goods. Much of the time is spent on the boat's upper deck, watching the scenery glide by, knocking back beers, and talking and laughing over the ever-blasting music. The middle deck is where hammocks are slung, providing a place to read, nap or practice Portuguese with your neighbor. Night falls quickly and decisively, and night skies on the river can be spectacular.

For most people a two- to three-day trip is plenty. For all its romantic appeal, riverboat travel can get rather tedious, especially with the constant pounding of the music and engine. There's virtually no chance of seeing wildlife and boats typically travel far from shore. Consider taking a boat for one leg, and flying the others: air and boat fares can be surprisingly comparable, and you'll have more time for tours and other activities.

The two-day boat trip between Belém and Santarém is an interesting one, passing through the tidal zone around Belém, the narrows of Breves, the high bluffs around Monte Alegre and finally the main channel near Santarém. (The Santarém–Manaus leg, by contrast, follows the main channel only.) The Rio Negro, especially the upper regions, has fairly little boat traffic, and winds through massive archipelagos. Porto Velho to Manaus, along the Rio Madeira, is another good choice, a scenic backdoor route to the Amazon.

GRAHAM MULROONEY/ALAMY STOCK PHOTO ©

GVICTORIA/SHUTTERSTOCK ©

OTORONGO/SHUTTERSTOCK ©

1. Amazon riverboat, Santarém (p590)
2. Riverboats, Rio Negro, Manaus (p606)
3. Hammocks on a riverboat

Top Tips

➡ You'll need a hammock and rope, as well as a light sheet in case the temperature drops. Most boats have a few private cabins, with bunks, private bathrooms and air-conditioning, though for the price you may as well fly.

➡ Get to the boat early to secure a good hammock spot. Away from the restrooms is best.

➡ Buffet-style meals are sold (or included) on all boats, but are notoriously unsanitary. Instead, stick with made-to-order burgers and sandwiches sold from the boat's grill.

➡ Bring water, dry snacks and extra toilet paper.

➡ Theft isn't rampant, but foreigners make tempting targets. Be especially alert when the boat stops in port, which can be in the middle of the night.

➡ Never leave cameras, cell phones or other valuables unattended in your hammock, and keep your backpack zipped and locked.

➡ Make friends with the passengers around you, as they can keep an eye on your gear.

➡ Bring a thin cable and lock to secure your bag to one of the boat's center poles.

➡ Some thieves will snatch a promising piece of luggage and jump overboard; an accomplice waiting in a motorboat fishes thief and bag from the river and zips away to salvage whatever's not waterlogged. Victims can't jump in after them and captains will not stop or turn around.

Airlines

Azul (☎0800-887-1118, 91 4003-1118; www.voeazul.com.br) Flights to Santarém, Macapá, Altamira, Cuiabá, Campinas, Fortaleza and Belo Horizonte among other destinations. Also flies to Miami.

Gol (☎91 3210-6312, 0800-704-0465; www.voegol.com.br) Serves numerous domestic and international destinations.

LATAM (☎91 3212-2166; www.latam.com) Extensive domestic and international network.

MAP (☎in Manaus 92 2125-5000; www.voemap.com.br) Flies to Altamira and Santarém.

Surinam Airways (☎91 3222-4831, 91 3210-6432; www.flyslm.com) Flies to Cayenne (French Guiana) and Paramaribo (Suriname).

TAP (Air Portugal; ☎0800-727-2347; www.flytap.com) Flights to Lisbon.

BOAT

All long-distance boats leave Belém from the handsomely renovated **Terminal Hidroviária** (Av Marechal Hermes). You can purchase tickets from the booths inside the terminal, but an easier and more reliable option is to contact Amazon Star Turismo (p577), whose multilingual staff can book boat tickets, including over the phone or internet, for trips to or from Belém, for no extra cost.

AR Transporte (☎91 3224-1225; www.artransporte.com.br) and **San Marino** (☎in Manaus 93 99179-1222; www.facebook.com/Ferryboat.sanmarinoll) offer boat service to and from Manaus and most points along the way. At last check, boats to Manaus left Wednesday and Saturday, plus every other Tuesday, at 6pm with stops at Monte Alegre (hammock/hammock with air-con/cabin with air-con/cabin with air-con and bathroom R$200/230/750/950, three days), Santarém (R$230/270/800/1000, four days), Parintins (R$330/370/950/1100, five days), and Manaus (R$370/400/1000/1200, six days); cabins rates are for two people. Meals are not included, but you can purchase food on board.

Arapari Navigação (☎91 3241-4977; Siqueira Mendes 120) and **Rodofluvial BANAV** (☎91 3269-4494; www.banav.com.br) alternate service to Ilha de Marajó, with daily ferries from Belém to Camará, (R$25 standard, R$40 'VIP' with air-con and airplane-style seating, three hours) at 6:30am and 2:30pm Monday to Saturday, and 10am on Sunday.

BUS

Belém's **long-distance bus station** (Av Almirante Barroso) is 3km east of the town center. Major destinations may be served by several lines, while *leito* and *semi-leito* (overnight sleeper) seats are available on some longer routes.

In addition to the long-distance bus services, **Sinprovan** (☎91 3226-5879) operates frequent services to Marudá (R$36, 3½ hours) in air-conditioned minibuses.

Getting Around

The long-distance bus station is on the corner of Av Almirante Barroso and Av Governador José Malcher, 3km east of the city center. To get there from the center, take any 'Guama – P Vargas' bus (316) from Av Presidente Vargas. To get from the station into town, turn right out of the terminal and cross to the diagonally opposite corner; buses line up on the AV Borroso in order to turn right onto Av Governador José Malcher, toward Praça de República. A taxi from the bus terminal costs R$20 to R$25.

TO/FROM THE AIRPORT

Aeroporto Internacional Val de Cãns is 8km north of the center on Av Júlio César. The 'Pratinha – Pres Vargas' bus (638) runs between the airport and Av Presidente Vargas (R$3, 40 minutes); the 'E Marex' bus also goes there, but you may have to change buses at the depot (no charge). Arriving by plane, turn left as you leave the terminal; buses stop at the traffic circle about 50m past the end of the terminal. A taxi between the airport and center is a fixed R$50 when booked inside the terminal; you may be able to catch one for less at the bus stop, though they pass somewhat infrequently.

BUSES FROM BELÉM

DESTINATION	COST FROM (R$)	DURATION (HRS)	COMPANY
Altamira	197	14	Boa Esperança (www.viajeboaesperanca.com.br)
Brasília	255	35	Rápido Marajó (www.rapidomarajo.com.br)
Fortaleza	170	24	Guanabara (www.expressoguanabara.com.br), Itapemirim (www.itapemirim.com.br)
Salvador	489	35	Itaperim (www.itaperim.com.br)
São Luís	146	13	Boa Esperança (www.viajeboaesperanca.com.br), Rápido Marajó (www.rapidomarajo.com.br)

BOOKS ABOUT THE AMAZON

Countless books have been written about the Amazon. Notable ones available in English include:

- *The Cloud Forest* (Peter Matthiessen; 1961)
- *The Burning Season: The Murder of Chico Mendes and the Fight for the Amazon Rain Forest* (Andrew Revkin; 1990)
- *The Smithsonian Atlas of the Amazon* (Michael Goulding et al; 2003)
- *The River of Doubt: Theodore Roosevelt's Darkest Journey* (Candice Millard; 2005)
- *Tree of Rivers: The Story of the Amazon* (John Hemming; 2008)
- *The Thief at the End of the World: Rubber, Power, and the Seeds of Empire* (Joe Jackson; 2008)
- *Fordlandia: The Rise and Fall of Henry Ford's Forgotten Jungle City* (Greg Grandin; 2009)
- *The Lost City of Z: A Tale of Deadly Obsession in the Amazon* (David Grann; 2009)
- *The Last of the Tribe: The Epic Quest to Save a Lone Man in the Amazon* (Monte Reel; 2016)

Algodoal

0XX91 / POP 1500

The small fishing village of Algodoal on Ilha de Maiandeua exchanges cars and paved roads for expansive views over firm, windswept beaches and a sometimes turbulent sea. A popular getaway for young *belenenses*, Algodoal is jam-packed during a few frenetic months in the summer and over certain holidays, and quiet and virtually abandoned during down periods. If you catch it when it's quiet, it's one of northern Brazil's best hideaways. It's 180km northeast of Belém.

Sights

Praia da Caixa d'Água is the long beach in front of town. Across a tidal canal is **Praia do Farol**, a broad attractive beach that's good (and convenient) for swimming and sunbathing. Further on, past a rocky outcrop, is **Praia da Princesa** with a cluster of beach restaurants followed by 7km of lovely white sand. Across an even stronger canal is **Praia do Mupéua**, extending another 7km to Fortalezinha village.

Activities & Tours

You can canoe (R$3) up the canal at Praia do Farol to spot birds and sometimes monkeys (best at sunset), visit Lago de Princesa (best April to June), walk or boat to the village of Fortalezinha, or even walk around the island.

Sunset is the best time to spot birds and wildlife, including the timid but radiant guará (scarlet ibis). However, high tide is when the canals are deepest and canoes can penetrate the furthest. Ideally, you'll be visiting when sunset and high tide happen to coincide! At high tide, you can canoe clear to Praia do Mupéua on the other side of the island (and from there walk back to town, about 7km) or else return along another canal to Porto do Mamede, Algodoal's main dock.

Partway up the canal from Praia do Farol, a path cuts through the forest and low sand dunes to Lago da Princesa and onward to Praia da Princesa (2km to 3km total). Boatmen can drop you at the path, and you can visit the lake, then return by foot along the beach (4km). The lake is just a small lagoon, and worth visiting only when full (April to June).

Another option is visiting Fortalezinha, a small village on the other side of the island, where you can walk the beach and grab lunch at one of several small restaurants. The boat ride from Algodoal to Fortalezinha is scenic but pricey (R$100); alternatively, you can catch a canoe (R$4 per person) from Porto do Mamede to the nearby community of Camboinha and follow well-marked paths from there.

From Fortalezinha it's possible to walk counter-clockwise back to Algodoal. (The reverse is much less pleasant, as you'll be walking against the wind.) It's a long (14km) but scenic walk. However, there's a powerful *furo* (tidal inlet) about halfway around that should never be crossed on foot. Wait for a fisherman to ferry you across or else turn back.

On any trip, be sure to bring mosquito repellent, water and sun protection.

Guided trips range from R$50 to R$200 per person, depending on what you do. For simple trips, boatmen can be hired at the mouth of the canal at Praia do Farol. Many hotels can recommend guides; Pousada Marhesias has the most in-depth information, including simple maps of the island.

Sleeping & Eating

Algodoal is awash with pousadas of all shapes and sizes. They fill to capacity during high season and holidays, but are empty – or simply closed – otherwise.

★ **Pousada Marhesias** POUSADA $
(91 9112-3461, 91 3854-1129; www.marhesias.com; Bertoldo Costa 47; s R$120-150, d R$150-180;) This well-run hotel has artsy guestrooms facing a leafy garden. All have air-con and TV; suites are larger with private verandas. A large common deck has views of the sea and beach. Excellent restaurant and bar, and wi-fi in the common areas. It's located at the far end of town, closest to the Praia do Farol.

Pousada Ponta do Boiador HOTEL $
(91 99215-9939; Bertoldo Costa 44; d standard/ste from R$150/180;) Suites here are newer, larger and better appointed, with breezy patios with hammocks. Standards are simpler and quite small, though their all-wood construction lends a clean, dry air. All have air-conditioning, hot showers and sea views. Best of all, the Boiador has direct beach access and a large waterfront deck with meal service, cold beers and occasional live music.

Hotel Bela Mar POUSADA $
(91 3854-1128; www.facebook.com/pousadabelamar; Magalhães Barata; s/d with fan R$65/90, with air-con R$80/120;) A clean, reliable choice, this is the first hotel you reach from the boat drop-off. A dozen tidy rooms are arranged around a pretty central garden, all with high ceilings and attractive decor. An ample breakfast spread is served in the hotel's spacious restaurant.

Restaurante La Izla BRAZILIAN $$
(Bertolda Costa; mains R$15-37; 11am-11pm) This family-run choice has a few tables on a sunny patio and a few more inside the owners' clapboard home. The menu is painted on the wall and consists of the Brazilian basics: a choice of fried fish, chicken or beef, plus rice, *feijão* (beans) and *farofa* (manioc flour sautéed with butter).

Pousada Marhesias BRAZILIAN $$
(Bertoldo Costa 47; mains R$12-48; 7pm-10:30pm) This place serves a little of everything, from fish and seafood to pasta and pizza, all freshly made and served in a large second-floor dining area with a high peaked ceiling and tasteful decor. You can count on hearing some great jazz over your meal – it's almost all they play. Open for lunch for hotel guests only.

Information

DANGERS & ANNOYANCES

The island has several tidal channels, known as *furos* (meaning 'punctures' in Portuguese) that connect inland lagoons to the ocean. They rise and fall, and even change directions, according to the tide. The one between Praia do Farol and Praia da Princesa (known as Furo Velho) is especially treacherous and should never be crossed on foot. Fishermen are usually around and can ferry you across.

INTERNET ACCESS

Most hotels have wi-fi. There's also free community wi-fi, though finding a strong signal can be tough.

MEDICAL SERVICES

Farmacias Kadosh (7:30am-8pm Mon-Sat, to 7pm Sun) A small pharmacy selling sunscreen, bug spray, condoms, medicine and more.

MONEY

There is no ATM on the island or even in Marudá, and not all hotels accept credit cards. Best to bring cash from Belém.

Getting There & Away

Access to Algodoal is via the mainland village of Marudá. Boats leave for Algodoal (R$10, 40 minutes) at 9am, 11am, 1:30pm, 3:30pm and 5pm daily, plus 8:30pm Friday. Buses from Belém drop off (and pick up) passengers at the port, but vans only go as far as the bus station, which is five long blocks away, or R$15 in a taxi.

Arriving at Algodoal, a slew of donkey-cart drivers will vie for the chance to take you to your hotel (per person R$12). Some drivers will try to convince you to go to certain hotels where they earn a commission; always insist on going to the one of your choosing.

Boats return to the mainland at 6am, 8am, 10:30am and 1:30pm daily, plus 3pm Friday, and 3pm and 5pm Saturday and Sunday. Buses for Belém wait for passengers from the boat to leave, though you may need to make your way quickly to Marudá's bus station to catch them.

Ilha de Marajó

☎0XX91 / POP 48,000

The 50,000-sq-km Ilha de Marajó, slightly larger than Switzerland, lies at the mouth of the Amazon River and is generally considered to be the largest river island in the world; writer Peter Matthiessen once described it as the Amazon's cork. (Some argue Marajó doesn't qualify because part of the island faces the open ocean.) It was the ancient home of the Marajoaras indigenous culture, notable for their large ceramic burial urns. Marajó remains a world apart, where bicycles outnumber cars and water buffalo graze around town.

Only the island's eastern shore is accessible to tourists, with three small towns: Joanes (the smallest), Salvaterra (with the best beach but not much else) and Soure (the laid-back 'capital' of Marajó). The island's interior is wetland, home to thousands of birds, including the graceful *guará* (scarlet ibis). Be aware that Marajó is very wet from January to June.

Getting There & Away

Arapari Navigação (p584) and Rodofluvial BANAV (p584) – standard R$25, 'VIP' service with air-con and airplane-style seating R$40, three hours – leave Belém's main boat terminal at 6:30am and 2:30pm Monday to Saturday and 10am on Sunday, arriving at a port south of Joanes called Foz do Rio Camará, or Camará for short. They return from the same port at 6:30am and 3pm Monday to Saturday, and 3pm Sunday.

Getting Around

Buses and minivans meet ferries arriving from Belém at Camará, Marajó island's main port. Each has a sign to its destination; simply look for the place you're going to and get on. It's R$8 to Joanes, Salvaterra or the Foz do Rio Camará ferry port, and R$11 to R$18 to Soure, including the barge across the river and drop-off at your hotel. (The full-sized buses don't do hotel drop-offs, however.)

Moto-taxis are common in all three towns, and cost R$5 around town, R$5 to R$15 to outlying beaches, and R$30 between Joanes and Salvaterra.

Salvaterra and Soare are separated by the wide mouth of the Rio Paracauari; boats connect the two. Boats also go from Soare to the car-ferry pier (8km from Salvaterra, R$1) or you can hop on the ferry itself for free.

Joanes

☎0XX91 / POP 300

It may be just across the river from Belém, but sleepy Joanes is all about total isolation. The essence of its appeal is simple: a lovely hotel and beach, the remains of a 17th-century Jesuit church and hardly a soul in sight. There are very few services here, and no one accepts credit or debit cards. Just the way we like it.

Sleeping & Eating

Pousada Vila Joanes POUSADA **$**
(☎91 99217-2248; Segunda; d/tr R$140/170;) Overlooking the water like any self-respecting Joanes accommodation should, the whitewashed Pousada Vila Joanes is suitably simple, lovely and quiet, and gets consistently good reviews from travelers. No credit cards.

Pousada Ventania do Rio-Mar POUSADA **$$**
(☎91 3646-2067; www.pousadaventania.com; Quarta Rua; s/d R$165/203;) Atop a breezy headland overlooking the shore. Large, simple rooms have whimsical decor and oversized paintings, bathrooms (but no TV or air-con) and open onto a large patio. The beach is just steps away, and the staff can arrange a variety of excursions, including canoeing and fishing with local guides. Cash only.

Jacaré SEAFOOD **$**
(mains R$12-28; 7am-10pm) One of a handful of beach restaurants serving the Marajoana favorites of grilled fish and buffalo steaks. The atmosphere is very laid-back and you may find yourself lingering long after you finish your meal.

Getting There & Away

Ferries operate once or twice daily between Belém and Camará (standard/VIP R$25/40, three hours); the VIP seating includes air-con and airplane-style seating.

Shuttles to/from the ferry at Camará cost R$8 (20 to 30 minutes). There are two morning shuttles from Joanes to Salvaterra and the boat pier (R$12, 7am and 9:30am) but no return service. Taxis charge R$70 for the same trip, while moto-taxis are R$30 (but carry only one person, of course). Biking is possible, but can be a long, hot haul.

Salvaterra

☎0XX91 / POP 9650

Salvaterra has Ilha de Marajó's best and longest beach, the aptly named Praia

PREHISTORIC AMAZONIA

Most researchers agree that human occupation of the Amazon Basin began around 11,000 to 14,000 years ago, based on studies of ancient cave paintings near Monte Alegre, in Pará state. Around 6000 years ago, the Tapajoara people, living near present-day Santarém, started creating simple clay urns, the oldest known pottery in the Americas, and other indigenous Amazonians began mastering rudimentary agriculture.

By the last few centuries of the pre-Christian era, the Amazon was home to numerous cohesive communities, numbering in the thousands and led by chiefs. They produced good-quality pottery and cultivated maize and manioc intensively. It was during this time that the techniques of agriculture still used today were first developed, including selective burning, crop rotation and allowing the land periodic 'rest periods' to regenerate.

The Marajoara were among the most sophisticated pre-colonial Christian-era Amazonians, flourishing between AD 400 and 1350 on the wetlands of present-day Ilha de Marajó. They built massive earth platforms called *aterros* – the largest were 6m high and 250m long – to escape the annual floods. They buried their dead in elaborate urns, considered to be the most sophisticated ceramics produced in pre-colonial Brazil.

Interestingly, early human occupation of the Amazon has emerged as a proxy for today's environmental debates. Conservationists have long argued that large-scale occupation and development is incompatible with a healthy rainforest. However, recent research suggesting the early Amazon may have been far more populated than previously thought has been used by some to argue that greater exploitation of the rainforest is not only harmless, but has been part of its history for millennia.

Grande, a short walk outside town. The town itself is at once compact (which creates a sense that it is busier than it actually is) and laid-back in the finest tradition of Brazilian coastal towns.

Sights

Praia Grande BEACH

Praia Grande is, as the name suggests, a big beach: it's a long wide swathe of golden-brown sand about 500m south of Salvaterra proper. A slew of beach restaurants perched on stilts overlook the first section of the beach, but the far end is virtually deserted, save for one large resort. Stingrays may be present but are easily scared off if you shuffle your feet as you enter and leave the water.

Sleeping & Eating

Pousada Bosque dos Aruãs POUSADA $

(☎91 3765-1115; Segunda Rua; s/d R$90/110, ste R$165-190; ❄📶) On an oceanfront lot shaded by mango trees, long wood cabins have two guestrooms apiece, each with small private patio, bright interior paint, TV and aircon. Two standalone suites are larger with slightly nicer amenities, like glass showers and veranda, and are nearest the water. Somewhat shabby overall, but very peaceful. Praia Grande is a 10-minute walk away.

The hotel's restaurant is one of Salvaterra's best.

Hotel Beira-Mar HOTEL $

(☎91 3765-1400; Frei Romão; r with fan/air-con R$55/80; ❄📶) A short walk from the center and Praia Grande; rooms here are of the large and plain variety, with graying tile floors, TV and thin mattresses and linens. Wi-fi signal is spotty.

Restaurante Umuarama SEAFOOD, PIZZA $

(☎91 98300-1330; Terceira; mains R$10-32; ⏲11am-3pm & 7-10:30pm) This low-key, open-air restaurant serves shrimp, fish and buffalo dishes during the daytime and pizza at night. Located a short walk from Praia Grande, this is a popular and less-expensive alternative to restaurants right on the beach, but you'll still catch a sea breeze.

Pousada Bosque dos Aruãs BRAZILIAN $$

(mains R$25-$60; ⏲noon-3pm & 6-10pm) True, dishes like fish with shrimp sauce or breaded buffalo steak can be had anywhere on the island, but the food and presentation at this pousada are surprisingly refined and well worth the somewhat higher prices. It's open to guests and nonguests alike, with service on the hotel's small wooden patio.

Information

The **post office** (⏲8am-noon & 2-5pm Mon-Fri) is along the main drag.

Getting There & Away

BANAV (91 3269-4494; 8-11am) sells ferry tickets from its office in Salvaterra, but ferries leave from Foz do Rio Camará, south of Joanes. Otherwise, buy tickets on the shuttle or at the port. Motorized canoes connect downtown Salvaterra with Soure (R$3). Alternatively, take the ferry from the pier at the end of Salvaterra's main road (R$2, 15 minutes, 7am to 6pm); you can bring bicycles on board the latter.

Soure

0XX91 / POP 25,500

The 'Capital of Marajó,' Soure is located on the far side of the Rio Paracauari. Although it's the biggest town on the island, Soure has a very laid-back vibe, with horses and water buffalo grazing on the soccer fields and double-wide streets, many of them dirt or grass with a bike path weaving down the middle.

Sights

The beaches near Soure, which have a mix of salt- and freshwater, are often covered with fantastic seeds washed down from the Amazonian forests. If you enter the water, shuffle your feet to scare away stingrays.

Praia do Pesqueiro is Soure's most popular beach, a broad swathe of soft beige sand, backed by thatch-roofed restaurants. Pesqueiro is further from town (about 12km north) than the other beaches, but along the way you can spot buffalos wallowing in marshes and catch a glimpse of Marajó's lush interior. A moto-taxi runs R$15 each way, while cabs charge R$40 for up to four people.

Praia Barra Velha and **Praia de Araruna** are narrow beaches edged by thick mangrove stands and separated from each other by a wide tidal channel. Barra Velha has several small restaurants, while Praia de Araruna is virtually deserted. High tide can reduce both shorelines to a thin strip of sand, but otherwise they're pleasant and easy to reach by foot, bike or taxi. To get there, follow Travessa 14 east of town for about 4.5km to a fork in the road; to the right is a walkway leading to Praia Barra Velha, while to the left and a short distance further is a footbridge across the channel to Praia de Araruna.

Praia Garrote is a completely undeveloped beach at the mouth of the Rio Paracauari. To get there, follow Travessa 9 east out of town; the road makes a sharp right-hand turn and continues to a tidal inlet. Fishers can ferry you across, and the beach is a short distance further.

Activities & Tours

A bicycle is a great way to get around Soure. A guy named **Bimba** (Rua 4, btwn Travessas 18 & 19; per hour/day R$4/25) rents bikes from his house; it's the one with a stone facade, next to a hardware shop. Near Pousada O Canto do Francês, a local family also has **bikes for rent** (Travessa 8, btwn Ruas 6 & 7; per hour/day R$4/28; 8am-8pm).

Three nearby *fazendas* (ranches) make for interesting half-day trips. **Fazenda Bom Jesus**, **Fazenda São Jerônimo** and **Fazenda Araruna** offer the same basic activities, including riding water buffaloes, visiting mangroves and beaches, and spotting birds, monkeys and other animals. Bom Jesus is the most adventurous of the three – the grounds look more like a nature preserve than a ranch – though at São Jerônimo you can ride a buffalo in the surf.

Morning boat rides up Rio Paracauari can also be arranged, including passing through a mangrove 'tunnel' and a chance to see birds and pink dolphins. There are also city tours, with visits to local artisans and beach-hopping tours. Prices start at R$80 to R$120 per person.

Hotels like Pousada O Canto do Francês and Hotel Casarão da Amazônia can provide additional details and make reservations for all of these activities. The latter also has multiday all-inclusive *fazenda* packages; check the website for details.

Festivals & Events

Círio de Nazaré RELIGIOUS

(2nd Sun in Nov) Soure has its own **Círio de Nazaré** (2nd Sun in Oct) with a beautiful procession. Hotels can be booked up at this time.

Sleeping

Pousada O Canto do Francês POUSADA $

(91 3741-1298; www.ocantodofrances.blogspot.com.br; cnr Rua 6 & Travessa 8; s/d incl breakfast R$150/170;) Nine spacious, attractive suites have whitewashed walls, fine woodwork and comfortable beds. Lunch and dinner can be ordered, though service is slow. Meals are served in the hotel's shaded patio and are a nice way to meet fellow guests. It's far from the center, but a nearby family rents bikes.

★**Hotel Casarão da Amazônia** HOTEL $$

(91 3741-1988; www.casaraoamazonia.com.br; cnr Rua 4 & Travessa 9; s/d from R$244/282;) Occupying a beautifully restored

19th-century *casarão* (mansion), rooms here have high ceilings, flat-screen TVs and small but stylish bathrooms; some units are oddly narrow, but still comfortable. A newer garden annex has slightly larger rooms, with patios and hammocks. The hotel's large pool is heaven on a hot day, and the restaurant is one of the island's best.

Pousada Restaurante Ilha Bela POUSADA **$$**
(☎91 3741-1313; www.ilhabelamarajo.blogspot.com; cnr Rua 1 & Travessa 13; s/d R$120/190; ❄📶) A short distance from Soare's ferry dock, this reliable guesthouse and restaurant has spotless rooms with updated amenities and includes a wonderful breakfast. Quads have patios with views of the river. Festivals and other events are sometimes held in the plaza directly in front, and could make sleeping tough if you happen to visit then. The hotel's restaurant is worth checking out.

Eating

Pousada Restaurante Ilha Bela BRAZILIAN **$**
(☎91 3741-1313; cnr Rua 1 & Travessa 13; R$18-38; ⏲7am-3pm & 6-11:30pm Wed-Mon) Fresh typical Marajoara fare, including fried fish and buffalo steak, served in a breezy corner dining area. There's live music on Friday evenings.

Hotel Casarão da Amazônia INTERNATIONAL **$$**
(☎91 3741-1988; www.casaraoamazonia.com.br; cnr Rua 4 & Travessa 9; R$20-55; ⏲11am-3pm & 7-10pm) It's no surprise that the island's nicest hotel (p589) also has its most sophisticated restaurant. It's not easy to attract experienced staff to this culinary hinterland, but the Italian owner's efforts have paid off. The kitchen prepares everything from local specialties to international staples. Seating is on a covered terrace.

Café de Soare FRENCH **$$**
(Rua 3, btwn Travessas 14 & 15; mains R$15-45; ⏲6:30-10pm Mon-Sat) Run by an earnest French expat, this small but excellent restaurant has a handful of tables in its attractive dining area and a few more on the sidewalk. The buffalo steak with Gorgonzola sauce is a favorite, as are the mouthwatering crepes and mixed salads.

Shopping

Cerâmica Mbara-yo CERAMICS
(www.facebook.com/ceramica.mbarayo; Travessa 20, btwn Ruas 3 & 4; ⏲8am-noon & 2-6pm Mon-Sat, 8am-noon Sun) This is the modest shop of ceramicist Carlos Amaral, who combines traditional Aruã and Marajoara ceramic traditions with award-winning results. You can have a short tour of the workshop to see how the pieces are made. Numerous small, affordable pieces are for sale, and each has a particular tale or significance behind it.

Information

MEDICAL SERVICES

Drogaria Big Farm (Rua 4, at Travessa 16; ⏲7am-9pm Mon-Sat, 8am-noon Sun) Pharmacy and mini-mart.

MONEY

Banco do Brasil (Rua 3, btwn Travessas 17 & 18; ⏲10am-3pm Mon-Fri) Has an ATM and foreign exchange.

Bradesco (Rua 2, btwn Travessas 15 & 16; ⏲10am-3pm Mon-Fri) Central ATM.

POST

Post Office (Rua 2, btwn Travessas 13 & 14; ⏲9am-noon & 2-5pm Mon-Fri)

Getting There & Away

The main bus and passenger ferry stops near the corner of Travessa 11 and Rua 1. Motorized canoes shuttle to downtown Salvaterra (R$3) and to the passenger ferry dock (R$2), leaving Soare from a long pier at Travessa 14 and Rua 1.

For transport between Camará and Soare, **Edgar Transporte** (☎91 3741-1763, 91 9634-0722; edgar-transporte@hotmail.com; Travessa 15 935, btwn Ruas 6 & 7; per person R$18) is a professionally run shuttle service that has modern, air-conditioned vehicles and confirmed reservations for just slightly more than the standard service. Boat tickets, including VIP, can be purchased on the shuttle. Reserve one to three days in advance, especially in high season.

Santarém

☎0XX93 / POP 296,302

Santarém is a terrific destination, a languid riverside town with a breezy waterfront promenade, parks and several good restaurants. More than that, it's a fine gateway to several quintessential Amazon experiences – getting to primary rainforest, in the Floresta Nacional (FLONA) do Tapajós, is much easier here than from Manaus, and Santarém has its very own 'meeting of the waters,' where the Rio Tapajós flows into the Amazon. Not far to the east, Lago Maicá is a gorgeous floodplain rich in birds and other wildlife, including pink dolphins and sloths.

Santarém

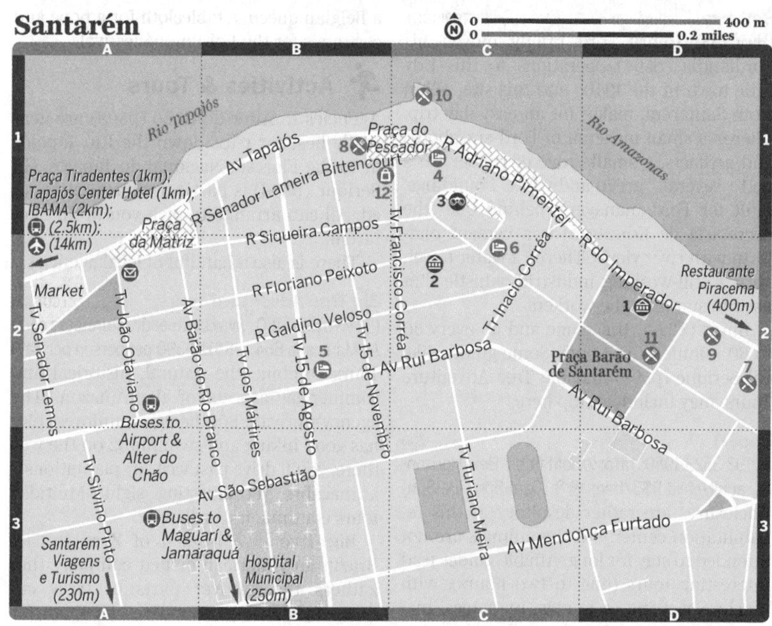

Just a short bus ride away is Alter do Chão, a cool little town with white-sand river beaches and a laid-back vibe. And this area is steeped in history, from ancient petroglyphs in nearby Monte Alegre to the boom and bust of Amazonian rubber in Fordlândia.

History

The Santarém region has been a hub of human settlement for many thousands of years; some of the oldest remains of human settlement were discovered in Monte Alegre a short distance downstream. A Jesuit mission was established at the meeting of the Tapajós and Amazon rivers in 1661, and officially named Santarém in 1758.

The later history of Santarém was marked by the rubber boom and bust, and a series of gold rushes that started in the 1950s. The economy today is based mainly on soy and hardwoods and, increasingly, on gold and bauxite mining, whose severe environmental impact make them controversial.

Sights

★Lago Maicá LAKE

The floodplains east and southeast of Santarém are among the Amazon's most rewarding excursions. Flooded for much of the year, the plains are home to fabulous birdlife (including toucans and macaws), pink dolphins, howler monkeys, sloths and anacondas. The sunrise and sunset views are pure magic and there's a real sense of tranquility out here. Take an overnight boat trip, go canoeing through the flooded forest and relax far from the tourist hordes. Gil Serique (p598) organizes especially enjoyable excursions here.

Santarém

Sights

1 Museu de Santarém D2
2 Museu Dica Frazão C2
3 Praça Mirante do Tapajós C1

Sleeping

4 Hotel London Santarém C1
5 Hotel Palace Santarém B2
6 Hotel Sandis Mirante C2

Eating

7 Açaí Santarém D2
8 Bar Mascote B1
9 La Tasca D2
10 Massabor C1
11 Quiosque da Praça D2

Shopping

12 Loja Regional Muiraquita B1

Belterra HISTORIC SITE

(Hwy 163) Henry Ford briefly moved his Fordlândia (p594) operations to this tidy little town in the 1940s and this site, 40km from Santarém, makes for an easy day trip. There's a small museum of Ford-era photos and artifacts, a small grove of rubber trees and several green-and-white buildings, built for Ford managers; behind one (the Secretária de Educação) is a cement platform with river views. There's a water tower, with a still-working industrial whistle that used to summon the workers.

Buses ($3.50; 1hr) come and go every 30 to 60 minutes, until 9pm. Some guides, like Gil Serique (p598) and Big Tree Adventure Tours, may include a stop here.

ZooFIT ZOO

(☎93 3523-1989; http://zoofit.fit.br; Belo Horizonte; adult/child R$3/free; ⏰8:30am-5pm Tue-Sun) Enclosures are rather desultory at this rehabilitation center, but the animals are not intended to stay for long. Affable guides lead interesting tours (one to two hours), with up-close viewing of pumas, manatees, macaws and more, and occasionally a chance to hold or feed them. It's especially fun for kids. Reachable by taxi or bus.

Praça Mirante do Tapajós VIEWPOINT

This pleasant oval-shaped plaza and viewpoint has two open-air food stalls and good river views. An observation tower affords an even better view, including of Santarém's own 'meeting of the waters.' Look for a set of stairs just east of Brisa Hotel.

Museu de Santarém MUSEUM

(Centro Cultural João Fona; Rua do Imperador, Praça Barão de Santarém; by donation; ⏰8am-5pm Mon-Fri, to 1pm Sat) Housed in a large yellow waterfront mansion, this museum is also known as the Centro Cultural João Fona, after the Pará artist who painted the frescoes on its interior walls. It features, among other things, an excellent collection of stone and clay artifacts from the Tapajoara culture that flourished in this area more than 6000 years ago.

Museu Dica Frazão MUSEUM

(Floriano Peixoto 281; by donation; ⏰8am-6pm Mon-Sat) Dona Dica Frazão spent three-quarters of a century making clothing and fabrics from natural fibers, including grasses and wood pulp. She died aged 96 in 2017, but the museum continues with a display room of her creations, including a dress made for a Belgian queen, a tablecloth for a pope and costumes for the Boi-Bumbá festival.

Activities & Tours

Agencies in Alter do Chão (p598) are generally best for trips down the Rio Tapajós or to the Floresta Nacional do Tapajós. Gil Serique (p598) is particularly recommended. All can arrange to pick you up in Santarém.

There is also a handful of local agencies.

Big Tree Adventure Tours ECOTOUR

(☎93 9195-3160; www.bigtreeadventuretours.com; Av Maracana 664; US$110-390 per person per day) Tours combine the natural, historical and commercial aspects of the Amazon. The agency's private 800 hectare rainforest plot has good hiking and swimming; on the way there, you'll drive past vast soy plantations – a macabre yet arresting sight. Multiday tours continue to Fordlândia.

Big Tree is a branch of Zero Impact Brazil, an American-owned company that gathers the leftover parts of trees cut down by developers and resells them for specialty use, from pool cues to high-end guitars. Ask about visiting ZIB's sawmill in Santarém, with its incredible array of Amazonian timber, including 'tiger wood' and 'purpleheart.'

Santarém Viagens e Turismo ADVENTURE

(☎93 3523-2037; www.santaremviagenseturismo.weebly.com; Travessa Silvino Pinto 860) All the usual tours including to Lago Maicá (p591) and Floresta Nacional do Tapajós (p596). Pierre Schwartz is a promising young guide who speaks English.

Festivals & Events

Dia de São Pedro RELIGIOUS

(⏰Jun 29) Boats decorated with flags and flowers sail in procession before the city in honor of São Pedro, the patron saint of fisherfolk.

Sleeping

Hotel Sandis Mirante HOTEL $

(☎93 99239-2488; www.hotelsandismirante.com.br; Coronel Joaquim Braga 180; s/d/tr R$130/145/180) This attractive place up on the hill just back from the waterfront has clean, modern rooms, some with river views, although why they built such small windows we'll never understand. It's an otherwise excellent choice.

Hotel Palace Santarém HOTEL $

(☎93 3523-2052; www.hotelpalacesantarem.com.br; Av Rui Barbosa 726; s/d from R$120/150) A recent change of owner here has brought more professionalism and style to this place – rooms are comfortable and among the best in town, but with budget prices. It's right in the heart of town too.

Hotel London Santarém HOTEL $$

(☎93 3523-2328; www.hotellondonsantarem.com.br; Senador Lameira Bittencourt 41; s/d R$160/188; ❄📶) The rooms here are a little small and don't take advantage of the location – it's just across the road from the waterfront in the heart of town – but they're comfortable, especially if you've been out in the forest for a while. The highlight is the rooftop bar-restaurant with fine river views. Decent breakfast too.

Tapajós Center Hotel HOTEL $$

(☎93 3522-5353; Av Tapajós 1827; s/d/tr R$120/170/200, superior s/d/tr R$170/22/250; P❄📶) Spacious rooms have warm accents, firm beds, modern TVs and air-conditioning, spotless bathrooms and (best of all) large verandas with bracing views of the river. The hotel's main drawback is that it's a mile (1.5km) from the center of town; the waterfront can be a pleasant (albeit hot) walk and taxis are plentiful when you feel like a ride.

Eating

★Quiosque da Praça STREET FOOD $

(Praça Barão de Santarém; from R$8; ⏲7am-1pm & 4-11pm) This small kiosk just west of the center serves the best *tacacá* (local soup with shrimp) we've tasted in Brazil. A late-afternoon bowl of this local favorite will set you up nicely for the night ahead.

★Massabor PIZZA $

(☎93 3522-0509; Av Tapajós; pizza R$33-43, mains R$15-50; ⏲5-11pm) Occupying a raised pier over the water, this open-air restaurant opposite Praça do Pescador has nice breezes and gorgeous river views; watch for dolphins. The menu is mostly pizza, but there is a page dedicated to local dishes, including *tacacá*. The food is fine if unremarkable – it's all about atmosphere as the sun goes down.

Açaí Santarém BRAZILIAN $

(☎93 3522-1464; www.facebook.com/acaistm; Travessa Pedro Texeira 41; 250/500ml bowl from R$8/16; ⏲7am-7pm) Brazil's growing obsession with *açaí*, a berry indigenous to the Amazon and rich in antioxidants, is old news here – they serve up great bowls of the stuff. We like it plain, as is the tradition, but you can also add everything from fish powder and shrimp to bananas and condensed milk.

Opening hours sometimes vary, as supplies sometimes run low.

> **LOCAL KNOWLEDGE**
>
> **STREET FOOD: TACACÁ**
>
> Mention *tacacá* to any person from the Brazilian Amazon, and you may see them drool. Originally a dish from indigenous communities, it's a glutinous broth made from wild manioc, small yellow peppers, dried shrimp and *jambu* (a local flowering herb). It's a particular favorite in Santarém; drink it steaming hot from a bowl between the hours of 4pm and 7pm as a precursor to the main meal. Our favorite *tacacá* is served at Quiosque da Praça – eat it here and you're halfway to being a local – and they also serve it at Massabor.

★Restaurante Piracema BRAZILIAN $$

(☎93 3522-7461; www.restaurantepiracema.com.br; Av Mendonça Furtado 73; R$25-80; ⏲11am-11:30pm Tue-Sat, to 3pm Sun) Considered by many to be the best restaurant in town, Piracema uses regional ingredients and flavors to create dishes you'll find nowhere else. The specialty is the *peixe á Piracema,* a spherical construction of layered smoked *pirarucú* (a freshwater fish), banana and cheese. It's strange but delicious, and large enough for two.

La Tasca BRAZILIAN $$

(☎93 98405-8532; Rua do Imperador; snacks from R$8.50, mains R$23-80; ⏲7pm-midnight) La Tasca is a lively place in the evening, and we love the mix of tapas-style plates. Signature dishes include *bacalhau espiritual* (a creamy, Portuguese-style cod dish) or the bite-sized *camarão do imperador* (a battered prawn served with cheddar or Gorgonzola).

Bar Mascote BUFFET, SEAFOOD $$

(☎93 99216-8546; www.facebook.com/restaurantemascote; Praça do Pescador; buffet per kilo R$46, plate of the day R$32, mains R$30-70; ⏲6-11pm Tue-Fri, from 11am Sat, 5-11pm Sun) The lunch buffet is tasty, the *prato feito* (plate of the

WORTH A TRIP

FORDLÂNDIA

History buffs will enjoy a trip to Fordlândia, where you can explore the remains of Henry Ford's ill-fated Amazonian enterprise. You can wander cavernous factories, climb the town's iconic 36-meter-high water tower and more. That said, it's a long way to go (and come back) for just a half-day of sights – travelers short on time or lacking a burning interest in early-20th-century industrial history may consider giving it a pass.

Rubber was (and is) absolutely essential to the manufacture of automobiles. In the early 1900s, Britain had a near monopoly on the world's rubber supply, having smuggled rubber tree seeds out of the Amazon and grown them, with great success, in plantations in Asia. Fordlândia, founded in 1928, was Henry Ford's attempt to establish his own source of rubber. But in typical Ford fashion, the project was as much sociological as it was economic or horticultural. Ford forbade workers from drinking, smoking or visiting prostitutes (rules they circumvented by paddling out to barges moored offshore). He insisted American-style homes and dormitories be built, but their thick walls and asbestos roofs turned them into ovens. Worst of all, virtually no one sent from company headquarters in Dearborn, Michigan, had experience with the Amazon or its trees. Tens of thousands of rubber trees were planted only to die from blight because they'd been planted too close together. (In the wild, rubber trees always grow widely spaced apart.) Operations were moved briefly to Belterra (p592) (which can be visited as a day trip from Santarém) but in 1945, with synthetic rubber rapidly supplanting the natural product, the company sold Fordlândia back to Brazil for a loss, in today's dollars, of over $200 million. Ford himself never visited.

Fordlândia today is a rather downbeat town, and surprisingly little has been done to preserve or promote the town's unique history. Two of the main sights are visible right from the pier: the *caixa de água* (water tower) which you can climb via a narrow ladder, and two huge factories, known locally as *casonas* (big houses) filled with abandoned machinery, vehicles and random parts, many stamped *Michigan*. Further afield are Fordlândia's cemetery, the collapsed remains of the town's once-grand hospital, and Vila Americana, a row of American-style houses, some of which can be visited.

The boat schedules are such that you'll need to stay at least a night. **Pousada Americana** (☎93 3505-3073; www.pousada-americana.blogspot.com; Av Boa Vista 31; s/d R$120/140; ❄📶) has spacious rooms, sparkling bathrooms, and air-con in most units. A newer annex has a large patio with hammocks, and the property's fruit trees are home to numerous birds, including several talkative parrots. From the ferry, bear left 500m. The owners also happen to be Fordlândia's go-to tour guides. A four-hour tour, including vehicle, is R$60 to R$100 per group.

From Santarém, there are daily departures for Fordlândia by speedboat (R$70, five hours, 1pm) and slow boat (R$55; 12 to 15 hours, 4pm Monday to Saturday, 2pm Sunday; take the Itaituba boat). Returning, the speedboat passes by at 2pm to 3pm, and the slow boat around 8pm to 10pm (earlier on Sundays); check schedules before setting out from Santarém. You'll enjoy good views of the verdant forest, especially going upriver, when the boat hugs the shore.

day) is especially good value and the air-conditioned dining room is a welcome respite on a hot day. The outdoor patio is good for drinks and a light appetizer.

Shopping

Loja Regional Muiraquita GIFTS & SOUVENIRS
(☎93 98801-6748; Senador Lameira Bittencourt 131; ⏲9am-7pm Mon-Fri, to 6pm Sat) Santarém has a large collection of souvenirs. There's a lot of tat and not much that's original here, but you might uncover the occasional nice item.

Information

EMERGENCY

Ambulance (☎192)

Police (☎190; Praça Barão de Santarém)

INTERNET ACCESS

Cyber Cafe (Av Tapajós; per hr R$5; ⏲8am-7pm Mon-Fri, to 4pm Sat)

LAUNDRY

Lavandería Estoril (☎93 3523-1329; Travessa Turiano Meira 167; wash & dry per kg R$25, plus iron per kg $30; ⏰8am-6pm Mon-Sat) Same-day service if you drop off clothes in the morning.

MEDICAL SERVICES

Hospital Municipal (cnr Avs Presidente Vargas & Barão do Rio Branco; ⏰24hr) Large public hospital.

MONEY

Bradesco (Av Rui Barbosa; ⏰9am-3pm Mon-Fri) Foreign exchange.

Santander (Av Rui Barbosa) Most reliable ATMs in town.

POST

Main Post Office (Siqueira Campos; ⏰9am-5pm Mon-Fri)

TOURIST INFORMATION

IBAMA (ICMBio) (☎93 3523-2964; www.icmbio.gov.br; Av Tapajós 2267, Santarém; ⏰8am-noon & 2-6pm Mon-Fri) Local office of IBAMA, including the division that oversees FLONA Tapajós. Located 2km west of the center.

TRAVEL AGENCIES

Santarém Tur (☎93 3522-4847; www.santaremtur.com.br; Adriano Pimentel 44; ⏰8am-6pm Mon-Fri, to noon Sat) Arranges plane tickets, tour packages (including city tours), day trips to Alter do Chão by boat or car, and overnight riverboat tours to FLONA.

Getting There & Away

AIR

Aeroporto de Santarém – Maestro Wilson Fonseca is 14km west of town. It handles flights to/from Manaus and Belém. To go just about anywhere else you'll need to change in one of these cities.

Azul (☎93 3523-3287; www.voeazul.com.br)

GOL (☎93 3522-3386, 0800-704-0465; www.voegol.com.br)

MAP (☎93 3529-0308, in Manaus 92 2125-5000; www.voemap.com.br)

LATAM (☎93 3523-9744; www.latam.com) Serves Brasília.

BOAT

There are two official ports for passenger boats, though an explosion of river traffic means virtually the entire waterfront can be crowded with vessels. Look for large signs or banners indicating each boat's destination and departure times. Be aware that times listed here are subject to change.

For Fordlândia and Monte Alegre, consider taking *a lancha rápida* (speedboat) offering comfortable airplane-style seating and half the travel time for just a few dollars more. Various independently owned boats use three nearly side-by-side piers just east of **Praça Tiradentes**; signs indicate which boat leaves on a given day. Altogether, there are daily departures for Fordlândia (R$65, five hours, 1pm) and Monte Alegre (R$60, three hours, 4pm; plus 9am Tuesday and Saturday).

Docas do Pará

The main port, **Docas do Pará**, is located 2.5km west of the center. There you can catch a slow boat to Belém (hammock R$200, double cabin R$600 to R$800, 48 hours) at 10am Friday and every second Sunday, and 11am Monday, which stops at Monte Alegre (hammock R$50, five to seven hours) along the way; to Manaus (hammock R$180, double cabin R$600, 40 to 48 hours) at noon Monday to Wednesday, Friday and Saturday, and at 11am on Thursday, all with a stop at Parantins (hammock R$80, 20 hours); or to Fordlândia (R$50; 12 to 15 hours) at 4pm Monday to Saturday and 2pm Sunday – take the Itaituba boat. Meals are not included, but can be purchased on board. Buy your ticket in advance, especially in high season, to be sure you get a spot. Note you can only board during designated time slots: 6am to 7am, 10am to 10:30am, noon to 12:15pm, and 1pm to 2pm.

Praça Tiradentes

The port Praça Tiradentes is located 1km west of the center on Av Tapajós and is used for boats to less-common destinations, including Macapá (hammock R$150 including meals, 36 hours, 6pm daily), Monte Alegre (hammock R$45, five to seven hours; take the 6pm Macapá boat) and Alenquer (hammock R$35, seven hours, 8pm Sun-Fri, noon Sat).

BUS

The **bus station** (☎93 3523-4940; Hwy BR-163) is 2.5km west of town. Catch a bus here to Belterra ($3.50; one hour); they come and go every 30 to 60 minutes until 9pm.

There are almost no long-distance bus services to/from Santarém – the roads are appalling.

Buses to Alter do Chão (R$3.50, 60 minutes) stop on **Av Rui Barbosa** near Av Barão do Rio Branco roughly every hour between 5am and 10pm (until 6:30pm on Sundays).

Buses to Maguarí and Jamaraquá (R$12, two to three hours, 11am Monday to Saturday, 6:30am Sunday) depart from **Av São Sebastião** (Av São Sebastião) in Santarém. Return buses depart Jamaraquá at 4:30am and 6am Monday to Saturday, 4:30pm Sunday). The Sunday bus is air-conditioned.

Getting Around

Apart from walking, moto-taxis are the best way to get around town. Most trips cost R$5.

Around Santarém

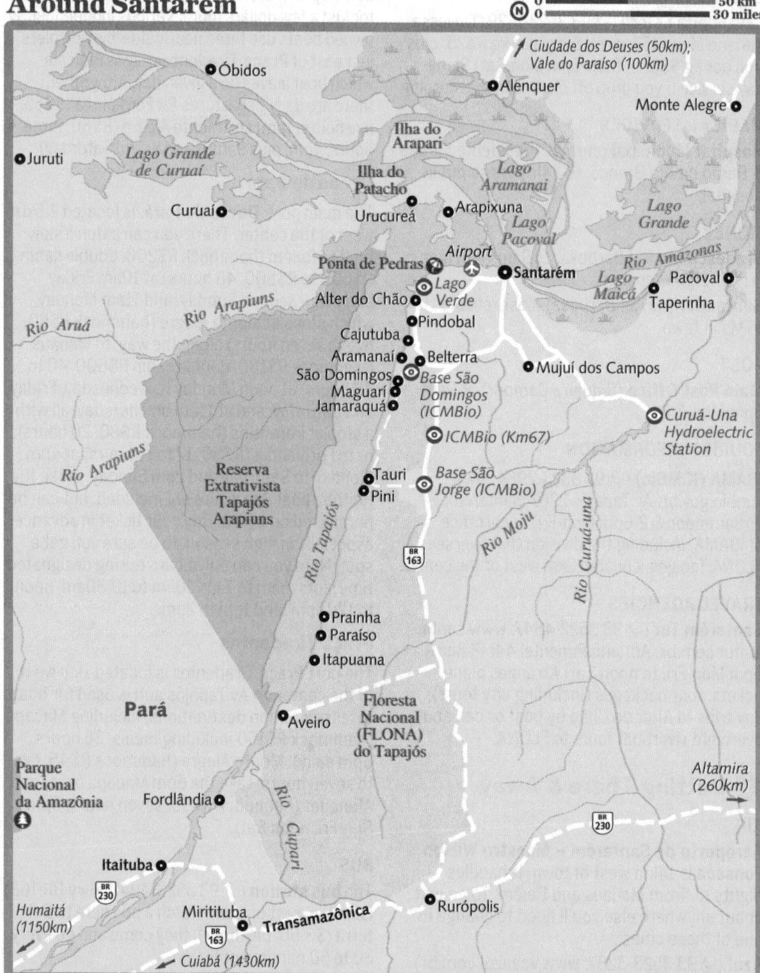

Floresta Nacional do Tapajós

One of the last and most accessible stretches of primary rainforest in the region, this protected **area** (FLONA do Tapajós) is the Amazon rainforest you always imagined. Behemoth samaúma and other trees, some with trunks too big for even 20 people to stretch their arms around, are a highlight of this 5440-sq-km reserve on the east side of the Rio Tapajós. Visit with a guide and it's likely to be one of your most memorable experiences. Wildlife includes numerous species of birds (king vultures are a highlight), while the forest is also home to elusive cats (including jaguar and ocelot, although they're rarely seen), as well as howler monkeys, squirrel monkeys and capuchins.

Sights

The riverside villages of **Maguarí** and **Jamaraquá** have been hosting travelers the longest and have the most established accommodations, tours and other services. A third village, **São Domingo**, is at the entrance to the reserve and has modest tourist options as well.

The only problem with making these villages a focal point of your visit is that the primary rainforest, and hence the really big trees, are a two-and-a-half-hour hike away.

Tours

All three villages have well-maintained forest trails. There are some lovely *igarapés* (inlets), too, with good canoeing and possibly animal-spotting when the water is high. Tour prices include: a four- to five-hour hike and a one- to two-hour canoe trip costs R$100 to R$150 per group (up to six people). Overnight trips (per person R$150 to R$200) and private boat service to and from Alter do Chão (per person R$250) can be arranged.

You can get also get to FLONA by boat, leaving from Alter do Chão. Freelance boatmen do day trips for around R$100 per person, but it's a tiring three hours each way in a small motorized canoe, and does not include guide service. The tour agencies charge R$200 to R$250 per person, including a local guide and using faster and more comfortable motorboats. The agencies also do overnight trips to FLONA, sleeping on board a river boat. Try Mãe Natureza (p599) and Areia Branca Ecotour (p599) in Alter do Chão.

To experience the primary rainforest, as opposed to the river villages, we recommend the tours by Gil Serique (p598), whose family once lived in the forest. Tours (from US$150 per person per day) can be day tours or overnight versions where you sleep in a camp deep in the forest. Ask Gil to also take you up into the canopy via the 45m-high tower built by NASA.

Sleeping & Eating

Lodging is available in simple pousadas run by local families, who also arrange tours. The bus driver can drop you right in front of each of these places. Gil Serique (p598) can arrange an overnight stay deep in the primary rainforest.

Tours here should include meals (always ask what is included before handing over any money), while the village pousadas can also cook up simple meals for guests.

Pousada Jamaraquá POUSADA $
(☎93 99124-5750, 93 99179-9569; Transtapajós s/n; d incl meals R$125) Accommodations are in a large riverside structure, with a breezy deck for hammocks and a couple of very basic rooms. There's a pleasant sandy beach when the water's low, and you can swim from the deck when it's high. On the downside, the bathrooms are located at the back at the main house, about 100m away. The bus stops in front.

Pousada Floresta do Tapajós POUSADA $
(☎93 99113-8458; www.pousadaflorestadotapajos.wordpress.com; Transtapajós S/N; per person R$50) Better known as 'Pousada de Bata' for its austere but highly knowledgeable owner and main tour guide, this guesthouse has an airy hammock area, decent bathrooms and a welcoming family atmosphere. It's located in a quiet leafy plot about 500m past the main village center; if arriving by bus, ask the driver to drop you here.

Pousada São Domingo POUSADA $
(☎93 99212-0072; Transtapajós s/n; R$50 per person incl breakfast) Less a guesthouse than just a guy who lets people crash at his place, there's an open-air hammock area and outdoor showers set in a large shady plot. Guests can use the owner's bathroom. The owner used to work for tour operators in Alter do Chão, and guides hiking and boat tours right from his property.

Pousada Maguary POUSADA $
(☎93 99115-9540; Transtapajós s/n; incl breakfast R$50, additional R$20 for lunch or dinner) You feel like part of the family here, and no wonder: the warm, elderly owners were among the first in FLONA to open their home to community tourism. Unfortunately, the dim, low-ceiling hammock area and run-down toilets make this a less appealing option for many visitors.

Information

ICMBio (☎93 3522-0564; www.icmbio.gov.br/flonatapajos; Av Tapajós 2267, Santarém) The federal environmental agency oversees the reserve and has a handful of outposts at various points around the park, including in São Domingo and this one at the entrance (Km 67), as well as an office in Santarém. Boats and buses entering the reserve stop to allow tourists to register, but there is no entrance fee.

Getting There & Away

BOAT

It's best to visit on a guided tour run by a reputable travel agency in Alter do Chão, but it is possible to arrange a private boat transfer from the docks in the town for around R$100 per person return.

BUS

Buses to Maguarí and Jamaraquá (R$12, two to three hours, 11am Monday to Saturday, 6:30am Sunday) depart from downtown Santarém. Return buses depart Jamaraquá at 4:30am and 6am Monday to Saturday, 4:30pm Sunday. The Sunday bus is air-conditioned.

CAR & MOTORCYCLE

The most accessible access point to the primary rainforest is at Km 67 along Rte 163 south of Santarém, although we strongly advise against visiting this section on your own. Take a guided tour with Gil Serique.

Alter do Chão

☎0XX93 / POP 7500

Alter do Chão, 33km west of Santarém, is an appealing, languid riverside town that's popular with visitors from Santarém on weekends and during holiday periods. It's best known for its Ilha do Amor (Island of Love), a picturesque island ringed by a white-sand beach directly in front of town.

But Alter do Chão is much more than a beach town. The lagoon it fronts (Lago Verde) can be explored by canoe or stand-up paddle board. It's also the departure point for boat tours to nearby forest reserves and isolated communities, and has one of the best indigenous art stores in the Amazon region.

Sights

In addition to Ilha do Amor and Praia do Cajueiro, there are several beaches further afield best reached in a car or on a beach-hopping tour, including **Pindobal** (8km), **Cajutuba** (16km), **Aramanai** (26km) and **Ponta de Pedras** (28km). These beaches are quite built up with waterfront restaurants; if you're looking for an isolated beach experience, talk to a tour agency.

Ilha do Amor BEACH

A small slice of paradise just offshore from Alter do Chão, the 'Island of Love' is especially striking when the water is low (August to December) and beach restaurants and cool, calm water make it a great place to chill out. In high water, the island is much smaller but still worth a visit. When the water is low, you can wade from the waterfront to Ilha do Amor. Otherwise, rowboats will take you across for R$5 per person.

Praia do Cajueiro BEACH

A few blocks west of the town center along the waterfront promenade is this pleasant beach, wrapping around to the Tapajós River.

Lago Verde LAKE

This huge three-fingered lake is surrounded by forest and has places to swim, snorkel with fish and spot wildlife (including a resident family of monkeys). Tour agencies do good boat tours (per person R$50 to R$75, two to three hours, two to six people) or you can hire one of the yellow-shirted freelance boatmen on the waterfront; the latter are cheaper, but may not have the same service or equipment that agencies do.

Ponta do Cururú NATURAL FEATURE

Most afternoons, large numbers of pink and grey dolphins congregate just offshore from this sandy point near the mouth of the Rio Tapajós for an evening snack. It's a great place to go for sunsets and dolphin-spotting, and many guides combine tours of Lago Verde or Canal do Jarí with a stop here.

Activities

Adventure sports are a natural fit for many visitors here. Rewarding options include stand-up paddling (SUP), windsurfing, kayaking, mountain biking and tree climbing (*arbolismo* in Portuguese). Ask at Mãe Natureza, Areia Branca Ecotour or Gil Serique for prices and availability.

Tours

Besides short trips around Alter do Chão (Lago Verde, Ponta do Cururú, beach-hopping) there are some great options for longer multiday tours. These include canoeing the animal-rich **Canal do Jarí**, hiking and visiting villages in Floresta Nacional (FLONA) do Tapajós (p596) and the Reserva Extrativista (RESEX) Tapajós-Arapiuns (p623), river trips up the **Rio Arapiuns**, and adventure routes into the **Parque Nacional da Amazônia**. Discuss details with tour agencies in town; prices range from R$180 to $300 per person per day, all-inclusive.

★**Gil Serique** ECOTOUR

(☎93 99130-5298; www.gilserique.com; Av Copacabana 45, at PA-457; per person per day US$150) Gil is a true character, a lithe teller of tales and one of the area's top naturalists. Born and raised nearby, Gil's tours are part history, part ecology and part family lore, related with infectious enthusiasm and near-perfect English. Visits to Lago Maicá (p591), a gorgeous floodplain teeming with birds and other wildlife, are especially memorable. Pricier than others, but worth it.

From the bus drop-off, walk down to the plaza and bear right along the waterfront. It's the house at the end, painted with travel-related logos. Gil can often offer discount lodging, airport pickup and other help; enquire in advance.

Areia Branca Ecotour ECOTOUR
(93 3527-1386, 93 99121-5646; www.areiabrancaecotour.com.br; Lago Verde; 8am-noon & 2-7pm Mon-Fri, to 1pm Sat & Sun) Located on the waterfront a short distance from the plaza, this small agency is run by multilingual siblings. Tours are available to all the standard destinations, but the specialty here is multiday packages to less-visited communities like Santi in RESEX Tapajós-Arapiuns and Marituba and Bregança in FLONA Tapajós.

Mãe Natureza ECOTOUR
(93 3527-1264, 93 99131-9870; www.maenaturezaecoturismo.com.br; Praça 7 de Setembro; 8:30am-1pm & 4-11pm) Agency run by genial Argentinean expats. Be sure to ask about week-long adventure tours to remote indigenous areas and the Brinco das Moças waterfall, deep in RESEX Tapajós-Arapiuns, although confirm first they have guides that speak your language. Day trips including tree-climbing, kite-surfing and stand-up paddling can also be arranged.

Festivals & Events

Festa do Cairé RELIGIOUS
(2nd week Sep) The Festa do Çairé is the major folkloric event in western Pará. The Çairé is a standard held aloft to lead a flower-bedecked procession; its origins may go back to symbols used by early missionaries to help convert indigenous groups.

Sleeping

★ **Pousada Vila Alter** POUSADA $
(93 99173-9772; Everaldo Martins 603; s/d/tr R$80/120/140;) The pick of the many new pousadas opening around town, the welcoming Vila Alter has a colorful little garden and tidy rooms. The whole feel here is one of intimacy and warmth, and the price is terrific value. It's far enough up the hill to avoid the evening noise, but it's just five minutes away on foot.

Pousada do Tapajós Hostel HOSTEL $
(93 99210-2166; www.pousadatapajos.com.br; Lauro Sodré 100; dm R$50, d/tr/q R$180/190/200;) Dorms here are clean and comfortable, though a bit cramped, with sturdy bunks and large lockers. Private rooms are sparkling, modern and well removed from the dorm area. There's an ample breakfast, open kitchen and large backyard with hammocks. It's five blocks west of the center.

Hotel Belo Alter HOTEL $$
(93 3527-1230; www.beloalter.com.br; Pedro Teixeira 500; s/d/tr R$220/330/450;) This aging hotel has a leafy setting and rooms with a hint (just a hint, mind you) of style, featuring wood rather than tiled floors. It's secluded and quiet, but a long walk into town. You wouldn't want to do it after dark.

Hotel Borari HOTEL $$
(93 3527-1152; Dom Marcedo Costa; s/d/tr/ste R$180/220/280/400;) One of the few places with running hot water, the Borari is arguably the best hotel in town, although it lacks the warmth of some of the pousadas. Rooms are smallish but tidy, and the suite has a balcony.

Pousada Vila Da Praia HOTEL $$
(93 9197-7214, 93 3529-1909; www.viladapraiapousada.blogspot.com; PA-457; s/d R$160/190;) Amiable service, simple but comfortable rooms, and a great location make this a recommendable option. Rooms vary considerably: some have colorful cement walls, others wood paneling; some are oddly small, others sleep up to six. All come with TVs, air-conditioning, floral prints and a substantial breakfast, served in an open-air dining area. Just a block from the waterfront.

Eating

★ **Siria** VEGETARIAN $
(93 99217-2034; Travessa Agostinho Lobato s/n; mains R$20-30; noon-4pm;) The lovely chef-owner, Betania, prepares just one dish per day, announced on a sandwich board out front. From chickpea omelets to vegetable tarts, count on it being outstanding, served with brown rice, fresh salad and creative drinks, like hibiscus and *maracujá* (passion fruit) iced tea, plus dessert. Dishes are vegan or vegetarian, depending on the sauce. Attractive outdoor dining area.

Barraca de Tapioca BRAZILIAN $
(Lauro Sodré; mains R$6-12; 2-8pm) Perched on a rise overlooking the water, this cara-

van-and-plastic-chair place serves tapioca pancakes with a mix of sweet and salty fillings. It's that simple, and that good.

★ Espaço Gastronômico BRAZILIAN $$
(☎93 98401 6144; www.espacoalter.com.br; Lauro Sodré 74; mains R$25-60; ⏰7-11pm; 📶) What a fabulous place! It's made almost entirely from recycled wood and other materials, with a commitment to using local ingredients and indigenous sauces, which might include Brazil nuts, honey and manioc, or ceviche with mango. Upstairs is the place to be, with diaphanous curtains blowing in the sea breeze. Joana is a marvelous host.

Arco-Iris da Amazônia BRAZILIAN $$
(☎93 3527-1182; arcoirisdaamazonia@bol.com.br; Praça 7 de Setembro; mains R$25-55; ⏰6-11pm Wed-Mon) Art and jewelry store by day, fine restaurant by night. One of three side-by-side places serving dinner and drinks right on the plaza, the Arco-Iris' dishes are expertly prepared with fresh sophisticated flavors, from lamb to crepes to hamburgers. Portions are on the small side, but there's definitely a quality over quantity argument to be made here. Prompt service.

Tribal BRAZILIAN $$
(Travessa Antônio Lobato; dishes R$30-60; ⏰11am-4pm & 7-11pm) *Churrasco* plates come with a spear of steak, sausage, chicken and tongue, while well-prepared fish dishes serve two easily, with potato salad to spare. This spacious two-floor open-air dining area is located a block and a half up from the plaza.

Entertainment

★ Espaço Gastronômico LIVE MUSIC
(☎93 98401 6144; www.espacoalter.com.br; Laura Sodré 74; cover from R$20; ⏰10pm-4am Sat Jul-Feb; 📶) There's always something worth seeing at this cool music-restaurant space at the east end of the waterfront promenade. There's live *carimbó* Saturday nights in season, and guest bands play rock, *forró*, samba, reggae and more; check Facebook or the chalkboard out front for the latest. Great restaurant too.

Shopping

★ Araribá Cultura Indígena ARTS & CRAFTS
(☎93 3527-1324; www.araribah.com.br; Travessa Antônio Lobato; ⏰9am-9pm Mon-Sat, to 7:30pm Sun) Arguably the best indigenous art store in the region, representing communities throughout the Amazon Basin. Items range from inexpensive necklaces to museum-quality masks and ceremonial costumes. Shipping available; credit cards accepted.

Information

DANGERS & ANNOYANCES

Stingrays are a concern around Ilha do Amor, Lago Verde and the Tapajós River, especially in the afternoon and evening. Fortunately they're very skittish, so it's generally safe to swim and wade where other people are doing the same. It's also a good idea to shuffle your feet whenever entering and exiting the water (here or anywhere in the Amazon); this kicks up a cloud of sand in front of you and scares rays away.

MEDICAL SERVICES

Farmacia Primavera (☎93 3527-1105; PA-457; ⏰9am-8pm) A pharmacy is a few blocks up from the waterfront.

MONEY

Accessing money and the internet can be a real headache in Alter do Chão. There was only one ATM in Alter do Chão at the time of writing, and it was pretty unreliable – better to bring cash from Santarém. Most hotels accept credit cards, but not all.

Banco do Brasil (inside Mini-Center Mingote, Praça 7 de Setembro; ⏰6:30am-8:30pm Mon-Sat, to 7:30pm Sun) The ATM here sometimes works, but don't count on it.

POST OFFICE

Post office (cnr PA-457 & Rua Professor Juvencio Navarro; ⏰9am-noon & 2-5pm Mon-Fri) A few blocks up from the waterfront.

Getting There & Away

Buses from Alter do Chão to Santarém (R$3.50, one hour) depart hourly from the **bus station** (Everaldo Martins) 5:30am to 11pm, except on Sunday, when services end around 6pm. Catch the bus a block up from Praça 7 de Setembro, at the corner of **Rua Dom Macedo Costa and Travessa Antônio A Lobato** (cnr Rua Dom Macedo Costa & Travessa Antônio A Lobato). If arriving in Santarém on the bus, there's a handy stop along **Rua Dom Macedo Costa** (Rua Dom Macedo Costa), which means a shorter walk down into town.

There is no bus to the Santarém airport from Alter do Chão, unfortunately. It's possible to take the bus as far as the airport turnoff, and wait for the airport bus from Santarém to pass, usually within 30 to 60 minutes. Otherwise, a taxi to the airport (or to Santarém or the riverboat ports) costs a painful R$100.

WORTH A TRIP

MONTE ALEGRE

The hills close to the dusty provincial town of Monte Alegre shelter one of the Amazon's most important archaeological sites – the rock paintings here, which may date back more than 13,000 years, have changed the way that historians understand the human history of the region. You'll need at least a two-day round-trip from Santarém, which is 120km upstream, to make the trip here worthwhile. The town itself is a fairly unappealing place, and it sees very few tourists.

Sights

The hot sandstone hills behind Monte Alegre are dotted with caves and bizarre rock outcroppings. They, in turn, are adorned with dozens of rock paintings from ancient Amazonians. The paintings are red, yellow and brown, and depict human and animal figures, handprints and geometric designs. Studies conducted in the 1990s by pioneering archaeologist Anna Roosevelt, a great-granddaughter of Theodore Roosevelt, suggest the caves at Monte Alegre were occupied from anywhere between 10,900 to 13,150 years ago – thousands of years earlier than previously thought. (Artifacts in Chile and central Brazil have returned similar dates.) This caused quite a ruckus and forced archaeologists to rethink when and how ancient people first arrived in South America. Most still believe the first migrants arrived from Asia across the Bering Strait to Alaska, but rather than spreading gradually southward from there, it appears at least some Paleoindian groups made their way to Central and South America fairly quickly, probably using boats and hugging the coastline, reaching as far south as Patagonia. From those southbound groups, splinter parties must have cut eastward and inland (or even turned the corner at Tierra del Fuego), eventually populating the Amazon and the rest of the interior.

Monte Alegre's cave paintings are quite accessible from Santarém. The best-known site is Serra do Paituna, with a distinctive ridge-top rock formation called Pedra do Pilão and the stunning Pedra Pintada cavern, where Roosevelt's primary excavations took place. Two other sites, Serra do Ererê and Serra de Itauajuri, are harder to reach (especially in rainy season) but have excellent paintings as well. All three require a vehicle and guide (the area has been designated as a state park), and include moderately strenuous hiking. Bring sturdy shoes and plenty of water.

Tours

Nelsí Sadeck (☎93 98421-2928; nelsi.sadeck@gmail.com) is an amiable former teacher who assisted Roosevelt's excavations and is Monte Alegre's go-to guide. He speaks Portuguese only, so English-speaking visitors to Monte Alegre will want to contact **Ilivaldo Luz** (ilivaldoluz@gmail.com). Reach out to the guides a few days in advance of your visit. Tours are R$150 to R$200 per day (up to four people); the use of a truck runs an additional R$300 per day.

Sleeping & Eating

Hotel Shekinah (☎93 3533-1489; www.hotelshekinah.com; 7 de Setembro 74; s/d R$80/120; ❄☎✉) Rooms here are bright, clean and reasonably spacious, with colorfully painted walls. There's even a swimming pool, though it's in need of some shade and a good scrubbing. The hotel is just two blocks from the central plaza, with various restaurant options nearby.

Getting There & Away

The easiest way to visit Monte Alegre is to organize a tour with one of the tour operators in Santarém or Alter do Chão; Gil Serique (p598) is an excellent choice.

Your best bet for traveling by boat to Monte Alegre is to ask around the port in Santarém a few days before you wish to travel. From Monday to Friday, there's a speedboat that departs Santarém at 4pm to Santana do Tapará (R$27, 1¼ hours); a public bus to Monte Alegre (R$10) *usually* meets the arriving boat. There's also an irregular slow boat service from Santarém, but the schedule is such you'll need to stay two or more nights to have sufficient time to see anything.

TOCANTINS

The state of Tocantins was created in 1989 from what was previously the northern half of Goiás. It's in a transition zone between the Amazon rainforest to the north and the cerrado (savanna) in the southeast. This makes for plenty of outdoor opportunities, and the state is making a concerted effort to portray itself as Brazil's next ecotourism hot spot. It certainly has the potential, from easy-to-reach hiking and waterfalls around Taquarussú to vast protected areas like **Parque Estadual do Jalapão** (www.jalapao.to.gov.br) and Ilha do Bananal, a Pantanal-like wetland.

Palmas

0XX63 / POP 295,000

Thirty years ago, the broad valley bisected by the Rio Tocantins held just a scattering of rural *fazendas* (ranches). Starting in 1989, a new state capital was built from scratch, and construction, the state government and economic incentives brought thousands of Brazilians to this unlikely landscape, 1000km north of Brasília and 1600km south of Belém. The city itself is sure to strike most first-timers as sterile and shadeless, but it has a way of growing on you, with a number of good outdoorsy options nearby.

We wouldn't cross the country to visit, and until neighboring Taquarussú really takes off as an ecotourism destination, there aren't that many reasons to come here, although it does have a certain appeal as a study in custom-made, modern urban architecture.

Sights

Most of the sights of interest are around Praça Girossóis, one of the largest municipal squares in the world.

Cathedral CATHEDRAL
(Praça Girossóis) Palmas' main cathedral has a modern look, with a low sloping exterior and a long interior nave. It lacks the gravitas of Brazil's older houses of worship, but is worth a quick look.

Memorial Coluna Prestes MEMORIAL
(Praça Girossóis; 8am-6pm Tue-Sun) FREE Housed in a curious white tubular structure near Palacio Araguaia, the Memorial Coluna Prestes tells the life story of Captain Luis Carlos Prestes, who led 1500 rebel soldiers against the military dictatorship in 1924. The 25,000km march lasted three years and is credited with helping bring democracy to Brazil, especially its long-isolated interior.

Palacio Araguaia PALACE
(63 3218-1000; Praça Girossóis; 8am-6pm) FREE Built on the only hill in town, the state capitol building looks over the plaza and Palmas itself. The lobby has huge colorful mosaics and, in one corner, an impressive scale model of Praça Girossóis. No shorts or tank tops; the 2nd floor closed on weekends.

Tours

Jalapão Extremo ECOTOUR
(63 99968-1166, 63 3322-7990; www.jalapaoextremo.com.br; Jalapao Eco Tour, 409 Norte, AL 29, Lote 13, Plano Diretor Norte) This youthful and adventurous agency runs tours of Parque Estadual do Jalapão, Taquarussu and around, from one to seven days (R$150 to R$3000 per person). Tours include visiting remote waterfalls and Jalapão's famous sand dunes. Travel is by 4WD vans; lodging includes camping and modest hotels. Guides are excellent; the clientele is mostly Brazilian. The extreme heat and strenuous excursions may prove challenging for some.

Sleeping

Hotel Serra Azul HOTEL $
(63 3215-1505; Rua NO-03; s/d R$125/150;) Clean rooms, affordable prices and convenient location make this Palmas' best budget option. Rooms are small with few frills, but face onto a sunny courtyard with a quaint dining room where breakfast is served. It's close to the bus stop for those who don't have a car, and has secure parking for those who do.

Pousada das Artes Hotel HOTEL $$
(68 3219-1500; 103 Sul, LO-01 Av 78; s/d from R$148/168;) This well-located upscale hotel lives up to its name, with artsy rooms and architecture. Both are the handiwork of Graça Arnús, who designed the building and painted the intriguing artwork in the guestrooms and common areas. Accommodations are comfortable and modern; the small pool a welcome bonus. The hotel hosts occasional art expositions.

Pousada dos Girassóis HOTEL $$
(68 3219-4500; www.pousadadosgirassois.com.br; Av NS-01; s/d from R$120/150;) Rooms at this longtime favorite have details like modern paintings, glass showers and a

Palmas

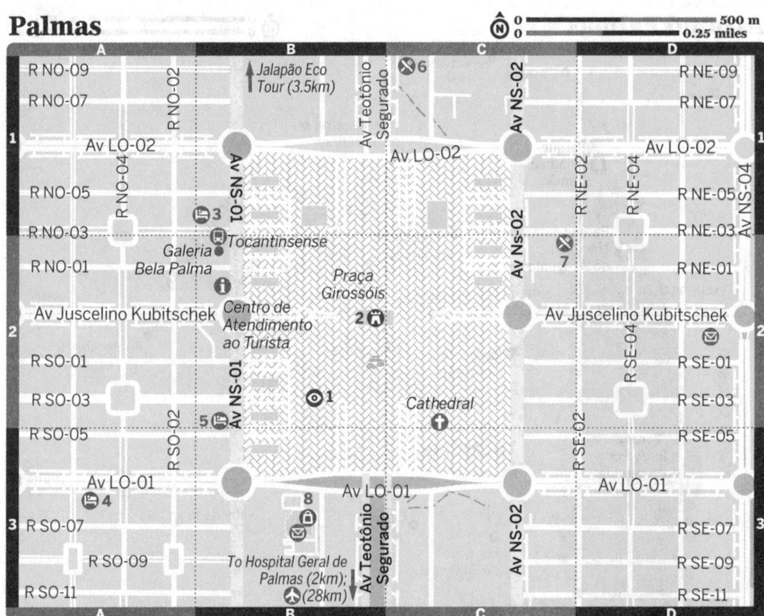

writing desk with a leather chair. Large windows and private verandas make some units feel more spacious. The pool area is oddly small and uninviting.

Eating

Restaurante Seara BUFFET $

(☎63 3225-8157; www.facebook.com/seararestaurante; Rua NE-03, btwn Av NS-02 & Rua NE-02; per kg R$40; ⏰11am-3pm Mon-Sat) Large bustling per-kilo place that's popular with workers at nearby government offices. Welcoming service and well-prepared food; best of all it's open until 3pm, when it seems every other self-service restaurant is dead and gone.

Churrascaría Portal do Sul BRAZILIAN $$

(☎63 3225-8744; 102 Norte, Conj 01, Lote 04; rodízio R$65; ⏰11:30am-2:30pm) Come hungry and treat yourself to the all-you-can-eat *rodízio* (a buffet of fresh meat) at this large place north of the plaza. The dining area won't win any awards for decor; then again, the only looking around you'll be doing is to see which aromatic skewer is coming next.

Information

EMERGENCY

Ambulance (☎192)

Police (☎190)

Palmas

Sights

1 Memorial Coluna Prestes.................. B2
2 Palacio Araguaia.............................. B2

Sleeping

3 Hotel Serra Azul................................ B1
4 Pousada das Artes Hotel.................. A3
5 Pousada dos Girassóis...................... B2

Eating

6 Churrascaría Portal do Sul................ C1
7 Restaurante Seara............................. C2

Shopping

8 Palmas Shopping.............................. B3

LAUNDRY

Quality Lavandería (☎63 3215-5060; cnr Avs NS-01 & LO-01; wash/dry per kg R$12, plus ironing per kg R$20; ⏰8am-6:30pm Mon-Fri, 9am-1pm Sat) Can do your laundry the same day if you drop it off early, and will deliver loads of 2kg or more to your hotel.

MEDICAL SERVICES

Droganita (☎63 3228-5804; Rua NO-03; ⏰24hr) One of several pharmacies in Galeria Bela Palma.

Hospital Geral de Palmas (☎63 3218-7802; Quadra 201 Sul, Av LO-5) Between Av Teotônio

Around Palmas

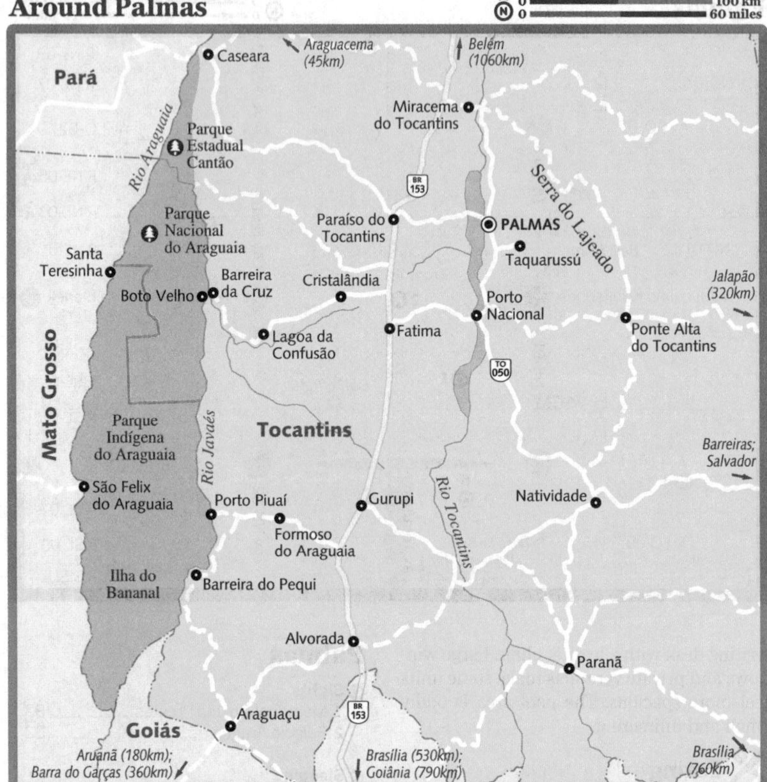

Segurado and Av NS-01, this is the city's main public hospital; 24-hour emergency room.

Hospital Oswaldo Cruz (63 3219-9000; Quadra 501 Sul, Av NS-01) Between Av LO-09 & Av LO-11, this recommended private hospital is in Palmas' medical district; 24hr emergency room.

MONEY

Both of the main banks have ATMs. Otherwise, there are ATMs located at **Palmas Shopping** (www2.palmasshopping.com.br; Praça Girossóis; 10am-9pm), a small, busy mall on the south side of Praça Girossóis.

Banco do Brasil (Quadra 103-Sul, cnr Avs Juscelino Kubitschek & NS-01; 9am-3pm Mon-Fri)

Bradesco (Quadra 104 Nte, cnr Avs Juscelino Kubitschek & NS-02; 9am-3pm Mon-Fri)

POST

Post Office (Palmas Shopping; 10am-9pm Mon-Fri, to 1pm Sat) Central post office.

Post Office (Av JK, btwn Rua SE-04 & Av NS-04; 9am-5pm Mon-Fri) Not quite as central as the main post office but less busy.

TOURIST INFORMATION

Centro de Atendimento ao Turista (CATUR; 63 2111-2771; www.palmas.to.gov.br; Quadra 103, cnr Avs NS-01 & Juscelino Kubitschek; 8am-4pm Mon-Fri) Useful tourist office for Palmas and the surrounding area.

Getting There & Away

AIR

The **Aeroporto de Palmas** (63 3219-3700; www4.infraero.gov.br) is 26km south of the city center.

Azul (63 3219-3872, 63 4003-1118; www.voeazul.com.br) To/from Brasília.

GOL (63 3219-3794, 0800-704-0465; www.voegol.com.br) Connects Palmas with Brasília and São Paulo.

LATAM (63 4002-5700, 63 3219-3784; www.latam.com) To/from Brasília and São Paulo.

Passaredo (63 3219-3840, 0800-770-3757; www.voepassaredo.com.br) Palmas to/from Goiânia and Araguaina.

BUS

Most long-distance buses do not enter Palmas, stopping instead in the highway-side town of Paraíso do Tocantins, 15km west of Palmas; note that departures listed here are from Paraíso. To get between Paraíso and Palmas, minibuses operated by **Tocantinsense** (☎63 3214-4194; www.tocantinense.com.br) loop around every 30 to 60 minutes (R$15, 45 minutes) from roughly 6:30am to 10pm, with reduced services on weekends. Catch inbound shuttles at the Paraíso bus station, outbound ones at the bus stop in front of **Galeria Bela Palma** (Rua NO-03; ⏰9am-6pm Mon-Fri) in Palmas.

Buses connect Palmas with Belém (R$200, 18 hours), Brasília (R$165, 13 hours) and São Paulo (R$295).

For Taquarussú, take any bus (including Bus 01 or 90 in front of Galeria Bela, R$5) to the Terminal Urbano, where you can transfer to Bus 45.

CAR

Car-rental agencies include **Avis** (☎63 3215-3336, airport 63 3219-3802; cnr Ruas SO-03 & SO-04), **Hertz** (☎63 3219-3859; Aeroporto de Palmas) and **Localiza** (☎0800-979-2020; Aeroporto de Palmas). Each has an office at the airport.

Taquarussú

☎0XX63 / POP 5500

This cozy town is nestled in the green Serra do Carmo hills, 30km southeast of Palmas, in an area studded with waterfalls and blanketed in forest. The state and local tourism boards have dedicated themselves to making Taquarussú an ecotourism destination, though things have a stalled somewhat in recent times. Guides are needed for most outings, and it's helpful to rent a car in Palmas.

 Activities

Exploring the region's waterfalls, swimming holes and forested areas is the main ways to get active, although a guide is mandatory as there's little you can do independently. The tourist office has a list of guides – count on R$150 per person per day, although rates are negotiable. Jalapão Extremo (p602) in Palmas is an excellent place to start.

Sleeping & Eating

Pousada Lokau POUSADA $

(☎63 3554-1238; Rua 8; r per person R$50; ❄📶) Part art gallery, part guesthouse, the Lokau has five clean, comfortable rooms opening onto a pleasant garden. They can be a bit musty at first, but high ceilings and stand-up fans help.

Restaurante Mandala BRAZILIAN $

(☎63 3554 1387; Av Belo Horizonte; R$11-23; ⏰noon-3pm daily, 6-9pm Wed-Sun) This restaurant is right around the corner from the plaza, on the road toward Fazenda Encantada. The fixed-plate lunch comes with pasta, rice, beans, salad, *farofa* (manioc flour sautéed with butter) and a choice of meat, all for R$16.

EXPLORING BEYOND TAQUARUSSÚ

There are 80 identified waterfalls, caves and pools in the area, of which 10 to 15 are open and accessible to the public during most of the year. The tourist office (p606) encourages visitors to use guides for all the sites, though several of the most popular ones are easy enough to visit on your own. Before setting out, discuss with your guide what type of falls you'd like to see, how much hiking and driving you want, and whether the car you have is adequate for all sites (some require 4WD, especially in the rainy season).

Cachoeira de Roncadeira is the tallest waterfall in the area (70m), and **Cachoeira Escorrega Macaco**, just 100m away, is almost the same height (60m). Both tumble picturesquely down sheer rust-brown cliffs, fringed by green vegetation, into small pools good for wading and swimming. The falls are located 1.5km down a well-marked trail; follow signs toward Hotel Fazenda Encantada and look for a large turnoff and parking area as the road ascends just out of town.

Cachoeira Taquaruçú is a muscular cascade with a choppy swimming hole that can get crowded on hot summer weekends. Look for the large roadside parking area along the highway from Palmas, about 4.5km before reaching Taquarussú; the falls are a 150m walk from there. A R$5 per person trail fee applies if you come without a guide.

Other popular spots that are best visited with a guide include the **Cachoeira do Rappel**, on the Fazenda Encantada grounds and used for rappelling, and **Vale do Vai-Quem-Quer**, a broad valley with a series of falls and good swimming spots.

Information

MONEY

There's a Banco do Brasil ATM next to the tourist office.

TOURIST INFORMATION

The **Centro de Atendimento ao Turista** (CATUR; 63 3554-1515; Rua 20-A; 8am-noon & 2-6pm Mon-Fri, to 4pm Sat & Sun), near the plaza, is the best place for information about the area and to hire a guide.

Getting There & Away

If driving from Palmas, take Hwy TO-010 past the bus station and follow the signs, passing first through the town of Taquaralto.

From Palmas, take any bus (including Bus 01 or 90 in front of Galeria Bela, R$5) to the Terminal Urbano, where you can transfer to Bus 45 for Taquarussú.

AMAZONAS

Welcome to the heart of the Amazon. Amazonas is Brazil's largest state, spanning almost 1.6 million sq km. You could fit four Germanys within its borders with room left over for, say, Greece. It is here that the massive Solimões, Negro and Madeira rivers converge to form the Rio Amazonas, the granddaddy of them all. Manaus is where it all begins, a logical base for coming and going, and there are some genuinely rewarding tours, sights and urban amenities.

But Amazonas – not to mention Amazonia as a whole – is an incredibly big chunk of earth, and Manaus, with its outstanding tours, is merely a starting point. True, deep-immersion Amazon experiences, from Mamirauá Reserve to Reserva Extrativista Baixo Rio Branco-Jauaperi, from the Rio Urubu to the Rio Javari, are where you'll encounter the Amazon of which you always dreamed.

Manaus

0XX92 / POP 2.2 MILLION

Manaus is the Amazon's largest city, an incongruous urban metropolis in the middle of the jungle and a major port for seafaring vessels that's 1500km from the ocean. The Amazonian rainforest has a population density half that of Mongolia's, but the journey there invariably begins in (or passes through) this gritty, bustling city. Don't be surprised if you feel a little out of whack.

Manaus is no architectural gem, but does have some genuinely rewarding sights, including a leafy zoo and a rewarding beach-and-museum combo. It's a place to stock up on anything you forgot to pack, make reservations and begin your journey out into the jungle, or refill your tank with beer and internet after a week in the forest.

Another bit of advice: don't get stuck here! Manaus is best enjoyed as a starting point for your Amazon adventure, not the end of your road into the Amazon.

Sights

City Center

★ Teatro Amazonas THEATER

(92 3232-1768; Praça São Sebastião; guided tour R$20; 9:15am-5pm, tours every 30 mins until 4pm) This gorgeous theater was built at the height of the rubber boom, using European designers, decorators and even raw materials. The original driveway was Brazilian, though, made of Amazonian rubber to soften the clatter of late-arriving carriages. The theater's performance schedule includes an excellent opera festival (p610) in April and May. Hour-long guided tours offer an up-close look at the theater's opulent construction.

Centro Cultural Usina Chaminé MUSEUM

(92 3633-3026; Av Lourenço da Silva Braga; 8am-2pm Tue-Fri, 9am-1pm Sat) FREE Also known as the Museu dos Cinco Sentidos (Museum of the Five Senses), this innovative museum uses the five senses to evoke and illustrate indigenous and Caboclos life and culture. You can hear recordings of native languages, smell Amazonian spices, admire indigenous folk art and more.

Museu Amazônico MUSEUM

(92 3234-3242; Ramos Ferreira; 8am-noon & 2-5pm Mon-Fri) FREE Housed in a converted mansion, the Museu Amazônico has a small but excellent collection of indigenous items and artifacts from around the Amazon, many from ongoing archaeological studies in Amazonas state.

Palacete Provincial MUSEUM

(Praça da Polícia; 9am-5pm Tue & Wed, to 7pm Thu-Sat, 4-8pm Sun) FREE The 'Image and Sound' center at this handsome cultural complex has a huge collection of films, including century-old documentaries by Portuguese filmmaker Silvino Santos, some of the earliest recordings of Amazonian native people. The art gallery is decent too, but the police and archaeology displays are snoozers. Young eager guides are available for tours.

Outside the City Center

★Encontro das Águas RIVER

(Meeting of the Waters) Just beyond Manaus, the warm dark Rio Negro pours into the cool creamy Rio Solimões, but because of differences in temperature, speed and density, their waters don't mix, instead flowing side by side for several kilometers. The bicolor phenomenon occurs throughout the Amazon, but nowhere as dramatically as here. Day trips always include a stop here, and many tour operators at least pass by en route to their lodges. Never disappoints.

★Jardim Botânico Adolpho Ducke PARK

(☎92 3582-3188; www.jardimbotanicodemanaus.org; Av Margarita s/n; R$10, incl tower R$30; ⊙8am-noon & 1-4:30pm Tue-Sun, last entry 4pm) FREE Spanning over 100 sq km, this 'garden' is actually the world's largest urban forest. There's a network of five short trails (guides and closed shoes required, two to three hours, free with admission) and an open-air museum that includes rotating exhibits on Amazonian flora and fauna and a spectacular 42-meter-high observation tower. It's busier on weekends and free on Tuesday.

Comfortable shuttles (92 99286-9888, R$30 roundtrip, 45 minutes) leave from outside the tourist office (CAT) at 9am and 4pm. Otherwise, catch Bus 676 (R$3, one hour) from Praça da Matriz.

Museu do Seringal Vila Paraíso MUSEUM

(Rubber Museum; ☎92 3631-3632, 92 99275-4646; São João Afluente do Tarumã Mirim; R$5; ⊙8am-4pm Tue-Fri, 9am-1pm Sat & Sun) Located on the grounds of a former rubber-baron estate, this museum includes tours of the historic townhouse, a replica rubber-tapper shack and smokehouse, and a leafy trail showing how rubber trees are tapped. Sounds gimmicky, but is instead intriguing. Consider combining it with a stop at Praia da Lua, Manaus' best beach.

Boats to the museum (R$12, 25 minutes, via Praia da Lua) leave frequently from Marina Davi, just past the Hotel Tropical in Ponta Negra. From the center, take bus 120 or 121 (R$4, 20 minutes) to the end of the line, then walk or catch a free 'Especial' bus to the marina.

WORTH A TRIP

BOI-BUMBÁ

Tens of thousands of people descend on **Parantins** on the last weekend of June for the **Boi-Bumbá Festival** (⊙Jun) festival, an Amazonian version of the Northeast's Bumba Meu Boi, and one of the Amazon's largest parties. The festival centers on rivalry between two 'clans,' the Caprichoso, who dress all in blue, and Garantido, who dress in red. Parintins' hotels are booked months in advance, but travelers can usually score hammock space on one of the hundreds of riverboats that head there from Manaus and elsewhere.

Centro Cultural dos Povos da Amazônia MUSEUM

(☎92 2123-5300; Praça Francisco Pereira da Silva s/n; ⊙9am-4pm Mon-Fri) FREE At the heart of this massive cultural complex is the excellent Museu do Homem do Norte (Museum of Northern Man), which contains an incredible array of artifacts and multimedia exhibits on Amazonian indigenous groups. From the center, buses 625, 711 and 705 all pass by, or ask a taxi to take you to the 'Bola da Suframa.'

Bosque da Ciência (INPA) ZOO

(Forest of Science; ☎92 3643-3192; http://bosque.inpa.gov.br; Av Otávio Cabral; R$5; ⊙9am-noon & 2-4pm Tue-Fri, 9am-4pm Sat & Sun) Occupying a lush forest plot within the city, Bosque da Ciência (aka INPA, for the research institution that runs it) has enclosures for rescued manatees, giant otters and more. There are many smaller animals simply roaming around, such as squirrel monkeys, sloths and anteaters.

To get there from Praça da Matriz, the 810 'Especial' minibus (R$4) stops right outside the gates, while bus 519 (R$3) stops a half-block away. A taxi costs R$45.

Praia da Lua BEACH

Manaus' best beach has fine white sand and tea-colored water, and can be coupled with a visit to the Museu do Seringal for a nice city escape. Like all river beaches, Lua is biggest when the water is low (September to December). Beach shacks serve fish and beer at tables set up along the water.

Catch a boat to Praia da Lua (R$5, 10 minutes) from Marina Davi, just past Ponta Negra. Take bus 120 or 121 (R$3, 20 minutes) to the turnaround, and then walk or wait for the free 'Especial' bus to the marina.

Manaus

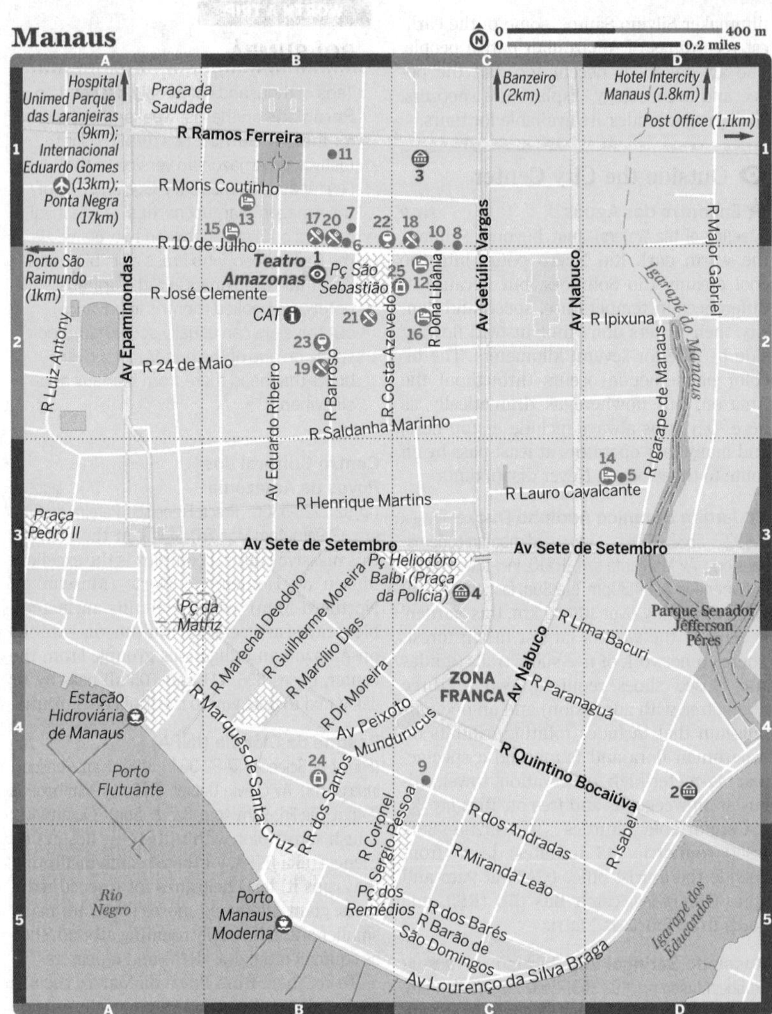

Parque Ecologico Januari NATURE RESERVE

As close as you'll get to experiencing a real Amazonian ecosystem on a half-day trip from Manaus, this 9000-acre park has flooded forests, giant water lilies, large trees, fishing opportunities and a smattering of Amazonian wildlife. It's fairly tame compared to the real thing, with raised wooden walkways and even a restaurant, but it's still a worthwhile introduction.

All tour operators in Manaus can organize visits here, often combining them with visits to the Encontro das Águas (p607) and other nearby attractions.

Tours

A cadre of registered guides run personalized tours of Manaus' main sights, including the port area, the fish and fruit markets, the opera house, and more – it's a good way to see a lot in a short time. Most are friendly and knowledgeable, and some speak several languages; look for them around the northwest corner of Praça São Sebastião. Rates average R$50 per group for three to five hours; taxi or boat fare is additional.

Manaus

Top Sights
1 Teatro Amazonas ... B2

Sights
2 Centro Cultural Usina Chaminé ... D4
3 Museu Amazônico ... C1
4 Palacete Provincial ... C3

Activities, Courses & Tours
5 Amazon Antonio Jungle Tours ... D3
6 Amazon Eco Adventures ... B1
7 Amazon Gero Tours ... B1
8 Amazon Green Tours ... C1
9 Amazonas Indian Turismo ... C4
10 Iguana Turismo ... C1
11 Swallows & Amazons ... B1

Sleeping
12 Boutique Hotel Casa Teatro ... C2
13 Go Inn Manaus ... B1
14 Hostel Manaus ... D3
15 Hotel Villa Amazônia ... B1
16 Local Hostel ... C2

Eating
17 Delícias Caseiras ... B1
18 Delicias da Marlene ... C1
19 Restaurante Castelinho ... B2
20 Tacacaria Amazônia ... B1
21 Tambaqui De Banda ... B2

Drinking & Nightlife
22 Bar do Armando ... B1
23 Mao Bar ... B2

Entertainment
Teatro Amazonas ... (see 1)

Shopping
24 Comercial São Bento ... B4
25 Galeria Amazônica ... C2

★**Amazônia Expeditions** ECOTOUR
(☎92 3671-2731; www.amazoniaexpeditions.com.br; Rua Miguel Ribas 1339) This experienced operator has decades of experience leading tour groups as well as prestigious scientific expeditions. They're one of few groups that goes up the Rio Negro to the Reserva Extrativista Baixo Rio Branco-Jauaperi (p623), and guides are professional and knowledgeable about wildlife and botany.

★**Amazon Eco Adventures** ECOTOUR
(☎92 98831-1011; www.amazonecoadventures.com; 10 de Julho, at Tapajós) Amazon Eco Adventures is an excellent choice, offering tours with small groups, comfortable speedboats, their own overnight boat and top guides. You'll go swimming at the meeting of the waters, and activities like visiting indigenous villages don't have a voyeuristic feel. Their trips to Presidente Figueiredo are equally rewarding, forgoing the touristy waterfalls for caves and falls where few visitors go.

They also have a lodge up on the Rio Urubu. Although they're pricier than others, they're well worth it.

★**Amazon Antonio Jungle Tours** ECOTOUR
(☎92 3234-1294, 92 99961-8314; www.antonio-jungletours.com; Hostel Manaus, Rua Lauro Cavalcante 231) Taking travelers to the scenic, wildlife-rich (and, in the north, mosquito-free) Rio Urubu, Antonio Gomes runs some of the region's best tours. Depending on water levels, you can hike deep into primary forest, canoe quietly through the flooded forest, visit local communities, fish for piranhas and spend time out on the Amazon itself.

He has two excellent lodges and a range of flexible packages that can last anywhere from a couple of days to a week. Slightly pricier, but worth it.

Lo Peix ECOTOUR
(☎92 98182-4793; www.lopeix.com; Av Coronel Teixera Puerto, Ponta Negra; per person R$435-1680, 3-12 days) The Spanish-Brazilian owners spent years exploring the Amazon in a riverboat before starting a tour company offering the same thing. Tours go further up the Rio Negro than other Manaus-based groups and hit places like the Anavilhanas Archipelago, Jaú National Park, prehistoric sites near Airão Velho and more, with frequent stops for canoeing, hiking, snorkeling and visiting local communities.

Amazon Green Tours ECOTOUR
(☎92 99106-5650, 92 98817-0325; www.amazongreentours.com; 10 de Julho 718) A husband and wife, both jungle-born, are the heart of this small, highly professional agency. Survival tours are a specialty, but even day hikes are imbued with interesting info and demonstrations. A spacious new lodge has comfortable air-conditioned rooms, plus chalets and a hammock area. The owners run workshops to help locals learn English and other skills; ask about participating.

Amazon Tree Climbing ECOTOUR
(☎92 8195-8585; www.amazontreeclimbing.com; Caravelle 22a, Tarumã) Yellow-shirted guides lend a youthful vibe to this outfit, whose tours range from half-day trips near Manaus with views of the Meeting of the Waters to all-day excursions that may also include visiting an indigenous village. Getting to the top of the massive trees can be quite challenging physically, but the experience is unforgettable.

Amazonas Indian Turismo ECOTOUR
(☎92 99240-5888; amazonasindian@hotmail.com; Andradas 311) This longtime budget agency has a rustic camp on the Rio Urubu, with latrine toilets and no electricity. You won't spend much time there, though, as the operator specializes in multiday hikes through the forest, sleeping in makeshift camps, with hammocks slung between two trees. It's notable for being indigenous-owned and operated; most guides are Wapixano, and all speak English.

Amazon Gero Tours ECOTOUR
(☎92 99198-0111, 92 99983-6273; www.amazongerotours.com; Tapajós 27) The effusive Gero Mesquita, an all-round good guy, runs a popular lodge in the Juma-Mamori area with comfortable dorms and private rooms, and a cadre of skilled guides (several former guides have opened agencies of their own). Besides standard tours, Gero arranges multiday treks into untouched forest and organizes 'social sustainability' programs where travelers work on needed community projects.

Swallows & Amazons ECOTOUR
(www.swallowsandamazonstours.com; Ramos Ferreira 922) This long-established South African–Brazilian agency specializes in riverboat tours, with different boats available for different levels of comfort, from open-air hammocks to air-conditioned cabins. Tours mostly go up the Rio Negro, including to the Anavilhanas Archipelago and Jaú National Park, exploring smaller tributaries along the way, with plenty of hiking, canoeing and fishing. Online booking recommended.

Iguana Turismo ECOTOUR
(☎92 99351-3630; www.amazonbrasil.com.br; Hotel Dez de Julho, 10 de Julho 663) This well-oiled operator has comfortable dorms and cabins at its Juma Lake lodge, a youthful vibe and accessible rates. Large groups can lend a cattle-herd feel, but you can't expect true isolation at budget rates. Tours are decent, guides get high marks and there's good swimming, canoeing and dolphin-spotting from the lodge's pier.

Festivals & Events

Manaus Opera Festival MUSIC
(Festival Amazonas de Ópera; ⏲late Apr–early May) Inaugurated in 1997, the annual Manaus Opera Festival brings high-quality opera deep into the rainforest at the Teatro Amazonas (p615). The three-week gala usually takes place in late April and early May, and tickets (R$5 to R$80) are available at the Teatro Amazonas several weeks before the festival opens.

Audience apparel ranges from tuxedos and ballroom gowns to jeans and T-shirts that have obviously done duty in the jungle (they do draw the line at shorts, tank tops and flip-flops).

Amazon Film Festival FILM
(Praça São Sebastião; ⏲Nov) In November, this increasingly popular film festival screens dozens of movies related to the Amazon, from rare Brazilian features filmed in Manaus to foreign documentaries about the

WORTH A TRIP

PRESIDENTE FIGUEIREDO

Self-named the 'Terra de Cachoeiras' (Land of Waterfalls), this dusty little town is surrounded by dozens of cascades and caves. Among the most impressive are Iracema, Cachoeira da Onza, Caverna do Maroaga, Gruta Judéia, Santuario, Asaframa and Pedra Furada (the most distant of the falls, 60km from town). You need a vehicle to visit the waterfalls here. You can rent a car from Manaus (125km south) or take the bus and hire a guide in Presidente Figueiredo; there's a tourist kiosk a short distance from the bus station. Several agencies in Manaus offer tours in this area too, notably Amazon Eco Adventures (p609) and **Tropical Tree Climbing** (☎92 99245-3669; www.tropicaltreeclimbing.com; Hwy BR-178, Km 144). Be aware that this is the only major leisure spot easily accessible by road from Manaus, and so it gets obscenely packed most weekends.

WORTH A TRIP

RIO URUBU

To get a taste of the Amazon in all its remote and wild glory usually means a multiday excursion from Manaus – the rainforest surrounding the Amazon's largest city long ago disappeared under the weight of human settlements and resource extraction. All of which is what makes the Rio Urubu such a wonderful surprise.

Just two hours by road from Manaus (although you'll need additional boat journeys to reach the lodges), the Rio Urubu is largely mosquito-free and has remarkably intact rainforest ecosystems with plentiful wildlife – we saw four species of monkey, a tayra (a large member of the weasel family), an anteater and stunning birdlife in just one day of exploring. Activities such as jungle hikes, canoe trips through dense flooded forest, visits to local communities, fishing and overnight forest camping are all possible, although what's on offer varies a little with the time of year and changing water levels.

Two operators in particular offer tours here. Amazonas Indian Turismo has a rustic lodge in the area, while Amazon Antonio Jungle Tours (p609) has two excellent places to stay.

Amazon Antonio's Lodge (☎92 99961-8314; www.antonio-jungletours.com; Rio Urubu; per person in dm/room with private bathroom incl meals from R$330/375; ❄) Antonio Gomes, who also runs Amazon Antonio Jungle Tours (p609), has built a splendid lodge on the mosquito-free banks of the Rio Urubu, surrounded by a pristine tract of riverine forest rich in wildlife and tall trees. There's a hammock dorm, a bunk-bed dorm and a range of wooden chalets and bungalows. The rooms are outstanding, especially the chalets with expansive terrace and hammocks. The communal dining area is open-sided and overlooks the river, while the three-story observation tower has glorious views, especially at sunset. Activities include fishing, jungle hikes, canoe trips and overnight camping.

Pousada Cumaru (☎92 99961-8314; www.antonio-jungletours.com; Rio Urubu; per person in dm/d with shared bathroom incl meals R$360/400; P) This small pousada does get more mosquitoes than the lodges upriver, but it's still a terrific choice. Simple but large wooden rooms with shared bathrooms and balconies overlook the river, and it offers a lovely dining area and meals cooked by a local family. It's run by Amazon Antonio Jungle Tours and a visit here can be combined with a visit to their other lodge upriver. All the usual activities are available, and you'll also emerge from the narrow river channels into the wide Amazon itself.

destruction of the rainforest. Headliners are shown in Teatro Amazonas (p615), but you can see films every night for free at a large outdoor screen set up right in the Praça São Sebastião.

Festival Folclórico do Amazonas CULTURAL
(⌚Jun) This June festival features a wide variety of regional folklore performances, including rehearsals of the Parintins Boi-Bumbá teams. The festival culminates on June 29 with the Procissão Fluvial de São Pedro (St Peter River Procession), when hundreds of riverboats parade on the Rio Negro before Manaus to honor the patron saint of fishers.

Sleeping

★Hostel Manaus HOSTEL $
(☎92 3233-4545; www.hostelmanaus.com; Lauro Cavalcante 231; dm with fan/air-con R$46/52, s with air-con & shared bathroom R$65, d with private/shared bathroom from R$121/93; ❄@☜) Manaus' first hostel is still its best. Spacious, warmly decorated common areas with colorful artworks and a rooftop dining area set it apart from other hostels, and there's a highly recommended tour operator on site. Large dorms and tidy private rooms are well looked after, and the whole place is a refuge from busy Manaus streets and professionally run.

There's kitchen access and self-service laundry. The addition of a lovely heritage building next door has only increased the hostel's charm.

Local Hostel HOSTEL $
(☎92 3213-6079; www.localhostel.com.br; Marçal 72; dm R$40-50, d R$120-140; ❄) A great hostel in almost every way: it's a block from the opera house, there are youthful staff and clientele, and clean, comfortable dorms with privacy curtains, reading lights and individual power outlets. Spiffy private rooms are a worthwhile splurge.

JUNGLE TRIPS

Getting away from Manaus and out into the jungle should be the goal of every visitor to the Amazon. Although day trips from the city are possible, including to the Encontro das Águas or to waterfall-rich Presidente Figueiredo, to truly experience the jungle, you'll need to venture a little further. The longer you're away from Manaus, the more you're likely to see and to feel as if you've done more than scratch the surface of this vast and extraordinary region.

Jungle Tour Operators

Manaus has dozens of operators who can take you out into the wild. Quality varies enormously, and paying more doesn't necessarily guarantee you a good experience. The majority of trips sold on the street, and even at some of the reputable tour agencies, are consolidated onto huge cattle boats; bargain hard for these because there's really not much bang for your buck.

But there are also some excellent companies run by professional staff and led by knowledgeable guides. Talk with other travelers to get a feel for what's possible, especially at the budget end of things. There are also some terrific operators in Novo Airão (p620).

What Sort of Trip?

While anything's possible, the most common trip is three to five days based at a jungle lodge or on a riverboat, with day trips for hiking, canoeing, fishing for piranha, spotting caiman at night and visiting local villages. Sleeping in hammocks in the forest for a night or two is usually possible, but not required. Some operators also offer so-called survival tours, which are spent mostly or entirely in forest camps.

Thinking carefully about what sort of trip you want can help determine which operator is best for you. How much do you want to rough it? Do you want a bed or a hammock? What about sleeping aboard a boat? Private bathroom, shared or pit toilet? Do you want to spend a night or two in the forest or do day trips from the lodge? How much do mosquitoes bother you? Do you prefer hiking or canoeing? There is no shame in choosing more or less comfort – you are there to enjoy yourself, after all.

There are also a few questions to ask the tour operator: does the guide speak English (or a language you understand)? How long will you spend getting there? What is the trip itinerary? How much hiking and/or canoeing will you do? How large are the groups? Ask to see recent pictures of the accommodations and activities, and a guest comment book.

And talk to other travelers! Virtually every foreigner you see in Manaus is planning a trip or returning from one, and they are a good source of honest, up-to-date info.

What to Bring

Bring shoes or boots for hiking, sandals for around the lodge, long-sleeved shirts and pants, mosquito repellent, a hat and sunscreen, rain gear, flashlight, roll of toilet paper, daypack and a water bottle. And binoculars! Even a small pair makes a big difference, yet few operators have extra pairs. Plastic bags, including a heavy-duty one large enough for your entire pack, are useful for rainstorms and leaky boats. Leave whatever you don't need at your hotel in Manaus – virtually all offer free, secure luggage storage.

Chez les Rois POUSADA **$**

(☎92 3584-5130; www.chezlesrois.com.br; Pérola Negra 1 Quadra G1, Conjunto Manauense, Barrio Vieiralves; r from R$110; ❄@🛜🏊) Occupying an attractive colonial home in a swanky neighborhood, Chez les Rois has handsome woodwork and great common areas, with little nooks where you can read or soak up the sun, plus a welcoming pool. Guestrooms are smallish, and you'll probably need a taxi to get around, but the overall ambience is worth a few bumped elbows and extra reais.

Hotel Intercity Manaus HOTEL **$$**

(☎92 3303-1330; www.intercityhoteis.com.br; Prof Márciano Armond 544; standard s/d from R$205/235, superior s/d from R$230/260; ❄🛜🏊) One of Manaus' better hotels, the Intercity has large, well-appointed rooms with a sitting area, rustic wooden floors and fine views from some rooms. The only real difference between standard and superior rooms is that the latter are found on the 8th floor or above. The restaurant is a disappointment.

When to Go

You can visit the Amazon year-round, but when you visit will have a big impact on the kind of experience you'll have.

From May to October, give or take a month at either end depending on the year, rivers overflow their banks. This means you'll spend much of your time paddling through the flooded forest. It's a terrific time to see monkeys such as squirrel monkeys, capuchins, saki monkeys and howler monkeys, as well as plenty of birdlife. Caiman are more commonly spotted on night tours at this time. To have a better chance of seeing cats, big snakes or deep-forest monkey species such as spider monkeys, you'll need to find dry land and hike into the forest, although even then these species can be elusive.

From November through to May, especially early in this period, flooded forest is less widespread, meaning river beaches are exposed and accessible and it's easier to see wildlife along the river margins. On the downside, the magic of floating through the flooded forest is more difficult to experience, and rain is an ever-present possibility.

Wildlife

The Amazon is teeming with animals, but seeing them can be quite hard. (It's a much better place to be wowed by the flora and the river itself, rather than wildlife.) On a typical trip, you are very likely to see pink and grey dolphins and a slew of birds, including herons, parrots and possibly macaws and toucans. Monkeys, sloths, anacondas, boa constrictors and caimans are relatively common, but seeing them is no sure thing. River otters and tapirs are even more elusive, and you're almost certain to not see jaguars, ocelots or manatees – they are extremely hard to spot.

'White water' areas tend to have more animals, but they also have more mosquitoes and thicker vegetation. State and national reserves have more (and less skittish) wildlife. The biggest factor in seeing animals is luck, followed by the quality of the forest and the diligence of your guide. Refrain from chatting unnecessarily.

Jungle Lodges

Most agencies have a small lodge or jungle camp where guests stay and activities such as canoeing, hiking and fishing are launched.

A handful of these are luxurious; they cater to an upscale client base and while the activities are usually the same as those offered by operators in Manaus, the lodging, food and service tend to be somewhat more refined (and the prices substantially higher). Prices at these places can easily surpass US$1000 per person per day.

Elsewhere, the majority of jungle lodges have amenities such as electricity and flush toilets, but not all. Prices usually include meals, lodging, transport and guides, and range between R$150 to R$350 per person per day; this normally includes time spent traveling to and from the lodge, not just the time you're actually there. Prices vary primarily by the type of accommodations: hammocks with shared toilets are the cheapest option, followed by dorms and private rooms, then riverboats and specialized tours.

Hotel Adrianópolis All Suites APARTMENT **$$**
(☎92 2101-2000; www.hoteladrianopolis.tur.br; Salvador 195; apt from R$220; ❄📶🍽) Outrageously good value, these modern apartments have smallish bedrooms, but size doesn't matter here because there's a kitchen and sitting area to relax in. It's a R$20, ten-minute taxi ride from the Praça São Sebastião.

Go Inn Manaus HOTEL **$$**
(☎92 3306-2600; www.atlanticahotels.com.br/hotel/manaus/go-inn-manaus; Monsenhor Coutinho 560; s/d R$185/220; ❄📶) A bit plastic, perhaps, but still a welcome oasis of business-class comfort amid Manaus' mostly gritty downtown options. Rooms are smallish but very comfortable and clean, with modern bathrooms and technology. There's an extra-large restaurant and well-stocked convenience store, plus a lobby business area, a small fitness room and a kids' playroom. No swimming pool.

Boutique Hotel Casa Teatro HOTEL **$$**
(☎92 3633-8381; www.casateatro.com.br; 10 de Julho 632; s/d R$210/250, with shared bathroom

R$120/150;) Rooms are modern and cute, but *really* small – basically, boutique walk-in closets. Standards have bunks and shared bathrooms, while en-suite rooms at least have double beds, though still not much floor space. Common areas are truly lovely, including cozy sitting rooms and a rooftop patio with views of the opera house. Great location and service, but brace yourself for the sardine treatment.

★Hotel Villa Amazônia HOTEL **$$$**
(☎92 3347-7829; www.villaamazonia.com; 10 de Julho 315; r from R$550;) Arguably Manaus' only top-end hotel worthy of the name, Hotel Villa Amazônia is wonderfully central, with large stylish rooms, muted accents and personal service. The building it inhabits is similarly stunning. Some rooms look on to a verdant garden.

Eating

Delicias da Marlene BRAZILIAN **$**
(☎9298192-6092; 10 de Julho 625; mains from R$10; ⏲11am-11pm Tue-Sun) Simple, no-nonsense cooking with buffet lunches (R$10 per plate) that range from rice and spaghetti to salads and grilled meats, plus tacacá (p593) and local fish dishes. It's hugely popular with locals.

Delícias Caseiras BRAZILIAN, SELF-SERVICE **$**
(☎92 3232 9202; 10 de Julho 499; lunch per kg R$30, mains R$20-45; ⏲11am-3pm & 6:30-9:30pm Mon-Sat) The tables are crammed together and the fans are blowing full blast to accommodate the scads of loyal clients at this great hole-in-the-wall just off Praça São Sebastião. Lunch self-serve is outstanding, especially for the price, but it's also open for dinner, serving home-style classics.

★Amazônico Peixaria Regional SEAFOOD, BRAZILIAN **$$**
(☎92 3236-0546; www.amazonico.com.br; Av Darcy Vargas 222; mains R$36-98; ⏲noon-3pm & 6:30-11pm Mon-Sat, 11:30am-4pm Sun) However you get your *tambaqui* (perhaps the tastiest of all Amazonian fish) prepared here – stewed, grilled, ribs – the execution is perfect. They serve all manner of other fish and steak dishes, and fab desserts too. The atmosphere is casual, the service attentive and the cooking top-notch. It's one of the best meals you'll have in the Amazon.

Even once you factor in the taxi fare both ways, it's terrific value.

Tacacaria Amazônia BRAZILIAN **$$**
(☎92 99112-3730; www.facebook.com/TacacariaAmazonia; 10 de Julho 503; mains R$20-45; ⏲10:30am-10:30pm Mon-Sat, from 3pm Sun) This bright, appealing place serves a range of local dishes, specializing in tacacá (p593) and well-prepared fish from the Amazon, including *tambaqui* and *pirarucú*. English is spoken and they're good at putting an order together without the hard sell.

Tambaqui De Banda BRAZILIAN **$$**
(☎92 3622-8162; www.tambaquidebanda.com.br; Praça São Sebastião; mains for two R$50-80; ⏲11am-11pm) The look is plastic, the location is ideal and the food surprisingly good. Bring some friends – nearly all dishes are for two or more people and the group-friendly menu makes for a boisterous ambience. Outdoor tables face the opera house. The specialty is grilled boneless *tambaqui* (a local fish), served with all the fixings.

Restaurante Castelinho BUFFET **$$**
(☎92 3633-3111; www.facebook.com/CastelinhoRestaurante; Barroso 317; per kg R$45; ⏲11am-3pm Mon-Fri) The food and service at this popular per-kilo lunch-only place are perfectly good, but the highlight has to be the building itself: a beautiful, high-ceilinged rubber-era mansion that served as a private residence, doctor's office and foreign consulate before being converted into a restaurant. You'll find everything from tapioca and fish to lasagna.

★Coco Bambu Manaus BRAZILIAN, SEAFOOD **$$$**
(☎92 3667-7430; www.cocobambu.com; Ponta Negra Shopping Center, Av Coronel Teixeira 5705; mains R$45-120; ⏲11:30am-3pm & 8pm-midnight Sun-Thu, 11:30am-5pm & 8pm-1am Fri & Sat) In a shopping center on the way to Ponta Negra west of town, this place deserves its consistently good reviews. Professional service and artfully prepared seafood and steaks are fabulous, but leave room for the brilliant desserts. The cocktails are similarly worth crossing town for.

Banzeiro BRAZILIAN **$$$**
(☎92 3234-1621; www.restaurantebanzeiro.com.br; Libertador 102, NS das Gracas; mains R$75-140; ⏲11:30am-3pm & 7-11pm, to 10pm Sun) One of Manaus' top gourmet restaurants, especially for fish. Varieties such as *pirarucú, tambaqui* and other Amazonian specialties are served in various preparations, from cheese and banana to parsley and *formigas* (ants). Pricey but truly one-of-a-kind. Online reservations recommended.

Drinking & Nightlife

Bar do Armando BAR

(92 3232-1195; www.facebook.com/bardoarmando; 10 de Julho 593; 5pm-2am) Near the opera house, this is a traditional rendezvous for Manaus' intellectual and bohemian types, but all sorts of people crowd around the outdoor tables for beers and conversation.

Mao Bar BAR

(92 3345-4550; Barroso; 5pm-late Tue-Sat) This bar is super-cool – a moodily lit, semi-subterranean spot on the basement level with great music and drinks and a laid-back backpacker vibe. Occasional live music and movie screenings.

Copacabana Chopperia CLUB

(92 3584-4569; www.facebook.com/Oficial.Copacabana; Estrada do Turismo, Tarumã; 7pm-3am Thu-Sun) Rio-style bar and dance club, with a semi-open-air bar, performance stage and dance floor, with room for 7000 revelers! DJs spin everything from samba and MPB (Música Popular Brasileira) to electronica and funk. Check out the club's Facebook page for details and deals. Located on Estrada do Turismo, a long avenue near Ponta Negra with numerous bars and restaurants.

Entertainment

★**Porão do Alemão** LIVE MUSIC

(92 3239-2976; www.poraodoalemao.com.br; Av São Jorge 1986; R$30; 10:30pm-late Wed-Sat) This longtime bar and club features Brazilian and international rock and pop, and has a safe, lively scene popular with tourists and locals alike. There's a VIP area upstairs (R$40).

Teatro Amazonas LIVE MUSIC

(92 3622-1880; Praça São Sebastião; free to R$80; 8pm, except Mon) Performances at Manaus' iconic theater are all over the place: professional opera, jazz combos, student guitar, dance and more. Quality varies but the setting is superb: some shows are terrific, others barely tolerable, most are free. A line starts forming at 7pm, but you can usually arrive right before the show starts to snag a balcony or rear seat.

JUNGLE TRIP SCAMS

Most travelers to the Amazon have a wonderful time. But Manaus is teeming with scammers and touts, and it helps to know how to avoid them. Most peddle cut-rate tours that turn out to be woefully uninspired: awful accommodations, surly guides, and sad, damaged forest with no wildlife. Tourists have been seriously injured, and a few even killed, on tours with unscrupulous or inexperienced guides. Mainly, though, they get duped: swindled out of their time, money and a chance to really enjoy the Amazon. Here are some tips and pointers to avoid getting scammed.

Don't be naive. The smooth-talking guy who approaches you at the airport, on the street or at the door of your hostel, with promises of an epic adventure at a rock-bottom price, is most likely scamming you.

Do not tell touts what hotel or tour agency you're considering. They're trying to squeeze a commission out of the hotel or operator. The magic words are 'I already have a reservation,' whether it's true or not. Touts only get paid for bringing people without reservations or prior bookings.

No legitimate tour agency 'fishes' for clients at the airport. Those that do are cut-rate operators trying to snag unsuspecting tourists. Some touts shamelessly lie about who they work for, claiming to have been sent there to pick you up. Many legit agencies do offer airport pickups, but they send someone with your name on a sign.

Never pay for a tour anywhere except at the agency's main office. Touts often pretend they are with a legitimate agency but steer you to a cafe or airport bench to make the deal. They even make phony phone calls to convince you the main office is closed, or that you must commit right away to get the best price or the 'last seat on the boat.' These are all scams.

Above all, don't risk your life to save a little time or money. In the end, it's tourists who keep scammers in business by booking with them. There are legitimate established agencies for all budgets and tastes; take the time to find one that works for you.

Shopping

★Galeria Amazônica ARTS & CRAFTS

(☎92 3203 3633; galeria@waimiriatroari.org.br; Costa Azevedo 272; ⏲8am-8pm Mon-Sat) Right on Praça São Sebastião, this is Manaus' top shop for genuine-article Amazonian handiwork, including gorgeous basketwork, pottery and folk art, as well as T-shirts, jewelry and a handful of Portuguese-language books. Prices are on the high side, but so is the quality.

Comercial São Bento SPORTS & OUTDOORS

(☎92 3234-4000; Miranda Leão 133; ⏲8am-5:30pm Mon-Fri, to 4pm Sat) One of several *casas de redes* (hammock shops) clustered around this corner; this one has a monster selection and amiable service. For riverboat trips, suitable cloth hammocks start at R$30, while larger, prettier and more durable ones go for R$60 to R$200. If you'll be sleeping in the jungle, consider getting a mosquito net (R$14 to R$30) as well.

Information

EMBASSIES & CONSULATE

Venezuelan Consulate-General (☎92 3584-3813; Río Jamary 10, Conj Vieiralves, Nossa Senhora das Graças)

EMERGENCY

Police stations are located across from the bus station on Praça da Matriz and inside the main boat terminal (Estação Hidroviária).

Ambulance (☎192)

State Police (☎190; Praça da Matriz) There's a station across from the bus station on Praça da Matriz.

Tourist Police (☎92 3231-1998; Av Eduardo Ribeiro) Alongside the Centro de Atendimento ao Turista.

LAUNDRY

Most hotels have laundry services for guests, but high per-piece rates add up fast.

Lavandería Central (☎92 3631-1322; Quintino Bocaiúva 607; per piece R$2.50; ⏲8am-noon & 2-5pm Mon-Fri, to 1pm Sat) Located a block east of Av Nabuco. Add R$1 per piece for ironing. Quick service.

LEFT LUGGAGE

Most hotels store bags for free while you're on a jungle trip. The airport and long-distance bus station have luggage storage for a small fee that varies according to size and the length of time you'll need it.

MEDICAL SERVICES

Fundação de Medicina Tropical (Tropical Medicine Foundation; ☎92 2127-3555; Av Pedro Teixeira 25) Also known as Hospital de Doenças Tropicais, this well-regarded hospital specializes in tropical diseases. Free yellow fever vaccines available.

Hospital Unimed Parque das Laranjeiras (☎0800-702-9088, 92 3633-4431; www.unimedmanaus.com.br; Av Professor Nilton Lins 3259) One of the best private hospitals in the city.

MONEY

Banco do Brasil (Guilherme Moreira 315; ⏲9am-3pm Mon-Fri) Has an ATM.

Bradesco (Av Eduardo Ribeiro 475, at Saldanha Marinho; ⏲9am-3pm Mon-Fri) Reliable ATM in the town center.

POST

Post Office (☎92 3215-2540; Av Silves 363; ⏲8am-4pm Mon-Fri, 8am-noon Sat)

TOURIST INFORMATION

CAT (☎92 3182-6250; www.visitamazonas.am.gov.br; Av Eduardo Ribeiro 666; ⏲8am-5pm Mon-Fri, to noon Sat & Sun) Branch of the state tourism agency, located on the southwest corner of Praça São Sebastião. Doesn't have a lot to offer, with no brochures.

Getting There & Away

AIR

Airport

Manaus is an important air hub for the Amazonas region. The main airport, **Aeroporto Internacional Eduardo Gomes** (☎92 3652-1210; www4.infraero.gov.br/aeroportos/aeroporto-internacional-de-manaus-eduardo-gomes/; Av Santos Dumont 1350), is located 13km north of the city center. Modern, spiffy and cavernous – thank you World Cup 2014! – it has info kiosks, ATMs (but no foreign exchange desk at the time of writing), luggage lockers, restaurants, shopping and wi-fi. Charter planes and smaller regional airlines may use a separate terminal (known as 'Eduardinho'), about 600m east of the main one.

Airlines

American Airlines (☎92 3652-1911, 0300-789-7778; www.aa.com) Direct flights between Manaus and Miami.

Azul (☎92 3652-1830, 92 4003-1118; www.voeazul.com.br) Connects Manaus with Boa Vista, Tefé, Tabatinga, Belo Horizonte, São Paulo, Santarém and Fortaleza.

Copa Airlines (☎92 3652-1442, 0800-771-2672; www.copaair.com) International flights to/from Manaus, including Panama City, Miami and Bogota.

Gol (☎0800-704-0465, 92 3652-1593; www.voegol.com.br) Manaus to/from Boa Vista, Porto Velho, Santarém, Belém, Brasília and São Paulo.

LATAM (☎92 4002-5700, 92 3652-1211; www.latam.com) Direct flights between Manaus and

Boa Vista, Sao Paulo, Rio de Janeiro, Brasília, Fortaleza and Belém, with extensive onward domestic and international connections.

MAP (☎92 3652-1931, 92 2125-5000; www.voemap.com.br) Connects Manaus with smaller airports across the Amazon and beyond, including Barcelos, São Gabriel da Cachoeira, Eirunepé, Tefé, Coari, Lábrea, Itaituba, Parintins and Porto Trombetas.

TAP (☎092 3652-1973, 0800-727-2347; www.flytap.com) Has an office in Manaus, but no flights into the city.

BOAT

The main port's **ticket office** (☎92 3233-7061, 92 3088-5764; Marquês de Santa Cruz; ⏲6:15am-5:45pm) sells passage for most long-distance riverboats. It is not recommended to buy tickets from the men with desks along the sidewalk in front of the boat terminal; although they're slightly cheaper, you're the first to be bumped if the boat is full.

RIO SOLIMÕES

Large passenger boats plying the Rio Solimões use Manaus' main passenger port, **Estação Hidroviária de Manaus** (☎92 3233 7061; www.portodemanaus.com.br; Porto Flutuante). Speedboats use the smaller **Porto Manaus Moderna** (behind Mercado Municipal Adolfo Lisboa) Headed up the Rio Solimões, boats call at Tefé, Benjamin Constant and Tabatinga.

DESTINATION	TYPE OF BOAT	DEPARTURE	DURATION	HAMMOCK OR SEAT (R$)	CABIN, 2 PAX (R$)
Tefé	Riverboat	5-6am Tue-Thu, Sat & Sun	36 hrs	175	650
Tefé	Speedboat	6am Tue	13 hrs	270	-
Tabatinga	Riverboat	noon Wed, Fri & Sat	7 days	400	1620
Tabatinga	Speedboat	6am Tue, Thu, Fri & Sun	36 hrs	600	-

RIO NEGRO

Both slow (river) boats and speedboats going up the Rio Negro use **Porto São Raimundo** (Coração de Jesus), a seedy port about 1.5km northwest of the center. If traveling by speedboat, bring a camping pad if you've got one: many passengers lie in the aisle to get some sleep.

DESTINATION	TYPE OF BOAT	DEPARTURE	DURATION (HRS)	HAMMOCK OR SEAT (R$)	CABIN, 2 PAX (R$)
Novo Airão	Riverboat	8pm Tue & Thu	9-10	48	-
Barcelos	Riverboat	6pm Tue, Wed & Fri	25-30	140	350
Barcelos	Speedboat	3pm Tue & Fri	12	180	-
São Gabriel da Cachoeira	Riverboat	5pm & 6pm Fri	72	390	-
São Gabriel da Cachoeira	Speedboat	3pm Tue & Fri	24	450	-

RIO AMAZON & RIO MADEIRA

Passenger boats going downstream to Belém depart from the Estação Hidroviária de Manaus and usually make stops in Itacoatiara, Parintins, Santarém and Monte Alegre. Boats to Porto Velho take the Rio Madeira, making stops at Manicoré and Humaitá.

DESTINATION	DEPARTURE	DURATION	HAMMOCK (R$)	CABIN, 2 PAX (R$)
Belém	11am Wed & Fri	4 days	from 350	from 1100
Porto Velho	6pm Tue	4 days	240	660
Santarém	11am Mon-Sat	36 hrs	180	from 800

WORTH A TRIP

JUMA LAKE

One of the most popular excursions into the wider Amazon region from Manaus is to Juma Lake. Although the wider area south of the Amazon River is increasingly populated and areas of pristine forest are shrinking, the lake and its immediate surrounds remain worth visiting. While here, you can, depending on the time of year, canoe through the flooded forest or hike through the jungle, as well as go caiman spotting by night or piranha fishing by day. Wildlife is pretty scarce these days, but the birdlife is good.

The journey there from Manaus takes more than three hours by boat, meaning that we recommend a minimum stay of one night, preferably more. Although most operators in Manaus can arrange your visit to Juma Lake, we recommend booking directly through the lodges themselves.

Amazon Lodge (☎92 93308-1181; www.amazonlodgeamazonas.com.br; per person per night US$250-600) A homey floating lodge in a secluded corner of the lake. Standard rooms are small but comfortable, while larger suites have private outdoor showers. None have private toilets, however.

Juma Lodge (☎92 3232-2707; www.jumalodge.com; 1 night all-inclusive s R$2245-3265, d R$3326-4838) The deluxe lakefront cabins here stand dramatically on 15m stilts, connected by wood walkways, with huge screened windows and private patios. West-facing units can get hot in the late afternoon, but that's when you might be sipping a caipirinha in the lodge's shady deck or spacious communal dining area. Tours make use of comfortable motorized canoes, though groups can be large. Per-night rates fall the longer you stay.

Dolphin Lodge (☎92 3663-0392, 92 99431-4991; www.dolphinlodge.tur.br; 2 nights all-inclusive s/d R$920/1500) Not on the lake but nearby, this was once the preferred lodge of an agency selling upscale group packages. It operates independently now, with comfortable rooms and unblemished views from its perch atop a high riverbank in the Mamori-Juma area. The affable owner ably runs the lodge and tours.

BUS

Eucatur (☎92 3301-5800; www.eucatur.com.br) has services to Boa Vista (R$170, 10 to 12 hours, 10am, 6pm, 7pm and 11pm). If you plan to continue directly to Venezuela, take the 6pm or 7pm buses from Manaus in order to have the best chance of catching the one and only bus to the border, which leaves Boa Vista at 7am.

Asatur (☎in Boa Vista 95 3224-2630; www.asaturturismo.com.br) also serves Boa Vista (R$170 to R$230, 7pm; 11¾ hrs); there are two departures at 7pm, one of which is 'VIP' with nearly fully reclining seats and on-board wi-fi.

Aruanã (☎92 3642-5757) Aruanã has seven daily buses from Manaus to Presidente Figueiredo (R$35, two hours), leaving from Manaus at 6am, 10am, 12:30pm, 4pm, 6pm, 8pm and 11pm) and to Itacoatiara (R$55, four hours, six daily).

CAR

Rental agencies at the airport include **Localiza** (☎92 3652-1176), **Unidas** (☎92 3652-1327; www.unidas.com.br), **Avis** (☎92 3652-1579; www.avis.com.br) and **Hertz** (☎92 3652-1421; www.localizahertz.com/brasil/pt-br).

Getting Around

Bus fare is R$3.80 on most routes. Taxis are plentiful, but rather expensive – from R$20 within the center and more for destinations beyond that or if you get mired in traffic.

TO/FROM THE AIRPORT

Buses 306 'Aeroporto' (R$3.80) and 813 'Aeroporto-Ejecutivo' (R$8) run about every half-hour between the airport and Praça da Matriz in the center of town; the latter is air-conditioned, less crowded and definitely worth the extra reais. At the airport, turn right out of the main doors and walk to the bus stop at the end of the terminal. In town, the most convenient stops are Praça da Matriz and on Av Getúlio Vargas near Rua José Clemente.

Taxis at the airport charge a fixed R$75 for the 20-minute ride into town, while the return trip costs around R$65; some hotels have an arrangement with taxi drivers whereby you pay R$50 if going from the hotel to the airport. In any case, always be sure to agree on a price before setting off.

Around Manaus

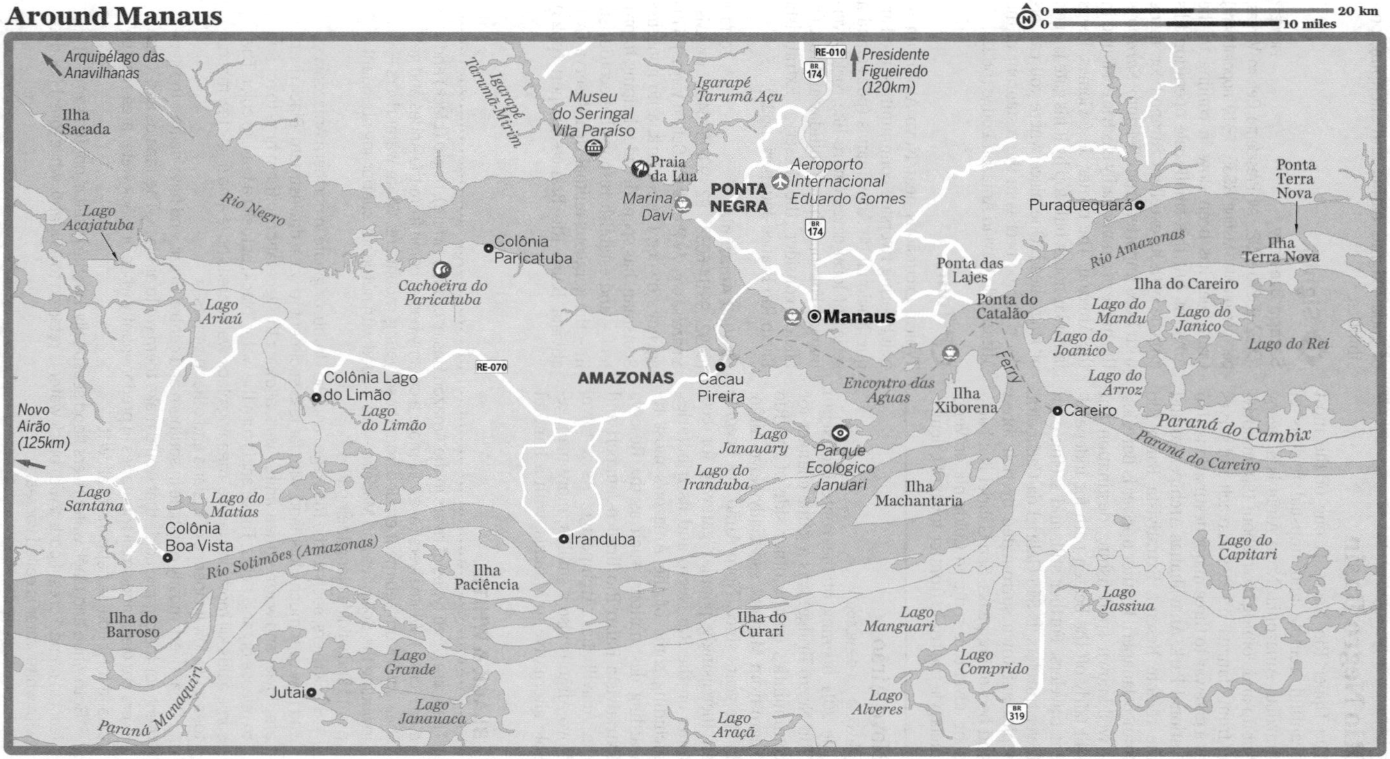

0 20 km
0 10 miles
Arquipélago das Anavilhanas
Ilha Sacada
Igarapé Tarumã-Mirim
Museu do Seringal Vila Paraíso
Igarapé Tarumã Açu
RE-010
BR 174
Presidente Figueiredo (120km)
Praia da Lua
Aeroporto Internacional Eduardo Gomes
PONTA NEGRA
Marina Davi
BR 174
Ponta Terra Nova
Puraquequara
Ilha Terra Nova
Rio Amazonas
Rio Negro
Lago Acajatuba
Colônia Paricatuba
Cachoeira do Paricatuba
Ponta das Lajes
Ilha do Careiro
Lago do Mandu
Lago do Janico
Lago do Rei
Ponta do Catalão
Lago do Joanico
Lago do Arroz
Manaus
Lago Ariaú
RE-070
AMAZONAS
Cacau Pireira
Colônia Lago do Limão
Lago do Limão
Encontro das Aguas
Ilha Xiborena
Ferry
Careiro
Paraná do Cambix
Paraná do Careiro
Novo Airão (125km)
Lago Janauary
Parque Ecologico Januari
Lago do Iranduba
Ilha Machantaria
Lago Santana
Lago do Matias
Colônia Boa Vista
Iranduba
Lago do Capitari
Rio Solimões (Amazonas)
Ilha Paciência
Lago Jassiua
Ilha do Barroso
Ilha do Curari
Lago Manguari
Lago Grande
Lago Comprido
Jutai
Lago Alveres
Lago Janauaca
Lago Araçã
BR 319
Paraná Manaquiri

Rio Negro Basin

The Upper Rio Negro is one of the most beautiful, remote and unusual regions of Brazilian Amazonia. Novo Airão is a sleepy but up-and-coming town about 180km upriver from Manaus; it's easy to reach and serves as a gateway to three major destinations: Jaú National Park, Anavilhanas Archipelago and the remote Reserva Extrativista Baixo Rio Branco-Jauaperi. Further upriver is Barcelos, a well-known sport-fishing destination but still fairly off the beaten path for independent travelers. Further still, and seeing even fewer travelers, is São Gabriel da Cachoeira, a pleasant town surrounded by rich forest and beckoning peaks. São Gabriel is a back-door adventure route to Colombia or Venezuela, via the triple-frontier town of Cucuí.

Novo Airão

☎0XX92 / POP 18,600

The 2011 opening of the Ponte Rio Negro (Rio Negro Bridge) was a game changer for communities on the other side of the Rio Negro from Manaus, especially Novo Airão. In the years since, Novo Airão has become an increasingly popular gateway for eco-tours on the Rio Negro and its tributaries, including some of the Amazon's most rewarding destinations, such as the Reserva Extrativista Baixo Rio Branco-Jauaperi and the Anavilhanas Archipelago. As a town, Novo Airão is also a smaller, more manageable alternative to Manaus, with a handful of good lodging, eating and shopping possibilities.

Sights

Sarapo Brewery BREWERY

(☎92 99270-9792; Av Presidente Getulio Vargas; per person incl tasting R$35; ⏲by appointment) Craft beer has been slow in coming to the Amazon, but this small-scale operation fills a niche with its excellent Sarapo beer, made with hops imported from Belgium. *Sarapo* is the name of a non-deadly electric eel found in the Amazon. The owner, José Gomes, keeps irregular hours, but stop by if his gate is open or ring ahead. One place where you can order a Sarapo beer is in the restaurant of the Mirante do Gavião Amazon Lodge (p622).

Tours

Typical excursions near Novo Airão run to neighboring riverside communities, the Parque Nacional de Anavilhanas (p624), and a series of local caves (more like rocky overhangs). For something multiday and further afield, consider the Reserva Extrativista Baixo Rio Branco-Jauaperi (p623).

★**Visit Amazônia** ECOTOUR

(☎92 99114-6038, 92 99215-1648; www.visitamazonia.org; Av Presidente Getulio Vargas) This agency's owner, Chris Clark, a no-nonsense Scotsman, has spent decades helping to protect – and establish responsible ecotourism in – the gorgeous animal-rich Reserva Extrativista Baixo Rio Branco-Jauaperi (p623),

BLACK & WHITE

There are three types of rivers in the Amazon Basin: *branco* (white), *negro* (black) and *claro* (clear). White rivers (actually more a creamy beige) come from the Andes and get their color from sediment eroded from those 'young' mountains. White-water rivers – including the Solimões and Madeira – are loaded with nutrients, supporting abundant plants and wildlife along their paths.

Black rivers, such as the Rio Negro and Rio Urubu, originate in northern Amazonia and flow over much older land, with far less sediment to wash downstream. Black rivers are slower and warmer than white rivers, allowing the vegetation in them time to rot and to release organic acids. Those acids turn the water 'black', actually a tea-like color. The same acids kill mosquito larvae, meaning black-water areas have amazingly few mosquitoes and a low incidence of malaria and other diseases.

Clear rivers mostly originate in southern and central Brazil, and have neither the sediment nor the organic acids that would make them white or black. The Tapajós and Xingu rivers are clear, and small tributaries in predominantly white or black water areas can be clear if their course happens to allow it.

Both white and black water rivers flood seasonally, but the result is not the same, at least in name. Forest flooded with black water is referred to as *igapó*, while forest flooded with white water is called *várzea*.

also known as Xixuaú-Xipariná. He still specializes in highly recommended trips there but also runs tours from Novo Airão to the Anavilhanas Archipelago and elsewhere.

Plan on at least a week if going to the Xixuaú, two weeks for the Xipariná.

★Expedição Katerre ECOTOUR
(☎92 3365-1644; www.katerre.com; Francisco Cardoso) This excellent operator runs high-quality expeditions from one to eight days to the marvelous Reserva Extrativista Baixo Rio Branco-Jauaperi (p623); as they like to say, they begin their Amazon journeys where many other operators end theirs. Their boats are among the Amazon's best, and they're flexible in meeting individual or group needs. Based out of the Mirante do Gavião Amazon Lodge.

Em Cantos da Amazônia ECOTOUR
(☎92 3365-1023, 92 9229-6667; www.emcantosdaamazonia.com; Pousada Bela Vista, Av Presidente Getulio Vargas 47, at Av Ajuricaba) Day trips with this amiable operator based out of the Pousada Bela Vista explore the islands and waterways of the Anavilhanas Archipelago, the Madada Caves and nearby riverside villages, while more expensive excursions, including multiday trips, go as far as Jaú National Park (p624).

Ama Boto WILDLIFE
(☎93 99337-6510; Antenor Carlos Frederico; adult/child R$15/7.50; ⏲8am-5pm) This dolphin-feeding operation helped put Novo Airão on the map. Such is its popularity that now, thankfully, swimming with the dolphins has been stopped, but watching them feed makes for a fine photo opportunity. Visits begin on the hour (except 1pm) with a 15-minute, Portuguese-only presentation on pink dolphins, followed by the feeding.

Located 500m upriver from Pousada Bela Vista, just past the marina.

Sleeping

Pousada Lanna POUSADA $
(☎92 3365-1765; Av Ajuricaba 8; d/tr/q R$50/60/70; ❄📶) Stay here only if you must, or if price is everything. Cell-like rooms at this basic hotel are small, many have no windows and reception is often nowhere to be found. But they do have televisions, wi-fi that sometimes works, and air-con. Alas, the showers are cold and breakfast is not included. They rent rooms by the hour on weekend nights...

★Pousada Bela Vista POUSADA $$
(☎92 99229-6667, 92 3365-1023; www.pousadabelavista.com; Av Presidente Getulio Vargas 47; s/d/tw/tr incl breakfast R$210/260/310/360; ❄📶🏊) Easily Novo Airão's best midrange guesthouse and a wonderful place to take a break from life on the road, Pousada Bela Vista is run by a German-Brazilian couple and features comfortable rooms adorned with richly colorful paintings by a local artist, as well as a swimming pool and the town's best Rio Negro views. It has great meal and bar service too.

There's outdoor gym equipment or hammocks, depending on your needs, as well as colorfully painted children's playground equipment.

An in-house tour operator, Em Cantos da Amazônia, runs day trips and multiday excursions.

★Mirante do Gavião Amazon Lodge LODGE $$$
(☎92 3365 1181; www.mirantedogaviao.com.br; Francisco Cardoso; s incl breakfast R$1031-1526, d incl breakfast R$1788-2662; ❄📶🏊) This lodge at Novo Airão's northern end is a real stunner. Everything here is architecturally striking, from its tree-house rooms to those that resemble the upturned hulls of local fishing boats, which maximize natural airflow. Rooms are large and supremely comfortable; tree-house rooms are the smallest, but have the best Rio Negro views. There's an outstanding open-sided restaurant (p622) by the water.

Everything here is built from sustainable local wood, and there's an observation tower and riverside games room. A planned expansion will only bring the number of rooms to ten, ensuring that the sense of personal service remains.

Their in-house tour operator, Expedição Katerre, is similarly excellent, and all-inclusive packages are possible.

Anavilhanas Jungle Lodge LODGE $$$
(☎92 98111-4298, Manaus 92 3622-8996; www.anavilhanaslodge.com; 2-night, 3-day all-inclusive package s R$3540-5544, d R$5600-8360; P❄📶) This well-run lodge has stylish modern rooms with hardwood floors, electric lighting, private bathrooms and even air-conditioning. Even better, the rich forest and winding waterways of the namesake Anavilhanas Archipelago are directly across the water, just outside the

front door. Tours include canoeing, hiking and multiday expeditions. Popular with families, it's located on a secluded spot just downriver from town.

There's a minimum two-night stay. Transfers by seaplane from Manaus can be arranged, as can excursions around the surrounding area.

Eating

Saloon Aljunicaba BRAZILIAN $
(☎95 3365-1614; cnr Av Ajuricaba & Rua Barbosa; burgers R$8-12; ⏲2-11pm Mon-Fri, 11am-10pm Sat & Sun) If you spot the red VW Beetle outside, you'll know you've found this simple yet appealing bar-restaurant. Locals swear (and we agree) that these are the best burgers in town. It's the top pick for a drink away from the river.

★Mirante do Gavião Amazon Lodge BRAZILIAN $$
(☎92 3365 1181; www.mirantedogaviao.com.br; Francisco Cardoso; mains R$45-78; ⏲noon-9pm; 🌶) This classy restaurant in the lodge of the same name has an extensive menu, focusing on local ingredients with a few innovative riffs; the iconic *pirarucú* fish is grilled with sweet potatoes, coconut milk, lemon and ginger. It's open to nonguests, but you'll need to call ahead to make a reservation. There are plenty of vegetarian options too. The riverside setting is lovely.

★Flor do Luar BRAZILIAN $$
(☎93 99418-0865; Av Presidente Getulio Vargas; mains R$26-45; ⏲9am-5pm Fri-Sun) One of the Amazon's best restaurants, Flor do Luar sits on a floating pontoon on the Rio Negro and serves fabulous food and cold beers. The specialty is the *banda de tambaqui assada*, a local fish cooked on the grill with plantains, but start with the brilliant *dadinho de tapioca* (deep-fried tapioca croquettes). You can even swim from the waterfront platform.

Pousada Bela Vista BRAZILIAN $$
(☎92 3365-1023; www.pousada-belavista.com; Av Presidente Getulio Vargas 47; mains R$26-40; ⏲11:30am-9pm; 📶) The welcoming bar-restaurant at the Pousada Bela Vista has elevated Rio Negro views, decent service and nicely prepared food, from salads to steak and grilled fish. It's a small but carefully chosen menu. Nonguests welcome.

Shopping

★Fundação Almerinda Malaquias ARTS & CRAFTS
(FAM; ☎92 99398-6331, 92 3365-1000; www.fundacaoalmerindamalaquias.org; off Av Ajuricaba; ⏲7-11am & 1-5pm Mon-Fri, 8am-noon & 2-5pm Sat & Sun) 🌿 The shop for this local foundation, set up to help local community projects, has an excellent choice of mostly wooden crafts, from carved animals and canoes to notebooks. We especially liked the tiny box of 20 different Amazonian woods. If you come on weekdays and (sometimes) Saturday mornings, you'll see the local craftspeople at work.

Arte Waimiri Atroari ARTS & CRAFTS
(Av Presidente Getulio Vargas; ⏲8am-noon & 2-5pm Mon-Sat) This small shop at the entrance to the port sells crafts from the Waimiri Atroari indigenous people who live a day's journey north of Novo Airão, along the Rio Jauaperi. It's mostly basketwork, bows and arrows, hammocks and a handful of Portuguese-language books about the Waimiri Atroari.

Todo Mosaico ART
(☎92 98435-7331; buyehelen@gmail.com; Av Presidente Getulio Vargas; ⏲3-7pm Mon-Fri, from 9am Sat & Sun) This one-room showroom exhibits the eye-catching paintings (parrots are a recurring theme) of local artist Buy Chaves and the wood-sculpted furnishings of Helen Rossy. It's next to the entrance of Pousada Bela Vista and well worth a look.

Information

Banco Bradesco (Av João Paulo II; ⏲9am-3pm Mon-Fri, ATM 24hr) The town's only ATM.

Getting There & Away

BOAT

Riverboats travel a few times a week between Novo Airão and Manaus (R$48, nine to ten hours). From Manaus, they leave around 8pm on Tuesday and Friday. Going the other way, they depart Novo Airão's impressive (albeit rather under-used) port around 8pm on Sunday, Monday and Thursday.

BUS & SHARED TAXI

Collective taxi services (referred to locally as *taxi lotação*) are quick and plentiful, zipping between Manaus and Novo Airão ($60, 2½ hours) many times per day. The taxi stop in Manaus is on the westbound side of AM-070,

THE WAIMIRI ATROARI

The story of Brazil's relationship with the indigenous peoples of the Amazon is told in part through the story of the Waimiri Atroari people, whose 28,500 sq km Reserva Indígena Waimiri Atroari straddles Roraima and Amazonas states. Their homeland also sits just across the river from the Reserva Extrativista Baixo Rio Branco-Jauaperi, north of the Rio Negro.

When the first explorers, settlers and miners arrived in the territory of the Waimiri Atroari in the late 19th century, their population was close to 6000. Encroachment by outsiders and government efforts to 'civilize' indigenous groups saw increasing conflict throughout the 20th century as the local population fought for survival. This developed into open warfare in the late 1960s and early 1970s when the Brazilian government began construction of the BR-174 highway, which would ultimately connect Manaus with Boa Vista. As the conflict escalated, massacres of the Waimiri Atroari occurred with impunity – a 2014 government report found that the Waimiri Atroari population fell from 3000 in 1972 (the year that the road's construction began) to just 1000 in 1974. Disease, a tin mine and the building of the Balbina Dam all contributed further to this massive loss of life. By 1988, just 388 Waimiri Atroari people were believed to survive.

And yet, there is some evidence that the situation may have turned around through a combination of more enlightened government policies and growing self-reliance within the community. Intruders have been driven from Waimiri Atroari land, health and education infrastructure has been developed with the use of Waimiri Atroari staff, and, since 2016, the community closes the Manaus-Boa Vista highway from 6pm to 6am (an exception is made for buses) every night to protect the region's wildlife and wandering bands of hunters; the Roraima state government is currently suing the community for this act. Money is also flowing into the community thanks to government compensation schemes and a growing market for indigenous handicrafts: you can purchase Waimiri Atroari handicrafts at Galeria Amazônica (p616) in Manaus and Arte Waimiri Atroari in Novo Airão. A 2014 estimate suggested that the Waimiri Atroari population had recovered to 1749, with rumors that the number may be higher, with uncontacted bands of Waimiri Atroari living deep inside the reserve's dense forest.

about 700m before the bridge; taxis depart as soon as there are four passengers, from roughly 6am to 5pm, and will drop you at your hotel. Leaving **Novo Airão** (Av Ajuricaba), the stop is on the main drag at the northern (river) end of town; hotel drop-off in Manaus costs an extra R$40. Alternately, **Arauná buses** (✆92 3615-1110, Manaus 92 3642-5757; Av Ajuricaba) leave Manaus' bus station at 11:30am and 4pm, and leave Novo Airão at 5:30am and 4pm (R$50, four hours).

Reserva Extrativista Baixo Rio Branco-Jauaperi

This massive swathe of protected **rainforest** (Xixuaú-Xipariná) is a fantastic ecotourism destination and one of the best places to see wildlife in the Amazon. You'll need at least a week to get the best out of it, but expect to see up to ten primate species, giant river otters, dolphins, caimans and, if you're really lucky, jaguars, margays and ocelots.

The reserve is located 500km upstream from Manaus and stretches from the banks of the Rio Negro north for almost 400km. The Jauaperi River is the main access point and is accessible from Novo Airão. To the east, the Terra Indígena Waimiri-Atroari is safely locked away, while the Rio Branco National Park is to the west, linking a vast chain of protected areas across Brazil's northern Amazon region. The reserve remains one of the most pristine corners of the Amazon.

History

A reserve of some description was first proposed back in the 1980s in recognition of the region's intact forest and riverine ecosystems. Despite significant opposition, a decree was finally issued on June 5, 2018, granting status as an 'extractive reserve' (*reserva extratavista*, or RESEX). First imagined by Chico Mendes, extractive reserves allow locals to live inside the protected area and take what they need for subsistence, but not for commercial purposes. No more than 500 people live inside the reserve's boundaries.

Activities

Excursions include hiking and canoe trips through the flooded forest. You'll spend more time doing either one or the other depending on the water level and time of year. The forests tend to be flooded from February through to April with little dry land. Fishing is possible year-round.

This is an excellent area to spot wildlife. Commonly spotted animals include howler, capuchin, squirrel and saki monkeys; marmosets and tamarins; pink and gray dolphins; manatees; anacondas and boa constrictors; and macaws and toucans.

Tours

Although technically in southern Roraima state, the reserve is accessible via Novo Airão and the upper Rio Negro. Most tours here are handled by the excellent Visit Amazônia (p620), based in Novo Airão.

A week is the recommended minimum stay, but it's possible to visit for a shorter time if you come and go by speedboat. Visits start at €140 per person per day, and vary depending on length of stay, size of your group and mode of transport. In the far northern reaches of the reserve, the Xiparinã is even more of a lost world with manatees and all manner of other wildlife. A trip up here is a serious expedition, requiring at least two weeks from Manaus and costing €180 per person per day.

Other groups offering tours here include Expedição Katerre (p621) and Amazônia Expeditions (p609).

Sleeping & Eating

If you're traveling with Visit Amazônia (p620), accommodations are in simple stilted cabins across the water from Xixuaú village; rooms come with a shared toilet and mosquito nets, although malaria has been eradicated from the area. Larger groups can be accommodated in boats, which is where visitors from other tour companies stay.

As you'll need to join a tour to visit here, all your meals will be included in the price of your package. There are no restaurants or grocery stores, although you can catch your own fish or sometimes purchase fish from local fishers.

Getting There & Away

The only way to arrive here is on an organized tour. The main Xixuaú base is an eight-hour speedboat ride north from Novo Airão, although most boat trips take much longer.

Barcelos

0XX92 / POP 27,745

Quiet riverside Barcelos is no secret to fisherfolk, foreign and Brazilian alike, who flock to the small town for *tucanaré* (peacock bass) package tours. Fleets of yachts and riverboats serve eager khaki-clad anglers, and locals earn good money as guides and boat crew. Non-fishing tourism, however, is relatively rare, though not for lack of potential. Barcelos provides access to the world's largest river archipelago and Brazil's highest waterfall.

NATIONAL PARKS OF THE RIO NEGRO

Parque Nacional de Anavilhanas Stretching along the Rio Negro for almost 130km and with 400 islands, this national park, centered on the Anavilhanas Archipelago, is one of the most rewarding excursions in the Rio Negro Basin. When water levels are high, its flooded forests are most often visited on a day trip from Novo Airão. At other times, island beaches appear and camping overnight becomes possible.

The best tours here are run by Visit Amazônia (p620) and Expedição Katerre (p621).

Parque Nacional do Jaú Spanning nearly 23,000 sq km, Jaú is Brazil's second-biggest national park, and one of the largest tracts of protected tropical rainforest on earth. It stretches west from the Rio Negro along the Jaú and Carabinani rivers. The Unesco-listed park has a number of waterfalls, important stands of primary forest and a handful of access rivers. All of that said, visiting is less rewarding than the Reserva Extrativista Baixo Rio Branco-Jauaperi (p623).

Wildlife – including numerous primate species, big snakes, dolphins and sloths, as well as forest birdlife – is more difficult to see here than in some other areas, although the forest is impressive. There are no lodges in the park, so it's best to visit with a tour outfit that specializes in riverboat tours, such as Swallows & Amazons (p610) or Lo Peix (p609) in Manaus, or Em Cantos da Amazônia (p621) in Novo Airão. Advance booking is essential, as the operator must obtain special permission to enter the park.

Barcelos is adjacent to Mariuá Archipelago, the largest fluvial archipelago in the world (Anavilhanas is second) with over 750 islands and excellent beaches, canoeing and camping.

A word of warning: on our last trip here, very few independent tourists had been passing through and organizing excursions upon arrival had become quite difficult – try and line something up before you arrive in town.

Sights

★Serra do Aracá State Park WATERFALL, PARK

Although this state park was established in 1990 to preserve the unique canyons carved out by the Rio Aracá, it wasn't until recently that the massive waterfall at its heart was officially measured and certified. Turns out, Cachoeira do El Dorado is Brazil's highest waterfall, plunging 353m over a sandstone cliff into a mist-swept pool below.

Adventure tours to the waterfall take a minimum of 10 days and cost around R$250 to R$350 per person per day. Ask at Hostel Barcelos about arranging a trip; at least one month advance planning is required.

Arquipélago Mariuá NATURE RESERVE

(per person per day R$150) Hostel Manaus arranges engaging tours of various lengths to this massive collection of islands, the largest river archipelago in the world, southeast of Barcelos. You'll ply the winding waterways, visit island communities, sleep on the beach or in local homes, and look out for otters, macaws and other wildlife.

Praia Grande BEACH

This is Barcelos' biggest and most accessible beach. It's on an island directly opposite town and is a short boat ride (R$4) from the main dock. Shacks serve hot meals and cold drinks, especially on summer weekends. There are many smaller, more secluded beaches a bit further away, where boatmen can drop you off for a few hours.

Tours

Untamed Angling FISHING

(☎11 98181 8703; www.marieriver.com) This upscale fishing operator run tours into the Marié Fishing Reserve, centered on indigenous territory on the Marié River, close to the Colombia border west of Barcelos. They have their own guides, booking service and luxury accommodation boat; you'll need to book directly with them well in advance of your visit. Most trips fly in directly from Manaus.

Amazonas Mataverde ECOTUR

(☎92 9185-6071; per person per day R$150, food & lodging only R$75) Four hours by motorized canoe from Barcelos, this simple camp has good hiking and even better canoeing. You'll explore the islands and waterways of the labyrinthine Mariuá Archipelago, with a chance to see birds, turtles, dolphins, even river otters. It's operated by a young Spaniard and his Brazilian wife, who grew up in a nearby village; contact them directly or through Hostel Barcelos.

Sleeping & Eating

Hotel Rio Negro HOTEL $

(☎97 3321-1260; hotelrionegrobarcelos@hotmail.com; Av Mariuá 51; s/d R$90/130; ❄) An attractive, reliable choice that has large clean rooms with TV and air-conditioning; rear units have views of the river. The hotel also has its own pier and can arrange short fishing trips for people not interested in the big multiday packages.

Hostel Barcelos HOSTEL $

(☎97 99157-5271; www.hostelbarcelos.com; Anauali 46; hammock R$20, dm with fan $30, s/d with air-con R$40/80; 📶🏊) Comfortable rooms, a swimming pool, a laid-back vibe and an affable Luxembourger who serves a mean fruit-juice cocktail all make this the go-to spot for independent travelers arriving in Barcelos. Guests can make use of bicycles, kayaks, wi-fi and a collection of international movies. It's located near the airport; reservations essential.

The owner has info on a variety of guided and DIY excursions, including visiting an observation tower, ornamental fish farms, turtle breeding grounds and fruit farms with great birdwatching.

Camaleón Beach Grill BRAZILIAN $

(Tenheiro Aranha; mains R$12-45) A wooden stairway leads from the plaza down to platforms where umbrella-shaded tables have views overlooking the river and Praia Grande beyond. Grilled fish and meat are served with standard sides.

Information

MONEY

Banco do Brasil (Av Mariuá s/n; ⏲9am-2pm Mon-Fri) Central bank with forex facilities.

Bradesco (Av Mariuá s/n; ⏲9am-2pm Mon-Fri) Has an ATM.

TOURIST INFORMATION

Tourist Office (Av Mariuá s/n; ⌚ hours vary) Very limited assistance.

Getting There & Away

AIR

The **airport** is 1.5km southeast of the town center. MAP (p617) had temporarily stopped flights connecting Barcelos with Manaus and São Gabriel da Cachoeira at the time of writing. Check online to see if they've resumed.

BOAT

Various companies provide slow boat and speed-boat services between Porto São Raimundo (p617) in Manaus and Barcelos; be sure you're buying tickets from the correct operator for the day and time you want!

Slow boats leave Manaus for Barcelos (hammock/cabin R$140/350, 25 to 30 hours) on Tuesday, Wednesday and Friday at around 6pm, returning to Manaus on Monday, Wednesday, Thursday and Friday (various departure times). Speedboats with airplane-style seating make the same trip in about 12 hours, departing Manaus on Tuesday and Friday at 3pm (R$180) and leaving Barcelos the same days at 7pm.

São Gabriel da Cachoeira

☎0XX97 / POP 44,600

São Gabriel da Cachoeira is the Upper Rio Negro's largest town, but you'd never guess from its pleasant, laid-back vibe. The town sits on a lovely bend of the Rio Negro river, with a long series of rapids tumbling picturesquely by, and sandy beaches lapped by the Negro's blood-orange water. Outside São Gabriel, several buttes jut up from the rainforest, including a three-peaked mountain known as Bela Adormecida (Sleeping Beauty). The town has long been the jumping-off point for 10-day journeys up Brazil's highest peak, Pico da Neblina (2994m).

> **WARNING**
>
> Most of the forest around São Gabriel is Yanomami indigenous land and makes for great hiking and boating, but official permission is required to enter. The situation changes frequently, but at the time of research, guides in São Gabriel were having considerable difficulty getting permits. Yanomami leaders reportedly want tourists to use only indigenous guides, at an added cost. Some freelance guides will enter without permission, but you run a serious risk of being detained and possibly fined. Alternatively, there are a handful of places that do not require permission but still offer rewarding hiking, canoeing and wildlife-spotting. In any case, advance inquiries are strongly suggested.

Activities

Climbing mountains in the middle of the Amazon is a pretty cool reason to come to São Gabriel da Cachoeira. Forest excursions, including hiking and swimming, are also possible in the surrounding area. Pousada Pico da Neblina is a good place to inquire about trips of all kinds.

Mountain Climbing

Climbing **Bela Adormecida** (four to five days, R$250 per person per day, two person minimum) is the most popular excursion, and includes motoring up the ink-black Rio Curicuriari, with its picturesque rapids and rock formations, visiting Yanomami villages and hiking through towering rainforest to reach the thousand-meter peaks.

And don't forget **Pico da Neblina** (2994m), a rocky wedge awhirl in freezing fog, though the bureaucratic challenges of getting a permit to do so deter all but a few mountaineers.

Hiking & Swimming

If permission to enter Yanomami territory is not forthcoming, **camping trips** (from R$250 per person per day) can be arranged in non-indigenous areas, including hiking through animal-rich forest and swimming in low, chunky waterfalls.

Ilha do Sol is a long sandy island in the middle of the river opposite Barrio Praias. Boats ferry beach-goers from the shore to the island (R$3, five minutes), where you'll find a small restaurant and great swimming. Sundays are especially busy.

Sleeping & Eating

★ **Pousada Pico da Neblina** POUSADA $
(☎97 99511-1456; Capitão Euclides, Barrio da Praia; s/d R$45/70; ❄📶) Occupying a grand old mansion with views of São Gabriel's best beach, Pico da Neblina is used mostly for long-term rentals but reserves one room for travelers, with air-conditioning and wi-fi. Breakfast isn't included, but there are

several places to eat nearby. The breezy exterior passageways are nice for hanging up a hammock, and the Australian owner arranges excellent tours.

Hotel Deus Me Deu HOTEL $

(☎97 3471-1395; Av Presidente Castelo Branco 313; s/d R$70/120; ❄) This family-run hotel has clean rooms in the rear that are basic but perfectly acceptable; some have air-conditioning. The 2nd-floor reception area has a sunny patio with tables and chairs, overlooking the street.

La Cave Du Conde BRAZILIAN $$

(☎97 3471-1738; Brig Eduardo Gomes 444; mains R$14-48; ⏰7-10:30pm Tue-Sat) The refined menu, bar service and warm rustic ambience make this a pleasant surprise in the middle of the Amazon, but the main reason to come is to sample authentic regional and indigenous dishes, including São Gabriel's famous ant soup, made from fish, veggies, spices and a handful of bugs.

Information

MONEY

Banco do Brasil (Av Presidente Castelo Branco s/n; ⏰8am-1pm Mon-Fri)

Bradesco (Av Presidente Castelo Branco; ⏰8am-1pm Mon-Fri)

POST

Post Office (31 de Março; ⏰7:30am-noon & 1:30-4pm Mon-Fri)

Getting There & Away

AIR

The **Aeroporto de São Gabriel da Cachoeira** (☎97 3471-1343) is 15km east of town.

MAP (☎97 3471-2244, in Manaus 92-2125-5000; www.voemap.com.br) has flights between Manaus and São Gabriel da Cachoiera on Wednesday and Sunday.

BOAT

Both slow boats and speedboats travel along the Rio Negro between Manaus' Porto São Raimundo (p617) and São Gabriel da Cachoeira. Slow boats leave Manaus for São Gabriel (hammock R$390, 72 hours) at 5pm and 6pm on Fridays only. Speedboats leave from the same port on Tuesday and Friday at 3pm (R$450, 24 hours).

The return is slightly quicker, with slow boats departing São Gabriel Fridays at 8am and 9am on Tuesdays, and speedboats departing Tuesday and Friday at 9am.

Tefé

☎0XX97 / POP 64,000

A gritty, bustling city overlooking a massive lake, Tefé is best known as the jumping-off point to Reserva de Desenvolvimento Sustentável Mamirauá (Mamirauá Reserve), one of the best eco-destinations in the Amazon. But city leaders are working hard to convince Mamirauá-bound tourists to spend time in and around town, with options for hiking, boating and visiting local villages, including in the newly established Floresta Nacional de Tefé (FLONA Tefé). A trip to Mamirauá is still the best reason to visit Tefé, but travelers with an extra day or two will find some worthwhile ways to spend them here.

Sights

Floresta Nacional de Tefé FOREST

(FLONA Tefé) Spanning over a 10,000 sq km, Floresta Nacional de Tefé can be visited through various community-based tours. Most begin with a long boat ride across Tefé lake to small riverside communities within the reserve. Depending on the season, you'll have a chance to see and learn about essential activities like *farinha* (flour) production, açaí processing, Brazil nut collection and bee-keeping. Hike through the forest to encounter huge tropical trees and hopefully some monkeys and other wildlife.

Encontro das Aguas RIVER

(Meeting of the Waters) Tefé has a small Encontro das Aguas, where an offshoot of the creamy-brown Solimões merges with the red-black water pouring out of Lago de Tefé. It's an excellent place to spot pink dolphins.

Seminario San José ARCHITECTURE

(The Seminary; Praça Tulio Avevêdo) In town, Seminario San José is a striking structure that occupies the entire northern side of Praça Tulio Avevêdo. It was once a seminary and is now used for cultural and educational events.

Sleeping

★**Pousada Multicultura** POUSADA $

(☎97 99142-5340; www.multiculturatur.com; 15 de Junho 136; s R$85-150, d R$120-200; ❄📶) The UK-Brazilian couple who took over management of this popular guesthouse are maintaining all its best features – large comfortable rooms, tourist info for visitors – while making some great additions, including new tours and a restaurant-bar with views of Tefé lake.

Stylo's Hall Hotel HOTEL $
(☎97 3343-2337; www.facebook.com/styloshall; Rua Duque de Caxias 10; s R$90-150, d R$120-180) Wow! Every room here is beautifully decorated in the theme of a different country or city: Paris, Los Angeles, Israel and so on. Rooms are huge, with firm new beds and spotless bathrooms, and have gorgeous views of the river. It's located within steps of the speedboat pier, on the top floor of a shopping center.

Egas Hotel HOTEL $
(☎97 3343-6299; egashotel@hotmail.com; cnr Ruas Getúlio Vargas & Daniel Servalho; s R$115, d R$150-200; ❄📶) Large clean rooms, most opening onto breezy corridors, and a convenient location near both parks and opposite a bank and internet cafe.

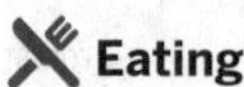

Eating

Restaurante Grão de Mostarda BRAZILIAN $
(☎97 3343-3730; www.facebook.com/restauranteepizzariagraodemostarda; Hermes Tupinambá; per kg R$41, mains R$15-36; ⏲11am-midnight Thu-Tue) Terrific per-kilo restaurant, with a breezy open-air dining room on the second floor and an air-conditioned area above that. Good-quality food and service make it popular with locals and visitors alike. Serves mostly pizza at night.

Restaurante Stylo BRAZILIAN $
(Floriano Peixoto 190; mains R$16-43; ⏲10am-11pm Mon-Sat) The most reliable place to eat in the center, with hefty, well-prepared dishes served at outdoor tables right on the street corner. The menu includes all the standards, plus a few less common ones, such as *lingua na brasa* (grilled tongue).

Restaurant Ki-Papo SELF-SERVE, BRAZILIAN $
(Av Juruá; per kg R$34; ⏲11am-3pm) Low-key per-kilo place with OK food and a fine panoramic view of Lago de Tefé. A short walk west of the center.

Information

EMERGENCY

Ambulance (☎192)
Police (☎190)

INTERNET ACCESS

There's free, reasonably reliable wi-fi in Praça Tulio Azevêdo, across from Banco do Brasil.

MEDICAL SERVICES

Hospital São Miguel (☎97 3343-2469; Bexiga) Public hospital.

MONEY

Banco do Brasil (Olavo Bilac, at Praça Tulio Azevêdo; ⏲9am-2pm Mon-Fri) Centrally located.

THE MAMIRAUÁ STORY

Nearly enclosed by the Solimões and Japurá rivers, Mamirauá is Brazil's largest area of intact *várzea*, a unique forest ecosystem defined by sediment-rich seasonal flooding. When the water is high (May to July), there is no exposed ground in the 11,400 sq km reserve. As the water recedes, it can leave behind (or strip away) a meter or more of soil. Huge islands – there are more than 1200 in the reserve – form and disappear seasonally, and a house that's built on 8-foot stilts may be at ground level in just a few years. Trees and plants have adapted to live for several months underwater, while normally ground-dwelling animals (from insects to jaguars) spend the same period exclusively in the treetops.

Mamirauá abuts two extractive reserves to the north and west, and the massive Amanã Reserve to the east, which in turn borders Jaú National Park (p624). Altogether, they span around 67,000 sq km – nearly the size of Ireland – and form the second-largest block of protected tropical rainforest in the world. (The largest is also in the Amazon, along the Guyana Shield.) Add in Indian reserves and the Reserva Extrativista Baixo Rio Branco-Jauaperi (p623) on the north bank of the Rio Negro, and the so-called mosaic of protected areas across the Central Amazon is starting to take on epic proportions.

Mamirauá was Brazil's first 'sustainable development reserve' (there are now more than 20) and is ably managed by the Instituto Mamirauá (www.mamiraua.org.br) in Tefé. Sustainable reserves are designed to ensure conservation and scientific research, while promoting sustainable practices and employment for the local population, including ecotourism. There are numerous small communities within the Mamirauá Reserve whose residents work part-time as tour guides, cooks, boat drivers, research assistants and nature wardens without abandoning traditional work such as fishing, planting and hunting. Management of the reserve and its primary lodge is due to revert to local control in 2022.

(Continued on page 637)

MARCUSVDT/SHUTTERSTOCK ©

Amazon Wildlife

A huge variety of animals call the Amazon home: piranha and pink dolphins ply the waters, macaws fill the air in squawking flight, squirrel monkeys dart through the trees, and tarantulas and poison dart frogs lurk in the underbrush. The lush rainforest and murky water can make spotting animals quite hard, but all the more rewarding when you do.

Contents

- Land Mammals
- Birds
- Aquatic Animals
- Reptiles, Insects & Amphibians

Above Harpy eagle (p633)

MYIMAGES - MICHA/SHUTTERSTOCK ©

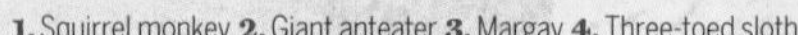

1. Squirrel monkey **2.** Giant anteater **3.** Margay **4.** Three-toed sloth

LUCIANO QUEIROZ/SHUTTERSTOCK ©

Land Mammals

Jaguar The Americas' largest cat, though Amazonian jaguars are smaller than those elsewhere. During the wet season, they can live for months entirely in the treetops, munching mainly on sloths. Where to see: Mamirauá, FLONA Tapajós, Upper Rio Negro

Margay Small cat that's a master climber, with paws that can rotate 180 degrees. Where to see: Mamirauá, Upper Rio Negro

Three-Toed Sloth A fairly common sight, sloths (or *preguiça* in Portuguese) are a favorite prey of jaguars and harpy eagles. Where to see: throughout the Amazon

Squirrel Monkey Aptly named, squirrel monkeys are tiny and agile, living in clans numbering into the hundreds. Where to see: throughout the Amazon

Capuchin Monkey Early explorers thought this small monkey's brown fur looked like the hooded cape of Capuchin friars. Where to see: throughout the Amazon

Howler Monkey The male howler's deathly cry can be heard for miles, though spotting the brown or black tree-dwellers can be tough. Where to see: Mamirauá, around Manaus

Coati Related to raccoons and similarly clever, coati have long tails and long, sensitive noses, which they use to forage for insects, lizards and other small prey. Where to see: throughout the Amazon

Giant Anteater Distantly related to sloths, Amazonian giant anteaters are skilled climbers, a trait useful for feeding on insect nests built in tree trunks. Where to see: throughout the Amazon, but difficult to spot

Brazilian Tapir Up to a meter tall and weighing over 200kg, tapirs are a prized but challenging prey for jaguars, caiman, even anaconda, and of course humans. Where to see: throughout the Amazon, but difficult to spot

Spider Monkey The largest and most intelligent of Amazon monkeys, spider monkeys are also among the most sensitive to human intrusion. Where to see: primary forest areas

HANS WAGEMAKER/SHUTTERSTOCK ©

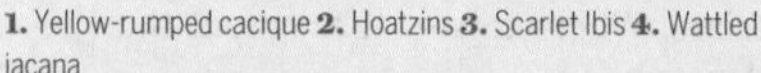

1. Yellow-rumped cacique **2.** Hoatzins **3.** Scarlet Ibis **4.** Wattled jacana

GUENTERMANAUS/SHUTTERSTOCK ©

Birds

Toucan Its long, colorful beak allows the toucan to crack hard nuts, but makes long flight difficult. Its distinctive whistle lets you know ones near. Where to see: throughout the Amazon

Ibis With long, curved beaks, the brilliant scarlet ibis, or *guará,* prefers mangroves and estuaries, while the larger green ibis is common further inland. Where to see: Algodoal, Ilha Marajó, around Manaus, Mamirauá

Macaw Known as *araras,* Amazonian macaws can be scarlet, green or blue. Macaws mate for life, and pairs can be seen (and heard) in long, squawking flights in the morning and evening. Where to see: throughout the Amazon

Amazon Parrot Catch-all name for various closely related species of parrots, mostly green with splashes of red, yellow or blue, and highly adept at mimicking human speech. Where to see: throughout the Amazon

Harpy Eagle Over a meter tall, harpy eagles are the Americas' largest raptors, known to snatch monkeys and sloths right out of trees. Where to see: throughout the Amazon, but difficult to spot

Hoatzin This pheasant-like bird may be a living link between dinosaurs and modern birds, with its reptilian appearance, poor flying, and claws on its chicks' wings. Where to see: Floresta Nacional do Tapajós, around Manaus, Upper Rio Negro, Mamirauá

Yellow-Rumped Cacique This talkative yellow-and-black bird is one of the most commonly seen birds in the Amazon, known for building its dangling bag-like nests near active wasps' nests. Where to see: throughout the Amazon

Wattled Jacana A common bird with a loud urgent call, found in wetlands throughout the Amazon. Male jacanas incubate the eggs, while females may maintain up to four active partners. Where to see: throughout the Amazon

1

2

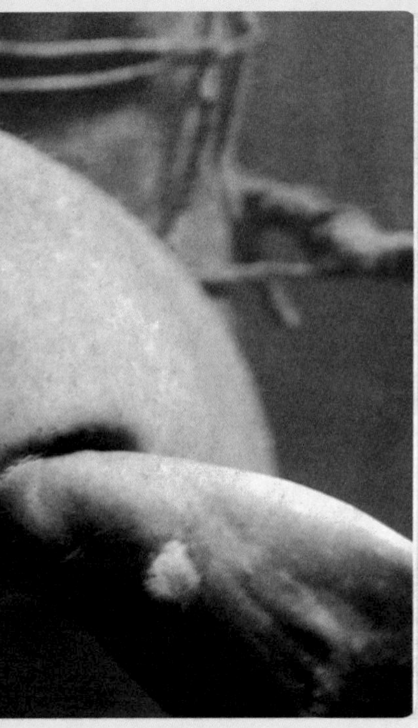

LUIZ FERNANDO SOUZA FERNANDES/GETTY IMAGES ©

1. Amazon manatee **2.** Boto **3.** Giant otter

Aquatic Animals

Giant Otter Up to 2m (6ft) long, giant otters are playful and social, though hunting and trapping (for their soft, extremely dense pelt) has reduced their numbers to critical levels. Where to see: Xixuaú-Xiparina Reserve, Upper Rio Negro

Boto The Amazon's famous pink dolphins are easy to spot, occurring in large numbers throughout the river system. Unlike other dolphins, *botos* can bend their necks and paddle backward, adaptions that help them navigate the flooded forest without getting stuck. Where to see: throughout the Amazon

Tucuxi The Amazon's 'other' dolphin looks and behaves much like a bottlenose dolphin, but grows to just 1.5m (5ft). Unlike *botos*, *tucuxi* do not venture into the flooded forest to feed. Where to see: throughout the Amazon

Amazon Manatee Although they grow to nearly 3m (10ft) and up to 450kg (1000lb), manatees are extremely difficult to spot in the wild and their precise numbers are unknown. Manatees gorge on aquatic plants during the wet season, and may fast for several months when the water is low. Where to see: Mamirauá

Pirarucú The world's largest scaled fish, *pirarucú* (also known as arapaima, outside the Amazon) can grow to 3m (10ft) and 220kg (480lb) and breathe air from the surface. Where to see: around Manaus, Mamirauá

Stingray Most Amazonian rays have distinctive spots and a nasty sting if you step on them. They are more closely related to Pacific rays than Atlantic ones, one of the clues that the Amazon originally flowed east to west. Where to see: throughout the Amazon

Piranha The Amazon's most famous fish is found through the river system, and ranges from 14cm to 26cm (5.5in to 10in). There are at least 30 species of piranha, including the small but aggressive red-bellied piranha. Contrary to myth, piranha rarely bite humans. Where to see: throughout the Amazon

Blue morpho buttterfly

Reptiles, Insects & Amphibians

Caiman Caiman are related to alligators and live throughout the Amazon. The largest type, black caiman, can grow to 6m (20ft), but most are 2m (7ft) or less. Where to see: throughout the Amazon

Anaconda The world's largest snake is known to grow up to 11m (37ft) and weigh more than 225kg (500lb), though stories of much larger ones abound. They live mostly in swamps and river channels, and eat fish, turtles, and occasionally caiman or land animals such as deer and rodents. Where to see: around Manaus, Mamirauá, but difficult to spot

Poison Dart Frog Most poison dart frogs are tiny (around 1.5cm) and brightly colored. Some secrete a powerful toxin, which indigenous Amazonians used to make their blow darts even more potent. Where to see: throughout the Amazon, but difficult to spot

Tarantula The Amazon has several species of huge, hairy arachnids, including one with a leg span of more than 33cm (13in). Most tarantulas live in burrows, and hunt insects, frogs, even small birds. Where to see: throughout the Amazon

Morpho Butterfly The brilliant metallic blue wings of the morpho butterfly have a way of brightening up any forest path. They can grow up to 20cm (8in) across, though most are somewhat smaller. Where to see: throughout the Amazon

Ants A single acre of Amazonian rainforest can have more than 3.5 million ants, and collectively ants make up 10% to 30% of the Amazon's total animal biomass. There are dozens of species, including leaf-cutter ants and aggressive bullet ants. Where to see: throughout the Amazon

(Continued from page 628)

Bradesco (cnr Ruas Getúlio Vargas & Daniel Servalho) A reasonably reliable ATM.

POST

Post Office (Estrada Aeroporto; ⌚8am-4pm Mon-Fri)

TOURIST INFORMATION

Instituto Mamirauá (☎97 3343-9700; www.mamiraua.org.br; Quintino do Caiúva; ⌚8am-noon & 2-6pm Mon-Fri, 8am-noon Sat) Oversees the Mamirauá Reserve and Pousada Uacari; stop in or call for info and reservations. English spoken.

TRAVEL AGENCIES

Pousada Multicultura (☎97 3343-5837; www.multiculturatur.com; 15 de Junho 136) The multilingual owners can purchase boat and plane tickets to and from Tefé for a 15% service fee, and have information about Mamirauá Reserve and other area tours and sights.

Getting There & Away

AIR

The **Aeroporto de Tefé** (www4.infraero.gov.br) is 5km southwest of the town center.

Azul (☎97 3343-9580; www.voeazul.com.br) Flies between Tefé and Manaus three times a week.

MAP (☎in Manaus 92 2125-5000; www.voemap.com.br) Has twice-weekly flights between Tefé and Manaus or Eirunepé.

BOAT

Slow boats between Manaus and Tefé (hammock R$175, double cabin R$650, 36 hours) depart in both directions five to seven days per week. Boats to and from Tabatinga (R$195, 40 to 48 hours) don't dock in Tefé proper; instead, take a boat to the village of Nogueira and taxi from there to Alvarães. Do the reverse if arriving from Tabatinga, but be aware that taxis and boats are available only during the daytime.

AJATO (☎97 3343-5306, in Manaus 92 3622-6047; ajatonavegacao@r7.com) has comfortable speedboat service to and from Manaus (R$270, 13 hours), with departures a few times per week at around 6am, and to and from Tabatinga ($460, 23 to 24 hours), with four departures weekly.

Advance reservations are recommended, especially for speed boats.

Mamirauá Reserve

The remarkable Mamirauá Sustainable Development Reserve has pristine rainforest, abundant animal life and fairly easy access, located just 1½ hours by boat from Tefé, with its reliable air and boat service. The primary lodge in the reserve runs outstanding tours and has comfortable accommodations – it's one of the Amazon's best ecotourism operations.

Activities

Boat safaris, traditional fishing and visits to local communities are all possible, alongside hiking or canoeing through the flooded forest; which of the latter two depends on the time of year and water levels.

Mamirauá is home to 35 mammal species, including 11 primate species, and 377 recorded bird species. Mamirauá's wildlife is more abundant and less skittish than that in other places. The reserve's signature creature is the uacari (wah-CAR-ee) monkey. However, you're much more likely to see howler, capuchin and the endemic black-faced squirrel monkeys, plus sloths, caimans, dolphins and

THE WHITE UAKARI MONKEY

One of the Amazon's most unusual inhabitants, the white uakari monkey, with its distinctive bald head and shaggy white coat, is one of the main reasons to visit Mamirauá Reserve. Indeed, its protection was a defining motive for setting up the reserve in the first place. Found nowhere else on earth, the white uakari monkey is more shy than either howler or squirrel monkeys, but it's nonetheless possible to see them on jungle hikes or along river margins, particularly close to sunrise or sunset.

Officially listed as endangered, the white uakari has a crimson or scarlet face and a very short tail. It inhabits the treetops and can travel almost 5km in a day through the canopy of the flooded forest on its quest for the seeds and fruits that dominate its diet. It is a particularly skilled jumper and such is its dependence upon an intact canopy that it is especially susceptible to deforestation. The monkeys live in groups of between five and 30 and can live for up to 30 years. Historically, their nickname among the local people was the 'English monkey,' so closely did their bright red faces resemble the sunburned faces of Anglo explorers!

MAMIRAUÁ'S JAGUARS

Mamirauá actually has Brazil's second-largest jaguar population, with a relatively stable population of approximately 1000 in the reserve alone. Sighting them is difficult, not least because of the sheer size and forest density of the reserve, and wildlife-watching takes place only in the reserve's far southeast. Even so, Pousada Uacari has a 'Jaguar Package.' Running only during a short window in June or July, when the forest is fully flooded and jaguars live in much smaller territories in the treetops, the package makes use of the radio collars placed on jaguars by research scientists. Sightings aren't guaranteed, but chances are high. At other times of the year, jaguar sightings are possible, but rare.

dozens of bird species, such as macaws, toucans and hoatzin. Manatees live in the reserve's waterways, too, while the margay (an arboreal cat) inhabits both the flooded and dry-land forest, but both are rarely spotted.

High water here is May to July, when the forest is completely flooded and you glide through the water in canoes. (This is not to be confused with rainy season, which runs from December to April.) This is when monkeys and sloths are most visible, and tends to be the busiest time. During low water, roughly September to November, hiking is possible and aquatic animals, especially fish and caimans, are more concentrated.

Tours

Untamed Angling FISHING
(☎11 98181 8703; www.untamedangling.com) This upscale fishing operator recently partnered with Pousada Uacari to host exclusive fly-fishing tours from September to November. Anglers stay at Uacari, but have their own guides and excursions, primarily targeting *pirarucú* (arapaima), the world's largest scaled fish, growing up to 3m (10ft) and 220kg (480lb). Book directly with the agency.

Sleeping

Pousada Casa do Caboclo LODGE $$
(☎97 99199-7822, 97 98804-8134; www.casadocaboclo.com; Boca de Mamirauá; per person per day R$300) The first and only authorized alternative to Pousada Uacari for travelers visiting the reserve. Simple rooms, shared toilets and not-so-comfy boats don't compete with Pousada Uacari for comfort or polish (especially during the midday heat), but it's a great option for budget travelers or those looking for a less-touristed spot.

It's located in Boca de Mamirauá, an aptly named community at the mouth of the reserve, and all tours are within the protected area. That means you'll see the same animals and vegetation. Guests can also can climb three observation towers left behind by a Japanese film crew – an unusual bonus.

It's run by an amiable local couple who spent years working as staff and guides at Uacari.

★ **Pousada Uacari** LODGE $$$
(☎97 3343-4160; www.uakarilodge.com.br; all-inclusive 3/4/7 nights s R$2740/3210/4410, d R$4980/5840/8020; 📶) Mamirauá Reserve's primary ecolodge is built entirely on floating logs and parked on a lovely river bend well into the reserve. Spacious bungalows have hot-water bathrooms, fans and a small patio with hammock; generous, delicious meals are served in a large common area. Guided excursions include paddling through the forest, dolphin-spotting trips, and visiting a local community, while researchers give interesting lectures.

An English-speaking naturalist is at the main lodge at all times (and accompanies some excursions), but most guides speak Portuguese only. There are special packages for jaguar spotting, birdwatching and photography that include a private guide and a superior room.

Getting There & Away

Transfers from Tefé's airport or river port are included in most packages offered by the pousadas.

The Triple Frontier

Tabatinga

☎0XX97 / POP 59,000

The Brazilian town of Tabatinga is most notable as the place where the Amazon River enters Brazil. Tabatinga and the Colombian town of Leticia lie side by side on the eastern bank of the Amazon river, about 1100km west of Manaus, while the far bank belongs to Peru. A logical travel hub, the 'triple frontier' also happens to be a good area for taking jungle trips, particularly to remote areas up the Rio Javari (the Brazil–Peru border) and further up the

Amazon in Colombia. Most travelers stay in Leticia, which is more pleasant and better equipped than Tabatinga or the small villages on the Peruvian side.

Sights

Centro de Interpretación Natütama MUSEUM

(by donation; 8am-noon & 2-5pm Wed-Mon) The Centro de Interpretación Natütama has a fascinating museum with nearly 100 life-sized wood carvings of Amazonian flora and fauna. There's also a small turtle hatchery outside. Located on the riverfront just east of the docks.

Sleeping

Novo Hotel HOTEL $

(97 3412-3846; novohoteltbt@hotmail.com; Pedro Texeira 9; s/d/tr R$55/80/110;) Conveniently located just three blocks from Porta da Feira, this welcoming, clean option is perfect if you're catching an early boat.

Hotel Takana HOTEL $

(97 3412-3557; Oswaldo Cruz 970; s/d R$95/125, ste R$150-170;) Tabatinga's best hotel has modern rooms, with hot water, air-conditioning, TV and minibar, plus a lush central courtyard. A bit removed from the main drag, but that's not necessarily a bad thing. Suites are larger and have king-size beds. Some rooms are a little sterile, with white-tiled floors and aging wooden bedheads. Others are stylish, with chessboard floors and bold colors.

Eating

Restaurante Tres Fronteiras do Amazonas BRAZILIAN, PERUVIAN $

(97 3412-2341; Rui Barbosa; mains R$20-45; 7am-9pm) This attractive palm-thatched open-air restaurant has a wide choice of fish and meat dishes, plus a selection of drinks, including cheap caipirinhas. The food is an odd Brazilian-Colombian-Peruvian hodgepodge and the menu is in Portuño – an unsystematic mixture of Portuguese and Spanish. Located 200m west of Av da Amizade.

Churrascaria Tia Helena BRAZILIAN $$

(97 3412 2165; Marechal Mallet 12; buffet R$32; noon-9pm) At this delicious all-you-can-eat restaurant, waiters bring skewered meats directly from the grill and carve them up at the table in classic Brazilian fashion. The place is no-frills; think cement floors and fluorescent lights.

The Triple Frontier

★ São Jorge PERUVIAN $$

(97 3385-1274; Av da Amizade 1941; mains R$18-45; 9am-9:30pm Mon-Sat, to 6pm Sun) Residents on both sides of the border rave about the authentic ceviche at this simple Peruvian-run spot: the mountainous pile of excellent citrus-cooked fish and onions served on a bed of sweet potatoes and chunky corn feeds two. It seems strange to walk from Colombia to Brazil for Peruvian ceviche, but that's the beauty of the tri-border!

Drinking & Nightlife

Bar Mirador BAR

(Rua T-11; noon-9pm) A dead-simple Brazilian drinking den that is a spectacular spot for a cold sunset beer overlooking the Amazon. It's about 50m up the hill from the Posto Policial (Police Post) in Barrio Dom Pedro, just south of the floating dock. You have to walk through somebody's ramshackle backyard to enter!

Scandalos CLUB

(97 3412-2712; cnr Av da Amizade & Rua Pedro Texeira; cover R$10; 9pm-4am Fri & Sat) Some people in Tabatinga told us this club was 'un-Christian, immoral and homosexual,' which means, of course, it's awesome! Located about five blocks from the border, it attracts a young, sexy crowd dancing till dawn.

A QUESTION OF TIME

Tabatinga is the same time zone as Manaus (GMT minus four hours), which is technically an hour ahead of Leticia. In practice, however, most businesses in Tabatinga adjust their official hours to fall into line with Leticia. Always check carefully if you're counting on a particular set of opening hours.

Information

EMBASSIES & CONSULATES

Colombian Consulate (97 3412-2104; http://tabatinga.consulado.gov.co; Sampaio 623; 7am-1pm Mon-Fri)

EMERGENCY NUMBERS

Police (190)

ENTRY & EXIT FORMALITIES

Polícia Federal (97 3412-2180; Av da Amizade 26; 8am-6pm) One hundred meters south of Rua Duarte Coelho.

MEDICAL SERVICES

Hospital de Guarnição de Tabatinga (97 3412-2403, 192; Duarte Coelho, at Av da Amizade) Large public hospital.

MONEY

Bradesco (Av da Amizade, at Av Marechal Mallet; 9am-2pm Mon-Fri) Reliable ATM.

POST

Post Office (97 3412-2442; Av da Amizade 1087; 8am-5pm Mon-Fri)

TOURIST INFORMATION

Tourist Information Center (Centro de Informação Turística; Av da Amizade s/n; 8am-6pm Mon-Fri, to noon Sun) Limited help.

Getting There & Away

AIR

The **airport** (97 3412-1100; www4.infraero.gov.br) is 4km south of Tabatinga; coming from Leticia, catch one of the *coletivos* marked 'Comara.'

Azul (97 3412-1124, reservations 0800-887-1118; www.voeazul.com.br) is the only airline operating here, with one flight most days to and from Manaus.

BOAT

Slow boats to Manaus (hammock/cabin R$400/1620; seven days) leave from the Porto Fluvial every Wednesday and Saturday, plus some Tuesdays, between 8am and 2pm. Arrive early to stake out good hammock space, as boats can be quite crowded.

AJATO speedboats (92 3412-2227, in Manaus 92 3622-6047; 8am-5pm Mon-Fri, to noon Sat) leave Tabatinga for Manaus (R$600, 36 hours) on Tuesday, Thursday, Saturday, and Sunday mornings.

To get to Tefé, the Sunday and Thursday speedboats to Manaus now make a stop in Tefé proper. Otherwise, take a Manaus-bound slow boat as far as Alvarães (R$165, 44 to 48 hours), where you can catch a shared taxi to the village of Nogueira (R$12, 20 minutes) and then a motorboat (R$12, 20 minutes) into Tefé; note that taxis and local boats only operate during the day time.

Bear in mind that departure days and times change regularly; always check in advance.

Getting Around

For a *coletivo* (minibus) from the airport to town (R$3), walk to the left outside the airport terminal and down the approach road to the corner of the main road. Some continue into Leticia.

A taxi from the airport costs R$25 to R$30 to hotels in Tabatinga and R$40 to those in Leticia. Moto-taxis are ubiquitous and cheap (R$5 to R$10), but most cannot cross the international border.

Leticia (Colombia)

The capital city of the Amazonas province, Leticia is the largest settlement for hundreds of kilometers and yet still looks and feels very much like the small frontier town it is. Located on the Amazon River where Colombia, Brazil and Peru meet, Leticia is some 800km from the nearest Colombian highway. It's a bustling town abuzz with fleets of motorcycles, with a few minor sights to entertain you for a day or two.

Notwithstanding the oppressive heat, stultifying humidity and ferocious mosquitoes, Leticia is a pleasant enough town but not a destination in itself: it's a stepping stone for visiting the tropical rainforest that's right on your doorstep, with remote jungle lodges and indigenous communities just a short boat ride away along the Rio Amazonas.

Sights

★Mundo Amazónico GARDENS

(8-592-6087, 321-472-4346; www.mundoamazonico.com; Km7.7, Via Tarapacá; tours COP$10,000; 8am-3pm Mon-Sat) This 29-hectare reserve works as a center for environmental education and makes for a great place to get to know something of the plants, trees and inhabitants of the jungle before you set out on an expedition. The

BORDER CROSSINGS

To/From Colombia

The international border is marked by nothing more than a few moneychangers on the Brazilian side and a Colombian police officer directing traffic on the other side. You are free to move between Tabatinga and Leticia as much as you like, but if you plan to travel onward, even to Amacayacu National Park, you should clear immigration for both countries before leaving town. There's a Colombian Consulate (p640) in Tabatinga.

To/From Peru

High-speed passenger boats between Tabatinga and Iquitos (Peru) are operated by **Transtur** (in Iquitos 51 6529-1324; www.transtursa.com; Jirón Raymondi 384) and **Transportes Golfinho** (Iquitos 51 65-225-118; www.transportegolfinho.com; Marechal Mallet 306, Tabatinga). Boats depart Tabatinga's Porto da Feira daily around 5am, Brazilian time (boarding begins an hour earlier) arriving in Iquitos about 10 hours later; fares are US$75 each way. Be sure to get a Brazilian exit stamp the day before; you'll stop first at the island community of Santa Rosa, where the Policía Internacional Peruviano (PIP) handles Peruvian border control. If you're staying in Leticia, be aware that nighttime taxi rates are triple the daytime rate. Be warned, too, that there are slower, cheaper boats to Iquitos, but they are not comfortable and some are unsafe.

If you just want to get to Santa Rosa, small motorboats go back and forth frequently from Porto da Feria (R$4, five minutes) from around 6am to 6pm.

There's a Peruvian consulate in Leticia, Colombia.

extensive botanical gardens boast some 700 species of flora that can be visited on four differently themed tours (the botanical garden, sustainable processes, cultural presentations and the aquarium), each lasting between 30 and 45 minutes and leaving every hour until 2pm.

Museo Etnográfico Amazónico MUSEUM
(8-592-7783; Carrera 11 No 9-43; 8:30am-6pm Mon-Fri, 9am-1pm Sat) FREE This little museum has a small but thorough collection of indigenous artifacts. Learn about *malocas* (ancestral longhouses) and *chagras* (indigenous production systems) and peruse the musical instruments, textiles, tools, pottery, weapons and many ceremonial masks. Labeled in English, the museum makes a good introduction to the indigenous cultures of the region, such as the Huitotos, Yukunas and Ticunas.

Activities

Amazon Jungle Trips TOURS
(321-426-7757; www.amazonjungletrips.com.co; Av Internacional No 6-25) With more than 25 years of experience catering to backpackers, Amazon Jungle is one of the oldest and most reliable tour companies in Leticia. Owner Antonio Cruz Pérez speaks fluent English and can arrange individually tailored tours, including trips to the two very different reserves the company runs: **Zacambú** (321 426-7757; www.amazonjungletrips.com.co; COP$290,000 per person per day all inclusive) and **Tupana Arü Ü** (321-426-7757; www.amazonjungletrips.com.co).

Sleeping

★**Hostel Casa de las Palmas** HOSTEL $
(321-435-2114; www.casadelaspalmasleticia.com; Carrera 11 No 13-110; dm/r COP$25,000/65,000;) Designed with the comfort of backpackers in mind, this friendly hostel consists of a clutch of snug, spotless rooms, with a wonderful pool and garden area round back, fresh fruit and coffee for breakfast and plenty of helpful advice from the staff. Their jungle tours get glowing reports from the guests, too.

★**Pirañita Hostel** HOSTEL $
(313-209-2671; Calle 8 No 6 - 42; dm/s/d COP$24,000/65,000/75,000;) Sociable without being a crush-your-beer-can-against-your-forehead party hostel, the 'Little Piranha' features the eponymous fish motif throughout its spotless rooms and greenery-festooned common areas. Air-con is a boon in sweaty Leticia and the friendly bilingual owners are happy to organize group activities, from guest barbecues to jungle trips. Walls are on the thin side.

Leticia (Colombia)

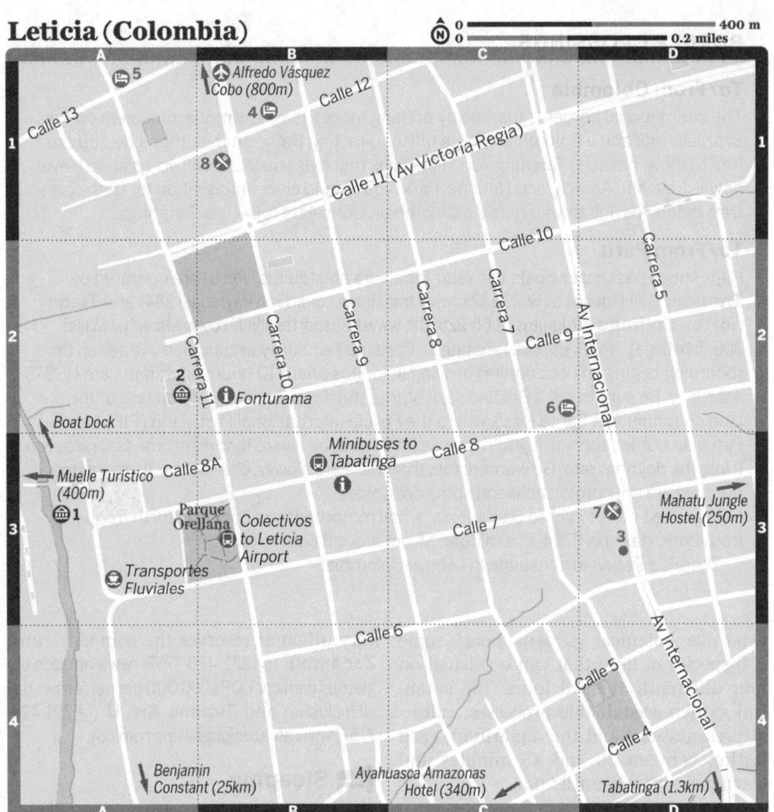

Leticia (Colombia)

Sights

1 Centro de Interpretación Natütama........A3
2 Museo Etnográfico Amazónico........A2

Activities, Courses & Tours

3 Amazon Jungle Trips........D3

Sleeping

4 Amazon B&B........B1
5 Hostel Casa de las Palmas........A1
6 Pirañita Hostel........C2

Eating

7 El Cielo........D3
8 El Santo Angel........B1

Ayahuasca Amazonas Hotel HOTEL $$
(☎316-373-1359, 8-592-4356; ayahuascaamazonas hotel@yahoo.es; Carrera 10 No 3-28; r/bungalow from COP$130,000/160,000; ❄📶) Despite being named for the hallucinogenic indigenous brew, this is no retreat for self-discovery, just an immaculately clean and friendly family-run hotel in a bustling residential neighborhood by the Brazilian border. While the owners speak no English, they look after their guests very well, and can arrange tours and expeditions into the rainforest. There's also a hot tub to relax in.

★ **Amazon B&B** B&B $$$
(☎8-592-4981; www.amazonbb.com; Calle 12 No 9-30; s/d incl breakfast COP$165,000/228,000, cabaña d/tr/f COP$280,000/350,000/420,000; ❄📶) Leticia's most charming and stylish option, this hotel comprises six cabañas and four rooms surrounding a gorgeous tropical garden. The cabañas are spacious and come with high ceilings, well-stocked minibars and small, enclosed terraces with hammocks. Big discounts are available out of season, but note that only two rooms have air-con; the others are fan-cooled.

Eating

There are a number of good restaurants in Leticia, although they mostly open only in the evenings. Leticia's specialty is fish, including the delicious *gamitana* and *pirarucú*, which is best avoided out of season as some locals ignore bans on catching the species when spawning. Prices can be higher than in 'mainland' Colombia, but many restaurants serve cheap set meals.

★ **El Cielo** AMAZONIAN $$
(☎320-454-4569; Av Internacional No 6-11; mains COP$17,000-33,000; ⊙4-11pm Mon & Wed-Sat, 11am-5pm Sun;) The pinnacle of culinary sophistication in Leticia, this cool, creative space serves *casabes* (mini-pizzas made from yuca instead of flour) with imaginative toppings, including *pirarucú* (a popular local fish) and *tucupi* (a cassava extract). Despite the busy location on the main road, its pleasantly lit gravel garden is a lovely place for a meal.

★ **El Santo Angel** INTERNATIONAL $$
(☎8-592-3866; www.facebook.com/elsantoangeld; Carrera 10 No 11-119; mains COP$15,000-37,000; ⊙4pm-midnight Tue-Sun;) With one of the most varied and interesting menus in town, Santo Angel is a popular place for an evening meal. Diners spill out all over the street, and there's often live (but not ear-splitting) musical entertainment. On offer are wraps, nachos, salads, grills, pita bread, burgers and pizza, as well as German beers.

Information

CONSULATES

Brazilian Consulate (☎8-592-7530; Calle 9 No 9-73; ⊙8am-5pm Mon-Fri) Obtain Brazilian visas here.

Peruvian Consulate (☎8-592-7755; Calle 11 No 5-32; ⊙8am-noon & 2-4pm Mon-Fri) If you're coming from or going to Iquitos, head here to get your entry or exit stamp.

EMERGENCY

San Rafael de Leticia Hospital (☎8-592-7826; www.esehospitalsanrafael-leticia-amazonas.gov.co; Carrera 10 No 13-78) Basic medical services; for anything serious, it's best to fly to Bogotá.

A yellow fever vaccination is recommended 10 days before arrival; make sure to bring your yellow fever certificate with you.

INTERNET ACCESS

Sluggish internet speeds plague Leticia, though nearly every hotel and most restaurants have free wi-fi.

MONEY

There are ATMs in the town center, especially along Carrera 10 between Calles 7 and 10, and *casas de cambio* on Calle 8 between Carrera 11 and the market. Shop around; exchange rates vary.

TOURIST INFORMATION

Leticia's small **tourist office** (Secretaría de Turismo y Fronteras; ☎8-592-4162; Calle 8 No 9-75; ⊙8am-noon & 2-5pm Mon-Fri, 8am-1pm Sat) is helpful and friendly.

Fonturama (Fondo de Promoción y Desarrollo Turístico del Amazonas; ☎8-592-4162; www.fonturamazonas.org; Carrera 11 No 9-04; ⊙9am-noon & 2-7pm Mon-Sat) has info on sustainable tourism in the region.

Getting There & Away

AIR

All foreigners must pay a COP$32,000 tourist tax upon arrival at Leticia's airport, **Aeropuerto Internacional Alfredo Vásquez Cobo** (Carrera 10), to the north of town. Taxis into town cost around COP$10,000; if traveling light, hop on a moto-taxi.

Avianca (www.avianca.com) and Latam (www.latam.com) have several daily flights to Bogotá.

Tabatinga International Airport has flights to Manaus daily with Azul (www.voeazul.com.br). The airport is 4km south of Tabatinga; *colectivos* (shared taxis, minivans, or midsize buses) marked 'Comara' from Leticia will drop you nearby. Don't forget to get your Colombian exit stamp at Leticia's airport and, if needed, a Brazilian visa before departure.

When departing Leticia's airport, all foreigners must check in at **Migración Colombia** (☎8-592-7189; www.migracioncolombia.gov.co; Aeropuerto Internacional Alfredo Vásquez Cobo; ⊙7am-6pm Mon-Fri, 7am-4pm & 7pm-10pm Sat & Sun) before proceeding through airport security, regardless of whether they're leaving Colombia or not; you'll be directed there after check-in if you haven't done it already – it's a painless and free procedure that takes a matter of seconds.

BOAT

Buy tickets for Puerto Nariño and other points upriver from one of the three agencies at **Transportes Fluviales** (☎311-486-9464, 311-532-0633; Malecon Plaza, Carrera 12 No 7-36). Boats to Puerto Nariño depart from Leticia's **Muelle Turístico** at 7am, 9am, noon and 2pm daily (COP$31,000, two hours). Arrive in good time for your boat, as the dock can be hard to find. You'll need your passport when buying tickets.

If you're departing from Tabatinga, be aware that it is one hour ahead of Leticia. Don't miss your boat!

UNCONTACTED

Anthropologists believe there may be more than 150 uncontacted indigenous groups worldwide (defined as a group with no peaceful contact with mainstream society). Nearly two-thirds of these live in the Brazilian and Peruvian Amazon.

Arriving at those numbers and estimating how many people belong to each group is difficult but not impossible. Contacted tribes often tell of uncontacted families living in remote areas of their territories. Occasionally members of an uncontacted group will emerge from the jungle, having left or been expelled from their land. Experts believe most groups have seen or even encountered outsiders – and have probably seen and heard airplanes. Funai, Brazil's federal indigenous affairs agency, employs researchers who study footprints, abandoned huts and other clues to track uncontacted groups and produce a rough census. Funai policy is that although they seek evidence of such groups' existence, they have not sought to make contact with them for the past three decades. Even so, conflicts are common and massacres of previously uncontacted groups continue to be reported across the Amazon.

Officially, 107 uncontacted groups are believed to live in Brazil's Amazonas and Rondônia states. In the latter, at least three are thought to remain in the Uru-eu-Wau-Wau indigenous reserve, in the center of the state. The reserve suffers rampant illegal mining and logging, and uncontacted groups have retreated ever deeper into the forest. Rondônia is also home to an indigenous man believed to be the last member of an unknown tribe. Described as 'the world's loneliest man,' he is possibly the only survivor of an attack on his people by farmers in 1995. He has refused all contact, despite being surrounded by pastures and plantations. He is sometimes called the 'man in the hole' because he has a hole in his hut, protected by sharp spikes, where he hides when outsiders approach. After gunmen attempted to kill him in 2009 (presumably ranchers or their henchmen) Funai allotted the man a 4000-hectare territory and restricted all future contact. For the complete account, pick up a copy of Monte Reel's excellent book *The Last of the Tribe* (2010). In 2018, Funai released covertly filmed footage of the man to prove that he was still alive, a prerequisite to continuing the restrictions upon encroachment by farmers and others who surround the reserve.

In August of the same year, a Funai expedition into the remote Vale do Javari, close to the Rio Javari, filmed 16 people from what is believed to an uncontacted group moving through a forest clearing. An estimated 11 such groups are believed to inhabit this remote area in Amazonas state.

For information on uncontacted groups generally, see **Survival International** (www.survivalinternational.org).

Getting Around

The main mode of public transportation is moto-taxis, with folks on motorcycles who zip around town with an extra helmet. The base rate is COP$2500. Frequent *coletivos* (COP$2500 to COP$7000) link Leticia with Tabatinga and the 'Kilometer' villages north of Leticia's airport. There are **minibuses to Tabatinga** (Cnr Carrera 10 & Calle 8) and **colectivos to Leticia airport** (Parque Orellana).

Puerto Nariño (Colombia)

The Amazonian village of Puerto Nariño, 75km upriver from Leticia, is an inspiring example of human coexistence with nature. Here, cars are banned (the only two vehicles are an ambulance and a truck for collecting recyclables), rainwater is pooled in cisterns for washing and gardening, and electricity comes from the town's fuel-efficient generator, which runs only until midnight. Every morning, citizen brigades fan out to tidy up the town's landscaped sidewalks, and Puerto Nariño's ambitious recycling and organic-waste management programs would put most world cities to shame. As a contrast to dirty and polluted Leticia, it couldn't be more stark.

The majority of Puerto Nariño's residents are indigenous Ticuna, Cocoma and Yagua peoples. Their community experiment in ecological living has made ecotourism an important source of income, and this tranquil place is a great base from which to visit beautiful Lago Tarapoto and the Amazon in general.

Sights & Activities

Communing with nature is the main activity here. You can rent a kayak for around COP$15,000 and go in search of river dolphins, and jungle guides can take you on day treks and night walks. Your accommodations can help organize any of these.

★ Lago Tarapoto LAKE

Lago Tarapoto, 10km west of Puerto Nariño, is a beautiful jungle lake fed by the Río Amazonas, and is home to pink dolphins, a tiny population of manatees and massive water lilies. A half-day trip to the lake in a *peque-peque* (a low-slung wooden boat) from Puerto Nariño (around COP$50,000 for up to four people for around four hours) is the main draw for visitors, who usually take a dip in the gorgeously clear water. Piranha fishing is also possible here.

Mirador Nai-pata VIEWPOINT

(Calle 4; adult/child COP$5000/3000; ⊙7am-6pm Mon-Fri, 8am-5pm Sat & Sun) For a bird's-eye view of the village and the surrounding jungle and Amazon, climb this impressive wooden tower (*'nai-pata'* means 'treehouse' in the Ticuna tongue), on the top of a hill in the center of the village. Cool down afterwards with an ice cream next to the tower.

Sleeping & Eating

★ Alto de Aguila - Cabañas del Fraile CABAÑAS $

(☎314-201-3154, 311-502-8592; altodelaguila@hotmail.com; dm COP$20,000, r per person with/without bathroom COP$30,000/25,000) In the jungle outside the village, friar Hector José Rivera and his delightful monkeys run this hilltop oasis overlooking the Amazon. The complex includes several simple huts, shared facilities and a lookout tower. Between the monkeys, turkeys, dogs and macaws roaming about, there's a real menagerie to enjoy, along with utter isolation and free use of canoes on the Amazon.

★ Maloca Napü GUESTHOUSE $

(☎314-437-6075, 315-607-4044; www.malocanapu.com; Calle 4 No 5-72; dm COP$20,000, r per person with/without balcony COP$30,000/25,000; @) Perhaps the most charming guesthouse in Puerto Nariño, Maloca Napü has the look and feel of a tree-house fort, surrounded as it is by a thickly forested garden. The rooms are simple but comfortable, with fans, shared bathroom with super-refreshing rain-style showers, and fully equipped kitchen. Everyone who works here is above-and-beyond friendly.

Las Margaritas COLOMBIAN $$

(☎311-276-2407; Calle 6 No 6-80; set-price meals COP$15,000; ⊙noon-3pm) Under a huge *palapa* (thatched roof) just beyond the soccer pitch, lunch-only Las Margaritas is the best restaurant in Puerto Nariño, even if it's rather pricey by local standards and aimed almost entirely at visiting tour groups. The all-you-can-gobble buffet-style meals are delicious, though, and involve fish, chicken, *patacones* (fried plantains) and salad.

Information

INTERNET ACCESS

What little internet exists here is snail-slow and will remind you of the bad old days of dial-up.

MONEY

There are no banks or ATMs in Puerto Nariño, and credit cards are not accepted anywhere, so bring plenty of cash from Leticia if you plan to do excursions into the jungle from here, as costs can add up quickly.

TOURIST INFORMATION

There's a small **tourist office** (cnr Carrera 6 & Calle 5; ⊙8am-noon & 2-5pm Mon-Fri) inside the town hall.

Getting There & Away

High-speed boats to Puerto Nariño depart from Leticia's dock at 7am, 9am, noon and 2pm daily (COP$30,000, two hours); return-trip boats to Leticia depart at 7am, 10am, 1:30pm and 3:30pm.

You can purchase tickets at **Transportes Fluviales** (☎8-592-6752; Muelle Turistico). In Leticia boats can get very full, so buy your tickets early or the day before.

RORAIMA

The tropical rainforest that blankets Roraima's southern half (bisected by the equator) gives way to broad savanna in the middle of the state, and remote and beautiful mountains in the north. The state includes most of the Brazilian territories of the Yanomami, one of the country's largest surviving indigenous peoples. This could be one of the Amazon's most varied playgrounds, but it's yet to really take off – the state capital, Boa Vista, still doesn't make the itinerary of most travelers and opportunities for getting beyond city limits are limited. Also, the troubled

UP RIVER, DOWN RIVER

For 150 million years after South America and Africa went their separate ways, the Amazon river actually flowed east to west, the opposite direction to which it flows today. That's why Amazonian stingrays are most closely related to Pacific species, and how telltale sediment from eastern South America ended up in the middle of the rainforest. It was only 15 to 20 million years ago that the Andes shot up and blocked the river's westward exit. Around the same time, a smaller ridge of land, now called the Purus Arch, rose like a spine in the middle of the continent.

East of the Purus Arch the river started draining into the Atlantic Ocean, but west of there, the water was trapped and a huge inland sea formed. Sediment deposited during that period form the sandy soil typical of the Amazon today. Eventually the water poured over the Purus Arch, gouging a deep channel near present-day Óbidos – still the narrowest and deepest part of the river – and the Amazon returned to being a river, but now flowing west to east.

situation in Venezuela across the border means that tourism has taken a back seat for now.

Roraima is home to Monte Roraima (2875m), and although this intriguing flat-topped mountain sits right on the Brazil-Venezuela-Guyana border, the best way up is from the Venezuelan side.

Boa Vista

☎0XX95 / POP 325,000

Unless you're on your way to Guyana or Venezuela, there's little reason to visit Boa Vista. It's a pleasant enough riverside town with all the comforts and facilities of a medium-sized Brazilian city. But with Venezuela in a state of turmoil and considerable numbers of Venezuelans fleeing the country, Boa Vista's infrastructure was under considerable strain as of our last visit. When Venezuela returns to peace, Boa Vista will once again be a way station en route to Venezuela's beautiful high plains.

Sights

Cathedral CATHEDRAL

(Av Ville Roy) The soaring concave facade and gleaming white paint make this modern church hard to miss, especially as it faces Boa Vista's main plaza.

Praia Grande BEACH

A tawny sandbar beach emerges on the far bank of the Rio Branco during low water, roughly December to April. Known as Praia Grande, it is indeed big and beachy, and makes for a pleasant afternoon visit. Its transitory existence means there is no shade – bring an umbrella or consider waiting until the afternoon. **Porto do Babazinho** (☎95 3624-8382; Av Major Williams 1) runs a ferry service for R$5 round-trip, and can provide food and drinks. Be alert for stingrays. It's opposite Boa Vista.

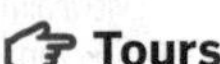

Tours

Sebastião de Souza e Silva ADVENTURE

(☎95 9111-3511; babazinhorr@yahoo.com; Av Major Williams 1) Porto do Babazinho is the home base for longtime local guide Sebastião de Souza e Silva (aka Babazinho), who leads and arranges a variety of adventure outings, from windsurfing lessons and rentals to daylong and multiday hiking, canoeing and animal-spotting excursions, all at reasonable rates.

Roraima Adventures TOURS

(☎95 3624-9611; www.roraima-brasil.com.br; Coronel Pinto 97; ⌚8am-noon & 2-6pm Mon-Fri, 8am-noon Sat) Organizes professional multiday camping tours all over Roraima, including Serra do Tepequém and Mt Roraima in Venezuela, and even into the Yanomami Reserve (provided that permits can be secured).

Sleeping

Hotel Euzébio's HOTEL $

(☎95 2121-0300; www.hoteleuzebios.com.br; Cecília Brasil 160; s/d standard R$92/126, superior R$138/172; ❄📶🏊) Standard rooms are clean but small; superiors are bigger, more cheerful and come with hot water and minibar. All rooms have air-con and TV, and the swimming pool is a treat. It's a bit removed from the center, but close to the appealing walkways and nighttime restaurants on Av Capitan Ene Garcez. There's a 10% to 15% discount for paying in cash.

Hotel Farroupilha HOTEL **$**
(☎95 3624-4226; Av das Guianas 1400; s/d R$75/100; ❄📶) This basic hotel is opposite the bus terminal; it's a reliable option if you're just passing through, less so if you're planning to stay a while. Rooms are clean and reasonably comfortable, with air-conditioning but no hot water. Breakfast is decent but ends early (8:30am) and is not served at all on Sunday. Wi-fi is spotty.

Boa Vista Eco Hotel HOTEL **$$**
(☎95 3621-7100; http://boavistaecohotel.com; Av Glaycon De Paiva 1240; s/d R$231/275; ❄📶) It may not be saying much, but the Eco Hotel is arguably the pick of Boa Vista's hotels. Simple, modern rooms are best if you can get the upper floors; there's a decent on-site restaurant. It's a fair walk into town.

Eating

Open-Air Food Court BRAZILIAN **$**
(Av Capitan Ene Garcez; mains R$5-28; ⏲5pm-midnight) A busy open-air food court occupies part of the long narrow park between the split lanes of Av Capitan Ene Garcez. A slew of mom-and-pop restaurants have tables set up under a high awning, serving cheap, delicious Brazilian fare. There's occasionally music, but the lively, family-friendly ambience is the real draw here.

THE YANOMAMI

The Yanomami are one of the most populous indigenous peoples of Amazonia, their lands spanning much of northern Amazonia, including across the Venezuelan border. Despite their numbers – estimated at around 15,000 – they remained relatively undisturbed until the 1970s. That's when the Brazilian government decided to build Hwy BR-210, abruptly exposing the Yanomami to hundreds of construction workers and other outsiders. Predictably, the Yanomami began dying of measles, influenza and venereal diseases; several villages were wiped out entirely.

A decade later, a gold rush sent some 40,000 miners swarming into Yanomami territory, polluting rivers and destroying the forest anew. In 1988 the government attempted to strip the Yanomami of 70% of their traditional territory in order to open it to mining. National and international uproar forced the government to back off, but the plight of the Yanomami remained dire. Nearly a fifth of the group's population died between 1986 and 1993, mostly of disease.

In 1991 the Venezuelan government officially recognized its portion of the Yanomami territory as a special indigenous reserve. Brazil followed suit a month later, creating the 96,650-sq-km **Terra Indígena Yanomami**, Brazil's largest single indigenous territory.

The focal point of each Yanomami community is the *yano*, a large, round timber-and-thatch structure where each family has its own section facing onto an open central area used for communal dance and ceremony. Each family arranges its own area by slinging hammocks around a constantly burning fire that forms the center of family life.

Their traditional diet includes monkey, tapir, wild pig and a variety of insects, plus fruits, yams, bananas and manioc. The Yanomami hold elaborate ceremonies and rituals and place great emphasis on intertribal alliances, primarily to minimize feuds. When nearby soil and hunting grounds are exhausted, the *yano* is dismantled and the village moves to a new site.

Disease is cured with shaman dances, healing hands and various herbs, including *yakoana* (a hallucinogenic herbal powder). When a tribe member dies, the body is hung from a tree until dry, then burned to ashes. The ashes are mixed with bananas, which are then eaten by friends and family of the deceased to incorporate and preserve the spirit.

Anthropologist Napoleon Chagnon lived with the Yanomami off and on for three decades and described them in his best-selling book *The Fierce People* as aggressive and living in a state of 'chronic warfare.' He received acclaim when the book was published in 1968, but his methods and findings have come under increased scrutiny over the years, including accusations that he knowingly exacerbated a measles outbreak and that he greatly exaggerated the degree of violence within the community. The controversy highlighted the ethical dilemmas inherent in studying isolated indigenous groups and the importance, above all, of emphasizing nuance over grand (and usually Western-centric) proclamations.

Boa Vista

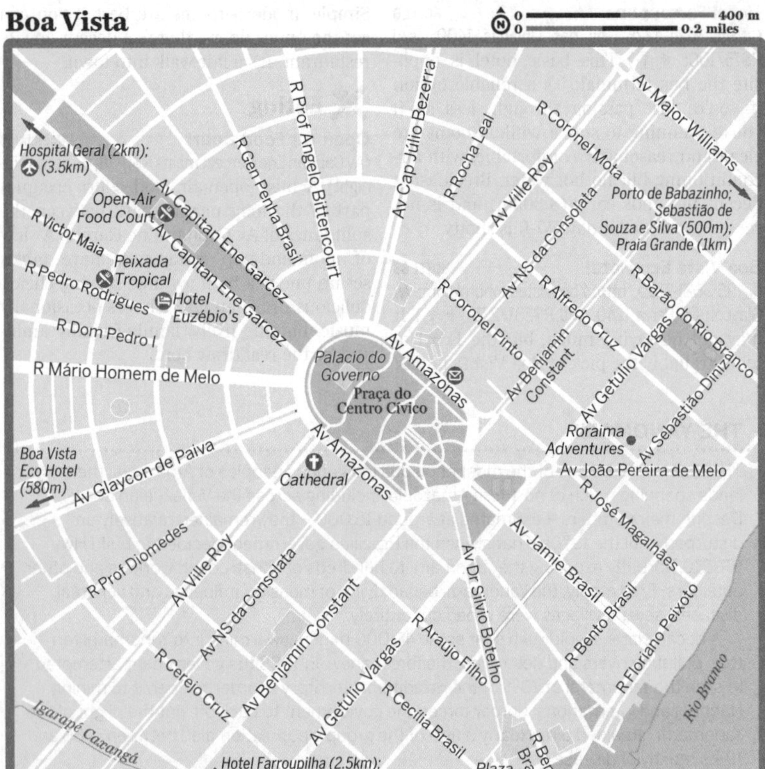

Peixada Tropical SEAFOOD **$$**
(☎95 3224-6040; www.facebook.com/peixada-tropical; cnr Ajuricaba & Pedro Rodrigues; mains for two R$36-60; ⌚10am-midnight) Another popular open-air lunch spot serving fish in every way imaginable, from Portuguese fish stew to Bahian style (fried and spicy). Closed some Sundays.

Information

DANGERS & ANNOYANCES

If you go to Praia Grande, watch for stingrays – use a long stick to poke the shallow water in front of you.

EMBASSIES & CONSULATES

Venezuelan Consulate (☎95 3623-6612; Av Benjamin Constant 968; ⌚8am-noon Mon-Fri) Travelers of many nations need to obtain a Venezuelan tourist card before entering the country by land. The process can be completed in Boa Vista and usually takes about 30 minutes, although check the prevailing situation in Venezuela before crossing the border.

EMERGENCY

Ambulance (☎192)

Police (☎190)

MEDICAL SERVICES

Hospital Geral (☎95 2121-0620; Av Brg Eduardo Gomes 1364) Main public hospital, located 2km northwest of the center of town toward the airport. It has a 24-hour emergency room.

MONEY

Banco do Brasil (Av Glaycon de Paiva 56; ⌚8am-2pm Mon-Fri) Changes euro and US dollars.

Bradesco (cnr Av Sebastão Diniz & Rua Inácio Magalhães) Reliable ATMs.

POST

Main Post Office (☎95 3621-3535; cnr Avs Amazonas & NS da Consolata; ⌚8am-4:30pm Mon-Fri, to noon Sat)

TRAVEL AGENCIES

Timbó Turismo (☎95 3224-4077; timbotur@osite.com.br; cnr Av Benjamin Constant & Rua Araújo Filho; ⏰8am-noon & 2-6pm Mon-Fri, to noon Sat) Sells plane and bus tickets.

Getting There & Away

AIR

The **airport** (☎95 3198-0119; www4.infraero.gov.br; Praça Santos Dumont 100) is 3.5km northwest of the city center.

Frequent promotions mean flying is often only slightly more expensive than the bus. There was no direct air service from Boa Vista to Guyana or Suriname at the time of research; connect through Belém instead.

Azul (☎95 3198-0171; www.voeazul.com.br) Flights to/from Manaus.

GOL (☎0800-704-0465, 95 3198-0135; www.voegol.com.br) Flights to/from Manaus, Belém and Brasília.

LATAM (☎95 3198-0140; www.latam.com) Flights to/from Manaus and Brasília.

BUS

The **bus station** (Av das Guianas, Bairro São Vicente) is 2.5km southwest of the center.

Eucatur (☎0800-455-050, 95 3623-1318; www.eucatur.com.br) and **Amatur** (☎95 3224-0004; www.amatur.com.br) both have multiple daily buses to Manaus (R$170 to R$230, 10 to 12 hours).

Getting Around

Around town, taxis marked 'Lotação' operate like buses, following fixed routes and carrying up to four passengers (R$5).

To get to the airport, you can take a 'Carana-Aeroporto' bus 206 (R$4, 6am to 11:15pm) from the bus terminal on Av Dr Silvio Botelho. Taxis to/from the airport charge R$35 to R$40.

Several buses go to/from the bus station, including '214-Jockei Clube' and '215-Nova Ciudad' (all R$4, every 20 to 30 minutes, 5:30am to midnight). A taxi from the center to the bus station costs about R$20; a *lotação* cab is R$5.

BORDER CROSSINGS

To Guyana

Amatur has daily buses to Bonfim on the Guyana border (R$25, 1½ hours, four daily). From there, you cross the border to Lethem and catch a bus to Georgetown (R$125 from Boa Vista, 15 to 16 hours, five daily).

To Venezuela

If you're traveling onward to Venezuela, you need to first get to the Brazilian border town of Pacaraíma; from the bus station, there's one daily bus (R$28, 3½ hours, 7am) and numerous collective taxis (R$42, 2½ hours). You'll need a Venezuelan tourist card to enter the country.

RONDÔNIA

It may not be the Brazilian Amazon's greatest prize, but Rondônia does serve as something of a gateway to some intriguing attractions on the rainforest's southern fringe. Porto Velho has excellent air and boat connections – the trip from Porto Velho to Manaus along the Rio Madeira is one of the least traveled river journeys of the Amazon Basin – while Guajará-Mirim is where Brazil meets Bolivia.

Porto Velho

☎0XX69 / POP 448,000

Porto Velho is a vital link in Brazil's agricultural economy, as soybeans and other products are shipped on huge barges from here down the Rio Madeira and transferred directly to ocean liners headed abroad. That same ride – albeit on a boat not a barge – draws some travelers up from Cuiabá and the Pantanal on the slow route to Manaus and the Amazon. The city itself has a few bright spots, but mostly serves as a transfer point.

Sights & Activities

The broad Rio Madeira forms the western boundary of Porto Velho. With headwaters in the Bolivian Andes, it's 3200km long and has a peak average flow of 1.4 billion liters a minute – it's the sixth-largest river in the world. It enters the Amazon River 150km downstream from Manaus.

At 5:30pm on weekdays, and hourly from 8am to 6pm on weekends, **riverboats** make 50-minute cruises along the Rio Madeira from the dock in front of the Madeira-Mamoré train station (R$18 per person). While not exactly thrilling, this is a reasonable way to idle away an hour or so – with luck you'll see a few pink dolphins. You can buy snacks and drinks on board.

Porto Velho

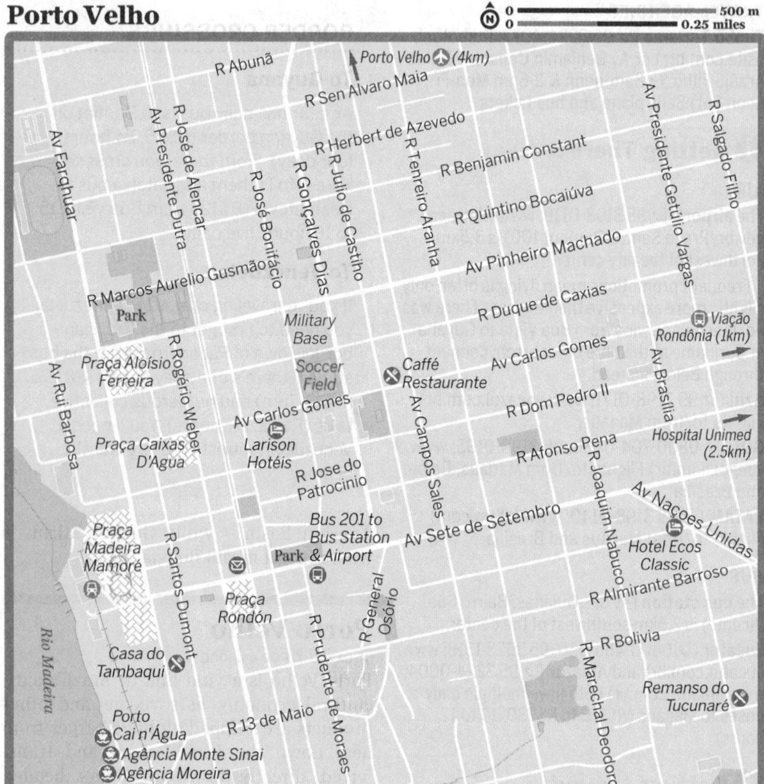

Sleeping

Hotel Ecos Classic HOTEL $

(☎69 2182-0707; Paulo Leal 611; s/d R$120/141; ❄☜) Rooms here have a touch of style that you rarely find in the Brazilian Amazon. It's understated but unmistakable, with wood paneling or designer wallpaper. Professional service is another plus, as is the gym, although it's a fair walk into the center.

Larison Hotéis HOTEL $

(☎69 3229-0509; www.larisonhoteis.com.br; Av Carlos Gomes 756; s/d from R$110/133; ❄☜) Large, spotless rooms with firm beds, luxurious linens, modern bathrooms and reliable air-con and internet make this a gem in Porto Velho's sometimes dreary hotel selection. The hotel caters to business travelers, so weekend rates can be a serious steal.

Eating

Caffé Restaurante BUFFET $

(☎69 3224-3176; Av Carlos Gomes 1097; per kg from R$40; ⌚11am-3pm Mon-Sat) The excellent buffet includes a wide selection of mains – from shepherd's pie to fried fish – a slew of sides and a refrigerated case full of succulent desserts, all served in a cool dining area. It's popular with professionals, but still reasonably priced.

Casa do Tambaqui BRAZILIAN $$

(☎69 3224-1022; www.facebook.com/CasadoTambaqui2015; Av Farquar 1008; mains for two R$44-70; ⌚11:30am-10pm) *Tambaqui* is a huge river fish with succulent white meat, often served grilled and *sem espinhas* (without bones). That's the specialty here, with dishes for two to five people. The menu has no individual plates, so come with a friend (or else very hungry). The dining room looks across the street to the old railway station and the Rio Madeira.

Remanso do Tucunaré BRAZILIAN $$
(☎69 3301-6217; Av Brasília 1506; dishes R$19-43; ⏲11am-3pm & 6-10pm) The good fish dishes serve two easily; try a delicious *caldeirada de tucunaré* (river-fish stew) or *tambaqui* (big fish chunks boiled with onion and tomatoes in a soup-like sauce, accompanied by rice). Decor is decidedly downmarket, but that's part of the charm.

Information

EMERGENCY

Ambulance (☎192)

Police (☎190)

LAUNDRY

Lavandería Mamoré (☎69 3221-3266; cnr Av Pinheiro Machado & Rua Deodoro; per piece R$2-9; ⏲8am-6pm Mon-Sat) Quick and professional, but prices are high. You can save a bit by forgoing ironing.

MEDICAL SERVICES

Drogaria Natal (Av Pinheiro Machado, at Julio de Castiho; ⏲7am-1am) Large pharmacy and convenience store.

Hospital Central (☎69 3224-5225; Julio de Castiho 149) Large public hospital with an emergency room.

Hospital Unimed (☎69 3216-6800; Av Rio Madeira 1618) Private hospital.

MONEY

Bradesco (Av Sete de Setembro; ⏲9am-3pm Mon-Fri) Reliable ATMs.

POST

Post Office (☎69 3217-3667; cnr Avs Presidente Dutra & Sete de Setembro; ⏲8am-5pm Mon-Fri, 9am-noon Sat)

TOURIST INFORMATION

IBAMA (☎69 3217-2700; Av Jorge Teixeira 3559; ⏲8am-noon & 1:30-5pm Mon-Fri) Useful for updates and general information on the region's reserves and indigenous territories.

Getting There & Away

AIR

The **Aeroporto Internacional de Porto Velho** is 7km north of town.

Azul (☎69 3219-7454; www.voeazul.com.br) Flights to/from Manaus, Belo Horizonte and Cuiabá.

GOL (☎0800-704-0465, 69 3219-7498; www.voegol.com.br) Flights to/from Manaus, Rio Branco, Brasília, São Paulo, Fortaleza and more.

LATAM (☎0800-123-200, 69 3219-7502; www.tam.com.br) Flights to/from São Paulo and Brasília.

BOAT

Slow boats down the Rio Madeira to Manaus (R$290 hammock, double cabin with fan/air-con R$790/1020, 2½ days) leave Tuesday, Wednesday and Saturday at 2pm from **Porto Cai n'Água** at the end of Rua 13 de Maio. You'll need your own hammock, and meals are available for purchase. Buy tickets from one of the brokers at the port, including **Agência Monte Sinai** (☎69 99346-7101, 69 3223-1987; transportesmontesinai@hotmail.com; ⏲8am-6pm Mon-Sat) and **Agência Moreira** (☎69 99211-4987, 69 99235-2525; Porto Cai n'Água; ⏲8am-6pm Mon-Sat). You can claim a spot and sleep on board two to three days before departure.

BUS

The **bus station** (cnr Avs Jorge Teixeira & Carlos Gomes) is 2km east of the center.

Eucatur (☎69 3222-2233; www.eucatur.com.br) runs daily buses to Rio Branco (R$115, nine to ten hours, four daily) and Cuiabá (R$220 to R$369; 26 hours, eight daily), with connections to Brasília and beyond.

Viação Rondônia (☎69 3225-2891; Av Gov Jorge Teixeira 1296) runs seven daily buses to Rio Branco (R$115, nine to ten hours).

Collective taxis serve Guajará-Mirim (per person R$120, four hours). The price is based on a minimum of four passengers, so you may have to wait for the car to fill up.

Getting Around

Bus 201 with signs reading 'Almirante' or 'Hospital de Base via Aeroporto' run between the city center and the bus station and the airport, passing each every 30 minutes (every hour on weekends). Pick it up at the bus station or airport terminal (in both cases, the stop is to your right as you leave the main doorway), or along Av Sete de Setembro.

A taxi between the bus station and town costs R$15; to or from the airport is R$40.

Guajará-Mirim

☎0XX69 / POP 44,700

This low-key town on the Rio Mamoré came into existence as the southern terminus of the Madeira–Mamoré railway. Both Guajará-Mirim and Bolivian Guayaramerín across the river are free-trade zones with a steady stream of shopping tourists. For travelers, it's mainly a border-crossing point, with little of interest to detain you.

Guajará-Mirim

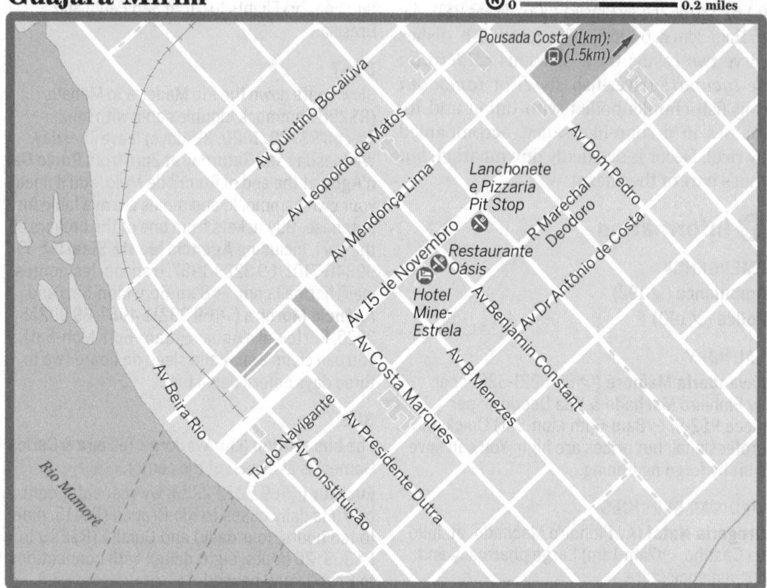

Sleeping & Eating

Pousada Costa POUSADA $
(69 3541-6516; Av Tiradentes 236; s/d R$75/110;) Colorful decor and warm service from the live-in owners make this an agreeable choice. Rooms are smallish, but have hot water and air-conditioning. It's a bit removed from the port and center, but the owners are happy to call for a moto-taxi or cab (or you can walk a block to the main drag).

Hotel Mine-Estrela HOTEL $
(69 3541-1206; Av 15 de Novembro 460; s/d R$60/100;) Has large basic rooms with cable TV, internet and a location that's convenient to restaurants and passing taxis for getting to the port or bus station. Maintenance seems to have suffered in recent years, but it remains a reliable budget choice if you're just passing through.

Restaurante Oásis BUFFET $
(69 3541-1621; Av 15 de Novembro 460; per kg R$39; 11am-3pm Wed-Mon) This longtime favorite in Guajará-Mirim can be counted on for a well-prepared lunch buffet, including freshly grilled meats. The airy dining area gets some street noise, but it's still a pleasant and convenient place for a midday break.

Lanchonete e Pizzaria Pit Stop PIZZA $
(69 3541-7178, 69 3541-4213; Av 15 de Novembro 620; mains R$15-28; 6-10pm) A popular if somewhat sterile place serving decent pizzas. It has a huge wide-screen TV, so you're sure not to miss a moment of the latest *novela* (soap) or soccer game.

Getting There & Away

The **bus station** (Av 15 de Novembro) is 2km east of the center; taxis from there into town cost R$30 to R$40, moto-taxis are R$18. **Viação Rondônia** (Porto Velho 69 3225-2891) runs seven daily buses to Porto Velho (R$80, six to seven hours) at 1am, 6:30am, 10am, 1pm, 2pm, 6pm and 11:55pm; the 1pm and 11:55pm departures are direct and about an hour quicker.

ACRE

Spread across the southern reaches of the Brazilian Amazon close to the borders with Bolivia and Peru, Acre is an interesting experience. For a start, it was the home state of martyred union and environmental leader Chico Mendes, and was a key battleground for the conflict over deforestation. And thanks to those struggles, today a full third of the state is under environmental protection or designated as indigenous lands. Your best chance for exploring the forest is from Xapuri, Mendes' former home town.

Remember that Acre is in a different time zone (one hour behind) than Porto Velho and Manaus.

Rio Branco

☎0XX68 / POP 370,000

Rio Branco, the capital of Acre, was founded in 1882 by rubber-tappers on the banks of the Rio Acre. Once a brash, uneasy town, Rio Branco has transformed itself into a genuinely pleasant place, with several excellent cultural outlets and easy access to some interesting sites, including Xapuri, the hometown of the environmentalist Chico Mendes.

Sights

★Mercado Velho MARKET

(Praça Bandeira) Not only a great place for a meal or late-afternoon beer, Rio Branco's refurbished riverside Mercado Velho is a favorite spot for city-sponsored cultural events, including live music, dance performances, poetry readings and comedy troupes, usually held evenings and weekends.

Museu da Borracha MUSEUM

(Rubber Museum; ☎68 3223-1202; Av Ceará 1441; ⏲8am-6pm Tue-Fri) FREE The long-standing Rubber Museum is well worth a look for its fascinating history of rubber-tapping in Acre. The museum's three rooms have displays ranging from how tappers learned to extract the milky sap without killing the tree (a tool called a *cabrita,* meaning 'little goat', was key) to the life and work of Chico Mendes and the Rural Workers Union. Portuguese only.

Palacio Rio Branco HISTORIC BUILDING

(Praça Povos da Floresta; ⏲8am-6pm Tue-Fri, 4-6pm Sat & Sun) FREE Acre's first capitol building, the imposing Palacio Rio Branco, is now mostly a tourist attraction. A maze of interconnected rooms contain informative, well-done displays on prehistoric artifacts, indigenous communities, Chico Mendes and the Acrean Revolution.

Cathedral CATHEDRAL

(☎68 3224-1932; Praça da Catedral 8) Rio Branco's main cathedral, built in 1959, has a single soaring bell tower and three long, spacious naves lined with 36 stained-glass windows.

Memorial dos Autonomistas MEMORIAL

(Autonomists Memorial; ☎68 3224-2133; Praça Eurico Dutra; ⏲8am-6pm Tue-Fri, 4-8pm Sat & Sun) FREE In its spiffy home on the main plaza, the Memorial dos Autonomistas has a permanent display on Acre's battle for statehood, plus space for rotating art exhibits. It's also where José Guiomard dos Santos is buried. Though not Acrean by birth, Guiomard served as federal administrator of the region and later, as a senator, helped pass legislation giving Acre its statehood.

Sleeping

Hotel do Papai HOTEL $

(☎68 3223-2044; Floriano Peixoto 849; s/d R$90/135; ❄📶) The Papai's huge reception area gives way to clean rooms with updated TVs and air-conditioning. Large colorful scenes of Amazonia are painted on the high walls of the rooms, making up somewhat for the oldish beds and bathrooms, and lack of natural light. The elderly and charmingly grumpy owner tends the desk.

Nobile Suites Gran Lumni HOTEL $$

(☎68 3212-3100; www.nobilehoteis.com.br; Av Ceará 2156; s/d R$148/175; ❄📶🏊) It's a 15-minute hike into the town center, but the Gran Lumni has some of Rio Branco's best rooms – they're actually stylish with muted accents, rather than the stark, white-tiled approach of most midrange hotels in the Brazilian Amazon.

Holiday Inn Express HOTEL $$

(☎68 3302-2300; www.ihg.com; Rio Grande do Sul 332; r from R$185; ❄@📶🏊) Rio Branco's best hotel is an easy walk from the city center. The rooms are warmly hued and the service is excellent.

Hotel Guapindaia Praça Business HOTEL $$

(☎68 3224-7677; Rui Barbosa 354; s/d R$100/175; ❄📶🏊) Rooms are pretty tiny at this business-minded hotel, though you can't beat the location, a block from a leafy plaza and the city's narrow central park. The large air-conditioned lobby and professional service are a breath of fresh air, and guestrooms are spotless, if not spacious.

Eating

★Mercado Velho MARKET $

(Praça Bandeira; dishes from R$6; ⏲7am-10pm) Dubbed the 'Old Market,' this is actually part of a highly successful urban-renewal effort. An old port building was transformed into an attractive food market where you can

Rio Branco

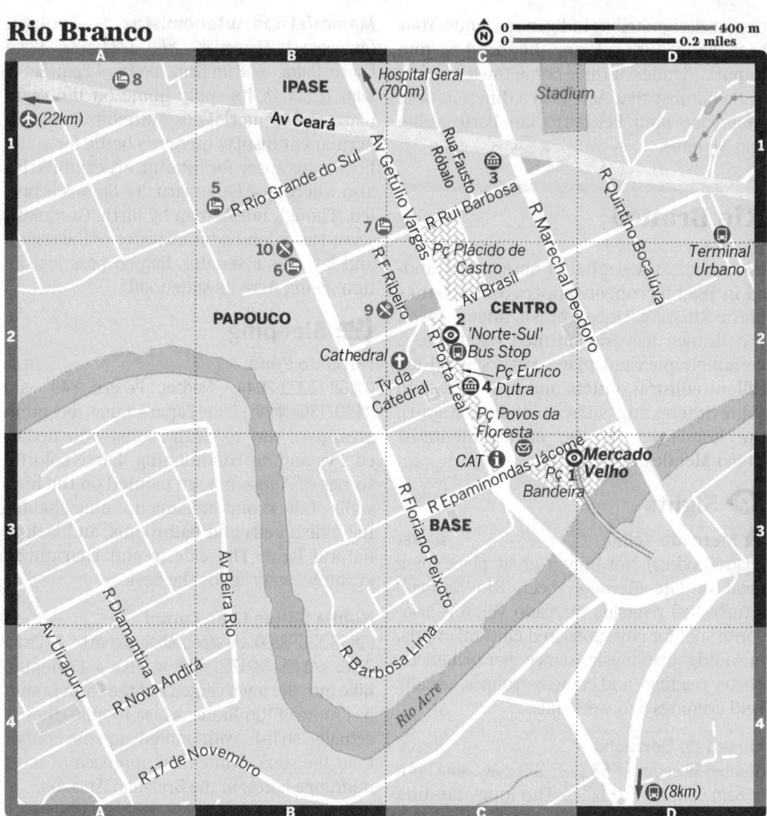

Rio Branco

Top Sights

1 Mercado Velho C3

Sights

2 Memorial dos Autonomistas C2
3 Museu da Borracha C1
4 Palacio Rio Branco C2

Sleeping

5 Holiday Inn Express B1
6 Hotel do Papai B2
7 Hotel Guapindaia Praça Business B1
8 Nobile Suites Gran Lumni A1

Eating

9 AFA Bistrô D'Amazônia B2
10 Churrascaria Triângulo B2
Mercado Velho .... (see 1)

Entertainment

Mercado Velho .... (see 1)

order anything from grilled comfort food to complete entrees, served at indoor booths or at tables overlooking a tidy riverfront plaza. Especially popular in the evenings, when there's live music.

AFA Bistrô D'Amazônia BUFFET **$$**

(Ribeiro 99; per kg R$65 Mon-Fri, R$82 Sat & Sun; ⏲11am-2:30pm) An unassuming exterior belies a fancy-pants bistro that's town's favorite lunch spot. The city's professional classes pack in for fresh (albeit pricey) salad combinations, tender meat and fish dishes, and irresistible desserts. Sundays feature *frutas do mar*.

Churrascaria Triângulo BRAZILIAN **$$**

(☎68 3224-9265; Hotel Triângulo, Floriano Peixoto 727; per kg R$43, rodízio from R$50; ⏲11am-3pm daily, 7-10pm Mon-Sat) The ambience here is lacking, but if you're famished and in the mood for meat, you're sure to leave satisfied. The *rodízio* (all-you-can-eat buffet) is especially filling.

Entertainment

Mercado Velho LIVE MUSIC

(Praça Bandeira; ⏲5-11pm) Many of the eating options in this attractive riverfront market have evening and nighttime service, from cool beers to full meals. It's a popular and pleasant place to while away a few hours, listening to music (there's usually at least one singer or guitarist) and contemplating the pedestrian bridge, bathed in a hypnotic blue light.

Information

EMERGENCY

Police (☎190; Epaminondas Jácome)

MEDICAL SERVICES

Hospital Geral (Emergency Room; ☎68 3223-3080, 192; cnr Av Nações Unidos & Hugo Carneiro) Has an emergency room.

MONEY

Banco do Brasil (Porta Leal 85; ⏲9am-3pm Mon-Fri) In the city center.

Bradesco (Porta Leal 83; ⏲9am-3pm Mon-Fri) Has an ATM.

POST

Post Office (Epaminondas Jácome 447; ⏲7am-4pm Mon-Fri, 8am-noon Sat)

TOURIST INFORMATION

CAT (Centro de Atendimento ao Turista; Praça Povos da Floresta; ⏲8am-9pm Mon-Sat, 9am-noon Sun) Not terribly helpful, but a good place to start.

TRAVEL AGENCIES

Discovery Viagens (☎68 9238-9495; AFA Hotel, Ribeiro 109; ⏲8am-5pm Mon-Fri) Local tour operator offering guided excursions of all sorts, including bike tours in Xapuri and visits to the Yawanawá indigenous community and Serra do Divisor National Park. Has an info desk in the lobby of the AFA Hotel.

Getting There & Away

Paved roads connect Rio Branco with Porto Velho and Brasiléia, but people generally fly. Most of Acre's roads are unpaved, and can be difficult or impassable during the rainy season, usually October to May (ie most of the year).

AIR

The small **Aeroporto de Rio Branco** (☎68 3211-1000; www4.infraero.gov.br/aeroportos/aeroporto-de-rio-branco-placido-de-castro; Av Plácido de Castro) is 22km northwest of town on Hwy BR-364.

GOL (☎68 3211-1070, 0800-704-0465; www.voegol.com.br) Three daily flights to/from Brasília, and one to/from Porto Velho.

LATAM (☎68 3211-1092, 68 4002-5700; www.latam.com) Two daily flights to/from Brasília, with extensive onward connections.

BOAT

The Rio Acre is navigable all the way to the Peruvian border at Assis Brasil but there's little river traffic (and none that follows a schedule). Headed the other direction, it's possible to catch a boat down the Rio Purus from the town of Boca do Acre, north of Rio Branco, theoretically all the way to Manaus. That said, if Manaus is your destination, there's a much more frequent and reliable boat service on the Rio Madeira, leaving from Porto Velho.

BUS

Long-distance buses leave from the **Rodoviária Internacional de Rio Branco** (☎68 3221-3693; Hwy BR-364, Km 125), a sleek new bus terminal 8km southwest of town. **Petroacre** (☎68 3221-1452) has services to Xapuri (R$38, 3½ hours, 6am and 1:45pm), Brasiléia (R$48, four hours, 6am, noon and 2:45pm), Assis Brasil (R$60, six hours, 6am and noon) and Cruzeiro do Sol ($128, 12 to 14 hours, 7:15am and 7:30pm).

Eucatur (☎68 3233-3741; www.eucatur.com.br) and **Viação Rondônia** (☎68 3224-4293) have three to four departures daily to Porto Velho (R$115, nine to ten hours) usually once in the morning and the rest nonstop overnighters.

CAR & MOTORCYCLE

Highway BR-364 is paved and well maintained between Rio Branco and Porto Velho, and as far as Sena Madureira, 170km west of Rio Branco. Likewise, the road from Rio Branco to Brasiléia (235km) and Assis Brasil on the Peruvian border is also paved.

Getting Around

At Rio Branco's bustling **Terminal Urbano** (City Bus Terminal; Sergipe, btwn Av Ceará & Benjamin Constant) you pay your fare at a bank of turnstiles and buses come and go from clearly marked platforms. At least three different city buses run between the downtown terminal and the Rodoviária Internacional; they are marked either '**Norte-Sul**,' 'Parque Industrial' or 'Jacarandá' (R$3.50, 20 to 30 minutes, every 15 minutes). A taxi to or from the city center costs R$40, a moto-taxi R$20.

Xapuri

☎0XX68 / POP 11,670

This little town of neat wooden houses along broad streets is one of the more rewarding spots in the Brazilian Amazon. It was home to

CHICO MENDES & HIS LEGACY

In the mid-1970s an ambitious military-government plan to tame the Amazon attracted a flood of developers, ranchers, logging companies and settlers into Acre, who clear-cut rubber and Brazil trees to make room for ranches. Francisco Alves Mendes Filho, better known as Chico Mendes, was a 30-something rubber-tapper, but one of the few who could read and write, and had long taken an interest in improving the lives of fellow *seringueiros* (rubber-tappers). In 1977, he cofounded the Sindicato dos Trabalhadores Rurais de Xapuri (Xapuri Rural Workers' Union) to defy the violent intimidation and dispossession practiced by the newcomers.

Mendes organized *empates* (stoppages), nonviolent human blockades to stop the clear-cutting. But Mendes was not initially an environmentalist – his motivation was to help rubber-tappers, whose livelihood happened to depend on a healthy, intact forest. Likewise, the environmental movement (largely based in the US at the time) was focused on preserving 'virgin' forest, which it assumed to be empty of humans save for a few indigenous tribes.

The joining of those groups – rubber-tappers and American environmentalists – was one of Mendes' key accomplishments. He convinced rubber-tappers to see themselves as stewards of the forest and allies of indigenous peoples. And he helped conceive of 'extractive reserves,' to this day an important means of protecting land and people there. He won numerous international awards in the process, including election to the UN Environment Organization's Global 500 Honor Roll in 1987.

Mendes' fame abroad made life increasingly dangerous at home. Killings of rural workers and activists, including priests and lawyers, jumped from single digits in the 1960s, to over a hundred in 1980, to nearly 500 between 1985 and 1987, according to Amnesty International.

In December 1988 Mendes moved to establish his birthplace, Seringal Cachoeira, as an extractive reserve, defying a local rancher and strongman, Darly Alves da Silva, who claimed the land. Mendes had already denounced Silva to the police for threatening his life and for the murder of a union representative earlier that year. Mendes received numerous death threats, but resisted the urging of colleagues to flee Acre state. On December 22, 1988, Mendes stepped onto the back porch of his home in Xapuri and was shot at close range by men hiding in the bushes. He staggered into the house, where his wife and children were watching TV, and bled to death.

Mendes' murder was the first of hundreds to be thoroughly investigated and prosecuted, owing to the massive international reaction to his killing. Darly Alves da Silva and his son Darci Pereira da Silva were sentenced to 19 years in prison for ordering and committing the crime. Both da Silvas escaped from jail in 1993, apparently just walking free, suggesting complicity among the guards, but were recaptured in 1996, after another outcry, and returned to jail. The men completed their sentences in 2009; Darci reportedly lives in the Pantanal region, but Darly has remained in the area, and can be seen around Xapuri to this day.

Mendes' life and death brought unprecedented international attention to the environmental crisis in the Amazon – read Andrew Revkin's excellent *The Burning Season* (1990) for a fine overview of Mendes' life and death.

But activism on behalf of the forest and people who live there remains a dangerous undertaking. On February 12, 2005, a US-born nun named Dorothy Stang was gunned down in the small town of Anapú, in the soy and cattle country of Pará state, by two men reportedly acting on the orders of rancher Vitalmiro Bastos de Moura, who Stang had accused of illegally clearing land. The gunmen were quickly caught and convicted, but holding Bastos de Moura accountable has proved difficult. He was sentenced to 30 years in prison three times, and all three times his conviction was overturned and he was released. A second rancher was convicted of the crime in 2010, but released in 2012. Bastos de Moura was re-tried and re-convicted in 2013, and is in prison again – for now. The prospects of finding justice for scores of other murder victims, whose deaths will never attract the international attention that Mendes' and Stang's did, are decidedly bleak.

environmental and labor hero Chico Mendes, and therein lies its primary appeal, with a museum, Mendes' former house and some of the region's best places to base yourself.

Sights & Activities

★Casa Chico Mendes HISTORIC BUILDING
(Batista de Moraes 494; ⏲8:30am-4:30pm Tue-Fri, 9am-1pm Sat) FREE This simple wood house is where Chico Mendes lived with his family until his murder on the back steps in 1988. Tours include a graphic description of the moment he was shot, with bloodstains still on the walls. Across the street, the Chico Mendes Foundation center has poster-sized photos of Mendes and a collection of personal items and international awards.

Museu do Xapuri MUSEUM
(C Brandão; ⏲8:30am-5:30pm Tue-Sat, 9am-1pm Sun) FREE This small but intriguing museum tells how Xapuri, located at the confluence of two rivers, was once a major transport hub for rubber, nuts, wood and other products, and a favorite of Middle Eastern merchants peddling everything from shovels to perfume. It's housed in an attractive mansion that served as the city hall from 1929 to 2000.

★Pousada Ecológica Seringal Cachoeira ECOTOUR
(☎68 99943-4747; www.facebook.com/seringalcachoeira; per person R$50-100) Various guided hikes are available at this comfortable lodge, 32km from Xapuri. One hike leaves at 4am for a fascinating real-life look at how workers collect latex and Brazil nuts, with good opportunities to spot wildlife (primarily birds) too. There's also tree-climbing and a canopy tour, with 500m of rope bridges and zip lines. Open to guests and nonguests; reserve ahead.

Sleeping

★Pousada Ecológica Seringal Cachoeira LODGE $
(☎68 99943-4747; www.facebook.com/seringalcachoeira; dm R$75, d R$150, all incl breakfast; ❄) This ecolodge is set in a working rubber forest and has cozy accommodations plus guided hikes and activities. Lodging is in large dorms or comfortable stand-alone 'chalets,' while meals (lunch and dinner R$30) are served in the spacious main building. It's 32km north of Xapuri where Chico Mendes first tapped rubber trees and collected Brazil nuts.

On Hwy BR-317, look for a turnoff 4km south of the Xapuri junction; from there it's another 16km by well-maintained dirt road to the lodge. A taxi from Xapuri costs R$120.

Pousada das Chapurys POUSADA $
(☎68 3542-2253; www.facebook.com/pousadachapurys; Sadala Koury 1385; s/d/tr R$80/120/150; ❄📶) A short walk from the bus terminal, this is the old standby of Xapuri's hotels, and still a pleasant and convenient place to stay. The owners were close friends of Chico Mendes, and have fascinating stories, photos and memorabilia in the hotel's dining area. Rooms are large and comfortable but dated.

Eating

Pizzaria Tribos PIZZA $
(☎68 3542-2531; C Branbão; mains R$18-38; ⏲dinner) One of a handful of kiosks in a small park a block off the main plaza, Tribos serves delicious pizzas at small outdoor tables and gets kudos for playing a good mix of rock.

Information

MONEY

Banco da Amazona (C Bradão; ⏲9am-3pm Mon-Fri) Next to the gas station.

TOURIST INFORMATION

Tourist Information Kiosk (⏲7am-noon & 2-5pm Mon-Fri) Opposite the bus station, this place has more handicrafts than tourist information, but does have amiable attendants and a handy brochure about Xapuri.

Getting There & Away

Xapuri lies about 12km northwest of Hwy BR-317, the main road between Rio Branco (241km away) and Brasiléia (74km away).

Petroacre (p655) has a bus service from Xapuri to Rio Branco (R$38, 3½ hours, 6am and 1:45pm). There's only one bus from Xapuri to Brasiléia (R$15, two hours) departing at 10am. Alternatively, you can catch a cab to the *trocamento* (junction) on Hwy BR-317 (R$18) and catch a passing Rio Branco or Brasiléia bus there.

Brasiléia

☎0XX68 / POP 23,400

The border town of Brasiléia is separated from Cobija, Bolivia, by the meandering Rio Acre and Igarapé Bahia. There's precious little to do here, unless you're in the market for a computer or DVD player – for that, you can join the crowds crossing into Cobija to take advantage of the lower prices and a duty-free border. Otherwise, it's simply a way station for those passing through.

BORDER CROSSINGS

To/From Peru

Access to Peru is through the village of Assis Brasil, 110km west of Brasiléia. Once an adventure route, the road is now paved and has daily bus services. Complete Brazilian immigration procedures in Brasiléia, and Peruvian immigration at the border town of Iñapari.

To/From Cobija, Bolivia

You are free to cross back and forth between Cobija and Brasiléia without passing through immigration, provided you're going for a short period. If you plan to continue inland, or stay longer than a couple of days, you ought to clear immigration officially.

A bridge over the Igarapé Bahia connects Epitaciolândia to Cobija, and is the official border crossing, with immigration offices for both countries nearby. A smaller, more convenient bridge spans the Rio Acre, making it possible to walk from one downtown to the other in just a few minutes. The smaller bridge – which is dedicated to Wilson Pinheiro, a rubber-tapper union president and friend of Chico Mendes who was assassinated in July 1980 – is at the end of Av Prefeito R Moriera; there is a customs post there, but no immigration officers.

Bolivian immigration (☎546-5760; Plaza General Germán Busch, Cobija; ⏰9am-noon & 2-5pm Mon-Fri) faces Cobija's main plaza. There's also a checkpoint on the main international bridge, which is open round the clock. In Brazil, the Polícia Federal (p658) handle immigration procedures; the office is in Epitaciolândia, just across the main international bridge. In Cobija, the **Brazilian consulate** (☎842-2110; Av Chelio Luna Pizarro, Cobija; ⏰8:30am-12:30pm Mon-Fri) is a half-block from the main plaza, on Av General Rene Barrientos, next to the Banco Mercantil de Bolivia.

Sleeping & Eating

Pousada Las Palmeras POUSADA $
(☎68 3546-3302; www.facebook.com/pousadalaspalmeras.brasileia; Odilon Pratagi 125, at Geny Assis; s/d R$60/80; ❄📶) Brasiléia's most appealing hotel also has to be its unluckiest – it's been flooded several times when the Rio Acre tops its banks, including in March 2015. The hardworking owner has rebuilt each time, and so Las Palmeras is open once again, with narrow singles and spacious doubles, all with air-con, TV, minibar and hot water.

Saborella BRAZILIAN $
(Odilon Pratagi s/n; mains R$15-36; ⏰11am-3pm daily, 5-10pm Tue-Sun) Daily specials make ordering easy at this small restaurant, one of few genuinely agreeable places in town. Located half a block from the bus station, you'll find all the Brazilian staples, with rice, beans and burgers in abundance.

Information

EMBASSIES & CONSULATES

Bolivian Consulate (☎68 3546-5760; Hilário Meireles 236; ⏰8am-noon & 2-4pm Mon-Fri)

Brazilian Consulate (Av Ismael Montes, Cobija; ⏰8am-1pm Mon-Fri) Across the border in Cobija.

EMERGENCY

Police (☎68 3546-3207, 190; Av Prefeito R Moreira No 456; ⏰24hr)

Policia Federal (☎68 3546-3204; ⏰8am-7pm)

MONEY

Banco do Brasil (Av Prefeito R Moreira 470; ⏰9am-3pm Mon-Fri) Also has an ATM.

POST

Post Office (Av Prefeito R Moreira; ⏰8am-noon & 2-5pm Mon-Fri)

Getting There & Away

The bus station is 500m from most of the hotels and the main commercial strip; a taxi in either direction costs R$10. Petroacre has daily departures to Rio Branco (R$35, four hours) plus services to Xapuri (R$15, two hours) and Assis Brasil (R$15, two hours). You can usually catch a collective taxi to any of these, which are pricier but much quicker.

Getting Around

Hwy BR-317 from Rio Branco approaches Brasiléia from the southeast, through the adjacent but independent town of Epitaciolândia. The Brasiléia bus station is just across a small bridge; from there it's a 500m walk (or R$10 taxi ride) to the center of town. If you do walk, bear right out of the bus terminal, and follow Rua Odilon Pratagi to Av Prefeito R Moreira, which roughly approximates to the town center.

Understand Brazil

BRAZIL TODAY 660

Brazil faces many challenges, including political corruption, economic woes and the rise of far-right demagogues.

HISTORY 662

Portuguese royals, repressive military dictatorships and socially minded visionaries have all shaped Brazil's complicated past.

LIFE IN BRAZIL 674

A portrait of Brazil's cultural diversity, its divergent lifestyle and social challenges of today.

BRAZILIAN RHYTHMS 677

The Brazilian soundtrack includes samba, bossa nova, Música Popular Brasileira (MPB), *tropicália,* hip-hop and rock.

FOOTBALL 682

A look at Brazil's extraordinary footballing legacy.

CINEMA & LITERATURE 685

Iconic movies and novels by Brazil's top filmmakers and writers.

ARCHITECTURE 687

Home to baroque churches and modernist masterpieces, Brazil has some surprising architectural treasures.

THE NATURAL WORLD 690

An overview of Brazil's rich ecosystems and its incredible plant and animal life.

Brazil Today

Brazil has suffered through hard times in recent years. A huge corruption scandal has caused the impeachment of the nation's first female president, sent numerous business leaders and politicians to jail (including former president Lula), and left deep scars on the economy. There are rays of hope, however, with Brazil's worst recession finally behind them, and continued investments in a greener, more sustainable future.

Best on Film

Tropa de Elite (Elite Squad; 2007) An action film of crime and corruption as an elite police squad and drug lords clash. Don't miss the sequel (The Enemy Within).

Central do Brasil (Central Station; 1998) Walter Salles' moving tale of a homeless boy and an older woman on a road trip across Brazil.

Reaching for the Moon (2013) Tragic love story between an American poet and Brazilian architect, set in 1950s Petrópolis.

Bel Borba Aqui (2012) Colorful documentary of an artist who uses Salvador as his canvas.

Ao Som As Redor (Neighboring Sounds; 2012) Critically acclaimed film dealing with the wealthy and the underclass in Recife.

Best in Print

Brazil on the Rise (Larry Rohter; 2010) Insightful portrait of the politics, culture and challenges of the South American nation.

The Lost City of Z (David Grann; 2009) Gripping journey into the Amazon to retrace the steps of lost explorer Colonel Fawcett.

Death in Brazil (Peter Robb; 2005) Well-written travelogue that delves into history, culture and corruption.

A Fateful Election

In 2018 Brazilians went to the polls to vote in a presidential election that was unlike any in the past. Two years prior, their previous incumbent, Dilma Rousseff, had become Brazil's first democratically elected president to be impeached and removed from office. Meanwhile, Rousseff's predecessor and Workers' Party founder, Luiz Inácio Lula da Silva, was only a few months into his 12-year prison sentence. Despite the charges – money laundering and passive corruption – he remained extremely popular with Brazilians. He even attempted to run for president that year. His efforts, however, were thwarted when the Superior Electoral Court barred him from running.

Anger against the ruling political class led to the rise of far-right demagogues like Jair Bolsonaro (often described as the Brazilian Donald Trump). A former military officer, Bolsonaro praised strong-arm rulers like Augusto Pinochet and promised to bring law and order back to Brazil. His fiery rhetoric earned him many enemies, and he was stabbed during a campaign rally in Minas Gerais. The wound, however, didn't stop Bolsonaro, who won the election and promised a hard-line agenda in the months ahead. The tack to the far right was the most radical political change since Brazil's restoration of democracy in the 1980s.

Deep-Rooted Corruption

If there's one central theme made shockingly clear in the most recent election cycle, it's the pervasive level of corruption plaguing Brazilian politics. Even a people accustomed to this endemic problem were shocked at the vast size of the scandals that have rocked the country in the last few years. The magnitude of the scandal exposed by Operação Lava Jato (Operation Car Wash), which first came to light in 2014, boggles the imagination. This colossal kickback scheme was tied to Petrobras, Brazil's state-run oil company, as well as Odebrecht, the massive multinational construction firm headquartered in Brazil. The money laundering involved more than US$5 billion in bribes, and led to the convictions of over 200 of the country's top executives and politicians – including former president Lula and Rio state governor Sergio Cabral.

Economic Woes

The repercussions from the scandal have sent shockwaves rippling through the county, and beyond, with at least 10 other countries involved. Brazil was already reeling from a crippling recession (in part brought on by overspending on the 2014 World Cup and 2016 Olympics), and the scandal only made things worse – undermining investor confidence and leading to mass layoffs by the scandal-plagued industries. The economy contracted by more than 3.5% in both 2015 and 2016 – its longest recession in history. As unemployment surged and the currency collapsed, the number of Brazilians living in poverty grew by a whopping 33% (an estimated six million people fell below the poverty line between 2014 and 2018). With prices rising and wages falling, workers have taken to the streets in mass protests; in 2018 one trucker strike left the country paralyzed for nearly two weeks. Huge budget cuts to schools, hospitals and other public institutions have also had devastating effects; a raging fire destroyed most of the collection inside Brazil's National History Museum, a 200-year-old icon that housed some of the most important archeological collections in South America.

A Glimmer of Hope

The good news is that after three years of crisis, Brazil's economy was finally climbing out of the red by late 2018. Business investment was on the rise as the political scandal (somewhat) subsided, and production rose significantly across many sectors (agriculture, electronics and the automotive sectors, among them). Meanwhile, Brazil has continued to invest in renewable energy, and today sustainable sources meet more than 70% of Brazil's energy needs (some months reaching above a whopping 86% of Brazil's domestically produced electricity). Recent years have seen the opening of massive solar farms – including two in 2017 that are among the largest on the continent. Wind power has also grown in leaps and bounds, with installed capacity of 13.1 MW in 2018 – a 35% increase from just three years prior. That said, oil production remains a huge part of the Brazilian economy, and finding the balance between green energy and petroleum will be one of the hot political topics in the years ahead – along with the challenge of preserving Brazil's natural environment (particularly the Amazon) amid relentless economic pressures, driven in part by the agriculture lobby.

POPULATION: **208 MILLION**

GDP: **$3.2 TRILLION**

INFLATION: **4.6%**

UNEMPLOYMENT: **12%**

ANNUAL FOREIGN TOURISTS: **6.6 MILLION**

if Brazil were 100 people

48 would be white
43 would be mixed race
8 would be black
1 would be Asian

belief systems

(% of population)

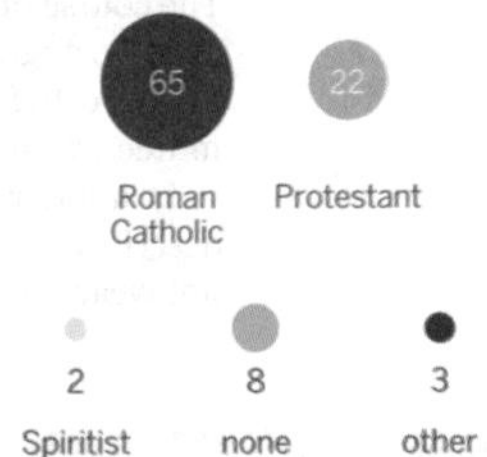

population per sq km

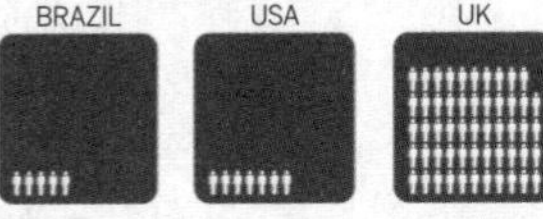

≈ 5 people

History

Brazil's population, the fifth biggest in the world, reached its lands from Africa, Asia, Europe and other parts of the Americas – diverse origins that have created one of the planet's most racially mixed societies. How they came, intermingled and developed the unique Brazilian identity that charms visitors today is a rough-and-tumble story of courage, greed, endurance and cruelty, eventually yielding a fitful progress toward the democracy the country now enjoys.

Before the Portuguese

It's generally believed that the early inhabitants of the Americas arrived from Siberia in waves between about 12,000 and 8000 BC, crossing land now submerged beneath the Bering Strait, then gradually spreading southward over many millennia. Some scholars, however, believe that humans arrived much earlier (25,000 to 35,000 BC) in groups that traveled by boat across the Pacific.

Researchers in the remote Serra da Capivara in the Northeastern state of Piauí have found some of Brazil's earliest evidence of human presence. The oldest traces of human life in the Amazon region can be seen on a detour from a river trip between Santarém and Belém: a series of rock paintings estimated to be 12,000 years old near Monte Alegre.

By the time the Portuguese arrived, there were probably between two and four million people, speaking an estimated 1000 languages, in what's now Brazil.

History Books

Brazil: Five Centuries of Change (2009), Thomas E Skidmore

The History of Brazil (1999), Robert Levine

A Concise History of Brazil (1999), Boris Fausto

Cabral & Chums

The course of Brazilian history was changed forever in 1500, when a fleet of 12 Portuguese ships carrying nearly 1200 men rolled up near what is today Porto Seguro. When they arrived, their indigenous reception committee was ready and waiting.

In a letter back to the Portuguese king, scribe Pero Vaz de Caminha described a group of around two dozen men who were brown-skinned, not wearing any clothes and carrying bows and arrows.

TIMELINE

c 12,000 BC

Early inhabitants of the Americas arrive from Siberia in waves from 12,000 to 8000 BC, crossing land now submerged beneath the Bering Strait, then gradually spreading southward over many millennia.

AD 1500

Pedro Álvares Cabral makes landfall around present-day Porto Seguro and claims possession of the land – believed at first to be an island – for the Portuguese crown.

1549

Tomé de Sousa is named Brazil's first governor. He centralizes authority and founds the city of Salvador, which will remain Brazil's capital for more than two centuries.

The festivities didn't last long. Having erected a cross and held Mass in the land they baptized Terra da Vera Cruz (Land of the True Cross), the Portuguese took to the waves once again. With lucrative spice, ivory and diamond markets in Asia and Africa to exploit, Portugal had bigger fish to fry elsewhere. It wasn't till 1531 that the first Portuguese settlers arrived in Brazil.

Brazil's Indigenous People

For Brazil's indigenous people, April 22, 1500, marked the first chapter in their gradual extermination. Sixteenth-century European explorers along the Amazon encountered large, widespread populations; some were practicing agriculture while others were nomadic hunter-gatherers. Coastal peoples fell into three main groups: the Guarani (south of São Paulo and in the Paraguai and Paraná basins inland), the Tupi or Tupinambá (along most of the rest of the coast) and the Tapuia (peoples inhabiting shorter stretches of coast in among the Tupi and Guarani). The Tupi and Guarani had much in common in language and culture. A European adaptation of the Tupi-Guarani language later spread throughout colonial Brazil and is still spoken by some people in Amazonia.

Over the following centuries a four-front war – cultural, physical, territorial and biological – was waged on the indigenous way of life. Many indigenous fell victim to the *bandeirantes* – groups of roaming raiders who spent the 17th and 18th centuries exploring Brazil's interior, pillaging indigenous settlements as they went. Those who escaped such a fate were struck down by the illnesses shipped in from Europe, to which they had no natural resistance. Others were worked to death on sugar plantations.

Rio de Janeiro got its name because the Portuguese arrived in January (Janeiro), 1502, and thought that Guanabara Bay on which it lies was the mouth of a *rio* (river).

The Unconquered (2011), written by Scott Wallace, provides a fascinating glimpse of one of the Amazon's mysterious and little-known peoples.

Sugar & Slavery

Brazil didn't boast the ivory and spices of Africa and the East Indies, and the only thing that had interested the Portuguese in the early years after they had found it was a rock-hard tree known as *pau brazil* (brazilwood), which yielded a valuable red dye. Merchants began sending a few ships each year to harvest brazilwood and take it back to Europe, and the colony changed its name to Brazil in tribute to the tree. Alas, the most accessible trees were rapidly depleted. But after colonization in 1531, the colonists soon worked out that Brazil was a place where sugarcane grew well. Sugar came to Brazil in 1532 and hasn't left since. It was coveted by a hungry European market, which used it for medicinal purposes, to flavor foods and even in wine.

1550

Facing a shortage of labor (as indigenous slaves die from introduced European diseases), Portugal turns to the African slave trade; open-air slave markets spread across the slowly growing colony.

1621

The Dutch West India Company sets up shop in Northeastern Brazil, heralding the beginning of the Dutch presence in Brazil. Its goal: to wrest control of the colony from Portugal.

1650s

Communities of runaway slaves, called *quilombos*, flourish in the countryside, eventually becoming targets of *bandeirantes*. Hundreds of these communities will later become towns following abolition in the late 1800s.

1695

Palmares, the largest *quilombo* in Brazil's Northeast – and home to more than 20,000 inhabitants – is destroyed following decades of attacks by Portuguese troops.

One of Brazil's great folk heroes is Chico Rei, an African king enslaved and brought to work in the mines, but who managed to buy his freedom and later the freedom of his tribe.

The Slave Trade

African slaves started to pour into Brazil's slave markets from about 1550. They were torn from a variety of tribes in Angola, Mozambique and Guinea, as well as the Sudan and Congo. Whatever their origins and cultures, their destinations were identical: slave markets such as Salvador's Pelourinho or Belém's Mercado Ver-o-Peso. By the time slavery was abolished in Brazil in 1888, around 3.6 million Africans had been shipped to Brazil – nearly 40% of the total that came to the New World.

Africans were seen as better workers and less susceptible to the European diseases that had proved the undoing of so many indigenous people. In short, they were a better investment. Yet the Portuguese didn't go out of their way to protect this investment. Slaves were brought to Brazil in subhuman conditions: taken from their families and packed into squalid ships for the monthlong journey to Brazil.

BRAZIL'S INDIGENOUS PEOPLE TODAY

When the Portuguese arrived in 1500, there were, by the most common estimates, between two and four million indigenous people already living in Brazil, in over 1000 different tribes. Five centuries later there are an estimated 900,000 indigenous left, living in a little over 200 tribes. Slavery, disease, armed conflict and loss of territory all took a savage toll on Brazil's native peoples, to the point where in the 1980s indigenous numbers were under 300,000 and it was feared they might die out completely. Since then there has been a marked recovery in the indigenous population, partly thanks to international concern about groups such as the Yanomami, who were threatened with extermination by disease and violence from an influx of gold prospectors into their lands. Government policy has become more benign and huge areas of Brazil are now Terra Indígena (Indigenous Land). Just over 1 million sq km – more than 12% of the whole country – is now either officially registered as Indigenous Land or in the process of registration

There are those who think that 12% of national territory reserved for 0.25% of the national population is too much and fail to respect indigenous rights to these lands. Disputes between indigenous groups and loggers, miners, homesteaders, hunters, road builders and reservoir constructors are still common, and sometimes violent.

It's thought there may still be more than 60 uncontacted tribes, mostly small groups in the Amazon forests – home to about 60% of Brazil's indigenous (and almost all of the existing Indigenous Lands).

Most of Brazil's indigenous still live traditional lifestyles, hunting (some still with blowpipes and poisoned arrows) and gathering and growing plants for food, medicine and utensils. Their homes are usually made of natural materials such as wood or grass. Ritual activity is strong, body- and face-painting is prevalent, and most indigenous people are skilled in making pottery, basketry, masks, headdresses, musical instruments and other artisanry with their hands.

1696

News of the discovery of gold in Brazil reaches Lisbon. In ensuing years, tens of thousands of migrants stream into present-day Minas Gerais, Mato Grosso, Goiás and southern Bahia.

1750

The Spanish concede to the Portuguese the Treaty of Madrid, which hands over 6 million sq km to the Portuguese and puts Brazil's western borders largely where they are today.

1750s

Gold (and later diamonds) begin to define the colonial economy. In Minas Gerais the population explodes from 30,000 in 1710 to 500,000 by the end of the century.

1763

With gold flowing from Minas Gerais through Rio de Janeiro, the city grows in wealth and population; the Portuguese court transfers the capital of Brazil from Salvador to Rio.

Masters & Slaves

For those who survived the ordeal of the journey, arrival in Brazil meant only continued suffering. A slave's existence was one of brutality and humiliation. Kind masters were the exception, not the rule, and labor on the plantations was relentless. Slaves were required to work as many as 17 hours each day, before retiring to the squalid *senzala* (slave quarters), and with as many as 200 slaves packed into each dwelling, hygiene was a concept as remote as the distant coasts of Africa. Dysentery, typhus, yellow fever, malaria, tuberculosis and scurvy were rife; malnutrition a fact of life. Syphilis also plagued a slave population sexually exploited by its masters.

The sexual exploitation of slaves by white colonists was so common that a large mixed-race population soon emerged. Off the plantations there was a shortage of white women, so many poorer white colonists lived with black or indigenous women.

Gilberto Freyre's *The Masters and the Slaves* (1933), a book about the relationship between slaves and masters on Pernambuco's sugar plantations, revolutionized Brazilian thinking about the African contribution to Brazilian society.

Resistance & the Quilombos

Resistance to slavery took many forms. Documents of the period refer to the desperation of the slaves who starved themselves to death, killed their babies or fled. Sabotage and theft were frequent, as were work slowdowns, stoppages and revolts.

Other slaves sought solace in African religion and culture. The mix of Catholicism (made compulsory by slave masters) and African traditions spawned a syncretic religion on the sugar plantations, known today as Candomblé. The slaves masked illegal customs with a facade of Catholic saints and rituals.The martial art capoeira also grew out of the slave communities. Enslaved peoples also built their own churches. Places like the Igreja NS do Rosário dos Pretos in Salvador served as the epicenter for their communities.

Many slaves escaped from their masters to form *quilombos,* communities of runaway slaves that quickly spread across the countryside. The most famous, the Republic of Palmares, which survived through much of the 17th century, was home to some 20,000 people before it was destroyed by federal troops.

As abolitionist sentiment grew in the 19th century, many (unsuccessful) slave rebellions were staged, the *quilombos* received more support and ever-greater numbers of slaves fled the plantations. Only abolition itself, in 1888, stopped the growth of *quilombos.*

Quilombo (1984), directed by Cacá Diegues, is an epic history flick in which the vast Palmares *quilombo* – a community of runaway slaves led by the legendary Zumbi – is reconstructed in Rio's Baixada Fluminense.

The Bandeirantes & the Gold Rush

The *bandeirantes,* too, were keen to make inroads into Brazil. These bands of raiders roamed Brazil's interior in search of indigenous slaves, mapping out territory and bumping off the odd indigenous community along the way.

1789

The first organized movement toward independence springs to life. Tiradentes and 11 other conspirators organize the Inconfidência Mineira to overthrow the Portuguese. The plot fails, however, and Tiradentes is executed.

1807

Napoleon invades Portugal and the Portuguese prince regent (later known as Dom João VI) and his entire court of 15,000 flee for Brazil. The royal coffers shower wealth upon Rio.

1815

Dom João VI declares Rio the capital of the United Kingdom of Portugal and Brazil. The same year, a mounting financial crisis forces the king to return to Portugal.

1822

Left in charge of Brazil after his father Dom João VI returns to Portugal, the prince regent Dom Pedro I declares independence from Portugal and crowns himself 'emperor' of Brazil.

The *bandeirantes* took their name from the trademark flag-bearer who would front their expeditions. During the 17th and 18th centuries, group after group of *bandeirantes* set out from São Paulo. The majority were bilingual in Portuguese and Tupi-Guarani, born of Portuguese fathers and indigenous mothers. They benefited from both indigenous survival techniques and European weaponry.

By the mid-17th century they had journeyed as far as the peaks of the Peruvian Andes and the Amazon lowlands. It was the exploits of these marauders that stretched Brazil's borders to their current extent. In 1750, after four years of negotiations with the Spanish, their conquests were secured. The Treaty of Madrid handed more than 6 million sq km to the Portuguese and put Brazil's western borders more or less where they are today.

The *bandeirantes* were known for more than just their colorful flags. Protected from arrows by heavily padded cotton jackets, they waged an all-out war on Brazil's indigenous people, despite the fact that many of them had indigenous mothers. Huge numbers of indigenous people fled inland, searching for shelter from the raiders in the Jesuit missions. But there were few hiding places – it is thought the *bandeirantes* killed or enslaved well in excess of 500,000 people.

With great mineral wealth flowing out of Brazil, it's no surprise that piracy surged during the epoch. Islands such as Ilha Grande, with its sheltered bays and fresh water supply, made convenient launchpads on gold-laden Portuguese vessels.

Gold

In 1500 Pero Vaz de Caminha wrote to his king, describing the uncertainties of wealth in the interior, and the possibility that there might be gold, silver or another type of valuable material.

Though it wasn't discovered until nearly two centuries later, there certainly was gold in Brazil. Unsurprisingly, it was the *bandeirantes* who discovered it in the 1690s in the Serra do Espinhaço in Minas Gerais.

For part of the 18th century Brazil became the world's greatest gold 'producer,' unearthing wealth that helped build many of Minas Gerais' historic cities. Boom towns like Ouro Prêto, Sabará, Mariana and São João del Rei sprang up in the mountain valleys. Wealthy merchants built opulent mansions and bankrolled stunning baroque churches, many of which remain to this day.

Gold produced a major shift in Brazil's population from the Northeast to the Southeast. When gold was first discovered, there were no white colonists in the territory of Minas Gerais. By 1710 the population had reached 30,000, and by the end of the 18th century it was 500,000 – the vast majority arriving from Portugal. An estimated one-third of the two million slaves brought to Brazil in the 18th century were sent to the goldfields, where their lives were often worse than in the sugar fields.

But the gold boom didn't last. By 1750 the mining regions were in decline and coastal Brazil was returning to center stage. Many of the gold hunters ended up in Rio de Janeiro, which grew rapidly.

1831

Brazil's first home-grown monarch, Dom Pedro, proves incompetent and abdicates the throne. His son Pedro II takes power in 1840 and ushers in a long period of growth and stability.

1835

Inspired by the successful Haitian Revolution some years earlier, Brazilian slaves in Salvador stage an uprising – Brazil's last big slave revolt – which narrowly fails.

1865

Brazil, allied with Uruguay and Argentina, wages the 'War of the Triple Alliance' on Paraguay. South America's bloodiest conflict leaves untold thousands dead, and wipes out half of Paraguay's population.

1888

Slavery is abolished in Brazil, the last country in the New World to do so. The law is signed by Princesa Isabel.

Dom João VI

Brazil became a temporary sanctuary to the Portuguese royal family in 1807. Running scared from Napoleon, whose army was at that moment advancing on Lisbon, some 15,000 court members fled to Rio de Janeiro, led by the prince regent, Dom João.

Like so many *estrangeiros* (foreigners) arriving in Brazil, the regent fell in love with the place and granted himself the privilege of becoming the country's ruler. He opened Rio's Jardim Botânico (Botanical Gardens) to the public in 1822, and they remain there to this day in the upmarket Jardim Botânico neighborhood.

Even after Napoleon's defeat at Waterloo in 1815, Dom João showed no sign of abandoning Brazil. When his mother, Dona Maria I, died the following year, he became king and declared Rio the capital of the United Kingdom of Portugal and Brazil. Brazil became the only New World colony ever to have a European monarch ruling on its soil.

The hilarious film *Carlota Joaquina, Princesa do Brasil* (1995) is about a Spanish princess married to the future Dom João VI, who flees with the entire Portuguese court to Brazil to escape Napoleon.

Independence

Independence eventually came in 1822, 30 years after the Inconfidência Mineira (the first organized movement toward independence, organised by Tiradentes and 11 other conspirators to overthrow the Portuguese). Legend has it that on the banks of São Paulo's Ipiranga river, Brazil's then regent, Dom João's son Pedro, pulled out his sword, bellowing, '*Independência ou morte!*' (Independence or death!). With the same breath he declared himself Emperor Dom Pedro I.

The Portuguese quickly gave in to the idea of a Brazilian empire. Without a single shot being fired, Dom Pedro I became the first emperor of an independent Brazil. The *povo brasileiro* (Brazilian people), however, were not as keen on Pedro as he was about their newly born nation. From all accounts he was a blundering incompetent, whose sexual exploits (and resulting string of children) horrified even the most permissive of Brazilians. After nine years of womanizing he was forced to abdicate, leaving his five-year-old son, Dom Pedro II, to take over.

A period of crisis followed: the heir to the throne was, after all, just a child. Between 1831 and 1840 Brazil was governed by so-called *regências* (regencies), a time of political turmoil and widespread rebellions. The only solution was the return of the monarchy and a law was passed to declare Dom Pedro II an adult, well before his 18th birthday.

Aged just 15, Dom Pedro II received the title of Emperor and Perpetual Defender of Brazil (so began the so-called 'Império Brasil', aka 'Brazilian Empire'), precipitating one of the most prosperous spells in the country's history, barring the war with Paraguay in 1865. Invaded by its neighbor,

The bloodiest and most radical of the 1830s revolts was the Cabanagem War in Pará. Rebels held Belém for a year before being evicted and decimated by government troops.

1889

A military coup, supported by Brazil's wealthy coffee farmers, overthrows Pedro II. The monarchy is abolished and the Brazilian Republic is born. Pedro II goes into exile in Paris.

1890

Demand for rubber skyrockets with the start of the US automobile industry. Brazil, the world's only natural exporter until 1910, fuels boom times in Amazonian cities like Belém and Manaus.

1890s

With slavery abolished, Brazil opens its borders to meet its labor needs. Over the next four decades, millions arrive from Italy, Portugal, Spain, Germany and later Japan and other countries.

1920

The rubber boom goes bust as the Dutch and English plant their own rubber trees in the East Indies. Brazil's monopoly on the world rubber market deflates.

Brazil teamed up with Argentina and Uruguay and thrashed the Paraguayans back across the border.

Paraguay was left crippled – its population of about half a million slashed to just 200,000, of whom around 180,000 were women. Brazil, too, suffered heavily: around 100,000 men died, many of them slaves sent to war in the place of wealthier Brazilians.

A masterpiece of Brazilian literature, *Rebellion in the Backlands* (1902) vividly describes the Canudos massacre. Author Euclides de Cunha witnessed the end of Canudos as a correspondent for a São Paulo newspaper.

Abolition & the Republic

Since the 16th century, slavery had formed the backbone of a brutally unequal society in Brazil. In 1880 the noted abolitionist Joaquim Nabuco wrote about the grave injustices woven into Brazilian society.

To undo something so deeply ingrained into the Brazilian way of life was never likely to be easy. Brazil prevaricated for nearly 60 years before any sort of resolution was reached. The 19th century was punctuated by a series of half-hearted legislative attempts to lay the slave industry to rest. Such laws repeatedly failed.

Slave trafficking to Brazil was banned in 1850, but continued clandestinely. Not until May 13, 1888 – 80 years after Britain had freed its slaves – was slavery itself officially banned in Brazil. Unsurprisingly, this didn't make a huge immediate difference to the welfare of the 800,000 freed slaves, who were largely illiterate and unskilled. Thousands were cast onto the streets without any kind of infrastructure to support them. Many died, while others flooded to Brazil's urban centers, adding to the cities' first slums. Still today, the black community overall experiences higher poverty and lack of access to educational resources.

'Order and Progress,' the slogan on Brazil's flag, comes from French philosopher Auguste de Comte (1797–1857), whose elevation of reason and scientific knowledge over traditional religious beliefs influenced the young Brazilian republic.

Not far out of the door behind slavery was the Império Brasil. In 1889 a military coup, supported by Brazil's wealthy coffee farmers, decapitated the old Brazilian empire and the republic was born. The emperor went into exile, where he died a couple of years later.

A military clique ruled Brazil for the next four years until elections were held, but because of ignorance, corruption, and land and literacy requirements, only about 2% of the adult population voted. Little changed, except that the power of the military and the now-influential coffee growers increased, while it diminished for the sugar barons.

Open Borders

In the final decade of the 19th century, Brazil opened its borders. Millions of immigrants – from Italy, Japan, Spain, Germany, Portugal and elsewhere – streamed into Brazil to work on the coffee *fazendas* (farms), and to make new lives in the rapidly growing cities, especially Rio and São Paulo, adding further textures to Brazil's ethnic mixture and confirming the shift of Brazil's economic center of gravity from the Northeast to the Southeast.

1930

Getúlio Vargas comes into power. Inspired by European fascists, President Vargas presides over an authoritarian state, playing a major role in Brazilian politics until his fall from power in 1951.

1937

Getúlio Vargas announces a new constitution for what he calls the 'Estado Novo' (New State); he passes minimum-wage laws in 1938, expands the military and centralizes power.

1942

Initially maintaining neutrality, Brazil enters WWII on the side of the Allies, providing raw materials, plus 25,000 troops (the only Latin American nation to do so).

1950

Newly constructed Maracanã Stadium in Rio plays center stage in the FIFA World Cup. Brazil dominates until the final, when, before 200,000 fans, it suffers a stunning loss to Uruguay.

Over the next century, immigrants continued to flood into Brazil. The country became a haven for Jews fleeing persecution at the hands of the Nazis, as well as Nazis looking to avoid being put on trial for war crimes. Arabs, universally known as *turcos* by the Brazilians, also joined the influx of newcomers. Many of the traders you'll meet at Rio de Janeiro's Rua Uruguaiana flea market hail from the Middle East.

PRINCESA ISABEL: LIBERATOR OF SLAVES

Princesa Isabel's parents didn't leave much space on their daughter's birth certificate. Born at the Palácio de São Cristóvão to Pedro II and Teresina Cristina on July 29, 1846, she found herself the proud owner of no less than 10 names. Isabel Cristina Leopoldina Augusta Micaela Gabriela Rafaela Gonzaga de Bragança e Bourbon. She's better known today, however, by this memorable title: the liberator of slaves.

For over 300 years Brazilian society had been defined by the slave trade. Keen to cover their tracks, slave traders destroyed many documents relating to their line of work. But it is believed that around 3.6 million slaves were shipped from Africa to Brazil between 1550 and 1888, used as free labor for the sugar (and later coffee) plantations.

The first real steps toward abolition came in 1826 when the English, having themselves banned slavery in 1807, forced Brazil to outlaw slave-trafficking. Yet over the following decades the numbers of slaves entering Brazil only rose. A series of equally ineffective laws proceeded, of which – as is often the case in Brazil – not a single one '*pegou*' (caught on).

On May 13, 1888, after nearly 80 years of prevarication and crossed words with the pro-abolition English, Isabel put pen to paper on the document that would define her life – the Lei Aurea. The document contained less than 200 words but its implications were huge. 'Slavery,' it pointed out, 'is now extinct in Brazil.'

Increasingly, however, historians look at her actions with cynicism. Abolition eradicated an unquestionable evil from Brazilian society, but what would Brazil's 800,000 freed slaves, largely illiterate, unskilled and unemployed, now do to support themselves?

Isabel seems not to have anticipated this particular question. Thousands of ex-slaves were cast out onto the streets without any kind of infrastructure to support them. Many died, while others flooded to Brazil's urban centers, adding to the city's first favelas.

Rio's world-famous Mangueira samba school marked the centenary year of the Lei Aurea with a scathing critique of the law, entitled '100 years of freedom, reality or illusion?' 'Could it be that the Lei Aurea so dreamt about, signed so long ago, was not the end of slavery?' it asked.

A visit to the impoverished Mangueira favela in Rio's North Zone, in which many of the inhabitants are paid miserable wages to work as porters and maids for the city's better off, shows the answer is a resounding yes. As the samba points out, Princesa Isabel freed black Brazilians from 'the whips of the *senzala*' but left them stranded 'in the misery of the favela'.

1954

Following an explosive political scandal, the military calls for the resignation of President Getúlio Vargas. He pens a melodramatic letter then shoots himself through the heart at his Rio palace.

1956

Juscelino Kubitschek de Oliveira (better known as JK), is elected president, and builds a new capital – Brasília. JK had to borrow heavily to finance the project, leading to inflation that will dog the economy for decades.

1958

Brazil wins its first football World Cup. The team catapults to victory over Sweden, largely on the skills of a precocious 17-year-old unknown by the name of Pelé.

1960

The capital is officially moved from Rio de Janeiro to Brasília. Architects Oscar Niemeyer and Lúcio Costa play a starring role in building hypermodern Brasília from scratch in just 41 months.

Getúlio Vargas, Populist Dictator

The Vargas era began in 1930 when members of the newly formed Liberal Alliance party decided to fight back after the defeat of their candidate, Getúlio Vargas, in the presidential elections. The revolution kicked off on October 3 in Rio Grande do Sul and spread rapidly through other states. Twenty-one days later President Júlio Prestes was deposed and on November 3 Vargas became Brazil's new 'provisional' president.

From 1980 to 1994, Brazilians suffered devastating hyperinflation, which peaked above 2000% for several years. At this rate, rent doubled every 10 weeks, food and clothes went up 40% a month and credit cards charged 25% a month interest.

The formation of the Estado Novo (New State) in November 1937 made Vargas the first Brazilian president to wield absolute power. Inspired by the fascist governments of Salazar in Portugal and Mussolini in Italy, Vargas banned political parties, imprisoned political opponents and censored artists and the press.

Despite this, many liked Vargas. The 'father' of Brazil's workers, he introduced new labor laws and remained popular throughout his tenure. In 1951 he was elected president, this time democratically. But Vargas' new administration was plagued by the hallmark of Brazilian politics – corruption. Amid calls from the military for his resignation, Vargas responded dramatically. He penned a note saying, 'I leave this life to enter into history,' and on the following morning, August 24, 1954, fired a single bullet through his own heart.

The Generals Take Over

In 1964 the left-leaning president João Goulart was overthrown in a so-called *revolução* (revolution) – really a military coup, which many Brazilians believed was backed by the US government. President Lyndon Johnson did nothing to dampen such theories when he immediately cabled his warmest wishes to the new Brazilian administration.

Set during the military dictatorship, Bruno Barreto's film *Four Days in September* (1998) is based on the 1969 kidnapping of the US ambassador to Brazil by leftist guerrillas.

Brazil's military regime was not as brutal as those of Chile or Argentina – a reality that led to the somewhat-unkind saying, 'Brazil couldn't even organize a dictatorship properly.' Yet for the best part of 20 years, freedom of speech was an unknown concept and political parties were banned.

The Brazilian economy flourished. Year after year in the late 1960s and early 1970s, the economy grew by over 10% as Brazil's rulers borrowed heavily from international banks. But in the absence of rural land reform, millions moved to the cities, where favelas filled up the open spaces.

During this time, Brazil's obsession with 'megaprojects' was born. Under the quick-spending regime, construction began on numerous colossal (and mostly ill-fated) plans, including the Transamazônica highway, the Rio-Niterói Bridge and the Ilha do Fundão, which was to house Rio's Federal University.

1964
President Goulart is overthrown by a military coup – with strong evidence of US involvement. So begins the era of dictatorship, with generals running the show for the next 20 years.

1968
The government passes the repressive Ato Institutional 5 law, which purges opposition legislators, judges and mayors from public office; most political parties are banned. Protests erupt nationwide.

1968
The Brazilian economy booms, averaging an incredible 10% growth for the next six years. Rapid income growth continues into the 1970s.

1972
The era of megaprojects and skyrocketing deficits begins, with the opening of the 5300km Transamazônica highway. It costs nearly US$1 billion, but never achieves its goal of colonizing the Amazon.

The Workers Organize

By the late 1970s, the economic boom was dying and opposition to the regime began to spread from the educated middle class to the working class. A series of strikes in the São Paulo car industry signaled the intent of the militant new workers' movement. At the helm was charismatic Luíz Inácio 'Lula' da Silva, who famously lost one *dedo* (finger) in a factory accident.

The Partido dos Trabalhadores (PT; Workers' Party), Brazil's first-ever mass political party to speak for the poor, grew out of these strikes, and helped pave the way toward *abertura* (opening), a cautious return to civilian rule between 1979 and 1985. With popular opposition gathering force, the military announced gradual moves toward a democratic Brazil.

Although it's set in Britain in the future, Terry Gilliam's dystopian film *Brazil* (1985) pulls themes from real 1980s Brazil, and other military dictatorships, showing an Orwellian world of crushing bureaucracy.

THE ORIGINS OF THE FAVELA

In the 1870s and '80s, terrible droughts coupled with the decline of the sugar industry brought economic devastation. Offering a vision of hope, messianic movements became popular among Brazil's poor. The most famous was that of Canudos, led by itinerant preacher Antônio Conselheiro (Antônio the Counselor), who wandered for years through the backlands preaching and prophesying the appearance of the Antichrist and the end of the world. He railed against the new republican government and in 1893 eventually settled with his followers at Canudos, in the interior of northern Bahia. Within a year and a half Canudos had grown to a city of 35,000.

The republican government sensed plots in Canudos to return Brazil to the monarchy. It took them several attempts, however, before a federal force of 8000 well-supplied soldiers – many of whom hailed from Rio – took Canudos after vicious, hand-to-hand, house-to-house fighting. It was a war of extermination that nearly wiped out every man, woman and child from Canudos; the settlement was then burned to the ground to erase it from the nation's memory.

The surviving soldiers and their wives returned to Rio, where they were promised land in exchange for their victory. The government, however, reneged on the promise, and the soldiers occupied the nearby hillside of Morro da Providência. Oddly enough, as the first tenants put up makeshift shelter and settled in, they came across the same hardy shrub they found in the arid lands surrounding Canudos. Called *favela,* this plant caused skin irritations to all who came in contact with it – according to some accounts, the protective shrub even helped repel the army's initial invasions. Hillside residents began calling their new home the Morro da Favela, and the name caught on. Soon the word *favela* was used to describe the ever-increasing number of informal communities appearing around Rio, which quickly gathered a mix of former slaves and poverty-stricken inhabitants from the interior, who came to the city seeking a better life.

1979–80

The consistent decline of workers' wages leads to strikes across the country. Unions call for justice and young workers join with intellectuals and activists to form Partido dos Trabalhadores (PT; Workers' Party).

1984

The Movimento Sem Terra (MST; Landless Workers' Movement) – an organization calling for land reform – is founded. The fringe organization of 6000 families grows to more than 1.5 million today.

1988

Amazonia rubber-tappers' leader and environmentalist Chico Mendes is murdered by a local rancher and his son. The public outcry following Mendes' death forces the government to create extractive reserves.

1994

Following the impeachment of President Collor, Vice President Itamar Franco takes power. He introduces a new currency, the real, which stabilizes the economy and ushers in an economic boom.

Democracy & Corruption

In 1985 a presidential election took place, though the only voters were members of the national congress. Unexpectedly, Tancredo Neves, opposing the military candidate, came out on top, and millions of Brazilians took to the streets to celebrate the end of military rule.

Australian Peter Robb weaves the whole of Brazil's history, and most of its literature, into his account of the alleged widespread corruption of the Collor de Mello regime, *A Death in Brazil* (2003).

Immediately a spanner was thrown in the works: Neves died from heart failure before he could assume the presidency. His vice-presidential candidate, the whiskered José Sarney, took over. Sarney – who had supported the military until 1984 – held office until 1989, a period in which runaway inflation helped Brazil rack up a gargantuan foreign debt.

In the 1989 direct presidential election, the first ever that could be called democratic, it was a Northeastern political climber by the name of Collor who was victorious, beating Lula, the PT's candidate, by the smallest of margins.

Fernando Collor de Mello, former governor of the small state of Alagoas, revolutionized consumer laws. Sell-by dates, however, couldn't save him from disgrace. An ever-lengthening list of scandals involving Collor and his intimate associate PC Farias – alleged corruption on a vast scale, alleged drug deals, family feuds – led to a congressional inquiry, huge student protests and eventually the president's impeachment.

Brazil's Boom Days

The first favela (slum) appeared on Rio's landscape in 1897, but it wasn't until 1994 that the communities (which today number over 600) were included on maps.

Following Collor's impeachment, Vice President Itamar Franco found himself in the hot seat. Despite his reputation as an eccentric, his administration was credited with competence and integrity. Franco's greatest achievement was to stabilize Brazil's violently erratic economy, introducing a new currency, the real. Pegged to the US dollar, the real caused inflation to plummet from a rate of over 5000% in late 1993 to under 10% in 1994.

The Plano Real sparked an economic boom that lasted two decades, though it was Franco's successor, former finance minister Fernando Henrique Cardoso, who presided through the mid-1990s over a growing economy and record foreign investment. He is often credited with laying the groundwork that put Brazil's hyperinflation to bed, though often at the neglect of social problems.

Come the 2002 election, Lula, at the fourth time of standing, toned down his socialist rhetoric, and promised to repay Brazil's international debts. This propelled Lula to a convincing victory over the center-right candidate Jose Serra. For the first time ever, Brazil had a government on the left of the political spectrum and a president who really knew what poverty was like. One of 22 children born to a dirt-poor illiterate

2002

After four unsuccessful attempts, Luíz Inácio 'Lula' da Silva is elected president. The former union leader serves a moderate first term, despite upper-class fears of radical agendas.

2003

President Lula launches Bolsa Família, a program of cash payments to Brazil's 11 million poorest families. The social program is credited with reducing poverty by 27% during Lula's first term.

2011

Dilma Rousseff is sworn in as president of Brazil, becoming the first woman ever to hold the office. As Lula's handpicked successor, she largely continues the policies of her predecessor.

2014

Brazil hosts the 2014 FIFA World Cup, spending around US$12 billion in preparation for the event, which is staged at 12 different cities across the country.

farmworker from Brazil's stricken Northeast, Lula had worked as a shoeshine boy, then a mechanic, then a trade-union leader.

His accession initially alarmed investors, who had envisioned a left-leaning renegade running the economy amok. In fact, he surprised friends and foes alike with one of the most financially prudent administrations in years, while still addressing Brazil's egregious social problems.

When Lula left office in 2010, Brazil's economic prosperity was clear. Brazil became a net foreign creditor for the first time in 2008 and the country weathered the economic recession at the end of the decade better than any other developing country. He also helped achieved notable success in antipoverty measures, and helped millions to enter the middle class – all of which helps explain why Lula was rated Brazil's most popular president in history; in his final months in office his approval rating was above 80%.

The Accidental President of Brazil, by Fernando Henrique Cardoso, is an elucidating memoir by one of Brazil's most popular presidents, a former sociology professor vaulted into power.

Bye-Bye Brasil is a classic Brazilian film that follows a traveling circus across Brazil's Northeast, charting the profound changes in Brazilian society that characterized the second half of the 20th century.

Trouble Ahead

Riding Lula's coattails, fellow party member Dilma Rousseff was elected Brazil's first female president in 2010. A former Marxist guerilla, Dilma came down hard on corruption – at least initially. During her first year in office, six of her government ministers lost their positions due to their involvement in corruption scandals. Her second term, however, imploded when high-ranking members of her own party were linked to a massive corruption scandal. Yet even before this came to light, Rousseff's popularity was tanking, owing in part to anger over the obscene amount of money being spent on the 2014 FIFA World Cup – money that protestors said would be better spent on health, education and poverty reduction. To make matters worse, the burgeoning Brazilian economy stalled, with GDP growth averaging a mere 2% per year during her first term, and outright shrinking in her second term (by a staggering 3.6% in 2016).

With huge protests rocking the country, and the country in the grip of its largest recession in history, Rousseff was headed for a fall, and in 2016 she was impeached and removed from office for budgetary violations. Her vice-president, Michel Temer, took over. He too, however, proved unable to curb Brazil's grave problems: its surging unemployment, weakening currency and high crime rates rocking cities across the country – not to mention the endless scourge of corruption (Temer was also under investigation for accepting bribes and money laundering). Presidential elections were held in 2018, bringing a host of unlikely candidates to the fore.

Two recent books look at one of Brazil's most popular presidents: Richard Bourne's *Lula of Brazil: The Story So Far* (2008), and *Lula and the Workers Party in Brazil* (2003) by Sue Branford.

2014

News emerges of Brazil's largest corruption scandal in history. High-ranking politicians and oil-company executives are linked to a US$5 billion scheme that shakes the country to its core.

2015

In the run-up to the Summer Olympics, Rio spends US$13 billion on stadiums, infrastructure and civic beautification, adding a new metro line, a downtown light rail and new museums.

2016

Brazil's first female president is impeached for breaking budgetary laws. Her vice-president, Michel Temer, assumes office. The following year he is charged with accepting bribes, and his approval rating plummets to 7%.

2018

Presidential elections veer toward chaos, with its most popular candidate (Lula) behind bars, its extreme right-wing candidate (Bolsonaro) violently stabbed during a campaign rally, and two other candidates under criminal investigation.

Life in Brazil

Brazil is a nation of astounding diversity, forged from African, European and indigenous influences, along with the tens of millions of immigrants who flooded into the country in the late 19th and early 20th centuries. Brazilians of today represent a complicated portrait of colors and creeds and hail from a wide range of socioeconomic backgrounds. The lifestyle is no less diverse – not surprising for a country that's home to both age-old indigenous cultures and modern metropolises.

Multiculturalism

Dozens of uncontacted indigenous groups still live in the Amazon. In 2018 FUNAI (Brazil's National Indian Foundation) released drone images of a tribe that had no known contact with the outside world. FUNAI estimates there are at least eight different uncontacted indigenous peoples living in the area.

Brazilian identity has been shaped not only by the Portuguese, who provided its language and main religion, but also by the indigenous population, Africans and the many immigrants who arrived over the years from Europe, the Middle East and Asia.

Indigenous culture, though often ignored or denigrated by urban Brazilians, has helped shape modern Brazil and its legends, dance and music. Many indigenous foods and beverages, such as tapioca, manioc (cassava), potatoes, *maté* and guaraná (a shrub whose berry is a stimulant; also a popular soft drink) have become staples.

The influence of African culture is also evident, especially in the Northeast. The slaves imported by the Portuguese brought with them their religion, music and cuisine, all of which have become a part of Brazilian identity.

Brazil had several waves of voluntary immigration. After the end of slavery in 1888, millions of Europeans were recruited to work in the coffee fields. The largest contingent was from Italy (some one million arrived between 1890 and 1920), but there were also many Portuguese and Spaniards, and smaller groups of Germans and Russians.

Immigration is only part of the picture when considering Brazil's diversity. Brazilians are just as likely to mention regional types, often accompanied by their own colorful stereotypes. Caboclos, who are descendants of local indigenous groups, live along the rivers in the Amazon region and keep alive the traditions and stories of their ancestors. *Gaúchos* populate Rio Grande do Sul, speak a Spanish-inflected Portuguese and can't quite shake the reputation for being rough-edged cowboys. By contrast, *baianos,* descendants of the first Africans in Brazil, are stereotyped for being the most extroverted and celebratory of Brazilians. *Mineiros* (residents of Minas Gerais state) are considered more serious and reserved than Brazil's coastal dwellers, while *sertanejos* (residents of the backlands – called *sertão* – of the Northeast) are dubbed tough-skinned individuals with strong folk traditions. *Cariocas* (residents of Rio city) are superficial beach bums according to *paulistanos* (residents of São Paulo city), who are often denigrated as being workaholics with no zeal for life – a rivalry that anyone who's lived in LA or New York can understand.

Japanese immigration began in 1908, and today São Paulo has the world's largest Japanese community outside of Japan.

Today there are dozens of terms to describe the various racial compositions of Brazilians, and it is not uncommon for apparently white Brazilians to have a mix of European, African and indigenous ancestors. Yet, despite appearances of integration and racial harmony, underneath is a brutal reality. Although black and multiracial people account for 45% of the population, they are sorely underrepresented in government and business, and often see little hope of rising out of poverty. Indigenous people are even more openly discriminated against, continuing a cycle that began with the genocidal policies of the first Europeans.

Population

Brazil is the world's fifth-most-populous country, but it also has one of the smallest population densities, with around 24 people per sq km. Most of Brazil's population lives along the coast, particularly in the South and Southeast, home to 75% of the country's inhabitants. Until the mid-20th century, Brazil was largely a rural country – today its population is more than 80% urban. The population in cities has exploded in the last half-century, though growth is slowing.

The Northeast has the highest concentration of Afro-Brazilians, with Salvador as its cultural capital. In the Amazon live Caboclos (literally 'Copper-Colored'), the descendants of indigenous peoples and the Portuguese. In the South is the most European of the Brazilian population, descendants of Italian and German immigrants.

While there is much more mixing between races, Brazil is a long way from being a color-blind society. Afro-Brazilians make up the bulk of low-paid workers, and are far more likely to live in favelas than in middle-class neighborhoods. More than 40% of Afro-Brazilians live in poverty (twice the rate of whites). Afro-Brazilians die younger than whites, earn less and have a greater risk of going to prison. Barely 2% of Afro-Brazilians attend university, though a quota system approved by the supreme court in 2012 aims to address the long-standing racial imbalance. Black political representatives and even high-ranking black employees are rarities – clear examples of the lack of opportunities for black people in Brazil.

The indigenous population today numbers more than 900,000, comprising 240 tribes. Although this is a fraction of the estimated two million or more in Brazil at the time of European arrival, the indigenous population has shown a remarkable resurgence in recent years: the population has tripled since 1970. Customs and beliefs vary widely from tribe to tribe – as do the strengths of these traditions in the face of expulsion from traditional lands, declining numbers, missionary activity and other influences.

After centuries of genocidal attacks, slavery, dispossession and death from imported diseases, Brazil's indigenous population is growing again but still faces a host of problems. Most of them live in the Amazon rainforest, and therefore the threats that the rainforest faces – logging, mining, ranching, farming, roads, settlements, dams, hydroelectric schemes – also threaten the indigenous whose way of life depends on it.

Lifestyles

Constructing a portrait of the typical Brazilian is a complicated task, given the wide mix of social, cultural and economic factors in play. One thing that everyone agrees on is the huge chasm separating the rich from the poor.

The country's middle and upper class live in comfortable apartments or houses, with all the trappings of the developed world, including good health care in private clinics, cars, vacation homes and easy access to the latest gadgets and trends (though prices for luxury goods are much higher here). The wealthiest send their children to private schools and abroad to university. Maids are common – even among middle-class Brazilians – and some families have chauffeurs and cooks. Depending on where one lives in the country, crime is likely to be of high concern. Those who can take extra precautions, opting for high-security buildings or even hiring bodyguards.

The 1979–83 droughts in the Northeast were among the worst the country has ever experienced, leaving between 250,000 and one million people dead.

The Ukrainian community in Brazil numbers 550,000, the majority of whom live in the South. Prudentopolis is a city of Orthodox churches and Slavic features, with 75% of the population of Ukrainian descent.

How to Be a Carioca (1992), by Priscilla Ann Goslin, is a humorous portrait of the Rio dweller, with tongue-in-cheek riffs on beach-going, driving, soap operas, football and *carioca* slang.

WOMEN IN BRAZIL

Brazil had one of the earliest feminist movements in Latin America, and women were among the first in the region to gain the right to vote, in 1932. Today there is a growing number of feminist NGOs, dedicated to educating women about their legal rights and family planning, while also training police how to handle cases of domestic violence. In Brasília there's even a feminist lobby.

Dilma Rousseff, who became Brazil's first female president in 2011, served as a major icon for breaking down barriers for women. Sadly, her tenure ended abruptly when she was impeached and removed from office in 2016 for budgetary violations. Some of her supporters feel that she was the victim of an antifeminist backlash; her fall from power was particularly stinging given that many of the parliamentarians who voted to remove her from office were under investigation for far more serious offenses than Rousseff.

Regardless of advances, many *machista* (chauvinist) stereotypes persist, and women are still sorely underrepresented in positions of power. Women occupy only around 11% of seats in the National Congress. As of 2018 this makes Brazil the lowest ranked in all of Latin America (where women on average make up around 29% of the legislature).

In other spheres, women represent around 43% of the workforce – a big leap from decades past but still below the average in Latin America (where women comprise 54% of the workforce). Unfortunately, the wage gap remains high. Depending on the industry, men earn anywhere from 22% to 36% more than women of the same age and income level.

Women receive 120 days of paid maternity leave (men receive five days of paternity leave). Abortions are still illegal in Brazil (except in cases of rape and maternal-health risks), and an estimated one million are performed each year, often with substantial health risks. More than 250,000 women each year are hospitalized from clandestine abortions. In 2018 the supreme court was considering a plan to decriminalize abortion, and the issue was a hot topic in the presidential election that year.

Somewhere below the elite are working-class folks struggling to put food on the table and pay the rent; the children tend to live at home until they are married. Couples tend to marry younger.

At the bottom of the socioeconomic ladder are *favelados* (residents of the favelas), who live in self-constructed housing (usually boxy concrete or brick dwellings) in crowded makeshift communities. Ranging in size from a few thousand inhabitants to over 70,000, favelas are found in nearly every urban area in Brazil. Most residents have electricity and running water, though open sewers run through many favelas. Access to education, adequate health care, transportation and other essential infrastructure can often be limited, though this is slowly changing under government-funded favela-improvement schemes.

Benedita da Silva: An Afro-Brazilian Woman's Story of Politics and Love (1997) is the memoir of Brazil's first Afro-Brazilian female senator, detailing her rise from the favelas to becoming an important political voice.

In the countryside, conditions for the poor can be even worse. Unequal land distribution dating back to the colonial era means that thousands of homeless rural families are left to squat on vacant land or work long hours as itinerant laborers for low wages.

Regardless of socioeconomic background, most Brazilians have a healthy appreciation for a good party (Carnaval is but one manifestation). This joie de vivre can be seen in football matches, on the beaches, in the samba clubs and on the streets. The flip side of this trait is *saudade,* that woeful manifestation of longing or deep regret, given much play on old bossa nova records.

Brazilian Rhythms

Shaped by the mixing of varied influences from three continents, Brazilian popular music has always been characterized by great diversity. The *samba canção* (samba song), for example, is a mixture of Spanish bolero with the cadences and rhythms of African music. Bossa nova was influenced by samba and North American music, particularly jazz. *Tropicália* mixed influences ranging from bossa nova and Italian ballads to blues and North American rock. Brazil is still creating new and original musical forms today.

Samba & Choro

The birth of modern Brazilian music essentially began with the birth of samba, first heard in the early 20th century in a Rio neighborhood near present-day Praça Onze. Here Bahian immigrants formed a tightly knit community in which traditional African customs – music, dance and the Candomblé religion – thrived. Such an atmosphere nurtured the likes of Pixinguinha, one of samba's founding fathers, as well as Donga, one of the composers of 'Pelo Telefone,' the first recorded samba song (in 1917) and an enormous success at the then-fledgling Carnaval.

Samba continued to evolve in the homes and *botequims* around Rio. The 1930s are known as the golden age of samba. Sophisticated lyricists such as Dorival Caymmi, Ary Barroso and Noel Rosa popularized samba *canção,* melody-driven samba laid over African percussion. Songs in this style featured sentimental lyrics and an emphasis on melody (rather than rhythm), foreshadowing the later advent of cool bossa nova.

The 1930s were also the golden age of samba songwriting for Carnaval. *Escolas de samba* (samba schools or clubs), which first emerged in 1928, soon became a vehicle for samba songwriting, and by the 1930s samba and Carnaval would be forever linked.

Great *sambistas* (samba singers) continued to emerge in Brazil over the next few decades, although other emerging musical styles diluted their popularity. Artists such as Cartola, Nelson Cavaquinho and Clementina de Jesus made substantial contributions to both samba and styles of music that followed from samba.

Traditional samba went through a rebirth a little over a decade ago with the opening of old-style *gafieiras* (dance halls) in Lapa. Today Rio is once again awash with great *sambistas.* Classic *sambistas* such as Alcione and Beth Carvalho still perform, while stars such as Teresa Christina and Grupo Semente are intimately linked to Lapa's rebirth. Other talents include Diogo Nogueira, the deep-voiced samba son of legendary singer João Nogueira, and Mart'nália, daughter of samba icon Martinho da Vila.

Another popular artist still active in Rio is Maria Rita, the talented singer and songwriter whose voice is remarkably similar to that of her late mother, Elis Regina – one of Brazil's all-time greats. Rita's album *Samba Meu Samba Meu* is still one of her best.

Choro is a relative of samba. Characterized by its jazzy sound, melodic leaps and sometimes rapid-fire tempo, *choro* is mostly instrumental music and highly improvisational. It's played on the *cavaquinho* or guitar alongside a recorder or flute. The flutist Pixinguinha (1898–1973) is one of the great legends of *choro.*

The Brazilian Sound, by Chris McGowan and Ricardo Pessanha, is a well-illustrated, readable introduction to Brazilian music, with insight into regional styles and musicians (big-name and obscure). Useful discography included.

Bossa Nova

In the 1950s came bossa nova (literally new wave), sparking a new era of Brazilian music. Bossa nova's founders – songwriter and composer Antônio Carlos (Tom) Jobim and guitarist João Gilberto, in association with the lyricist-poet Vinícius de Moraes – slowed down and altered the basic samba rhythm to create a more intimate, harmonic style. This initiated a new style of playing instruments and of singing.

Bossa Nova: The Story of the Brazilian Music that Seduced the World, by Ruy Castro, is an excellent book that captures the vibrant music and its backdrop of 1950s Rio.

Bossa nova's seductive melodies were very much linked to Rio's Zona Sul, where most bossa musicians lived. Songs such as Jobim's 'Corcovado' and Roberto Menescal's 'Rio' evoked an almost nostalgic portrait of the city with their quiet lyricism. Bossa nova was also associated with the new class of university-educated Brazilians, and its lyrics reflected the optimistic mood of the middle class in the 1950s.

By the 1960s bossa nova had become a huge international success. Bossa nova classics were adopted, adapted and recorded by such musical luminaries as Frank Sinatra, Ella Fitzgerald and Stan Getz, among others.

In addition to the founding members, other great Brazilian bossa nova musicians include Marcos Valle, Luiz Bonfá and Baden Powell. Bands from the 1960s such as Sergio Mendes & Brasil '66 were also quite influenced by bossa nova, as were other artists who fled the repressive military dictatorship to live and play abroad. More recent interpreters of the seductive bossa sound include the Bahian-born Rosa Passos and *carioca* (resident of Rio de Janeiro) Paula Morelenbaum.

Tropicália

One of Brazil's unique artistic movements, emerging in the late 1960s, *tropicália* was a direct response to the dictatorship that held power from 1964 to 1984. Leading the movement were Caetano Veloso and Gilberto Gil, making waves with songs of protest against the national regime. In addition to penning defiant lyrics, *tropicalistas* introduced the public to electric instruments, fragmentary melodies and wildly divergent musical styles.

Important figures linked to *tropicália* include Gal Costa, Jorge Ben Jor, Maria Bethânia, Os Mutantes and Tom Zé. Although *tropicália* wasn't initially embraced by the public, who objected to the electric and rock elements (in fact, Veloso was booed off the stage on several occasions), by the 1970s its radical ideas had been absorbed and accepted, and lyrics of protest were ubiquitous in songwriting of the time.

While 'pure' *tropicália* bands aren't around any more, the influence can still be heard in the music of groups such as AfroReggae, one of Rio's leading funk bands.

Música Popular Brasileira (MPB)

Música Popular Brasileira (MPB) is a catchphrase to describe all popular Brazilian music after bossa nova. It includes *tropicália*, *pagode* and Brazilian pop and rock. All Brazilian music has roots in samba; even in Brazilian rock, heavy metal, disco or pop, the samba sound is often present.

MPB first emerged in the 1970s along with talented musicians such as Edu Lobo, Milton Nascimento, Elis Regina, Djavan and dozens of others, many of whom wrote protest songs not unlike the *tropicalistas*. Chico Buarque is one of the first big names from this epoch, and is one of Brazil's best songwriters. His music career began in 1968 and spanned a time during which many of his songs were banned by the military dictatorship – in fact, his music became a symbol of protest during that era.

Jorge Ben Jor is another singer whose career, which began in the 1960s, has survived up to the present day. Highly addictive rhythms are omnipresent in Ben Jor's songs, as he incorporates African beats and elements of funk, samba and blues in his eclectic repertoire. The celebratory

TOP SOUNDS FROM BRAZIL

One of the world's great music cultures, Brazil has an astounding array of talented musicians. A list of our favorite songs could fill a small book, but we've limited our highly subjective pick to 24 songs from 24 different artists.

- 'Sampa' – Caetano Veloso
- 'Alvorada' – Cartola
- 'Calice' – Chico Buarque & Milton Nascimento
- 'Aguas de Março' – Elis Regina (written by Tom Jobim)
- 'Hoje é Dia da Festa' – Elza Soares
- 'Namorinho de Portão' – Gal Costa
- 'Quilombo, o El Dorado Negro' – Gilberto Gil
- 'Desafinado' – João Gilberto
- 'Mas Que Nada' – Jorge Ben Jor
- 'A Procura da Batida Perfeita' – Marcelo D2
- 'Novo Amor' – Maria Rita
- 'Carinhoso' – Marisa Monte (written by Pixinguinha)
- 'Besta é Tu' – Novos Baianos
- 'Panis et Circenses' – Os Mutantes
- 'Beira Mar' – Raimundo Fagner and Zeca Baleiro
- 'Carolina' – Seu Jorge
- 'Acenda o Farol' – Tim Maia
- 'Garota de Ipanema' – Tom Jobim
- 'Não me deixe só' – Vanessa da Mata
- 'Felicidade' – Vinícius de Moraes
- 'Boca do Ceu' – Ava Rocha

album *África Brasil* and his debut album, *Samba Esquema Novo* (with recognizable hits such as 'Mas, Que Nada!'), are among his best.

Carlinhos Brown continues to make immeasurable contributions to Brazilian music, particularly in the realm of Afro-Brazilian rhythms. Born in Bahia, Brown has influences that range from *merengue* (fast-paced dance-hall music originating in the Dominican Republic) to Candomblé music to straight-up funk in the style of James Brown (the US artist from whom Carlinhos took his stage name). In addition to creating the popular percussion ensemble Timbalada, he has a number of excellent albums of his own (notably *Alfagamabetizado*). Involved in many diverse projects, Brown was even nominated for an Oscar in 2012 for best original song ('Real in Rio' for the film *Rio*), which he and Sergio Mendes composed.

Brazilian Rock, Pop & Hip-Hop

MPB tends to bleed into other genres, particularly into rock and pop. One artist who moves comfortably between genres is Bebel Gilberto (the daughter of João Gilberto), who blends bossa nova with modern beats on jazz-inflected bilingual albums like *All in One* (2009). Another heiress of Brazilian traditions is the Rio-born Marisa Monte, popular at home and abroad for her singing and songwriting. Mixing samba, *forró* (traditional, fast-paced music from the Northeast), pop and rock, Marisa has created a number of fine solo albums (*Barulinho Bom – A Great Noise* in English – is one of her best) and has performed on many others. Her brief collaboration with Arnaldo Antunes and Carlinhos Brown resulted in the fine album

Tribalistas (2003). Other notable young singers who hail from a bossa line include Roberta Sá, whose albums blend elements of bossa, jazz and even reggae. Her 2016 album *Delírio no Circo* was nominated for a Grammy in 2017. Fernanda Porto, whose music is often described as drum 'n' bossa, blends electronica and bossa grooves; check out her 2009 album *Auto-Retrato*.

The expat singer-songwriter and performance artist Cibelle incorporates a mix of pop, folk and Brazilian sounds in her lush (mainly English-language) recordings, like those on *The Shine of Dried Electric Leaves* (2006) and the more electro-oriented *Unbinding (*2014). She came to prominence as the main vocalist on Suba's noteworthy album *São Paulo Confessions* (1999). With a host of Grammy nominations to her name, Céu has many fans both at home and abroad. She has recorded three albums over the last seven years, creating dreamlike melodies with elements of *tropicália*, samba, reggae and jazz. Her album *Caravana Sereia Bloom* (2012), is a colorful work with songs inspired by a road trip across Brazil. Her critically acclaimed fourth album, *Tropix* (2016), won in two different categories at the 2017 Latin Grammy awards.

Top Music Blogs

- The Saudade Project (www.saudadeproject.com)
- Slipcue (www.slipcue.com/music/brazil/brazillist.html)
- Brazilian Music Day (brazilianmusicday.org)
- The Brazilian Sound (http://thebraziliansound.blogspot.com)

Brazilian hip-hop emerged from the favelas of Rio sometime in the 1980s, and has been steadily attracting followers ever since. Big names such as Racionais MCs first emerged out of São Paulo, but Rio has its share of more recent success stories. One of the best on the scene is Marcelo D2 (formerly of Planet Hemp), earning accolades for albums like *A Procura da Batida Perfeita* (2003) and *A Arte do Barulho* (2008).

Better known to international audiences is Seu Jorge, who starred in the film *Cidade de Deus* and performed brilliant Portuguese versions of Bowie songs on Wes Anderson's film *The Life Aquatic*. His best solo work is *Cru* (2005), a hybrid of hip-hop and ballads, with politically charged beats.

Most of today's hip-hop artists hail from São Paulo. A few names to look out for include Emicida, a rapper admired for his cutting improvisational rhymes. Check out his funk-laden single 'Triunfo,' one of his early breakthrough hits. Rael de Rima is a fast-rapping lyricist with a strong sense of musicality, often performing with guitar and a full back-up band (a rarity for many hip-hop artists). MC Criolo, whose songs tackle urban violence, police brutality and racism, has become a huge hit in the favelas.

Brazil gets its share of megarockers on world tours. It also has a few homegrown talents. The group Legião Urbana from Brasília remains one of the all-time greats among rock lovers. The band (which folded shortly after the death of lead singer Renato Russo in 1996) enjoyed enormous success in the 1980s and early 1990s, and has sold over 15 million records. Raul Seixas, Skank, O Rappa, Os Paralamas Sucesso and the Rio-based Barão Vermelho are other essential names. The versatile and original Ed Motta, from Rio, injects soul, jazz and traditional Brazilian music into rock.

CANNIBALISM BRAZILIAN-STYLE

The eating of human flesh, as practiced by a few pre-Columbian tribes, contributed to some notion of Brazilian identity. In the 1920s the intellectual movement of anthropophagy (a fancy word for cannibalism) came to denote Brazil's lust for new ideas and culture from abroad that would be consumed and transformed into something uniquely Brazilian.

In music, bossa nova incorporated (ingested) American jazz, blues and classical music, but created something entirely new. A few years later, along came the *tropicalistas*, who were open admirers of Oswald de Andrade's 1928 *Manifesto Antropofágico* (Cannibalistic Manifesto). *Tropicália* devoured elements of American rock and roll, blues, jazz and British psychedelic styles, as well as samba and even bossa nova, and produced a powerful new sound entirely Brazilian in its construction.

This notion of cultural cannibalism has been used to explain the prodigious output of Brazil not only in music, but also in fiction, painting and even filmmaking.

In other genres, indie-rock favorites Los Hermanos were a top band that created catchy albums before breaking up in 2007. Check out *Ventura* (2003) or *Bloco do Eu Souzinho* (2001), one of the seminal pop-rock albums of its time. Vanguart, somewhere in the folk-rock genre, are also a group to watch. Their self-titled debut album (2007) channels samba, blues and classic rock. Other breakout successes include girl-band CSS, which stands for 'Cansei de Ser Sexy' ('Tired of Being Sexy'), who blend '80s new wave and electro-pop with irreverent lyrics (sung in English) and up-tempo beats.

Tropical Truth: A Story of Music and Revolution in Brazil, by Caetano Veloso, describes the great artistic experiment of *tropicália* in 1960s Brazil. Although digressive at times, Veloso captures the era's music and politics.

Rising stars in the music scene include BaianaSystem, a Salvador-based group who channel traditional Northeastern rhythms with accents from West Africa, the Caribbean and beyond on albums like *Outras Cidades* (2017). Another Salvadoran to be reckoned with is the singer and composer Lucas Santtana, whose 2017 album *Modo Avião* has earned him comparisons with João Gilberto and other legendary Brazilian artists from the past. Delving into experimental sounds, the artist Thiago Nassif creates playful melodies, fractured rhythms and amorphous sonic textures on *Três*, an album he produced with Arto Lindsay in 2015, which Nassif rereleased in 2018. The acclaimed singer-songwriter Ava Rocha incorporates both traditional Brazilian rhythms (samba, bossa nova, *tropicália*) as well as rock, pop and funk on her eclectic albums. *Trança* (2018) is one of her best.

Regional Music

The Northeast has perhaps the most regional musical and dance styles. The most important is *forró,* a lively, syncopated music centered on the accordion and the *zabumba* (an African drum). Although a few artists, such as Luiz Gonzaga and Jackson do Pandeiro, have achieved national status, *forró* was long dismissed by urbanites as unsophisticated. The 2000 film *Eu, Tu, Eles* (Me, You, Them) brought down-home *forró* to center stage, aided in part by Gilberto Gil singing the hit *Esperando na Janela*.

Raul Seixas (1945–89) is often called the father of Brazilian rock. Many of his wild rock anthems are well known, and it's not uncommon to hear shouts of '*toca Raul!*' (play Raul!) at concerts. Curiously, Paulo Coelho (the bestselling New Age author) cowrote many of his songs.

The *trio elétrico,* also called *frevo baiano,* began more as a result of a change in technology than in music. It started as a joke when, during Carnaval in Salvador in the 1950s, a group of musicians spearheaded by innovative musical talents Dodo and Osmar (aka Adolfo Nascimento and Osmar Alvares Macedo) got on top of a truck and played *frevo* with electric guitars. The *trio elétrico* is not necessarily a trio, but it's still the backbone of Salvador's Carnaval, when trucks piled high with speakers – with musicians perched on top – drive through the city surrounded by dancing mobs. Another important element of Carnaval on the streets of Salvador is the *bloco afro* (Afro-Brazilian percussion group). Filhos de Gandhi and Grupo Olodum are the most famous of these: Filhos has deep African roots and is strongly influenced by Candomblé; Olodum invented samba-reggae.

Mangue beat (also known as *mangue bit*), from Recife, combines folkloric and regional styles with international influences as diverse as hip-hop, neo-psychedelic and *tejano* (instrumental folk music with roots in northern Mexico and southern Texas). The early leaders of the genre were Chico Science and Nação Zumbi – the title of their 1996 masterpiece, *Afrociberdelia,* kind of summed up what its music was about.

Axé is a label for the profuse samba-pop-rock-reggae-funk-Caribbean fusion music that emerged from Salvador in the 1990s. Taking its cue from Salvador's older Carnaval forms, *axé* was popularized by the powerful, flamboyant Daniela Mercury. Other exponents include the groups Ara Ketu and Chiclete com Banana. At its best it's great, superenergetic music – hear Daniela sing 'Toda Menina Baiana' (Every Bahian Girl) – but some bands overcommercialized it at the end of the '90s.

The influence of Brazilian indigenous music was absorbed and diluted, as was so much that derived from Brazil's cultures. The *carimbó* music of the Amazon region (where the majority of the indigenous population lives today) is influenced primarily by the black communities of the coastal zones.

Football

Brazilians, quite simply, are football mad. No one goes to work on big international game days, with everyone packing into neighborhood bars or on the sidewalks out front to watch the game. After a big win, the whole country erupts with a rowdy night of partying. And should the team lose, the sadness in the air is palpable. Everyone cheers for the national team, but for most of the year, the local club team is the one that matters most.

The Game, the Fans

Most of the world generally acknowledges that Brazilians play the world's most creative, artistic and thrilling style of football. They are also generally known as lousy defenders, but no one seems to mind since they make the attack so exciting. The fans, too, are no less fun to watch. Skillful moves and adroit dribbling past an opponent receive a Spanish bullfight-style 'olé!' while fans do their best to rev up the action by pounding drums (or the backs of the chairs), waving huge flags, setting off fireworks and smoke bombs or sometimes launching nefarious liquids over the grandstands of opposing fans.

Futebol by Alex Bellos (2002), is a fascinating and humorous look at the culture behind Brazil's nationwide obsession, with stories of the legendary players and the way that football has shaped Brazilian society.

Legends of the Sport

Brazil has raised many world-famous players through its ranks, from the Afro-Brazilian player Leonidas da Silva – who helped break down racial barriers (and scored the only bicycle-kick goal ever in World Cup history in 1938) – to Romario, a powerful striker who scored more than 900 goals during his career. The greatest of all though is Pelé, sometimes referred to simply as 'O Rei' (The King).

The Clubs

Brazil has a staggering number of league teams – more than 400 according to the Brazilian Football Confederation (CBF) – with 20 top-level pro teams (part of the so-called Campeonato Brasileiro Série A). Apart from a couple of short breaks for the Christmas–New Year holiday and Carnaval, professional club competitions go on all year. There are a bewildering number of competitions with hotly contested state championships, particularly in Rio (the Campeonata Carioca) and São Paulo (the Campeonata Paulista). Expect intense and bitter matches, especially when historic hometown rivals face off, such as Flamengo versus Fluminense in Rio; Palmeiras versus Corinthians in São Paulo; Atlético Mineiro versus Cruzeiro in Belo Horizonte; and Grêmio (Gisele Bündchen's favorite team) versus Internacional in Porto Alegre.

Flamengo

The most successful among Rio's big four, Flamengo have an enormous fan base both in Rio and around the world – an estimated 36 million followers, which makes them the most popular football club in Brazil. Flamengo certainly does not lack for cash flow, with annual revenue of over R$650 million. Famous players who have donned the iconic red-and-black jerseys include Zico, often hailed as the best player never to win a World Cup; Leonidas, leading scorer at the 1938 World Cup; Bebeto, Mario Zagallo and Romario.

Fluminense

Founded by sons of the elite in Rio back in 1902, Fluminense has contributed a number of top players to the national team. They have also been hailed as the 'champion of the century', for winning the largest number of Campeonato Carioca titles in the 20th century (28 in all). Current stars include Fred (aka Frederico Chaves Guedes), who scored the fastest goal in Brazilian history (finding the net 3.17 seconds after the game's start). Like Flamengo, Fluminense play their home games at Maracanã stadium.

Santos

This port city 80km southeast of São Paulo has a legendary footballing reputation. Santos has won eight national championships and has nurtured the talents of some of Brazil's all-time greats, including Pelé, who played on the team from 1957 to 1974. On the World Cup teams of 1962 and 1970, eight of the 11 starting players came from Santos. The club's most recent star was Neymar, whose youth (he scored his 100th goal as a professional in 2012 at age 20) and skill earned him comparisons to Lionel Messi and Pelé. In both 2011 and 2012, Neymar won the South American Footballer of the Year award. Unable to resist bigger fame (and income) abroad, Neymar signed a five-year contract with FC Barcelona in 2013, then he moved to Paris St-Germain in 2017.

For insight into what's happening in the Brazilian football scene – from player news to upcoming matches – visit www.sambafoot.com.

Corinthians

The most popular of São Paulo's three big teams, Corinthians are also Brazil's most valuable club team with an estimated worth of over US$460 million. The team vaulted to fame in 2012, winning both the Copa Libertadores and the FIFA Club World Cup (defeating English superpower Chelsea 1–0 in the final). Their archrivals are Palmeiras, a team they face (and often defeat) in the legendary Derby Paulista. Fans are noted for their die-hard loyalty. Over 30,000 supporters made the trip to Japan for the 2012 Club World Cup final.

BRAZILIAN FOOTBALL: THE CLUBS

If you get a chance, see a game live; there's no experience quite like it. Many stadiums went through upgrades in preparation for the World Cup. Here's a short list of top teams to catch.

CLUB	CITY	STADIUM (CAPACITY)	JERSEYS
Bahia	Salvador	Fonte Nova (57,000)	white
Botafogo	Rio de Janeiro	João Havelange (47,000)	black & white stripes
Corinthians	São Paulo	Arena Corinthians (68,000)	white; black collar
Cruzeiro	Belo Horizonte	Mineirão (65,000)	blue
Flamengo	Rio de Janeiro	Maracanã (78,000)	red; black hoops
Fluminense	Rio de Janeiro	Maracanã (78,000)	red, green & white stripes
Grêmio	Porto Alegre	Arena do Grêmio (61,000)	blue, black & white stripes
Internacional	Porto Alegre	Beira-Rio (60,000)	red
Náutico Capibaribe	Recife	Arena Pernambuco (46,000)	red & white stripes
Palmeiras	São Paulo	Arena Palestra Itália (60,000)	green
Santos	Santos	Vila Belmiro (26,000)	white
São Paulo	São Paulo	Morumbi (67,000)	white; red & black hoops
Vasco da Gama	Rio de Janeiro	São Januário (35,000)	white; black slash

PELÉ

One of the world's most famous players – still widely considered to be the greatest ever to have played the game – is Pelé. Not just a legendary footballer, he was also Brazil's first black government minister (for sport, from 1995 to 1998) and he has been knighted by Queen Elizabeth II.

Pelé has come a long way since he was born Edson Arantes do Nascimento in a humble Minas Gerais town on October 23, 1940. Yet despite his stardom, his public image remains impeccable. He's never smoked, has never been photographed with a drink in hand, and has never been involved with drugs.

In a 22-year career, the teams on which Pelé played gained 53 titles, including three World Cups (the first, in Sweden in 1958, when he was just 17 years old) and back-to-back World Club Championships (with Santos in 1962 and 1963), among many others. Despite lucrative offers to play in Europe, Pelé never did so – in fact, President Janio Quadros had Pelé declared a national treasure in 1971 so that he could not be transferred to a European club.

Pelé retired from the Brazilian team in 1971 and from Santos in 1974. In 1975 the New York Cosmos coaxed him north to the US, where he played until 1977, when the team won the American championship. He finally retired for good at the end of that year, after a game between the Cosmos and Santos in which he played the first half for the Cosmos and the second half with Santos.

In 1366 games (112 for the Brazilian national team), he scored 1282 goals, making him Brazil's all-time highest goal scorer. When he scored his 1000th goal in 1969 in Maracanã stadium, he dedicated it to the children of Brazil.

Pelé, who maintains an oceanfront home in Rio, continues to be a goodwill ambassador for sport, and still commands enormous respect – as evidenced by the roar of the crowd when he made a surprise appearance at the end of the Summer Olympics in London in 2012. In Brazil, Pelé is known simply as 'O Rei' (the king).

The first time Brazil hosted the World Cup, in 1950, the national team lost in a dramatic final against Uruguay before some 200,000 fans in Rio's Maracanã Stadium. The unforgettable day of infamy was later called '*Maracanaço*' (the Maracanã stadium debacle) and is still in common parlance.

The World Cup

Brazil, the most successful football nation in the history of the games (with five World Cup victories), became the fifth country to host the World Cup twice. Aside from Rio, where the final took place, 11 other cities across the country staged games. Brazil spent around R$26 billion in preparation for the 2014 event, including stadium construction, upgrades to airports, roads and other infrastructure. Unfortunately, dreams for a grand victory celebration were crushed when Brazil suffered an embarrassing 7-1 loss to a far superior Germany team in the semifinals. The game was held in Estádio Mineirão in Belo Horizonte, and the scandalous defeat (in the first half Germany scored four goals in six minutes) was later dubbed *Mineiraço* (the Mineirão stadium debacle). Many Brazilians were so disappointed that they even booed their own players as they left the field. The 2018 World Cup started off promisinglu for Brazil, but the Seleção (the team's nickname, meaning 'the Squad') was knocked out of the competition by Belgium in the quarter finals.

Cinema & Literature

Brazil has a flourishing film industry, though many productions don't see screen time beyond the country's borders. Key periods in Brazilian cinema include the avant-garde Cinema Novo movement of the 1960s and the hard-hitting socially conscious films of the last decade, with a new crop of talented directors emerging on the scene. In the realm of literature, Brazil has produced a handful of great writers, including the Bahian legend Jorge Amado, globally renowned Paolo Coelho and the brilliant modernist Clarice Lispector.

Cinema

In the 1960s the Cinema Novo movement emerged in Brazil, focusing on the country's bleak social problems. Young filmmakers, influenced by Italian neorealism and the French new wave, set about making a series of experimental films embracing the avant-garde filming techniques of the time. One of the great films made during this epoch was Anselmo Duarte's 1962 *O Pagador de Promessas* (The Payer of Vows), a poetic story about a man who keeps his promise to carry a cross after the healing of his donkey. It won the Palme d'Or at the Cannes film festival. Another great pioneer of Cinema Novo is the director Glauber Rocha. In *Deus é o Diabo na Terra do Sol* (Black God, White Devil; 1963), Rocha explored the struggle, fanaticism and poverty of Northeastern Brazil. It's one of the great films of the period.

The 1964 military coup stymied much creative expression in the country, and Cinema Novo died out just as its filmmakers were entering their prime. The first significant film to be made after the 1960s was Carlos Diegues' *Bye Bye Brasil* (1980). It chronicles the adventures of a theater troupe as it tours the country, witnessing the profound changes in Brazilian society in the second half of the 20th century.

In the 1980s, Hector Babenco emerged as one of Brazil's rising stars. In *Pixote* (1981), Babenco brought to life the yawning chasm between haves and have-nots in a story about a homeless child who gets swept from innocent waif to criminal by the currents of the underworld. Two decades later, his film *Carandiru* (2003) offered an inside look at São Paulo's hellish state penitentiary of the same name.

Brazilian Cinema, edited by Randal Johnson and Robert Stam, provides a fascinating overview of the great movements that have shaped the industry, exploring Cinema Novo, tropicalism and other important influences.

Fernando Meirelles earned his credibility with *Cidade de Deus*, the 2002 film based on a true story by Paolo Lins. The film, which showed brutality and hope coexisting in a Rio favela (slum), earned four Oscar nominations. More importantly, it brought much attention to the urban poor in Brazil.

Set in 1970 during the height of the military dictatorship, *O Ano em Que Meus Pais Saíram de Férias* (The Year My Parents Went on Vacation; 2006), directed by Cao Hamburger, is a poignant coming-of-age story. Brazil's official Oscar entry for best foreign film in 2007 tackles complex issues with sensitivity in the story of a young boy left adrift in a working-class neighborhood of São Paulo. Political repression, the World Cup of 1970 and Jewish culture all form the backdrop of Hamburger's remarkably well-made film.

One of the most talked-about films of recent years is the 2007 *Tropa de Elite* (Elite Squad), which depicts police brutality in the favelas; it also makes a very clear link between middle-class college kids who buy drugs and the deaths of young children in the favelas, who are recruited by drug lords to help meet the demand for cocaine and other substances. It was

TOP FILMS

- *O Som ao Redor* (Neighboring Sounds; 2012), by Kleber Mendonça Filho
- *Tropa de Elite* (Elite Squad; 2007), by José Padilha
- *Casa de Areia* (House of Sand; 2005), by Andrucha Waddington
- *Carandiru* (2003), by Hector Babenco
- *Cidade de Deus* (City of God; 2002), by Fernando Meirelles
- *Madame Satã* (2002), by Karim Aïnouz
- *Central do Brasil* (Central Station; 1998), by Walter Salles
- *Pixote* (1981), by Hector Babenco
- *O Que é Isso Companheiro* (Four Days in September; 1998), by Bruno Barreto
- *Bye Bye Brasil* (1980), by Carlos Diegues
- *O Pagador de Promessas* (The Payer of Vows; 1962), by Glauber Rocha
- *Orfeu Negro* (Black Orpheus; 1959), by Marcel Camus

made by José Padilha, the acclaimed director of the disturbing documentary *Bus 174* (2002), which depicts a high-profile bus hijacking that took place in Rio de Janeiro in 2000.

Walter Salles is Brazil's best-known director, whose Oscar award-winning *Central do Brasil* (1998) should be in every serious Brazilianist's film library. Salles' film *Diarios de Motocicleta* (The Motorcycle Diaries; 2004) chronicles the historic journey of Che Guevara and Alberto Granada across South America, while *On the Road* (2012) is a colorful adaptation of the Jack Kerouac classic. His first feature film, *Terra Estrangeiro* (Foreign Land; 1995), holds an important place in the renaissance of Brazilian cinema.

Tristes Tropiques (1955), by Claude Lévi-Strauss, is both a well-written travelogue and one of the most important anthropological studies of some of Brazil's indigenous peoples.

In the last decade, the Brazilian industry has produced thought-provoking films and documentaries. Felipe Barbosa's *Casa Grande* (2014) is a coming-of-age story set in Rio about a privileged high-school student who is suddenly thrust into a life of poverty when his father's business collapses. *Laerte-Se* (2017) is a documentary about the triumphs and struggles of one of Brazil's top cartoonists, Laerte Coutinho, who after living as a man for over 50 years decides to reintroduce herself to the world as a woman.

Literature

Brazil's most famous writer is Jorge Amado, who died in August 2001. Born near Ilhéus in 1912, and a longtime resident of Salvador, Amado wrote colorful romances about Bahia's people and places. His early work was strongly influenced by communism. His later books are lighter in subject, but more picturesque and intimate in style. The two most acclaimed are *Gabriela, Cravo e Canela,* which is set in Ilhéus, and *Dona Flor e Seus Dois Maridos*, set in Salvador. *Tent of Miracles* explores race relations in Brazil, and *Pen, Sword and Camisole* laughs its way through the petty worlds of military and academic politics. *The Violent Land* is an early Amado classic.

An Anthology of Twentieth-Century Brazilian Poetry (1972) is a fine introduction to Brazilian poets. It's edited by American poet Elizabeth Bishop, who planned a short trip to Santos and ended up staying 15 years.

Clarice Lispector (1920–77), one of Latin America's great 20th-century novelists, is surprisingly little known outside the country. Her existentialism-influenced writings focus on human isolation, alienation and moral doubt, and convey a deep understanding of women's feelings. The short-story collections *Family Ties* and *Soulstorm* are among her best works.

One of the world's top-selling authors hails from Brazil. Paulo Coelho (b 1947) earned a global following for his classic New Age fables like *The Pilgrimage* and *The Alchemist*. The latter focuses on the adventures of an Andalusian shepherd and touches on the topics of fate and destiny. The novel, one of more than 30 books written by Coelho, has sold more than 65 million copies and has been translated into 80 different languages.

Architecture

Brazilian architecture encompasses a wide variety of styles and influences, from glittering 400-year-old baroque churches to futuristic art museums from the era of modernism. Highlights include colonial town centers like those in Ouro Preto and Salvador, as well as groundbreaking designs in Brasília, Rio and São Paulo. Architectural surprises lurk everywhere in Brazil, including a lavish theater of eclectic style in the heart of the Amazon and art deco beauties in the southernmost reaches of the country.

Indigenous & Colonial Architecture

Although little is known of pre-Columbian architecture, numerous Amazonian tribes still use traditional designs and locally sourced materials in the building of houses and communal spaces. Designs vary from region to region, with groups like the Yanomami living in huge circular communal dwellings known as *yanos*, which can house up to 400 people. Each family maintains its own hearth where meals are prepared. In the center of the *yano*, a huge open-air plaza is used for communal gatherings, games and rituals.

In the early days of European colonization, architecture meant strong buildings that could withstand the elements, and fortresses built in strategic locations along the coast. The earliest Portuguese constructions, built in wood and earthworks, were later transformed into imposing stone citadels, a handful of which still survive. Overlooking the entrance to Baía de Guanabara, the Fortress of Santa Cruz da Barra was originally built over the improvised redoubt built by the French in the mid-1500s. During Portuguese rule the fort served as the most important defense system in the colony, and proved instrumental in defenses against French and later Dutch invasions. Around 300m off the coast of Salvador, the fort of São Marcelo, built in the early 1600s, stands atop a bank of reefs and is one of the only circular forts in the country.

As small colonial outposts grew into villages and towns, the church took on a prominent role, sponsoring the construction of learning centers, hospitals and missions. In the 1600s the Jesuits built a series of missions in parts of present-day Rio Grande do Sul as well as Paraguay and Argentina. The brick buildings, with baroque details and carved wood interiors, were built by indigenous craftsmen, though nothing of the interiors survives. In ruins today, these eerie remains provide an astonishing record of the past, and were declared a Unesco World Heritage site in 1983.

The mannerist style of early colonial buildings was characterized by largely geometric facades with square-shaped windows and triangular pediments. This style was visible in buildings like the Mosteiro São Bento in Rio and the Igreja dos Santos Cosme e Damião in Pernambuco. As riches flowed through Brazil in the 18th century, this fairly austere design gave way to the excesses of the baroque. Newly constructed churches and convents featured ornamental facades, while interiors had elaborately carved wooden details, hand-painted azulejos (Portuguese tiles) and an abundance of gold leaf.

Architecture In Print

The Curves of Time: The Memoirs of Oscar Niemeyer (2000), Oscar Niemeyer

When Brazil Was Modern: A Guide to Architecture, 1928–1960 (2003), Lauro Cavalcanti

Roberto Burle Marx: The Lyrical Landscape (2001), Marta Iris Montero

Architectural Guide, Brazil (2015), Laurence Kimmel et al

Salvador, as the capital of colonial Brazil, became the backdrop to many impressive buildings still standing today – including works like the Igreja e Convento São Francisco with exuberant gilded woodwork covering nearly every surface. As elsewhere in Brazil, enslaved peoples helped construct many buildings in the historic Cidade Alta as well as creating some of its most stunning artworks. Artists like O Cabra spent years working on his spectacular *Senhor Morto* (the Dead Christ) for the Ordem Terceira do Carmo.

Other stunning colonial architecture blankets the streets of Olinda, which is essentially an 18th-century city. Its architectural wealth and unique atmosphere stem from its 20 baroque churches and many convents, chapels and houses. In São Luís, the entire street plan of the late 17th-century heart of the city survives, along with many historic buildings including fine mansions with colorful tiled facades.

Some of the finest buildings from the colonial period are found in the inland state of Minas Gerais. Fueled by the gold rush of the 1700s, lavish wealth was bestowed upon the town of Ouro Preto. Hilly cobblestone streets wind past some 150 architecturally significant buildings, including nearly two dozen baroque churches. It's Brazil's greatest concentration of baroque buildings, some of which were designed or embellished by the genius of Brazilian baroque, Aleijadinho. Lovely Ouro Preto is joined on the World Heritage List by Diamantina, founded by 18th-century diamond hunters. Other Minas towns, such as Tiradentes and São João del Rei, also have significant colonial buildings.

All across Brazil, many of the finest colonial building were built by enslaved people. Although not allowed to enter the beautiful churches they built for white colonists, slaves managed to build a few important gathering spaces for their own communities, some of which still stand today: Igreja de Santa Efigênia dos Pretos, in Ouro Preto; Igreja NS do Rosário dos Pretos, in Salvador; and Igreja NS do Rosário dos Homens Pretos, in Olinda.

Neoclassicism

In the early 19th century, a group of architects, artists and composers was selected by the Portuguese crown to bring new life to Brazil. Now that Rio de Janeiro was the imperial seat of power, it needed a makeover to suit the royal entourage. The French Artistic Mission arrived in 1816 and introduced a whole new design aesthetic to the budding Brazilian empire. Neoclassicism became the official style and was formally taught in the newly founded Imperial Academy. The works built during this period were grandiose and monumental, dominated by classical features such as elongated columns and wide domes. Among the many fine examples of this period are Rio's Museu Nacional de Belas Artes, the Theatro Municipal and the Casa França-Brasil.

Over the next three decades, neoclassicism spread to other parts of Brazil as builders left the heavy colonial-style aesthetic behind and embraced the new design principles inspired by classical antiquity. Grand buildings from this period include the Palácio dos Leões in Maranhão, the Teatro da Paz in Belem, the Assembleia Legislativa da Província de Pernambuco in Recife, and Dom Pedro II's former summer palace in Petrópolis.

Eclecticism

The end of the 19th century brought new elements to the rigid strictures of neoclassicism. True to its name, eclecticism embraced a wide range of influences, bringing a new form of monumentality, more decorative facades and exotic elements. It also pulled from the past, using Romanesque, Gothic, Moorish and even baroque flourishes. At the same time, technological innovations allowed builders to use materials in new ways, such as cast-iron frames, which were making their appearance in Europe and the US. Eclectic architecture was used in theaters, parliamentary halls and colleges.

Dating from this time are grandiose buildings like the Teatro Amazonas in Manaus, which is famed for both its grandeur (including Murano glass chandeliers and Carrara marble stairs) as well as unusual elements like the ceramic tile dome featuring the colors of the Brazilian flag. In

Rio, the Real Gabinete Português de Leitura (Royal Reading Room) shows inspiration from the much earlier manueline period (early 1500s), with a Gothic facade and the highlighting of its metallic structure.

Art Deco

In the 1930s the art deco movement was characterized by clean geometric facades featuring obvious symmetry and a lack of ornamentation. In comparison to eclecticism, art deco created a more simplified, streamlined aesthetic. It was also better suited to the increasingly vertical urban landscapes as population growth began to rapidly accelerate in Brazilian cities. Art deco design became widespread in Brazil. A few outstanding examples from that time include the Palácio do Comércio in Porto Alegre, the Estação Dom Pedro II (aka Central Station) in Rio de Janeiro and the Elevador Lacerda, connecting the lower and upper towns in Salvador.

Modernism

The 1930s also saw the emergence of a new generation of Brazilian architects, led by Oscar Niemeyer and influenced by the modernist ideas of Le Corbusier. Niemeyer was pivotal in breaking away from the neoclassical style and designing without ornamentation, using steel and glass in elemental, aesthetically pleasing shapes. He is considered one of the great pioneers of modernism, and his reach is global.

Niemeyer's best-known project wasn't a building but rather an entire city. The nation's new capital, Brasília, was created in the 1950s and early 1960s from scratch by Niemeyer, urban planner Lúcio Costa and landscape architect Burle Marx. Although Brasília has its critics, it's still considered one of the world's most audacious urban-design projects. Its wild, airplane-shaped street plan has many iconic building, including the crown-shaped cathedral, the Santuário Dom Bosco, and dramatic government buildings, such as the Palácio do Itamaraty and Palácio da Justiça. Outside the capital, Niemeyer created many innovative designs (often featuring his trademark curves), such as the Museu do Arte Contemporânea (MAC) in Niterói. Its fluid form and delicate curves are reminiscent of a flower in bloom (though many simply call it a spaceship on the launchpad).

The Contemporary Scene

Many other talented architects emerged in the second half of the 20th century. Lina Bo Bardi (1914–1992), born in Rome, immigrated to Brazil following WWII. Highly active in Brazil's intellectual life, her first project was São Paulo's Casa de Vidro (Glass House; 1951), a Zen-like cube atop slender columns that melds into the surrounding landscape. She went on to expand on the idea of weight and levity in her design for the Museu de Arte de São Paulo (MASP), a bold design featuring two huge red concrete frames that suspend the interior glass structure above the ground. She remained active in the design world until the 1990s, both as a practitioner and a theorist, collaborating in numerous projects. Her many admirers remark on her 'anthropological architecture', design based on a respectful attitude toward the user.

One of Brazil's best-known living architects is Paulo Mendes da Rocha (born 1929). In 2006 the São Paulo–based architect won the Pritzker Prize (the Nobel of the architecture world) for his 'deep understanding of the poetics of human space'. Part of the avant-garde group of 'brutalist' architects, Mendes da Rocha designs with simple materials and formats that are readily available and easily constructed. There's also an ethical dimension to his work that focuses on the harmony between indoor and outdoor space. His work can be seen in São Paulo's Praça do Patriarca, a revitalized public space with a curved steel canopy that appears to float overhead.

Iconic Brazilian Designs

Museu de Arte de São Paulo, São Paulo

Congresso Nacional, Brasília

Sítio Burle Marx, Rio de Janeiro

Teatro Amazonas, Manaus

The Natural World

Home to the world's largest rainforest, as well as some of the greatest wetlands, Brazil boasts some of the most astounding plant and animal life on earth. More known species of plants, freshwater fish, amphibians and mammals are found in Brazil than in any other country in the world. Unfortunately, Brazil is also renowned for the destruction of its natural environment. Conservation remains a hot topic, and protecting Brazil's natural wonders is increasingly seen as pivotal for Brazil's future.

Above Epiphyte, Atlantic Rainforest

The Land

Brazil is the world's fifth-largest country (after Russia, China, Canada and the USA). Its 8.5 million sq km occupy almost half of South America. Brazil has five principal biomes (major regional plant and animal groupings): Amazonia, Atlantic rainforest, caatinga (semiarid land), cerrado (the central savanna) and the wetlands of the Pantanal.

Amazonia

Covering over 4 million sq km (almost half the country), Brazilian Amazonia incorporates 30% of the world's tropical forest. It's home to around 45,000 plant species (some 20% of the world total), 311 mammal species (about 10% of the world total), 1000 bird species (15%), 1800 types of butterfly and around 2000 species of fish (in contrast, Europe has about 200). The forest still keeps many of its secrets: to this day, major tributaries of the Amazon River remain unexplored, thousands of species have not yet been classified and dozens of human communities have eluded contact with the outside world.

Including a further 2 million sq km in neighboring countries, the entire Amazon Basin holds 20% of the world's freshwater and produces 20% of the world's oxygen.

Seasonal rainfall patterns mean that the water levels of the Amazon River and its tributaries rise and fall at different times of the year. This produces dramatic alterations in the region's geography. Water levels routinely vary by 10m to 15m between low and high marks; during high-water periods, areas totaling at least 150,000 sq km (about the size of England and Wales together) are flooded.

Forest Layers

The rainforest is stratified into layers of plant and animal life. Most of the animal activity takes place in the canopy layer, 20m to 30m above ground, where trees compete for sunshine, and butterflies, sloths and the majority of birds and monkeys live. Here hummingbirds hover for pollen, and macaws and parrots seek out nuts and tender shoots. A few tall trees reaching up to 40m, even 50m, poke above the canopy and dominate the forest skyline. These 'emergent trees' are inhabited by birds such as the harpy eagle and toucan and, unlike most other rainforest plants, disperse their seeds by wind.

The dense foliage of the canopy layer blots out sunlight at lower levels. Below the canopy is the understory. Epiphytes (air plants) hang at midlevels, and below them are bushes, saplings and shrubs growing up to 5m in height. Last is a ground cover of ferns, seedlings and herbs – plants adapted to very little light. Down here live ants and termites, the so-called social insects. The *saubas* (leaf-cutter ants) use leaves to build underground nests for raising fungus gardens, while army ants swarm through the jungle in huge masses, eating everything in their path. Insects, fungi and roots fight for access to nutrients, keeping the forest floor quite tidy.

The forest's soils are typically shallow. Many trees have buttress roots that spread over wide patches of ground to gather more nutrients.

The Amazon on Film

Amazon: Land of the Flooded Forest, National Geographic

Amazon – River of the Future, Jacques Cousteau

Amazon – Journey to a Thousand Rivers, Jacques Cousteau

The Burning Season: The Chico Mendes Story, John Frankenheimer

Atlantic Rain Forest

Brazil's 'other' tropical rainforest, the Mata Atlântica (Atlantic rain forest), is actually older than the Amazon forest and evolved independently. It once extended along the country's southeast-facing coast, from Rio Grande do Norte to Rio Grande do Sul. Today three-quarters of Brazil's population and all its main industrial cities are located in what used to be the Mata Atlântica, and only 7% of the original forest remains.

Along the coast, there are still long stretches of this luxuriant forest. Some areas boast what may be the highest biodiversity levels on earth. The Atlantic rain forest also contains many unique species. You'll find 26 primate species (21 of which are found only here), 2000 butterfly species (including 900 found nowhere else) and some 600-plus bird species – with many endemics among them. Unsurprisingly, many of these species are endangered, including the four types of lion tamarin and the two woolly spider monkeys (the largest primates in the Americas).

Caatinga, Lajedo de Pai Mateus (p518)

Caatinga

Caatinga is semiarid land, with hardy vegetation composed mainly of cacti and thorny shrubs adapted to a shortage of water and extreme heat – the natural environment of much of the interior of the Northeast region, the *sertão*. Rainfall (300mm to 800mm a year) is irregular, and often torrential when it comes (in the first half of the year). Most rivers rising here are dry for half the year. Despite this, the caatinga harbors surprising biodiversity. When it does rain, the trees break into leaf and the ground turns green. 'Islands' of humidity and fertile soils around the mountain ranges are known as *brejos*. Caatinga is a habitat unique to Brazil, although less than one-tenth of it is in its natural state.

The Brazilian version of the yeti is the Mapinguari, a legendary animal of the Amazon that grows to 2m, is covered in red hair and can rip apart palm trees.

Cerrado

Cerrado covers the central high plains of Brazil – 2 million sq km in a rough triangle from southern Minas Gerais to Mato Grosso to southern Maranhão, nearly a quarter of the country in all. Typical cerrado is open savanna grassland dotted with trees, though it can edge into scrub, palm stands or even fairly thick forest. Over 800 bird species are known to live here and plant diversity is great – 10,000 species, of which 45% are found nowhere else in the world. Many plants are used to produce cork, fibers, oils, handicrafts, medicines and food. Medicinal plants native to cerrado include arnica and golden trumpet.

Pantanal

The Pantanal is a vast swampy wetland in the center of South America, about half the size of France – some 210,000 sq km spread across Brazil, Bolivia and Paraguay. It's the largest inland wetland on earth, and 140,000 sq km of it lies in Brazil, in the states of Mato Grosso and Mato Grosso do Sul.

Parque Nacional da Chapada dos Veadeiros (p358), Cerrado

During the wet season, from October to March, the waters from the higher surrounding lands run into the Pantanal, inundating as much as two-thirds of it for half the year. The Pantanal, though 2000km upstream from the Atlantic Ocean, is only 100m to 200m above sea level and drains very slowly.

This seasonal flooding has made systematic farming impossible, severely limiting human impact on the area, and it creates an enormously rich feeding ground for wildlife. It is the best area to head for in all Brazil if you want to see wildlife, boasting greater visible numbers of animals and at least as much variety of creatures as Amazonia, with which it shares many species. The Pantanal supports numerous species, including iconic creatures like the giant anaconda, the jaguar, the puma, the giant anteater, the hyacinth macaw, the giant otter, and the black howler and brown capuchin monkeys - and millions of caimans. The most visible mammal is the capybara, the world's largest rodent, which is often seen in family groups or even large herds.

One hectare (10,000 sq meters) of well-conserved caatinga can be home to 200 different ant species.

Wildlife

Brazil's teeming flora and fauna make it one of the planet's best destinations for nature lovers.

Mammals

Anteaters & Sloths

The giant anteater (up to 2m long) lives off termites and ants. Its meat is prized in some areas of Brazil, and it's a threatened species. The collared or lesser anteater, up to 1.4m long, is yellow and black, mainly nocturnal, and often climbs trees.

The giant ground sloth, which grew to the size of an elephant, once inhabited much of Brazil. It was easy prey for prehistoric hunters and was presumably hunted to extinction 10,000 years ago.

Sloths have strong arms and legs, and spend most of their time hidden (and sleeping) in trees. You have a good chance of seeing some if you get a bit off the beaten track in Amazonia: from a moderate distance they look like clumps of vegetation high in trees. The species you're most likely to see is the brown-throated three-toed sloth.

Monkeys

About 80 of the world's approximately 300 primate species (which also include marmosets and tamarins) are found in Brazil, many of them unique to the country. Southeast Brazil's two species of woolly spider monkey, the southern *muriqui* and northern *muriqui,* with their thick brown fur, are the largest primates in the Americas and both are endangered, the northern species critically so and down to a population of under 300.

Howler monkeys are known for their distinctive roar. They live in groups of up to 20 that are led by a single male. In Amazonia you're most likely to encounter the red howler monkey. Further south, including in the Pantanal, the black howler monkey is the local species. The brown howler monkey inhabits the small remaining areas of the Mata Atlântica.

The two types of uakari monkey, the black-headed and the bald, inhabit Amazonian flooded forest. The bald uakari has a red or pink bald head and thick, shaggy body fur ranging from chestnut-red to white (giving rise to the popular names red uakari and white uakari).

The bald uakari's red complexion and lack of head hair have earned it the nickname *macaco-inglês* (English monkey).

Felines

Many visitors dream of sighting a wild jaguar, but few have the luck of seeing one in the wild. The elusive and splendid jaguar is widely but thinly distributed in Brazil, occurring in Amazonia and the Pantanal among other regions. Jaguars hunt at night, covering large distances. They prey on a wide variety of animals, in trees, in water and on the ground, including sloths, monkeys, fish, deer, tapirs, capybaras and agoutis – but rarely people.

The puma, almost as big as the jaguar and similarly elusive, is the same beast as North America's cougar or mountain lion. As well as preying on deer, it sometimes attacks herds of domestic animals, such as sheep or goats.

Dolphins, Manatees & Whales

On many rivers in the Amazon Basin you should catch glimpses of the pink dolphin. It's most often seen where tributaries meet larger rivers, and is most active in the early morning and late afternoon. Sightings are tantalizing – and getting good photos virtually impossible – as the dolphin surfaces unpredictably, for just a second or so at a time, to breathe. Often it won't even lift its head above the surface. The pink dolphin has a lumpy forehead, a long beak and no dorsal fin (just a ridge). Adults are 1.8m to 2.5m long, weighing 85kg to 160kg.

Amazonian myth has it that the pink dolphin can turn itself into a handsome man able to seduce young women.

Amazonian rivers are also home to the gray dolphin, a bit smaller than the pink and often found together with it. Unlike the pink dolphin, the gray also inhabits the sea, in coastal waters from Florianópolis to Panama. When it surfaces it usually lifts its head and part of its body out of the water.

Larger than the dolphin is the Amazon manatee, a slow-moving vegetarian that is illegally hunted for its meat and in danger of extinction. Prospects are even poorer for the marine West Indian manatee, of which there are just 500 left in coastal waters from the state of Alagoas northward.

Top Golden lion tamarin

Bottom Marmosets

JANTROYKA/GETTY IMAGES ©

Hyacinth macaws

Seven whale species occur off Brazil's coasts, with good sightings off Praia do Rosa between June and October. The rare humpback whale breeds in the same months in the Parque Nacional Marinho de Abrolhos, off the coast of southern Bahia.

Fish

Amazonia is home to at least 2000 freshwater fish species, and the Pantanal to around 300 species. The biggest Amazonian fish is the enormous *pirarucu*, or *arapaima*, which can weigh well over 100kg. The pirarucu is a voracious hunter of other fish and a rich food source for humans. To try to preserve the shrinking population, catching it is banned if it's less than 1.5m in length or during the October-to-March spawning season.

The pirarucu has gills, but they are basically useless. It breathes with lungs instead and has to surface for air about every 10 minutes or it will drown.

The most important food fish of central Amazonia is the little *jaraqui*, which swims in shoals of thousands. Another food fish, the *tambaqui*, is of the same family as piranhas. The rotund *tambaqui* can reach 1m in length and weigh up to 25kg. Normally it lives on nuts (which it can crack with its jaws) and seeds, but when the waters recede it can turn carnivorous.

Amazonia harbors at least 100 species of catfish, named for the long bristles that help them search for food on river bottoms. One aggressive catfish, the *piraíba*, grows up to 3m long and weighs as much as 200kg. It will even attack water birds. The dourado, up to 1m long with pale-gold sides, is common in the Pantanal as well as Amazonia, and is a popular dish in restaurants throughout the country.

MAN BITES PIRANHA

Why are people scared of piranhas? Humans eat piranhas a billion times more often than piranhas eat people. They're reasonably tasty, if a bit small and bony. A standard activity on an Amazon jungle trip is catching your own piranha lunch.

A piranha is not just a piranha, of course. It could be any of about 40 species of the *Serrasalmo* genus. Piranhas are found in the basins of the Amazon, Orinoco, Paraguay and São Francisco Rivers and in the rivers of the Guianas. Some live on seeds and fruits, some on other fish, and only a handful of species are potentially a risk to larger creatures. These types are most dangerous when stuck in tributaries, meanders or lakes that get cut off from main rivers in the dry season. When they have eaten all the other fish, the piranhas will attack more or less anything, including wounded mammals entering their waters. The scent of blood or bodily fluids in the water can whip a shoal into a feeding frenzy. Confirmed accounts of human fatalities caused by piranhas are extremely few, but plenty of Amazonian river folks have scars or missing fingers to testify just how sharp and vicious those little triangular teeth can be.

Birds

With its diverse habitats and extraordinary number of species, Brazil is a major hot spot for bird-watchers.

Birds of Prey

Much like great cats, birds of prey command respect and are always an object of fascination. Brazil has around 40 species of eagle, hawk, falcon, kite, caracara and kestrel, some quite common, and they're not very easy to tell apart.

The largest bird of prey in the Americas is the ferocious harpy eagle, with claws bigger than human hands. It eats sizable mammals (including monkeys) and nests at least 25m above the ground in large jungle trees. Although a few harpies still inhabit Mata Atlântica, the bird is found chiefly in Amazonia.

Amazon Books

- *Tree of Rivers, John Hemming*
- *The Smithsonian Atlas of the Amazon, Michael Goulding*
- *The Last Forest, Mark London and Brian Kelly*
- *One River, Wade Davis*
- *The Lost Amazon, Isabel Kuhl*

Parrots

These are the kinds of bird that have come to symbolize tropical rainforests, and people travel from all over the world to see some of Brazil's dozens of species.

The name scarlet macaw is given to two large, gloriously colored species: *Ara chloroptera,* also called the red-and-green macaw, which grows up to 95cm long, with blue-and-green wings and a red-striped face; and *Ara macao,* which is a bit smaller with blue-and-yellow wings. The latter bird is restricted to Amazonia, but the red-and-green macaw also inhabits the Pantanal, cerrado and even caatinga.

The blue-and-yellow macaw, about 85cm long, is also widely distributed. The yellow covers its underside, the blue its upper parts.

Toucans

Among the most colorful groups of Latin American birds are toucans, which despite their large beaks are able to fly with a surprising agility. Toucans live at forest treetop level and are often best seen from boats. Brazil's biggest is the toco toucan, whose habitat ranges from Amazonia to the cerrado to the Pantanal. Around 55cm long, including its bright-orange beak, the toucan's plumage is black except for a white neck area. In Amazonia you may see the white-throated toucan or the yellow-ridged toucan. Both are fairly large birds, with black beaks.

Rufescent tiger-heron

Waterfowl

Highly visible birds in the Pantanal and Amazonia include herons, egrets, storks, ibises, spoonbills and their relatives. The tiger heron, with its brown and black stripes, is particularly distinctive. The sight of hundreds of snowy egrets gathering in a waterside rookery looks like a sudden blooming of white flowers in the treetops.

Of the storks, one of the most striking is the tall black-headed and scarlet-necked jabiru found in the Pantanal and Amazonia. In the Pantanal, also look for the similarly sized maguari stork, which is mainly white with a pinkish face, and the smaller wood stork, with its black head and beak with a curved end. The beautiful pink roseate spoonbill is another Pantanal resident. The spectacular scarlet ibis lives in flocks along the Northeast coast.

For 15 years Mark Plotkin devotedly tracked down Amazonian shamans to understand some of their encyclopedic knowledge of medicinal plants. His *Tales of a Shaman's Apprentice* (1993) is both a travelogue and adventure story.

Plants

The last ice age did not reach Brazil and the rainforests have never suffered long droughts, so the area has had an unusually long period of time to develop plant species that are found nowhere else in the world.

Though estimates run at around 45,000, it would be impossible to determine an exact number of plant species in the Amazon, let alone in the whole of Brazil, as new plants are being discovered all the time and, unfortunately, others are disappearing with frightening frequency. The great majority of the plants in Brazil's rainforests are trees – estimated at some 70% of the total vegetation. Many rainforest trees look similar even though they are of different species, but a trained eye can distinguish more than 400 species of tree per hectare in some areas.

Jabiru stork

National Parks & Protected Areas

Much of Brazil is, officially at least, under environmental protection. Over 1000 areas, covering some 1.3 million sq km (around 15% of the whole country), are protected. Some of these are run by the federal government, some by state governments and some by private individuals or nongovernmental organizations (NGOs).

Terras Indígena (Indigenous Lands) occupy about 12% of Brazilian territory, nearly all in the Amazon. Though they are not explicitly dedicated to nature conservation, their inhabitants tend to use them with minimal environmental impact.

Environmental Issues

Sadly, Brazil is as renowned for its forests as it is for destroying them. At last count more than one-fifth of the Brazilian Amazon rainforest had been completely destroyed. Cutting down forests for cattle ranches and to grow crops (namely soybeans) and illegal logging are among the chief threats to the Amazon. The rate of deforestation has had ups and downs in recent years, falling year-on-year from 2005 to 2015. It surged again in the last few years, with the rate of deforestation rising by 22% from mid-2017 to mid-2018.

Big development projects are also affecting the Amazon. The government has some 30 large hydroelectric dams in the works for the Amazon region. The biggest is the massive Belo Monte dam on the Rio Xingu in Pará, which flooded nearly 500 sq km of rainforest, and displaced at least 20,000 people, including thousands of indigenous people who have resided along the river for centuries. At the time of writing, half of its 24 turbines were operational. It's expected to be fully operational by 2020.

Field Guides

Birds of Brazil, Ber van Perlo

Medicinal and Useful Plants of the Upper Amazon, James L Castner

Neotropical Rainforest Mammals, Louise Emmons

A Neotropical Companion, John Kricher

Brazil: Amazon and Pantanal, David L Pearson and Les Beletsky

TOP RESERVES & NATIONAL PARKS

Fernando de Noronha archipelago (p502) Fabulous marine park of islands, 350km from Natal.

Floresta Nacional do Tapajós (p596) Lush Amazonian rainforest preserve.

Ilha de Marajó (p587) Huge river island in the mouth of the Amazon.

Ilha Grande (p129) Hilly island covered by virgin Atlantic rainforest, a few hours from Rio.

Mamirauá Reserve (p637) Amazonian floodplain reserve teeming with wildlife; excellent ecotourism program.

Pantanal (p375) Vast wetlands that are one of Brazil's best places to see wildlife.

Parque Estadual da Pedra Azul (p220) Dramatic 1822m blue-tinged rock formation with natural pools and forest.

Parque Estadual de Itaúnas (p216) Sand dunes, beaches and a sea-turtle preserve.

Parque Nacional da Chapada Diamantina (p462) Large mountainous park in Bahia with stunning scenery, waterfalls and rivers.

Parque Nacional da Chapada dos Guimarães (p371) Waterfalls, canyons and bizarre rock formations.

Parque Nacional da Chapada dos Veadeiros (p358) High-altitude cerrado (savanna) with picturesque landscapes near Brasília.

Parque Nacional da Serra da Capivara (p555) Park in southern Piauí with thousands of prehistoric paintings and unique rock formations.

Parque Nacional do Itatiaia (p146) Ruggedly beautiful mountainous park, 150km from Rio.

Parque Nacional do Iguaçu (p289) Brazilian side of the spectacular waterfalls.

Parque Nacional dos Lençóis Maranhenses (p564) Enormous expanse of sand dunes and clear rain pools.

Praia do Rosa (p312) Beach town in Santa Catarina that's a famed whale sanctuary.

The Pantanal wetlands also face serious threats, including the rapid spread of intensive soy, cotton and sugarcane farming on Brazil's central plains, which are the source of most of the Pantanal's water. The sugarcane is the raw material of ethanol motor fuel, the international growth of which has led to the creation of dozens of new ethanol distilleries in Mato Grosso do Sul. Herbicides, fertilizers and other chemicals from the plantations drizzle their way into Pantanal waters, and forest clearance on the plains leads to erosion and consequent silting of Pantanal rivers. The growing cities around the Pantanal (many of which lack adequate waste-treatment plants) and ongoing industrial development also pose serious risks to this region.

The International Ecotourism Society (www.ecotourism.org) is a great source of ideas, news, facts and recommendations on sustainable travel the world over, Brazil included.

On Brazil's coasts, growth of cities and burgeoning tourism developments threaten many delicate coastal marine ecosystems, despite the creation of protected areas on extensive tracts of land and sea.

Survival Guide

DIRECTORY A–Z....702
Accessible Travel....... 702
Accommodations....... 702
Customs Regulations............ 703
Electricity............. 703
Embassies & Consulates........... 703
Food.................... 704
Health.................. 704
Insurance.............. 706
Internet Access......... 706
Legal Matters...........707
LGBT+ Travelers.........707
Maps.....................707
Money....................707
Opening Hours......... 708
Public Holidays......... 708
Safe Travel............. 708
Shopping.............. 708
Telephone............. 709
Time.................. 709
Toilets................. 709
Tourist Information............ 709
Visas.................. 709
Volunteering............710

TRANSPORTATION...711
GETTING THERE & AWAY.................711
Entering the Country......711
Air........................711
Land......................712
River.....................713
Sea.......................713
GETTING AROUND.........713
Air........................713
Bicycle...................714
Boat......................714
Bus.......................714
Car & Motorcycle........715
Hitchhiking..............715
Local Transportation..........716
Train.....................716

LANGUAGE........ 717
Glossary................722

Directory A–Z

Accessible Travel

Wheelchair users don't have an easy time in Brazil, but in the large cities there is a concerted effort to keep people mobile. Problems you'll encounter include immensely crowded public buses, and restaurants with entrance steps. It pays to plan your trip through contact with some of the relevant organizations.

Rio is probably the most accessible city in Brazil for travelers with disabilities to get around in, but that doesn't mean it's always easy. The metro system has electronic wheelchair lifts, but these aren't always operational. The streets and sidewalks along the main beaches have curb cuts and are wheelchair accessible, but most other areas do not have cuts. For transport around Rio, contact **Especial Coop Taxi** (☎21 3295-9606, WhatsApp 21 99776-5347; www.facebook.com/especialcoop). In São Paulo, contact the the government's **Central de Atendimento do Táxi Acessível** (☎11 3740-5544).

Most newer hotels have wheelchair-accessible rooms, and some cable TV is closed captioned.

Accommodations

Brazilian accommodations range from battered, windowless cells to sumptuous seaside guesthouses, with many possibilities in between. Nearly every *pousada* (guesthouse), hostel and hotel serves some form of *café da manha* (breakfast).

Private rooms with communal bathrooms are called *quartos*. Rooms with a private bathroom are *apartamentos*.

Reservations

In tourist centers, especially Rio, it's wise to make reservations during July (school holidays), and from Christmas to Carnaval. The same holds for any vacation mecca (eg Búzios, Ilhabela, Morro de São Paulo) on weekends, and anywhere during major festivals. For prime peak times (eg Carnaval), make contact months ahead.

Hotels

Brazil's hotels range from the good, modern and luxurious, to the shabby and moldy. At the more expensive places, taxes of 15% are often added to the price. Prices typically rise by about 30% during the high season, and room rates double or even triple during Carnaval and around New Year's Eve. During those times, minimum stays of four to seven days are fairly common. Hotels in business-oriented cities such as São Paulo, Curitiba, Porto Alegre and Brasília usually give discounts for stays on weekends.

Pousadas

A pousada typically means a small family-owned guesthouse, though some hotels call themselves 'pousadas' to improve their charm

SLEEPING PRICE RANGES

The following price ranges refer to a double room with bathroom in high season (December to March). Unless otherwise stated, breakfast is included in the price.

$ less than R$160

$$ R$160–R$350

$$$ more than R$350

The price range for Rio, São Paulo and Brasília is higher:

$ less than R$200

$$ R$200–R$500

$$$ more than R$500

quotient. Pousadas can cost as little as R$160 for a rustic double and as much as R$600 for a lavish option.

Hostels

Youth hostels in Brazil are called *albergues da juventude*. Hostelling International Brasil (www.hihostelbrasil.com.br) has more than 50 hostels in the country, all with links on the website. There are also scores of private hostels. Rio is by far the country's hostel capital, with over 90 at last count. Quality varies considerably, but they're generally good places to meet Brazilian and foreign travelers. A dorm bed in a hostel costs between R$40 and R$80.

Jungle Lodges

One popular type of remote-area accommodations is the jungle lodge, which caters to tourists in or on the edge of the forest. Though they're sometimes pricey, you're paying for the experience of lodging in the rainforest, rather than amenities – which are midrange at best. The largest number of jungle lodges are found outside of Manaus.

Rental Accommodations

It's possible to rent holiday, short- or long-term apartments through a local holiday-rental agencies. Airbnb has thousands of listings across Brazil.

Customs Regulations

Travelers entering Brazil can bring in 2L of alcohol, 400 cigarettes, and one personal computer, video camera and still camera. Newly purchased goods worth up to US$500 are permitted duty-free. Meat and cheese products are not allowed.

BOOK YOUR STAY ONLINE

For more accommodations reviews by Lonely Planet authors, check out http://lonelyplanet.com/brazil/hotels/. You'll find independent reviews, as well as recommendations on the best places to stay. Best of all, you can book online.

Electricity

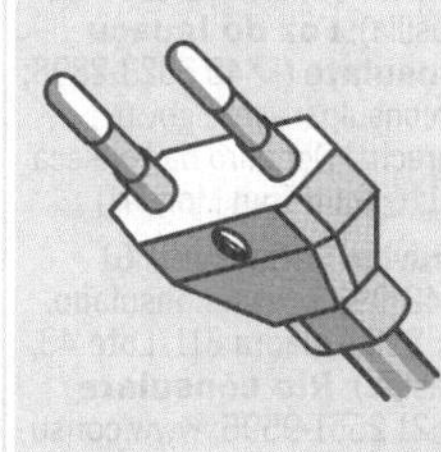

127V/220Hz/60Hz

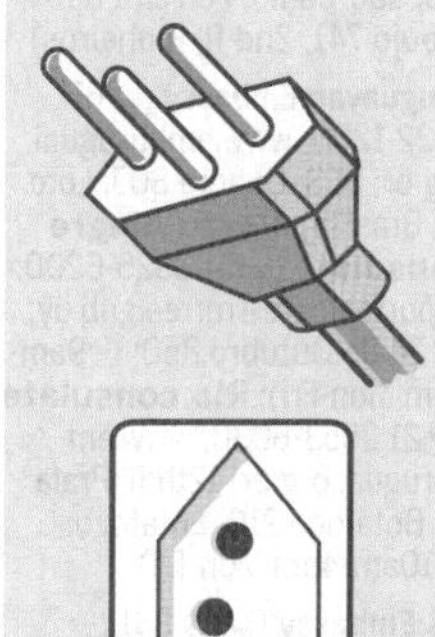

127V/220Hz/60Hz

Embassies & Consulates

The embassies are all in Brasília, but many countries have consulates in Rio and São Paulo, and often other cities as well. For addresses in Brasília, SES stands for Setor de Embaixadas Sul.

Argentine Embassy (☎61 3212-7600; www.ebras.cancilleria.gov.ar; SES Quadra 803, Lote 12, Brasília); **Foz do Iguaçu consulate** (☎45 3574-2969; http://cfdig.cancilleria.gov.ar; Travessia Bianchi 26; ⏰10am-3pm Mon-Fri); **Porto Alegre consulate** (☎51 3321-1360; http://caleg.cancilleria.gov.ar; Coronel Bordini 1033); **São Paulo consulate** (☎11 3897-9522; www.cpabl.mrecic.gov.ar; Av Paulista 2313, Jardins)

Australian Embassy (☎61 3226-3111; www.brazil.embassy.gov.au; SES, Quadra 801, Lote 7, Brasília); **Rio consulate** (☎21 3824-4624; www.dfat.gov.au; 23rd fl, Av Presidente Wilson 231, Centro; ⏰10am-4pm Mon-Fri)

Bolivian Consulate (☎61 3366-4448; www.embolivia.org.br; SES, Quadra 809, Lote 34, Brasília); **Brasiléia consulate** (☎68 3546-5760; Hilário Meireles 236; ⏰8am-noon & 2-4pm Mon-Fri); **Corumbá consulate** (☎67 3231-5605; www.cancilleria.gob.bo; 7 de Setembro 47; ⏰visas 8:30-9:30am Mon-Fri); **Guajará-Mirim consulate** (☎69 3541-8622; 15 de Novembro 255; ⏰8am-noon & 2-6pm Mon-Fri); **Rio consulate** (☎21 2552-5490; www.consuladodeboliviaenrio.org.br; No 101, Av Rui Barbosa 664, Flamengo; ⏰9am-2pm Mon-Fri)

Canadian Embassy (☎61 3424-5400; www.brazil.gc.ca; SES, Quadra 803, Lote 16, Brasília); **Rio consulate** (☎21 2543-3004; www.brasil.gc.ca; 13th fl, Av Atlântica 1130, Copacabana; ⏲8am-12:30pm & 1:30-5pm Mon-Thu, 8am-12:30pm Fri); **São Paulo consulate** (☎11 5509-4321; www.canadainternational.gc.ca; Av das Nações Unidas 12901, 16th fl, Torre Norte, Brooklin Paulista)

Colombian Embassy (☎61 3214-8900; http://brasil.embajada.gov.co; SES, Quadra 803, Lote 10, Brasília); **Tabatinga consulate** (☎97 3412-2104; http://tabatinga.consulado.gov.co; Sampaio 623; ⏲7am-1pm Mon-Fri)

Dutch Embassy (☎61 3961-3200; www.holandaevoce.nl; SES, Quadra 801, Lote 05, Brasília); **Rio consulate** (☎21 2157-5400; www.nederlandenu.nl; 6th fl, Av Ataúlfo de Paiva 204, Leblon; ⏲8:30am-4pm Mon-Thu, to noon Fri)

French Embassy (☎61 3222-3999; www.br.ambafrance.org; SES, Quadra 801, Lote 04, Brasília); **Rio consulate** (☎21 3974-6699; http://riodejaneiro.ambafrance-br.org; Av Presidente Antônio Carlos 58, Centro; ⏲8:30am-12:30pm Mon-Fri by appointment, 2:30-4pm Tue & Wed)

German Embassy (☎61 3442-7000; www.brasilia.diplo.de; SES, Quadra 807, Lote 25, Brasília); **Rio consulate** (☎21 3380-3700; www.rio-de-janeiro.diplo.de; Av Presidente Antônio Carlos 58, Centro; ⏲8:30-11:30am Mon, Tue, Thu & Fri, 1-3pm Wed)

Guyanese Embassy (☎61 3248-0874; www.embguyana.org.br; SHIS, QI 5, Conjunto 19, Casa 24, Brasília)

Irish Embassy (☎61 3248-8800; www.embaixada-irlanda.org.br; SHIS QI 12 Conjunto 5, Casa 9, Brasília)

Israeli Embassy (☎61 2105-0500; www.embassies.gov.il; SES, Quadra 809, Lote 38, Brasília)

New Zealand Embassy (☎61 3248-9900; www.mfat.govt.nz; SHIS QI 9, Conjunto 16, Casa 1, Brasília); **New Zealand Consulate São Paulo** (☎11 3898-7400; www.mfat.govt.nz/en/countries-and-regions/latin-america; 12th fl, Bela Paulista Bldg, Av Paulista 2421)

Paraguayan Embassy (☎61 3242-3020; www.mre.gov.py; SES, Quadra 811, Lote 42, Brasília); **Foz do Iguaçu consulate** (☎45 3523-2898; fozconsulpar@mre.gov.py; Marechal Deodoro da Fonseca 901; ⏲9am-1pm Mon-Fri)

Peruvian Embassy (☎61 3242-9933; www.consulado.pe; SES, Quadra 811, Lote 43, Brasília); **Rio consulate** (☎21 2551-9596; www.consuladoperurio.com.br; 2nd fl, Av Rui Barbosa 314, Flamengo; ⏲9am-3pm Mon-Fri)

UK Embassy (☎61 3329-2300; www.reinounido.org.br; SES, Quadra 801, Lote 08, Brasília); **Rio consulate** (☎21 2555-9600; www.reinounido.org.br; 2nd fl, Praia do Flamengo 284, Flamengo; ⏲8:30am-12:30pm & 1:30-4:30pm Mon-Fri); **São Paulo consulate** (☎11 3094-2700; www.gov.uk/world/organisations/british-consulate-general-sao-paulo; Ferreira de Araújo 741, 2nd fl, Pinheiros)

Uruguayan Embassy (☎61 3322-1200; www.emburuguai.org.br; SES, Quadra 803, Lote 14, Brasília); **Porto Alegre consulate** (☎51 3325-6200; cgportoalegre@mrree.gub.uy; Av 24 de Outubro 850; ⏲9am-3pm Mon-Fri); **Rio consulate** (☎21 2553-6030; www.emburuguai.org.br; 12th fl, Praia de Botafogo 210, Botafogo; ⏲10am-4pm Mon-Fri)

US Embassy (☎61 3312-7000; https://br.usembassy.gov; SES, Quadra 801, Lote 3, Brasília); **Rio consulate** (☎21 3823-2000; www.brazil.usembassy.gov; Av Presidente Wilson 147, Centro; ⏲8am-5pm Mon-Fri); **Salvador consulate** (☎71 3113-2090; Room 1401, Av Tancredo Neves 1632, Salvador Trade Center, Caminho das Árvores); **São Paulo consulate** (☎11 3250-5000; https://br.usembassy.gov/embassy-consulates/saopaulo; Henri Dunant 500, Chácara Santo Antônio)

Venezuelan Embassy (☎61 2101-1010; http://brasil.embajada.gob.ve; SES, Quadra 803, Lote 13, Brasília); **Boa Vista consulate** (☎95 3623-6612; Av Benjamin Constant 968; ⏲8am-noon Mon-Fri); **Manaus consulate** (☎92 3584-3813; Río Jamary 10, Conj Vieiralves, Nossa Senhora das Graças); **Rio consulate** (☎21 2554-5955; 14th fl, Av Presidente Vargas 463, Centro; ⏲9am-1pm Mon-Fri)

Food

Brazil has incredible variety when it comes to cuisine. Every region has its own specialties, from delectable freshwater fish from the Amazon and the Pantanal, to the unique African-influenced dishes in Bahia. You'll find European influences in the south (German, Italian) and down-home comfort classics (beans, pork) from Minas Gerais. If you're a foodie, São Paulo, which has 14 Michelin-starred restaurants, should figure high on your itinerary. Rio de Janeiro also has many standout dining rooms.

Health

For an ambulance in Brazil, call ☎192, or an emergency number.

EATING PRICE RANGES

The following price ranges refer to a main course.

$ less than R$30

$$ R$30–R$75

$$$ more than R$75

Good medical care is available in the larger cities but may be difficult to find in rural areas. Medical care in Brazil may be extremely expensive.

Each Brazilian pharmacy has a licensed pharmacist. Most are well supplied.

Before You Go

HEALTH INSURANCE

If your health insurer doesn't cover you for medical expenses incurred abroad, you'll need to purchase extra travel insurance. Find out in advance if your travel insurer will make payments directly to providers or reimburse you later for overseas health expenditures.

RECOMMENDED VACCINATIONS

Since most vaccines don't produce immunity until at least two weeks after they're given, visit a physician four to eight weeks before departure. Ask your doctor for an International Certificate of Vaccination (otherwise known as the yellow booklet), which will list all the vaccinations you've received. This is mandatory for countries that require proof of yellow-fever vaccination upon entry, but it's a good idea to carry it wherever you travel.

In Brazil

AVAILABILITY & COST OF HEALTH CARE

Good medical care is available in the larger cities but may be difficult to find in rural areas. Medical care in Brazil may be extremely expensive.

Each Brazilian pharmacy has a licensed pharmacist. Most are well supplied.

INFECTIOUS DISEASES

The diseases of most concern are mosquito-borne infections, including malaria, yellow fever and dengue fever, which are not a significant concern in temperate regions.

ZIKA VIRUS: WARNING FOR PREGNANT TRAVELERS

Brazil has experienced several outbreaks of Zika virus since 2015. Transmitted by mosquitoes, Zika rarely causes illness – only one in five infected people will experience the flu-like symptoms. However, the virus has been linked to microcephaly (abnormally small head size with possible brain damage) in babies born to women who were infected while pregnant. Check the latest warnings with the US Centers for Disease Control (CDC) before you travel. If there's an outbreak, pregnant women should consider postponing travel to Brazil.

DENGUE

Found throughout Brazil, dengue is transmitted by aedes mosquitoes, which bite preferentially during the daytime and are more common in densely populated, urban environments.

Dengue usually causes flu-like symptoms, including fever, muscle aches, headaches, nausea and vomiting, often followed by a rash. There is no vaccine or treatment for dengue fever except to take analgesics such as acetaminophen/paracetamol and to drink plenty of fluids.

HEPATITIS A

Hepatitis A is the second-most-common travel-related infection after traveler's diarrhea. It's a viral infection of the liver that is usually acquired by ingestion of contaminated water, food or ice, though it may also be acquired by direct contact with infected persons. The illness occurs throughout the world, but the incidence is higher in developing nations. Symptoms may include fever, malaise, jaundice, nausea, vomiting and abdominal pain. Most cases resolve without complications, though hepatitis A occasionally causes severe liver damage. There is no treatment.

The vaccine for hepatitis A is extremely safe and highly effective. If you get a booster six to 12 months later, it lasts for at least 10 years. You really should get it before you go to Brazil or any other developing nation. Because the safety of hepatitis A vaccine has not been established for pregnant women or children under the age of two, they should instead be given a gamma globulin injection.

MALARIA

Malaria is transmitted by mosquito bites, usually between dusk and dawn. The main symptoms are high spiking fevers, which may be accompanied by chills, sweats, headache, body aches, weakness, vomiting or diarrhea. Severe cases may involve the central nervous system and lead to seizures, confusion, coma and death.

Taking prophylactic malaria pills is strongly recommended for forested areas within the nine states of the Amazonia region.

If you develop a fever after returning home, see a physician, as malaria symptoms may not occur for months.

TYPHOID

Typhoid fever is caused by ingestion of food or water contaminated by a species of salmonella known as *Salmonella typhi*. Fever occurs in virtually all cases. Other symptoms may include headache, malaise, muscle aches, dizziness, loss of appetite, nausea and abdominal pain. Either diarrhea or constipation may occur.

PRACTICALITIES

Newspapers The biggest Portuguese-language daily newspapers are *Jornal do Brasil* (www.jbonline.com.br) and *O Globo* (www.globo.com.br), both from Rio, and *O Estado de São Paulo* (www.estadao.com.br) and *Folha de São Paulo* (www.folha.uol.com.br), out of São Paulo. The weekly *Veja* (www.veja.abril.com.br) is a current-affairs magazine, and in Rio and São Paulo it comes with a good pullout guide to what's happening locally. For English-language news in Rio, check out the *Rio Times* (www.riotimesonline.com).

TV Programming revolves around sports, comedy shows and the nightly *telenovelas* (soap operas); *O Globo* is the largest nationwide TV network. Brazil uses the PAL system for video/DVD.

Smoking Banned in restaurants and bars; some hotels have smoking rooms.

Weights & Measures The metric system is used.

Unless you expect to take all your meals in major hotels and restaurants, typhoid vaccine is a good idea.

YELLOW FEVER

Yellow fever is a life-threatening viral infection transmitted by mosquitoes in forested areas. The illness begins with flu-like symptoms, which may include fever, chills, headache, muscle aches, backache, loss of appetite, nausea and vomiting. These symptoms usually subside in a few days, but one person in six enters a second, toxic phase characterized by recurrent fever, vomiting, listlessness, jaundice, kidney failure, and hemorrhage, leading to death in up to half of the cases. There is no treatment.

The yellow-fever vaccine is strongly recommended for all travelers to Brazil, except those visiting only Rio de Janeiro, São Paulo and the coastal areas south of São Luís. Proof of vaccination is no longer required from travelers arriving from a yellow-fever-infected country in Africa or the Americas.

INSECT BITES & STINGS

To prevent mosquito bites, wear long sleeves, long pants, hat and shoes (rather than sandals). Bring along a good insect repellent, preferably one containing DEET, which should be applied to exposed skin and clothing, but not to eyes, mouth, cuts, wounds or irritated skin.

For additional protection, you can apply permethrin to clothing, shoes, tents and bed nets. Permethrin treatments are safe and remain effective for at least two weeks, even when items are laundered. Permethrin should not be applied directly to skin.

Don't sleep with the window open unless there is a screen in the window frame. If the sleeping area is not otherwise protected, use a mosquito coil, which will fill the room with insecticide throughout the night.

TAP WATER

Tap water in Brazilian cities such as Rio and São Paulo is generally safe to drink, but it tastes awful. In remote areas, tap water may be suspect. Many hotels and guesthouses filter their water – be sure to inquire about the status where you're staying. Vigorous boiling for one minute is the most effective means of water purification, though you can also use a water filter, ultraviolet light (such as a steripen) or iodine pills.

Insurance

A travel-insurance policy to cover theft, loss and medical problems is a good idea. The policies handled by STA Travel and other student-travel organizations are usually good value. Some policies offer lower and higher medical-expense options; the higher ones are chiefly for countries such as the USA that have extremely high medical costs. There is a wide variety of policies available, so check the fine print.

Some policies specifically exclude 'dangerous activities,' which can include scuba diving, motorcycling and even hiking.

You may prefer a policy that pays doctors or hospitals directly rather than you having to pay on the spot and claim later. If you have to claim later, make sure you keep all documentation.

Check that the policy covers ambulances or an emergency flight home.

Worldwide travel insurance is available at www.lonelyplanet.com/bookings. You can buy, extend and claim online any time – even if you're already on the road.

Internet Access

Most hostels and hotels, as well as many cafes and restaurants, provide wi-fi access. It's usually free, although pricier hotels sometimes charge for it.

Internet cafes have largely disappeared from the Brazilian landscape. If you do manage to find one, expect to pay between R$5 and R$10 an hour.

Legal Matters

If something is stolen from you, report it to the police. No big investigation is going to occur, but you will get a police report to give to your insurance company.

In recent years, Brazil has gotten quite strict about drink driving. Police checkpoints stop cars at random.

The penalties for drug possession are harsh, and you don't want to end up in a Brazilian prison – so it's wise to stay away from drugs in any form. Some police checkpoints are set up outside nightclubs to stop taxis and give the full pat down to club-goers on their way home (hint, don't carry anything!). Police along the coastal drive from Rio to Búzios and Rio to São Paulo are notorious for hassling young people and foreigners. Border areas are also a danger, particularly around the Bolivian border.

If you are arrested, know that you have the right to remain silent, and that you are innocent until proven guilty. You also have the right to be visited by your lawyer or a family member.

A large amount of cocaine is smuggled out of Bolivia and Peru through Brazil. Be very careful with drugs. If you're going to buy, don't buy from strangers and don't carry anything around with you.

Marijuana is illegal in Brazil. Nevertheless, it's plentiful and widely used. Like many other things in Brazil, everyone except the military and the police has a rather tolerant attitude towards it. Bahia seems to have the most open climate.

If you're coming from one of the Andean countries and have been chewing coca leaves, be especially careful to clean out your pack before arriving in Brazil. Sentences are stiff even for possession of coca leaves.

LGBT+ Travelers

Brazilians are pretty laid-back when it comes to most sexual issues, and homosexuality is more accepted here than in any other part of Latin America. That said, the degree to which you can be out in Brazil varies greatly by region, and in some smaller towns discrimination is prevalent.

Rio is the gay capital of Latin America, though São Paulo and to a lesser extent Salvador also have lively scenes. Gay and lesbian bars are disappearing (blame it on dating/hooking-up apps like Grindr). Those still around are all-welcome affairs attended by GLS (Gays, Lesbians e Simpatizantes), a mixed heterosexual and homosexual crowd far more concerned with dancing and having a good time than anything else.

There is no law against homosexuality in Brazil, and the age of consent is 18, the same as for heterosexuals.

Useful resources include the following:

Mix Brasil (www.mixbrasil.org.br) The largest Brazilian LGBT site.

ABGLT (Associação Brasileira de Lésbicas, Gays, Bissexuais, Travestis, Transexuais e Intersexos; www.abglt.org)

ACAPA (Associação Brasileira de Gays, Lésbicas, Bissexuais, Travestis e Transexuais; www.disponivel.uol.com.br/acapa)

Maps

The Quatro Rodas series, which includes good regional maps (Norte, Nordeste etc), are the best available maps of Brazil and can be found throughout the country. Quatro Rodas also publishes the *Atlas Rodoviário,* useful if you're driving, as well as excellent street atlases for the main cities.

Money

The Brazcurrency is the real (hay-*ow;* often written R$); the plural is reais (hay-*ice*). One real is made up of 100 centavos.

It might be handy to keep cash in reserve, though you'll want to be exceptionally cautious when traveling with it. Cash should be in US dollars or euros.

FRAUD WARNING

Credit-card and ATM fraud is widespread in Brazil, especially in the Northeast. Card cloning (*clonagem* in Portuguese) is the preferred method: an entrepreneurial opportunist sticks a false card reader into an ATM that copies your card and steals the PIN when you come along and withdraw money. Shazam! A few hours later, $1500 disappears from your account in Recife while you and your card are safe and sound sipping caipirinhas on the beach in Natal!

To combat fraud, restaurants will bring the credit-card machine to your table or ask you to accompany them to the cashier to run a credit-card transaction. Never let someone walk off with your card. Other tips:

- Use high-traffic ATMs inside banks during banking hours only.
- Always cover the ATM keypad when entering personal codes.
- Avoid self-standing ATMs whenever possible and never use an ATM that looks tampered with.

ATMs

ATMs are the easiest way of getting cash in big cities and are common. In many smaller towns, ATMs exist but don't always work for non-Brazilian cards. Make sure you have a four-digit PIN (longer PINs may not work). In general, Citibank, Banco do Brasil and Bradesco are the best ATMs to try.

Bargaining

A little bargaining for hotel rooms should become second nature. Before you agree to take a room, ask for a better price: '*Tem desconto?*' (Is there a discount?) and '*Pode fazer um melhor preço?*' (Can you give a better price?) are the phrases to use. There's sometimes a discount for paying *à vista* (cash).

You should also bargain when shopping in markets. And if you're about to ride in unmetered taxis, be sure to agree on the price before departing.

Credit Cards

You can use credit cards for many purchases and to make cash withdrawals from ATMs and banks. Visa is the most widely accepted card, followed by MasterCard. Amex and Diners Club cards are less useful. Visa cash advances are widely available, even in small towns with no other currency-exchange facilities; you'll need your passport, and the process can be time consuming, especially at the ubiquitous but bureaucratic Banco do Brasil.

Opening Hours

Banks 9am–3pm Monday–Friday

Bars 6pm–2am

Cafes 8am–10pm

Nightclubs 10pm–4am Thursday–Saturday

Post offices 9am–5pm Monday–Friday; some open Saturday morning

Restaurants Noon–2:30pm and 6–10:30pm

Shops 9am–6pm Monday–Friday and 9am–1pm Saturday

Public Holidays

April 19, the Dia do Índio (Indigenous Day), is not a national holiday but is nevertheless marked by festivities in indigenous villages around the country.

New Year's Day January 1

Carnaval February/March (the two days before Ash Wednesday)

Good Friday & Easter Sunday March/April

Tiradentes Day April 21

May Day/Labor Day May 1

Corpus Christi Late May/June (60 days after Easter Sunday)

Independence Day September 7

Day of NS de Aparecida October 12

All Souls' Day November 2

Proclamation of the Republic November 15

Christmas Day December 25

Safe Travel

Brazil receives plenty of bad press about its violence and high crime rate. Unfortunately, the security situation remains a big concern, and you need to take basic precautions wherever your travel. This means not taking anything of value with you to the beach, carrying only the cash you need for the day, and leaving expensive (and expensive-looking) items at home.

Scams & Robbery Techniques

Distraction is a common tactic employed by street thieves. The aim is to throw potential victims off guard so that they're easier prey. It may be something as simple as asking you for a cigarette or a light so that you slow down and take your attention off other people around you.

There have also been reports of druggings, including spiked drinks. While you're temporarily unconscious or semiconscious as a result of some noxious substance being slipped into your beverage, you're powerless to resist thieves. If you start to feel unaccountably dizzy, disoriented, fatigued or just mentally vacant not long after imbibing, your drink may have been spiked. If you suspect this to be the case, call for help, quickly extricate yourself from the situation and try to get to a safe place – your hotel room.

Exercise extreme caution when someone you don't know or trust offers you a drink of any kind or even cigarettes, sweets etc. If the circumstances make you suspicious, the offer can be tactfully refused by claiming stomach or other medical problems.

Cut-Rate Tour Operators & Touts

In Manaus, Cuiabá and other parts of the Amazon and the Pantanal, there's a major problem with freelancers and shady operators selling cut-rate tours that turn out to be ecologically unsound, awful and/or unsafe. As a rule, never book a tour (or even accept help) from someone who approaches you unsolicited at the airport or on the street. Go directly to the offices in town, or book on websites ahead of time.

Shopping

Handicrafts and artwork make fine souvenirs and are best purchased directly from the artist or artisan. For genuine indigenous arts and crafts, have a look in the Artíndia stores of Funai (the government indigenous agency) and museum gift shops.

Artisans in the Northeast produce a rich assortment of artistic items. Salvador and nearby Cachoeira are most notable for their rough-hewn wood sculptures. Ceará specializes in fine lace. The interior of Pernambuco, in particular Caruaru, is famous for wildly imaginative ceramic figurines.

Telephone

Cell Phones

Brazil uses the GSM 850/900/1800/1900 network, which is compatible with North America, Europe and Australia, but the country's 4G LTE network runs on 2500/2690 (for now), which is not compatible with many North American and European smartphones.

Cell phones have nine-digit numbers starting with a 9. Mobiles have city codes, just like landlines, and if you're calling from another city, you have to use them. Tim (www.tim.com.br), Claro (www.claro.com.br), Oi (www.oi.com.br) and Vivo (www.vivo.com.br) are the major operators.

Foreigners can purchase a local SIM with a passport instead of needing a Brazilian CPF (tax ID number) – a major bureaucratic roadblock dismantled. Local SIM cards can be used in unlocked European and Australian phones, and in US phones on the GSM network.

CITY CODES & CARRIERS

Brazil has several rival long-distance telephone carriers. When making a long-distance call (either between cities or internationally), you have to select a carrier and include its two-digit *código de prestadora* (code) in the number you dial. Brazilian city codes are commonly quoted with an xx representing the carrier code, eg 0xx21 for Rio de Janeiro or 0xx71 for Salvador.

This construction may look complicated, but in practice it's straightforward. For one thing, you can use the main carriers, **Embratel** (☎21) or **Oi Telemar** (☎31) for any call; for another, other major carriers usually have their names and codes widely displayed in their localities, particularly on public phones.

For example, to call from Rio de Janeiro to Fortaleza (city code 0xx85), in the state of Ceará, you dial 0 followed by 21, 23, 31 or 85 (the codes of the four carriers that cover both Rio and Ceará), followed by 85 for Fortaleza, followed by the number.

For an international call, dial 00 followed by either 21, 23 or 31 (the international carriers), followed by the country code, city code and number.

Time

Brazil has four time zones:

Most of the country is GMT/UTC minus three hours. This includes Rio, São Paulo, the South, Northeast, Brasília and half of the Amazon.

Mato Grosso, Mato Grosso do Sul and most of the Amazon are one hour behind Brasília time (GMT/UTC minus four hours).

A tiny part of Amazonas state and all of Acre are two hours behind Brasília time (GMT/UTC minus five hours).

The Fernando de Noronha archipelago is one hour *ahead* of Brasília time (GMT/UTC minus two hours).

Brazilian daylight saving time runs from mid-October to mid-February, during which period clocks are advanced one hour – but only in the Southeast, South and Central West.

Toilets

Public toilets are not common but can be found at every bus station and airport in most cities and towns; there's usually a charge of around R$1 to R$2. People will generally let you use the toilets in restaurants and bars. As in other Latin American countries, toilet paper isn't flushed. There's usually a basket next to the toilet to put paper in.

Tourist Information

Tourist offices in Brazil are a mixed bag. Some offices have dedicated, knowledgeable staff, while others have little interest in helping tourists.

Embratur (www.visitbrasil.com), the Brazilian tourism institute, provides limited online resources.

Visas

Brazil has a reciprocal visa system, so if your home country requires Brazilian nationals to secure a visa, then you'll need one to enter Brazil. US, Canadian and Australian citizens need visas, but UK, New Zealand, French and German citizens do not. You can check your status with the Brazilian embassy or consulate in your home country.

If you do need a visa, arrange it well in advance. Visas are not issued on arrival; and you won't be permitted into the country without one. Applying for a visa got easier in 2018, however, when Brazil rolled out its new e-visa system, which is available to citizens from the US, Canada, Australia and Japan. The application fee is US$40, plus an online service fee of US$4.25. The

GOVERNMENT TRAVEL ADVICE

The following government websites offer travel advisories and information on the security situation in Brazil and elsewhere.

Australian Department of Foreign Affairs & Trade (www.smarttraveller.gov.au)

British Foreign Office (www.gov.uk/foreign-travel-advice)

Canadian Department of Foreign Affairs (www.travel.gc.ca/travelling/advisories)

US State Department (http://travel.state.gov)

service is valid for both tourists and business travelers.

To apply, visit the official website endorsed by Brazil's Ministry of Foreign Affairs: VFS Global (www.vfsglobal.com/Brazil-eVisa). You will need to upload a passport photograph and a scanned image of your passport bio page, and fill in other required details on the application. E-visas are valid for two years, for stays of up to 90 days per year.

Once all the documents have been submitted, the processing times for the visa is around five business days. Unfortunately, the online application process does not currently run very smoothly. Many applicants have had problems uploading photos – or having their photos rejected – experience website crashes. It's wise to apply well in advance of your departure.

After your visa has been approved, you will receive a pdf of your e-visa. Print this out and take it with you on your trip. Without the printed copy, you may not be allowed to board your flight, and may also be denied entry into the country.

Old-fashioned consular visas are also still available. These are pricier and you'll have to apply in person to a Brazilian consulate in your home country.

Applicants under 18 years of age wanting to travel to Brazil must also submit a notarized letter of authorization from a parent or legal guardian.

Visa Extensions

Brazil's Polícia Federal, who have offices in the state capitals and border towns, handle visa extensions for those nationalities allowed to extend (Schengen-region passport holders, for example, must leave for 90 days before reentering for a second 90-days – extending is not an option).

Entry & Exit Cards

On entering Brazil, all tourists must fill out a *cartão de entrada/saida* (entry/exit card); immigration officials will keep half, you keep the other. They will also stamp your passport and, if for some reason they are not granting you the usual 90-day stay in Brazil, the number of days you are allowed to stay will be written in your passport.

When you leave Brazil, the second half of the entry/exit card will be taken by immigration officials. Don't lose your card while in Brazil, as it could cause hassles and needless delays when you leave.

Passports

By law you must carry a passport with you at all times, but many travelers opt to carry a photocopy (preferably certified) when traveling about town and to leave their passport securely locked up at their hotel.

Volunteering

Atados (Map p249; www.atados.com.br; Rua Teçaindá 81, Pinheiros) Supports several hundred volunteer organizations involved in social work, the environment and health care. Headquartered in São Paulo.

Iko Poran (☎21 3217-1474; www.ikoporan.org) Rio-based service linking volunteers with needy organizations. Iko Poran also provides housing for volunteers. Rio based.

Regua (www.regua.org; Reserva Ecológica de Guapi Assu) Accepts volunteers from all over the world for reforestation and other conservation work.

Task Brasil (www.taskbrasil.org.uk) UK-based organization that places volunteers in Rio.

Transportation

GETTING THERE & AWAY

Most travelers start their Brazilian odyssey by flying into Rio, but the country has several other gateway airports, as well as land borders with every country in South America except Chile and Ecuador. Flights and tours can be booked online at lonelyplanet.com/bookings.

Entering the Country

Immigration and customs formalities are fairly straightforward, though you'll want to be sure to have your visa in order if you're from a country (like the USA, Canada or Australia) that needs it.

Air

The most popular international gateways are Rio de Janeiro's **Galeão International Airport** (Aeroporto Internacional Antônio Carlos Jobim; ☎21 3004-6050; www.riogaleao.com; Domestic Arrival Hall, Av Vinte de Janeiro) and São Paulo's **GRU Airport** (Aeroporto Guarulhos; ☎11 2445-2945; www.gru.com.br; Rod Hélio Smidt s/n). From both, connecting flights leave regularly to airports throughout the country. Salvador and Recife receive a few direct scheduled flights from Europe.

Though headquartered in Chile, **LATAM** (☎0300-570-5700; www.latam.com) is Brazil's largest international carrier, with flights to New York, Miami, Paris, London, Lisbon and seven South American cities. The US Federal Aviation Administration has assessed LATAM as Category 1, which means it is in compliance with international aviation standards.

Tickets

For high-season travel, roughly from mid-December to the end of February, tickets to Brazil cost about US$300 more than they do during the rest of the year.

INTERNATIONAL AIR PASSES

If you're combining travel in Brazil with other countries in southern South America, air passes can be decent value if you're covering a lot of ground in 30 days and don't mind a fixed itinerary.

The Visit South America air pass offered by airlines of the Oneworld Alliance (www.oneworld.com) allows stops in more than 60 cities in 10 South American countries. Prices are calculated on a per-flight, per-distance basis. Sample fares include US$300 from Rio de Janeiro to Lima (Peru), US$310 from São Paulo to Buenos Aires (Argentina), and US$280 from Santiago (Chile) to Lima (Peru).

The Gol South America air pass is valid for travel on the **Gol** (☎0300-115-2121; www.voegol.com.br) network,

CLIMATE CHANGE & TRAVEL

Every form of transport that relies on carbon-based fuel generates CO_2, the main cause of human-induced climate change. Modern travel is dependent on airplanes, which might use less fuel per mile per person than most cars but travel much greater distances. The altitude at which aircraft emit gases (including CO_2) and particles also contributes to their climate change impact. Many websites offer 'carbon calculators' that allow people to estimate the carbon emissions generated by their journey and, for those who wish to do so, to offset the impact of the greenhouse gases emitted with contributions to portfolios of climate-friendly initiatives throughout the world. Lonely Planet offsets the carbon footprint of all staff and author travel.

including routes between Brazil and Chile, Argentina, Paraguay, Uruguay, Peru and Bolivia. Fares start at US$680 plus tax for four flights, US$840 for five flights; each additional flight is US$160.

Land

There's direct land access to Brazil from nine countries. Several border towns can also be reached by river from Bolivia or Peru. If arriving overland from Colombia or Venezuela, you no longer need to have a certificate of a yellow-fever vaccine to enter Brazil (but you'll still need a visa!).

Border Crossings

ARGENTINA

The main border point used by travelers is Puerto Iguazú–Foz do Iguaçu, a 20-hour bus ride from Buenos Aires. Further south, you can cross from Paso de los Libres (Argentina) to Uruguaiana (Brazil), which is also served by buses from Buenos Aires.

Direct buses run between Buenos Aires and Porto Alegre (R$335, 21 hours) and Rio de Janeiro (R$550, 42 hours). Other destinations include Florianópolis (R$458, 25 hours), Curitiba (R$385, 32 hours) and São Paulo (R$467, 44 hours).

BOLIVIA

Brazil's longest border runs through remote wetlands and forests, and is much used by smugglers. The main crossings are at Corumbá, Cáceres, Guajará-Mirim and Brasiléia.

The busiest crossing is between Quijarro (Bolivia) and Corumbá (Brazil), which is a good access point for the Pantanal. Quijarro has a daily train link with Santa Cruz (Bolivia). Corumbá has bus connections with Bonito, Campo Grande, São Paulo, Rio de Janeiro and southern Brazil.

Cáceres, in Mato Grosso (Brazil), has a daily bus link with Santa Cruz (Bolivia) via the Bolivian border town of San Matías.

Guajará-Mirim (Brazil) is a short river crossing from Guayaramerín (Bolivia). Both towns have onward bus links into their respective countries (Guayaramerín also has flights), but from late December to late February heavy rains can make the northern Bolivian roads a very difficult proposition.

Brasiléia (Brazil), a 4½-hour bus ride from Rio Branco, stands opposite Cobija (Bolivia), which has bus and plane connections into Bolivia. Bolivian buses confront the same wet-season difficulties.

CHILE

Although there is no border with Chile, direct buses run via Argentina between Santiago and Brazilian cities such as Porto Alegre (R$486, 40 hours), São Paulo (R$465, 57 hours) and Rio de Janeiro (R$560, 63 hours).

BOLIVIAN ENTRY REQUIREMENTS

Any US citizen entering Bolivia is required to have a visa, which costs US$160. Citizens from most other nations receive free 30-day entry. Although technically it's possible to obtain a visa at the border, it's wise to secure this beforehand – particularly if arriving overland, as long delays are likely. Bolivian Immigration has a whole host of other requirements, including a certificate of yellow-fever vaccine, proof of financial solvency, and more. Visit www.bolivia-usa.org for the latest.

COLOMBIA

Leticia, on the Rio Amazonas in far southeast Colombia, is contiguous with Tabatinga (Brazil). You can cross the border on foot or by Kombi van or taxi. From within Colombia, Leticia is only really accessible by air. Tabatinga is a quick flight (or a several-day Amazon boat ride) from Manaus or Tefé.

FRENCH GUIANA

The Brazilian town of Oiapoque, a rugged 560km bus ride from Macapá, stands across the Rio Oiapoque from St Georges (French Guiana). A road connects St Georges to the French Guiana capital, Cayenne, with minibuses shuttling between the two. (Get there early in the morning to catch one.)

GUYANA & SURINAME

From Boa Vista, there are daily buses to Bonfim, Roraima (R$26, 1½ hours), on the Guyanese border, a short motorized-canoe ride from Lethem in southwest Guyana.

Overland travel between Suriname and Brazil involves first passing through either French Guiana or Guyana.

PARAGUAY

The two major border crossings are Ciudad del Este (Paraguay)–Foz do Iguaçu (Brazil) and Pedro Juan Caballero (Paraguay)–Ponta Porã (Brazil). Direct buses run between Asunción and Brazilian cities such as Florianópolis (R$340, 22 hours), Curitiba (R$270, 14 hours), São Paulo (R$250, 20 hours) and Foz do Iguaçu (R$80, 6½ hours).

PERU

There is at least one daily bus connecting Rio Branco (Brazil) to Puerto Maldonado (Peru) via the border at Assis (Brazil)–Iñapari (Peru) on the US$2.75-billion Interoceanic Hwy. You can also reach Assis on daily buses from Epitáciolândia (R$20, two hours) and cross the Rio Acre to Iñapari.

URUGUAY

The crossing most used by travelers is Chuy (Uruguay)–Chuí (Brazil). This is actually one town, with the international border running down the middle of its main street. Other crossings are Río Branco (Uruguay)–Jaguarão (Brazil), Isidoro Noblia (Uruguay)–Aceguá (Brazil), Rivera (Uruguay)–Santana do Livramento (Brazil), Artigas (Uruguay)–Quaraí (Brazil) and Bella Unión (Uruguay)–Barra do Quaraí (Brazil). Buses run between Montevideo and Brazilian cities such as Porto Alegre (R$267, 12 hours), Florianópolis (R$290, 18 hours) and São Paulo (R$490, 32 hours).

VENEZUELA

From Manaus, five daily buses run to Boa Vista (R$170, 12 hours), from where you can connect to a 7am bus to Pacaraíma (R$28, 3½ hours) on the Venezuelan border.

Bus

International buses travel between Brazil and Argentina, Paraguay and Uruguay, along decent roads. Prices of bus tickets between countries are substantially more than you'd pay if you took a bus to the border, crossed on foot and caught another on the other side, but you'll lose a lot of time that way. If arriving by bus, make sure your papers are in order.

Car & Motorcycle

If you plan to take a vehicle into Brazil, be informed about essential documents, road rules, and info on fuel and spare parts. At the border you will be asked to sign a bond called a *termo de responsabilidade,* which lists the owner's identification details and home address, your destination, and a description of the vehicle (make, model, year, serial number, color and tag number). You will also be asked to pay a bank guarantee (the amount to be determined by customs) and sign a statement agreeing that if you stay for more than 90 days, you will contact customs in the area where the entry was registered to apply for an extension for the permit. This must be presented to customs at the time of departure. If your vehicle overstays its permitted time in Brazil, it is liable to be seized and the bank guarantee forfeited. It's illegal to sell the vehicle in Brazil.

All vehicles in Brazil must carry the registration document and proof of insurance. To take a vehicle into or out of Brazil, you might be asked for a *carnet de passage en douane,* which is a kind of vehicle passport, or a *libreta de pasos por aduana,* which is a booklet of customs passes. Contact your local automobile association for details about all documentation.

River

Bolivia

From Trinidad in Bolivia you can reach Brazil by a boat trip of about five days down the Río Mamoré to Guayaramerín, opposite the Brazilian town of Guajará-Mirim.

Peru

Fast passenger boats make the 400km trip (around US$75, 10 hours) along the Amazon River between Iquitos (Peru) and Tabatinga (Brazil). From Tabatinga you can continue 3000km down the river to its mouth.

Sea

Aside from a few organized commercial cruises with stops in Brazil, there are no regular voyages connecting the country with other international destinations.

GETTING AROUND

Air

Because of the great distances in Brazil, the occasional flight can be a necessity, and may not cost much more than a long-haul bus journey. If you intend to take more than just a couple of flights, a Brazil Airpass will probably save you money. Book ahead if traveling during busy travel times: from Christmas to Carnaval, around Easter, and July and August. Always reconfirm your flights, as schedules frequently change.

Airlines in Brazil

Brazil has two major national carriers, Gol and LATAM (a merger between the Chilean LAN and Brazilian TAM airlines), and a handful of smaller regional airlines. Brazil's main carriers:

Avianca (AV; ☎0300-789-8160; www.avianca.com)

Azul (☎0800-887-1118; www.voeazul.com.br)

Gol (☎0300-115-2121; www.voegol.com.br)

LATAM (☎0300-570-5700; www.latam.com)

Air Passes

A Brazil Airpass is a good investment if you're planning on covering a lot of ground in 30 days or less. Gol offers an air pass involving four/five domestic flights anywhere on its extensive network with prices starting at US$505/638, plus taxes and fees; each additional flight costs around US$120. Azul's air pass gives you up to four flights within a 21-day period for US$500.

Either of these passes must be purchased before you get to Brazil, and you have to book your air-pass itinerary at the time you buy it – or possibly pay penalties for changing reservations. Many travel agents sell the air pass, as does the Brazilian

Domestic Air Routes

travel specialist Brol (www.brol.com).

If for any reason you do not fly on an air-pass flight you have reserved, you should reconfirm all your other flights. Travelers have sometimes found that all their air-pass reservations had been scrubbed from the computer after they missed, or were bumped from, one flight.

Departure Tax

Departure tax is always included in the price of your ticket.

Bicycle

You don't see many long-distance cyclists in Brazil. Among the hazards are crazy drivers, roads without shoulder room, long distances and the threat of theft.

If you're determined to tackle Brazil by bike, go over your bike with a fine-tooth comb before leaving home and fill your repair kit with every imaginable spare part. There are several decent bike shops in Rio for buying equipment and gear as well as renting bikes (which average R$60 per day).

Boat

The Amazon region is one of the last great bastions of passenger river travel in the world. Rivers still perform the function of highways throughout much of Amazonia, with vessels of many shapes and sizes putt-putting up and down every river and creek that has anyone living near it.

Bus

Bus services in Brazil are generally excellent. Departure times are usually strictly adhered to, and most of the buses are clean, comfortable and well-serviced Mercedes, Volvo and Scania vehicles.

All major cities are linked by frequent buses – one leaves every 15 minutes from Rio to São Paulo during peak hours – and there is a surprising number of long-distance buses. Every big city, and most small ones, has at least one main long-distance bus station, known as a *rodoviária* (ho-do-vi-*ah*-ree-ya).

Brazil has numerous bus companies and the larger cities have several dozen rival agencies. ClickBus (www.clickbus.com.br) is a good app for consulting departures times, fares (which can be expensive) and purchases. Another good resource for searching national bus routes is Busca Ônibus (www.buscaonibus.com.br).

Classes

There are three main classes of long-distance bus. The ordinary *convencional* or *comum* is indeed the most common. It's fairly comfortable and usually has a toilet on board. An *executivo* or *semi-leito* is more comfortable (with reclining seats), costs about 25% more and stops less often. A *leito* (overnight sleeper) can cost twice as much as a *comum* and has fully reclining seats with blankets and pillows, air-con and sometimes an attendant serving sandwiches, coffee, soda and *água mineral* (mineral water).

With or without toilets, buses generally make pit stops for food and bathroom breaks every three or four hours.

Air-con on buses is sometimes strong; carry a light sweater or jacket to keep warm.

Buying Tickets

Usually you can go down to the bus station and buy a ticket for the next departing bus. In general, though, it's a good idea to buy the day before departure. On weekends, holidays and from December to February, advance purchase is always a good idea. If you have a PayPal account, you can buy tickets online at ClickBus (www.clickbus.com.br)

Car & Motorcycle

Especially in Rio, the anarchic side of the Brazilian personality emerges from behind the driver's wheel as lane dividers, one-way streets, sidewalks and pedestrians are disregarded.

Driver's License

Your home-country driver's license is valid in Brazil, but because local authorities probably won't be familiar with it, it's a good idea to carry an International Driving Permit (IDP) as well. This gives police less scope for claiming that you are not driving with a legal license. IDPs are issued by your national motoring association and usually cost the equivalent of about US$15. It is illegal for foreigners to drive motorbikes in Brazil unless they have a Brazilian license.

Fuel & Spare Parts

Ordinary gasoline (called *combustível* or *gasolina*) costs around R$4.60 per liter. Travelers taking their own vehicles need to check in advance what spare parts and gasoline are likely to be available.

Hire

A small four-door car with insurance and unlimited kilometers costs around R$100 a day (R$130 with air-con). You can sometimes get discounts for longer rentals.

To rent a car you must be 25 years old (21 with some rental firms, including Avis), have a credit card in your name and a valid driver's license from your home country (not just an IDP).

Minimum insurance coverage is always tacked onto the cost of renting, though you can get extra protection (a wise idea) for another R$20 to R$40 per day.

In Brazil, 4WD vehicles are hard to come by and can be quite expensive (over R$200 per day). Motorbike rental is even harder to find. Riders planning a long trip might have better luck purchasing a bike in Brazil and reselling it at the end of the trip.

Road Rules & Hazards

Brazil is a dangerous place to drive, with over 43,000 people killed in automobile accidents each year. Some roads are especially hazardous, such as the busy highways between Rio and São Paulo. The cult of speed is insatiable.

Owing to the danger of robbery, at night many motorists don't stop at red lights but merely slow down. This is particularly common in São Paulo. In big cities, keep your windows closed and doors locked when stationary.

Driving at night is particularly hazardous; other drivers are more likely to be drunk and, at least in the Northeast and the interior, the roads are often poor and unreliable. Poorly banked turns are the norm. To save a bit of fuel, some motorists drive at night with their headlights turned to low beam or turned off completely.

Brazilian speed bumps are quite prevalent. Always slow down as you enter a town.

Further headaches for drivers in Brazil are posed by poor signposting, impossible one-way systems, tropical rainstorms, drivers overtaking on blind corners, flat tires – common, but there are *borracheiros* (tire repairers) stationed at frequent intervals along the roads – and, of course, the police pulling you over for bogus moving violations.

For security, choose hotels with off-street parking; most midrange and top-end places offer this option.

Hitchhiking

Hitchhiking is never entirely safe in any country, and is not recommended. Travelers who decide to hitchhike should understand that they are taking a small but potentially serious risk. People who do choose to hitchhike will be safer if they travel in pairs and let someone know where they are planning to go.

Hitchhiking in Brazil, with the possible exception of the Pantanal and several other areas where it's commonplace among locals, is difficult. The Portuguese word for 'lift' is *carona*, so ask '*Pode dar carona?*' (Can you give us a lift?). The best way to hitchhike – practically the only way if you want rides – is to ask drivers when they're not in their vehicles; for example, by waiting at a gas station or truck stop. It's polite to offer to pay for your share of the gas in return for your lift.

Local Transportation

Bus

Local bus services tend to be decent. Since most Brazilians take the bus to work, municipal buses are usually frequent and their network of routes comprehensive. One-way fares range from R$3 to R$4.50.

In most city buses, you get on at the front and exit from the back, though occasionally the reverse is true. Usually there's a money collector sitting at a turnstile just inside the entrance.

Crime can be a problem: don't take valuables onto the buses, and think twice about taking informal minibuses in Rio and other urban areas, which have seen a recent increase in attacks.

Metro

Both Rio and São Paulo have excellent metro systems, with Rio's system expanded for the 2016 Olympics. These metros are a safe, cheap and efficient way of exploring the cities. One-way fares are R$4.30 in Rio and R$4 in São Paulo.

Taxi & Ride-Sharing Apps

Taxi rides are reasonably priced, and a taxi is the best option for getting around cities at night. Taxis in cities usually have meters that start around R$5.50 and rise by something like R$2.50 per kilometer (more at night and on weekends).

In small towns, taxis often don't have meters, and you'll have to arrange a price – beforehand.

If possible, orient yourself before taking a taxi, and keep a map handy in case you find yourself being taken on a wild detour.

The preferred app for local taxi drivers is 99Taxis (www.99app.com), and is more convenient and safer than calling for a taxi or hailing one in the street. Ride-share services like Uber (www.uber.com) and Cabify are widely available.

Train

Brazil's passenger-train services have been scaled down to almost nothing, though there are a few journeys well worth taking. One outstanding trip goes from Curitiba to Morretes through the coastal mountain range, with memorable views. The Belo Horizonte–Vitória run, via Santa Bárbara and Sabará, is also scenic. There's also one remaining line operating in the Northeast, which runs from São Luís south through the interior of Maranhão to the southern reaches of Pará state, getting you close to Parque Nacional Chapada das Mesas.

Steam trains are affectionately known as Marias Fumaça (Smoking Marys), and several still run as tourist attractions. There's a 13km ride from São João del Rei to Tiradentes in Minas Gerais. Another pleasant short trip, this time by electric train, is the 22km Ouro Preto–Mariana run.

Language

Portuguese is spoken by around 190 million people worldwide, 90% of whom live in Brazil. Brazilian Portuguese today differs from European Portuguese in approximately the same way that British English differs from American English. European and Brazilian Portuguese show some differences in spelling, pronunciation and, to some extent, vocabulary. For example, in Portugal, the word for 'train' is *comboio* and in Brazil you'd say *trem*.

Most sounds in Portuguese are also found in English. The exceptions are the nasal vowels (represented in our colored pronunciation guides by ng after the vowel), which are pronounced as if you're trying to make the sound through your nose; and the strongly rolled *r* (represented by rr in our pronunciation guides). Also note that the zh sounds like the 's' in 'pleasure'. The stressed syllables (generally the second-last syllable of a word) are indicated with italics. If you keep these few points in mind and read our pronunciation guides as if they were English, you'll have no problems being understood.

BASICS

Hello.	*Olá.*	o·*laa*
Goodbye.	*Tchau.*	tee·*show*
How are you?	*Como vai?*	*ko*·mo vai
Fine, and you?	*Bem, e você?*	beng e vo·*se*
Excuse me.	*Com licença.*	kong lee·*seng*·saa
Sorry.	*Desculpa.*	des·*kool*·paa
Please.	*Por favor.*	por faa·*vorr*
Thank you.	*Obrigado.* *Obrigada.*	o·bree·*gaa*·do (m) o·bree·*gaa*·daa (f)
You're welcome.	*De nada.*	de *naa*·daa
Yes.	*Sim.*	seeng
No.	*Não.*	nowng

What's your name?
Qual é o seu nome? kwow e o *se*·oo *no*·me

My name is ...
Meu nome é ... *me*·oo *no*·me e ...

Do you speak English?
Você fala inglês? vo·*se* *faa*·laa eeng·*gles*

I don't understand.
Não entendo. nowng eng·*teng*·do

WANT MORE?

For in-depth language information and handy phrases, check out Lonely Planet's *Brazilian Portuguese Phrasebook*. You'll find it at **shop.lonelyplanet.com**, or you can buy Lonely Planet's iPhone phrasebooks at the Apple App Store.

ACCOMMODATIONS

Do you have a ... room?	*Tem um quarto de ...?*	teng oom *kwaarr*·to de ...
double	*casal*	kaa·*zow*
single	*solteiro*	sol·*tay*·ro
twin	*duplo*	*doo*·plo

How much is it per night/person?
Quanto custa por noite/pessoa? *kwang*·to *koos*·taa porr *noy*·te/pe·*so*·aa

Can I see it?
Posso ver? *po*·so verr

campsite	*local para acampamento*	lo·*kow* *paa*·raa aa·kang·paa·*meng*·to
guesthouse	*hospedaria*	os·pe·daa·*ree*·a
hotel	*hotel*	o·*tel*
youth hostel	*albergue da juventude*	ow·*berr*·ge daa zhoo·veng·*too*·de

DIRECTIONS

Where is ...?
Onde fica ...? ong·de fee·kaa ...

What's the address?
Qual é o endereço? kwow e o eng·de·re·so

Could you please write it down?
Você poderia escrever num papel, por favor? vo·se po·de·ree·aa es·kre·verr noom paa·pel porr faa·vorr

Can you show me (on the map)?
Você poderia me mostrar (no mapa)? vo·se po·de·ree·aa me mos·traarr (no maa·paa)

at the corner	*na esquina*	na es·kee·naa
at the traffic lights	*no sinal de trânsito*	no see·now de trang·zee·to
behind ...	*atrás ...*	aa·traaz ...
in front of ...	*na frente de ...*	naa freng·te de ...
left	*esquerda*	es·kerr·daa
next to ...	*ao lado de ...*	ow laa·do de ...
opposite	*do lado oposto ...*	do laa·do o·pos·to ...
right	*direita*	dee·ray·taa
straight ahead	*em frente*	eng freng·te

EATING & DRINKING

What would you recommend?
O que você recomenda? oo ke vo·se he·ko·meng·daa

What's in that dish?
O que tem neste prato? o ke teng nes·te praa·to

I don't eat ...
Eu não como ... e·oo nowng ko·mo ...

Cheers!
Saúde! sa·oo·de

That was delicious.
Estava delicioso. es·taa·vaa de·lee·see·o·zo

Bring the bill/check, please.
Por favor traga a conta. porr faa·vorr traa·gaa aa kong·taa

I'd like to reserve a table for ...	*Eu gostaria de reservar uma mesa para ...*	e·oo gos·taa·ree·aa de he·zer·vaarr oo·maa me·zaa paa·raa ...
(eight) o'clock	*(às oito) horas*	(aas oy·to) aw·raas
(two) people	*(duas) pessoas*	(doo·aas) pe·so·aas

Key Words

bottle	*garrafa*	gaa·haa·faa
breakfast	*café da manha*	ka·fe daa ma·nyang
cold	*frio*	free·o
cup	*xícara*	shee·kaa·raa
dessert	*sobremesa*	so·bre·me·zaa
dinner	*jantar*	zhang·taarr
drink	*bebida*	be·bee·daa
entree	*entrada*	eng·traa·daa
fork	*garfo*	gaarr·fo
glass	*copo*	ko·po
hot (warm)	*quente*	keng·te
knife	*faca*	faa·kaa
lunch	*almoço*	ow·mo·so
market	*mercado*	merr·kaa·do
menu	*cardápio*	kaar·da·pyo
plate	*prato*	praa·to
restaurant	*restaurante*	hes·tow·rang·te
spicy	*apimentado*	aa·pee·meng·taa·do
spoon	*colher*	ko·lyerr

KEY PATTERNS

To get by in Portuguese, mix and match these simple patterns with words of your choice:

When's (the next flight)?
Quando é (o próximo vôo)? kwaang·do e (o pro·see·mo vo·o)

Where's the (tourist office)?
Onde fica (a secretaria de turismo)? ong·de fee·kaa (aa se·kre·taa·ree·aa de too·rees·mo)

I'm looking for (a hotel).
Estou procurando (um hotel). es·to pro·koorr·ang·do (oom o·tel)

Do you have (a map)?
Você tem (um mapa)? vo·se teng (oom maa·paa)

Is there (a toilet)?
Tem (banheiro)? teng (ba·nyay·ro)

I'd like (a coffee).
Eu gostaria de (um café). e·oo gos·taa·ree·aa de (oom kaa·fe)

I'd like to (hire a car).
Eu gostaria de (alugar um carro). e·oo gos·taa·ree·aa de (aa·loo·gaarr oom kaa·ho)

Can I (enter)?
Posso (entrar)? po·so (eng·traarr)

Could you please (help me)?
Você poderia me (ajudar), por favor? vo·se po·de·ree·aa me (aa·zhoo·daarr) por faa·vorr

Do I have to (get a visa)?
Necessito (obter visto)? ne·se·see·to (o·bee·terr vees·to)

Useful Telephone Phrases

I'd like to make an international call to...
Quero fazer uma ligação internacional para... ke·ro faa·*zerr* oo·maa lee·gaa·*sowng* eeng·terr·naa·syo·*now* paa·raa ...

I'd like to reverse the charges.
Quero fazê-la a cobrar. ke·ro faa·*ze*·la aa ko·*braarr*

I'm calling from a public/private phone in ...
Estou falando dum telefone público/particular no ... es·*to* faa·*laan*·do doom te·le·*fo*·ne *poo*·blee·ko/paarr·tee·koo·*laarr* no ...

The area code/number is...
O código/número é... o *ko*·dee·go/*noo*·me·ro e ...

Meat & Fish

beef	*carne de vaca*	*kaar*·ne de *vaa*·kaa
chicken	*frango*	*frang*·go
crab	*siri*	see·*ree*
fish	*peixe*	*pay*·she
lamb	*carneiro*	karr·*nay*·ro
meat	*carne*	*kaar*·ne
oyster	*ostra*	*os*·traa
pork	*porco*	*porr*·ko
seafood	*frutos do mar*	*froo*·tos do maarr
shrimp	*camarão*	ka·ma·*rowng*
tuna	*atum*	aa·*toong*
veal	*bezerro*	be·*ze*·ho

Fruit & Vegetables

apple	*maçã*	maa·*sang*
apricot	*damasco*	daa·*maas*·ko
avocado	*abacate*	aa·baa·*kaa*·te
cabbage	*repolho*	he·*po*·lyo
capsicum	*pimentão*	pee·meng·*towng*
carrot	*cenoura*	se·*no*·raa
cherry	*cereja*	se·*re*·zhaa
corn	*milho*	*mee*·lyo
cucumber	*pepino*	pe·*pee*·no
grapes	*uvas*	*oo*·vaas
lemon	*limão*	lee·*mowng*
lettuce	*alface*	ow·*faa*·se
mushroom	*cogumelo*	ko·goo·*me*·lo
onion	*cebola*	se·*bo*·laa
orange	*laranja*	laa·*rang*·zhaa
peach	*pêssego*	*pe*·se·go
pineapple	*abacaxí*	aa·baa·kaa·*shee*
potato	*batata*	baa·*taa*·taa
spinach	*espinafre*	es·pee·*naa*·fre
strawberry	*morango*	mo·*rang*·go
tomato	*tomate*	to·*maa*·te
watermelon	*melancia*	me·lang·*see*·aa

Other

bread	*pão*	powng
cake	*bolo*	*bo*·lo
cheese	*queijo*	*kay*·zho
chilli	*pimenta*	pee·*meng*·taa
eggs	*ovos*	*o*·vos
honey	*mel*	mel
ice cream	*sorvete*	sorr·*ve*·te
jam	*geléia*	zhe·*le*·yaa
lentil	*lentilha*	leng·*tee*·lyaa
olive oil	*azeite*	a·*zay*·te
pepper	*pimenta*	pee·*meng*·taa

Drinks

rice	*arroz*	a·*hoz*
salt	*sal*	sow
sauce	*molho*	*mo*·lyo
sugar	*açúcar*	aa·*soo*·kaarr
beer	*cerveja*	serr·*ve*·zhaa

CARIOCA SLANG

Cariocas (inhabitants of Rio de Janeiro) pepper their language with lots of interesting oaths and expressions.

Oi!	Hello!
Tudo bem?	Everything OK?
Tudo bom.	Everything's OK.
Chocante!	That's great!/Cool!
Merda!	That's bad!/Shit!
Ta ótimo!/Ta legal!	Great!/Cool!/OK!
Meu deus!	My God!
Ta louco!	It's/You're crazy!
Nossa!	Gosh! (lit: Our Lady)
Opa!	Whoops!
Oba!	Wow!
Falou!	You said it!
Eu estou chateado com ...	I'm mad at ...
Tem jeito?	Is there a way?
Sempre tem jeito.	There's always a way.

Signs

Banheiro	Toilet
Entrada	Entrance
Não Tem Vaga	No Vacancy
Pronto Socorro	Emergency Department
Saída	Exit
Tem Vaga	Vacancy

coffee	*café*	kaa·*fe*
fruit juice	*suco de frutas*	*soo*·ko de *froo*·taas
milk	*leite*	*lay*·te
red wine	*vinho tinto*	*vee*·nyo *teeng*·to
soft drink	*refrigerante*	he·free·zhe·*rang*·te
tea	*chá*	shaa
(mineral) water	*água (mineral)*	*aa*·gwaa (mee·ne·*row*)
white wine	*vinho branco*	*vee*·nyo *brang*·ko

EMERGENCIES

Help!	*Socorro!*	so·*ko*·ho
Leave me alone!	*Me deixe em paz!*	me *day*·she eng paas
Call ...!	*Chame ...!*	*sha*·me ...
a doctor	*um médico*	oom *me*·dee·ko
the police	*a polícia*	aa po·*lee*·syaa

It's an emergency.
É uma emergência. — e oo·maa e·merr·*zheng*·see·aa

I'm lost.
Estou perdido. — es·*to* perr·*dee*·do (m)
Estou perdida. — es·*to* perr·*dee*·daa (f)

I'm ill.
Estou doente. — es·*to* do·*eng*·te

It hurts here.
Aqui dói. — a·*kee* doy

I'm allergic to (antibiotics).
Tenho alergia à (antibióticos). — *te*·nyo aa·lerr·*zhee*·aa aa (ang·tee·bee·o·tee·kos)

Where are the toilets?
Onde tem um banheiro? — *on*·de teng oom ba·*nyay*·ro

SHOPPING & SERVICES

I'd like to buy ...
Gostaria de comprar ... — gos·taa·*ree*·aa de kong·*praarr* ...

I'm just looking.
Estou só olhando. — es·*to* so o·*lyang*·do

Can I look at it?
Posso ver? — *po*·so verr

How much is it?
Quanto custa? — *kwang*·to *koos*·taa

It's too expensive.
Está muito caro. — es·*taa* *mweeng*·to *kaa*·ro

Can you lower the price?
Pode baixar o preço? — *po*·de bai·*shaarr* o *pre*·so

There's a mistake in the bill.
Houve um erro na conta. — *o*·ve oom *e*·ho naa *kong*·taa

ATM	*caixa automático*	*kai*·shaa ow·too·*maa*·tee·ko
credit card	*cartão de crédito*	kaarr·*towng* de *kre*·dee·to
post office	*correio*	ko·*hay*·o
tourist office	*escritório de turismo*	es·kree·*to*·ryo de too·*rees*·mo

TIME & DATES

What time is it?
Que horas são? — kee *aw*·raas sowng

It's (10) o'clock.
São (dez) horas. — sowng (des) *aw*·raas

Half past (10).
(Dez) e meia. — (des) e *may*·aa

morning	*manhã*	ma·*nyang*
afternoon	*tarde*	*taar*·de
evening	*noite*	*noy*·te

yesterday	*ontem*	*ong*·teng
today	*hoje*	*o*·zhe
tomorrow	*amanhã*	aa·ma·*nyang*

Monday	*segunda-feira*	se·*goong*·daa·*fay*·ra
Tuesday	*terça-feira*	*terr*·saa·*fay*·raa
Wednesday	*quarta-feira*	*kwaarr*·taa·*fay*·raa
Thursday	*quinta-feira*	*keeng*·taa·*fay*·raa
Friday	*sexta-feira*	*ses*·taa·*fay*·raa
Saturday	*sábado*	*saa*·baa·do
Sunday	*domingo*	do·*meeng*·go

Question Words

How?	*Como é que?*	*ko*·mo e ke
What?	*Que?*	ke
When?	*Quando?*	*kwang*·do
Where?	*Onde?*	*ong*·de
Which?	*Qual?/Quais?* (sg/pl)	kwow/kais
Who?	*Quem?*	keng
Why?	*Por que?*	porr ke

January	*janeiro*	zha·*nay*·ro
February	*fevereiro*	fe·ve·*ray*·ro
March	*março*	*marr*·so
April	*abril*	aa·*bree*·oo
May	*maio*	*maa*·yo
June	*junho*	*zhoo*·nyo
July	*julho*	*zhoo*·lyo
August	*agosto*	aa·*gos*·to
September	*setembro*	se·*teng*·bro
October	*outubro*	o·*too*·bro
November	*novembro*	no·*veng*·bro
December	*dezembro*	de·*zeng*·bro

TRANSPORT

Public Transport

boat	*barco*	*baarr*·ko
bus	*ônibus*	*o*·nee·boos
plane	*avião*	aa·vee·*owng*
train	*trem*	treng

When's the ... (bus)?	*Quando sai o ... (ônibus)?*	*kwang*·do sai o ... (*o*·nee·boos)
first	*primeiro*	pree·*may*·ro
last	*último*	*ool*·tee·mo
next	*próximo*	*pro*·see·mo

a ... ticket	*uma passagem de ...*	oo·maa paa·*sa*·zheng de ...
1st-class	*primeira classe*	pree·*may*·raa *klaa*·se
2nd-class	*segunda classe*	se·*goom*·daa *klaa*·se
one-way	*ida*	*ee*·daa
return	*ida e volta*	*ee*·daa e *vol*·taa

What time does it leave/arrive?
A que horas sai/chega? aa ke *aw*·raas sai/*she*·gaa

Does it stop at ...?
Ele para em ...? *e*·le *paa*·raa eng ...

Please stop here.
Por favor pare aqui. poor faa·*vorr paa*·re aa·*kee*

bus stop	*ponto de ônibus*	*pong*·to de *o*·nee·boos
ticket office	*bilheteria*	bee·lye·te·*ree*·aa
timetable	*horário*	o·*raa*·ryo
train station	*estação de trem*	es·*taa*·sowng de treng

Numbers

1	*um*	oom
2	*dois*	doys
3	*três*	tres
4	*quatro*	*kwaa*·tro
5	*cinco*	*seeng*·ko
6	*seis*	says
7	*sete*	*se*·te
8	*oito*	*oy*·to
9	*nove*	*naw*·ve
10	*dez*	dez
20	*vinte*	*veeng*·te
30	*trinta*	*treeng*·taa
40	*quarenta*	kwaa·*reng*·taa
50	*cinquenta*	seen·*kweng*·taa
60	*sessenta*	se·*seng*·taa
70	*setenta*	se·*teng*·taa
80	*oitenta*	oy·*teng*·taa
90	*noventa*	no·*veng*·taa
100	*cem*	seng
1000	*mil*	*mee*·oo

Driving & Cycling

I'd like to hire a ...	*Gostaria de alugar ...*	gos·taa·*ree*·aa de aa·loo·*gaarr* ...
bicycle	*uma bicicleta*	*oo*·maa bee·see·*kle*·taa
car	*um carro*	oom *kaa*·ho
motorcycle	*uma motocicleta*	*oo*·maa mo·to·see·*kle*·ta

bicycle pump	*bomba de bicicleta*	*bong*·baa de bee·see·*kle*·taa
helmet	*capacete*	kaa·paa·*se*·te
mechanic	*mecânico*	me·*ka*·nee·ko
petrol/gas	*gasolina*	gaa·zo·*lee*·naa
service station	*posto de gasolina*	*pos*·to de gaa·zo·*lee*·naa

Is this the road to ...?
Esta é a estrada para ...? es·taa e aa es·*traa*·daa *paa*·raa ...

(How long) Can I park here?
(Quanto tempo) Posso estacionar aqui? (*kwang*·to *teng*·po) *po*·so es·taa·syo·*naarr* aa·*kee*

I have a flat tyre.
Meu pneu furou. *me*·oo pee·*ne*·oo foo·*ro*

I've run out of petrol.
Estou sem gasolina. es·*to* seng ga·zoo·*lee*·naa

GLOSSARY

afoxé – music of Bahia, which has strong African rhythms and close ties to Candomblé

albergue – lodging house or hostel

albergue da juventude – youth hostel

aldeia – originally a village built by Jesuits to convert *índios* to Christianity; now the term for any small, usually indigenous, village

apartamento – hotel room with a private bathroom

arara – macaw

artesanato – handcrafted workmanship

azulejos – Portuguese ceramic tiles with a distinctive blue glaze, often seen in churches

babaçu – versatile palm tree that is the basis of the rural economy in Maranhão

bairro – district

bandeirantes – bands of 17th- and 18th-century roaming adventurers who explored the vast Brazilian interior while searching for gold and *índios* to enslave; typically born of an *índio* mother and a Portuguese father

barraca – any stall or hut, including food and drink stands common at beaches, parks etc

beija-flor – literally 'flower kisser'; hummingbird; also the name of Rio's most famous samba school

berimbau – musical instrument that accompanies capoeira

bilheteria – ticket office

bloco – large group, usually numbering in the hundreds, of singing or drumming Carnaval revelers in costume, organized around a neighborhood or theme

boate – nightclub with a dance floor, sometimes featuring strippers; also boîte

bonde – cable car, tram or trolley

bossa nova – music that mixes North American jazz with Brazilian influences

boteco – small, open-air bar

boto – freshwater dolphin of the Amazon

Bumba Meu Boi – the most important festival in Maranhão, a rich folkloric event that revolves around a Carnavalesque dance/procession

caatinga – scrub vegetation of the *sertão*

Caboclo – literally 'copper-colored'; person of mixed Caucasian and *índio* ancestry

cachoeira – waterfall

Candomblé – Afro-Brazilian religion of Bahia

capivara – capybara; the world's largest rodent, which looks like a large guinea pig and lives in the Pantanal

capixaba – resident of Espírito Santo state

capoeira – martial art/dance developed by the slaves of Bahia

carioca – resident of Rio de Janeiro

casa grande – big house or plantation owner's mansion

casal – married couple; double bed

chapada – tableland or plateau that divides a river basin

churrascaria – restaurant featuring barbecued meat

cidades históricas – historic colonial towns

Círio de Nazaré – Brazil's largest religious festival, which takes place in Belém

coronel – literally 'colonel'; rural landowner who typically controlled the local political, judicial and police systems; any powerful person

correio – post office

delegacia de polícia – police station

Embratur – Brazilian Tourist Board

engenho – sugar mill or sugar plantation

escolas de samba – large samba clubs that compete in the annual Carnaval parade

estalagem – inn

estrangeiro – foreigner

fantasia – Carnavalesque costume

favela – slum, shantytown

favelado – resident of a favela

fazenda – ranch or farm, usually a large landholding; also cloth, fabric

fazendeiro – estate owner

feira – produce market

ferroviária – train station

festa – party

Filhos de Gandhi – Bahia's most famous Carnaval bloco

fio dental – literally 'dental floss'; Brazil's famous skimpy bikini

Flamengo – Rio's most popular football team; also one of Rio's most populated areas

Fluminense – native of Rio state; also the football team that is Flamengo's main rival

forró – popular music of the Northeast, recently enjoying a wave of nationwide popularity

frevo – fast-paced, popular music from Pernambuco

frigobar – minibar

Funai – Fundação Nacional do Indio; government *índio* agency

Fusca – Volkswagen Beetle, Brazil's most popular car

futebol – football

futevôlei – volleyball played without hands

gafieira – dance hall

garimpeiro – prospector or miner; originally an illegal diamond prospector

garimpo – mining camp

gaúcho – cowboy of southern Brazil

gringo – foreigner or person with light hair and complexion; can even refer to light-skinned Brazilians

gruta – grotto or cavern

hidrovia – aquatic freeway

hidroviária – boat terminal

hospedagem – cheap boardinghouse used by locals

Iemanjá – Afro-Brazilian goddess of the sea
igapó – flooded Amazon forest
igarapé – creek or small river in Amazonia
igreja – church
ilha – island
índio – indigenous person; translates as 'Indian'

jacaré – caiman
jangada – beautiful sailboat of the Northeast
jangadeiros – crews who use *jangadas*
jeito/jeitinho – possibly the most Brazilian expression, both a feeling and a form of action; from *dar um jeito*, meaning 'to find a way to get something done,' no matter how seemingly impossible, even if the solution may not be completely orthodox or legal

leito – sleeping berth
literatura de cordel – literally 'string literature'; popular literature of the Northeast
litoral – coastal region

machista – male chauvinist
mãe de santo – female Afro-Brazilian spiritual leader
malandro do morro – vagabond; scoundrel from the hills; a popular figure in Rio's mythology
maloca – *índio* dwelling
Maracanã – soccer stadium in Rio
mercado – market
mestiço – a person of mixed *índio* and European parentage
mineiro – resident of Minas Gerais
moço/a – waiter or other service industry worker
morro – hill; a person or culture of the favelas
mulato/a – person of mixed black and white parentage

novela – soap opera; Brazil's most popular TV shows
NS – Nosso Senhor (Our Lord) or Nossa Senhora (Our Lady)
orixá – deity of the Afro-Brazilian religions

pagode – popular samba music
pai de santo – male spiritual leader in Afro-Brazilian religions
palácio – palace or large government building
palafita – stilt or a house built on stilts
pampas – grassy plains of the interior of southern Brazil
parque nacional – national park
pau brasil – now-scarce brazilwood tree; a red dye made from the tree that was the colony's first commodity
paulista – resident of São Paulo state
paulistano – resident of São Paulo city
PCB – Communist Party of Brazil
pensão – guesthouse
posta restante – poste restante
posto – post; lifeguard posts along Rio de Janeiro's beaches, used as names for different sections of beach
posto de gasolina – a gas (petrol) station
posto telefônico – telephone office
pousada – guesthouse
praça – plaza or town square
praia – beach
PT – Partido dos Trabalhadores (Worker's Party); Brazil's newest and most radical political party

quarto – hotel room without a bathroom
quente – hot
quilombo – community of runaway slaves
Quimbanda – black magic
rápido – fast
real – Brazil's unit of currency since 1994; plural reais
rio – river

rodoferroviária – bus and train station
rodoviária – bus station
s/n – abbreviation for *sem número* (without number), used in some street addresses
sambista – samba composer or dancer
sambódromo – street with tiers of seating built for samba parades
senzala – slave quarters
serra – mountain range
sertanejo – resident of the *sertão*
sertão – the drought-prone backlands of the Northeast

telefonista internacional – international telephone operator
Terra da Vera Cruz – Land of the True Cross; the original Portuguese name for Brazil
terreiro – Afro-Brazilian house of worship
travessa – lane
travesti – transvestite; a popular figure throughout Brazil, considered by some to be the national symbol
trem – train
trio elétrico – three-pronged electrical outlet; electrically amplified bands that play atop trucks
tropicália – important cultural movement centered in Bahia in the late 1960s
Tupi – indigenous people and language that predominated along the coast at the time of the European invasion

Umbanda – white magic, a mixture of Candomblé and spiritism

vaqueiro – cowboy of the Northeast
várzea – Amazonian floodplain

zona da mata – bushland just inside the litoral in the Northeastern states

Behind the Scenes

SEND US YOUR FEEDBACK

We love to hear from travelers – your comments keep us on our toes and help make our books better. Our well-traveled team reads every word on what you loved or loathed about this book. Although we cannot reply individually to your submissions, we always guarantee that your feedback goes straight to the appropriate authors, in time for the next edition. Each person who sends us information is thanked in the next edition – the most useful submissions are rewarded with a selection of digital PDF chapters.

Visit **lonelyplanet.com/contact** to submit your updates and suggestions or to ask for help. Our award-winning website also features inspirational travel stories, news and discussions.

Note: We may edit, reproduce and incorporate your comments in Lonely Planet products such as guidebooks, websites and digital products, so let us know if you don't want your comments reproduced or your name acknowledged. For a copy of our privacy policy visit lonelyplanet.com/privacy.

OUR READERS

Many thanks to the travelers who used the last edition and wrote to us with helpful hints, useful advice and interesting anecdotes: Aida Bour, Clare Marsh, Jayelle Conway, Kier Hanson Santos, Léa Bianchini, Sarah Wotton, Urban Neudauer.

WRITER THANKS

Regis St Louis

Countless *cariocas* and expats provided help and friendship along the way, and I'm deeply grateful to Cristiano Nogueira, Jackki Saysell, Eduardo Cruxen, Ian Papareskos, Alberto Armendáriz, Bindu Mathur, Tom Lemesurier, German and Daniel Olano, Michael Nagy, Marcelo Esteves, André Paranhos, Toninho, Kevin Raub, Samantha Aquim, Gilson Martins, Antônia Leite Barbosa, and Lenny Niemeyer. As always, heartfelt thanks to Cassandra, Magdalena, Genevieve, Rothko and Kazimir for their continued support.

Gregor Clark

Muito obrigado to all the Brazilians who generously shared their smiles, thumbs-up and local knowledge – from Richard, Yara and Marina in Rio state to Ângela, José, Maira, Alex and Bia in Minas, and others too numerous to name. Muriqui-style *abraços* to my daughter Chloe for helping me test-taste *moquecas*, research hiking trails from Ilha Grande to Pedra Azul, and cheer Brazil on to three World Cup victories, and to Gaen, who always makes coming home the best part of the trip.

Anthony Ham

Heartfelt thanks to the following: Chris Clark and his family, Valdemar, Henrique Dolabella, Antonio Gomes, Gil Serique, Luciana V. Cobra and Letícia Galdino for their hospitality, insights and/or passion for the Amazon. Thanks also to Martin Scherbichler, Barbara Lockner, Aline Tiagor and Gergely Mohacsi. Thanks to Destination Editor Bailey Freeman, for sending me to such a wonderful corner of the earth. And all my love to my family, who tolerate my absences and welcome me home with such warmth – Marina, Carlota, Valentina and Jan. *Os quiero*.

Andy Symington

Very many people helped me along the road in Brazil and were generous with their time, information and company. I'd like to especially thank Wesley Simón de Silva, Jean Flávio, Charles Munn, Lindsay Kennon, Javiera Vargas, Júlio Ferreira, Rosana Guerra, Ana Paula, Priscilla Eilert, David Barnes and James Symington for various helpful deeds, plus Bailey Freeman and the LP team. And to the guys at Posto Paulista in Corumbá who wanted their gas station mentioned in the book...now it is.

Robert Balkovich

Thank you as always to my family – my mother, father, and sister – and friends for putting up with me never being able to make plans too far in advance. A special thanks to my friend Rafa and his family and friends for introducing me to Brazil and helping me feel welcome in their home when I was so far away from mine.

Alex Egerton

Huge gratitude to purveyor of fine anecdotes Camil Gemael Neto without whom this research trip would not have been possible, and to Adriana for endless advice and assistance. A shoutout for Bailey and Mr Raub for always being on call, and also to Laryssa in Alcântara, Frank in São Luis and all the other Brazilians that went above and beyond with their assistance. Big props for Olga Mosquera for keeping things running at home, and Nicholas Kazu for the patience.

Anna Kaminski

Huge thanks to Bailey for entrusting me with half of this beguiling country, to my fellow scribe Brendan and to everyone who's helped me along the way. In particular: Jose and the Graffiti Tour folks in Medellin, Tony in Popayán, Soledad and the mountain biking folk of Salento, Kolibri Hostel in Pereira, Gloria in Guatape, Finca El Maco and Pacho in San Agustín, plus the driver who successfully navigated the Trampolin de la Muerte.

Kevin Raub

Thanks to Bailey Freeman, Regis St. Louis, Alex Edgerton and all my fellow partners in crime at LP. On the road, Adriana Schmidt, Teresa Rocha, Siddy Hall, Patricia Moll Novaes, Lucas Terribili, Flavia Baldi, Paulo Yoller, Lúcia Rodrigues, Renato Nascimento, Pedro Rodrigues, Vini Fiore, Tulio Fiore, Pedro Albuquerque and Malu Sabatino.

ACKNOWLEDGEMENTS

Climate map data adapted from Peel MC, Finlayson BL & McMahon TA (2007) 'Updated World Map of the Köppen-Geiger Climate Classification', Hydrology and Earth System Sciences, 11, 1633-44.

Cover photograph: The Amazon Rainforest, Brazil, Filipe Frazao/Shutterstock ©

THIS BOOK

This 11th edition of Lonely Planet's *Brazil* guidebook was researched and written by Robert Balkovich, Gregor Clark, Alex Egerton, Anthony Ham, Anna Kaminski, Kevin Raub, Regis St Louis and Andy Symington. Regis, Gregor, Anna and Kevin also worked on the previous edition along with Gary Chandler and Bridget Gleeson. This guidebook was produced by the following:

Destination Editor
Bailey Freeman

Senior Product Editor
Saralinda Turner

Regional Senior Cartographer
Corey Hutchison

Product Editor Jessica Ryan

Book Designer Gwen Cotter

Assisting Editors Sarah Bailey, Nigel Chin, Michelle Coxall, Trent Holden, Gabrielle Innes, Rosie Nicholson, Charlotte Orr, Susan Paterson, Monique Perrin, Christopher Pitts, Tamara Sheward, Sam Wheeler

Assisting Cartographer
Rachel Imeson

Cover Researcher
Wibowo Rusli

Thanks to Shona Gray, Andi Jones, Sandie Kestell, Amy Lynch, Genna Patterson, Claire Rourke, Angela Tinson, Juan Winata

Index

A

accessible travel 702
accommodations 702-3, *see also individual locations*
Acre 652-8
activities, *see individual activities, individual locations*
addresses 346
adventure 26
agriculture 364
air travel 711-12, 713-14, **714**
  scenic flights 565
Aiuruoca 203-4
Alagoas 58, 464-81, **465**
  accommodations 464
  climate 464
  food 464
  highlights 465, **465**
  history 465-6
  travel seasons 464
Alcântara 564, **25**
Aleijadinho 190, 192-3
Algodoal 585-6
Alta Floresta 373-5
Alter do Chão 18, 598-600, **18**
Alto Paraíso de Goiás 359-61
Amado, Jorge 444
Amazon Basin 569, 620
Amazon River 646
Amazon, the 58, 568-658, 629-36, **570-1**
  accommodations 568
  climate 568
  food 49, 568
  highlights 570-1, **570-1**
  history 569-72, 588
  travel seasons 568
  travel to/from 572
  travel within 572
Amazonas 606-45
amusement parks 311
anacondas 636
Anchieta Palace 214
Anhangabaú 227-8
animals, *see individual animals*, wildlife
anteaters 631, 693-4, **630-1**
ants 636
aquariums 70, 385, 466
Aracaju 466-70
architecture 16, 338-9, 345, 627, 687-9, **16**, **338-9**
area codes 21, 709
Armação 303-4
Arraial d'Ajuda 450-3
Arraial do Cabo 161, 162-3, **161**
art galleries, *see* museums & galleries
ATMs 708
Avenida Paulista 232-3, **244-5**
azulejos 562

B

Bahia 57, 400-63, **401**
  accommodations 400
  climate 400
  food 49, 400
  highlights 401, **401**
  history 401-2
  tours 434-5, 441, 451
  travel to/from 402
  travel seasons 400
Balneário Camboriú 310-12
bandeirantes 665-6
Barcelos 624-6
bargaining 708
Barra 407
Barra da Lagoa 300-1
Barra da Tijuca 77-8, 96
Barra do Superagüi 281
Barra Funda 232
Barra Grande 439-41
Basílica Santuario de Nazaré 576
bathrooms 709
beaches
  Alagoas 470, 471, 476, 477-8
  Amazon, the 585, 588, 589, 598, 607, 625, 646
  Atins 547
  Bahia 434, 437, 439, 441, 444, 447-9, 451, 456
  Búzios 168
  Ceará 537, 543-4
  Copacabana Beach 65, **112-13**
  Fernando de Noronha 503, 504-5, **505**
  Guarapari 218
  Icaraí de Amontada 547, **546**
  Ipanema Beach 61
  Jacumã 520
  Jericoacoara 547, **546**
  João Pessoa 514
  Natal 519-20
  Paraná 277, 279
  Paraty 139
  Pernambuco 495
  Praia da Pipa 526-30
  Praia de Caetanos **546**
  Rio de Janeiro 61, 67, 78, 113, **112-13**
  Rio de Janeiro State 139, 159, 160, 168
  Rio Grande do Norte 530-1
  Rio Grande do Sul 331
  Salvador 409
  Santa Catarina 19, 298, 299, 300, 301, 303, 312-13, **19**
  São Luís 560
  São Paulo State 263, 264
  Sergipe 467
beer 13, 51, 306, 310, **13**
Belém 572-814, 584, **574-5**, **581**, **34**
  accommodations 578-9
  drinking 580
  entertainment 580
  festivals 577-8
  food 579
  history 572-3
  nightlife 580
  shopping 580
  sights 573, 576-7
  tours 577
  tourist information 580-1
  travel to/from 581, 584
  travel within 584
Belo Horizonte 171-2, 174-82, **176**
  accomodations 175, 177
  drinking 179-80
  entertainment 180
  food 177-9
  nightlife 179-80
  shopping 180-1
  sights 174-5
  travel to/from 181-2
Bento Gonçalves 320-1, **322**
berimbau **423**
Beto Carrero World 311
bicycling 127, 714
  Amazon, the 589
  Paraná 279
  Rio de Janeiro 79, 127
  Vale Europeu 308-9, **308-9**
birds 282, 633, 697, **287**, **628**, **632-3**
bird-watching 163, 282, 372, 374, 395, 633
Biribiri 206
Blumenau 13, 306-10, **307**, **309**
Boa Vista 646-9, **648**
boat travel 713, 714
  Amazon, the 582-3, 649, **582-3**
  Fernando de Noronha 503-6
  Paraná 279, 290, 291
  Rio de Janeiro State 162

Map Pages **000**
Photo Pages **000**

Rio Grande do Sul 316, 332
Santa Catarina 305
Boi-Bumbá 28, 607
Boipeba 437-8
Bom Jardim 372-3
bonde 77, 113, **113**
Bonito 16, 393-8, **393**, **16**
books 660, 682, 685-6
Amazon, the 697
architecture 687
history 662-3, 665, 668
music 677, 678
politics 672, 673, 676
border crossings 712-13
Argentina 290
Bolivia 391, 658, 712
Colombia 641
Guyana 649
Paraguay 290, 396
Peru 641, 658
Uruguay 333
Venezuela 649
bossa nova 678
Botafogo 66-7, 90-1, 105-7, 116-17, 123-4, **86-7**
botos 635, **634**
Brasiléia 657-8
Brasília 16, 57, 334, 335-49, **340-1**, **335**, **344**, **16**
accommodations 334, 344-5
climate 334
drinking 347-8
enertainment 348
food 334, 345-7
highlights 335, **335**
history 336
information 348-9
nightlife 347-8
shopping 348
sights 336-39, 342-3
tourist information 348-9
tours 343
travel to/from 349
travel within 349
travel seasons 334
breweries 151, 309, 310, 620
buggy rides 433, 519, 524, 531, 550
Bumba Meu Boi 28, 561
bus travel 713, 714-15
business hours 708
butterflies 636, **636**
Búzios 164-9, **165**, **166**, **161**

C

caatinga 692, **692**
cable cars 77, 113, 406, **113**
Cabo Frio 163-4
Cachoeira 427-30, **428-9**
caciques 633, **632**
caiman 636
Camamu 439
Cambará do Sul 328-31
Campeche 303
Campo Grande 384-9, **386-7**
Canasvieiras 299
Candomblé 412-13, 665, **413**
cangaceiros 512
Canoa Quebrada 543-5, 547, 548, **547**
canoeing, *see* kayaking & canoeing
Canudos 671
canyons 328-9
capoeira 409, 422-3, 550, **423**
cathedrals, *see* churches & cathedrals
car travel 713, 715
driver's licenses 715
rental 715
road rules 715
Caraíva 455-6
Caravelas 456
Carmo 406
Carnatal 29, 520
Carnaval 17, 27, 37-42, **17**
Alagoas 471
Mato Grosso do Sul 391
Olinda 42, 499, **42**
Ouro Preto 187
Paraty 142
Recife 490
Rio de Janeiro 17, 37-41, **41**, **17**, **39**
Salvador 41-2, 411, **40**
cashew trees 522
Catedral Metropolitana 337, 338, **339**
Catete **86-7**
cats 694
caving 372, 395
Diamantina 206
Paraná 277
São Paulo State 266
Caxambu 202
Ceará 58, 532, 533-56, **534-5**, **536**, **546**
accommodations 532
climate 532
food 532
highlights 534-5, **534-5**
history 533
travel seasons 532
travel to/from 533
travel within 533
cell phones 20, 709
Centro (Rio de Janeiro) 69-73, 91, 107-8, 117, 124, **92-3**
Centro Cultural Banco do Brasil 174, 228, 343
Centro Cultural São Francisco 513-14
Chapada dos Guimarães 369-71
Chico-Rei 186, 664
children, travel with 53-4, 79
chimarrão 319
choro 677
churches & cathedrals
Catedral Metropolitana 337. 338, **339**
Igreja da Sé 497
Igreja de NS da Corrente 478
Igreja de São Francisco de Assis 186, 194
Igreja de São Gonçalo Garcia 478
Igreja e Convento São Francisco 405
Igreja Matriz de Santo Antônio 197
Igreja NS da Lapa do Riberão 303
Igreja NS do Bonfim 406
Igreja São Francisco da Penitência & Convento de Santo Antônio 72
Mosteiro São Bento 228
Cidade Baixa 406-7
Cidade de Goiás 352-4, **353**
Cinelândia 92-3, **92-3**
cinema 685-6, *see also* films
Círio de Nazaré 29, 577-8
climate 20, *see also individual regions*
coati 631
Congonhas 192-3
Congresso Nacional 337
Conselheiro Antônio 671
consulates 703-4
Convento da Penha 214
Convento de São Francisco e Igreja NS dos Anjos 478
convents 214
Copacabana 65-6, 89-90, 103-5, 113, 114-16, 123, **74-5**
Copacabana Beach 65, 113, **112-13**
corruption 660-1, 672-3
Corumbá 389-93, **390**
Costa de Dentro 304
Costa Verde 129-45
courses
capoeira 409-10
cooking 83, 144, 410
dance 83, 409-10
language 83, 410-11
music 83
credit cards 708
Cristo Luz Statue 311
Cristo Redentor 68-9, 113, **112**
Cuiabá 365-9, **366-7**
Curitiba 269-74, **270**
currency 20
customs regulations 703
cycling, *see* bicycling

D

dams 282
dance 119-20, 121
courses 83, 409-10
dangers *see* safety
Delta do Parnaíba 554-5
dengue 705
Diamantina 204-8, **205**
dictatorship 670
distilleries 140-1, 197-9
diving 43, 46, **504**
Alagoas 481
Bonito 395
Búzios 165
Fernando de Noronha 505-8, **504**
Rio de Janeiro State 133
dolphins 527, 635, 694-6, **634**
Dom João 667
Domingos Martins 219-20
drinking 48-52, *see also individual locations*, **52**
breweries 151, 309, 310, 620
distilleries 140-1, 197-9
wineries 331-322, **322-3**, **326**
drinks 50-2
beer 13, 51, 306, 310, 13
chimarrão 319
guarana 51-2
maté 51
driving, *see* car travel

Dunas de Genipabu 519
dune buggies & rides 433, 519, 524, 531, 550

E

eagles 633, **629**
economy 660-1, 672-3
ecotourism
  Chapada dos Guimarães 369-70
  Floresta Nacional do Tapajós 598-9
  Manaus 609-10, 620-1
  Paraty 142
  Parque Nacional da Chapada Dos Veadeiros 358-9
  Reserva Extrativista Baixo Rio Branco-Jauaperi 625
  Rio Branco 657
embassies 703-4
Embu das Artes 255
Encontro das Águas 607
environment 699-700
Escadaria Selarón 76, **112**
Espírito Santo 56, 172-3, 212-21, **172-3**
  accommodations 170
  climate 170
  food 170
  highlights 172-3
  history 171
  travel to/from 171
  travel within 171
  travel seasons 170
exchange rates 21

F

favelas 84, 669, 671
Fernando de Noronha 14, 502-13, **506-7**, **14**, **504-5**
  accommodations 509-10
  activities 503-9
  beaches 503
  drinking 511-13
  food 510-11
  nightlife 511-13
  planning 502-3
  sights 503
  tourist information 512
  transportation 512-13
festivals & events 26, *see also* Carnaval, *individual locations*
  Boi-Bumbá 28, 607, **28**
  Bumba Meu Boi 28, 561, **28**
  Festa do Divino Espírito Santo 27, 355
  Festival de Dança 305
  Natal Luz 326
  Rio International Film Festival 29
  São Paulo 236-7
  Semana Santa 27, 142, 189, 352
  SP-Arte – São Paulo International Art Festival 236
  Vesperata 206
films 660, 665, 667, 670, 673
fish 696
fishing 47, 625, 638
Flamengo 68-9, 91, 107, 117, 124, **86-7**
Floresta Nacional de Tefé 627
Floresta Nacional do Tapajós 596-8
Florianópolis 295-8, **296**
Floripa, *see* Florianópolis
food 24-5, 48-52, 593, 704, **49**, **51**, *see also individual locations*
  cooking courses 83, 144, 410
  glossary 50
  markets 97
  pizza 241, 240-1
  tacacá 593
football 81, 174, 180, 254, 541, 682-4, **80-1**
  stadiums 77, 525, 541, **80-81**
  museums 174, 232
Fordlândia 594
Fortaleza 533-43, **538-9**
  accommodations 538-40
  beaches 537
  climate 532
  drinking 541
  festivals 537-8
  food 540-1
  history 533, 537
  shopping 541
  sights 537
  tourist information 542
  tours 537
  travel seasons 532
  travel to/from 542-3
Forte dos Reis Magos 518-19
forts
  Forte de Coimbra 390-1
  Forte de Copacabana 65
  Forte Defensor Perpétuo 137-8
  Forte do Presépio 573
  Forte dos Reis Magos 518-19
  Forte dos Remédios 503
  Forte Duque de Caxias 66
  Forte São Mateus 163
fountains 199
Foz do Iguaçu 282-5, 288-9 **285**
fraud 707
frogs 636
Funai people 644

G

Galinhos 523
galleries *see* museums & galleries
Galos 523
gardens, *see* parks & gardens
Gávea 64-5, 89-96, 101-3, 114, 123, **66-7**
gay travelers *see* LGBT+ travelers
Glória **92-3**
Goiânia 350-2
Goiás 57, 334, 349-61, **335**
  accommodations 334
  climate 334
  food 334, 351, 360
  highlights 335, **335**
  travel seasons 334
Gold Rush, the 665-6
Gramado 326-8, **327**
Guajará-Mirim 651-2, **652**
guaraná 51-2
Guarapari 218-19
Guarda do Embaú 312

H

hang gliding 43, 47, 79, 83, **47**
Hawaizinho 442
health 704-6
  insurance 705
  vaccinations 705
Higienópolis 232
hiking 43, 44
  Amazon, the 624, 626
  Bahia 462-3
  Diamantina 206
  Espírito Santo 216
  Fernando de Noronha 509
  Goiás 359
  Lençóis 458-60
  Maranhão 564-5
  Mato Grosso 371
  Minas Gerais 187, 199, 209, 212
  Paraná 291
  Parque Nacional do Itatiaia 146, 148
  Rio de Janeiro 78-9
  Rio de Janeiro State 132-3, 146-8, 149
  Rio Grande do Sul 329-30
  Salvador 431
  São Paulo State 266
  Visconde de Mauá 149
hip-hop 680
history 26, 662-73, *see also individual regions*
hitchhiking 715-16
hoatzins 633, **632-3**
holidays 708
horse riding 47, 142, 220
hot-air ballooning 332
Humaitá 66-7, **86-7**

I

ibis 633, **632**
Icaraí de Amontada 547, 549-50, **546**
Icaraizinho, *see* Icaraí de Amontada
Igreja da Sé 497
Igreja de NS da Corrente 478
Igreja de São Francisco de Assis 186, 194
Igreja de São Gonçalo Garcia 478
Igreja e Convento São Francisco 405
Igreja Matriz de Santo Antônio 197
Igreja NS da Lapa do Riberão 303
Igreja NS do Bonfim 406
Igreja São Francisco da Penitência & Convento de Santo Antônio 72
Iguaçu Falls 11, 282-91, 286-7, **283**, **11**, **286-7**
Iguape 267
Ilha Anchieta 259-60
Ilha das Couves 259
Ilha de Cabo Frio 162
Ilha de Itamaracá 500
Ilha de Itaparica 407
Ilha de Marajó 587-90
Ilha de Paquetá 84
Ilha de Santa Catarina

Map Pages **000**
Photo Pages **000**

293-304, **294**
Ilha do Mel 277-82, **278**
Ilha dos Aquários 450
Ilha Grande 12, 129, 132-7, 161, **132**, **12**, **160**
Ilhabela 263-7
Ilhéus 443-7, **445**
immigration 711
independence 667
indigenous people 5, 643, 644, 674, 687
infectious diseases 705-6
Instituto de Arte Contemporânea Inhotim 175
Instituto Moreira Salles 64, 233,
insurance 705, 706
internet resources 21, 703, 706, 710
Ipanema 61, 64, 85, 88-9, 96-100, 102, 111, 121-3, **66-7**
Itacaré 441
Itaipu Dam 282
Itatiaia region 146
Itaúnas 215-18
itineraries 30-6, **30-6**

J

jacanas 633, **633**
Jacumã 520
jaguars 14, 382, 631, 638, **14**
Jardim Botânico 64-5, 89, 101-3, 114, 123, **71**
Jardins 232-3, 234, 236, **244-5**
Jericoacoara 550-6
  accommodations 551-2
  activities 550-1
  drinking 553-4
  entertainment 554
  food 552-3
  nightlife 553-4
  tourist information 554-5
  tours 551
  travel to/from 555-6
João Pessoa 513-17, **514**, **516**
jogging 78
Joinville 304-6
Juma Lake 618
jungle tours 14, 612-13, 615, 641, **15**
Jurerê 299

K

kayaking & canoeing 46-7, 132, 527
kitesurfing 46, 530, 544, 549, 551

L

Lago Negro 326
Lagoa 64-5, 89, 101-3, 114, 123, **71**
Lagoa da Conceição 301-2
Lagoa Rodrigo de Freitas 64
lakes
  Lago Maicá 591
  Lago Negro 326
  Lago Tarapoto 645
  Lago Verde 598
  Lagoa da Conceição 301-2
  Lagoa Rodrigo de Freitas 64
Lampião 512
language 20
  courses 83, 410-11
Lapa 76-7, 95-6, 109-10, 118-19, 124-5, **92-3**
Laranjeiras 467
Lavras Novas 192
Leblon 61, 64, 85, 88-9, 100-1, 102, 111, 114, 121-3, **66-7**
legal matters 707
Leme 65-6, 89-90, 103-5, 114-16, 123, **74-5**
Lençóis 457-62, **459**, **547**
  accommodations 460-1
  activities 458-60
  festivals 460
  food 461
  hiking 458-60
  history 457
  sights 457-8
  tourist information 461-2
  tours 460
  travel to/from 462
  travel within 462
lesbian travelers *see* LGBT+ travelers
Leticia (Colombia) 640-4, **642**
LGBT+ travelers 707
  Florianópolis 298
  Rio de Janeiro 115
  Salvador 419
  São Paulo 252
Liberdade 229
literature 685-6, *see also* books
Litoral Gaúcho 331-3
Luz 229

M

macaws 633
Maceió 470-7, **472-3**
  accommodations 471-3
  beaches 470
  drinking 475
  festivals 471
  food 473-5
  nightlife 475
  shopping 475
  sights 470
  tourist information 476
  travel to/from 476
  travel within 476
Malaria 705
Mamirauá 628
Mamirauá Reserve 637-8
manatees 635, 694-6, **634-5**
Manaus 606-18, **608**, **619**, **34**
  accommodations 611-14
  drinking 615
  entertainment 615
  festivals 610-11
  food 614
  nightlife 615
  shopping 616
  sights 606-8
  tourist information 616
  tours 608-10
  travel to/from 616-18
  travel within 618
Mangue Seco 432-4
maps 707
Maracanã Stadium 77, 81, **98-9**, **80-1**
Maragogi 480-1
Maranhão 58, 532, 556-67, **534-5**
  accommodations 532
  climate 532
  food 532
  highlights 534-5, **534-5**
  history 533
  travel to/from 533
  travel seasons 532
Marechal Deodoro 477
margays 631, **630**
Mariana 190-2
maté 51
Mato Grosso 57, 362, 364-75, **363**
  accommodations 362
  climate 362
  food 362
  highlights 363, **363**
  history 364
  tours 371-2
  travel seasons 362
Mato Grosso do Sul 57, 362, 384-99, **363**
  accommodations 362
  climate 362
  food 362
  highlights 363, **363**
  history 364
  tours 391, 393-5
  travel seasons 362
media 706
Mendes, Chico 656, 657
Mercado Municipal 226-7
milagres 480
military coups 670
Minas da Passagem 191
Minas Gerais 56, 170, 212, **172-3**
  accommodations 170
  climate 170
  food 170
  highlights 172-3, **172-3**
  history 171
  travel to/from 171, 197
  travel seasons 170
Mineirão & Museu Brasileiro do Futebol 174
mines 186
mission sites 324-5
mobile phones 20, 709
monasteries 497, 513-14
money 20, 661, 707-8
monkeys 213, 631, 637, **630**, **695**
Monte Alegre 601
Morretes 274-5
Morro de São Paulo 434-7
Mosteiro São Bento 228
motorcycle travel 713, 715
mountain climbing 626
multiculturalism 674-5
museums & galleries
  Art Izu 391
  Casa da Imagem 227
  Casa do Carnaval da Bahia 403
  Casa do Maranhão 558-9
  Casa do Nhôzinho 559
  Centro Cultural Usina Chaminé 606
  Embaixada dos Bonecos Gigantes 486
  Fundação Casa de Jorge Amado 405

museums & galleries *continued*
Instituto de Arte Contemporânea Inhotim 175
OM.art 64
Memorial Minas Gerais Vale 174
Mineirão & Museu Brasileiro do Futebol 174
Museo Pomerano 308
Museu Afro-Brasil 233
Museu Cais do Sertão 486
Museu da Borracha 653
Museu da República 69
Museu das Bandeiras 352
Museu das Cavalhadas 354-5
Museu das Culturas Dom Bosco 385
Museu de Arte de São Paulo 232
Museu de Arte do Rio 70
Museu de Arte do Rio Grande do Sul 316
Museu de Arte Moderna (Rio de Janeiro) 72-3
Museu de Arte Moderna (São Paulo City) 233
Museu de Biologia Professor Mello Leitão 217
Museu de História do Pantanal 389
Museu de Santarém 592
Museu do Divino 355
Museu do Estado do Pará 573
Museu do Mamulengo 497
Museu do Negro 559
Museu do Seringal Vila Paraíso 607
Museu Histórico de Santa Catarina 295
Museu Histórico Nacional 70
Museu Imperial 151
Museu Nacional 338-9, 34, **339**
Museu Náutico da Bahia 407
Museu Oceanográfico 333
Museu Oscar Niemeyer 271
Oficina Cerâmica Francisco Brennand 487
Palácio Antonio Lemos & MABE 573
Palácio Museu Olímpio Campos 466
Pina_Luz 229
Planetário 65
Museu Nacional 338-9, 342, **339**
music 490, 677-81
Música Popular Brasileira (MPB) 678-9

N

Natal 517-26, **519**, **521**
accommodations 522
beaches 519-20
drinking 524-5, 529
entertainment 525
festivals 520
food 522-4, 528-9
history 518
nightlife 529
shopping 525
sights 518-19
tourist information 525
tours 520
travel to/from 525-6, 530
travel within 525-6
national parks & reserves 699-700
Arquipélago Mariuá 625
Cristalino Lodge 374
Estação Biológica de Caratinga 213
Mamirauá Reserve 637-8
Mundo Amazónico 640-1
Pantanal Matogrossense National Park **7**
Parque Ecologico Januari 608
Parque Estadual da Guarita 332
Parque Municipal Lagoa da Peri 304
Parque Nacional da Chapada Diamantina 17, 462-3, **17**
Parque Nacional da Chapada Dos Guimarães 371-2
Parque Nacional da Chapada Dos Veadeiros 358-9, **44**
Parque Nacional da Serra da Bocaina 136
Parque Nacional da Serra da Capivara 555, **25**
Parque Nacional da Serra do Cipó 209-10
Parque Nacional da Serra Geral 329
Parque Nacional da Tijuca 64
Parque Nacional de Anavilhanas 624
Parque Nacional de Aparados da Serra 328-9
Parque Nacional de Brasília 343
Parque Natural do Caraça 210-11
Parque Nacional de Monte Pascoal 455
Parque Nacional de Sete Cidade 554
Parque Nacional de Ubajara 544
Parque Nacional do Iguaçu (Brazil) 286-7, 289-91, **286-7**
Parque Nacional do Jaú 624
Parque Nacional do Superagü 281
Parque Nacional dos Lençóis Maranhenses 18, 564, **18**
Parque Nacional Iguazú (Argentina) 291
Parque Nacional Marinho de Abrolhos 457
Parque Nacional Marinho de Fernando de Noronha 502
Parque Nacional Serra dos Órgãos 152, 156
Parque Unipraias 310-11
Reserva Extravista Baixo Rio Branco-Jauaperi 623-4
Reserva Natural Vale 217
Santuário de Vida Silvestre Vagafogo 355
Niemeyer, Oscar 232, 271, 338-9
Niterói 84
Nova Friburgo 157-9
Novo Airão 620-3

O

Oktoberfest 29, 306, 309, **28**
Olinda 18, 497-502, **498**, **18**
accommodations 499-500
drinking 501
festivals 499
food 500-1
nightlife 501
shopping 501
sights 497-8
tourist information 502
tours 499
travel to/from 502-13
Olivença 446
Olodum 421
opening hours 708
otters 635, **635**
Ouro Preto 13, 182-90, **184-5**, **13**
accommodations 178-8
drinking 188
entertainment 188
festivals 187
food 188-9
nightlife 188
sights 183-7
tourist information 190
tours 187
travel to/from 190
travel within 190

P

Pacaembu 232
Paço do Frevo 486
paddleboarding 45
Palace Hotel 415
Palácio Conde dos Arcos 352
Palácio da Alvorada 342-3, **338-9**
Palácio do Itamaraty 342
Palácio do Planalto 337
Palácio dos Leões 560
Palacio Rio Branco 653
Palácio Tiradentes 72
Palmas 602-5, **603**
Pantanal, the 7, 14, 375-84, **378**, **7**, **14**
accommodations 375, 379
climate 375
geography 375
planning 375, 379, 380
tours 379
Pântano do Sul 304
Pão de Açúcar 11, 67, **11**
Pará 572-600
paragliding 544, **547**, *see also* hang gliding
Paraíba 58, 482, 513-17, **484-5**
accommodations 482
climate 482
food 482

Map Pages **000**
Photo Pages **000**

highlights 484-5, **484-5**
travel to/from 483
travel seasons 482
Paraná 56, 268-91, **269**
accommodations 268
climate 268
food 268
highlights 269, **269**
history 269
travel seasons 268
Paranaguá 275-7, **276**
Paranapiacaba 260
Paraty 19, 137-46, 161, **138**, **140-1**, **19**
accommodations 143-144
activities 141-2
drinking 145
entertainment 145
festivals 142
food 144-5
sights 137-41
tourist information 145
tours 142
travel to/from 145
parks & gardens
Instituto Reserva Kautsky 219
Jardim Botânico Adolpho Ducke 607
Parque Cão Sentado 157
Parque da Catacumba 65
Parque da Cidade 65
Parque das Nações Indígenas 385
Parque do Flamengo 69
Parque Estadual da Pedra Azul 220
Parque Estadual da Serra dos Pirineus 355
Parque Estadual de Itaúnas 216
Parque Estadual de Vila Velha 272
Parque Estadual do Alto do Ribeira 266
Parque Ibirapuera 233
Parque Estadual Serra do Intendente 210
Parque Lage 65
Parque Natural do Caraça 210
Parque Vila Germânica 306
Quinta da Boa Vista 77
Serra do Aracá State Park 625
Sítio Burle Marx 78
Parque Ibirapuera 233
Parque Nacional da Chapada Diamantina 17, 462-3, **17**
Parque Nacional da Chapada dos Guimarães 371-2
Parque Nacional da Chapada dos Veadeiros 358-9, **44**
Parque Nacional da Serra da Capivara 555, **25**
Parque Nacional da Serra do Cipó 209-10
Parque Nacional de Caparaó 211-12
Parque Nacional do Iguaçu (Brazil) 286-7, 289-91, **286-7**
Parque Nacional do Itatiaia 146-8
Parque Nacional dos Lençóis Maranhenses 18, 564, **18**
Parque Nacional Iguazú (Argentina) 286-7, **286-7**
Parque Nacional Marinho de Fernando de Noronha 502
Parque Natural do Caraça 210-11
parrots 633, 697, **696**
passports 710, 711
Pataxó, the 458
Paulista Coast 259-67
Pedra Azul 220-1
Pelé 682, 684
Pelourinho 403
Penedo 150-1, 478-80
Pernambuco 58, 482, 483-513, **484-5**
accommodations 482
climate 482
food 482
highlights 484-5, **484-5**
travel to/from 483
travel seasons 482
Petrópolis 151-5, **154-5**
Piauí 58, 532, 554-5, **534-5**
accommodations 532
climate 532
food 532
highlights 534-5, **534-5**
history 533
travel to/from 533
travel seasons 532
Pinheiros 234, **249**
Pinto Bandeira 326
piracy 666
piranhas 635, 697
pirarucú 635
Pirenópolis 354-8, **356-7**
Piri, *see* Pirenópolis
pizza 241, **240-1**
Planetário 65
planning 20-22, 705, *see also individual regions*
basics 20-1
children, travel with 53-4, 79
itineraries 30-6, **30-6**
outdoor activities 43-7
travel seasons 20
plants 698
Poconé 373
politics 660-1
Ponta Porã 398-9
Pontal de Coruripe 479
pop music 679-81
population 661, 675
pororoca 577
Porto Alegre 316-20, **317**
Porto Seguro 447-50, **448**
Porto Velho 649-51, **650**
ports 390
Praça da Bandeira 110
Praça da República 228-9
Praça da Sé 223-7
Praça dos Três Poderes 336
Praça Mauá 69-73, 91, 107-8, 117, 124
Praia Brava 299
Praia da Lagoinha 299
Praia da Pipa 526-30
Praia da Carro Quebrado 476
Praia do Espelho 453
Praia do Forte 430-2
Praia do Francês 477-8
Praia do Gunga 471
Praia do Morro 476
Praia do Rosa 312-13
Praia Lopes Mendes 132
Praia Tabula 476
Presidente Figueiredo 610
Princesa Isabel 669
public holidays 708
public transport 716
Puerto Nariño (Colombia) 644-5

Q

quilombos 665

R

rainforest 691-3, **690**
Recife 18, 483, 486-97, **488-9**, **492**
accommodations 491
activities 489-90
drinking 493-4
entertainment 494
festivals 490
food 491-3
nightlife 493-4
shopping 494
sights 486-7
tourist information 495-6
travel to/from 496-7
Recôncavo 427-30, **414**
Redonda 548
Reserva Extrativista Baixo Rio Branco-Jauaperi 623-4
Reveillon 29
Ribeirão da Ilha 303
Rio Branco 653-5, **654**
Rio de Janeiro 55, 60-127, **62-3**
accommodations 60, 85-91, 95-6
activities 78-83
Barra da Tijuca 77-8, 96
Botafogo 66-7, 90-1, 105-7, 116-17, 123-4, **86-7**
Catete **86-7**
Centro 69-73, 91, 107-8, 117, 124, **92-3**
children, travel with 53, 79
climate 60
Copacabana 65-6, 89-90, 103-5, 113, 114-16, 123, **74-5**, **112-13**
drinking 110, 1149-19
emergencies 125
entertainment 119-21
festivals 17, 85, 37-41, **41**, **17**, **39**
Flamengo 68-9, 91, 107, 117, 124, **86-7**
food 50, 60, 97-110
Gávea 64-5, 89, 101-3, 114, 123, **66-7**
Glória **92-3**
highlights 62-3, **62-3**
history 61
Humaitá 66-7, **86-7**
Ipanema 61, 64, 85, 88-9, 96-100, 102, 111, 121-3, **66-7**
Jardim Botânico 64-5, 89, 101-3, 114, 123, **71**
Lagoa 64-5, 89, 101-3, 114, 123, **71**
Lapa 76-7, 95-6, 109-11, 118-21, 124-5, **92**

Leblon 61, 64, 85, 88-9, 100-1, 102, 111, 114, 121-3, **66-7**
Leme 65-6, 89-90, 103-5, 114, 123, **74-5**
media 125
medical services 125
money 125
nightlife 110, 114-19
Praça Mauá 69-73, 91, 107-8, 117, 124
safety 125
Santa Teresa 73, 76, 95-6, 109, 118, 124-5, **92-3**
São Cristóvão 98-9
shopping 121-127
sights 61, 64-23, 76-78
tourist information 126
tours 84-5
travel to/from 126-7
travel seasons 60
Urca 67, 90-1, 105-7, 116-17, 123-4
walking tours 83, **83**
Zona Norte 77
Rio de Janeiro State 55, 128-69, **130-1**
accommodations 128
climate 128
food 128
highlights 130-1, **130-1**
history 129, 137
travel seasons 128
Rio Grande 333
Rio Grande do Norte 58, 482, 517-31, **484-5**
accommodations 482
climate 482
food 482
highlights 484-5, **484-5**
travel to/from 483
travel seasons 482
Rio Grande do Sul 57, 314-33, **315**
accommodations 314
climate 314
food 314
highlights 315, **315**
history 315
travel seasons 314
Rio Negro Basin 620-7
Rio Negro **583**
Rio Urubu 611
Rio Vermelho 420

Map Pages **000**
Photo Pages **000**

robbery 708
rock climbing 43, 46, 220
rock music 679-81
Rondônia 649-52
Roraima 645-9
ruins 431

S

Sabará 183
safety 23, 705, 708
fraud 707
hitchhiking 715-16
Salvador 12, 402-11, 414-22, **404**, **408-9**, **417**, **12**, **42**
accommodations 414-17
beaches 409
climate 400
courses 409-11
drinking 420
entertainment 420-4
festivals 411, 414
food 417-19
history 403
nightlife 420
safety 424-5
shopping 424
sights 403-7
tourist information 424-5
tours 431
travel with 425-7
travel seasons 400
samba 39-41, 677, *see also* Carnaval
Santa Catarina 19, 56, 292-313, **293**, **19**
accommodations 292
climate 292
food 292
highlights 293, **293**
history 293
travel seasons 292
Santa Teresa 73, 76, 95-6, 109, 118, 124-5, **92-3**, **113**
Santarém 590-5, **591**, **596**
Santo Amaro 425
Santo Antônio de Lisboa 298-9
Santuário Dom Bosco 343
Santuário Santa Paulina **309**
São Cristóvão 98-9
São Felix 427-30, **428-9**
São Gabriel da Cachoeira 626-7
São João del Rei 193-6, **195**

São Jorge 361
São Luís 556-64, **557**, **558**
accommodations 560-1
beaches 560
drinking 562
entertainment 562
festivals 560, 561
food 561-2
history 557-8
shopping 562-3
sights 558-60
tourist information 563
travel within 563-4
São Miguel do Gostoso 530-1
São Miguel dos Milagres 476
São Paulo City 15, 56, 223-59, **226**, **230-1**
Avenida Paulista 232-3, **244-5**
Barra Funda 232
courses 236
festivals 236-7
food 50
Higienópolis 232
history 223
Jardins 232-3, 234-6, **244-5**
Liberdade 229
Luz 229
Pacaembu 232
Parque Ibirapuera 233
Pinheiros 234, **249**
Praça da República 228-9
sights 223-36
tourist information 253-6
tours 236
travel to 256
travel within 256-9
Ubatuba 259-67
Vila Madalena 234, **249**
walking tours 234-5, 236, **235**
São Paulo State 222-67
accommodations 222
climate 222
food 222
highlights 224-5, **224-5**
travel seasons 222
São Sebastião 262-7
São Thomé das Letras 203
Saquarema 159, 161, 163, **160**
scams 708
scenery 24
scenic flights 565

sculptures 192-3
Semana Santa 27
Cidade de Goiás 352
Ouro Preto 189
Rio de Janeiro 142
Sergipe 58, 464-81, 466-9, **445**
accommodations 464
climate 464
food 464
highlights 465
history 465-6
travel to/from 466
Serra da Mantiqueira 258
Serra Gaúcha 320-8
Serra Verde Express 275
Serro 208-9
sertão, the 518
shopping 708-9
slavery 416, 663-6
sloths 631, 694, **631**
smoking 706
snorkeling 43, 46, 372, 393-5, 505, 508, **504**
see also diving
snowsports 326
soccer, *see* football
songs 679
stand-up paddleboarding 45
stingrays 635
Sugarloaf Mountain 11, 67, **11**
superquadras 345
surfing 43, 44-5, 550, 577
Bahia 441
Fernando de Noronha 509
Rio de Janeiro 83
Rio Grande do Sul 332
Santa Catarina 301, 313
swimming 359, 395, 460, 605, 626
Paraty 141-2
Visconde de Mauá 148-9

T

Tabatinga 638-40
Tabuleiro 210
tacacá 593
tapirs 631
Taquarussú 605-6
tarantulas 636
Teatro Amazonas 606
Tefé 627-37
telephone services 20, 709
Templo da Boa Vontade 337
Teresópolis 155-7
Theatro Municipal 227-8

time 640, 709
Tiradentes 17, 196-202, **198**, **17**
Tocantins 602-6
toilets 709
Torres 331-3
toucans 633, 697
tourist information 709
tours, *see also* walking tours
- Brasília 343
- buggy 433, 519, 524, 531, 550
- Goiás 359
- jungle tours 14, 612-13, 615, 641, **15**
- Maceió 470-1
- Paraná 275, 282-3
- Rio Grande do Sul 316
- scams 615
- Sergipe 467-8
- walking 82, 234-5, 236, **82**, **234-5**

touts 708
train travel 716
Trancoso 453-5
Transpantaneira 376-7, **376-7**
travel advisories 710
travel to/from Brazil 711, **714**
travel within Brazil 713-16
trekking, *see* hiking
Triângulo 227-8
Triple Frontier, the 638-45, **639**
tropicália 678
turtles 431
typhoid 705-6

U

Ubatuba 259-62
Urca 67, 90-1, 105-7, 116-17, 123-4

V

vacations 708
vaccinations 705
Vale do Amanhecer 337
Vale do Matutu 203
Vale dos Vinhedos 321-5, **322-3**
Vale Europeu 308-9, **308-9**
Valença 438-9
Vargas, Getúlio 670
Vila do Abraão 129, 132-37, **134**
Vila Madalena 234, **249**
Vila Velha 272
visas 20, 709-10
Visconde de Mauá 148-50
Vitória 213-15, 407
volunteering 710

W

Waimiri Atroari people 623
walking, *see* hiking
walking tours
- Rio de Janeiro 82, **82**
- São Paulo 236, **235**

water parks 451
waterfalls
- Barcelos 625
- Bom Jardim 372
- Bonito 393-4
- Manaus 610
- Paraná 289-90
- Parque Nacional da Pirenópolis 355
- Chapada dos Guimarães 371
- Iguazu Falls 11, 282-91, **283**, **11**, **286-7**
- Rio de Janeiro state 148
- Taquarussú 605

waterfowl 698, **698**, **699**
weather 20, *see also individual regions*
whales 694-6
whale-watching 313
wildlife 24, 376-7, 621, 637-8, 690-700, **629**, **630-1**, **632-3**, **634-5**, **636**, **377**
- Amazon, the 629-36

wildlife reserves 355, 431
wildlife-watching 43, 508-9
- Pantanal, the 379-80, 382, 383
- Paraná 281

windsurfing 45-6, 530, 549, 550-1
wineries 321, 323, 326, 322-3, **322-3**
wolf-watching 211
women in Brazil 676
World Cup (football) 684

X

Xapuri 655-7

Y

Yanomami, the 647
yellow fever 706

Z

Zika virus 705
zip-lining 434
Zona Norte 77
zoos 577, 592, 607

Map Legend

Sights
- Beach
- Bird Sanctuary
- Buddhist
- Castle/Palace
- Christian
- Confucian
- Hindu
- Islamic
- Jain
- Jewish
- Monument
- Museum/Gallery/Historic Building
- Ruin
- Shinto
- Sikh
- Taoist
- Winery/Vineyard
- Zoo/Wildlife Sanctuary
- Other Sight

Activities, Courses & Tours
- Bodysurfing
- Diving
- Canoeing/Kayaking
- Course/Tour
- Sento Hot Baths/Onsen
- Skiing
- Snorkeling
- Surfing
- Swimming/Pool
- Walking
- Windsurfing
- Other Activity

Sleeping
- Sleeping
- Camping
- Hut/Shelter

Eating
- Eating

Drinking & Nightlife
- Drinking & Nightlife
- Cafe

Entertainment
- Entertainment

Shopping
- Shopping

Information
- Bank
- Embassy/Consulate
- Hospital/Medical
- Internet
- Police
- Post Office
- Telephone
- Toilet
- Tourist Information
- Other Information

Geographic
- Beach
- Gate
- Hut/Shelter
- Lighthouse
- Lookout
- Mountain/Volcano
- Oasis
- Park
- Pass
- Picnic Area
- Waterfall

Population
- Capital (National)
- Capital (State/Province)
- City/Large Town
- Town/Village

Transport
- Airport
- Border crossing
- Bus
- Cable car/Funicular
- Cycling
- Ferry
- Metro station
- Monorail
- Parking
- Petrol station
- Subway/Subte station
- Taxi
- Train station/Railway
- Tram
- Underground station
- Other Transport

Routes
- Tollway
- Freeway
- Primary
- Secondary
- Tertiary
- Lane
- Unsealed road
- Road under construction
- Plaza/Mall
- Steps
- Tunnel
- Pedestrian overpass
- Walking Tour
- Walking Tour detour
- Path/Walking Trail

Boundaries
- International
- State/Province
- Disputed
- Regional/Suburb
- Marine Park
- Cliff
- Wall

Hydrography
- River, Creek
- Intermittent River
- Canal
- Water
- Dry/Salt/Intermittent Lake
- Reef

Areas
- Airport/Runway
- Beach/Desert
- Cemetery (Christian)
- Cemetery (Other)
- Glacier
- Mudflat
- Park/Forest
- Sight (Building)
- Sportsground
- Swamp/Mangrove

Note: Not all symbols displayed above appear on the maps in this book

Robert Balkovich
Bahia, Sergipe, Alagoas Robert was born and raised in Oregon, but has called New York City home for almost a decade. When he was a child and other families were going to theme parks and grandma's house, he went to Mexico City and toured Eastern Europe by train. He's now a writer and travel enthusiast seeking experiences that are ever so slightly out of the ordinary to report back on. Follow him on Instagram @oh_balky.

Alex Egerton
Ceará, Piauí & Maranhão; Pernambuco, Paraíba & Rio Grande do Norte A news journalist by trade, Alex has worked for magazines, newspapers and media outlets on five continents. He spends most of his time on the road checking under mattresses, sampling suspicious street food and chatting with locals as part of the research process for travel articles and guidebooks. Alex has hiked through remote jungles in Colombia, explored isolated tributaries of the mighty Mekong and taken part in the first kayak descent of a number of remote waterways in Nicaragua. When not on the road, you'll find him at home amongst the colonial splendor of Popayán in southern Colombia.

Anna Kaminski
Colombia (The Amazon) Originally from the Soviet Union, Anna grew up in Cambridge, England. She graduated from the University of Warwick with a degree in Comparative American Studies, a background in the history, culture and literature of the Americas and the Caribbean, and an enduring love of Latin America. Her restless wanderings led her to settle briefly in Oaxaca and Bangkok and her flirtation with criminal law saw her volunteering as a lawyer's assistant in the courts, ghettos and prisons of Kingston, Jamaica. Anna has contributed to almost 30 Lonely Planet titles. When not on the road, Anna calls London home.

Kevin Raub
Paraná, Rio Grande do Sul, Santa Catarina, São Paulo State Atlanta native Kevin started his career as a music journalist in New York, working for Men's Journal and Rolling Stone magazines. He ditched the rock 'n' roll lifestyle for travel writing and has written over 70 Lonely Planet guides, focused mainly on Brazil, Chile, Colombia, USA, India, the Caribbean and Portugal. Raub also contributes to a variety of travel magazines in both the USA and UK. Along the way, the self-confessed hophead is in constant search of wildly high IBUs in local beers. Follow him on Twitter and Instagram @RaubOnTheRoad.

OUR STORY

A beat-up old car, a few dollars in the pocket and a sense of adventure. In 1972 that's all Tony and Maureen Wheeler needed for the trip of a lifetime – across Europe and Asia overland to Australia. It took several months, and at the end – broke but inspired – they sat at their kitchen table writing and stapling together their first travel guide, *Across Asia on the Cheap*. Within a week they'd sold 1500 copies. Lonely Planet was born.

Today, Lonely Planet has offices in Franklin, London, Melbourne, Oakland, Dublin, Beijing and Delhi, with more than 600 staff and writers. We share Tony's belief that 'a great guidebook should do three things: inform, educate and amuse'.

OUR WRITERS

Regis St Louis

Rio de Janeiro City Regis grew up in a small town in the American Midwest – the kind of place that fuels big dreams of travel – where he developed an early fascination with foreign dialects and world cultures. He spent his formative years learning Russian and a handful of Romance languages, which served him well on journeys across much of the globe. Regis has contributed to more than 50 Lonely Planet titles, covering destinations across six continents. His travels have taken him from the mountains of Kamchatka to remote island villages in Melanesia, and to many grand urban landscapes. When not on the road, he lives in New Orleans. Follow him on Instagram @regisstlouis. Regis also wrote the Plan Your Trip, Understand and Survive chapters.

Gregor Clark

Minas Gerais, Espirito Santo, Rio de Janeiro State Gregor is a US-based writer whose love of foreign languages and curiosity about what's around the next bend have taken him to dozens of countries across five continents. Chronic wanderlust has also led him to visit all 50 states and most Canadian provinces during countless road trips through his native North America. Since 2000 Gregor has regularly contributed to Lonely Planet guides, with a focus on Europe and the Americas.

Anthony Ham

The Amazon Anthony is a freelance writer and photographer who specializes in Spain, East and Southern Africa, the Arctic and the Middle East. When he's not writing for Lonely Planet, Anthony writes about and photographs Spain, Africa and the Middle East for newspapers and magazines in Australia, the UK and US. Now living in Australia, Anthony continues to travel the world in search of stories.

Andy Symington

Brasilia & Goiás, Mato Grosso & Mato Grosso do Sul Andy has written or worked on over a hundred books and other updates for Lonely Planet (especially in Europe and Latin America) and other publishing companies, and has published articles on numerous subjects for a variety of newspapers, magazines, and websites. He part-owns and operates a rock bar, has written a novel and is currently working on several fiction and non-fiction writing projects. Originally from Australia, Andy moved to Northern Spain many years ago. When he's not off with a backpack in some far-flung corner of the world, he can probably be found watching the tragically poor local football side or tasting local wines after a long walk in the nearby mountains.

OVER PAGE MORE WRITERS

Published by Lonely Planet Global Limited
CRN 554153
11th edition – Jun 2019
ISBN 978 1 78657 475 6
© Lonely Planet 2019 Photographs © as indicated 2019
10 9 8 7 6 5 4 3 2 1
Printed in Singapore

Although the authors and Lonely Planet have taken all reasonable care in preparing this book, we make no warranty about the accuracy or completeness of its content and, to the maximum extent permitted, disclaim all liability arising from its use.

All rights reserved. No part of this publication may be copied, stored in a retrieval system, or transmitted in any form by any means, electronic, mechanical, recording or otherwise, except brief extracts for the purpose of review, and no part of this publication may be sold or hired, without the written permission of the publisher. Lonely Planet and the Lonely Planet logo are trademarks of Lonely Planet and are registered in the US Patent and Trademark Office and in other countries. Lonely Planet does not allow its name or logo to be appropriated by commercial establishments, such as retailers, restaurants or hotels. Please let us know of any misuses: lonelyplanet.com/ip.